1987 CRB Commodity Year Book

EDITORIAL BOARD

Senior Editors
SUSAN BUCHANAN
SEYMOUR GAYLINN

Contributing Editors
MORTON BARATZ
CHRISTINE DEWAN
ERIC NADELBERG
GEORGE PARKER
WALTER SPILKA

PREPARED AND PUBLISHED BY

 **Commodity Research Bureau**
a Knight-Ridder Business Information Service
100 CHURCH ST., SUITE 1850
New York, N.Y. 10007

INTRODUCTION

1987 Commodity Year Book is designed to provide a review of recent activity affecting supply/demand trends and prices of commodities, financial futures, and foreign currencies. We have included text covering the economic and other factors influencing these markets in 1986 and 1985, tables, charts, and graphs of historical data.

Commodity prices trended lower in 1986, mainly because of large U.S and global supplies and sluggish economic conditions at home and worldwide. Inflation in the U.S. was subdued during the year, reflecting low prices of petroleum and agricultural products. The value of the dollar declined, yet the U.S. trade deficit reached a record $19 billion in November. During 1986, the discount rate was reduced four times, and this heightened enthusiasm for stock index and interest rate futures. However, an easier Federal Reserve Bank policy failed appreciably to help the U.S. economy, which grew at the annual rate of 2.1 percent in the second half of 1986, versus 2.2 percent in the first six months.

The steady growth in financial futures continued during 1986. Of the leading futures markets (those with 1986 volume over 100,000 contracts), interest rate and stock index futures together accounted for nearly 53 percent of volume, while currencies provided another 10 percent. The most active financial futures were contracts in Treasury bonds, the S&P 500 Index, Eurodollars, and the German mark. Agricultural commodities provided another 21 percent of volume in 1986, followed by metals with nine percent, and petroleum and products with seven percent. Corn, soybeans, and live cattle continued to be the most active farm futures. In metals, gold and silver remained the major markets, although trading in platinum rose 230 percent over the 1985 level. In the petroleum markets, crude oil and heating oil were the dominant contracts, and substantial volume increases occurred in both. Trading in crude oil more than doubled over the 1985 level, while volume in heating oil expanded by nearly 50 percent.

An important development during 1986 was the start of trading in the CRB Futures Price Index contract in June, on the New York Futures Exchange. The Index, which now reflects prices of 26 non-financial futures, is used as an analytical tool in assessing commodity price trends and in gauging inflation. (See "The Commodity Price Trend," page 5T.)

Included in this edition of the year book is a timely feature study, "Spreads in Financial Futures," by Phillip Tiger, which examines: principal spreads in interest rate, currency and stock index futures; factors affecting spread movements; profit opportunities; and analytical tools that help in evaluating spreads. The author is Vice President and Commodity Manager at the Washington, D.C. office of E.F. Hutton. A leading expert on spread trading, Mr. Tiger publishes a semi-monthly newsletter devoted to analysis of futures spreads.

Our second feature article, "The U.S. Agricultural Dilemma and Prospects for Change," by Richard Loewy, considers the causes of the current U.S. farm crisis, the recent performance of the U.S. in world agricultural markets, and the U.S. grains and oilseeds supply situation. The article also discusses domestic agricultural policies and offers suggestions for policy changes to help the farm sector. Richard Loewy is Senior Grains and Oilseeds Analyst at Prudential-Bache Securities, Inc., in New York and was formerly an economist with the U.S. Department of State.

We wish to express our appreciation for the assistance provided us by government agencies, particularly the U.S. Department of Agriculture and U.S. Bureau of Mines, various trade associations and publications, and other organizations. We have attempted to list these institutions on page 4T.

The Editorial Board
March 1987

TABLE OF CONTENTS

ACKNOWLEDGMENTS

The editors wish to thank the following for source material:

Aluminum Association
American Bureau of Metal Statistics
American Gas Association
American Iron and Steel Institute
American Metal Market
American Paper and Pulp Association
American Petroleum Institute
Atomic Industrial Forum, Inc.
Chicago Board of Trade
Chicago Mercantile Exchange
Citrus Associates of the N.Y. Cotton Exch., Inc.
Coffee, Sugar & Cocoa Exch., Inc.
Commodity Exchange, Inc.—N.Y.
Commodity Futures Trading Commission
Edison Electric Institute
Exxon Corp.
F. W. Dodge Corp.
Federal Power Commission
Federal Reserve Board
Futures Industry Association
Johnson Matthey Ltd.
General Services Administration
Gill & Duffus Ltd.
Handy & Harman
International Cotton Advisory Committee
International Monetary Market (Chicago)
International Tea Committee
Kansas City Board of Trade
MidAmerica Commodity Exchange
Minneapolis Grain Exchange

National Coffee Association of U.S.A., Inc.
New York Cotton Exchange
New York Futures Exchange
New York Mercantile Exchange
Newsprint Service Bureau
Nuclear Exchange Corp.
Nuclear Regulatory Commission
Oil World
Portland Cement Association
Random Lengths
Rubber Manufacturers Association
Rubber Study Group
Society of the Plastics Industry, Inc.
Leather Industries of America, Inc.
Tea Council, Inc.
Textile Economics Bureau, Inc.
Textile Organon
U.N. Food and Agriculture Organization
U.S. Department of Agriculture
U.S. Department of Commerce
U.S. Department of Energy
U.S. Department of Interior
U.S. Department of Labor
U.S. Bureau of Mines
U.S. Tariff Commission
U.S. Treasury Department
The Wall Street Journal
Winnipeg Commodity Exchange
Wool Services Co.
Zinc Institute, Inc.

The editors wish to thank the following for their contributions to the 1987 edition:

Barbara Lahey, production manager

Wanda Hardy, editorial production
Albert Marin, chart production
Rita Pacelli, statistical production
Candace Tettamanti, editorial production
Luis Vazquez, chart production

The Commodity Price Trend

U.S. inflation was subdued in 1986: commodity prices weakened, producer prices slipped, and consumer prices rose slightly. The CRB Futures Price Index, on a mostly-steady downtrend from 1984 to mid-1986, fell to the nine-year low of 196.9 in July. The Index reflects futures prices of 27 non-financial commodities[1] and was strongly pressured by declines in agricultural prices and petroleum values.

The Producer Price Index for finished goods fell by 1.9 percent during December, 1985–November, 1986. There was a substantial drop in the sub-index for fuels and related products and a slip in the farm products sub-index. The PPI has also been on a downtrend in recent years.

The CPI-U continued its long-term rise at a very sluggish rate. In December, 1985–November, 1986, the CPI rose by 1.2 percent—the smallest change for the period since 1962. During early 1986, the CPI registered the largest dip in over three years, because petroleum prices fell.

CRB Futures Price Index

The industrials group index ended 1986 nearly unchanged from a year ago. The major development was the spring plunge in crude oil prices. Nearby futures prices plummeted from $26/bbl. in early 1986 to below $10/bbl. in April. An August OPEC accord on quotas hiked crude prices to $15/bbl. In late December, OPEC agreed to cut production and to raise crude prices to about $18/bbl.

Cotton price activity was dramatic. Futures were pressured by a reduction in the government loan rate and implementation of a certificate program to bring U.S. prices down to international levels. Values tumbled for the first seven months of the year, then rebounded as the export pace improved significantly and mill use increased.

Fears of cut-off South African supplies sent platinum prices soaring in the summer; lack of a serious disruption took some buoyancy out of values. Silver futures fell to the lowest levels since 1982. World surplus and steady production by Mexico and Peru weighed on prices. Copper prices strengthened in early 1986, but later slumped with a sluggish U.S. economy and ample inventories.

The metals group index (gold, silver, platinum) registered sharp gains in August–October and ended 1986 above the year-before level. Gold prices improved in the first half of 1986, and rose on platinum's coattails in August, helped by rising investor demand for coins. The metal's price showed signs of weakness in October and the emergence of the Soviets as large sellers pressured the market. Prices worked down to $380 per ounce from $445. By year's end, gold prices had steadied.

The grains group index was significantly affected by changes in the Farm Bill. Government loan rates

for wheat, corn, barley and oats were lowered in 1986. Under other farm-program changes, a large number of certificates redeemable for government-owned grain were issued. As these were redeemed, grain released in the market exerted a downward influence on prices.

U.S. wheat output has fallen from the 1981–82 peaks; exports have also dropped sharply. As a result, stocks have reached record levels in the past two years. Moreover, the absence of the Soviets in the U.S. wheat market has had a bearish impact.

The 1986 corn crop was down from the previous year, but still the third-largest on record. As U.S. corn exports have fallen since 1979 and 1980, stocks have risen substantially.

The oilseeds group index (Chicago soybeans, Winnipeg rapeseed and flaxseed) suffered a sharp decline in 1986. The U.S. loan rate for soybeans was reduced, lowering the "floor" for market prices. U.S. soybean exports have retreated from peak levels in the early 1980s; domestic stocks have reached an all-time high.

Winnipeg rapeseed and flaxseed continued to trend lower in 1986. Canadian exports increased only slightly; extra production added to large stocks.

The livestock group index (cattle, hogs and pork bellies) had a volatile year, but ended about unchanged from a year ago. Cattle futures worked lower in second quarter 1986. Cow slaughters increased significantly under the Dairy Termination Program; declines in fed-cattle availability in the summer helped prices.

Hog prices made striking gains in 1986. Herd sizes declined, mainly because of producers' financial difficulties. USDA's bullish June hogs and pigs report showed lower-than-expected numbers and sent prices soaring.

The imported group index fell sharply. Coffee prices catapulted to near-record levels in late 1985–early 1986, but later slipped on evidence of ample world supplies and subdued consumption levels.

Cocoa prices lost ground with two years of record crops. World grindings were unable to keep pace with production gains; global stocks continued to rise. Prices advanced in August–September on successful International Cocoa Agreement negotiations and deteriorating Ivory Coast crop conditions, but later retreated.

World sugar prices gained in April–March with improving global consumption, some stock drawdowns, and concerns about the nuclear accident in Chernobyl. Later, world crop prospects brightened and stock use was less than expected, causing prices to slip.

Outlook

Most analysts are anticipating a slight pickup in the inflation rate in 1987, with a projected hike in petroleum prices. The Reagan administration forecasts the GNP deflator at 3.6 percent in 1987, and estimates that the CPI will rise by 3.8 percent. The commodity price trend may not keep up with the increase in inflation.

[1] The CRB Futures Price Index was adjusted March 2, 1987. Potato futures, which have traded on the New York Mercantile Exchange, will be delisted in May, 1987. The Index is therefore now an unweighted geometric average of the daily closing prices of 26 non-financial futures.

COMMODITY RESEARCH BUREAU   FUTURES PRICE INDEX
(1967 = 100)

(Weekly High, Low & Close)

27 FUTURES COMMODITIES

BARLEY	ORANGE JUICE
CATTLE (LIVE)	PLATINUM
COCOA	PORK BELLIES
COFFEE	POTATOES
COPPER	RAPESEED
CORN	RYE
COTTON	SILVER (N.Y.)
CRUDE OIL (N.Y.)	SOYBEANS
FLAXSEED	SOYBEAN MEAL
GOLD (COMEX)	SOYBEAN OIL
HEATING OIL (NO. 2)	SUGAR "11" (WORLD)
HOGS	WHEAT (CHI.)
LUMBER	WHEAT (MPLS.)
OATS (CHI.)	

1976 1977 1978 1979 1980 1981 1982 1983 1984 1985 1986 1987

Monthly CRB Futures Price Index   (High, Low & Close 1967 = 100)

Year		Jan.	Feb.	Mar.	Apr.	May	June	July	Aug.	Sept.	Oct.	Nov.	Dec.	Range
1982	High	267.2	268.6	257.5	257.3	253.3	242.0	242.4	238.4	239.8	234.3	236.3	235.7	268.6
	Low	256.0	256.5	248.7	252.5	244.9	231.5	233.2	227.1	227.9	225.8	231.2	231.1	225.8
	Close	267.2	256.5	250.1	253.1	244.9	239.3	233.7	235.4	227.9	229.9	235.7	234.0	—
1983	High	242.7	245.1	242.1	247.3	252.7	249.5	261.7	281.6	283.8	275.4	275.6	277.6	283.8
	Low	234.8	232.1	232.8	244.7	247.2	244.2	245.2	263.5	272.5	264.6	265.9	270.4	232.1
	Close	242.7	232.1	242.1	246.7	249.7	246.2	259.9	278.7	273.5	264.6	273.9	277.6	—
1984	High	278.3	276.1	283.0	283.2	284.2	280.3	268.3	259.8	256.3	254.8	258.7	253.2	284.2
	Low	273.2	266.1	274.7	275.1	275.3	268.4	249.4	253.3	250.3	252.0	252.7	244.0	244.0
	Close	273.6	272.5	283.0	275.1	280.1	271.0	249.4	257.1	251.4	254.8	253.8	244.2	—
1985	High	247.9	248.1	245.2	247.1	239.7	233.8	228.0	221.7	224.5	225.6	227.7	231.1	248.1
	Low	241.7	236.6	238.2	239.3	230.9	226.6	219.3	217.7	217.2	221.9	223.8	227.6	217.2
	Close	247.1	238.2	244.4	239.3	232.3	226.6	220.7	219.7	222.9	225.6	227.7	229.2	—
1986	High	231.1	216.6	216.5	213.5	216.1	205.7	203.7	207.1	212.3	213.4	213.3	212.0	231.1
	Low	219.9	209.9	209.4	203.0	205.5	201.6	196.9	201.0	208.2	209.7	208.4	207.5	196.9
	Close	219.9	209.9	209.6	213.5	205.5	201.6	200.1	207.1	210.9	211.3	210.7	209.1	—
1987	High	213.9	213.7											
	Low	208.3	204.2											
	Close	212.6	205.4											

Source: Commodity Research Bureau

T.006A

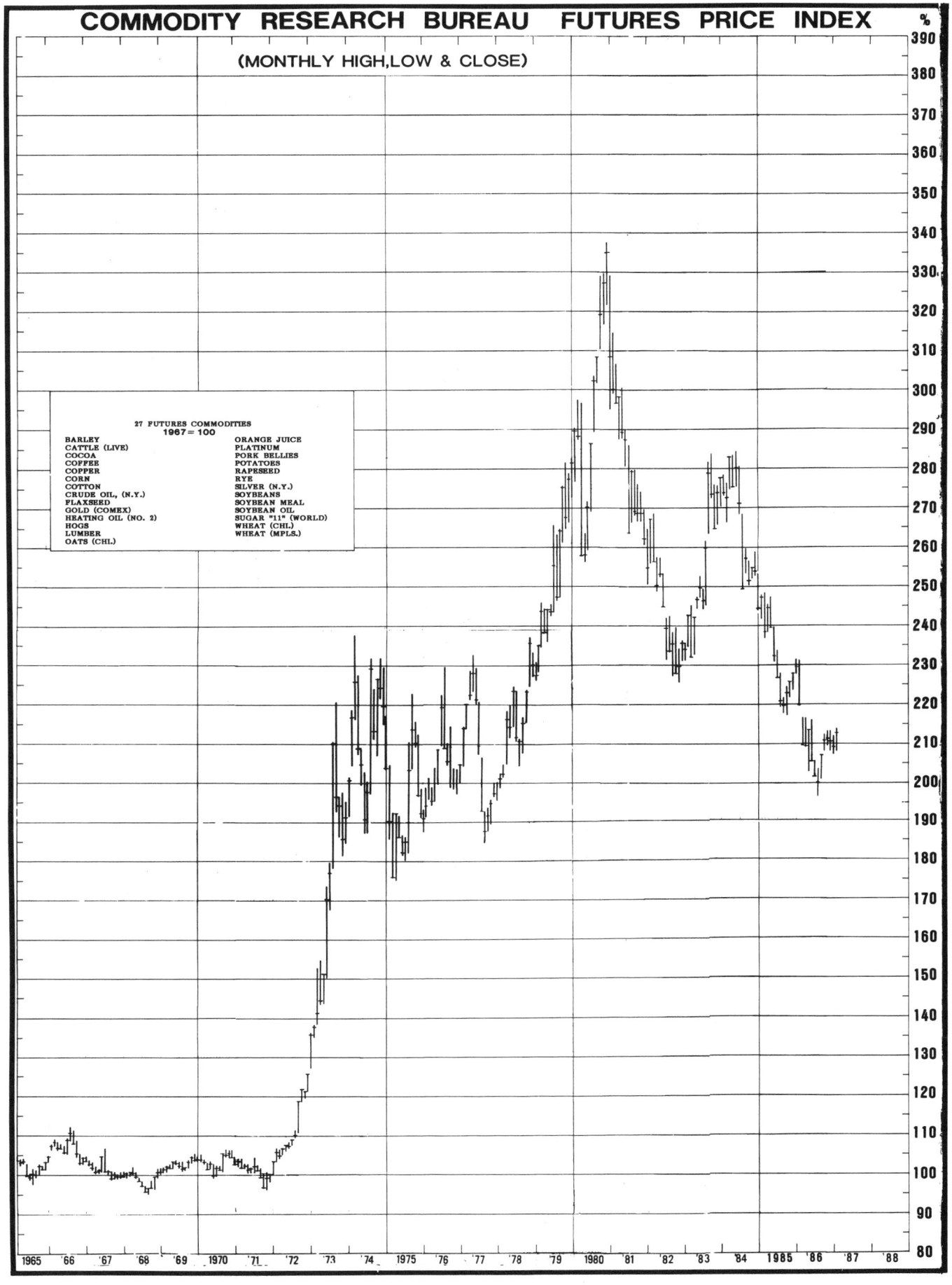

COMMODITY RESEARCH BUREAU FUTURES PRICE INDEX

(MONTHLY HIGH, LOW & CLOSE)

27 FUTURES COMMODITIES
1967 = 100

BARLEY	ORANGE JUICE
CATTLE (LIVE)	PLATINUM
COCOA	PORK BELLIES
COFFEE	POTATOES
COPPER	RAPESEED
CORN	RYE
COTTON	SILVER (N.Y.)
CRUDE OIL, (N.Y.)	SOYBEANS
FLAXSEED	SOYBEAN MEAL
GOLD (COMEX)	SOYBEAN OIL
HEATING OIL (NO. 2)	SUGAR "11" (WORLD)
HOGS	WHEAT (CHI.)
LUMBER	WHEAT (MPLS.)
OATS (CHI.)	

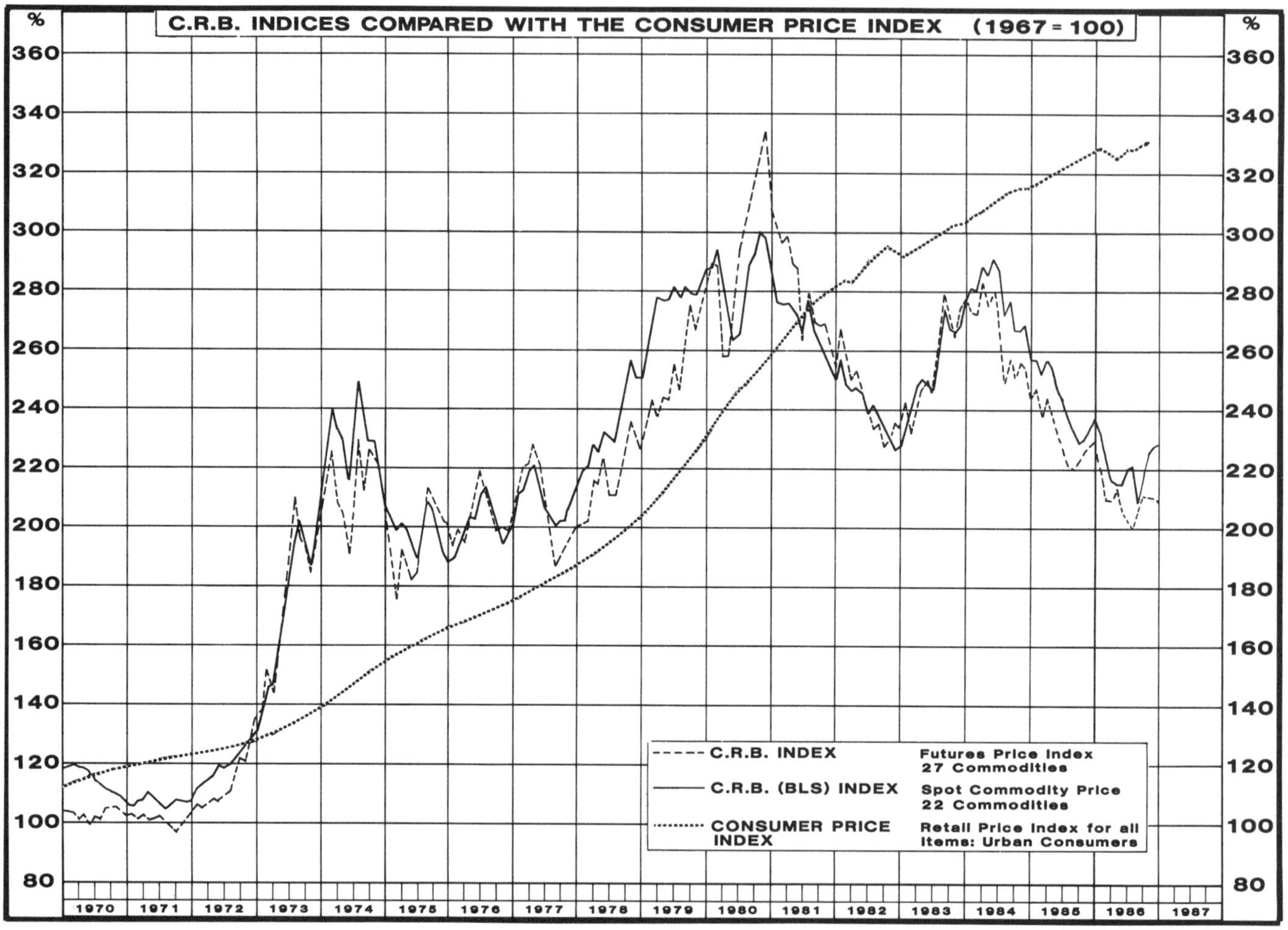

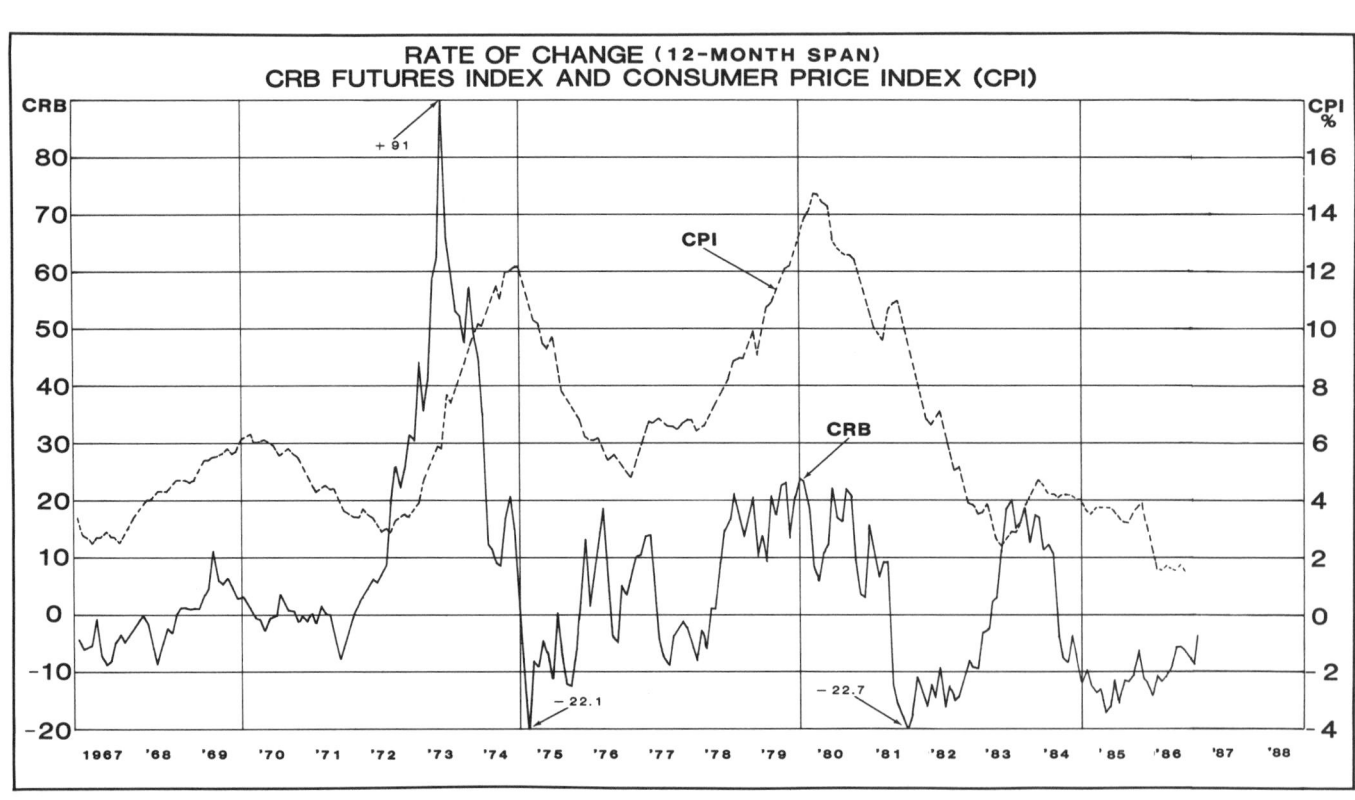

C.R.B. INDICES COMPARED WITH THE CONSUMER PRICE INDEX (1967 = 100)
%
360
340
320
300
280
260
240
220
200
180
160
140
120
100
80
C.R.B. INDEX
Futures Price Index 27 Commodities
C.R.B. (BLS) INDEX
Spot Commodity Price 22 Commodities
CONSUMER PRICE INDEX
Retail Price Index for all Items: Urban Consumers
1970
1971
1972
1973
1974
1975
1976
1977
1978
1979
1980
1981
1982
1983
1984
1985
1986
1987

RATE OF CHANGE (12-MONTH SPAN)
CRB FUTURES INDEX AND CONSUMER PRICE INDEX (CPI)
CRB
CPI %
80
70
60
50
40
30
20
10
0
-10
-20
16
14
12
10
8
6
4
2
0
2
4
+ 91
CPI
CRB
− 22.1
− 22.7
1967
'68
'69
'70
'71
'72
'73
'74
'75
'76
'77
'78
'79
'80
'81
'82
'83
'84
'85
'86
'87
'88

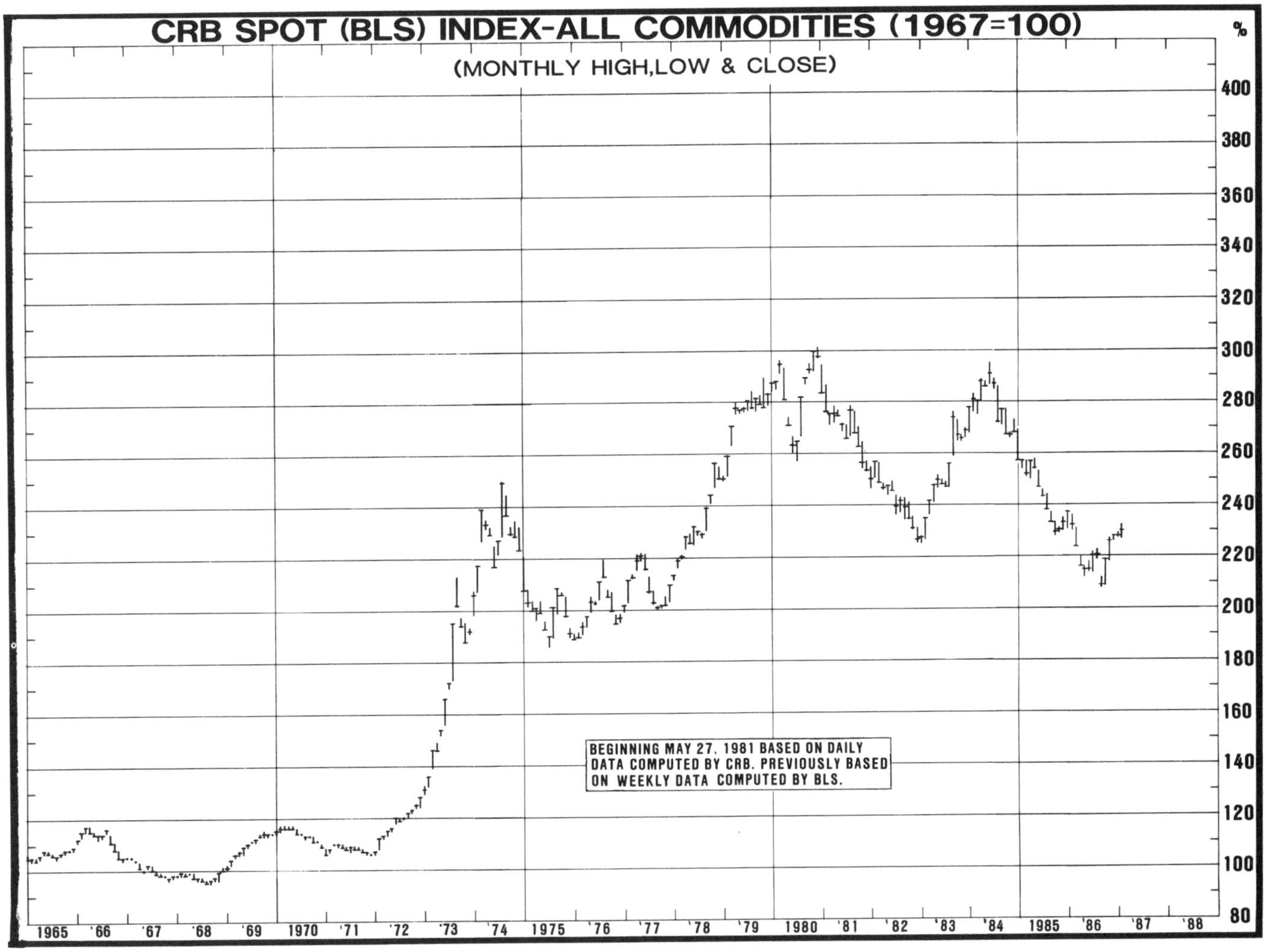

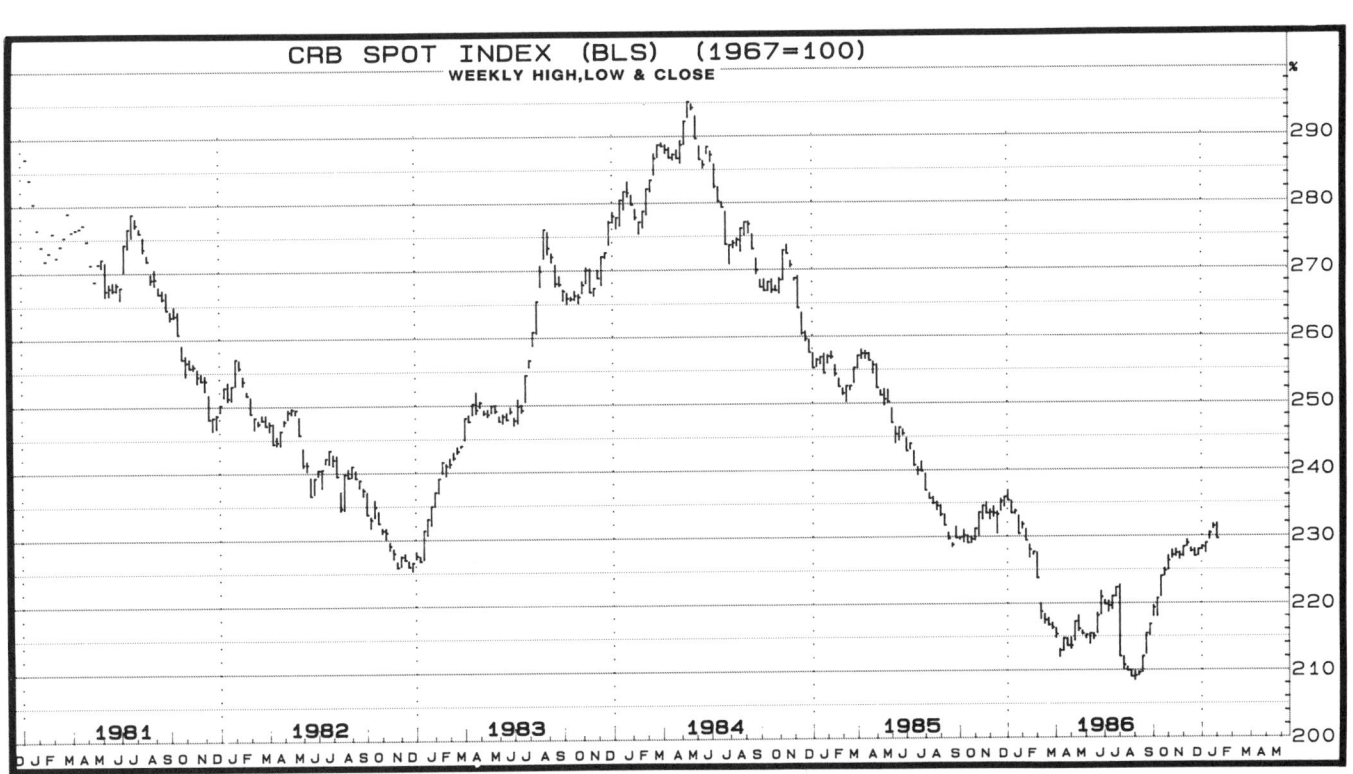

CRB SPOT (BLS) INDEX-ALL COMMODITIES (1967=100)
(MONTHLY HIGH, LOW & CLOSE)

BEGINNING MAY 27, 1981 BASED ON DAILY
DATA COMPUTED BY CRB. PREVIOUSLY BASED
ON WEEKLY DATA COMPUTED BY BLS.

CRB SPOT INDEX (BLS) (1967=100)
WEEKLY HIGH, LOW & CLOSE

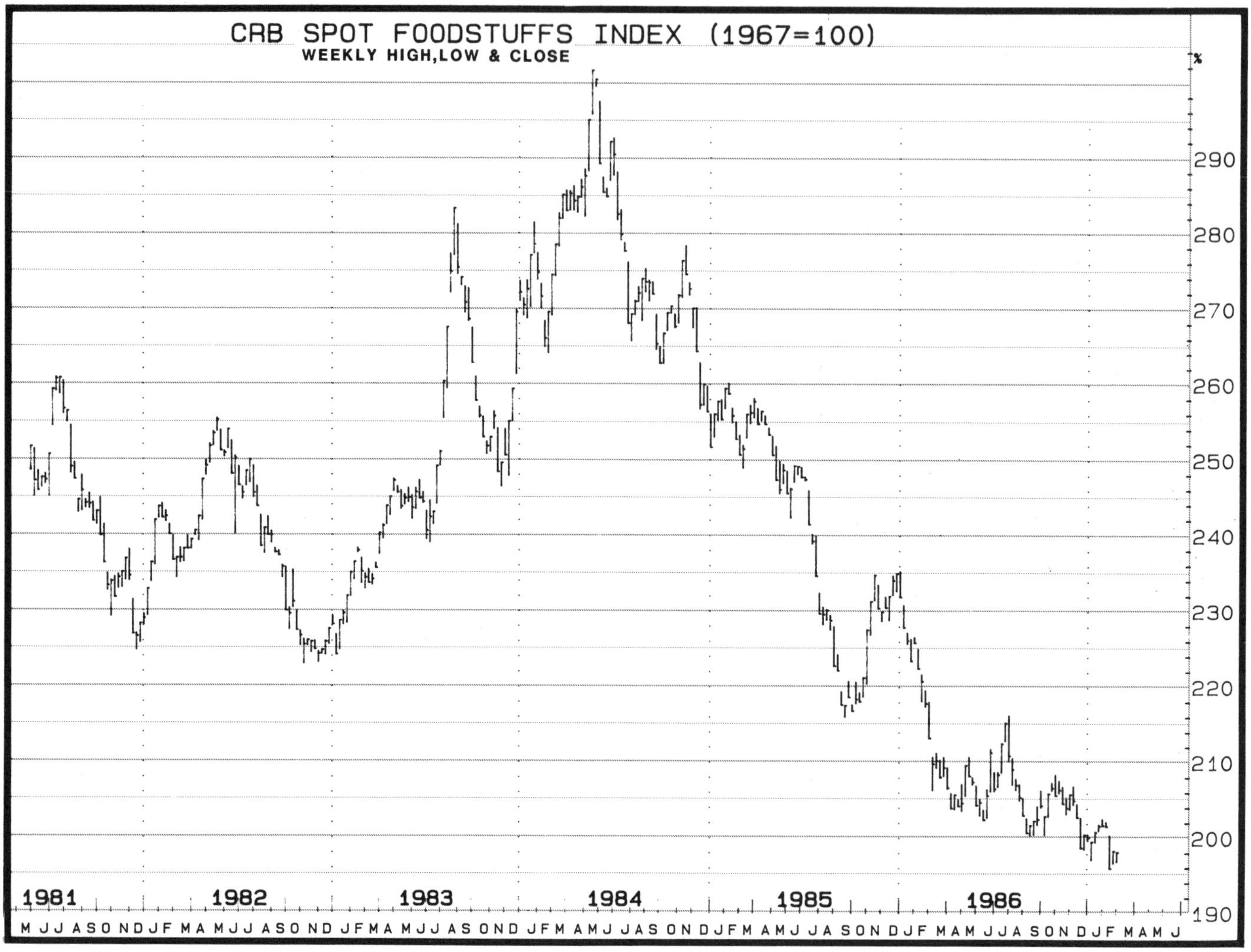

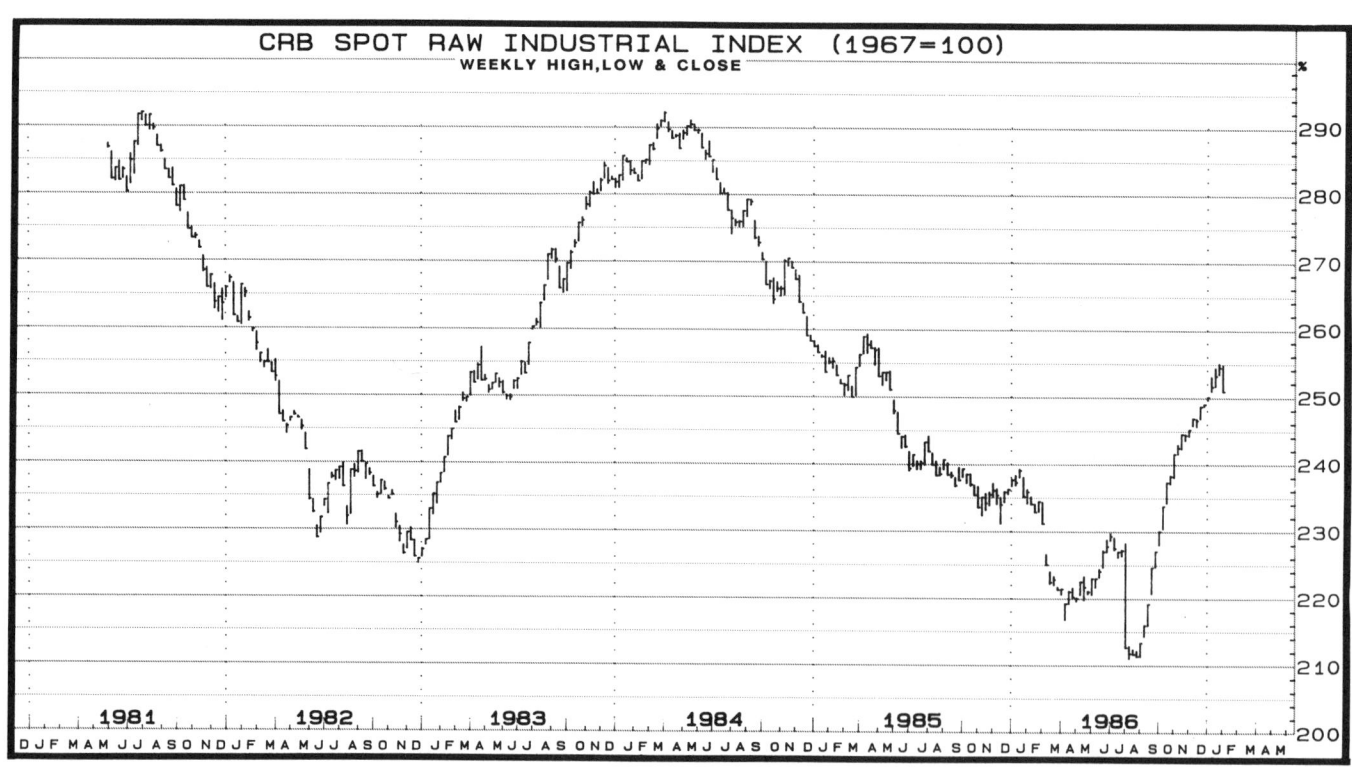

CRB SPOT FOODSTUFFS INDEX (1967=100)
WEEKLY HIGH,LOW & CLOSE
%
290
280
270
260
250
240
230
220
210
200
190
1981
1982
1983
1984
1985
1986
M J J A S O N D J F M A M J J A S O N D J F M A M J J A S O N D J F M A M J J A S O N D J F M A M J J A S O N D J F M A M J J A S O N D J F M A M J

CRB SPOT RAW INDUSTRIAL INDEX (1967=100)
WEEKLY HIGH,LOW & CLOSE
%
290
280
270
260
250
240
230
220
210
200
1981
1982
1983
1984
1985
1986
D J F M A M J J A S O N D J F M A M J J A S O N D J F M A M J J A S O N D J F M A M J J A S O N D J F M A M J J A S O N D J F M A M J J A S O N D J F M A M

CRB IMPORTED FUTURES INDEX (1967=100)
Weekly High, Low & Close

%

440
420
400
380
360
340
320
300
280
260
240

1983   1984   1985   1986

J J A S O N D J F M A M J J A S O N D J F M A M J J A S O N D J F M A M J J A S O N D J F M A M J J A S O N D J F M A

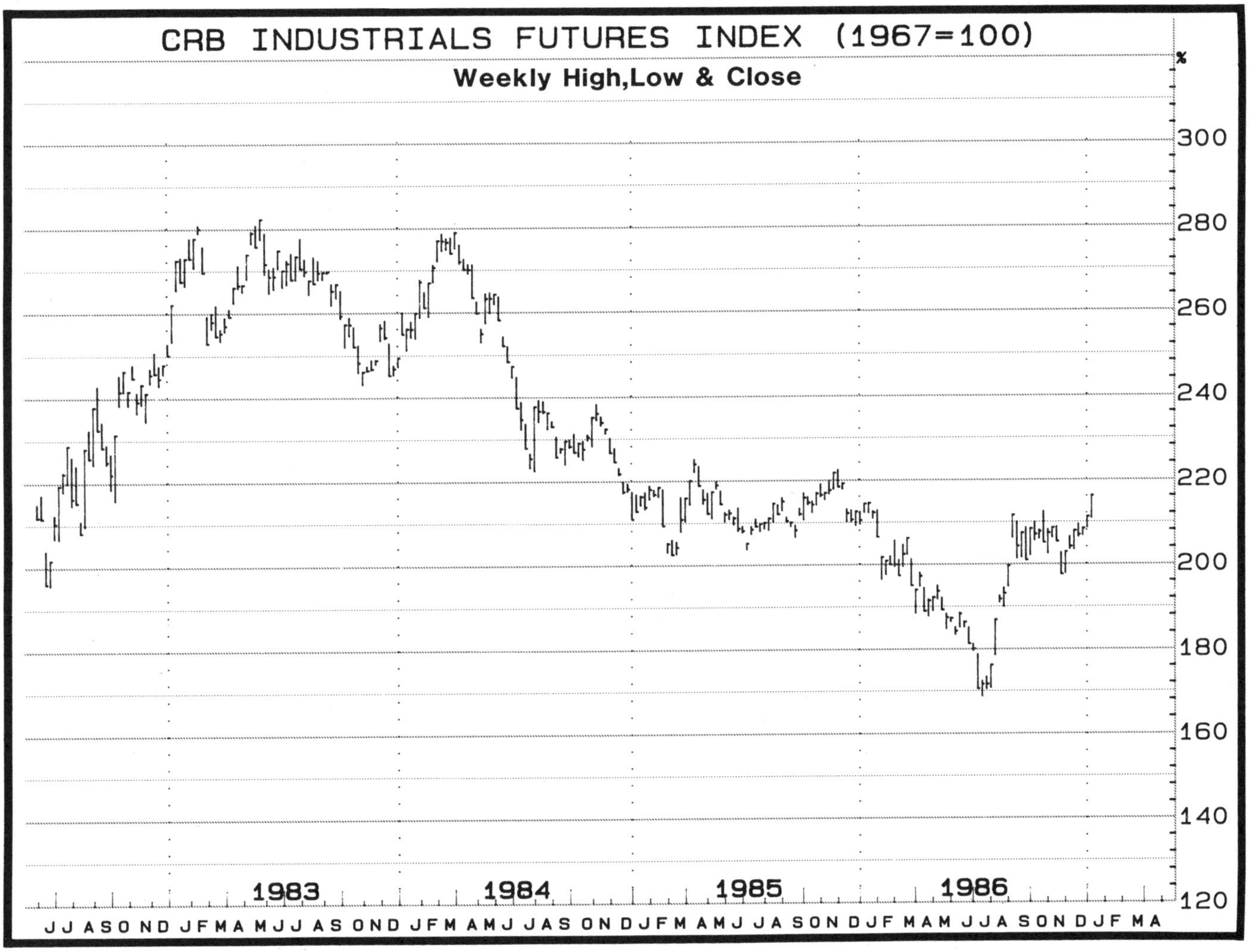

CRB INDUSTRIALS FUTURES INDEX (1967=100)
Weekly High, Low & Close

%

300
280
260
240
220
200
180
160
140
120

1983   1984   1985   1986

J J A S O N D J F M A M J J A S O N D J F M A M J J A S O N D J F M A M J J A S O N D J F M A M J J A S O N D J F M A

11T

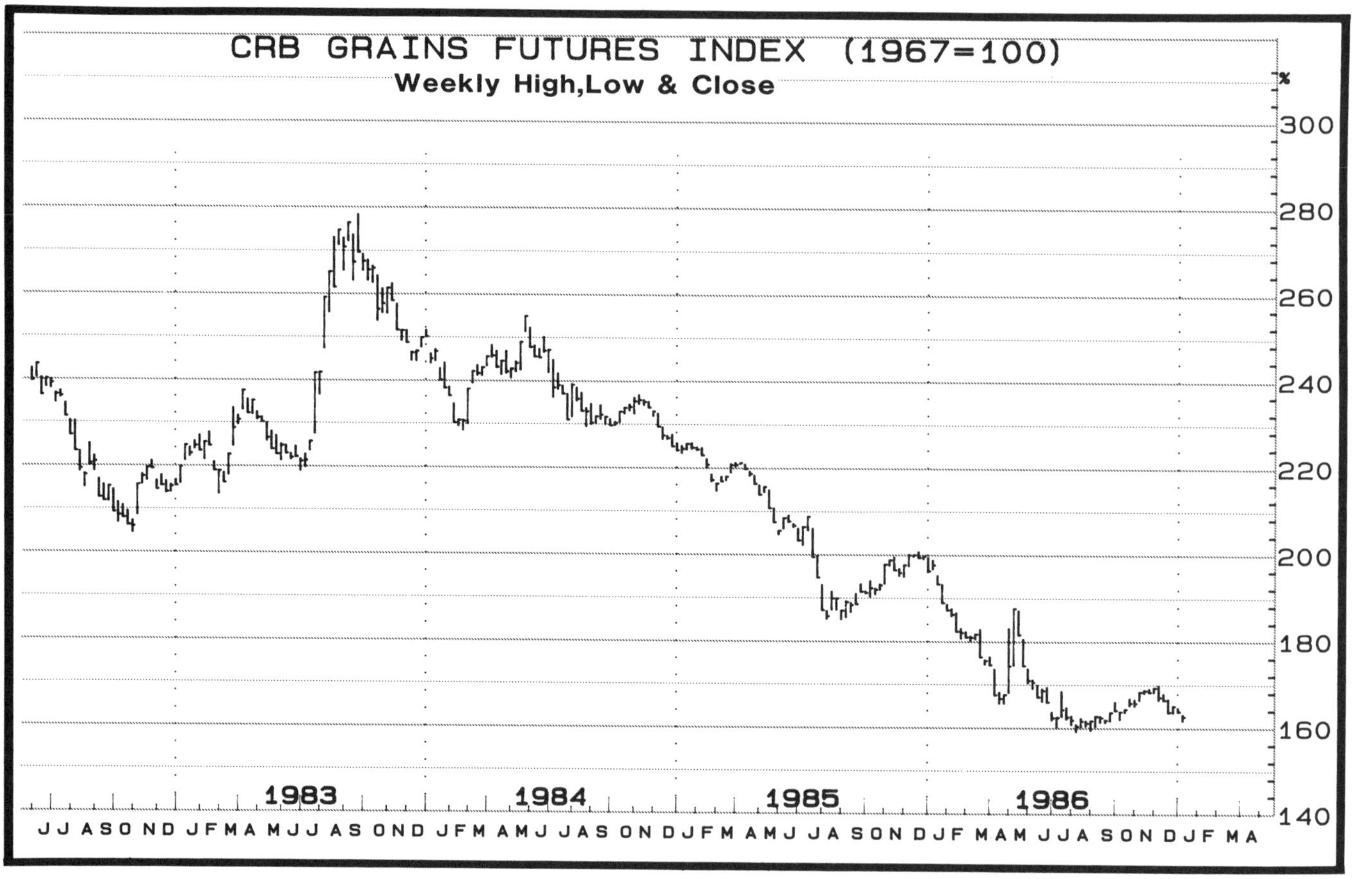
CRB GRAINS FUTURES INDEX (1967=100)
Weekly High,Low & Close
%
300
280
260
240
220
200
180
160
140
1983
1984
1985
1986
J J A S O N D J F M A M J J A S O N D J F M A M J J A S O N D J F M A M J J A S O N D J F M A M J J A S O N D J F M A

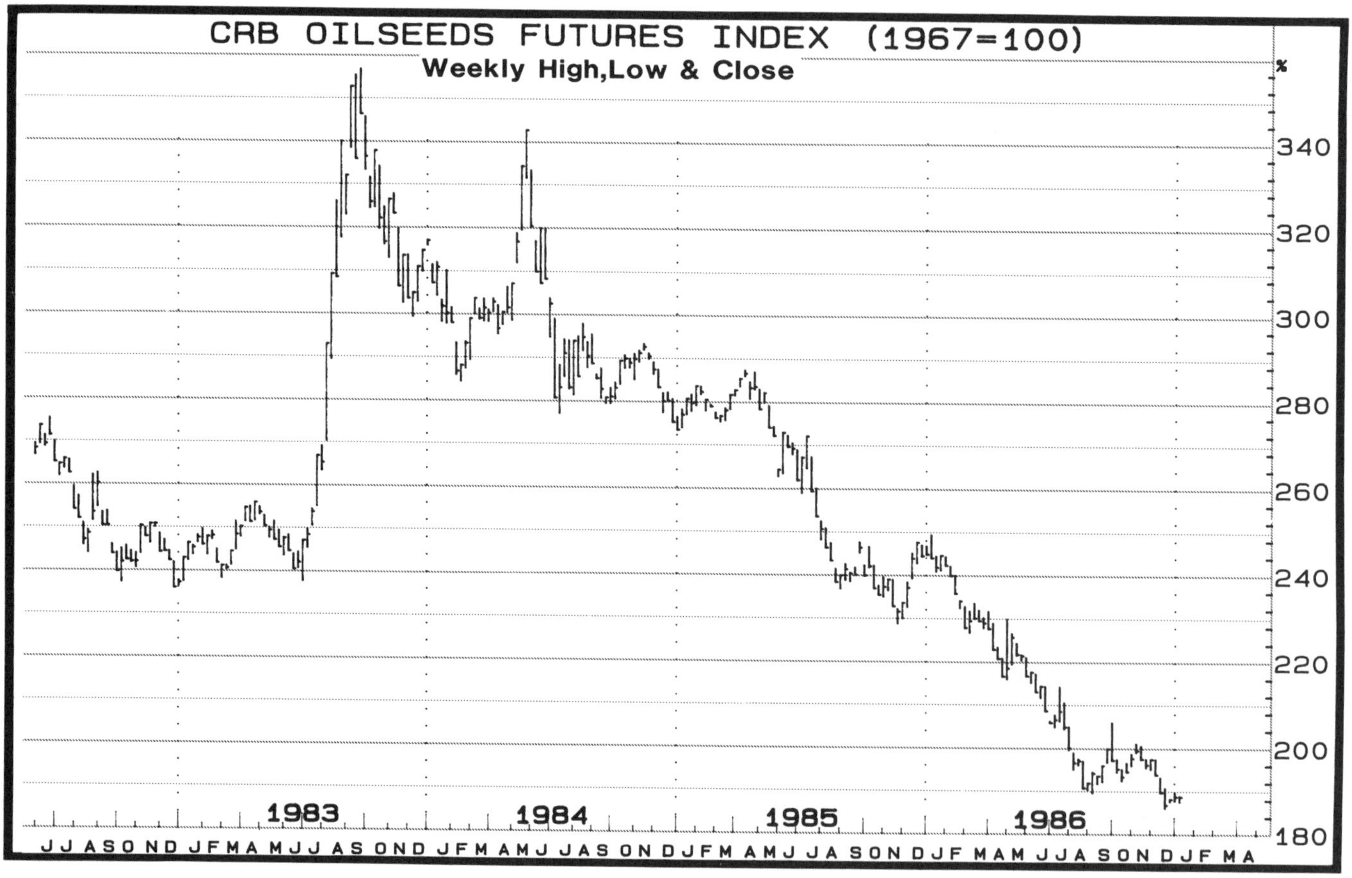
CRB OILSEEDS FUTURES INDEX (1967=100)
Weekly High,Low & Close
%
340
320
300
280
260
240
220
200
180
1983
1984
1985
1986
J J A S O N D J F M A M J J A S O N D J F M A M J J A S O N D J F M A M J J A S O N D J F M A M J J A S O N D J F M A

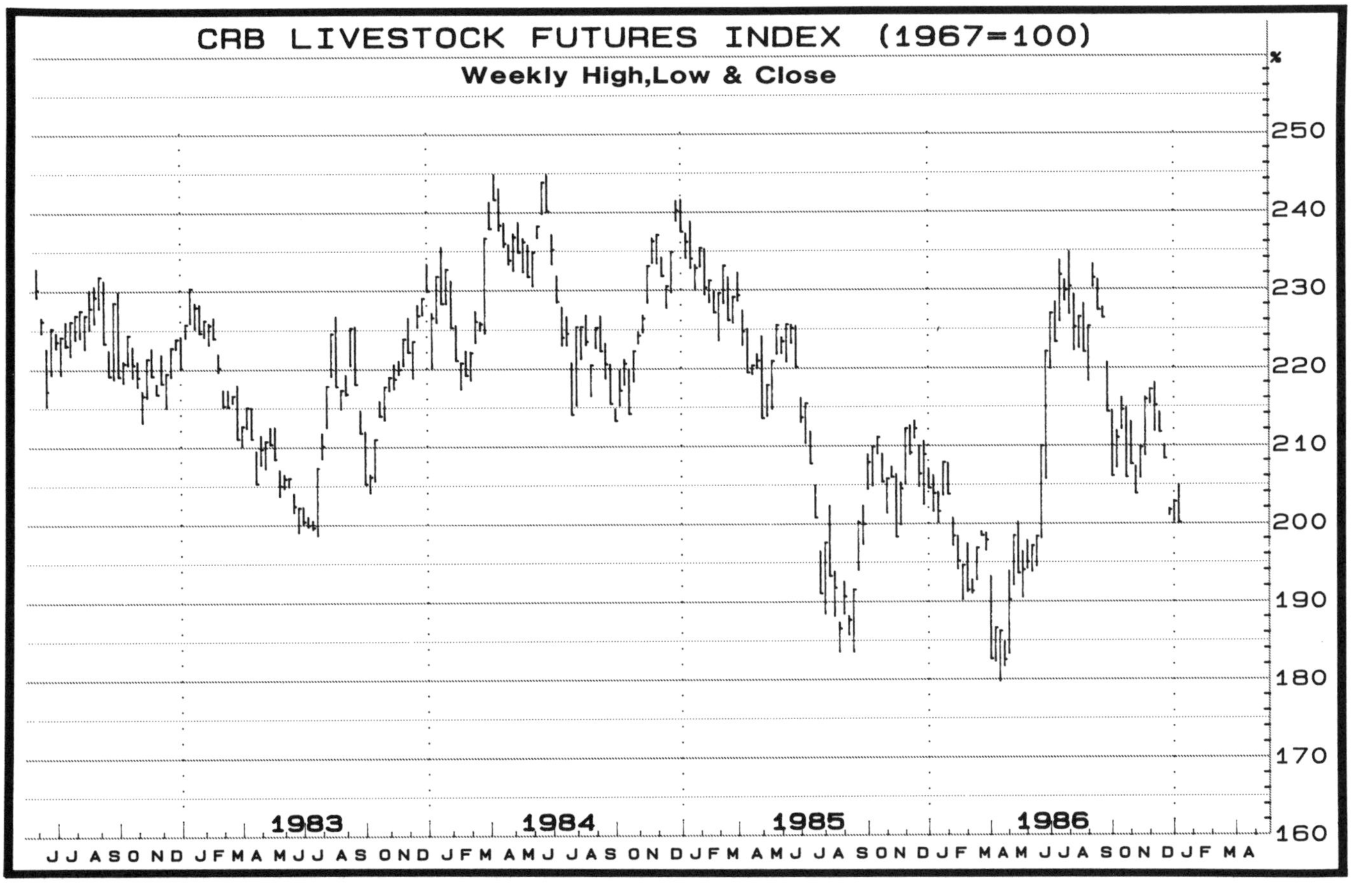

CRB LIVESTOCK FUTURES INDEX (1967=100)
Weekly High, Low & Close

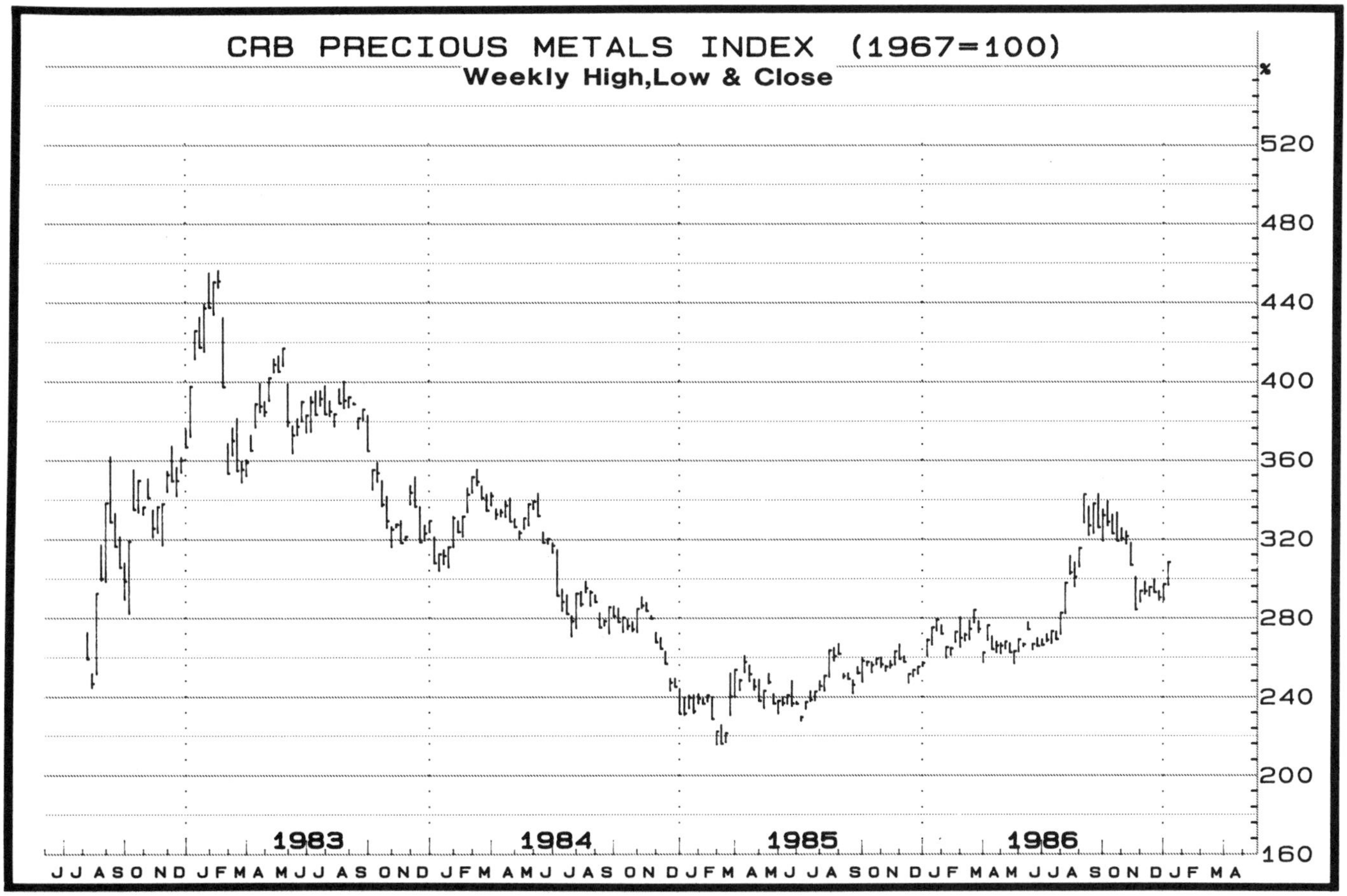

CRB PRECIOUS METALS INDEX (1967=100)
Weekly High, Low & Close

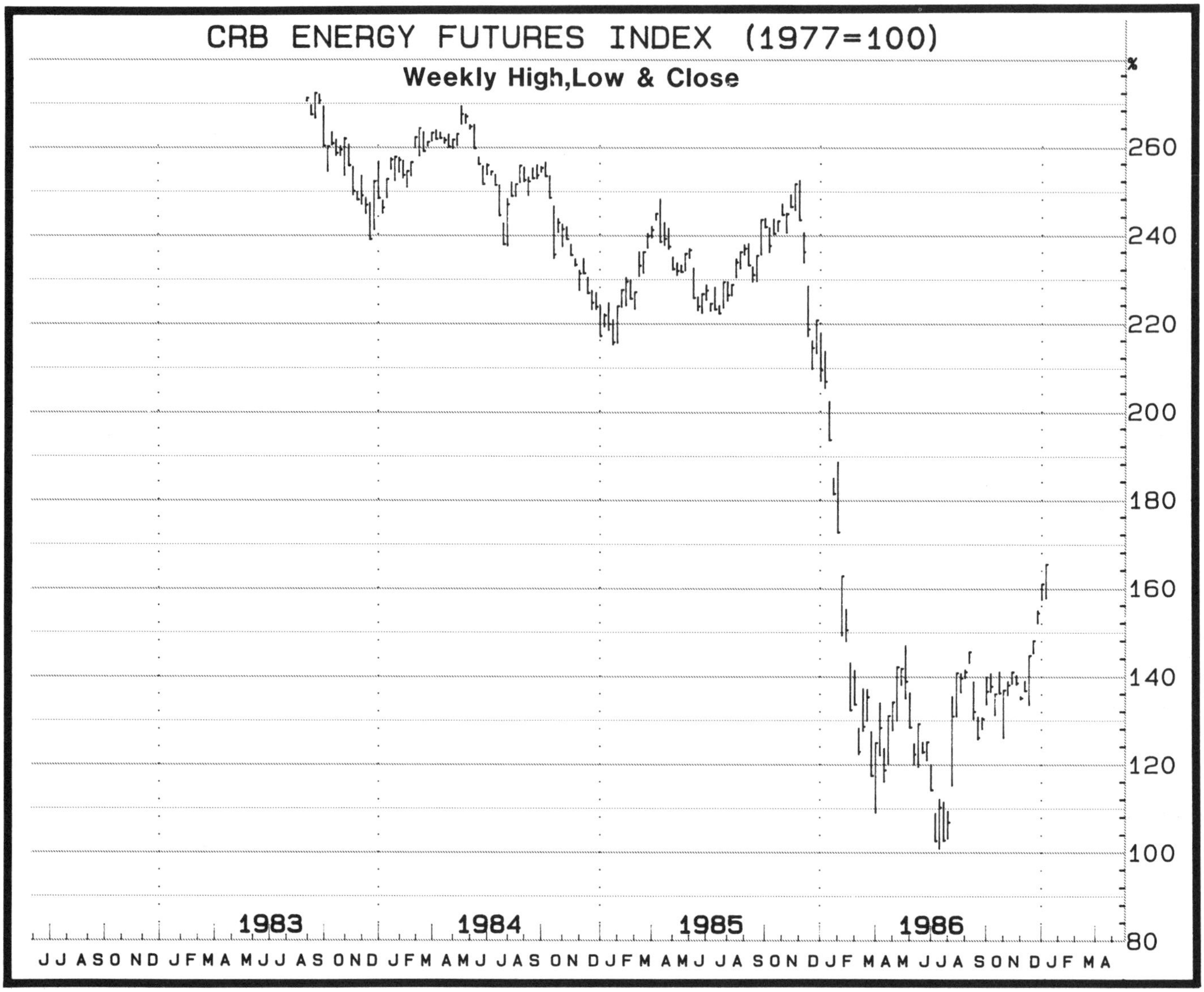

CRB ENERGY FUTURES INDEX (1977=100)
Weekly High, Low & Close

1983   1984   1985   1986

J J A S O N D J F M A M J J A S O N D J F M A M J J A S O N D J F M A M J J A S O N D J F M A

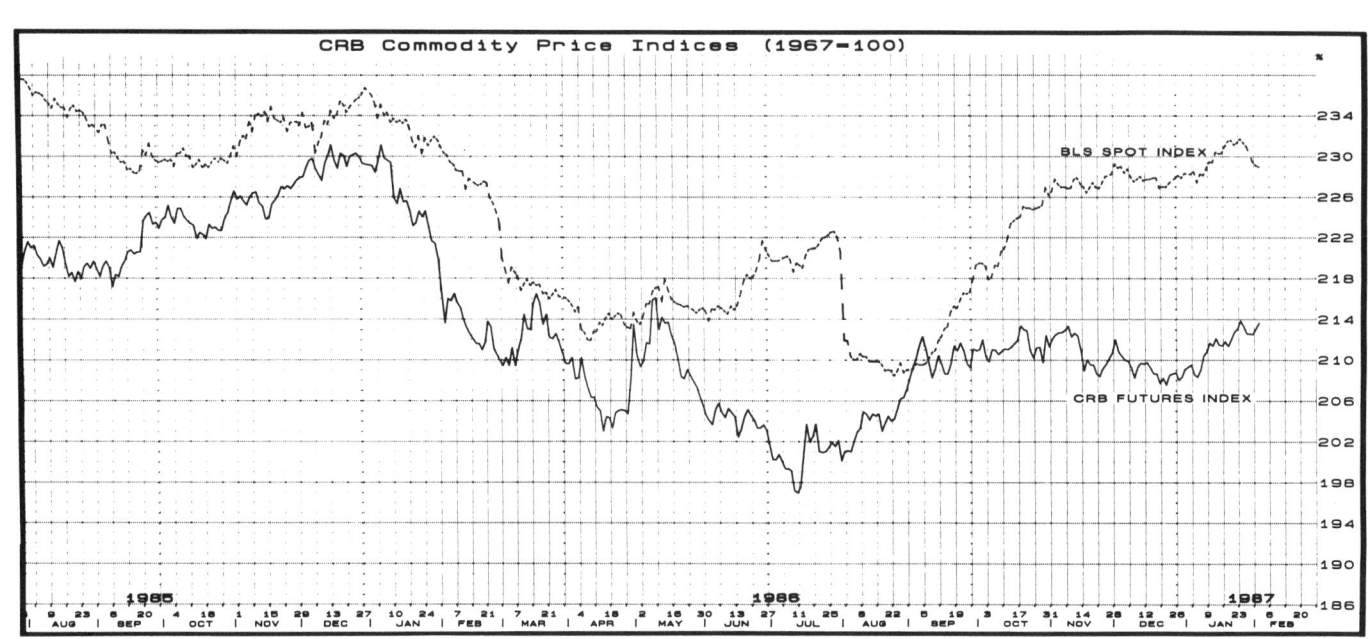

CRB Commodity Price Indices (1967=100)

BLS SPOT INDEX

CRB FUTURES INDEX

1985   1986   1987

9 23 | 6 20 | 4 18 | 1 15 29 | 13 27 | 10 24 | 7 21 | 7 21 | 4 18 | 2 16 30 | 13 27 | 11 25 | 8 22 | 5 19 | 3 17 31 | 14 28 | 12 26 | 9 23 | 6 20
| AUG | SEP | OCT | NOV | DEC | JAN | FEB | MAR | APR | MAY | JUN | JUL | AUG | SEP | OCT | NOV | DEC | JAN | FEB |

THE U.S. AGRICULTURAL DILEMMA AND PROSPECTS FOR CHANGE

BY RICHARD A. LOEWY

The U.S. agricultural sector has been beset by problems since the early 1980s, which have made a uniform, stable, long-term farm policy necessary. The array of problems contributing to the sector's current depression-like situation includes: lingering expectations of high inflation in the early 1980s; high domestic interest rates; bloated U.S. land values leveraged at the upper limit; recently tight Federal Reserve monetary policy and concurrent supply-side economics of the Reagan Administration; increasingly hard-nosed lending practices of agricultural banks; domestic support and set-aside programs that provide farmer incentives not to plant, while current law encourages planting of the full amount allowable; and the pattern of lower U.S. agricultural exports and loss of market share since 1981. In addition, U.S. prices have been dragged downward by burdensome stocks of grain and lower support prices specified by the 1985 Farm Bill.

The U.S. agriculture sector currently accounts for 18 percent of domestic GNP. About 2 percent is accounted for by the farming sector; 2 percent by the input sector (including equipment, supplies, feed, seed, fertilizer and labor); and the remaining 14 percent by downstream sectors of storing, processing, transporting, manufacturing, distribution, retailing and exporting. In the late 1920s, prior to the Depression, the farm sector contributed 25 percent of domestic GNP.

The demise of the farm sector began in the late 1970s, when farmers were caught up in the prevailing psychology of continuing double-digit inflation. Ownership of hard assets was the route to build up an estate, and this sometimes offset pragmatic planning.

Land values, which were bloated and reached their peak in 1981, were used as collateral to borrow money from banks at exorbitant interest rates in order to purchase more farmland or to augment input utilization. Good demand for U.S. exports and higher price levels, fanned by an inflationary bonfire, further encouraged optimism in the 1970s.

Paul Volcker, architect of Federal Reserve policy during the 1980s, successfully implemented a tight U.S. monetary policy designed to reduce double-digit inflation, strengthen the U.S. dollar, lower interest rates to single digits, raise domestic GNP, and promote a strong rally in the stock and bond markets. Commodity prices spiraled downwards and supply-side economic policy, in conjunction with Fed policies, produced record budget and trade deficits.

President Reagan's commitment not to raise taxes, along with overly optimistic GNP forecasts by his economic advisors, caused larger-than-forecast budget deficits. The strong dollar weakened U.S. exports and encouraged imports. In fact, during 1986, there was an unprecedented, three-consecutive-month U.S. farm trade deficit, which served to underscore the gravity of the trade problem.

U.S. farmers were suddenly caught in a serious financial bind in the 1980s. Land values plummeted, so they could not borrow on assets. The interest rate spread between lending and current rates (up to a 15-percent differential) put producers in a continual cash-flow squeeze; debt-service requirements soared and incomes stagnated. Rapid price declines for farm machinery and equipment frustrated efforts to reduce debt loans by selling assets. At the same time, banks were compelled to clamp down on extending further loans to farmers and became the focus of bankruptcy proceedings. (Table 1)

By contrast, those farmers who were not heavily indebted maintained their net income with the aid of government programs for major crops, in spite of low price levels.

The farm sector's problems have been exacerbated by various government programs, which have often impeded the farmer from exercising sound, market-oriented decisions. Production of a program crop such as wheat, feedgrains, cotton or rice, allows placement of the product in a nine-month loan program at Commodity Credit Corporation's (CCC) prevailing interest rates. At the expiration of the period, the farmer forfeits the crop under loan to the CCC if market prices are too low, or places product in a Re-

Table 1
U.S. Agricultural Land Values
(dollars per acre)

State	1981	1982	1983	1984	1985	1986	% Chg. 1981/1986[1]
Pennsylvania	1,568	1,513	1,520	1,642	1,510	1,458	−7.0
Minnesota	1,281	1,272	1,165	1,083	823	609	−52.5
Ohio	1,831	1,629	1,504	1,444	1,126	1,013	−44.7
Indiana	2,031	1,804	1,610	1,594	1,259	1,058	−47.9
Illinois	2,188	2,023	1,837	1,800	1,314	1,143	−47.8
Iowa	1,999	1,889	1,684	1,499	1,064	841	−57.9
Missouri	990	945	856	659	659	606	−38.8
Nebraska	729	730	701	617	444	364	−50.1
South Carolina	972	980	946	927	899	872	−10.3
Missouri	1,034	981	894	939	835	752	−27.3
National Average	819	823	788	782	679	596	−27.2

[1] The largest land value declines from 1981–1986 were in the highest yielding farm states.
Source: Economic Research Service, USDA.

serve program, which then removes the product for up to three years, unless a trigger-release price is reached. These market-removing mechanisms usually have a positive price impact and at least encourage prices to trend toward the loan rates. (1986/87 corn prices are a strong exception.) Further financial inducements have been provided if farmers set aside land or enter a paid diversion program. However, price support and set-aside programs have often postponed adjustments to underlying market realities.

Government programs tend to discourage farmers from concentrating on maximizing cost-efficiency and provide little incentive for aggressive marketing of products. Fixed costs constitute a high proportion of total costs in farming and, in most cases, returns from additional output exceed the variable costs of production. To minimize losses, farmers will continue producing as long as returns exceed out-of-pocket costs at the margin. This makes it difficult to reduce supplies.

In addition, farmers are compelled to plant excessively in spite of acreage-reduction programs, since eligibility for income support payments is tied to entry in government programs. This creates an environment that approximates centralized planning, and discourages farmers from planting for more sound economic reasons. The situation might be remedied by the transition payment "decoupling" concept proposed by Senator Boschwitz of Minnesota (discussed in a later section).

The 1973 U.S. Farm Act permitted farmers to receive deficiency payments based on their allotments, regardless of how many acres they planted. In too

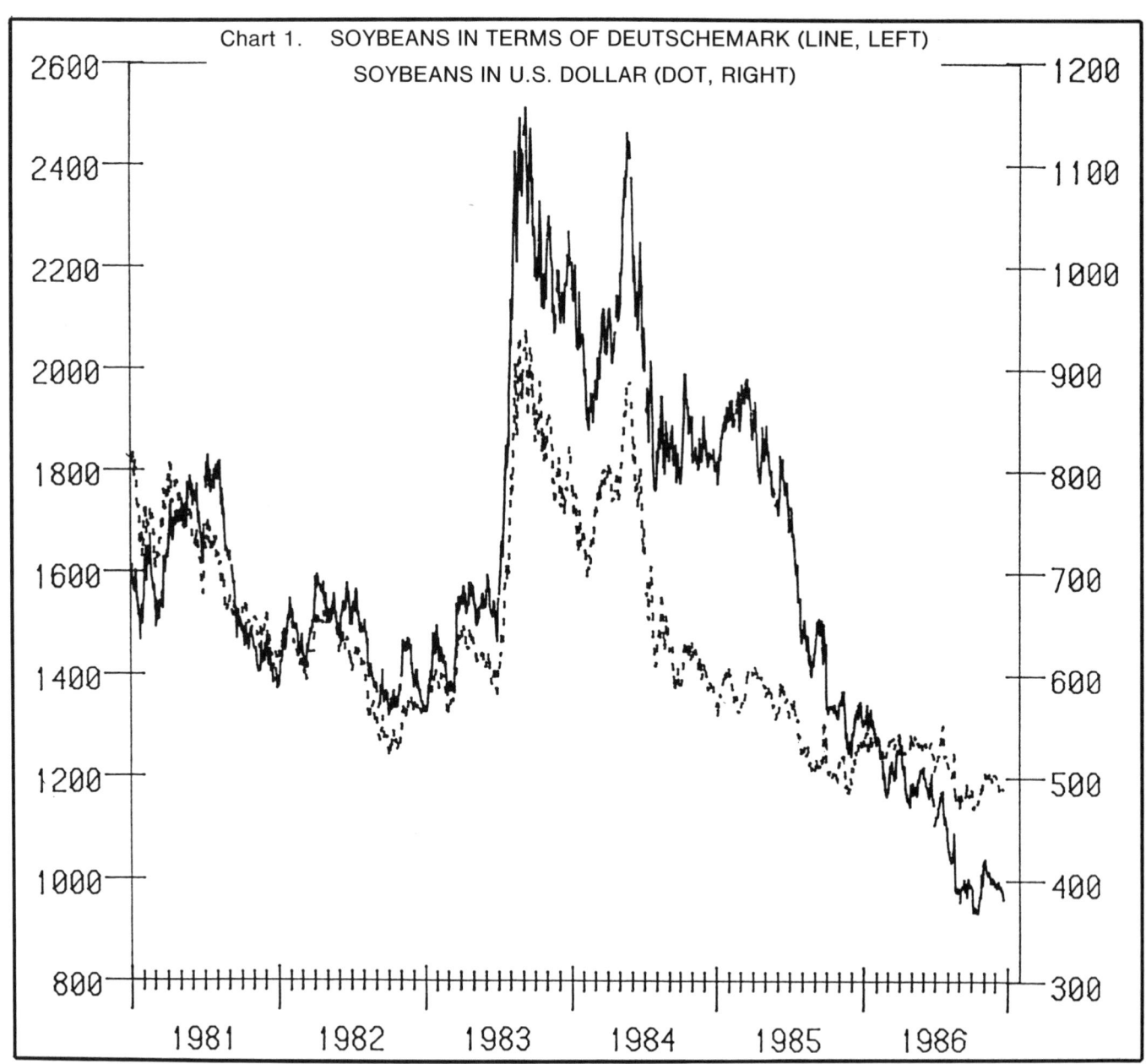

Source: Prudential-Bache Securities Inc.

many cases, however, allotments were out of line with current planting patterns. The 1977 Act replaced allotments with the current planting concept. Deficiency payments were to be based on normal production from current plantings. Set-aside programs during 1978 and 1979 did, in fact, reduce wheat acreage to some extent. Strong exports eliminated the need for further acreage-control programs until 1982, the first year under the Agriculture and Food Act of 1981. The 1981 Act continued the target price deficiency payment program, Farmer-Owned Reserve program and set-aside program authority. Unfortunately, target prices were based on higher-than-anticipated forecasts of inflation. The higher deficiency payments contributed to increased planted acreage for wheat during the 1980s.

The U.S. in the World Market

U.S. exports began to decline during the 1981/82 crop year. From 1981/82–1985/86, losses in the U.S. share of the wheat export market were 18.4%; coarse grains—18.5%; soybeans—8.9%; soybean meal—6.0%; and soybean oil—8.8%. The U.S. soybean complex market-share loss would have been worse had the Brazilian soybean drought not occurred in 1985/86. In the same year, the weak U.S. dollar helped to improve U.S. exports of soybeans and soybean meal to the European Community (EC) and Asian countries.

The chart on the preceding page reveals the impact of currency shifts between the U.S. dollar and West German mark on the price of a bushel of soybeans. Note that the strong U.S. dollar versus the mark (from 1981 to 1985) was a determining factor in lower U.S. exports of soybeans. The trend reversed itself in September, 1985. (Chart 1, Table 2)

The much-publicized U.S. grain embargo, imposed on the USSR in 1979 by the Carter administration, indicated to the world that the U.S. can and will turn off the food spigot. The U.S. has since been treated as a residual supplier by the Soviet Union, which has also prompted other importing countries to secure non-U.S. sources of grains. Another impact of the embargo is that the Soviet Union has not directly purchased U.S. soybean meal since 1979.

High domestic support prices of the 1981 Farm Bill—corn ($2.55), wheat ($3.30) and soybeans ($5.02)—led other export nations (Canada, Australia, Argentina for wheat; the EC, Argentina and Brazil for soybeans; and Argentina for corn) to key off higher U.S. support prices, on a C.I.F. (cost, insurance, freight) basis and to undercut U.S. prices. This has been a principal determining factor in the loss of U.S. market share.

The international debt crisis, which began in 1982 and particularly involved the Latin countries of Brazil, Argentina, and Mexico, triggered declining U.S. exports and rising U.S. imports from Latin America, and resulted in a negative U.S. trade balance. In order to obtain dollars to pay interest on their external debt, nations began reducing purchases of all U.S. exports. At the export peak in 1981, Latin American purchases of U.S. farm products totaled $6.9 billion, or 15 percent of total U.S. farm exports. In the wake of the debt crisis, however, U.S. agricultural exports tumbled one-third below their 1981 level, to $4.5 billion. Nearly 20 percent of the total decline in U.S. farm exports during those four years

was the result of dwindling sales to Latin America. (Tables 3 and 4)

In 1982, Mexico announced it was unable to pay interest on its debt obligations. It became increasingly apparent that Mexico was not alone in its financial difficulties; total Latin American debt was in excess of $318 billion, with annual interest of $38.5 billion. About 85 percent of the total debt was owed to private creditors, and one-third of that to U.S. commercial banks.

Table 2

U.S. Exports of Major Agricultural Commodities (million metric tons)

Product	Year	U.S. Exports	Total World Trade	U.S. Market Share (percent)
Wheat & Wheat Flour	1981/1982	48.2	101.3	47.6
	1982/1983	39.9	98.7	40.4
	1983/1984	38.9	102.0	38.1
	1984/1985	38.1	106.9	35.6
	1985/1986	25.0	85.5	29.2
Coarse Grains	1981/1982	60.0	96.6	62.1
	1982/1983	53.0	89.9	59.0
	1983/1984	56.6	91.9	61.6
	1984/1985	56.6	100.7	56.2
	1985/1986	36.1	82.8	43.6
Soybeans	1981/1982	25.28	29.32	86.2
	1982/1983	24.63	28.59	86.1
	1983/1984	20.21	26.15	77.3
	1984/1985	16.28	25.20	64.6
	1985/1986	20.14[1]	26.06	77.3
Soybean Meal	1981/1982	6.27	20.78	30.2
	1982/1983	6.45	23.29	27.7
	1983/1984	4.86	21.40	22.7
	1984/1985	4.46	22.28	20.0
	1985/1986	5.45[1]	22.49	24.2
Soybean Oil	1981/1982	.94	3.50	26.9
	1982/1983	.92	3.81	24.1
	1983/1984	.83	3.97	20.9
	1984/1985	.75	3.66	20.5
	1985/1986	.57	3.15	18.1

[1] U.S. soybeans and soybean meal exports were higher-than-normal due to the Brazilian drought.
Source: USDA, FAS/ERS trade data.

Table 3

Exports/Imports of Latin America (billion U.S. dollars)

	1981	1982	1983	1984	1985[1]
Total Exports	108.2	97.6	97.6	103.9	93.3
Total Imports	119.3	96.5	75.9	75.1	50.2
Trade Balance	−11.1	1.1	21.7	28.8	43.1
U.S. Exports	42.1	33.6	25.7	29.7	31.0
U.S. Imports	40.8	39.6	43.6	50.1	49.1
U.S. Trade Balance with Latin America	1.3	−6.0	−17.9	−20.4	−18.1

[1] Annualizing first 6 months data
Source: International Monetary Fund.

Table 4

U.S. Exports to Major Latin American Debtor Nations
(thousand metric tons)

	SOYBEANS		SOYMEAL		SOYOIL		CORN		WHEAT	
	81/82	85/86	81/82	85/86	81/82	85/86	81/82	85/86	81/82	85/86
Argentina										
Bolivia									0	114
Brazil	146	198			8	0	0	1158	3115	722
Chile					1	0	306	0	1020	463
Dom Rep	26	48	37	61	42	6	178	154	145	232
Ecuador	19	0	0	0	41	24			304	392
Mexico	251	809	10	64	83	56	476	1446	767	0
Peru	7	0	23	41	50	0	481	222	946	153
Uruguay							0	6	0	0
Venezuela	82	160	515	591	47	12	403	0	829	612
Total	531	1215	585	757	272	98	1844	2986	7126	2688

Source: USDA, U.S. Export Sales.

U.S. officials devised a strategy to insure debtor countries would continue servicing their debts and to prevent serious damage to the U.S. banking system. The priority of protecting the banking system sometimes came at the expense of the U.S. farmer. The strategy involved four objectives: debtor nations would increase exports and cut imports to generate money to service their debts; loans would be restructured to allow more time to repay maturing loans; commercial banks would make new loans to keep debtor nations from falling behind on interest payments; and the International Monetary Fund (IMF) would monitor debtors to insure implementation of essential economic reforms.

Partly as a result of these activities, the three largest debtor nations (Mexico, Brazil and Argentina) increased export volume by 62 percent, 56 percent, and 47 percent, respectively. However, the consequent drop in commodities prices, precipitated by increased production and exports, limited export revenue increases (Mexico—34 percent, Brazil—25 percent, and Argentina—3 percent).

International lending institutions, to which the U.S. is the leading monetary contributor, have, over time, assisted developing countries in agriculture by providing financial assistance to increase exports, and by giving financial and technical assistance to augment acreage and yields and to develop an infrastructure for the integration of developing countries' agricultural systems. Multilateral institutions have had an impact on improving the agricultural sectors of some developing countries that have been significant importers of U.S. grains and oilseeds, such as China, India, Mexico, Pakistan, Bangladesh, and the principal U.S. soybean export competitor, Brazil.

Due to the efforts of such groups as the American Soybean Association, Congress and other U.S. farm groups have become more aware of the problems involved in providing assistance to nations that directly compete with U.S. exports. Increasing Congressional pressure may be brought to bear on foreign loans that could result in competition with U.S. exports. (Several examples of controversial development loans are noted below.[1])

[1] A $350 million World Bank loan to Argentina in April, 1986, was intended to raise Argentina's exports of soybeans, corn, wheat, sorghum and sunflower. The World Bank stated that reforms would help Argentina earn an additional $1 billion a year in foreign

Technological progress and efforts toward self-sufficiency in principal producing and importing nations have resulted in increased yield and production levels and have caused a shift in terms of trade away from the U.S.

China's increasingly capitalistic approach of providing market incentives to producers in recent years has motivated farmers to raise productivity. Wheat yields have increased from 1.84 metric tons per hectare in 1978/79 to an estimated 3.01 in 1986/87 (a 64-percent rise). In the same time, harvested acreage rose by only 400 thousand hectares, from 29.2 to 29.6 million hectares. Production rose from 53.8 to a prospective-record 89.0 million metric tons, an increase of 65 percent. Chinese wheat imports averaged 13.3 million metric tons from 1981–1983; prospective

exchange by 1989. The aim was to permit Argentina to raise export revenue to pay its foreign debt by shifting its tax burden from exports to a land-based system. The Argentines will strive to raise production, since taxation will not increase with rises in production and exports, as it does with per-unit export taxes. (The best current example is the impact of Argentina's planted wheat acreage. Argentinian planting intentions, prior to the World Bank loans, were to lower wheat acreage by at least 20 percent, from 5.3 million hectares to 4.2 million. The 12-percent decline in the export tax—from 27 to 15 percent—prompted the Argentines to reduce planting by only 4 percent, to 5.1 million hectares. Similarly, what might have been a nominal increase in soybean plantings, 2–3 percent, will probably result in a 10–12 percent increase.)

From 1965 to 1975, the World Bank, the Inter-American Development Bank and the Asian Development Bank made 32 loans, totaling over $300 million, for augmenting palm oil production in developing countries. Twenty of the loans were approved after 1970. Substantial loans have continued to the present and have contributed to a worldwide glut of vegetable oils. U.S. imports of palm oil, which compete with domestic soybean oil, will be approximately 75 percent greater in 1986 than last year. A record world palm oil production figure of 4.8 million metric tons can be anticipated for 1986/1987 and steady annual growth of up to 10–12 percent is forecast until the year 2000. Unfortunately, the excessive palm oil production capacity in the world exists due to multilateral financing at interest rates below what were available in the U.S.

A 15-year, $200 million variable interest loan to Brazil was approved, in February, 1986, to improve the railway systems north of the states expanding soybean production. This will further lower the Brazilian export price of soybeans. Fortunately for the U.S., Brazil has embarked on a long-term plan of increasing acreage to feed the Brazilian people (which signifies greater domestic incentives to plant feedgrains, rice, black beans, etc., than to promote the export market of the soybean complex). This has occurred in the southern soybean producing states, where acreage has shifted out of soybeans into alternative crops. Lower world prices of soybeans have been an additional factor in curtailed acreage plantings in the South.

1986/87 imports are a diminished 6.5 million metric tons, with the strong probability that China will not buy wheat from the U.S. The increased domestic utilization of wheat of 35 million metric tons, from 1978/79 to 1986/87, has freed up some coarse grain production for export. Coarse grain production has been relatively stable over the past few years. From 1978/79 to 1983/84, China's exports ranged from 100 to 500 thousand metric tons. In the last 3 years, average exports have been around 6.27 million tons. Market incentives have also prompted a 15-percent expansion in corn production and a 20-percent increase in rice production.

The Soviet Union relies on sales of gold and crude petroleum at recently lower prices for grain purchases. This has prompted the USSR to be more judicious in optimizing imports and has spurred a drive for greater efficiency in the agricultural sector. The total Soviet 1986/87 grain crop of 210 million metric tons, the largest since 1978, probably reflects excellent moisture conditions during the critical growing periods, rather than innovative, short-term, technological advances by the Gorbachev Administration. The Administration is apparently determined to increase yields and to overhaul the entire antiquated agricultural system, but years of change must occur before any profound impact on the sector is evident. The Soviets continue to strive for self-sufficiency and are jealously monitoring agricultural progress in China. The USSR will have imported only 19 million metric tons of grains during 1986/87, versus the prior 5-year average of 38.7 million tons.

The European Community (EC) has successfully encouraged increased wheat plantings to attain self-sufficiency by implementing the Common Agricultural Policy (CAP). European farmers, unlike their American counterparts, are paid to increase their plantings. EC wheat production levels rose from 40 million to 82.9 million metric tons, a 107-percent increase. Yields have increased 51 percent, from 3.66 to 5.52 metric tons per hectare.

There are other, less dramatic examples of this trend toward self-sufficiency. India will be a net exporter of 500,000 metric tons of wheat this year; the next step will be acreage expansion and increased productivity of oilseeds. Pakistan is now close to self-sufficiency. Argentine wheat production has doubled, with government priority for agricultural production at the expense of a diminishing livestock sector in the Pampas. Brazil will continue to increase soybean production in the Northern states (Cerrados region) where 50 million hectares could be developed. In this region, there is access to limestone supplies (indispensable for alleviating acidity in the soil). Also, stable moisture from the Amazon region has greatly benefited yields. Thailand's feed grain output has nearly tripled; Australia and Canada have had major production increases, as well.

Foreign countries often have implemented export subsidies successfully. However, the U.S. frequently stumbles, and bears the brunt of adverse international public opinion, when it implements an export subsidy. A case in point was the recent implementation of the Export Enhancement Program (EEP), which combines wheat volume from commercial sources at market prices and cheaper-priced CCC stocks at price levels required to undercut other nations in the export market. With the program, the U.S. has been successful in obtaining additional export business in Egypt, Turkey, Morocco, Tunisia, Algeria and Iraq. However, the implementation of this program infuriated some long-term, high-volume U.S. grain customers not chosen to participate. The U.S. offered EEP wheat to the Soviet Union, but was rejected, in part because the USSR had a large crop, but also because it was not included on the original EEP list. The U.S. government recently offered one million metric tons of EEP wheat to China; as of mid-March, 1986, the country had purchased over 800,000 tons under the program.

The flexibility of some competitor countries in implementing export policy has been disadvantageous to the U.S. Brazil and Argentina recently converted their respective currencies—to the cruzado (from the cruzeiro) and to the austral (from the peso)—to lower inflation and to spur economic growth. Unfortunately, when the U.S. dollar was strong against foreign currencies, from 1981–1985, Brazil and Argentina undercut the U.S. in export markets. Both the cruzado and the austral are now pegged to the U.S. dollar, which (since 1985) has not provided the U.S. with an export advantage over these two nations. Furthermore, both countries have the flexibility of devaluing their currencies before large import tenders, which is an additional competitive export price advantage.

The Current U.S. Supply Situation

The U.S. is projectd to register record-breaking carryover levels in the 1986/87 season for wheat, corn, and soybeans. Commensurately, average prices to farmers are likely to decline further. (Tables 5, 6, & 7)

Burdensome stocks of the three principal U.S. cash crops have resulted from large crops, declining export demand, and stable-to-slightly-higher domestic use. In spite of declining wheat acreage in four of the last five years, and falling corn and soybean areas in three of those five years, excellent yields (except for wheat) have propped up the supply figures. A record soybean yield (1985/86 crop) and record corn yield (1986/87 crop) have been the culprits, under a lower-trend scenario for planted acreage, in not allowing production levels to fall enough. Sharply lower average farmer price levels projected for 1986/87 are as follows: wheat $2.20–$2.50; corn $1.20–$1.70; and soybeans $4.50–$5.10. These are due to the prospective record carry-over levels of all products and lower support prices established in the 1985 Farm Bill. Crop loan rates and target prices from 1986 to 1990, as specified by the new farm legislation are displayed below (Table 8).

The formula loan rates for 1986 wheat and corn were set at $3.00 and $2.40, respectively. The Secretary of Agriculture, through the Findley Amendment, dropped both rates 20 percent—to $2.40 and $1.92, respectively. The Gramm-Rudmann-Hollings 4.3-percent budget reduction further lowered final loan rates for wheat (to $2.30) and for corn (to $1.84). Historically, U.S. support prices define floor prices, and this will apply for the 1986/87 wheat and soybean crops. Corn has already trended some 34 cents below the loan rate, because of burdensome stocks and the fact that it has been the main crop taken in payment-in-kind (PIK) certificate redemptions.

Farm Policy and the Boschwitz/Boren Plan

The problems affecting the agriculture sector will require strong remedies. A significant first step has been the implementation of the 1985 Farm Bill.

The precepts of the 1985 Farm Bill were principally established through the efforts of Senator Rudy Boschwitz (Minnesota) and Senator David Boren (Oklahoma). Three main goals underlie the Bill: to protect farm income during an eight-year transition period; to promote full production and allow farmers to make decisions based on economic signals, not government programs; and, to enhance the competitiveness of U.S. exports.

The Boschwitz/Boren plan was to replace traditional systems of acreage reduction and target prices with a transition payment giving farmers adequate cash flow, as U.S. agricultural exports regain their competitiveness on world markets. For wheat, corn, cotton and rice, a transition payment would be established to provide farmers at full production the same income over variable costs as was earned in the 1985 acreage reduction program. Loan rates would be reduced and the transition payment would bring income to that level. (For example, if a farm had a 200-acre corn base and a 100-bushel-per-acre yield, it would receive $0.94 multiplied by 20,000 bushels. The total payment would be $18,800.)

The transition payment would be made regardless of what was produced on the land during 1986

Table 5

U.S. Wheat Supply/Demand Balance
June/May Crop Year
(million bushels)

	1982/83	1983/84	1984/85	1985/86	USDA 1986/87	Pru-Bache 1986/87	Pru-Bache 1987/88
Beginning stocks on June 1	1,159	1,515	1,399	1,425	1,905	1,905	1,942
Imports	8	4	9	15	10	10	10
Production	2,765	2,420	2,595	2,425	2,077	2,077	2,015[3]
Total supply	3,932	3,939	4,003	3,865	3,992	3,992	3,967
Food	616	635	650	678	690	710	
Seed	97	100	93	93	90	90	
Feed/Seed/Residual	195	376	411	273	350	325[1]	
Total domestic use	908	1,111	1,154	1,045	1,130	1,125	
Exports	1,509	1,429	1,424	915	975	925[2]	
Total use	2,417	2,540	2,578	1,960	2,105	2,050	
Ending stocks May 31	1,515	1,399	1,425	1,905	1,887	1,942	
Ending stocks as % of total:							
Use	63	55	55	97	90	95	
Production	55	58	55	79	91	94	

[1] Based on negative domestic wheat feed estimate Oct.–May.
[2] Assumes no U.S. exports to USSR or PRC.
[3] Based on planted acreage of 65.5 million acres, harvested acreage of 55.6 million, yield of 36.2/bu/acre.
Source: USDA, Prudential-Bache Inc.

Table 6

U.S. Corn Supply/Demand Balance
September/August Crop Year
(million bushels)

	1982/83	1983/84	1984/85	1985/86	USDA 1986/87	Pru-Bache 1986/87	Pru-Bache 1987/88
Beginning stocks on Sept. 1	2,537	3,523	1,006	1,648	4,038	4,038	5,611
Production	8,235	4,175	7,674	8,865	8,223	8,145[1]	7,245[4]
Imports	1	3	4	11	3	3	3
Total Supply	10,773	7,701	8,684	10,524	12,264	12,186	12,859
Feed Use	4,521	3,818	4,116	4,116	4,200	4,350	
Food/Seed/Industrial	895	975	1,055	1,129	1,150	1,175[2]	
Domestic Use	5,416	4,793	5,171	5,245	5,350	5,525	
Exports	1,834	1,902	1,865	1,241	1,125	1,505[3]	
Total Use	7,250	6,695	7,036	6,486	6,475	6,575	
Ending Stocks August 31	3,523	1,006	1,648	4,038	5,789	5,611	
Ending Stocks as Pct of Total:							
Use	49	15	23	62	89	85	
Production	43	24	22	46	70	69	

Notes: [1] Based on harvested acreage of 68,951 million acres and record yield of 118.1 bu/acre.
[2] Based on rising trend of domestic ethanol and high fructose corn syrup demand.
[3] Assumes no U.S. exports to USSR.
[4] Based on planted acreage of 69 million acres, harvested acreage of 63 million and trend yield of 115 bu/acre.
Source: USDA, Prudential-Bache Inc.

Table 7

U.S. Soybean Supply/Demand Balance

September/August Crop Year

(million bushels)

	1982/83	1983/84	1984/85	1985/86	USDA 1986/87	Pru-Bache 1987/88	Pru-Bache 1987/88
September 1							
Stocks	254	345	176	316	536	536	493
Production	2,190	1,636	1,861	2,099	2,009	1,987[1]	1,904[3]
Total Supply	2,444	1,861	2,037	2,415	2,545	2,523	2,397
Crush	1,108	983	1,030	1,053	1,080	1,090[2]	
Exports	905	740	598	740	760	850	
Seed/Feed/Residual	86	82	93	86	90	90	
Total Use	2,099	1,805	1,721	1,879	1,930	2,030	
Ending Stocks August 31	345	176	316	536	615	493	
Ending Stocks As Pct of Total:							
Use	16	10	18	29	32	24	
Production	16	11	17	26	31	25	

Notes: [1] Based on planted acreage of 61,835 million acres, harvested acreage of 59,513 million acres, and yield of 33.4 bu/acre.
[2] Based on Sept-Dec crush rate estimate of 383 million bu.
[3] Based on planted acreage estimate of 61.0 million acres, harvested acreage estimate of 59.5 million acres and trend yield of 32 bu/acre.
Source: USDA, Prudential-Bache Inc.

through 1990. Senator Boschwitz calls this approach "decoupling." Farmers receiving payments would be free to make planting decisions based on the market environment and would not have to plant anything. However, if no crop were produced, an acceptable cover crop or conservation practice would have to be established to qualify for the transition payment.

Table 8

Crop Loan Rates and Target Prices

(U.S. dollars)

Year	Wheat (BU.)	Corn (BU.)	Cotton (LB.)	Rice (CWT.)
1986				
Target loan	$4.38	$3.03	$.81	$11.90
Basic loan	$3.00	$2.40	$.55	$ 7.20
Announced loan	$2.40	$1.92		
1987				
Target loan	$4.38	$3.03	.794	$11.66
Basic loan	$2.85	$2.28	.5225	$ 6.84
Announced loan	$2.28	$1.82		
1988				
Target loan	$4.38	$3.30	.77	$11.30
Basic loan	$2.71	$2.17*		
Announced loan				
1989				
Target loan	$4.16	$2.88	.745	$10.95
Basic loan	$2.57	$2.06		
Announced loan				
1990				
Target loan	$4.00	$2.75	.729	$10.71
Basic loan	$2.44*	$1.96*		
Announced loan				

*Projected minimum rate.
Source: USDA

The concept of full production is to encourage farmers to make market decisions based on economic viability and not on government crop-reduction programs. Transition payments would not be forthcoming for crops grown on 30 million acres of highly erodible land, as defined by the Secretary of Agriculture, unless an approved soil conservation service plan were being followed. Of the 30 million acres, at least 20 million would be accepted into a ten-year conservation acreage reserve by competitive bids. Former wetlands now producing crops could be bid into the Reserve and later revert to wetlands. Land would be in the Reserve for ten years. Farmers would bid to receive either a lump sum payment in the first year of the Reserve or annual payments through the first five years.

Of all the goals of the Farm Bill, the promotion of U.S. exports is most important. Lower support prices are expected to help the competitiveness of U.S. exports over time, as foreign countries curtail planted acreage because of lower world prices. The U.S. would, in fact, impose a market-oriented economy on the rest of the world. Foreign government subsidy incentives to farmers might dissipate over time, beginning with the European Community.

One goal of the 1985 Farm Bill is to establish a "green dollar" program to increase exports by using CCC stocks as a bonus to exporters. The Secretary of Agriculture would accept bids from exporters for the amount of green-dollar certificates needed to complete an export sale. After the shipment had been made, the exporter would redeem his green dollars by exchanging them for CCC-owned commodities, which must be traded on world markets. It is hoped that implementation of this program would occur in a way that would not be offensive to well-established commercial clients, as has been the case with the Export Enhancement Program.

The CCC-stock-reduction program is another method of encouraging U.S. exports. Under this program, the Secretary of Agriculture would take an inventory of all commodities owned by the CCC. About

20 percent of those stocks would be exported for credit program use, provided the commodities were not required to operate the green dollar program. The CCC-owned commodities would be utilized for the intermediate credit programs (GSM-301 and GSM-201), which develop foreign countries' infrastructure for importing and using agricultural commodities, and to expand livestock production. Overseas donations of CCC-owned commodities would also be emphasized.

Conclusion: A More Unified Farm Policy Needed

In the judgment of this writer, the underlying features of the 1985 Farm Bill are well conceived and, if allowed to be carried to fruition through the phase-out period, would allow a market-oriented farm economy that has an excellent chance to succeed. There are, however, some caveats.

A new majority Democratic Congress in both Houses convened in January, 1987, and may be prepared to dismantle some features of the Farm Bill, particularly in view of the Reagan Administration's continuing problems over the Iranian arms deal. A Congress bent on flexing its muscles could provide the impetus for mandatory production controls, higher support prices, and protectionism.

Costs of the 1986 farm program were in the range of $25.6 billion. There is strong political momentum to curtail expenditures, especially given unrealistically high revenue projected by the Gramm-Rudman-Hollings group. A quick-fix would be to reduce target price levels by at least 10 percent, but that would mean less income support for farmers.

Congressional justification to alter the Farm Bill could come from the continuing demise of the U.S. in the export market. Time seems to be on the side of the U.S. in regaining its export market share in the next few years. However, if foreign countries perceive that the U.S. government is shifting away from the precepts of the 1985 Farm Bill, they may see the U.S. as incapable of pursuing an agricultural policy and might opt to expand acreage levels.

The U.S. must promote a unified agricultural policy in order for the farm sector to manage its significant problems. This writer believes that, in addition to the 1985 Farm Bill, a commission should be chosen to study the establishment of an independent agricultural entity, designed to function in a way similar to the Federal Reserve. The presiding officer of the new entity could be appointed to a 12-year term. USDA would carry out the policy of this entity and would not have to contend with inter-agency strife, since decision-making would originate from an outside, independent body.

The U.S. farm policy process has become overwhelming, as increasingly more agricultural committees have sprung up in the House and Senate and in the Office of Management and Budget. This has fragmented the participants and caused significant delays in implementing new legislation. In addition, special interest groups have garnered more power, which has further fragmented the political process. The creativity and efficiency of a more market-oriented sector, as espoused by Senators Boren and Boschwitz, is an indispensable piece to help this important sector of the economy out of its current dilemma.

SPREADS IN FINANCIAL FUTURES

BY PHILLIP E. TIGER

Commodity futures trading has been a factor in the economic activities of the U.S. since the opening of the Chicago Board of Trade (CBT) in 1848. Yet, the most dramatic growth story in futures has been in the past decade, as stock index, currency and interest rate futures have become the volume leaders in trading. (Table 1)

Those who trade futures—hedgers, professional traders, and speculators—have moved to the commodities which have shown consistency, volatility and liquidity; all of these characteristics have been evident in financial futures. Opportunities for the spread trader have developed, as various combinations in the financial markets have demonstrated tradable relationships providing profit potential and hedging advantages.

Currencies were the first to begin trading in 1972. In August, 1971, the Bretton Woods Currency Agreement was dismantled and currencies were allowed to float. This provided an environment where hedging and price speculation in currencies became possible and the International Monetary Market (IMM) of the Chicago Mercantile Exchange (CME) was born. Trading in currencies was somewhat eclipsed in the early 1970s by the dynamic bull markets in agricul-

tural commodities. But, as bullishness began to fade in farm commodities and concurrent activity in other financial markets increased, currency futures and then interest rate futures came into their own. The growing inflation in the U.S. during the middle to late 1970s was a major contributor to currency and interest rate trade; volatility increased greatly during the period and hedging became more a necessity than an option for those involved in international trade, banking and finance.

The principal currencies (in order of January, 1987, open interest and volume) are the West German mark, the British pound, the Japanese yen and the Swiss franc. The Canadian dollar trades actively, though at a fraction of the volume and open interest of the others. The Mexican peso was actively traded until successive devaluations negated its trading appeal (though it is still listed).

Spreads in currencies usually include one versus the other (inter-commodity), such as Deutschemark versus Swiss franc. Inter-delivery currency spreads are not practical for most speculative interests and outside traders, due to their low volatility and very poor volume and open interest beyond the first delivery month (except near the expiration of the lead delivery).

Interest rate futures began with the GNMA contract in 1975 and were followed by Treasury Bills in 1976. The rapid success of GNMAs and T-Bills led to the introduction, in 1977, of the 90-day Commercial Paper contract (which never gained much popularity) and the long-term (30-year) Treasury Bond contract. In the 1980s, the T-Bond contract became the most popular and actively traded futures contract.

The 10-year T-Note contract on the CBT was introduced in May, 1982, and gained popularity fairly rapidly, primarily as a spreading vehicle against T-Bonds. Futures in Certificates of Deposit and Eurodollars were introduced in 1980 on the IMM. Eurodollars have, in the past five years, become the most actively traded contract on the IMM. The Municipal Bond Index was introduced on the CBT in 1984 and gained in popularity as a spreading vehicle against T-Bonds.

Some evolution in interest rate futures has occurred, due to domestic economic conditions. One example is the reduced popularity of the GNMA contract. When mortgage interest rates rose in the late 1970s and peaked in 1981, rates accelerated to nearly double the 8% rate of the GNMA contract and, in many cases, beyond the ability of buyers to afford new houses. The concept of "creative financing" resulted, whereby the seller takes back the first and second trust at or below market rates. The disparity between "real" mortgage rates and stated rates negated some of the appeal of the GNMA contract for hedgers and the T-Bond contract gained in popularity. Also, the 1976 tax law changed the way spreads were viewed for tax purposes and reduced activity in the more distant deliveries, i.e., lowered liquidity. Eurodollars gained in popularity at the expense of T-Bills during 1982–1986 as interest rates and volatility declined (though much of the volume in T-Bills and Euros is on a spread basis).

Table 1

Volume and Open Interest of Selected Financial Futures, 1977–1987[1]

(thousands)

Year	Deutschemark Vol./Open Int.	Japanese Yen Vol./Open Int.	S&P 500 Vol./Open Int.
1977	0.49/n.a.	nil	——
1978	0.71/n.a.	1.99/n.a.	——
1979	1.16/5.23	0.81/2.92	——
1980	2.24/11.29	0.63/2.71	——
1981	2.90/10.20	1.09/7.45	——
1982	5.74/10.73	5.63/12.94	——
1983	8.04/21.20	11.28/27.26	24.13/12.59
1984	11.98/21.98	17.98/29.93	32.15/25.44
1985	12.88/33.77	2.69/13.54	32.30/42.19
1986	27.43/53.65	23.71/32.48	53.23/62.49
1987	21.61/44.91	11.01/24.10	80.49/94.13

Year	T-Bonds Vol./Open Int.	T-Bills Vol./Open Int.	Eurodollars Vol./Open Int.
1977	——	1.13/n.a.	——
1978	0.15/n.a.	1.56/n.a.	——
1979	1.86/41.07	5.08/58.2	——
1980	18.00/90.68	7.33/36.50	——
1981	33.00/243.60	14.72/42.79	——
1982	75.00/221.69	22.67/30.07	——
1983	65.00/185.69	13.55/48.57	1.60/18.21
1984	95.00/174.12	13.57/41.76	5.42/46.43
1985	100.0/202.49	6.81/42.52	17.50/86.65
1986	140.0/302.44	3.55/33.41	23.28/122.62
1987	150.0/231.18	8.19/37.06	34.77/94.13

[1] All figures based on the second day of trading in the year noted.

Principal spreads in interest rates include the Yield Curve (inter-delivery spreads) in T-Bills and T-Bonds, as well as the NOB spread (T-Notes versus T-Bonds) and the TED spread (T-Bills versus Eurodollars). T-Bonds are spread against GNMAs and the Muni Bond Index against T-Bonds (MOB spreads).

The third group of financial futures is stock index futures, which differ markedly from interest rate futures in some ways. Stock indices respond to economic stimuli much as interest rate futures do, but tend to be very volatile and may be subject to intraday and closing aberrations attributed to program trading. There are two noteworthy stock index spreads. First, is the spread between the Value Line Index (Kansas City Board of Trade, KC) and the Standard & Poors 500 Index (CME). The second is the New York Stock Exchange Composite Index (New York Futures Exchange, NYFE) versus the S&P Index. Several other traded indices may soon be candidates for inter-market spreading, among them CRB Index (NYFE), the Maxi Index (CBT), the S&P 100 Index (CME) and the U.S. Dollar Index (New York Cotton Exchange, NYCE).

Types of Spreads

The concept of spreading is often seen as complex, but the idea is as simple as that of a net buy or sell trade. The spread trader simply tries to take advantage of a change in the relationship between the spread components. The trader executes a simultaneous buy and sell; the objective is for the bought component ("leg") of the spread to gain on the one which is sold.

The first and most common type of spread is the inter-commodity spread—in this case, between two different financial instruments, but usually in the same delivery month and usually on the same exchange. Some examples would be the NOB spread (T-Notes versus T-Bonds), both traded on the CBT and normally involving the same delivery month, or the TED spread (Treasury Bills versus Eurodollar futures), both traded on the IMM and normally involving the same delivery month.

A second type of spread is the inter-delivery spread using the same commodity and same exchange, but different delivery months. These are sometimes known as yield curve spreads in the financial markets as they reflect changes in the perceived yield curve or the period in question. These spreads will also include a carrying charge component, represented by a discount (increased yield) relative to the time difference between deliveries and relative to current expectations with respect to yield.

A third type of spread is the inter-market spread, involving the arbitrage between the same commodity and delivery month in different markets, such as T-Bonds in London versus T-Bonds in Chicago. Arbitrage spreads tend to be specialized and are traded almost exclusively by arbitrageurs based in the principal trading countries. Another spread in this category is T-Bills versus T-Bonds; this is a way of spreading short-term rates against long-term rates and is usually done in a ratio of 2.5:1 (T-Bills/T-Bonds). Note that T-Bills do not have a carrying charge component. They are 90-day Bills and the deliveries in T-Bills are 90 days apart, so that each T-Bill contract is not deliverable against any other delivery month.

There are other contracts available, though their volume is relatively small. These include the "mini" contracts (usually half-size) traded on the Mid-America Commodity Exchange (MidAm) in Chicago and including all major currencies, T-Bills, and T-Bonds. There are also currency contracts on the Philadelphia Board of Trade (PBOT) the European Currency Unit contracts on the IMM, NYCE and PBOT, and Certificates of Deposit on the IMM.

Spread Analysis

The approaches to spread analysis are not particularly different from those used for net-trade analysis. However, the perspectives used must be adapted to the needs of the spreader (i.e., differences in relationships rather than absolute value).

The four essential areas of analysis include:

1. Fundamental analysis—Supply/demand analysis; carrying charges; the influence of news events; economic data, etc.
2. Technical analysis—Chart interpretation, including definition of trend, support and resistance areas, and projected risk and profit objectives.
3. Cyclic analysis—The examination of long- and short-term cycles, both in terms of underlying economic factors and in terms of price behavior.
4. Historical analysis—The determination of undervalued and overvalued price levels (what is "cheap" and what is "expensive") or deflation over relatively long time periods.

Fundamental Analysis

Fundamental analysis is virtually a daily necessity for traders of financial futures. Each day economic data are released which often have an immediate and measurable effect on all components of financial futures. Weekly figures include U.S. money supply, monthly statistics on new car sales, unemployment, housing starts, producer and consumer price indices, retail sales, manufacturers' inventories, industrial production, consumer credit, GNP, index of leading economic indicators and others.

There are also quarterly refunding packages, whereby the U.S. government refinances debt through issuance of one-year through 30-year debt instruments. The quantities and time spans of the refunded debt will have an effect on the market as well as on the results of the refunding, which will indicate how well the package was received by the buyers and will provide an indication of interest-rate levels for the various terms of debt. These factors have a significant effect on spread relationships.

One must also be aware of the price movements of commodities which have a direct effect on inflation/deflation (the petroleum complex) or which are indicators of perceptions about economic conditions (precious metals).

Market psychology is an important aspect of the financial futures markets. These markets, more than most others, tend to reflect perceptions rather than realities. Much of this can be attributed to the broad media play given to interest rates, balance of trade and currency fluctuations, and the stock market. One is more likely to hear of these items in daily news broadcasts than to hear news of agricultural or industrial commodities. News analysis and interpretation are given whether or not market conditions have changed. Thus, a prominent market analyst whose comments are relayed to the public may, in fact, prompt movement. This was quite evident in 1981 when rates were peaking and the popular analysts were predicting even higher rates, thereby discouraging selling and perhaps extending rate peaks.

The problem facing all fundamental analysts is the tendency to be most bullish at the top of the market and most bearish at the bottom. This is caused, at least in part, by the gap in time between knowledge of supply and knowledge of demand. Supply tends to be anticipated. One example is government refunding; issues and maturity dates are announced well beforehand (supply), but how well the market takes the refunding package and the resultant rates (demand) are not known until the refunding takes place.

Technical Analysis

Technical analysis is the interpretation of chart patterns. The assumption is that previous areas of support and resistance will hold when prices reach those areas. Therefore, areas of resistance will become areas of support when prices move above them and vice versa. The greatest utility of charts is in the graphic definition of trends. Technicians use many filters to "fine tune" their analyses, including moving averages, oscillators (measurements of differences between prices and moving averages), and applications of wave theory. However, the primary function of the chart is to define trend, support and resistance. "Chart points" become significant to some degree as self-fulfilling prophecies simply because so many traders are using the same numbers. Spread traders will find chart analysis to be of identical utility in defining trend, support and resistance. The "fine tuning," however, is of less import due to the inherently lower volatility of spread relationships.

Cyclic Analysis

Cyclic analysis can involve anything from a long-term cycle (such as the Kondratieff Wave of 55 to 60 years) to 15-minute cycles in daily trading activity. The usefulness of cycle analysis is in the anticipation of tops and bottoms, as well as price momentum. Cycles are also useful in determining seasonal trends, although financial futures have been trading for a relatively short time. However, each year increases the statistical reliability of seasonal analysis for net and spread trades. The seasonal spread index (Tiger on Spreads) was developed to represent the seasonal tendencies of spreads or specific delivery months regardless of price. This is done by reducing all price work for the years under study to percentages of contract highs and lows (e.g., contract low equals zero; contract high equals 100) and then averaging the years under study. The resulting chart will depict the tendency of a spread or net position to move up or down at a particular time of year. Those markets which have traded for six years or more will often display a reliable cyclical tendency.

Historical Analysis

Historical analysis is an approach to determination of value. A 1987 dollar has considerably less buying power than a 1971 dollar. A 1987 dollar (at this writing) also has considerably less buying power than a 1986 or 1985 dollar in terms of Continental currencies or the Japanese yen. Traders examine the effects of inflation/deflation and currency fluctuations in order to determine whether current price values or spread differentials are expensive (high) or inexpensive (low), relative to analogous situations in previous years.

The net or spread trader has an obligation to "do his homework" when approching a trade. A good analytical approach coupled with a disciplined money-management technique, while not a guarantee of profits, should at least weigh the probabilities in the trader's favor.

The above four-method analytical approach has proven successful for many traders. When three out of four analytical modes support a trade, it should stand a better chance of being successful. A trading discipline that restricts losses will complete the methodology.

Principal Spreads in Financial Futures

A market-by-market examination follows and focuses on the principal spread trades and the factors that make them move. These markets are interrelated; factors affecting one spread are likely to affect the others. Also, as has occurred during the past decade, one can anticipate shifts in emphasis between markets. T-Bonds are today's leaders, based on open interest and volume but, just as GNMAs declined in popularity during the late 1970s and T-Bills have given way to Eurodollars, market leadership can change. Each spread under scrutiny here is being studied based on current conditions. Traders must examine these descriptions and make appropriate adjustments for what has transpired since.

Currency Spreads

There are three principal inter-commodity spreads in the currency market: a) Swiss franc versus Deutschemark; b) D-mark (or Swiss franc) versus Japanese yen; and, c) D-mark (or Swiss franc) versus British pound. Each currency has a set of fundamental circumstances related to the issuing country. (Table 2.)

The Deutschemark/Swiss franc spread.—The D-mark/Swiss spread was maintained at a D-mark premium until the early 1970s, when the Bretton Woods agreement was dissolved and currencies were allowed to float. Recent history has demonstrated a tendency for the Swiss franc to maintain an 18–20 percent premium to the D-mark. Since March, 1985, the Swiss franc has been gaining on the D-mark as the dollar has weakened. The spread had a low on February 26, 1985, of 510 points Swiss premium. The D-mark low was 28.81 and the Swiss franc low was 34.08, a Swiss-franc premium of 18.3%. Recent highs in the Swiss franc and the D-mark (January 14, 1987) were at 65.75 and 55.20, respectively—a difference of 19.1%. (Table 2a.)

The long D-mark/short Swiss approach is appropriate during periods of dollar strength, when the Swiss premium approaches or exceeds 20 percent, or both. The reverse approach is appropriate during periods of dollar weakness or when the Swiss premium approaches or is below 18 percent. Note that, while this percentage relationship has been reliable during the past decade, any significant change in either the

Table 2

Fundamentals Affecting Selected Currencies

Great Britain — Member of European Community (EC), but pound tends to function to some degree as a petro-currency based on North Sea oil. Economy is essentially mediocre to weak.

West Germany — Strongest member of the EC. Major trading partner with both Japan and United States, but weaker members of the EC tend to act as a "drag" on the West German currency.

Switzerland — Not a member of the EC, but landlocked and dependent on EC members for much of its trade. Seen as a safe money haven and politically secure.

Japan — Major trading partner of all nations with expanding international economic growth. Economy tends to be more controlled and efficient than those of Western nations. Suffers from poor domestic natural resource base and need to have ever-expanding international trade to guarantee growth.

Swiss franc or D-mark's currency alignments or domestic interest rates could affect the spread.

The D-mark (or Swiss franc)/Japanese yen spread. This is essentially a spread between East and West. Japan's economic situation and world trading status are, for the most part, independent of those of the common market, Switzerland or the U.S.; Japanese policies and needs tend to be quite different from those of its trading partners. Nevertheless, there are always agreements (e.g., GATT) and disagreements (Japan's auto exports) that will tend to inflate or deflate the yen against the other currencies. This spread is therefore very volatile and requires greater emphasis on technical aspects than other spreads. Note again, the comparison between February 26, 1985, and January 14, 1987, as well as the yen low of November 4, 1982 (Table 2a).

One can see the lack of correlation and volatility inherent in the relationship. This dictates that each year be treated as a separate entity, although levels of historic premiums and discounts should be noted.

The D-mark (or Swiss franc)/British pound spread—These spreads are similar in character to the yen/Continental currency spreads in that there is no consistent pattern to the relationship. However, as the British pound functions somewhat as a petro-currency (rising and falling with the price of oil), even though petroleum represents less than 10% of Great Britian's GNP, some British pound/D-mark, Swiss franc, or yen trading is initiated in anticipation of rising or falling oil prices.

There are two ways to spread against the pound. Due to the different contract sizes, the pound can be spread against the other currencies on a contract-value basis. For example, the D-mark contract at 54 cents (1.85 dollar ratio) is worth $67,500, the British pound at 1.49 is worth $37,250, so a spread of 3 British pounds versus 2 D-marks would be approximately

Table 2a

Currency	11/4/82 (Low)	2/26/85 (Lows)	1/14/87 (Highs)
Japanese yen	3596	3816	6620
Swiss franc	4513 (+917)	3408 (−408)	575 (−45)
D-mark	3883 (+287)	2881 (−935)	5520 (−1100)

equal in dollar value. However, the IMM allows for preferential margin rates on inter-currency trades on a 1:1 basis, so the advantage for the spreader, in terms of return on equity, might favor the 1:1 spread rather than the closer contract-value relationship.

Interest Rate Spreads

A discussion of interest rate spreads logically begins with the inter-delivery spreads in T-Bills and T-Bonds. These spreads are often referred to as yield curve spreads.

The yield curve is the difference in yield on Treasury instruments measured over time. The further in the future a debt instrument matures, the greater the uncertainties relative to yields at the time of maturity. This uncertainty will result in the more distant instrument reflecting a somewhat higher yield. Also, one must allow some provision in the yield curve calculation for "carrying charges"—in the case of a debt instrument, the inherent cost of carrying such an instrument in inventory for the period of time in question. This would contribute to a higher yield for the more distant paper. Now, to this relatively orderly yield curve concept, market expectations are added. Readers will note that the past decade has brought both a large increase and a large decline in interest rates. One might expect significant changes in expectations as rates rose, topped out, then fell. These expectations can be seen graphically in the behavior of the yield curve spreads.

The first spread to examine is the inter-delivery T-Bond spread. The benchmark relationship is the one-year spread—March of one year versus the next, for example. Shorter-term spreads (March versus September, or March versus December) will display similar behavior to the one-year spread, but will be muted in terms of risk and profit potential by the shorter time frame. When the trader anticipates inflation or fears of inflation, the "back spread" approach is advisable; that is, selling the nearby month and buying the distant. When deflation or reduced inflation is anticipated, the forward spread is advisable (buying the nearby delivery, selling the more distant delivery).

Note the behavior of the one-year Bond spreads during the inflationary and deflationary cycles of the past decade. Inflation accelerated in the late 1970s and peaked in 1981. The March 1980/1981 T-Bond spread began at 16/32nds premium the nearby (higher yield expectation for the distant delivery) and declined to 4-0 (128/32nds) premium the distant delivery. The spread was acknowledging historically high rates of current return and anticipating some future change in the opposite direction. Then, look at the March 1984/85 spread and one can see the opposite—the tendency for the spread to favor the nearby contract over the more distant—anticipating higher yields or normal carrying charges for future deliveries, or both.

The 1984/1985 spread began (October 18, 1982,) at 8/32nds premium the 1985 Bond and peaked in January, 1984, at 2-09 (72/32nds) premium the nearby. That trend continued into 1986, when the one-year spreads reached 4-0 to 4-16 premium the nearby—an historical resistance area. The spread has behaved best, trended consistently, during periods of active increases or decreases in interest rates; it has exhibited broad trading ranges, but little trend, during periods of transition between rising and falling rate trends. One should also be aware of the tendency for inter-delivery interest rate spreads to become less volatile when rates are low and more volatile when rates are high. This is simply a function of rate of change, as a 1/8-percent move in rates is less significant at the higher rates than at the lower.

Inter-delivery T-Bond spreads should be viewed as a trading vehicle with strong trend potential during periods of trending interest rate changes. The one-year spread has notable historical resistance boundaries at 4-0 (128/32nds) premium in either direction. There is some modest seasonal behavior in the tendency for the nearby to gain on the distant delivery during the second quarter of the year. This tendency will be emphasized during periods of low or declining rates, or both.

Inter-delivery T-Bill spreads behave in a similar manner to the Bond spreads with a few exceptions. T-Bills are a much shorter-term instrument (90 days) and will tend to be a bit more responsive to short-term changes. However, the Bonds are the most popular of the interest rate futures; T-Bills rank fourth behind Bonds, Eurodollars, and 10-year T-Notes. Therefore, though the Bills should be the most responsive to fundamental changes, they will tend to lag Eurodollars and sometimes Bonds and Notes, in reaction to change.

Inter-commodity interest rate spreads focus on essential differences, rather than relative yields over time. Three spreads are worthy of discussion: the TED spread—T Bills versus Eurodollars; the NOB spread—T-Notes versus T-Bonds, and the MOB spread—Municipal Bonds Index versus T-Bonds.

The TED spread was very popular during the first half of the 1980s; it provided well-traded ranges and volatility, particularly during periods of large interest rate changes and international banking uncertainties. T-Bills are U.S. government-guaranteed securities, which are viewed as the safest of investments. Eurodollars are simply U.S. dollars on deposit in foreign banks and, as such, have no guarantees. Therefore, Eurodollar rates will *always* be higher than T-Bill rates or, in terms of futures (which are inverses of yield), T-Bill futures will always have a premium over Eurodollars. (Example: A T-Bill at 94.50 has a yield of 5½ percent. A Eurodollar at 93.50 has a yield of 6½ percent. Such a differential would be the TED spread at 100—this is T-Bills at a 100-point premium over Eurodollars.)

There are two primary factors which will generate fluctuations in the TED spread. The first is the interest rate itself. Eurodollars will tend to reflect a "percentage premium" in yield over T-Bills. Therefore, when interest rates are high or rising, or both, T-Bill futures will tend to gain on Eurodollar futures as the "Euros" maintain their higher interest rates by a percentage differential (usually 10 percent–20 percent) over T-Bills; that is, Eurodollar rates will be rising faster than T-Bills. The opposite will occur when rates are low and/or falling, as the percentage differences become a smaller absolute number and the difference between the two instruments narrows.

The second motivating factor in the TED spread is confidence in the dollar and/or foreign debt service. When the threat of foreign bank default or refinancing needs surfaces, it tends to weaken the dollar versus foreign currency markets and to increase the yield on Eurodollars (unguaranteed dollar deposits in foreign banks) versus T-Bills (guaranteed by the U.S. government).

The TED spread has suffered somewhat during the 1980s, as volatility in the spread has declined with falling interest rates. The spread has, in fact, stabilized in the area of 75 to 80 points T-Bill premium, as this is being written. Should interest rates decline further and no problems regarding Third World debt or other foreign deposits arise, the differential between T-Bills and Eurodollars may decline further, but *by a slower rate of change*. If interest rates increase or problems arise with dollar debtor nations, or both, then T-Bill futures will gain on Eurodollar futures once again and *probably at a faster rate of change*. Therefore, the viability of the TED spread for most traders will depend on reversing the trend seen since 1981 of declining interest rates (possibly in conjunction with debtor nations' problems in the servicing of their dollar obligations).

Historical analysis of the TED spread to date has shown the area of 65-85 T-Bills premium to be primary support, and the 115 to 135 area to be resistance. But, history for this spread has been too short to weigh such values too heavily.

The NOB spread (T-Notes versus T-Bonds) is perhaps the most popular and notable of interest rate spreads. Though the spread should reflect simply the differences between medium-term and longer-term rates, the behavior patterns have been much more erratic than warranted by that fact alone. This is due to several factors. One is the reluctance of longer-term rates to react quickly to changes in shorter-term rates. This creates a "rubber-band" effect, whereby pressure builds for Bond rates to change until they do so rather sharply. An example of this was in the 1985–1986 period when Bond rates followed short-term rates very reluctantly until a major up move in Bonds occurred. The June, 1986, T-Note/T-Bond spread traded between 9-0 and 10-16 for all of 1985. Then, as 1986 began, the spread began to favor Bonds and, in the period from early February through late March, 1986, the spread moved nearly 8-0 points (256/32nds) in favor of Bonds. This was a dramatic move and a very profitable trade for those who anticipated lower long-term rates.

Another factor in the volatility of the NOB spreads is their technical reliability. The spread tends to trend in both the long and short term, and support and resistance areas have demonstrated their validity. (Note that support becomes resistance and vice versa when such areas are penetrated by price action.) This serves to create and sustain trending moves as traders will recognize these factors and act to help the market become a "self-fulfilling prophesy," at least over the shorter term.

T-Notes almost always have a premium over T-Bonds, as the long-term instrument will reflect the increased yields due to the longer term and the carrying cost. The historical support and resistance areas of recent years are T-Note premiums of 9-0 to 11-0, 5-0 to 7-0, 3-0 to 5-0 and 0 to 2-0. Even a trading range within a support/resistance area is broad enough to generate some excellent spread trading opportunities. These spreads will have preferential margin rates (also true for TED and MOB spreads), which can mean a greater return on committed equity than for an outright long or short position. Of course, if potential is greater, risk can be greater too, and disciplined money management is of critical importance.

The general behavior pattern of the NOB spread is for Notes to gain on Bonds in times of increasing interest rates or inflationary fears, and for Notes to lose to Bonds during times of declining interest rates or deflationary fears. A major difference in the NOB spread, versus the TED spread, is the ability of the NOB spread virtually always to generate a potentially profitable trading range (i.e., $1,000 or more in value); the TED spread—particularly during periods of low interest rates—will generate very small ranges ($300 or less in value) making it difficult to trade.

A third inter-commodity spread which has been gaining in popularity is the Muni-Bond Index/T-Bond (MOB) spread. Here, the maturities of the underlying instruments are similar, but the natures of the instruments are different. The MOB spread will function to a large degree on changes in relative supply of Munis and of T-Bonds. Therefore, for example, T-Bonds which tend to weaken into quarterly refundings will also tend to weaken against the Muni-Bond Index at such times. This will be accentuated when the supply of Munis coming to market is concurrently light. Conversely, post-refunding Bond rallies will also be reflected in a long Bond/short Muni spread and will be abetted at times of heavy Muni supply (new issues coming to market).

The MOB spread is less volatile than the NOB spread due to the similarity of the Muni and T-Bond contracts. The Muni Bond Index is also too new as of this writing to have generated much historical or cyclic information. (The Muni Bond Index began trading in June, 1985.) However, the MOB spread has demonstrated its tradability and seems likely to increase in popularity over time.

Stock Index Spreads

There are two primary spreads in the stock index markets. They are inter-commodity spreads of the S&P 500 (CME) versus the Value Line Index (KC) and the S&P 500 versus two contracts of the NYSE Composite Index (NYFE). There is also modest but active trade in the Major Market Index (CBT); however, this Index is not now actively spread against the other indices. An understanding of the different indices is important to an understanding of the spread relationships. (Table 3.)

The S&P/Value Line Spread. This is perhaps the most popular index spread. The fundamental difference between the two indices is that the S&P tends to be a higher-quality (blue chip) stock index, while the Value Line Index is broader and includes many lesser (secondary) issues. The bull market of 1982–1987 has been primarily a blue-chip-led rally and, as one might expect, the S&P has had a tendency to gain on the Value Line after the initial stages of this bull market. There is no price-limiting differential between the two indices. The 5-year bull market witnessed a Value Line high premium of 3900 points (June, 1983) and a Value Line low (S&P premium) of −3140 (January, 1987).

There are few fundamental tools that will help to evaluate this spread. The spread is very volatile and this limits the effectiveness of fundamental analysis, which tends to be longer-term. Some assistance comes from observing the differentials between the cash (spot) index and the nearest futures trading month. Value Line futures have been running at a consistent discount to cash, while S&P futures have been running at a consistent premium to cash. When futures gain on cash, it tends to be a bullish indicator and vice versa, so a trader may be able to anticipate a change in trend by watching cash/futures differentials.

The most reliable analytical tools for stock index spreads appear to be technical methods. Trends have been consistent and support/resistance levels have also proven useful. There are no reliable historical parameters; recent market action has taken place in new high ground. Cyclical analysis is somewhat useful over the shorter term. There appears to be a three-day cycle operating in the spread which can be useful, at least for initiating and exiting orders.

Those trading the S&P/Value Line spread should watch the charts closely and trade with the trend on pullbacks to congestion areas. However, a 200- to 300-point range in the spread in any given trading day is very possible ($1000–$15000 spread); this spread is therefore only for the well-margined account.

The S&P/NYSE spread. The S&P/NYSE spread is more docile than the S&P/Value Line. The spread, two NYSE contracts versus one S&P contract, will move in a ratio of approximately ⅓ of the volatility of S&P/Value Line (i.e., 300 points of S&P/Value Line movement will equate with about 100 points of 2 NYSE/1 S&P). The two indices are somewhat similar in behavior, as well. Here too, technical tools are the most valuable, and day-to-day fundamentals and historical levels must be viewed as secondary indicators.

Note that the same stock market theorists propose that the maturing phase of a bull market will reflect greater activity in secondary issues as opposed to "blue chip," and vice versa for a bear market. This can be applied through use of the index spreads. However, as the action of the 1980s shows, one should not expect too much correlation between market action and theory, particularly over the short term.

Table 3

Index	Components	Nature of Contract	Point Value/ Futures
Value Line	1700 stocks/90% NYSE	secondary stock index	1 = $5.00
S&P 500	weighted 500 NYSE stocks	acts as a "blue chip" index	1 = $5.00
NYSE Composite	all NYSE issues	approximately half the value of the S&P & Value Line	1 = $5.00
Major Market Index	selected NYSE issues	acts as a "blue chip" index, tracks the Dow Jones Industrial Average	.05 = $12.5

Conclusion

The dynamics of financial futures, the fastest-growing segment of the commodity markets, have been demonstrated time and again in recent years. The ability of these markets to respond to moment-by-moment changes in domestic and world economics has attracted all types of traders—hedgers, professional and speculative traders, and commercial interests. Members of these groups have been able to find trading postures appropriate to their individual needs within these markets. Spread traders have a potpourri of combinations to trade in currencies, interest rate futures and stock indices.

These markets have been very responsive to the dramatic changes of the past decade. Contracts receiving great interest only a few years ago (e.g., GNMAS) have been eclipsed by new stars, while relatively new contracts, such as the Muni Bond Index, show promise for increased popularity. Each change in emphasis creates new opportunities for both net and spread traders.

Financial futures appear destined to be the "leaders of the pack" for some time. Spread trading is likely to increase as knowledge of these markets expands and as the potential for greater risk management and cyclical trading available to spreaders becomes known. Money management, risk definition, and discipline will continue to be the keys to growth and preservation of capital. A knowledge of financial futures, and particularly financial futures, spreads should help traders capitalize on the opportunities provided in this marketplace.

FUTURES VOLUME HIGHLIGHTS
1986 in Comparison with 1985

Ranks	Contracts With Volume Over 100,000	1986 Contracts	%	1985 Contracts	%	Rank
1.	T-Bonds, CBT	52,598,811	28.53	40,448,357	25.49	(1)
2.	S&P 500 Index, CME	19,505,273	10.58	15,055,955	9.49	(2)
3.	Eurodollar, CME	10,824,914	5.87	8,900,528	5.61	(3)
4.	Gold, COMEX	8,400,175	4.56	7,773,834	4.90	(4)
5.	Crude Oil, NYMEX	8,313,529	4.51	3,980,867	2.51	(11)
6.	DeutscheMark, CME	6,582,145	3.57	6,449,384	4.06	(6)
7.	Corn, CBT	6,160,298	3.34	6,392,812	4.03	(7)
8.	Soybeans, CBT	6,133,668	3.33	7,392,128	4.66	(5)
9.	Swiss Franc, CME	4,998,430	2.71	4,758,159	3.00	(9)
10.	Live Cattle, CME	4,690,538	2.54	4,437,327	2.80	(10)
11.	T-Notes (6½–10 yr), CBT	4,426,476	2.40	2,860,432	1.80	(15)
12.	Japanese Yen, CME	3,969,777	2.15	2,415,094	1.52	(19)
13.	Silver (5,000 oz), COMEX	3,849,687	2.09	4,821,206	3.04	(8)
14.	Sugar #11, CSC	3,583,814	1.94	3,012,929	1.90	(14)
15.	No. 2 Heating Oil, NYMEX	3,275,044	1.78	2,207,733	1.39	(21)
16.	Soybean Oil, CBT	3,182,963	1.73	3,647,408	2.30	(12)
17.	NYSE Composite Index, NYFE	3,123,668	1.69	2,833,614	1.79	(16)
18.	Soybean Meal, CBT	3,049,005	1.65	3,339,268	2.10	(13)
19.	British Pound, CME	2,701,330	1.47	2,799,024	1.76	(17)
20.	Wheat, CBT	2,090,316	1.13	2,127,962	1.34	(22)
21.	Live Hogs, CME	1,936,864	1.05	1,719,861	1.08	(24)
22.	Copper, COMEX	1,872,209	1.02	2,444,552	1.54	(18)
23.	T-Bills (90-day), CME	1,815,162	0.98	2,413,338	1.52	(20)
24.	MMI Maxi, CBT	1,738,916	0.94	422,091	0.27	(39)
25.	Platinum, NYMEX	1,624,635	0.88	693,256	0.44	(31)
26.	Pork Bellies (frozen), CME	1,100,339	0.60	1,457,386	0.92	(25)
27.	Coffee "C", CSC	1,073,142	0.58	650,768	0.41	(33)
28.	Cotton #2, NYCE	1,015,392	0.55	636,492	0.40	(34)
29.	Value Line Index, KCBOT	953,985	0.52	1,204,659	0.76	(26)
30.	Municipal Bond Index, CBT	906,980	0.49	334,691	0.21	(41)
31.	Leaded Reg. Gasoline, NYMEX	829,733	0.45	667,172	0.42	(32)
32.	Cocoa, CSC	777,765	0.42	800,573	0.50	(29)
33.	Wheat, KCBOT	744,023	0.40	735,447	0.46	(30)
34.	Canadian Dollar, CME	734,071	0.40	468,996	0.30	(36)
35.	Soybeans, MIDAM	680,156	0.37	843,231	0.53	(28)
36.	Silver (1,000 oz), CBT	511,239	0.28	1,034,830	0.65	(27)
37.	Lumber, CME	502,530	0.27	581,548	0.37	(35)
38.	T-Bonds, MIDAM	467,639	0.25	297,033	0.19	(43)
39.	Unleaded Gasoline, NYMEX	439,352	0.24	132,611	0.08	(48)
40.	Feeder Cattle, CME	411,441	0.22	455,881	0.29	(38)
41.	Corn, MIDAM	406,694	0.22	456,661	0.29	(37)
42.	Wheat, MIDAM	344,749	0.19	347,355	0.22	(40)
43.	Wheat, MGE	283,900	0.15	297,509	0.19	(42)
44.	Orange Juice (frozen), NYCE	211,543	0.11	190,758	0.12	(44)
45.	Dollar Index, NYCE	166,494	0.09	——	——	——
46.	Palladium, NYMEX	145,562	0.08	133,223	0.08	(47)
47.	Oats, CBT	140,952	0.08	——	——	——
48.	Gold, (Kilo) CBT	124,546	0.07	168,527	0.11	(45)
49.	Swiss Franc, MIDAM	102,019	0.06	110,047	0.07	(49)
	Contracts With Volume Over 100,000 Contracts [1]			2,201,971	1.38	
	Contracts With Volume Under 100,000 Contracts	832,603	0.45	1,142,090	0.72	
TOTAL		184,354,496	100.00	158,696,578	100.00	

[1] Contract over 100,000 traded in 1985 but not over 100,000 in 1986.

COMMODITY FUTURES CONTRACTS TRADED 1982 – 1986

	Contract Unit	1986	1985	1984	1983	1982
Wheat	5,000 bu.	2,090,316	2,127,962	2,974,886	3,886,914	4,031,584
Corn	5,000 bu.	6,160,298	6,392,812	9,108,526	11,924,576	7,948,257
Oats	5,000 bu.	140,952	99,024	155,110	359,825	424,595
Soybeans	5,000 bu.	6,133,668	7,392,128	11,362,691	13,680,324	9,165,520
Soybean Oil	60,000 lb.	3,182,963	3,647,408	4,009,548	3,858,558	3,049,313
Soybean Meal	100 tons	3,049,005	3,339,268	3,822,179	3,872,453	2,784,423
Plywood	76,032 sq. ft.			4,466	50,424	100,001
Silver	5,000 oz.				21,470	77,682
Silver	1,000 oz.	511,239	1,034,830	1,887,257	2,643,166	775,136
Gold	100 oz.				4,133	19,515
Gold	kilo	124,546	168,527	302,717	302,745	
GNMA mrtges, CDR	$100,000	24,078	84,396	862,450	1,692,017	2,055,648
GNMA II	$100,000			37,615		
Cash Settle GNMA	$100,000	7,351				
T-Bonds	$100,000	52,598,811	40,448,357	29,963,280	19,550,535	16,739,695
T-Notes (2-year)	$100,000				562	
T-Notes (6½–10 yr)	$100,000	4,426,476	2,860,432	1,661,862	814,505	881,325
Domestic CD (90-day)	$1,000,000					145,360
Unld. Reg. Gasoline	1,000 bbl.				51,573	8,736
Crude Oil	1,000 bbl.			628	94,591	
Heating Oil	1,000 bbl.				3,152	
Municipal Bond Index	$1,000 × Indx.	906,980	334,691			
Major Market Index	$100 × Indx.	36,292	2,062,083	1,514,737		
MMI Maxi	$250 × Indx.	1,738,916	422,091			
NASDAQ-100	$250 × Indx.	3,743	139,888			
CHICAGO BOARD OF TRADE		81,135,634	70,553,897	67,667,952	62,811,523	48,206,790
Fresh Eggs	22,500 dz					18
Potatoes	80,000 lb.					9
Live Hogs	30,000 lb.	1,936,864	1,719,861	2,169,030	2,790,746	3,560,974
Pork Bellies, Fzn.	38,000 lb.	1,100,339	1,457,386	1,908,045	2,403,277	2,811,674
Live Cattle	40,000 lb.	4,690,538	4,437,327	3,553,270	4,248,152	4,440,992
Feeder Cattle	42,000 lb.	411,441	455,881	316,985	537,173	603,769
Broilers	30,000 lb.					2,118
Lumber	130,000 bd. ft.	502,530	581,548	753,568	731,003	516,619
Plywood	152,064 sq. ft.					35
Gold	100 oz.		7	8,841	994,132	1,533,466
Leaded Reg. Gas	1,000 bbl.			4,045		
No. 2 Fuel Oil	1,000 bbl.			4,601		
T-Bills (90-day)	$1,000,000	1,815,162	2,413,338	3,292,817	3,789,864	6,598,848
Domestic CD (90-day)	$1,000,000	3,062	84,106	928,662	1,079,580	1,556,327
Eurodollar (3-month)	$1,000,000	10,824,914	8,900,528	4,192,952	891,066	323,619
European Curr. Unit	125,000	43,826				
British Pound	25,000	2,701,330	2,799,024	1,444,492	1,614,993	1,321,701
Canadian Dollar	100,000	734,071	468,996	345,875	558,741	1,078,467
DeutscheMark	125,000	6,582,145	6,449,384	5,508,308	2,423,508	1,792,901
Japanese Yen	12,500,000	3,969,777	2,415,094	2,334,764	3,442,262	1,762,246
Mexican Peso	1,000,000		12,737	15,364	40,308	65,036
Swiss Franc	125,000	4,998,430	4,758,159	4,129,881	3,766,130	2,653,332
Dutch Guilder	125,000				162	128
U.S. Silver Coins	$5,000					1
French Franc	250,000	2,685	9,335	8,388	26,348	16,474
S&P 500 Index	$500 × Indx.	19,505,273	15,055,955	12,363,592	8,101,697	2,935,532
S&P 100 Index	$200 × Indx.	3,514	1,662	166,202	390,902	
S&P OTC 250	$500 × Indx.	5,270	94,919			
CHICAGO MERCANTILE EXCHANGE		59,831,171	52,115,247	43,449,682	37,830,044	33,574,286

	Contract Unit	1986	1985	1984	1983	1982
Rice, Milled	120,000 lb.				275	5,262
Rice, Rough Old	200,000 lb.		9	2,978	11,964	11,253
Rice, Rough New		3,095				
Cotton	50,000 lb.				1,004	8,388
Cotton Short Staple	50,000 lb.	3	1,751			
Soybeans	5,000 bu.				197	1,998
Corn	5,000 bu.				102	971
CHICAGO RICE & COTTON EXCHANGE		3,098	1,760	2,978	13,542	27,872
Coffee "C"	37,500 lb.	1,073,142	650,768	499,133	427,441	556,435
Sugar # 11	112,000 lb.	3,583,814	3,012,929	2,449,549	3,201,968	2,037,020
Sugar # 12	112,000 lb.	19,058	99,851	109,448	84,120	51,093
Sugar # 14	112,000 lb.	72,526	17,433			
Cocoa	10 M tons	777,765	800,573	1,127,752	1,162,540	607,964
CPI-W	$1,000 × Indx.	8,776	1,324			
COFFEE SUGAR & COCOA EXCHANGE		5,535,081	4,582,878	4,185,882	4,876,069	3,252,512
Copper	25,000 lb.	1,872,209	2,444,552	2,506,365	3,186,914	2,362,625
Silver	5,000 oz.	3,849,687	4,821,206	6,742,508	6,432,982	2,868,639
Gold	100 oz.	8,400,175	7,773,834	9,115,504	10,382,805	12,289,448
Aluminum	40,000 lb.	52,627	77,063	82,661	11,896	
COMMODITY EXCHANGE		14,174,698	15,116,655	18,447,038	20,014,597	17,520,712
Wheat	5,000 bu.	744,023	735,447	956,668	942,971	964,815
Value Line Index	$500 × Indx.	953,985	1,204,659	910,956	724,979	528,743
Mini Value Line	$100 × Indx.	18,678	19,032	30,179	25,092	
KANSAS CITY BOARD OF TRADE		1,716,686	1,959,138	1,897,803	1,693,042	1,493,558
Wheat	1,000 bu.	344,749	347,355	404,508	334,413	243,640
Corn	1,000 bu.	406,694	456,661	604,992	629,678	274,324
Oats	1,000 bu.	2,169	1,746	7,067	11,797	12,981
Soybeans	1,000 bu.	680,156	843,231	1,301,916	1,171,294	527,411
Soybean Meal Old	20 tons	3,231	10,981			
Soybean Meal New		2,256				
Live Cattle	20,000 #	58,752	64,510	81,112	88,349	107,329
Live Hogs	15,000 #	80,818	74,388	112,877	108,069	175,624
Refined Sugar	40,000 lb.			24	3,306	24,000
Silver	1,000 oz.	649	4,510	19,497	96,611	125,409
New York Silver	1,000 oz.	9,342	57,886	12,611	30,833	3,810
Gold	33.2 oz.	0	76	41,690	349,044	383,499
New York Gold	33.2 oz.	21,111	31,467	19,285		
Platinum	25 oz.	5,944	1,368	213		
Copper	12,500 lbs.	892	4,043	492		
Copper High Grade		1,753				
T-Bonds	$50,000	467,639	297,033	251,300	267,259	419,277
T-Bills	$500,000	34,690	36,904	30,486	37,755	100,417
British Pound	12,500	17,270	21,239	8,901	884	
Swiss Franc	62,500	102,019	110,047	99,385	19,632	
DeutscheMark	62,500	74,662	85,439	67,507	6,607	
Japanese Yen	6,250,000	47,601	32,912	34,677	10,835	
Canadian Dollar	$50,000	6,150	3,370	3,315	171	
MIDAMERICA COMMODITY EXCHANGE		2,368,547	2,485,166	3,101,855	3,166,537	2,397,721
Wheat	5,000 bu.	283,900	297,509	338,487	379,603	346,226
White Wheat	5,000 bu.	686	3,402	2,245		
Sunflower Seeds	100,000 lb.				4	38
MINNEAPOLIS GRAIN EXCHANGE		284,586	300,911	340,732	379,607	346,264

	Contract Unit	1986	1985	1984	1983	1982
Cotton	50,000 lb.	1,015,392	636,492	1,137,141	1,550,117	1,255,792
Orange Jce. Fzn. Conc.	15,000 lb.	211,543	190,758	317,364	124,267	207,070
Propane	100,000 gal.	11,966	13,724	22,005	28,721	16,919
European Curr. Unit	100,000	72,195				
Dollar Index	$500 × Indx.	166,494	74,573			
NEW YORK COTTON & CITRUS		1,477,590	915,547	1,476,510	1,703,105	1,479,781
T-Bonds	$100,000				18	4,464
Domestic CD (90-day)	$1,000,000					132
NYSE Composite Index	$500 × Indx.	3,123,668	2,833,614	3,456,798	3,506,439	1,432,913
NYSE Financial Index	$1,000 × Indx.				3,828	13,933
CRB Index Futures*	$500 × Indx.	59,324				
NEW YORK FUTURES EXCHANGE		3,182,992	2,833,614	3,456,798	3,510,285	1,451,442
Palladium	100 oz.	145,562	133,223	159,019	241,224	63,829
Platinum	50 oz.	1,624,635	693,256	571,127	1,053,282	669,024
Imported Lean Beef	36,000 lb.					7
Potatoes	50,000 lb.				17,115	67,322
Potatoes (Cash Settlement)	100,000 lb.	16,558	16,903	26,595	16,650	
# 2 Heating Oil, NY	1,000 bbl.	3,275,044	2,207,733	2,091,546	1,868,322	1,745,526
# 2 Heating Oil, Gulf	1,000 bbl.					74
Leaded Reg. Gas., NY	1,000 bbl.	829,733	667,172	653,630	406,843	104,082
Leaded Reg. Gas., Gulf	1,000 bbl.					77
Unleaded Gas., NY	1,000 bbl.	439,352	132,611	2,736		
Crude Oil	1,000 bbl.	8,313,529	3,980,867	1,840,342	323,153	
NEW YORK MERCANTILE EXCHANGE		14,644,413	7,831,765	5,344,995	3,926,589	2,649,941
TOTAL FUTURES		184,354,496	158,696,578	149,372,225	139,924,940	112,400,879
PERCENT CHANGE (%)		16.17	6.24	6.75	24.49	

* Based on the Commodity Research Bureau (CRB) Futures Price Index.

Source: Futures Industry Association

Alcohol

Salient Statistics of Alcohol in the United States   In Millions of Gallons[3]

Year	Ethyl Alcohol & Spirits		Denatured Alcohol[2]				Produc-tion of Methanol (Synthetic)
	Produc-tion[5]	Stocks Dec. 31	Consumption				
			Produc-tion	Total	For Fuel Use	Stocks Dec. 31	
1976	498.8	85.3	225.3	225.6	—	3.2	940.1
1977	498.3	71.4	223.8	224.6	—	2.6	971.8
1978	506.7	71.2	227.7	228.8	—	2.7	970.4
1979	570.3	53.6	260.7	260.9	—	4.1	1,109.5
1980	643.2	72.0	301.2	281.5	14.5	10.1	1,077.3
1981	571.2	83.3	230.7	227.1	5.7	5.4	1,291.7
1982	601.1	95.0	284.9	277.9	41.9	6.6	1,137.7
1983	698.5	78.6	354.4	356.7	65.8	6.6	1,202.1
1984	631.3	132.5	416.9	410.5	116.7	24.5	1,232.8
1985[1]	680.7	47.1	507.7	513.8	222.9	26.5	900.5
1986[4]	624	50	416	452	237	27	906

[1] Preliminary.   [2] At denaturing plants.   [3] Ethyl alcohol in proof gallons; denatured alcohol in wine gallons.   [4] Forecast.   [5] Represents alcohol and spirits of 190° of proof and over.   *Source: Alcohol and Tobacco Division*   T.1

U.S. Production of Ethyl Alcohol[1] & Spirits   In Millions of Tax Gallons[2]

Year	Jan.	Feb.	Mar.	Apr.	May	June	July	Aug.	Sept.	Oct.	Nov.	Dec.	Total
1973	57.1	52.5	57.1	58.4	58.1	55.9	54.2	57.4	59.9	62.7	62.2	56.4	692.1
1974	49.9	49.9	45.3	55.5	52.8	40.8	45.3	52.4	59.5	61.0	48.6	54.8	618.2
1975	52.0	40.4	44.5	41.4	39.8	39.1	41.3	40.1	39.6	53.8	46.4	48.0	526.4
1976	41.6	36.2	44.0	39.3	36.0	37.0	45.5	46.0	43.3	39.3	42.8	47.7	498.8
1977	36.5	37.7	42.8	39.2	43.5	43.2	40.3	40.9	41.0	44.7	48.9	39.7	498.3
1978	35.8	41.1	50.4	42.2	31.3	48.7	42.5	45.4	50.5	40.3	38.0	40.7	506.7
1979	42.8	41.3	49.3	47.3	42.9	48.2	43.8	46.0	53.7	49.4	51.0	54.6	570.3
1980	57.4	52.7	55.3	55.2	54.2	45.7	52.8	46.4	57.3	64.6	47.9	53.7	643.2
1981	49.2	44.3	49.3	51.0	44.0	42.2	45.1	55.8	53.1	44.0	47.8	45.4	571.2
1982	42.9	39.8	48.2	37.6	41.9	52.6	51.9	44.3	53.3	61.9	61.7	65.0	601.1
1983	60.9	58.6	59.4	46.1	56.6	60.2	63.8	56.9	59.2	55.6	53.9	47.2	698.5
1984	49.3	45.9	54.1	58.2	50.9	49.7	48.4	48.3	51.8	60.5	50.4	63.7	631.2
1985	64.1	45.0	60.5	55.6	56.2	63.6	58.4	55.4	59.4	64.1	51.8	47.1	680.7
1986[3]	45.6	51.5	56.5	52.5	55.6	50.1							

[1] At industrial alcohol plants.   [2] A "tax gallon" is the alcoholic equivalent of a U.S. gallon at 60 degrees Fahrenheit, containing 50% of ethyl alcohol by volume.   [3] Preliminary.   *Source: Internal Revenue Service*   T.3

Average Wholesale Price Index of Ethyl Alcohol, in N.Y.   Dec. 1973 = 100

Year	Jan.	Feb.	Mar.	Apr.	May	June	July	Aug.	Sept.	Oct.	Nov.	Dec.	Average
1974	113.1	115.4	123.6	129.9	133.0	148.9	152.5	154.2	167.5	180.9	189.4	193.9	150.2
1975	201.6	206.3	219.2	219.2	217.8	218.0	216.8	214.6	215.8	217.1	218.2	216.6	215.1
1976	217.2	230.2	233.0	233.6	233.0	233.0	233.0	232.5	233.0	233.0	232.3	233.0	231.4
1977	231.6	233.0	232.3	232.3	232.3	233.0	238.8	244.9	243.6	243.1	242.5	243.9	237.6
1978	243.9	231.0	230.3	226.4	226.4	225.8	226.4	226.6	226.4	218.8	226.4	226.5	227.9
1979	234.8	239.2	239.2	243.6	248.1	249.4	260.1	265.4	277.6	284.3	291.5	292.2	260.5
1980	311.7	319.6	325.0	338.4	361.4	369.4	370.3	369.2	369.2	369.3	369.2	369.2	353.9
1981	369.2	369.2	370.3	370.3	368.5	368.5	387.3	387.3	387.3	396.8	392.0	383.3	379.2
1982	382.2	353.5	349.6	346.4	N.A.	338.7	341.1	345.2	336.6	335.5	335.9	N.A.	346.5
1983	336.4	335.2	334.4	333.3	333.2	333.2	337.2	337.1	337.0	337.0	340.4	340.4	336.2
1984	341.1	340.5	340.5	339.7	339.9	340.0	346.9	344.0	341.7	341.0	342.4	342.4	341.7
1985	339.3	334.2	326.2	326.0	326.0	326.0	325.7	328.1	327.3	324.6	325.3	324.9	327.8
1986	323.8	261.5	317.3	316.3	316.3	315.7	313.5	313.5	309.7	312.0			

Source: Bureau of Labor Statistics (0614-0341.04)   T.2

1

Aluminum

Aluminum prices were relatively stable during 1986. They started around 56.5 cents a pound and ended the period near 54.5 cents. World production levels were estimated at 15 million tonnes, the same as last year and near all-time highs. The U.S. was the largest producer, accounting for approximately 21 percent of the total. The USSR was a distant second with 14 percent of the total, followed by Canada with nine percent.

In the U.S., primary production for the first nine months of 1986 was 2.32 million tonnes, 13 percent below that for the comparable period in 1985, while estimated imports were up 44 percent for the same period at 1.53 million tonnes.

The domestic aluminum market has gone slightly stagnant, as the impact of competing materials has been felt across the broad spectrum of uses. Domestic consumption in 1986 was sluggish with apparent off-take near early-year estimates of 4.7 million tonnes, down from 1985's 4.9 million tonnes. Mirroring that trend, domestic production has fallen as well. As of June, 1986, there were only 22 domestic smelters operating about 78 percent of 4.9 million tonnes of capacity. Beyond closing for loss of consumption, domestic smelters are not as competitive as foreign producers, due to high operating costs. While U.S. productive capacity, relative to the rest of the world, has decreased from 36.5 percent in 1950 to 26.5 percent in 1985, imports relative to total consumption have changed little, if at all.

Over the past decade, the only nations to show increased or newly developed aluminum production capacity have been low-cost energy producers such as Canada, Australia, Venezuela, and Brazil. At one point in 1986, U.S. imports of plates and bars increased by almost 70 percent as a result of a large increase in receipts from Venezuela.

In October, 1986, the Office of the United States Trade Representative and the Government of Japan negotiated a memorandum of understanding on trade in aluminum. Japan agreed to drop its tariff on unwrought aluminum to one percent from nine percent, and to three percent from 9.2 percent on other forms of the metal. The full measure will be implemented on January 1, 1988, with decreases to five percent and 6.1 percent to be effective April 1, 1987. A semi-annual review of the arrangements has also been instituted.

During the year, major aluminum producers in Australia and Canada purchased the Goldendale, Washington and Sebree, Kentucky aluminum reduction plants, respectively, from domestic corporations divesting metal operations. Private investors and employees purchased the Colombia Falls, Montana aluminum reduction plant in September.

Aluminum consumption centers around the east-central United States. In 1985, packaging accounted for an estimated 38 percent of domestic consumption, transportation accounted for 21 percent and building for 16 percent. The Bureau of Mines has estimated that, from a 1983 base, apparent U.S. demand for aluminum will rise at an average annual rate of 4.6 percent through 1990. High operating costs of domestic aluminum reduction plants are expected to preclude future expansions and to lower increased imports and scrap recovery.

World Production of Aluminum   In Thousands of Metric[3] Tons

Year	Aus-tralia	Aus-tria	Canada	China	France	West Germany	Hun-gary	Italy	Japan	Nor-way	Spain	Switzer-land	Brazil	United Kingdom	United States	USSR	World Total
1977	273	101	1,073	385	440	818	79	287	1,310	686	233	88	184	386	4,539	1,810	15,189
1978	290	101	1,156	400	431	816	79	298	1,166	704	234	88	205	382	4,804	1,840	15,578
1979	297	102	904	400	436	817	79	297	1,114	732	286	91	263	396	5,023	1,930	16,044
1980	335	104	1,177	400	476	806	81	299	1,203	720	426	95	287	413	5,130	1,940	16,944
1981[3]	379	94	1,116	350	436	729	74	274	771	634	397	82	256	339	4,489	1,800	15,079
1982	381	94	1,065	380	390	723	74	233	351	638	367	75	299	241	3,274	1,875	13,408
1983	478	94	1,091	400	361	743	74	196	256	715	358	76	401	252	3,353	2,000	13,910
1984[1]	758	95	1,227	400	342	777	74	230	287	761	381	79	455	288	4,099	2,100	15,664
1985[2]	851	94	1,282	410	293	745	74	245	227	724	370	73	540	275	3,500	2,200	15,289

[1] Preliminary.   [2] Estimate.   [3] Data prior to 1981 are in thousands of short tons.   *Source: Bureau of Mines*   T.4

U.S. Production of Primary Aluminum (Domestic & Foreign Ores)   In Thousands of Metric Tons

Year	Jan.	Feb.	Mar.	Apr.	May	June	July	Aug.	Sept.	Oct.	Nov.	Dec.	Total[1]
1982	318	282	305	289	291	272	269	260	246	249	241	249	3,274
1983	253	223	248	245	265	261	284	297	299	320	318	340	3,353
1984[2]	342	324	350	348	365	351	349	344	329	338	325	334	4,099
1985[2]	329	289	312	295	304	288	292	289	280	285	265	271	3,499
1986[2]	273	251	281	275	284	241	231	230	225				

[1]Final annual totals.   [2] Preliminary.   *Source: Bureau of Mines*   T.9

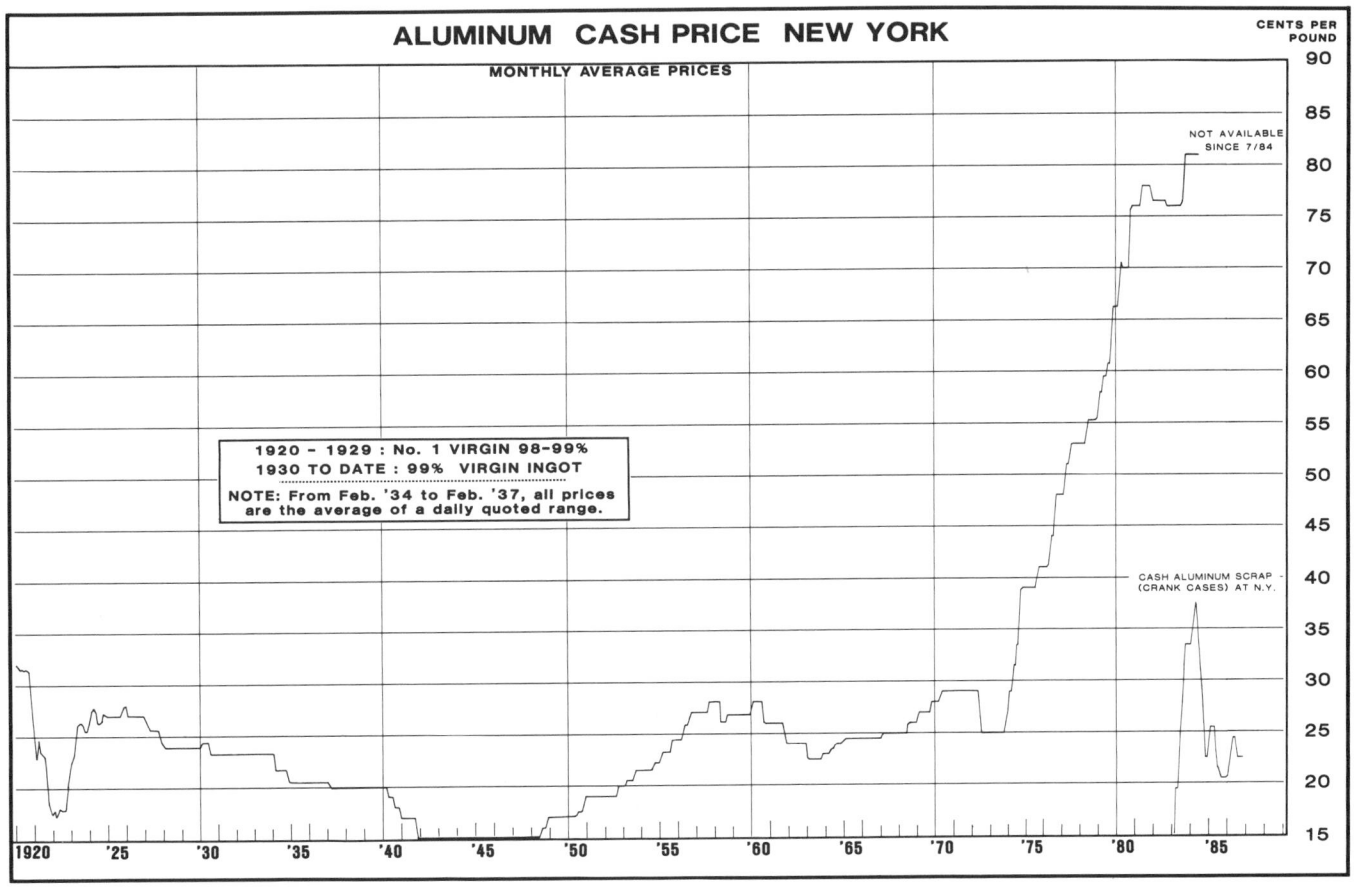

ALUMINUM CASH PRICE NEW YORK

MONTHLY AVERAGE PRICES

CENTS PER POUND

NOT AVAILABLE SINCE 7/84

1920 – 1929 : No. 1 VIRGIN 98-99%
1930 TO DATE : 99% VIRGIN INGOT
NOTE: From Feb. '34 to Feb. '37, all prices are the average of a daily quoted range.

CASH ALUMINUM SCRAP (CRANK CASES) AT N.Y.

Salient Statistics of Aluminum in the U.S.   In Thousands of Metric[8] Tons

Year	Net Import Reliance as a % of Apparent Consumption	Total Production Primary	Secondary	Primary Ship- ments[1]	Recovery from Scrap Old	New	Apparent Con- sump- tion	Plate, Sheet, Foil	Rolled Struc- tural Shapes[2]	Ex- truded Shapes[3]	All	Perma- nent Mold	Die	Sand	All	Total All Net Ship- ments
1978	11	4,804	1,323	7,143	575	1,098	6,045	3,643	583	1,311	5,673	229	666	126	1,044	6,717
1979	4	5,023	1,401	6,922	614	1,163	5,888	3,592	618	1,263	5,615	241	635	143	1,040	6,655
1980	7	5,130	1,389	6,003	680	1,058	5,065	3,346	606	1,165	5,242	193	443	121	769	6,011
1981[8]	7	4,489	1,394	5,644	758	1,031	4,614	3,097	472	1,079	4,689	132	524	108	826	5,515
1982	7	3,274	1,466	5,090	782	884	4,370	2,749	391	871	4,094	108	480	81	728	4,823
1983	17	3,353	1,564	5,857	820	953	5,035	3,249	423	1,038	4,798	137	592	76	861	5,659
1984	7	4,099	1,760	6,509	825	935	5,279	3,259	451	1,182	5,003	161	679	90	990	5,994
1985[4]	12	3,500	1,762	6,385	850	912	5,172	3,289	379	1,240	5,024	152	565	121	874	5,898
1986[6]		3,100			540		5,600									

Net Shipments[5] by Producers — Wrought Products. Castings.

[1] To Domestic Industry.   [2] Also rod, bar & wire.   [3] Also rod, bar, tube, blooms & tubing.   [4] Preliminary.   [5] Consists of total shipments less shipments to other mills for further fabrication.   [6] Estimate.   [7] Net exports.   [8] Data prior to 1981 are in thousands of short tons.
Source: U.S. Bureau of Mines

T.8

U.S. Supply and Distribution of Aluminum   In Thousands of Metric Tons

Year	Apparent Con- sump- tion	Production Primary	From Old Scrap	Im- ports	Ex- ports	Inventories (Dec. 31) Private	Govern- ment	Year	Apparent Con- sump- tion	Production Primary	From Old Scrap	Im- ports	Ex- ports	Inventories (Dec. 31) Private	Govern- ment
1981	4,615	4,489	758	848	787	2,996	2	1984	5,279	4,099	825	1,477	734	2,653	2
1982	4,370	3,274	782	878	748	2,812	2	1985[1]	5,172	3,500	850	1,420	908	2,343	2
1983	5,035	3,353	820	1,091	776	2,265	2	1986[2]	5,600	3,100	540	2,100	720	2,300	2

[1] Preliminary   [2] Estimate   *Source: U.S. Bureau of Mines*

T.8A

ALUMINUM

High, Low & Closing Prices of December Aluminum Futures in New York   In Cents Per Pound

| Year of Delivery | | Yr. Prior to Delivery | | Jan. | Feb. | Mar. | Apr. | May | June | July | Aug. | Sept. | Oct. | Nov. | Dec. | Life of Delivery Range |
		Nov.	Dec.													
1985	High	61.30	57.10	54.60	54.15	53.70	53.35	52.30	49.30	48.20	47.30	45.50	45.70	45.25	53.25	85.70
	Low	57.15	51.10	50.45	51.70	51.75	50.60	46.85	44.90	45.05	45.45	43.05	41.80	41.90	44.05	41.80
	Close	54.95	51.10	53.20	52.70	52.70	50.60	48.85	45.45	46.00	45.55	44.30	41.90	44.40	51.25	—
1986	High	49.50	57.15	59.35	58.60	61.75	61.75	58.10	55.55	54.00	53.25	54.90	52.90	50.65	50.70	61.75
	Low	46.30	48.80	54.60	54.90	57.55	54.05	52.65	52.75	51.00	51.60	52.15	49.60	48.05	48.50	46.15
	Close	48.90	55.50	56.20	57.90	58.50	54.05	54.50	53.60	52.60	52.60	52.50	50.15	48.70	50.70	—
1987	High	51.90	52.00													
	Low	50.45	50.45													
	Close	50.75	52.00													

Source: Commodity Exchange, Inc. (Comex)—N.Y.   T.11A

Month-End Open Interest of Aluminum Futures at New York   In Contracts

Year	Jan.	Feb.	Mar.	Apr.	May	June	July	Aug.	Sept.	Oct.	Nov.	Dec.
1984	3,304	3,006	3,262	2,278	2,678	1,868	3,141	3,017	2,974	4,058	5,269	4,220
1985	4,102	3,727	2,710	2,460	2,264	1,803	1,686	1,507	1,749	1,873	1,687	2,044
1986	2,386	2,179	2,476	1,717	1,444	1,098	1,215	869	854	948	781	977

Source: Commodity Exchange, Inc. (Comex)—N.Y.   T.11B

Volume of Trading of Aluminum Futures at New York   In Contracts

Year	Jan.	Feb.	Mar.	Apr.	May	June	July	Aug.	Sept.	Oct.	Nov.	Dec.	Total
1984	8,599	7,743	5,059	5,997	3,893	3,802	5,291	8,567	4,231	9,190	14,086	6,203	82,661
1985	10,788	9,222	4,935	7,353	4,935	6,609	4,159	9,052	3,342	3,166	6,934	6,568	77,063
1986	8,409	9,600	7,982	8,572	3,250	4,475	2,218	2,855	1,600	1,104	1,699	863	52,627

Source: Commodity Exchange, Inc. (Comex)—N.Y.   T.11C

Average Price of Cast Aluminum Scrap (Crank Cases)[1] in New York   In Cents per Pound

Year	Jan.	Feb.	Mar.	Apr.	May	June	July	Aug.	Sept.	Oct.	Nov.	Dec.	Average
1982	20.50	20.50	19.85	19.50	19.25	16.32	16.00	16.00	16.00	16.00	14.95	14.50	17.45
1983	15.12	17.50	19.50	19.50	23.50	25.50	27.65	31.80	33.50	33.50	33.50	33.50	26.17
1984	34.83	35.50	36.59	37.50	35.64	32.98	30.50	29.11	25.55	23.07	22.50	23.67	30.62
1985	25.50	25.50	25.50	25.50	23.23	21.50	21.40	20.50	20.50	20.50	20.50	22.55	22.55
1986	21.23	22.50	23.60	24.50	24.50	23.36	22.50	22.50	22.50	22.50	22.50	22.50	22.89

[1] Dealers' buying prices.   *Source: American Metal Market*   T.12

Aluminum Products (Ingot & Mill Products) Shipments[1] in the U.S.   In Million Pounds

Year	Jan.	Feb.	Mar.	Apr.	May	June	July	Aug.	Sept.	Oct.	Nov.	Dec.	Total
1982	862	946	1,074	1,014	972	1,127	881	1,114	1,016	980	959	1,099	12,039
1983	971	972	1,185	1,054	1,224	1,205	1,077	1,212	1,202	1,103	1,141	1,275	13,622
1984[2]	1,100	1,263	1,384	1,129	1,297	1,288	1,107	1,236	1,128	1,282	1,140	1,207	14,655
1985[2]	1,132	1,097	1,254	1,209	1,287	1,208	1,199	1,234	1,264	1,278	1,123	1,032	14,462
1986[2]	1,174	1,168	1,379	1,323	1,369	1,201							

[1] Mill products & pig & ingot (net shipments).   [2] Preliminary.   *Source: Bureau of the Census*   T.10

U.S. Aluminum Inventories, Total (Ingot, Mill Prod. & Scrap)   In Million Pounds

Year	Jan. 1	Feb. 1	Mar. 1	Apr. 1	May 1	June 1	July 1	Aug. 1	Sept. 1	Oct. 1	Nov. 1	Dec. 1
1982	6,607	6,644	6,722	6,639	6,665	6,664	6,557	6,607	6,490	6,415	6,412	6,373
1983	6,180	6,140	6,075	5,870	5,723	5,558	5,418	5,451	5,353	5,236	5,273	5,191
1984[1]	4,994	5,200	5,225	5,295	5,435	5,579	5,618	5,775	5,794	5,881	5,889	5,922
1985[1]	5,850	5,759	5,678	5,657	5,600	5,712	5,595	5,579	5,512	5,439	5,324	5,241
1986[1]	5,165	5,161	5,158	5,054	5,097	5,045	5,047					

[1] Preliminary.   *Source: Bureau of Mines*   T.5

Aluminum Exports (Metal & Alloys, Crude) from the U.S.   In Thousands of Metric Tons[1]

Year	Jan.	Feb.	Mar.	Apr.	May	June	July	Aug.	Sept.	Oct.	Nov.	Dec.	Total
1982	22.1	18.8	46.0	26.6	19.9	48.5	24.2	42.6	23.6	59.5	42.1	27.3	401.2
1983[1]	50.9	12.2	14.0	46.4	8.2	14.9	37.1	33.2	44.5	27.4	50.8	24.1	360.7
1984	24.5	20.1	19.9	7.6	23.4	24.0	22.1	37.5	23.9	17.9	32.9	32.3	286.2
1985	43.9	34.6	24.9	31.0	32.8	58.8	41.8	28.5	29.6	21.4	20.5	13.1	383.0
1986	24.1	28.1	20.0	14.1	18.7	12.6	12.1	17.2					

[1] Data prior to 1983 are in thousands of short tons.   *Source: Bureau of the Census*   T.7

Aluminum General Imports (Metal & Alloys, Crude) into the U.S.   In Thousands of Metric Tons[1]

Year	Jan.	Feb.	Mar.	Apr.	May	June	July	Aug.	Sept.	Oct.	Nov.	Dec.	Total
1981	55.8	55.7	75.6	50.2	67.8	55.9	63.9	67.0	60.5	55.2	41.5	49.3	710.7
1982	38.5	65.9	61.7	61.0	51.0	66.5	42.2	78.2	52.8	52.7	60.1	47.8	679.4
1983[1]	48.2	42.6	33.2	66.9	84.6	82.9	72.1	65.7	56.6	58.2	63.6	40.3	714.9
1984	70.9	94.9	114.3	68.8	108.8	73.9	66.8	68.0	89.9	93.0	68.6	57.4	975.3
1985	75.6	62.7	88.9	73.2	80.4	84.8	75.9	80.4	103.4	95.0	76.7	64.0	960.9
1986	90.5	110.9	140.9	144.4	167.3	137.0	131.2	136.1					

[1] Data prior to 1983 are in thousands of short tons.   *Source: Bureau of the Census*   T.6

Antimony

Judging from U.S. Bureau of Mines' data for the first nine months of 1986, total output of antimony from domestic smelters during the year was about 16,600 short tons, one percent higher than in 1985. Domestic production of secondary antimony was sharply lower in 1986 at 11,500 tons, down nearly 15 percent from 1985. Imports—in the form of ore and concentrate, metal, and oxide—were running in 1986's first three quarters at an annual rate of 18,400 tons, down 12 percent from the year before. Total domestic supply of antimony during 1986 was an estimated 46,500 short tons, up nine percent from 1985.

Industrial consumption of primary antimony falls into three broad categories: metal products, non-metal products, and flame retardants. In 1986, retardants accounted for 65 percent of industrial usage; the chief applications were in plastics and textiles.

Most of industry's consumption of primary antimony was in the form of oxide, with the balance in metal. Total industrial consumption in 1986 was an estimated 11,900 tons, which was only marginally higher than in 1985. Exports of metals, alloys, scrap, and oxide combined were estimated at 1,150 tons, little changed from the previous year.

With consumption and production roughly equivalent, the New York dealer price for 99.5 percent to 99.6 percent metal, c.i.f. U.S. ports, hovered during 1986's first half at an average of $1.32 per pound, only slightly above the average of $1.31 in 1985. Prices softened, however, during the third quarter of 1986. The average dealer price fell to $1.083 per pound and Asarco, Inc. lowered its published prices for high-tint and antimony oxide from $1.40 to $1.35 per pound.

World Mine Production of Antimony (Content of Ore)   In Short Tons

Year	Australia	Bolivia	Austria	China[1]	Czecho-slovakia	Italy	Mexico[2]	Morocco	Peru[5]	Turkey	South Africa	United States	USSR	Yugo-slavia[4]	World Total[1]
1983[3]	582	10,969	726	16,500	550	0	2,777	500	786	926	6,947	838	10,000	1,047	55,526
1984[1]	550	10,700	720	16,500	550	440	2,200	550	770	900	9,900	557	10,300	990	58,857
1985[1]		10,000		16,500			2,000				9,000			1,500	58,600

[1] Estimate.   [2] Includes antimony content of miscellaneous smelter products.   [3] Preliminary.   [4] Metal.   [5] Recoverable.
Source: Bureau of Mines   T.13

Salient Statistics of Antimony in the United States   In Short Tons

Year	Net Import Reliance as a % of Apparent Consumption	Ship-ments of Mine	Production Mine (Primary[2])	Production Smelter (Primary[2])	Secondary (Alloys)[2]	Imports[5] Ore Gross Weight	Imports[5] Ore Sb Content	Imports[5] Metal Gross Weight	Ex-ports[3]	Ores & Concen-trates	Industry Stocks, Dec. 31[2] Metallic	Industry Stocks Oxide	Industry Stocks Sulfide	Industry Stocks Resi-dues & Slag	Total[6]	Prod. of Anti-monial Lead[2]
1983	54	878	838	14,557	14,204	6,305	2,770	1,282	304	446	805	2,614	19	51	3,935	N.A.
1984[1]	58	711	557	16,979	14,806	9,891	4,299	3,898	511	1,304	603	4,926	14	69	6,916	N.A.
1985[4]				16,449	13,572		6,638	5,129	362	1,164	800	3,954	16	99	6,033	
1986[4]				16,600	8,860		5,760	7,440	560	1,120	813	3,900	20		5,800	

[1] Preliminary.   [2] Antimony content.   [3] Antimony ore, metal & compounds.   [4] Estimate.   [5] Imports for consumption.   [6] Including primary antimony residues & slag.   *Source: Bureau of Mines*   T.15

Industrial Consumption of Primary Antimony in the United States   In Short Tons (Antimony Content)

Year	Ammu-nition	Metal Products Anti-monial Lead	Metal Products Sheet & Pipe	Metal Products Bearing Metal & Bearings	Metal Products Cable Cover-ing	Metal Products Solder	Metal Products Type Metal	Metal Products Total All Metal Products	Flame Retar-dant	Ammun. primers	Non-Metal Products Ceramics & Glass	Non-Metal Products Rubber Pdt's.	Non-Metal Products Pig-ments	Non-Metal Products Plas-tics	Non-Metal Products Total	Grand Total
1983	175	926	43	143	31	154	10	1,562	6,204	16	1,252	70	198	993	2,652	10,418
1984[1]	N.A.	845	80	169	N.A.	228	31	1,701	7,959	21	1,292	21	178	1,108	2,787	12,447
1985[2]	410	568		179		338	31	1,642	7,530	20	1,187	25	147	998	2,529	11,701
1986[2]		468		90		170		1,248	6,000		900		200	730	2,000	9,160

[1] Preliminary.   [2] Estimated coverage based on 77% of the industry.   *Source: Bureau of Mines*   T.16

Antimony Imported (for Consumption) into the U.S. and Price Ranges

Year	Imported for Consumption Antimony Ore Value Ths. $	Needle or Liquated Antimony Gross Weight Sh. Tons	Needle or Liquated Antimony Value $ Ths.	Antimony Metal Short Tons	Antimony Metal Value $Ths.	Antimony Oxide Short Tons	Antimony Oxide Value $ Ths.	Foreign Metal (Duty Paid Delivery New York) ¢ Lb.	Antimony Trioxide ¢ Lb.	Metal[2] ¢ Lb.	Domestic (Based on Antimony in Alloy)
1983	2,335	47	58	1,282	1,987	10,604	13,318	78–135	100–120	91.3	200
1984[1]	6,798	72	157	3,898	8,037	17,884	26,348	120–177	116–180	151.2	200
1985[1]		112		5,129		8,815				131.1	200
1986[1]		400		7,440		11,400				124.0	200

[1] Preliminary.   [2] N.Y. Dealer Price, 99.5% to 99.6%, C.I.F. U.S. ports.   *Source: Bureau of Mines*   T.17

Apples

World Production of Apples (Dessert & Cooking)   In Thousands of Metric Tons

Year	Mex-ico	Argen-tina	Aus-tralia	Spain	Belg-Lux.	Canada	France	West Germany	Italy	Japan	Nether-lands	Turkey	United Kingdom	United States[2]	Yugo-slavia	World Total
1974	213	786	368	1,038	209	406	1,610	1,281	1,886	850	385	950	340	2,964	370	14,895
1975	230	608	368	1,091	268	460	2,125	2,035	2,127	989	430	900	338	3,415	370	16,910
1976	329	576	275	1,008	241	409	1,598	1,487	2,143	879	380	1,000	388	2,936	483	15,501
1977	297	820	301	672	120	411	1,186	1,176	1,828	959	315	900	234	3,057	381	13,934
1978	313	810	258	1,015	273	452	1,768	1,783	1,874	844	510	1,000	342	3,446	381	16,589
1979	338	972	345	1,097	322	435	1,769	1,951	2,023	853	450	1,350	334	3,694	428	16,605
1980	282	908	345	859	330	553	1,802	1,880	1,966	960	450	1,100	321	4,005	483	17,179
1981	280	804	294	1,008	134	422	1,502	773	1,773	846	260		227	3,517	508	14,099
1982	394	817	301	891	270	478	1,978	2,637	2,642	925	440		340	3,684	746	18,419
1983[1]	302	934	281	1,047	203	485	1,573	1,313	2,056	1,048	364		293	3,798	557	16,212
1984[3]	437	950	320	1,049	230	455	1,930	1,799	2,075	986	380		312	3,758	607	17,354
1985[3]														3,606		
1986[3]														3,510		

[1] Preliminary.   [2] Commercial crop.   [3] Estimate.   *Source: Foreign Agricultural Service, U.S.D.A.*   T.18

Salient Statistics of Apples[1] in the United States

Year	Production Total	Production Util-ized	Western Avg. Auction Price N.Y. $ Per Box Golden Delicious	Western Avg. Auction Price N.Y. $ Per Box Red Rome	Fresh	Canned	Dried	Frozen	Juice & Cider	Other[3]	Avg. Farm Price ¢ Per Lb.	Farm Value Million $	Foreign Trade[4] Domestic Exports Fresh	Foreign Trade[4] Domestic Exports Dried[5]	Imports Fresh & Dried[5]	Fresh Per Capita Con-sump-tion Lbs.
1974	6,580	6,530	8.81	7.04	3,691	1,226	197	182	1,031	204	8.40	551.6	106.1	3.7	37.8	16.5
1975	7,530	7,103	8.22	5.16	4,357	1,027	230	207	1,192	91	6.50	460.9	102.3	3.7	57.8	19.1
1976	6,472	6,467	7.57	3.67	3,916	920	229	220	1,109	73	9.10	586.5	123.7	4.6	55.7	17.1
1977	6,740	6,710	8.76	7.28	3,860	1,076	226	161	1,267	121	10.60	708.6	142.4	8.2	63.6	16.9
1978	7,597	7,544	9.77	6.00	4,210	1,224	221	207	1,495	186	10.40	781.4	154.8	7.3	78.5	17.5
1979	8,126	8,101	N.A.	N.A.	4,289	1,337	256	137	1,954	130	10.90	881.2	237.3	5.5	71.2	17.5
1980	8,818	8,800			4,934	1,202	195	168	2,137	165	8.70	761.3	311.3	7.6	76.8	19.0
1981	7,740	7,693			4,442	1,002	190	173	1,798	87	11.10	851.1	269.2	8.3	128.3	16.8
1982	8,122	8,110			4,537	1,249	210	191	1,808	116	10.00	809.0	261.8	16.1	98.7	17.9
1983	8,379	8,358			4,621	1,204	283	170	1,985	95	10.50	879.0	228.7	12.0	126.0	18.4
1984[2]	8,331	8,316			4,664	1,177	289	198	1,886	102	11.20	926.4	——209.4——			18.3
1985[2]	7,949	7,861			4,234	1,276	253	174	1,849	75	11.60	850.2	——152.8——			18.1
1986[2]	7,738															

Utilization of Quantities Sold — Processed[5] — Millions of Pounds — Metric Tons

[1] Commercial crop.   [2] Preliminary.   [3] Mostly crushed for vinegar, jam, etc.   [4] Year beginning July.   [5] Fresh weight basis.
Source: Statistical Reporting Service, U.S.D.A.   T.19

U.S. Price[1] of Apples Received by Growers (for Fresh Use)   In Cents per Pound

Year	Jan.	Feb.	Mar.	Apr.	May	June	July	Aug.	Sept.	Oct.	Nov.	Dec.	Average
1974	7.110	7.370	6.066	6.650	8.500	N.A.	N.A.	N.A.	8.213	9.793	N.A.	8.320	7.753
1975	8.193	9.500	10.000	9.580	11.783	14.081	N.A.	N.A.	N.A.	7.261	7.272	7.440	9.457
1976	7.217	8.437	8.250	8.750	7.752	8.070	N.A.	N.A.	N.A.	9.610	9.008	9.785	8.542
1977	N.A.	10.900	10.030	9.794	9.725	9.935	N.A.	N.A.	N.A.	9.960	9.000	8.020	9.417
1978	11.183	11.280	11.305	N.A.	N.A.	N.A.	N.A.	N.A.	N.A.	N.A.	21.612	14.000	13.876
1979	13.500	14.000	14.000	14.500	13.500	13.750	N.A.	N.A.	N.A.	12.750	14.500	15.250	13.972
1980	15.750	15.667	16.750	16.750	16.750	19.000	N.A.	N.A.	N.A.	12.500	12.000	12.000	15.240
1981	12.000	12.250	13.500	12.583	12.875	13.500	N.A.	N.A.	N.A.	16.000	15.125	15.500	13.704
1982	15.125	16.000	16.833	15.000	N.A.	N.A.	N.A.	N.A.	N.A.	13.500	13.000	14.000	14.780
1983[1]	11.8	12.3	12.8	11.3	11.4	10.5	11.2	14.4	18.0	16.5	15.3	14.6	13.3
1984	14.4	15.2	15.3	15.0	15.1	14.7	18.6	18.3	20.7	18.4	17.3	17.8	16.7
1985	14.7	14.5	15.0	14.9	13.6	12.3	17.5	18.2	17.7	17.3	17.5	17.7	15.9
1986[2]	17.0	17.9	18.4	17.3	21.1	24.2	25.4	26.8	22.3	20.1	18.5		

[1] Prior to 1983, data are in dollar per tray ctn. of "Delicious" in the U.S.   [2] Preliminary.   *Source: Bureau of Labor Statistics* (0111-0215.99)
T.20

Arsenic

Substantial resources of arsenic occur in copper ores in Peru and the Philippines, in copper-gold ores in Chile, and in gold ores in Canada. The global resource base has been estimated at 1.5 million tonnes.

World production data for 1986 were not available at this writing, but total output was probably in line with 1984 and 1985, when it averaged 36,000 tonnes per year. The bulk of the world's annual production comes from the USSR (22 percent of the total), Sweden (16 percent), France (14 percent), Mexico (13 percent) and Chile (10 percent). In the U.S., a plant in Tacoma, Washington that produced crude arsenic trioxide and arsenic metal closed in 1985, allegedly because of costs associated with compliance with environmental regulations. A firm in Georgia refines low-grade arsenic trioxide for use in certain wood preservatives and a Wyoming company makes arsenic acid for similar applications.

The U.S., the world's largest consumer of arsenic and its derivatives, uses 40 percent of global output, chiefly in wood preservatives and agricultural herbicides. The principal sources of U.S. supply are Sweden and Canada, each of which accounts for 29 percent of total imports, followed by Mexico and France. Until January 1, 1987, only arsenic trioxide and sulfide entered the U.S. duty-free. After that date, imports of arsenic metal from most-favored nations also became tariff-free, and the impost on other compounds from such nations fell to 3.7 percent *ad valorem*. Since January, 1986, there has been a tariff of 6 cents per pound on arsenic metal imported from non-most-favored nations and of two percent *ad valorem* on other arsenic compounds. Imported trioxide carried an average year-end price in 1985 of 42 cents per pound, as against only 33 cents per pound for domestic trioxide.

Synthetic organic compounds, such as paraquat, are substitutes for arsenic herbicides; pentacholorophenol and creosote may be used instead of chromated copper arsenate as wood preservatives. However, in most of these cases, the substitute is higher in cost and inferior in quality to arsenic.

World Production of White Arsenic (Arsenic Trioxide)   In Metric[4] Tons

Year	Portugal	Boivia	Brazil	Canada	Chile	France	West Germany	USSR	Japan	Mexico	Peru	Rep. of Korea	Sweden	Namibia[3]	World Total
1974	290		20	—	—	9,000	401	8,050	213	10,477	2,175	18	16,190	7,319	54,153
1975	282		14	—	—	7,300	350	8,100	66	6,747	1,461	110	12,884	7,345	44,659
1976	306		0		—	8,023	400	8,200	66	6,062	879	1,028	7,411	5,646	38,021
1977	245		—		—	6,661	400	8,300	131	6,332	1,507	713	6,613	2,882	33,784
1978	279				—	6,500	400	8,400	100	6,884	1,457	604	6,700	2,647	33,971
1979[4]	345				—	5,550	—	7,700	182	6,537	1,415	590	5,080	2,221	29,620
1980	200	81			—	5,300	360	7,700	284	6,932	2,475	N.A.	6,500	1,288	31,199
1981	196	127	—	—	—	5,200	360	7,750	95	6,517	2,164	170	6,900	1,370	30,870
1982	200	261	—	—	—	5,100	360	7,800	100	4,740	1,663	306	7,200	1,895	29,625
1983[1]	190	107	—	—	—	4,700	360	7,900	300	4,557	1,110	560	5,300	1,126	26,210
1984[2]	180	130	—	1,000	3,500	5,000	360	8,000	500	4,500	1,100	N.A.	5,900	2,504	32,674
1985[2]					3,500	6,000		8,000		4,500	1,000		6,000	2,500	39,000

[1] Preliminary.   [2] Estimate.   [3] Output of Tsumeb Corp. Ltd. only.   [4] Data prior to 1979 are in short tons.   *Source: Bureau of Mines*   T.21

Salient Statistics of White Arsenic in the U.S.   In Metric[5] Tons

Year	Trioxide (As₂O₃)	Metallic Arsenic	Arsenic Acid	Sulfide	Arsenic Compounds	Trioxide Mexican 99.13% As₂O₃ ¢ lb.[3]	Value of Imports Thous. $	Trioxide Domestic[4] 95% As₂O₃ — ¢ lb. 12/31 —	Metal Domestic 99% As	Peru	Canada	France	Mexico	South Africa	Sweden	Bel-Lux.	Exports (compounds) Gross Weight
1974	13,742	707			43		2,449			24	—	480	6,185	145	6,889		
1975	12,013	483			77	16.5	4,426	13.1	160	66	—	595	3,174	970	7,172		
1976	4,262	288			355	17	1,528	13.1	175	—	—	462	3,793	—		3	
1977	5,981	357	382	—	1,109	18	1,962	13.1	190	—	22	1,352	3,089	—	1,323		
1978	10,306	369	565	—	473	27	5,918	23¼	190	—	136	5,077	2,603	—	2,281	189	
1979	12,325	405	176	39	1	30	7,728	24¼	190	477	277	3,242	3,125	—	5,014	184	969
1980	12,528	266	271	11	1	46	9,190	31¾	300	—	486	2,780	3,720		4,770	388	1,518
1981[5]	17,199	294	1,511	—	4	78	17,742	40	275	50	5,581	749	3,566	17	4,902	1,251	523
1982	14,599	136	699	18	362	59	18,205	40	245	—	3,352	1,992	2,276	—	4,192	1,030	2,658
1983	10,186	243	2,385	1,127	26	45	13,920	33	225	—	2,525	667	2,531	17	3,430	946	85
1984[2]	13,985	304	2,506	20	35	42	14,581	33	210		4,767	1,261	3,115	—	3,914	843	76
1985[1]	18,000					42		33	210								200

[1] Estimate.   [2] Preliminary.   [3] F.O.B. Laredo, TX.   [4] F.O.B. Tacoma, Wash.   [5] Data prior to 1981 are in short tons.   *Source: Bureau of Mines*   T.22

Barley

World production of barley in 1986/87 is projected by USDA to reach 175.6 million tonnes, down one percent from a year ago. The Soviet Union and the European Community (EC) are the largest producers, each accounting for about 25 percent of the world total; the U.S. grows about seven percent of the world crop. Most of the decline in world production will take place in the EC, where output is expected to fall by eight percent. Canada had an excellent growing season; its crop of 14.7 million tonnes is almost 19 percent larger than a year ago.

World use of barley in 1986/87 is expected to total 173.6 million tonnes, nearly unchanged from a year ago. World trade is likely to decline, as most importers reduce purchases. The USDA projects world barley exports at 17.6 million tonnes, eight percent less than last season. The U.S. will buck this trend by increasing exports. Saudi Arabia is the major market, accounting for nearly 37 percent of world trade.

Global ending stocks of barley are projected to increase five percent to 26.7 million tonnes. The U.S. will hold almost 29 percent of the total.

U.S. barley production in 1986/87 was a record 600 million bushels, a slight increase over last season. While yields were off marginally, to 50 bushels per acre, harvested acreage of 12 million acres was the highest since the 1962/63 season. Planting of barley has been trending higher since 1979/80. With carrying stocks of 325 million bushels, the total supply of barley is projected by USDA to reach 930 million bushels. This represents a 10-percent increase from the previous season.

Domestic use of barley is estimated by USDA at 475 million bushels, a drop of five percent from a year ago. Last season, record amounts of barley were fed; this season should see a decline due to ample corn supplies. Exports of barley are estimated to improve substantially. The USDA projects 1986/87 exports at 100 million bushels, much above year-ago's 22 million bushels. While the major export markets for the U.S. are Japan and Taiwan, sales of barley under the Export Enhancement Program to Saudi Arabia have been very strong. Should the export projection be obtained, 1986/87 would be the best export season since 1981/82.

Total use of barley is estimated to increase 10 percent, to 575 million bushels, but huge stocks will mean increase in supplies. Carryout stocks on May 31, 1987, are projected to reach 355 million bushels, a nine-percent increase from a year ago.

U.S. Government Price Support

The price support loan rate for barley in 1987 is $1.49, while the target price remains at $2.60. In 1986, the loan rate was $1.56. For barley producers to qualify for the 1987 program, they must reduce base acreage by 20 percent. A paid diversion of 15 percent of acreage is optional.

Futures Market

Feed barley futures are traded on the Winnipeg Commodity Exchange (WCE).

World Barley Supply and Demand   In Millions of Metric Tons

Crop Year	Exports						Imports		Production	Utilization				Stocks[2]		
	Aus-tralia	Can-ada	EC-12	Total Non-U.S.	U.S.	Total Ex-ports	U.S.S.R.	Total Imports	Pro-duction	West Europe	Non-U.S.	U.S.	Total Util-ization	Non-U.S.	U.S.	Total Stocks
1980–81	1.5	4.0	4.6	12.4	1.8	14.2	4.0	14.2	164.0	52.0	157.2	7.6	164.8	14.1	3.0	17.1
1981–82	1.7	5.5	3.5	12.0	2.0	14.1	3.6	14.1	157.0	48.3	149.1	8.1	157.2	13.7	3.2	17.0
1982–83	.6	6.1	3.9	12.5	1.0	13.4	2.2	13.4	166.9	49.5	152.6	8.9	161.5	15.6	4.7	20.3
1983–84	3.7	4.2	3.8	13.3	2.1	15.4	.5	15.4	164.8	49.1	160.5	9.8	170.4	16.2	4.1	14.7
1984–85	4.7	2.5	8.0	17.2	1.2	18.4	4.7	18.4	174.2	50.2	157.0	10.3	167.4	16.2	5.4	21.6
1985–86	3.8	4.8	7.9	18.5	.8	19.2	3.0	19.2	177.0	48.1	163.0	10.9	173.9	17.6	7.1	24.7
1986–87[1]	2.4	5.5	6.0	15.4	2.2	17.6	2.8	17.6	175.6	48.3	163.2	10.3	173.6	19.0	7.7	26.7

[1] Preliminary.   [2] End of crop year season.   *Source: Foreign Agricultural Service, U.S.D.A.*   T.29A

World Production of Barley   In Thousands of Metric Tons

Crop Years	China	United States	Austr-alia	Canada	Rep. of Korea	Den-mark	Moroc-co	France	India	Japan	USSR	West Ger-many	Spain	Turkey	United King-dom	World Total
1979–0	7,500	8,334	3,703	8,460	1,508	6,657	1,886	11,196	2,142	406	47,900	8,184	6,252	5,000	9,609	160,200
1980–1	7,600	7,859	2,682	11,259	859	6,044	2,210	11,758	1,624	375	43,400	8,826	8,705	5,300	10,326	164,000
1981–2	7,500	10,436	3,450	13,724	749	6,044	1,039	10,231	2,293	383	37,500	8,687	4,757	5,900	10,230	157,000
1982–3	7,000	11,233	1,939	13,966	749	6,357	2,334	10,036	1,993	390	43,000	9,460	5,269	6,400	10,954	166,900
1983–4	6,800	11,081	4,890	10,209	815	4,423	1,228	8,865	1,867	380	50,000	8,944	6,662	5,400	9,980	164,800
1984–5[1]	7,300	13,046	5,554	10,296	804	6,072	1,405		1,787	396	41,800	10,284	10,000	6,000	11,100	174,200
1985–6[2]	6,200	12,900	4,913	12,443							46,500					177,000
1986–7[2]	6,400	13,100	3,600	14,700							48,000					175,600

[1] Preliminary.   [2] Estimated.   *Source: Foreign Agricultural Service, U.S.D.A.*   T.23

BARLEY

U.S. Barley Acreage and Prices

Year Begin-ning June 1	Acreage (Million Acres) National Pro-gram	Set-aside	Planted	Harvest-ed for Grain	Yield per Harvest-ed Acre In — Bushels —	Re-ceived by Farm-ers[1]	Seasonal Prices Minneapolis or Better Feed (No. 2)	Malt-ing (No. 3) Dollars per Bushel	Port-land No. 2 Western	Govt. Price Support Operations Na-tional Avg. Loan Rate	Sup-port or Target Price	Placed Under Loan (Mil. Bu.)	Total Pay-ments to Partici-pants[6] (Mil. $)
1978–9	7.5	.8	10.0	9.2	49.2	1.92	1.80	2.38	2.10	1.63	2.25	67.6	97[9]
1979–0	7.8	.7	8.1	7.5	50.9	2.29	2.16	2.87	2.69	1.71	2.40	30.0	22[8]
1980–1	8.7	—	8.3	7.3	49.7	2.84	2.60	3.64	3.34	1.83	2.55	31.2	31[7]
1981–2	10.2	—	9.6	9.0	52.4	2.44	2.21	3.06	2.87	1.95	2.60	60.5	63[8]
1982–3	—	.4	9.5	9.0	57.2	2.22	1.76	2.53	2.52	2.08	2.60	92.6	60[10]
1983–4	—	1.1	10.4	9.7	52.3	2.50	2.48	2.84	2.91	2.16	2.60	32.4	72[3]
1984–5	—	.5	12.0	11.2	53.4	2.26	2.09	2.55	2.59	2.08	2.60	55.0	50[10]
1985–6[4]	—	.7	13.2	11.6	51.0	2.00	1.53	2.24	2.22	2.08	2.60		150[10]
1986–7[5]	—	1.8	13.0[2]	12.0	50.0	1.50	1.20	1.80	1.89	1.56	2.60		304[3]

[1] Excludes support payments. [2] Prospective plantings. [3] Deficiency & diversion payments. [4] Preliminary. [5] Estimate. [6] Available for total feed grains only. [7] Disaster payments. [8] Deficiency & disaster payments. [9] Deficiency, disaster & diversion payments. [10] Deficiency payments. *Source: Economic Research Service, U.S.D.A.*

T.24

High, Low & Closing Prices of May Barley Futures at Winnipeg In Canadian Dollars per Tonne

Year of Delivery		June	July	Aug.	Sept.	Oct.	Nov.	Dec.	Jan.	Feb.	Mar.	Apr.	May	Life of Delivery Range
1981	High	131.50	139.50	139.60	143.50	150.30	165.00	166.50	162.90	156.90	153.30	153.90	153.50	166.50
	Low	121.40	126.50	130.00	137.50	137.20	149.60	141.90	150.70	151.40	145.30	146.20	145.50	121.40
	Close	128.00	138.10	139.50	141.60	149.30	164.00	160.80	150.80	151.60	146.80	153.90	145.50	—
1982	High	144.00	144.20	141.90	133.10	134.70	133.00	130.80	133.20	132.90	128.20	125.50	133.00	144.2
	Low	133.60	136.20	128.50	127.50	129.00	127.00	126.60	128.80	126.80	118.00	121.30	121.80	118.0
	Close	134.60	142.30	131.00	129.50	132.90	127.50	129.10	131.50	127.00	125.30	122.00	125.80	—
1983	High	127.90	127.50	116.80	108.70	105.00	110.50	107.10	111.30	109.50	107.50	109.20	108.20	127.90
	Low	127.90	114.80	106.30	102.50	100.70	101.50	105.50	104.90	101.90	100.00	104.80	100.30	100.00
	Close	127.90	115.70	107.80	104.80	101.50	105.80	106.20	108.50	103.60	106.80	107.30	101.20	—
1984	High	109.00	110.50	131.00	142.10	141.00	138.00	137.00	137.00	133.00	132.00	134.60	149.00	149.00
	Low	107.30	107.50	116.20	128.50	128.80	132.30	131.70	131.80	124.80	128.30	127.60	132.10	107.30
	Close	107.50	110.50	128.60	137.20	134.00	133.90	136.20	132.60	128.90	132.00	133.00	142.00	—
1985	High	136.00	138.50	137.00	134.30	135.20	138.80	139.10	138.10	137.80	138.20	142.00	149.00	149.00
	Low	130.10	124.30	129.80	129.70	132.20	133.80	136.50	136.20	130.40	134.00	138.20	128.50	124.30
	Close	131.50	137.50	130.10	134.20	134.20	138.10	137.10	137.80	134.80	138.00	142.00	129.60	—
1986	High	—	131.10	120.40	117.00	116.90	116.20	115.60	114.40	105.40	102.60	102.30	116.00	131.10
	Low	—	121.90	113.70	111.10	113.00	114.50	112.60	104.50	100.40	98.70	84.60	87.80	84.60
	Close	—	122.00	114.10	113.70	115.70	115.45	113.60	104.90	100.90	102.20	92.80	115.10	—
1987	High	—	86.50	85.50	89.90	88.20	87.40	85.40						
	Low	—	85.30	83.50	83.20	83.20	82.70	84.00						
	Close	—	85.30	83.60	88.90	84.00	85.10	84.40						

Source: Winnipeg Commodity Exchange

T.26

Production of Barley in the United States, by States In Millions of Bushels

Year	Ari-zona	Cali-fornia	Colo-rado	Ida-ho	Kan-sas	Minne-sota	Mary-land	Okla-homa	Montana	North Dakota	Oregon	Pennsyl-vania	Utah	South Dakota	Wash-ington	Wyo-ming
1979	3.2	47.4	18.7	54.9	2.3	40.8	3.8	2.5	40.6	75.9	8.3	4.0	10.4	20.8	17.0	8.7
1980	4.5	44.1	15.9	59.0	2.1	34.6	3.4	1.7	44.1	48.0	10.1	3.8	10.8	15.2	32.3	8.6
1981	4.1	40.3	18.6	63.1	1.7	57.7	5.0	1.6	56.8	105.6	11.7	4.1	11.1	20.1	44.1	9.0
1982	3.8	38.4	15.9	75.9	2.5	51.0	5.4	1.1	76.4	103.4	15.5	3.4	12.9	23.4	49.4	9.4
1983	2.8	29.4	16.5	67.0	4.6	43.5	5.0	1.5	77.7	114.7	16.5	3.6	11.4	23.1	54.4	10.0
1984	5.4	29.0	20.2	88.4	6.7	61.8	5.5	2.1	59.1	153.7	17.4	3.6	11.6	30.3	63.7	10.4
1985	6.0	24.8	21.8	71.9	7.5	71.0	5.5	1.9	30.0	184.3	19.3	4.3	11.8	32.4	56.6	10.6
1986[1]	3.1	22.8	23.3	67.7	11.0	55.0	5.2	1.8	92.0	189.8	20.1	3.9	11.5	34.8	41.4	10.9

[1] Preliminary. *Source: Crop Reporting Board, U.S.D.A.*

T.25

Average Cash Price of No. 2 (or better) Feed Barley, in Minneapolis   In Cents Per Bushel

Year	June	July	Aug.	Sept.	Oct.	Nov.	Dec.	Jan.	Feb.	Mar.	Apr.	May	Average
1977–8	176	163	150	158	166	165	165	165	165	166	191	190	168
1978–9	184	171	168	177	181	188	179	171	169	186	189	196	180
1979–0	216	239	215	222	234	211	215	209	204	206	212	209	216
1980–1	215	248	239	243	277	303	275	281	290	263	251	239	260
1981–2	209	226	235	221	226	231	206	220	227	216	216	224	221
1982–3	212	185	172	169	154	158	159	163	172	173	201	195	176
1983–4	196	195	242	261	260	253	239	255	256	265	274	277	248
1984–5	259	218	213	205	210	206	188	198	199	197	205	205	209
1985–6[1]	190	166	146	140	141	149	160	157	—	—	—	131	153
1986–7[1]	123	116	113	127	150	163							

[1] Preliminary.   *Source: Economic Research Service, U.S.D.A.*   T.27

Month-End Open Interest of Barley Futures at Winnipeg   In Contracts (20 Tonne)

Year	Jan.	Feb.	Mar.	Apr.	May	June	July	Aug.	Sept.	Oct.	Nov.	Dec.
1979	16,704	18,864	18,579	23,142	17,635	23,336	26,643	25,193	24,230	20,466	22,107	21,468
1980	19,105	17,631	14,848	14,027	15,842	17,658	18,224	18,724	21,082	16,574	16,173	13,496
1981	14,560	13,335	13,836	16,380	14,252	12,968	15,101	16,620	16,086	10,971	10,591	8,832
1982	8,485	7,838	7,096	6,684	6,774	6,298	7,019	7,427	8,148	8,697	8,697	7,826
1983	9,952	10,972	9,535	10,458	11,064	12,592	12,688	18,486	19,110	17,099	15,083	10,673
1984	10,279	10,698	9,693	12,649	10,439	13,752	12,451	14,125	15,380	9,836	11,345	9,334
1985	10,984	11,828	9,622	8,152	9,187	9,187	8,808	9,529	9,948	10,166	9,948	7,624
1986	7,702	9,550	8,679	9,275	8,109	8,286	8,223	8,729	9,709	8,605	8,771	8,121

Source: Winnipeg Commodity Exchange   T.28

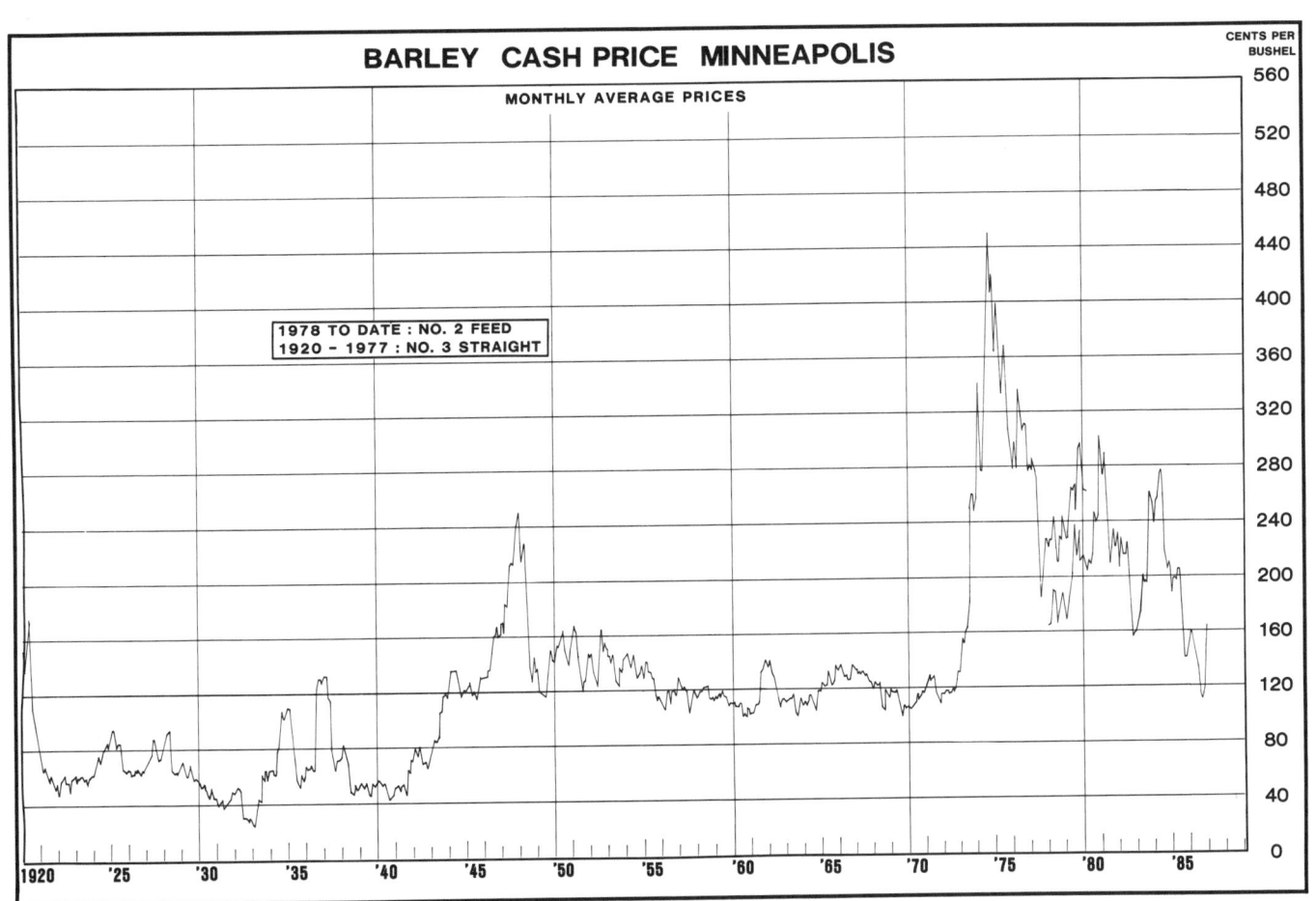

BARLEY CASH PRICE MINNEAPOLIS

MONTHLY AVERAGE PRICES

1978 TO DATE : NO. 2 FEED
1920 – 1977 : NO. 3 STRAIGHT

BARLEY

Salient Statistics of Barley in the United States   In Millions of Bushels

Year Begin. June 1	Begin- ning Stocks	Produc- tion	Im- ports	Total Supply	Food	Alc. Bever- ages	Seed	Feed & Residual	Total	Ex- ports	Total Disapp.	Gov't. Owned[1]	Privately Owned[2]	Total Stocks
1978–9	173.1	454.8	10.5	638.4	6.0	147.5	13.6	217.6	384.7	25.7	410.4	2.5	225.5	228.0
1979–0	228.0	383.2	11.8	623.0	7.0	150.9	14.0	204.2	376.1	54.8	430.9	3.2	188.9	192.1
1980–1	192.1	361.1	10.2	563.4	7.0	155.3	13.2	173.9	349.4	76.7	426.1	3.4	133.9	137.3
1981–2	137.3	473.5	9.6	620.4	6.9	150.9	16.3	198.4	372.5	100.1	472.6	3.3	144.5	147.8
1982–3	147.8	515.9	10.7	674.4	7.2	145.5	17.4	240.4	410.5	47.2	457.7	6.0	210.7	216.7
1983–4	216.7	508.9	7.1	732.7	7.0	142.5	19.9	282.4	451.8	91.5	543.3	11.9	177.5	189.4
1984–5	189.4	599.2	10.1	798.7	7.0	142.0	21.2	304.2	474.4	76.9	551.3	14.6	232.8	247.4
1985–6[3]	247.4	591.4	9.0	847.8	——147.2——		19.6	334.6	501.4	21.8	523.2	57.4	267.2	324.6
1986–7[4]	324.6	599.8	5.0	929.4	——174.4——			300.0	474.4	100.0	574.4	30.0	325.0	355.0
1987–8[4]	355.0													

[1] Uncommitted inventory.   [2] Includes quantity under loan & farmer-owned reserve.   [3] Preliminary.   [4] Estimate.
Source: Economic Research Service, U.S.D.A.

T.29

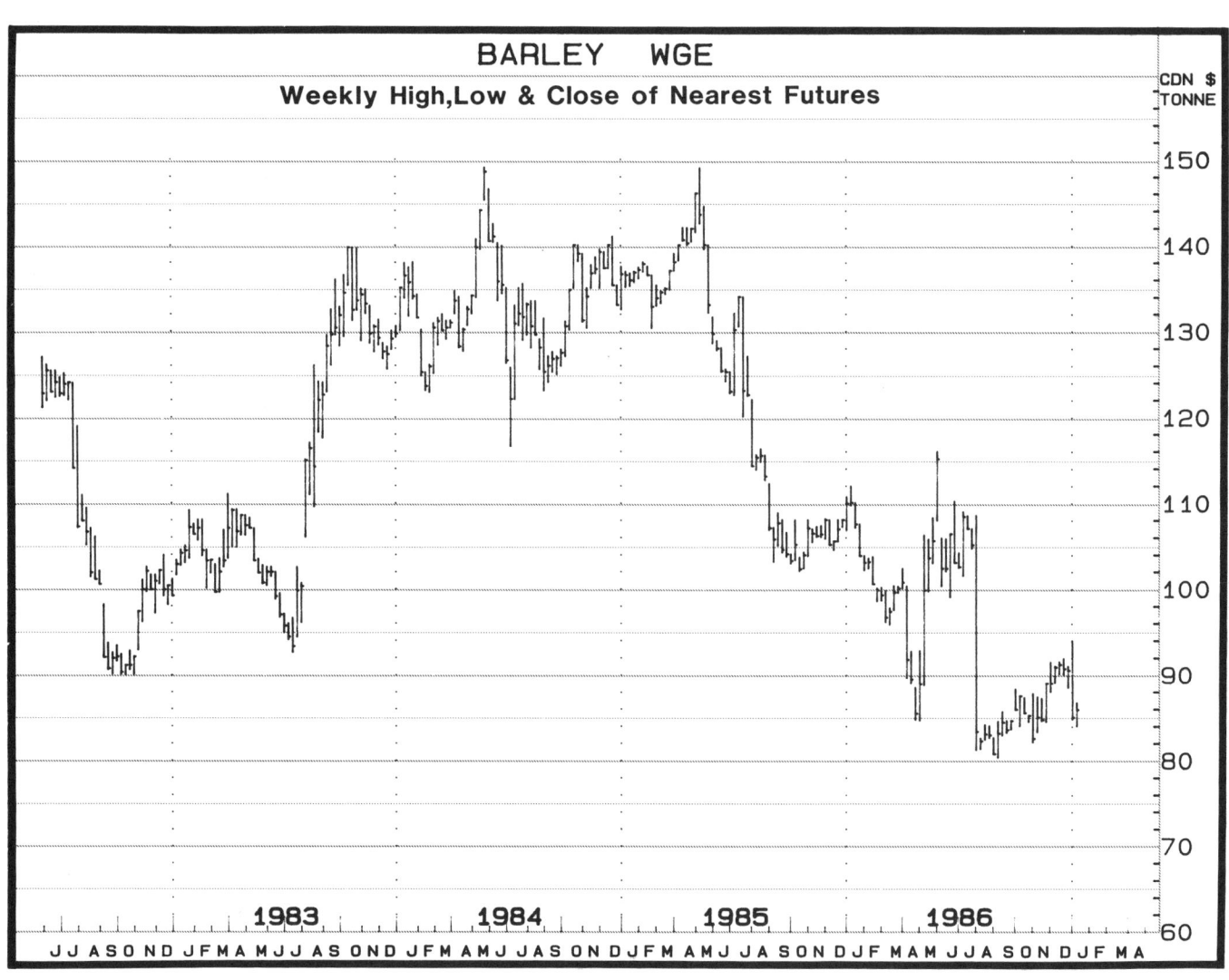

BARLEY   WGE
Weekly High, Low & Close of Nearest Futures

CDN $ / TONNE

1983   1984   1985   1986

Bauxite

The U.S. bauxite mining industry is in a state of decline. Third-quarter 1986 domestic bauxite production of 106,000 tons was the lowest third-quarter figure since 1940. Production for that period was off 39 percent from the comparable year-ago period; high-quality reserves in the U.S. are virtually depleted and are used strictly for non-metal purposes. For 1986, domestic production through the third quarter was 370,000 tons, off 30 percent from the first nine months of 1985. Production trends in earlier quarters were poor, with second-quarter production characterized by the Bureau of Mines as the lowest quarterly production level since 1932.

Bauxite ore is refined into alumina, which is reduced to aluminum. Four nations produce the bulk of the world's bauxite; Jamaica is the leader, followed by Brazil, Guinea and Australia. But the sources of bauxite are diverse. Production in 17 nations listed as "other," including the U.S., totaled 20 percent of world production in 1985. Currently, Guinea is the largest source of bauxite ore for the U.S. and supplies almost 50 percent of total U.S. imports. Australia, which produces more than 33 percent of the world's supply, is the source of 10 percent of U.S. bauxite imports. However, the U.S. is importing less bauxite and more alumina, as offshore suppliers seek to reduce transportation costs, process bauxite ore locally, and export the value-added commodity. The conversion from bauxite to alumina is 2.3 pounds of bauxite to make one pound of alumina. Global reserves of bauxite are estimated at 23.2 million tons, with Guinea's share of that totaling more than 25 percent, Australia's about 20 percent, and Brazil's about 13 percent. Total resources are put at 55 to 75 billion tons, with the bulk in South America and Africa.

The U.S. was the world's largest producer of alumina until 1975, when it was surpassed by Australia. Currently, Australia accounts for most of the increase in world alumina production over the last 15 years and supplies about 68 percent of U.S. alumina imports. Except for Japan, which has decreased alumina production, most of the major producers have kept output fairly constant over the last 15 years. The widespread production of alumina tends to insure secure supplies at competitive prices.

The continued general weakness in domestic production, compared with prior years, is chiefly attributable to low prices and weak demand for primary aluminum and alumina-based refractories, chemicals and abrasives. Steep declines in bauxite output forecast for 1986 were correct and further erosion is likely. To stem the tide, some aluminum producers have engaged in expanding or diversifying this research into advanced materials, such as ceramics, composites and laminates, and polymers, as well as toward advanced manufacturing systems. These product and manufacturing advances, when allied with aggressive marketing programs, are expected to allow producers to maintain and possibly to expand revenues.

World Production of Bauxite   In Thousands of Metric Tons

Year	Australia	Brazil	China	France	Greece	Guinea	Guyana[2]	Hungary	Indonesia	Jamaica[3]	Malaysia	Surinam	USSR[3]	U.S.[3]	Yugoslavia	World Total
1976	24,084	827	1,300	2,330	2,551	10,848	2,686	2,918	940	10,296	660	4,613	4,500	1,989	2,033	77,417
1977	26,086	1,120	1,500	2,059	2,885	10,841	2,731	2,949	1,301	11,390	616	4,805	4,600	2,013	2,044	81,931
1978	24,293	1,160	1,500	1,978	2,663	11,527	2,425	2,899	1,008	11,739	615	5,188	4,600	1,669	2,565	80,975
1979	27,583	2,388	1,500	1,969	2,812	11,326	2,312	2,976	1,052	11,618	387	5,010	4,600	1,821	3,012	85,522
1980	27,179	5,538	1,500	1,921	3,286	11,862	1,844	2,950	1,249	12,054	920	4,646	4,600	1,559	3,138	89,220
1981	25,441	5,770	1,500	1,827	3,216	11,112	1,681	2,914	1,203	11,682	701	4,006	4,600	1,510	3,249	85,347
1982	23,625	6,289	1,500	1,662	2,853	11,827	1,783	2,627	700	8,361	589	4,205	4,600	732	3,668	79,318
1983	24,372	7,199	1,600	1,663	2,455	12,421	1,087	2,917	778	7,683	502	3,400	4,600	679	3,500	78,644
1984[1]	32,182	6,433	1,600	1,607	2,296	13,160	1,333	2,994	1,003	8,734	680	3,454	4,600	856	3,347	88,173
1985[2]	32,400	6,650	1,650	1,484	2,500	13,100	1,675	2,815	830	6,239	540	3,000	4,600	674	3,250	85,133

[1] Preliminary.   [2] Estimate.   [3] Dry Bauxite equivalent of ore processed.   *Source: Bureau of Mines*   T.30

U.S. Salient Statistics of Bauxite   In Thousands of Metric Tons

Year	Net Import Reliance as a % of Apparent Consumption	Av. Price F.O.B. Mine $ per Ton	Mine Production Crude	Mine Production Dried Equivalent	Value ($1,000)	Recovery[1] of Processed Bauxite Crude Ore Treated	Recovery[1] Recovered[1] Total	Recovery[1] Recovered[1] Dried Equiv.	Dry Equivalent Imports[2] (for Consumption)	Dry Equivalent Exports[2]	Consumption	Stocks, Dec. 31 Producers & Processors	Stocks, Dec. 31 Consumers	Stocks, Dec. 31 Govt.	Stocks, Dec. 31 Total
1976	91	5–15	2,420	1,989	26,645	366	175	289	12,749	15	14,039	526	4,923	15,308	20,756
1977	91	5–15	2,436	2,013	27,555	419	169	294	12,989	26	14,528	685	7,264	15,087	23,036
1978	93	5–15	2,066	1,669	23,185	379	154	236	13,847	13	14,738	556	7,806	14,661	23,023
1979	93	5–15	2,186	1,821	24,875	466	235	336	13,780	15	15,697	620	7,958	14,661	23,239
1980	94	6–16	1,869	1,559	22,353	355	179	277	14,087	21	15,962	662	7,681	14,661	23,004
1981	94	8–20	1,847	1,510	26,489	419	187	328	12,802	20	13,525	897	7,395	14,661	22,953
1982	96	8–20	896	732	12,334	234	120	184	10,122	49	9,217	614	6,548	16,326	23,488
1983	96	13–20	826	679	11,309	293	140	225	7,601	74	9,100	552	5,061	16,326	21,939
1984	96	13–20	1,054	856	15,643	361	168	294	10,228	82	10,519	499	4,382	17,338	22,219
1985[3]	97	13–20	787	674	12,855	329	166	284	7,944	56	8,206	413	3,431	18,357	22,201

[1] Calcined, or sintered.   [2] Including concentrates.   [3] Preliminary.   *Source: Bureau of Mines*   T.31

Bismuth

Domestic bismuth consumption gained sharply in 1986. Consumption through the third quarter of 1986 totaled 2.31 million pounds, compared with total 1985 usage of 2.64 million pounds. If fourth-quarter 1986 consumption remains at the current quarterly average of 770,365 pounds, total 1986 off-take would approximate 3.0 million pounds, or about 15 percent more than 1985's usage. This would be a record level of consumption.

Part of the gain is attributable to price elasticity. Prices fell to $2.80–$2.90 a pound from $3.80–$3.90 a pound in the fourth quarter of 1985, and were dramatically down from 1984's $6.55–$6.75 levels. Other consumption gains are the result of new technologies coming on stream in the steel industry, where the use of bismuth in the commercial production of free-machining alloy bar steel has brought on increased demand. Most of the gains, however, came from chemical applications of the metal in pharmecuticals, where it is used in the preparation of stomach remedies and in industrial chemicals.

U.S. production is estimated to have remained steady over the past three years. Figures are not available because there is only one domestic producer and the Bureau of Mines withholds production statistics to avoid disclosing proprietary company data.

The gap between consumption and domestic production is met with imports, which, in line with apparent consumption increases, were also up for 1986.

Through the third quarter, bismuth imports totaled 1.86 million pounds, compared with all of 1985's 1.99 million pounds.

Based on the figures for the first six months of 1986, imports from Belgium and Luxembourg, Japan, and South Korea substantially exceeded the quantities for the comparable six months of 1985, while imports from the Federal Republic of Germany were considerably lower.

World mine production estimates for 1986 had not been released as of this writing, but production trends over the past five years have been steady, averaging about 8.5 million pounds a year. Production in 1985 is generally estimated to have been 8.1 million pounds, with Australia producing about 35 percent of the total.

Bismuth in the U.S. is expected to be recovered as a byproduct from domestic and imported lead ores and concentrates. Other potential sources include byproduct recovery from molybdenum and tungsten ore. Large, unmeasured quantities of bismuth are also present in Mexico, Bolivia, Peru, Australia, China and the Korean Peninsula.

While there are substitutes for bismuth in most of its uses, they are generally uncompetitive on the basis of cost and quality. From a 1983 base, demand for bismuth is expected to increase at an annual rate of 1.4 percent through 1990. Reliance on imports is expected to remain strong.

World Mine Production of Bismuth   In Thousands of Pounds

Year	Romania (Ore)	Australia (concentrates)	Bolivia (concentrates)	Canada	China (Ore)	France (Metal)	South Korea (Metal)	Yugo-slavia (Metal)	Japan (Metal)	Mexico (Metal)	Peru (Metal)	West Germany (Ore)	USSR (Metal)	World Total
1977	180	2,054	1,435	363	500	115	293	163	1,538	1,607	1,420	24	140	9,872
1978	180	2,324	677	320	530	N.A.	269	29	1,375	2,156	1,347	20	150	9,412
1979	180	2,200	22	306	570	N.A.	192	51	1,010	1,662	1,162	22	160	7,548
1980	180	2,650	24	377	570	N.A.	271	183	745	1,698	1,096	0	160	7,954
1981	180	2,600	24	370	570	N.A.	220	225	1,054	1,446	1,409	0	170	8,268
1982	180	3,310	11	417	570	N.A.	209	108	1,071	1,336	1,351	0	170	8,733
1983[1]	180	3,100	13	445	570	N.A.	200	99	1,263	1,202	1,179	—	180	8,431
1984[2]	180	3,310	10	440	570	N.A.	200	88	1,240	1,300	1,160	—	180	8,675
1985[2]		3,200	100	400			200		1,100	1,000	1,000			8,100

[1] Preliminary.   [2] Estimate.   *Source: Bureau of Mines*   T.35

U.S. Salient Statistics of Bismuth   In Thousands of Pounds

Year	Experimental	Metallurgical Additives	Other Alloys	Fusible Alloys	Chemicals[4]	Other Uses	Total Consumption	Consumer Stocks Dec. 31	Exports of Metal & Alloys	Imports Peru	Imports Mexico	Imports Japan	Imports Total	Price[1] $ Per Pound
1977	.6	461.6	18.6	611.2	1,274.5	13.1	2,379.6	436.1	95.3	632.4	182.2		2,013.3	6.01
1978	.6	485.3	21.8	836.0	1,149.7	18.6	2,511.9	781.9	96.3	334.7	535.3		2,657.8	3.38
1979	3.2	703.8	22.0	721.0	1,248.7	28.5	2,727.2	629.7	427.8	648.7	604.8	185.5	2,167.3	3.01
1980	1.2	467.9	26.5	650.9	1,115.6	26.7	2,288.8	674.0	128.7	619.1	860.4	138.4	2,217.4	2.64
1981	.2	307.0	26.0	657.0	1,387.6	15.0	2,392.7	509.0	78.7	859.3	724.1	124.1	2,436.2	2.32
1982	.5	124.6	21.4	571.6	1,144.8	13.6	1,876.4	541.6	52.8	864.1	699.5	41.4	2,026.2	1.61
1983	1.7	522.8	20.0	622.8	1,103.7	13.0	2,285.3	577.5	306.1	653.7	706.6	68.3	1,972.0	1.72
1984[2]	—	424.5	20.0	608.8	1,573.0	22.0	2,648.4	480.0	311.5	391.8	430.5	209.2	1,948.4	4.27
1985[2]	—	668.2	21.0	610.1	1,325.0	19.3	2,643.5	507.1	268.7	173.3	678.2	99.4	1,998.9	5.38
1986[3]	—	770.0	30.0	650.0	1,600.0	10.0	3,100.0	560.0	100.0	150.0	700.0	200.0	2,500.0	3.00

[1] N.Y., average ton lots; effective Oct. 1981, domestic producers' list price was suspended. Major foreign producer price is recorded.   [2] Preliminary.   [3] Estimate.   [4] Includes pharmaceuticals.   *Source: Bureau of Mines*   T.36

Broilers

1986 U.S. broiler production is estimated to be four percent higher than in 1985. The number of broilers slaughtered was up 3.9 percent, while average marketing weights increased 1.2 percent. USDA has projected 1986 broiler consumption at 57 pounds per person, up 1.5 pounds from last year. This would be the highest consumption rate in the past six years and reflects an increase of 21 percent since 1980. Exports of whole young chickens and chicken parts totaled 388 million pounds for the first three quarters of 1986, up 26 percent. Japan was the largest importer of U.S. young chickens, accounting for 33 per-

cent of exports. Due to the Export Enhancement Program, Egypt's imports in the third quarter, 1986, rose 638 percent from the year-ago period.

Broiler prices this year have benefited from increased demand from fast-food chains, as many have added more chicken items to their menus. With prospects for less red meat production in 1987, broiler prices are expected to remain relatively high, though below the peaks seen in 1986. USDA has estimated that young chicken production and per capita consumption should increase about six percent in 1987. Exports are projected to remain unchanged.

Broiler Supply and Prices in the United States

Year & Quarters	Number (Mil.)	Federally Inspected Slaughter Avg. Wt. (Lbs.)	Liveweight Pounds (Mil. Lbs.)	Certified RTC Wt. (Mil. Lbs.)	Total Production RTC[2] (Mil. Lbs.)	Per Capita Consumption (Lbs.)	Prices Farm (Cents/Lb.)	City[4] (Cents/Lb.)
1981	4,076	4.01	16,350	11,906	11,981	48.6	28.5	46.3
1982	4,068	4.04	16,456	12,039	12,175	50.0	26.9	44.0
1983	4,133	4.09	16,984	12,389	12,400	50.8	29.2	50.4
1984[1]	4,272	4.17	17,801	12,999	13,011	53.0	33.7	55.5
1985[3]	4,439	4.20	18,623	13,569	13,762	55.5	30.2	50.7
I	1,056	4.21	4,440	3,229	3,272	13.2	30.6	51.5
II	1,146	4.21	4,820	3,513	3,562	14.4	30.0	50.6
III	1,153	4.14	4,771	3,484	3,536	14.3	30.1	50.8
IV	1,085	4.23	4,593	3,344	3,392	13.6	30.0	50.0
1986[3]	1,500	4.24	19,000	14,000	14,350	57.0		
I	1,099	4.36	4,722	3,414	3,451	13.8	29.9	50.4
II	1,189	4.24	5,045	3,673	3,722	14.8	31.6	54.2
III	1,188	4.17	4,958	3,599	3,647		42.0	69.4
IV								

[1] Preliminary. [2] Total production equals fed, inspec. slaughter plus other slaughter minus cut-up & further processing condemnation. [3] Forecast. [4] 12-city weighted average.   *Source: Economic Research Service, U.S.D.A.*   T.38

Salient Broiler Statistics in the United States

Year	Commercial[2] Production Number (Millions)	Live weight (Mil. Lbs.)	Average Live weight Per Bird (Lb.)	Farm Price (¢ Lb.)	Gross Income (Mil. $)	Total Chickens[2] Supply & Distribution Commercial Broilers	Other Chickens	Total (In Millions of Pounds)	Storage Stocks Jan. 1	Export & Shipments	Consumption—Civilian Military	Total	Per Capita (in Lbs.)
1981	4,148	16,520	4.01	28.4	4,699	11,992	743	12,736	136	920	36	11,767	51.6
1982	4,149	16,760	4.04	26.9	4,502	12,175	744	12,919	149	675	36	12,222	53.1
1983	4,184	17,038	4.09	28.6	4,873	12,400	715	13,115	135	591	36	12,510	53.8
1984	4,282	17,863	4.17	33.7	6,018	13,011	696	13,707	139	580	36	13,065	55.7
1985[1]	4,479	18,851	4.20	30.1	5,680	13,762	636	14,398	171	582	36	13,748	58.0
1986[3]						14,344	668	15,012	135	676	37	14,335	59.9

[1] Preliminary. [2] Ready-to-cook basis. [3] Estimate.   *Source: Economic Research Service, U.S.D.A.*   T.39

Average Wholesale Broiler[1] Prices RTC   In Cents Per Pound

Year	Jan.	Feb.	Mar.	Apr.	May	June	July	Aug.	Sept.	Oct.	Nov.	Dec.	Avg.	4-Region Ave. Retail	Hens-N.Y.[2] 8–16 Lbs.
1981	49.5	50.3	48.2	44.4	46.3	49.3	50.2	47.3	43.6	43.7	42.5	40.1	46.3	73.7	59.7
1982	45.2	44.5	44.8	42.6	45.8	47.0	46.1	43.4	43.6	42.3	40.3	42.0	44.0	71.6	60.8
1983	43.1	45.2	41.9	40.9	46.9	49.1	52.8	54.2	54.5	50.4	56.3	57.1	49.4	72.8	60.5
1984	62.1	61.2	62.0	56.0	57.6	55.5	57.3	51.5	53.6	48.8	52.1	49.0	55.6	81.4	74.4
1985	52.8	51.9	49.7	47.8	50.9	53.4	50.2	50.1	52.2	48.3	53.7	48.7	50.8	76.3	75.5
1986	51.7	49.0	50.3	50.0	54.6	58.3	69.1	69.7	61.0	61.6					

[1] Ice packed, ready-to-cook. [2] In retail stores (urban areas), whole or cut-up ready to cook.   *Source: Bureau of Labor Statistics*   T.37

15

Burlap and Jute

Jute, a strong, coarse fiber from tiliaceous plants, is used to make burlap and cords. World production of jute and jute-like fibers was 6.98 million tonnes in 1985, according to the U.N. Food and Agriculture Organization. (Estimates of 1986 world output were not available at this writing.) China, India, Bangladesh, and Thailand account for nearly all world production.

China, the leading producer, has consistently had the highest jute yields per hectare. In 1985, China's crop was about 3.2 million tonnes, which reflected a large increase over previous seasons. China's average yield was 3.8 tonnes/hectare in 1985. While India and Bangladesh each devotes more area to jute than China, their crops are smaller. India produces about 1.5 million tonnes a year and Bangladesh about 1 million tonnes.

Bangladesh is the main exporter, shipping 350,-000–450,000 tonnes of jute a year. China exports about 40,000 tonnes annually. Leading importers are the European Community (EC), Pakistan, and Thailand. The U.S. typically imports 10,000–15,000 tonnes each year.

The price of jute FOB Bangladesh averaged $531/tonne in 1984 and rose to $583 in 1985. By January, 1986, the price had retreated to $310/tonne, as a result of large world supplies. The price of burlap in New York at year-end 1985 was $0.25/40-inch yard; at year-end 1986, it was $0.23.

Average Producer Price Index of Raw Jute, Bang Tossa C., Landed, at New York   1967 = 100'

Year	Jan.	Feb.	Mar.	Apr.	May	June	July	Aug.	Sept.	Oct.	Nov.	Dec.	Average
1980	N.A.	N.A.	N.A.	N.A.	N.A.	N.A.	N.A.	N.A.	29.00	28.50	29.00	29.00	28.80
1981	N.A.	27.35	27.35	N.A.	29.00	N.A.	29.00	29.00	29.00	29.00	24.00	22.55	27.30
1982	23.50	23.40	23.15	24.50	N.A.	N.A.	23.20	25.50	25.50	25.50	25.50	25.50	24.53
1983[1]	154.60	154.60	154.60	154.60	154.60	154.60	154.60	154.60	154.60	154.60	154.60	154.60	154.60
1984	154.60	154.60	154.60	178.90	178.90	178.90	178.90	178.90	178.90	178.90	288.10	N.A.	182.20
1985	N.A.	N.A.	N.A.	N.A.	N.A.	N.A.	N.A.	N.A.	N.A.	N.A.	N.A.	N.A.	N.A.
1986[2]	102.90	102.00	102.00	102.00	102.00	102.00	106.40	106.40	106.40	106.40	106.40		

[1] Data Prior to 1983 are in *Cents Per Pound*.   [2] Data beginning Jan. 1986 are for jute & linen goods including yarns & fabrics with June 1985 = 100 as the index.   *Source: Bureau of Labor Statistics* (0391-0101.99)   T.41

Average Wholesale Price of Burlap (40 Inch—10 Oz.) at New York   In Cents Per Yard

Year	Jan.	Feb.	Mar.	Apr.	May	June	July	Aug.	Sept.	Oct.	Nov.	Dec.	Average
1980	N.A.	39.80	40.00	38.50	N.A.	N.A.	N.A.	N.A.	33.50	33.50	N.A.	33.00	36.40
1981	N.A.	27.35	27.35	N.A.	29.00	N.A.	29.00	29.00	29.00	29.00	24.00	22.55	27.36
1982	23.50	23.40	23.15	24.50	N.A.	23.30	23.20	23.35	25.25	26.75	25.50	24.30	23.29
1983	22.65	24.25	26.35	26.20	24.40	25.20	24.75	25.50	26.25	26.95	29.65	31.70	26.15
1984	31.25	30.55	30.55	30.55	29.70	29.70	32.85	33.85	36.05	37.95	39.85	39.40	33.52
1985	39.60	37.25	36.05	35.80	36.40	34.25	31.15	31.15	26.50	24.90	23.75	25.10	31.83
1986	N.A.	N.A.	N.A.	N.A.	N.A.	N.A.	N.A.	N.A.	N.A.	N.A.	N.A.	N.A.	N.A.

Source: Bureau of Labor Statistics (0337-0461.01)   T.42

Butter

Early projections of world butter production during 1986 put the figure near what it was in 1985. Output was expected to be higher than a year earlier in China, India, Mexico and New Zealand, but gains in those countries were projected to be offset by lowered rates of production in the U.S. and the European Community (EC). Little change was foreseen in global demand for butter. With such major producers as New Zealand, the EC and the U.S. competing aggressively for export sales, prices on international markets promised to remain near the levels that prevailed in 1985.

In the domestic market, the major event of the year was implementation of the Dairy Termination Program (DTP) under the provisions of the 1985 Farm Bill. DTP offered dairy farmers sizable monetary incentives in return for agreeing to dispose of their herds either by slaughter or export and for committing themselves to forego dairy farming for at least five years. In anticipation of the program's onset in April, 1986, output of milk products, including butter, surged. In the first quarter of the year, more than 375 million pounds of butter were produced, a level almost 15 percent higher than in the same period the year before. Net removals of butter by the USDA amounted to more than 171 million pounds during January through March, 1986, 33 percent more than in first quarter 1985. Commercial disappearance of creamery butter also spurted during the early months of 1986, largely because sellers were accumulating inventories in expectation of a substantial decline in the supply of fluid milk from pre-program levels, thereby inducing price increases. This expectation proved to be correct, and by mid-summer 1986, but-

ter prices had climbed to the sell-back price of the Commodity Credit Corporation (CCC). Some five million pounds of the product were sold back to the industry during August alone. Even so, the CCC's uncommitted inventory of butter as of September, 1986, was almost 219 million pounds, some 73 percent higher than at 1985's start and 46 percent more than the year before.

Rising commercial usage and continuing removals of butter by the CCC combined with the prospect of reduced output to push up butter prices as 1986 progressed. The wholesale price index number for butter advanced from 217.1 (1967=100) at the close of 1985 to 234.7 in August, 1986. By the same token, the wholesale price of a pound of Grade A butter at Chicago rose from $1.3912 in December, 1985, to $1.5386 in August, 1986. Curiously, however, the retail price index number for butter moved slightly downward during the same period.

Projections of supply, demand and prices of butter during 1987 are difficult compared with earlier years, because of uncertainty about the effect of the Dairy Termination Program. Butter supplies will be reduced if farmers who are not participating in the Program only modestly expand their production of milk, butter and other dairy products. That eventuality, and further growth in commercial usage of butter, would push product prices still higher—and that is a key objective of the Program. If, on the other hand, non-participants in the Program uniformly try to enlarge their production, output could surge to or even beyond pre-Program levels. That would mean a tendency toward burgeoning stocks, falling prices and increased acquisition of butter by the CCC.

Supply and Distribution of Butter in the United States   In Millions of Pounds

Year	Supply			Cold Storage Stocks[1] Jan. 1[2]	Imports	Domestic Disappearance — Civilian —		Military	Exports & Shipments[4]	Dept. of Agr.			Total Use	93 Score — Wholesale Prices	
	Production					Total	Per Capita —Lbs.—			Jan. 1 Stocks[5]	Dec. 31 Stocks[5]	Removed by U.S.D.A. Programs		Calif. AA	Chi. AA
	Creamery	Farm	Total											$ Lb.	
1978	994	—	994	185	2	969	4.4	3	5	151	192	112	969	1.2666	1.1058
1979	985	—	985	207	2	1,011	4.5	6	5	192	153	82	1,016	1.4327	1.2374
1980	1,145	—	1,145	178	2	1,017	4.5	5	3	153	268	257	1,020	1.6135	1.4079
1981	1,228	—	1,228	305	3	974	4.3	4	132	268	382	352	1,106	1.6855	1.4897
1982	1,257	—	1,257	429	3	1,011	4.3	20	212	382	439	382	1,223	1.7187	1.4839
1983	1,299	—	1,299	467	3	1,150	4.9	16	120	439	464	413	1,270	1.7229	1.4832
1984	1,103	—	1,103	499	3	1,162	4.9	16	133	464	260	203	1,295	1.7459	1.5088
1985[3]	1,248	—	1,248	297	4	1,164	4.9		181	260	169	334	1,345		
1986[6]	1,240	—	1,240	206						169	180	300			

[1] Commercial.   [2] Includes stocks held by U.S.D.A.   [3] Preliminary.   [4] Includes U.S.D.A. shipments to Territories.   [5] Includes butteroil.
[6] Estimate.   *Source: Department of Agriculture*

T.43

17

BUTTER

World (Total) Butter[1] Production In Thousands of Metric Tons

Year	Aus- tralia	Bra- zil	Cana- da	China	Czech- oslovakia	Argen- tina	Den- mark	France	Ire- land	W. Ger- many	Nether- lands	N. Zea- land	India	Po- land	Swe- den	USSR	South Africa	United Kingdom	United States
1979	105		106	95		32	131	596	132	568	202	255	475	293	65	1,409	18	161	447
1980	84	100	111	95	128	29	113	618	124	578	179	265	480	294	66	1,388	17	168	519
1981	79	60	125		127	32	108	599	125	545	183	247	620	260	64	1,318	15	170	557
1982	76	70	134		138	37	121	624	140	556	216	248	650	265	70	1,403	17	216	570
1983	88	70	118		149	32	131	637	164	627	271	252	670	300	73	1,562	19	240	589
1984	111	70	119		152	28	104	621	171	572	241	287	690	322	77	1,588	18	205	500
1985[2]	114	70	108		150	32	110	595	163	515	229	293	700	308	74	1,596	17	202	585
1986[3]	105	65	106		150	33	110	630	154	560	265	301	720	285	66	1,630	17	212	540

[1] Factory (including creameries and dairies) & farm. [2] Preliminary. [3] Forecast. *Source: Foreign Agricultural Service, U.S.D.A.* T.44

Production of Creamery Butter in Factories in the United States In Millions of Pounds

Year	Jan.	Feb.	Mar.	Apr.	May	June	July	Aug.	Sept.	Oct.	Nov.	Dec.	Total
1980	105.7	99.9	101.1	112.2	116.6	93.9	83.7	75.3	77.0	91.4	84.7	103.6	1,145
1981	123.1	108.4	115.5	117.3	115.5	95.9	82.7	82.3	85.2	99.5	93.4	109.5	1,228
1982	127.3	115.9	123.4	———334.0———			———256.4———			———300.0———			1,257
1983	139.1	119.2	123.6	124.0	120.7	103.7	91.4	84.6	84.7	100.5	98.1	109.6	1,299
1984	127.3	108.9	107.6	103.0	105.1	81.8	72.7	70.2	67.5	84.4	79.8	95.1	1,103
1985[1]	118.4	107.5	105.9	111.4	112.9	95.6	92.4	92.1	92.1	109.3	99.4	115.4	1,248
1986[1]	135.8	119.4	120.2	121.7	116.0	92.0	81.5	72.3	79.2	84.6			

[1] Preliminary. [2] Estimate. *Source: Crop Reporting Board, U.S.D.A.* T.45

Commercial Disappearance of Creamery Butter in the U.S. In Millions of Pounds

Year	Jan.	Feb.	Mar.	Apr.	May	June	July	Aug.	Sept.	Oct.	Nov.	Dec.	Total
1979	83.1	78.3	88.5	70.7	64.2	68.1	72.5	66.2	63.4	78.4	84.4	78.7	895.0
1980	75.0	86.1	88.8	47.7	54.2	59.4	73.2	78.8	77.3	66.3	78.1	93.5	878.8
1981	———188.9———			———214.2———			———222.9———			———243.2———			869.2
1982	———211.4———			———217.6———			———217.3———			———251.0———			897.3
1983	———209.5———			———198.6———			———217.0———			———256.6———			881.7
1984[1]	———194.0———			———241.3———			———215.6———			———251.9———			902.7
1985[1]	———200.0———			———203.9———			———241.5———			———272.9———			930.5
1986[1]	———193.7———			———224.4———			———237.6———						

[1] Preliminary. *Source: Economic Research Service, U.S.D.A.* T.46

Cold Storage Holdings of Creamery Butter in the U.S., on First of Month In Millions of Pounds

Year	Jan.	Feb.	Mar.	Apr.	May	June	July	Aug.	Sept.	Oct.	Nov.	Dec.
1980	177.8	191.0	205.6	217.2	238.1	281.7	295.9	308.0	306.4	302.9	301.5	302.7
1981	304.6	332.1	372.3	407.4	450.4	473.6	507.5	515.5	515.6	489.5	470.0	451.1
1982	429.2	430.3	440.4	447.8	—	—	541.6	—	—	510.0	—	—
1983	466.8	485.4	522.0	529.0	555.7	576.1	589.6	588.4	581.8	552.3	523.9	506.7
1984	499.4	510.6	532.5	529.3	532.4	538.5	516.7	489.6	462.7	426.3	374.3	335.9
1985	296.6	277.3	289.4	291.7	272.7	283.2	286.8	280.7	264.6	247.0	231.6	206.9
1986[1]	205.5	206.3	245.5	283.3	304.8	333.8	342.8	337.6	304.4	279.6	253.3	221.1

[1] Preliminary. *Source: Crop Reporting Board, U.S.D.A.* T.47

Wholesale Price of 92 Score Creamery (Grade A, Bulk) Butter at Chicago In Cents Per Pound

Year	Jan.	Feb.	Mar.	Apr.	May	June	July	Aug.	Sept.	Oct.	Nov.	Dec.	Average
1980	130.2	130.3	130.4	134.3	136.9	139.0	139.3	144.5	145.1	147.1	147.6	147.7	139.3
1981	147.3	147.3	147.3	147.3	147.3	147.5	147.9	148.0	148.5	150.6	148.9	148.1	148.0
1982	147.5	147.5	147.8	147.4	147.3	147.3	147.6	148.1	148.4	147.4	148.2	147.9	147.7
1983	147.3	147.3	147.3	147.3	147.3	147.3	147.8	151.0	147.6	147.3	143.1	143.1	147.3
1984	140.4	141.3	142.1	142.9	142.9	150.0	155.6	150.6	158.1	158.1	158.1	145.6	148.8
1985	141.5	141.3	141.3	141.9	141.9	141.9	141.5	140.7	141.2	141.6	139.5	139.1	141.1
1986	—	138.3	—	—	———138.9———			———150.6———					

Source: Economic Research Service, U.S.D.A T.48

Cadmium

Cadium prices stabilized around the $1.20-a-pound mark by the third quarter of 1986, a gain from levels earlier in the year of about $1.00 a pound. Domestic cadmium refinery production continued to fall short of domestic demand. Only five cadmium refineries operate in the U.S.; as a result, the industry is forced to rely heavily on imports. While imports of cadmium in the third quarter of 1986 decreased significantly from those of the previous quarter, imports for the first nine months of 1986 remained well above the comparable 1985 period. 2,412 tons of cadmium were imported in the first three quarters of 1986, compared with full-year 1985 imports of 1,987 tons.

World refinery production in 1986 is expected to equal 1985's 17,500 tons, while domestic production of cadmium metal in the third quarter of 1986 was 22 percent below the level of the previous quarter, according to the U.S. Bureau of Mines. (No. U.S. production figures were released on a quarterly basis.) The Bureau of Mines said that production of cadmium metal for the first nine months of 1986 was 19 percent below that for the comparable 1985 period.

Japan, the U.S., Canada, and Australia are the four major cadmium producing nations. Annual production is about 2,400 tons, 1,600 tons and 1,200 tons and 1,200 tons, respectively.

U.S. cadmium consumption is expected to continue to grow at an average annual rate of 1.7 percent a year through 1990, with the largest growth area coming from use in nickel-cadmium sulfide and cadmium telluride in solar photovoltaic cells.

Cadmium is a toxic metal. Concerns about the environmental impact of cadmium refinery waste disposal have brought about increased cadmium recovery at smelters and have reduced the amount of cadmium released into the ecosystem through industrial pollution.

World resources of cadmium are estimated at 9 million tons, or about 0.3 percent of global zinc reserves, of which cadmium is a geochemical byproduct. Large resources of cadmium are contained in the zinc-bearing coals mid-continental America and in similar deposits elsewhere. Undiscovered cadmium reserves are estimated to be between 5 and 50 million tons, depending upon which economic model is used for the projections.

World Smelter Production of Cadmium Metal   In Metric Tons

Year	Australia[4]	Belgium	Canada[4]	China	Finland	France	W. Germany	Italy	Japan	Mexico[4]	Norway	Poland	Un. King.	USSR	United States[3]	Zaire	World Total
1976	649	1,200	1,314		428	532	1,275	436	2,500	710	80	750	190	2,700	2,047	266	16,998
1977	670	1,440	1,185		527	790	1,336	448	2,844	908	97	754	295	2,750	1,999	246	18,288
1978	747	1,164	1,265		611	694	1,182	378	2,531	897	120	761	291	2,800	1,653	186	17,310
1979	804	1,440	1,455		590	689	1,266	527	2,597	830	115	773	424	2,850	1,823	212	18,679
1980	1,012	1,524	1,303	250	581	789	1,194	568	2,173	778	130	698	375	2,850	1,578	168	18,238
1981	1,031	1,176	1,298	270	621	663	1,192	489	1,977	590	117	580	278	2,900	1,603	230	17,381
1982	1,010	996	809	300	566	793	1,030	475	2,034	607	104	570	354	2,900	1,007	281	16,378
1983	1,100	800	1,107	300	616	540	1,095	456	2,214	642	117	570	340	3,000	1,052	308	16,725
1984[2]	1,200	850	1,200	300	600	500	1,100	400	2,400	650	110	570	340	3,000	1,686	310	17,687
1985[2]	1,200	850	1,200						2,400	650					1,568		17,500

[1] Preliminary.   [2] Estimate.   [3] Primary & secondary metal.   [4] Refined.   *Source: Bureau of Mines*   T.49

Salient Statistics of Cadmium in the United States   In Metric Tons of Contained Cadmium

Year	Net Import Reliance as a % of Apparent Consumption	Production — Primary — Producers — Metallic	Production — Primary — Producers — Shipments	Production — Primary — Producers — Value Mil. $	Cadmium Sulfide[3]	Imports (for Consumption) — Metallic	Imports (for Consumption) — Flue Dust[3]	Imports (for Consumption) — Total	Price[5] $ per lb.	Exports — Cadmium Metal, Alloys, Dross, Flue Dust	Exports — Value Ths. $	Consumption[4]	Stocks, Dec. 31 — Industry — Metallic	Stocks, Dec. 31 — Industry — Compounds	Stocks, Dec. 31 — Distributors
1975	41	1,990	742	4.2	895	2,375	314	2,689	3.36	180	589	3,055	1,881	121	
1976	64	2,047	2,707	10.5	729	3,094	223	3,317	2.66	229	713	5,381	1,242	148	
1977	51	1,999	1,837	7.1	639	2,332	13	2,345	2.96	107	316	3,818	1,452	72	255
1978	63	1,653	1,957	5.9	698	2,881	—	2,881	2.45	326	864	4,510	1,152	45	296
1979	64	1,823	2,468	9.5	813	813	—	2,572	2.76	211	550	5,099	517	52	327
1980	55	1,578	1,271	5.2	801	2,617	—	2,617	2.84	236	464	3,534	841	42	439
1981	63	1,603	1,382	3.8	527	3,090	—	3,090	1.93	239	332	4,378	1,077	68	215
1982	73	1,007	1,832	2.6	374	2,305	—	2,305	1.11	11	126	3,728	635	167	150
1983	72	1,052	1,495	1.8	670	2,196	—	2,196	1.13	170	351	3,763	209	49	91
1984[2]	50	1,686	1,811	2.6	771	1,889	—	1,889	1.69	106	208	3,371	208	59	52
1985[2]	55	1,603	1,791		727	1,988	—	1,988	1.20	86		3,500	136	111	59
1986[1]		1,275	2,000			3,000	—	3,000		50			240	76	11

[1] Estimate.   [2] Preliminary.   [3] Cd content.   [4] Apparent Primary cadmium in all forms.   [5] Sticks & Balls in 1 to 5 short ton lots.
Source: Bureau of Mines   T.50

Castor Beans

World production of castorseed in 1986/87 (October/September) was estimated by *Oil World,* at the beginning of the season, to be 1.02 million tonnes, 9 percent below 1985/86 production. Output in India was expected to rise about 10 percent from 1985/86, while production in Brazil was expected to decrease 34 percent. Bahia is the main producing state in Brazil, and most of the crop there is harvested in May–September. Production in China was forecast to be down 3 percent from the year-ago figure, and output in the Soviet Union was estimated to be unchanged.

Global castor oil production was forecast to have increased less than one percent in 1986, to about 375,000 tonnes. Large increases in production were seen in Brazil and China, while output in India declined sharply. World stocks of castor oil, at the start of the 1986/87 season, were projected to be almost 7 percent above opening stocks for the year-ago period. Major increases in stocks were expected in the Soviet Union, India, and Brazil, while large decreases were expected in the European Community. West Germany and Japan are usually the major importers of castorseed. France, the Soviet Union and the U.S. are normally the world's largest importers of castor oil.

U.S. imports of castor oil in 1985/86 were nearly 10 percent lower than in the previous season. Although castor oil prices continued to be weak during much of 1986, consumption in the U.S. declined. To some extent, this may have reflected substitution of synthetic oils for castor oil in industrial uses. U.S. consumption of castor oil in inedible products dropped 11 percent in 1985/86 from the previous year. U.S. stocks of castor oil as of November 1, 1986, were estimated at 14,500 tonnes, sharply above the 8,900 tonnes on hand a year earlier.

World Production of Castorseed Beans   In Thousands of Metric Tons

Crop Year	China	Brazil	Ecuador	Ethiopia	India	Romania	Paraguay	Israel	Mexico	Pakistan	Thailand	USSR	Philippines	Sudan	World Total
1982–3	156	192	5	1	345	8	20		5	26	34	89	14	2	922
1983–4[1]	179	172	6	1	405	6	17		4	24	25	65	18	2	949
1984–5[2]	164	225	6	1	469	8	16		4	17	23	58	24	1	1,040
1985–6[2]	175	386	6	1	350	7	15		4	19	26	60	22	1	1,096

[1] Preliminary.   [2] Estimate.   *Source: Foreign Agricultural Service, U.S.D.A. "The Oil World."*   T.51

Castor Oil Consumption[1] in the United States   In Thousands of Pounds

Crop Year	Oct.	Nov.	Dec.	Jan.	Feb.	Mar.	Apr.	May	June	July	Aug.	Sept.	Total
1982–83	5,143	6,486	6,307	6,551	7,223	6,216	6,281	6,122	4,642	3,849	5,725	7,488	72,033
1983–84	5,488	4,749	4,965	4,764	4,990	5,296	5,599	6,723	5,663	7,958	7,859	6,812	70,866
1984–85[2]	6,937	5,581	4,178	4,519	5,178	5,930	5,169	7,480	7,158	5,320	5,816	3,839	67,105
1985–6[2]	4,807	3,614	3,840	2,833	5,016	4,935	4,528	5,282	5,602	7,054	6,084	6,111	59,706
1986–7[2]	6,983												

[1] In inedible products (Resins, Plastics, etc.).   [2] Preliminary.   *Source: Bureau of the Census.*   T.52a

Castor Oil Stocks in the United States   In Thousands of Pounds

Crop Year	Oct. 1	Nov. 1	Dec. 1	Jan. 1	Feb. 1	Mar. 1	Apr. 1	May 1	June 1	July 1	Aug. 1	Sept. 1
1982–83	6,874	5,922	7,820	6,722	6,278	6,742	4,966	9,155	6,493	4,837	8,975	4,766
1983–84	5,501	5,688	6,086	4,860	5,096	2,101	N.A.	N.A.	N.A.	N.A.	N.A.	N.A.
1984–85[1]	6,998	7,432	5,669	11,734	10,403	11,129	18,518	24,952	19,072	21,623	16,652	16,001
1985–6[1]	14,632	17,087	28,477	21,031	24,754	25,586	26,263	19,739	30,125	24,740	29,809	26,919
1986–7[1]	22,212	27,279										

[1] Preliminary.   *Source: Bureau of the Census.*   T.52b

Monthly Average Wholesale Prices of Castor Oil[1] at New York   In Cents per Pound

Year	Jan.	Feb.	Mar.	Apr.	May	June	July	Aug.	Sept.	Oct.	Nov.	Dec.	Average
1982	42.80	43.30	43.30	43.30	44.70	45.90	46.50	45.50	45.50	45.50	45.50	45.50	44.78
1983	45.50	45.50	45.50	46.80	49.50	49.50	53.40	61.80	78.50	78.50	78.50	78.50	59.29
1984	78.50	78.50	78.50	78.50	78.50	73.70	69.00	77.30	65.00	65.00	65.00	65.00	72.71
1985	65.0	65.0	65.0	65.0	65.0	36.0	36.0	36.0	36.0	36.0	36.0	34.0	47.92
1986	34.5	34.5	34.5	34.5	33.4	32.3	32.4	32.6	31.7				

[1] Average wholesale, tank cars, imported Brazil.   *Source: Foreign Agricultural Service, U.S.D.A.*   T.53

Cattle & Calves

Mid-1986 appeared to mark the end of an extended and extremely difficult inventory-adjustment period for the cattle industry. Return to a typical cyclical inventory movement is not likely until the 1990s, as external factors continue to mute biological adjustments. Major adjustments occurred in the 1970s; an unprecedented build-up in the cattle inventory peaked at a record 132 million head in 1975 and was followed by a huge liquidation, which ended in 1979 and left the inventory at 110.9 million. Cattle inventory rose to 115.4 million head in 1982. However, 1982 through summer 1986 continued downward adjustments. As 1987 began, the cattle inventory declined another four percent from a year earlier, but third-quarter 1986 figures indicated that the cattle liquidation was drawing to a close.

Beef production in 1987 is expected to decline because of herd reductions since 1982, less slaughter under the Dairy Termination Program (DTP), and more retention of animals for inventory. However, already-large total meat supplies are expected to expand in 1988 from the moderately lower level of 1987. The impact of these larger meat supplies will be to slow markedly the rate of beef-herd expansion at least through the early 1990s.

Cattle on feed on October 1, 1986, was the third-smallest inventory for this date since 1970, despite a three-percent increase from the record low a year earlier. Near-record-high placements and marketings in summer 1986 were partially offsetting and resulted in continuing low fed-cattle inventories. Cattle on feed on July 1 were eight percent below the year earlier, but third-quarter 1986 fed-cattle marketings declined by only two percent. Increased marketings occurred as cattle continued to be placed on feed at heavy weights, many in fleshy, grass-fed condition. A record-large 74 percent of cattle on feed at the beginning of the third quarter were marketed.

Placements onto feedlots in mid-1986 were almost record-large at 61 million head, the most since 1978. Fall placements were expected to remain high, as fed cattle prices rose and grain prices continued well below the year before.

Feeder cattle supplies were drawn down sharply in summer 1986; competition between feeders and stocker operators for the reduced supply was expected to intensify. Feeder cattle supplies outside feedlots on October 1, 1986, were seven percent below the year before. Continued declines in the calf crop resulted in a four-percent drop in the feeder calf supply. Nonfed steer and heifer slaughter was also large in summer 1986, due to dairy heifers slaughtered under the DTP and to some grass-fed feeder cattle going directly to slaughter.

Beef production in 1987 was expected to drop by five to seven percent below the 1986 level. Sharpest year-to-year declines were forecast to occur in the second and third quarters (due mainly to the large DTP slaughter during the spring and summer of 1986). Total production was expected to decline, with nearly all of the drop in the nonfed slaughter categories. Total fed cattle marketings were expected to remain in the 25.5 to 26 million head range, which

has existed since 1983. Sharpest year-to-year declines should occur in cow slaughter, given the lower beef and dairy cow numbers and expectations that the beef breeding herd will begin to stabilize. A stronger economy or greater price impact from reduced beef supplies in 1987 could result in even lower nonfed slaughter and more steers and heifers being placed on feed. Slaughter weights should remain near record-large in 1987. Fed cattle should represent a larger proportion of the slaughter mix, which suggests even heavier weights. But, cow slaughter weights are likely to drop as the dairy proportion declines, offsetting the increase in fed cattle in the slaughter mix.

1986 prices for Choice fed steers at Omaha rose from $54 per cwt. in June to about $60 in October. During this period, 400–500 pound calves and 600–700 pound yearlings at Kansas City rose from $65 to $73 and from $58.50 to $66, respectively. Utility cow prices at Omaha averaged near $38 in 1986. Prices dropped to $36 per cwt. in April as the DTP was announced, but soon recovered and remained fairly stable through the rest of the year.

Total meat supplies should remain large, as poultry supplies continue to rise. Larger supplies of relatively lower-priced poultry should hold down gains, particularly as beef prices rise. Retail prices may increase to the low $2.40s in 1987, up from about $2.32 in 1985 and 1986. Thus, beef prices may return to near the average of the early 1980s, when per capita beef supplies were four to five pounds higher.

In late 1986, feeder cattle prices were expected to average about $4 per cwt. above the year before, due to the smaller supply, lower grain prices and increased demand from feedlot and stock interests. However, stronger fed cattle prices during spring 1987 should support further price increases for feeder cattle.

Moderate cattle price increases and continuing financial problems in many areas should hold down the rate of herd expansion. Many producers who liquidated their herds in recent years to reduce debt and to improve cash flow were not likely to have the additional cash flow necessary to afford the large capital investment required to reenter the cattle sector.

On balance, fed cattle prices could rise to the middle $60/cwt in spring 1987, but price strength beyond that, even with reduced beef supplies, will be difficult as supplies of competing meats expand. Moreover, consumer demand for beef continues to be held in check owing to publicity in recent years over the possible benefits of a diet low in red meat. The cattle/beef industry, however, began to advertise more aggressively during 1987 and to emphasize the advantages of red meat. For 1987 as a whole, prices may average in the range of $62–$68 per cwt.

Futures Markets

Live beef cattle futures and options against futures are traded at the Chicago Mercantile Exchange (CME) and at the MidAmerica Exchange. A feeder cattle futures contract is traded at the CME.

CATTLE AND CALVES

Cattle Supply and Distribution in the United States   In Thousands of Head

Year	Cattle & Calves on Farms Jan. 1	Imports	Calves Born	Total Supply	Livestock Slaughter—Cattle and Calves Commercial Federally Inspected	Other[2]	All Commercial	Farm	Total Slaughter	Deaths on Farms	Exports	Total Disappearance
1983	115,001	921	43,925	159,847	37,614	2,111	39,725	411	40,136	5,501	56	45,693
1984	113,700	753	42,500	156,955	38,910	1,969	40,879	411	41,290	5,475	71	46,805
1985	109,749	836	44,045	151,030	34,631	1,657	36,288			5,030	125	45,200
1986[1]	105,468											

[1] Preliminary.   [2] Wholesale and retail.   *Source: Economic Research Service, U.S.D.A.*   T.56

U.S. Cattle on Feed in 13 States, Quarterly   In Thousands of Head

Year		I	II	III	IV	Year		I	II	III	IV
1983	Number on Feed[1]	10,271	9,153	9,070	8,465	1985	Number on Feed[1]	10,653	9,688	8,670	7,937
	Placed on Feed	5,027	5,894	5,583	7,272		Placed on Feed	5,315	5,206	5,480	7,325
	Marketings	5,694	5,527	5,891	5,436		Marketings	5,907	5,787	5,969	5,224
1984	Number on Feed[1]	9,908	9,340	8,700	9,000	1986[1]	Number on Feed[1]	9,694	8,915	7,950	8,197
	Placed on Feed	5,511	5,562	6,252	7,559		Placed on Feed	5,260	5,181	6,326	
	Marketings	5,714	5,620	5,684	5,507		Marketings	5,723	5,771	5,846	5,404

[1] Beginning of Period.   [2] Preliminary.   *Source: Economic Research Service, U.S.D.A.*   T.56a

United States Beef Supply and Utilization

Year		Commercial production	Farm production	Beginning stocks	Imports	Total supply	Exports	Shipments	Military purchases	Ending stocks	Total disappearance	Per capita disappearance	Retail weight per capita	Population
		--------- Million Pounds ---------										---- Pounds ----		Million
1983	I	5,527	64	294	527.89	6,412.89	66.81	10.35	28	299	6,008.73	25.95	19.20	231.50
	II	5,556	27	299	516.67	6,398.67	61.96	10.27	34	254	6,038.44	26.02	19.22	232.00
	III	6,015	28	254	539.04	6,836.04	71.62	9.14	34	268	6,453.28	27.74	20.53	232.60
	IV	5,962	64	268	347.47	6,641.47	71.71	10.47	25	325	6,209.29	26.66	19.73	233.20
	Year	23,060	183	294	1,931.07	25,468.07	272.10	40.23	121	325	24,709.74	106.23	78.61	232.60
1984	I	5,708	61	325	470.5	6,564.5	90.0	10.8	24	326	6,113.6	26.16	19.36	233.70
	II	5,819	26	326	371.0	6,542.0	70.5	13.2	36	303	6,119.3	26.13	19.34	234.20
	III	5,949	26	303	513.7	6,791.7	86.6	14.2	27	320	6,343.9	27.03	20.00	234.70
	IV	5,933	61	320	467.9	6,781.9	81.6	9.1	25	358	6,308.2	26.74	19.78	236.00
	Year	23,418	171	325	1,823	25,746	328.8	47.3	112	358	24,901	106.05	78.48	234.80
1985	I	5,692	60	358	420	6,530	82	12	28	334	6,074	26	19	236.20
	II	5,923	26	334	534	6,817	77	12	31	296	6,401	27	20	236.80
	III	6,167	25	296	633	7,121	91	12	30	308	6,680	28	28	237.40
	IV	5,775	60	308	481	6,624	78	15	26	317	6,188	26	19	237.90
	Year	23,557	171	358	2,068	26,154	328	51	115	317	25,342	107	79	237.00
1986[1]	I	5,769	60	317	502	6,648	102	13	24	297	6,212	26	19	238.50
	II	6,247	26	297	482	7,052	83	12	33	322	6,603	28	20	239.00
	III	6,275	25	322	640	7,237	144	15	29	292	6,757	28	20	239.60
	IV													
	Year[2]	23,941	171	317	2,125	26,554	500	55	122	325	25,552	107	79	239.30

[1] Preliminary. [2] Forecast.   *Source: Economic Research Service, U.S.D.A.*   T.56b

World Cattle and Buffalo Numbers   In Millions of Head

Year	Argen- tina	Aus- tralia	Brazil	Canada	China	Colom- bia	France	W. Ger- many	India	Poland	Turkey	Mexico	South Africa	USSR	Un. King- dom	United States	World Total[1]
1981	58.8	25.2	93.0	12.2	95.0	24.4	23.6	15.1	245.6	11.3	16.9	34.0	13.2	115.1	13.1	114.4	943
1982	57.9	24.6	93.0	12.1	N.A.	24.2	23.5	15.0	260.0	11.5	17.0	34.7	13.1	115.9	13.0	115.4	959
1983	58.0	22.5	93.0	11.7		24.0	23.7	15.1	263.7	11.0	16.5	33.9	12.5	117.2	13.2	115.0	957
1984	58.6	22.2	93.3	11.4		22.4	23.5	15.6	267.5	11.1	16.0	33.9	12.1	119.6	13.1	113.7	960
1985	58.8	22.8	94.7	11.0		21.9	23.1	15.7	271.4	10.9	15.5	33.9	12.0	121.1	13.0	109.7	963
1986[2]	57.6	23.2	95.2	10.6		20.5	22.8	15.6	275.3	10.8	15.0	33.7	11.8	120.8	12.7	105.5	958
1987[1]	56.5	23.3	96.0	10.3		19.2	22.6	15.4	273.6	10.6	14.5	34.2	12.0	122.0	12.8	101.8	952

[1] Forecast.   [2] Preliminary.   *Source: Foreign Agricultural Service, U.S.D.A.*   T.54

U.S. Cattle on Feed in 7 States   In Thousands of Head

Year	Jan. 1	Feb. 1	Mar. 1	Apr. 1	May 1	June 1	July 1	Aug. 1	Sept. 1	Oct. 1	Nov. 1	Dec. 1	Average
1983	8,316	8,052	7,604	7,268	7,221	7,331	7,278	6,861	6,704	6,951	7,683	7,814	8,316
1984	8,006	7,917	7,515	7,568	7,376	7,318	7,125	6,811	6,747	7,442	8,221	8,544	8,006
1985	8,635	8,169	7,877	7,814	7,495	7,444	7,057	6,404	6,155	6,461	7,582	7,892	8,635
1986	7,860	7,624	7,262	7,263	7,077	7,076	6,523	6,321	6,404				

Source: Economic Research Service, U.S.D.A.   T.54a

U.S. Cattle Placed on Feedlots in 7 States   In Thousands of Head

Year	Jan.	Feb.	Mar.	Apr.	May	June	July	Aug.	Sept.	Oct.	Nov.	Dec.	Total
1982	1,457	1,320	1,798	1,565	1,853	1,420	1,205	1,731	1,994	2,660	1,785	1,533	20,261
1983	1,509	1,179	1,394	1,566	1,843	1,595	1,174	1,582	2,003	2,358	1,711	1,736	19,744
1984	1,566	1,301	1,764	1,515	1,798	1,445	1,323	1,680	2,265	2,546	1,945	1,624	20,772
1985	1,449	1,342	1,594	1,417	1,666	1,267	1,078	1,510	1,988	2,779	1,776	1,480	19,346
1986	1,581	1,210	1,650	1,555	1,746	1,142	1,544	1,812	2,083				

Source: Economic Research Service, U.S.D.A.   T.54b

U.S. Cattle Marketings in 7 States   In Thousands of Head

Year	Jan.	Feb.	Mar.	Apr.	May	June	July	Aug.	Sept.	Oct.	Nov.	Dec.	Total
1982	1,522	1,413	1,547	1,414	1,413	1,510	1,482	1,689	1,575	1,527	1,485	1,430	18,007
1983	1,643	1,506	1,593	1,470	1,583	1,570	1,497	1,651	1,682	1,626	1,459	1,425	18,701
1984	1,569	1,621	1,594	1,523	1,637	1,544	1,553	1,683	1,489	1,657	1,501	1,414	18,785
1985	1,782	1,540	1,559	1,603	1,589	1,572	1,670	1,670	1,603	1,573	1,380	1,401	18,989
1986	1,740	1,470	1,563	1,621	1,615	1,128	1,682	1,659	1,617				

Source: Economic Research Service, U.S.D.A.   T.54c

Condition[1] of Pasture and Range Feed in the United States, on First of Month   In Percent of Normal

Year	Apr. 1	May 1	June 1	July 1	Aug. 1	Sept. 1	Oct. 1	Nov. 1	Dec. 1
1983	84	80	85	88	76	63	66	73	N.A.
1984	74	75	79	80	75	70	66	74	N.A.
1985	79	83	81	77	70	75	76	79	N.A.
1986	N.A.	76	80	83	76	79	83	85	

[1] Indicates current supply of feed for grazing on non-irrigated pastures & ranges relative to that expected from existing stands under very favorable weather conditions. [80 & over, good to excellent; 65–79, poor to fair; 50–64, very poor; 35–49, severe drought; under 35, extreme drought.]
Source: Statistical Reporting Service, U.S.D.A.   T.57A

CATTLE AND CALVES

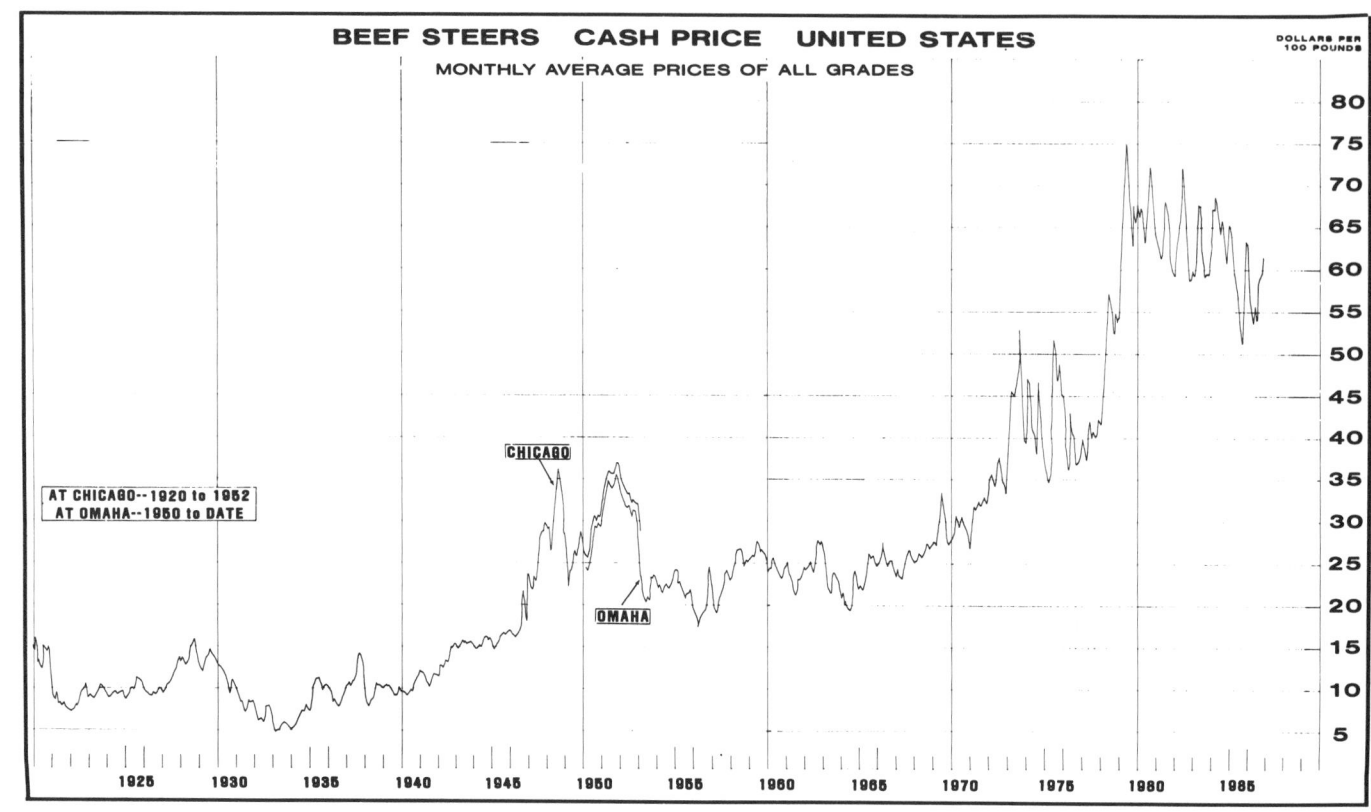

BEEF STEERS CASH PRICE UNITED STATES

MONTHLY AVERAGE PRICES OF ALL GRADES

DOLLARS PER 100 POUNDS

CHICAGO

OMAHA

AT CHICAGO--1920 to 1952
AT OMAHA--1950 to DATE

Average Wholesale Prices of Beef Steers at Omaha, Choice (900–1100 Lbs.)   In Dollars Per 100 Pounds

Year	Jan.	Feb.	Mar.	Apr.	May	June	July	Aug.	Sept.	Oct.	Nov.	Dec.	Average
1981	63.08	61.50	61.40	64.92	66.86	68.26	67.86	66.37	65.37	61.45	59.81	59.24	63.84
1982	60.75	63.54	65.80	69.11	72.10	70.18	66.18	65.14	61.25	58.78	58.91	59.82	64.22
1983	59.33	61.20	64.03	67.70	67.51	65.90	62.22	61.27	59.19	59.58	59.41	62.85	62.52
1984	67.08	67.07	68.60	67.86	65.89	64.28	65.79	64.36	62.68	60.85	64.24	65.32	65.33
1985	64.35	62.80	59.58	58.72	57.58	56.69	53.26	51.94	51.29	58.02	63.30	62.94	58.37
1986	59.69	56.42	55.55	53.69	55.79	54.08	58.27	59.04	59.43				

Source: Economic Research Service, U.S.D.A.   T.65

Average Prices of Steers (Stocker & Feeder) Kansas City   In Dollars Per 100 Pounds

Year	Jan.	Feb.	Mar.	Apr.	May	June	July	Aug.	Sept.	Oct.	Nov.	Dec.	Average
1981	68.56	68.41	65.47	66.28	63.10	63.51	61.51	64.15	64.58	62.52	61.77	58.96	64.26
1982	59.22	62.37	63.96	64.72	66.07	63.70	64.17	66.42	63.55	62.21	61.24	59.17	62.79
1983	63.70	66.34	66.71	65.90	63.88	60.41	58.21	59.58	55.81	56.97	58.12	61.00	61.39
1984	64.39	65.97	66.30	64.15	60.82	59.28	62.17	61.34	62.01	62.74	63.96	64.26	63.11
1985	66.00	67.02	66.66	66.06	64.25	59.11	57.43	57.81	56.27	59.12	60.05	62.04	62.08
1986	61.34	61.68	59.99	56.68	62.21	53.69	57.98	62.20	61.51				

Source: Economic Research Service, U.S.D.A.   T.61

Federally Inspected Slaughter of Cattle in the United States   In Thousands of Head

Year	Jan.	Feb.	Mar.	Apr.	May	June	July	Aug.	Sept.	Oct.	Nov.	Dec.	Total
1983	2,894	2,554	2,828	2,615	2,820	3,000	2,737	3,220	3,156	3,099	2,899	2,994	34,816
1984	2,951	2,836	2,954	2,728	3,169	3,062	2,996	3,260	2,903	3,313	2,923	2,784	35,880
1985[1]	3,134	2,661	2,761	2,848	3,052	2,770	3,023	3,089	2,877	3,097	2,669	2,778	34,765
1986[1]	3,204	2,613	2,726	3,086	3,123	3,017	3,213	3,101	3,019				

[1] Preliminary.   *Source: Crop Reporting Board, U.S.D.A.*   T.66

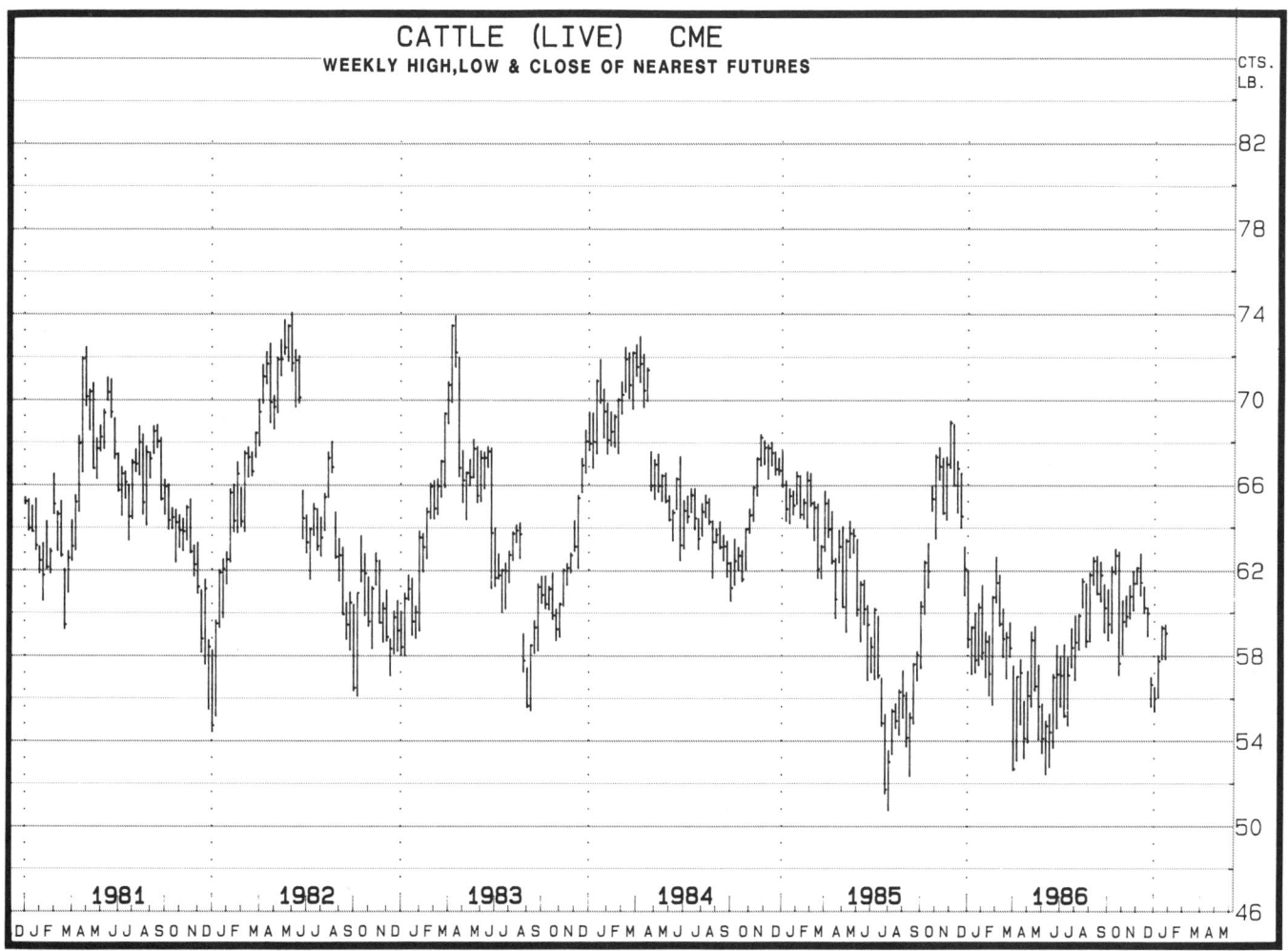

CATTLE (LIVE) CME
WEEKLY HIGH,LOW & CLOSE OF NEAREST FUTURES

High, Low & Closing Prices of June Live Beef Cattle Futures at Chicago   In Cents per Pound

Year of Delivery		Year Prior to Delivery									Delivery Year						Life of Delivery Range
		Apr.	May	June	July	Aug.	Sept.	Oct.	Nov.	Dec.	Jan.	Feb.	Mar.	Apr.	May	June	
1982	High	72.30	71.90	70.40	67.95	66.97	67.35	66.72	66.05	63.55	61.60	64.75	66.87	70.10	73.65	74.00	74.00
	Low	70.40	68.05	66.85	64.82	64.02	64.42	64.60	61.80	54.75	56.00	60.65	62.72	66.20	69.30	69.57	54.75
	Close	70.40	69.80	67.00	67.02	65.37	65.27	65.20	63.30	55.77	61.40	62.92	66.42	69.57	73.37	70.00	—
1983	High	—	65.50	63.30	64.55	63.72	63.25	62.50	61.80	62.00	63.90	66.47	69.77	71.15	68.05	67.70	71.15
	Low	—	63.90	60.00	60.50	61.77	58.40	58.02	58.52	58.55	60.75	62.90	64.80	65.10	64.30	65.75	58.02
	Close	—	64.10	62.75	62.85	62.30	59.27	59.62	60.80	61.10	62.72	65.27	69.62	66.12	66.05	66.85	—
1984	High	—	—	62.25	64.65	66.55	65.70	65.55	66.30	67.65	68.35	69.35	69.85	69.70	67.35	67.25	69.85
	Low	—	—	61.35	61.10	62.95	63.00	63.20	63.60	65.05	65.45	65.10	67.00	65.62	64.60	63.32	61.10
	Close	—	—	61.80	64.15	63.25	64.90	63.75	65.45	67.05	66.05	69.10	68.70	66.17	64.62	66.05	—
1985	High	—	—	66.55	67.35	67.40	67.70	67.10	68.15	68.10	69.00	69.50	67.75	66.92	64.27	61.47	69.50
	Low	—	—	66.00	65.00	65.00	65.70	65.20	66.30	66.50	66.35	66.55	64.60	62.32	59.05	56.80	56.80
	Close	—	—	66.55	65.00	67.37	66.40	66.75	67.70	67.85	68.35	67.37	67.20	62.65	60.10	56.80	—
1986	High	—	66.60	66.05	64.55	62.75	62.25	63.40	62.45	63.05	63.15	62.50	60.52	57.55	59.35	57.10	66.60
	Low	—	65.60	63.00	58.10	59.10	56.25	60.00	59.90	60.15	58.65	57.40	58.20	53.17	53.40	52.42	52.42
	Close	—	65.90	63.35	60.20	59.60	62.22	61.47	62.42	61.40	61.97	61.37	58.25	57.20	54.07	56.97	—
1987	High	57.50	57.00	57.95	60.00	58.75	59.25	57.45	58.07	57.50							
	Low	53.35	53.70	53.30	55.85	57.00	56.30	55.25	56.50	54.90							
	Close	56.35	54.20	55.60	58.30	58.75	56.82	57.05	57.20	55.55							

Source: Chicago Mercantile Exchange   T.62

CATTLE AND CALVES

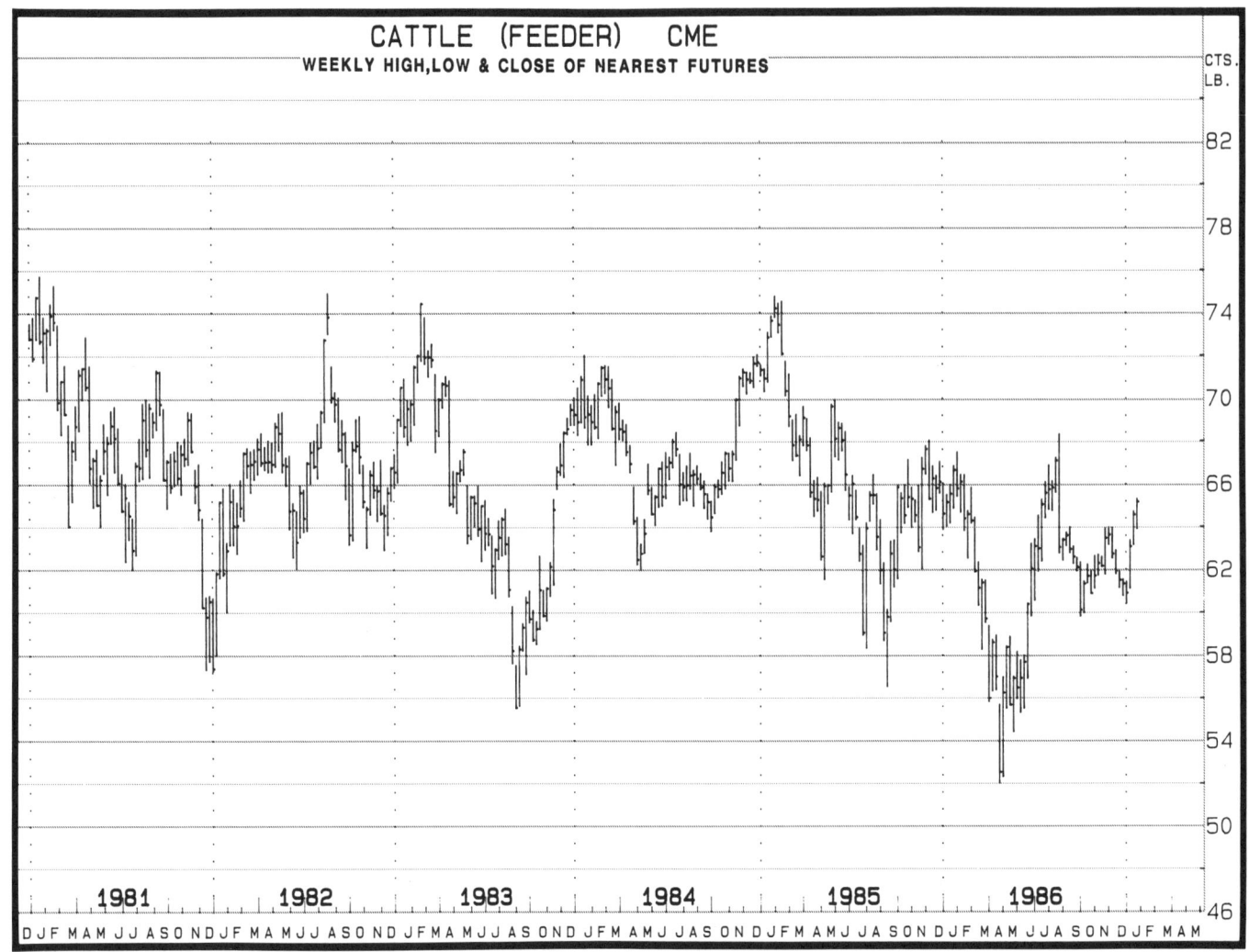

CATTLE (FEEDER) CME
WEEKLY HIGH,LOW & CLOSE OF NEAREST FUTURES

1981　　1982　　1983　　1984　　1985　　1986

Month-End Open Interest of Live Beef Cattle Futures at Chicago　In Contracts

Year	Jan.	Feb.	Mar.	Apr.	May	June	July	Aug.	Sept.	Oct.	Nov.	Dec.
1980	57,192	60,701	50,406	55,582	53,319	59,162	67,059	57,314	58,815	58,009	64,570	45,864
1981	45,325	45,425	48,336	54,045	48,667	50,162	44,597	53,142	51,267	54,025	61,763	51,226
1982	51,036	51,082	61,160	58,383	61,341	48,314	44,024	44,645	42,694	42,412	44,085	45,115
1983	49,014	56,500	59,992	59,771	58,548	47,307	42,292	49,524	52,174	48,215	49,014	51,629
1984	54,669	57,351	59,793	50,190	44,142	41,790	38,689	37,064	38,416	45,984	64,085	57,242
1985	58,769	57,744	63,236	57,324	56,216	49,594	45,674	48,583	50,888	65,037	68,592	59,361
1986	53,559	55,203	52,551	52,245	55,736	58,420	66,835	64,662	60,580	57,668	64,658	56,421

Source: Chicago Mercantile Exchange　　　　　　　　　　T.64

Volume of Trading of Live Beef Cattle Futures at Chicago　In Thousands of Contracts

Year	Jan.	Feb.	Mar.	Apr.	May	June	July	Aug.	Sept.	Oct.	Nov.	Dec.	Total
1980	646.0	545.5	562.0	568.6	499.5	460.7	604.3	443.8	461.1	461.0	348.3	395.2	5,997.0
1981	354.8	347.8	430.7	416.4	350.0	361.0	320.8	329.3	348.9	327.7	335.3	359.7	4,282.4
1982	387.2	332.5	434.3	355.8	389.3	458.4	340.2	326.0	353.1	421.2	337.4	305.6	4,441.0
1983	370.4	332.7	455.8	489.0	389.1	328.9	302.2	324.9	344.1	335.4	297.9	277.9	4,248.2
1984	457.4	397.6	404.2	323.2	256.4	215.5	265.3	202.6	181.0	245.9	345.7	258.5	3,553.3
1985	340.7	290.3	327.9	304.3	412.0	317.2	440.5	370.2	400.2	445.3	405.0	383.8	4,437.3
1986	492.6	381.0	408.2	462.1	424.2	374.5	448.7	373.0	387.1	376.9	289.4	273.0	4,690.5

Source: Chicago Mercantile Exchange　　　　　　　　　　T.63

555

5555555555

555555555555

Beef Steer-Corn Price Ratio at Omaha[1]

Year	Jan.	Feb.	Mar.	Apr.	May	June	July	Aug.	Sept.	Oct.	Nov.	Dec.	Average
1981	19.2	19.3	19.4	20.0	20.6	21.4	21.5	23.8	26.0	25.2	25.0	25.0	22.2
1982	24.6	25.9	26.5	26.5	27.2	26.5	26.1	29.2	27.5	27.7	25.1	25.2	26.5
1983	24.5	23.4	22.7	21.9	21.8	21.2	19.6	18.1	17.8	18.4	18.3	19.8	20.6
1984	21.6	22.1	21.1	20.4	19.7	19.1	20.4	20.7	21.3	22.5	24.6	25.6	21.6
1985	24.8	24.1	22.2	21.5	21.5	21.0	20.6	21.7	21.8	25.7	27.8	26.7	23.3
1986	25.6	24.4	24.0	22.9	22.8	22.3	29.0	36.6	42.4				

[1] Bushels of No. 2 yellow corn equal in value to 100 pounds liveweight of choice slaughter steers, 900–1100 lbs.
Source: Economic Research Service, U.S.D.A.

T.56c

Farm Value, Income & Wholesale Prices of Cattle & Calves

Year	Per Head $	Total Million $	Gross Income From C. & C.[2] Million $	Prime	Steers[3] Choice	Good	Heifers Good	Choice	Feeder Steers All Weights at K.C.	Cows, Utility Omaha	Vealers, Choice So. St. Paul	Cows, Commercial Omaha	Steer, Choice	Heifer, Choice	Cow[5] Canners[6]
1980	502	55,831	32,452	N.A.	67.05	62.16	61.22	64.90	71.30	45.72	75.52	44.91	104.39	101.86	92.45
1981	475	54,292	30,139	N.A.	63.84	59.83	59.46	62.05	64.26	41.93	77.25	41.59	99.85	97.48	84.06
1982	415	47,967	30,390	N.A.	64.22	59.47	59.82	62.79	62.79	39.96	77.70	40.35	101.68	98.54	78.96
1983	406	46,769	29,240	N.A.	62.52	56.99	56.75	61.45	61.39	39.35	72.97	39.40	97.87	94.45	78.48
1984[1]	396	44,976	31,159		65.34	59.14	58.73	64.59	63.11	39.81	63.98	40.75	100.17	96.62	74.70
1985[1]	402	44,139			58.37	53.25	59.79	57.64	62.08	38.32	58.28	37.91	N.A.	N.A.	N.A.
1986[1]	391	41,280													

At Omaha — *Beef, Dressed (Car Lots)* — Dollars Per 100 Pounds

[1] Preliminary. [2] Excludes interfarm sales & Gov't. payments. Cash receipts from farm marketings + value of farm home consumption.
[3] Weighted average prices of beef steers, sold out of first hands for slaughter. [5] All weights. [6] & cutter.
Source: Statistical Reporting Service, U.S.D.A.

T.60

Average Price Received by Farmers for Beef Cattle In Dollars Per 100 Pounds

Year	Jan.	Feb.	Mar.	Apr.	May	June	July	Aug.	Sept.	Oct.	Nov.	Dec.	Average[1]
1980	63.80	67.00	64.40	60.60	60.70	61.10	63.20	64.40	63.00	62.10	60.00	59.40	62.40
1981	60.40	59.40	58.20	61.00	60.50	61.40	60.50	59.70	55.60	53.80	52.60	52.50	56.70
1982	53.50	56.30	58.60	60.10	62.60	61.10	55.80	54.20	52.30	51.70	51.20	54.50	55.50
1983	54.30	57.10	59.70	60.10	58.60	57.60	57.60	56.60	55.70	54.10	54.80	57.00	57.30
1984	57.20	59.70	61.70	60.10	58.60	57.60	57.60	56.60	55.70	54.10	54.80	57.00	57.30
1985	57.40	58.50	57.30	56.20	55.30	53.60	50.20	49.40	49.10	52.10	54.70	53.70	53.70
1986[2]	53.20	53.00	52.40	50.30	51.00	50.10	52.90	54.40	54.60	54.40	54.70		

[1] Weighted average by quantities sold. [2] Preliminary. *Source: Crop Reporting Board, U.S.D.A.*

T.68

Average Price Received by Farmers for Calves In Dollars Per 100 Pounds

Year	Jan.	Feb.	Mar.	Apr.	May	June	July	Aug.	Sept.	Oct.	Nov.	Dec.	Average[1]
1980	86.90	90.90	82.60	75.50	75.40	76.90	75.40	75.60	74.30	73.90	72.10	70.30	76.80
1981	70.40	70.60	68.80	69.60	66.00	66.30	62.00	62.30	61.40	59.00	59.40	57.70	64.00
1982	57.00	58.90	61.90	62.10	64.20	61.70	60.40	61.80	59.00	58.30	58.10	58.80	59.80
1983	62.40	66.50	68.40	66.70	66.20	64.30	60.30	57.40	56.10	57.20	59.40	60.60	61.70
1984	61.10	63.90	63.70	62.30	60.80	59.20	59.10	59.10	56.60	58.20	59.40	59.40	59.90
1985	64.10	65.40	65.90	65.40	65.60	62.60	60.00	61.40	58.30	60.20	61.40	58.80	62.10
1986[2]	60.10	62.80	61.90	58.90	58.00	58.10	59.40	61.10	63.40	62.70	62.20		

[1] Weighted average by quantities sold. [2] Preliminary. *Source: Crop Reporting Board, U.S.D.A.*

T.69

Federally Inspected Slaughter of Calves & Vealers in the U.S. In Thousands of Head

Year	Jan.	Feb.	Mar.	Apr.	May	June	July	Aug.	Sept.	Oct.	Nov.	Dec.	Total
1980	212	187	201	185	161	154	186	182	198	229	185	214	2,294
1981	215	192	213	190	159	175	204	198	228	236	217	254	2,478
1982	——702——			——609——			——692——			——726——			2,729
1983	221	204	246	202	194	211	214	262	258	259	266	262	2,798
1984	253	236	264	226	233	218	258	294	245	282	275	247	3,030
1985[1]	270	236	261	252	246	221	274	272	271	298	268	298	3,168
1986[1]	289	256	276	284	257	240	281	262	263				

[1] Preliminary. *Source: Crop Reporting Board, U.S.D.A.*

T.67

Cement

U.S. Bureau of Mines estimates 1986 domestic production at 82 million tons; estimated consumption is 92 million tons. Cumulative imports through October, 1986, were 13 percent above the same 1985 period.

Domestic shipments of finished portland cement through October, 1986, were 76.1 million tons, five percent above the year-ago period. Leading producing states were California, Texas, Pennsylvania, Michigan, and Missouri. Major consuming states were California, Texas, Florida, Illinois and New York. Cumulative masonry cement shipments, through October, 1986, were 3.15 million tons, eight percent above the year-ago period.

Average monthly price for bulk cement in 20 cities was reported in *Engineering News Record* through October, 1986, as $65.02 per short ton; the high was posted in May at $66.70. October, 1986 average price of $63.43 was the low for the period.

U.S. cement demand increased about seven percent in 1985, with improved industrial, commercial, and residential construction activity. The largest increases were in New England (17 percent) and the Middle Atlantic (10 percent). From a 1983 base, the Bureau of Mines has estimated demand will rise at an annual rate of two percent through 1990.

In 1985, the U.S. relied more heavily on imports to meet cement requirements. Import reliance as a percentage of consumption was 15 percent, surpassing the nine-percent record in 1979. This trend is expected to continue.

World Production of Hydraulic Cement by Selected Countries   In Millions of Short Tons

Year	Rep. of Korea	Brazil	Canada	China	France	West Germany	India	Italy	Japan	Poland	Spain	South Africa	Turkey	United Kingdom	United States	USSR	World Total
1982	19.7	28.3	9.3	103.7	28.8	33.2	24.8	43.8	88.9	17.7	32.6	8.8	17.4	14.3	64.3	136.3	978.4
1983	23.5	23.0	8.7	119.3	27.0	33.6	28.0	43.2	89.2	17.9	33.8	8.7	15.0	14.8	71.3	141.3	1,010.1
1984[1]	22.5	27.6	9.5	133.5	25.0	31.9	32.0	41.6	86.9	18.4	28.0	9.0	17.3	14.9	78.7	143.5	1,045.5
1985[2]	22.5	29.8	10.5	157.1	25.4	32.0	36.4	44.0	80.3	16.5	28.1	7.8	17.6	14.7	78.9	144.0	1,071.2

[1] Preliminary.   [2] Estimate.   *Source: Bureau of Mines*   T.70

Salient Statistics of Cement in the United States

Year	Net Import Reliance as a % of Apparent Consumption	Production Portland (Million Tons)	Production Others[2] (Million Tons)	Production Total (Million Tons)	Capacity Used[3] %	Shipments From Mills Total Mil. Tons	Shipments From Mills Value[4] $ Mil.	Average Value (F.O.B. Mill) $ per Ton	Stocks at Mills Dec. 31 (Million Tons)	Imports[5] (Million Tons)	Exports[5] (Million Tons)	Apparent Consumption	Cement Rock	Lime-stone[6]	Clay & Shale	Gypsum & Anhy.	Total (All)
1982	5	61.1	2.3	63.4	58.7	64.1	3,264	50.94	6.8	2.9	.2	65.6	18.6	71.3	8.3	3.1	107.1
1983	6	67.5	2.9	70.4	64.6	70.9	3,543	49.95	6.7	4.2	.1	73.4	21.6	73.1	8.7	3.5	113.5
1984	10	74.4	3.3	77.7	71.8	80.2	4,152	51.80	6.9	8.7	.1	84.3	27.0	78.5	9.1	4.0	124.8
1985[1]	15	74.6	3.3	77.9	73.0	83.0	4,286	51.61	7.2	14.1	.1	87.5	24.3	77.6	8.8	4.0	121.4

[1] Preliminary.   [2] Masonry, natural & pozzolan (slag-line).   [3] At Portland-cement mills.   [4] Value received f.o.b. mill, excluding cost of containers.   [5] Hydraulic & clinker cement.   [6] Including oyster shells.   *Source: Bureau of Mines*   T.71

Index of Wholesale Price of Portland Cement   Base Per Ton 1967 = 100

Year	Jan.	Feb.	Mar.	Apr.	May	June	July	Aug.	Sept.	Oct.	Nov.	Dec.	Average
1982	336.3	338.2	341.4	341.1	341.8	341.8	339.5	337.9	337.1	334.5	334.8	328.9	337.9
1983	326.4	332.4	330.2	339.1	339.6	340.9	340.5	346.3	347.9	346.8	340.5	340.5	339.1
1984	337.3	345.0	354.6	351.5	357.0	352.8	353.5	355.9	354.1	353.2	356.5	358.8	352.5
1985	356.9	359.7	361.1	359.6	365.4	363.8	360.5	360.9	358.5	357.1	355.2	356.8	359.6
1986[1]	359.0	360.7	360.4	360.4	355.0	353.4	350.5	349.2	349.7	352.3			

[1] Preliminary.   *Source: Bureau of Labor Statistics* (1322-0131.99)   T.74

Shipments of Finished Portland Cement from Mills in the United States   In Millions of Barrels

Year	Jan.	Feb.	Mar.	Apr.	May	June	July	Aug.	Sept.	Oct.	Nov.	Dec.	Total[1]
1982	15.1	17.8	25.7	28.2	31.0	35.4	34.5	36.0	35.4	34.1	27.4	22.7	343.6
1983	18.9	17.7	25.4	28.4	33.6	39.4	37.3	41.9	39.5	39.1	32.8	22.2	376.9
1984[2]	20.4	25.6	29.2	34.3	41.5	43.1	42.1	46.9	39.9	43.3	36.5	25.7	435.8
1985[2]	21.8	21.7	31.7	39.4	44.2	42.6	45.9	46.9	43.3	46.0	33.2	26.7	445.1
1986[2]	28.9	23.7	32.3	41.5	43.2	44.8	46.9	46.6					

[1] Does not necessarily agree with monthly figures. These are compiled from producers' annual reports and are final.   [2] Preliminary
Source: Bureau of Mines   T.73

Cheese

Preliminary figures indicate that domestic output of cheese continued a long-term uptrend in 1986. Increased production occurred in the face of declining milk output, brought about by three major changes in government policy: reduction of dairy price supports under the 1985 Farm Bill; lowered appropriations for price-support payments to dairy farmers as a result of the Gramm-Rudman-Hollings Act; and depletion of dairy herds through the federal Dairy Termination Program. The rise in cheese production was achieved at the expense of output of other dairy products, notably butter and whole milk.

The specifics of production in 1986, based on a mixture of statistics and extrapolations, are these: American cheese up approximately five percent from 1985; other kinds of cheese up 10 percent; cottage cheese (creamed and low-fat combined) up one percent. Imports were slightly lower during 1986—and in 1985 were lower than in 1984.

The force behind increased production was strong demand. Data comparing January–July, 1986, with the same period a year before show that sales of American cheese had risen nearly six percent, sales of other types almost nine percent, and sales of cottage cheese one percent. Reflecting changes in dietary habits, sales of Mozzarella and low-fat cottage cheese were particularly brisk during 1986.

Statistics covering the larger part of 1986 show that commercial stocks of American cheese fell to a level not touched (except possibly in 1982) since 1973. Cheese makers apparently sold large amounts to the Commodity Credit Corporation, rather than adding to inventories, partly because many underestimated seasonal price increases. Stocks of other types of cheese also dipped to low levels during 1986.

With roughly equivalent growth in both the demand for and supply of cheese, prices rose only modestly during 1986. Between New Year's Day and midsummer 1986, the retail price index for all types of cheese edged upward 0.5 percent. The retail price of American cheese advanced from $2.53 per pound in December, 1985, to $2.60 per pound at the end of July, 1986. Fragmentary data covering later months tend to confirm this upward tendency.

It is possible that 1987 milk output will be lower than in 1986, because of federal policies. But, the impact of that development upon production of cheese may be minimal, as it apparently was in 1986. In that event, continuing strong demand should exert further upward pressure on prices. Prices could also be enhanced if imports of cheese fell markedly in reaction to the appreciation of major currencies against the dollar and the sharpening trade "war" between the U.S. and the European Community.

Two tendencies are virtually certain to persist, if not intensify, during 1987. One, mentioned above, is the shift in consumer preferences toward low-fat cheese products at the expense of those containing whole milk. The impact upon prices of this development, which affects the composition of output as opposed to total volume, is difficult to assess. The second ongoing trend is the rising usage of cheese substitutes fortified by the milk protein called casein. These substitutes, lower in price than many kinds of natural cheese, are widely used in such prepared foods as frozen pizza.

World Cheese (Total[1]) Production   In Millions of Metric Tons[3]

Year	Argentina	Australia	Brazil	Canada	China	Czechoslovakia	Denmark	France	West Germany	Italy	Netherlands	New Zealand	USSR	Sweden	Switzerland	United Kingdom	United States
1980	245	154		177	270	109	221	1,146	421	615	443	106	648	101	125	237	1,807
1981	226	130	217	177		113	243	1,168	448	610	465	84	656	103	128	241	1,940
1982	229	153	220	170		120	245	1,200	446	645	481	112	699	108	129	244	2,060
1983	209	158	200	185		123	249	1,245	446	656	485	114	744	115	135	244	2,186
1984	210	161	200	193		130	293	1,287	465	661	515	110	780	116	130	245	2,120
1985[2]	220	160	205	208		131	253	1,306	480	700	522	115	785	115	128	256	2,279
1986[3]	215	164	205	213		132	253	1,343	482	690	530	126	800	115	130	265	2,400

[1] Farm & factory production.   [2] Preliminary.   [3] Estimate.   *Source: Foreign Agricultural Service, U.S.D.A.*   T.75

Supply and Distribution of All Cheese in the United States   In Millions of Pounds

Year	Production Whole Milk[2]	Production All Cheese[3]	Supply Jan. 1 Commercial Stocks	Imports[4]	Total Supply	Cheese 40-Lb. Blocks Wisc. Assembly Points ¢ per lb.	Exports & Shipments[5]	Jan. 1 Stocks	Dec. 31 Stocks	Amer. Cheese Removed by U.S.D.A. Programs	Total Disap.	Domestic Disapp. Military	Domestic Disapp. Civilian	Civilian Per Capita
1980	2,376	3,984	513	231	4,728		46	3	169	350	4,038	16	3,976	17.6
1981	2,642	4,278	691	248	5,169	139.44	45	169	515	563	4,239	12	4,182	18.4
1982	2,752	4,542	976	269	5,677	138.27	85	515	647	643	4,722	15	4,633	20.1
1983	2,928	4,820	1,065	286	6,171	138.28	94	647	793	833	4,904	18	4,792	20.6
1984[1]	2,648	4,674	1,267	306	6,267	137.96	78	793	621	447	5,185	18	5,088	21.7
1985[1]	2,854	5,025	1,062	303	6,374	127.72		621	595	629			4,900	22.0
1986[6]	3,000	5,300	944			128.00		595		540			5,000	

[1] Preliminary.   [2] Whole milk American cheddar.   [3] All types of cheese except cottage, pot and baker's cheese.   [4] Imports for consumption.   [5] Commercial.   [6] Estimate.   *Source: Department of Agriculture*   T.76

CHEESE

Cheese Production in the United States   In Millions of Pounds

Year	American Whole Milk	American Part Skim	American Total	Swiss, Including Block	Munster	Baick	Limburger	Neufchatel	Cream Cheese	Italian Varieties	Blue mold	All Other Varieties	Total of All Cheese[2]	Cottage Cheese Low-Fat	Cottage Cheese Curd[4]	Cottage Cheese Creamed[5]
1977	2,043	4.1	2,047	189.3	55.4	15.9	1.7	3.3	173.1	793.5	34.8	44.4	3,359	139.0	684.5	878
1978	2,074	4.9	2,079	209.4	59.3	16.9	1.6	3.9	194.3	875.7	35.3	44.2	3,520	153.1	688.4	871
1979	2,190	4.4	2,194	213.3	63.6	14.4	1.6	5.2	207.1	929.1	34.6	54.1	3,717	150.4	668.5	840
1980	2,376	5.4	2,381	218.9	70.0	15.4	1.6	4.3	224.3	982.7	33.0	52.9	3,984	179.8	667.4	825
1981	2,642	5.9	2,664	214.4	67.4	13.9	1.2	—241.3—		994.4	30.2	66.6	4,278	208.3	647.5	773
1982	2,752	6.9	2,759	221.1	71.7	14.3	1.5	—262.8—		1,087.8	31.0	92.4	4,542	217.6	628.9	749
1983	2,928	4.1	2,932	209.5	69.6	14.2	1.1	—270.0—		1,200.2	31.5	90.6	4,820	215.9	618.2	743
1984[1]	2,648	2.7	2,649	208.0	76.0	16.0	1.2	—276.5—		1,318.8	34.1	92.2	4,674	227.6	603.5	734
1985[3]			2,854	—————————————2,171—————————————									5,025	—	965.4	—

[1] Preliminary.   [2] Excludes full-skim cheddar and cottage cheese.   [3] Estimated.   [4] Includes cottage, pot, and baker's cheese with a butterfat content of less than 4%.   [5] Includes cheese with a butterfat content of 4 to 19%.   *Source: Agricultural Marketing Service, U.S.D.A.*   T.77

Wholesale Price of American Cheese, Fresh Single Daisies at Chicago   In Cents Per Pound

Year	Jan.	Feb.	Mar.	Apr.	May	June	July	Aug.	Sept.	Oct.	Nov.	Dec.	Average
1977	114.0	114.0	115.2	119.3	119.3	119.4	119.4	119.4	120.5	120.6	121.1	122.4	118.7
1978	122.9	124.1	124.6	125.9	125.9	125.9	126.0	132.1	134.0	139.4	140.0	141.0	130.1
1979	141.0	135.0	135.6	137.4	137.6	138.9	140.9	145.8	148.8	146.6	144.7	144.4	141.4
1980	146.7	147.2	150.8	153.5	154.2	154.8	155.5	157.0	161.5	165.3	164.1	164.1	156.2
1981	164.0	164.0	166.9	167.0	167.8	167.9	167.8	167.8	167.8	168.5	169.2	168.4	167.2
1982	168.4	168.4	168.4	168.4	168.4	168.4	168.4	168.4	168.3	168.6	168.6	168.6	168.4
1983	168.0	166.6	166.6	166.6	167.5	168.4	168.4	168.4	169.1	169.9	169.9	168.4	168.2
1984	168.9	168.9	168.9	168.9	168.9	168.8	170.0	172.1	175.9	174.4	169.9	169.1	170.4
1985	168.3	166.7	166.0	163.1	167.7	166.7	158.2	165.1	155.6	155.6	155.6	155.6	162.0
1986	155.6	155.6	155.6	155.7	155.8	155.8	157.2	159.6	159.7				

Source: Statistical Reporting Service, U.S.D.A.   T.79

United States Total Cheese Production[1]   In Millions of Pounds

Year	Jan.	Feb.	Mar.	Apr.	May	June	July	Aug.	Sept.	Oct.	Nov.	Dec.	Total
1977	265.6	252.5	299.7	304.7	326.1	316.0	280.2	275.7	251.7	256.9	247.8	281.6	3,359
1978	271.1	259.9	314.4	303.7	332.9	331.9	293.6	286.5	265.0	279.3	279.7	301.4	3,520
1979	292.5	272.2	323.0	318.8	340.4	343.8	318.8	309.0	290.7	308.0	289.4	308.7	3,717
1980	312.3	303.1	339.7	336.6	360.5	359.9	332.7	317.6	317.0	332.1	317.2	354.4	3,984
1981	342.8	317.8	374.1	379.5	394.2	390.9	353.0	340.6	334.4	343.4	334.1	372.7	4,278
1982	351.3	331.0	391.7	—	1,203	—	—	1,121	—	—	1,143	—	4,542
1983	384.8	359.3	425.3	413.1	439.4	444.7	402.1	381.3	373.0	391.9	389.3	415.4	4,820
1984	382.1	366.0	412.3	409.9	432.9	415.4	379.9	371.2	357.8	381.1	368.9	396.3	4,674
1985[2]	390.6	355.3	411.5	423.8	451.1	441.3	429.3	422.7	399.6	428.0	411.8	437.5	5,025
1986[2]	425.9	398.7	462.7	461.0	480.5	459.1	439.3	424.9					

[1] Excludes cottage and full skim American.   [2] Preliminary.   *Source: Statistical Reporting Service, U.S.D.A.*   T.78

Cold Storage Holdings of All Varieties of Cheese in the U.S., on First of Month   In Millions of Pounds[2]

Year	Jan.	Feb.	Mar.	Apr.	May	June	July	Aug.	Sept.	Oct.	Nov.	Dec.
1977	478.4	485.7	471.2	485.8	510.3	557.2	583.7	592.9	592.9	553.9	502.8	479.8
1978	468.6	459.6	442.0	430.0	447.1	462.5	500.2	498.5	489.7	476.6	455.2	431.0
1979	436.4	436.6	446.2	448.6	462.2	495.3	519.9	555.3	548.5	540.6	526.9	528.2
1980	512.1	515.8	508.9	495.1	510.5	544.4	582.7	620.0	613.8	610.6	590.9	565.4
1981	578.8	601.7	596.3	593.6	632.4	649.8	685.7	714.2	719.4	694.3	682.4	677.5
1982	709.6	711.7	696.4	722.4	—	—	803.9	—	—	864.3	—	—
1983	963.5	1,032	1,088	1,118	1,132	1,138	1,162	1,194	1,231	1,248	1,235	1,215
1984	1,205	1,201	1,220	1,217	1,182	1,208	1,193	1,186	1,148	1,115	1,078	1,044
1985[1]	986.2	968.9	944.4	907.7	898.6	911.0	954.2	963.5	962.9	941.0	891.8	877.5
1986[1]	852.9	835.8	811.2	836.7	838.4	873.3	892.4	915.6	911.7	854.5	805.0	759.6

[1] Preliminary.   [2] Quantities are given in "net weight."   *Source: Crop Reporting Board, U.S.D.A.*   T.80

Chromite

Chromite is the source of chromium, which is used to harden steel alloys and to produce stainless steel. The U.S. is entirely dependent upon imports for its chromium needs. Although some resources do exist, the ore is not extracted due to its low commercial potential. South Africa supplies approximately two-thirds to three-quarters of U.S. needs, depending on demand and the type (either chromite ore used in the refractory, chemical and ferroalloys industries, or high- and low-carbon ferrochromium used in steel making).

For the first three quarters of 1986, imports of chromite were 336,410 tons, compared with all of 1985's 414,370 tons. Imports of ferrochromium in the same 1986 period were 322,910 tons, compared with total 1985 imports of 331,065 tons.

South Africa supplied 240,350 tons of chromite to the U.S., over 70 percent of the total for the first nine months of 1986, valued at $10.7 million. Turkey and the Philippines were other major suppliers.

South Africa supplied 60 percent of U.S. imports of high carbon ferrochromium, or 171,510 tons. 39 percent of the low-carbon ferrochromium imports to the U.S. during January–September, 1986, came from South Africa, or 13,875 tons of the nine-month total which was 35,500 tons.

U.S. chromium consumption for the first nine months of 1986 totaled 308,670 tons, compared with all of 1985's 560,421 tons. Use of ferrochromium in the same period totaled 244,316 tons, compared with full-year 1985's 349,548 tons.

The U.S. is one of the world's major consumers of chromium. Some 86 percent of domestic usage is in the chemicals and metallurgical industries; the remainder is used in the refractory industry. The total value of the chromite used as chromium and ferrochromium was estimated at $180 million in 1985; this declined in 1986 due to lower prices for South African ore.

1986 world chromite production is not expected to change much from 1985's estimated 10.6 million tonnes. South Africa mines about one-third of the world's chromite and is a major exporter to the U.S. From a 1983 base, the Bureau of Mines estimates that chromium use will increase about 6.4 percent a year through 1990.

World resources total about 36 billion tons of shipping-grade ore, but more than 90 percent of those resources are located in volatile southern Africa—26 billion tons in South Africa and 11 million tons in Zimbabawe. Alternate sources of supply reserves are not considered commercially viable.

In 1986, Diamond Shamrock Corp., the larger of two domestic chromium-chemicals producers, was sold as part of a corporate merger to Occidental Petroleum Corp. for about $850 million.

World Mine Production of Chromite   In Thousands of Short Tons

Year	Albania	Brazil	Cuba	Finland	Greece	India	Japan	Pakistan	Philippines	Zimbabwe	Turkey	South Africa	Iran	USSR	Madagascar	World Total[1]
1977	970	342	22	443	46	389	20	9	593	746	560	3,372	257	2,400	182	10,415
1978	1,090	1,056	32	449	41	293	10	12	595	527	420	3,466	218	3,640	152	12,064
1979	827	375	31	480	50	342	13	3	613	597	410	3,634	150	2,535	141	10,277
1980	840	345	31	399	46	352	15	3	547	610	411	3,763	90	3,200	198	10,915
1981	783	261	23	454	27	369	12	2	484	591	442	3,164	35	3,200	110	10,018
1982	744	304	30	380	32	374	12	4	355	476	499	2,385	45	3,240	49	9,026
1983	755	171	37	271	30	465	9	7	294	463	381	2,460	55	3,240	50	8,829
1984[2]	794	282	41	492	68	466	8	3	286	525	537	3,314	55	3,240	66	10,312
1985[1]	909	303	44	500	68	610	13	4	284	551	496	3,682	55	3,240	66	10,951

[1] Estimate.   [2] Preliminary.   *Source: Bureau of Mines*   T.81

U.S. Salient Statistics of Chromite   In Thousands of Short Tons

Year	% Net Import Reliance of Apparent Consumption	Shipments from Gov't Stockpiles	Exports	Imports (For Consumption)	Re-exports	Consumption by Primary Consumer Groups (Gross Weight) Total	Metallurgical	Refractory	Chemical	Stocks, Dec. 31 Metallurgical	Refractory	Chemical	Total Stocks	$ Per Metric Ton South Africa[2]	Turkish[4]
1977	91	517	187	1,293	61	1,000	578	208	214	900	174	264	1,338	59	137
1978	91	—	23	1,013	29	1,010	534	237	239	755	185	361	1,301	56	105
1979	90	—	27	1,024	28	1,214	774	198	242	416	161	330	907	56	110
1980	91	—	6	982	44	977	577	160	240	219	128	370	728	55	110
1981	90	—	71	898	67	889	503	148	238	230	128	370	728	55	110
1982	85	—	8	507	57	558	283	80	195	120	113	313	546	52	110
1983	76		11	190	5	320	64	72	184	140	76	239	456	52	110
1984	81		55	305	4	512	226	97	189	24	70	233	327	52	110
1985[1]	73			101	414	4	560	273	65	222	44	49	207	300	42	110

[1] Preliminary.   [2] Cr_2O_3, 44% (Transvaal).   [3] Estimate.   [4] 48% Cr_2O_3.   *Source: Bureau of Mines*   T.82

31

Coal

Some 889 million short tons of coal were produced during 1986, up 0.6 percent from 1985. Imports were 2.1 million tons, compared with 1.95 million in 1985. Exports came to 90 million short tons, as against 92.7 million tons the year before. Domestic supply was near 800 million tons, up 7 million tons.

Aggregate demand for coal, including domestic consumption and exports, was an estimated 880 million short tons, 3.4 percent lower than in 1985. Measured in Btu, coal consumption aggregated to 17.5 quadrillion (10 to the 15th power) Btu, virtually unchanged from 1985. 83 percent of total consumption was by electric utilities and 16 percent by industrial enterprises. Residential usage of coal ended for all practical purposes during the 1940s and usage in the transportation sector ceased in the 1950s. Coal was the primary energy source for some 56 percent of the 2.5 trillion kilowatt hours of electricity produced in the United States during 1986. 90 percent of coal used for that purpose was of the bituminous variety.

Along with two other fossil fuels (heavy oil and natural gas) used in steam-electric utility plants, coal's average cost fell to $1.60 per million Btu from $1.648 in 1985. Coal maintained its substantial price advantage over two rivals: the average cost of heavy oil began 1986 at $3.926 per million Btu, but dropped to $1.843 in July; the average cost of natural gas declined from $3.15 per million Btu in January to $2.172 in July. The outlook for 1987 is for no significant change in any of the key market variables.

World Production of All Coal[3]   In Millions of Metric Tons

Year	Australia	East Germany	Canada	Czecho-slovakia	France	West Germany	Greece	India	Japan	China	Poland	South Africa	United Kingdom	United States	U.S.S.R.	Yugo-slavia
1983	143	278	45	129	20	214	30	142	17	688	234	139	119	712	642	59
1984[2]	160	296	57	131	19	211	32	152	17	736	242		51	808	637	59
1985[1]	165	300	60	128	17	208	33	155	15	750	246		55	800	650	60

[1] Estimate. [2] Preliminary. [3] Includes anthracite, subanthracite, bituminous, subbituminous, lignite & brown coal.   *Source: United Nations.* T.83

Bituminous Coal Production[1] in the United States   In Millions of Short Tons

Year	Jan.	Feb.	Mar.	Apr.	May	June	July	Aug.	Sept.	Oct.	Nov.	Dec.	Total
1983	62.5	60.4	68.6	61.6	62.9	61.4	54.9	72.9	69.9	71.3	68.3	63.4	778.0
1984	67.9	73.7	81.6	71.7	79.8	75.3	73.9	89.7	78.0	68.6	63.4	62.6	891.8
1985[2]	68.0	67.0	77.7	76.5	78.2	73.0	69.3	79.2	73.6	79.7	68.9	69.6	878.9
1986[2]	78.3	72.7	77.6	74.9	73.1	72.7	67.0	74.1	73.6	76.8	68.7		

[1] Includes small amount of lignite.   [2] Preliminary.   *Source: Bureau of Mines*   T.88

Pennsylvania Anthracite Coal Production[1]   In Thousands of Short Tons

Year	Jan.	Feb.	Mar.	Apr.	May	June	July	Aug.	Sept.	Oct.	Nov.	Dec.	Total
1983	277	260	343	285	293	352	309	400	385	414	412	359	4,089
1984	284	249	278	228	377	293	384	435	423	349	332	323	4,162
1985[2]	282	279	329	249	335	420	338	409	381	447	386	396	4,708
1986[2]	261	243	260	300	294	297	294	325	328	431	373		

[1] Represents production in Pennsylvania only. Production outside which is small, is included in Bituminous Production series.   [2] Preliminary.   *Source: Bureau of Mines*   T.92

U.S. Stocks of Bituminous Coal for All Industrial & Retail Dealers, at End of Month   In Million Short Tons

Year	Jan.	Feb.	Mar.	Apr.	May	June	July	Aug.	Sept.	Oct.	Nov.	Dec.
1983	185.7	185.4	186.1	187.2	190.8	190.7	174.9	168.6	167.2	172.6	172.7	162.1
1984	156.4	163.0	167.7	175.3	184.7	187.4	186.0	193.5	201.3	200.4	195.3	190.4
1985[1]	176.7	170.2	172.5	177.9	180.5	181.3	172.1	168.8	168.8	172.8	170.4	163.0
1986[1]	158.0	156.4	159.0	166.1	170.0	168.6						

[1] Preliminary.   *Source: Bureau of Mines*   T.87

Average Wholesale Price of Bituminous[1] Coal (Screenings, Industrial Use)   (1967 = 100)

Year	Jan.	Feb.	Mar.	Apr.	May	June	July	Aug.	Sept.	Oct.	Nov.	Dec.	Average
1983	531.5	529.2	534.6	534.3	532.0	530.8	531.3	533.2	534.6	534.9	539.1	540.7	533.8
1984	538.1	541.5	543.1	538.9	544.4	541.1	545.1	547.0	546.1	545.9	545.6	544.6	543.5
1985	544.8	546.4	545.6	544.5	545.1	544.3	546.7	547.0	545.6	540.4	534.2	537.1	543.5
1986[2]	537.7	535.4	538.3	536.5	535.6	535.1	535.2	533.7	533.9	532.4	530.9		

[1] Prices are for Screenings, industrial use, f.o.b. mine.   [2] Preliminary.   *Source: Bureau of Labor Statistics* (0512)   T.90

Salient Statistics of the Bituminous Coal Industry in the United States

Year	Production Under-ground (Millions Net Tons)	Production Sur-face (Millions Net Tons)	Total Pro-duction (Millions Net Tons)	Value Total Million $	Value Avg. Per Ton $	Num-ber of Mines	Thous. of Men Em-ployed	Aug. Tons Per Miner Per Hr. Under-ground	Aug. Tons Per Miner Per Hr. Sur-face	Aug. Tons Per Miner Per Hr. Total	Im-ports	Grand Total	Exports to: Canada (Thousands of Short Tons)	Exports to: Europe	Exports to: Asia
1980	337	487	824	21,580	24.52	5,598	224.9	1.21	3.27	1.94	1,194	89,882	17,039	40,414	25,481
1981	316	503	818	21,505	26.29	5,569	226.3	1.29	3.50	2.11	1,043	110,243	17,856	56,130	31,010
1982	338.6	495.0	833.5	22,621	27.14	5,363	214.4	1.37	3.48	2.14	742	105,244	18,205	51,211	29,957
1983	299.9	478.1	778.0	20,111	25.85	4,265	173.5	1.62	3.87	2.52	1,271	76,870	16,809	32,979	21,895
1984[1]	351.5	540.3	891.8	22,750	25.51	4,902	175.7	1.72	4.10	2.65	1,286	80,793	20,140	32,766	21,306
1985[2]	350.1	528.9	878.9								1,952	91,361	16,112	44,677	21,803

[1] Preliminary. [2] Estimate. *Source: Energy Information Administration* T.84

United States Production of Coal by Principal States   In Millions of Short Tons

Year	Anthra-cite Pennsyl-vania	Bituminous Alabama	Colo-rado	Illinois	Indiana	Ken-tucky	Mon-tana	Ohio	Pennsyl-vania	Vir-ginia	West Vir-ginia	Ten-nessee	Wyo-ming	Total Bitu-minous	Total U.S.
1981	5.4	24.5	19.9	51.9	29.3	157.6	33.6	37.4	78.1	42.0	112.8	10.5	103.0	818.4	823.8
1982	4.6	26.6	18.3	60.3	31.8	150.2	27.9	36.5	74.8	39.8	128.5	7.5	108.4	833.5	838.1
1983	4.1	23.8	16.7	56.8	31.8	131.2	28.9	33.8	65.7	35.0	115.0	6.6	112.2	778.0	782.1
1984	4.2	27.1	18.0	63.8	37.6	159.5	33.0	39.3	73.3	40.4	131.0	7.3	130.9	891.8	895.9
1985[2]	4.7	27.8	17.2	59.2	33.3	152.3	33.3	35.6	66.7	40.9	127.8	7.4	140.7	878.9	883.6
1986[1]	3.7	26.4	17.7	64.1	34.2	156.3	34.6	35.4	70.7	44.2	129.4	7.8	139.8	908.0	911.7

[1] Estimate. [2] Preliminary. *Source: Bureau of Mines* T.85

U.S. Consumption & Stocks of Bituminous Coal & Lignite   In Millions of Short Tons

Year	Stocks—Dec. 31 Electric Power Utilities	Oven Coke Plants	Steel & Rolling Mills	Other Indus-trials	Producers & Distrib.	Total	Consumption Electric Power Utilities	Coke Plants Beehive	Coke Plants Ovens	Steel & Rolling Mills	Other Indus-trials	Retail De-liveries[2]	Total
1980	178.3	9.0	—11.8—		23.9	223.0	568.3	—66.5—		—59.3—		4.9	699.1
1981	163.4	6.4	— 9.8—		23.8	203.4	595.6	—60.9—		—66.6—		5.4	728.5
1982	175.1	4.6	— 9.4—		36.1	225.2	592.6	—40.9—		—63.5—		6.6	703.6
1983	149.1	4.3	— 8.6—		33.4	195.4	624.2	—37.0—		—65.6—		7.1	733.9
1984[3]	173.0	6.2	—11.2—		33.5	223.9	663.3	—44.0—		—73.2—		7.7	788.2
1985[3]	149.2	3.4	—10.4—		32.7	195.7	692.8	—41.0—		—74.8—		6.5	815.1

[1] Preliminary. [2] To other consumers. (Residential & Commercial) [3] Estimate. *Source: Energy Information Administration* T.86

Statistical Trends in the Pennsylvania Anthracite Industry

Year	Production (Millions of Net Tons) Total	Sur-face	Under-ground	Value of Produc-tion Million $	Avg. Value Per Net Ton	Stocks (Dec. 31) Electric Utilities	Prod. & Distrib.	Exports to: Total	Canada	France	Nether-land	South Korea	Appar-ent Con-sump-tion	Avg. No. of Men Work-ing Daily (1,000)	Num-ber of Mines	Avg. Tons Per Miner Per Hr.
1980	6.1	5.5	.6	259.3	42.51	4,741	432	1,795	421	266	127		3,667	3.6	306	1.11
1981	5.4	4.8	.6	239.1	44.28	5,537	370	2,249	361	77	22		4,084	3.1	232	.92
1982	4.6	4.0	.6	229.3	49.85	6,080	672	980	316	57	—	550	3,349	2.7	220	.59
1983	4.1	3.6	.5	214.4	52.29	6,507	498	776	296	58	30	357	2,823	2.1	224	1.01
1984[1]	4.2	3.6	.6	202.5	48.22	6,710	565	680	301	—	52	292	3,092	2.1	149	1.02
1985[2]	4.7	4.0	.7			7,189	416	1,286	277	19	32	535	2,914			

[1] Preliminary. [2] Estimate *Source: Energy Information Administration* T.91

Average Wholesale Price of Anthracite Coal (Chestnut—F.O.B. Mine)   Index—1967 = 100

Year	Jan.	Feb.	Mar.	Apr.	May	June	July	Aug.	Sept.	Oct.	Nov.	Dec.	Average
1980	435.7	435.7	435.7	459.7	459.7	459.7	462.1	469.8	478.2	479.6	491.1	497.9	463.7
1981	508.7	542.9	542.8	545.2	552.8	572.0	589.7	597.3	619.9	629.1	642.5	643.7	582.2
1982	643.7	643.7	645.5	648.1	639.0	637.5	637.5	637.4	637.4	637.4	638.0	638.0	640.3
1983	636.0	635.9	634.2	621.7	603.1	605.1	613.3	610.4	610.4	610.4	612.0	612.3	617.1
1984	612.2	612.0	611.2	610.4	611.1	610.8	610.8	610.8	610.8	615.2	615.5	614.7	611.3
1985	615.0	615.0	615.0	614.9	614.9	614.8	614.8	614.8	615.2	615.5	622.9	622.9	616.3
1986[1]	645.9	646.4	646.4	635.1	635.1	636.1	635.8	635.8	635.5	635.5	635.8		

[1] Preliminary. *Source: Bureau of Labor Statistics* (0511-0101.02) T.89

Cobalt

Domestic cobalt mining ceased in 1971 and the last refinery, AMAX's Louisiana plant, closed at the end of 1985. Consequently, the U.S. is entirely dependent on imports for its cobalt requirements.

Cobalt production is centered in central Africa; Zaire and Zambia account for about 65 percent of the world's production. The Soviet Union and Australia also produced commercially significant amounts. World production figures for 1986 are not currently available, but industry expectations are that 1986 production levels will match 1985's 35,101 tons.

For the first 10 months of 1986, imports into the U.S. were 4,826 tons, compared with 1985's full-year total of 8,000 tons. Canada was the leading supplier to the U.S. with 28 percent of the total; Zambia was second with 23 percent and Norway third-largest with 19 percent.

Domestic consumption of cobalt metal, oxide, chemical compounds, scrap and other in the period January to October, 1986, totaled 8,795 tons, compared with 9,074 for the same period in 1985. Slight decreases in metals and compounds consumption were mainly responsible for the drop. Total 1985 consumption of all types was 13,541 tons.

According to industry sources, on November 20, 1986, Zaire and Zambia, the world's largest cobalt producers, entered into a cartel to try to stabilize the cobalt market. The aim of the cartel was to establish a uniform price near $7.00 a pound. However, the softness of the market forced the cartel to adjust its price ideas. Zaire and Zambia have reached other agreements to control the price of cobalt in the past, but have not had notable success. Most recently, they had come to an agreement in 1984, but Zairian producers immediately began to undercut the posted price and Zambia was forced to follow suit.

Because the $7.00-a-pound price is considered reasonable by consumers, many industry analysts believe that this agreement has a better-than-ordinary chance to survive for a prolonged period of time. However, they also note that cobalt prices can vary a great deal, mostly because they are a function of how well Zambian and Zairian producers cooperate on pricing.

U.S. demand for cobalt is expected to grow in coming years, with consumption forecast at a three percent annual growth rate from a 1983 base, according to the U.S. Bureau of Mines.

Other than nickel, there are few effective substitutes for cobalt, which is one reason why the U.S. government has a regular purchase program in place for the National Strategic Stockpile. Currently, cobalt stocks in the program total 25,552 tons. The adequacy of future cobalt supplies is largely dependent upon political and economic conditions in foreign countries which have tended to be unstable or hostile. Identified world cobalt resources are placed by the Bureau of Mines at 12 million tons, found in nickel-bearing laterite deposits, nickel-copper sulfide deposits and sedentary copper deposits. In addition, vast hypothetical resources exist in nodules and crusts on the ocean floor.

World Mine Production of Cobalt — In Short Tons of Recovered Cobalt Content

Year	Australia	Zaire	USSR	France[3]	Canada	Cuba	Philippines	Finland	W. Germany[3]	Japan[3]	Norway[3]	Morocco	Zambia	New Caledonia	World Total
1980	2,177	17,000	2,300	745	1,767	1,778	1,467	1,141	330	3,160	1,405	924	4,850	395	34,538
1981	1,616	17,000	2,400	493	2,293	1,890	1,099	1,140	160	2,669	1,592	870	4,410	407	33,895
1982	1,631	12,460	2,500	545	1,548	1,650	516	1,026	160	2,141	1,094	770	3,584	299	26,754
1983[1]	1,500	12,460	2,600	—	1,747	1,820	639	1,000	110	1,512	996	—	3,527	300	26,445
1984[2]	1,400	18,700	2,900	—	2,200	1,690	140	1,000	110	998	990	—	5,090	280	35,635
1985[2]	1,500	18,000	3,000		2,200	1,800	400	1,000					5,000	300	35,100

[1] Estimate. [2] Preliminary. *Source: Bureau of Mines*   T.93

U.S. Salient Statistics of Cobalt — In Thousands of Pounds of Contained Cobalt

Year	Net Import Reliance as a % of Apparent Consumption	Cobalt Pdt's Production	Consumer Stocks Dec. 31	Imports for Consumption	Consumption By End Uses										Total	Price $ Per Pound[3]
					Steel Full Alloy	Stainless & Heat Resisting	Catalysts[4]	Super Alloys	Tool Steel	Magnetic Alloys	Non-ferrous Alloys	Drier in Paints, etc.[5]	Cutting & Wear Resistant Mater.	Welding & Hard Facing Rods		
1980	93	3,274	2,540	16,302	116	47	1,656	6,285	321	2,267	150	1,331	1,344	620	15,321	25
1981	92	3,302	1,411	15,594	141	35	1,279	4,195	170	1,687	131	1,378	1,076	488	11,680	14.58
1982	92	2,863	1,327	12,870	114	51	789	3,319	161	1,544	175	1,114	638	446	9,468	8.56
1983	95	3,232	1,441	17,221	82	54	1,064	4,034	248	1,711	169	1,503	666	472	11,319	5.76
1984[1]	95	3,499	1,368	25,310	31	74	1,296	4,766	353	2,209	176	1,258	831	399	12,994	10.40
1985[2]	95		1,131	17,800	90	76	1,250	4,700	315	2,500	100	1,700	820	600	13,544	11.50
1986[2]			1,300			85		4,400	330	2,400	90	1,800	800		10,000	

[1] Preliminary. [2] Estimate. [3] Annual spot for cathodes. *Source: Bureau of Mines*   T.94

Cocoa

USDA forecast 1986/87 world cocoa bean production (December, 1986) at 1.97 million tonnes, slightly above record levels of the past two years. Expanded production areas, improved agricultural practices, favorable weather conditions, and attractive prices were likely in Malaysia (up 13 percent) and Ghana (up 10 percent). World production was hampered by less favorable growing conditions in portions of West Africa, notably the Ivory Coast and Nigeria.

Output in the Ivory Coast, the world's largest producer, is forecast to decline in 1986/87. USDA estimated that drier-than-usual weather during July and August will likely result in reduction in output of eight percent from last year. Reduced bean size is also likely; new plantings and young trees increasing in productivity are expected partially to offset the effects of unfavorable weather. Ivory Coast is likely to account for 28 percent of 1986 U.S. cocoa bean imports and 26 percent of world production.

Brazil, second-largest producer of cocoa beans, accounts for about 20 percent of world production. 1986/87 Brazilian output is forecast to be up one percent, reflecting favorable growing conditions for the Bahian main crop. Arrivals of the 1986 Bahia temporaro crop, were somewhat disappointing, with an 11-percent drop from last year. Currently, emphasis is on increasing area. Brazil contributes about 13 percent of U.S. cocoa bean imports.

World cocoa grindings continue to lag the expansion in production, and stocks are expected to increase for the third consecutive year. Grindings in 1986 were estimated to be down one percent from the year before, at 1.81 million tonnes, with stocks increasing by 134,000 tonnes. Brazilian grindings were down, due in part to a brief industrial-dispute stoppage in early August and, more importantly, because of reduced export demand. In West Africa, a combination of operating problems and slack demand from consumer countries kept grindings down. Ecuador's grindings fell when the government withdrew special incentives to the local processing industry. Grindings in non-origin countries were also down, with the exception of the Netherlands. In Britain, cocoa bean grindings during the first three quarters of 1986 were 63,195 tons, 11 percent lower than January–September, 1985 period. West German grindings for the same period totaled 146,873 tons, down four percent; in the U.S. they were down six percent. However, if higher 1986/87 production estimates are realized, USDA forecasts that grindings could rise to 1.85 million tonnes in 1987.

U.S. imports of cocoa and its products dropped in both volume and value for the first half of 1986, compared with 1985. Measured by volume, intake of cocoa beans, sweetened and unsweetened chocolate, cocoa butter, and sweetened and unsweetened cocoa were down 13 percent from the same period in 1985. Measured by value, imports were about 14 percent below the comparable year-ago figure. Particularly steep volume declines were seen in sweetened cocoa powder (off 72 percent), cocoa beans (off 28 percent) and chocolate confectionary (off 23 percent). Imports of confectioner's coatings, on the other hand, were 36 percent higher than last year.

The largest importers of cocoa beans are France, West Germany, the Netherlands, Great Britain, and the U.S. Second-quarter 1986 cocoa prices in these countries were an average 29 percent lower than in the same quarter of 1985. Consumer spending on cocoa, rose only three percent in these countries. Overall, the largest consumers of cocoa are Switzerland, Austria, Belgium, Norway and West Germany.

At the Fifth Session of the U.N. Cocoa Conference in Geneva during July, 1986, agreement was reached on principal elements of the new International Cocoa Agreement (to replace the 1980 ICCA, which expired September 30, 1986). The new pact includes the Ivory Coast, which was not a member of the 1980 agreement, but it does not include the United States, the world's largest consumer. After a four-month transition period, the new ICCA will be in effect for three years. The cornerstone of the agreement is still a 250,000-ton capacity buffer stock, of which 100,000 tons of cocoa are to be carried over from the 1980 pact. To allow for currency fluctuations, prices in the new pact are to be based on SDR's (Special Drawing Rights), rather than individual currencies. It is too early to predict the impact of the new agreement, but membership of the Ivory Coast could improve significantly.

Futures Markets

Cocoa futures are actively traded on the Coffee, Sugar & Cocoa Exchange in New York and on the London Terminal Market.

World Cocoa Supply and Demand   In Thousands of Metric Tons

Crop Year[1]	Stocks Oct. 1	Net World Crop[2]	Total Availability	Seasonal Grindings	Closing Stocks	Stock Change	Crop Year[1]	Stocks Oct. 1	Net World Crop[2]	Total Availability	Seasonal Grindings	Closing Stocks	Stock Change
1978–9	390	1,478	1,868	1,457	411	+ 21	1983–4	606	1,502	2,108	1,720	388	−218
1979–0	411	1,611	2,022	1,488	534	+123	1984–5[3]	388	1,931	2,319	1,795	524	+136
1980–1	534	1,644	2,178	1,592	586	+ 52	1985–6[3]	524	1,907	2,431	1,803	628	+104
1981–2	586	1,719	2,305	1,600	705	+119	1986–7[4]	628	1,903	2,531	1,841	690	+ 62
1982–3	705	1,521	2,226	1,620	606	− 99							

[1] Crop year season is Oct.–Sept.   [2] The Net World Crop is obtained by adjusting the Gross World Crop for one percent loss in weight.   [3] Preliminary.   [4] Forecast.   *Source: Gill and Duffus, Ltd.*

T.95

35

COCOA

World Production of Cocoa Beans in Principal Producing Countries   In Thousands of Metric Tons

Crop Year (Oct.–Sept.)	Brazil	Cameroon	Colombia	Dominican Rep.	Ecuador	Equatorial Guinea[1]	Ghana	Indonesia	Ivory Coast	Malaysia	Mexico	Papua New Guinea	Nigeria	Sierra Leone	Togo	Venezuela	World Total
1980–1	351	120	36	33	85	8	258	13	417	49	30	27	160	10	16	14	1,694
1981–2	315	120	39	43	88	8	225	17	465	61	41	29	183	9	11	15	1,737
1982–3	339	106	40	43	55	9	179	20	360	68	34	29	160	9	10	15	1,543
1983–4	309	109	41	42	55	9	159	23	411	90	36	28	125	8	21	12	1,544
1984–5	415	120	42	39	128	8	175	32	565	100	42	30	170	11	7	11	1,963
1985–6[3]	395	117	44	37	100	8	215	36	570	130	41	31	135	10	12	11	1,964
1986–7[2]	400	120	45	40	100	8	240	38	525	150	43	30	125	10	15	12	1,974

[1] Includes Fernando Po & Rio Muni.   [2] Forecast.   [3] Preliminary.   *Sources: Foreign Agricultural Service; U.S.D.A.*   T.96

World Absorption (Consumption) of Cocoa[2]   In Thousands of Metric Tons

Year	Japan	Australia	Belgium	Brazil	Canada	Colombia	France	W. Germany	Netherlands	Spain	Italy	Switzerland	USSR	United King.	United States	World Total
1980	25	11	23	200	12	31	48	158	133	35	34	17	130	65	142	1,510
1981	29	12	29	195	17	35	52	167	141	37	35	18	120	85	190	1,599
1982	32	9	29	170	16	38	52	175	148	37	39	18	130	88	199	1,607
1983	34	8	33	198	16	39	53	180	157	38	36	18	145	77	194	1,652
1984	34	6	36	214	22	33	52	194	161	35	40	19	150	90	209	1,750
1985[1]	34	2	36	234	21	39	42	207	167	39	47	20	160	91	205	1,830
1986[3]	34	1	37	200	20	41	40	200	175	39	45	19	160	85	205	1,812

[1] Preliminary.   [2] Figures represent the "absorption," "disappearance" or "grindings" of cocoa beans in each country—in other words, net imports of cocoa beans adjusted for changes in stock.   [3] Estimate.   [4] Forecast.   *Source: Gill & Duffus, Ltd.*   T.98

World Exports of Cocoa Beans by Principal Producing Countries   In Thousands of Metric Tons

Year	Brazil	Costa Rica	Dominican Repub.	Ecuador	Equatorial Guinea	Cameroon	Ghana	Malaysia	Ivory Coast	Papua New Guinea	Nigeria	Sao Tome & Principe	Trinidad & Tobago	Venezuela	Togo	Grand Total
1980	123.6	2.2	23.4	14.1	6.0	80.5	218.6	30.6	305.3	28.8	133.9	7.0	2.1	7.8	14.5	1,046
1981	125.2	2.0	27.3	24.1	7.5	82.4	180.9	42.4	437.2	27.8	109.0	6.0	3.0	8.0	17.2	1,146
1982	143.5	1.9	38.2	38.0	7.5	66.4	217.1	57.7	326.3	28.2	136.7	6.0	2.4	9.5	10.1	1,138
1983	152.8	.7	38.3	7.0	8.0	80.1	177.3	57.2	286.4	26.3	152.3	3.1	2.0	9.5	9.5	1,076

[1] Preliminary.   *Source: Foreign Agricultural Service, U.S.D.A.*   T.100

Raw Cocoa Grindings in Selected Countries   In Thousands of Metric Tons

Year	Total	1st Quarter	2nd Quarter	3rd Quarter	4th Quarter	Total	1st Quarter	2nd Quarter	3rd Quarter	4th Quarter	Total	1st Quarter	2nd Quarter	3rd Quarter	4th Quarter
	France					Germany (West)					Holland				
1980	43.1	12.5	10.9	9.1	10.7	151.2	40.2	35.4	32.9	42.6	132.6	35.1	31.4	29.5	36.7
1981	47.0	12.6	12.0	9.6	12.9	159.4	41.7	37.6	35.4	44.7	141.0	36.0	34.3	32.7	38.0
1982	45.5	13.1	12.3	9.7	10.4	167.0	45.1	39.9	35.8	46.3	148.4	38.4	34.9	33.7	41.3
1983	47.6	12.2	12.9	10.9	11.7	179.5	45.7	41.0	43.0	49.8	156.9	40.5	37.9	35.2	43.4
1984	47.2	14.0	12.5	11.1	9.7	193.5	49.9	48.6	42.4	52.6	161.4	44.4	40.0	35.0	42.1
1985	42.5	12.4	10.6	8.3	11.2	206.8	57.0	51.7	44.0	54.0	167.4	44.6	41.7	37.0	44.1
1986[1]		10.9					53.6	50.6				46.2	45.1		
	Italy					United Kingdom					United States				
1980	33.8	8.0	8.4	8.1	9.3	65.3	15.5	16.1	15.5	18.2	142.2	33.5	31.5	34.9	42.4
1981	35.1	8.6	8.1	5.8	12.6	85.3	21.7	21.3	19.2	23.1	190.2	48.4	46.0	48.8	47.1
1982	39.2	9.6	10.1	6.0	13.6	88.1	25.3	21.1	19.6	22.1	199.1	47.7	50.6	50.1	50.7
1983	36.4	8.4	7.9	8.1	12.0	76.7	19.8	18.1	17.4	21.3	193.6	45.9	46.7	47.8	53.2
1984	39.8	8.0	5.6	9.8	16.5	89.6	22.3	21.9	21.1	24.2	164.4	42.4	41.6	40.9	39.5
1985	47.4	11.1	10.5	8.8	17.0	91.3	26.5	24.5	20.0	20.3	153.8	39.0	37.5	40.5	36.8
1986[1]		10.9					21.1	21.9				33.8	37.0		

[1] Preliminary.   *Source: Gill and Duffus, Ltd.*   T.97

Imports of Cocoa Butter—Selected Countries   In Metric Tons

Year	Argentina	Australia	Austria	Belgium	Canada	Finland	France	West Germany	Italy	Japan	Netherlands	Norway	Sweden	Switzerland	UK	USA	USSR	Yugoslavia
1980	1,868	4,532	2,485	12,388	3,717	2,057	14,285	22,790	1,211	6,264	16,445	1,855	4,155	9,117	29,597	34,658	—	1,054
1981	1,923	4,410	3,461	11,960	4,505	2,228	14,170	29,358	1,667	10,352	11,021	1,875	4,234	10,208	19,549	43,196	—	1,965
1982	1,734	5,419	3,382	12,281	4,860	2,333	14,008	30,564	1,631	10,615	16,225	2,083	4,451	9,982	25,820	37,325	—	1,009
1983	720	6,067	3,535	12,128	5,313	2,428	16,690	30,581	2,151	9,947	20,224	1,892	4,704	10,224	31,581	47,981		653
1984	1,175	6,445	3,763	13,451	5,437	2,156	17,325	35,241	2,337	8,436	25,072	2,139	5,103	9,798	30,203	51,711	4,200	248
1985[1]	N.A.	8,538	3,682	15,416	5,535	2,039	19,908	33,378	3,056	8,632	24,595	1,957	4,929	11,175	31,372	70,146	N.A.	N.A.
1986[2]		9,000	4,000	13,000	5,200	2,000	20,000	27,000	2,500	8,100	18,000	2,000	4,800	12,000	40,000	75,000		

[1] Preliminary.   [2] Estimate.   *Source: Gill & Duffus Group PLC*   T.97a

Imports of Cocoa Liquor and Cocoa Powder (Selected Countries)   In Metric Tons

	Cocoa Liquor							Cocoa Powder								
Year	France	West Germany	Netherlands	Poland	UK	USA	USSR	Belgium	France	West Germany	Italy	Japan	Netherlands	Sweden	UK	USA
1978	16,282	741	3,901	7,485	3,859	43,679	—	3,079	3,529	6,912	3,955	1,558	2,096	2,469	1,022	79,263
1979	15,872	795	4,136	25,755	4,784	47,828	5,000	3,642	4,368	10,846	5,266	2,215	2,970	2,656	1,747	64,080
1980	15,688	1,922	7,634	23,822	1,928	43,796	5,200	3,335	5,905	10,693	6,142	2,656	3,018	3,457	1,885	65,606
1981	15,457	2,151	9,262	26,835	1,914	33,109	16,000	3,503	7,963	12,935	6,478	2,616	3,255	3,551	2,393	77,879
1982	13,871	2,196	13,519	12,642	2,283	31,419	8,700	3,770	7,609	13,524	6,673	2,832	2,974	3,872	3,284	60,563
1983	15,164	2,288	14,216	20,442	3,829	45,477	15,425	3,895	8,527	13,886	7,964	3,157	3,009	3,806	3,014	78,968
1984	20,268	3,075	13,622	N.A.	2,184	45,547	32,000	4,204	9,652	13,554	7,462	3,260	3,574	3,996	3,654	89,978
1985[1]	24,031	3,570	14,822	N.A.	3,400	53,042	N.A.	4,586	8,269	16,624	N.A.	3,841	4,669	3,928	2,591	81,775
1986[2]	30,000	2,500	13,000		5,000	60,000		5,000	9,000	18,000		4,000	4,700	4,000	3,000	90,000

[1] Preliminary.   [2] Estimate.   *Source: Gill & Duffus Group PLC*   T.97b

United States Imports of Cocoa (Includes Shells)   In Thousands of Long Tons

Year	Jan.	Feb.	Mar.	Apr.	May	June	July	Aug.	Sept.	Oct.	Nov.	Dec.	Total
1978	19.4	20.3	27.9	20.5	16.5	12.4	16.1	14.7	7.3	15.9	18.6	20.2	209.7
1979	27.3	26.7	14.6	12.8	8.8	13.7	11.8	15.7	5.7	10.1	10.0	8.0	165.2
1980	11.1	9.2	8.0	19.5	15.4	12.0	16.9	9.6	8.2	9.6	9.4	19.9	148.5
1981	13.5	27.8	19.2	30.4	27.1	24.1	19.3	22.0	20.3	24.1	5.8	11.5	245.0
1982	10.0	29.0	17.6	15.3	16.8	11.9	13.0	20.3	14.3	14.4	14.4	17.4	194.2
1983	46.0	42.7	19.0	36.4	14.4	11.1	9.6	7.2	6.1	5.3	7.7	8.2	181.0
1984[1]	15.5	21.3	28.7	16.9	24.7	15.3	13.3	10.8	10.4	5.0	10.8	18.2	190.9
1985[1]	42.2	43.7	39.1	9.9	30.5	15.6	13.9	12.5	10.9	10.2	12.6	25.0	266.1
1986[1]	29.4	17.1	15.1	9.3	19.0	16.1	21.2	22.5					

[1] Preliminary.   *Source: Department of Commerce*   T.102

Bahia (Brazil) Crops   In Thousands of Bags of 60 Kilos

Year	Total Crop Brazilian Crop Year	Temporao Brazilian Crop Year	Main- Mid March (Arrivals)	Main Crop (Oct.–Apr.)	Temporao International Crop Year	Total Crop International Crop Year
1977–78	3,989	2,102	1,769	1,887	2,524	4,411
1978–79	4,329	2,524	1,762	1,805	3,129	4,934
1979–80	5,387	3,129	2,158	2,257	2,383	4,640
1980–81	5,041	2,383	2,646	2,658	2,892	5,550
1981–82	4,609	2,892	1,718	1,718	3,170	4,888
1982–83	5,284	3,170	2,114	2,114	3,084	5,198
1983–84	5,876	3,084	2,792	2,792	1,786	4,578
1984–85[1]	5,030	1,786	3,244	3,244	3,126	6,370
1985–86[1]	6,027	3,126	2,901			

[1] Preliminary.   *Source: Gill & Duffus Group PLC*   T.102a

COCOA

New York Cocoa Bean Futures[1] Prices   In Cents Per Pound

Year	Jan.	Feb.	Mar.	Apr.	May	June	July	Aug.	Sept.	Oct.	Nov.	Dec.	Average
1977	173.0	190.3	207.5	198.3	199.3	199.3	199.3	199.3	256.0	250.0	250.0	250.0	214.4
1978	165.0	140.0	178.0	179.0	170.0	155.0	161.0	175.0	189.0	183.0	199.0	196.0	174.2
1979	193.0	177.0	176.0	157.5	165.0	172.0	158.0	157.0	166.0	159.0	154.5	155.0	160.4
1980	163.8	173.5	157.0	147.0	135.0	125.3	134.5	120.0	122.0	119.0	120.0	108.0	135.4
1981	109.5	110.0	112.0	115.0	104.0	89.0	108.5	112.0	117.0	113.0	103.0	109.0	108.5
1982	116.0	107.0	102.0	99.0	94.0	80.0	83.0	86.0	87.0	88.0	82.0	85.0	92.4
1983[2]	77.6	83.9	80.1	81.4	89.8	99.8	99.6	99.7	93.0	91.3	97.1	112.0	92.1
1984	115.2	110.8	113.0	112.8	118.8	108.2	97.1	98.6	104.3	99.8	100.6	95.5	106.2
1985	98.3	100.0	98.9	101.6	96.1	91.5	95.7	98.2	101.3	102.5	97.9	102.0	98.7
1986	100.6	95.5	91.0	84.9	81.4	81.4	87.6	89.1	95.6				

[1] Avg. of the daily closing price of the nearest 3 active futures trading month converted to ¢ per lb.   [2] Prices prior to 1983 are for spot cocoa bean (ACCRA) in N.Y.   *Source: Bureau of Labor Statistics* (0191-0221); *N.Y. Cocoa Exchange.*   T.105

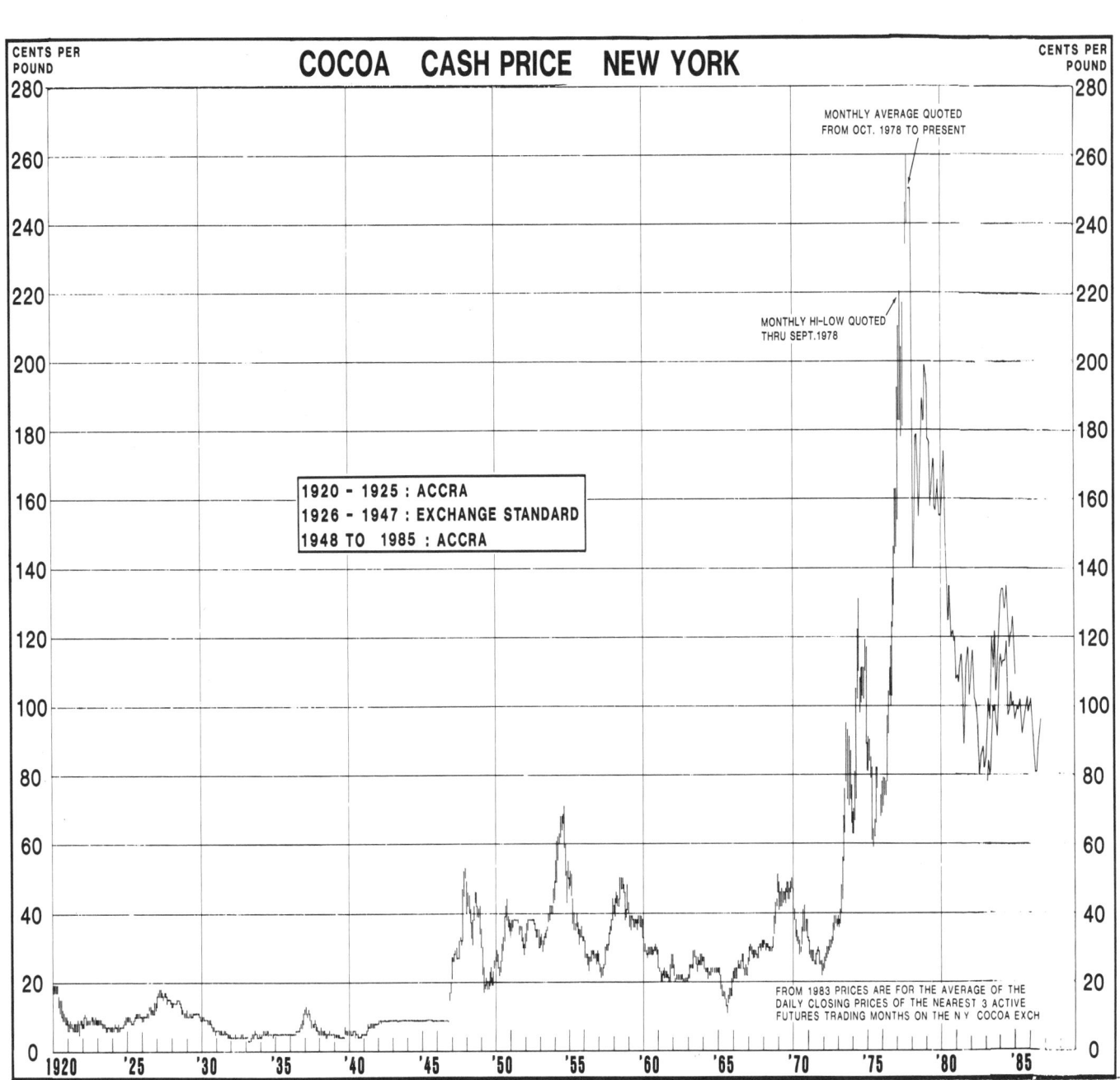

COCOA   CASH PRICE   NEW YORK

MONTHLY AVERAGE QUOTED FROM OCT. 1978 TO PRESENT

MONTHLY HI-LOW QUOTED THRU SEPT.1978

1920 - 1925 : ACCRA
1926 - 1947 : EXCHANGE STANDARD
1948 TO 1985 : ACCRA

FROM 1983 PRICES ARE FOR THE AVERAGE OF THE DAILY CLOSING PRICES OF THE NEAREST 3 ACTIVE FUTURES TRADING MONTHS ON THE N.Y. COCOA EXCH

Visible Stock of Cocoa in Philadelphia (Delaware River) Warehouses, at End of Month In Ths. of Bags

Year	Jan.	Feb.	Mar.	Apr.	May	June	July	Aug.	Sept.	Oct.	Nov.	Dec.
1981	38.1	15.5	15.4	45.7	189.7	227.4	246.6	255.8	307.5	271.9	234.6	231.3
1982	190.1	163.4	174.1	163.2	154.0	125.7	104.6	64.2	51.8	64.3	69.3	98.5
1983	123.6	192.4	281.5	356.5	344.7	338.9	297.7	258.5	204.5	119.8	69.2	43.0
1984	59.5	69.9	105.4	98.8	148.3	168.0	158.3	187.6	165.3	99.7	83.6	217.1
1985	221.3	282.0	333.6	420.9	416.4	389.1	315.9	323.9	320.7	316.3	289.1	280.6
1986	281.3	276.4	258.8	255.8	237.9	201.3	208.7	182.0	209.5	137.1	136.7	188.5
1987	209.8											

Source: Coffee, Sugar & Cocoa Exchange, Inc.

T.107

Visible Stock of Cocoa in New York Warehouses[1], at End of Month   In Thousands of Bags

Year	Jan.	Feb.	Mar.	Apr.	May	June	July	Aug.	Sept.	Oct.	Nov.	Dec.
1981	37.5	14.9	29.3	66.5	120.3	93.1	75.8	115.3	84.6	62.1	55.5	66.2
1982	33.4	61.3	66.7	57.3	99.0	98.6	115.8	137.7	108.8	97.1	96.1	68.9
1983	64.7	80.1	80.0	88.9	136.4	184.8	178.7	173.5	138.6	109.5	103.0	93.9
1984	59.3	53.2	52.3	52.5	70.7	57.2	93.8	99.9	109.2	62.8	36.3	32.4
1985	34.7	22.0	13.2	36.4	167.8	170.9	161.3	155.7	164.6	150.6	131.8	107.1
1986	99.2	96.9	95.6	89.7	87.4	90.3	88.9	103.6	102.1	87.5	70.6	59.9
1987	51.9											

[1] In licensed & unlicensed warehouses of storage companies licensed by the Coffee, Sugar & Cocoa Exch.   Source: Coffee, Sugar & Cocoa Exch., Inc.

T.106

U.S. Spot Cocoa Prices for Selected Origins of Cocoa Beans and Products   (Dollars per metric ton)

Crop Year (Oct.–Sep.)	Cocoa Beans				Chocolate Liquor		Cocoa Butter		Cocoa Cake 10–12% Fat
	Ivory Coast	Brazil	Dominican Republic	Ecuador	Ecuador	Brazil	African	Other	
1982/83	2,031	1,999	1,815	1,886	2,310	2,440	4,294	4,191	872
1983/84	2,569	2,611	2,361	2,477	3,025	3,119	5,281	5,178	1,610
1984/85	2,433	2,407	2,197	2,239	2,784	2,919	5,331	5,276	951
1985/86	2,281	2,207	2,020	2,048	2,552	2,720	4,940	4,897	825
June '86	2,032	1,958	1,756	1,805	2,236	2,411	4,350	4,307	746
July '86	2,196	2,097	1,904	1,960	2,440	2,598	4,712	4,660	821
Aug. '86	2,203	2,127	1,940	1,985	2,491	2,642	4,744	4,679	873
Sept. '86	2,354	2,278	2,095	2,138	2,732	2,866	5,104	5,033	969

Source: The Cocoa Merchants Association. All prices are nominal net ex dock or ex warehouse, U.S. Eastern seaboard North of Hatteras, for merchandise physically available in interstate commerce, in truckload quantities, regular commercial quality. Foreign Agricultural Service, U.S.D.A.

T.99a

Month–End Open Interest of Cocoa Futures at New York   In Contracts

Year	Jan.	Feb.	Mar.	Apr.	May	June	July	Aug.	Sept.	Oct.	Nov.	Dec.
1980	8,314	7,723	6,744	6,639	8,114	6,682	8,900	9,529	13,548	14,282	13,210	11,978
1981	14,269	14,064	16,209	13,721	13,929	11,853	16,328	16,897	17,042	18,823	15,388	14,137
1982	14,554	14,421	15,129	14,036	15,563	14,083	15,954	14,678	16,439	18,615	17,600	19,988
1983	25,989	22,401	22,155	24,796	29,457	29,403	28,447	29,275	28,282	27,890	29,266	29,153
1984	29,712	26,116	26,511	22,277	26,795	23,817	23,691	23,397	22,106	22,505	21,253	20,936
1985	25,616	23,817	27,701	23,588	21,103	21,515	20,487	19,106	20,720	20,224	17,981	16,044
1986	19,259	19,521	21,341	19,654	24,246	23,100	26,017	25,781	25,636	25,189	22,577	26,109

Source: Coffee, Sugar & Cocoa Exchange, Inc.

T.103

Volume of Trading of Cocoa Futures at New York   In Contracts

Year	Jan.	Feb.	Mar.	Apr.	May	June	July	Aug.	Sept.	Oct.	Nov.	Dec.	Total
1980	23,600	40,410	25,066	23,897	26,170	29,673	34,158	27,265	45,437	43,945	39,770	28,954	388,971
1981	32,916	43,352	37,056	52,875	32,691	54,479	55,525	53,557	43,764	63,751	53,674	39,011	562,651
1982	42,498	44,744	52,468	52,591	38,332	50,693	45,504	45,457	61,137	67,652	48,243	56,744	607,964
1983	88,429	96,636	82,115	91,851	83,275	135,536	102,212	112,031	103,023	70,032	97,781	98,619	1,162,540
1984	151,282	113,788	102,622	103,415	113,757	107,219	75,180	101,732	75,294	69,322	74,357	33,927	1,127,752
1985	86,748	83,988	94,863	72,564	64,716	62,989	74,583	57,842	52,912	58,358	53,056	37,954	800,573
1986	52,774	61,836	70,859	74,249	57,525	77,335	79,029	65,963	75,673	64,729	54,090	43,703	777,765

Source: Coffee, Sugar & Cocoa Exchange, Inc.

T.104

COCOA

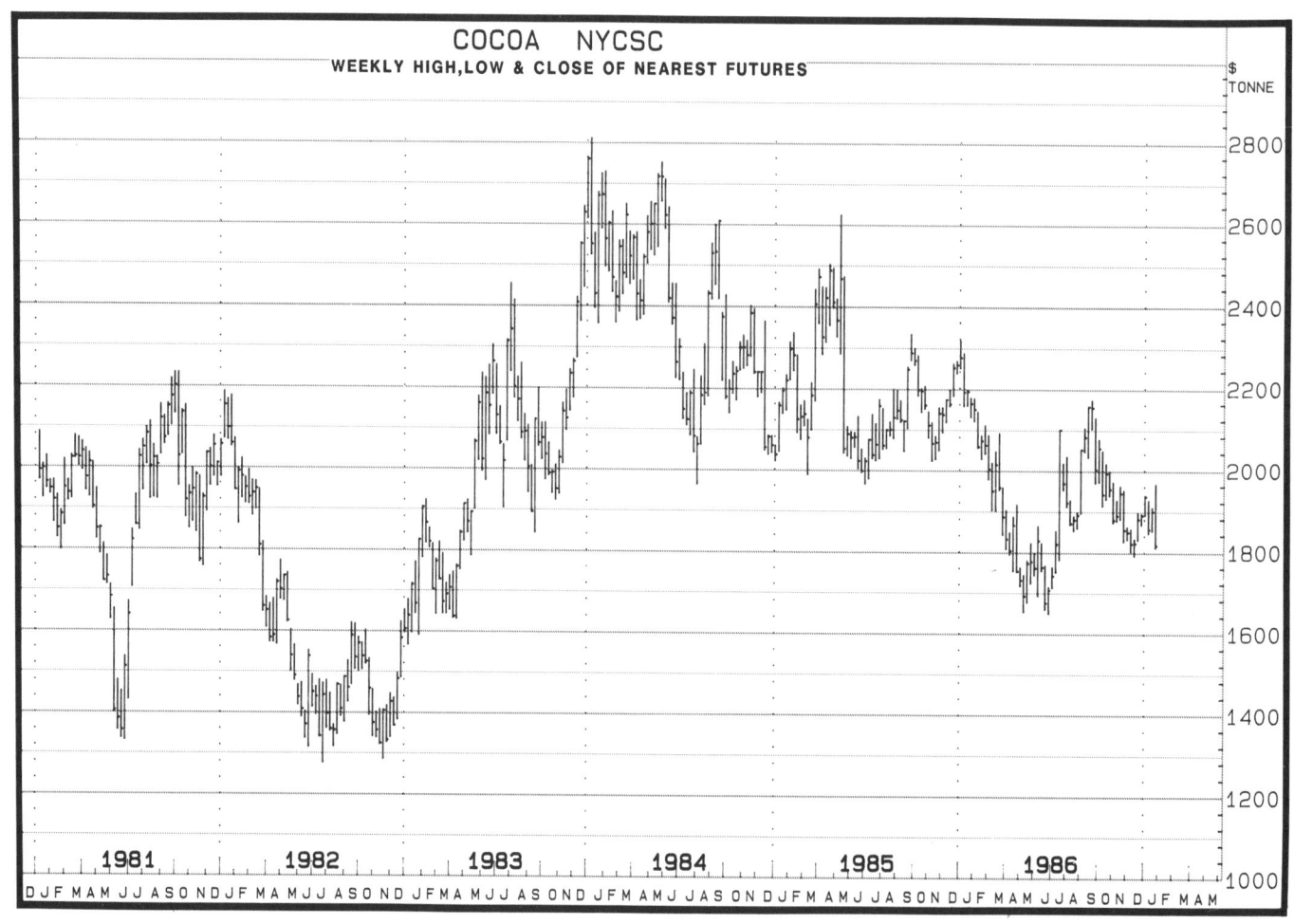

COCOA NYCSC
WEEKLY HIGH, LOW & CLOSE OF NEAREST FUTURES

High, Low & Closing Prices of March Cocoa Futures at New York   In Dollars per Tonne

Year of Delivery		Feb.	Mar.	Apr.	May	June	July	Aug.	Sept.	Oct.	Nov.	Dec.	Jan.	Feb.	Mar.	Life of Delivery Range
						Year Prior to Delivery							Delivery Year			
1983	High	2145	2105	1875	1835	1663	1640	1604	1696	1669	1495	1650	1840	1919	1816	2295
	Low	2071	1840	1738	1657	1508	1485	1451	1534	1435	1383	1447	1565	1640	1688	1383
	Close	2071	1854	1802	1660	1605	1518	1527	1604	1467	1465	1603	1826	1704	1691	—
1984	High	2015	1958	1990	2325	2390	2460	2440	2195	2124	2272	2759	2805	2626	2645	2805
	Low	1785	1790	1780	1895	2070	2055	2080	1907	1953	1967	2175	2353	2355	2425	1653
	Close	1838	1835	1990	2168	2224	2369	2113	2089	1989	2224	2755	2521	2462	2617	—
1985	High	2455	2510	2500	2560	2430	2234	2305	2350	2248	2291	2133	2309	2332	2210	2602
	Low	2240	2350	2343	2401	2230	1998	1990	2150	2118	2056	2034	2018	2071	1985	1985
	Close	2363	2489	2435	2401	2280	2000	2275	2199	2224	2117	2052	2271	2140	2139	—
1986	High	2135	2190	2170	2105	2048	2207	2295	2392	2365	2239	2305	2315	2140	2059	2392
	Low	2000	1955	2025	1980	1967	1991	2125	2170	2173	2117	2180	2118	1975	1899	1899
	Close	2028	2150	2027	2041	2013	2153	2262	2336	2191	2214	2298	2146	2000	2011	—
1987	High	2283	2200	2106	1960	2007	2098	2176	2248	2076	2003	1937				
	Low	2148	2015	1931	1884	1825	1895	1970	2011	1920	1876	1837				
	Close	2165	2039	1952	1906	1904	2034	2176	2034	1927	1886	1935				

Source: Coffee, Sugar & Cocoa Exchange, Inc.

T.108

Coconut Oil and Copra

Copra is the dried meat of the coconut and is crushed to produce coconut oil and copra meal. The USDA projects world production of copra at 5.32 million tonnes, an increase of nearly two percent over 1985/86. Copra production has increased substantially since 1983/84, with the Philippines and Indonesia accounting for approximately two-thirds of world production. The key development in this market came with the change in the Philippine government; the coconut industry monopoly has been dissolved. While this has favorable long-term possibilities, the USDA notes there are a number of factors which could have an important influence on the course of the industry. These include aging coconut palm trees, export competition for coconut oil from palm oil, and uncertainty among coconut producers about the policies implemented by the new government. Copra exports are minimal at 410,000 tonnes, up slightly from a year ago. Most copra is exported from Pacific islands where crushing facilities are lacking. The major importer of copra is West Germany. Ending stocks of copra are estimated by USDA to reach 310,000 tons, an increase of 55 percent from last season.

The copra crush is projected by USDA to fall six percent to 5.07 million tonnes. World production of coconut oil is forecast at 3.17 million tonnes, down six percent from 1985/86. The Philippines and Indonesia produce two-thirds of the world supply. Coconut oil exports are projected at 1.32 million tonnes, 16 percent less than a year ago. The Philippines are by far the major exporters, while Indonesia uses its production in the domestic market. Part of the reason for reduced coconut oil exports is the competition from palm oil. Since coconut and palm oil are substitutes in many uses, low palm oil prices have cut into coconut oil markets.

World coconut oil consumption in 1986/87 is projected by USDA to reach 3.24 million tonnes, over a four-percent increase from last season. The major users of coconut oil are Indonesia, the U.S., India and West Germany. World imports have expanded, due mostly to low prices compared with competing oils. The U.S. is the major importer of coconut oil, and consumes more in inedible products than in edible products. U.S. imports of coconut oil were estimated at 551,842 tonnes for the 12 months ending September, 1986. This is a 27-percent increase from the same year-ago period. The USDA indicates that U.S. imports from the Philippines are on a rising trend, apparently due to somewhat limited substitutability of other oils for coconut oil. World ending stocks of coconut oil are projected by USDA at 270,000 tonnes compared to 340,000 tonnes a year ago.

World production of copra meal in 1986/87 is expected to total 1.69 million tonnes, a decline of six percent from 1985/86. The major copra producers are the Philippines and Indonesia, with about 90 percent of world output, and the main destination of copra meal is Western Europe. World trade in copra meal in 1986/87 is projected to decline to 1.03 million tonnes, compared to 1.17 million tonnes a year ago. World ending stocks of copra meal will be minimal at 7,000 tonnes.

World Copra Production by Principal Countries   In Thousands of Metric Tons

Crop Year	Naupu	Fiji	India	Indonesia	Jamaica	Malaysia	Mexico	Mozambique	Papua-New Guinea	Philippines	Solomon Isl.	Sri Lanka	Tanzania	Thailand	Ivory Coast	New Hebrides	Vietnam	World Total
1978–9	35	22	317	1,040	28	213	130	65	159	1,823	33	166	27	50	14	49	39	4,367
1979–0	46	25	329	1,158	29	210	120	68	145	1,960	32	93	29	50	21	34	39	4,553
1980–1	42	25	329	1,284	25	208	130	55	158	2,256	33	128	29	30	24	47	39	4,986
1981–2	42	25	335	1,205	28	206	100	50	132	2,077	33	174	29	35	26	44	40	4,790
1982–3	42	25	268	1,091	29	208	110	50	120	2,015	31	131	29	30	27	45	40	4,600
1983–4[1]	42	25	300	1,205	30	212	100	50	125	1,417	33	72	29	40	27	47	41	3,960
1984–5[2]	42		338	1,203		220	100	50	128	2,000	33	129				47		4,820
1985–6[2]																		5,230
1986–7[2]																		5,320

[1] Preliminary.   [2] Forecast.   *Source: Foreign Agricultural Service, U.S.D.A.*   T.109

World Coconut Oil Exports by Principal Countries   In Thousands of Metric Tons

Crop Year	Sri Lanka (Ceylon)	Singapore[2]	Indonesia	Malaysia[2]	Philippines Registered	Ivory Coast	Netherlands	Mozambique	EC-10	Fiji	Papua New Guinea	Total Oceania	World Total
1978–9	32	42	2	66	795	9	31	5	165	17	28	70	1,092
1979–80	3	35	41	65	914	9	35	4	133	18	34	75	1,204
1980–1	21	63	4	64	1,047	13	41		67	15	29		1,338
1981–2	39	50	0	60	949	16	33		82	15	33		1,260
1982–3	38	30	8	69	1,020	16	35		65		22		1,320
1983–4[1]	40	24	20	65	586	20	20		52		22		900
1984–5[3]			3	66	949				63				1,170
1985–6[3]													1,580
1986–7[3]													1,320

[1] Preliminary.   [2] Net exports.   [3] Forecast.   *Source: Foreign Agricultural Service, U.S.D.A.*   T.110

COCONUT OIL AND COPRA

Supply & Distribution of Coconut Oil in the United States   In Millions of Pounds

Year Begin. Oct. 1	Imports[2]	Stocks Oct. 1[3]	Total Supply	Exports & Shipments	Disappearance			Production of Coconut Oil (Refined)				
					Total Domestic	Edible Pdt's.	Inedible Pdt's.	Total	Jan.–March	April–June	July–Sept.	Oct.–Dec.
1979–0	810	157	967	30	785			595.6	183.9	137.4	143.8	129.7
1980–1	1,122	152	1,274	38	1,032	337.6	452.1	644.7	146.1	153.4	156.0	196.1
1981–2	960	204	1,164	29	976	337.9	411.5	700.3	193.3	175.3	171.9	159.8
1982–3	882	160	1,042	21	876	340.0	493.9	665.7	162.1	162.4	168.7	172.5
1983–4	916	145	1,061	50	901	299.0		692.6	163.1	186.0	167.1	176.4
1984–5[1]	891	110	1,001	20	904	27.0	376.0	616.2	161.3	175.7	145.1	134.1
1985–6[1]	1,217	77	1,294	22	966	306.5		564.0	130.7	133.9	147.6	151.8
1986–7[1]	1,050	306	1,356	22	1,100				197.9	182.1	155.4	

[1] Preliminary. [2] Imports for consumption. [3] Includes G.S.A. stockpile & in U.S. bond. *Sources: Bureau of the Census; Agricultural Marketing Service*
T.112

U.S. Consumption of Coconut Oil in End Products (Edible & Inedible Pdts.)   In Millions of Pounds

Year	Jan.	Feb.	Mar.	Apr.	May	June	July	Aug.	Sept.	Oct.	Nov.	Dec.	Total
1976	80.3	78.4	88.1	83.3	84.9	90.3	80.2	82.6	80.8	79.2	87.1	75.1	990.3
1977	73.4	69.9	82.6	73.0	73.9	79.1	63.1	71.9	73.1	76.3	77.4	65.0	878.7
1978	69.3	71.0	81.5	88.9	87.6	76.1	73.6	79.0	72.4	84.0	75.4	55.4	914.2
1979	72.7	66.3	83.3	69.1	69.9	62.0	50.4	58.5	58.0	54.4	55.3	48.5	748.5
1980	55.9	49.9	59.5	55.8	58.1	56.3	56.2	51.0	62.5	66.9	63.1	58.3	693.5
1981	67.6	65.0	71.1	68.2	64.0	70.4	58.0	70.4	66.7	73.2	59.8	52.2	786.6
1982	63.3	59.6	61.7	58.5	64.7	64.2	62.2	63.9	66.1	60.2	70.5	60.6	755.5
1983	62.0	64.8	61.1	64.8	80.2	74.9	70.5	61.2	64.3	68.4	66.2	61.0	799.4
1984	71.5	68.5	66.0	67.0	72.6	70.9	61.8	70.7	48.1	63.4	56.6	45.3	762.4
1985	53.4	57.1	46.1	52.5	51.7	52.8	53.2	57.2	61.2	53.1	57.7	50.0	646.0
1986[1]	67.5	43.8	44.7	51.5	45.7	50.0	49.5	67.2	52.8	78.7	67.5		

[1] Preliminary.   *Source: Bureau of the Census*
T.114

Stocks of Coconut Oil (Crude & Refined) in the United States[2]   In Millions of Pounds

Year	Jan. 1	Feb. 1	Mar. 1	Apr. 1	May 1	June 1	July 1	Aug. 1	Sept. 1	Oct. 1	Nov. 1	Dec. 1
1977	123.0	163.9	152.0	156.3	170.7	162.7	150.5	160.5	178.8	136.7	128.6	114.6
1978	133.7	146.5	176.7	173.6	166.8	140.2	146.0	132.6	130.6	144.8	123.1	120.2
1979	154.6	211.3	216.0	89.1	47.5	156.4	119.5	132.2	138.7	167.1	235.0	218.8
1980	309.7	357.7	248.4	246.5	211.2	211.9	220.6	191.6	210.1	182.6	225.6	264.6
1981	300.1	309.2	359.6	322.5	309.5	289.5	285.1	265.8	260.3	227.7	170.0	168.7
1982	173.1	153.6	186.0	160.7	153.0	170.8	194.8	184.3	166.9	159.7	144.5	144.5
1983	127.2	143.8	144.7	144.0	162.9	168.9	123.6	127.7	131.8	145.3	162.5	175.6
1984	175.2	215.5	193.8	165.0	150.2	121.8	78.7	90.9	100.2	111.0	119.8	107.3
1985	121.5	127.9	91.9	81.3	74.9	85.9	116.0	121.7	140.5	130.0	177.4	162.8
1986[1]	206.5	252.8	262.0	285.3	246.3	289.3	275.0	273.4	273.8	308.0	295.4	316.9

[1] Preliminary.   [2] Includes coconut oil held in U.S. customs bond.   *Source: Bureau of Census*
T.115

Average Price of Coconut Oil (Crude)[1] at New York[2]   In Cents Per Pound

Year	Jan.	Feb.	Mar.	Apr.	May	June	July	Aug.	Sept.	Oct.	Nov.	Dec.	Average
1977	25.6	27.4	34.7	37.3	34.3	29.9	24.8	21.8	22.9	23.9	24.9	26.4	27.8
1978	26.4	27.1	31.9	30.5	29.9	32.4	32.9	32.3	39.2	41.6	42.6	42.6	34.1
1979	46.3	47.2	47.0	49.9	53.2	57.3	57.3	53.7	44.8	42.5	42.4	40.2	48.5
1980	40.8	40.6	37.5	34.1	29.3	29.5	30.4	29.9	29.1	27.9	29.4	27.8	32.1
1981	26.3	25.0	23.9	24.3	26.0	27.4	28.1	26.4	24.3	26.6	26.6	25.4	25.9
1982	24.8	24.8	22.9	23.0	23.3	23.1	21.1	19.3	19.8	20.0	N.A.	N.A.	22.2
1983	N.A.	20.3	21.0	25.6	28.4	35.8	33.7	N.A.	N.A.	N.A.	N.A.	44.9	27.5
1984[2]	49.2	54.3	53.0	50.8	63.0	69.9	73.3	70.0	64.6	65.6	56.2	52.6	60.2
1985	42.2	40.2	41.0	41.0	N.A.	N.A.	31.7	27.5	25.0	24.0	22.8	17.4	31.3
1986	20.6	18.0	15.6	15.5	13.8	13.9	13.8	13.0	13.3				

[1] Tank cars, f.o.b. mill. Includes 1¢ import duty.   [2] Prior to 1984, prices are at the U.S. Pacific Coast.   *Source: Bureau of Labor Statistics* T.116

Coffee

Some 56 countries in the southern half of the globe contributed to world coffee output in 1986/87, but the bulk of production came from a few. Heading the list were Brazil with 20 percent of total output and Colombia with 15 percent. Indonesia was a distant third with seven percent, followed closely by the Ivory Coast (six percent) and Mexico (six percent). Uganda and Ethiopia contributed approximately four percent each.

For the 1986/87 crop year, world output has been estimated at 81 million 60-kilo bags. This figure is roughly 16 percent below last year's and reflects the lowest level of production since 1979/80. Most of the decline in output was attributable to Brazil, where there was a severe drought during the summer of 1985. Brazilian production fell from 33 million bags in 1985/86 to only 13.9 million in 1986/87, a slide of almost 58 percent. Output in Colombia was estimated to be down six percent from 1985/86 at 11.8 million bags. In Latin countries, in general, production was down. The primary causes of this decline were poor weather, low prices, and increased production costs. Despite the decline in output, the total world coffee supply for 1986/87, estimated at 130 million bags, was only one percent lower than the previous crop year. Beginning stocks amounting to more than 46 million bags, the highest in over 10 years, provided a substantial cushion for total supply.

Somewhat more than one-half of available world supplies were exported in the form of beans, while another two percent were exported in soluble form. Virtually all remaining supplies were either consumed domestically (17 percent) or held as stocks. These percentages differ only modestly from those of earlier years.

USDA has estimated that global consumption during 1986/87 was approximately 93.1 million 60-kilo bags, compared with 89.6 million bags the year before. Although expected consumption exceeded estimated output by 12 million bags, or roughly 15 percent, the carry-in of over 46 million bags more than covered the apparent deficit.

After soaring during November, 1985–January, 1986 on Brazilian drought concerns, prices of coffee futures were on a steep downtrend in most of 1986. The retreat in price was mostly due to evidence of ample inventories.

Wholesale and retail prices of coffee receded during the latter months of 1986. After advancing swiftly from $2.586 per pound in November, 1985, to $3.506 in May, 1986, the price of a one-pound can of ground roast coffee in the United States retreated to $3.344 in December.

By early December, 1986, the key indicator price of the International Coffee Agreement (ICO) slipped below $1.45 a pound, causing the ICO to convene a special meeting to discuss reintroduction of export quotas as a price-control device. The meeting was adjourned after a single session, presumably without results.

In September, 1986, Brazil hoped to preserve its share of the global market (and its customary export quota of 30% of the ICO's total) by seeking 1.5 million 60-kilo bags of Robusta coffee on the European market. The purchases ended by the time Brazil had bought 600,000 bags, because prices had risen. Starting in April, 1987, Brazil plans to sell the coffee over a period of weeks so that the markets can absorb it. 500,000 bags were in warehouses in Trieste and another 100,000 bags were in containers at the Brazilian port of Paranagua.

Given generally weak roaster demand and sharp differences among the exporting and importing countries about what price level should be sought and how it should be attained and maintained, the prospect for the coming months is for stable-to-slowly-rising output and further price declines.

Futures Markets

Washed Arabica coffee futures are traded on the Coffee, Sugar, and Cocoa Exchange, Inc. (CSCE) in New York. Robusta coffee futures are traded in London and also in Paris.

World Coffee Supply and Distribution   In Thousands of 60 Kilo Bags

Country by Time Period	Beginning Stocks	Production	Imports	Total Supply Distribution	Domestic Use	Exports Beans	Exports RSTD/GRND	Exports Soluble	Exports Total	Ending Stocks
1977/78	25,612	70,696	613	96,921	18,764	47,704	183	897	48,784	29,373
1978/79	29,373	78,978	729	109,080	19,466	61,906	222	2,433	64,561	25,059
1979/80	25,053	81,789	690	107,532	19,973	59,244	217	2,573	62,034	25,525
1980/81	25,525	86,261	653	112,439	20,595	56,835	166	2,821	59,822	32,022
1981/82	32,022	98,189	769	130,980	21,232	60,584	223	4,059	64,866	44,882
1982/83	44,882	82,778	790	128,450	20,686	62,101	202	2,488	64,791	42,973
1983/84	42,973	90,049	779	133,801	21,228	65,188	337	2,772	68,297	44,276
1984/85[1]	44,276	90,357	614	135,247	21,500	67,824	300	3,310	71,434	42,313
1985/86[2]	42,313	98,647	611	141,571	22,328	67,562	324	2,873	70,759	48,484

Note: Total may not add because of rounding.   [1] Preliminary.   [2] Estimate.   *Source: Foreign Agricultural Service, U.S.D.A.*   T.117a

COFFEE

World Green Coffee (Total) Production   In Thousands of 60 Kilo Bags (132.276 Lbs. Per Bag)

Crop Year	Angola	Brazil	Camer-oon	Colom-bia	Costa Rica	Ethi-opia	Guate-mala	India	Indon-esia	Ivory Coast	Mexico	Salva-dor	Uganda	Zaire (Congo, K)	World Total
1978–9	613	20,000	1,634	12,600	1,749	3,142	2,827	1,842	4,788	4,742	4,022	3,423	1,944	1,293	79,074
1979–0	260	22,000	1,658	12,712	1,522	3,188	2,647	2,495	4,803	3,973	3,600	3,322	2,042	1,316	81,908
1980–1	586	21,500	1,959	13,500	2,140	3,264	2,702	1,977	5,365	6,090	3,862	2,940	2,133	1,526	86,344
1981–2	392	33,000	1,850	14,342	1,782	3,212	2,653	2,540	5,785	4,160	3,900	2,886	2,885	1,425	98,189
1982–3	330	17,750	1,830	13,300	2,300	3,670	2,530	2,170	4,750	4,510	4,530	3,100	3,000	1,354	82,778
1983–4	260	30,000	1,000	13,000	2,070	3,990	2,340	1,667	5,500	1,420	4,530	2,600	3,200	1,350	90,049
1984–5[1]	260	27,000	2,100	11,000	2,516	2,600	2,703	2,917	5,400	4,900	4,250	2,700	3,300	1,503	90,357
1985–6[1]	250	33,000	1,900	12,500	2,013	3,150	2,530	2,334	5,750	5,000	4,480	2,600	3,000	1,540	98,647

[1] Preliminary.   *Source: Foreign Agricultural Service, U.S.D.A.*   T.117

World Green Coffee (Exportable)[3] Production   In Thousands of 60 Kilo Bags

Crop[2] Year	Angola	Brazil	Camer-oon	Colom-bia	Costa Rica	Ethi-opia	Guate-mala	Indon-esia	Ivory Coast	Kenya	Mexico	Salva-dor	Uganda	Zaire (Congo, K)	World Total
1978–9	568	12,000	1,606	10,970	1,533	1,432	2,517	3,738	4,677	1,181	2,915	3,226	1,905	1,123	60,028
1979–0	220	14,000	1,626	10,962	1,311	1,555	2,336	3,723	3,908	1,468	2,310	3,122	2,001	1,141	62,258
1980–1	545	13,500	1,926	11,675	1,932	1,664	2,381	4,137	6,026	1,648	2,362	2,740	2,090	1,346	66,064
1981–2	350	24,500	1,815	12,492	1,539	1,596	2,328	4,630	4,095	1,434	2,450	2,686	2,840	1,240	77,311
1982–3	287	9,750	1,785	11,445	2,077	2,108	2,195	3,636	4,445	1,501	2,830	2,900	2,954	1,159	62,366
1983–4	216	21,500	945	11,140	1,837	2,355	2,000	4,375	1,355	2,186	3,030	2,400	3,153	1,096	69,127
1984–5[1]	215	18,500	2,045	9,135	2,281	700	2,373	4,440	4,835	1,460	2,530	2,500	3,252	1,253	69,097
1985–6[1]	204	24,000	1,845	10,630	1,778	1,300	2,210	4,650	4,930	2,105	2,710	2,400	2,950	1,275	76,563

[1] Preliminary.   [2] Coffee marketing year begins in July in some countries & in others about Oct.   [3] Exportable production represents total harvested production minus estimated domestic consumption.   *Source: Foreign Agricultural Service, U.S.D.A.*   T.118

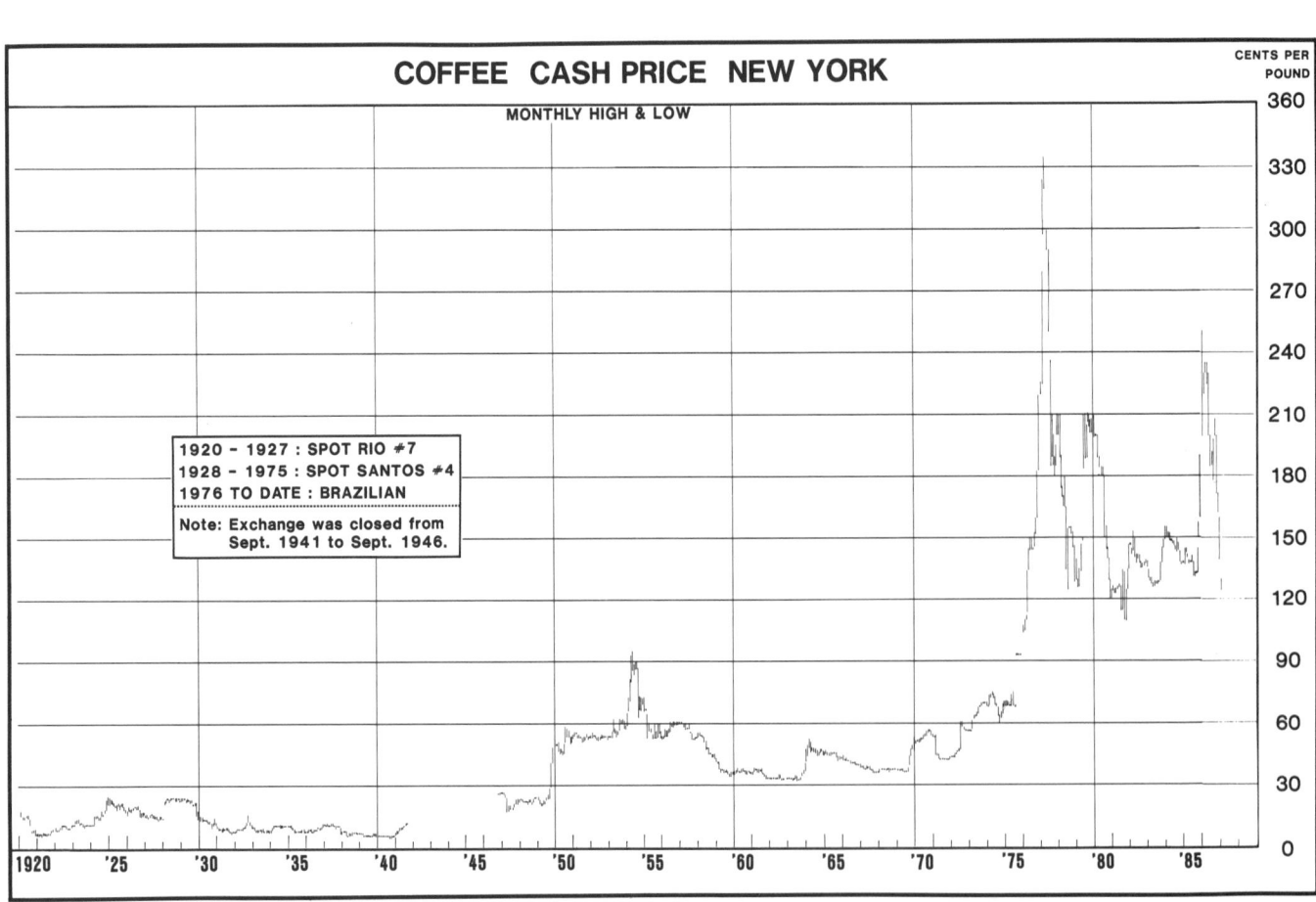

COFFEE CASH PRICE NEW YORK

CENTS PER POUND

MONTHLY HIGH & LOW

1920 - 1927 : SPOT RIO #7
1928 - 1975 : SPOT SANTOS #4
1976 TO DATE : BRAZILIAN

Note: Exchange was closed from Sept. 1941 to Sept. 1946.

44

Origin of Coffee Imports (for Consumption) into the U.S.   In Thousands of 60 Kilo Bags

Year	Angola	Brazil	Colombia	Costa-Rica	Domin. Repub.	Ecuador	Ethi-opia	Guate-mala	Indon-esia	Ivory Coast	Mexico	Peru	Phil-ippines	Salva-dor	Vene-zuela	Grand Total
1972	1,297	6,152	2,711	294	401	490	965	689	744	977	1,070			391	243	20,769
1973	1,693	4,596	2,868	284	507	435	1,062	1,110	626	1,150	1,641			1,047	174	21,789
1974	2,396	2,725	3,090	268	381	512	505	1,096	942	749	1,324			1,111	246	19,245
1975	1,202	3,748	3,400	192	336	694	533	874	765	966	1,662	432		1,018	182	20,289
1976	871	3,092	2,688	179	551	767	703	749	1,082	1,330	1,869	461	44	1,045	288	19,788
1977	49	2,453	1,951	272	585	505	288	832	860	673	1,406	654	6	1,037	155	14,808
1978	304	2,694	2,808	334	461	1,044	461	942	1,177	775	1,390	954	62	627	239	18,133
1979	40	1,890	3,891	516	548	638	549	1,123	1,294	834	1,934	565	96	1,123	121	19,396
1980	120	3,505	3,404	298	343	539	406	1,374	1,315	438	1,337	573	179	1,374	35	18,153
1981	21	3,243	1,727	226	359	701	547	645	1,516	602	1,393	439	270	779	27	16,555
1982	63	3,372	1,710	248	500	773	578	844	1,118	998	1,377	513	308	919	16	17,416
1983	27	3,417	1,755	226	430	857	519	887	1,079	674	1,495	439	276	1,214	26	16,449
1984	5	3,866	2,170	258	447	961	423	1,118	1,030	1,144	1,553	557	296	1,052	88	17,734
1985[1]	27	4,148	2,554	360	439	974	195	1,054	1,041	951	1,812	543	407	1,366	107	18,698
1986																

[1] Preliminary.   *Source: U.S. Department of Commerce*   T.122

Total Coffee Imports (for Consumption) into the U.S.   In Thousands of 60 Kilo Bags

Year	Jan.	Feb.	Mar.	Apr.	May	June	July	Aug.	Sept.	Oct.	Nov.	Dec.	Total
1972	2,547	2,172	1,137	1,146	1,784	1,452	1,434	1,947	2,149	2,057	1,643	1,288	20,757
1973	1,996	1,844	2,101	2,050	2,494	1,710	1,573	1,731	1,399	1,624	1,624	1,652	21,799
1974	2,182	2,022	2,457	2,264	1,873	1,529	1,499	1,152	821	740	1,159	1,550	19,248
1975	1,852	1,656	1,535	1,448	1,365	1,736	1,626	1,868	2,533	1,784	1,587	1,299	20,289
1976	1,664	1,744	2,311	1,636	1,546	1,864	1,909	1,637	956	1,013	1,649	1,858	19,788
1977	1,994	1,707	1,839	1,824	1,224	1,137	756	695	678	635	972	1,347	14,808
1978	1,682	1,575	1,707	1,557	1,345	1,249	1,316	1,124	1,337	1,901	1,689	1,651	18,133
1979	1,747	1,353	1,631	2,037	1,619	1,617	1,597	1,404	1,632	1,273	1,593	1,893	19,396
1980	2,020	1,366	1,421	1,642	1,566	1,663	1,533	1,386	1,062	1,292	1,386	1,715	18,153
1981	1,858	1,738	1,395	1,299	1,356	1,026	922	1,213	1,150	1,487	1,565	1,547	16,555
1982	1,287	1,195	1,490	1,147	1,476	1,335	1,282	1,602	1,640	2,005	1,356	1,602	17,416
1983	1,556	1,332	1,373	1,253	1,502	1,034	1,319	1,230	1,532	1,685	1,380	1,253	16,449
1984	1,598	1,299	1,440	1,905	1,615	1,059	1,722	1,735	1,432	1,614	1,127	1,187	17,734
1985	1,622	1,681	1,702	1,430	1,324	1,751	1,217	1,757	1,773	1,385	1,272	1,785	18,698
1986	2,360	1,836	1,645	1,667	1,810	1,286	1,549	1,513	1,641	1,535			

Source: U.S. Dept. of Commerce   T.121

Average Spot Price of Coffee (Brazilian[1]) at N.Y.   In Cents Per Pound

Year	Jan.	Feb.	Mar.	Apr.	May	June	July	Aug.	Sept.	Oct.	Nov.	Dec.	Average
1972	N.A.	N.A.	N.A.	46.3	48.0	48.5	N.A.	62.5	59.0	48.0	56.0	57.0	54.4
1973	57.0	62.0	65.5	65.0	65.0	67.0	70.0	70.0	72.5	72.3	73.0	72.0	67.6
1974	72.0	71.0	75.0	75.5	76.5	74.0	72.0	63.0	60.0	64.0	69.0	70.0	70.2
1975	67.5	68.0	———————————No Quotations———————————										67.8
1976	———No Quote———			93.5		———No Quote———			152.0		———No Quote———		122.8
1977	—————————————————No Quote—————————————————												
1978	—————————————No Quote—————————————							135.0	154.0	154.0	153.0	146.0	148.4
1979	146.0	127.0	136.0	138.0	148.0	180.0	209.0	201.0	206.0	208.0	205.0	212.0	176.3
1980	189.0	213.0	205.0	208.0	218.0	211.0	195.0	206.0	206.0	210.0	210.0	208.0	206.6
1981	218.0	218.0	218.0	218.0	129.0	115.5	115.5	127.0	127.0	129.5	147.0	150.0	159.4
1982	151.0	136.0	136.0	145.0	145.0	145.0	145.0	145.0	145.0	145.0	133.0	133.0	142.0
1983	133.0	133.0	133.0	141.5	141.5	141.5	141.5	143.0	143.0	143.0	143.0	143.0	140.0
1984[1]	150.0	151.0	151.0	148.0	148.0	147.0	145.0	145.0	146.0	140.0	138.0	138.0	145.6
1985	140.0	145.0	141.0	138.0	138.0	140.0	134.0	133.0	133.0	137.0	155.0	175.0	142.4
1986	241.0	226.0	235.0	228.0	218.0	193.0	188.0	185.0	193.0	187.0	167.0	146.0	200.6

[1] Prices prior to 1984 are for Santos No. 4 at N.Y.   *Sources: Bureau of Labor Statistics (0191-0101.01); Wall St. Journal*   T.120

COFFEE

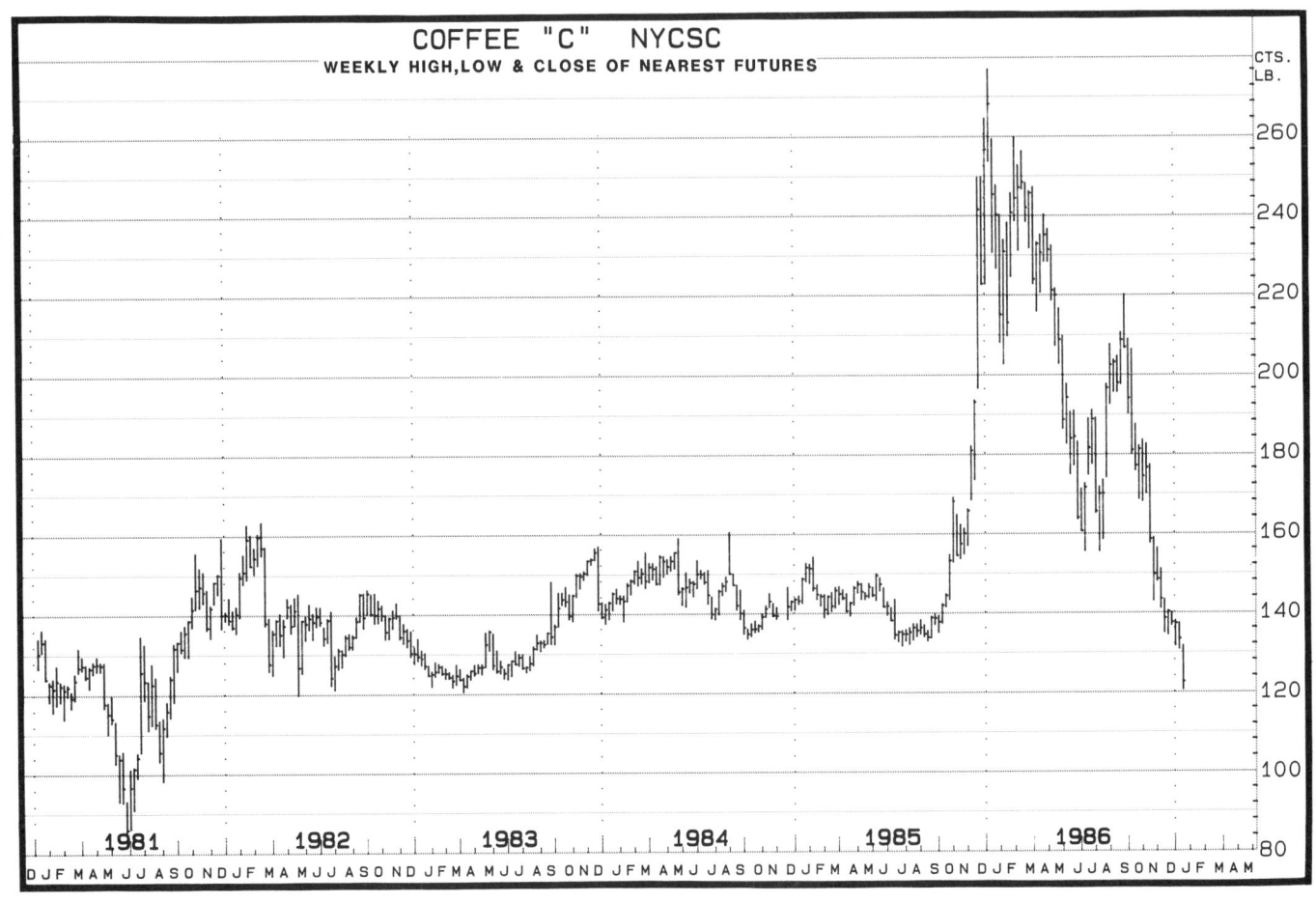

COFFEE "C" NYCSC
WEEKLY HIGH, LOW & CLOSE OF NEAREST FUTURES

CTS.
LB.

High, Low & Closing Prices of May Coffee Futures in New York   In Cents per Pound

Year of Delivery		Mar.	Apr.	May	June	July	Aug.	Sept.	Oct.	Nov.	Dec.	Jan.	Feb.	Mar.	Apr.	May	Life of Delivery Range
					Year Prior to Delivery									Delivery Year			
1981	High	190.75	187.50	198.00	198.60	181.40	162.00	157.00	138.00	128.50	130.40	137.00	127.00	131.40	129.25	127.90	198.60
	Low	176.25	176.10	177.40	169.00	138.47	135.25	129.75	128.25	114.75	116.00	123.30	115.55	117.65	121.50	113.00	113.00
	Close	179.69	178.54	190.60	179.75	146.59	143.78	134.65	128.55	123.25	127.81	127.25	121.00	128.66	126.48	113.00	—
1982	High	126.25	124.00	123.87	111.00	126.75	120.25	123.50	130.25	138.00	133.80	137.88	147.30	149.00	143.75	144.95	149.00
	Low	120.10	117.50	111.50	80.50	81.25	98.28	96.10	123.00	124.25	122.23	128.75	137.25	124.50	129.20	135.10	80.50
	Close	122.60	122.25	112.50	87.50	121.45	98.28	123.00	129.00	126.23	133.63	137.88	141.26	128.56	141.72	138.25	—
1983	High	116.50	118.50	117.50	121.25	117.50	114.00	131.00	131.15	135.40	132.30	127.90	123.95	126.90	126.85	135.17	135.40
	Low	114.00	107.50	109.25	113.50	103.51	107.50	111.00	124.00	126.25	121.60	120.25	118.90	120.35	120.10	124.55	103.51
	Close	114.76	113.00	118.51	118.28	108.25	113.10	129.45	130.49	131.78	125.00	120.60	120.12	123.23	124.80	134.17	—
1984	High	117.00	117.75	126.00	124.50	124.00	127.25	130.05	137.30	139.90	144.10	139.65	145.00	152.30	154.23	158.50	158.50
	Low	109.50	113.00	116.00	121.50	121.60	122.25	125.25	129.30	134.50	134.30	134.25	132.75	141.90	147.00	147.80	108.50
	Close	115.13	116.75	123.38	122.51	122.26	125.80	129.25	135.50	138.78	135.94	137.05	144.84	151.37	152.20	154.00	—
1985	High	131.50	138.50	152.00	146.28	140.15	146.00	143.15	135.35	139.15	140.25	147.90	150.70	146.20	147.30	147.50	152.00
	Low	125.28	130.00	137.50	137.75	132.90	133.25	132.75	131.31	134.50	135.60	138.65	139.85	139.25	138.85	143.00	122.01
	Close	131.38	138.50	142.25	137.76	133.48	144.15	133.80	135.05	135.72	140.25	147.24	139.96	144.43	145.80	143.50	—
1986	High	142.50	145.00	144.50	148.75	143.50	142.13	144.45	161.18	171.45	214.09	272.62	261.00	257.00	243.70	234.25	272.62
	Low	136.59	137.00	141.55	142.28	136.20	137.75	137.15	136.20	155.25	174.90	217.80	207.78	231.15	215.25	202.00	130.25
	Close	141.75	143.00	144.00	144.88	138.65	140.75	140.60	161.18	171.45	241.09	218.51	246.96	246.44	229.07	204.09	—
1987	High	265.00	265.00	261.00	210.50	198.50	205.00	219.50	189.00	173.00	150.50						
	Low	247.00	247.00	237.00	177.00	169.95	165.50	173.00	165.38	149.26	132.50						
	Close	265.00	265.00	247.38	180.25	184.50	199.50	192.78	169.38	151.25	138.00						

Source: N.Y. Coffee, Sugar & Cocoa Exchange, Inc.   T.125

46

Month-End Open Interest of Coffee Futures at New York   In Contracts

Year	Jan.	Feb.	Mar.	Apr.	May	June	July	Aug.	Sept.	Oct.	Nov.	Dec.
1978	4,413	4,191	3,942	3,661	3,733	2,952	3,152	3,926	4,004	4,767	5,951	6,581
1979	7,113	7,965	8,799	9,751	10,279	8,761	10,214	12,014	12,479	14,808	15,974	15,988
1980	13,077	13,113	12,990	11,288	16,975	15,854	13,576	10,767	11,824	11,155	9,489	8,848
1981	8,218	8,624	9,931	10,043	8,969	8,093	9,182	8,182	9,223	9,084	8,922	9,823
1982	11,236	9,647	9,249	8,753	7,949	8,358	7,791	8,393	9,677	8,876	9,152	9,273
1983	10,752	10,336	11,739	11,752	11,317	7,885	8,042	9,351	9,439	9,420	8,600	7,706
1984	8,086	10,963	13,012	11,649	9,841	9,437	10,303	10,405	10,300	10,400	10,143	12,431
1985	14,435	12,454	12,973	13,230	12,606	10,561	11,783	10,148	10,066	11,873	11,776	13,167
1986	13,062	15,758	15,611	16,285	16,765	15,492	17,011	15,908	19,171	18,769	15,081	14,928

Source: N.Y. Coffee, Sugar & Cocoa Exchange, Inc.   T.124

Volume of Trading of Coffee "C" Futures at New York   In Contracts

Year	Jan.	Feb.	Mar.	Apr.	May	June	July	Aug.	Sept.	Oct.	Nov.	Dec.	Total
1978	11,125	10,341	17,202	12,049	12,194	11,112	11,346	18,526	13,526	14,615	14,589	17,334	163,959
1979	21,463	25,243	24,205	36,298	35,885	39,137	43,944	43,046	40,088	50,054	51,949	38,488	449,799
1980	70,277	77,143	112,558	93,108	145,830	87,149	80,217	66,054	69,731	37,528	35,310	32,029	906,944
1981	38,671	34,086	44,963	29,766	39,384	46,094	50,759	50,482	44,368	44,235	49,468	41,757	515,302
1982	47,560	50,976	63,168	52,708	51,062	44,428	42,779	38,457	44,583	39,967	46,247	37,500	556,435
1983	30,567	32,884	44,211	37,399	44,917	45,575	26,065	32,818	22,579	38,999	34,428	36,999	427,441
1984	33,327	44,890	46,793	46,833	51,174	42,891	34,956	48,979	43,159	29,703	37,457	36,094	499,133
1985	48,733	54,809	52,365	58,531	38,755	54,725	42,222	39,425	23,615	58,870	83,845	94,671	650,768
1986	113,305	95,509	76,787	82,308	75,176	87,323	78,670	106,366	93,465	112,685	89,713	61,835	1,074,142

Source: N.Y. Coffee, Sugar & Cocoa Exchange, Inc.   T.123

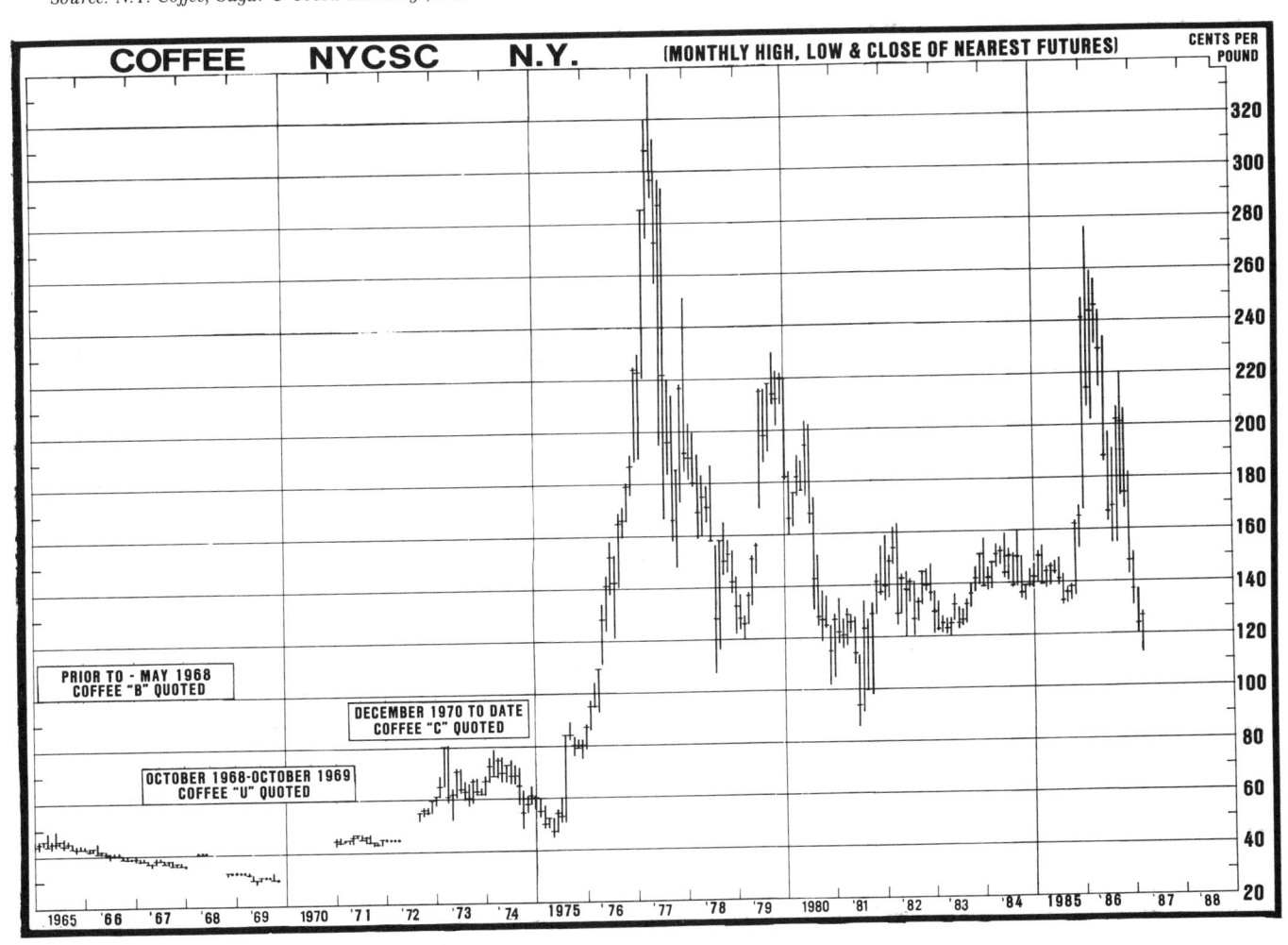

Coke

U.S. Salient Statistics of Coke   In Thousands of Short Tons

Year	Prod- uct- ion[2]	Domestic Consump- tion	Producers' Stocks—Jan. 1 Total	Oven Coke at Plants Mer- chant	Oven Coke at Plants Fur- nace	Petrol- eum Coke	Ex- ports	Im- ports	Exports to Can- ada	Exports to Mex- ico	Exports to Bel./ Lux.	Exports to Neth- erlands	Exports to Korea Rep.	Exports to Tur- key	Exports to Vene- zuela	Avg. Price of Coke Exports $ SH. Ton
1977	53,509	54,144	6,487	314	6,173	2,127	1,241	1,829	634.9	49.4						
1978	49,009	56,948	6,444	136	6,308	2,050	693	5,722	299	37.4						
1979	52,943	53,826	3,534	184	3,350	2,214	1,440	3,974	598	61.0						
1980	46,132	41,278	5,185	595	4,590	1,042	2,071	659	812	75.0						
1981	42,786	44,046	8,627	1,106	7,521	846	1,170	527								
1982	28,115	25,776	6,724	403	6,324	900	993	120	449.7	72.0	99.3	132.7	4.5	—	40.1	61.81
1983	25,808	29,850	8,190	331	7,858	1,344	665	35	471.2	55.8	24.7	24.0	—	—	7.0	68.53
1984	30,561	29,899	3,518	286	3,233	1,096	1,045	582	477.0	72.8	106.4	150.2	64.8	80.1	65.8	66.48
1985[1]	28,651	29,270	3,716	353	3,363	968	1,130	578	407.3	97.3	108.8	68.0	.1	57.6	42.6	68.40
1986[3]	29,000	29,500	2,553	404	2,148	1,232	1,179	440								80.00

[1] Preliminary.   [2] Beehive and oven, coke & breeze.   [3] Estimate.   *Source: Bureau of Mines*   T.127

Oven Coke Production in the United States   In Thousands of Short Tons

Year	Jan.	Feb.	Mar.	Apr.	May	June	July	Aug.	Sept.	Oct.	Nov.	Dec.	Total
1977	4,412	4,267	4,696	4,666	4,822	4,686	4,639	4,249	4,069	4,289	4,186	4,077	53,060
1978	3,603	2,741	2,661	3,753	4,398	4,362	4,455	4,379	4,346	4,512	4,383	4,645	48,238
1979	4,469	4,031	4,679	4,419	4,585	4,352	4,414	4,440	4,366	4,466	4,252	4,453	52,943
1980	4,394	4,204	4,444	4,396	4,238	3,686	3,370	3,387	3,295	3,470	3,565	3,683	46,132
1981	———	11,178	———	———	9,853	———	———	11,175	———	———	10,580	———	42,786
1982	———	8,828	———	———	7,507	———	———	6,270	———	———	5,509	———	28,115
1983	———	5,579	———	———	6,451	———	———	6,753	———	———	7,025	———	25,808
1984	———	7,696	———	———	8,227	———	———	7,522	———	———	7,115	———	30,561
1985[1]	———	7,211	———	———	7,601	———	———	7,150	———	———	6,689	———	28,651
1986[1]	———	7,252	———	———	7,156	———							

[1] Preliminary.   *Source: Bureau of Mines*   T.128

Coke (Oven-Coke) Stocks at Plants   In Thousands of Short Tons

Year	Jan. 1	Feb. 1	Mar. 1	Apr. 1	May 1	June 1	July 1	Aug. 1	Sept. 1	Oct. 1	Nov. 1	Dec. 1
1977	6,487	6,950	7,231	7,283	7,038	6,736	6,468	6,516	6,281	6,192	6,554	6,526
1978	6,444	5,937	5,209	3,460	3,189	2,993	2,964	2,845	2,989	3,065	3,131	3,339
1979	3,534	3,548	3,509	3,339	3,495	3,459	3,200	3,253	3,322	3,754	4,228	4,630
1980	5,185	5,531	5,781	5,832	6,063	6,698	7,426	8,133	8,676	9,018	9,011	9,040
1981	8,267	—	—	7,586	—	—	4,990	—	—	5,198	—	—
1982	6,724	—	—	7,455	—	—	7,871	—	—	7,969	—	—
1983	8,190	—	—	5,781	—	—	4,569	—	—	3,875	—	—
1984	3,518	—	—	3,153	—	—	2,966	—	—	3,441	—	—
1985[1]	3,716	—	—	3,471	—	—	3,279	—	—	3,217	—	—
1986[1]	2,553	—	—	2,319	—	—	2,174	—	—			

[1] Preliminary.   *Source: Bureau of Mines*   T.131

Index of Wholesale Price of Oven Foundry Coke F.O.B. at Birmingham, Ala.   Base Per Ton 1967 = 100

Year	Jan.	Feb.	Mar.	Apr.	May	June	July	Aug.	Sept.	Oct.	Nov.	Dec.	Average
1980	439.6	439.6	439.6	439.6	439.6	439.6	439.6	439.6	439.6	439.6	439.6	434.0	439.1
1981	434.0	434.0	434.0	434.0	478.9	478.9	478.9	478.9	478.9	478.9	478.9	478.9	463.9
1982	478.9	485.2	485.2	N.A.	485.2	454.8	467.4	465.9	465.7	463.4	463.4	463.4	470.8
1983	460.5	460.5	452.7	452.7	433.6	433.6	426.8	448.9	448.9	448.1	448.8	410.7	443.8
1984	413.6	433.0	434.1	437.8	436.6	437.2	437.0	432.4	430.8	427.6	427.9	430.2	431.5
1985	434.8	434.5	428.2	425.3	424.8	424.3	423.8	423.7	423.7	422.4	422.1	419.2	425.6
1986[1]	411.6	412.6	412.3	407.0	406.5	402.3	401.6	402.3	402.3	401.5	390.0		

[1] Preliminary.   *Source: Bureau of Labor Statistics* (0522-0101.99)   T.130

Copper

The Bureau of Mines' data for the first nine months of 1986 suggests U.S. mine production of recoverable copper was approximately 1.14 million metric tons, about 10 percent higher than output in the year before. The apparent upturn was not shared, however, by other types of copper production. Domestic smelter output of primary copper was roughly six percent smaller in 1986 than in 1985; refinery output (electrolytic and electrowon combined) was down an estimated 25 percent. Production of secondary copper declined across the board: refined by three percent; brass ingots by 26 percent; brass mill products by 23 percent; other items by 25 percent.

U.S. domestic supplies of unmanufactured copper were augmented by 1986 imports estimated at 470,-000 metric tons of refined copper, about 25 percent above 1985's rate. As usual, Chile and Canada were the main suppliers. The former's share of total U.S. imports was about 50 percent, the latter's about one-third. U.S. exports of ore and concentrate also rose in 1986, increasing by roughly 13 percent above 1985. The same was true of unalloyed copper scrap. Exports of refined copper, such as bars and ingots, were substantially smaller in 1986 than exports of ores, and concentrate rose in volume by an estimated 11 percent.

Extrapolation of incomplete 1986 data from the Bureau of Mines reveals that total apparent consumption of copper during the year amounted to approximately 2.10 million metric tons. That represented a decline of about 25 percent from the 1985 level. Similarly, total consumption of refined copper was down modestly for the year, compared with the year before. Usage of purchased copper-base scrap was virtually unchanged on a year-over-year basis.

With demand for copper lower in 1986 than in 1985, prices of various copper products weakened. By October, 1986, the average U.S. producers' delivered price of both cathode and wirebar was 63.46 cents per pound, as against 66.97 in 1985. By the same token, the October cash price per pound for standard grade copper on the London Metals Exchange averaged 58.29 cents, versus 63.19 cents in 1985; the average price of Grade A copper in October was 59.71 cents, compared with 64.29 cents in 1985.

In several other respects, 1986 was an eventful year for the domestic copper industry. Heading the list was widespread restructuring of the industry, chiefly through spin-offs of subsidiaries and injection of foreign (mainly, Japanese) investment in domestic enterprises. Key producers also came to terms with different environmental regulators. The chief case in point was Phelps Dodge Corporation, which was allowed by the state of Arizona to continue to operate its smelter in Douglas, Arizona during 1986, in return for the company's agreement to shut the plant down in early 1987; Phelps Dodge had concluded that it would be financially unsound to invest in anti-pollution devices.

The Commodity Futures Trading Commission approved the Commodity Exchange's (COMEX) application to trade high-grade copper cathode futures in 1986. A high-grade contract was also approved for the MidAmerica Exchange (MidAm).

Futures Markets

Copper futures are traded on COMEX in New York, the London Metals Exchange (LME), and the MidAm in Chicago.

World Mine Production of Copper (Content of Ore) In Thousands of Metric Tons

Year	Australia	Canada[3]	Chile	China	Finland	Japan	Mexico	Peru	Zambia	Poland	Zaire	South Africa	Philippines	United States[3]	USSR	World Total[1]
1979	237.6	636.4	1,063	200	41.1	59.1	107.1	390.7	588.3	325.0	430.4	190.6	298.3	1,444	855[4]	7,691
1980	243.5	716.4	1,068	165.0	36.8	52.6	184.1	366.8	595.8	346.1	539.5	200.7	304.5	1,181	590.0	7,405
1981	231.3	691.3	1,081	170.0	38.5	51.5	232.9	342.1	588.0	294.6	555.1	199.4	302.3	1,538	570.0	7,777
1982	245.3	612.4	1,242	175.0	37.8	50.7	229.2	356.6	567.8	376.0	519.0	188.7	292.1	1,147	560.0	7,619
1983	261.5	653.0	1,258	175.0	39.3	46.0	196.0	322.2	574.5	402.3	536.5	205.0	271.4	1,038	570.0	7,712
1984[2]	236.0	712.8	1,291	180.0	31.3	43.3	303.5	375.1	541.0	431.0	520.0	198.2	233.4	1,103	590.0	7,986
1985[1]	258.0	724.4	1,356	185.0	30.0	43.2	290.0	397.2	483.0	431.3	560.0	202.3	226.2	1,106	600.0	8,114

[1] Estimate. [2] Preliminary. [3] Recoverable. [4] Smelter Production. *Source: Bureau of Mines* T.132

Commodity Exchange Inc. (COMEX) Warehouse Stocks of Copper In Thousands of Short Tons

Year	Jan. 1	Feb. 1	Mar. 1	Apr. 1	May 1	June 1	July 1	Aug. 1	Sept. 1	Oct. 1	Nov. 1	Dec. 1
1979	179.2	170.8	156.4	133.6	118.3	89.9	70.7	61.5	56.8	57.0	64.9	71.3
1980	107.8	114.1	132.0	145.7	149.8	155.5	167.3	181.7	190.8	185.4	178.6	170.9
1981	179.6	179.3	179.8	173.3	182.4	175.5	170.6	168.8	167.5	171.6	173.1	171.4
1982	187.6	189.3	193.6	195.7	198.5	201.5	202.2	207.4	211.8	207.1	210.3	246.3
1983	274.4	278.5	293.6	306.1	325.9	336.5	347.4	360.1	374.5	389.3	396.1	404.2
1984	409.2	417.7	409.9	403.2	392.3	372.5	361.6	335.6	320.6	310.8	300.7	288.1
1985	276.3	258.2	238.8	224.8	214.3	201.0	186.4	167.7	155.0	149.0	136.4	124.6
1986	120.3	120.1	118.5	116.4	114.5	108.5	103.4	95.7	90.6	86.6	81.0	84.0
1987	93.3											

Source: Commodity Exchange, Inc. N.Y. (COMEX)

T.144

COPPER

U.S. Salient Statistics of Copper   In Thousands of Metric Tons

Year	New Copper Produced — From Domestic Ores — Mines	Smelters	Refineries	From Foreign Ores[2]	Total New	Secondary Recovered[7]	Imports[3] Unmanufactured	Refined	Exports Ore, Concentrate[4]	Refined[5]	Stocks—Dec. 31 N.Y. Commodity Exch.	Primary Producers (Refined)	Blister & Materials in Solution	Appar. Consumption[6] Refined Copper (Reported)	Primary & Old Copper[8]
1975	1,282	1,247	1,167	143	1,309	335	294	133	305	156	91	187	283	1,191	1,526
1976	1,457	1,326	1,291	106	1,396	380	485	346	218	102	182	172	291	1,656	2,036
1977	1,364	1,265	1,280	77	1,357	410	396	351	91	47	167	212	314	1,622	2,032
1978	1,358	1,270	1,327	122	1,449	502	532	403	187	92	163	153	263	1,819	2,321
1979	1,447	1,313	1,413	104	1,517	604	282	204	231	74	90	64	275	1,735	2,432
1980	1,181	994	1,126	89	1,215	613	555	427	107	14	163	49	272	1,862	2,179
1981	1,538	1,295	1,419	125	1,544	592	447	331	151	24	170	151	277	2,025	2,292
1982	1,147	941	1,050	176	1,227	518	525	258	195	31	248	268	233	1,658	1,761
1983	1,038	888	1,028	154	1,182	449	675	460	50	81	371	154	174	1,804	2,014
1984	1,103	990	1,090	75	1,165	461	552	445	69	91	251	122	245	2,123	2,107
1985[1]	1,106	942	1,004	54	1,057	503	444	378	130	38	109	311	146	1,906	2,153
1986[9]	1,150	900			1,055		500			15	80	200	120	2,000	2,150

[1] Preliminary.   [2] Also from matte, etc., refinery reports.   [3] For consumption.   [4] Blister (copper content)."   [5] Ingots, bars, etc.   [6] Withdrawals from total supply on domestic account.   [7] From old scrap only.   [8] Old scrap only.   [9] Estimate.   *Source: Bureau of Mines*   T.133

Consumption of Refined Copper[2] in the United States   In Thousands of Metric[4] Tons

Year	Cathodes	By-Products Wire Bars	Ingot & Ingot Bars	Cakes & Slabs	Billets	Other	By Class of Consumer Wire Mills	Brass Mills	Chemical Plants	Secondary Smelters	Foundries	Miscellaneous	Total Consumption
1975	527.9	722.8	72.5	97.7	75.7	4.1	1,061.3	439.0	.5	4.5	14.0	15.3	1,534.5
1976	846.0	768.0	93.5	123.8	84.0	8.6	1,346.0	574.9	.5	3.1	15.4	19.7	1,991.9
1977	965.5	861.3	90.2	115.0	103.3	11.2	1,511.2	628.6	N.A.	6.6	N.A.	N.A.	2,185.0
1978[4]	1,026.1	794.7	111.9	117.1	114.6	24.9	1,517.4	619.2	.4	7.5	12.4	32.3	2,189.3
1979	1,099.0	701.9	92.1	105.6	129.5	30.4	1,499.6	610.2	.4	6.3	11.9	30.1	2,158.4
1980	960.2	583.0	67.6	84.3	117.4	49.7	1,308.9	511.6	.3	5.0	10.9	25.3	1,862.1
1981	1,198.9	489.2	66.7	121.8	101.9	46.7	1,449.6	536.2	.4	5.4	11.3	22.2	2,025.2
1982	1,211.0	195.1	45.1	92.4	82.2	32.4	1,232.8	393.2	.4	4.4	7.6	19.7	1,658.1
1983	1,448.1	77.4	53.2	115.3	101.8	8.2	1,269.9	500.3	.6	3.2	11.3	18.8	1,803.9
1984[1]	1,635.4	72.1	74.4	127.7	118.5	8.2	1,416.3	578.1	.6	6.9	16.0	18.2	2,122.7
1985[3]							1,378.6	485.3		—————41.7—————			1,905.6

[1] Preliminary.   [2] Primary & secondary.   [3] Estimate.   [4] Data prior to 1978 are in thousands of short tons.   *Source: Bureau of Mines*

T.134

U.S. Mine Production of Recoverable Copper, by Selected States   In Thousands of Metric Tons

Year	Arizona	California	Colorado	Idaho	Michigan	Missouri	Montana	Nevada	New Mexico	Pennsylvania	Tennessee	Utah	Maine	Other States[2]	Total
1976	929.3	.3	2.2	3.1	39.7	10.0	82.7	52.8	156.4	—	10.1	168.2	1.6	.2	1,456.6
1977	838.0	.2	1.7	3.7	38.4	10.6	78.2	60.8	149.4	—	5.6	176.1	1.2	.3	1,304.4
1978	891.4	N.A.	1.2	3.9	N.A.	10.8	67.3	20.5	127.8	—	11.3	186.3	—	37.1	1,357.6
1979	949.0	N.A.	.4	3.6	N.A.	13.0	69.9	N.A.	164.3	—	N.A.	193.1	—	53.3	1,446.6
1980	770.1	N.A.	.5	3.1	N.A.	13.6	37.7	N.A.	149.4	—	N.A.	157.8	—	48.9	1,181.1
1981	1,040.8	N.A.	N.A.	4.2	N.A.	8.4	62.5	N.A.	154.1	—	N.A.	211.3	—	56.8	1,538.2
1982	769.5	N.A.	.6	3.1	N.A.	7.9	65.0	N.A.	N.A.	—	N.A.	189.1	—	111.8	1,147.0
1983	678.2	N.A.	N.A.	3.6	—	7.7	33.3	N.A.	N.A.	—	N.A.	169.8	—	145.5	1,038.1
1984	746.5	N.A.	N.A.	3.7	—	5.8	N.A.	N.A.	N.A.	—	N.A.	N.A.	—	317.6	1,091.3
1985[1]	796.6			3.6		13.4	15.1							277.1	1,105.8
1986[3]	800.0					20.0								330.0	1,150.0

[1] Preliminary.   [2] Also includes N.A. States.   [3] Estimate.   *Source: Bureau of Mines*   T.135

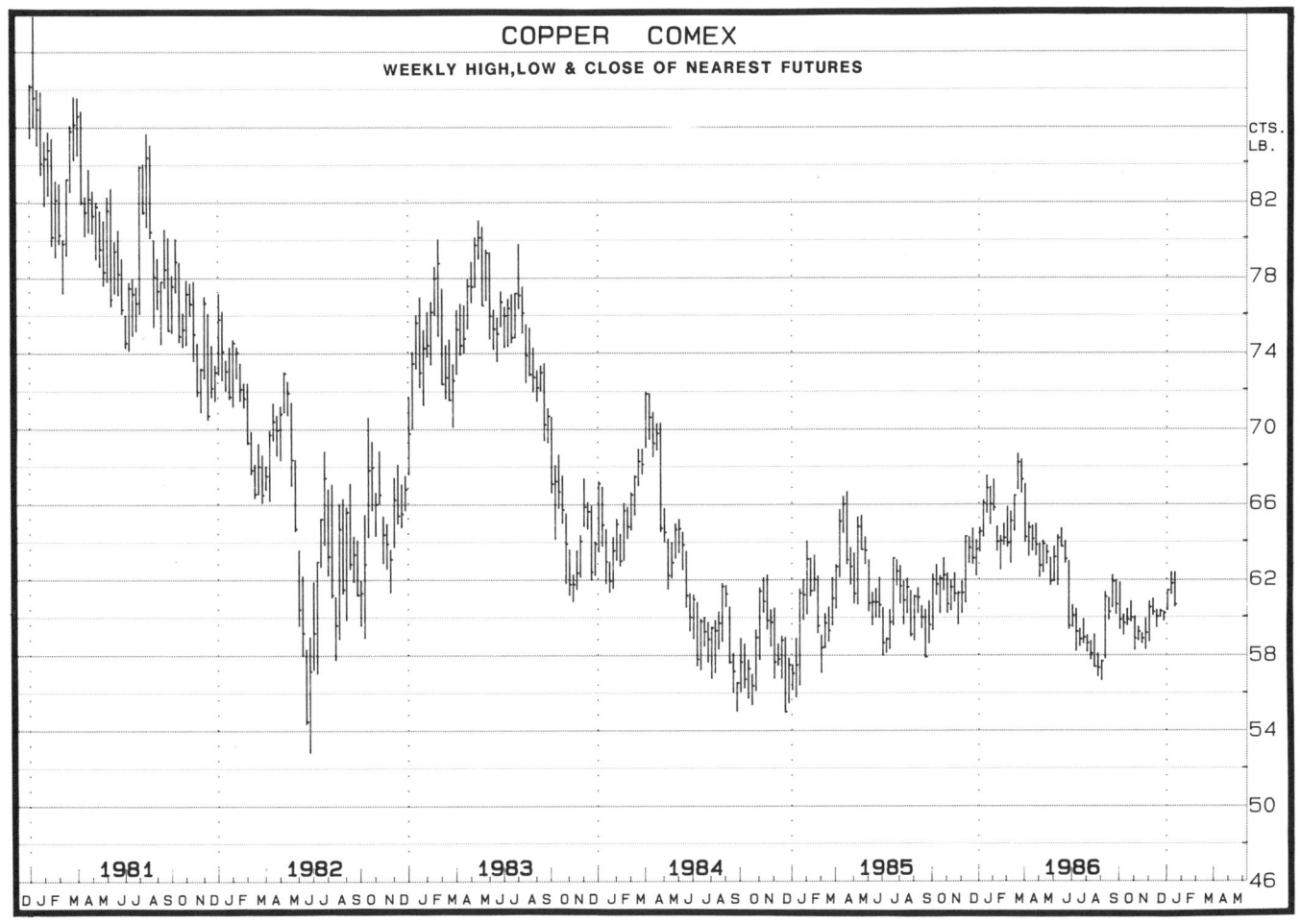

COPPER COMEX
WEEKLY HIGH, LOW & CLOSE OF NEAREST FUTURES

High, Low & Closing Prices of May Copper Futures on the Commodity Exch., Inc., N.Y. (COMEX) ¢ Lb.

Year of Delivery		Mar.	Apr.	May	June	July	Aug.	Sept.	Oct.	Nov.	Dec.	Jan.	Feb.	Mar.	Apr.	May	Life of Delivery Range
1981	High	135.00	105.50	101.90	100.00	107.70	103.90	106.80	102.00	100.00	96.80	94.20	87.95	88.30	87.40	81.85	153.00
	Low	98.40	93.60	94.00	90.40	97.20	92.00	94.00	97.20	94.90	82.30	84.75	81.80	79.30	80.10	77.50	77.50
	Close	99.20	100.50	98.40	97.80	99.00	94.35	97.30	98.10	96.20	89.20	87.00	82.55	86.40	81.15	77.85	—
1982	High	100.00	99.65	96.00	94.10	92.80	95.50	87.40	84.90	81.70	80.50	77.70	76.25	71.75	71.25	72.90	115.20
	Low	92.80	94.00	91.35	86.70	85.20	85.80	79.80	79.40	74.85	74.00	73.00	71.10	66.70	66.10	66.65	66.10
	Close	98.85	95.20	93.20	86.80	93.10	87.45	82.10	81.65	77.35	77.30	76.35	71.10	67.55	70.00	66.70	—
1983	High	82.25	81.20	82.70	71.30	75.60	72.00	71.90	71.50	70.85	72.65	77.95	81.45	78.40	78.70	80.90	108.30
	Low	77.00	76.80	73.00	60.80	65.35	63.25	62.40	62.00	64.30	67.00	71.00	75.00	70.80	73.80	76.70	62.00
	Close	78.00	80.70	72.60	67.60	68.65	67.20	62.95	67.95	68.90	70.70	76.60	75.20	75.15	77.40	78.05	—
1984	High	85.40	86.00	87.60	83.80	85.05	83.00	78.95	71.70	70.65	69.40	68.10	67.30	71.80	71.75	65.65	88.60
	Low	78.05	81.70	83.70	80.25	80.60	77.30	69.80	64.90	64.00	64.60	62.50	63.90	65.60	63.90	61.40	61.40
	Close	82.60	84.30	84.80	81.25	82.45	77.60	70.25	66.10	69.15	68.30	65.70	66.10	71.75	64.45	64.55	—
1985	High	71.80	79.10	73.35	71.75	67.10	66.60	65.15	62.75	62.70	60.90	64.40	64.20	63.15	66.55	65.30	92.00
	Low	65.60	72.00	69.10	65.35	61.80	62.00	58.90	58.45	59.05	56.40	56.20	57.95	59.10	60.80	60.60	56.20
	Close	71.75	72.40	70.95	67.35	61.90	66.05	60.55	62.75	59.85	57.85	63.15	59.60	62.60	60.95	62.20	—
1986	High	65.65	68.50	68.00	64.35	66.15	64.70	62.90	63.85	63.45	65.35	68.00	67.50	69.15	66.30	63.95	69.15
	Low	62.80	63.55	63.00	61.65	61.50	61.60	60.00	61.15	60.80	61.60	64.50	64.55	63.60	62.15	61.60	60.00
	Close	65.65	63.55	63.95	62.00	63.45	63.05	60.55	61.50	62.10	64.45	67.15	66.05	66.15	62.25	62.85	—
1987	High	70.00	67.75	65.55	65.50	62.10	60.95	63.45	61.55	61.85	62.00						
	Low	66.00	63.80	63.65	61.30	59.90	58.60	57.75	59.25	59.65	60.40						
	Close	68.00	63.80	64.35	61.60	60.10	59.40	61.80	59.80	61.55	61.75						

Source: Commodity Exchange, Inc. of N.Y. (COMEX)

T.141

COPPER

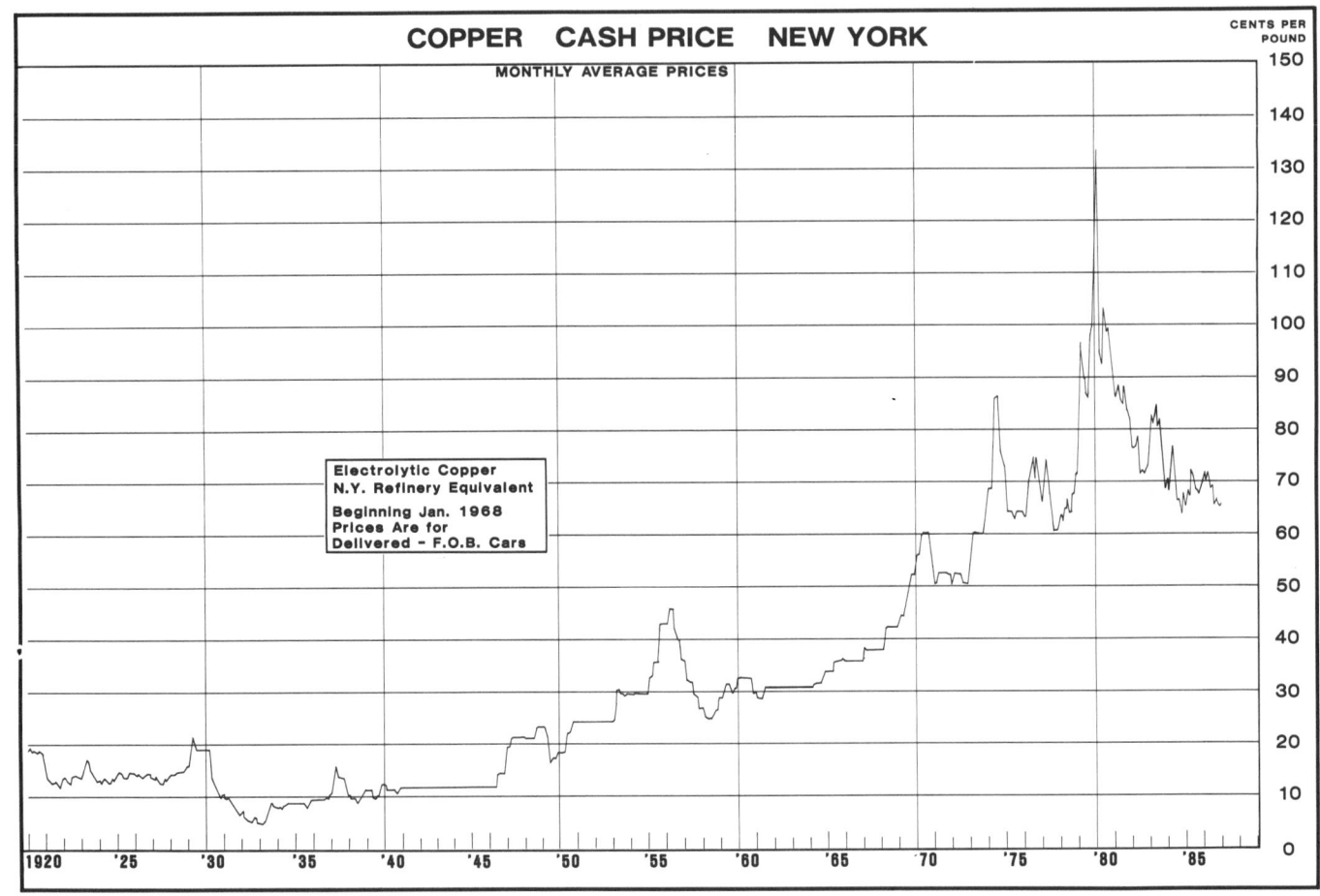

COPPER CASH PRICE NEW YORK

MONTHLY AVERAGE PRICES

CENTS PER POUND

Electrolytic Copper
N.Y. Refinery Equivalent

Beginning Jan. 1968
Prices Are for
Delivered – F.O.B. Cars

Producers' Prices of Electrolytic (Wirebar) Copper, Delivered U.S. Destinations   In Cents Per Pound

Year	Jan.	Feb.	Mar.	Apr.	May	June	July	Aug.	Sept.	Oct.	Nov.	Dec.	Average
1977	66.13	68.63	72.54	74.41	72.77	70.13	68.10	63.89	60.63	60.63	60.63	62.11	66.72
1978	63.63	63.59	62.35	64.63	64.90	66.78	63.99	67.34	67.63	70.13	71.68	71.73	66.53
1979	76.15	89.41	94.65	98.66	91.04	87.66	86.02	89.94	95.07	98.84	98.44	106.08	92.75
1980	118.05	133.83	106.23	94.61	93.16	92.39	103.10	100.60	98.73	99.41	96.98	89.20	102.19
1981	88.64	86.07	87.32	88.44	86.33	85.68	84.71	87.98	85.63	83.28	82.09	80.94	85.59
1982	79.42	79.35	76.45	76.99	78.78	71.43	71.78	71.83	71.37	71.92	72.28	73.17	74.56
1983	79.03	82.72	81.09	82.44	84.80	80.90	81.81	79.80	76.75	71.58	68.64	70.43	78.33
1984	69.08	69.51	74.18	76.58	71.56	69.19	66.34	66.44	65.39	63.92	67.71	65.28	68.77
1985	66.23	68.32	67.19	72.17	71.89	68.86	68.53	68.32	67.66	68.60	68.37	70.10	68.85
1986	71.57	70.21	71.78	70.55	68.69	69.15	65.47		66.82	65.61	65.06	65.91	67.91

Source: American Metal Market   T.136

Month-End Open Interest of Copper Futures at COMEX   In Contracts

Year	Jan.	Feb.	Mar.	Apr.	May	June	July	Aug.	Sept.	Oct.	Nov.	Dec.
1979	53,776	56,481	55,719	48,857	45,572	43,992	39,372	58,966	63,825	58,451	62,659	64,363
1980	63,132	60,834	41,546	31,618	31,923	32,454	37,303	38,497	46,737	54,201	52,666	44,225
1981	47,300	47,641	48,699	49,784	52,527	52,325	54,011	54,781	57,153	58,054	52,654	52,226
1982	56,469	60,458	62,817	67,700	74,353	65,938	66,049	64,615	69,845	79,365	85,824	92,146
1983	113,044	121,875	116,706	105,451	99,198	101,350	109,829	106,882	108,357	104,204	104,087	106,898
1984	115,648	100,663	107,730	96,293	92,254	82,836	82,946	84,991	83,606	88,418	83,433	86,502
1985	94,398	82,182	82,195	85,676	82,369	84,913	78,227	75,187	77,106	75,868	76,106	77,790
1986	89,213	79,497	91,606	73,828	71,286	65,698	62,060	60,118	65,370	70,396	74,353	77,988

Source: Commodity Exchange, Inc. of N.Y. (COMEX)   T.142

U.S. Imports (for Consumption) of Copper (Unmanufactured), by Sources and Types
In Thousands of Metric Tons

Year	Ore & Concentrates	Blister	Matte	Refined	Scrap	Australia	Canada	Mexico	W. Germany	Chile	Peru	Philippines	Yugoslavia	Zaire	Zambia	South Africa	Total U.S. Imports
1978	20.9	78.7	10.7	414.7	21.4	10.0	77.3	5.8	8.5	175.8	94.8	12.0	10.9	1.8	79.8	15.5	546.4
1979	22.4	68.1	.4	215.2	22.2	2.1	89.0	8.5	6.1	116.2	52.8	15.4	3.4	1.5	15.9	2.0	328.3
1980[2]	52.4	44.5	.4	426.9	22.8	5.4	152.4	8.3	.5	126.6	52.5	8.9	4.5	5.0	64.9	2.2	547.0
1981	39.1	30.1	2.7	330.6	27.0	1.5	108.5	23.8	—	137.8	52.0	20.4	2.4	24.7	44.1	—	429.6
1982	118.1	97.4	4.1	258.4	28.1	3.7	111.0	64.4	—	233.0	26.8	27.1	—	19.6	10.5	—	506.0
1983	90.6	46.4	3.3	459.6	23.1	—	153.8	44.7	—	292.4	38.9	11.4	—	29.1	24.7	14.0	622.9
1984[1]	11.1	38.9	2.1	444.7	23.0	3.8	177.6	9.5	—	149.4	63.0	6.7	—	28.0	59.5	.5	519.8
1985[3]	2.9	13.0	4.0	377.7	44.2												441.7
1986[3]	3.7			470.0													

Note: Includes refined; black, blister, & converter; scrap; & copper content of ore, matte, and regulus. [1] Preliminary. [2] Prior to 1980, data are for general imports. [3] Estimate. *Source: Department of Commerce; Bureau of Mines* T.137

United States Exports of Refined Copper[1] to Selected Countries   In Thousands of Metric Tons

Year	Total U.S. Exports	United Kingdom	China Mainland	Belgium	Brazil	Canada	France	W. Germany	India	Italy	Netherlands	Taiwan	Sweden	Mexico	Japan
1978	91.9	13.8	3.0	2.5	3.3	5.1	7.0	18.1	—	19.0	3.0	.9	4.2	1.0	10.0
1979	73.7	6.5	3.1	2.5	6.2	4.5	12.5	3.5	—	11.4	6.6	1.2	2.8	.5	2.0
1980	14.5	2.0	—	.6	1.5	2.9	1.9	.8	.1	1.4	.6	.3	.1	.9	.8
1981	24.4	1.3	—	—	.8	6.4	1.1	1.1	—	.7	—	—	—	7.2	3.9
1982	30.6	1.3	16.1		.4	2.8	1.1	1.9	.1	.1	3.3	—	—	—	.8
1983	81.4	.4	2.2	.7	—	1.7	.6	2.2	—	—	60.6	1.0	.1	5.3	5.7
1984	91.4	.7	.1	—	—	2.9	.8	1.2	—	—	6.4	3.2	—	2.8	71.2
1985[2]	37.9	.7	—	.5	—	3.5	.3	1.3			17.3	1.5		4.2	5.0
1986[3]	15.0	2.3				4.0	.5	1.3							

[1] Bars, ingots or other forms. [2] Preliminary. [3] Estimate. *Source: Department of Commerce* T.138

Dealers' Buying Price of No. 2 Heavy Copper Scrap at N.Y.   In Cents Per Pound

Year	Jan.	Feb.	Mar.	Apr.	May	June	July	Aug.	Sept.	Oct.	Nov.	Dec.	Average
1976	36.98	37.92	39.76	41.95	44.10	43.66	46.93	45.73	43.71	38.48	35.00	34.10	40.69
1977	34.00	35.73	41.50	40.63	39.62	35.91	35.00	34.04	33.00	33.00	33.00	33.00	34.23
1978	34.00	35.61	35.59	39.73	39.18	41.77	40.50	41.89	42.50	44.70	45.40	44.75	40.47
1979	47.07	58.82	65.46	68.93	63.14	59.05	57.79	58.85	62.03	62.89	62.25	65.00	60.94
1980	74.91	82.35	70.30	60.18	57.60	56.50	65.36	64.88	64.21	65.37	66.08	58.36	65.51
1981	57.60	55.50	57.14	59.50	58.20	55.32	52.68	53.50	53.00	50.16	48.08	46.00	53.89
1982	57.43	57.20	53.76	53.99	53.38	43.24	47.12	46.49	47.83	48.79	48.61	50.75	50.73
1983	42.55	46.71	51.50	51.50	53.74	54.50	54.50	53.54	51.74	48.12	43.30	42.50	49.52
1984	41.17	40.60	43.59	44.50	43.30	42.21	39.36	38.50	38.08	36.20	34.50	35.67	39.81
1985	37.50	37.50	37.50	37.50	37.50	37.50	37.50	37.50	37.50	37.50	37.50	37.50	37.50
1986	38.23	39.50	39.50	39.50	39.50	39.50	39.50	37.79	37.50	37.50	37.50	37.50	38.59

Source: American Metal Market T.140

Volume of Trading of Copper Futures at COMEX   In Contracts

Year	Jan.	Feb.	Mar.	Apr.	May	June	July	Aug.	Sept.	Oct.	Nov.	Dec.	Total
1978	75,219	88,765	119,423	112,834	117,745	135,363	98,274	160,456	95,360	158,815	151,284	95,150	1,408,688
1979	154,378	228,837	234,044	234,554	212,934	186,097	139,912	210,387	208,869	200,123	163,074	145,732	2,301,033
1980	243,069	205,232	185,692	121,708	102,054	130,678	148,698	125,062	169,370	132,850	127,110	156,556	7,848,080
1981	116,295	131,960	143,662	140,605	104,376	158,396	125,109	190,763	148,456	114,960	144,453	128,345	1,647,380
1982	112,118	166,562	135,434	179,854	174,157	249,276	197,828	245,973	169,909	231,771	273,546	226,257	2,362,625
1983	306,001	381,645	320,574	278,655	226,482	309,540	213,832	295,470	188,201	230,063	289,111	147,340	3,186,914
1984	199,461	259,881	217,635	269,765	196,382	223,551	152,424	215,226	149,465	170,568	279,151	172,856	2,514,311
1985	254,052	261,784	167,686	310,487	215,079	209,506	146,396	195,882	138,803	178,728	200,142	166,007	2,444,552
1986	190,983	206,513	197,818	240,770	106,750	200,547	89,818	145,468	123,779	121,361	162,963	85,439	1,872,209

Source: Commodity Exchange, Inc. of N.Y. (COMEX) T.143

COPPER

Exports of Refined Copper from the United States   In Thousands of Short Tons

Year	Jan.	Feb.	Mar.	Apr.	May	June	July	Aug.	Sept.	Oct.	Nov.	Dec.	Total
1975	19.7	20.8	14.3	24.9	21.3	13.5	9.8	6.7	11.5	12.5	9.0	8.4	172.4
1976	11.2	8.5	10.8	10.9	8.6	9.4	8.7	9.4	10.0	11.5	7.3	6.8	113.1
1977	3.7	1.8	3.6	5.2	5.2	5.2	5.5	1.6	4.4	4.6	5.0	6.9	52.7
1978	4.7	4.9	11.9	7.3	11.4	10.1	7.2	10.2	22.2	5.3	5.3	8.8	109.3
1979	9.8	9.4	11.6	10.0	8.9	8.7	4.8	2.9	2.9	2.7	7.3	1.5	88.7
1980	1.0	1.4	1.9	1.5	1.5	2.0	1.9	.9	.4	.5	1.0	3.4	17.2
1981	2.9	2.5	5.8	1.2	.9	3.5	1.3	1.7	3.0	.7	2.1	1.8	28.1
1982	.4	.6	.9	1.0	1.6	1.6	2.9	5.4	9.9	8.6	.8	1.1	35.0
1983	13.4	.7	1.5	2.0	3.2	2.9	18.1	13.4	4.1	14.2	2.8	11.2	87.5
1984	17.5	14.4	8.9	6.8	14.7	1.6	14.0	2.3	2.2	1.9	2.8	6.9	93.9
1985[1]	2.0	3.3	7.7	3.7	1.3	3.9	5.7	6.3	1.0	1.3	.9	1.1	48.1
1986[1]	1.3	1.5	1.2	1.0	2.4	.9	.8	1.8	1.7	.6			

[1] Preliminary.   Source: Department of Commerce

T.139

Refined Copper Stocks in the U.S.A.   In Thousands of Short Tons (Recoverable Copper Content)

Year	Jan. 1	Feb. 1	Mar. 1	Apr. 1	May 1	June 1	July 1	Aug. 1	Sept. 1	Oct. 1	Nov. 1	Dec. 1
1975	194.9	242.7	259.2	297.8	320.6	334.6	338.2	349.5	341.8	312.3	314.9	324.6
1976	360.7	363.4	370.9	347.8	343.0	325.2	317.1	350.4	355.8	356.1	372.8	416.5
1977	473.8	469.3	487.0	472.3	442.1	447.6	435.0	408.9	370.6	409.4	418.0	456.9
1978	471.1	488.7	491.6	470.2	480.5	465.5	464.0	430.9	418.0	405.9	416.4	408.9
1979	367.0	318.4	287.5	262.1	237.4	197.8	176.0	174.6	158.0	154.6	148.6	167.3
1980	186.3	203.5	228.2	237.1	269.1	277.3	295.7	310.6	301.0	274.6	265.0	246.0
1981	253.0	261.6	249.4	236.8	245.5	243.4	264.7	276.9	276.0	275.5	281.6	301.2
1982	338.6	351.9	375.9	387.3	409.8	422.5	448.1	463.7	449.9	436.2	438.2	470.8
1983	484.5	489.6	501.6	508.9	524.1	519.4	498.7	509.0	522.7	509.1	514.2	505.2
1984	475.3	497.8	499.6	483.3	478.3	463.4	483.2	493.4	490.7	467.1	475.2	457.3
1985	469.7	452.9	380.9	368.2	358.4	363.2	344.1	331.4	310.9	275.7	257.3	264.1
1986[1]	270.7	271.0	261.6	242.0	231.1	201.4	188.0	209.6	214.4	188.1	189.0	211.3
1987[1]	238.7											

[1] Preliminary.   Source: American Bureau of Metal Statistics, Inc.

T.145

Refined Copper Stocks Outside the U.S.A.   In Thousands of Short Tons (Recoverable Copper Content)

Year	Jan. 1	Feb. 1	Mar. 1	Apr. 1	May 1	June 1	July 1	Aug. 1	Sept. 1	Oct. 1	Nov. 1	Dec. 1
1975	591.2	628.8	624.5	655.8	723.1	766.0	784.7	861.5	933.4	1,007	1,072	1,108
1976	1,135	1,150	1,149	1,086	1,048	1,045	1,040	1,080	1,112	1,102	1,102	1,141
1977	1,117	1,158	1,200	1,166	1,183	1,185	1,195	1,210	1,229	1,247	1,240	1,225
1978	1,201	1,231	1,139	1,139	1,104	1,099	1,052	1,059	1,001	960.2	962.0	963.1
1979	942.2	878.2	862.4	765.1	758.8	756.7	727.2	687.1	696.6	648.2	635.4	641.3
1980	619.5	598.3	560.9	534.6	516.5	525.9	531.2	530.9	553.2	527.9	489.1	472.6
1981	476.2	485.2	471.0	463.0	458.8	449.8	446.0	454.9	454.7	433.4	419.4	403.0
1982	432.5	446.3	448.4	459.6	452.0	458.7	479.3	492.0	503.6	522.7	575.1	642.9
1983	699.9	760.8	766.4	759.1	795.5	780.0	722.2	683.0	757.4	767.2	765.2	810.4
1984	832.5	817.5	730.0	653.0	618.5	519.3	551.9	526.5	516.0	493.9	483.9	430.0
1985	425.0	420.7	385.7	361.9	364.6	380.4	368.8	464.0	546.7	558.4	533.6	486.6
1986[1]	502.8	501.3	447.9	435.9	423.1	422.0	399.2	422.7	453.7	450.7	464.2	462.0

[1] Preliminary.   Source: American Bureau of Metal Statistics, Inc.

T.150

Refined Copper Production Outside the U.S.A. In Thousands of Short Tons (Recoverable Copper Content)

Year	Jan.	Feb.	Mar.	Apr.	May	June	Refined July	Aug.	Sept.	Oct.	Nov.	Dec.	Total	Crude Primary	Secondary
1977	358.1	352.1	380.2	363.0	383.5	386.7	361.7	379.7	372.0	367.4	388.5	393.5	4,486	—5,046—	
1978	387.3	344.0	395.9	348.7	401.9	388.1	371.9	348.4	350.0	381.9	364.5	351.5	4,434	—4,868—	
1979	359.8	347.9	360.1	336.9	345.1	364.9	358.1	377.2	366.5	400.9	388.0	382.6	4,388	—4,791—	
1980	384.2	382.8	408.4	398.3	418.7	396.8	392.2	402.9	386.1	394.4	371.8	389.9	4,727	—4,968—	
1981	359.7	347.9	393.6	390.0	388.0	391.4	377.0	377.7	378.8	379.9	366.9	393.8	4,545	—4,891—	
1982	398.2	381.0	442.6	391.8	365.2	403.9	368.4	365.8	386.1	405.8	411.8	372.6	4,693	—5,065—	
1983	386.8	366.3	411.8	400.0	401.2	418.0	381.9	404.3	395.9	404.5	393.1	409.5	4,773	—5,201—	
1984	380.3	376.9	412.4	375.1	374.1	382.5	357.4	381.5	373.8	405.2	380.8	358.7	4,559	—5,114—	
1985	371.6	338.8	388.5	376.1	377.4	351.4	384.2	385.6	380.4	387.6	385.5	394.9	4,522	—5,217—	
1986[1]	366.3	349.4	398.7	409.8	384.0	355.5	368.8	384.2	398.0	402.2	384.0				

[1] Preliminary.   *Source: American Bureau of Metal Statistics, Inc.*   T.148

Refined Copper Production in the U.S.A. In Thousands of Short Tons (Recoverable Copper Content)

Year	Jan.	Feb.	Mar.	Apr.	May	June	Refined July	Aug.	Sept.	Oct.	Nov.	Dec.	Total	Crude Primary	Secondary
1977	140.9	140.9	162.3	150.6	166.2	152.4	52.2	46.3	124.4	120.6	137.3	113.0	1,507	—1,386—	
1978	129.0	112.5	143.2	141.0	145.3	135.1	96.1	138.9	144.9	163.4	162.4	133.3	1,645	—1,434—	
1979	135.6	135.8	152.2	149.8	154.6	149.4	132.3	144.9	137.5	148.7	170.0	155.5	1,766	—1,542—	
1980	161.0	149.5	162.3	170.4	158.7	167.2	52.4	28.7	27.3	61.0	85.8	136.9	1,361	—1,205—	
1981	133.5	116.3	152.2	155.8	135.0	158.3	131.7	124.0	140.5	127.3	124.9	147.9	1,647	—1,429—	
1982	117.5	123.4	121.5	116.4	107.5	108.6	81.8	77.6	80.6	80.1	92.1	90.8	1,198	—1,026—	
1983	97.3	100.6	131.9	125.5	112.2	114.5	73.1	90.6	91.2	110.4	89.1	100.2	1,237	—1,077—	
1984	98.8	100.7	117.1	120.5	127.9	125.6	123.0	126.1	101.8	119.5	95.4	101.4	1,358	—1,270—	
1985	113.5	101.2	118.8	122.4	124.1	100.8	99.9	96.8	93.0	112.9	119.7	106.7	1,310	—1,387—	
1986[1]	109.5	98.3	103.5	115.0	122.4	112.1	109.3	108.9	106.7	114.4	116.6	137.4	1,354	—1,325—	

[1] Preliminary.   *Source: American Bureau of Metal Statistics, Inc.*   T.149

Refined Copper Deliveries to Fabricators in the U.S.A.
In Ths. of Short Tons (Recoverable Copper Content)

Year	Jan.	Feb.	Mar.	Apr.	May	June	July	Aug.	Sept.	Oct.	Nov.	Dec.	Total
1977	166.6	138.2	202.0	195.6	185.3	192.4	104.5	100.6	100.5	145.7	135.9	141.0	1,808
1978	137.7	141.3	190.2	148.7	175.9	159.8	133.4	168.9	179.2	170.4	177.7	179.7	1,963
1979	191.1	174.8	193.5	182.4	204.7	192.4	166.4	179.3	157.4	190.4	161.4	156.7	2,151
1980	173.5	153.7	193.5	167.8	176.3	175.0	98.7	85.0	83.7	106.6	128.7	154.5	1,697
1981	153.0	154.2	196.5	165.1	169.1	158.8	150.6	152.7	157.5	159.5	131.6	131.2	1,880
1982	134.6	112.2	131.5	114.2	121.0	111.4	106.2	110.6	131.8	113.3	78.4	119.2	1,384
1983	126.2	141.1	185.3	156.0	165.9	164.4	91.0	105.2	141.2	137.1	110.2	145.3	1,669
1984	118.3	146.1	185.7	184.4	190.7	163.8	150.7	159.3	166.0	167.1	151.5	124.2	1,906
1985	170.2	188.7	159.8	153.0	144.3	135.2	122.3	130.0	153.3	151.5	137.9	120.7	1,767
1986[1]	123.8	120.1	146.1	155.2	173.8	136.0	112.3	126.4	160.1	133.8	113.9	124.8	1,626

[1] Preliminary.   *Source: American Bureau of Metal Statistics, Inc.*   T.147

Refined Copper Deliveries to Fabricators Outside the U.S.A.
In Ths. of Short Tons (Recoverable Copper Content)

Year	Jan.	Feb.	Mar.	Apr.	May	June	July	Aug.	Sept.	Oct.	Nov.	Dec.	Total
1977	331.6	305.6	405.0	342.6	364.9	360.0	326.5	344.9	339.8	350.7	374.0	390.8	4,236
1978	338.5	370.0	422.6	372.1	400.8	426.0	362.4	402.9	382.7	376.8	360.2	376.8	4,592
1979	424.2	395.9	460.4	342.0	349.1	383.3	376.8	346.7	408.5	390.2	377.6	386.4	4,658
1980	386.2	403.2	400.0	407.6	396.9	376.6	357.3	346.7	389.5	406.5	374.4	375.8	4,653
1981	336.8	353.7	383.2	385.4	380.8	382.7	346.0	355.9	393.4	369.5	373.9	364.5	4,426
1982	373.4	380.1	423.6	387.4	348.3	365.4	341.4	342.8	354.9	343.5	331.3	301.6	4,294
1983	303.2	322.9	371.1	325.7	392.2	454.4	407.4	308.3	360.7	389.4	350.2	397.4	4,383
1984	375.0	448.8	477.8	377.1	453.1	358.8	372.5	371.5	382.7	394.6	420.7	360.6	4,793
1985	356.6	372.1	408.2	369.8	379.8	395.9	300.4	319.9	384.6	422.0	419.6	375.9	4,505
1986[1]	364.5	398.5	397.8	403.1	374.4	378.6	349.0	337.9	377.8	376.6	377.8		

[1] Preliminary.   *Source: American Bureau of Metal Statistics, Inc.*   T.146

Corn

1986/87 world coarse grains production (corn, sorghum, barley, oats, millet, mixed grains) is projected by USDA at 830.4 million tonnes, down two percent from last season. 1985/85 production was a record 847.5 tonnes. Corn is the world's most widely produced coarse grain; world production in 1986/87 is placed at 479 million tonnes, down less than one percent from last year's record. The U.S. is still the largest producer; its market share of 44 percent is down from 47 percent last season. China is the second-largest producer, with 15 percent of the market, and is followed by Eastern Europe.

World corn utilization continues in an uptrend, as countries make improvements in diet. USDA projected 1986/87 global corn use at 438.5 million tonnes, up almost four percent from a year ago. The U.S. takes almost 31 percent of the world total.

World trade is estimated at 56.4 million tonnes, up over four percent from a year ago. Most of the increase is accounted for by the U.S., where exports will improve some. Argentina and South Africa are also expected to increase exports. Among the major importers, Japan is projected to purchase 15.6 million tonnes, an increase of six percent from a year ago. Soviet production and imports remain key variables in the world grain outlook; grain production this season has been larger than estimates. Coarse grain production is estimated by USDA at 108 million tonnes, up eight percent from a year ago. The Soviets continue to upgrade diets by increasing livestock production; imports will decline with larger crops. Coarse grain imports are placed at 8 million tons, down 42 percent from a year ago.

1986/87 world carryover stocks are projected by USDA to reach a record 163.1 million tonnes, up 33 percent from a year ago. Over 87 percent of world stocks will be held by the U.S.

U.S. corn production in 1986/87 was 8.22 billion bushels, down seven percent from last year's record crop. Planted acreage was 76.6 million acres, eight percent less than a year ago, while harvested acreage totaled 69 million. Record participation in the government's acreage reduction program contributed to the decline in plantings. Producers left marginal acreage idle and the national average yield reached a new record of over 119 bushels per acre, despite devastating drought in the Southeast. Corn yields have been higher for several years and show no signs yet of leveling off.

Despite the decline in production, record carry-in stocks of 4.04 billion bushels mean total supply this season is a record 12.3 billion bushels, 16 percent more than a year ago. Domestic corn use is projected by USDA to reach 5.35 billion bushels, a small increase from last season. Usage of corn has been trending mostly sideways since 1980. Feeding is the largest source of disappearance, accounting for an average 60 percent of total use. This season, feeding is estimated by USDA at 4.2 billion bushels or about 65 percent of total use. Poultry production is expected to expand as consumers continue to switch out of red meats. Offsetting this is reduced production of hogs, though profitable feeding ratios could mean future herd expansion. The impact of the new tax laws on cattle feeding remains a question. Corn used for food, seed, and industrial purposes is expected to increase almost two percent to 1.15 billion bushels. In recent years, the growth rate in this sector has been very high, due primarily to increased use of corn sweeteners. Corn has also found a use in ethanol production to boost octane ratings in gasoline. Future growth in these industries is expected to be slower as market saturation is reached.

U.S. corn exports in 1986/87 are projected by USDA to decline nine percent to 1.125 billion bushels; exports have been trending lower since 1979/80. The primary reason is the larger grain crop in the Soviet Union. The major export outlets for U.S. corn are Japan, USSR, Taiwan, Spain and Mexico. Competition remains intense as exporters like Argentina and South Africa seek to increase market share. Additional competition will come from ample world supplies of feed grade wheat and barley. With a larger crop, the Soviet Union may opt to purchase only minimal amounts of U.S. corn.

Total use is estimated at 6.47 billion bushels, about the same as a year ago. Corn stocks at August 31, 1987, are projected at 5.79 billion bushels, 43 percent more than a year ago and a record carryout. Much of the crop should be entered in the loan program. While this will reduce free stocks, extensive use of generic certificates in lieu of cash payments will free up some supplies.

U.S. Government Price Support

The price support loan rate for 1987 is $1.82; the target price is $3.03. In 1986, the price support was $1.92, while the target price was $3.03. To qualify for program benefits, producers must reduce base acreage by 20 percent. A paid diversion on an additional 15 percent of acreage is optional.

Futures Markets

Corn futures and options trade on the Chicago Board of Trade (CBOT); futures are also traded on the MidAmerica Commodity Exchange (MidAm).

World Production of Corn or Maize   In Millions of Metric Tons

Crop Year	United States	Agrentina	Brazil	Mexico	South Africa	France	China	India	Italy	Bulgaria	Hungary	Yugoslavia	Romania	Indonesia	USSR	World Total
1982-3	209.2	9.0	19.5	7.0	4.1	10.4	60.3	6.5	6.8	3.4	7.8	11.1	12.6	3.2	14.7	439.9
1983-4	106.0	9.2	21.0	9.3	4.4	10.4	68.2	7.9	6.7	3.3	6.5	10.7	12.0	5.1	13.3	347.5
1984-5[1]	194.9	11.5	22.0	9.9	7.8	10.0	73.4	7.2	6.9	3.1	6.5	11.0	11.0	4.0	13.6	458.3
1985-6[2]	225.2	12.3	20.0	10.5	8.0		63.8								14.4	481.6
1986-7[2]	208.8	12.5	22.5	10.0	9.0		70.0								16.5	479.0

[1] Preliminary.   [2] Estimated.   *Source: Foreign Agricultural Service, U.S.D.A.*   T.151

World Coarse Grains Supply & Demand   In Millions of Metric Tons/Hectares

Crop Year	Area Harvested	Yield	Production	World Trade[1]	Utilization Total[2]	Ending Stks[3]	Stocks as % of Util
1980/81	342.4	2.14	732.9	108.0	745.1	90.6	12.2
1981/82	349.9	2.19	766.0	96.6	737.7	120.7	16.4
1982/83	339.7	2.31	784.4	89.9	752.6	152.5	20.3
1983/84	335.3	2.05	687.7	91.9	762.2	77.9	10.2
1984/85	335.3	2.43	813.5	100.6	783.4	108.0	13.8
1985/86[4]	337.8	2.51	847.5	83.8	776.8	178.8	23.0
1986/87[5]	334.7	2.48	830.4	84.8	786.4	222.8	28.3

Note: "Stocks as percent of utilization" represent the ratio of marketing year ending stocks to total utilization.   [1] Trade data as expressed in this table exclude intra-EC trade. The trade year is October/September.   [2] For countries for which stocks data are not available (excluding the USSR) utilization estimates represent "apparent" utilization, i.e., include annual stock level adjustments.   [3] Stocks data are based on an aggregate of differing local marketing years and should not be construed as representing world stock levels at a fixed point in time. Stocks data are not available for all countries and exclude those such as the People's Republic of China and parts of Eastern Europe. World Stock Levels have been adjusted for estimated year-to-year changes in USSR grain stocks, but do not purport to include the absolute level of USSR grain stocks.   [4] Preliminary.   [5] Projection.   *Sources: Prepared or estimated on the basis of official statistics of foreign governments, other foreign source materials, reports of U.S. Agricultural Attaches and Foreign Service Officers, results of Office Research and Related Information.*   150a

Acreage and Supply of Corn in the United States   In Millions of Bushels

Year Beginning Sept.[5]	Planted All Purposes	Harvested For Grain	Harvested For Silage	Harvested For Forage	Yield, Per Harv. Acre-Bus.	Carry-over, Sept. 1[5] On Farms	Carry-over, Sept. 1[5] Off Farms	Carry-over, Sept. 1[5] Others[3]	Carry-over, Sept. 1[5] Total	Grain Production	Imports[2]	Total (All Supply Grain)
		In Millions of Acres										
1979-0	81.4	72.4	8.0	.4	109.5	794.5	— 509.5—		1,304	7,928	1.1	9,233
1980-1	84.0	73.0	9.3	.6	91.0	920.5	— 696.6—		1,617	6,639	1.2	8,258
1981-2	84.1	74.5	8.3	.4	108.9	489.9	— 544.4—		1,034	8,119	1.2	9,154
1982-3	81.9	72.7	8.3	.3	113.2	1,243.3	— 930.7—		2,174	8,235	.9	10,410
1983-4	60.2	51.5	7.8	.3	81.1	1,510.4	—1,609.5—		3,120	4,175	2.5	7,297
1984-5	80.5	71.9	7.5	.3	106.7	347.9	— 375.4—		723	7,674	3.3	8,401
1985-6[1]	83.3	75.1	7.2	.3	118.0	678.9	— 701.8—		1,381	8,865	1.8	10,248
1986-7[4]	76.6	69.0			119.2	2,049		1,989	4,038	8,223	3.0	12,264

[1] Preliminary.   [2] Includes grain equivalent of cornmeal & flour.   [3] Interior mills & elevators and terminal mkts.   [4] Estimate.   [5] Data prior to 1986-7 are as of Oct 1.   *Source: Economic Research Service, U.S.D.A.*   T.152

U.S. Corn Supply and Disappearance   In Millions of Bushels

Year & Periods Begin. Sept. 1	Supply Beginning Stocks	Supply Production	Supply Imports	Supply Total Supply	Disappearance / Domestic Use Food, Alcohol & Industrial	Seed	Feed & Residual	Total	Exports	Total Disappearance	Ending Stocks Gov't. Owned[1]	Ending Stocks Privately Owned[2]	Ending Stocks Total
1983-4	3,523	4,175	2.7	7,701	956.0	18.9	3,818	4,793	1,902	6,694	201.5	804.8	1,006
Sep.–Nov.	3,523	4,175	.5	7,698	238.6	—	1,311	1,550	497.0	2,047	1,227	4,425	5,652
Dec.–Feb.	5,652	—	.6	5,652	222.8	—	1,056	1,279	508.5	1,787	1,214	2,651	3,865
Mar.–May	3,865	—	1.0	3,866	247.3	16.6	939.7	1,204	517.3	1,721	195.0	1,950	2,145
June–Aug.	2,145	—	.6	2,146	247.3	2.3	511.1	760.7	378.7	1,139	201.5	804.8	1,006
1984-5[3]	1,006	7,674	3.5	8,684	1,035	19.4	4,116	5,170	1,865	7,036	224.9	1,423	1,648
Sep.–Nov.	1,006	7,674	.9	8,681	249.7	—	1,294	1,544	506.2	2,050	206.7	6,424	6,631
Dec.–Feb.	6,631	—	.4	6,632	241.5	—	1,183	1,424	583.9	2,008	209.7	4,414	4,623
Mar.–May	4,623	—	1.1	4,624	267.8	15.6	1,027	1,310	478.9	1,789	221.7	2,614	2,836
June–Aug.	2,836	—	1.1	2,837	276.2	3.8	612.0	892.0	296.4	1,188	224.9	1,423	1,648
1985-6[4]	1,648	8,865	10.6	10,524	1,110	18.6	4,116	5,245	1,241	6,486	546.0	3,492	4,038
Sep.–Nov.	1,648	8,865	1.0	10,514	271.5	—	1,210	1,482	417.7	1,900	388.6	8,226	8,615
Dec.–Feb.	8,615	—	1.3	8,616	259.0	—	1,305	1,564	465.3	2,029	509.4	6,078	6,587
Mar.–May	6,587	—	2.3	6,589	286.5	15.4	1,095	1,397	204.4	1,601	550.9	4,438	4,989
June–Aug.	4,989	—	6.0	4,995	293.0	3.2	506.4	802.6	153.8	956.4	546.0	3,492	4,038
1986-7[4]	4,038	8,223	3.0	12,264	—1,150—		4,200	5,350	1,300	6,650	1,020	4,594	5,614
Sep.–Nov.	4,038	8,223											

[1] Uncommitted inventory.   [2] Includes quantity under loan & farmer-owned reserve.   [3] Preliminary.   [4] Estimate.
Source: Economic Research Service, U.S.D.A.   T.154

CORN

Corn Production Estimates and Cash Prices in the U.S.

Crop Year	Aug. 1	Sept. 1	Oct. 1	Nov. 1	Dec. 1	Final	St. Louis No. 2 Yellow	Gulf Ports No. 2 Yel. (Export)	Los Angeles No. 2 Yel.	Season Farm Avg. Price[1]	K.C. White No. 2	Value of Production (Million Dollars)
			In Thousands of Bushels						$ per bushel			
1978–9	6,503,190	6,797,650	6,823,720	6,890,310	7,081,849	7,267,827	2.46	2.75	3.39	2.25	2.93	16,281
1979–0	7,108,938	7,268,175	7,390,365	7,585,535	7,763,771	7,928,139	2.68	2.98	3.74	2.52	4.70	19,904
1980–1	6,645,842	6,534,370	6,466,622	6,461,244	6,647,534	6,639,396	3.40	3.59	4.48	3.11	4.96	20,571
1981–2	7,734,941	7,940,421	8,081,444	8,097,231	8,200,951	8,118,650	2.63	2.87	3.92	2.50	2.60	20,406
1982–3	8,315,088	8,318,678	8,314,938	8,329,808	8,397,334	8,235,101	2.87	3.06	3.93	2.68	3.35	22,070
1983–4	5,236,558	4,390,443	4,259,408	4,120,983	4,203,777	4,174,678	3.49	3.67	4.22	3.25	4.70	13,568
1984–5	7,667,721	7,551,991	7,497,831	7,527,206	7,649,995	7,674,020	2.81	3.00		2.62		20,106
1985–6[2]	8,265,554	8,468,504	8,602,994	8,716,534	8,865,006		2.37	2.52		2.35		20,833
1986–7[2]	8,316,156	8,268,141	8,220,201	8,222,576						1.80		14,801

[1] Includes an allowance for unredeemed loan & purchase agreement deliveries valued at the average loan rate.   [2] Preliminary.
Source: Economics Research Service; Crop Reporting Board, U.S.D.A.   T.153

Production of Corn (For Grain) in the United States, by States   In Millions of Bushels

Year	Illinois	Indiana	Iowa	Kansas	Kentucky	Michigan	Minn.	Missouri	Nebraska	No. Car.	Ohio	Pa.	South Dakota	Wisconsin	Texas
1978	1,240	669.6	1,478	153.0	119.9	194.4	643.8	200.1	762.8	121.6	379.1	115.9	177.6	294.0	144.0
1979	1,414	675.4	1,664	172.0	132.6	237.5	606.0	240.0	822.3	128.4	417.5	121.6	210.9	317.2	132.3
1980	1,066	602.9	1,463	110.9	103.6	247.0	610.1	109.7	603.5	103.8	440.7	96.0	121.9	348.4	117.0
1981	1,454	654.0	1,759	148.1	149.0	273.6	744.7	213.4	791.2	140.9	360.0	134.4	180.6	378.0	127.5
1982	1,499	790.0	1,578	139.1	154.5	293.2	734.5	199.0	748.0	155.4	456.0	126.1	193.7	361.8	119.7
1983	624.1	340.9	743.9	85.6	46.1	165.6	367.1	72.9	470.5	76.8	224.0	72.5	104.4	223.1	104.8
1984	1,247	705.5	1,445	119.4	146.0	220.1	689.1	154.4	806.2	145.8	460.2	148.5	186.3	344.5	144.2
1985	1,535	756.5	1,707	140.4	159.1	286.7	724.5	272.8	953.6	128.4	511.8	151.8	252.0	358.5	156.5
1986[1]	1,421	725.4	1,620	168.8	138.2	244.8	684.0	273.7	890.5	91.1	473.6	139.4	232.2	359.6	137.5

[1] Preliminary.   *Source: Crop Reporting Board, U.S.D.A.*   T.157

Corn (Shelled & Ear) Stocks in the United States   In Millions of Bushels

Year	On Farms Jan. 1	Apr. 1	June 1	Sept. 1[2]	Off Farms Jan. 1	Apr. 1	June 1	Sept. 1[2]	Total Stocks Jan. 1	Apr. 1	June 1	Sept. 1[2]
1978	3,824	2,517	1,849	659	1,679	1,360	989	445	5,503	3,877	2,837	1,104
1979	4,638	3,178	2,318	794	1,681	1,322	969	509	6,319	4,500	3,287	1,304
1980	5,036	3,437	2,552	920	1,844	1,416	1,093	697	6,880	4,854	3,644	1,617
1981	4,139	2,640	1,817	490	1,718	1,346	956	544	5,857	3,986	2,773	1,034
1982	4,986	3,592	2,734	1,243	1,934	1,506	1,146	931	6,921	5,098	3,880	2,174
1983	5,936	4,242	3,094	1,510	2,269	1,956	1,830	1,610	8,205	6,198	4,924	3,120
1984	3,080	1,934	1,213	348	1,833	1,318	932	375	4,913	3,251	2,145	723
1985	4,304	2,834	2,008	N.A.	1,560	1,132	828	N.A.	5,864	3,966	2,836	1,648
1986[1]	5,525	3,980	3,142	2,049	2,366	1,965	1,847	1,989	7,891	5,945	4,989	4,038

[1] Preliminary.   [2] Prior to 1986, data are for Oct. 1.   *Source: Crop Reporting Board, U.S.D.A.*   T.156

Distribution of Corn in the United States   In Millions of Bushels

Year Beg. Sept.	Wet-Milled Products HFCS	Glucose & Dextrose	Starch	Alcohol Fuel	Beverage[2]	Dry-Milled Products Alcohol Fuel	Beverage	Alkaline Cooked Pdt's.	Total Shipments	Seed	Livestock Feed[3]	Exports (Incl. Grain Equiv. of Pdt's.)	Total Utilization	Domestic Disappearance
1979–0	127	170	130	10	20	0	20	158	640	20.0	4,549	2,415	7,604	5,189
1980–1	165	183	120	20	20	15	20	160	718	20.2	4,157	2,408	7,283	4,875
1981–2	185	183	130	55	30	25	10	162	797	19.4	4,169	2,010	6,975	4,966
1982–3	215	188	127	100	30	40	10	170	895	14.5	4,521	1,834	7,249	5,416
1983–4	256	191	145	120	30	40	10	164	975	18.9	3,818	1,902	6,694	4,793
1984–5	309	188	142	120	30	80	10	160	1,055	19.4	4,116	1,865	7,036	5,170
1985–6[1]	330	190	150	140	30	100	10	161	1,130	18.6	4,116	1,241	6,486	5,245
1986–7[4]	335	195	150	145	30	105	10	161	1,150	19.0	4,200	1,300	6,650	5,350

[1] Preliminary.   [2] Also includes nonfuel industrial alcohol.   [3] Feed & waste (residual, mostly feed).   [4] Forecast.
Source: Economics Research Service, U.S.D.A.   T.155

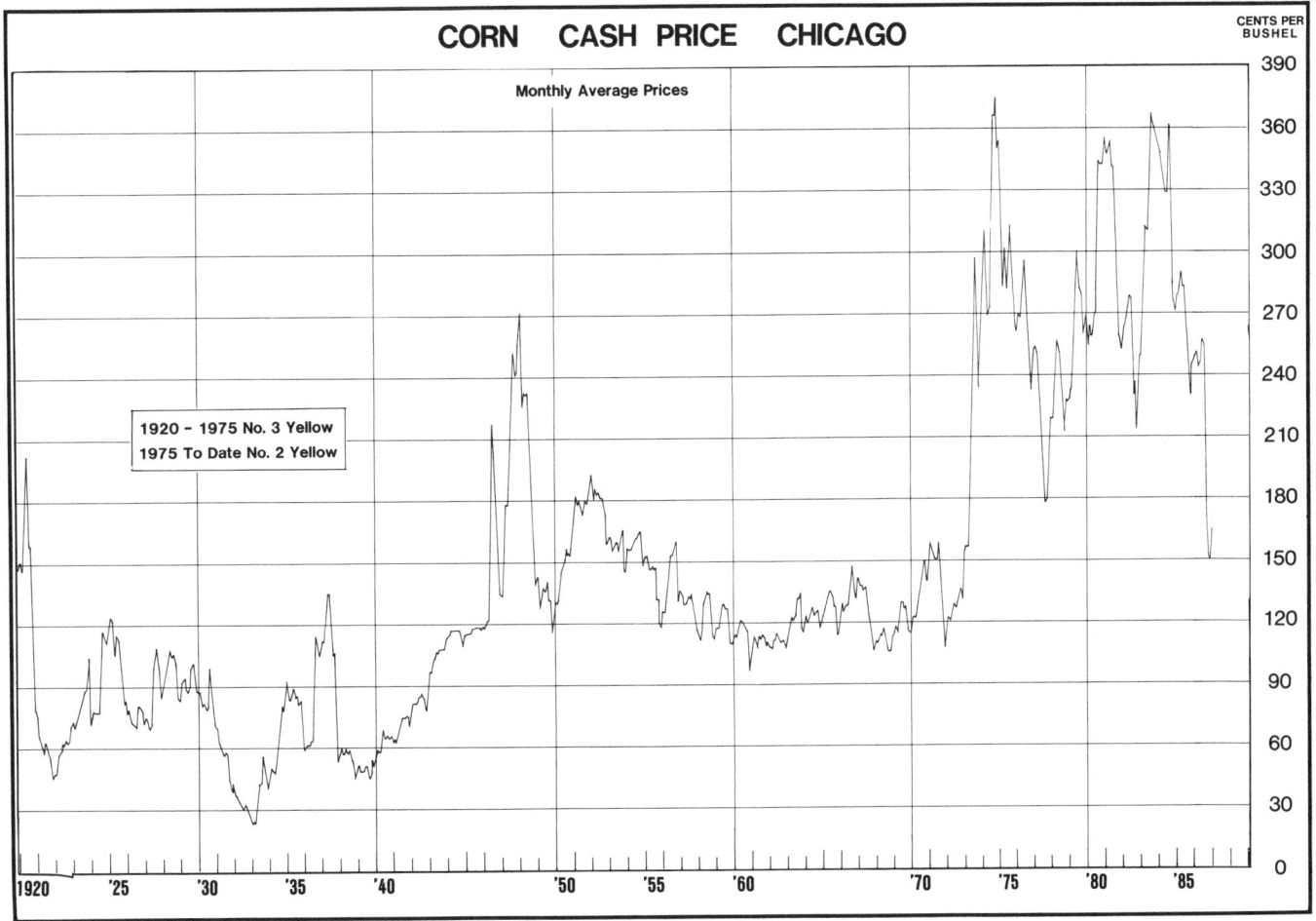

Average Cash Price of Corn, No. 2 Yellow (15 Days) at Chicago In Cents Per Bushel

Year	Oct.	Nov.	Dec.	Jan.	Feb.	Mar.	Apr.	May	June	July	Aug.	Sept.	Average[1]
1978–9	222	228	227	229	235	242	253	266	283	300	282	278	249
1979–0	273	259	269	254	265	260	261	270	270	308	336	344	275
1980–1	343	343	354	356	349	348	353	347	341	341	309	272	344
1981–2	261	260	252	263	263	267	269	273	272	261	236	217	263
1982–3	207	238	244	254	274	298	312	311	328	333	360	352	298
1983–4	347	351	338	330	329	352	361	361	362	345	323	295	346
1984–5	281	279	272	279	279	284	290	285	283	276	250	231	279
1985–6[2]	226	246	250	251	249	245	246	255	252	198	168	149	235
1986–7[2]	151	167											

[1] Weighted average by carlot sales.   [2] Preliminary.   *Source: Economic Research Service, U.S.D.A.*   T.161

Average Cash Price of Corn, No. 2 Yellow at Omaha In Dollars Per Bushel

Crop Year	Oct.	Nov.	Dec.	Jan.	Feb.	Mar.	Apr.	May	June	July	Aug.	Sept.	Average
1979–80	2.37	2.32	2.36	2.26	2.33	2.23	2.32	2.43	2.50	2.81	2.98	3.01	2.44
1980–81	3.16	3.34	3.30	3.29	3.18	3.17	3.24	3.24	3.19	3.15	2.79	2.51	3.17
1981–82	2.44	2.39	2.37	2.47	2.45	2.48	2.61	2.65	2.65	2.54	2.23	2.23	2.48
1982–83	2.12	2.35	2.37	2.42	2.62	2.82	3.09	3.10	3.11	3.18	3.39	3.32	2.73
1983–84	3.23	3.24	3.17	3.11	3.03	3.25	3.33	3.35	3.37	3.22	3.11	2.94	3.23
1984–85	2.71	2.61	2.55	2.60	2.61	2.68	2.73	2.68	2.70	2.61	2.39	2.35	2.65
1985–86	2.26	2.28	2.36	2.33	2.31	2.31	2.34	2.43	2.42	2.01	1.61	1.41	2.25
1986–87	1.40	1.52											

Source: Economic Research Service, U.S.D.A.   T.161a

CORN

Weekly Outstanding Export Sales & Accumulated Exports—U.S. Corn   In Thousand Metric Tons

Marketing Year 1986/87 Week Ending	1986/87 Outst. Sales	Accum. Exports	Marketing Year 1985/86 Week Ending	1985/86 Outst. Sales	Accum. Exports	1984/85 Outst. Sales	Accum. Exports
Sept. 4	6,309	72	Oct. 3	9,449	202	16,489	276
11	6,547	381	10	9,439	746	16,937	913
18	6,728	926	17	9,122	1,631	17,121	1,708
25	6,912	1,497	24	8,992	2,389	16,581	2,941
Oct. 2	6,850	2,255	31	9,950	3,110	16,106	4,195
9	6,712	2,924	Nov. 7	9,618	4,350	15,386	5,384
16	6,504	3,699	14	9,579	5,428	14,357	6,958
23	6,336	4,491	21	8,864	6,831	13,627	8,262
30	5,880	5,307	28	8,602	8,229	12,765	10,084
Nov. 6	6,005	5,842	Dec. 5	8,458	9,352	12,058	11,321
13	5,997	6,536	12	7,992	10,523	11,252	12,573
20	5,968	7,274	19	8,806	11,652	9,923	14,018
27	5,751	7,936	26	8,389	12,203	9,113	15,154
Dec. 4	5,536	8,790	Jan. 2	8,116	12,852	9,357	16,262
11	5,454	9,466	9	7,306	14,109	10,002	17,923
18	5,868	9,901	16	6,765	15,079	9,512	18,839
25			23	6,759	15,964	8,726	19,945
Jan. 1			30	6,313	16,887	7,712	21,010
8			Feb. 6	5,658	17,944	8,966	21,786
15			13	5,255	18,693	8,529	22,731
22			20	4,878	19,491	7,850	23,683
29			27	4,178	20,410	7,778	24,955
Feb. 5			Mar. 6	3,790	21,027	7,537	25,905
12			13	3,507	21,682	7,877	26,876
19			20	3,073	22,071	8,343	27,856
26			27	2,714	22,594	8,322	28,854
Mar. 5			Apr. 3	2,465	23,123	8,135	30,046
12			10	2,334	23,534	7,897	30,946
19			17	2,301	23,771	6,743	31,992
26			24	2,353	24,016	6,616	32,881
Apr. 2			May 1	2,661	24,361	6,010	33,833
9			8	3,162	24,538	5,586	34,625
16			15	2,856	24,773	5,096	35,471
23			22	2,836	25,094	4,879	36,203
30			29	2,836	25,341	4,765	36,978
May 7			June 5	3,061	25,787	4,960	37,529
14			12	2,799	26,173	5,210	37,986
21			19	2,851	26,370	5,089	38,499
28			26	2,789	26,697	4,762	38,994
			July 3	2,923	27,094	4,655	39,696
			10	2,874	27,353	4,377	40,187
			17	2,746	27,623	4,317	40,799
			24	2,902	27,701	4,281	44,221
			31	2,832	28,001	4,233	44,665
			Aug. 7	2,855	28,270	4,055	42,171
			14	2,614	28,688	3,433	42,987
			21	2,667	28,835	3,535	43,503
			28	2,543	29,227	3,016	43,901

Source: U.S.D.A. Export Sales Report (U.S.D.A.)   T.161b

U.S. Exports[2] of Corn (Including Seed), By Country of Destination   In Thousands of Metric Tons

Yr. Begin. October	USSR	China	Canada	Egypt	West Germany	Greece	Israel	Italy	Japan	Mexico	Nether-lands	Korea	Spain	United Kingdom	Total Exports
1980–1	4,947	725	551	1,129	1,264	718	547	1,859	12,586	3,790	1,773	2,304	2,651	1,395	59,368
1981–2	7,499	1,117	320	1,348	1,136	734	403	655	10,588	554	1,428	2,690	4,000	1,091	49,609
1982–3	3,082	2,161	250	1,516	332	221	420	89	13,179	3,987	421	3,904	2,132	755	47,105
1983–4[1]	6,283	0	166	1,303	(EC-3,927)				13,775	2,806		2,971	1,972		46,985

[1] Preliminary.   [2] Exports of grain only. Does not include corn exported under the food for relief or charity program.
Source: Foreign Agricultural Service, U.S.D.A.   T.165

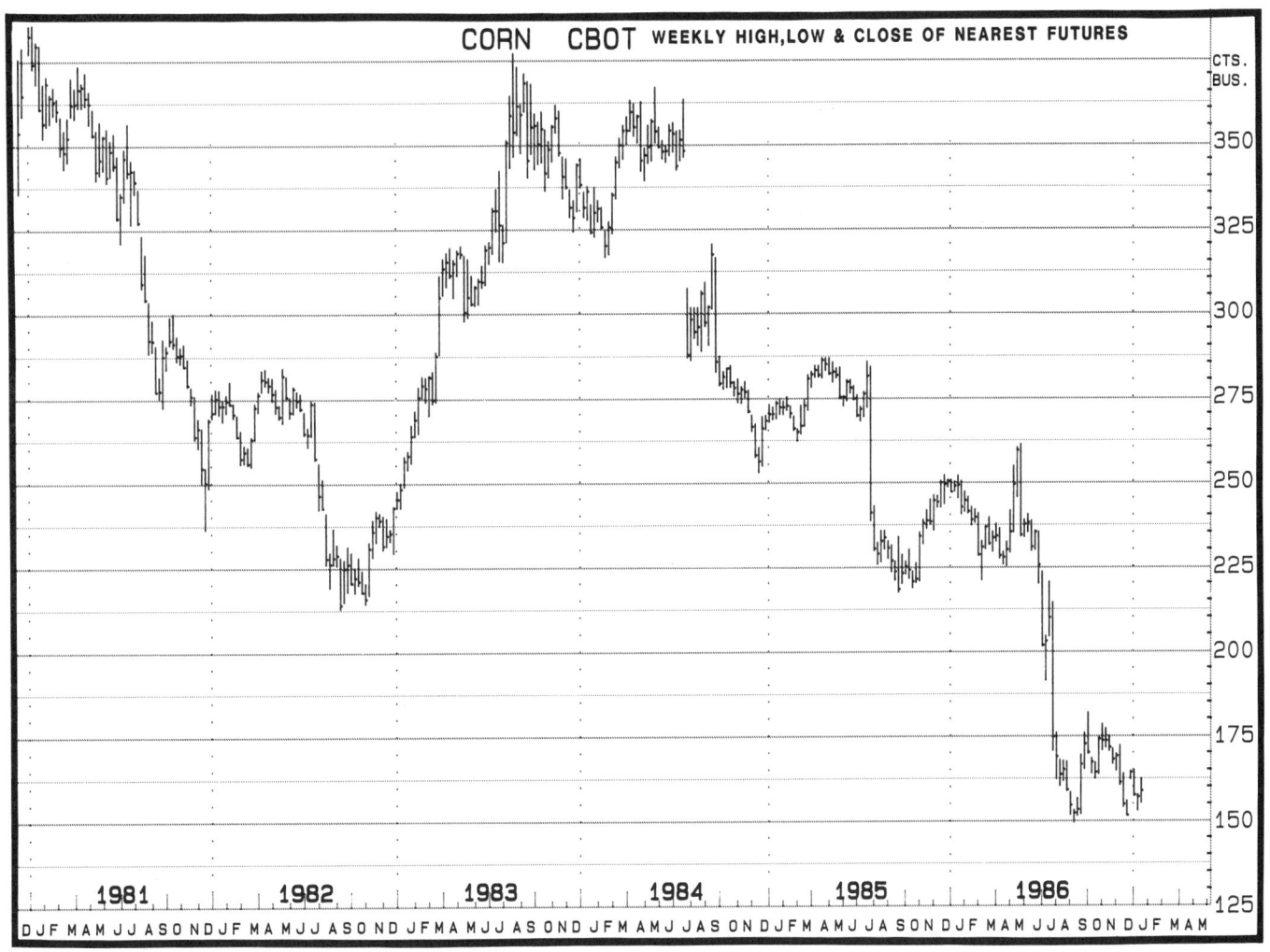

Volume of Trading of Corn Futures at Chicago   In Millions of Bushels

Year	Jan.	Feb.	Mar.	Apr.	May	June	July	Aug.	Sept.	Oct.	Nov.	Dec.	Total
1979	1,734	2,281	2,739	3,302	3,751	5,705	5,806	3,999	3,135	4,522	3,794	2,592	43,359
1980	3,287	3,227	3,493	3,690	3,265	3,362	6,722	7,310	6,287	6,609	6,455	6,027	59,735
1981	4,848	4,495	5,036	5,222	3,867	4,785	5,459	5,019	3,626	3,127	3,913	3,978	53,375
1982	2,802	3,390	3,634	3,355	2,754	3,538	3,122	3,552	3,127	3,239	5,734	2,594	39,741
1983	3,638	3,114	5,355	4,440	3,943	4,511	5,627	7,431	5,882	5,180	5,734	3,518	59,623
1984	3,518	3,866	4,248	4,407	4,259	4,111	4,868	3,975	3,289	2,883	3,619	2,439	45,543
1985	2,406	2,369	2,746	2,608	2,346	2,494	3,231	2,743	2,629	2,597	3,545	2,248	31,964
1986[1]	2,929	2,153	2,203	2,840	3,029	2,390	2,605	2,217	2,486	3,103	2,591	2,555	30,801

[1] Preliminary.   *Source: Chicago Board of Trade*

T.164

CORN

Month-End Open Interest of Corn Futures at Chicago In Millions of Bushels

Year	Jan.	Feb.	Mar.	Apr.	May	June	July	Aug.	Sept.	Oct.	Nov.	Dec.
1980	838.9	799.0	789.8	787.7	766.7	721.6	1,048.8	1,382.4	1,398.0	1,587.9	1,575.5	1,315.0
1981	1,216.5	1,107.5	1,002.4	846.5	737.5	572.6	568.8	637.8	637.7	724.7	674.6	630.7
1982	708.0	625.6	650.0	610.0	594.5	552.6	581.8	596.6	594.7	663.5	712.1	657.8
1983	776.9	778.5	872.5	832.4	760.0	727.2	792.5	1,127.1	1,134.4	1,163.4	1,138.0	1,062.1
1984	1,022.3	964.0	1,034.3	901.5	776.8	717.8	704.0	712.2	730.6	738.4	657.8	649.4
1985	659.2	588.2	629.0	587.6	507.9	499.2	603.1	661.4	605.7	698.0	714.4	622.1
1986	587.2	545.1	559.5	574.2	574.0	564.3	558.7	594.0	671.7	792.1	677.4	605.5

Source: Chicago Board of Trade T.163

High, Low & Closing Prices of May Corn Futures at Chicago In Cents per Bushel

Year of Delivery		Year Prior to Delivery										Delivery Year					Life of Delivery Range
		Mar.	Apr.	May	June	July	Aug.	Sept.	Oct.	Nov.	Dec.	Jan.	Feb.	Mar.	Apr.	May	
1983	High	317½	322½	313½	307	294¼	281	259¼	253	258	255	278	292	315½	318¾	319¼	322½
	Low	310	313¼	303	291¾	274½	250¾	243½	236¼	242¾	242¾	251	273	282¼	304¼	297¼	236¼
	Close	316	313¼	303	292¾	276½	255¾	248	236¼	247¾	253	277	281½	312¾	317¼	311	—
1984	High	325	324½	320	301½	347	390	385½	359¾	361½	346	338¾	336	357¼	362¼	366	390
	Low	297½	312¼	296¼	286¼	285	341½	345½	337	335¾	329½	324¾	320	331	340	338½	285
	Close	317¾	316¼	297¼	289¾	342½	374½	358½	341¼	340¼	340¼	332¾	332½	353¼	344½	365¾	—
1985	High	312¾	322	321	330	328¼	302¾	301¼	295¾	292¼	285¼	280¼	281	282	286	284¾	330
	Low	300	310	304¾	309¾	289¾	291¼	286½	285½	283¼	272¾	274	269¾	270	280¼	279	269¾
	Close	309¼	314	316½	326¾	297¼	295½	286½	287½	284½	276	278½	271¼	281¼	283¼	283	—
1986	High	282¾	284	279½	274½	264¾	242	243½	247¾	250¾	256½	255¼	245¾	235¾	241	260½	291¼
	Low	274¾	275½	264½	262½	238½	231	231½	238¼	241	242½	243	226¾	222½	224¾	233	222½
	Close	282¾	279	267½	263¾	240½	235	240¾	246½	243½	252¼	244¾	227	234¾	238¼	257	—
1987	High	225½	223¼	226½	212½	198¼	192½	193½	192½	192	184½						
	Low	214	207	207½	195¾	185½	182¾	180	180¼	183¾	167						
	Close	219	223¼	208¼	196	186¾	183	191½	187¼	184	167½						

Source: Chicago Board of Trade T.162

Corn Price Support Data in the United States

Year Begin. Oct.1	National Avg. Loan Rate	Grain Reserve Loan Rate	Target Price	Placed Under Loan	% of Production	Acquired by CCC	Taotl Deliv-eries[2]	Stocks at Close of Mkt. Year (Aug. 30): CCC Inven-tory	Under CCC Loan	Farmer Owned Reserve	"Free" Stocks	Total Stocks	CCC Inventory As of Dec. 31: CCC Owned	Under CCC Loan
	¢ Bush.			Millions of Bushels										
1980-1	225	240	235	840	12.6	1	42	237.8	100.8	185.4[4]	424	1,034	256.4	966.0
1981-2[1]	240	255	240	1,978	24.1	172	45	302.4			336	2,537	248	1,234
1982-3[1]	255	290	270	1,585	18.9	349	0	1,150			440	3,120	429	2,400
1983-4[1]	265		286	162	3.9	3		201				1,006	1,230	1,450
1984-5[1]	255		303	1,100	14.4	105		265				1,648	296	1,056
1985-6[1]	255		303									3,413		
1986-7[1]	192		303									4,013		

[1] Preliminary. [2] Includes "delivered to CCC" from original program and deliveries from reseal program and over-deliveries as determined by weight of farm-stored grain when delivered to CCC. [3] Less than 500,000 bushels. [4] Called Reserve Corn under extended loan.
Source: Agricultural Stabilization and Conservation Service, U.S.D.A. T.159

Corn Under Price Support through the End of the Month (Cumulative Total from Current Season's Crop) In Millions of Bushels

Crop Year	Aug.	Sept.	Oct.	Nov.	Dec.	Jan.	Feb.	Mar.	Apr.	May	June	July	Aug.	Sept.
1980-1		2.3	44.6	145.0	386.0	746.7	795.2	816.0	830.6	836.0	838.1			
1981-2		13.5	81.9	418.7	1,049	1,642	1,826	1,903	1,940	1,951	1,962			
1982-3		15.5	76.2	334.5	870.2	1,369	1,505	1,551	1,561	1,567	1,572			
1983-4		.4	14.6	58.1	98.3	138.0	149.1	158.3	160.2	161.1	161.3			
1984-5		2.3	47.2	278.5	631.5	969.6	1,028	1,055	1,063	1,068	1070			
1985-6	11.1	56.9	369.8	1,069	2016	2,055	2,828	2,916	2,996	3,278	3,040			
1986-7	8.1	59.2	535.6	1,583										

Source: U.S. Department of Agriculture T.158

CORN OIL

Supply & Distribution of Corn Oil   In Millions of Pounds

Year Beginning Oct.	Supply				Disappearance									Total Domestic Disappearance	Total Exports & Shipments
					Food Uses					Non-Food Uses					
	Production	Imports	Stocks Oct. 1	Total Supply	Shortening	Margarine	Salad & Cooking Oil	Other	Total Food Uses	Foots & Loss	Other	Total Non-Food Uses			
1976-7	669	10	41	720	3	235	303	2	543	37	1	38	605	59
1977-8	695	3	46	744	4	243	288	—	510	45	1	46	580	88
1978-9	737	—	73	810		223	314						619	121
1979-0	791	—	70	861		222	335						654	141
1980-1	864	—	66	930		217	383		625				673	181
1981-2	872	—	76	948		217	357		593				689	206
1982-3	983	—	53	1,036		217	395		637				723	224
1983-4	1,053	—	89	1,142		196	458		693				762	310
1984-5[1]	1,195	—	71	1,266		206	511		774				930	260
1985-6[2]	1,241	—	75	1,316		181							887	340
1986-7[2]	1,295	—	90	1,385									920	385

[1] Preliminary.   [2] Forecast.   *Source: Economic Research Service, U.S.D.A.*   T.166

Crude Corn Oil Production in the United States   In Millions of Pounds

Crop Year	Oct.	Nov.	Dec.	Jan.	Feb.	Mar.	Apr.	May	June	July	Aug.	Sept.	Total
1976-7	62.0	50.4	51.3	48.1	49.0	59.2	55.6	58.1	57.9	64.0	59.3	53.7	668.6
1977-8	58.9	58.0	50.1	54.9	51.6	58.7	57.1	68.0	64.7	60.5	59.7	63.8	695.5
1978-9	65.4	59.8	55.8	47.6	54.9	69.4	67.4	69.7	60.6	61.5	63.9	60.3	736.3
1979-0	61.8	63.3	63.0	62.3	60.0	70.7	64.3	68.3	65.1	66.2	69.9	76.2	791.1
1980-1	80.6	68.0	59.0	65.8	63.6	76.2	69.6	74.3	76.1	76.2	76.4	77.8	863.6
1981-2	81.4	69.2	66.5	56.7	64.9	76.4	71.6	77.1	73.9	76.5	79.3	78.0	871.5
1982-3	79.2	72.6	78.4	78.9	73.1	88.2	79.8	85.9	83.6	82.7	92.0	88.2	982.6
1983-4	87.0	85.7	83.2	92.1	87.5	91.1	88.5	94.5	84.4	90.6	86.4	82.0	1,053
1984-5	88.8	75.5	89.6	87.7	84.2	107.3	107.0	110.1	107.7	130.1	101.9	104.0	1,194
1985-6[1]	114.2	101.5	97.1	72.8	97.9	102.5	109.8	118.4	106.3	108.6	119.9	104.1	1,253
1986-7[1]	127.6	114.8											

[1] Preliminary.   *Source: Economic Research Service, U.S.D.A.*   T.167

U.S. Corn Oil Consumption in Refining   In Millions of Pounds

Crop Year	Oct.	Nov.	Dec.	Jan.	Feb.	Mar.	Apr.	May	June	July	Aug.	Sept.	Total
1983-4	82.4	82.4	81.6	72.6	64.2	91.8	75.1	85.9	74.6	85.1	93.0	86.5	1,053
1984-5	82.1	86.7	91.0	84.0	71.3	89.4	75.5	106.0	97.4	109.1	96.2	90.8	1,080
1985-6[1]	106.0	95.8	87.1	94.1	84.0	100.9	95.0	103.4	91.2	105.2	97.4	98.1	1,158
1986-7[1]	100.5												

[1] Preliminary.   *Source: Bureau of the Census*   T.167

Corn Oil Spot Price, Crude, Wet Mill at Chicago   In Cents Per Pound

Year	Oct.	Nov.	Dec.	Jan.	Feb.	Mar.	Apr.	May	June	July	Aug.	Sept.	Average
1976-7	27.1	27.5	26.0	28.0	36.0	36.0	34.5	35.5	31.0	27.5	23.5	23.2	29.7
1977-8	26.5	31.5	35.0	40.0	44.0	43.0	36.5	35.3	33.0	33.3	31.5	35.5	35.4
1978-9	34.0	35.0	31.0	35.0	34.0	33.3	32.1	33.0	30.0	31.0	32.3	32.5	32.8
1979-0	32.8	29.9	33.3	27.5	29.0	26.0	20.0	23.0	22.0	27.3	29.8	28.0	27.4
1980-1	28.0	27.5	28.0	26.3	25.0	23.8	25.5	24.4	24.5	25.8	22.3	21.5	25.2
1981-2	20.0	21.0	25.0	24.0	29.0	25.0	25.0	24.0	23.5	23.0	20.5	21.0	23.4
1982-3	23.0	23.8	24.0	22.5	24.5	21.5	21.0	22.5	22.0	20.0	25.0	36.0	23.8
1983-4	27.5	28.0	25.8	27.0	25.3	26.5	30.0	38.8	35.7	26.0	23.8	29.0	26.6
1984-5[1]	30.5	34.2	30.7	28.7	30.0	31.0	32.5	31.5	30.8	N.A.	N.A.	N.A.	31.1
1985-6[1]	20.9[2]	20.2	20.1	20.8	18.7	17.1	17.8	18.0	17.3	17.0	16.7	16.7	17.0

[1] Preliminary.   [2] Prior to Oct. 1985 prices are for F.O.B. Decatur (tank cars).   *Source: Economic Research Service, U.S.D.A.*   T.168

Cotton

1986/87 world cotton production is projected by USDA to reach 70.45 million bales, 11 percent lower than 1985/86. A sharp fall in U.S. production accounts for most of the decline, as well as smaller crops in the USSR, India and Pakistan. The Soviet crop of 11.2 million bales will be the smallest since 1973/74, due partly to lack of irrigation water. China, the world's largest producer, will have a crop of 17.2 million bales, about a quarter of world production, and the smallest since the 1982/83 season.

World mill consumption of cotton is estimated by USDA to reach a record 77.1 million bales, up over three percent from 1985/86. Much of the increase is due to cotton's low price relative to manmade fibers and to growing consumer preference for cotton clothing. Countries expected to show the largest increase in mill use are Taiwan, the U.S., Hong Kong and Pakistan. China, the world's largest consumer of cotton, is expected to show no change in mill use.

The USDA expects 1986/87 expansion of world trade in cotton. World exports are expected to reach 23.02 million bales, up almost 14 percent from a year ago. The increase in world exports will be accounted for by the U.S. Among other major exporters, including the USSR, China and Pakistan, no increase or some decline in shipments will occur.

With a smaller world crop and record consumption, world ending stocks of cotton will drop. The USDA now projects 41.03 million bales, 15 percent less than last season's stocks of 48.3 million. China will hold a 37-percent share of world stocks. The U.S. will carry about 13 percent of the world supply.

The 1986/87 U.S. cotton crop is estimated by USDA at 9.8 million bales, a 27-percent decline from 1985/86. Harvested acreage fell to 8.7 million acres; participation in the 25-percent acreage reduction program was over 90 percent. The national average yield was 539 pounds per acre, somewhat below the five-year average. Much of the production decline occurred in the drought-stricken Southeast, in Texas where a poor harvest resulted in lower yields.

Domestic mill use in 1986/87 is projected to increase to 7 million bales, over nine percent above last year's use of 6.4 million bales. Cotton's share of domestic fiber consumption began rising in the late 1970s, reflecting changes in consumer tastes. While lower oil prices have benefited manmade fibers, this has not been enough to offset the impact of sharply lower cotton prices. Imports of textiles and apparel continue to grow, but restrictions on some textile imports, scheduled to be effective in 1987, will benefit domestic mills.

1986/87 U.S. cotton exports are projected by USDA to stage a dramatic rebound from last season's depressed levels. Exports are now estimated at 6.8 million bales, much above the 2 million bales of last season. This level of exports, slightly above the average of the last five years, is due to lower sharply prices for U.S. cotton, as well as to reduced export competition. Much of the increased export activity is with traditional customers like Japan, Taiwan and South Korea.

Ending stocks of U.S. cotton are currently estimated by USDA to reach 5.5 million bales, a significant decline from last season's 9.4 million bales.

Government Support Program

The 1985 Farm Bill made significant changes in the cotton program. An important feature of the program allows producers to repay price support loans at the lower level of the loan rate or world price of cotton as calculated by USDA. If the world price of cotton is below the loan rate, producers may repay the lower of the two. Loans may not be repaid at less than 80 percent of the loan. These changes are significant in that they bring U.S. prices in line with world prices and make exports more price competitive. The 1986 target price is 79.4 cents per pound, down slightly from 81 cents in 1986. The loan rate for 1987 is set at 52.25 cents per pound, the lowest rate allowed under the Farm Bill. To participate in the 1987 program, producers must reduce acreage by 25 percent, the same as in 1985.

Futures Market

Cotton futures are traded on the New York Cotton Exchange (NYCE).

Supply and Distribution of All Cotton in the United States   In Thousands of (480-Lb. Net Weight) Bales

Crop Year Beginning Aug. 1	At Mills	In Public Storage	Else-where	Total	CCC Held	Total Stocks	Current Crop[2] Less Ginnings	New Crop[3]	Total[4]	Imports	City Crop	Total	Mill Consumption	Exports	Total
1978–9	1,120	3,806	400	4,057	1,232	5,326	10,405	72	10,477	4	0	15,807	6,352	6,180	12,532
1979–0	928	2,604	250	3,145	635	3,782	14,190	200	14,390	5	0	18,177	6,506	9,229	15,735
1980–1	955	1,822	250	2,485	542	3,027	10,627	44	10,671	27	1	13,897	5,891	5,926	11,817
1981–2	883	1,688	25	1,943	652	2,595	15,106	40	15,146	26	0	17,767	5,264	6,567	11,831
1982–3	830	5,269	300	2,640	3,759	6,399	11,486	2	11,488	20	0	17,907	5,512	5,207	10,719
1983–4	792	6,978	167	7,837	4,766	7,561	7,502	163	7,665	12	0	15,235	5,928	6,786	12,714
1984–5	830	1,839	106	2,775	590	2,906	12,382	70	12,452	24	0	15,379	5,540	6,215	11,755
1985–6[1]	768	3,070	264	4,102	1,809	4,088	12,918	147	13,065	33	0	17,181	6,410	1,969	8,375
1986–7[5]	812	8,502	36	9,350	6,829	9,041	9,309	84	9,393	10	3	18,465	7,010	6,750	13,760

[1] Preliminary.   [2] Less ginnings prior to Aug. 1.   [3] Ginnings prior to Aug. 1 end of season.   [4] Includes inseason ginnings.   [5] Estimate.
Source: Economic Research Service, U.S.D.A.

T.170

Cotton World Supply and Demand   In Thousands of 480-lb. Bales

Yr. Begin. Aug. 1	Beginning Stocks				Production				Consumption				Exports			
	US	USSR	PR China	World Total	US	USSR	PR China	World Total	US	USSR	PR China	World Total	US	USSR	PR China	World Total
1978–9	5,347	2,465	2,500	26,158	10,856	11,907	9,950	59,639	6,352	9,075	13,100	63,286	6,180	3,756	15	19,790
1979–0	3,958	1,895	1,460	21,735	14,629	12,833	10,100	65,736	6,506	9,100	14,100	66,155	9,229	3,770	12	23,244
1980–1	3,000	2,154	1,548	21,177	11,122	13,498	12,400	64,996	5,891	9,150	15,100	65,969	5,926	4,070	6	19,713
1981–2	2,668	2,585	2,392	21,193	15,646	13,277	13,600	71,190	5,264	9,150	16,200	66,138	6,567	4,295	0	20,233
1982–3	6,632	2,527	1,892	25,192	11,963	11,932	16,500	68,050	5,513	9,200	16,400	68,245	5,207	3,890	75	19,427
1983–4	7,937	1,845	3,017	25,043	7,771	12,065	21,300	67,655	5,928	9,150	16,000	68,726	6,786	3,202	800	19,198
1984–5	2,775	2,341	7,767	24,983	12,982	11,876	28,700	88,113	5,540	9,500	15,500	69,826	6,215	2,920	1,200	20,397
1985–6[1]	4,102	2,616	19,752	43,039	13,432	12,095	19,000	78,918	6,399	9,600	17,500	74,558	1,960	3,000	2,750	20,268
1986–7[2]	9,348	2,756	18,403	48,304	9,792	11,200	17,200	70,445	7,010	9,700	17,500	77,083	6,750	2,800	2,750	23,023

[1] Preliminary.   [2] Estimate.   *Source: Foreign Agricultural Service, U.S.D.A.*   T.168a

World Production of Cotton   In Thousands of Bales[3]

Year Begin. Aug. 1	Argentina	Brazil	PR. China	Egypt	India	Iran	Mexico	Pakistan	Israel	Sudan	Colombia	Turkey	United States	USSR	World Total
1977–8	1,011	2,116	9,411	1,832	5,656	817	1,620	2,640	294	911	642	2,639	14,389	12,468	63,836
1978–9	797	2,519	9,958	2,014	6,194	607	1,563	2,174	363	637	373	2,191	10,856	11,830	59,482
1979–0	667	2,629	10,158	2,221	6,274	458	1,509	3,343	346	523	573	2,191	14,629	12,410	64,938
1980–1	384	2,825	12,433	2,428	6,090	290	1,620	3,282	359	441	531	2,290	11,122	13,165	64,484
1981–2	696	2,939	13,632	2,291	6,473	338	1,440	3,438	420	706	406	2,244	15,641	13,012	70,542
1982–3	511	2,985	16,525	2,115	6,320	427	840	3,775	399	915	153	2,241	11,963	12,193	67,743
1983–4	827	2,554	21,300	1,839	5,878	409	1,038	2,149	425	1,003	352	2,398	7,771	12,282	67,479
1984–5	786	4,423	28,700	1,840	7,925	512	1,240	4,628	400	945	575	2,664	12,982	11,876	88,113
1985–6[1]	505	3,766	19,000	1,999	8,400	459	960	5,700	455	681	523	2,379	13,432	12,095	78,918
1986–7[2]	500	3,375	17,200	2,000	7,800	475	675	5,400	300	725	500	2,065	9,792	11,200	70,445

[1] Preliminary.   [2] Estimate.   [3] U.S. is in running bales (500 lbs.); all others are 478 pound net weight bales.
Source: International Cotton Advisory Committee; Foreign Agricultural Service, U.S.D.A.   T.169

World Consumption[3] of All Cottons in Specified Countries   In Thousands of Bales (478 Pounds Net[2])

Yr. Beg. Aug. 1	Argentina	Brazil	PR. China	Egypt	Poland	France	W. Germany	India	Italy	Japan	Mexico	Pakistan	Un. Kingdom	United States	USSR	World Total
1977–8	478	2,241	12,050	1,295	697	846	807	5,298	837	2,988	737	1,892	413	6,509	8,834	60,825
1978–9	503	2,440	12,747	1,319	727	822	777	5,626	975	3,286	757	1,942	447	6,352	8,888	63,105
1979–0	468	2,589	13,564	1,295	782	846	789	5,925	1,047	3,386	757	1,972	400	6,506	8,916	65,315
1980–1	382	2,526	15,078	1,498	752	767	792	6,313	971	3,285	759	2,061	220	5,891	8,971	66,102
1981–2	359	2,619	16,094	1,340	697	743	795	5,789	994	3,423	708	2,351	207	5,264	8,984	65,843
1982–3	423	2,639	16,405	1,199	699	765	928	6,233	1,000	3,275	630	2,549	208	5,513	9,039	67,844
1983–4	497	2,553	16,300	1,196	638	745	989	6,614	1,125	3,298	528	2,208	206	5,926	9,083	69,182
1984–5	514	2,616	16,200	1,369	712	724	1,000	7,117	1,212	3,187	556	2,437	202	5,540	9,322	70,507
1985–6[1]	484	2,800	17,800	1,418	726	715	942	7,156	1,171	3,160	675	2,503	208	6,389	9,600	74,292
1986–7[4]	528	3,200	18,000	1,500	726	725	950	7,390	1,150	3,127	600	2,664	215	7,000	9,800	76,629

[1] Preliminary.   [2] Except for the U.S. which are in running bales.   [3] Includes estimates for hand spinning in some countries. Excludes cotton burned or otherwise destroyed.   [4] Estimate.   *Source: International Cotton Advisory Committee*   T.173

Consumption of American and Foreign Cotton in the United States   In Thousands of Bales[1]

Year	Aug.	Sept.	Oct.	Nov.	Dec.	Jan.	Feb.	Mar.	Apr.	May	June	July	Total
1978–9	459	569	482	595	435	603	471	506	584	484	489	503	6,180
1979–0	472	482	630	482	436	604	507	513	622	496	478	487	6,209
1980–1	443	456	597	458	475	435	446	539	435	441	531	385	5,641
1981–2	429	517	448	403	400	378	398	493	410	392	460	317	5,038
1982–3	386	474	416	391	425	404	430	549	431	441	543	369	5,259
1983–4	453	560	459	446	468	469	448	548	430	442	503	354	5,580
1984–5[2]	416	494	415	377	407	399	418	519	419	439	525	369	5,197
1985–6[2]	458	560	562	477	486	595	499	492	620	503	489	522	6,263
1986–7	534	526											

[1] American cotton, running bales; foreign cotton, equivalent 500 lb. bales.   [2] Preliminary.   *Source: Bureau of the Census*   T.188

COTTON

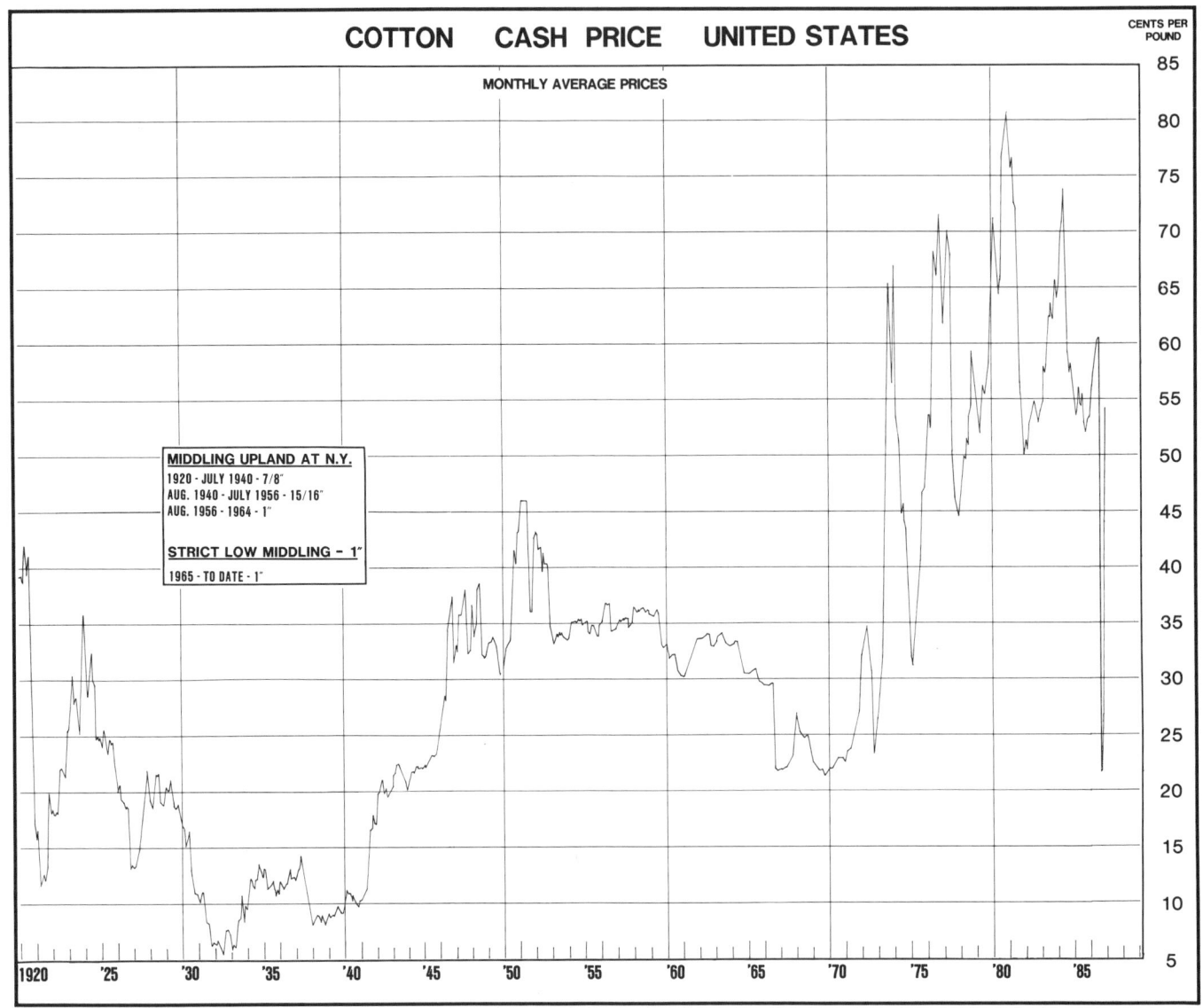

COTTON CASH PRICE UNITED STATES

MONTHLY AVERAGE PRICES

CENTS PER POUND

MIDDLING UPLAND AT N.Y.
1920 - JULY 1940 - 7/8"
AUG. 1940 - JULY 1956 - 15/16"
AUG. 1956 - 1964 - 1"

STRICT LOW MIDDLING - 1"
1965 - TO DATE - 1"

Average Spot Cotton Prices,[2] C.I.F. Northern Europe   In Cents Per Pound (Equivalent U.S. ¢/Lb.)

| Crop Year (Aug.-July) | M 1" | | Guate-mala SM | U.S. Memphis Terr. SM | Greece SM | Egypt Giza[81]/[69] FG | SM 1 1/16–3/32" | | | | USSR Pervyi 31/32 MM | Tanza-nia A.A. No. 1/2 | Turkey Izmir (12 MIR) | SM 1 1/8" U.S. Calif. | Austr-alian M-1 3/32 |
	U.S. Orleans/ Texas	Pakistan N.T. Sind					Mexico SM	Nicara-gua SM	Syria SM						
1978–79	63.23		75.23	72.52	83.09		72.94	70.21	72.08	72.55		73.46	77.99	
1979–80	75.36	75.41	83.63	87.49	84.00	136.37	85.86	86.13	83.50	85.89	92.33	90.25	90.69	
1980–81	89.14	84.94	93.47	101.23	83.80	137.66	94.91	92.46	101.00	92.80	103.25	96.65	101.85	
1981–82	66.76	65.65	72.87	76.30	81.00	115.73	75.28	72.17	79.82	73.02	88.08	77.55	79.79	
1982–83	68.11	65.59	76.14	77.94	85.74	110.07	76.39	75.70	81.10	71.00	87.50	83.44	84.99	
1983–84	78.41	75.20	86.81	87.09	94.37	134.07	87.42	86.02	90.00	91.15	95.14	92.74	94.90	90.83
1984–85	65.92	55.96	66.96	73.47	74.32	136.06	70.00	N.A.	75.15	—	77.18	74.18	75.88	67.62
1985–86[1]	52.55	37.44	51.38	58.50	50.98	111.27	53.02	N.A.	47.00	48.09	55.89	54.21	59.65	50.34
July '86	29.70	28.30		38.05	37.10	111.75	43.80			36.15	45.00	44.70	41.90	
Aug. '86	29.44	27.94		37.75	36.80	111.75	43.06			36.44	46.30	44.75	44.31	
Sept. '86	34.54	33.25		44.69	46.00	111.75	46.00			43.63	50.00	53.30	56.50	
Oct. '86	43.55	40.20		52.35	53.85	111.75	54.75			53.20	54.00	54.35	67.40	

[1] Preliminary.   [2] Generally for prompt shipment.   *Source: International Cotton Advisory Committee*   T.172

Average Price of Strict Low Middling, 1¹/₁₆″, Cotton at Designated U.S. Markets   ¢/Lb. (Net Weight)

Year	Aug.	Sept.	Oct.	Nov.	Dec.	Jan.	Feb.	Mar.	Apr.	May	June	July	Average
1978–9	59.78	60.04	64.08	65.65	64.39	61.48	60.59	58.70	58.05	60.90	63.38	61.87	61.58
1979–0	62.08	62.15	62.88	63.40	66.20	72.40	80.66	79.24	79.05	78.27	72.41	79.01	71.48
1980–1	85.60	87.51	85.78	87.05	87.23	85.11	83.30	81.52	81.15	78.46	78.12	75.08	82.99
1981–2	66.44	60.81	60.63	57.47	55.11	57.82	57.26	59.73	62.03	62.44	61.10	64.96	60.48
1982–3	60.38	58.98	58.58	58.20	59.65	60.16	61.72	66.05	65.33	66.88	70.74	70.27	63.08
1983–4	72.93	71.68	72.01	73.41	73.04	70.55	71.38	74.89	75.64	79.44	75.00	67.35	55.00
1984–5	63.01	61.17	61.15	60.43	60.45	59.97	58.65	60.18	61.71	60.11	59.76	59.55	60.51
1985–6	57.87	56.38	56.14	56.03	56.25	58.39	59.81	61.75	62.62	63.95	65.24	65.73	60.01
1986–7	26.81	33.56	43.95	45.74	54.18								

Note: Grade 41.   *Source: Department of Agriculture*   T.190

Average Spot Cotton, 1³/₃₂″, Price (SLM) at Designated U.S. Markets   In Cents Per Pound (Net Weight)

Year	Aug.	Sept.	Oct.	Nov.	Dec.	Jan.	Feb.	Mar.	Apr.	May	June	July	Average	1¹/₃₂″	1″
1978–9	60.01	60.27	64.31	65.94	64.68	61.77	60.88	59.03	58.44	61.30	63.79	62.26	61.89	59.92	55.24
1979–0	62.47	62.54	63.28	63.81	66.58	72.78	81.05	79.63	79.44	78.66	72.80	79.40	71.87	69.53	63.39
1980–1	86.00	87.91	86.18	87.45	87.63	85.57	83.70	81.92	81.55	78.86	78.52	75.48	83.39	80.95	75.70
1981–2	66.84	61.22	61.08	57.91	55.52	58.24	57.70	60.12	62.41	62.82	61.48	N.A.	60.89	58.28	54.13
1982–3	60.76	59.36	58.97	58.57	60.02	60.53	62.09	66.43	65.72	67.31	71.20	70.73	63.47	61.17	56.41
1983–4	70.52	69.29	69.49	70.82	70.44	68.03	68.98	72.56	73.37	77.18	72.74	65.11	73.55	70.71	66.32
1984–5	63.45	61.60	60.71	59.99	60.01	59.52	58.21	59.74	61.27	59.67	59.32	59.99	60.29	58.30	55.98
1985–6	57.40	55.89	55.66	55.55	55.77	57.92	59.34	61.28	62.15	63.48	64.77	66.20	59.62	57.87	55.81
1986–7	27.39	35.56													

Source: Agricultural Marketing Service, U.S.D.A.   T.191

Average Spot Prices of U.S. Cotton,[1] 1¹/₁₆ inches—(SLM) at Designated Markets   In Cents Per Pound

Yr. Begin. Aug. 1	At-lanta	Au-gusta	Charles-ton	Dallas	Fresno	Gal-veston	Green-ville	Green-wood	Houston	Little Rock	Lubbock	Mem-phis	Mont-gomery	Phoenix	Aver-age
1978–9	—	62.50	—	58.33	67.66	—	62.09	61.84	59.45	—	58.27	61.68	61.92	61.98	61.58
1979–0	—	73.92	—	66.91	73.76	—	73.24	72.73	—	—	66.43	72.55	72.57	71.98	71.48
1980–1	—	85.21	—	80.65	82.80	—	84.54	84.30	—	—	79.66	83.81	84.28	81.70	82.99
1981–2	—	61.87	—	58.32	61.02	—	61.57	61.34	—	—	57.96	61.00	61.34	59.93	60.48
1982–3	—	—	—	61.62	64.49	—	63.50	63.35	—	—	60.84	63.33	63.50	63.17	63.08
1983–4	—	—	—	70.79	77.02	—	73.28	73.14	—	—	70.35	73.25	72.93	74.13	73.11
1984–5	—	—	—	58.94	61.29	—	61.08	60.98	—	—	58.93	60.73	60.56	61.57	60.51
1985–6	—	—	—	58.96	60.35	—	60.52	60.69	—	—	59.17	60.40	60.17	59.84	60.01

[1] Mixed Lots, Net Weight, uncompressed in warehouse.   *Source: Agricultural Marketing Service, U.S.D.A.*   T.177

Avg. Price[1] Received by Farmers for Upland Cotton in the U.S.   In Cents Per Pound

Year	Aug.	Sept.	Oct.	Nov.	Dec.	Jan.	Feb.	Mar.	Apr.	May	June	July	Average[1]
1978–9	57.4	56.2	59.6	61.1	59.0	57.0	55.6	53.5	54.7	56.0	58.8	61.9	58.1
1979–0	59.2	57.3	61.2	61.0	59.8	60.9	64.9	62.9	61.0	63.6	62.2	71.5	62.3
1980–1	73.7	73.9	75.3	77.6	80.9	76.6	70.8	71.9	72.7	72.5	71.2	70.4	74.4
1981–2	65.0	58.1	63.2	61.1	51.5	50.3	49.1	50.4	54.3	55.8	58.1	59.9	54.0
1982–3	52.7	56.0	60.9	61.0	57.7	57.0	57.7	62.2	60.4	63.6	62.6	67.1	59.1
1983–4	64.6	62.8	63.1	67.0	66.2	62.7	65.0	70.1	67.2	72.7	68.0	65.9	66.0
1984–5	67.3	65.6	64.4	62.0	56.1	52.2	49.5	56.1	57.0	57.5	60.3	60.5	57.8
1985–6[2]	56.6	55.9	57.3	56.5	53.7	54.0	56.9	58.1	59.2	58.5	58.5	61.5	56.8
1986–7[2]	47.2	47.4	47.1	52.9	55.4								

[1] Weighted average by sales.   [2] Preliminary.   *Source: Crop Reporting Board, U.S.D.A.*   T.187

COTTON

High, Low & Closing Prices of May Cotton Futures at New York   In Cents per Pound

Year of Delivery		Year Prior to Delivery										Delivery Year					Life of Delivery Range
		Mar.	Apr.	May	June	July	Aug.	Sept.	Oct.	Nov.	Dec.	Jan.	Feb.	Mar.	Apr.	May	
1980	High	67.90	65.70	66.40	68.25	67.00	70.00	69.00	68.90	73.00	76.40	86.00	90.42	90.70	87.40	84.40	90.70
	Low	66.00	64.10	63.00	63.90	64.55	65.90	66.25	66.40	68.20	70.82	73.97	80.70	77.52	79.50	80.90	64.15
	Close	65.65	65.45	64.15	65.60	66.05	69.20	67.70	68.22	71.77	75.95	85.37	86.77	85.12	81.99	83.75	—
1981	High	80.60	77.60	78.42	75.00	85.70	94.50	96.87	93.50	93.12	97.67	96.50	93.70	89.80	89.20	85.20	97.67
	Low	74.50	74.30	74.92	72.80	75.50	81.65	87.00	88.20	86.70	88.40	88.35	86.00	84.75	83.75	80.65	71.00
	Close	77.00	75.05	75.00	74.80	84.80	93.92	90.40	90.20	92.08	95.60	90.90	90.14	86.12	84.00	80.45	—
1982	High	84.90	85.35	83.66	82.50	81.27	79.40	73.80	71.90	70.45	67.40	67.95	67.65	66.75	68.95	68.50	87.50
	Low	82.75	83.20	81.80	78.70	79.10	71.45	68.55	68.30	64.40	63.11	65.55	64.65	64.01	65.40	67.50	63.11
	Close	84.20	83.26	82.90	79.00	79.30	69.15	69.15	69.45	65.29	65.70	67.82	64.94	65.92	68.30	68.43	—
1983	High	74.65	76.75	76.50	77.50	77.50	74.90	72.15	69.25	68.15	68.90	68.40	71.25	76.42	75.30	71.60	77.50
	Low	73.50	74.20	73.74	69.45	74.50	69.50	66.75	65.80	65.81	66.20	66.35	66.26	70.30	70.25	69.77	65.80
	Close	74.53	76.40	73.30	76.60	74.66	69.90	67.25	67.42	66.62	67.41	67.33	71.20	75.32	71.08	71.03	—
1984	High	74.60	75.50	80.00	83.40	82.70	83.80	83.40	82.15	83.80	82.05	78.25	78.79	81.85	82.54	84.40	84.40
	Low	70.60	73.25	73.20	79.25	78.20	80.30	78.15	78.70	80.31	78.35	74.75	74.05	77.70	77.90	81.50	66.75
	Close	73.80	73.80	80.00	80.00	81.00	82.80	79.30	81.65	80.98	78.42	77.13	78.09	81.74	82.39	82.39	—
1985	High	81.85	78.00	79.25	79.15	75.25	71.80	69.00	72.05	71.30	67.66	68.20	66.85	68.25	70.45	68.98	79.25
	Low	77.70	75.80	77.45	75.00	69.60	68.74	67.60	67.36	66.45	66.20	65.70	63.28	63.26	64.75	66.10	63.26
	Close	81.74	78.00	78.60	75.00	69.75	69.15	68.00	69.85	66.95	66.95	65.76	64.18	67.60	66.40	66.33	—
1986	High	67.55	67.88	66.65	64.25	62.90	61.10	60.90	62.39	63.45	62.10	63.60	64.48	65.85	67.25	68.05	70.55
	Low	66.35	66.52	61.86	62.00	59.95	59.30	59.25	60.45	60.50	59.60	58.80	59.50	61.90	60.70	66.00	58.80
	Close	67.55	66.52	63.13	63.00	60.25	60.05	60.48	67.34	60.75	62.06	60.32	63.45	65.69	66.80	67.20	—
1987	High	46.70	41.85	40.55	37.30	35.25	38.40	48.90	50.90	52.96	59.50						
	Low	40.50	38.30	36.70	33.60	31.56	32.40	35.44	45.51	46.35	52.60						
	Close	41.00	40.70	36.73	33.93	34.40	38.40	47.50	47.00	52.96	59.25						

Source: N.Y. Cotton Exchange   T.184

Month–End Open Interest of Cotton Futures at New York   In Contracts

Year	Jan.	Feb.	Mar.	Apr.	May	June	July	Aug.	Sept.	Oct.	Nov.	Dec.
1980	54,046	57,891	44,363	38,596	31,753	27,276	39,711	46,814	49,370	45,433	40,208	38,022
1981	32,078	34,782	25,882	24,108	26,793	27,286	26,009	30,014	32,121	31,671	29,157	28,584
1982	30,296	31,740	30,230	31,422	27,665	24,675	24,978	25,052	27,047	26,070	26,949	26,581
1983	29,544	34,165	36,109	33,990	35,026	33,851	31,402	33,981	31,531	29,272	30,868	30,758
1984	32,246	28,060	34,212	29,596	30,569	22,239	21,734	21,576	20,419	22,547	19,211	16,614
1985	19,790	17,660	18,678	14,101	16,481	15,381	19,386	20,861	21,011	22,889	23,196	21,748
1986	23,326	20,824	20,112	20,121	23,702	22,505	25,321	27,642	23,406	24,432	20,534	23,035

Source: N.Y. Cotton Exchange   T.182

Volume of Trading of Cotton Futures at New York   In Contracts

Year	Jan.	Feb.	Mar.	Apr.	May	June	July	Aug.	Sept.	Oct.	Nov.	Dec.	Total
1980	286,058	278,901	290,133	206,682	191,067	128,393	175,619	188,542	224,323	186,615	173,081	173,133	2,523,447
1981	156,303	166,292	150,297	117,653	90,157	117,249	99,175	95,312	96,956	120,301	115,833	89,985	1,415,213
1982	100,242	104,444	103,697	106,892	95,597	151,068	116,211	99,674	101,119	94,265	98,597	83,988	1,255,202
1983	97,947	123,620	139,032	132,447	139,953	153,932	143,116	156,680	121,972	113,759	137,472	90,187	1,550,117
1984	124,735	133,891	127,448	126,780	139,988	111,050	71,522	51,941	39,519	83,631	86,729	39,907	1,137,141
1985	61,860	57,034	61,921	65,709	47,606	47,604	41,069	40,524	42,747	55,046	63,829	51,543	636,492
1986	73,576	77,152	57,433	74,520	54,479	64,742	75,545	94,025	130,989	111,356	113,812	84,618	1,015,250

Source: N.Y. Cotton Exchange   T.183

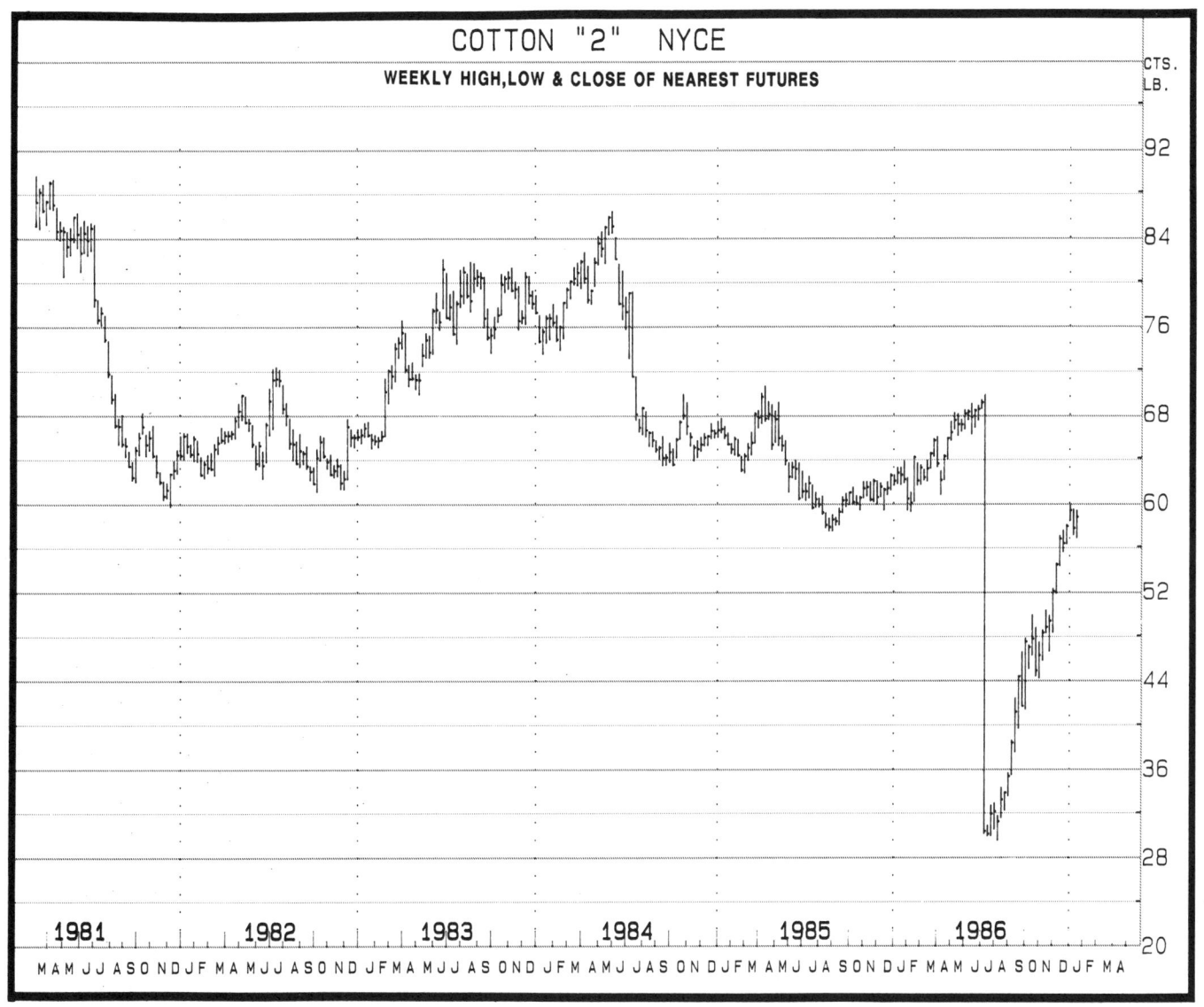

COTTON "2" NYCE

WEEKLY HIGH,LOW & CLOSE OF NEAREST FUTURES

CTS.
LB.

1981 1982 1983 1984 1985 1986

M A M J J A S O N D J F M A M J J A S O N D J F M A M J J A S O N D J F M A M J J A S O N D J F M A M J J A S O N D J F M A M J J A S O N D J F M A

United States Government Crop Forecasts and Actual Cotton Crops

	Forecasts of Production (1,000 Bales of 480 Lbs.[1])					Actual Crop	Forecasts of Yields (In Lbs. Per Harv. Acre)					Actual Yield
Year	Aug. 1	Sept. 1	Oct. 1	Nov. 1	Dec. 1		Aug. 1	Sept. 1	Oct. 1	Nov. 1	Dec. 1	
1976	10,734	10,375	10,251	9,891	10,264	10,581	466	451	445	435	451	465
1977	13,535	13,302	13,317	13,832	14,496	14,389	506	495	500	503	525	520
1978	11,820	11,155	10,873	10,981	10,841	10,856	462	425	429	418	421	420
1979	13,710	14,245	14,356	14,544	14,527	14,629	497	525	528	535	534	547
1980	12,812	11,689	11,589	11,224	11,125	11,122	461	421	419	408	411	404
1981	14,789	15,507	15,476	15,560	15,733	15,646	515	540	540	543	546	543
1982	11,143	11,029	11,365	11,947	12,102	11,963	563	569	587	605	613	590
1983	7,810	7,776	7,550	7,497	7,725	7,771	503	501	487	504	506	508
1984	12,569	13,276	13,272	13,271	13,292	12,982	583	615	620	613	610	600
1985	13,780	13,655	13,638	13,875	13,810	13,432	638	632	633	644	644	630
1986	10,676	10,506	10,006	9,875	9,792		573	565	539	546	539	

[1] Net Weight bales.   *Source: Crop Reporting Board, U.S.D.A.*   T.175

COTTON

United States Production of Cotton (Upland) & American-Pima
In Thousands of 480-Pound Net Weight Bales

Year	Upland														Total Amer. Pima
	Ala-bama	Ari-zona	Arkan-sas	Cali-fornia	Geor-gia	Loui-siana	Missis-sippi	Mis-souri	No. Car.	Okla-homa	So. Car.	Ten-nessee	Texas	New Mex-ico	
1978	291	1,068	660	1,940	111	478	1,378	188	45	355	115	235	3,792	101	93.4
1979	324	1,280	606	3,408	152	690	1,437	157	43	522	116	171	5,515	104	98.6
1980	275	1,354	444	3,109	86	460	1,143	177	52	205	77	200	3,320	107	104.2
1981	422	1,556	604	3,535	159	742	1,565	168	95	440	164	315	5,663	141	79.6
1982	460	1,095	534	3,073	235	870	1,760	204	102	238	155	339	2,700	78	98.7
1983	183	725	323	1,971	112	532	900	73	43	145	53	151	2,380	70	94.7
1984	447	1,097	612	2,913	281	1,056	1,650	187	120	183	170	337	3,680	87	130.4
1985	545	928	703	3,114	370	742	1,655	204	117	285	180	419	3,910	71	155.1
1986[1]	330	680	605	2,250	200	680	1,200	197	110	240	87	400	2,500	68	201.5

[1] Preliminary. Source: Crop Reporting Board, U.S.D.A.   T.176

Gross Entries of Cotton into U.S. Government Loan Program   In Thousands of Running Bales

Crop Year	Aug.	Sept.	Oct.	Nov.	Dec.	Jan.	Feb.	Mar.	April	May[1]	June[1]	July[1]	Seasonal Total
1978-9	0	5	26	89	215	584	352	189	68	16	14	[2]	1,560
1979-0	0	[2]	23	294	319	600	316	110	51	35	8	[2]	1,759
1980-1	0	[2]	8	253	528	912	343	204	36	28	16	[2]	2,328
1981-2	0	9	132	293	1,081	2,796	1,120	473	117	39	21	2	6,083
1982-3	0	46	143	674	1,857	1,590	4,503	4,160	43	23	13	3	5,062
1983-4	0	0	165	227	253	513	188	264	127	9	32	5	1,765
1984-5	0	1	11	98	563	776	1,057	324	62	44	32	5	2,977
1985-6	31	202	771	1,497	1,406	2,375	781	159	61	12	40	60	7,365
1986-7	22	136	775	1,146	1,124								

NOTE: Seasonal totals are net, due to allowances for rejections.   [1] Entries after April 30 represent late reporting.   [2] Less than one thousand bales. Sources: N.Y. Cotton Exchange; Commodity Credit Corporation   T.178

Average Wholesale Price of Cotton Yarn[1] (30/1, Combed, Knitting) on Cones   Index 1967 = 100

Year	Jan.	Feb.	Mar.	Apr.	May	June	July	Aug.	Sept.	Oct.	Nov.	Dec.	Average
1978	153.2	155.2	157.5	158.1	160.1	162.7	163.7	163.7	163.7	165.0	165.0	165.6	161.1
1979	165.6	166.3	165.6	165.6	165.9	166.9	166.9	167.3	167.9	169.9	172.8	176.3	168.1
1980	180.6	198.3	200.0	203.0	204.6	202.7	203.3	206.3	206.3	207.6	210.6	211.6	202.9
1981	212.9	214.6	214.6	212.6	211.9	211.9	210.3	207.0	203.0	199.0	196.7	192.1	207.2
1982	244.0	243.6	242.8	242.2	242.7	240.3	240.4	240.1	239.0	237.4	237.1	236.4	240.0
1983	234.8	234.1	234.2	236.1	236.1	236.7	237.5	239.7	241.5	242.6	243.6	244.3	238.4
1984	244.9	246.2	246.7	248.2	248.1	247.8	248.0	244.9	242.9	242.0	240.9	239.7	245.0
1985	239.5	237.3	237.1	235.5	235.7	235.3	235.1	232.3	231.7	231.8	231.7	231.6	234.6
1986[2]	227.5	228.4	228.6	229.7	230.0	229.5	229.7	227.5	226.3	225.5			

[1] Natural stock, f.o.b. mill.   [2] Preliminary.   Source: Bureau of Labor Statistics (0326-01)   T.181

U.S. Daily Rate of Upland Cotton Mill Consumption[2] on Cotton-System Spinning Spindles
In Thousands of 480 Lb. Running Bales[3]

Crop Yr.	Aug.	Sept.	Oct.	Nov.	Dec.	Jan.	Feb.	Mar.	Apr.	May	June	July	Average
1978-9	22,941	22,780	24,090	23,809	21,735	24,114	23,567	25,306	23,358	24,193	24,454	20,127	23,373
1979-0	23,617	24,177	25,188	24,099	21,813	24,160	25,353	25,654	24,899	24,781	23,883	18,473	23,836
1980-1	22,130	22,816	23,884	22,885	19,000	21,773	22,312	21,544	21,741	22,060	21,260	19,250	26,066
1981-2	21,448	20,679	22,420	20,138	15,985	18,898	19,885	19,720	20,476	19,580	18,382	15,980	19,466
1982-3	19,295	18,954	20,794	19,526	17,009	20,211	21,505	21,966	21,525	22,042	21,739	18,444	20,251
1983-4[3]	22.6	22.4	22.9	22.3	18.7	23.5	22.4	21.9	21.5	22.1	20.1	17.7	21.6
1984-5	22.2	21.1	22.2	20.2	17.6	20.7	21.7	21.6	21.8	22.8	21.8	19.2	21.1
1985-6[1]	23.8	23.3	25.6	24.8	20.2	24.7	25.9	25.6	25.8	25.7	25.4	21.6	24.4
1986-7[1]	27.7	27.4											

[1] Preliminary.   [2] Not seasonally adjusted.   [3] Data prior to 1983 are in running bales.   Source: Bureau of the Census; U.S.D.C.   T.180

Exports of American Cotton from the United States   In Thousands of Running Bales

Year	Aug.	Sept.	Oct.	Nov.	Dec.	Jan.	Feb.	Mar.	Apr.	May	June	July	Total
1976-7	274	342	217	265	376	354	509	536	548	400	462	282	4,564
1977-8	181	200	149	333	496	521	502	704	640	510	528	456	5,218
1978-9	524	388	283	355	464	517	577	574	602	542	614	410	5,849
1979-0	463	428	390	630	902	737	1,025	1,150	916	911	686	540	8,778
1980-1	402	393	237	436	541	669	2,352	733	498	458	320	264	7,303
1981-2	990	261	262	478	737	653	754	873	676	484	498	396	7,062
1982-3	342	351	293	382	377	438	368	487	612	464	831	409	5,354
1983-4	383	322	261	441	632	663	719	896	723	607	422	365	6,434
1984-5[1]	452	264	292	484	629	766	766	625	544	426	353	252	5,853
1985-6[1]	193	187	207	223	187	396	180	176	163	76	55	21	2,064
1986-7[1]	261												

[1] Preliminary.   Source: Foreign Agricultural Service, U.S.D.A.   T.185

U.S. Exports of American Cotton to Countries of Destination   In Thousands of 480-Pound Bales

Yr. Beg. Aug. 1	Bangla-desh	Can-ada	Hong Kong	France	W. Ger-many	India	Italy	Japan	Nether-lands	Spain	Swe-den	United King-dom	Rep. of Korea	P.R. China	Tai-wan	USSR	World Total
1976-7	122	187	358	45	36	273	85	973	12	86	17	66	913	0	436		4,565
1977-8	46	214	479	80	65	1	77	1,028	21	64	21	59	1,172	443	490		5,219
1978-9	116	222	427	63	96	1	146	1,342	18	65	23	72	1,278	648	454		6,180
1979-0	71	272	636	92	204	0	185	1,588	11	131	21	72	1,484	2,268	728		9,229
1980-1	33	267	205	42	112	—	54	1,139	1	60	10	38	1,303	1,375	351		5,926
1981-2	50	167	243	58	119	—	106	1,626	2	57	17	43	1,412	848	777	0	6,567
1982-3	88	238	158	45	163	0	105	1,286	7	72	23	50	1,322	20	378	192	5,207
1983-4	135	227	283	154	195	—	252	1,709	6	114	28	67	1,269	12	495	351	6,785
1984-5	60	195	125	132	195	—	301	1,464	4	118	22	72	1,257	6	513	329	6,211
1985-6[1]	14	98	1	8	85		91	520	1	29	15	35	513	0	46	0	1,958

[1] Preliminary.   Source: Bureau of the Census   T.189

U.S. Exports of Cotton Cloth (Raw Cotton Equivalent)   In Thousands of Bales (Net Weight—480 Lbs.)

Year	Jan.	Feb.	Mar.	Apr.	May	June	July	Aug.	Sept.	Oct.	Nov.	Dec.	Total
1976	42.8	41.6	54.6	48.0	41.1	47.8	39.0	39.0	45.8	57.5	45.6	53.2	556.0
1977	42.8	51.6	47.1	47.2	36.9	36.5	29.4	31.0	40.2	24.8	26.3	46.3	460.1
1978	32.2	35.2	37.1	35.2	34.5	33.0	31.4	35.9	37.9	44.8	50.1	50.4	457.9
1979	45.6	45.4	56.7	44.1	50.5	57.0	46.2	47.1	55.8	59.0	62.3	58.1	627.7
1980	50.6	54.2	52.4	45.2	42.4	47.2	34.6	44.3	48.0	42.0	38.4	40.9	540.2
1981	34.8	28.2	35.8	35.7	30.9	30.8	21.7	25.9	25.8	27.5	26.6	21.9	345.6
1982	18.2	18.6	20.4	20.6	24.3	24.8	22.7	15.7	18.4	20.7	18.4	16.4	239.2
1983	20.1	15.1	18.2	17.2	14.2	15.9	12.7	14.0	15.4	16.0	15.3	14.8	188.8
1984	14.2	12.3	13.6	13.4	14.2	16.9	13.5	12.8	15.7	16.7	14.1	13.5	170.9
1985[1]	18.7	15.2	19.8	21.2	17.3	18.6	65.7	21.6	24.7	17.4	15.6	14.7	220.5
1986[1]	17.5	20.1	23.6	23.5	27.4	23.6							

[1] Preliminary.   Source: Bureau of the Census   T.193

United States Cotton Ginnings

Crop Year	Aug. 1	Aug. 16	Sept. 1	Sept. 16	Oct. 1	Oct. 15	Nov. 1	Nov. 15	Dec. 1	Dec. 15	Jan. 1	Jan. 15	Feb. 1	Total Crop
						Ginnings to: (In Thousands of Running Bales)								
1978-9	144	N.A.	672	788	1,490	2,904	4,659	5,890	6,668	8,096	9,317	9,723	10,049	10,549
1979-0	72	N.A.	539	697	916	2,105	4,799	7,287	9,937	11,772	12,728	13,439	13,832	14,262
1980-1	200	N.A.	582	745	1,312	2,566	4,600	6,698	7,841	8,808	9,873	10,430	10,676	10,826
1981-2	44	N.A.	427	645	1,725	3,299	5,541	7,688	10,156	12,023	13,460	14,276	14,778	15,150
1982-3	40	N.A.	453	578	1,529	2,660	5,288	7,202	8,823	9,627	10,574	10,974	11,300	11,526
1983-4	2	N.A.	315	397	763	1,748	3,348	4,638	6,003	6,880	7,209	7,389	7,476	7,504
1984-5	163	N.A.	634	780	1,175	2,277	4,321	7,025	8,972	10,478	11,079	11,682	12,319	12,545
1985-6	70	N.A.	681	1,073	2,431	4,342	6,246	8,216	10,052	11,372	12,365	12,785	12,953	12,988
1986-7[1]	147	N.A.	624	1,023	2,408	3,621	5,291	6,375	7,495	8,273	8,590			

[1] Preliminary.   Source: Bureau of Census   T.171

COTTON

Cotton Government Loan Program in the United States

Crop Yr. Beginning Aug.	Acreage — Prospective Planting Intentions (Thousand Acres)	Acreage — Harvested (Thousand Acres)	Loan Rate — Avg. at Spot[2] Mkts. (¢ Per Lb.)	Loan Rate — Target Price (¢ Per Lb.)	Stocks—Aug. 1 — Gov't Owned	Stocks—Aug. 1 — Loan	Stocks—Aug. 1 — Total Stock	Loan Entries	Total Supply	Loan Cotton Repossessed	Total Distribution
1980–1	14,843	13,215	48.00	58.40	—	542	542	2,328	2,870	2,218	2,218
1981–2	14,484	13,841	52.46	70.87	—	652	652	6,082	6,734	2,975	2,975
1982–3	12,599	9,734	57.08	71.00	2	3,757	3,759	5,056	8,815	4,049	4,049
1983–4	9,281	7,348	55.00	76.00	334	4,432	4,766	1,782	6,416	5,958	5,958
1984–5	10,759	10,379	55.00	81.00	121	469	590	2,974	3,564	1,755	1,755
1985–6[1]	10,957	10,229	57.30	81.00	152	1,657	1,809	7,396	9,205	2,376	2,376
1986–7[3]	9,711	8,492	55.00	81.00	766	6,063	6,829	4,500	11,329	5,500	5,500

[1] Preliminary. [2] Strict low middling, 1¹/₁₆″ at 10 markets. [3] Estimate. *Source: Department of Agriculture* T.174

Purchases Reported by Exchanges in Designated U.S. Spot Markets   In Running Bales

Year Beginning August 1	Aug.	Sept.	Oct.	Nov.	Dec.	Jan.	Feb.	Mar.	Apr.	May	June	July	Total
1979	284,889	229,192	529,677	1,499,688	2,498,483	2,901,588	1,068,127	642,337	333,008	139,875	123,119	110,892	10,360,875
1980	107,920	92,769	499,579	961,488	1,565,792	1,143,395	878,913	576,871	268,136	243,096	142,885	121,300	6,602,144
1981	115,017	201,791	468,124	821,205	1,606,620	2,049,345	1,163,850	877,323	403,824	449,948	277,553	420,336	8,854,936
1982	122,082	150,629	375,083	717,258	1,160,522	1,139,575	793,071	829,016	356,510	434,794	478,658	247,150	6,804,348
1983	236,607	270,662	688,534	1,022,458	1,639,279	1,697,601	750,963	424,475	162,863	171,484	59,012	126,720	7,250,658
1984	258,511	154,557	271,195	558,999	1,153,086	1,015,087	570,259	287,483	303,501	159.540	123,089	131,035	4,986,342
1985	166,725	152,795	258,891	395,097	570,460	671,758	389,436	416,654	487,813	626,319	968,185	690,947	5,795,080
1986	585,628	638,356	392,451	422,542	1,353,241								

[1] Purchases are for 10 markets; commencing February 1980 purchases are for nine markets; and commencing March 28, 1983 purchases are for eight markets. *Source: Agricultural Marketing Service: U.S.D.A.* T.190a

Raw Cotton Equivalent of U.S. Textile Exports   In Thousands of Pounds

Year and month	Semi-Manufactured — Yarn	Semi-Manufactured — Sewing thread crochet, darning and embroidery cotton	Semi-Manufactured — Fabric standard constructions	Semi-Manufactured — Other fabric	Semi-Manufactured — Total all	Manufactured Products — Blankets, spreads, pillow cases, and sheets	Manufactured Products — Towels	Wearing Apparel — Knit	Wearing Apparel — Other than knit	Manufactured Products — Other household and clothing articles	Manufactured Products — Floor covering	Manufactured Products — Industrial products	Manufactured Products — Total all	Grand total exports
1982	17,981	11,277	71,570	13,186	114,838	14,092	6,222	34,713	45,321	15,918	N.A.	14,277	138,506	253,342
1983	18,854	11,577	51,667	7,747	90,636	8,725	5,705	27,957	44,113	13,736	13,986	11,601	128,977	219,614
1984	11,186	8,369	55,848	5,997	82,047	9,008	4,470	25,904	42,360	13,894	9,813	15,014	124,032	206,081
Jan. 1985	1,133	499	6,916	391	8,981	707	312	2,014	1,977	1,309	834	1,132	8,552	17,533
Feb.	534	930	5,506	306	7,306	785	238	2,242	2,254	1,275	384	1,189	8,558	15,863
Mar.	957	855	7,347	296	9,524	837	234	2,708	2,523	874	686	1,600	9,692	19,217
Apr.	1,147	833	7,719	427	10,160	815	367	2,554	3,381	700	736	1,688	10,482	20,643
May	1,459	645	5,776	395	8,319	891	335	2,236	2,303	777	740	1,186	8,642	16,961
June	1,616	886	5,992	431	8,943	838	323	1,590	2,087	859	713	1,456	8,244	17,187
July	1,099	257	5,775	383	7,530	923	429	1,557	2,252	807	686	975	7,779	15,309
Aug.	1,570	761	7,297	687	10,367	948	356	1,999	2,307	537	740	1,613	8,666	19,033
Sept.	4,342	1,119	6,026	336	11,867	707	165	2,062	2,517	805	608	1,262	8,348	20,215
Oct.	1,170	579	6,056	492	8,360	835	350	2,174	3,054	983	688	1,677	10,041	18,401
Nov.	1,029	569	5,242	590	7,481	646	237	2,498	3,335	1,122	744	1,439	10,291	17,771
Dec.	787	533	5,267	400	7,054	870	236	1,692	2,168	989	596	1,324	8,037	15,091
Total	16,843	8,466	74,919	5,134	105,892	9,802	3,582	25,326	30,158	11,037	8,155	16,541	107,332	213,224
Jan. 1986	935	497	6,469	446	8,404	491	342	1,801	2,060	933	636	1,438	7,827	16,231
Feb.	749	347	7,864	599	9,651	533	325	1,754	2,934	839	581	1,905	9,056	18,707
Mar.	680	1,056	8,985	604	11,341	776	415	2,737	3,397	917	774	1,821	11,043	22,384
Apr.	709	275	9,698	545	11,296	938	281	2,348	3,054	3,274	889	1,941	12,974	24,270
May	764	922	10,914	488	13,145	526	459	2,093	3,996	1,182	820	1,752	11,073	24,218
June	929	311	9,599	485	11,350	498	345	2,061	3,935	819	814	1,645	10,414	21,763
July	561	377	6,699	588	8,293	590	300	2,035	3,486	771	731	2,381	10,507	18,800

Source: Bureau of the Census

Cotton Cloth[1] Production in the United States   In Millions of Linear Yards

Year	First Quarter	Second Quarter	Third Quarter	Fourth Quarter	Total Year	Year	First Quarter	Second Quarter	Third Quarter	Fourth Quarter	Total Year
1979	1,018	998	914	927	3,858	1983	1,068	1,052	1,032	1,040	4,192
1980	1,226	1,182	987	1,062	4,456	1984	1,069	1,031	947	955	4,002
1981	966	961	942	987	3,856	1985[2]	1,014	982	933	955	3,921
1982	979	961	868	987	3,794	1986[2]	1,045	944			

[1] Cotton broadwoven goods over 12 inches in width.   [2] Preliminary.   *Source: Bureau of the Census*   T.192

U.S. American Upland Cotton—Ginnings, by Staple Length   In Thousands Running of Bales

Year beginning August	($^{13}/_{16}$'') 26 & under	($^7/_8$'') 28	($^{29}/_{32}$'') 29	($^{15}/_{16}$'') 30	($^{31}/_{32}$'') 31	(1'') 32	(1$^1/_{32}$'') 33	(1$^1/_{16}$'') 34	(1$^3/_{32}$'') 35	(1$^1/_8$'') 36 & Over	All staple lengths
1978	1	9	89	432	877	1,335	1,090	2,497	3,113	1,017	10,459
1979	4	24	126	650	1,453	1,775	1,239	1,462	4,378	3,056	14,166
1980	7	51	164	452	798	1,040	903	1,670	3,318	2,322	10,724
1981	2	25	155	805	1,924	1,700	1,124	2,725	4,419	2,194	15,073
1982	2	16	78	412	935	676	454	985	3,509	4,362	11,430
1983	3	22	65	251	482	471	513	1,012	2,531	2,063	7,413
1984[1]	7	45	122	414	761	719	715	1,149	2,858	5,630	12,419

[1] Preliminary.   *Source: Agricultural Marketing Service, U.S.D.A.*   T.179

Raw Cotton Equivalent of U.S. Textile Exports   In Thousands of Pounds

Year and month	Yarn, Thread, and Woven Fabric — Yarn	Woven Fabric — 100 percent cotton	Blends	Total All	Pile fabrics and mfrs.	Bed clothes and towels	Gloves, hosiery, and hdkf.	Other wearing apparel	Lace fabric and articles	House-hold and clothing articles	Misc. products	Floor cover-ing	Total All	Grand total imports
1982	27,264	218,619	41,518	288,645	6,342	64,060	22,652	487,867	4,046	10,628	10,053	2,408	608,537	897,182
1983	40,881	274,467	64,108	380,706	7,721	70,067	25,383	597,423	5,957	11,855	14,335	7,526	740,631	1,121,337
1984	52,897	360,701	90,126	505,533	12,572	106,468	26,609	733,111	9,651	18,652	18,992	14,649	941,193	1,446,726
Jan. 1985	2,592	21,340	4,927	29,004	1,547	9,766	2,492	61,663	980	1,400	2,011	1,299	81,342	110,346
Feb.	3,611	31,859	5,253	40,956	1,256	11,024	2,244	75,427	743	1,035	1,861	1,424	95,198	136,154
Mar.	3,175	30,214	7,587	41,262	1,491	12,212	3,191	75,505	1,365	1,227	2,161	1,985	99,283	140,543
Apr.	4,235	25,916	6,726	37,087	1,374	9,495	2,344	56,918	894	1,234	1,669	1,600	75,709	112,797
May	3,902	29,293	11,706	45,117	2,055	11,420	1,939	71,308	1,203	1,865	1,707	1,908	93,526	138,642
June	3,732	26,534	8,589	39,140	2,168	10,505	2,614	72,970	1,029	1,699	1,962	1,244	94,344	133,490
July	5,028	25,398	8,326	38,975	1,420	10,649	2,479	85,042	1,303	1,277	1,714	1,294	105,439	144,414
Aug.	3,878	23,742	7,158	34,861	1,702	9,993	3,444	68,919	920	1,184	1,386	1,539	89,346	124,107
Sept.	5,277	29,577	9,061	44,066	1,512	11,927	3,004	82,090	433	2,880	1,034	1,384	104,146	148,511
Oct.	5,658	30,019	9,923	45,823	1,040	-9,212	2,590	69,560	469	1,940	479	1,436	86,924	132,748
Nov.	6,968	33,269	7,075	47,469	1,213	10,587	2,071	72,454	379	1,933	4,282	1,373	94,475	141,943
Dec.	5,762	34,735	7,238	48,114	1,138	10,704	1,640	73,620	654	2,007	899	1,498	92,325	140,439
Total	53,818	341,896	93,569	491,874	17,916	127,494	30,052	865,476	10,372	19,681	21,165	17,984	1,112,262	1,604,134
Jan. 1986	6,473	41,232	7,959	55,851	1,961	11,269	2,244	89,130	588	2,220	3,798	1,467	112,893	168,743
Feb.	8,184	35,354	8,553	52,380	1,664	9,962	1,932	91,202	562	2,072	4,758	1,404	113,916	166,295
Mar.	9,468	41,967	10,181	61,873	1,729	13,340	3,169	87,533	674	2,541	4,177	1,698	115,174	177,046
Apr.	8,805	36,960	10,016	55,981	1,658	13,380	2,098	68,393	493	2,328	3,434	1,434	93,635	149,617
May	8,641	33,452	8,809	51,103	1,594	10,570	2,340	76,971	604	2,292	3,756	1,724	100,210	151,313
June	8,369	32,599	9,122	50,339	2,109	9,227	2,166	89,172	598	3,106	3,766	1,422	111,877	162,216
July	11,408	39,826	9,547	61,029	1,804	10,689	1,772	96,365	615	2,600	4,072	1,701	119,962	180,991

Source: Bureau of the Census

Cottonseed and Products

Cottonseed, a byproduct of cotton ginning, is not directly affected by domestic and international supply/demand factors. World production for 1986/87 was estimated by USDA at 26.71 million tonnes, down more than 12 percent from the 1985/86 estimate of 30.4 million tonnes. Output in China, now the world's largest producer, was estimated to be off 16 percent from 1985/86, due primarily to reduced acreage as farmers shifted to other crops. Output in the USSR, the next major producer, was estimated to be down over seven percent; U.S. production was forecast to be off 27 percent. The drop in U.S. production was mainly due to the large participation of farmers in the cotton acreage reduction program.

World cottonseed trade was expected to increase only slightly in 1986/87 and to account for less than one percent of world production. Mexico is the most important market for U.S. cottonseed, accounting for more than 96 percent of U.S. shipments. Japan is expected to remain the world's largest import market for cottonseed in 1986/87, with Denmark the world's largest importer of cottonseed meal.

Global production of cottonseed oil in 1986/87 was forecast by USDA at 3.1 million tonnes, 12 percent lower than in 1985/86, primarily because of reduced output in the U.S. and China. World consumption is forecast to be down two percent; a drawdown in stocks will be required to meet needs. Consumption in Egypt is expected to be up seven percent and the country's imports are projected to expand by 14 percent. The leading importer of cottonseed oil, Egypt has been purchasing larger quantities to meet the needs of its growing population. The U.S. is the world's major exporter; over 55 percent of production is exported, with Venezuela, Egypt, and Japan the main destinations.

World Production of Cottonseed   In Thousands of Metric Tons

Crop Year	Sudan	Argentina	Brazil	China	Egypt	India	Mexico	Pakistan	Peru	Turkey	South Africa	USSR	United States	World Total
1980–1	192	315	1,133	4,602	844	2,749	590	1,429	151	800	116	5,082	4,056	24,807
1981–2	306	170	1,164	5,046	805	2,961	525	1,497	130	781	72	5,279	5,803	27,493
1982–3	421	290	1,198	6,117	769	3,047	313	1,648	60	782	53	5,094	4,304	26,647
1983–4	438	220	995	7,883	680	2,647	377	1,021	100	835	73	4,815	2,791	26,084
1984–5	435	294	1,758	10,639	664	3,447	450	2,014	130	928	100	4,740	4,671	33,875
1985–6[1]			1,500	7,050	698	3,650		2,470		810		4,810	4,789	30,390
1986–7[2]			1,340	6,360	690	3,390		2,410		760		4,470	3,504	27,360

[1] Preliminary.   [2] Estimated.   *Source: Foreign Agricultural Service, U.S.D.A.*   T.194

Salient Statistics of Cottonseed in the United States

Year Begin. Aug.	Farm Value of Production Mil. $	Exports	Seed for Planting	Residual[2]	Crushings	Oil	Meal	Linters[5]	Hulls	Other[3]	Oil	Meal	Linters	Hulls	Farm Price $ Per Ton
			— In Thousands of Short Tons —					In Million Pounds					In Pounds		
1980–1	574.5	133	—	922 —	4,076	1,195	3,580	1,097							129.00
1981–2	549.0	45	— 1,394 —		4,575	1,551	4,380	1,210							86.00
1982–3	366.2	12	— 1,342 —		3,800	1,134	3,176	1,029							77.00
1983–4	511.5	50	— 698 —		2,583	777	2,268	699							166.00
1984–5[1]	512.9	60	— 1,285 —		3,514	1,174	3,464								100.00
1985–6[1]	343.1	9	— 1,912 —		3,417	1,070	3,058								65.00
1986–7[4]	272.8	25	— 1,569 —		2,500	800	2,292								70.00

[1] Preliminary.   [2] Mainly used on farms for feed & fertilizer.   [3] Including loss; and also motes, grabbots & hullfibers.   [4] Forecast.
[5] In thousands of running bales.   *Source: Economic Research Service, U.S.D.A.*   T.195

Supply & Distribution of Cottonseed Oil in the United States   In Millions of Pounds

Crop Year[3] Beginning Oct.	Production	Imports for Consumption	Stocks Oct. 1	Total Supply	Exports	Total	Domestic	Per Capita Consumption in Lbs.	Shortening	Margarine	Salad & Cooking Oils	Other	Total	Foots & Loss	Other	Total
1981	1,551	—	80	1,631	847	1,527	680		167	22	402	12	603			
1982	1,134	2	104	1,240	546	1,150	604		142	31	444	16	634			
1983	777	18	90	885	303	835	532		143	35	366	17	562			
1984[1]	1,174	—	50	1,224	433	1,117	684		156	77	399	33	607			
1985–6[2]	1,070	—	107	1,177	442	1,087	645		191		342		579			
1986–7[2]	800	—	90	890	350	840	490									

[1] Preliminary.   [2] Estimate.   *Source: Economic Research Service, U.S.D.A.*   T.201

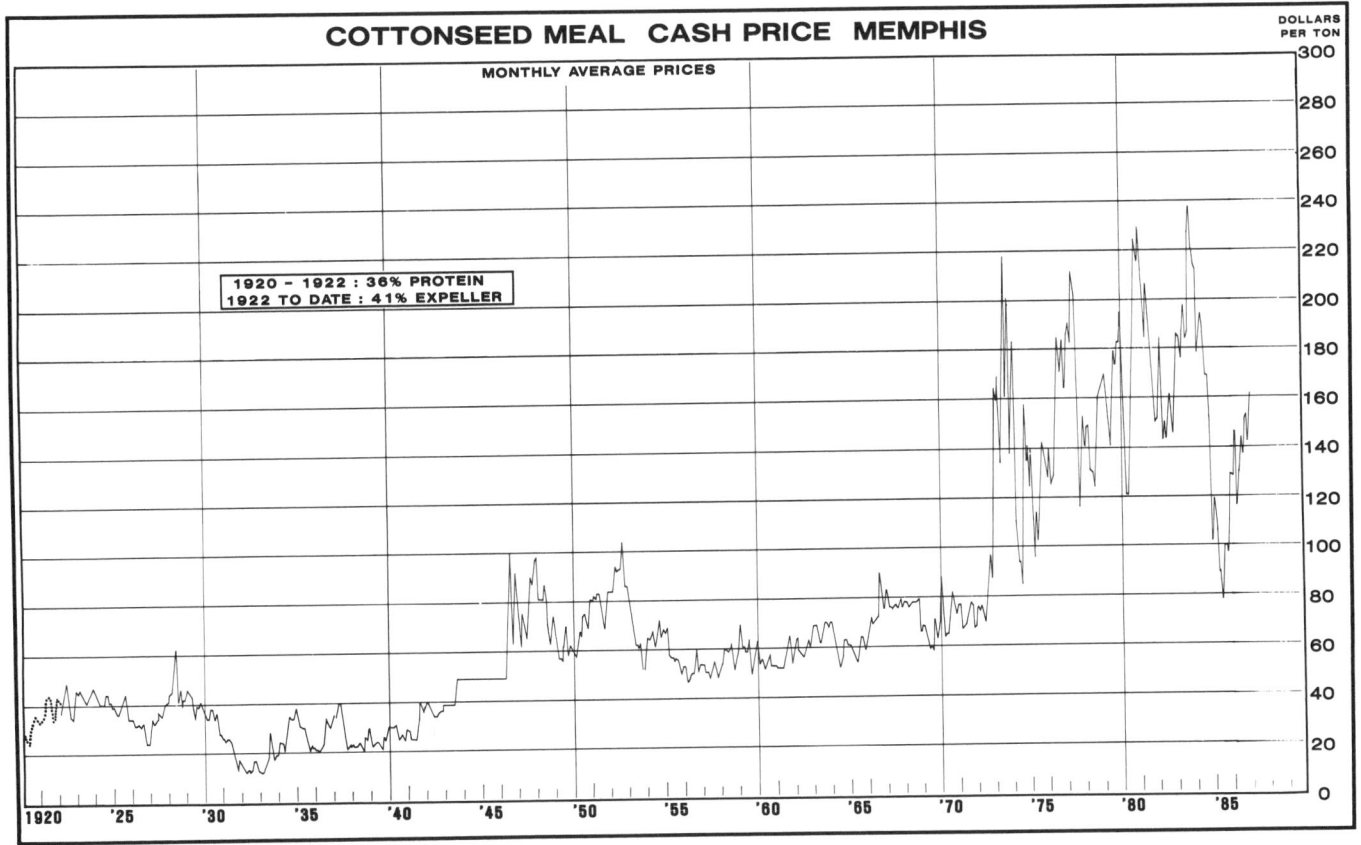

COTTONSEED MEAL CASH PRICE MEMPHIS

MONTHLY AVERAGE PRICES

DOLLARS PER TON

1920 – 1922 : 36% PROTEIN
1922 TO DATE : 41% EXPELLER

U.S. Consumption of Cottonseed Oil in End Products[1]   In Millions of Pounds

Year	Aug.	Sept.	Oct.	Nov.	Dec.	Jan.	Feb.	Mar.	Apr.	May	June	July	Total
1981–2	43.4	46.5	44.8	58.6	55.0	45.7	40.3	56.8	51.7	56.0	52.5	42.2	593.5
1982–3	54.1	50.4	47.3	56.1	60.0	49.0	53.2	52.0	53.0	56.6	59.1	54.7	645.5
1983–4	54.3	42.4	39.7	46.8	46.9	47.5	55.5	52.1	48.8	57.3	50.1	45.6	587.0
1984–5	43.1	35.5	42.8	55.1	63.5	54.2	58.4	59.2	52.3	64.0	50.2	45.2	623.4
1985–6[2]	40.4	44.8	58.8	50.5	49.1	53.0	61.0	53.2	50.8	53.2	50.8	63.6	629.2
1986–7[2]	50.5	47.9	56.0										

[1] Includes small amount exported but does not include imported oil.   [2] Preliminary.   *Source: Bureau of the Census*   T.206

U.S. Exports of Cottonseed Oil (Crude & Refined)   In Millions of Pounds

Year	Jan.	Feb.	Mar.	Apr.	May	June	July	Aug.	Sept.	Oct.	Nov.	Dec.	Total
1981	77.0	29.3	66.7	82.1	72.2	85.7	46.9	35.9	46.5	42.2	37.4	80.5	702.3
1982	41.2	146.2	110.6	68.6	74.5	67.0	63.7	47.3	68.4	52.2	60.0	54.7	854.4
1983	41.8	58.8	97.0	25.8	53.0	23.8	42.5	15.5	20.6	10.5	18.4	21.8	429.5
1984	36.4	39.9	31.8	32.9	46.5	12.8	29.9	8.8	13.1	11.0	37.1	77.3	377.5
1985	47.1	72.7	37.7	38.9	22.9	20.6	17.5	13.1	36.2	19.1	30.1	65.6	421.5
1986[1]	21.9	39.6	32.6	52.6	59.6	27.3	25.1	46.7	19.8				

[1] Preliminary.   *Source: Dept. of Commerce*   T.205

Average Wholesale Price of Cottonseed Meal (41% Solvent) at Memphis   In Dollars Per Short Ton

Year	Jan.	Feb.	Mar.	Apr.	May	June	July	Aug.	Sept.	Oct.	Nov.	Dec.	Average
1982	184.70	159.40	138.00	148.10	143.75	150.00	158.75	161.50	150.00	145.60	161.70	166.25	155.65
1983	169.40	165.60	153.00	173.40	167.50	164.90	186.90	227.00	237.50	245.00	219.20	214.00	232.34
1984	212.60	178.10	187.30	194.10	190.00	177.50	169.30	168.90	151.60	114.90	101.60	119.40	163.78
1985	109.75	105.60	89.10	82.75	78.10	94.40	99.75	100.00	96.90	116.50	128.75	127.82	102.45
1986	146.25	128.75	115.60	129.25	133.75	132.50	137.00	150.60	152.50	141.90	157.50		

Source: Economic Research Service, U.S.D.A.   T.196

COTTONSEED AND PRODUCTS

Cottonseed Crushed (Consumption) in the United States   In Thousands of Short Tons

Year	Aug.	Sept.	Oct.	Nov.	Dec.	Jan.	Feb.	Mar.	Apr.	May	June	July	Total
1980–1	330	306	365	426	400	440	378	372	314	278	248	218	4,076
1981–2	191.6	186.2	323.5	455.5	473.3	478.8	446.6	482.3	424.1	426.7	357.1	329.6	4,575
1982–3	290.3	285.8	391.5	481.7	432.6	435.6	368.7	321.7	240.5	214.6	164.2	172.3	3,800
1983–4	166.6	120.7	187.9	301.8	296.6	347.8	289.7	294.7	205.6	173.2	124.3	74.1	2,579
1984–5	70.2	72.6	274.3	423.1	424.2	453.4	394.5	395.3	316.2	279.5	219.6	191.3	3,514
1985–6[1]	194.6	197.0	338.0	411.4	368.8	431.5	361.0	349.8	281.3	213.8	154.5	115.3	3,417
1986–7[1]	141.7	167.7	208.5	258.6									

[1] Preliminary.   *Source: Bureau of Census*   T.197

Production of Cottonseed Cake and Meal in the United States   In Thousands of Short Tons

Year	Aug.	Sept.	Oct.	Nov.	Dec.	Jan.	Feb.	Mar.	Apr.	May	June	July	Total
1980–1	152.3	144.0	170.3	202.1	191.1	204.9	176.3	173.4	145.5	130.8	114.2	104.2	1,909
1981–2	88.3	88.7	152.1	220.2	219.0	226.9	206.5	220.3	195.3	195.9	164.4	150.2	2,128
1982–3	129.8	129.3	173.5	219.4	197.3	195.1	167.0	146.7	107.8	97.1	71.4	78.9	1,713
1983–4	78.8	55.3	86.7	144.5	140.9	162.4	134.7	136.2	95.1	76.7	55.9	35.8	1,203
1984–5	32.2	32.6	127.3	198.4	198.7	207.7	180.4	181.6	145.0	128.8	99.1	86.2	1,619
1985–6[1]	87.9	90.7	153.1	187.6	169.4	199.1	166.4	159.1	128.6	97.5	71.5	51.9	1,563
1986–7[1]	64.4	77.7	95.0	119.2									

[1] Preliminary.   *Source: Bureau of Census*   T.198

U.S. Production of Crude Cottonseed Oil   In Millions of Pounds

Year	Aug.	Sept.	Oct.	Nov.	Dec.	Jan.	Feb.	Mar.	Apr.	May	June	July	Total
1980–1	104.9	93.1	116.4	130.6	122.3	131.7	118.9	115.4	100.8	88.7	77.4	69.6	1,270
1981–2	62.1	60.9	111.2	153.5	161.8	154.1	145.6	155.9	138.4	140.1	117.5	105.9	1,507
1982–3	92.0	88.8	129.8	157.3	143.3	137.6	117.7	102.6	75.8	69.0	53.1	55.7	1,223
1983–4	54.6	37.1	58.6	94.6	93.6	109.5	91.3	96.6	69.3	55.4	40.1	24.4	825
1984–5	21.7	21.6	84.3	132.5	132.5	141.5	124.3	123.3	96.3	87.0	67.7	62.9	1,096
1985–6[1]	60.9	60.7	105.6	129.8	117.1	136.4	115.6	112.0	93.5	69.6	50.1	37.8	1,089
1986–7[1]	48.0	54.5	64.5	82.2									

[1] Preliminary.   *Source: Bureau of Census*   T.199

United States Production of Refined Cottonseed Oil   In Millions of Pounds

Year	Aug.	Sept.	Oct.	Nov.	Dec.	Jan.	Feb.	Mar.	Apr.	May	June	July	Total
1980–1	96.2	94.8	94.1	119.8	125.1	131.3	99.6	102.1	113.0	82.9	79.1	73.7	1,212
1981–2	56.9	53.1	84.7	129.3	144.6	110.2	121.2	135.7	124.9	128.9	121.8	104.8	1,316
1982–3	91.3	76.7	91.5	127.3	124.5	119.2	113.4	103.1	82.6	78.0	60.1	56.5	1,124
1983–4	55.2	39.2	54.6	91.1	97.7	99.7	98.4	100.6	89.1	71.5	43.4	30.5	871
1984–5	25.7	27.8	64.5	121.4	117.6	135.8	122.2	101.9	93.3	95.4	74.6	68.2	1,043
1985–6[1]	55.9	57.0	87.5	117.1	112.0	119.3	109.3	112.9	99.9	63.7	54.9	42.4	1,032
1986–7[1]	60.3	51.2	73.1										

[1] Preliminary.   *Source: Bureau of Census*   T.202

U.S. Stocks of Cottonseed Oil (Crude & Refined) at End of Month   In Millions of Pounds

Year	Aug.	Sept.	Oct.	Nov.	Dec.	Jan.	Feb.	Mar.	Apr.	May	June	July
1980–1	138.6	121.9	122.5	152.8	170.1	183.5	200.1	202.4	165.9	160.1	121.7	113.0
1981–2	109.4	80.0	102.6	127.2	133.1	165.7	148.3	152.0	160.1	147.8	144.5	154.1
1982–3	115.2	103.6	121.1	148.9	172.2	175.3	175.1	158.1	164.6	130.4	113.6	108.9
1983–4	96.7	89.6	82.5	108.6	144.6	152.5	152.1	172.6	167.4	131.7	111.5	86.1
1984–5	61.2	49.8	57.6	74.6	79.4	89.6	98.6	114.2	114.7	107.7	105.8	124.4
1985–6[1]	131.2	106.9	106.2	127.9	129.4	162.0	184.1	197.7	179.7	168.0	154.5	110.4
1986–7[1]	90.4	84.9	77.2									

[1] Preliminary.   *Source: Bureau of Census*   T.203

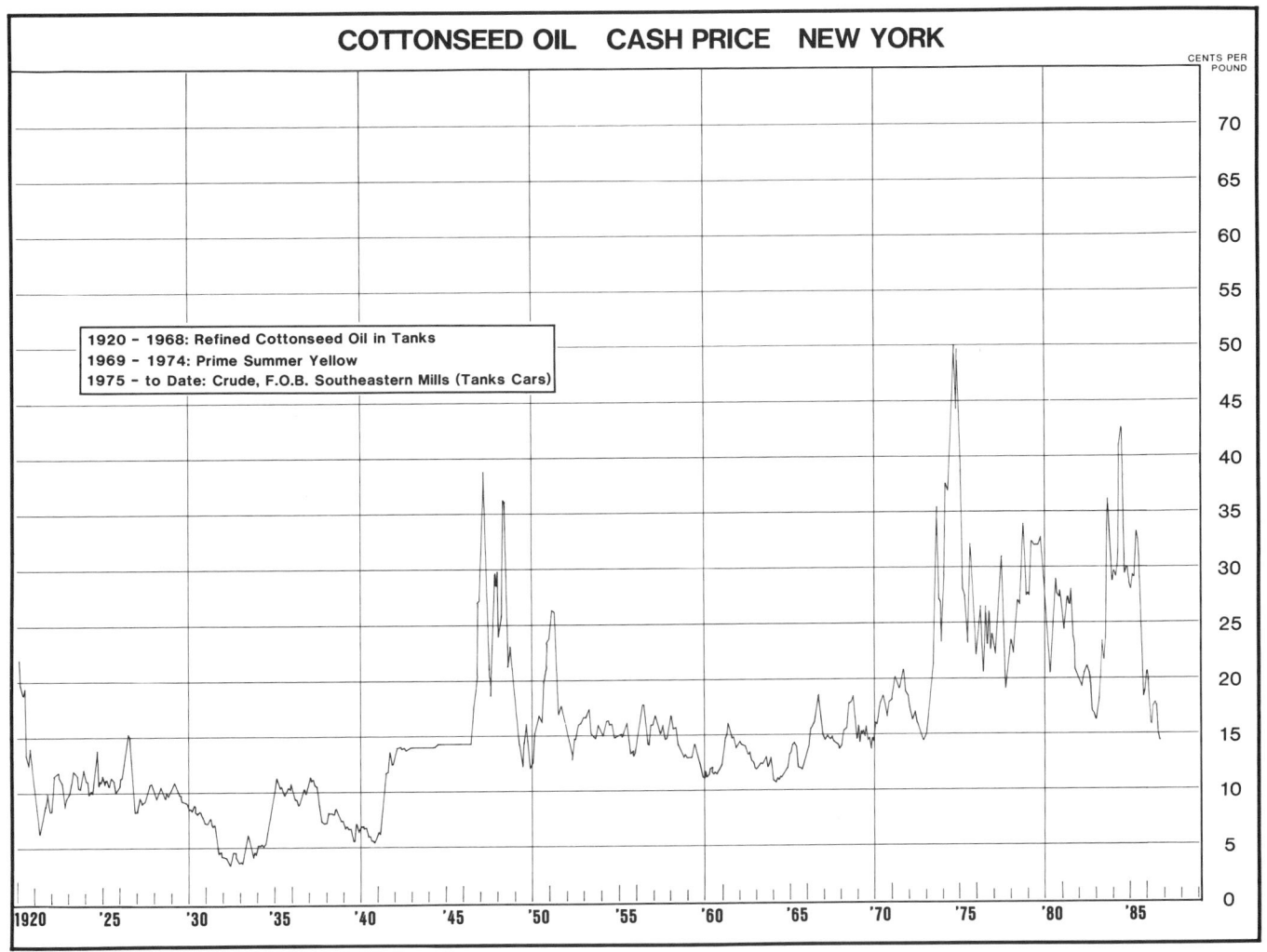

COTTONSEED OIL   CASH PRICE   NEW YORK

CENTS PER POUND

1920 – 1968: Refined Cottonseed Oil in Tanks
1969 – 1974: Prime Summer Yellow
1975 – to Date: Crude, F.O.B. Southeastern Mills (Tanks Cars)

Average Price of Crude Cottonseed Oil, F.O.B. Southeastern Mills (Tank Cars)   In Cents Per Pound

Year	Jan.	Feb.	Mar.	Apr.	May	June	July	Aug.	Sept.	Oct.	Nov.	Dec.	Average
1979	27.3	32.0	32.5	32.0	32.0	32.0	32.0	32.0	32.9	29.7	27.6	26.2	30.7
1980	24.3	23.8	22.4	20.4	20.9	22.3	27.8	29.0	27.5	27.2	27.8	27.0	25.0
1981	25.3	24.2	25.3	27.3	26.7	26.6	27.9	24.6	20.7	20.5	20.4	19.8	24.1
1982	19.9	19.5	19.1	20.4	21.0	21.1	20.9	20.3	18.0	16.9	16.8	16.3	19.2
1983	16.3	17.8	18.3	21.4	23.4	21.6	23.6	33.3	36.2	31.7	29.0	28.7	25.1
1984	29.8	29.1	30.1	31.4	41.1	42.6	36.3	32.7	31.0	30.6	31.0	29.3	32.9
1985	27.4	30.1	30.2	32.3	33.3	32.6	29.1	23.8	20.7	18.3	18.9	20.6	26.4
1986	19.9	17.6	15.8	17.5	17.7	17.9	17.6	15.1	14.3				

Source: Economic Research Service, U.S.D.A.   T.204

U.S. Exports of Cottonseed Oil to Important Countries   In Thousands of Metric Tons

Crop Year	Canada	Costa Rica	Dom. Rep.	Egypt	W. Germany	Guatemala	India	Iran	Japan	Korea	Netherlands	South Africa	Turkey	United Kingdom	Venezuela	Total
1979–0	5.3	1.9	28.4	157.1	—	0	0	—	23.0	1.9	5.2		3.0	.5	72.3	330.2
1980–1	2.5	1.0	33.2	75.6	—	0	27.2	0	40.2	2.5	5.8		—	1.5	109.1	321.9
1981–2	4.3	3.1	27.3	156.2	2.3	9.9	0	0	41.2	3.0	10.2		0	3.5	91.2	384.4
1982–3	4.3	.5	6.6	66.3	3.3	15.3	0	0	34.6	2.5	5.1	1.2	0	1.5	73.8	247.5
1983–4	3.5	0	4.5	31.2	7.9	1.1	—	—	16.7	2.9	2.1	1.8	—	3.0	55.4	137.4
1984–5[1]	3.3	1.0	3.9	55.9	—	9.8	—	—	22.8	1.8	5.8	2.0	—	1.5	70.0	196.2
1985–6[1]	2.7	—	5.9	37.8	4.9	11.1	—	—	26.3	4.5	8.0	1.6	—	.5	48.6	200.7

[1] Preliminary.   *Source: U.S. Bureau of the Census*   T.202A

Currencies

Throughout most of 1986, the U.S. dollar continued to fall against major currencies. The decline in U.S. interest rates, the Reagan Administration's desire to preempt protectionist legislation by improving the U.S. trade deficit, and market perceptions of a sluggish U.S. economy continued to exert pressure on the greenback.

In the first and second quarters, the dollar's weakness was primarily a carryover from the decline ushered in by the Plaza Agreement. In September, 1985, finance ministers from the U.S., Japan, West Germany, England and France met in New York to discuss coordinated actions to curb the dollar's strength. It was understood that the five countries, known as the Group of Five (G-5), would refrain from taking individual actions which would inject undue volatility into the monetary market. It was also agreed that the value of the dollar should decline.

Initially, the value of the dollar changed little against a number of other currencies and, in fact, appreciated against some Far Eastern currencies. Moreover, U.S. imports from Japan were not curtailed, despite a record-high yen. Japanese manufacturers reacted to an unfavorable swing in the yen by absorbing the foreign exchange loss and accepting lower profits. Later, however, there was a long slide in the dollar on broad perceptions that the U.S. economy's growth was sluggish and apt to remain so; this indicated the need for still-lower U.S. interest rates.

Discord in the G-5 began to surface in summer 1986, when West Germany and Japan failed to make interest rate cuts in line with those in the U.S. When the finance ministers—the number had increased to seven with Canada and Italy—met again in Washington in September, 1986, the focus was on the scale of the trade imbalance (i.e., huge deficits in the U.S. and record surpluses in Japan and Germany). There were fears that the imbalance could not be sustained without pushing the dollar lower and eventually bringing on a worldwide recession. Following those meetings, the Japanese yen moved sharply lower in October, 1986.

The Japanese economy slowed in 1986, especially within its manufacturing sector. The yen soared to a record high against the dollar in September, but then retreated considerably. Japan lowered its key lending rates during 1986, but further action appeared necessary to stimulate the economy. Additional rate cuts, if implemented, could restrain the yen's value against the dollar.

West Germany resisted U.S. pressure to lower its key lending rate in 1986. With a forecast of four to five percent growth in GNP (the forecast was later lowered to three percent), the Bundesbank wished to avoid overheating the economy. The mark made a high in September. After a brief interlude of decline, which occurred in tandem with the yen, the currency surged once more as the dollar slumped subsequent to the disclosure of arms sales to Iran.

The sharp increase in the mark's value during 1986 did not impede Germany's exports of durable goods, particularly automobiles to the U.S. The alignment of the mark within the European Monetary System in early January, 1987, was initially expected to have a limited impact on the dollar's value; the opposite occurred as the action tended to highlight economic problems in the U.S. and to underscore the strength of the West German economy. There was considerable interest in whether West Germany would lower its key lending rates. In January, 1987, the Bundesbank cut the Lombard rate by 0.5 percent to five percent; this tempered the mark's rise.

Futures Markets

The International Monetary Market (IMM) of the Chicago Mercantile Exchange lists futures contracts in the British pound, Canadian dollar, Deutschemark, Japanese yen, Swiss franc, Dutch guilder, French franc, and Mexican peso.

Monthly Close of the CRB Currency Futures Index   1977 = 100

Year	Jan.	Feb.	Mar.	Apr.	May	June	July	Aug.	Sept.	Oct.	Nov.	Dec.
1979			Not calculated prior to Sept 1979.						125.1	120.2	121.3	122.9
1980	122.9	120.5	115.1	120.2	122.7	123.6	121.7	124.5	125.0	123.8	121.9	122.5
1981	118.7	115.2	116.3	112.9	109.3	107.2	103.1	104.2	106.4	109.8	112.7	111.6
1982	109.4	105.6	104.7	106.6	104.0	99.7	100.2	93.9	97.7	96.2	98.8	102.4
1983	99.4	98.8	98.8	99.8	99.0	98.5	96.8	95.7	97.4	97.1	96.3	96.2
1984	93.9	97.1	97.7	95.1	94.1	92.2	88.8	89.8	86.2	86.5	84.3	83.1
1985	81.6	78.0	84.2	83.4	84.8	85.5	91.4	90.3	93.9	95.9	98.7	98.8
1986	99.5	103.9	103.3	108.5	104.3	109.6	112.4	113.2	112.3	109.2	112.0	114.4
1987	118.5	119.5										

Source: Commodity Research Bureau.

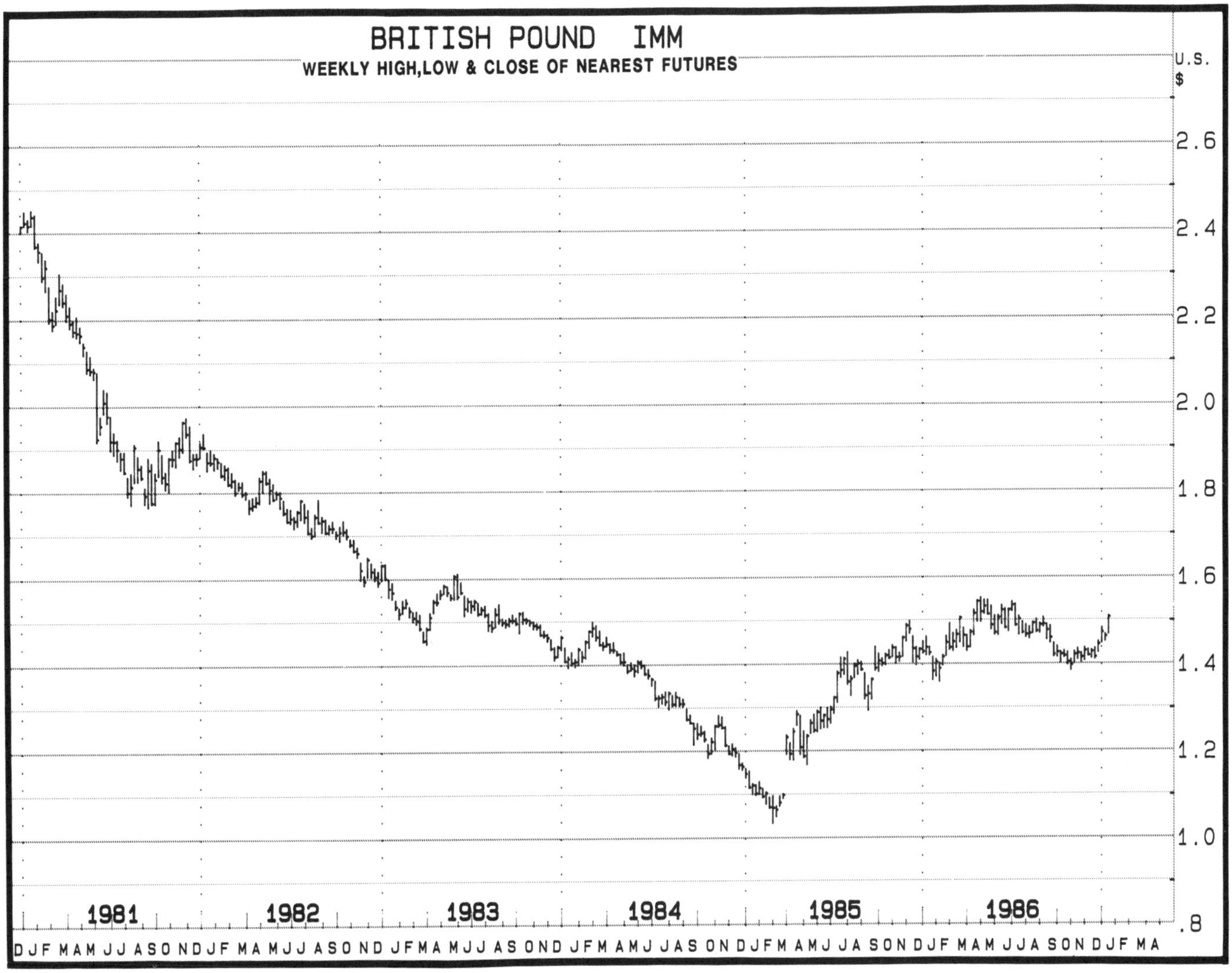

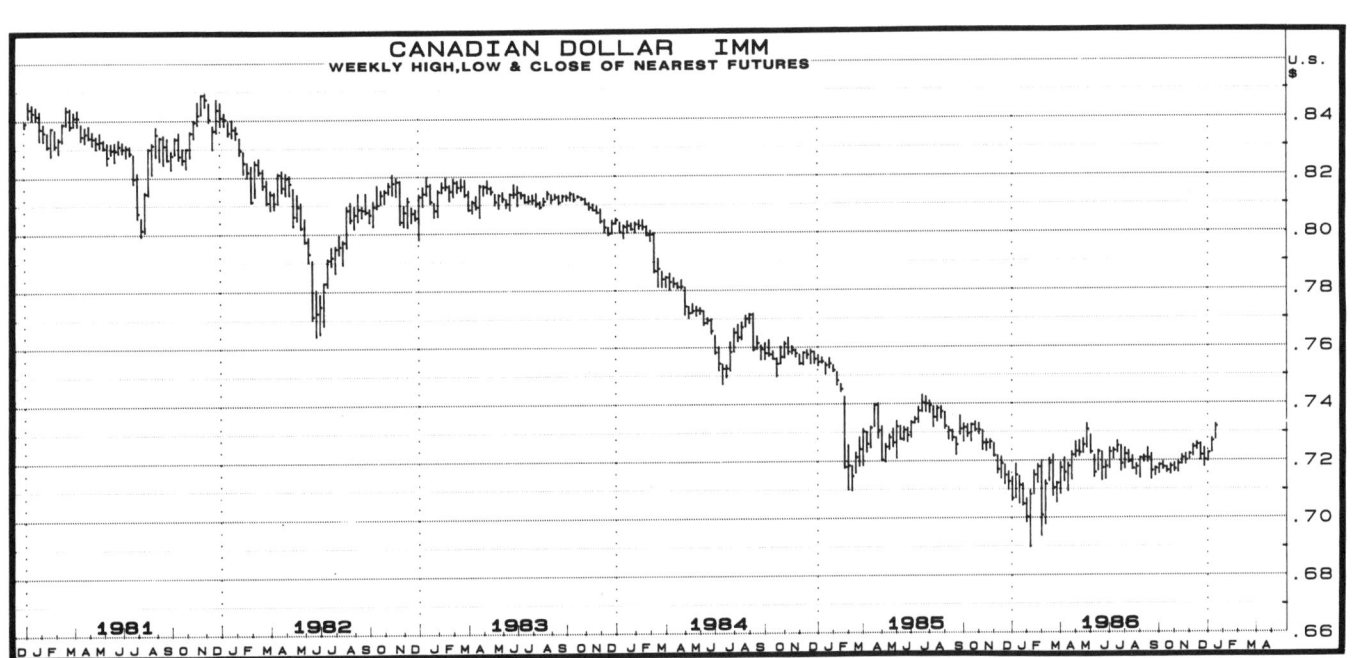

BRITISH POUND   IMM
WEEKLY HIGH, LOW & CLOSE OF NEAREST FUTURES

U.S. $

2.6

2.4

2.2

2.0

1.8

1.6

1.4

1.2

1.0

.8

1981   1982   1983   1984   1985   1986

D J F M A M J J A S O N D J F M A M J J A S O N D J F M A M J J A S O N D J F M A M J J A S O N D J F M A M J J A S O N D J F M A M J J A S O N D J F M A

CANADIAN DOLLAR   IMM
WEEKLY HIGH, LOW & CLOSE OF NEAREST FUTURES

U.S. $

.84

.82

.80

.78

.76

.74

.72

.70

.68

.66

1981   1982   1983   1984   1985   1986

D J F M A M J J A S O N D J F M A M J J A S O N D J F M A M J J A S O N D J F M A M J J A S O N D J F M A M J J A S O N D J F M A M J J A S O N D J F M A

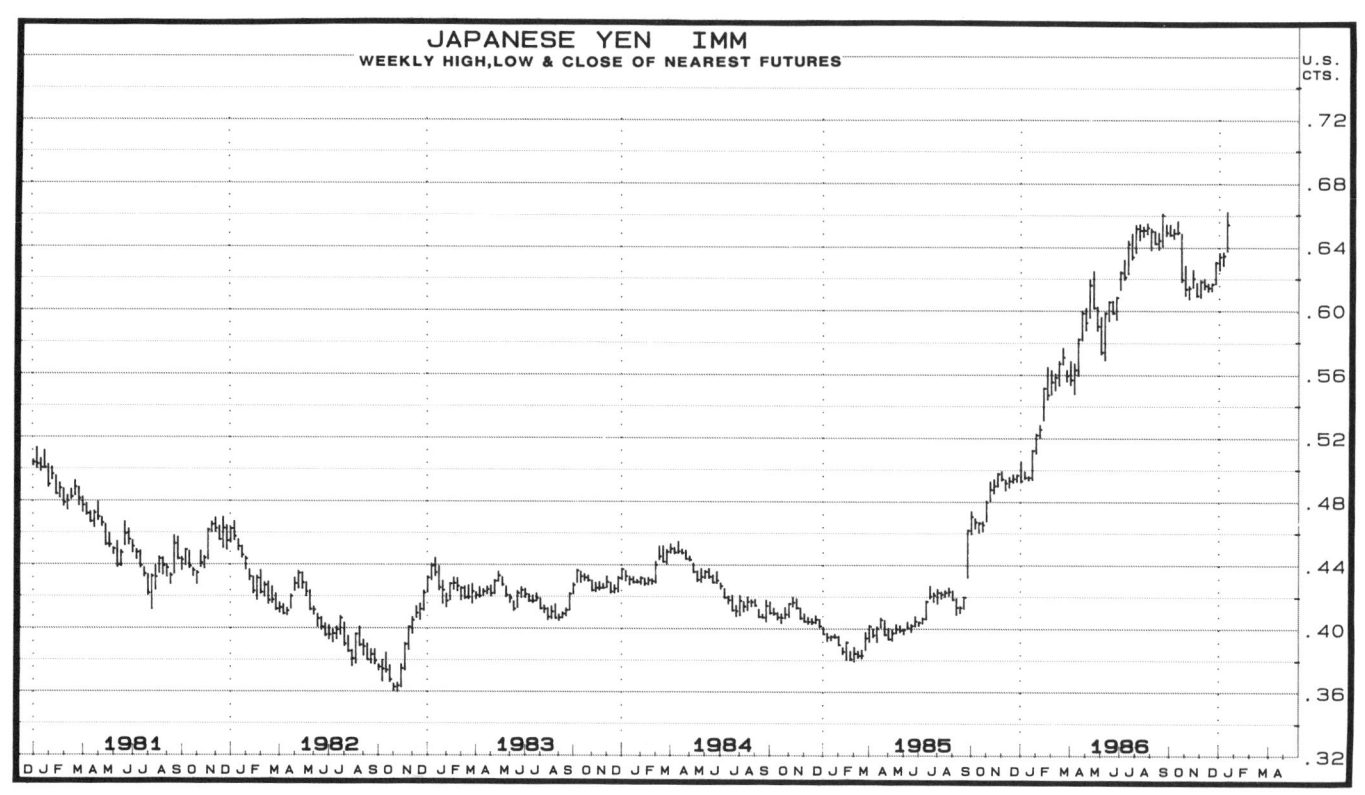

JAPANESE YEN   IMM
WEEKLY HIGH, LOW & CLOSE OF NEAREST FUTURES

U.S. CTS.

.72
.68
.64
.60
.56
.52
.48
.44
.40
.36
.32

1981   1982   1983   1984   1985   1986

D J F M A M J J A S O N D J F M A M J J A S O N D J F M A M J J A S O N D J F M A M J J A S O N D J F M A M J J A S O N D J F M A M J J A S O N D J F M A

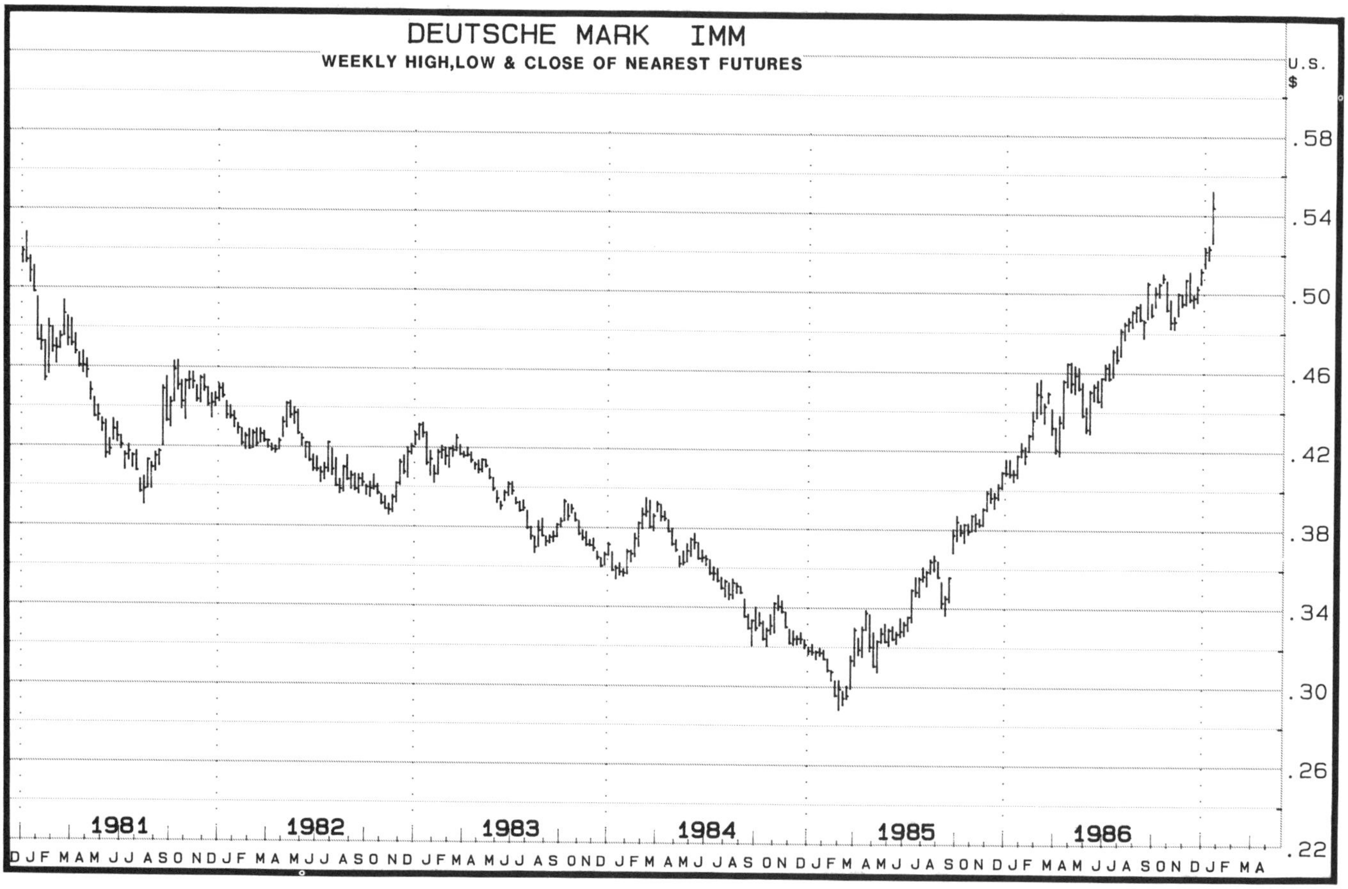

DEUTSCHE MARK   IMM
WEEKLY HIGH, LOW & CLOSE OF NEAREST FUTURES

U.S. $

.58
.54
.50
.46
.42
.38
.34
.30
.26
.22

1981   1982   1983   1984   1985   1986

D J F M A M J J A S O N D J F M A M J J A S O N D J F M A M J J A S O N D J F M A M J J A S O N D J F M A M J J A S O N D J F M A M J J A S O N D J F M A

80

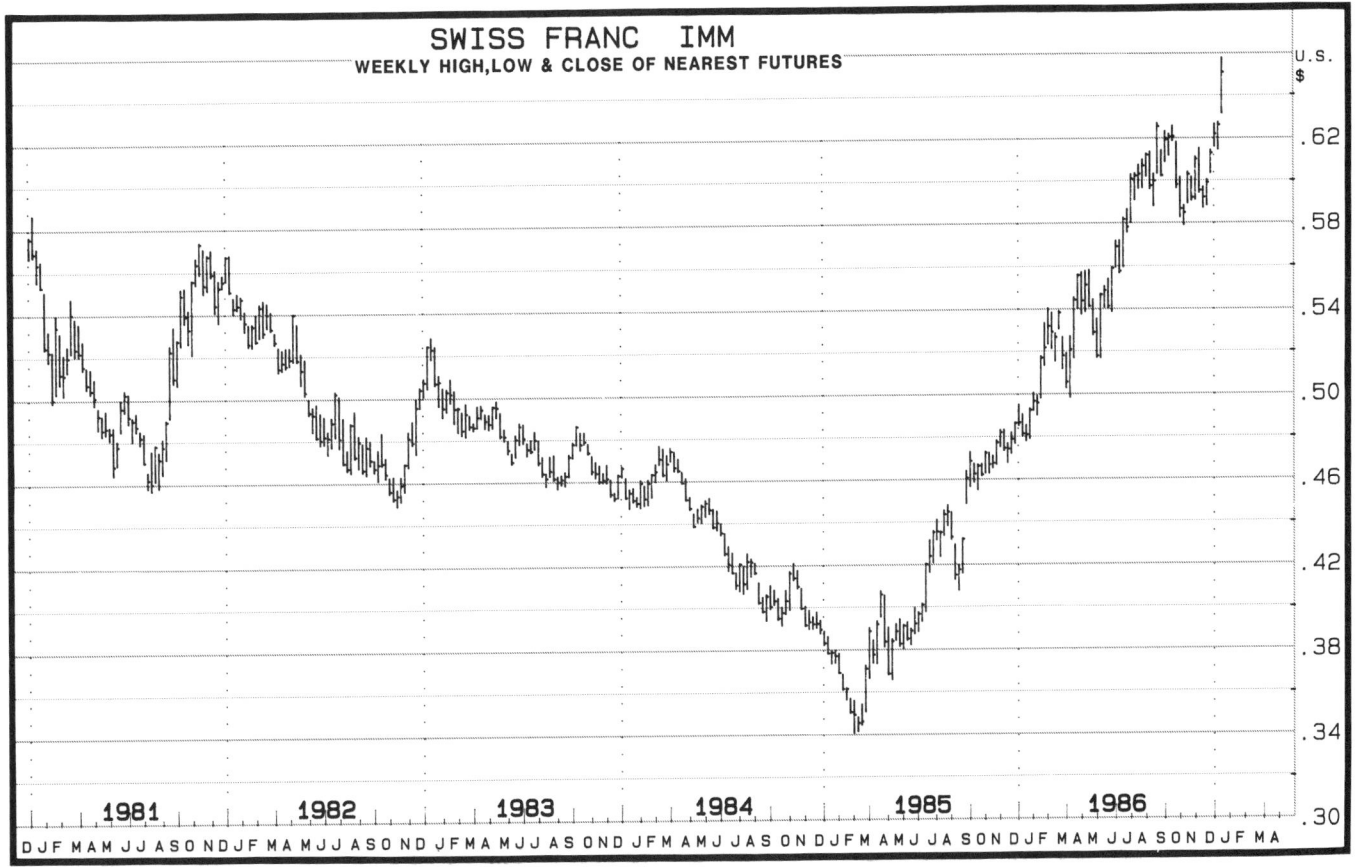

SWISS FRANC IMM
WEEKLY HIGH, LOW & CLOSE OF NEAREST FUTURES

Canadian Dollars per U.S. Dollar

Year	Jan.	Feb.	Mar.	Apr.	May	June	July	Aug.	Sept.	Oct.	Nov.	Dec.	Average
1982	1.192	1.214	1.220	1.230	1.225	1.275	1.268	1.250	1.234	1.229	1.226	1.238	1.233
1983	1.228	1.227	1.226	1.232	1.228	1.232	1.233	1.233	1.232	1.232	1.237	1.247	1.232
1984	1.248	1.248	1.269	1.279	1.294	1.304	1.323	1.303	1.314	1.318	1.316	1.320	1.295
1985	1.324	1.354	1.383	1.364	1.375	1.367	1.352	1.357	1.369	1.366	1.376	1.395	1.365
1986	1.407	1.404	1.400	1.387	1.375	1.389	1.386	1.388	1.387				

Source: Economic Research Service, U.S.D.A.   T.0581

German Marks per U.S. Dollar

Year	Jan.	Feb.	Mar.	Apr.	May	June	July	Aug.	Sept.	Oct.	Nov.	Dec.	Average
1982	2.293	2.365	2.379	2.397	2.308	2.430	2.464	2.477	2.502	2.530	2.555	2.419	2.427
1983	2.389	2.428	2.408	2.439	2.465	2.548	2.590	2.673	2.670	2.601	2.682	2.749	2.553
1984	2.810	2.698	2.596	2.647	2.746	2.738	2.848	2.882	3.028	3.066	2.997	3.102	2.846
1985	3.169	3.300	3.296	3.087	3.103	3.062	2.906	2.792	2.836	2.643	2.594	2.511	2.942
1986	2.437	2.330	2.276	2.268	2.263	2.232	2.148	2.060	2.040				

Source: Economic Research Service, U.S.D.A.   T.0582

Japanese Yen per U.S. Dollar

Year	Jan.	Feb.	Mar.	Apr.	May	June	July	Aug.	Sept.	Oct.	Nov.	Dec.	Average
1982	224.7	235.1	240.7	244.9	236.5	251.0	255.1	258.8	262.6	271.3	265.1	241.0	248.8
1983	232.5	236.1	238.0	237.6	234.7	240.0	240.4	244.4	242.9	232.3	234.9	234.3	237.5
1984	233.7	233.5	225.2	225.2	230.4	233.4	243.0	242.0	245.3	246.7	243.5	247.8	237.5
1985	254.1	260.2	257.8	251.5	251.6	248.8	241.1	237.3	236.2	214.6	203.8	202.7	238.3
1986	199.8	184.8	178.6	174.7	166.9	167.4	158.1	154.1	154.6				

Source: Economic Research Service, U.S.D.A.   T.0583

CURRENCIES

British Pound Per U.S. Dollar

Year	Jan.	Feb.	Mar.	Apr.	May	June	July	Aug.	Sept.	Oct.	Nov.	Dec.	Average
1982	.5300	.5410	.5536	.5638	.5521	.5685	.5760	.5791	.5837	.5890	.6119	.6180	.5722
1983	.6341	.6525	.6706	.6505	.6358	.6456	.6539	.6654	.6669	.6675	.6766	.6971	.6592
1984	.7102	.6931	.6864	.7036	.7190	.7257	.7572	.7608	.7954	.8197	.8066	.8428	.7517
1985	.8861	.9141	.8903	.8066	.8001	.7817	.7241	.7226	.7329	.7031	.6946	.6919	.7790
1986	.7014	.6999	.6809	.6671	.6564	.6625	.6631	.6726	.6809				

Source: Economic Research Service, U.S.D.A.

T.0580

Month–End Open Interest of British Pound Futures in Chicago   In Contracts

Year	Jan.	Feb.	Mar.	Apr.	May	June	July	Aug.	Sept.	Oct.	Nov.	Dec.
1982	11,622	18,839	20,374	17,621	11,478	19,464	12,580	15,022	15,459	15,155	20,083	14,854
1983	20,803	24,311	19,495	24,032	32,900	21,098	22,643	23,505	19,183	18,641	23,105	16,968
1984	20,972	27,563	17,939	20,035	17,876	13,072	15,710	15,105	15,473	18,921	21,701	15,624
1985	22,230	23,911	29,487	31,486	50,437	38,496	46,123	41,685	24,982	28,699	35,562	25,082
1986	38,235	40,880	28,187	39,520	30,584	24,702	26,211	27,788	37,506	36,992	34,127	23,145

Source: International Monetary Market (Chicago)

T.0584

Month–End Open Interest of Canadian Dollar Futures in Chicago   In Contracts

Year	Jan.	Feb.	Mar.	Apr.	May	June	July	Aug.	Sept.	Oct.	Nov.	Dec.
1982	8,540	11,001	15,770	10,920	16,098	18,895	15,503	17,811	12,434	14,057	17,534	18,033
1983	21,733	15,270	13,594	13,015	11,695	13,608	12,453	10,466	5,764	6,544	6,979	5,131
1984	5,624	5,607	9,572	12,306	10,484	7,684	8,244	8,197	6,397	7,737	10,641	7,775
1985	9,248	12,208	11,132	10,503	12,479	8,145	8,817	9,461	4,771	4,801	8,516	13,929
1986	18,922	15,075	9,748	13,670	14,977	9,400	13,739	17,501	9,358	12,377	14,648	14,937

Source: International Monetary Market (Chicago)

T.0585

Month–End Open Interest of Deutschemark Futures in Chicago   In Contracts

Year	Jan.	Feb.	Mar.	Apr.	May	June	July	Aug.	Sept.	Oct.	Nov.	Dec.
1982	13,411	12,974	13,824	16,874	13,293	11,917	13,903	14,025	14,600	14,491	22,873	19,792
1983	16,806	16,653	18,195	22,944	25,382	23,269	27,585	23,531	30,077	24,460	23,385	22,804
1984	24,830	38,569	37,871	33,228	34,665	25,166	29,713	34,871	37,068	42,785	44,888	33,746
1985	49,483	45,759	48,190	47,318	52,909	50,400	56,977	54,966	42,696	50,796	57,347	53,525
1986	56,622	70,411	53,054	58,819	58,486	38,698	50,631	57,849	45,708	47,807	58,346	44,292

Source: International Monetary Market (Chicago)

T.0586

Month–End Open Interest of Japanese Yen Futures in Chicago   In Contracts

Year	Jan.	Feb.	Mar.	Apr.	May	June	July	Aug.	Sept.	Oct.	Nov.	Dec.
1982	11,761	12,880	14,784	18,407	15,405	10,171	18,328	12,289	14,996	13,883	22,627	25,777
1983	26,913	31,388	23,095	31,378	39,661	28,279	32,731	27,510	37,616	36,891	34,976	32,998
1984	28,988	34,456	42,730	30,390	28,035	16,121	18,197	20,172	15,431	21,592	19,828	13,542
1985	13,755	16,206	21,333	17,893	18,251	22,258	37,861	35,896	32,581	37,658	39,605	28,058
1986	31,732	33,792	31,305	38,348	38,363	37,443	47,528	49,571	30,463	43,062	41,052	23,172

Source: International Monetary Market (Chicago)

T.0587

Month–End Open Interest of Swiss Franc Futures in Chicago   In Contracts

Year	Jan.	Feb.	Mar.	Apr.	May	June	July	Aug.	Sept.	Oct.	Nov.	Dec.
1982	11,493	10,637	14,772	13,318	15,956	12,217	16,935	15,642	15,768	15,793	24,881	25,906
1983	28,628	29,288	22,848	30,877	33,679	26,930	29,997	25,367	31,106	23,808	26,793	21,450
1984	23,067	30,948	25,407	25,118	25,548	18,402	19,093	21,229	18,812	21,485	23,562	17,861
1985	24,406	28,898	22,446	27,144	32,175	27,891	34,160	35,850	25,988	28,190	35,047	27,351
1986	29,412	39,151	28,521	34,855	30,766	32,254	35,466	44,717	26,619	32,621	34,495	23,138

Source: International Monetary Market (Chicago)

T.0588

Index of Trade-Weighted Dollar Exchange Rates for Soybeans—April 1971 = 100

Year		Jan.	Feb.	Mar.	Apr.	May	June	July	Aug.	Sept.	Oct.	Nov.	Dec.
1983	Nominal	NOT			141.0	140.9	143.7	145.8	149.1	149.3	148.8	152.3	155.3
	Real	AVAILABLE			85.4	85.9	88.2	90.2	92.2	91.9	89.9	91.7	93.4
1984	Nominal	157.5	155.1	152.9	155.0	162.1	162.4	166.8	168.0	172.6	175.6	175.2	180.6
	Real	94.6	92.1	89.3	90.4	93.2	93.4	96.5	97.4	100.7	101.6	99.6	102.1
1985	Nominal	185.1	191.9	194.5	187.8	190.3	197.3	203.2	201.4	209.7	210.2	229.2	113.8
	Real	103.4	107.4	107.3	101.8	102.4	101.9	98.7	96.5	97.6	92.4	91.6	84.4
1986[1]	Nominal	112	107	105	105	103	103	161	250	266	280	294	
	Real	82	79	76	76	74	75	75	75	75	75	76	

[1] Preliminary. *Nominal* values are percentage changes in currency units per dollar, weighted by proportion of agricultural exports from the United States. An increase indicates that the dollar has appreciated. *Real* values are computed in the same way as the nominal series, adjusted for CPI changes in the countries involved. *Source: Economic Research Service, U.S.D.A.*   T.0590

Index of Trade-Weighted Dollar Exchange Rates for Wheat—April 1971 = 100

Year		Jan.	Feb.	Mar.	Apr.	May	June	July	Aug.	Sept.	Oct.	Nov.	Dec.
1983	Nominal	NOT			1,003	1,085	1,158	1,290	1,444	1,553	1,713	1,843	1,973
	Real	AVAILABLE			96.9	97.3	98.2	100.0	103.6	102.5	101.5	102.2	102.2
1984	Nominal	2,126	2,334	2,588	2,803	3,018	3,305	3,645	3,958	4,395	4,612	5,378	5,865
	Real	102.7	102.2	101.1	102.3	103.5	104.1	104.4	104.5	105.5	105.2	106.4	106.9
1985	Nominal	6,598	7,285	7,988	9,093	996.1	11,012	11,996	13,008	14,116	15,607	17,029	18,368
	Real	108.9	109.6	108.8	109.0	110.1	111.5	110.6	110.0	110.8	109.0	108.9	103.8
1986[1]	Nominal	20,580	23,953	26,425	26,457	26,533	26,449	26,499	26,501	26,512	26,714	27,006	
	Real	102	102	102	101	100	101	100	101	102	103	105	

[1] Preliminary. *Nominal* values are percentage changes in currency units per dollar, weighted by proportion of agricultural exports from the United States. An increase indicates that the dollar has appreciated. *Real* values are computed in the same way as the nominal series, adjusted for CPI changes in the countries involved. *Source: Economic Research Service, U.S.D.A.*   T.0590A

Index of Trade-Weighted Dollar Exchange Rates for Corn—April 1971 = 100

Year		Jan.	Feb.	Mar.	Apr.	May	June	July	Aug.	Sept.	Oct.	Nov.	Dec.
1983	Nominal	NOT			308.8	320.9	333.0	354.5	382.1	400.4	424.5	448.3	471.1
	Real	AVAILABLE			89.0	89.2	91.4	94.0	95.9	95.5	93.7	95.3	96.6
1984	Nominal	497.1	526.7	563.2	598.6	640.6	684.1	740.4	789.2	860.0	897.8	1,013	1,093
	Real	97.7	95.4	92.7	93.6	96.5	96.5	99.4	100.3	103.2	104.1	102.5	104.7
1985	Nominal	1,212	1,326	1,438	1,599	1,740	1,905	2,067	2,227	2,403	2,627	2,865	2,903
	Real	106.1	109.4	109.4	104.4	105.2	104.7	102.3	100.3	101.5	97.0	96.8	86.9
1986[1]	Nominal	3,227	3,720	4,081	4,086	4,095	4,083	4,172	4,297	4,320	4,369	4,430	
	Real	85	81	79	78	77	77	78	79	80	79	80	

[1] Preliminary. *Nominal* values are percentage changes in currency units per dollar, weighted by proportion of agricultural exports from the United States. An increase indicates that the dollar has appreciated. *Real* values are computed in the same way as the nominal series, adjusted for CPI changes in the countries involved. *Source: Economic Research Service, U.S.D.A.*   T.0591

Index of Trade-Weighted Dollar Exchange Rates for Cotton—April 1971 = 100

Year		Jan.	Feb.	Mar.	Apr.	May	June	July	Aug.	Sept.	Oct.	Nov.	Dec.
1983	Nominal	NOT			155.5	155.7	155.9	157.0	158.9	159.9	163.4	180.2	181.4
	Real	AVAILABLE			89.0	88.9	89.9	90.9	91.9	91.7	91.6	92.6	93.3
1984	Nominal	182.5	181.4	180.4	184.0	185.8	187.2	190.3	191.1	195.5	197.0	197.6	207.0
	Real	93.6	92.8	91.6	92.1	93.3	94.2	95.6	96.1	97.0	97.8	98.0	99.1
1985	Nominal	209.3	211.5	212.9	211.3	212.8	212.8	213.3	213.0	215.1	212.8	214.8	216.4
	Real	100.0	101.6	102.3	101.0	101.7	101.1	99.9	99.8	100.6	98.4	97.5	97.3
1986[1]	Nominal	216	214	228	227	226	233	231	230	233	236	237	
	Real	97	95	94	93	92	92	91	90	91	92	93	

[1] Preliminary. *Nominal* values are percentage changes in currency units per dollar, weighted by proportion of agricultural exports from the United States. An increase indicates that the dollar has appreciated. *Real* values are computed in the same way as the nominal series, adjusted for CPI changes in the countries involved. *Source: Economic Research Service, U.S.D.A.*   T.0591A

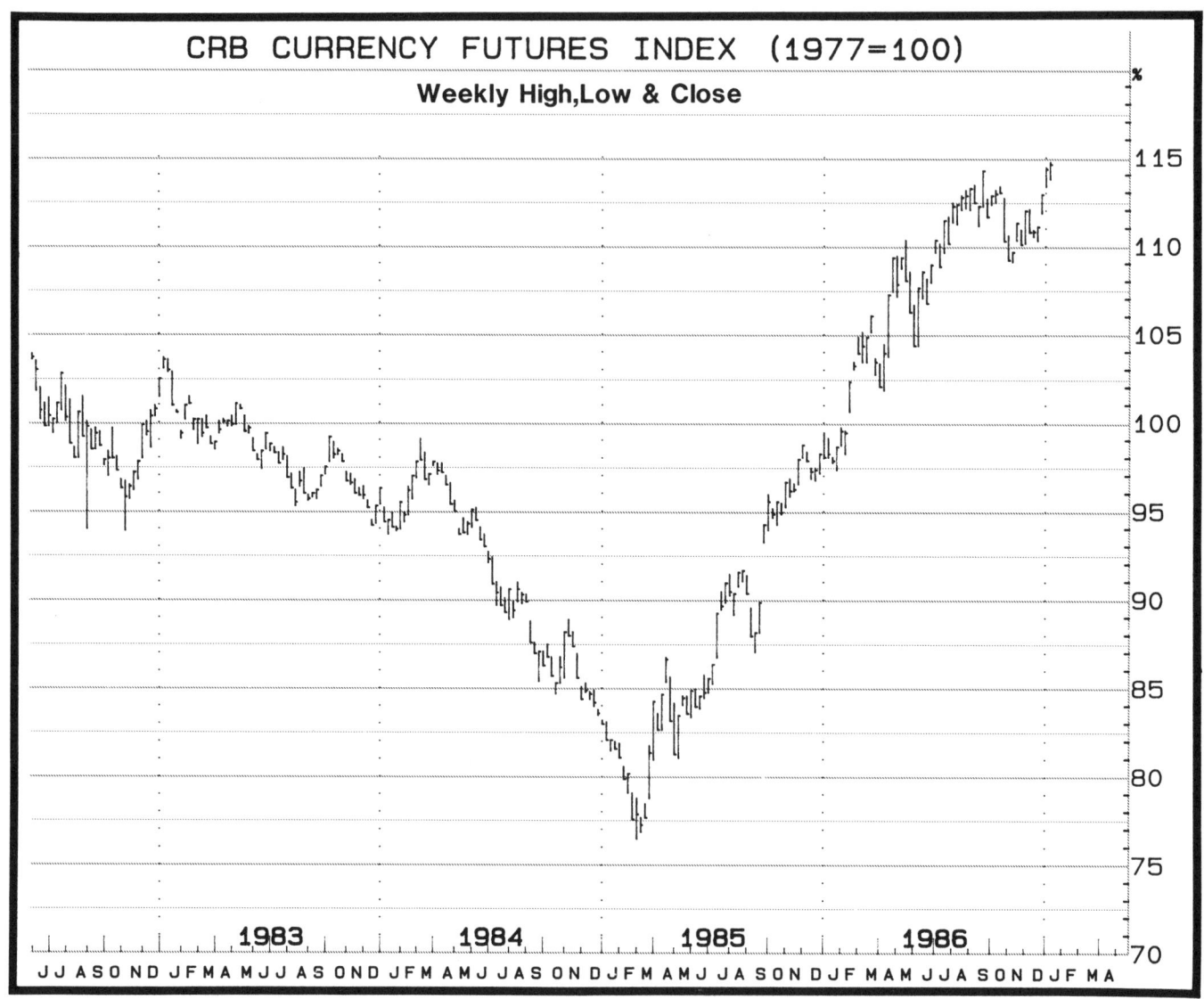

CRB CURRENCY FUTURES INDEX (1977=100)
Weekly High, Low & Close

Index of Trade-Weighted Dollar Exchange Rates for Total Agriculture   April 1971 = 100

Year		Jan.	Feb.	Mar.	Apr.	May	June	July	Aug.	Sept.	Oct.	Nov.	Dec.
1983	Nominal	NOT			304.6	318.0	329.2	354.4	384.1	403.2	429.8	454.4	478.4
	Real	AVAILABLE			91.2	91.4	93.0	94.9	97.2	96.5	95.0	96.2	97.3
1984	Nominal	505.7	538.8	580.4	618.9	661.8	710.1	770.3	823.2	899.3	938.9	1,067	1,152
	Real	97.2	96.5	94.4	95.6	97.8	98.0	100.2	100.6	102.9	103.5	102.5	104.2
1985	Nominal	1,282	1,404	1,526	1,707	1,861	2,042	2,217	2,392	2,583	2,830	3,083	3,183
	Real	106.1	108.5	108.3	104.6	105.2	105.5	103.3	101.9	103.1	99.3	99.1	91.6
1986[1]	Nominal	3,544	4,093	4,495	4,500	4,511	4,498	4,567	4,661	4,680	4,729	4,791	
	Real	90	88	86	85	84	85	85	86	87	87	89	

[1] Preliminary.   *Nominal* values are percentage changes in currency units per dollar, weighted by proportion of agricultural exports from the United States. An increase indicates that the dollar has appreciated.   *Real* values are computed in the same way as the nominal series, adjusted for CPI changes in the countries involved.   *Source: Economic Research Service, U.S.D.A.*   T.0589

Eggs

Statistics covering the first nine months of 1986 indicate that the year's domestic output of eggs was about the same as in 1985, roughly 5.7 billion dozens. The total number of layers on farms was running modestly ahead of 1985's average of 277 million, because producers were adding more replacement pullets to the laying flock. However, this did not result in enlarged output, because slaughter of light-type mature chickens remained well above the low level that prevailed during 1985. The output of eggs per layer during 1986 also was little changed from the prior year, when it amounted to 247.

Imports increased in 1986; shell eggs and shell equivalent of egg products totaled 98 million dozen during 1986's first three quarters, up more than 25 percent from the same 1985 period. The largest foreign supplier to the U.S. was Canada, which provided 2.4 million eggs, compared with 5 million during 1985. Most of Canada's exports were in the form of egg products. The second-largest supplier, the Netherlands, exported 2 million shell eggs to the U.S.

Domestic consumption of shell eggs and shell egg equivalent of egg products dipped in 1986 to about 252 eggs per capita, as against 255 per person in 1985. In 1986's first half, to be specific, per capita usage of shell eggs decreased by 1.7 eggs and all egg consumption fell by 1.9 eggs.

U.S. egg exports were expected to rise in 1986 over the previous year, due to a decline in the U.S. dollar. Japanese purchases of American egg exports amounted to more than 21 million dozens during April–June, 1986, compared with 10.7 million dozens during the same period a year before. All told, nearly three-fourths of U.S. exports of eggs and egg product went to Japan. Canada accounted for another 10 percent and Hong Kong for six percent more.

Throughout the first three quarters of 1986, egg prices were well above year-earlier levels, due mainly to rising exports. Farm prices per dozen averaged about 53 cents; in the same 1985 period, the average on-farm price was roughly 47 cents. The national average retail price for large Grade A eggs during January–September, 1986, was 86.4 cents per dozen; in the same span of 1985, the average was 78 cents. The consumer price index for eggs, which registered 161.3 (1967=100) in January, 1985, was 186.0 in September, 1986, a jump of more than 15 percent.

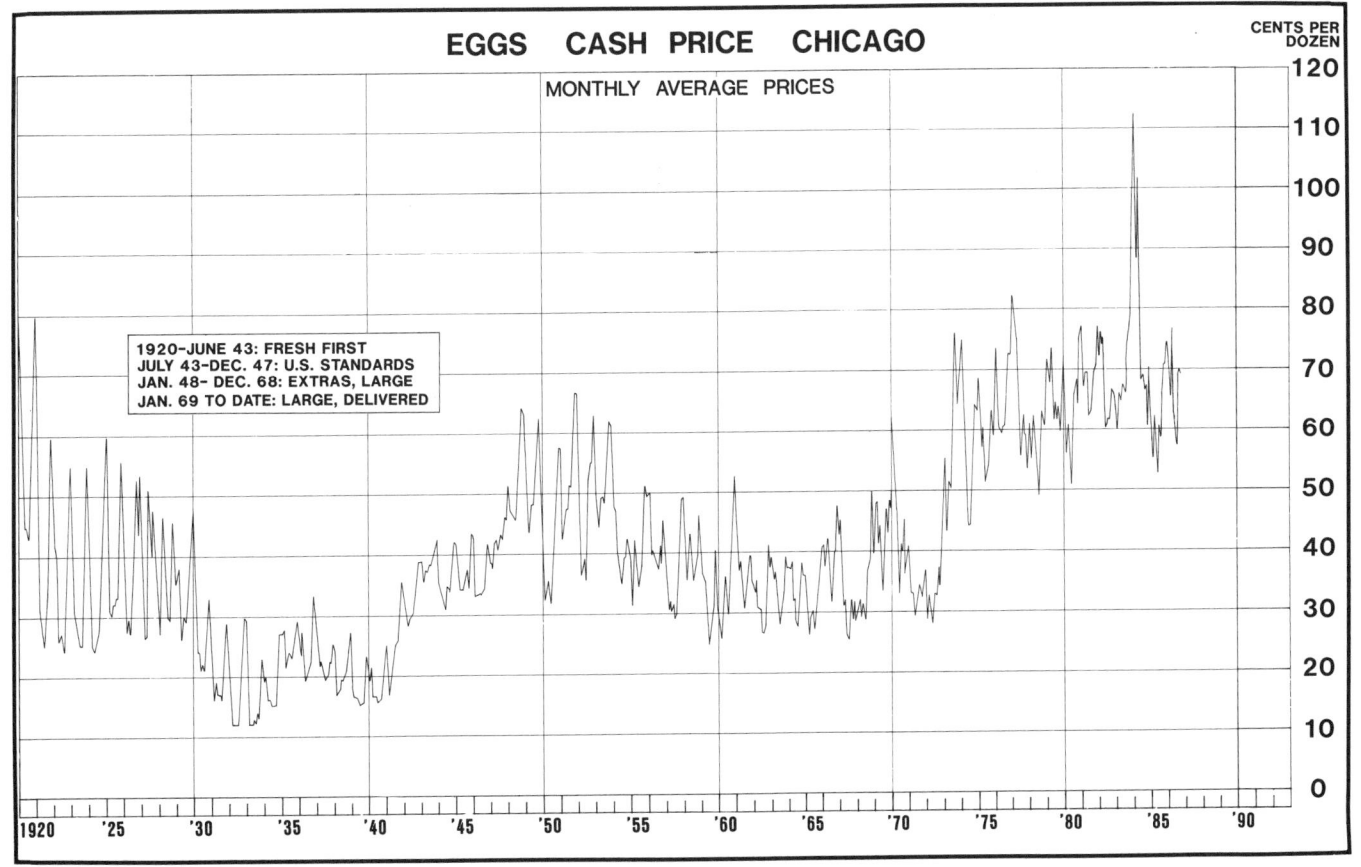

EGGS CASH PRICE CHICAGO

CENTS PER DOZEN

MONTHLY AVERAGE PRICES

1920-JUNE 43: FRESH FIRST
JULY 43-DEC. 47: U.S. STANDARDS
JAN. 48- DEC. 68: EXTRAS, LARGE
JAN. 69 TO DATE: LARGE, DELIVERED

EGGS

World Production[2] of Eggs   In Billions of Eggs

Year	Argentina	Australia	Bel. & Lux.	Brazil	Canada	Israel	France	West Germany	Italy	Japan	Netherlands	Poland	Spain	South Africa	USSR	United Kingdom[3]	United States
1978	3.3	3.5	3.8	6.6	5.5	1.8	13.5	14.3	11.0	32.8	7.0	8.5	10.1	3.9	64.5	14.3	67.3
1979	3.4	3.4	3.5	7.2	5.6	1.8	13.8	13.3	11.0	33.2	8.2	8.7	11.0	3.1	65.6	15.0	69.2
1980	3.4	3.4	3.3	9.6	5.9	1.6	14.5	13.7	10.7	33.4	9.0	8.9	11.7	2.4	70.9	14.0	69.7
1981	3.3	3.6	3.3	10.2	5.9	1.4	15.2	13.2	11.4	33.3	9.8	8.8	11.8	2.6	70.9	13.7	69.9
1982	3.2	3.4	3.3	10.2	5.9	1.8	15.9	13.1	11.2	34.3	10.7	7.6	12.4	3.1	72.4	13.5	69.6
1983	3.3	3.5	3.2	9.0	6.1	1.8	15.0	13.0	10.9	34.8	10.7	7.6	12.2	3.3	75.1	13.2	67.9
1984	3.2	3.5	3.1	8.5	5.9	2.1	14.9	13.1	10.8	35.5	11.1	8.2	10.1	3.3	76.5	13.0	68.5
1985[1]	3.2	3.3	3.1	9.0	5.9	2.1	14.9	13.2	10.9	35.7	11.1	8.6	10.2	3.2	77.0	13.1	68.3
1986[4]	3.2	3.2	3.0	10.0	5.9	1.5	14.8	13.0	10.9	36.3	11.0	8.3	10.2	3.3	77.5	13.1	68.9

[1] Preliminary.   [2] Relates to farm production in Canada and the United States. Information for many countries is not explicit on this point.   [3] Farm production, years ending May.   [4] Forecast.   *Source: Foreign Agricultural Service, U.S.D.A.*   T.210

Salient Egg Statistics in the United States

Year	Hens & Pullets On Farms Dec. 1[2] (Millions)	Avg.[9] Number During Year (Millions)	Rate of Lay Per Layer During Year[3] Number	Eggs Farm Prod. (Billions)	Price Per Dozen	Consumed[4] on Farms (Billions)	Sold (Billions)	Gross Income[5] Billion $	Total Egg Prod.[6]	Imports[7]	Exports[8] and Shipments (Million Dozen)	Used for Hatching (Million Dozen)	Civilian Consumption Total	Civilian Consumption Per Capita Eggs
1978	293.3	281.5	239	67.1	52.2	.46	66.68	2.92	5,608	11	120	466	5,009	273
1979	294.9	288.6	240	69.2	58.3	.45	68.76	3.36	5,777	10	104	498	5,162	278
1980	294.1	287.7	242	69.7	56.3	.45	69.23	3.27	5,806	5	167	499	5,122	272.4
1981	293.8	287.7	243	69.8	63.1	.44	69.38	3.67	5,825	5	257	507	5,043	265.5
1982	289.6	286.3	243	69.7	59.5	.43	69.27	3.46	5,802	3	185	506	5,071	265.3
1983	278.5	276.1	247	68.2	61.1	.42	67.75	3.47	5,659	23	112	500	5,056	261.2
1984[1]	285.8	278.0	245	68.2	72.3	.39	67.80	4.11	5,708	32	86	530	5,105	260.9
1985[1]	279.8	276.7	247	68.4	57.1	—N.A.—		3.25	5,688	13	101	548	5,031	254.6
1986[10]		277.0	248						5,650	15	120	565	5,000	250.6

[1] Preliminary.   [2] Of laying age.   [3] Number of eggs produced during the year divided by the average number of hens & pullets of laying age on hand during the year.   [4] Consumed in households of farm producers.   [5] Value of sales plus value of eggs consumed in households of producers.   [6] Farm production, plus nonfarm output estimated at 10% of farm through 1954; thereafter, 1 percentage point less each year.   [7] Shell-egg equivalent of eggs and egg products.   [8] Shell eggs & shell equivalent of frozen & dried egg products.   [9] Average number of layers on farms during the year.   [10] Estimate.   *Source: Agricultural Marketing Service, U.S.D.A.*   T.211

Average Wholesale Prices of Shell Eggs (Large) Delivered, Chicago   In Cents Per Dozen

Year	Jan.	Feb.	Mar.	Apr.	May	June	July	Aug.	Sept.	Oct.	Nov.	Dec.	Average
1978	55.2	62.8	62.0	57.0	52.0	49.3	61.2	61.8	63.2	60.8	67.2	71.6	60.3
1979	71.3	67.7	73.5	68.7	61.9	64.8	61.9	64.0	62.0	59.7	66.3	72.4	66.2
1980	59.9	56.3	60.6	56.8	50.8	54.6	63.2	65.9	68.8	64.3	75.7	77.3	62.8
1981	71.4	67.2	66.6	69.7	62.2	62.9	67.5	68.7	70.7	71.3	77.3	72.1	69.0
1982	76.2	74.2	75.2	68.3	60.4	60.8	61.7	61.6	65.9	66.8	66.2	64.1	66.8
1983	60.2	62.7	66.2	64.9	68.4	68.0	66.2	74.4	76.2	77.9	88.4	98.6	72.7
1984	112.3	102.6	88.3	101.8	74.3	68.1	69.0	66.5	67.2	60.7	70.4	62.2	78.6
1985[1]	58.4	55.1	62.3	57.3	52.9	60.8	58.6	66.4	70.5	70.7	74.6	73.2	63.4
1986[1]	70.6	65.7	76.9	62.6	62.0	57.3	69.4	70.0	69.4	66.3	74.1		

[1] Preliminary.   *Source: Economic Research Service, U.S.D.A.*   T.212

Total Egg Production in the United States   In Millions of Eggs

Year	Jan.	Feb.	Mar.	Apr.	May	June	July	Aug.	Sept.	Oct.	Nov.	Dec.	Total[2]
1978	5,743	5,106	5,700	5,559	5,723	5,460	5,541	5,574	5,495	5,751	5,685	5,948	67,157
1979	5,892	5,290	5,909	5,721	5,862	5,648	5,798	5,810	5,653	5,881	5,797	6,064	69,209
1980	6,047	5,595	5,956	5,715	5,798	5,582	5,708	5,753	5,725	5,948	5,795	6,054	69,686
1981	6,020	5,421	6,009	5,761	5,855	5,608	5,799	5,835	5,685	5,919	5,859	6,079	69,825
1982	5,958	5,333	——17,557——			——17,231——			——17,419——			6,030	69,718
1983	5,931	5,354	5,928	5,622	5,711	5,526	5,666	5,639	5,493	5,699	5,570	5,772	68,169
1984	5,685	5,326	5,796	5,643	5,742	5,525	5,750	5,766	5,622	5,856	5,747	6,040	68,230
1985[1]	5,950	5,293	5,923	5,670	5,721	5,499	5,661	5,686	5,545	5,761	5,658	5,883	68,250
1986[1]	5,862	5,295	5,903	5,651	5,781	5,593	5,690	5,706	5,560	5,810	5,674		

[1] Preliminary.   [2] Dec. 1 previous year thru Nov. 30.   *Source: Crop Reporting Board, U.S.D.A.*   T.219

Total Eggs—U.S. Supply and Distribution   In Millions of Dozen

Year & Quarters	Supply				Ending Stocks[1]	Utilization — Domestic Disappearance				
	Production	Imports[1]	Beginning Stocks[1]	Total Supply		Exports & Shipments[1]	Eggs Used for Hatching	Military	Civilian[1]	
									Total	Per Capita (Number)
1982 I	1,444	.5	17.5	1,447	14.4	53.1	128.4	5.9	1,260	65.9
II	1,441	.3	14.4	1,437	18.2	36.9	132.4	4.8	1,263	65.9
III	1,436	1.6	18.2	1,434	22.3	37.6	120.4	6.4	1.270	66.1
IV	1,480	.1	22.3	1,483	20.3	57.3	124.5	5.3	1,296	67.3
1983 I	1,434	5.0	20.3	1,442	18.1	30.2	128.4	6.3	1,277	66.2
II	1,405	2.9	18.1	1,409	17.4	29.2	129.2	6.9	1,243	64.3
III	1,400	7.4	17.4	1,411	13.2	26.7	120.1	6.5	1,258	64.9
IV	1,420	8.2	13.2	1,432	9.3	26.4	122.4	5.4	1,278	65.8
1984 I	1,401	13.9	9.3	1,414	10.2	17.5	133.0	4.2	1,259	64.6
II	1,409	7.6	10.2	1,413	13.7	15.3	138.0	5.3	1,255	64.2
III	1,428	7.2	13.7	1,436	13.4	26.7	128.4	3.7	1,277	65.2
IV	1,470	3.4	13.4	1,476	11.1	26.5	130.2	4.4	1,315	66.9
1985[2] I	1,431	2.2	11.1	1,433	11.0	24.5	136.1	5.1	1,267	64.4
II	1,408	3.3	11.0	1,410	11.9	24.5	139.7	5.6	1,240	62.8
III	1,408	2.3	12.2	1,409	13.1	25.0	133.7	4.5	1,246	63.0
IV	1,442	4.9	13.1	1,449	10.7	27.0	138.6	5.0	1,279	64.5
1986[2] I	1,422	3.6	10.7	1,436	8.7	33.4	138.5	4.6	1,250	62.9
II	1,419	4.0	8.7	1,432	11.9	28.2	144.6	4.2	1,243	62.4
III	1,413		11.9		11.4		140.9			
IV										

[1] Shell eggs & the approx. shell-egg equivalent of egg product.   [2] Preliminary.   *Source: Economic Research Service, U.S.D.A.*   T.213

Shell Eggs: Civilian Per Capita Disappearance in the United States   Number of Eggs

Year	Jan.	Feb.	Mar.	Apr.	May	June	Shell Equivalent July	Aug.	Sept.	Oct.	Nov.	Dec.	Total[1]	Pro-cessed[2]	Total
1977	20.9	17.9	20.1	19.2	19.4	18.1	19.1	19.1	19.0	20.7	20.2	21.4	235	37	272
1978	21.1	18.6	20.8	20.0	20.3	18.8	19.7	19.8	19.7	20.9	20.7	21.9	242	36	278
1979	21.3	18.5	21.0	20.0	20.1	19.2	20.1	19.9	19.8	20.2	20.2	21.8	242	36	278
1980	21.1	19.0	20.9	19.4	19.8	18.7	19.0	19.6	19.4	19.8	20.0	20.7	237.3	35	272
1981	———58.5———			———56.7———			———57.3———			———60.7———			233.1	33	265
1982	———58.6———			———57.0———			———56.5———			———59.1———			231.2	34	265
1983	———57.8———			———55.5———			———55.0———			———57.6———			225.9	35	261
1984	———55.7———			———54.8———			———55.2———			———57.7———			223.4	38	261
1985[3]	———55.6———			———52.4———			———52.8———			———55.0———			215.7	39	255
1986[3]	———54.4———			———51.9———											

[1] Monthly totals do not necessarily add to yearly figures due to rounding.   [2] Liquid, frozen, & dried egg (egg solids) converted to shell egg equivalent.   [3] Preliminary.   *Source: Economic Research Service, U.S.D.A.*   T.214

Egg-Feed Ratio[1] in the United States

Year	Jan.	Feb.	Mar.	Apr.	May	June	July	Aug.	Sept.	Oct.	Nov.	Dec.	Average
1976	8.6	8.2	7.4	7.3	7.5	6.8	6.8	7.6	7.7	7.8	8.7	9.1	7.9
1977	8.5	8.1	7.3	6.8	5.9	5.8	6.7	7.2	7.6	7.1	7.3	7.4	7.1
1978	6.7	7.5	7.4	6.7	6.3	5.6	6.4	7.0	7.3	7.0	7.5	8.0	7.0
1979	7.8	7.7	8.0	7.4	6.9	6.7	6.1	6.1	6.4	6.1	6.8	7.3	6.9
1980	6.6	6.0	6.4	6.0	5.4	5.6	5.7	6.0	6.2	5.7	6.0	6.6	6.0
1981	5.9	5.7	5.6	5.9	5.2	5.2	5.5	5.8	6.4	6.5	7.2	6.7	6.0
1982	6.6	6.8	7.1	6.6	5.6	5.3	5.7	5.4	6.0	6.3	6.3	6.0	6.2
1983	5.7	5.8	6.1	5.8	6.0	5.8	5.7	6.1	6.0	6.2	6.9	7.7	6.0
1984[2]	8.8	8.5	7.4	8.6	6.5	5.8	5.8	5.8	5.9	5.7	6.5	6.2	6.9
1985[2]	5.5	5.6	6.2	5.7	5.5	5.8	5.8	6.5	7.0	7.3	7.4	7.4	6.3
1986[2]	7.2	6.9	—	6.5	—	—	6.8	—	—	7.0			

[1] Pounds of laying feed equivalent in value to one dozen eggs.   [2] Preliminary.   *Source: Economic Research Service, U.S.D.A.*   T.215

EGGS

Hens and Pullets of Laying Age in the U.S., First of Month In Millions

Year	Jan. 1	Feb. 1	Mar. 1	Apr. 1	May 1	June 1	July 1	Aug. 1	Sept. 1	Oct. 1	Nov. 1	Dec. 1
1979	291.7	292.1	290.2	288.6	285.5	283.4	283.7	285.1	287.2	290.2	291.7	294.9
1980	296.0	293.1	288.7	285.3	280.8	279.5	279.9	282.2	287.9	291.7	292.8	294.1
1981	295.2	292.4	291.3	286.3	284.5	282.5	280.9	284.5	283.8	287.2	290.5	293.8
1982	291.7	290.1	288.4	—	—	282.7	—	—	281.9	—	—	289.6
1983	285.8	283.3	280.5	276.9	273.0	271.8	270.1	269.7	271.5	272.2	276.4	278.5
1984[1]	277.2	276.5	277.0	278.9	276.1	276.2	276.5	274.3	277.8	280.5	282.2	285.8
1985[1]	286.9	281.7	279.0	276.1	272.5	269.2	269.8	271.3	273.8	276.2	280.7	279.8
1986[1]	280.9	280.4	279.8	—	—	273.4	—	—	273.0	—	—	280.1

[1] Preliminary. *Source: Crop Reporting Board, U.S.D.A.* T.216

Eggs Laid Per Hundred Layers in the United States In Number of Eggs

Year	Jan.	Feb.	Mar.	Apr.	May	June	July	Aug.	Sept.	Oct.	Nov.	Dec.	Average
1979	2,018	1,817	2,042	1,994	2,062	1,992	2,038	2,030	1,958	2,021	1,976	2,052	
1980	2,053	1,923	2,075	2,019	2,070	1,996	2,031	2,018	1,976	2,035	1,975	2,054	2,422
1981	2,049	1,857	2,081	2,018	2,065	1,991	2,051	2,053	1,991	2,049	2,005	2,083	2,426
1982	2,048	1,850	——6,159——			——6,112——			——6,105——			2,097	2,435
1983	2,084	1,899	2,127	2,045	2,096	2,039	2,099	2,084	2,021	2,078	2,008	2,078	2,468
1984	2,054	1,925	2,085	2,032	2,079	1,999	2,086	2,088	2,013	2,080	2,023	2,109	2,046
1985[1]	2,092	1,887	2,138	2,067	2,119	2,024	2,099	2,096	2,018	2,069	2,018	2,097	2,059
1986[1]	2,086	1,890			2,108		2,095	2,093					

[1] Preliminary. *Source: Crop Reporting Board, U.S.D.A.* T.221

Egg-Type Chicks Hatched by Commercial Hatcheries in the United States In Millions

Year	Jan.	Feb.	Mar.	Apr.	May	June	July	Aug.	Sept.	Oct.	Nov.	Dec.	Total
1979	39.9	39.5	50.1	52.4	55.9	47.8	42.8	41.9	36.6	39.5	37.5	36.4	519.0
1980	38.1	42.1	46.5	47.9	47.6	42.3	37.9	38.0	37.4	37.3	33.8	35.8	484.6
1981	37.8	36.1	44.5	48.3	46.1	40.5	32.3	33.8	32.3	35.9	33.7	33.1	454.2
1982	36.7	36.4	44.2	46.6	47.3	39.4	35.4	33.5	31.2	32.3	30.2	31.1	444.4
1983	32.6	33.0	39.3	36.7	38.3	37.5	30.5	30.9	31.8	32.3	29.6	34.4	406.9
1984	36.9	37.5	45.7	47.9	49.0	46.5	38.4	34.8	33.1	31.4	30.1	27.1	458.5
1985[1]	28.3	28.4	36.9	40.9	39.0	33.8	32.1	32.5	33.6	33.6	33.6	34.6	407.3
1986[1]	34.4	34.7	39.7	42.7	42.7	37.4	33.5	33.4	32.5	32.5	27.8		

[1] Preliminary. *Source: Crop Reporting Board, U.S.D.A.* T.220

U.S. Cold Storage Holdings of Shell Eggs, 1st of Month In Thousands of Cases (One Case = 30 Dozen)

Year	Jan.	Feb.	Mar.	Apr.	May	June	July	Aug.	Sept.	Oct.	Nov.	Dec.
1979	38	22	18	24	20	27	24	32	28	31	24	24
1980	38	47	24	22	30	47	51	39	28	39	15	19
1981	31	28	18	31	31	25	41	39	20	19	21	38
1982	35	28	19	39	—	—	32	—	—	29	—	—
1983	34	35	25	18	23	32	44	24	25	25	45	18
1984	13	28	17	36	35	41	42	29	31	23	37	35
1985	31	30	29	23	26	30	21	30	20	22	23	28
1986[1]	24	28	21	20	32	44	38	25	33	29	20	29

[1] Preliminary. *Source: Crop Reporting, Board U.S.D.A.* T.217

U.S. Cold Storage Holdings of Frozen Eggs, 1st of Month In Millions of Pounds[1]

Year	Jan.	Feb.	Mar.	Apr.	May	June	July	Aug.	Sept.	Oct.	Nov.	Dec.
1979	25.3	25.5	24.5	21.1	21.7	21.6	22.8	25.9	24.7	24.1	25.6	23.4
1980	23.4	22.1	23.8	23.4	25.9	26.6	28.6	29.4	30.7	29.7	29.2	25.3
1981	24.3	24.3	24.2	22.3	21.9	22.7	24.2	26.9	27.2	25.5	25.6	23.7
1982	21.6	21.2	19.4	17.4	—	—	22.7	—	—	28.3	—	—
1983	25.4	25.5	25.7	23.1	22.5	21.2	21.1	20.4	19.0	16.4	14.2	13.4
1984	11.8	11.0	11.4	12.0	12.7	12.8	16.4	17.5	16.6	16.7	17.9	16.2
1985	13.4	14.9	13.9	13.5	13.2	14.4	15.3	18.0	18.4	16.4	15.1	13.8
1986[2]	13.2	12.7	12.8	10.7	12.5	11.3	14.2	15.1	15.0	14.0	14.0	13.1

[1] Converted on basis 39.5 pounds frozen eggs equals 1 case. [2] Preliminary. *Source: Crop Reporting Board, U.S.D.A.* T.218

Electric Power

Year by year, the amount of electricity generated in the U.S. has grown. Based on incomplete data, output in 1986 was near 2.575 billion kilowatt hours, four percent larger than in 1985. About 55 percent of total electricity generation was derived from bituminous coal. Nuclear plants contributed 16 percent of the total, hydroelectric units 12 percent, natural gas 10 percent, and petroleum six percent.

The contribution to total production by nuclear power plants rose. At the end of August, 1986, the number of operable reactors had reached 99, up by four from the end of December, 1985. Two more reactors were in the start-up phase and construction permits had been granted for another 25. Nuclear-based electricity generation, which amounted to about 191 million net kilowatt hours in 1976, was closing in on 400 million net kwh a decade later.

In mid-1986, consumption of electric power was running at an annual rate of 2.39 billion kwh, or roughly 93 percent of yearly output. Indicated consumption in 1986 was about 3.5 percent larger than in 1985, and almost 29 percent greater than 10 years before. Approximately 35 percent of the power consumed in 1986 was for residential usage, 34 percent for industrial purposes, 27 percent in commercial establishments, and the remaining four percent for governmental units, railways, street-lighting agencies, and the like. This distribution of final demand has prevailed for many years. Consumption of nuclear electric power has grown apace of rising nuclear gen-

eration. In 1986, it was running at the annual rate of 4.31 quadrillion (10 to the 15th power) Btu, as against 4.16 quadrillion in 1985.

In 1986, as in every year since 1981, the cost of fossil fuels delivered to steam-electric utility plants fell. At the beginning of the 1980s, the average cost was $2.256 per million Btu for all fossil fuels; cost was averaging $1.711 per million around year-end 1985, a slide of more than 24 percent. The principal cause for this development was declining prices of heavy oil. Where the average cost of heavy oil to a steam-electric plant was $5.334 per million Btu in 1981 and $4.812 at the close of 1984, it had dipped to only $1.843 in July, 1986, a reduction over five years of more than 65 percent. By contrast, the average cost of delivered coal stood at $1.57 per million Btu in July, 1986, as against $1.647 in 1981 and $1.61 in December, 1985. The price of natural gas fell only slightly between 1981 and 1986, dropping from $2.805 at the period's start to $2.172 near its conclusion, down 22 percent.

In 1986, retail electricity prices continued their slow uptrend. The average price to residential users stood at 8.2 cents per kilowatt hour in August, 1986, compared with 7.44 cents in December, 1985. Similarly, the average retail price for commercial consumers stood at 7.5 cents per kwh in August, 1986, and at 7.3 cents in December, 1985. The average price to industrial buyers rose from 5.2 cents in December, 1985, to 5.3 cents in mid-1986.

World Electricity Production   In Billions of KWH

Year	Australia	Brazil	Canada	Czechoslov.	France	West Germany	Italy	Japan	Norway	Poland	Sweden	Switzerland	South Africa	United Kingdom	United States	USSR
1978	86.2	112.5	345.2	69.1	226.7	353.4	175.0	564.0	81.0	115.6	90.3	42.3	84.5	287.7	2,286	1,200
1979	92.1	126.5	363.2	68.1	241.1	374.2	180.5	589.6	89.1	117.5	92.4	42.7	90.3	299.9	2,319	1,238
1980	96.3	139.5	377.5	72.6	243.3	368.8	185.7	577.5	84.1	121.9	93.4	46.6	95.0	284.9	2,354	1,295
1981	102.5	142.2	390.9	74.1	260.8	368.0	181.8	583.2	92.8	115.0	100.0	48.0	97.4	277.7	2,359	1,325
1982	104.9	152.0	387.5	74.7	262.2	366.9	183.7	581.1	91.9	117.6	96.6	50.8	119.9	272.1	2,302	1,367
1983	109.2	162.0	408.4	76.0	297.2	371.8	180.7	555.5	104.7	125.9	105.9	50.8	108.3	276.2	2,368	1,396
1984[1]	115.8		424.8	78.3	302.5	394.3	180.3	580.4	106.6	135.3	119.6	47.7		282.4	2,416	1,493
1985[3]	120.0		430.0	80.0	305.0	400.0	185.0	585.0	108.0	133.0	114.0	50.0		285.0	2,500	1,505

[1] Preliminary.   [2] Estimate.   *Source: United Nations*   T.222

Installed Capacity, Capability & Peak Load of the U.S. Electric Utility Industry   In Millions of Kilowatts

Year	Total Electric Utility Industry	Installed Generating Capacity at Dec. 31 — Type of Prime Mover — Hydro	Gas Turbine & Steam	Nuclear Power	Internal Combustion	Type of Ownership — Investor Owned	Cooperatives	Sub-Total Gov't.	Municipal Utilities	Federal	Power Districts, State Projects	Capability at Winter Peak Load	Non-Coincident Winter Peak Load	Margin of Reserve (%)	Generation	Peak Load Factor (%)
1978	579.3	71.0	449.2	53.5	5.5	453.6	11.6	114.0	34.4	54.3	25.3	561.6	383.1	33.7	2,219	62.1
1979	598.4	75.4	463.0	54.6	5.5	464.1	13.8	120.5	34.5	58.3	27.6	554.3	368.9	36.9[2]	2,247	64.4
1980	613.7	76.4	475.3	56.5	5.6	477.1	15.4	121.2	34.6	59.1	27.5	572.2	384.6	23.5	2,293	61.1
1981	635.0	77.2	491.3	60.8	5.6	490.8	18.4	125.7	35.1	61.0	29.5	581.1	391.1	25.2	2,311	61.6
1982	650.1	78.1	503.8	63.0	5.1	499.1	21.5	129.5	35.8	62.5	31.2	596.9	373.3	29.2	2,241	62.1
1983	658.2	79.0	507.1	67.1	5.0	505.5	22.2	130.5	36.6	63.0	30.9	611.6	410.8	25.0	2,310	59.5
1984	672.5	80.6	516.5	70.5	4.8	514.9	24.7	132.9	36.7	63.3	32.8	622.1	436.4	25.3	2,416	59.7
1985[1]	688.7	83.0	520.3	80.4	5.0	530.4	24.6	133.8	37.0	63.7	33.0	636.5	423.7	25.9	2,470	62.0

[1] Preliminary.   [2] New series starting 1980.   *Source: Federal Power Commission*   T.223

ELECTRIC POWER

Available Electricity & Energy Sales in the United States   In Billions of Kilowatt Hours

	Generation						Sales to Ultimate Customers							
	Electric Utility Industry			Other		Total			Inter-				Other	Rail-
Year	Hydro	Steam	Nuclear	Total[5]	Sources[2]	Total	Million $	Total[4]	Residen-tial	Depart-mental	Comm-ercial	Indus-trial	Street & Highway	Public Author-ities	ways & Rail roads
1973	272.1	1,495	83.3	1,856	103	1,959	31,663	1,703	554.2	5.5	396.9	687.2	12.8	42.3	4.2
1974	301.0	1,446	113.7	1,866	102	1,968	39,127	1,701	555.0	5.4	392.7	689.4	13.3	40.7	4.3
1975	300.0	1,439	172.5	1,918	85	2,003	46,855	1,733	586.1	5.4	418.1	661.6	13.9	43.6	4.3
1976	283.7	1,558	191.1	2,038	87	2,125	53,463	1,850	613.1	6.4	440.6	725.2	14.4	45.6	4.3
1977	220.5	1,648	250.9	2,124	88	2,212	62,610	1,951	652.3	7.2	469.2	757.2	14.4	46.2	4.2
1978	280.4	1,645	276.4	2,206	79	2,300	69,853	2,018	679.2	7.1	480.7	782.1	14.8	49.5	4.3
1979	279.8	1,708	255.2	2,247	71	2,318	79,640	2,084	696.0	7.4	494.7	817.6	14.8	49.6	4.3
1980	276.0	1,756	251.1	2,283	68	2,351	95,462	2,126	734.4	6.4	524.1	793.8	14.8	48.3	4.3
1981	260.7	1,759	272.7	2,295	70	2,365	111,016	2,151	730.5	6.2	521.7	819.6	14.7	53.7	4.2
1982	309.2	1,647	282.8	2,238			121,584	2,100	732.7	5.4	517.0	770.4	14.2	55.7	4.3
1983	332.1	1,682	293.7	2,308			129,507	2,158	750.9	5.4	546.3	780.0	14.1	56.7	4.3
1984	321.2	1,766	327.6	2,415			142,281	2,286	780.7	5.8	583.8	836.1	14.1	61.0	4.5
1985[1]	281.1	1,803	383.7	2,468			148,892	2,318	794.4	5.8	613.2	821.7	14.4	64.3	4.7
1986[3]	290.0		400.0				149,000	2,300	800.0	6.0	610.0	810.0	15.0	65.0	2.5

[1] Preliminary.   [2] Includes generation of industrial and railway electric plants.   [3] Estimate.   [4] Also includes interdepartmental (averages about 600 million kwh).   [5] Includes internal combustion.   *Sources: Federal Power Commission; Edison Electric Institute*   T.224

Electric Power Production by Electric Utilities in the U.S.   In Billions of Kilowatt Hours

Year	Jan.	Feb.	Mar.	Apr.	May	June	July	Aug.	Sept.	Oct.	Nov.	Dec.	Total
1974	156.9	142.4	149.9	141.9	153.4	156.0	177.9	173.8	152.2	151.9	149.8	159.5	1,867
1975	164.3	147.1	155.5	146.2	153.2	162.4	176.8	179.7	155.2	154.9	152.8	169.4	1,918
1976	178.3	156.7	164.2	153.2	157.4	173.4	186.4	186.4	165.0	163.7	169.1	183.9	2,038
1977	196.4	162.7	169.1	156.9	169.3	180.8	198.9	196.1	176.2	166.4	167.1	184.2	2,124
1978	197.3	173.7	173.2	159.7	175.2	187.4	202.6	205.6	185.6	175.6	176.3	191.7	2,206
1979	209.7	186.3	182.8	170.0	178.1	186.7	202.3	204.9	180.8	179.7	177.5	188.7	2,247
1980	200.0	188.7	187.5	168.7	175.7	189.4	216.8	215.4	191.5	178.6	178.6	195.6	2,286
1981	206.5	179.6	185.6	172.5	177.8	202.7	220.4	210.4	186.8	181.4	175.6	195.6	2,295
1982	209.4	180.3	187.7	172.6	177.1	186.1	210.6	205.7	180.7	173.0	173.4	184.7	2,241
1983	195.6	172.5	182.5	170.4	174.4	191.0	220.2	230.0	195.6	182.9	182.9	212.3	2,310
1984	216.6	189.6	200.1	181.1	192.2	209.6	221.2	229.3	195.2	190.9	190.4	200.0	2,416
1985[1]	227.7	198.1	194.7	184.7	196.7	205.0	226.7	226.1	202.4	194.8	192.4	219.3	2,470
1986[1]	217.7	192.4	196.7	187.2	198.3	215.0	242.7	225.2					

[1] Preliminary.   *Source: Federal Power Commission*   T.225

Use of Fuels for Electric Generation in the United States

	Consumption of Fuel			Total Fuel in Coal Equivalent (Thousand Short Tons)	Net Gen-eration by Fuels[3] (Million Kw. Hr.)	Lbs. of Coal Per Kw. Hr. (Pounds)	% of Total Net Fuel Genera-tion	Average Cost of Fuel Per Kw. Hr. (¢)	Heat Rate BTU Per Kw. Hr.	Cost Per Million BTU Consumed (¢)
Year	Coal (Thousand Short Tons)	Fuel Oil (Thousand Barrels)[2]	Gas (Million Cubic Feet)							
1973	388,190	559,842	3,640,756	688,043	1,498,958	.918	96.1	.50	10,429	48.4
1974	392,344	536,140	3,429,072	685,115	1,449,079	.946	95.6	.93	10,481	89.0
1975	406,032	506,081	3,157,591	686,236	1,441,611	.952		1.12	10,383	108.3
1976	448,431	555,583	3,080,627	740,112	1,558,951	.950		1.20	10,369	115.3
1977	477,215	623,656	3,190,571	798,425	1,648,775	.969		1.38	10,449	131.8
1978	481,624	635,829	3,188,370	811,814	1,646,163	.986		1.53	10,495	145.3
1979	527,317	523,297	3,490,523	837,371	1,708,029	.981		1.62	10,470	155.4
1980	569,453	420,214	3,681,595	916,952	1,753,749	.980		2.07	10,489	197.0
1981	596,797	351,111	3,640,154	922,133	1,755,401	.992		2.42	10,506	230.2
1982	593,666	249,771	3,225,518	858,869	1,644,062	.996		2.46	10,517	234.0
1983	625,211	245,497	2,910,767	861,621	1,678,021	.993		2.40	10,539	227.1
1984[1]	664,399	204,479	3,111,342	909,156	1,758,882	.990		2.41	10,385	232.0
1985[1]	693,841	173,414	3,044,083	926,793	1,794,276	.990		2.27	10,426	217.7
1986[4]	680,000	230,000	2,800,000							

[1] Preliminary.   [2] 42-gallon barrels.   [3] Excludes wood & waste fuels.   [4] Estimate.   *Source: Federal Power Commission*   T.226

Fertilizer

The fertilizer industry produces nitrogenous, phosphatic and potassic (potassium) fertilizers. Nitrogen, phosphorous and potassium are the primary plant nutrients. The basic nitrogen fertilizer is ammonia, which is made from natural gas and nitrogen. Ammonia may be applied in liquid form below the surface of the soil or converted into solid nitrogenous fertilizers, such as urea or diamonium phosphate. Phosphoric acid, made from phosphate rock and sulfuric acid, is the source of most of the phosphorous used in agriculture. The major potassium fertilizer is potassium chloride, more commonly called potash. Fertilizer chemicals based on nitrogen account for 53 percent of total U.S. fertilizer consumption; those based on phosphorous, 26 percent; and potassium fertilizers, 21 percent.

The world's primary producers are the U.S., the USSR, China and Canada. The U.S. leads in phosphate production, followed by Morocco. The USSR is the foremost producer of ammonia, followed by China and the U.S. Canada and the USSR are the major potash producers.

The Bureau of Mines projected 1986 production of nitrogen to be 11.5 million short tons, 19 percent below last year's 14.1 million. U.S. consumption for 1986 was forecast at 13.3 million short tons, off 14 percent from the year before. Imports were down seven percent, estimated at 2.05 million short tons, while exports were down 47 percent, amounting to only 531,000 short tons for the year.

The Bureau of Mines projected 1986 phosphate rock production at 40.5 million tonnes, down over 20 percent from 1985. Although there were many factors which contributed to this sharp drop, the two largest were increased foreign competition and depressed prices. U.S. exports declined 24 percent in 1986 to an estimated 8.4 million tonnes. This may be the beginning of a new trend; due to production increases abroad, exports should continue to decline through 1987. Prices for phosphate rock were also very low. Reportedly, production costs actually exceeded selling prices at several times during the year.

U.S. potash production in 1986 was estimated at 1.17 million tonnes, off 17 percent from 1985. Large stocks, depressed prices and slow demand were factors which contributed to the decline. Demand for potash was projected to be off seven percent. Apparent domestic consumption totaled 5.14 million tonnes in 1986, with imports estimated at 4 million tonnes and exports at 500,000 tonnes.

The largest factor affecting the U.S. fertilizer industry has been the troubled agricultural economy. Because of the depressed price of farm commodities throughout much of 1986, the value of land decreased and the amount farmers were able to borrow from banks declined. Falling farm profits also made it difficult to pay off old loans, causing a sharp increase in defaults. All of these factors severely affected the demand for fertilizer. High participation in the acreage reduction program resulted in much fallow land during 1986 and thus a decrease in demand for fertilizer. The summer drought, heavy rains and large harvests also had a negative impact. The decline in demand, coupled with extensive stocks from 1985, resulted in sharply reduced prices throughout 1986. No immediate improvement is seen for 1987.

World Production of Ammonia   In Thousands of Short Tons of Contained Nitrogen

Year	Bulgaria	Canada	China	France	East Germany	West Germany	India	Italy	Japan	Mexico	Netherlands	Poland	Romania	United Kingdom	United States	USSR	Total
1979	.9	2.2	9.7	2.4	1.2	2.4	2.5	1.6	2.6	1.5	2.1	1.7	2.6	1.8	15.4	13.4	78.4
1980	.9	2.3	11.0	2.3	1.3	2.3	2.4	1.5	2.3	1.7	2.1	1.6	2.5	1.8	16.2	13.9	81.2
1981	1.1	2.4	13.4	2.5	1.3	2.2	3.5	1.3	2.0	2.0	2.0	1.5	2.6	2.0	15.7	14.2	84.8
1982	1.1	2.3	14.0	2.2	1.3	1.7	3.8	1.2	1.8	2.2	1.8	1.5	2.9	1.9	13.0	15.4	83.6
1983	1.2	3.2	15.2	2.1	1.3	1.9	3.9	1.2	1.7	2.1	1.9	1.6	3.0	1.9	11.3	16.0	86.6
1984[1]	1.3	3.9	15.4	2.2	1.3	2.2	4.4	1.2	1.8	2.0	2.5	1.6	3.0	2.0	13.4	16.5	93.0
1985[2]	1.5	3.9	16.5	2.3	1.3	1.7	4.5	1.3	1.8	2.0	2.5	1.4	3.0	2.0	13.2	17.1	94.3

[1] Preliminary.   [2] Estimate.   *Source: Bureau of Mines*   T.227

U.S. Salient Statistics of Nitrogen[1] (Ammonia)   In Thousands of Short Tons

Year	Net Import Reliance as a % of Appar. Con.	Production (Fixed)	Imports Fixed	Exports (Ammonia)	Apparent Consumption — Fixed (Ammonia)	Apparent Consumption — Elemental	Apparent Consumption — Fixed	Producer Stocks (Year End)	Average Price ($ Per Short Ton) — Urea F.O.B. Gulf[2] Coast	Average Price ($ Per Short Ton) — Urea Deliv. Corn Belt	Ammonium Nitrate: Deliv. Corn Belt	Ammonia F.O.B. Gulf Coast
1979	7	15,420	1,603	647		14,386	16,565	1,752	145–150	165–170	118–120	128–132
1980	9	16,244	1,921	681			17,754	1,483	170–175	155–170	110–115	120–125
1981	5	15,732	1,719	506			16,467	1,960	130–135	170–180	138–150	132
1982	8	13,029	1,737	610			14,145	1,970	122–125	135–145	125–145	120
1983	18	11,297	2,169	298			13,719	1,422	135–140	160–167	135–145	175
1984	13	13,368	2,699	438			15,346	1,705	147–149	168–200	135–150	147
1985[1]	8	13,238	2,306	1,010			14,439	1,800	82–95	110–137	112–133	135

[1] Elemental, Fixed, & Natural Nitrates.   [2] Prilled.   *Source: Bureau of Mines*   T.228

91

FERTILIZER

World Production of Phosphate Rock, Basic Slag & Guano   In Ths. of Metric Tons (Gross Weight)

Year	Algeria	Brazil	China	Christmas Island	Israel	Jordan	Morocco	Nauru Island	Senegal	South Africa	Syria	Togo	Tunisia	United States	USSR	World Total
1977	1,173	676	4,000	1,186	1,227	1,782	17,572	1,146	1,871	2,403	425	2,857	3,615	47,256	26,925	119,310
1978	1,136	1,096	4,695	1,400	1,725	2,303	19,713	1,999	1,759	2,699	800	2,827	3,712	50,037	23,900	125,022
1979	1,084	1,628	8,517	1,367	2,086	2,825	20,032	1,828	1,835	3,221	1,272	2,920	4,154	51,611	24,400	131,825
1980	1,025	2,612	10,726	1,713	2,307	3,911	18,824	2,087	1,632	3,185	1,319	2,933	4,582	54,415	30,300	144,193
1981	916	3,238	11,500	1,423	1,919	4,244	18,562	1,480	1,699	2,718	1,321	2,215	4,596	53,624	30,700	143,001
1982	947	2,732	11,720	1,328	2,148	4,390	17,754	1,359	1,182	3,161	1,455	2,800	4,196	37,414	31,300	127,385
1983	893	3,208	12,500	1,094	2,969	4,749	20,106	1,684	1,521	2,887	1,229	2,081	5,924	42,573	31,600	139,404
1984[1]	1,000	3,855	14,210	1,259	3,312	6,263	21,245	1,358	1,912	2,585	1,514	2,696	5,346	49,197	31,900	152,488
1985[2]	1,207	4,214	12,000	1,200	4,076	6,067	20,737	1,508	1,702	2,421	1,270	2,452	4,530	50,835	32,200	151,363

[1] Preliminary.   [2] Estimate.   *Source: Bureau of Mines*   T.229

U.S. Salient Statistics of Phosphate Rock   In Thousands of Metric Tons

Year	Mine Production	Marketable Production	Value Mil. $	Imports for Consumption	Exports	Apparent Consumption	Stocks, Dec. 31 (Producer)	Price—$ Avg. Per Metric Ton (f.o.b. Mine)	Avg. Price of Fla. & No. Car $ Tonne—F.O.B. Mine (−60% to +74) Domestic	Export	Average
1977	166,893	47,256	821.7	158	13,230	34,365	13,682	17.39			
1978	173,429	50,037	928.8	908	12,870	36,812	15,748	18.56			
1979	185,757	51,611	1,046	886	14,358	39,591	14,500	20.26	18.91	24.60	20.57
1980	209,883	54,415	1,257	486	14,276	40,791	13,709	23.10	21.01	30.03	23.51
1981	183,733	53,624	1,438	13	10,395	35,144	19,619	26.82	25.17	33.74	27.68
1982	104,135	37,414	950	31	9,842	28,760	18,287	25.40	28.78	28.92	25.93
1983	125,691	42,573	1,021	9	12,010	34,838	14,500	23.98	22.64	25.70	23.48
1984	163,012	49,197	1,182	9	11,528	41,758	11,897	24.03	22.67	26.28	23.48
1985[1]	175,058	50,835	1,203	34	10,284	36,384	15,534	23.67	22.41	25.35	23.08
1986[2]		43,000			9,000	34,000	16,000	22.00			

[1] Preliminary.   [2] Estimate.   *Source: Bureau of Mines*   T.230

U.S. Salient Statistics of Potash   In Thousands of Metric Tons (K_2O Equivalent)

Year	Net Import as % of Consumption	Production	Sales by Producers	Value Mil. $	Imports for Consumption	Exports	Apparent Consumption	Producer Stocks Dec. 31	$ per ton Avg. Value Per Ton of Product—$	Avg. Value of K_2O Equiv.	Average Price[2] $ Per Met. Ton
1976	61	2,177	2,268	210.8	4,168	857	5,578	471	50.37	92.93	73
1977	63	2,229	2,232	206.9	4,605	845	5,992	467	48.78	92.68	71
1978	64	2,253	2,307	226.5	4,707	809	6,205	414	51.97	98.16	76
1979	66	2,225	2,388	279.2	5,165	635	6,918	251	61.38	116.92	95
1980	65	2,239	2,217	353.9	4,972	840	6,349	273	82.98	159.63	133
1981	65	2,156	1,908	328.9	4,796	491	6,213	520	89.62	172.40	137
1982	65	1,784	1,784	265.6	3,858	519	5,123	520	78.42	148.87	109
1983	75	1,429	1,513	220.8	4,440	300	5,653	391	74.85	145.97	100
1984	74	1,564	1,639	241.8	4,829	446	6,022	312	75.95	147.55	109
1985[1]	77	1,296	1,266	178.4	4,593	513	5,346	336	71.22	140.89	95

[1] Preliminary.   [2] Unit of K_2O, standard 60% muriate f.o.b. mine.   *Source: Bureau of Mines*   T.232

World Production of Marketable Potash   In Thousands of Metric Tons (K_2O Equivalent)

Year	Canada (sales)	Chile	China	Congo (Brazz.)	France	Germany East	Germany West	Israel	Italy	Jordan	Spain	USSR	United States	United Kingdom	World Total
1976	4,996	15	150	254	1,603	3,161	2,036	680	330	—	630	8,310	2,177	41	24,386
1977	5,764	11	18	136	1,580	3,229	2,341	730	224	—	562	8,347	2,229	81	25,252
1978	6,340	17	21	—	1,795	3,323	2,470	744	196	—	613	8,193	2,253	157	26,122
1979	7,074	22	16	—	1,921	3,395	2,616	737	182	—	668	6,635	2,225	277	25,768
1980	7,532	25	12	—	1,894	3,422	2,737	797	156	—	658	8,064	2,239	321	27,857
1981	6,549	21	20	—	1,831	3,460	2,591	839	142	—	732	8,449	2,156	285	27,075
1982	5,309	21	26	—	1,704	3,434	2,056	1,004	146	9	692	8,079	1,784	245	24,509
1983	6,938	21	29	—	1,536	3,431	2,419	1,000	184	172	657	9,294	1,429	308	27,418
1984[1]	7,527	18	40	—	1,739	3,465	2,644	1,100	178	295	677	9,776	1,564	325	29,348
1985[2]	6,600	19	40		1,750	3,475	2,580	1,100	205	550	660	10,000	1,296	343	28,618

[1] Preliminary.   [2] Estimate.   *Source: U.S. Bureau of Mines*   T.231

Flaxseed and Linseed Oil

The USDA projects 1986/87 world flaxseed production at 2.79 million tonnes, a 10-percent increase from 1985/86. In Canada, the world's largest producer, the flaxseed crop has registered sharp increases over the last three seasons. In addition to expanded acreage, yields have also increased. The Canadian crop this year is estimated at 1.05 million tonnes, a 17-percent increase from a year ago. Argentina's crop of 550,000 tonnes is 15 percent larger than last season. The Soviet Union had a slightly larger crop, as did the U.S. with production of 220,000 tonnes.

World flaxseed demand has been declining over the last 25 years, due to synthetic fibers substituting for flax and alternative oils replacing linseed oil. Flaxseed producers have switched to other crops like sunflowers; the change in Canada and Argentina has not been successful. World demand of linseed oil appears to have stabilized over the last five years.

World flaxseed crush in 1986/87 is projected at 2.04 million tonnes, up slightly from 1985/86. World trade is expected by USDA to increase six percent to 720,000 tons. Ending stocks are projected to rise to 640,000 tons, a 68-percent increase.

Linseed oil production is projected at 690,000 tons, a marginal increase from a year ago. World exports should decline slightly to 230,000 tons. Argentina is the largest linseed oil exporter accounting for about 60 percent of world trade. Usage of linseed oil in 1986/87 is projected at 660,000 tons, down slightly from a year ago. Ending stocks should be small at 40,000 tons.

World production of linseed meal in 1986/87 is projected at 1.32 million tonnes, compared to 1.28 million in 1985/86. World exports should decline to 600,000 tonnes from 620,000 tonnes in 1985/86. Argentina is also the world's largest exporter of linseed meal; the major importers are Belgium, the Netherlands and West Germany. Consumption of meal is projected at 1.36 million tonnes, a five-percent increase from 1985/86. Ending stocks are expected to be 20,000 tonnes, the same as a year ago.

Futures Market

Flaxseed futures are traded on the Winnipeg Commodity Exchange (WCE).

World Production of Flaxseed   In Thousands of Metric Tons

Crop Year	Argentina	Australia	Czechoslovakia	Canada	Ethiopia	Egypt	France	Hungary	India	Mexico	Poland	Romania	Turkey	Uruguay	United States	USSR	World Total
1980–1	610	7	15	442		27	35	10	423	8	29	44	3	21	196	196	2,096
1981–2	600	7	12	468		18	18	11	483	12	24	38	2	14	185	165	2,086
1982–3	765	3	15	752		38	31	11	375	1	20	43	2	6	261	150	2,502
1983–4	703	4	15	447		16	29	11	440	4	25	23	2	11	175	259	2,130
1984–5[1]	550	5	15	690		17	35	12	390	3	20	42	2	12	178	250	2,310
1985–6[1]	480			900					450						211	200	2,440
1986–7[2]	550			1,050					450						220	230	5,320

[1] Preliminary.   [2] Estimate.   Source: Foreign Agricultural Service, U.S.D.A.   T.233

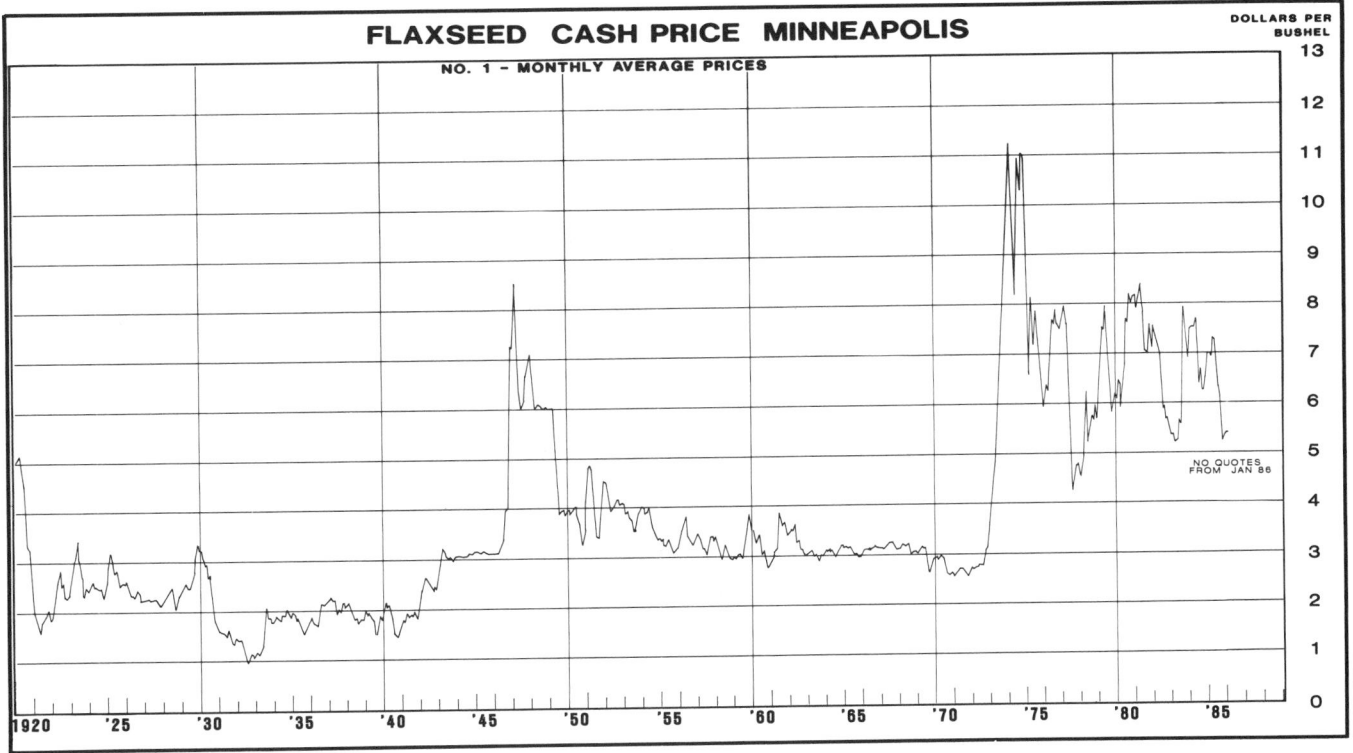

FLAXSEED CASH PRICE MINNEAPOLIS

NO. 1 – MONTHLY AVERAGE PRICES

DOLLARS PER BUSHEL

NO QUOTES FROM JAN 86

FLAXSEED AND LINSEED OIL

Production of Flaxseed in the United States   In Thousands of Bushels

| Year | Crop Production Estimates | | | | Minne-sota | Mon-tana | North Dakota | South Dakota | Texas | U.S. Total |
	Aug. 1	Sept. 1	Oct. 1	Dec. 1						
1977	15,466	16,011	16,249	16,105	3,190	35	7,500	4,290	90	14,280
1978	11,156	11,348	11,705	10,921	2,201	—	4,025	2,188	200	8,614
1979	11,847	12,501	13,255	13,539	2,219	—	5,980	3,770	45	12,014
1980	7,060	7,700	7,940	8,128	1,563	—	2,900	3,445	20	7,728
1981	8,083	8,083	7,893	7,799	1,300	—	4,250	2,249	—	7,289
1982	10,940	11,485	11,730	11,635	1,650	—	5,873	2,755	—	10,278
1983	8,295	7,535	7,413	7,363	938	—	4,600	1,365	—	6,903
1984	7,260	7,555	7,555	7,022	653	—	4,875	1,494	—	7,022
1985[1]	8,220	8,513	8,512	8,293	950	—	6,008	1,335	—	8,293
1986[1]	—	—	—	8,700						8,700

[1] Preliminary, December estimate.   *Source: Agricultural Board, U.S.D.A.*

T.234

U.S. Supply and Distribution of Flaxseed   In Thousands of Bushels

| Year Begin-ning June | Supply | | | | | | | Distribution | | | | Total Distri-bution |
| | Stocks, June 1 | | | Total Stocks | Imports | Pro-duction | Total Supply | Seed | Crushing | Exports | Other[2] | |
	Farm	Term-inal	All Other									
1977-8	1,070	—1,934—		2,961	859	14,280	18,100	557	11,615	1,001	—388	11,784
1978-9	2,890	—2,606—		5,315	1,557	8,614	15,486	724	13,009	91	—922	12,811
1979-0	977	—1,607—		2,584	1,916	12,014	16,514	650	12,425	174	—1,753	11,322
1980-1	2,681	—2,337—		5,018	2,510	7,728	15,256	547	11,927	76	—27	12,447
1981-2	1,136	—1,597—		2,733	3,502	7,289	13,524	691	11,231	11	—359	11,574
1982-3	1,175	— 775—		1,950	1,921	10,278	14,149	486	8,722	638	1,091	10,937
1983-4	1,956	—1,258—		3,212	4,756	6,903	14,871	438	12,733	52	—68	13,155
1984-5				1,716	3,796	7,022	12,534	511	9,935	238	0	10,684
1985-6[1]				1,850	2,927	8,293	13,070	517	10,313	250	0	11,080
1986-7[3]				1,990	2,575	8,700	13,265	515	10,500	250	0	11,265

[1] Preliminary. [2] Other disappearance represents cleaning loss, waste, and residual. [3] Forecasts. *Source: Agricultural Statistics Board, U.S.D.A.*

T.235

Average Price Received by Farmers for Flaxseed in the U.S.   In Cents Per Bushel

Year	July	Aug.	Sept.	Oct.	Nov.	Dec.	Jan.	Feb.	Mar.	Apr.	May	June	Average[1]
1977-8	514	415	420	456	420	432	421	407	441	485	532	589	454
1978-9	524	534	531	525	539	530	567	601	648	706	737	727	574
1979-0	690	642	634	556	544	561	551	579	585	551	604	588	597
1980-1	655	702	717	710	723	759	754	748	725	735	765	747	720
1981-2	723	708	644	621	664	684	690	691	680	669	660	665	673
1982-3	625	535	537	511	495	468	486	470	460	454	469	492	519
1983-4	496	594	714	700	692	655	686	701	710	708	720	691	677
1984-5	625	607	572	567	586	605	659	664	618	667	694	654	625
1985-6	610	572	539	501	480	478	477	493	495	488	487	497	510
1986-7	439	379	368	345	339	323							

[1] Season average includes an allowance for unredeemed loans.   *Source: Agricultural Statistics Board, U.S.D.A.*

T.236

Average Price of No. 1 Flaxseed at Minneapolis   In Dollars Per Bushel

Year	Aug.	Sept.	Oct.	Nov.	Dec.	Jan.	Feb.	Mar.	Apr.	May	June	July	Average[1]
1977-8	4.26	4.41	4.79	—	4.80	4.61	4.51	4.78	5.30	5.78	6.25	5.22	4.97
1978-9	5.47	5.76	5.70	5.99	5.75	6.17	6.63	7.22	7.54	7.51	7.98	7.23	6.58
1979-0	7.00	6.71	6.12	5.84	6.16	6.14	6.47	6.44	5.95	6.24	6.50	7.15	6.39
1980-1	7.70	7.65	7.82	8.23	8.04	8.17	8.19	7.93	8.11	8.42	8.06	7.85	8.01
1981-2	7.62	7.02	7.00	7.41	7.61	7.15	7.57	7.47	7.35	7.28	7.02	6.90	7.28
1982-3	5.90	5.93	5.70	5.71	5.52	5.36	5.37	5.23	5.22	5.25	5.66	5.58	5.54
1983-4	6.15	7.93	7.65	7.09	6.92	7.50	7.52	7.54	7.52	7.70	7.19	6.39	7.26
1984-5	6.68	6.25	6.26	6.51	6.76	7.00	7.00	6.91	7.31	7.29	7.01	6.61	6.80
1985-6	6.31	6.14	5.64	5.25	5.38	5.40	—	—	—	—	—	—	5.69

[1] Weighted average by carlot sales.   *Source: Agricultural Statistics Board, U.S.D.A.*

T.238

Supply and Distribution of Linseed Oil in the U.S. & World Production & Price   In Millions of Pounds

Year Beginning June	Supply — Stocks June 1	Supply — Production	Supply — Total	Exports & Shipments	Domestic Disappearance — Drying Oil Products — Paint & Varnish	Linoleum & Oilcloth	Resins & Plastics	Other In-edible	Total	Lubricants & Similar Oils	Total	Production in 1,000 tonnes — Total World	Argentina	India	U.S.	Rotterdam Ex-Tank $ Tonne
1978-9	70	259	329	54	127.7		29.5				231					601
1979-0	44	256	300	38	103.7		19.6				208	685	169	116	114	668
1980-1	54	251	305	51	69.6		23.3				198	627	162	140	108	694
1981-2	56	237	293	54	42.4		20.9				189	630	162	140	108	564
1982-3	50	182	232	21							176	650	221	108	82	456
1983-4[1]	35	265	300	51	56.5		27.7				201	740	206	128	120	556
1984-5[1]	48	194	242	15							194	710	170	146	88	639
1985-6[2]	33	205	238	15							184	680	145	130	96	475

[1] Preliminary.   [2] Estimate.   [3] Oil production calculated from assumed extraction rates.   *Source: Economic Research Service, U.S.D.A.*   T.239

U.S. Linseed Oil Consumption in Refining   In Millions of Pounds

Year	July	Aug.	Sept.	Oct.	Nov.	Dec.	Jan.	Feb.	Mar.	Apr.	May	June	Total
1979-0	18.4	19.9	15.8	24.3	14.9	11.4	11.7	12.3	14.6	17.1	11.6	12.2	184.2
1980-1	13.2	15.7	16.7	21.1	11.4	11.6	13.6	13.9	12.2	19.8	15.4	12.9	177.5
1981-2	21.0	16.0	15.3	15.2	N.A.	N.A.	6.5	9.6	11.5	17.5	9.9	9.0	131.5
1982-3	8.7	8.3	8.4	7.6	6.1	5.0	6.0	6.3	7.1	7.0	7.6	8.9	87.0
1983-4	11.7	11.9	12.4	16.5	10.6	10.0	13.5	12.6	21.8	8.0	N.A.	N.A.	129.0
1984-5	N.A.	N.A.	16.1	15.6	N.A.	N.A.	12.3	N.A.	N.A.	15.0	19.2	N.A.	78.2
1985-6[1]	16.0	9.9	15.3	14.3	12.2	9.2	9.4	N.A.	13.6	14.7	12.3	15.1	142.0
1986-7[1]	14.0	13.8	15.8	15.1									

[1] Preliminary.   *Source: Bureau of the Census*   T.242

Factory Shipments of Paints, Varnish and Lacquer in the U.S.   In Millions of Dollars

Year	Jan.	Feb.	Mar.	Apr.	May	June	July	Aug.	Sept.	Oct.	Nov.	Dec.	Total
1981	482.8	512.9	625.7	660.7	654.8	721.8	652.4	661.8	652.6	599.7	489.7	440.4	7,155
1982	486.9	509.1	616.1	633.4	664.3	736.0	631.6	671.5	653.8	545.2	479.8	419.7	7,047
1983	495.2	522.7	661.2	681.9	733.9	814.2	697.6	760.2	719.5	662.2	585.0	510.2	7,844
1984	628.7	676.7	764.2	758.2	843.4	844.0	789.4	838.1	749.7	771.0	638.5	571.3	8,818
1985[1]	669.5	661.2	806.2	925.5	996.0	942.9	925.5	855.2	797.0	811.0	665.4	564.1	9,173
1986[1]	717.4	698.4	766.2	920.5	916.1	900.0	871.0	860.8					

[1] Preliminary.   *Source: Bureau of the Census*   T.246

Wholesale Price of Raw Linseed Oil at Minneapolis in Tank Cars   In Cents Per Pound

Year	July	Aug.	Sept.	Oct.	Nov.	Dec.	Jan.	Feb.	Mar.	Apr.	May	June	Average
1979-0	30.0	30.0	32.0	32.0	32.0	32.0	32.0	28.8	28.8	27.8	26.6	27.0	29.9
1980-1	27.0	28.6	29.0	29.2	29.0	29.8	32.8	32.0	31.3	32.0	32.6	32.8	30.5
1981-2	32.8	32.3	31.8	30.8	30.0	27.6	29.5	28.5	28.2	28.0	28.0	27.0	29.5
1982-3	27.8	26.3	26.0	24.6	25.0	25.2	24.6	25.0	24.3	23.6	23.0	23.0	24.9
1983-4	22.8	25.5	31.6	34.0	31.5	32.0	32.0	32.0	31.8	32.0	33.0	34.5	31.1
1984-5	33.4	38.0	31.0	28.8	28.5	30.0	31.2	32.0	N.A.	N.A.	N.A.	N.A.	31.6
1985-6	34.6	33.3	33.0	30.0	30.0	27.6	30.0	30.0	30.0	30.0	30.0	29.4	30.7
1986-7	29.0	29.0	29.0	28.2									

Source: Department of Agriculture   T.240

U.S. Stocks of Linseed Oil (Crude & Refined) at Factories & Warehouses   In Millions of Pounds

Year	July 1	Aug. 1	Sept. 1	Oct. 1	Nov. 1	Dec. 1	Jan. 1	Feb. 1	Mar. 1	April 1	May 1	June 1
1979-0	49.1	39.9	47.7	62.9	46.4	43.6	35.6	41.8	36.3	48.2	65.6	53.5
1980-1	42.9	45.3	35.5	52.5	43.8	34.5	45.6	50.6	53.3	34.7	42.1	56.3
1981-2	67.1	57.4	65.7	71.4	72.1	64.3	56.3	62.7	57.0	64.6	66.7	50.4
1982-3	37.4	33.9	30.5	44.6	43.0	26.8	39.0	34.1	41.8	41.6	27.1	35.1
1983-4	54.7	46.5	41.7	50.4	46.0	34.9	34.1	38.0	40.3	41.5	55.2	47.6
1984-5	50.7	40.8	24.9	48.3	41.3	36.1	39.3	38.3	34.1	30.1	35.1	33.4
1985-6[1]	32.7	36.9	25.4	47.0	62.3	55.2	60.5	62.7	64.5	66.0	56.1	40.1
1986-7[1]	46.0	45.3	40.5	40.0	45.2	39.0						

[1] Preliminary.   *Source: Bureau of the Census*   T.245

FLAXSEED AND LINSEED OIL

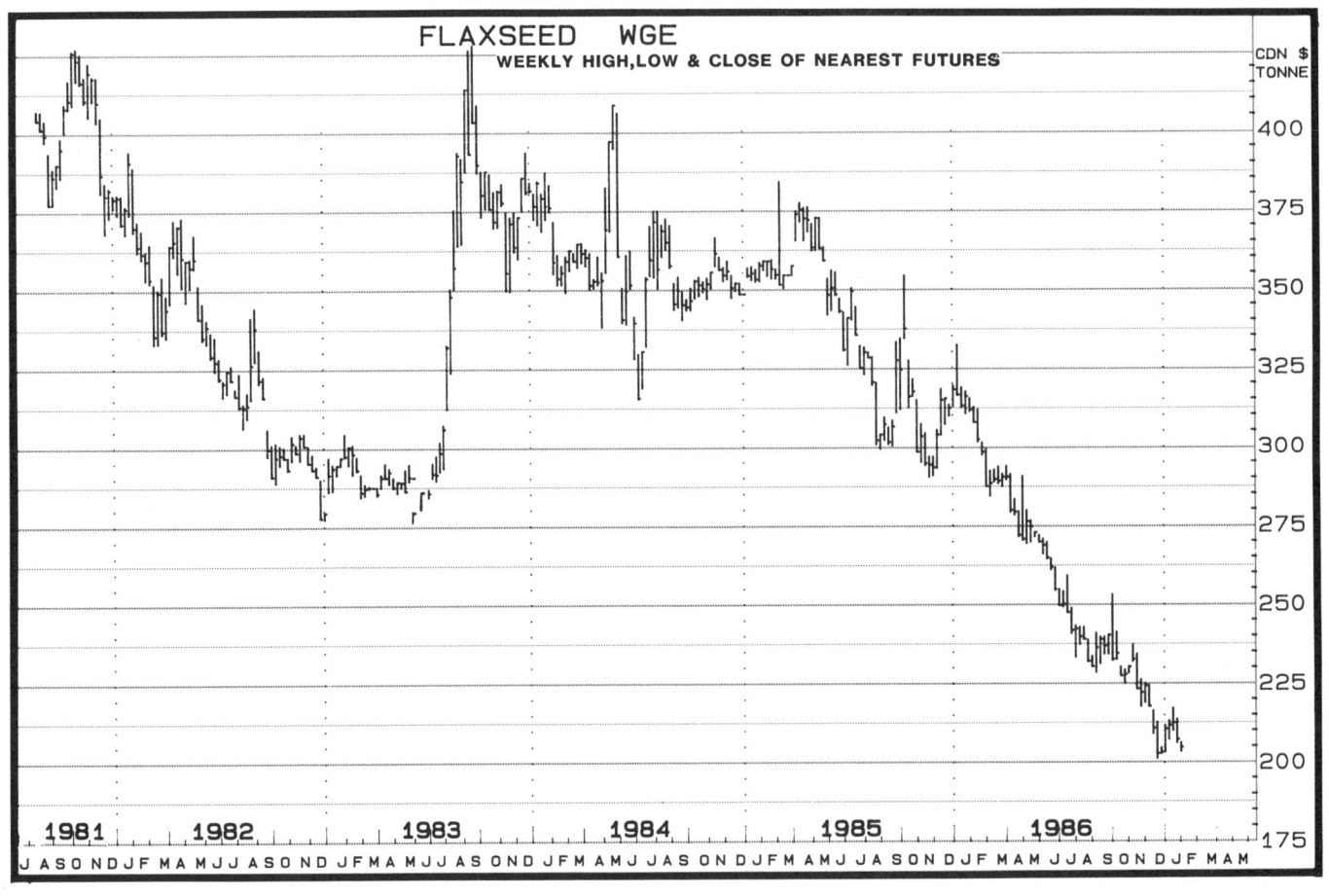

High, Low & Closing Prices of May Flaxseed Futures in Winnipeg   In Canadian Dollars per Tonne

Year of Delivery		June	July	Aug.	Sept.	Oct.	Nov.	Dec.	Jan.	Feb.	Mar.	Apr.	May	Life of Delivery Range
				Year Prior to Delivery							_Delivery Year_			
1984	High	—	—	409.0	454.0	416.0	402.9	408.0	390.1	386.2	366.0	362.3	408.0	454.0
	Low	—	—	352.0	407.0	391.5	369.0	377.5	370.0	350.0	353.0	347.0	337.5	337.5
	Close	—	—	408.0	415.5	391.5	381.0	392.6	382.5	353.0	359.0	347.5	376.5	—
1985	High	385.0	394.0	402.5	382.5	380.5	384.5	377.5	363.7	366.8	366.0	377.0	372.2	402.5
	Low	365.0	356.0	380.6	372.0	371.5	371.3	361.0	358.8	361.0	357.0	365.0	344.0	344.0
	Close	376.5	385.6	389.0	375.5	371.8	376.0	361.0	362.0	362.5	365.5	366.0	347.8	—
1986	High	375.0	373.1	353.9	340.0	349.0	313.0	333.0	334.0	319.3	300.5	293.5	282.0	378.5
	Low	374.2	350.3	318.2	318.0	316.0	303.5	309.1	317.0	295.3	290.3	270.1	269.0	269.0
	Close	366.0	350.3	324.4	328.5	317.5	308.5	325.0	318.0	295.5	293.5	290.4	269.5	—
1987	High	—	280.0	262.8	265.2	258.7	250.4	239.2						
	Low	—	268.0	248.0	247.5	242.1	231.5	212.8						
	Close	—	268.0	248.0	260.5	245.0	238.7	217.8						

Source: Winnipeg Commodity Exchange   T.243

Month–End Open Interest of Flaxseed Futures in Winnipeg   In Contracts

Year	Jan.	Feb.	Mar.	Apr.	May	June	July	Aug.	Sept.	Oct.	Nov.	Dec.
1983	4,759	5,261	4,128	5,039	4,552	3,697	3,321	2,520	3,953	3,345	6,282	6,091
1984	6,509	6,964	5,100	5,944	4,509	3,943	5,140	6,164	5,853	4,490	5,618	5,162
1985	5,408	5,927	6,281	5,783	6,321	5,848	5,016	5,913	5,815	4,315	4,186	4,024
1986	5,037	5,600	5,204	6,586	6,137	6,487	5,561	6,626	7,147	3,955	5,618	4,247

Source: Winnipeg Commodity Exchange   T.244

Gas

Preliminary figures suggest that during 1986 approximately 16 quadrillion (10 to the 15th power) Btu of dry natural gas were produced in the U.S. That amount was 19 quadrillion Btu below 1985 production. Domestic supplies were augmented by imports of 60 quadrillion Btu, down nearly one-third from 1985. Roughly 6.9 billion cubic feet of natural gas were in underground storage in late 1986, little changed from the prior year.

Consumption of natural gas (including supplemental gaseous fuels) fell to an estimated 16.65 quadrillion Btu, down 6.7 percent from 1985. About 28 percent of total consumption was by residential users, one-third by industrial consumers, and 15 percent each by commercial users and electric utilities. Most of the decline in consumption, year-over-year, is attributed to fuel-switching by industrial and commercial consumers. The sharp drop in fuel-oil prices in 1986 prompted appropriately-equipped consumers to substitute No. 2 distillate for natural gas.

Whereas the natural gas price per thousand cubic feet to residential consumers (nearly all of whom are unable to switch fuels on short notice) rose from an average of $5.71 in December, 1985, to $6.58 in July, 1986, the average price to commercial users during the same period *fell*, from $5.25 per thousand cubic feet to $5.06. The average price to industrial consumers also fell, from $3.79 to $2.80. Worth noting, as well, is the changed relationship between the prices of residential heating oil and residential natural gas during December, 1985–July, 1986. The average price of the former fuel, in 1972 dollars, skidded from 41.2 cents per gallon to 29.6 cents, while the average price for natural gas *increased*, from 234.5 cents per thousand cubic feet to 239.1 cents.

In 1987, output and consumption of gas should be modestly smaller than in 1986. Prices to residential consumers should creep up some more, while prices to commercial and industrial users will be unchanged or will drift slowly downward.

World Natural Gas Production (Marketed Production[3])   In Thousands of Terajoule[4]

Year	Argentina	Canada	China	France	Indonesia	West Germany	Iran	Italy	Mexico	Netherlands	Poland	Romania	United Kingdom	United States	USSR	Venezuela	Australia
1976	268	2,820		279	115	676	788	600	515	3,422	243	1,384	1,491	20,552	11,194	497	231
1977	271	2,962		299	162	673	743	524	538	3,067	249	1,465	1,536	18,921	12,102	510	264
1978	256	2,856	535	307	353	720	668	524	701	3,048	244	1,475	1,458	18,846	12,967	528	274
1979	303	3,041	566	303	482	729	700	581	832	3,100	224	1,409	1,470	19,415	14,160	601	303
1980	327	2,790	558	289	607	632	279	476	1,036	3,012	193	1,455	1,379	19,256	15,168	643	351
1981	340	2,748	496	277	653	680	247	536	1,033	2,664	187	1,532	1,374	19,057	16,215	647	406
1982	393	2,825	464	341	646	577	257	555	1,068	2,280	167	1,640	1,526	17,656	17,414	684	432
1983	457	2,740	475	379	844	629	264	498	1,048	2,422	193	1,680	1,577	15,880	18,628	644	443
1984[1]	498	2,964	478		1,669	587		533	1,095	2,445	210		1,590	17,116	20,469		470
1985[2]	505	3,000	500		1,690	580		540	990	2,450	225		1,650	16,850	21,000		490

[1] Preliminary.   [2] Estimate.   [3] Comprises all gas collected & utilized as fuel or as a chemical industry raw material, including gas used in oilfields and/or gasfields as a fuel by producers.   [4] Terajoule = 10^{12} Joule = approx. 10^9 BTU.   *Source: United Nations*   T.247

United States Recoverable Reserves and Deliveries of Natural Gas   In Billions of Cubic Feet

Year	Recoverable Reserves of Natural Gas Dec. 31[3]	Residential	Commercial	Lease & Plant Fuel	Carbon Black	Petroleum Refineries	Used as Pipeline Fuel	Industrial	Other Consumers	Total Deliveries	Electric Utility Plants[2]
1974	237,132	4,786	2,556	1,477	40	1,040	669	8,292		19,077	3,443
1975	228,200	4,924	2,508	1,396	26	946	583	6,968		17,558	3,158
1976	216,026	5,051	2,668	1,634	28	919	548	6,964	285	17,764	3,081
1977	208,878	4,821	2,501	1,659	28		533	6,815	257	17,329	3,191
1978	200,302	4,903	2,601	1,648			530	6,757	291	17,449	3,188
1979	200,987	4,965	2,786	1,499			601	6,899	301	18,141	3,491
1980	199,021	4,752	2,611	1,026			635	7,172		18,216	3,682
1981	201,730	4,546	2,520	928			642	7,128		17,834	3,640
1982	201,512	4,633	2,606	1,109			596	5,831		16,295	3,226
1983	200,247	4,381	2,433	978			490	5,643		15,367	2,911
1984	197,463	4,555	2,524	1,077			529	6,154		16,345	3,111
1985[1]		4,433	2,432	1,016			504	5,901		15,811	3,044
1986[4]		3,750	2,000				450	5,000		14,000	2,750

[1] Preliminary.   [2] Figures include gas other than natural (impossible to segregate); therefore, shown separately from other consumption.   [3] Estimated proved recoverable reserves.   [4] Estimated.   *Source: U.S. Dept. of Energy*   T.251

GAS

Gas Utility Sales in the United States by Types & Class of Service   In Trillions of BTU's[3]

Year	Total Utility Sales	No. of Cust. (Mil.)	Class of Service Resi-dential	Com-mercial	Indus-trial	Other	Revenue—Mil. $ Total	Resi-dential	Com-mercial	Indus-trial	Other
1973	164,799	44.2	49,936	22,808	83,708	8,347	12,987	6,247	2,172	4,197	371
1974	160,003	44.7	48,648	22,934	81,532	6,890	15,242	6,899	2,539	5,391	413
1975	148,629	44.8	49,910	23,868	68,371	6,480	19,101	8,445	3,303	6,745	608
1976	148,135	45.1	50,142	24,266	71,070	2,696	23,701	9,941	4,075	9,435	250
1977	143,409	45.7	49,463	24,094	67,107	2,746	28,303	11,541	4,980	11,455	328
1978	147,480	46.0	51,070	25,000	68,410	3,010	32,150	12,939	5,696	13,139	377
1979	154,400	46.7	50,830	24,860	75,550	3,160	38,947	14,833	6,624	17,045	446
1980[3]	15,413	47.4	4,826	2,453	7,957	177	48,303	17,432	8,183	22,215	473
1981	15,375	48.1	4,610	2,375	8,239	150	56,110	19,180	9,286	27,124	520
1982	14,183	48.5	4,770	2,471	6,794	147	63,200	23,700	11,666	27,200	634
1983	12,859	48.9	4,450	2,298	5,970	140	65,837	26,173	12,659	26,315	690
1984	13,162	49.5	4,628	2,396	5,991	146	67,496	27,485	13,205	26,093	713
1985[1]	12,612	50.4	4,515	2,345	3,684	133	63,316	26,868	12,753	15,559	625
1986[2]	12,800	51.0	5,000	2,750	3,100	150	61,500	31,200	14,200	12,000	680

[1] Preliminary.   [2] Estimate.   [3] Data prior to 1980 are in millions of therms.   *Source: American Gas Association*   T.253

Salient Statistics of Natural Gas in the United States

In Billions of Cubic Feet

Year	Supply Marketed Produc-tion	Stor-age With-drawals	Import (Con-sumed)	Total Supply	Disposition Con-sump-tion	Ex-ports	Stored	Extrac-tion Loss	Unac-counted For	Total Dispo-sition	Well-head Price	Imports	Avg. Value Delivered to Consumers— $ Per Ths. Cu. Ft. Resi-dential	Comm-ercial	Industrial	Electric Utilities
1973	22,648	1,533	1,033	25,213	22,049	77	1,974	917	196	25,213	.22	N.A.	1.29	.94	.50	.38
1974	21,601	1,701	959	24,260	21,223	77	1,784	887	289	24,260	.30	N.A.	1.43	1.07	.67	.71
1975	20,109	1,760	953	22,821	19,538	73	2,104	872	235	22,821	.45	N.A.	1.71	1.35	.96	.77
1976	19,952	1,921	963	21,983	19,946	65	1,756	854	216	22,837	.58	N.A.	1.98	1.64	1.24	1.06
1977	20,025	1,750	1,011	21,924	19,521	56	2,307	863	41	22,786	.79	N.A.	2.35	2.04	1.50	1.32
1978	19,974	2,158	966	22,245	19,627	53	2,278	852	287	23,097	.91	2.21	2.56	2.23	1.70	1.48
1979	20,471	2,047	1,253	22,964	20,241	56	2,295	808	372	23,772	1.18	2.60	2.98	2.73	1.99	1.81
1980	20,180	1,972	985	22,515	19,877	49	1,949	777	640	23,292	1.59	4.42	3.68	3.39	2.56	2.27
1981	19,956	1,930	904	22,191	19,404	59	2,228	775	501	22,967	1.98	4.84	4.29	4.00	3.14	2.89
1982	18,520	2,165	933	21,000	18,001	52	2,472	762	475	21,762	2.46	4.94	5.17	4.82	3.87	3.48
1983	16,822	2,270	920	19,354	16,835	55	1,822	790	642	20,144	2.59	4.51	6.06	5.59	4.18	3.58
1984	18,230	2,098	843	20,443	17,951	55	2,295	838	143	21,282	2.66	4.08	6.12	5.55	4.22	3.70
1985[1]	17,198	2,397	950	19,855	17,281	55	2,163	816	354	20,669	2.51	3.18	6.12	5.50	3.95	3.55
1986[2]	16,000	1,600	700	18,500	16,000	55	2,100	800	100	19,055	1.90	2.75	6.20	5.05	3.00	2.70

[1] Preliminary.   [2] Estimate.   [3] Total value of market production at the wellhead.   *Source: U.S. Dept. of Energy*   T.248

United States Marketed Production[1] of Natural Gas   In Billions of Cubic Feet

Year	Arkan-sas	Cali-fornia	Kan-sas	Alas-ka	Loui-siana	Missis-sippi	Mon-tana	New Mexico	Ohio	Okla-homa	Penn-sylvania	Texas	West Virginia	Wy-oming	Michigan
1972	167	487	889	126	7,973	104	33	1,216	90	1,807	74	8,658	215	375	
1973	158	449	893	131	8,242	100	56	1,219	94	1,771	79	8,514	209	358	
1974	124	365	887	129	7,754	79	55	1,245	92	1,639	83	8,171	202	327	
1975	116	318	844	160	7,091	70	41	1,217	85	1,605	85	7,486	154	316	102
1976	110	354	829	166	7,007	71	43	1,231	89	1,727	89	7,192	153	329	119
1977	104	311	781	188	7,215	83	47	1,203	99	1,770	92	7,051	153	330	130
1978	107	311	854	203	7,476	107	47	1,174	114	1,774	98	6,548	149	357	148
1979	109	248	798	221	7,266	144	54	1,181	123	1,835	96	7,175	151	414	160
1980[2]	112	264	732	226	6,937	165	54	1,142		1,892		7,169	152	382	153
1981															

[1] Comprises gas either sold or consumed by producers, including losses in transmission, quantities added to storage and increases of gas in pipelines.   [2] Preliminary.   *Source: U.S. Dept. of Energy*   T.250

Gasoline

Average daily production of motor gasoline in the U.S. during 1986 was about 6.7 million barrels, up an estimated five percent (300,000 barrels) from 1985. Another 300,000 barrels, on average, were added each day through imports; that figure was a hefty 21 percent lower than in 1985. Exports during the first 10 months of 1986 were only 40,000 barrels and during several months there were no exports whatever. The unleaded portion of total supply continued its slow-but-steady growth. In 1977, unleaded gasoline constituted under 28 percent of supply; the share had risen to 65 percent in 1985 and 69 percent in 1986. Ending stocks of motor gasoline averaged 227 million gallons during 1986, up slightly (2.7 percent) from 1985, but down five percent from 1984.

Although the number of automobiles on the road has increased about 9 million per year during the 1980s and the average number of miles travelled per car rose from 9,135 in 1980 to 9,827 in 1985, motor fuel consumption has grown less quickly. On average, 603 gallons of gasoline were burned per car; by 1985, the figure had dipped nine percent, to 549 gallons. Similarly, a passenger car, which in 1980 travelled an average of 15.2 miles per gallon of fuel, covered an average of 17.9 miles in 1985.

In 1986, retail prices of motor gasoline fell below $1.00 throughout most of the U.S. for the first time since 1979. The average retail price in urban areas for unleaded regular gasoline hit 84.3 cents per gallon in August, 1986. The average yearly price in 1985 was $1.202; a high of $1.378 per gallon occurred in 1981. In constant (1972) dollars, the average price at retail of leaded regular gasoline closed at 32.7 cents in mid-1986, compared with 60.5 cents for 1980 as a whole. The steep drop in prices during 1986 resulted from the near free-fall in crude oil prices that began in November, 1985, when Saudi Arabia ceased restricting output and literally turned its oil pumps loose. Within a matter of weeks, the price of oil crude had fallen by more than 50 percent, dragging down with it prices of oil products and by-products.

1987 domestic production and imports are likely to change only modestly from 1986's rates, with imports falling and production rising. Consumption should increase moderately, as the number of vehicles on the road continues to rise and consumers' enthusiasm for the most efficient cars continues to wane. The only real uncertainty is the retail price of gasoline, which depends on the degree to which OPEC succeeds in enforcing an agreement to lift prices well above 1986's average level.

Futures Market

Unleaded gasoline futures are traded on the New York Mercantile Exchange (NYMEX).

High, Low & Closing Prices of December Leaded Regular Gasoline Futures In N.Y.   In ¢ Per Gallon

Year of Delivery	Yr. Prior to Delivery Oct.	Nov.	Dec.	Jan.	Feb.	Mar.	Apr.	Delivery Year May	June	July	Aug.	Sept.	Oct.	Nov.	Life of Delivery Range
1983 High	99.25	96.50	87.15	84.05	79.70	77.50	82.00	81.00	82.75	83.50	84.10	81.90	80.40	81.70	99.25
Low	96.50	88.50	83.00	79.40	71.75	71.00	77.00	75.20	77.75	80.25	81.70	78.30	76.00	76.50	71.00
Close	96.50	88.50	83.00	79.40	72.00	76.50	80.00	78.70	81.60	83.30	81.95	78.53	79.98	76.86	—
1984 High	—	—	—	—	—	—	—	80.30	79.60	76.75	77.35	76.60	76.40	73.00	80.30
Low	—	—	—	—	—	—	—	79.20	75.80	71.40	73.05	74.90	69.08	67.30	67.30
Close	—	—	—	—	—	—	—	79.20	77.25	72.30	75.95	76.10	72.50	68.15	—
1985 High	78.10	74.00	72.50	68.90	71.45	74.75	76.00	70.60	70.60	70.60	72.40	74.05	78.45	80.10	
Low	72.20	69.61	67.55	65.35	68.80	69.75	70.00	68.75	66.40	68.25	68.80	67.40	72.70	77.00	
Close	73.25	71.05	69.50	68.70	69.25	74.75	70.00	70.15	69.90	69.40	70.45	73.61	79.02	77.94	—
Commodity Delisted in October 1986															

Source: N.Y. Mercantile Exchange

T.0575

High, Low & Closing Prices of December Unleaded Regular Gasoline Futures In N.Y.   In ¢ Per Gallon

Year of Delivery	Yr. Prior to Delivery Oct.	Nov.	Dec.	Jan.	Feb.	Mar.	Apr.	Delivery Year May	June	July	Aug.	Sept.	Oct.	Nov.	Life of Delivery Range
1985 High	—	—	—	—	—	77.00	78.00	72.45	71.60	71.65	72.65	75.10	80.50	81.00	81.00
Low	—	—	—	—	—	72.75	72.00	70.75	67.65	69.45	70.00	68.70	73.80	78.25	67.65
Close	—	—	—	—	—	77.00	72.00	71.25	70.90	70.70	71.60	74.50	80.20	79.00	—
1986 High	—	—	—	61.00	52.50	43.50	40.65	42.60	39.60	35.30	43.55	46.40	43.90	43.00	61.00
Low	—	—	—	55.10	40.80	34.00	34.56	36.50	36.00	30.32	31.00	34.55	37.70	40.00	30.20
Close	—	—	—	55.10	41.75	34.00	36.08	38.25	36.00	31.30	43.18	40.24	41.53	41.28	—
1987 High	—	—	51.00												
Low	—	—	49.25												
Close	—	—	51.00												

Source: N.Y. Mercantile Exchange

T.0575A

99

LEADED REG GASOLINE   UNLEADED GAS   NYMEX

WEEKLY HIGH,LOW & CLOSE OF NEAREST FUTURES

CTS.
GAL.

UNLEADED FROM
DEC. 3, 1984

1982   1983   1984   1985   1986

S O N D J F M A M J J A S O N D J F M A M J J A S O N D J F M A M J J A S O N D J F M A M J J A S O N D J F M A M J J A S O N D J F M A M

Month-End Open Interest of Unleaded Regular Gasoline Futures In New York   In Contracts

Year	Jan.	Feb.	Mar.	Apr.	May	June	July	Aug.	Sept.	Oct.	Nov.	Dec.
1984	FUTURES TRADING BEGAN DEC. 3, 1984											1,243
1985	2,429	1,464	3,411	4,977	4,406	4,923	5,685	4,599	3,910	4,921	3,922	3,150
1986	4,703	3,703	3,212	2,850	4,625	3,457	4,637	8,021	16,177	19,622	17,568	27,100

Source: N.Y. Mercantile Exchange

T.0576

Month-End Open Interest of Leaded Regular Gasoline Futures in New York   In Contracts

Year	Jan.	Feb.	Mar.	Apr.	May	June	July	Aug.	Sept.	Oct.	Nov.	Dec.
1982	1,228	970	1,051	1,334	2,694	3,232	2,668	2,713	3,803	4,503	3,887	4,732
1983	6,826	9,646	11,450	12,564	11,852	12,920	11,624	11,584	12,984	10,290	12,918	19,335
1984	20,248	18,212	18,013	14,455	15,423	15,523	11,988	11,747	10,391	7,826	7,966	9,230
1985	8,779	10,413	12,776	12,355	12,301	12,155	13,169	12,450	12,923	13,186	12,634	12,741
1986	14,836	14,353	18,477	22,147	22,122	21,713	14,721	9,980	1,926	166	Delisted	

T.0576A

Gold

The global reserve base of gold has been estimated at nearly 1.5 billion ounces, of which about 55 percent is located in South Africa. The world's estimated stock of gold above ground, excluding what is in industrial usage, stands at about 2.6 billion ounces. By-product resources account for between 15 percent and 20 percent of that amount.

Based on U.S. Bureau of Mines data for 1986's first seven months, the year's total extraction of recoverable gold in the U.S. came to roughly 2.22 million troy ounces, a figure which is about 10 percent below actual domestic production during 1985. In 1986, as in 1985, the bulk of domestic production came from Nevada mines, which yielded 55 percent of aggregate output. South Dakota mines were second in importance, contributing 13 percent of total extraction.

The domestic gold supply was significantly augmented by imports, which amounted to an aggregate of about 11.50 million ounces through August, 1986; that figure suggests an annual rate in the neighborhood of 17 million ounces. About 89 percent of imports were in the form of refined bullion. Dore and precipitate accounted for another 7.7 percent of imports, waste and scrap for 2.8 percent, and ore and concentrate for the small remainder. Exports of gold from the U.S. were substantial in absolute terms, but represented in combination barely 20 percent of total import volume. The bulk (62 percent) of exports were in the form of refined bullion, another 27 percent were waste and scrap, and 11 percent were dore and precipitates. The lion's share of U.S. imports came from Canada; a similar share of U.S. exports went to Canada.

Gold prices improved in the first half of 1986, due mainly to concerns over the U.S. trade and budget deficits and a weakening dollar. Prices rose on platinum's coattails in August and were helped by rising investor demand for gold coins. However, as the metal's price showed signs of weakness in October, the emergence of the Soviets as large sellers pressured the market. Prices worked down to $380/oz. from $445/oz. earlier. By year's end, gold prices had steadied, with indications of an oil price hike and continuing interest in gold bullion.

Available data at this writing were too skimpy to permit a confident forecast about supply of and demand for gold during 1987. Even so, the opening during 1986 of several new mines in the U.S., Australia and Canada, among other places, argued that producers have a generally optimistic attitude toward short- and intermediate-term prospects for profitable operations.

Futures Markets

Gold futures are traded in the U.S. on New York's Commodity Exchange (COMEX), and Chicago's International Monetary Market (IMM). Futures trading in gold also takes place on Canada's Winnipeg Commodity Exchange (WCE) and in Hong Kong and Sydney. Options on gold futures are also traded on COMEX.

World Mine Production of Gold   In Thousands of Fine Ounces (Troy Ounces)

Year	Australia	Zaire (Congo)	Canada	China	Colombia	Ghana	India	Japan	Mexico	Nicaragua	Papua N. Guinea	Philippines	Zimbabwe	South Africa	United States	USSR[1]	Total World[1]
1973	554	134	1,954		216	723	105	188	133	85		572	800	27,495	1,176	7,100	43,297
1974	513	131	1,698		265	614	101	140	134	83		538	600	24,388	1,127	7,300	40,124
1975	527	103	1,654		309	524	91	144	145	70		503	387	22,938	1,052	7,500	38,476
1976	503	91	1,692		300	532	101	138	163	76		501	402	22,936	1,048	7,700	39,024
1977	625	80	1,734		257	481	97	149	213	66	740	559	399	22,502	1,100	7,850	38,906
1978	648	76	1,735	150	246	402	89	145	202	74	751	587	388	22,649	999	8,000	39,057
1979	597	73	1,644	200	269	357	85	128	190	61	630	535	388	22,617	964	8,160	38,830
1980	548	41	1,627	225	510	353	79	102	176	60	452	644	368	21,669	970	8,300	39,179
1981	591	65	1,673	1,700	529	341	80	99	199	62	540	758	371	21,121	1,379	8,425	41,251
1982	867	61	2,081	1,800	473	331	72	104	214	54	589	834	426	21,355	1,466	8,550	43,127
1983	984	193	2,363	1,850	439	276	70	101	198	46	579	817	453	21,847	2,003	8,600	44,996
1984[2]	1,257	117	2,638	1,900	800	287	65	104	271	35	835	787	478	21,907	2,085	8,650	46,408
1985[1]	1,833	75	2,747	1,950	1,150	299	59	159	285	24	1,050	810	480	21,566	2,475	8,700	48,217
1986[1]															2,900		

[1] Estimated.   [2] Preliminary.   *Source: U.S. Bureau of Mines*

T.258

GOLD

SPOT GOLD — MONTHLY HIGH, LOW & CLOSE - N.Y. (HANDY & HARMAN)

Salient U.S. Gold Statistics   In Thousands of Troy Ounces

Year	Mine Produc- tion	Value Mil. $	Refinery Prod. New (Domestic)	Secondary[2]	Exports (Excl. coinage	Imports For Con- sumption	Stocks, Dec. 31 Treas. Dept.[5]	Futures Exch.	Ear- marked[6]	Industrial	Consumption Dental	Industrial[3]	Jewelry & Arts	Total	Price $ Per Troy Oz.[4]
1979	964	296.6	795	2,883	16,492	4,630	264.6	2.5	359.3	.9	646	1,406	2,688	4,785	307.50
1980	970	594.1	773	3,824	6,119	4,542	264.3	5.0	354.5	.9	341	1,287	1,505	3,215	612.56
1981	1,379	633.9	801	3,085	6,437	4,652	264.1	2.4	350.6	.6	314	1,210	1,730	3,276	459.64
1982	1,466	551.0	718	3,040	2,970	4,920	264.0	2.3	348.6	.8	358	1,102	1,954	3,423	375.91
1983	2,003	849.1	885	2,970	3,139	4,593	263.4	2.5	341.4	.6	360	1,032	1,666	3,061	424.00
1984	2,085	751.8	760	3,104	4,981	7,869	262.8	2.4	337.9	.8	363	1,084	1,709	3,164	360.66
1985[1]	2,475	786.3	620	2,735	3,967	8,226	262.7	2.1	377.4	.6	394	1,055	1,643	3,100	317.66

[1] Preliminary.   [2] Old & New Scrap.   [3] Including space & defense.   [4] Engelhard selling quotations.   [5] Includes gold in Exchange Stabilization Fund.   [6] Gold held for foreign & international official accounts at N.Y. Federal Reserve Bank.   *Source: Bureau of Mines*   T.260

Commodity Exchange Inc. (COMEX) Depository Warehouse Stocks of Gold   In Thousands of Ounces

Year	Jan. 1	Feb. 1	Mar. 1	Apr. 1	May 1	June 1	July 1	Aug. 1	Sept. 1	Oct. 1	Nov. 1	Dec. 1
1979	2,604	2,566	2,540	2,501	2,286	2,443	2,700	2,480	2,509	2,512	2,281	2,277
1980	2,253	2,445	2,575	2,897	3,097	3,291	3,386	3,597	3,619	3,832	4,873	5,099
1981	4,814	4,570	4,192	3,897	3,513	3,585	3,417	3,258	2,887	2,776	2,605	2,494
1982	2,366	2,339	2,267	2,196	2,198	2,181	2,047	1,980	1,982	1,971	1,985	2,137
1983	2,247	2,621	2,754	2,645	2,636	2,723	2,630	2,648	2,570	2,538	2,500	2,485
1984	2,481	2,472	2,408	2,452	2,412	2,426	2,376	2,395	2,387	2,391	2,349	2,366
1985	2,308	2,308	2,273	2,109	2,136	2,142	2,133	2,107	2,119	2,083	2,099	2,105
1986	2,109	2,352	2,580	2,593	2,567	1,986	1,992	1,621	1,664	1,726	1,787	2,193
1987	2,890											

Source: Commodity Exchange of N.Y. (COMEX)   T.263

High, Low & Closing Prices of December Gold Futures on COMEX   In Dollars per Ounce

Year of Delivery		Year Prior to Deliv.							Delivery Year								Life of Delivery Range
		Oct.	Nov.	Dec.	Jan.	Feb.	Mar.	Apr.	May	June	July	Aug.	Sept.	Oct.	Nov.	Dec.	
1983	High	503.0	486.0	505.5	553.0	553.5	467.5	472.0	472.5	442.8	455.0	441.0	429.0	408.8	408.8	404.0	554.7
	Low	433.0	437.5	470.0	486.5	453.4	431.5	444.5	432.0	414.0	423.0	418.5	401.0	378.0	373.0	372.0	366.7
	Close	465.0	486.4	489.0	551.7	453.4	442.4	453.5	432.6	432.3	427.4	424.8	407.8	378.8	403.0	379.0	—
1984	High	450.0	452.0	443.5	419.7	434.0	439.5	416.5	414.0	422.0	389.8	369.0	356.3	355.8	353.5	332.6	608.0
	Low	419.5	412.1	411.0	393.0	405.0	414.0	399.5	392.0	385.5	345.0	349.0	341.6	333.5	325.0	304.7	304.7
	Close	411.1	445.1	421.4	404.9	426.9	416.4	401.1	410.4	391.6	350.3	358.0	351.3	336.0	329.1	312.1	—
1985	High	398.0	389.0	364.5	332.0	327.0	357.0	353.0	342.3	339.0	339.0	339.0	350.2	336.5	335.7	328.2	489.5
	Low	370.0	355.0	330.0	317.8	301.5	306.0	328.0	319.0	320.5	315.5	326.5	318.2	324.9	322.1	313.0	301.5
	Close	372.2	360.7	333.9	325.2	307.5	349.2	329.9	327.4	325.3	335.2	339.8	327.1	326.7	322.9	326.7	—
1986	High	363.6	358.5	352.3	392.0	375.0	375.0	361.0	358.0	362.2	371.3	404.5	446.0	446.5	443.8	400.0	446.5
	Low	350.5	347.5	336.5	348.5	347.5	344.0	341.0	347.5	342.0	349.3	364.0	392.0	400.0	376.5	383.0	336.5
	Close	352.4	348.5	351.4	369.7	356.6	345.3	357.7	353.9	354.0	369.7	393.3	429.8	405.0	390.9	389.3	—
1987	High	483.9	434.0	425.0													
	Low	443.0	398.5	404.0													
	Close	443.0	410.9	424.6													

Source: Commodity Exchange of N.Y. (COMEX)   T.266

Gold Total Open Interest at New York (COMEX) & Chicago IMM[1]   In Thousands of Contracts

Year						At New York (COMEX)								At Chicago (IMM)[1]		
	Jan. 1	Feb. 1	Mar. 1	Apr. 1	May 1	June 1	July 1	Aug. 1	Sept. 1	Oct. 1	Nov. 1	Dec. 1	Jan. 1	Apr. 1	July 1	Oct. 1
1981	295.5	211.4	202.5	180.8	187.9	198.6	214.7	215.9	203.1	198.6	202.6	187.3	88.6	54.8	78.5	56.5
1982	175.6	153.0	145.8	134.8	134.6	131.2	139.1	119.0	119.0	110.6	112.6	121.8	33.1	18.7	14.1	8.0
1983	127.7	120.4	123.7	91.6	105.2	109.8	113.4	104.7	114.0	123.4	134.9	126.6	7.9	5.2	4.9	3.3
1984	139.7	121.6	140.8	120.8	134.3	147.0	134.9	132.2	139.4	141.7	161.0	158.2	1.4	.6	.2	.2
1985	170.3	135.0	145.7	119.2	130.2	126.0	131.3	122.5	135.4	122.8	123.1	128.3	2.4	1.9	2.4	2.2
1986	132.8	141.3	144.4	139.9	134.3	114.0	122.4	127.0	143.8	128.9	149.5	132.2	1.3	1.6	1.2	2.4
1987	140.9												1.4			

[1] Beginning Jan. 1, 1985 data are for "Kilo" gold at CBT. *Source: Commodity Exchange of N.Y. (COMEX), International Monetary Market of Chicago (IMM) & Chicago Board of Trade.*   T.261

Total Volume of Trading of Gold Futures at New York (COMEX)   In Thousands of Contracts

Year	Jan.	Feb.	Mar.	Apr.	May	June	July	Aug.	Sept.	Oct.	Nov.	Dec.	Total
1981	943.6	708.7	994.5	695.7	782.6	780.1	836.5	862.1	1,063.4	769.0	886.8	1,050.5	10,374
1982	922.4	669.0	1,264.7	966.3	708.7	943.3	1,153.5	1,182.7	1,224.7	1,074.1	1,044.2	1,116.6	12,289
1983	1,369.0	1,047.4	1,087.6	712.7	872.2	839.9	818.6	684.1	694.1	832.7	780.5	643.8	10,383
1984	749.3	786.5	829.8	563.2	833.7	737.8	1,006.9	791.3	753.2	671.4	814.9	577.7	9,122
1985	950.3	589.9	962.8	599.6	752.6	443.6	738.1	657.7	615.8	438.7	479.1	545.8	7,774
1986	1,126.2	574.2	703.9	617.9	482.2	451.6	527.6	711.1	1,054.7	846.9	724.3	579.6	8,400

Source: Commodity Exchange of N.Y. (COMEX)   T.265

U.S. Mine Production of Recoverable Gold   In Thousands of Troy Ounces

Year	Alaska	Arizona	California	Colorado	Idaho	Montana	Nevada	New Mexico	South Dakota	Utah	Other States	Total U.S.
1981	26.5	100.3	6.3	51.1	[2]	54.3	524.8	65.7	278.2	227.7	44.3	1,379.2
1982	30.5	61.1	10.5	64.6	[2]	75.2	757.1	[2]	185.0	174.9	106.8	1,465.7
1983	39.5	62.0	38.4	63.1	[2]	161.4	960.7	[2]	309.8	238.5	129.1	2,002.5
1984	19.4	54.9	85.9	60.0	[2]	181.2	1,020.5	[2]	310.5	[2]	352.2	2,084.6
1985[1]	44.7	52.1	165.1	43.3	[2]	160.3	1,276.1	45.0	356.1	135.5	197.2	2,475.4
1986[3]		45.0	250.0	33.0	60.0	155.0	1,590.0	46.0	363.0			2,900.0

[1] Preliminary.   [2] Included in "Other States."   [3] Estimate.   *Source: Bureau of Mines*   T.262

U.S. Monetary Stock of Gold at End of Month   In Billions of Dollars

Year	Jan.	Feb.	Mar.	Apr.	May	June	July	Aug.	Sept.	Oct.	Nov.	Dec.
1984	11.120	11.116	11.111	11.109	11.104	11.100	11.099	11.098	11.097	11.096	11.096	11.096
1985	11.095	11.093	11.093	11.091	11.091	11.090	11.090	11.090	11.090	11.090	11.090	11.090
1986	11.090	11.090	11.090	11.089	11.085	11.084	11.084	11.084	11.084			

Source: Federal Reserve Board   T.264

GOLD COMEX
WEEKLY HIGH, LOW & CLOSE OF NEAREST FUTURES

Monthly Average Gold Price (Handy & Harman at New York) $ Per Troy Ounce

Year	Jan.	Feb.	Mar.	Apr.	May	June	July	Aug.	Sept.	Oct.	Nov.	Dec.	Average
1979	227.5	246.1	242.2	238.9	257.4	279.2	295.3	301.6	357.0	392.7	392.2	461.0	307.59
1980	675.4	665.5	553.6	516.8	513.9	600.7	643.3	627.5	675.8	660.3	622.5	594.8	612.51
1981	557.4	500.3	498.8	494.9	479.8	460.8	408.8	411.0	444.1	437.2	413.7	408.7	459.61
1982	384.1	374.1	330.3	350.0	334.4	315.0	340.1	366.0	435.6	421.8	414.1	445.4	375.94
1983	479.9	490.4	419.7	432.2	437.6	412.8	423.1	416.3	411.5	393.2	382.3	387.1	423.83
1984	370.9	386.0	394.4	381.7	377.3	377.7	346.4	347.7	340.9	340.1	340.9	319.0	360.23
1985	302.8	298.8	303.9	324.9	316.1	316.5	317.8	330.2	322.6	326.0	325.5	322.4	317.31
1986[1]	345.5	339.3	345.4	340.6	342.5	342.8	348.9	376.9	419.0	423.6	398.8	390.0	367.5

[1] Preliminary.   *Source: U.S. Bureau of Mines; American Metal Market, Handy & Harman*   T.259

Grain Sorghum

1986/87 world production of sorghum is projected by USDA at 66.3 million tons, a seven-percent decline from a year ago. The U.S. is the world's largest producer, accounting for 34 percent of total output this season. India is the next-largest producer, accounting for 17 percent of world production. The U.S. is the dominant exporter, accounting for almost 60 percent of the projected trade total of 9 million tons. Australia and Argentiana export smaller amounts. Japan is the primary importer, taking 52 percent of world exports. World use of sorghum will almost match production at 63.7 million tons. World carryout stocks are projected at a record 19.9 million tons, 15 percent more than a year ago. The U.S. will hold 82 percent of world stocks.

U.S. production is estimated by USDA at 900 million bushels, 19 percent less that last season's record crop. While the crop is smaller, it is still larger than any crop in recent years. Harvested acreage is estimated at 13.5 million acres, the smallest area since 1983/84, when the Payment In Kind (PIK) program and drought cut acreage. The national average yield is 66.7 bushels per acre, the same as the year-ago record. Yields fell in the drought-damaged Southeast, but were excellent elsewhere.

With season's beginning stocks of 551 million bushels, the total U.S. supply of sorghum in 1986/87 will be a record 1.45 billion bushels, three percent more than a year ago. Usage of sorghum is projected at 780 million bushels, 10 percent less than a year ago. Feed use declined as a result of liquidation of livestock herds. The USDA projects exports at 175 million bushels, about the same as a year ago. The primary markets for the U.S. are Japan, Venezuela, Israel, Mexico and Taiwan.

Ending stocks are currently projected at 671 million bushels, some 22 percent more than last year and the largest in many years. Due to entries of sorghum into the price-support loan program, free stocks are expected to be tighter.

U.S. Government Price Support

For the 1987 crop, the loan rate is $1.74 per bushel, with a target price of $2.88. This past season, the loan rate was $1.82, while the target price was $2.88. To qualify for 1987 program benefits, producers must reduce base acreage by 20 percent. An optional paid diversion is available on 15 percent of acreage.

World Sorghum Supply and Demand   In Millions of Metric Tons

Crop Year	Exports Argentina	Exports Non-U.S.	Exports U.S.	Exports Total	Imports Japan	Imports U.S.S.R.	Imports Total	Total Production	Utilization China	Utilization Japan	Utilization Mexico	Utilization U.S.S.R.	Utilization Total	Stocks[3] Non-U.S.	Stocks[3] U.S.	Stocks[3] Total
1981–2	5.2	7.4	6.3	13.7	3.0	2.9	13.7	70.2	6.6	3.6	6.8	3.4	66.0	4.8	7.5	12.3
1982–3	4.9	6.2	5.4	11.6	2.7	2.3	11.6	65.1	6.9	2.8	6.1	2.9	63.4	3.5	11.2	14.6
1983–4	4.8	6.8	6.2	13.1	4.2	1.9	13.1	59.2	8.3	4.0	6.3	2.0	62.7	3.8	7.3	11.1
1984–5	3.4	5.6	7.5	13.1	4.6	1.5	13.1	66.0	7.2	4.7	6.4	1.5	65.9	3.6	7.6	11.3
1985–6[1]	2.2	4.7	4.1	8.8	5.1	.1	8.8	71.2	4.9	4.9	5.7	.6	65.1	3.3	14.0	17.3
1986–7[2]	1.7	3.9	5.1	9.0	4.7	.1	9.0	66.3	5.1	4.7	5.6	.1	63.7	3.5	16.4	19.9

[1] Preliminary.   [2] Estimate.   [3] End of crop year season.   Source: Foreign Agricultural Service, U.S.D.A.   T.272a

Salient Statistics of Grain Sorghum in the United States

Crop Year	Acreage Planted[2] for All Purposes 1,000 Acres	For Grain Acreage Harv. 1,000 Acres	For Grain Production 1,000 Bushels	For Grain Yield Per Harv. Acre Bushels	For Grain Price Cents Per Bushel	For Grain Produc. Value Million Dollars	For Silage Acreage Harv. 1,000 Acres	For Silage Production 1,000 Tons	For Silage Yield Per Harv. Acre Tons	For Forage Acreage Harv. 1,000 Acres	Feed Grains U.S. Exports Under Gov't. Programs Mutual Security (AID) (In Ths. Metric Tons)	Feed Grains U.S. Exports Under Gov't. Programs Total All (In Ths. Metric Tons)
1981–2	16,020	13,677	875,835	64.0	238	2,079	786	9,447	12.1	1,024	444	1,244
1982–3	16,138	14,137	835,083	59.1	252	2,091	603	7,403	12.3	914	323	732
1983–4	11,880	10,001	487,521	48.7	284	1,382	639	6,572	10.3	747	392	848
1984–5	17,254	15,355	866,241	56.4	237	2,039	609	6,472	10.6	679	793	1,395
1985–6[1]	18,285	16,672	1,112,571	66.7			515	6,261	12.2	796		
1986–7[1]	14,973	13,494	900,039	66.7								

[1] Preliminary.   [2] Grain and sweet sorghums for all uses including syrup.   Source: Crop Reporting Board, U.S.D.A.   T.267

Production of All Sorghum for Grain in the United States, by States   In Thousands of Bushels

Year	Iowa	Arizona	California	Colorado	Kansas	Missouri	Nebraska	New Mexico	North Carolina	Oklahoma	South Dakota	Texas	Arkansas
1982	885	1,185	5,390	10,230	207,700	63,910	128,480	13,160	3,000	20,400	17,250	305,250	15,780
1983	300	988	3,645	6,960	121,690	40,020	61,000	6,300	1,386	11,880	13,630	157,500	17,600
1984	660	1,360	3,936	15,910	216,750	91,770	121,600	15,400	3,025	18,000	18,565	209,350	42,480
1985	—	1,296	2,988	11,200	289,800	117,030	153,600	13,920	3,224	22,500	15,000	241,900	66,240
1986	—	870	2,210	10,920	292,000	88,290	127,500	10,120	1,400	20,250	16,100	214,600	35,700

[1] Preliminary.   Source: Crop Reporting Board, U.S.D.A.   T.268

GRAIN SORGHUM

U.S. Grain Sorghum Quarterly Supply and Disappearance   In Millions of Bushels

Year & Preiod Beginning Sept. 1	Begin. Stocks	Pro-duction	Im-ports	Total Supply	Food, Al-cohol & Industrial	Seed	Feed & Resid.	Total	Ex-ports	Total	Gov't. Owned[1]	Pri-vately Owned[2]	Total Stocks
	Supply				Disappearance — Domestic Use						Ending Stocks		
1983–4	439.1	487.5	0.1	926.7	7.7	2.1	384.9	394.7	244.6	639.3	102.8	184.6	287.4
Sep.–May	439.1	487.5	—	926.6	5.7	1.0	356.6	363.3	194.4	557.7	78.0	290.9	368.9
Jun.–Aug.	368.9	—	0.1	369.0	2.0	1.1	28.3	31.4	50.2	81.6	102.8	184.6	287.4
1984–5	287.4	866.2	0.1	1,153.7	15.3	2.5	538.8	556.6	269.9	853.5	112.1	188.1	300.2
Sep.–May	287.4	866.2	0.1	1,153.7	12.4	1.8	541.9	556.1	236.8	792.9	111.1	249.7	360.8
June–Aug.	360.8	—	—	360.8	2.9	.7	−3.1	.5	60.1	60.6	112.1	188.1	300.2
1985–6[3]	300.2	1,112.6	—	1,412.8	26.0	2.5	655.3	683.8	178.0	861.8	207.0	344.0	551.0
Sep.–May	300.2	1,112.6	—	1,412.8	22.1	1.8	619.7	643.6	140.3	783.9	181.4	447.5	628.9
June–Aug.	628.9	—	—	628.9	3.9	.7	35.6	40.2	37.7	77.9	207.0	344.0	551.0
1986–7[5]	551.0	900.0	—	1,451.0	—30.0—		575.0	605.0	200.0	805.0	250.0	396.0	646.0
Sep.–May	551.0	900.0											

[1] Uncommitted inventory.   [2] Includes quantity under loan & farmer-owned reserve.   [3] Preliminary.   [4] Less than 50,000 bushels.
[5] Estimate.   *Source: Economic Research Service, U.S.D.A.*   T.269

Average Price of Sorghum Grain, No. 2, Yellow at Kansas City   In Dollars Per 100 Pounds (Cwt.)

Year	Oct.	Nov.	Dec.	Jan.	Feb.	Mar.	Apr.	May	June	July	Aug.	Sept.	Average
1978–9	3.61	3.67	3.64	3.71	3.73	3.77	3.81	3.92	4.41	4.89	4.44	4.34	3.92
1979–0	4.42	4.41	4.57	4.21	4.35	4.20	4.15	4.31	4.49	5.36	5.71	5.61	4.54
1980–1	5.65	5.91	5.82	5.79	5.52	5.46	5.49	5.38	5.23	5.29	4.58	4.16	5.48
1981–2	4.14	4.14	4.27	4.44	4.26	4.28	4.45	4.48	4.50	4.38	4.02	4.06	4.29
1982–3	3.85	4.25	4.37	4.37	4.54	5.08	5.30	5.37	5.37	5.32	5.69	5.55	4.80
1983–4	5.37	5.25	5.16	5.09	5.03	5.40	5.36	5.39	5.40	4.95	4.74	4.46	5.22
1984–5	4.25	4.28	4.32	4.48	4.33	4.58	4.76	4.74	4.74	4.50	4.06	3.56	4.46
1985–6[1]	3.62	3.75	3.97	3.95	3.80	3.82	4.00	4.25	4.00	3.20	2.71	2.47	3.72
1986–7[1]	2.60	2.70											

[1] Preliminary.   *Source: Economic Research Service, U.S.D.A.*   T.271

U.S. Exports of Grain Sorghum, by Country of Destination   In Thousands of Metric Tons

Yr. Beg. October	Poland	Belg. & Luxem.	Port-ugal	Spain	W. Ger-many	India	Venezu-ela	Israel	Japan	Sene-gal	Nether-lands	Nor-way	Mexico	South Africa	Total All Exports
1978–9	136.4	—			.8	—		689.4	1,981.1	1.2	37.8	141.5	1,124.0	—	5,247.1
1979–0	107.5	.3			.3	—		348.0	3,972.7	12.5	69.1	232.8	2,255.2	—	8,199.2
1980–1	—	60.0			—	—	501	449.0	2,725.4	13.3	11.5	198.9	2,646.3	.3	7,701.6
1981–2	—	.4		790	.4	—	713	368.0	2,436.9	1.9	.4	201.2	544.2		6,289.8
1982–3	—	0		105		—	243	340.7	741.0	13.9	0	44.6	3,260.3	.2	5,402.6
1983–4[1]	—	—		465		—	206	574	1,504.8	145.0	.2	0	2,758.4	.2	6,226.0
1984–5[1]				45			1,093	587	2,726				1,958		6,996

[1] Preliminary.   *Source: Grain & Feed Division, U.S.D.A.*   T.270

Grain Sorghum Price Support Program & Market Prices

Year Beginning September	Quantity	% of Production	Acuired By CCC	Owned by CCC Sept. 30	Support Loan	Target Price	Kansas City	Fort Worth	Los Angeles	Gulf Ports
	Put Under Price Support		Price Support Operations (Million Cwt.)		— $ Per Cwt. — —		No. 2 Yellow ($ Cwt.)			
1978–9	51.6	12.3	17.1	24.4	3.39	4.07	3.92	4.31	5.44	4.55
1979–0	35.8	7.9	1.3	24.6	3.57	4.18	4.54	4.88	6.32	5.43
1980–1	18.1	5.6	.1	21.4	3.82	4.46	5.48	5.97	7.31	6.27
1981–2	155.0	31.5	6.5	24.0	4.07	4.55	4.29	4.87	6.18	5.03
1982–3	134.5	28.8	41.0	92.4	4.32	4.64	4.80	5.19	6.56	5.41
1983–4	7.6	2.8	1.2	50.0	4.50	4.86	5.22	5.53	6.69	5.77
1984–5	43.0	8.8	7.0	78.0	4.32	5.14	4.46	5.04		4.90
1985–6[1]					4.32	5.14	3.72	4.32		4.07
1986–7[2]					3.25	5.14				

[1] Preliminary.   [2] Estimate.   *Source: Economic Research Service, U.S.D.A.*   T.272

Hay

1986 hay production was forecast at a record 158 million tons, six percent above 1985. Nearly 61 million acres were harvested; average yield per acre was about 2.59. Records were set despite severe drought which cut the hay crop in Alabama, Georgia and South Carolina by over 50 percent of 1985's harvest. Offsetting much of this loss were large crops in the Dakotas and Montana.

Total 1986 U.S. supply was about 185 million short tons, compared with 176 million in 1985. Disappearance was expected to fall, given an ongoing decline in the population of roughage-consuming animals. The Dairy Termination Program, designed to reduce dairy herds and downtrends in the size of beef-cattle and sheep herds were two contributing factors.

Halfway through the 1986/87 season, the average price received by hay farmers was $61 per ton, as against $68.50 per ton in 1985 and almost $73 per ton in 1984. In the drought-stricken Southeast, the average price was well above the national average. Although the winter months promised to bring seasonal price increases, USDA forecast that prices in 1986/87 would average $5 to $10 per ton below those recorded in 1985/86.

Salient Statistics of All Hay in the United States

Year Beginning May	Acres Harvested 1,000 Acres	Yield Per Acre Tons	Production	Carry-over May 1	Disappearance	Supply Per Animal Unit	Disappearance	Animal Units Fed[2] Millions	Farm Price[3] $ Per Ton	Farm Produc. Value Million $	Alfalfa Seed (certified)	Timothy Seed	Red Clover Seed	Sudan-Grass
			— Million Tons —			— In Tons —				— Dollars Per Cwt. —			
1981-2	59,599	2.39	142.5	25.4	142.9	1.83	1.56	91.8	67.30	9,590	218.00	93.20	115.00	40.70
1982-3	59,812	2.50	149.2	25.0	146.1	1.93	1.62	90.2	69.30	10,340	207.00	67.80	124.00	45.10
1983-4	59,717	2.36	140.8	28.1	148.8	1.89	1.67	89.3	75.80	10,673	209.00	67.40	151.00	45.00
1984-5	61,445	2.45	150.6	20.1	143.8	1.99	1.67	85.9	72.70	10,949	220.00	69.60	147.00	42.40
1985-6[1]	60,553	2.46	149.0	26.9	149.1	2.11	1.79	83.4	68.50	10,207				
1986-7[1]	60,902	2.59	158.0	26.8		2.24		80.6						

Retail Price Paid by Farmers columns: Alfalfa Seed (certified), Timothy Seed, Red Clover Seed, Sudan-Grass.

[1] Preliminary.   [2] Roughage-consuming animal units fed annually.   [3] Price of hay sold baled, for year beginning July.
Source: Economic Research Service, U.S.D.A.   T.275

Production of All Hay in the United States by Important States   In Millions of Tons

Year	Calif.	Idaho	Ill.	Iowa	Mich.	Minn.	Mo.	No. Dak.	Nebr.	N.Y.	Ohio	Pa.	So. Dak.	Wis.	Texas
1983	7.4	4.9	2.7	5.9	4.5	8.3	5.4	4.5	7.6	5.3	3.2	4.6	7.6	12.2	7.5
1984	7.9	4.7	3.9	7.9	5.3	8.4	6.3	4.5	7.7	5.4	3.8	5.1	8.1	12.8	5.4
1985	8.0	4.1	4.1	7.1	5.7	8.0	6.5	3.8	6.8	5.3	4.6	5.3	4.8	11.1	8.2
1986[1]	8.6	4.6	3.7	8.6	6.3	9.3	6.2	5.9	6.7	5.3	4.7	5.4	9.0	13.7	7.3

[1] Preliminary.   *Source: Crop Reporting Board, U.S.D.A.*   T.277

U.S. Types of Hay Production & Farm Stocks   In Millions of Short Tons

Year	Alfalfa & Mixtures	All Other	All Hay	Corn for Silage[1]	Sorghum[1] Silage	Farm Stocks Jan. 1	May 1
		— Production —				— Farm Stocks —	
1982	88.4	60.9	149.2	117.8	7.4	99.2	25.0
1983	82.2	58.6	140.8	96.3	6.6	104.0	28.1
1984	90.1	60.5	150.6	104.6	6.5	89.3	20.1
1985	85.3	63.7	149.0	102.6	6.3	100.6	26.9
1986[2]	94.6	63.4	158.0			96.8	26.8

[1] Not included in all tame hay.   [2] Preliminary.   *Source: Crop Reporting Board, U.S.D.A.*   T.276

Average Price Received by Farmers for All Hay (Baled)   In Dollars Per Ton

Year	May	June	July	Aug.	Sept.	Oct.	Nov.	Dec.	Jan.	Feb.	Mar.	Apr.	Average[1]
1981-2	75.30	66.90	64.00	63.90	62.70	64.80	65.40	65.70	67.90	69.90	69.50	73.30	67.30
1982-3	77.50	69.60	66.10	65.00	66.80	67.10	68.70	68.60	70.30	73.20	69.90	74.00	69.30
1983-4	78.10	72.70	71.20	71.20	74.70	76.80	75.10	76.70	76.60	78.70	79.40	79.80	75.80
1984-5	82.50	76.10	72.40	70.40	70.70	73.10	71.40	73.40	73.00	73.10	72.20	72.50	72.70
1985-6[2]	77.00	72.10	67.90	66.70	66.90	66.00	66.00	67.20	67.80	67.30	68.00	69.20	68.50
1986-7[2]	70.90	62.40	58.70	58.30	58.40	57.40	56.50						

[1] Weighted average by sales.   [2] Preliminary.   *Source: Crop Reporting Board, U.S.D.A.*   T.278

Heating Oil

In 1986, average daily production of distillate fuel oil in the U.S. amounted to roughly 2.8 million barrels, about the same as in 1985. Imports augmented the domestic supply by the daily average of 222,000 barrels, putting aggregate daily supply in the vicinity of 2.9 million barrels. The latter figure, too, was virtually identical with that for 1985.

Consumption of distillates by the residential sector was little changed in 1986 from 1985, holding at approximately 2.6 quadrillion (10 to the 15th power) Btu. Usage in 1986 was only 60 percent of the level in the peak year 1977, even though the number of households and housing units in the U.S. grew markedly over the last nine years. The explanation for this phenomenon lies largely in conservation practices, such as improved efficiency of heating-oil equipment and better insulation of buildings. The drop in usage is also explained by substitution of other fuels, such as natural gas, for heating purposes. Specifically, there was a 25-percent decline in consumption of heating oil per housing unit between 1975–76 and 1985–86; natural gas replaced heating oil in an estimated 1.7–2.0 million homes between 1975 and 1985; and the fraction of single-family homes warmed by oil fell from approximately 10 percent of nationwide dwelling-completions during the late 1970s to 2–3 percent of completions in the 1980s.

The most dramatic event for buyers and sellers of heating oil in 1986 was the sharp skid in selling prices that began in late 1985, when Saudi Arabia decided to discipline its price-cutting counterparts by greatly enlarging its daily production of crude oil. The price charged by refiners for resale of No. 2 fuel oil fell from its November, 1985 peak of 8.49 cents per gallon to just 40 cents per gallon in August, 1986. The national average price of No. 2 distillate peaked at $1.086 per gallon in November, 1985, then receded steadily to only $0.66 in August of the following year.

All other things held constant, price changes of that magnitude should stimulate a more-than-proportional increase in consumption. But, that did not happen in heating oil, because its demand is price-inelastic: its consumption in the short run is a function, not so much of price, as of users' requirements for physical comfort; few residential and commercial consumers are able, on short notice, to switch fuels in response to price differentials. It is no surprise, then, that residential and commercial consumption of distillate fuel rose much less than proportionally to the change in its price during 1986.

Barring some unforeseeable development affecting heating oil's price and availability, consumption of the fuel is expected to remain little changed from 1986's level during 1987. Efforts should intensify among suppliers of crude oil to raise that product's price and, by extension, the prices of all its byproducts. But, as was observed above, those effects are unlikely to have more than a minor impact upon residential-commercial supply of or demand for heating oil during 1987.

Futures Markets

Heating-oil futures contracts are traded on the New York Mercantile Exchange (NYMEX). They are also traded under the name gas-oil on the International Petroleum Exchange in London.

High, Low & Closing Prices of January Heating Oil Futures[1] in N.Y.   In Cents per Gallon

Year of Delivery		Jan.	Feb.	Mar.	Apr.	May	Year Prior to Delivery[2] June	July	Aug.	Sept.	Oct.	Nov.	Dec.[2]	Life of Delivery Range
1981	High	—	—	—	94.00	93.25	91.00	86.50	82.00	87.50	90.25	99.00	97.25	99.00
	Low	—	—	—	88.00	90.25	85.90	81.50	78.45	79.00	83.15	88.50	89.25	78.45
	Close	—	—	—	92.50	91.00	86.60	81.55	81.12	84.55	89.50	95.62	96.90	—
1982	High	—	114.00	113.10	110.70	103.40	101.10	103.75	103.05	99.35	102.35	102.85	101.75	114.00
	Low	—	113.75	109.50	101.00	100.10	97.00	99.35	98.10	96.70	99.00	101.50	96.95	96.70
	Close	—	114.50	109.50	102.00	100.95	99.90	102.35	98.19	98.89	102.06	101.78	97.10	—
1983	High	—	—	85.00	95.75	100.40	98.75	93.60	96.65	101.95	104.20	99.20	90.60	104.20
	Low	—	—	82.00	85.50	94.00	90.61	89.25	90.70	95.55	97.10	84.20	79.81	79.81
	Close	—	—	85.00	94.40	97.00	91.08	90.80	96.30	99.79	98.29	86.52	82.81	—
1984	High	—	—	75.25	84.25	83.75	87.00	88.90	90.15	87.55	84.15	84.10	85.55	90.15
	Low	—	—	68.70	78.50	79.25	81.80	85.25	86.30	82.00	80.20	77.10	75.80	68.70
	Close	—	—	74.60	82.49	81.80	86.20	88.90	86.52	82.50	82.16	77.44	84.24	—
1985	High	—	—	83.75	84.40	87.45	87.40	83.25	84.05	86.10	85.45	81.05	79.25	87.45
	Low	—	—	83.15	82.30	82.20	81.75	76.05	76.90	80.80	75.75	74.75	72.25	72.25
	Close	—	—	83.75	83.00	86.87	83.00	76.30	82.55	84.80	79.98	76.61	72.40	—
1986	High	—	—	76.90	79.10	76.50	75.50	74.85	79.35	83.50	88.25	90.75	87.45	90.75
	Low	—	—	76.70	75.50	74.10	70.00	70.35	73.15	76.55	80.30	85.15	74.80	70.00
	Close	—	—	76.10	76.00	76.25	71.40	73.55	79.35	82.49	87.52	87.07	86.55	—
1987	High	57.60	54.00	46.15	44.65	47.10	44.45	40.70	47.80	49.00	46.25	46.75	49.20	57.60
	Low	56.50	44.50	37.60	36.20	41.60	40.20	33.85	36.40	33.53	38.95	41.90	42.35	33.53
	Close	56.50	44.50	37.60	41.33	41.60	41.33	36.20	47.36	44.57	43.08	42.89	48.90	

[1] No. 2 heating oil.   [2] Contract expires the last business day of the previous calendar month quoted.   *Source: N.Y. Mercantile Exchange* T.281

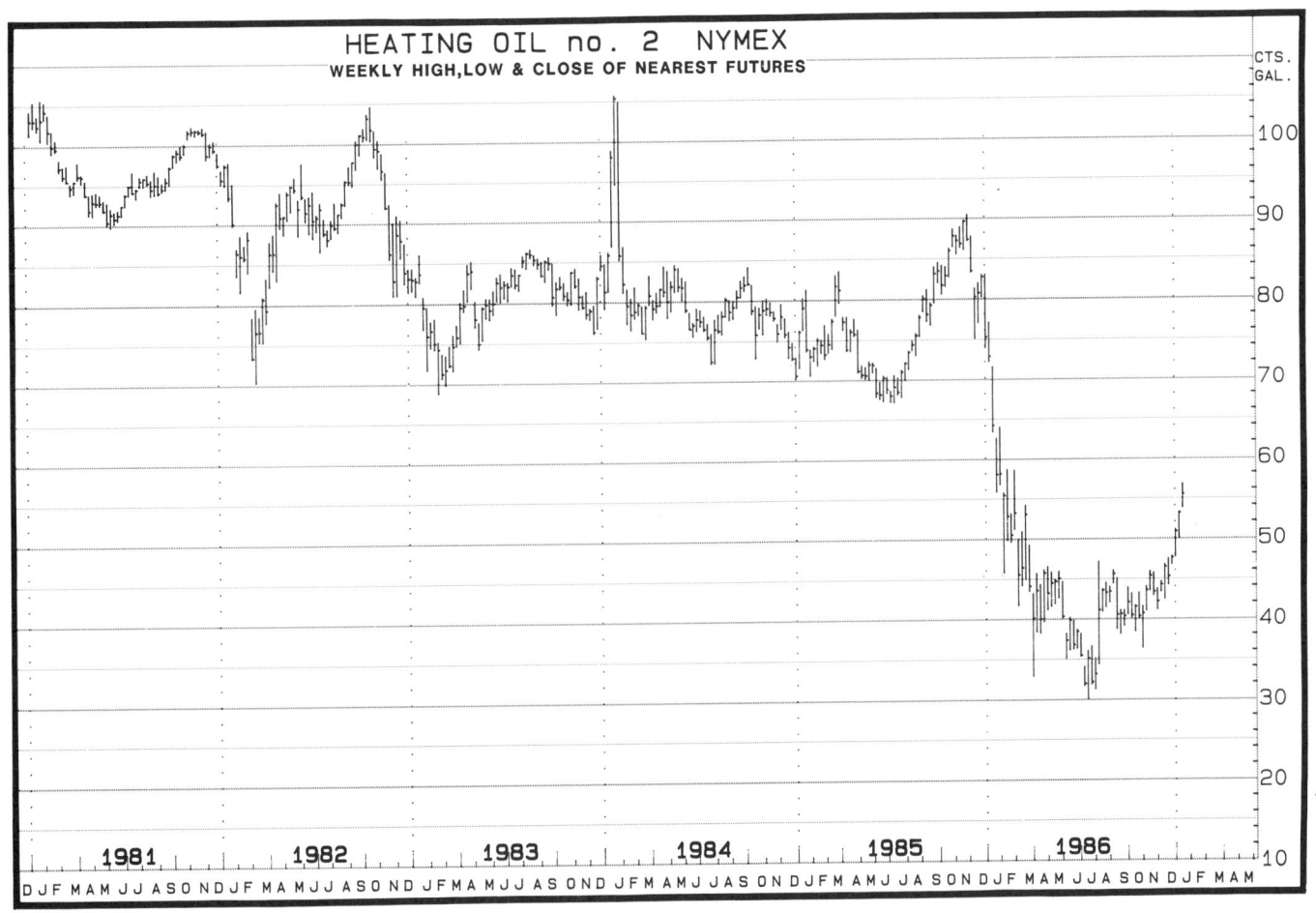

Month-End Open Interest of Heating Oil[1] Futures in New York   In Contracts

Year	Jan.	Feb.	Mar.	Apr.	May	June	July	Aug.	Sept.	Oct.	Nov.	Dec.
1979	327	200	118	299	370	485	1,165	1,280	1,894	1,952	2,221	1,973
1980	2,186	2,590	2,032	2,324	2,622	2,948	3,286	5,889	8,365	11,884	13,519	11,556
1981	11,792	12,040	13,256	14,893	17,919	16,822	19,220	28,102	36,996	35,519	33,517	31,585
1982	22,042	15,655	21,121	18,502	19,248	21,277	21,676	20,815	22,500	29,614	24,486	21,848
1983	19,642	23,307	18,980	22,868	27,797	29,320	34,414	32,276	37,856	36,164	36,230	30,916
1984	32,596	18,900	17,738	16,617	18,343	18,109	19,813	20,290	28,995	27,200	26,798	25,371
1985	19,122	16,552	17,351	15,796	17,660	19,698	22,993	25,731	30,127	33,438	36,793	31,172
1986	29,066	31,685	33,377	33,760	40,977	55,945	67,625	64,450	74,104	82,224	70,196	72,564

[1] No. 2 heating oil.   *Source: N.Y. Mercantile Exchange*   T.279

Volume of Trading of Heating Oil Futures[1] in New York   In Contracts

Year	Jan.	Feb.	Mar.	Apr.	May	June	July	Aug.	Sept.	Oct.	Nov.	Dec.	Total
1979	365	515	182	369	502	1,377	2,156	2,205	2,847	5,895	9,371	8,010	33,804
1980	8,512	8,427	5,146	4,798	3,421	5,923	6,074	11,564	27,430	40,525	53,098	63,366	238,284
1981	67,368	58,514	55,299	65,350	58,933	76,580	86,394	100,102	99,790	121,455	78,972	126,749	995,532
1982	165,079	148,794	176,373	146,821	98,440	135,181	107,102	118,496	120,830	167,439	177,832	183,139	1,745,526
1983	153,864	112,649	137,237	121,300	163,923	149,138	138,706	140,671	187,283	169,271	200,400	193,877	1,868,322
1984	254,788	209,802	144,326	144,041	161,689	144,182	120,668	153,913	137,011	281,183	182,005	163,938	2,091,546
1985	286,264	149,403	162,503	137,064	122,699	133,339	148,117	157,552	202,785	246,558	219,126	242,323	2,207,733
1986	274,057	221,156	214,501	207,387	223,943	247,552	309,465	282,636	285,246	387,054	271,497	349,992	3,275,044

[1] No. 2 heating oil.   *Source: N.Y. Mercantile Exchange*   T.280

HEATING OIL

U.S. Gross Input to Crude Oil Distillation Units   In Millions of 42-Gallon Barrels

Year	Jan.	Feb.	Mar.	Apr.	May	June	July	Aug.	Sept.	Oct.	Nov.	Dec.	Total
1974	373.2	326.5	368.7	371.6	400.4	398.8	414.1	409.1	380.0	398.3	386.0	404.9	4,632
1975	395.8	353.9	384.3	368.3	384.7	385.6	414.9	416.9	401.5	397.3	394.6	411.4	4,709
1976	403.6	388.1	412.2	396.4	413.4	427.7	446.1	446.3	425.3	428.0	437.3	457.0	5,081
1977	453.4	425.5	456.2	438.3	463.1	457.9	471.1	465.9	457.8	466.3	449.2	463.5	5,468
1978	450.1	401.4	448.3	426.6	472.4	451.5	470.5	483.8	462.2	475.9	470.6	487.6	5,501
1979	467.7	409.3	449.6	445.2	457.1	453.6	477.9	474.0	447.1	457.9	447.0	472.4	5,459
1980	453.6	421.7	433.8	413.5	423.4	421.7	422.5	412.3	408.2	402.9	403.4	432.4	5,049
1981	418.3	369.6	391.4	368.5	389.3	381.9	389.6	409.2	382.2	382.9	377.5	393.8	4,654
1982	371.5	325.1	361.4	353.1	379.1	388.1	399.6	378.0	376.7	376.8	364.4	368.8	4,443
1983	355.4	307.8	344.8	352.0	374.4	378.3	390.9	383.1	381.9	371.1	366.8	354.1	4,361
1984	364.8	356.0	374.2	362.3	385.5	372.5	377.5	388.6	374.2	376.7	367.7	371.0	4,471
1985[1]	359.2	321.6	356.7	359.0	381.4	372.7	392.6	378.9	362.9	383.3	378.9	395.1	4,440
1986[1]	389.5	338.0	364.3	377.1	411.6	400.2	402.8						

[1] Preliminary.   *Source: Bureau of Mines*   T.282

Average Price of Distillate (Middle) No. 2 Fuel Oil[1]   Index (1967 = 100)

Year	Jan.	Feb.	Mar.	Apr.	May	June	July	Aug.	Sept.	Oct.	Nov.	Dec.	Average
1973	113.9	124.1	129.1	130.1	133.8	137.4	141.8	143.3	145.6	147.7	157.3	171.7	139.7
1974	194.8	234.1	251.8	257.9	269.2	279.7	288.9	294.8	298.8	297.9	296.0	300.1	272.0
1975	299.1	297.5	294.6	294.9	296.1	301.3	308.3	312.9	318.2	322.9	330.8	336.3	309.4
1976	336.7	339.3	335.3	331.8	328.5	329.2	332.2	336.2	338.9	341.2	344.3	349.8	337.0
1977	359.2	369.6	378.0	384.4	387.5	387.5	388.6	389.1	389.3	389.6	392.4	394.4	384.1
1978	396.7	398.6	394.8	393.3	393.3	393.3	393.2	393.6	394.0	400.0	407.6	418.0	398.0
1979	425.7	432.6	451.9	477.9	504.8	542.3	593.1	632.8	680.6	709.9	715.3	719.9	573.9
1980	739.3	793.5	837.7	858.9	964.8	860.9	870.2	875.6	873.2	868.4	873.4	891.1	850.6
1981	935.4	1,000.3	1,082.8	1,105.4	1,092.5	1,092.2	1,079.8	1,076.7	1,067.8	1,056.1	1,047.5	1,060.6	1,058.1
1982	1,067.8	1,058.2	1,029.3	953.6	928.7	974.6	1,024.0	1,022.2	998.8	999.2	1,041.5	1,054.5	1,012.7
1983	985.3	927.4	874.2	813.4	838.1	879.4	876.3	883.0	894.3	912.2	901.8	892.1	889.8
1984	871.4	924.4	952.1	874.9	881.9	895.2	893.4	859.6	837.8	854.4	868.9	851.4	880.5
1985	835.7	810.3	809.9	820.3	851.0	797.7	754.9	743.6	800.5	841.3	887.5	905.5	821.5
1986[2]	830.2	631.6	519.1	504.3	476.4	452.9	371.7	406.5	469.0	436.0			

[1] Barge lots, f.o.b. refinery or terminal, excluding all fees & taxes.   [2] Preliminary.   *Source: Bureau of Labor Statistics* (0573)   T.283

Average Wholesale Price of Kerosene (Light Distillate)—No. 1 Fuel   Index (1967 = 100)

Year	Jan.	Feb.	Mar.	Apr.	May	June	July	Aug.	Sept.	Oct.	Nov.	Dec.	Average
1973	112.1	120.4	121.2	123.4	122.9	126.9	128.6	129.4	130.0	135.6	135.9	145.9	128.0
1974	154.3	184.8	198.7	209.4	217.6	233.2	241.7	250.2	256.8	254.7	261.4	257.9	226.7
1975	253.7	267.2	274.9	273.6	280.6	284.6	283.7	299.1	297.9	299.4	304.2	307.8	285.6
1976	310.5	316.2	313.9	311.2	306.7	303.8	305.4	309.2	311.5	316.0	320.2	323.2	312.3
1977	326.1	339.7	346.9	352.4	355.5	358.0	360.9	363.2	364.0	375.1	379.4	381.3	358.5
1978	383.0	388.2	388.4	387.9	390.7	391.4	393.1	394.4	395.8	397.6	398.4	403.0	392.7
1979	407.5	412.7	419.1	433.0	465.5	504.1	533.4	588.4	633.4	675.2	696.6	706.3	539.6
1980	733.9	776.9	834.6	862.5	870.5	878.4	892.7	903.1	903.2	896.3	896.8	911.4	863.4
1981	932.1	972.0	1,041.0	1,080.9	1,084.1	1,078.9	1,067.5	1,052.6	1,044.6	1,043.2	1,042.7	1,037.9	1,039.8
1982	1,044.3	1,034.3	1,027.9	1,009.1	975.9	974.2	984.4	983.0	976.3	969.7	985.9	992.1	996.4
1983	975.2	959.4	939.2	908.4	897.1	894.3	882.8	880.7	880.4	889.3	885.5	881.4	906.1
1984	872.2	885.8	903.5	879.2	876.8	876.5	874.3	863.0	853.2	854.4	857.1	847.5	870.3
1985[1]	840.8	833.3	827.5	824.5	826.9	803.1	779.8	780.3	780.6	795.2	806.3	812.7	809.3
1986[1]	795.6	750.2	684.6	584.8	523.8	504.4	452.9	413.3	426.8	423.9			

[1] Preliminary.   *Source: Bureau of Labor Statistics* (0572)   T.284

Stocks of Distillate Fuel in the U.S., First of the Month   In Millions of Barrels

Year	Jan.	Feb.	Mar.	Apr.	May	June	July	Aug.	Sept.	Oct.	Nov.	Dec.	Residual Fuel — Oil Stocks — Jan. 1	July 1
1976	208.8	165.5	150.5	138.3	137.3	147.1	165.1	190.9	218.0	232.3	235.6	223.7	74.1	64.3
1977	186.0	143.0	133.3	141.9	148.3	162.2	178.9	204.9	229.8	252.8	267.4	270.6	72.3	71.9
1978	250.3	213.3	165.7	137.9	136.2	144.6	157.3	180.5	200.2	220.7	233.1	233.2	90.0	72.0
1979	216.5	175.8	127.3	112.8	115.1	123.1	141.4	171.2	195.4	220.4	231.1	236.7	90.2	79.8
1980	228.7	212.4	191.7	177.9	177.2	183.4	196.6	213.8	226.3	232.4	225.7	222.4	95.6	87.8
1981	205.4	179.4	172.6	164.4	164.6	171.8	179.9	186.3	200.2	207.3	201.2	200.1	91.5	69.4
1982	191.5	164.4	147.4	126.3	108.0	113.6	123.7	148.2	158.7	161.2	170.1	185.6	78.0	60.7
1983	178.6	167.6	148.2	118.1	103.1	108.9	113.7	130.7	142.4	154.0	162.6	161.2	66.2	49.9
1984	140.3	119.3	132.2	109.6	97.7	98.1	112.8	124.4	133.3	142.9	152.2	161.0	48.5	46.9
1985[1]	161.1	141.8	121.5	99.4	97.1	104.7	109.7	115.7	113.8	117.4	123.4	139.7	53.0	40.2
1986[1]	143.7	139.0	112.8	99.3	95.3	97.8	108.8	122.8	138.1	152.6			50.4	43.0

[1] Preliminary.   *Source: Bureau of Mines*   T.285

U.S. Production of Distillate Fuel Oil   In Millions of Barrels

Year	Jan.	Feb.	Mar.	Apr.	May	June	July	Aug.	Sept.	Oct.	Nov.	Dec.	Total
1977	104.5	103.5	98.4	89.8	97.1	95.7	99.1	101.4	99.3	104.2	100.2	103.0	1,196.3
1978	95.1	82.7	93.5	88.8	100.8	93.3	96.8	102.2	95.6	102.3	101.0	104.2	1,156.1
1979	94.3	80.9	93.6	88.4	95.0	94.6	102.5	103.0	100.6	100.8	97.2	99.9	1,150.8
1980	93.4	80.2	79.3	73.8	76.7	79.4	83.4	76.3	80.6	80.3	81.1	89.6	974.1
1981	92.6	78.6	77.0	72.5	76.1	75.0	74.2	82.3	78.3	77.0	81.5	88.6	953.8
1982	80.3	67.9	70.9	70.7	81.2	81.9	84.8	77.7	79.7	88.0	85.8	82.3	951.3
1983	72.0	59.8	61.8	65.1	75.8	76.4	80.7	81.1	82.2	83.1	80.4	78.2	896.5
1984	80.3	83.1	76.8	70.3	81.3	86.4	84.3	82.5	81.2	83.4	84.8	86.7	981.2
1985[1]	80.9	69.8	69.6	74.2	82.8	79.4	82.0	80.4	77.8	90.0	93.1	98.4	980.9
1986[1]	89.9	71.8	82.0	83.7	88.6	82.0	84.1	90.7	85.8				

[1] Preliminary.   *Source: Dept. of Energy*   T.286

U.S. Imports of Distillate Fuel Oil   In Millions of Barrels

Year	Jan.	Feb.	Mar.	Apr.	May	June	July	Aug.	Sept.	Oct.	Nov.	Dec.	Total
1977	10.8	18.6	17.0	4.6	3.1	4.0	5.9	5.0	5.1	4.6	5.6	7.0	91.3
1978	6.1	5.9	6.0	3.0	3.9	4.4	4.6	4.4	4.9	5.5	6.7	7.9	63.3
1979	7.0	5.5	5.5	4.5	5.8	5.4	7.0	6.7	3.8	6.6	5.8	7.1	70.5
1980	5.5	6.9	6.0	4.6	3.9	3.2	3.6	2.4	3.0	3.6	4.0	5.2	51.9
1981	8.5	9.1	4.6	3.5	5.5	6.7	5.5	5.4	3.9	3.7	3.7	2.9	63.1
1982	3.0	3.7	1.5	1.8	2.3	3.1	3.9	2.5	1.8	2.8	4.4	3.4	34.0
1983	2.1	1.6	1.3	2.2	4.5	5.4	8.3	9.3	7.8	8.1	6.1	6.8	63.5
1984	9.3	13.2	3.6	6.6	7.8	7.7	6.2	8.0	8.7	13.0	9.5	5.9	99.4
1985[1]	8.4	4.2	4.8	7.3	6.3	4.6	3.0	2.5	6.7	8.1	8.4	8.9	73.1
1986[1]	9.7	3.6	6.7	4.4	4.5	4.9	9.1	11.0	7.2				

[1] Preliminary.   *Source: Dept. of Energy*   T.287

U.S. Domestic Consumption of Distillate Fuel Oil   In Millions of Barrels

Year	Jan.	Feb.	Mar.	Apr.	May	June	July	Aug.	Sept.	Oct.	Nov.	Dec.	Total
1977	158.2	131.8	106.7	88.1	86.2	83.1	79.1	81.6	81.4	94.1	102.6	130.4	1,223.3
1978	138.2	135.8	127.3	93.3	96.2	85.1	78.2	86.8	79.9	95.4	107.5	128.8	1,252.6
1979	142.0	134.7	113.6	90.5	92.9	81.2	79.4	85.6	79.4	96.7	97.4	114.9	1,208.5
1980	115.1	107.6	98.5	79.0	74.5	69.5	69.7	66.2	77.6	90.5	88.5	112.1	1,049.0
1981	127.4	94.5	90.0	76.0	74.7	73.9	73.7	74.0	75.4	86.9	86.4	99.6	1,032.5
1982	108.0	86.4	91.3	89.3	75.8	73.5	63.8	68.8	75.2	80.0	74.2	88.5	974.9
1983	86.7	77.8	91.4	80.9	73.0	75.7	70.4	77.3	77.3	80.9	86.2	104.3	981.9
1984	109.3	82.2	101.0	87.8	87.2	77.8	77.6	79.3	79.6	85.7	84.8	88.8	1,041.2
1985[1]	107.3	92.4	95.1	83.0	80.6	77.8	75.5	81.7	77.3	89.9	82.4	100.9	1,046.8
1986[1]	100.5	96.7	98.2	88.2	85.9	74.4	76.8	84.5	75.4				

[1] Preliminary.   *Source: Dept. of Energy*   T.288

Hides and Leather

World production of bovine hides and skins in 1986 was estimated at 4.3 million tonnes, down two percent from last year. The U.S. was the world's largest producer, making up 24 percent of total world output. Other major producers were the Soviet Union (22 percent), Brazil (eight percent), and Argentina (seven percent). Total world imports of hides and skins were estimated at 1.8 million tonnes, up four percent from 1985. The largest importers were Italy, Japan, Korea, and Czechoslovakia. World exports in 1986 were 1.6 million tonnes, unchanged from last year. The U.S. was the largest exporter, making up 42 percent of the total. The largest consumers were Italy, the U.S., Brazil and Argentina, accounting for 34 percent of total world utilization.

U.S. production of bovine hides and skins in 1986 was estimated at 1 million tonnes, unchanged from a year ago. The U.S. imported 35,000 tonnes, up three percent over the previous year; Canada supplied 85 percent of the import market. U.S. exports were 655,-000 tonnes, about the same as a year ago. The largest exporting markets were Japan and Korea, making up 27 percent and 26 percent of U.S. exports, respectively. Total domestic utilization of hides and skins was projected at 408,000 tonnes, off one percent from 1985. Production of hides and skins in 1987 is forecast to decline to 967,000 tonnes.

The quantity of leather shipped in 1986 was projected at 16.2 million equivalent cattle hide units. Domestic slaughter and production of leather goods declined from 1985 levels, but U.S. tanners increased exports because of the lower value of the dollar. As of August, 1986, U.S. exports of upper and lining leather had increased 17 percent from the year-before period. Over the long term, prospects for the U.S. leather industry appear positive. Hide supply is forecast to decline, pushing up leather prices somewhat. A weaker U.S. dollar and continued growth in export demand should enhance the level of shipments to other countries.

South Korea was expected to be the number-one market for U.S. hides and skins in 1986, replacing Japan, which has been the leader for more than 15 years. Korean leather footwear production in 1985 exceeded 70 million pounds, up 80 percent from 1984. This segment of the industry was expected to show 40–50 percent growth in 1986, based on the first six months of production data. The U.S. provided 91 percent of Korea's hide and skin imports and 15 percent of finished leather imports during January–May, 1986. Korea's annual imports in 1986 may exceed $600 million.

Italy's imports of hides and skins in 1986 were expected to decrease for the second year in a row because the fall in the dollar has reduced sales by leather producers; imports are forecast to remain unchanged in 1987.

World production of bovine hides and skins in 1987 is projected at 4.28 million tonnes, down marginally from 1986 levels. Countries expected to show increases are Brazil, the USSR, Mexico, New Zealand and Australia. Other major producers are expected to show slight to moderate declines, notably the U.S. Utilization in 1987 is projected to increase one percent to 4.57 million tonnes, led by higher demand in Brazil, Korea and Mexico. World imports of hides and skins in 1987 are expected to remain about equal to 1986.

World Production of Bovine Hides and Skins   In Thousands of Units of Metric Tons

Year	Argentina	Australia	Brazil	Canada	Colombia	France	Germany East	Germany West	Mexico	Italy	Poland	South Africa	Turkey	New Zealand	United Kingdom	United States	USSR
1980	322	149	280	91		EC-10 (698)						60		40		964	867
1981	333	142	291	96		EC-10 (683)						52		44		987	890
1982	293	155	308	98	92	179	44	149	138	96	75	53	56	46	106	1,019	867
1983	270	160	322	99	84	200	45	149	140	99	70	61	59	44	109	1,040	892
1984	290	129	310	94	87	190	45	164	145	101	73	60	60	37	113	1,066	917
1985	311	124	340	95	92	190	48	159	139	101	71		61	41	110	1,028	942
1986[1]	306	133	320	92	92	186	48	161	127	102	71		62	41	91	1,028	950

* Average   [1] Preliminary.   *Source: Foreign Agricultural Service, U.S.D.A.*   T.289

Salient Statistics of Hides & Leather in the United States

Year	New Supply of Cattle Hides — Domestic Slaughter — Federally Inspected	Uninspected[4]	Total Production	Net Exports	Total New Supply	Wholesale Prices—¢ lb. Heavy Cows[2]	Native[3] Steers	Production All U.S. Tanning	Cattle-Hide	Upper & Lining Leather Exports Ths. Sq. Ft.	Wholesale Leather Prices Cattle Hide[5]	Upper[6]	Footwear Production[7]	Export
			Thousands of Equivalent Hides					In Ths. Equiv. Hides			—1967 = 100—		—Mil. Pairs—	
1980	31,642	2,165	33,807	18,640	15,167	47.1	45.7	17,600	14,790	192,597	310.6	211.7	386.3	9.8
1981	32,819	2,134	34,953	18,701	16,252	46.1	44.2	19,184	15,520	192,193	319.8	214.4	372.0	9.7
1982	33,907	1,936	35,843	22,553	13,290	45.1	42.3	18,229	15,028	159,804	311.4	215.8	359.1	7.7
1983	34,816	1,833	36,649	21,205	15,444	53.5	50.2	18,610	15,430	155,808	330.7	223.4	344.3	6.2
1984[1]	35,880	1,702	37,582	25,194	12,388	67.0	61.0	16,940	14,021	163,373	372.3	219.2	301.4	6.2
1985[1]	34,765	1,528	36,293	24,398	11,895			15,230	12,550	131,505	353.2	223.5	266.0	9.2

[1] Preliminary.   [2] Heifers.   [3] Central U.S.   [4] Includes farm slaughter; diseased & condemned animals & hides taken off fallen animals.
[5] Finished cattlehide & kipside leather; sheep & lamb leather.   [6] Women's Leather Upper.   [7] Other than rubber.
Sources: Leather Industries of America; Bureau of Labor Statistics; Dept. of Commerce   T.290

U.S. Exports of Upper & Lining Leather   In Thousands of Square Feet

Year	Jan.	Feb.	Mar.	Apr.	May	June	July	Aug.	Sept.	Oct.	Nov.	Dec.	Total
1977	18,630	19,272	23,315	18,338	16,714	16,205	18,612	12,276	16,838	12,807	14,980	18,240	206,276
1978	17,364	15,308	16,408	16,720	18,899	21,427	14,160	19,726	16,224	17,438	17,947	17,176	208,799
1979	13,854	16,014	18,833	16,480	15,664	18,526	13,153	15,265	14,457	13,895	16,089	15,433	187,665
1980	15,769	16,873	18,710	13,024	12,652	15,483	15,481	15,215	15,818	19,051	20,880	13,641	192,597
1981	19,633	14,418	19,717	17,678	18,016	18,692	13,921	10,918	15,393	12,682	19,464	11,660	192,193
1982	10,849	10,343	13,696	15,534	17,449	18,610	18,486	12,065	10,417	11,842	9,726	10,786	159,804
1983	11,052	12,453	15,078	15,200	13,492	14,868	12,013	13,099	12,715	14,027	12,400	9,412	155,808
1984	13,624	13,015	17,787	14,772	19,514	14,294	12,907	14,046	11,219	11,533	10,231	10,431	163,373
1985[1]	10,266	8,855	11,023	11,637	12,112	16,233	9,919	10,763	8,085	12,310	12,452	7,824	131,505
1986[1]	12,032	10,849	13,050	13,652	14,560	13,945	11,902	16,769	11,502	13,043			

[1] Preliminary.   *Source: Leather Industries of America*   T.292

U.S. Production of All Footwear (Shoes, Sandals, Slippers, Athletic, Etc.)   In Millions of Pairs

Year	Jan.	Feb.	Mar.	Apr.	May	June	July	Aug.	Sept.	Oct.	Nov.	Dec.	Total
1977	34.8	34.5	37.6	34.3	35.5	36.9	26.9	37.5	35.6	36.4	35.9	33.2	418.1
1978	34.5	34.8	39.9	35.8	39.5	36.8	26.1	37.1	34.2	36.3	33.8	30.2	418.9
1979	37.3	34.9	38.7	33.4	37.3	31.9	25.4	33.9	31.1	35.0	31.3	28.7	398.9
1980	34.9	33.2	33.9	32.9	34.1	32.5	27.3	30.7	32.5	36.2	29.5	28.6	386.3
1981	31.1	30.4	34.1	32.6	31.6	30.0	26.8	30.4	32.6	34.7	30.3	27.4	372.0
1982	29.4	30.2	34.4	30.0	31.0	31.0	26.1	30.7	31.4	31.2	28.4	25.3	359.1
1983	28.1	32.1	31.8	27.3	30.3	28.8	22.8	30.7	29.7	29.4	28.0	25.2	344.3
1984	26.7	28.5	29.6	27.1	28.0	24.1	20.3	25.5	21.4	24.7	21.9	19.4	301.4
1985[1]	22.6	21.1	22.2	22.3	24.9	21.2	19.8	24.6	22.5	24.9	21.1	18.8	266.0
1986[1]	21.9	20.8	20.5	20.3	19.9	17.5	18.0	20.3	18.9				

[1] Preliminary.   *Source: U.S. Department of Commerce*   T.295

U.S. Imports and Exports of All Cattle Hides   In Thousands of Hides

Year	Imports Total	Imports From Canada	Total	Canada	France	W. Germany	Japan	Mexico	Nether-lands	Poland	Tai-wan	Spain	Romania	Korea Repub.	Czech.	Italy
1976	962	958	25,270	1,057	816	518	9,356	1,708	326	389		957	1,651	3,270	678	1,561
1977	932	926	24,489	859	769	435	8,425	1,967	417	433		940	1,472	3,611	680	1,048
1978	704	694	24,791	1,093	555	379	8,797	1,938	211	349		1,019	1,942	3,720	586	1,284
1979	673	643	23,731	1,248	691	454	7,396	2,428	324	513		892	1,317	2,526	682	2,248
1980	880	859	19,512	1,046	238	206	7,476	1,972	164	522		112	1,046	2,653	318	690
1981	1,028	881	19,703	1,212	137	319	7,512	2,485	94	203		394	680	3,579	334	486
1982	658	592	23,175	1,041	478	671	6,469	1,882	280	790		643	939	4,572	415	1,395
1983	665	570	21,281	1,235	332	343	6,413	1,296	174	303		246	1,318	4,635	489	823
1984	711	669	25,029	1,072	292	252	7,334	1,858	221	319	2,697	242	1,032	5,423	669	1,170
1985[1]	1,044	883	24,956	729	215	110	6,824	2,287	71	402	2,797	214	1,168	6,441	418	1,134

[1] Preliminary.   *Source: Leather Industries of America*   T.297

Average Factory Price of Footwear in the United States   In Dollars Per Pair

Year	Jan.	Feb.	Mar.	Apr.	May	June	July	Aug.	Sept.	Oct.	Nov.	Dec.	Average
1977	8.61	8.40	8.63	8.81	8.53	8.39	8.44	8.36	8.51	8.28	8.62	9.00	8.54
1978	8.50	8.39	8.76	9.35	9.51	9.37	9.41	8.66	9.40	9.37	9.61	10.31	9.20
1979	9.73	9.84	9.68	10.23	10.00	10.48	11.74	10.31	10.30	10.46	11.15	11.47	10.60
1980	11.67	11.83	11.81	12.27	12.16	11.37	11.40	11.94	11.08	11.25	11.45	11.41	11.63
1981	11.67	11.93	12.52	12.72	13.09	13.16	13.01	13.14	13.22	12.90	12.67	12.58	12.52
1982	12.96	12.32	12.49	12.74	12.76	13.30	14.13	13.34	13.12	13.10	13.56	14.08	13.14
1983	12.88	13.72	13.18	13.54	14.20	13.57	12.91	14.14	14.06	15.02	14.69	15.55	13.96
1984	14.95	14.19	14.00	14.99	15.20	14.43	14.88	14.59	15.11	14.56	15.00	15.62	14.79
1985	15.24	14.97	14.10	14.87	14.86	15.35	14.24	14.55	14.12	13.71	13.56	15.13	14.56
1986[1]	14.02	13.30	13.27	13.66	14.40	14.38	14.90	13.81	14.05	13.76			

[1] Preliminary.   *Source: Leather Industries of America*   T.298

HIDES AND LEATHER

Index Price[2] of Hides (Packer Heavy Native Steers[1])—F.O.B. Shipping Point   1967 = 100

Year	Jan.	Feb.	Mar.	Apr.	May	June	July	Aug.	Sept.	Oct.	Nov.	Dec.	Average
1973	34.0	33.5	28.3	38.3	36.3	33.8	36.3	38.3	35.5	36.3	32.8	28.2	34.3
1974	29.3	—	24.1	26.3	26.3	23.3	25.8	25.3	24.5	17.3	17.5	14.3	23.1
1975	11.8	12.5	16.3	27.5	25.3	25.8	25.3	25.3	25.8	28.0	30.8	26.3	23.4
1976	31.5	29.8	30.0	34.9	39.0	34.8	36.3	37.3	38.3	31.8	29.0	32.3	33.8
1977	35.8	36.3	37.3	40.1	41.3	36.3	38.1	36.8	34.8	33.8	34.8	38.0	37.0
1978	38.8	37.8	37.3	41.3	41.8	45.8	47.8	53.0	59.0	57.3	54.8	51.8	47.2
1979[2]	506.4	548.4	766.9	750.1	760.2	696.3	653.0	594.6	549.2	568.9	498.5	480.1	614.4
1980	496.7	409.3	331.5	320.5	283.6	321.0	369.0	448.0	361.4	412.9	455.9	420.6	385.9
1981	375.1	344.1	356.1	405.8	385.8	364.9	351.7	373.6	344.3	347.7	347.2	343.4	361.6
1982	353.6	346.0	325.8	339.3	353.5	342.1	342.1	349.7	343.5	336.4	324.7	312.9	339.1
1983	313.9	315.0	329.6	345.0	378.6	386.8	434.2	N.A.	447.5	450.2	469.9	489.6	396.4
1984	479.0	469.5	486.4	470.4	530.6	558.9	515.9	543.3	597.5	559.8	386.0	391.5	499.1
1985	416.2	378.5	370.8	466.8	494.4	490.7	465.5	428.6	N.A.	N.A.	N.A.	N.A.	435.1
1986[3]	502.3	508.5	502.8	520.0	524.8	531.6	526.1	506.3	496.9	517.7	533.0		

[1] Over 53 pounds.   [2] Data prior to 1979 are in *cents per pound*.   [3] Preliminary.   *Source: Bureau of Labor Statistics* (0411–0111.99)   T.296

HIDES   CASH PRICE   CHICAGO   CENTS PER POUND

MONTHLY AVERAGE PRICE

1964 TO DATE PACKERS' HEAVY NATIVE STEERS

1920-1963: PACKERS' LIGHT NATIVE COWS

Hogs

Hogs and pigs inventory in the ten major producing states totaled 39.7 million head on December 1, 1986, down 3 percent from 1985 and down 6 percent from 1984. Hogs kept for breeding totaled 5.1 million head, down 4 percent from 1985; hogs retained for market were 34.6 million head, versus 35.8 million in 1985. Hog numbers in the major producing states have been on a downtrend in recent years. The December 1 U.S. pig crop totaled 51 million head, off 3 percent from the 1985 level. Breeding and marketing totals were also down 3 percent. The 1986 U.S. pig crop totaled 82.3 million head, 4 percent below 1985 and 5 percent under 1984.

The hog-corn ratio and producers' returns rose sharply in mid-1986, but producers continued to reduce herds. The decline in sows farrowing has been moderated by the trend of record-high pigs per litter each quarter; there have been year-over-year increases for several consecutive quarters, mainly due to genetics and better management practices.

Profitability in hog production usually leads to expansion in the breeding herd and year-over-year increase in sows farrowing about two quarters later. Recently, response has been slower, and at a lower rate than in years past, because of some producers' financial difficulties and tighter credit practices.

Reduced costs and continuing cutbacks in hog production caused a sharp price rally in 1986. As a result, producers' returns were among the highest on record; such returns should trigger a double-digit increase in pork production by late 1987. However, due to a prolonged period of poor returns and financial problems, sharp increases in pork production may not occur before early 1988. Still, the outlook for relatively high returns continuing through most of 1987 should encourage producers to begin expanding output.

Hog slaughter in the first and second quarters of 1987 should be below 1986. Relatively cheap feed may encourage producers to feed barrows and gilts to heavier weights. The September 1, 1986, inventory of market hogs weighing under 60 pounds, from which first-quarter slaughter is primarily drawn, was down 8 percent. The June–August pig crop, normally slaughtered in the first quarter, was down 6 percent from a year ago. The five-year slaughter market hog inventory relationship indicates that commercial hog slaughter averages 137 percent of the ten-states market hog inventory.

Barrow and gilt prices at the seven major markets averaged $61 per cwt. in the third quarter of 1986 (compared with $44 in 1985) and were the highest since 1982. Government purchases of red meats for export and domestic feeding programs required by the Farm Bill contributed to higher prices.

Futures Markets

Live hog futures are traded at the Chicago Mercantile Exchange (CME) and the MidAmerica Exchange. Options are also traded against the CME contract.

World Hog Numbers in Specified Countries   In Millions of Head

Year	Brazil	Canada	Denmark	France	W. Germany	Hungary	Italy	Japan	Mexico	Philippines	Poland	Spain	China[3]	Un. Kingdom	United States	USSR	World
1980	36.5	10.1	9.5	11.4	22.4	8.4	8.8	10.0	12.8	7.9	21.0	10.5		7.8	67.3	73.9	
1981	35.0	10.2	9.7	11.7	22.6	8.3	8.9	10.1	15.4	7.6	18.7	11.0	305.4	7.8	64.5	73.4	708.7
1982	33.5	10.0	9.8	11.8	22.3	8.3	9.0	10.0	16.2	7.6	19.1	10.7	293.7	7.9	58.7	73.3	693.5
1983	33.5	10.1	9.5	11.7	22.5	9.0	9.1	10.3	16.5	8.0	17.6	11.7	300.8	8.2	54.5	76.7	700.1
1984	30.0	10.7	9.0	11.3	23.4	9.8	9.2	10.4	13.1	7.6	15.9	12.1	298.5	7.8	56.7	78.7	700.3
1985	30.0	11.0	9.0	11.0	23.6	9.2	9.0	10.7	12.3	7.3	17.2	11.8	306.8	7.8	54.1	77.9	705.3
1986[1]	30.5	10.7	9.1	11.0	24.3	8.3	9.1	11.1	13.1	7.7	19.2	11.9	331.5	7.9	52.3	77.6	728.9
1987[2]	31.2	10.9	9.4	10.8	24.8	8.3	9.2	11.2	13.1	7.1	19.0	12.0	343.3	8.0	50.0	77.5	740.1

[1] Preliminary.   [2] Estimate.   [3] Mainland.   *Source: Foreign Agricultural Service, U.S.D.A.*   T.300

Salient Statistics of Pigs and Hogs in the U.S.

Year	Spring[2] Sows Farrowed	Spring[2] Pigs Saved	Fall[3] Sows Farrowed	Fall[3] Pigs Saved	Total Pig Crop	Value of Hogs on Farms, Dec. 1 $ Per Head	Value of Hogs on Farms, Dec. 1 Total Million $	Hog Marketings Ths. Head	Quantity Produced (Live Wt.) Mil. Lbs.	Value of Production Mil. $	Commercial Federally Inspected	Commercial Other	Commercial Total	Farm	Total
	In Thousands of Head														
1979	7,176	50,571	7,322	52,241	102,792	56.00	3,775	92,499	22,617	9,424	85,425	3,674	89,099	1,070	90,169
1980	7,229	52,288	6,855	49,432	101,720	74.70	4,821	100,651	23,402	8,864	91,882	4,192	96,074	1,100	97,174
1981	6,440	47,605	6,268	46,248	93,853	70.10	4,114	95,986	21,813	9,532	87,851	3,724	91,575	895	92,470
1982	5,664	41,575	5,884	43,614	85,189	89.90	4,903	86,972	19,658	10,297	79,328	3,861	82,190	655	82,845
1983	6,301	47,409	6,176	45,746	93,155	58.80	3,331	89,129	21,195	9,899	84,762	2,823	87,584	517	88,101
1984	5,694	42,403	5,857	44,183	86,586	75.00	4,056	87,264	20,177	9,501	82,478	2,690	85,168	473	85,641
1985[1]	5,571	42,545	5,667	43,476	86,029	69.60	3,639				81,948	2,521	84,491		
1986[1]	5,236	40,313	5,163	39,755	82,283						77,000	2,200	79,200		
1987[4]	5,342	41,133													

[1] Preliminary.   [2] December–May.   [3] June–November.   [4] Breeding intentions; Estimates.   *Source: Statistical Reporting Service, U.S.D.A.* T.302

HOGS

Hogs and Pigs on U.S. Farms on December 1   In Thousands of Head

Year	Georgia	Illinois	Indiana	Iowa	Kansas	Kentucky	Minnesota	Missouri	Nebraska	No. Carolina	Ohio	South Dakota	Tennessee	Wisconsin	Total
1979	2,360	6,950	4,850	16,200	2,090	1,470	4,900	4,650	4,150	2,650	2,120	2,000	1,400	1,830	67,318
1980	3,250	6,600	4,600	16,100	1,900	1,220	5,100	3,980	3,900	2,460	2,050	1,860	1,140	1,680	64,462
1981	1,520	6,450	4,100	16,300	1,770	1,040	4,300	3,400	4,100	1,980	1,920	1,710	900	1,380	58,698
1982	1,450	5,600	4,400	14,400	1,670	960	4,000	3,500	3,800	2,150	1,920	1,580	750	1,220	54,534
1983	1,350	5,400	4,200	15,000	1,650	1,000	4,400	3,600	4,000	2,350	2,200	1,730	950	1,280	56,694
1984	1,200	5,400	4,300	14,200	1,600	880	4,300	3,450	3,700	2,300	1,970	1,600	1,100	1,300	54,073
1985[1]	1,150	5,400	4,150	13,500	1,520	800	4,100	3,050	3,900	2,350	1,980	1,610	950	1,250	52,313
1986[1]															50,960

[1] Preliminary.   *Source: Crop Reporting Board, U.S.D.A.*

T.301

Quarterly 10—U.S. State Hogs & Pigs Report   In Thousands of Head

Year[2]	Inventory[1]	Breeding[1]	Market[1]	Farrowings	Pig Crop	Year	Inventory[1]	Breeding[1]	Market[1]	Farrowings	Pig Crop
1983	44,150	5,638	38,512	9,735	72,733	1985	41,100	5,258	35,842	9,020	67,648
I	42,440	5,670	36,770	2,090	15,543	I	42,420	5,348	37,072	1,935	14,690
II	41,840	5,928	35,912	2,768	21,063	II	39,680	5,220	34,460	2,420	18,762
III	45,645	6,263	39,382	2,422	17,836	III	41,650	5,397	36,253	2,191	16,941
IV	46,030	5,839	40,191	2,377	17,663	IV	41,820	5,377	36,443	2,265	17,255
1984	42,420	5,348	37,072	9,020	67,680	1986					
I	44,150	5,638	38,512	1,964	14,288	I[3]	41,000	5,258	35,842	1,940	14,880
II	40,070	5,446	34,624	2,481	18,814	II[3]	38,600	4,988	33,612	2,161	16,878
III	41,915	5,771	36,144	2,259	17,158	III[3]	38,045	4,840	33,205	2,034	15,853
IV	43,180	5,550	37,630	2,316	17,420	IV[3]	39,585	4,840	34,745	2,060	

[1] Beginning of period.   [2] Quarters are Dec. preceding year—Feb. (I), Mar.–May (II), June–Aug. (III), & Sept.–Nov. (IV).   [3] Preliminary.   *Source: Crop Reporting Board, U.S.D.A.*

T.181a

U.S. Federally Inspected Hog Slaughter   In Thousands of Head

Week ended	1984	1985	1986	Week ended	1984	1985	1986
Jan. 1[1]	1,350	1,238	1,153	July 2	1,438	1,476	1,329
8	1,418	1,295	1,250	9	1,105	1,171	1,118
15	1,708	1,679	1,635	16	1,445	1,523	1,390
22	1,625	1,615	1,654	23	1,378	1,427	1,345
29	1,577	1,528	1,563	30	1,305	1,400	1,280
Feb. 5	1,543	1,565	1,506	Aug. 6	1,382	1,474	1,312
12	1,571	1,582	1,526	13	1,406	1,556	1,338
19	1,578	1,508	1,512	20	1,409	1,524	1,367
26	1,579	1,539	1,501	27	1,479	1,531	1,385
Mar. 5	1,656	1,608	1,606	Sept. 3	1,502	1,601	1,419
12	1,791	1,635	1,635	10	1,396	1,429	1,257
19	1,691	1,638	1,650	17	1,657	1,690	1,492
26	1,681	1,647	1,556	24	1,679	1,667	1,504
Apr. 2	1,695	1,642	1,579	Oct. 1	1,679	1,681	1,503
9	1,695	1,569	1,518	8	1,699	1,644	1,515
16	1,728	1,623	1,633	15	1,701	1,686	
23	1,642	1,676	1,651	22	1,754	1,620	
30	1,588	1,662	1,637	29	1,736	1,654	
May 7	1,635	1,702	1,619	Nov. 5	1,754	1,668	
14	1,664	1,699	1,606	12	1,742	1,654	
21	1,579	1,705	1,560	19	1,681	1,654	
28	1,578	1,580	1,518	26	1,446	1,697	
June 4	1,367	1,361	1,307	30	1,812	1,328	
11	1,591	1,592	1,471	Dec. 3	1,792	1,656	
18	1,541	1,561	1,459	10	1,692	1,566	
25	1,431	1,535	1,373	17	1,687	1,655	
				24	1,238	1,153	

[1] Corresponding dates—1984: December 31, 1983; 1985: December 29, 1984.   *Source: Economic Research Service, U.S.D.A.*

T.181b

Federally Inspected Hog Slaughter in the United States In Thousands of Head

Year	Jan.	Feb.	Mar.	Apr.	May	June	July	Aug.	Sept.	Oct.	Nov.	Dec.	Total
1979	6,393	5,693	7,113	6,962	7,284	6,678	6,734	7,662	6,840	8,736	8,097	7,234	85,425
1980	8,038	7,277	7,856	8,456	8,167	7,279	6,910	6,745	7,601	8,404	7,362	7,788	91,882
1981	7,768	6,873	7,988	7,993	7,004	6,682	6,540	6,580	7,320	7,872	7,308	7,923	87,850
1982	6,875	6,340	7,691	————20,043————			————18,310————			————20,068————			79,328
1983	6,421	5,762	7,350	7,086	6,905	7,028	6,362	7,082	7,268	7,829	8,152	7,515	84,762
1984	6,947	6,591	7,578	6,953	7,153	6,392	5,806	6,628	6,439	7,908	7,354	6,729	82,478
1985[1]	7,114	6,208	6,932	7,177	7,359	6,209	6,399	6,810	6,738	7,566	6,818	6,640	81,974
1986[1]	6,968	6,127	6,662	7,160	6,669	5,894	5,918	5,798	6,322	7,045	6,049		

[1] Preliminary. *Source: Statistical Reporting Service, U.S.D.A.* T.305

Average Live Weight of All Hogs Slaughtered Under Federal Inspection In Pounds Per Head

Year	Jan.	Feb.	Mar.	Apr.	May	June	July	Aug.	Sept.	Oct.	Nov.	Dec.	Average[1]
1979	241	237	238	240	243	246	246	240	240	242	245	246	242.0
1980	243	239	239	241	244	244	242	239	239	241	246	247	242.0
1981	246	242	241	242	244	245	242	239	240	243	246	247	243.0
1982	243	239	239	———243———			———242———			———247———			243.0
1983	244	241	241	243	246	247	245	242	240	243	246	244	243.5
1984[2]	242	241	240	243	246	247	245	242	240	243	246	244	243.5
1985[2]	245	242	242	245	247	248	245	243	242	246	248	247	245.0
1986[2]	246	244	244	245	246	245	245	244	245	248	250		

[1] Average is weighted by federally inspected slaughter. [2] Preliminary. *Source: Department of Agriculture* T.311

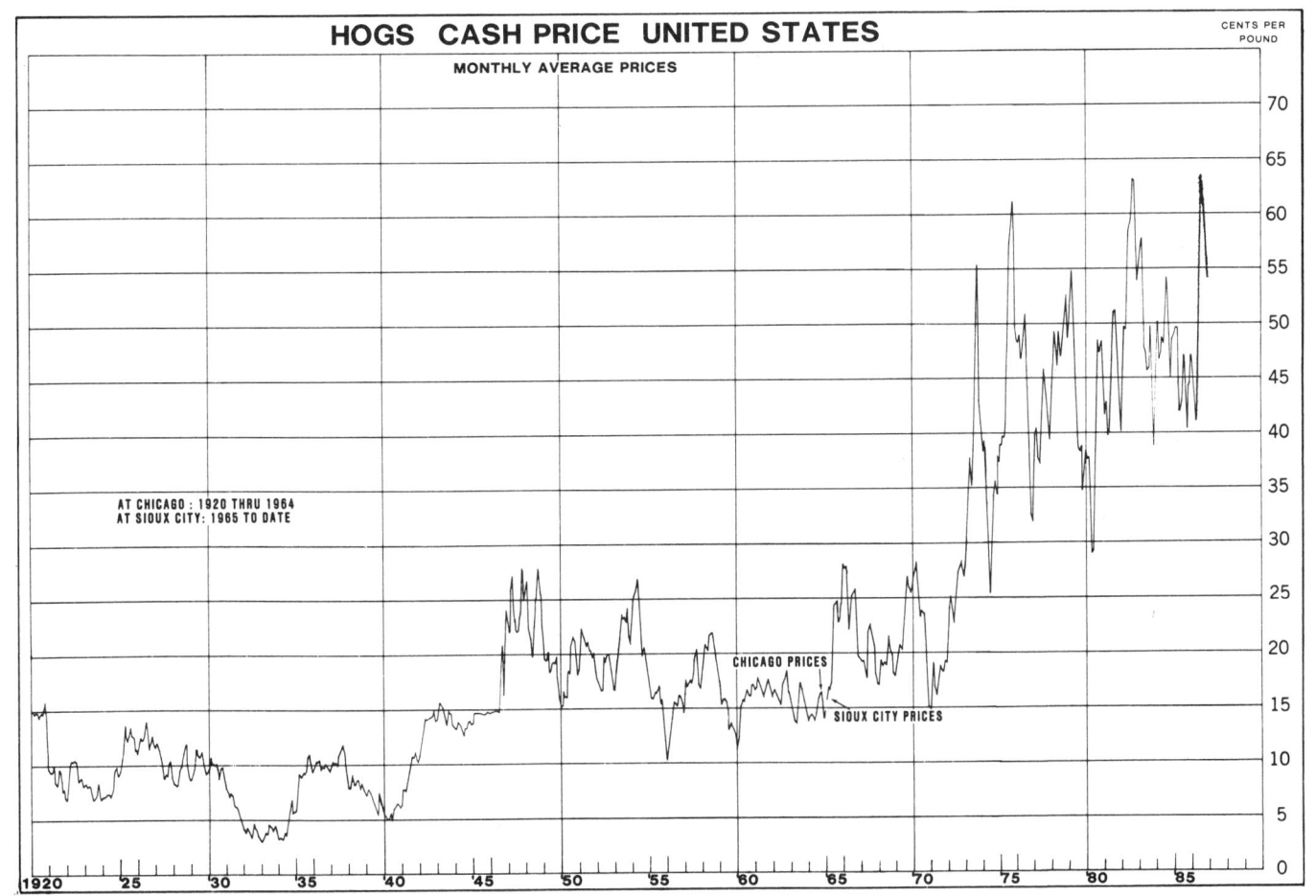

HOGS CASH PRICE UNITED STATES

MONTHLY AVERAGE PRICES

CENTS PER POUND

AT CHICAGO : 1920 THRU 1964
AT SIOUX CITY: 1965 TO DATE

CHICAGO PRICES

SIOUX CITY PRICES

HOGS

Average Price Received by Farmers for Hogs in the U.S.   In Cents Per Pound

Year	Jan.	Feb.	Mar.	Apr.	May	June	July	Aug.	Sept.	Oct.	Nov.	Dec.	Average[1]
1981	40.90	41.30	38.80	39.00	40.90	47.40	49.30	49.20	48.60	45.00	41.50	39.00	43.90
1982	43.40	48.30	48.60	51.20	56.70	57.50	57.80	61.20	61.30	55.80	52.50	53.60	52.30
1983	55.30	56.10	50.40	46.90	45.90	43.90	43.40	46.70	44.10	40.40	37.50	44.20	46.80
1984	48.40	45.40	45.80	47.50	47.20	49.00	52.00	50.50	46.30	43.60	47.00	48.60	47.10
1985	48.00	48.30	43.60	41.20	41.40	44.60	45.70	42.50	39.70	43.10	43.20	45.30	43.90
1986[2]	44.30	42.80	40.40	39.70	45.80	52.60	59.00	62.10	58.30	53.10	52.90		

[1] Weighted average by quantities sold.   [2] Preliminary.   *Source: Crop Reporting Board, U.S.D.A.*   T.306

Average Wholesale Price of Hogs, Average (All Weights) at Sioux City   In Dollars Per 100 Pounds

Year	Jan.	Feb.	Mar.	Apr.	May	June	July	Aug.	Sept.	Oct.	Nov.	Dec.	Average
1981	41.67	42.78	39.88	40.15	41.96	48.78	51.01	51.14	48.89	46.15	42.10	40.17	44.29
1982	45.77	49.70	49.50	52.16	58.35	59.01	59.70	63.18	63.12	57.27	53.90	55.23	55.21
1983	57.24	57.78	51.37	47.84	47.40	45.73	45.81	49.77	46.05	41.64	38.81	46.53	47.73
1984	50.14	46.68	47.36	48.69	48.22	50.04	54.25	52.57	47.86	45.01	48.55	49.03	49.03
1985	49.60	49.55	44.54	41.85	42.70	45.67	47.09	43.91	40.42	44.20	44.46	47.11	44.98
1986	45.60	43.80	41.08	40.59	46.43	54.95	61.59	63.66	59.59	54.86	54.44		

Source: Department of Agriculture   T.307

Hog-Corn Price Ratio[1] at Omaha

Year	Jan.	Feb.	Mar.	Apr.	May	June	July	Aug.	Sept.	Oct.	Nov.	Dec.	Average
1981	13.0	13.3	12.4	12.3	12.9	15.2	15.9	18.1	19.8	18.7	17.5	16.8	15.5
1982	18.4	20.1	19.8	19.8	21.8	22.1	23.3	27.9	28.1	27.2	22.8	23.0	22.9
1983	23.2	21.7	18.6	15.4	15.2	14.7	14.4	14.6	13.8	12.9	11.9	14.5	15.9
1984	16.0	15.3	14.5	14.5	14.3	14.8	16.6	16.8	16.0	16.4	18.4	19.6	16.1
1985[2]	18.8	18.7	16.4	15.2	15.7	16.9	17.9	18.2	17.1	19.5	19.3	19.8	17.8
1986[2]	19.0	19.0	17.6	17.2	19.5	22.4	30.3	39.3	42.9				

[1] Ratio computed by dividing average price packer and shipper purchases of barrows and gilts by average price No. 2 yellow corn both at Omaha. This ratio represents the number of bushels of corn required to buy 100 pounds of live hogs.   [2] Preliminary.   *Source: Economic Research Service, U.S.D.A.*   T.304

Cold Storage Holdings of Frozen Pork[1] in the U.S. on First of Month   In Millions of Pounds

Year	Jan.	Feb.	Mar.	Apr.	May	June	July	Aug.	Sept.	Oct.	Nov.	Dec.
1981	348.6	350.8	355.9	360.6	403.5	394.4	346.5	283.4	225.1	206.7	238.3	255.2
1982	264.4	247.3	246.3	274.1	—	—	264.1	—	—	183.0	—	—
1983	219.0	224.2	215.8	234.7	272.7	293.0	280.4	253.0	214.1	210.0	240.0	295.2
1984[2]	300.6	295.1	311.7	350.7	390.4	437.7	405.2	345.0	269.5	256.6	275.6	269.4
1985[2]	274.3	291.9	286.3	314.1	368.2	410.3	385.0	343.1	294.7	278.8	277.5	265.0
1986[2]	229.4	235.4	239.1	253.6	284.2	280.3	247.7	214.9	184.7	185.9	215.8	206.9

[1] Excludes lard.   [2] Preliminary.   *Source: Crop Reporting Board, U.S.D.A.*   T.303

High, Low & Closing Prices of June Live Hogs Futures at Chicago   In Cents per Pound

Year of Delivery		Year Prior to Delivery									Delivery Year						Life of Delivery Range
		Apr.	May	June	July	Aug.	Sept.	Oct.	Nov.	Dec.	Jan.	Feb.	Mar.	Apr.	May	June	
1984	High	47.75	47.75	46.50	50.50	56.00	55.00	52.15	54.25	53.75	56.00	53.20	57.27	58.00	56.20	54.80	58.00
	Low	46.75	45.40	43.90	43.80	48.90	49.90	49.00	52.20	52.00	52.30	50.40	51.30	54.20	51.35	51.47	43.80
	Close	46.75	45.80	45.15	49.80	53.55	50.05	51.97	53.55	53.05	52.75	51.70	56.12	54.42	51.60	54.17	—
1985	High	53.75	55.20	55.40	54.40	53.15	53.25	51.10	53.67	54.95	54.95	54.22	52.90	49.97	49.20	50.10	55.40
	Low	52.62	53.65	52.60	50.10	50.80	48.65	48.40	50.70	50.25	53.05	50.65	49.05	46.15	44.40	46.70	44.40
	Close	53.60	54.32	54.15	51.00	52.70	48.77	50.95	52.95	54.57	53.85	51.65	49.57	46.30	47.95	49.35	—
1986	High	48.95	48.65	49.00	47.60	44.40	43.75	43.97	44.70	46.45	47.00	45.50	45.90	46.87	50.10	59.72	59.72
	Low	47.55	46.80	46.90	41.75	40.05	39.80	42.25	42.20	43.25	43.65	42.10	42.05	40.25	45.52	49.75	39.80
	Close	48.70	48.25	47.75	43.57	40.82	43.00	42.65	44.65	45.85	45.27	42.80	43.82	46.60	49.77	59.65	—
1987	High	43.30	44.75	46.67	48.00	49.50	59.20	49.40	48.70	49.10							
	Low	39.90	39.90	40.60	43.80	46.10	41.20	46.00	45.45	45.50							
	Close	40.97	40.85	44.95	47.45	47.45	48.25	46.70	48.47	45.62							

Source: Chicago Mercantile Exchange   T.308

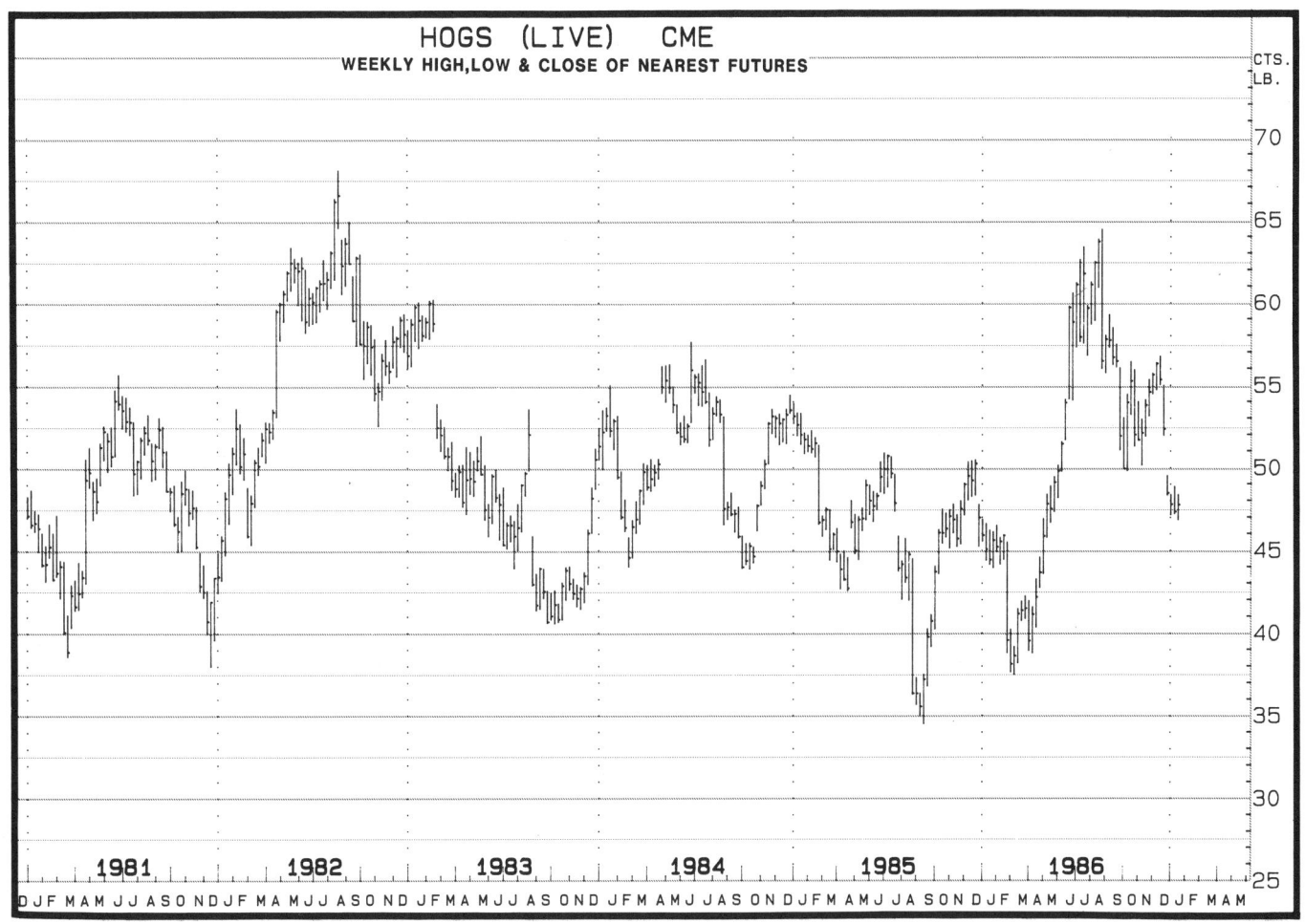

HOGS (LIVE) CME
WEEKLY HIGH, LOW & CLOSE OF NEAREST FUTURES

Month–End Open Interest of Live Hogs Futures at Chicago   In Contracts

Year	Jan.	Feb.	Mar.	Apr.	May	June	July	Aug.	Sept.	Oct.	Nov.	Dec.
1979	26,338	27,694	25,613	24,204	27,004	30,108	24,544	25,730	26,155	24,313	26,317	24,966
1980	27,387	27,765	21,857	24,795	25,814	29,011	27,635	28,725	31,696	36,962	38,534	26,816
1981	21,267	21,588	20,767	28,147	31,149	26,639	19,557	20,944	23,471	21,945	22,294	17,924
1982	27,528	29,960	43,387	51,056	63,760	46,002	42,884	51,530	48,263	48,751	47,067	43,791
1983	45,184	41,338	39,469	31,915	31,014	30,794	27,173	33,668	33,425	30.049	30,071	33,820
1984	33,049	35,159	35,289	33,122	34,148	30,517	23,579	24,061	21,048	20,689	26,975	24,037
1985	29,917	27,827	25,738	23,673	22,919	24,807	18,289	19,984	18,390	25,447	27,912	21,680
1986	22,125	21,639	17,123	19,037	25,497	26,878	32,704	32,643	32,479	27,447	30,980	23,620

Source: Chicago Mercantile Exchange   T.309

Volume of Trading of Live Hogs Futures at Chicago   In Thousands of Contracts

Year	Jan.	Feb.	Mar.	Apr.	May	June	July	Aug.	Sept.	Oct.	Nov.	Dec.	Total
1979	143.1	137.9	185.4	132.0	145.1	160.9	144.1	164.5	151.3	154.1	162.9	124.5	1,805.7
1980	152.9	122.3	138.3	158.8	133.8	170.8	189.7	188.6	239.1	258.1	195.3	201.4	2,153.8
1981	174.8	182.0	197.5	212.0	230.7	262.9	179.8	153.9	171.9	178.6	160.2	153.7	2,258.1
1982	178.7	195.6	262.6	222.6	288.0	408.3	300.1	344.5	347.2	383.4	324.9	305.1	3,561.0
1983	291.6	254.7	213.8	230.6	254.1	262.1	217.4	279.9	220.8	174.2	197.5	194.2	2,790.7
1984	232.2	212.7	243.8	172.3	211.0	192.6	189.2	143.9	109.1	140.7	181.0	140.5	2,169.0
1985	155.0	128.3	160.2	141.7	156.2	141.9	134.7	120.2	136.1	156.8	145.2	143.5	2,719.9
1986	156.3	108.5	113.7	153.6	157.4	160.8	224.3	168.8	196.5	183.4	171.0	142.5	1,936.9

Source: Chicago Mercantile Exchange   T.310

Honey

World honey production for 1986 is forecast at 950,000 tonnes, one percent higher than in 1985. Output in the USSR, the world's largest producer, is expected to remain about the same; there was a marginal decline in the number of bee colonies there. In North America, production is projected to increase 13 percent. Unfavorable weather conditions in Mexico's main producing area are likely to reduce output there by 9.6 percent in 1986. Canadian honey production should be up seven percent, thanks to good weather and improved field crops in the western provinces. South America will show a sharp drop in output, due mostly to Argentine declines; honey production in that country fell 44 percent, to the lowest level in eight years. Persistent November rains reduced the supply of nectar and pollen in flowers.

U.S. production is forecast at 91,000 tonnes, a 25-percent increase over last year. Favorable weather conditions are cited as the main reason for the rise. Beginning 1986 stocks in the U.S. were 97,932 tonnes, with projected growth of 45 percent for 1987. The increase is due, in part, to higher output and larger imports. Honey imports into the U.S. have shown a gradual rise of 44 percent from 1981 to 1985, with the total in 1985 at 62,706 tonnes. Honey exports, on the other hand, decreased 29 percent in the same period, with exports in 1985 at 2,949 metric tonnes. Total 1986 honey consumption in the U.S. is expected to rise by 19 percent over 1985.

Under the Food Security Act, the Secretary of Agriculture may set the loan repayment price at a level he determines will induce bee keepers to repay their loans, in order to minimize loan forfeitures, reduce stocks, and maintain the competitiveness of honey. In 1986, the loan repayment level for extra-light amber honey was 42 cents per pound, compared with an average support level of 64 cents per pound. According to the Census Bureau, the U.S. import price during most of 1986 averaged about 35.5 cents per pound, f.o.b.

World Production of Honey In Thousands of Metric Tons

Year	Argentina	Australia	Brazil	Canada	China (Mainland)	Ethiopia	France	West Germany	Japan	Mexico	Poland	Spain	Turkey	United States	U.S.S.R.	World Total
1977	22.0	14.9	14.0	25.4	60.0	19.0	8.2	20.0	6.2	60.0	10.0	12.0	21.7	81.0	208.0	798.3
1978	35.0	18.6	16.0	30.6	75.0	20.0	9.5	15.0	8.5	54.0	12.0	11.0	21.7	104.5	179.0	827.7
1979	30.0	25.0	18.0	32.9	110.0	20.0	14.4	9.9	7.5	52.0	13.0	12.0	23.7	107.8	189.0	880.1
1980	33.0	19.5	20.0	29.2	81.0	20.5	12.0	13.5	6.2	60.0	10.0	13.0	23.0	90.6	183.0	837.4
1981	30.0	24.8	24.0	32.9	110.0	21.0	10.0	14.0	6.0	60.0	10.0	13.0	23.0	84.3	184.0	873.8
1982	33.0	22.4	25.0	30.5	136.0		25.0	18.0	7.4	45.0				104.3	186.0	908.8
1983	30.0	25.0	25.0	38.8	143.3			19.0	6.9	68.0				93.0	210.0	970.0
1984[1]	35.0	28.0	26.5	43.3	147.5			16.0	6.8	60.0				75.0	193.0	945.0
1985[1]	45.0	25.0	28.0	35.2	150.0			11.0	7.2	52.0				68.0	190.0	940.0
1986[1]	25.0	27.3	26.9	37.8	150.0			18.0	5.0	47.0				91.0	190.0	950.0

[1] Preliminary. *Source: Foreign Agricultural Service, U.S.D.A.* T.312

Salient Statistics of Honey in the United States

Year	Number of Colonies Thous.	Yield Per Colony Lbs.	Total U.S.	California	Florida	Iowa	Minnesota	So. Dak.	Texas	Wisconsin	Domestic Disapp.	Imports For Consumption	Domestic Exports	Stocks Jan. 1	Extracted Florida Extra Light[2] ¢ Lb.	National Average Price Support ¢ Lb.	Per Capita Consumption Lbs.
			Honey Production; By States — In Millions of Pounds														
1977	4,346	41.0	178.1	13.7	14.4	6.1	12.0		9.0	9.6	240.8	63.9	5.5	34.3	40.6	32.7	1.09
1978	4,081	56.7	231.5	31.2	23.9	4.6	13.9		8.7	6.3	277.3	56.0	8.0	30.0	45.1	36.8	1.25
1979	4,155	57.4	238.7	17.1	27.3	6.6	15.8	17.3	11.4	8.8	282.7	58.6	8.8	32.2	50.2	43.9	1.26
1980	4,140	48.3	199.8	23.2	20.3	6.3	13.7	8.1	6.9	6.0	226.2	49.0	8.5	38.0	49.7	50.3	.99
1981[1]	4,213	44.1	185.9	9.0	24.1	3.4	8.2	9.2	11.4	4.1	232.0	77.3	9.2	52.1	52.7	57.4	1.01
1982[1]	4,250	54.1	230.0								250.8	92.0	8.5	74.1	54.5	60.4	1.08
1983[1]	4,275	48.0	205.0								277.9	109.8	7.5	136.8		62.2	1.19
1984[1]	4,300	38.4	165.1								251.8	124.0	7.6	214.8		65.8	
1985[1]	4,325	34.7	150.1								256.1	141.0	6.7	243.1		65.3	
1986[3]	4,350	46.0	200.1								292.1	130.4	7.4	274.2		64.0	

[1] Preliminary. [2] Amber, to Water White, Orange. [3] Forecast. *Source: Crop Reporting Board, U.S.D.A.* T.313

Interest Rates

Throughout 1986, the entire yield curve to maturity shifted downward, meaning that interest rates on credit instruments of varying lengths declined. The prime rate charged by banks on short-term business loans began the year at 9.5 percent, but fell steadily to 7.5 percent near year-end. The discount rate charged on loans to member banks by the Federal Reserve Bank of New York declined from 7.5 percent in December, 1985, to 5.5 percent 11 months later. The rate charged on loans by the federal intermediate credit banks decreased from 10.26 percent to 8.92 percent. Interest rates on conventional mortgages issued against new homes slid from an average of 10.44 percent to 9.46 percent late in the year.

The most prominent variable of demand was the sluggish pace of economic growth, brought about largely by near-depression conditions in agricultural and heavy-manufacturing sectors; both were hard hit by the slump in U.S. exports associated with the high value of the dollar against major overseas currencies. Mirroring the near-flatness of aggregate demand, the value of commercial and industrial loans was roughly $257 billion during 1986, just one percent above $255 billion in 1985. By contrast, real-estate loans were about $192 billion, as against $179 billion; the year-over-year increase came to more than seven percent. Were it not for real-estate loans and those the Federal Reserve System groups under the catch-all heading "Other Loans," many if not all of the rates in the structure would have been even lower.

The supply side of the interest-rate equation also contributed to the downward shift in the yield curve. The Federal Reserve System facilitated a steady increase in the money supply. Reserve bank credit outstanding rose about five percent, from $195 billion in late 1985 to more than $205 billion. Concurrently, member banks' reserve balances rose from an average of $28.6 billion in 1985 to an average of $32.1 billion in 1986, up over 12 percent. Free reserves of the member banks, which averaged −$204 million during 1985, averaged +$128 million in 1986. The pronounced slide in petroleum prices played a major role in the reduction of general price inflation; the premium demanded by leaders as a safeguard against inflation could be and was lowered.

Some analysts, assuming that spending by consumers, governments and domestic businesses will continue at or above 1986's rates and that exports will rise substantially as a result of the declining dollars, foresee acceleration in the general-inflation rate and significant upward movement in interest rates. This view is strengthened by the belief that oil-producing and exporting countries have learned that price-cutting does not reward them as much as price-fixing and that they will collaborate in restricting combined output in the interest of stabilizing, if not raising, the international market price of crude.

The opposing outlook holds that American exports are unlikely to increase much during 1987, even if the dollar remains devalued. The exchange rate is only one determinant of U.S. sales abroad; a true resurgence in exports will take time to develop. Moreover, many observers doubt that consumption spending, which has been debt-financed to a large degree, can continue at the torrid pace of 1983–86. There are well-grounded fears that the short-term economic effects of 1986's tax reforms will be more negative than positive. All these factors, it is argued, point toward further declines in interest rates or their stability at low levels in 1987.

U.S. Producer Commodity Price Index (Wholesale, All Commodities)   1967 = 100

Year	Jan.	Feb.	Mar.	Apr.	May	June	July	Aug.	Sept.	Oct.	Nov.	Dec.	Average
1980	254.9	260.2	261.9	262.8	264.2	265.6	270.4	273.8	274.6	277.8	279.1	280.8	268.8
1981	284.8	287.6	290.3	293.4	294.1	294.8	296.2	296.4	295.7	296.1	295.5	295.8	293.4
1982	298.3	298.6	298.0	298.0	298.6	299.3	300.4	300.2	299.3	299.8	300.3	300.7	299.3
1983	299.9	300.9	300.6	300.6	301.5	302.4	303.2	304.7	305.3	306.0	305.5	306.1	303.1
1984	308.0	308.9	311.0	311.3	311.5	311.3	311.9	310.7	309.3	309.4	310.3	309.8	310.3
1985	309.5	309.1	308.6	309.3	309.8	309.2	309.0	307.3	305.5	307.9	309.5	310.2	308.8
1986[1]	308.9	304.4	300.3	298.2	299.2	299.0	297.7	297.2	297.7	298.3			

[1] Preliminary.   *Source: Bureau of Labor Statistics*

T.315

U.S. Consumer Price Index   (Retail Price Index for All Items: Urban Consumers) 1967 = 100

Year	Jan.	Feb.	Mar.	Apr.	May	June	July	Aug.	Sept.	Oct.	Nov.	Dec.	Average
1980	233.2	236.4	239.8	242.5	244.9	247.6	247.8	249.4	251.7	253.9	256.2	258.4	246.8
1981	260.5	263.2	265.1	266.8	269.0	271.3	274.4	276.5	279.3	279.9	280.7	281.5	272.4
1982	282.5	283.4	283.1	284.3	287.1	290.6	292.2	292.8	293.3	294.1	293.6	292.4	289.1
1983	293.1	293.2	293.4	295.5	297.1	298.1	299.3	300.3	301.8	302.6	303.1	303.5	298.4
1984	305.2	306.6	307.3	308.8	309.7	310.7	311.7	313.0	314.5	315.3	315.3	315.5	311.1
1985	316.1	317.4	318.8	320.1	321.3	322.3	322.8	323.5	324.5	325.5	326.6	327.4	322.2
1986[1]	328.4	327.5	326.0	325.3	326.3	327.9	328.0	328.6	330.2	330.5			

[1] Preliminary.   *Source: Bureau of Labor Statistics*

T.316

INTEREST RATES

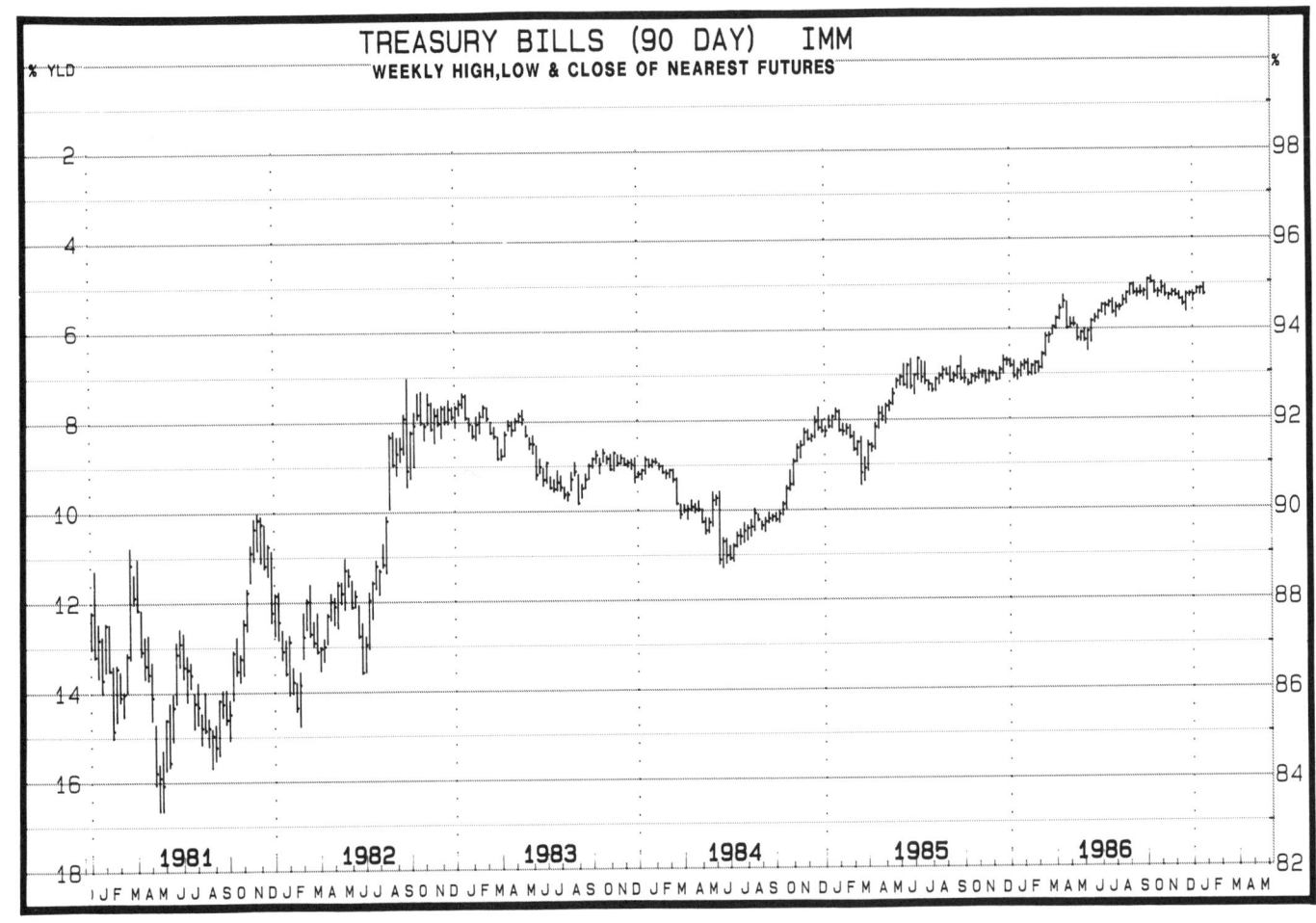

TREASURY BILLS (90 DAY) IMM
WEEKLY HIGH, LOW & CLOSE OF NEAREST FUTURES

Month–End Open Interest of 13 Wk.[1] Treasury Bill Futures in Chicago   In Thousands of Contracts

Year	Jan.	Feb.	Mar.	Apr.	May	June	July	Aug.	Sept.	Oct.	Nov.	Dec.
1980	30.2	25.0	28.5	28.2	24.7	25.2	22.9	23.1	21.4	24.2	39.2	42.9
1981	45.7	38.0	32.8	28.9	35.6	38.9	45.7	43.6	32.3	38.7	36.2	30.1
1982	33.9	33.0	36.5	43.9	52.5	41.4	52.2	59.6	51.1	45.8	50.1	49.0
1983	47.7	46.8	38.6	44.6	43.8	40.4	45.1	39.9	47.8	51.2	52.4	40.8
1984	48.7	50.8	48.8	55.8	52.4	47.5	43.4	44.9	36.8	47.8	45.7	40.7
1985	48.3	46.3	39.4	40.9	36.4	33.7	38.0	36.8	32.9	40.0	39.8	33.3
1986	37.9	47.6	49.2	47.6	39.9	39.0	40.7	39.6	35.0	37.0	37.6	37.6

[1] 90-day U.S. Treas. Bill.   *Source: International Monetary Market (Chicago)*   T.322

Volume of Trading of 13 Wk.[1] Treasury Bill Futures in Chicago   In Thousands of Contracts

Year	Jan.	Feb.	Mar.	Apr.	May	June	July	Aug.	Sept.	Oct.	Nov.	Dec.	Total
1980	237.5	245.4	290.3	350.1	321.2	250.7	224.4	204.9	231.1	274.3	287.7	401.1	3,338.8
1981	446.6	414.4	408.5	407.6	426.1	511.0	487.8	482.0	525.8	516.0	509.5	496.5	5,631.3
1982	503.5	465.5	638.7	529.1	595.4	546.0	615.2	738.4	628.6	521.4	442.4	374.7	6,598.8
1983	302.2	337.9	361.4	308.5	331.4	366.2	283.9	371.1	273.5	309.8	275.7	268.5	3,790.0
1984	200.0	213.4	304.9	300.2	489.1	342.8	315.1	242.5	201.6	203.6	264.0	215.5	3,293.0
1985	231.3	245.4	314.5	217.9	206.2	205.6	180.6	165.8	206.8	159.9	142.1	138.1	2,413.0
1986	175.0	215.4	149.5	212.8	169.7	152.9	117.8	135.7	160.8	114.2	106.3	105.1	1,815.0

[1] 90-day U.S. Treas. Bill.   *Source: International Monetary Market (Chicago)*   T.323

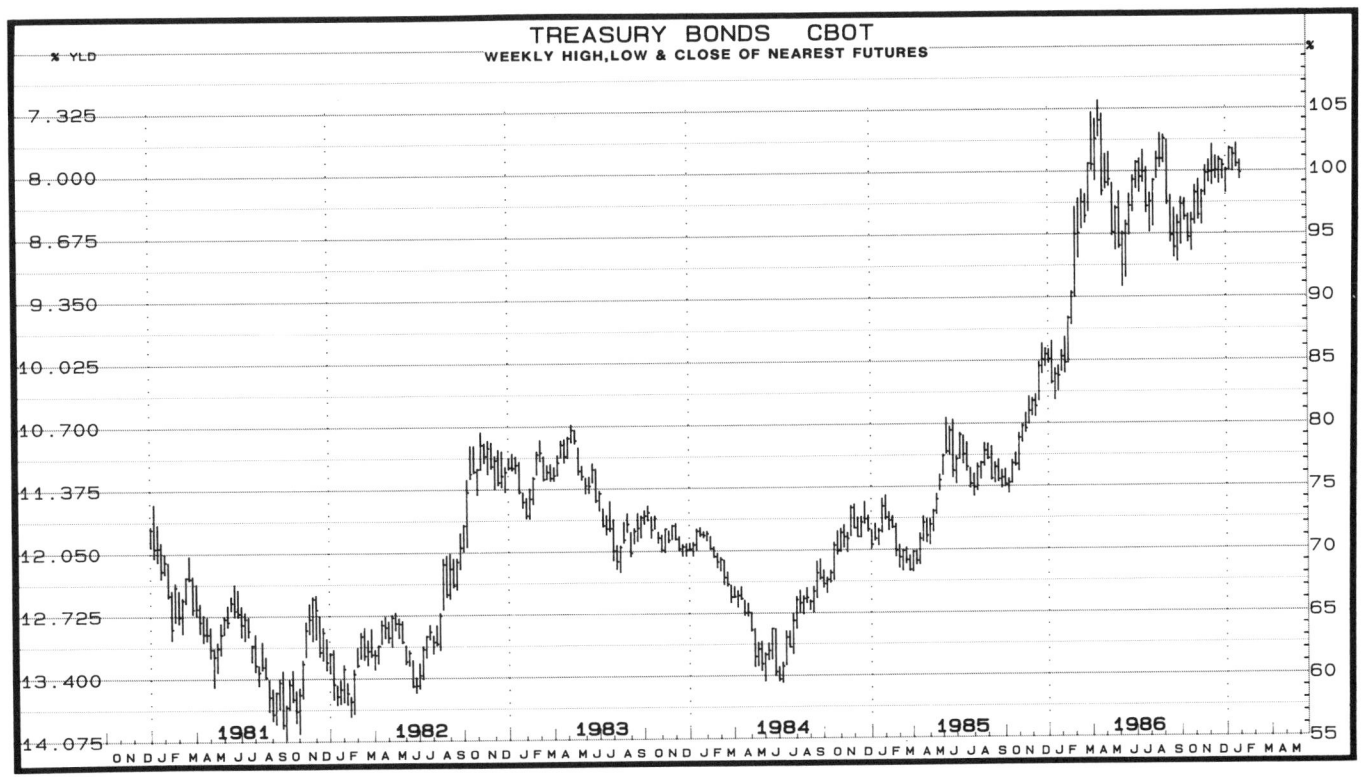

TREASURY BONDS CBOT
WEEKLY HIGH, LOW & CLOSE OF NEAREST FUTURES

Month–End Open Interest of Treasury Bond Futures in Chicago In Thousands of Contracts

Year	Jan.	Feb.	Mar.	Apr.	May	June	July	Aug.	Sept.	Oct.	Nov.	Dec.
1980	71.3	66.4	57.1	70.2	84.8	111.1	110.0	117.2	123.2	153.1	204.8	243.6
1981	240.7	223.6	226.1	230.4	241.3	290.9	315.1	295.4	240.5	257.7	248.7	221.7
1982	216.2	192.9	184.4	193.0	181.8	160.6	158.1	162.7	159.0	160.4	175.7	182.9
1983	177.6	142.9	147.5	142.1	130.3	144.5	165.1	142.5	150.0	172.9	193.4	183.7
1984	170.7	163.0	158.4	173.8	192.3	191.5	192.3	193.0	188.8	244.6	230.5	202.5
1985	208.3	224.2	214.1	220.2	210.8	197.6	223.1	215.8	234.5	309.1	306.3	300.6
1986	321.8	301.9	244.7	240.1	209.7	195.4	214.1	181.2	207.4	232.4	229.2	229.3

Source: Chicago Board of Trade   T.317

Volume of Trading of Treasury Bond Futures in Chicago In Thousands of Contracts

Year	Jan.	Feb.	Mar.	Apr.	May	June	July	Aug.	Sept.	Oct.	Nov.	Dec.	Total
1980	311.1	332.4	349.3	423.4	520.5	608.6	502.7	516.4	501.2	691.6	722.5	1,009.8	6,489.6
1981	846.7	868.6	975.9	998.9	1,178.1	1,094.4	1,081.8	1,191.5	1,313.7	1,289.1	1,691.5	1,377.9	13,908.0
1982	1,266.4	1,306.1	1,413.9	1,259.4	1,408.2	1,254.8	1,145.5	1,669.5	1,474.4	1,644.0	1,545.2	1,352.3	16,739.7
1983	1,333.9	1,447.8	1,600.4	1,262.9	1,679.2	1,704.8	1,579.0	2,312.7	1,605.7	1,839.4	1,687.0	1,497.8	19,551
1984	1,475.7	1,891.3	2,629.4	2,068.7	3,373.8	2,593.9	2,691.7	2,792.2	2,556.6	2,924.2	2,781.2	2,184.9	29,963
1985	2,974	3,250	2,906	2,272	3,339	3,755	3,308	3,409	3,149	3,558	4,118	3,965	40,448
1986	4,640	5,220	4,445	5,115	4,783	4,486	4,114	4,175	4,638	3,853	3,595	3,534	52,599

Source: Chicago Board of Trade   T.319

INTEREST RATES

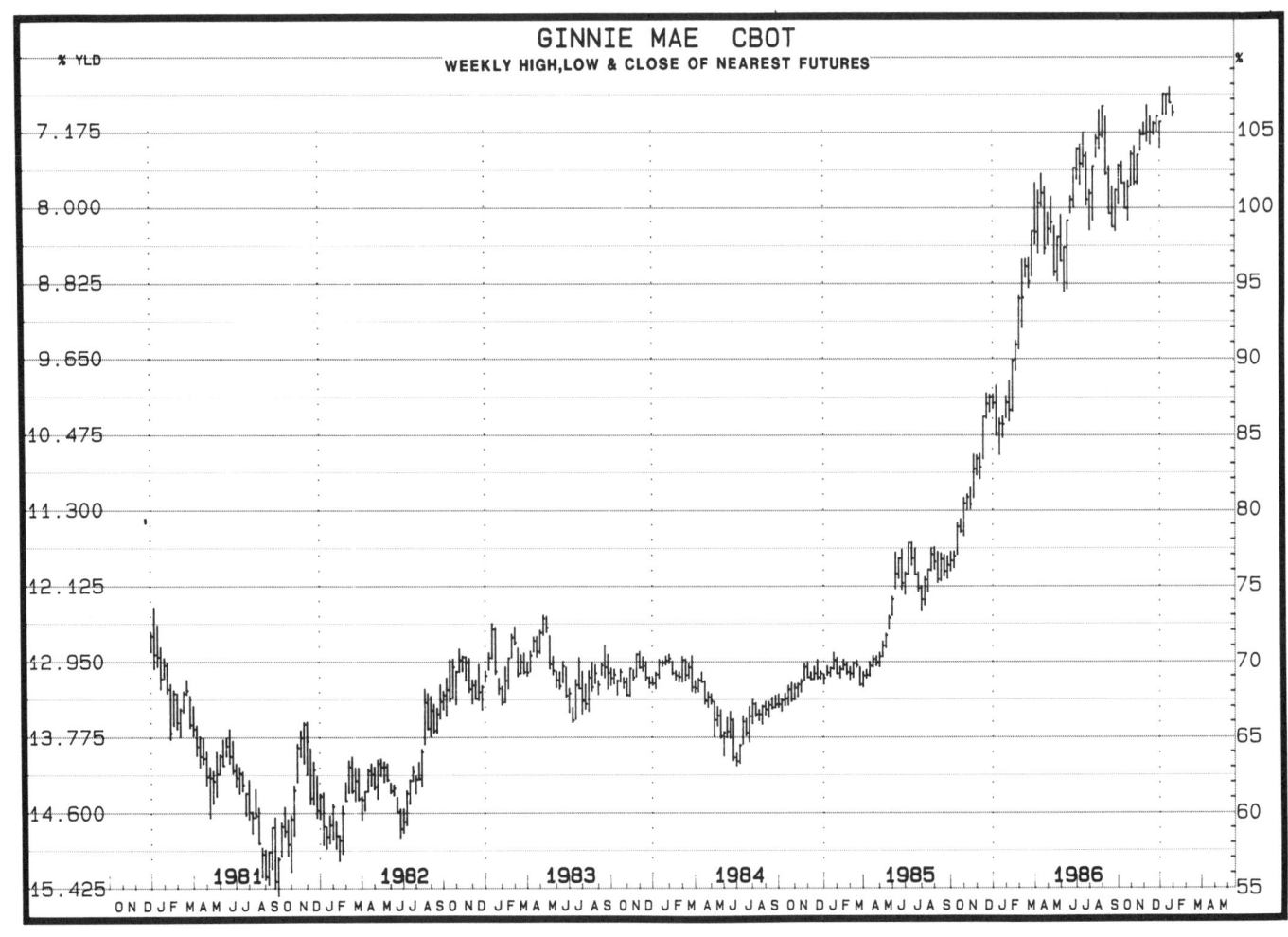

GINNIE MAE CBOT
WEEKLY HIGH, LOW & CLOSE OF NEAREST FUTURES

Month–End Open Interest of GNMA (CDR) Futures in Chicago   In Thousands of Contracts

Year	Jan.	Feb.	Mar.	Apr.	May	June	July	Aug.	Sept.	Oct.	Nov.	Dec.
1980	65.9	54.7	46.1	55.5	60.6	71.9	67.6	63.1	67.1	83.2	98.5	115.2
1981	97.0	97.1	99.8	105.7	107.5	121.0	133.9	116.6	96.5	95.2	82.7	77.2
1982	70.0	61.1	64.3	69.3	58.0	51.9	51.8	44.0	45.4	42.2	41.9	40.0
1983	34.9	35.4	45.6	41.3	42.4	44.9	50.0	52.4	45.6	42.2	43.4	37.4
1984	39.1	41.3	36.8	34.7	34.8	24.0	19.1	19.5	10.7	9.9	9.3	7.6
1985	7.4	5.4	3.4	4.1	4.5	3.1	4.5	4.3	4.2	4.3	4.4	2.9
1986	2.9	3.5	2.3	2.1	2.2	1.4	1.4	1.3	1.3	1.4	1.2	1.2

Source: Chicago Board of Trade   T.325

Volume of Trading of GNMA (CDR) Futures in Chicago   In Thousands of Contracts

Year	Jan.	Feb.	Mar.	Apr.	May	June	July	Aug.	Sept.	Oct.	Nov.	Dec.	Total
1980	170.0	155.5	156.3	190.3	219.7	248.4	162.0	151.6	133.9	205.0	214.5	318.7	2,326.3
1981	179.8	159.9	186.5	202.3	228.8	188.5	162.0	156.2	189.8	194.0	242.2	202.8	2,292.9
1982	188.8	184.1	182.6	140.6	159.3	156.3	154.8	222.7	170.5	218.3	143.6	134.0	2,055.6
1983	143.5	133.8	147.7	125.3	176.0	177.7	199.9	166.6	90.9	99.2	126.4	105.2	1,692.0
1984	67.3	118.2	168.9	80.6	97.4	96.4	57.6	62.7	48.6	24.6	23.9	16.2	862.5
1985	13.7	15.2	7.2	4.9	9.3	7.5	6.5	3.9	3.5	4.7	4.0	4.0	84.3
1986	2.5	4.0	2.7	3.5	3.3	1.6	1.0	1.1	1.4	.1	2.1	.1	24.1

Source: Chicago Board of Trade   T.324

High, Low & Closing Prices of June Treasury Bond Futures in Chicago   In 32nds of 100%

Year of Delivery		June	July	Aug.	Sept.	Oct.	Nov.	Dec.	Jan.	Feb.	Mar.	Apr.	May	June	Life of Delivery Range
				Year Prior to Delivery							Delivery Year				
1979	High	93–16	92–28	95–06	96–03	94–09	93–31	93–15	92–08	92–09	90–27	90–19	90–09	91–01	98–11
	Low	91–26	91–03	92–15	93–08	91–00	92–02	90–09	90–01	89–13	89–09	88–02	87–20	89–16	89–20
	Close	91–28	92–20	94–21	93–08	91–11	92–30	90–18	91–23	89–21	90–05	88–06	89–22	90–30	—
1980	High	92–13	92–12	91–18	89–18	87–13	84–14	85–00	82–24	75–07	71–24	77–27	83–20	87–07	95–31
	Low	89–24	89–27	89–09	87–05	78–11	78–15	80–20	74–07	63–15	64–30	67–12	77–00	78–09	63–15
	Close	91–27	90–20	89–11	87–21	80–12	83–01	82–29	75–04	69–00	67–27	77–02	79–14	85–25	—
1981	High	85–15	81–08	77–00	75–23	75–04	71–20	73–18	74–22	70–15	70–15	67–17	64–30	67–16	88–08
	Low	77–31	74–26	71–27	69–11	67–22	66–05	65–28	69–04	64–05	64–20	61–25	59–11	64–04	59–11
	Close	80–23	75–04	73–26	71–10	68–17	70–02	72–06	70–09	65–31	67–02	61–28	64–24	65–13	—
1982	High	69–29	66–23	64–30	62–04	61–09	66–24	66–14	62–16	62–26	64–08	64–27	65–05	62–18	74–20
	Low	65–28	62–28	59–04	56–08	56–12	58–30	60–20	58–05	57–10	60–22	61–05	62–15	59–01	56–08
	Close	65–30	63–01	59–17	57–03	59–05	65–21	62–04	61–01	61–14	61–30	63–06	62–27	59–24	—
1983	High	63–30	65–06	69–29	71–05	77–04	77–20	76–24	77–04	77–13	78–08	79–02	80–00	76–29	80–00
	Low	60–29	61–27	63–18	67–17	70–09	73–18	73–21	72–14	71–27	74–28	75–31	74–20	73–24	57–28
	Close	62–19	64–01	67–20	70–27	75–11	73–28	76–00	72–21	76–22	75–31	78–30	74–21	73–27	—
1984	High	74–29	73–05	71–12	72–02	75–15	70–31	70–20	71–06	70–26	68–22	67–00	64–31	63–21	77–28
	Low	72–00	67–26	66–28	68–09	69–18	68–23	68–05	68–30	67–22	65–22	64–17	59–16	60–11	58–28
	Close	73–03	68–16	68–12	71–23	69–19	70–17	69–15	70–07	68–07	66–07	64–22	60–05	61–19	—
1985	High	61–16	63–10	65–04	67–20	70–03	72–05	72–00	73–07	70–14	69–24	72–17	77–14	80–11	80–11
	Low	58–05	58–00	62–29	63–12	65–19	68–10	69–15	69–09	66–10	67–08	68–23	70–21	77–13	56–25
	Close	58–07	63–01	64–06	66–05	69–14	70–10	70–11	72–03	66–15	69–23	70–24	77–11	79–18	—
1986	High	76–07	76–00	75–05	74–29	76–17	79–25	84–25	85–10	96–01	102–12	105–15	101–11	98–01	105–15
	Low	72–10	71–09	71–19	71–26	72–04	75–15	78–04	80–20	82–26	92–06	97–29	93–19	90–22	56–29
	Close	74–05	72–09	74–02	73–14	76–01	79–15	84–08	84–03	94–00	102–10	100–24	93–28	96–13	—
1987	High	97–10	99–07	100–03	102–10	96–24	98–24	99–30							
	Low	88–12	92–16	93–01	89–17	91–21	93–24	96–24							
	Close	97–06	95–10	99–29	94–21	96–06	97–25	97–06							

Source: Chicago Board of Trade   T.320

High, Low & Closing Prices of June GNMA (CDR) Futures in Chicago   In 32nds of 100%

Year of Delivery		Apr.	May	June	July	Aug.	Sept.	Oct.	Nov.	Dec.	Jan.	Feb.	Mar.	Apr.	May	June	Life of Delivery Range
					Year Prior to Delivery								Delivery Year				
1979	High	92–15	91–18	89–23	90–08	91–31	92–16	91–13	90–29	90–17	89–16	89–22	88–20	88–09	87–16	88–19	96–20
	Low	91–12	89–10	88–06	87–31	89–24	90–11	88–26	89–15	87–21	87–17	87–12	87–19	85–27	85–14	86–23	85–14
	Close	91–15	89–10	88–07	89–31	91–14	90–24	89–00	90–02	87–30	89–04	87–26	88–00	85–31	86–28	87–20	—
1980	High	88–12	87–09	88–21	88–26	88–03	85–28	82–00	81–16	82–13	79–11	74–11	70–10	76–08	82–05	82–12	93–20
	Low	85–30	85–19	86–20	86–30	85–28	81–27	73–18	75–00	75–16	73–04	65–22	65–18	67–15	76–16	76–18	65–18
	Close	86–02	86–23	88–06	87–16	85–29	82–10	75–31	79–27	79–18	74–00	69–06	68–15	76–00	77–31	81–18	—
1981	High	77–00	82–12	82–02	77–22	74–24	73–15	73–12	70–20	73–04	74–07	70–15	69–16	67–01	64–00	65–16	91–02
	Low	69–02	76–07	76–06	72–23	69–28	68–11	67–06	66–13	65–31	69–00	65–14	65–19	61–30	59–21	63–03	58–21
	Close	76–16	77–15	77–15	73–03	71–14	70–05	67–31	69–07	71–27	70–08	66–21	66–21	62–01	63–23	63–22	—
1982	High	67–06	66–05	67–05	63–03	62–16	60–04	60–12	65–23	65–00	61–07	61–30	63–00	63–07	63–17	61–30	82–16
	Low	63–05	62–14	63–08	60–31	57–10	54–22	55–00	59–10	59–16	57–15	56–19	59–17	60–04	60–29	59–23	54–22
	Close	63–05	65–31	63–08	61–05	57–14	55–15	59–17	64–15	60–29	60–02	60–18	60–20	61–22	62–04	60–04	—
1983	High	62–15	62–23	60–15	61–27	66–12	67–11	69–10	70–00	68–21	71–19	70–27	71–10	72–00	73–00	69–30	73–00
	Low	59–17	60–16	57–21	58–14	60–07	63–19	65–16	65–30	65–22	66–15	66–04	68–04	69–09	68–09	67–01	54–28
	Close	61–03	60–25	59–05	60–28	63–31	66–04	68–11	66–02	68–11	66–22	70–12	69–07	71–27	68.10	67–05	—
1984	High	67–25	70–09	67–31	67–20	67–07	67–29	67–23	68–21	68–05	69–10	69–15	69–15	69–07	67–25	66–20	70–09
	Low	65–03	66–03	65–10	64–14	64–05	65–25	66–01	66–00	66–28	67–09	67–21	67–13	66–29	63–22	63–17	54–29
	Close	67–20	66–03	66–06	65–08	65–11	67–06	66–21	68–06	67–18	68–31	68–08	68–05	67–16	64–01	64–16	—
1985	High	66–02	64–16	62–13	64–05	64–13	66–14	67–13	68–20	68–17	68–12	69–14	69–08	70–10	74–06	77–10	77–10
	Low	64–07	59–29	60–16	60–25	63–19	63–29	65–11	66–11	67–07	66–26	68–07	68–03	68–27	69–21	74–23	57–12
	Close	64–09	60–05	60–22	63–12	64–04	65–18	66–12	67–15	67–22	67–26	68–09	69–00	69–23	74–01	76–28	—
1986	High	67–28	72–06	74–27	75–17	75–02	75–06	78–20	81–22	86–21	87–08	94–05	100–10	102–03	100–18	100–19	102–03
	Low	66–20	67–20	72–22	71–10	71–23	72–30	74–09	78–07	80–22	82–28	85–09	91–04	96–26	95–00	94–10	58–29
	Close	67–11	72–02	73–25	72–06	74–06	74–29	78–09	81–16	86–11	86–10	93–19	100–06	99–04	96–10	99–16	—

Source: Chicago Board of Trade   T.326

High, Low & Closing Prices of June 13 Wk. Treasury Bill Futures in Chicago   In Points of 100%

Year of Delivery		Year Prior to Delivery								Delivery Year						Life of Delivery Range
		Apr.	May	June	July	Aug.	Sept.	Oct.	Nov.	Dec.	Jan.	Feb.	Mar.	Apr.	May	June	
1978	High	93.59	93.31	93.69	93.57	93.50	93.51	93.28	93.28	93.29	93.17	93.15	93.33	93.49	93.48	93.41	93.80
	Low	92.52	92.53	93.19	93.01	92.95	93.10	92.80	92.92	92.95	92.63	92.78	93.00	93.03	93.09	93.20	92.26
	Close	92.60	93.22	93.61	93.15	93.38	93.29	92.97	93.25	93.13	92.99	93.13	93.02	93.13	93.21	93.23	—
1979	High	92.12	91.87	91.90	91.81	92.11	92.12	91.55	91.08	90.83	90.74	90.88	90.72	90.87	90.84	91.45	92.83
	Low	91.76	91.62	91.49	91.51	91.62	91.40	90.50	90.39	90.14	90.16	90.35	90.43	90.31	90.30	90.50	90.14
	Close	91.76	91.68	91.55	91.75	91.93	91.51	90.58	90.62	90.22	90.65	90.47	90.51	90.50	90.60	91.06	—
1980	High	90.91	91.55	92.59	92.50	92.30	91.65	91.41	91.22	91.01	90.50	89.05	86.40	89.94	92.73	93.97	93.97
	Low	90.51	90.48	91.34	91.54	90.93	90.36	88.10	88.85	89.21	88.37	86.06	84.20	85.40	89.75	92.00	84.20
	Close	90.62	91.46	92.32	91.89	91.11	91.03	89.29	90.55	90.17	88.84	86.49	85.82	89.90	92.30	92.12	—
1981	High	90.90	92.00	92.64	92.04	91.10	89.61	89.77	88.47	88.89	89.43	89.00	89.38	88.95	85.90	86.48	92.64
	Low	87.51	90.60	91.15	90.65	88.45	87.66	87.47	87.08	85.40	87.31	86.36	86.64	85.52	83.35	84.34	83.35
	Close	90.79	91.60	91.50	90.72	89.13	88.31	87.51	87.25	88.18	88.89	87.19	88.77	85.55	85.39	85.79	—
1982	High	89.20	87.81	88.47	87.86	87.52	87.00	87.61	89.54	89.42	87.85	87.48	88.32	88.16	88.94	88.46	91.26
	Low	87.09	86.03	87.40	86.91	85.95	85.48	85.53	87.42	86.93	85.85	85.45	86.46	86.67	87.41	87.16	85.45
	Close	87.10	87.73	87.92	87.21	86.08	85.60	87.55	89.19	87.76	86.90	86.92	86.83	87.88	88.57	87.18	—
1983	High	87.37	87.82	87.56	87.93	89.12	89.66	91.19	91.43	91.94	92.26	92.40	92.28	92.04	92.22	91.65	92.40
	Low	86.45	87.00	86.32	86.75	87.63	87.95	89.29	90.57	90.67	91.41	91.26	91.12	91.20	91.28	91.12	85.83
	Close	87.29	87.64	86.77	87.72	88.11	89.63	90.70	90.61	91.92	91.45	92.19	91.20	91.98	91.30	91.15	—
1984	High	91.23	91.47	90.60	90.44	90.06	90.51	90.66	90.57	90.47	90.82	90.78	90.48	90.18	90.36	90.37	91.47
	Low	90.63	90.33	90.11	89.55	89.30	89.57	90.32	90.13	90.00	90.32	90.28	89.79	89.77	89.44	90.12	86.50
	Close	91.23	90.34	90.39	89.60	89.59	90.46	90.39	90.39	90.44	90.72	90.38	89.97	89.94	90.18	90.28	—
1985	High	88.92	88.60	87.95	88.47	88.90	89.51	90.12	91.13	91.46	91.81	91.47	91.49	92.25	92.93	93.19	93.19
	Low	88.46	87.16	87.14	87.17	88.28	88.53	89.09	89.45	90.69	91.14	90.78	90.39	91.26	91.98	92.95	87.14
	Close	88.52	87.25	87.20	88.28	88.69	89.15	90.10	90.70	91.16	91.54	90.80	91.41	92.01	92.91	93.09	—
1986	High	90.64	91.68	92.24	92.41	92.17	92.32	92.59	92.91	93.30	93.18	93.53	94.07	94.71	94.20	93.74	94.71
	Low	89.86	90.36	91.58	91.50	91.51	91.74	92.03	92.41	92.72	92.63	92.93	93.38	93.96	93.68	93.48	86.43
	Close	90.37	91.66	91.89	91.62	91.93	92.19	92.51	92.91	93.14	93.13	93.39	94.07	94.11	93.71	93.49	—
1987	High	94.38	93.89	94.06	94.37	94.89	95.08	94.90	94.91	94.95							
	Low	93.55	93.17	92.94	93.91	94.22	93.46	94.50	94.55	94.62							
	Close	93.78	93.22	94.03	94.31	94.89	94.57	94.75	94.83	94.66							

Source: International Monetary Market (Chicago)   T.321

U.S. Industrial Production Index[1] (Seasonally Adjusted)   1977[3] = 100

Year	Jan.	Feb.	Mar.	Apr.	May	June	July	Aug.	Sept.	Oct.	Nov.	Dec.	Average
1978	140.0	140.3	142.1	144.4	144.8	146.1	147.1	148.0	148.6	149.7	150.6	151.8	146.1
1979	152.0	152.5	153.5	151.1	152.7	153.0	153.0	152.1	152.7	152.7	152.3	152.5	152.5
1980	153.0	152.8	152.1	148.2	143.8	141.4	140.3	142.2	144.4	146.6	149.2	150.4	147.0
1981	151.4	151.8	152.1	151.9	152.7	152.9	153.9	153.6	151.6	149.1	146.3	143.4	151.0
1982[3]	105.4	107.0	105.8	104.5	103.6	103.0	102.5	102.0	101.3	100.5	100.6	100.5	103.1
1983	102.5	103.3	104.2	105.6	106.9	107.8	109.8	111.6	113.7	114.4	114.8	115.5	109.2
1984	118.5	119.3	119.9	120.5	121.0	121.9	122.8	123.0	122.4	122.1	122.7	122.7	121.8
1985	122.7	123.2	123.4	123.3	123.6	123.6	123.4	124.4	124.3	123.6	124.8	125.6	124.5
1986[2]	126.2	125.3	123.6	124.7	124.2	124.2	124.9	125.1	125.2	125.2			

[1] Total Index of the Federal Reserve Index of Quantity Output.   [2] Preliminary.   [3] Data prior to 1982 are for 1967 = 100.
Source: Federal Reserve System   T.318

High, Low & Closing Prices of June Eurodollar Futures in Chicago   In Points of 100%

Year of Delivery		Year Prior to Delivery								Delivery Year						Life of Delivery Range
		Apr.	May	June	July	Aug.	Sept.	Oct.	Nov.	Dec.	Jan.	Feb.	Mar.	Apr.	May	June	
1985	High	87.35	86.89	86.18	87.03	87.47	88.30	88.94	89.92	90.23	90.88	90.50	90.25	91.31	92.25	92.59	92.59
	Low	86.74	84.83	85.17	85.27	86.78	86.69	87.66	88.85	89.39	89.83	89.42	88.97	90.03	91.00	92.18	84.83
	Close	86.80	84.99	85.30	86.82	86.99	87.82	88.87	89.47	89.88	90.57	89.45	90.23	91.05	92.24	92.44	—
1986	High	89.44	90.47	91.15	91.16	90.98	91.14	91.55	91.93	92.34	92.19	92.55	93.04	93.69	93.42	93.02	93.69
	Low	88.34	88.93	90.38	90.17	90.25	90.40	90.83	91.40	91.59	91.53	91.76	92.39	92.95	92.81	92.82	86.73
	Close	88.94	90.46	90.79	90.31	90.72	90.97	91.46	91.82	92.14	92.02	92.39	93.03	93.25	92.93	93.00	—
1987	High	93.20	92.81	92.90	93.28	94.02	94.13	94.02	94.08	94.15							
	Low	92.44	92.00	91.82	92.80	93.13	93.35	93.58	93.71	93.84							
	Close	92.65	92.10	92.84	93.28	94.08	93.66	93.91	94.01	93.86							

Source: International Monetary Market (IMM)—Chicago Mercantile Exchange   T.0564

Month-End Open Interest of Eurodollar Futures in Chicago   In Thousands of Contracts

Year	Jan.	Feb.	Mar.	Apr.	May	June	July	Aug.	Sept.	Oct.	Nov.	Dec.
1984	50.3	60.6	62.0	74.2	90.3	89.3	95.1	94.6	78.1	89.9	96.2	85.1
1985	105.5	105.5	98.4	110.0	130.7	116.3	128.9	131.4	122.0	144.2	165.3	121.5
1986	145.3	155.3	142.7	164.0	173.9	155.9	171.5	203.5	216.6	227.4	234.3	214.4

Source: International Monetary Market (IMM)—Chicago Mercantile Exchange   T.0564A

Volume of Trading of Eurodollar Futures in Chicago   In Thousands of Contracts

Year	Jan.	Feb.	Mar.	Apr.	May	June	July	Aug.	Sept.	Oct.	Nov.	Dec.	Total
1984	104.8	127.4	235.4	202.2	434.7	448.1	438.6	354.5	435.3	491.1	532.4	388.4	4,193
1985	524.7	723.6	877.2	764.7	753.7	891.5	798.0	697.5	769.1	694.3	695.4	710.7	8,901
1986	888.5	825.1	627.9	933.7	982.6	1,018.1	755.3	847.2	1,288.7	1,046.7	836.3	774.8	10,825

Source: International Monetary Market (IMM)—Chicago Mercantile Exchange   T.0564B

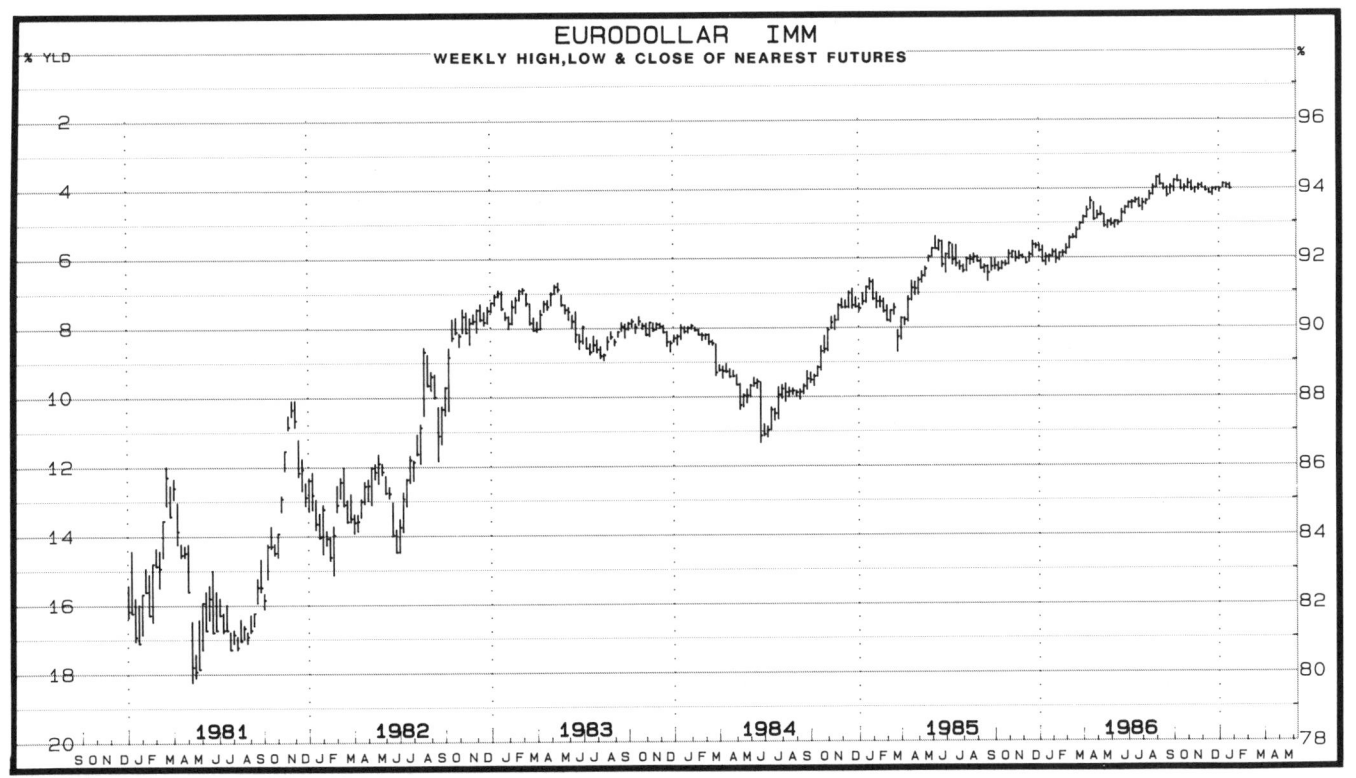

EURODOLLAR IMM
WEEKLY HIGH, LOW & CLOSE OF NEAREST FUTURES

INTEREST RATES

High, Low & Closing Prices of June T-Note Futures in Chicago   In 32nds of 100%

Year of Delivery		June	July	Aug.	Sept.	Oct.	Nov.	Dec.	Jan.	Feb.	Mar.	Apr.	May	June	Life of Delivery Range
				Year Prior to Delivery							**Delivery Year**				
1985	High	70–15	73–23	75–03	77–07	79–03	81–07	80–22	82–03	80–28	79–18	82–08	86–27	89–18	89–18
	Low	69–23	71–16	73–30	74–15	75–24	78–05	78–16	78–19	77–19	77–11	78–23	80–27	87–00	69–23
	Close	69–17	73–23	74–10	76–02	78–25	79–09	79–07	81–07	77–28	79–14	81–02	86–24	88–20	—
1986	High	85–17	84–29	84–24	84–15	86–10	88–19	92–17	92–21	100–03	102–26	105–08	102–13	101–02	105–08
	Low	81–15	81–00	81–14	82–18	82–31	85–23	87–22	89–05	91–00	97–05	100–18	97–12	95–19	74–30
	Close	82–30	81–27	83–27	83–26	85–28	88–13	92–02	92–07	98–15	102–24	102–08	97–23	100–06	—
1987	High	—	101–14	102–21	105–00	101–18	102–20	103–21							
	Low	—	98–00	98–29	97–31	99–00	100–12	102–00							
	Close	—	99–21	102–21	99–24	101–15	102–08	102–14							

Source: Chicago Board of Trade   T.0565

Month-End Open Interest of T-Note Futures in Chicago   In Thousands of Contracts

Year	Jan.	Feb.	Mar.	Apr.	May	June	July	Aug.	Sept.	Oct.	Nov.	Dec.
1984	19.6	23.3	21.8	28.1	32.5	32.3	36.5	32.8	30.3	34.7	33.7	36.0
1985	41.4	48.7	43.9	45.1	50.7	49.4	62.1	57.7	57.2	70.5	64.5	70.5
1986	79.1	76.5	66.3	63.8	74.5	66.7	67.7	54.8	55.1	61.6	61.6	53.7

Source: Chicago Board of Trade   T.0565A

Volume of Trading of T-Note Futures in Chicago   In Thousands of Contracts

Year	Jan.	Feb.	Mar.	Apr.	May	June	July	Aug.	Sept.	Oct.	Nov.	Dec.	Total
1984	59.7	110.5	126.8	105.3	199.1	145.1	147.2	162.8	139.5	149.2	166.0	150.7	1,662
1985	171.8	216.0	215.9	175.8	274.9	266.9	219.4	282.9	212.7	234.3	297.5	292.5	2,860
1986	269.7	401.4	383.1	381.7	434.8	470.3	309.7	363.1	459.5	319.9	328.1	305.2	4,426

Source: Chicago Board of Trade   T.0565B

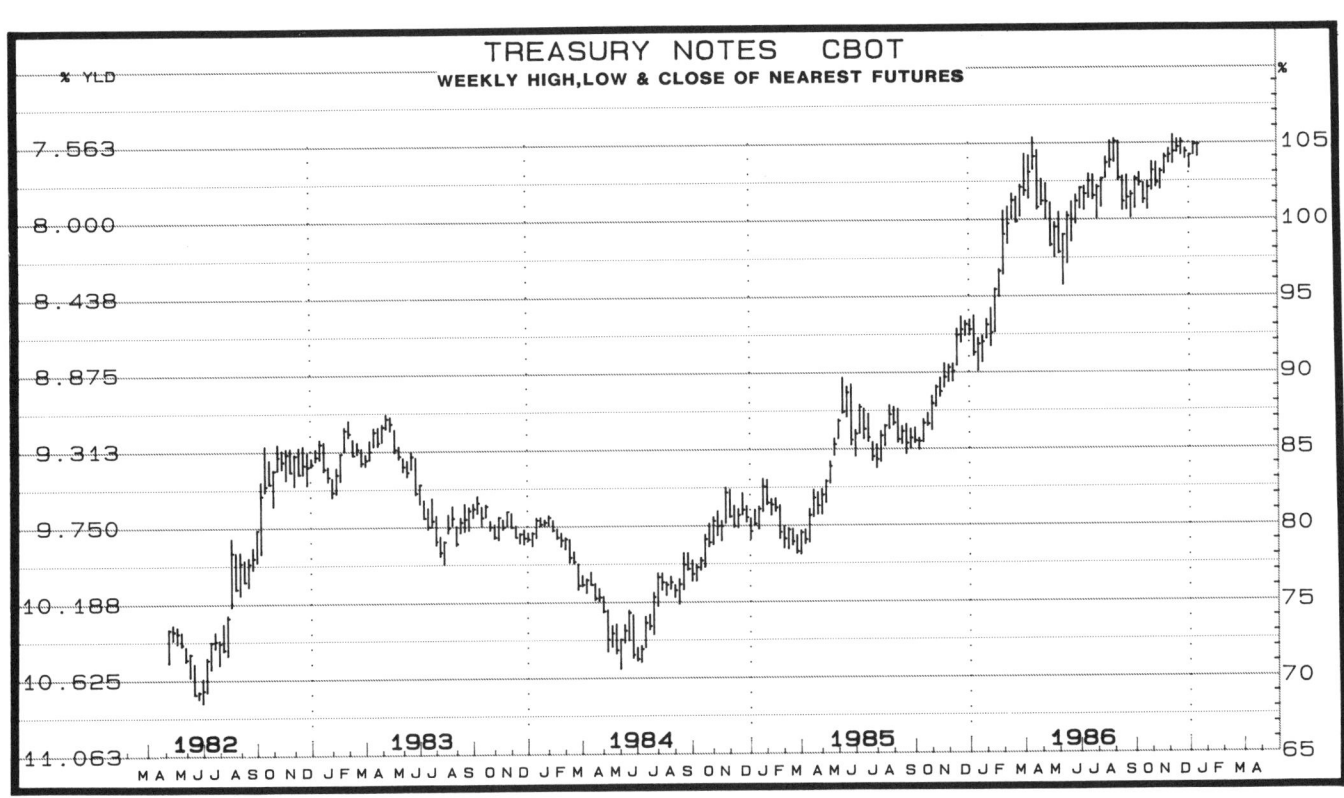

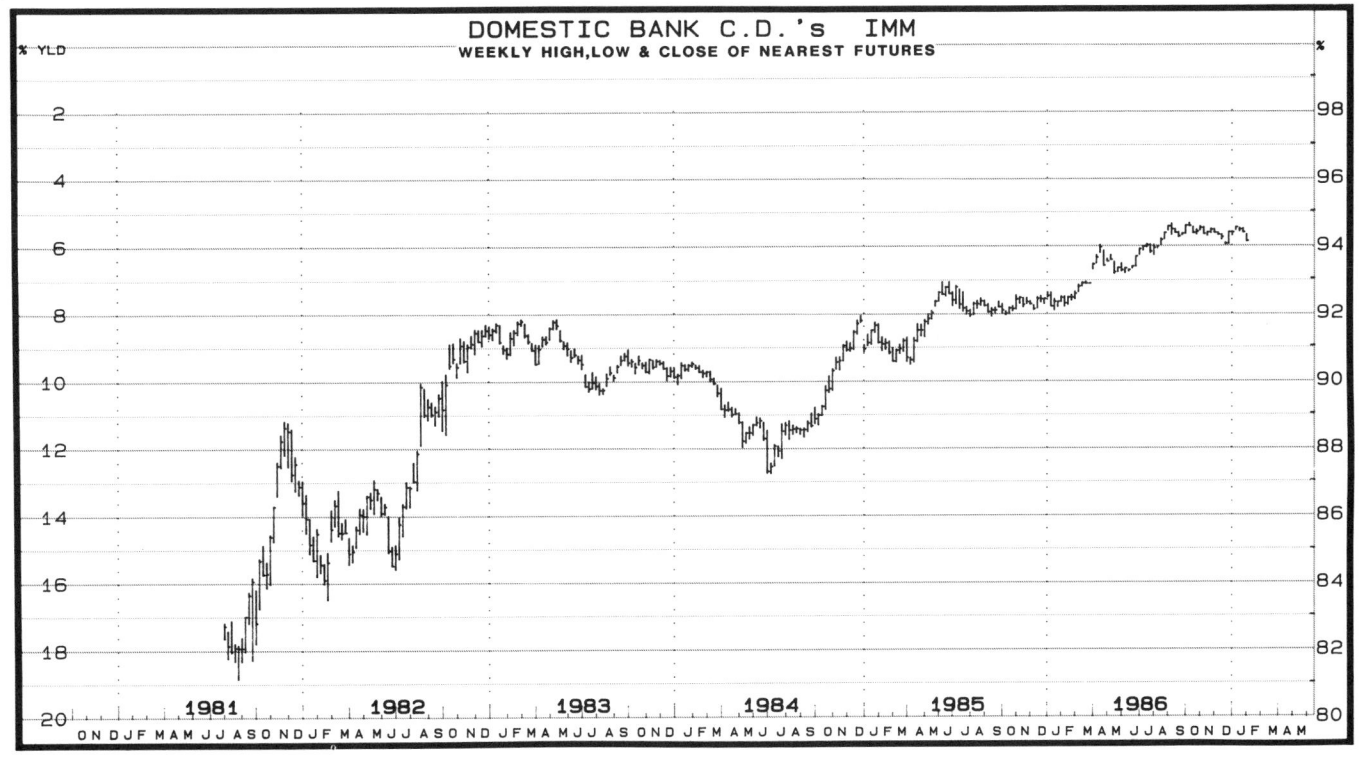

DOMESTIC BANK C.D.'s IMM
WEEKLY HIGH, LOW & CLOSE OF NEAREST FUTURES

U.S. Federal Funds Rate   In Percent

Year	Jan.	Feb.	Mar.	Apr.	May	June	July	Aug.	Sept.	Oct.	Nov.	Dec.	Annual
1976	4.87	4.77	4.84	4.82	5.29	5.48	5.31	5.29	5.25	5.03	4.95	4.65	5.05
1977	4.61	4.68	4.69	4.73	5.35	5.39	5.42	5.90	6.14	6.47	6.51	6.56	5.54
1978	6.70	6.78	6.79	6.89	7.36	7.60	7.81	8.04	8.45	8.96	9.76	10.03	7.93
1979	10.07	10.06	10.09	10.01	10.24	10.29	10.47	10.94	11.43	13.77	13.18	13.78	11.19
1980	13.82	14.13	17.19	17.61	10.98	9.47	9.03	9.61	10.87	12.81	15.85	18.90	13.36
1981	19.08	15.93	14.70	15.72	18.52	19.10	19.04	17.82	15.87	15.08	13.31	12.37	16.38
1982	13.22	14.78	14.68	14.94	14.45	14.15	12.59	10.12	10.31	9.71	9.20	8.95	12.26
1983	8.68	8.51	8.77	8.80	8.63	8.98	9.37	9.56	9.45	9.48	9.34	9.47	9.09
1984	9.56	9.59	9.91	10.29	10.32	11.06	11.23	11.64	11.30	9.99	9.43	8.38	10.23
1985	8.35	8.50	8.58	8.27	7.97	7.53	7.88	7.90	7.92	7.99	8.05	8.27	7.41
1986	8.14	7.86	7.48	6.99	6.85	6.92	6.56	6.17	5.89	5.85	6.04		

Source: U.S. Dept. of Commerce.

T.318a

LONG-TERM INTEREST RATES

PERCENT PER ANNUM

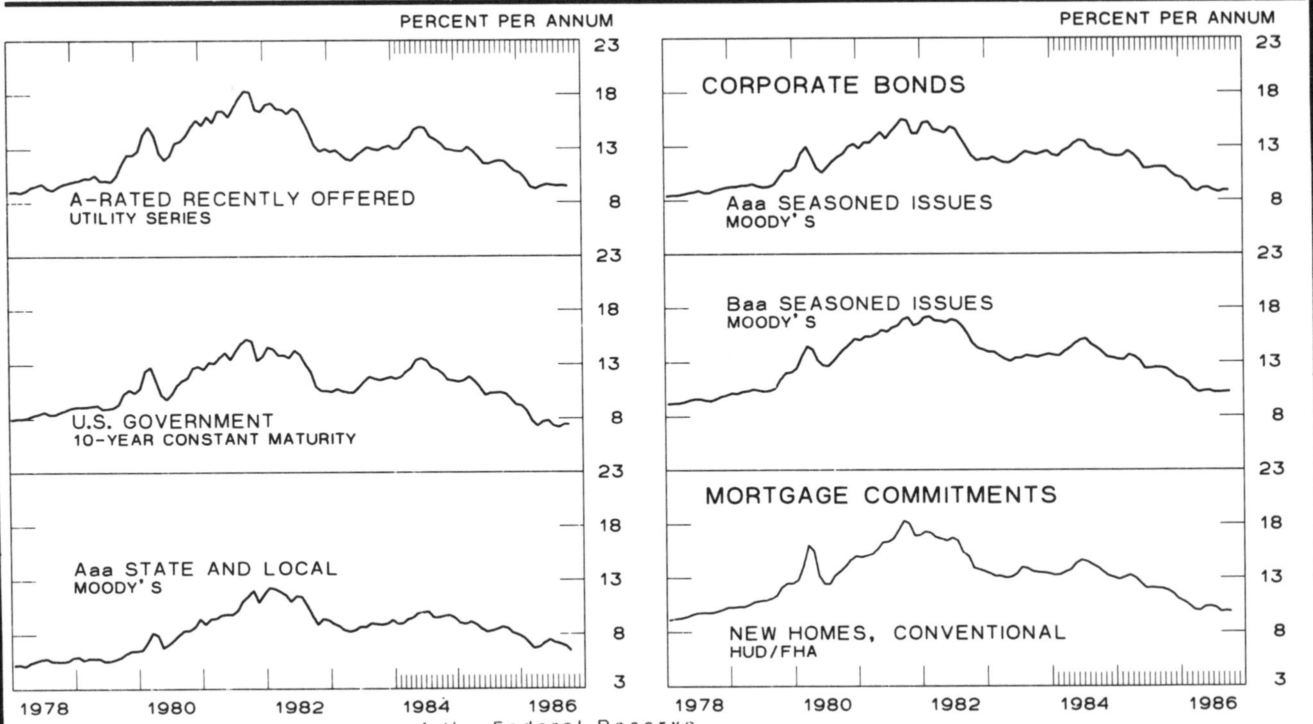

PERCENT PER ANNUM

A-RATED RECENTLY OFFERED
UTILITY SERIES

CORPORATE BONDS

Aaa SEASONED ISSUES
MOODY'S

U.S. GOVERNMENT
10-YEAR CONSTANT MATURITY

Baa SEASONED ISSUES
MOODY'S

Aaa STATE AND LOCAL
MOODY'S

MORTGAGE COMMITMENTS

NEW HOMES, CONVENTIONAL
HUD/FHA

1978   1980   1982   1984   1986

1978   1980   1982   1984   1986

SOURCE: Board of Governors of the Federal Reserve

SHORT-TERM INTEREST RATES

MONTHLY AVERAGES, EXCEPT FOR DISCOUNT AND PRIME RATES, WHICH ARE EFFECTIVE DATES OF CHANGE

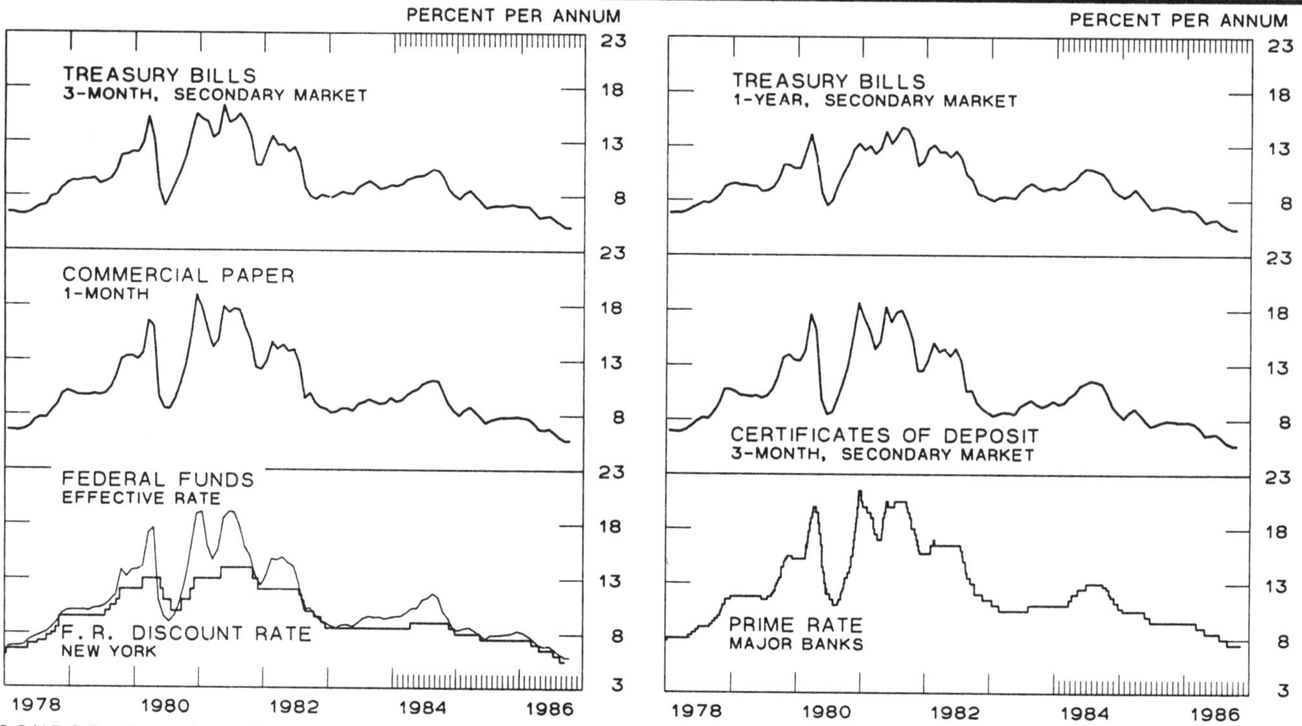

PERCENT PER ANNUM

PERCENT PER ANNUM

TREASURY BILLS
3-MONTH, SECONDARY MARKET

TREASURY BILLS
1-YEAR, SECONDARY MARKET

COMMERCIAL PAPER
1-MONTH

CERTIFICATES OF DEPOSIT
3-MONTH, SECONDARY MARKET

FEDERAL FUNDS
EFFECTIVE RATE

F.R. DISCOUNT RATE
NEW YORK

PRIME RATE
MAJOR BANKS

1978   1980   1982   1984   1986

1978   1980   1982   1984   1986

SOURCE: Board of Governors of the Federal Reserve

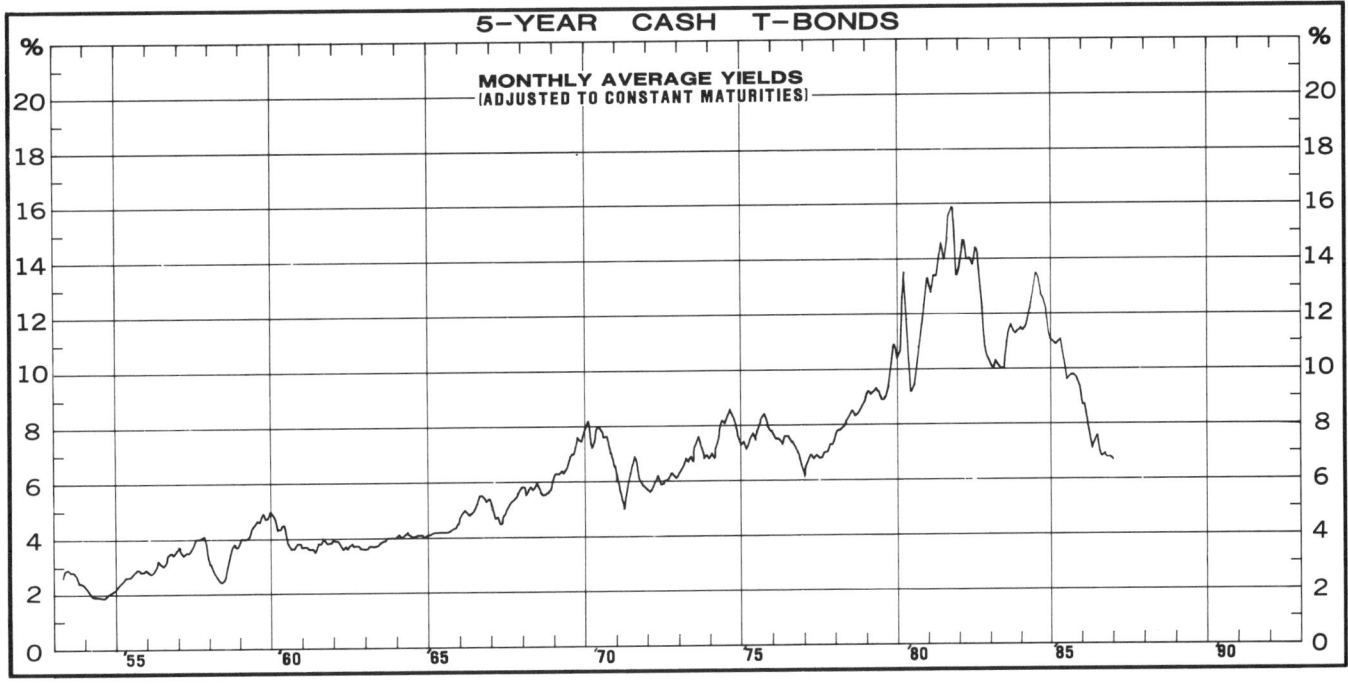

U.S. Money Supply M1 in 1982[2] Dollars   In Billions of Dollars

Year	Jan.	Feb.	Mar.	Apr.	May	June	July	Aug.	Sept.	Oct.	Nov.	Dec.	Average
1976	222.5	223.9	224.1	224.5	225.0	224.1	223.8	223.9	223.7	224.9	225.0	225.3	224.2
1977	221.2	220.9	221.0	221.5	221.2	220.9	221.2	221.2	221.8	222.6	222.8	223.1	221.6
1978	224.3	223.1	222.7	223.6	223.7	223.3	222.6	222.1	222.6	221.0	221.2	221.4	222.6
1979	222.4	220.8	220.6	221.9	219.6	219.7	219.3	218.3	216.8	215.0	213.4	211.9	218.3
1980	209.9	209.0	206.2	201.6	199.3	199.7	201.7	203.9	204.7	204.9	203.6	200.2	204.2
1981	200.5	200.0	200.3	202.0	199.9	198.2	197.1	196.5	194.9	194.3	194.8	196.4	197.8
1982	199.2	197.9	198.0	198.2	197.1	195.3	194.5	196.1	198.5	200.6	203.2	205.6	198.7
1983	206.7	209.2	211.4	211.5	213.4	214.6	215.8	216.6	216.7	217.4	217.6	217.7	213.8
1984[2]	501.7	502.2	503.9	504.3	506.4	508.8	507.1	506.2	507.5	504.9	508.2	510.8	506.6
1985	513.8	518.1	518.3	519.6	524.6	530.9	534.6	541.2	546.1	546.5	548.7	552.5	532.9
1986[1]	551.1	556.7	565.6	574.0	584.2	588.6	596.5	605.7	608.5	614.9			

[1] Preliminary.   [2] Data prior to 1984 are in 1972 dollars.   *M1*—This measure is currency, travelers checks, plus demand deposits at commercial banks and interest-earning checkable deposits at all depository institutions.   *Source: Federal Reserve System*   T.327

U.S. Money Supply M2 in 1982[2] Dollars   In Billions of Dollars

Year	Jan.	Feb.	Mar.	Apr.	May	June	July	Aug.	Sept.	Oct.	Nov.	Dec.	Average
1976	774.0	784.7	790.1	796.8	803.7	803.6	805.1	811.2	815.6	822.6	828.5	835.4	805.9
1977	840.1	841.9	845.1	848.3	852.7	853.7	856.1	859.2	861.7	865.3	866.5	868.1	854.9
1978	686.6	867.6	867.2	867.0	865.4	863.2	862.1	863.0	863.1	862.0	862.4	861.7	864.4
1979	860.7	857.4	856.8	857.0	853.9	853.2	850.7	848.9	845.5	838.7	833.0	827.7	848.6
1980	818.6	815.6	808.9	799.3	798.2	800.1	810.1	814.6	812.0	808.8	807.7	800.0	812.3
1981	787.2	786.3	788.3	793.8	790.9	788.5	784.9	786.4	784.2	787.9	792.0	798.6	789.1
1982	802.7	803.0	807.5	810.4	809.2	805.4	806.3	812.8	819.3	822.9	830.1	841.1	814.2
1983	857.2	873.5	879.7	880.0	883.2	887.1	889.0	890.6	893.0	898.0	900.7	902.4	888.7
1984[2]	2,079	2,087	2,092	2,098	2,108	2,114	2,115	2,120	2,129	2,135	2,153	2,171	2,117
1985	2,191	2,204	2,200	2,197	2,208	2,227	2,238	2,251	2,259	2,259	2,258	2,263	2,229
1986[1]	2,258	2,274	2,297	2,330	2,350	2,358	2,382	2,399	2,406	2,424			

[1] Preliminary.   [2] Data prior to 1984 are in 1972 dollars.   *M2*—This measure adds to M1 overnight repurchase agreements (RP's) issued by commercial banks and certain overnight Eurodollars (those issued by Caribbean branches of member banks) held by U.S. nonbank residents, general purpose and broker/dealer money market mutual fund shares (MMMF), and savings and small-denomination time deposits.
Source: Federal Reserve System   T.328

INTEREST RATES

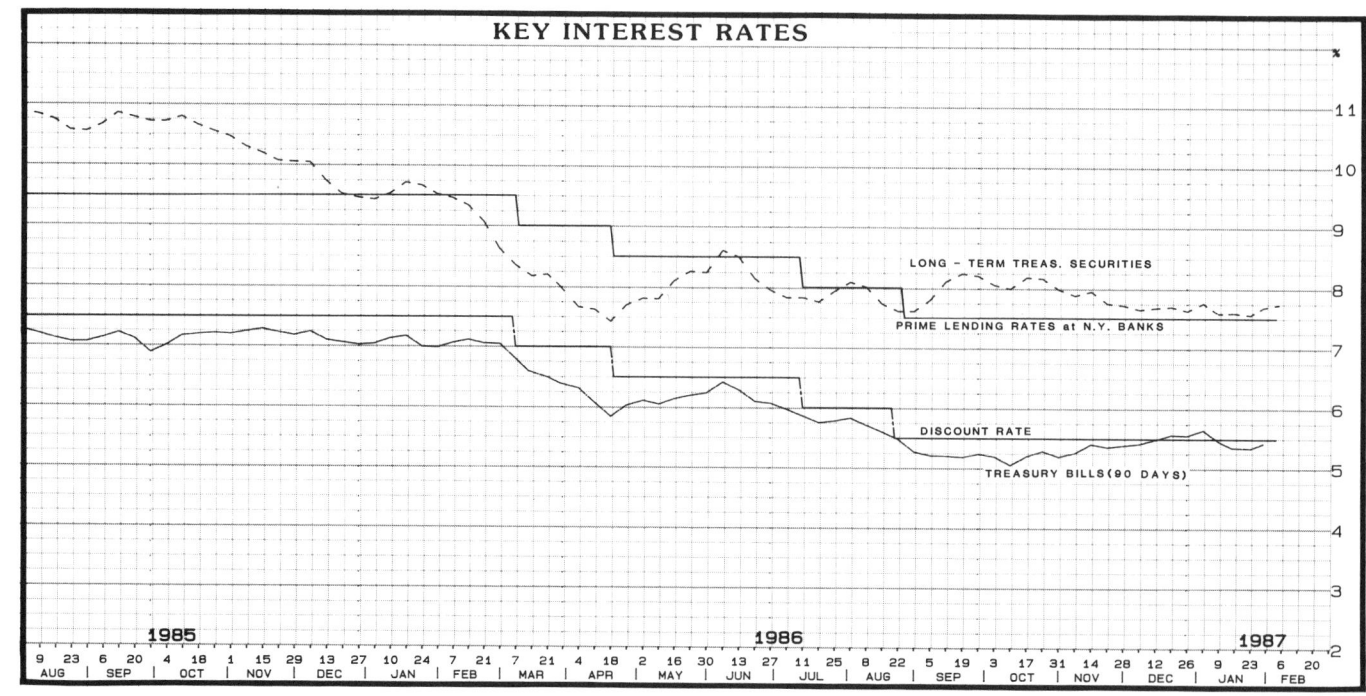

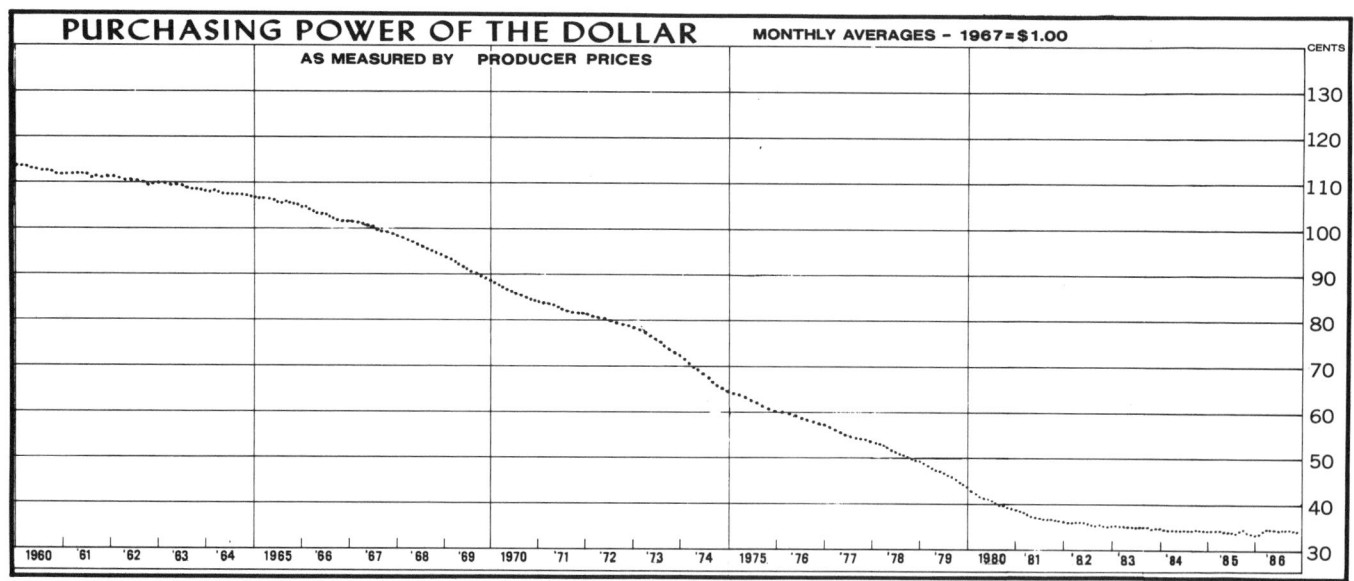

U.S. Gross National Product, National Income, and Personal Income   In Billions of Current Dollars[1]

Year	Gross National Product					National Income					Personal Income				
	I	II	III	IV	Annual Avg.	I	II	III	IV	Annual Avg.	I	II	III	IV	Annual Avg.
1977	1,835	1,895	1,954	1,989	1,918	1,471	1,528	1,585	1,618	1,551	1,476	1,514	1,558	1,604	1,538
1978	2,032	2,140	2,203	2,282	2,156	1,653	1,737	1,792	1,858	1,760	1,638	1,692	1,748	1,809	1,722
1979	2,336	2,378	2,455	2,503	2,418	1,907	1,941	1,994	2,025	1,967	1,872	1,917	1,982	2,034	1,951
1980	2,573	2,579	2,639	2,736	2,632	2,076	2,073	2,118	2,200	2,117	2,092	2,118	2,186	2,265	2,165
1981	2,979	3,018	3,100	3,114	3,053	2,388	2,415	2,483	2,487	2,444	2,441	2,485	2,568	2,591	2,521
1982	3,113	3,160	3,179	3,213	3,166	2,483	2,514	2,528	2,548	2,518	2,614	2,656	2,684	2,729	2,671
1983	3,266	3,367	3,444	3,546	3,406	2,599	2,686	2,742	2,852	2,720	2,753	2,813	2,847	2,942	2,839
1984	3,671	3,744	3,800	3,846	3,765	2,963	3,010	3,052	3,102	3,032	3,034	3,077	3,140	3,190	3,110
1985[2]	3,909	3,965	4,031	4,088	3,998	3,157	3,201	3,243	3,287	3,222	3,253	3,299	3,323	3,383	3,315
1986[2]	4,149	4,176	4,241			3,341	3,376	3,396			3,433	3,483	3,499		

[1] Seasonally adjusted at annual rates.   [2] Preliminary.   [3] Forecast.   *Source: U.S. Dept. of Commerce*

T.329

Iron and Steel

Strikes and bankruptcies littered the landscape of the iron and steel industry in 1986; 1987 is certain to be a year when the industry will wrestle with similar difficulties. The decline of the dollar on overseas financial markets may be the one bright spot where the industry can look to alleviate some of the pressing problems of undercapacity. But, domestic labor relations will continue to pose problems for both management and labor in the immediate future.

Domestic iron ore consumption for January–October, 1986, was only 47.6 million tons, down 11 percent from the same 1985 period. Total 1985 consumption was estimated to be 64.4 million tons; 1986's total is expected to be down as well.

U.S. production of iron ore for the first nine months of 1986 was 31.65 million tons, down some 18 percent from 1985's three-quarter total of 38.22 million tons. Iron ore imports in January–October, 1986, totaled 14.17 million long tons, versus 12.99 million for the comparable 1985 period, about a nine-percent gain. Canada was the leading shipper to the U.S. in the 10-month period, providing 7,244 million long tons. Venezuela, Brazil and Liberia were also major suppliers.

In May, 1986, the iron ore industry in the U.S. and Canada underwent major restructuring aimed at lowering pellet costs and improving the financial health of several of its members. In one instance, Bethlehem Steel Corporation became the largest shareholder of Iron Ore Company of Canada, the nation's largest producer. IOC's extensive facilities in Canada will help lower Bethlehem's costs.

On July 17, 1986, LTV Corp filed for bankruptcy, a decision which had far-reaching implications for the industry as a whole. LTV had been the steel industry's second-largest producer; it was the largest industrial corporation ever to file for bankruptcy.

Contract negotiations between USX (formerly United States Steel Corporation) and the United Steel Workers of America broke down in August, 1986, triggering the first nationwide work stoppage against that company in 27 years. The strike affected 22,100 workers at 16 locations in eight states. USX had started to shut down furnaces at its steel mills a week before in anticipation of the walkout.

USX is seeking significant wage, benefit, and work rule concessions from the union in order to remain competitive. Analysts estimate the steel component of USX is losing $43 million a month as a result of the job action, which was still continuing in 1987.

It is estimated that 1986 domestic production of raw steel will be 85 million tons, down from 1985's estimated 89 million tons. Apparent consumption of iron and steel in 1986 is estimated at 102 million tons, down from 1985's estimated consumption of 107.7 million tons. From a 1983 base, demand for steel is expected to increase at an average annual rate of about two percent through 1990.

1986 imports of steel were expected to be lower than 1985's estimated 25.5 million tons, as import restrictions took effect. As part of a five-year program to limit imports of steel, voluntary restraint agreements were negotiated with most major exporters and cases were pursued against unfairly priced steel.

World Production of Raw Steel (Ingots & Castings)   In Millions of Short Tons

Year	Belgium	Brazil	Canada	Czech-oslovakia	China	France	Italy	Japan	Rep. of Korea	Poland	Spain	South Africa	United Kingdom	United States	USSR	West Germany	World Total
1979	14.9	15.3	17.7	16.3	38.0	25.8	26.7	123.2	8.4	21.2	13.6	9.8	23.6	136.3	164.4	50.8	821.1
1980	13.7	16.9	17.5	16.8	40.9	25.5	29.2	122.8	9.4	21.5	13.9	10.0	12.4	111.8	163.1	48.3	789.5
1981	13.6	14.6	16.3	16.8	39.2	23.4	27.3	112.1	11.9	17.3	14.2	9.9	17.2	120.8	163.6	45.9	778.9
1982	10.9	14.3	13.0	16.5	41.0	20.3	26.4	109.7	13.0	16.3	14.5	9.1	15.1	74.6	162.2	39.6	709.7
1983	11.2	16.2	14.1	16.6	44.0	19.4	23.9	107.1	13.1	17.9	14.0	7.9	16.5	84.6	168.1	39.4	730.6
1984[1]	12.5	20.3	16.2	16.3	47.8	20.9	26.5	116.4	14.4	18.2	14.9	8.6	16.7	92.5	170.0	43.4	782.0
1985[2]	11.8	22.5	16.5	16.6	51.5	20.8	26.2	116.1	14.9	17.7	15.7	8.3	17.3	88.3	171.0	44.6	788.1

[1] Preliminary.   [2] Estimate.   *Source: Bureau of Mines*   T.330

Average Wholesale Prices of Iron and Steel in the U.S.   In Dollars Per Net Ton

Year	Pig Iron — Bessemer Neville Isl., Pa.	Iron Age Composite	No. 2 F.O.B. Birmingham	Steel Billets Pitts.	No. 1 Heavy Melting Steel Scrap — Pitts.	No. 1 Heavy Melting Steel Scrap — Chicago	Tin Plate (¼ Lb.)	Hot Rolled Sheet[2]	Steel Bars — Hot Rolled	Steel Bars — Cold Finished	Structural Shapes	Carbon Steel Plates	Cold Rolled Strip	Galvanized Sheets	Wire Rods-Chi. $Gr. Ton
1978	190.00	198.31	191.00	282.88	78.48	73.98	18.0–20.4	15.36	14.01	22.80	15.73	16.53	22.49	20.21	16.80
1979	190.00	203.00	191.00	302.00	100.77	96.69	19.1–23.4	17.05	16.20	25.07	17.36	18.46	24.13	22.40	17.22
1980	200.83	203.00	191.00	348.70	95.48	86.70	23.3–24.9	18.21	19.59	28.95	18.98	20.57	27.15	23.56	19.09
1981	209.67	204.66	205.33	358.00	100.57	91.76	24.9–26.7	20.13	16.95	29.45	21.32	23.04	30.23	26.05	20.27
1982	213.00	213.00	213.00	358.00	66.47	57.78	26.3–27.9	20.80	17.23	31.06	22.90	24.25	29.75	26.90	20.48
1983	213.00	213.00	213.00	358.00	76.99	72.42	27.7–29.3	22.16	20.25	28.50	22.90	25.45	33.45	28.23	20.48
1984	213.00	213.00	213.00	368.00	92.71	83.12	29.0–30.7	23.60	22.08	29.87	22.78	24.50	35.30	30.15	20.48
1985[1]	213.00	213.00	213.00	378.00	77.43	72.89	30.7–31.9	23.60	24.10	32.00	23.78	24.50	37.24	30.15	20.48
1986[3]					74.87	73.49									

Cents Per Pound at Pittsburgh (for Tin Plate through Galvanized Sheets columns)

[1] Preliminary.   [2] 10 gauge.   [3] Estimate.   *Source: American Metal Market*   T.337

IRON AND STEEL

Salient Statistics of Steel in the United States   In Millions of Short Tons

Year	Value of — Exports —(Million $)—	Value of — Imports —(Million $)—	Production — Steel Ingots and Castings — Basic Oxygen	Open Hearth Acid	Open Hearth Basic	Bessemer	Electric[3]	Total	Alloy Steel[2] Stainless	Alloy Steel[2] Other	Alloy Steel[2] Total	Shipments of Steel Products — Domestic Consumption	Shipments of Steel Products — Export
1977	2,284	5,936	77.4	5	20.0	5	27.9	125.3	1.9	15.3	17.2	88.0	3.1
1978	2,285	7,658	83.5	5	21.3	5	32.2	137.0	2.0	18.2	20.2	94.6	3.3
1979	2,804	7,823	83.3	5	19.2	5	33.9	136.3	2.1	18.0	20.1	98.3	2.0
1980	3,728	7,792	67.6	5	13.1	5	31.2	111.8	1.7	15.4	17.1	83.9	2.6
1981	3,649	11,286	73.2	5	13.5	5	34.1	120.8	1.7	17.6	19.3	88.5	1.8
1982	2,734	10,394	45.3	5	6.1	5	23.2	74.6	1.2	9.2	10.4	61.6	.8
1983	1,783	7,238	52.1	5	6.0	5	26.6	84.6	1.8	9.1	10.9	67.6	.5
1984	1,627	11,495	52.8	5	8.3	5	31.4	92.5	1.8	10.8	12.6	73.7	.4
1985[1]	1,476	11,019	51.9	5	6.4	5	29.9	88.3	1.7	9.9	11.6	73.0	

[1] Preliminary.   [2] Included under total steel production.   [3] Includes crucible steels.   [4] Estimate.   [5] No longer published.
Sources: American Iron & Steel Institute; U.S. Bureau of Mines   T.331

U.S. Production of Steel Ingots, Rate of Capability Utilization[1]   In Percent

Year	Jan.	Feb.	Mar.	Apr.	May	June	July	Aug.	Sept.	Oct.	Nov.	Dec.	Average
1978	77.2	80.1	83.1	88.5	91.5	91.1	85.1	86.3	88.6	89.8	89.4	87.7	86.8
1979	83.5	87.9	94.5	93.4	94.8	93.7	89.9	86.0	82.8	84.4	80.6	78.0	87.8
1980	82.7	85.3	88.4	83.0	69.6	58.4	53.1	54.4	62.6	72.2	79.5	77.8	72.8
1981	79.9	83.7	88.6	87.7	86.2	81.5	77.6	77.3	75.9	68.7	62.8	58.6	78.3
1982	59.3	60.9	61.7	55.2	50.9	47.7	43.8	42.4	41.9	40.2	35.9	34.0	48.4
1983	43.4	49.0	55.5	58.9	57.9	56.5	54.3	55.1	57.8	60.2	58.7	54.7	55.4
1984	69.6	76.0	79.1	80.8	79.8	71.4	65.3	60.5	57.7	58.4	57.8	52.4	68.4
1985[2]	60.9	66.1	72.1	71.6	68.9	66.3	62.1	63.2	63.4	65.2	64.7	59.7	66.1
1986[2]	69.4	71.8	71.9	73.5	69.5	63.5	59.2	52.8	54.3	56.8			

[1] Based on tonnage capability to produce raw steel for a full order book.   [2] Preliminary.   *Source: American Iron and Steel Institute*   T.332

United States Production of Steel Ingots   In Thousands of Short Tons

Year	Jan.	Feb.	Mar.	Apr.	May	June	July	Aug.	Sept.	Oct.	Nov.	Dec.	Total
1978	10,301	9,643	11,083	11,528	12,320	11,861	11,388	11,550	11,467	12,105	11,654	11,812	137,031
1979	11,105	10,562	12,576	12,196	12,789	12,230	11,821	11,309	10,541	10,810	9,997	9,996	136,341
1980	10,701	10,332	11,439	10,658	9,226	7,501	6,796	7,018	7,767	9,442	10,057	10,180	111,835
1981	10,590	10,028	11,744	11,243	11,423	10,451	10,160	10,120	9,618	9,003	7,962	7,672	120,828
1982	7,737	7,178	8,049	7,006	6,678	6,050	5,719	5,538	5,299	5,262	4,546	4,456	74,577
1983	5,570	5,676	7,127	7,292	7,412	6,993	6,921	7,020	7,134	7,692	7,263	6,991	83,379
1984	7,970	8,142	9,056	8,997	9,174	7,945	7,460	6,915	6,378	6,703	6,422	6,013	92,528
1985[1]	6,984	6,851	8,269	7,872	7,830	7,292	7,010	7,130	6,924	7,351	7,051	6,728	88,259
1986[1]	7,665	7,171	7,947	7,787	7,616	6,730	6,352	5,668	5,644	6,087			

[1] Preliminary.   *Source: American Iron and Steel Institute*   T.333

Shipments of Steel Products[1] by Market Classifications in the United States   In Thousands of Net Tons

Year	Appliances, Utensils & Cutlery	Auto-motive	Containers & Packaging	Construction	Contractors Products	Electrical Mach. & Equipment	Export	Machinery, Industrial Equip. & Tools	Oil and Gas	Rail Transportation	Steel for Converting & Processing[2]	Steel Service Center & Distributors	All Other[3]	Total Shipments
1977	2,129	21,490	6,714	7,553	4,500	2,639	1,076	5,566	3,650	3,238	3,679	15,346	13,567	91,147
1978	2,094	21,253	6,595	9,612	3,480	2,811	1,224	5,992	4,140	3,549	4,612	17,333	15,240	97,935
1979	2,141	18,624	6,770	10,058	4,021	2,821	2,010	6,027	3,738	4,127	4,728	18,263	16,934	100,262
1980	1,726	12,156	5,549	12,149	3,362	2,441	2,597	4,566	5,368	3,178	3,881	16,174	10,706	83,853
1981	1,775	13,154	5,292	8,446	3,230	2,600	1,844	4,624	6,238	2,162	2,338	17,637	16,672	87,014
1982	1,337	9,288	4,470	6,283	2,287	2,003	832	2,584	2,745	1,020	3,222	13,067	12,429	61,567
1983	1,618	12,320	4,532	7,271	2,703	2,335	544	2,486	1,296	937	1,211	16,710	13,621	67,584
1984	1,635	12,554	4,337	8,614	2,563	2,363	428	2,737	1,727	1,036	4,686	17,234	13,098	73,012
1985	1,182	12,725	4,069	6,407	2,663	1,845	494	2,129	1,745	1,059	4,971	17,548	15,861	72,698

[1] All grades including carbon, alloy & stainless steel.   [2] Net total after deducting shipments to reporting companies for conversion or resale.   [3] Includes agricultural; bolts, nuts, rivets & screws; forgings (other than automotive); shipbuilding & marine equipment; aircraft; mining, quarrying & lumbering; other domestic & commercial equipment machinery; ordnance & other direct military; & shipments of non-reporting companies.   *Source: American Iron and Steel Institute*   T.334

Net Shipments of Steel Products in the United States
(All Grades, Including Carbon, Alloy & Stainless Steel) In Thousands of Net Tons

Year	Cold Finished Bars	Rails & Accessories	Wire & Wire Products	Tin Mill Products	Plates	Sheets & Strip	Hot Rolled Bars	Pipe & Tubing	Shapes & Steel Piling	Reinforcing Bars	Hot Rolled Sheets	Cold Rolled Sheets	Semi-Finished	Alloy	Stainless
1981	1,620	1,458	1,694	4,927	7,397	36,924	6,628	10,286	4,903	4,371	13,451	14,396	5,598	10,595	1,163
1982	1,015	782	1,308	4,321	4,146	7,730[2]	4,757	5,026	3,563	4,049	9,052	11,132	3,693	6,726	894
1983	1,179	884	1,359	4,308	3,816	5,793[2]	5,129	3,242	3,622	4,275	11,619	13,781	3,861	6,154	1,137
1984[1]	1,158	1,239	1,222	4,062	4,342	8,357[2]	5,791	4,276	3,983	4,315	13,133	13,664	4,314	7,482	1,248
1985[1]	1,261	888	1,136	3,772	4,313	10,543[2]	5,526	4,096	4,843	4,444	12,952	13,574	4,350	7,422	1,251

[1] Preliminary. [2] Excludes Hot & Cold rolled sheets & strips. Shown elsewhere. *Source: American Iron & Steel Institute* T.335

U.S. Foreign Trade of Iron & Steel Products   In Thousands of Short Tons

	U.S. Imports of Iron & Steel Pdts.						Exports of Iron & Steel Pdts. from U.S.					
Year	Steel Mill Pdts.	Other Steel Pdts.	Iron Pdts. & Ferro-alloys	Grand Total Quantity	Mil. $	Iron & Steel Scrap	Steel Mill Pdts.	Other Steel Pdts.	Iron Pdts. & Ferro-alloys	Grand Total Quantity	Mil. $	Iron & Steel Scrap
1981	19,898	822	97	20,818	11,286	556	2,904	444	209	3,557	3,649	6,415
1982	16,536	745	104	17,385	10,394	474	1,842	342	183	2,367	2,734	6,804
1983	17,034	804	125	17,964	7,238	641	1,199	247	144	1,589	1,783	7,520
1984[1]	26,169	1,146	173	27,488	11,495	577	977	261	174	1,413	1,627	9,498
1985[2]	24,278	1,211	218	25,707	11,019	611	930	200	136	1,266	1,476	9,950

[1] Preliminary. [2] Estimate. *Source: U.S. Bureau of Mines; American Metal Market* T.336

World Production of Pig Iron (Excludes Ferro-Alloys)   In Millions of Short Tons

Year	Australia	Belgium	Brazil	Canada	China	Czech.	France	W. Germany	India	Italy	Japan	Luxembourg	Poland	Un. Kingdom	USSR	United States	World Total
1981	7.5	10.7	11.9	10.7	37.7	10.4	19.0	35.1	10.4	13.5	88.2	3.2	10.3	10.4	118.1	73.8	553.2
1982	6.6	8.6	11.9	8.8	39.2	10.5	16.6	30.4	10.6	12.7	85.6	2.9	9.4	9.2	117.0	43.3	504.0
1983	5.6	8.8	14.3	9.4	41.2	10.4	15.3	29.3	10.0	11.4	80.4	2.6	10.7	10.4	120.9	48.8	510.2
1984[1]	5.9	9.9	19.0	10.6	44.1	10.5	16.6	33.3	10.3	12.8	88.6	3.1	11.0	10.5	122.2	52.0	546.3
1985[2]	6.2	9.6	20.9	10.6	48.1	10.5	17.0	34.7	10.8	12.9	88.8	3.0	11.0	11.6	121.0	50.0	555.2

[1] Preliminary. [2] Estimated. *Source: Bureau of Mines* T.338

U.S. Pig Iron Production (Excluding Production of Ferro-Alloys)   In Thousands of Short Tons

Year	Jan.	Feb.	Mar.	Apr.	May	June	July	Aug.	Sept.	Oct.	Nov.	Dec.	Total
1981	6,603	6,108	7,193	6,755	6,938	6,408	6,268	6,259	5,889	5,419	4,782	4,750	73,570
1982	4,489	4,169	4,622	3,967	3,904	3,595	3,516	3,277	3,160	3,077	2,648	2,712	43,136
1983	3,192	3,264	4,206	4,333	4,376	4,060	4,213	4,245	4,159	4,317	4,119	4,084	48,706
1984	4,310	4,497	5,083	5,077	5,166	4,565	4,329	4,057	3,473	3,739	3,817	3,694	51,904
1985[1]	3,969	3,897	4,684	4,512	4,553	4,301	4,114	4,110	3,883	4,060	3,999	3,930	50,446
1986[1]	4,297	4,002	4,341	4,341	4,284	3,697	3,526	2,966	2,982	3,161			

[1] Preliminary. *Source: American Iron and Steel Institute* T.341

Salient Statistics of Ferrous Scrap & Pig Iron in the U.S.   In Millions of Short Tons

	Consumption: Ferrous Scrap & Pig Iron Charged To											Stocks—Dec. 31 Ferrous Scrap & Pig Iron at Consumers'		
	Mfg. of Pig Iron & Steel Ingots & Castings			Iron Foundries & Misc. Users			Mfg. of Steel Castings (Scrap)	All Uses			Imports of Scrap[2]	Exports of Scrap[3]			
Year	Scrap	Pig Iron	Total	Scrap	Pig Iron	Total		Ferr. Scrap	Pig Iron	Grand Total			Scrap	Pig Iron	Total Stocks
1981	68.3	73.0	143.6	14.2	2.0	16.2	2.6	85.1	75.0	162.1	.6	6.4	8.1	.9	9.0
1982	43.7	43.3	87.0	10.9	1.1	12.0	1.8	56.4	44.4	100.8	.5	6.8	6.4	.6	7.0
1983	49.0	49.0	98.0	11.4	1.0	12.4	1.5	61.8	50.1	111.9	.6	7.5	5.8	.3	6.1
1984[1]	51.8	52.0	103.8	12.3	1.2	13.5	1.6	65.7	53.2	118.9	.6	9.5	5.3	.3	5.6
1985[4]	53.2	49.8	103.0	15.2	1.5	16.7	2.1	70.5	51.4	122.0	.6	10.0	4.8	.3	5.1

[1] Preliminary. [2] Including tinplate scrap. [3] Excluding tinplate circles, strips, cobbles, etc. [4] Estimate. *Source: Bureau of Mines* T.342

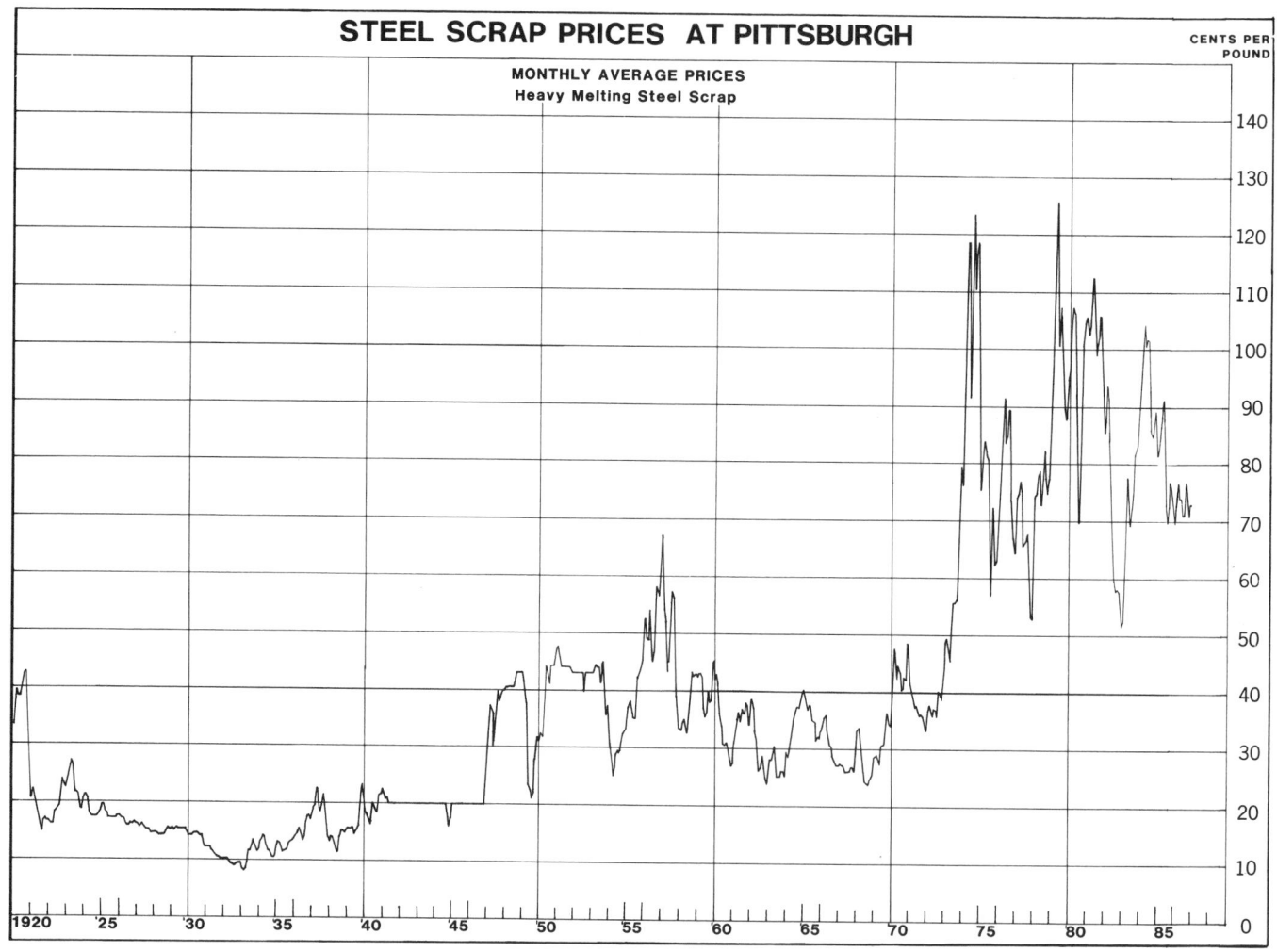

STEEL SCRAP PRICES AT PITTSBURGH

CENTS PER POUND

MONTHLY AVERAGE PRICES
Heavy Melting Steel Scrap

Consumption of Pig Iron in the U.S., by Type of Furnace or Equipment In Thousands of Net Tons

Year	Open Hearth	Electric	Cupola	Basic Oxy. Consen.	Air & Other Furn.	Direct Casting	Total	Year	Open Hearth	Electric	Cupola	Basic Oxy. Concen.	Air & Other Furn.	Direct Castings	Total
1978	13,444	1,440	1,056	69,028	398	3,055	88,420	1982	3,635	496	481	38,553	141	1,102	44,409
1979	12,865	905	1,026	68,526	397	3,738	87,458	1983	3,918	341	425	44,330	91	965	50,070
1980	8,606	855	698	56,414	299	2,182	69,053	1984[1]	5,720	368	469	45,551	92	1,002	53,202
1981	8,867	583	685	62,162	254	2,489	75,040	1985[2]	4,737	503	501	44,515	56	1,100	51,411

[1] Preliminary.   [2] Estimate.   *Source: Bureau of Mines*

T.340

Wholesale Price of No. 1 Heavy Melting Steel Scrap at Chicago In Dollars Per Gross Ton

Year	Jan.	Feb.	Mar.	Apr.	May	June	July	Aug.	Sept.	Oct.	Nov.	Dec.	Average
1977	69.00	69.00	69.65	70.79	64.62	58.36	57.00	57.00	55.00	49.00	43.95	59.26	60.21
1978	71.00	71.00	71.48	76.00	70.32	72.73	76.63	74.48	69.00	69.45	79.35	86.35	73.98
1979	93.00	103.00	121.73	110.10	91.91	106.62	98.62	89.96	86.00	86.22	91.00	91.28	96.69
1980	96.14	99.00	97.00	90.54	69.62	62.24	67.45	77.95	87.24	92.22	97.29	103.68	86.70
1981	95.00	91.11	105.14	107.55	97.50	88.00	88.45	97.76	92.52	82.64	75.00	74.41	91.76
1982	83.00	78.63	69.78	63.86	58.30	51.77	49.00	51.73	48.95	47.86	45.00	45.48	57.78
1983	56.14	67.00	77.70	70.33	65.00	70.52	70.08	74.00	78.00	78.00	78.30	84.00	72.42
1984	88.29	89.00	87.09	85.14	85.00	84.71	79.00	78.00	81.00	81.09	83.00	76.00	83.12
1985	78.86	82.16	84.76	79.59	68.00	62.00	64.24	73.00	72.00	71.87	69.00	69.19	72.89
1986	74.23	76.89	74.05	74.00	74.00	71.00	71.00	76.71	73.14	70.87	73.00	73.00	73.49

Source: American Metal Market

T.339

World Production of Iron Ore[3], by Specified Countries (Gross Weight)   In Millions of Long Tons

Year	Aus- tralia	South Africa	Brazil	Canada	Chile	China	France	Maur- itania	India	Liberia	Spain	Sweden	Peru	United States	USSR[1]	Vene- zuela	World Total[1]
1976	91.8	15.4	92.6	54.7	9.9	59.1	44.5	9.5	43.2	20.2	8.1	29.4	7.0	80.0	237.3	18.4	885.1
1977	94.4	26.1	80.7	56.7	7.5	49.2	36.1	9.6	41.9	17.4	8.2	24.4	6.2	55.8	238.0	13.5	827.8
1978	81.8	23.1	83.6	41.1	6.7	68.9	32.9	6.8	38.2	17.7	8.4	21.1	4.8	81.6	242.5	13.3	833.3
1979	90.3	31.1	102.4	58.9	7.0	65.0	31.1	9.2	39.2	18.1	8.7	25.8	5.4	85.7	237.9	15.0	888.8
1980	94.0	25.9	112.9	48.0	8.5	67.0	28.5	8.8	41.3	17.9	9.1	26.8	5.6	69.6	240.8	15.8	877.2
1981	83.3	27.9	97.9	51.2	7.6	65.0	21.3	8.6	40.7	19.4	8.4	22.9	6.0	73.2	238.6	15.3	843.2
1982	86.3	24.2	92.4	35.0	5.7	68.0	19.1	8.1	40.3	17.9	8.1	15.9	5.7	35.4	240.6	11.0	767.5
1983[2]	70.5	16.3	87.8	29.8	5.1	70.0	15.7	7.3	38.2	14.7	7.3	13.0	4.3	37.6	241.3	9.6	723.9
1984[2]	88.6	24.1	88.6	37.2	5.5	74.0	14.8	9.4	40.4	14.9	7.1	17.8	4.0	51.3	243.1	12.5	789.4
1985[1]	90	23	95	38		75	14		42	15		23		48	242	14	799

[1] Estimate.   [2] Preliminary.   [3] Iron ore, iron ore concentrates and iron ore agglomerates.   *Source: Bureau of Mines*   T.344

Salient Statistics of Iron Ore[2] in the U.S.   In Millions of Long Tons

Year	Net Import Reliance % of Apparent Consump- tion	Total[3]	Lake Superior	North- east	South- east	West	Ship- ments[4]	Value Mill. $ (at Mine)	Avg. Value $ at Mine Per Ton	Mines	Con- suming Plants	Lake Erie Docks	Im- ports	Ex- ports	Con- sump- tion	Manga- niferous Ship- ments[5]
1976	31	80.0	67.4	2.0	.1	9.7	77.1	1,871.1	24.28	14.0	56.2	4.8	44.4	2.9	125.4	.2
1977	48	55.8	44.1	1.2	.1	9.3	54.1	1,422.7	26.32	14.8	42.3	3.0	37.9	2.1	116.0	.2
1978	29	81.6	72.7	——— 8.9 ———			83.2	2,401.4	28.86	12.4	39.3	3.6	33.6	4.2	124.8	.3
1979	25	85.7	77.2	——— 8.6 ———			86.2	2,814.4	32.64	11.3	39.0	5.4	33.8	5.1	125.4	.2
1980	25	69.6	62.3	——— 7.3 ———			69.6	2,544.1	36.56	11.7	35.7	6.1	25.1	5.7	98.9	.2
1981	22	73.2	67.5	——— 5.7 ———			72.2	2,915.2	40.39	12.7	36.2	6.6	28.3	5.5	104.4	.2
1982	34	35.4	31.8	——— 3.6 ———			35.8	1,491.8	41.72	12.1	29.9	5.8	14.5	3.2	63.9	—
1983	37	37.6	35.6	——— 2.0 ———			44.6	1,945.0	43.61	4.1[6]	25.5	3.2	13.2	3.8	70.6	—
1984	19	51.3	49.7	——— 1.6 ———			50.9	2,247.7	44.17	5.3	24.0	2.9	17.2	5.0	72.5	.1
1985[1]	22	48.8	47.4	——— 1.1 ———			49.4	2,076.7	42.03	6.0	21.3	2.4	16.0	7.1	70.6	—

[1] Preliminary.   [2] Usable; less than 5% Mn.   [3] Includes by-product ore.   [4] Excludes by-product ore.   [5] Iron ore; 5 to 35% Mn.   [6] New classifi- cation.   *Source: Bureau of Mines*   T.345

U.S. Imports (for Consumption) of Iron Ore from Principal Countries   In Thous. of Long Tons

Year	India	Venezuela	Australia	Brazil	Canada	Chile	South Africa	USSR	Liberia	Sweden	Peru	Norway	Total
1976	130	9,001	617	5,388	24,962	608	162	44	2,153	441	716	151	44,390
1977	—	6,179	305	2,243	25,283	566	249	86	1,792	153	1,020	—	37,905
1978	—	6,083	264	3,979	19,236	390	94	—	2,170	256	818	302	33,616
1979	54	4,563	183	3,095	22,602	245	106	—	2,190	171	456	44	33,776
1980	—	3,602	—	1,995	17,311	322	6	—	1,590	33	193	—	25,058
1981	—	5,071	—	1,738	18,845	342	—	—	2,160	87	77	—	28,328
1982	—	1,643	—	972	9,281	47	52	—	2,399	71	35	—	14,501
1983	—	1,333	—	1,276	8,832	—	—	—	1,732	68	—	—	13,246
1984	—	1,524	—	2,533	11,190	—	—	—	1,745	84	7	—	17,187
1985[1]	—	2,068	—	2,540	8,557	164	—	—	2,206	65	121	—	15,771

[1] Preliminary.   *Source: Department of Commerce*   T.346

Total[1] Iron Ore Stocks at End of Month in the U.S.   In Millions of Long Tons

Year	Jan.	Feb.	Mar.	Apr.	May	June	July	Aug.	Sept.	Oct.	Nov.	Dec.
1977	73.5	72.2	70.1	68.5	67.7	68.5	69.7	67.2	65.9	63.5	60.7	59.4
1978	56.3	54.1	53.1	50.4	49.9	51.9	51.6	53.8	54.7	55.5	56.4	55.3
1979	53.0	50.7	47.8	46.7	46.6	48.0	51.0	51.5	52.0	54.2	57.7	56.1
1980	53.7	51.8	49.0	49.6	50.7	53.5	56.8	57.5	58.0	60.4	60.1	60.2
1981	54.5	53.2	50.8	49.8	51.4	53.7	56.4	58.8	59.6	60.4	60.1	60.2
1982	60.4	60.9	57.3	57.7	57.6	58.5	59.1	57.8	55.8	54.5	52.6	52.6
1983	45.5	42.6	39.6	37.5	37.2	37.4	37.0	35.3	35.7	34.7	33.8	32.6
1984[2]	30.1	28.4	26.3	26.2	27.4	29.2	30.9	31.6	32.2	33.3	33.7	32.1
1985[2]	30.4	28.9	25.1	28.0	29.0	29.8	29.6	30.7	31.2	30.6	29.9	29.4
1986[2]	27.3	26.2	25.1	24.0	25.0	25.1	24.9	23.4				

[1] All stocks at mines, furnace yards and at U.S. docks.   [2] Preliminary.   *Source: American Iron Ore Association*   T.347

Lard

World pork production in 1986 was estimated at 54.7 million tonnes, up about one percent from 1985. China was expected to show the largest increase. A moderate gain was anticipated for the European Community (EC); U.S. production was expected to decline. 1985/86 world output was projected to increase by about 1.8 percent as the trend to lower lard yields continued in many countries. Disappearance, excluding China, was estimated to increase marginally in 1985/86; China's was expected to increase in line with pork production gains. A five-percent increase in world stocks was projected for the fall of 1986, with gains expected in the EC and USSR. Unattrac- tive prices for lard, relative to many vegetable oils, were a negative factor for use early in 1985/86 and the latter part of 1984/85. World exports in 1985/86 were expected to show little change from the previous season.

U.S. production in 1985/86 was estimated at 404,200 tonnes, off five percent from 1984/85. Domestic disappearance of selected edible and inedible products was down four percent at 362,700 tonnes; consumption in baking and frying fats accounted for the bulk of edible use. U.S. exports increased 11 percent from 1984/85 totalling 51,100 tonnes; Mexico accounted for over 70 percent of total exports. U.S. imports for the same period were 700 tonnes, a 63-percent decline from last season. U.S. stocks at the end of the 1985/86 season were 9,800 tonnes, off 48 percent from the year earlier.

World pork production should continue its upward trend in 1987, with U.S. production up as well. A slight rise in global lard production is also expected.

Supply and Distribution of Lard in the United States   In Millions of Pounds

Year	Supply — Production — Commercial Federally Inspected	Other	Total	Farm	Total Production	Stocks Jan. 1[2]	Total Supply	Exports	Total Disappearance	Domestic Disappearance	Shortening	Margarine	Direct Use as Lard Civilian	Military	Per Capita Lbs.
1981	1,159	—	1,159	—	1,159	49	1,208	139	1,170	1,031	315	85	573	1	2.5
1982	1,011	—	1,011	—	1,011	37	1,048	103	1,111	1,008	251	28	586	1	2.5
1983	973	—	973	—	973	37	1,010	89	976	889	277	30	489	1	1.8
1984	939	—	939	—	939	34	973	89	935	846	264	40	491	1	2.1
1985[1]	927	—	927	—	927	39	966	105	930	825	274	62	423	1	1.8

[1] Preliminary.   [2] Factory & warehouse.   *Source: Economic Research Service, U.S.D.A.*   T.348

Lard Exports[2] of the United States by Selected Country of Destination   In Thousands of Metric Tons

Year	Asia	Belgium & Lux.	Canada	Belize	Bolivia	Neth. Antilles	Colombia	West Germany	Haiti	Mexico	Ecuador	Netherlands	Poland	United Kingdom	Yugoslavia	Total
1981	.1	—	9.0	1.8	2.1	.4	1.0	—	1.1	32.6	—	—	17.0	.6	—	67.9
1982	1.1	1.0	11.4	1.4	0	.6	.1	—	2.1	24.6	—	—	0	.6	—	46.7
1983	5.4	1.0	7.3	1.5	—	.4	.1	—	1.5	19.7	—	—	—	.4	—	40.2
1984[1]	.1	0	9.1	1.4	.1	.3	.1	—	.1	28.6	—	—	0	—	—	40.4

[1] Preliminary.   [2] Excludes exports for civilian relief & shipments by CARE.   *Source: Foreign Agricultural Service, U.S.D.A.*   T.352

United States Commercial[1] Production of Lard   In Millions of Pounds

Year	Jan.	Feb.	Mar.	Apr.	May	June	July	Aug.	Sept.	Oct.	Nov.	Dec.	Total
1981	100.0	87.0	99.0	104.0	95.0	91.0	89.0	86.0	96.0	104.0	99.0	104.0	1,155
1982	88.0	77.0	94.0			257.0			234.0			261.0	1,011
1983	73.0	66.0	84.0	81.0	79.0	79.0	73.0	81.0	84.0	90.0	94.0	88.0	973
1984	79.0	74.0	86.0	79.0	81.0	72.0	66.0	76.0	74.0	90.0	84.0	78.0	939
1985	81.0	70.0	78.0	81.0	83.0	70.0	72.0	77.0	76.0	85.0	78.0	76.0	927
1986[2]	80.0	68.0	76.0	81.0	76.0	67.0	67.0	66.0	71.0	80.0	69.0		

[1] Includes "Rendered Pork Fat."   [2] Preliminary.   *Source: Department of Agriculture*   T.354

Consumption (edible & inedible) of Lard in the United States   In Millions of Pounds

Year	Jan.	Feb.	Mar.	Apr.	May	June	July	Aug.	Sept.	Oct.	Nov.	Dec.	Total
1981	45.5	39.1	36.8	38.4	34.2	36.6	33.2	35.3	38.8	31.1	37.8	41.5	448
1982	35.3	25.4	28.6	33.4	31.2	28.1	24.2	22.2	22.4	21.6	23.3	26.3	322
1983	25.4	27.2	29.3	32.2	41.9	37.1	30.1	34.4	31.7	33.8	38.9	38.3	400
1984	33.9	27.6	30.5	29.3	33.4	26.0	25.8	26.2	23.1	31.1	37.5	30.5	355
1985	34.1	29.6	30.0	30.1	31.2	29.3	27.9	30.8	36.4	44.6	37.5	33.4	395
1986[1]	33.3	31.4	35.6	37.3	35.6	33.8	26.3	23.3	27.5	28.4	29.0		

[1] Preliminary.   *Source: Economic Research Service, U.S.D.A.*   T.349

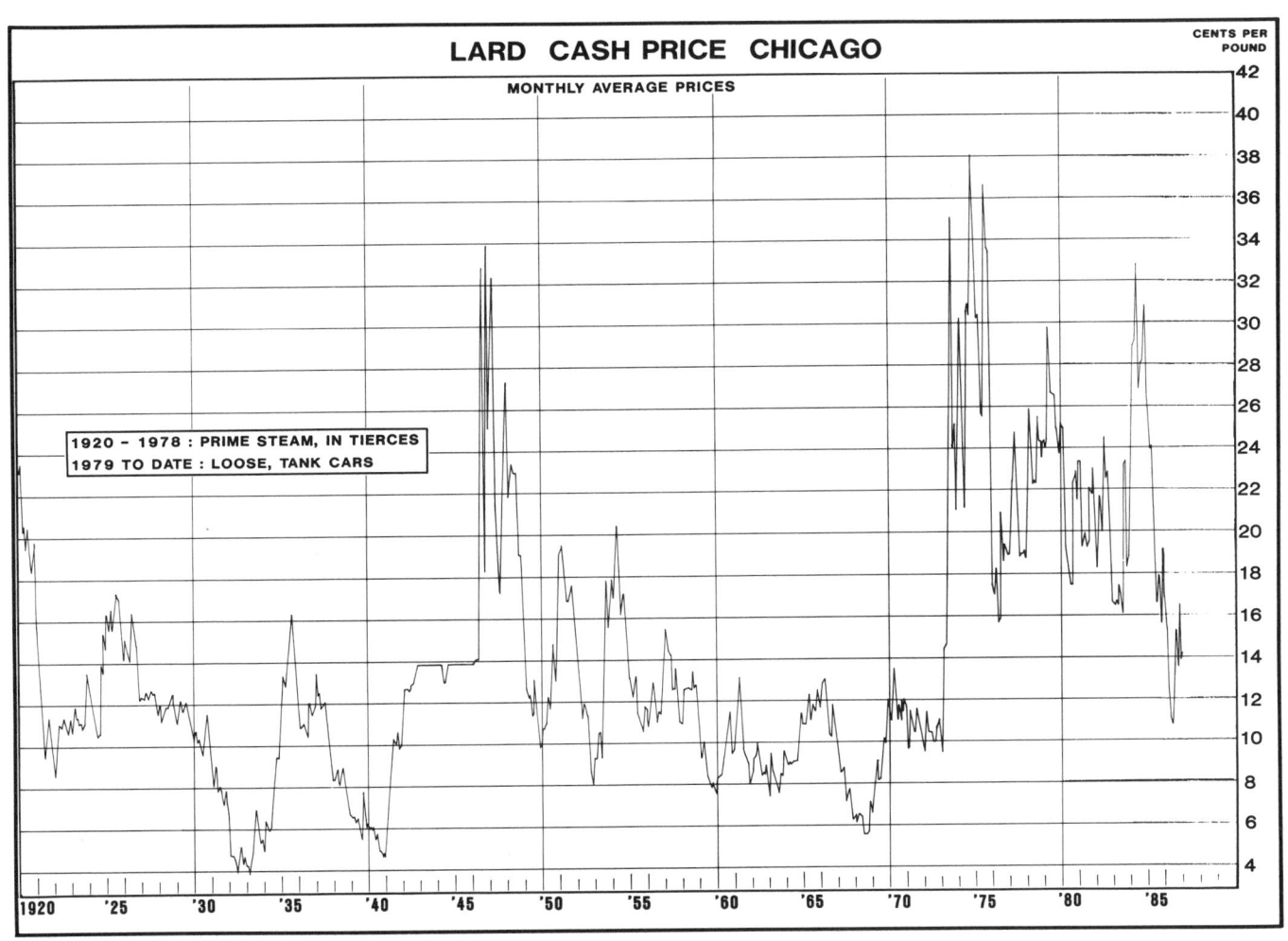

LARD CASH PRICE CHICAGO

MONTHLY AVERAGE PRICES

CENTS PER POUND

1920 – 1978 : PRIME STEAM, IN TIERCES
1979 TO DATE : LOOSE, TANK CARS

Average Wholesale Price of Lard—Loose, Tank Cars, Chicago   In Cents Per Pound

Year	Jan.	Feb.	Mar.	Apr.	May	June	July	Aug.	Sept.	Oct.	Nov.	Dec.	Average
1979	24.5	24.0	25.1	29.8	26.8	—	—	—	26.6	25.1	23.8	25.1	25.6
1980	22.0	21.6	19.3	19.0	18.0	17.5	17.5	22.5	23.0	21.6	23.3	23.3	20.7
1981	20.0	19.0	19.6	19.9	19.4	19.6	22.0	21.8	22.8	21.5	21.0	18.4	20.3
1982	20.0	21.5	20.0	22.0	23.0	24.6	22.6	22.8	21.3	21.0	17.3	16.5	21.1
1983	16.4	16.7	16.4	17.4	17.1	16.4	16.1	23.2	23.4	18.3	18.7	18.8	18.2
1984	25.9	26.3	28.9	29.1	32.8	29.5	26.8	28.1	28.2	30.5	30.8	26.4	28.6
1985	24.6	24.0	24.1	22.7	20.0	18.1	16.9	17.8	15.8	15.4	19.2	16.5	19.6
1986	16.0	15.5	12.3	11.3	10.6	11.3	14.9	15.2	13.6	16.5	13.9	14.2	13.8

Source: Economic Research Service, U.S.D.A.   T.350

United States Cold Storage Holdings of all Lard[1], on First of Month   In Millions of Pounds

Year	Jan.	Feb.	Mar.	Apr.	May	June	July	Aug.	Sept.	Oct.	Nov.	Dec.
1979	38.1	40.5	39.6	35.8	42.8	47.9	46.0	51.4	46.4	43.9	44.7	52.0
1980	49.9	54.4	61.3	62.5	57.9	51.7	59.1	57.1	55.0	43.5	44.6	48.7
1981	49.4	50.4	46.9	42.2	40.5	40.1	40.7	42.6	39.5	35.6	36.7	39.1
1982	37.0	35.3	32.5	34.0	32.7	31.8	31.4	25.5	32.2	24.2	29.5	39.0
1983	37.5	38.3	31.5	36.1	39.1	43.0	41.8	41.0	35.6	40.4	41.4	45.8
1984	34.2	34.1	28.5	29.1	31.2	38.1	34.4	32.9	33.1	29.9	37.8	33.1
1985	38.7	33.7	36.6	37.1	42.0	43.1	47.3	42.2	41.0	41.3	39.3	35.9
1986[2]	35.4	37.6	36.4	40.8	39.8	35.5	27.3	32.1	28.3	21.6	30.6	29.7

[1] Stocks in factories & warehouses (except that in hands of retailers).   [2] Preliminary.   *Source: Bureau of the Census*   T.351

Lead

Lead consumption for the first 10 months of 1986 held steady at 900,000 tons, in comparison to the same period of 1985. Total refinery production for the period was 313,686 tons, compared with full-year 1985 production of 484,444 tons. Total producer and consumer metal stocks continued to decline significantly, by more than 80,000 tons in the period from March to October, 1986. Domestic mine production of lead is estimated to be 400,000 tons in 1986, about unchanged from 1985's total.

Because of a drawdown in stocks, North American producer prices for lead rose steadily during the latter part of 1986. In May, 1986, the producer price was 19–20 cents a pound, and by October, 1986, the price had climbed to around 27–28 cents a pound. The average for the month of October (25.5 cents a pound) was the highest since August, 1984.

In the second week of 1986, ASARCO purchased a mine and mill in Missouri from Kennecott Copper Corp. If ASARCO reopens the mine and the mill, they will become a fully integrated lead producer, and only one of two in the U.S.

Lead ore imports in January–October, 1986, were 61,198 tons, compared with total 1985 imports of 42,665 tons. Refined metal imports for the first 10 months of 1986 were 109,659 tons, compared with total 1985 refined lead imports of 133,529 tons.

From a 1983 base, U.S. demand for lead is expected to increase at an average annual rate of about 1.3 percent through 1990. Growth in lead use is dependent upon the development of cost-competitive and reliable electrical vehicles for general and new industrial uses, major power supply load-leveling applications, and continuing high growth for uninterrupted power systems, according to the U.S. Bureau of Mines.

The U.S., Australia, and Canada are major world producers of lead; Australia leads, followed by the U.S. In recent years, significant reserves of lead have been discovered in association with zinc and silver ores in Alaska, Canada, Mexico, Australia, and South Africa. Identified world reserves are estimated at 1.4 billion short tons. Much of this is unrecoverable, but the likelihood of finding additional lead resources in commercial concentrations at a rate exceeding consumption is highly favorable, according to industry analysts.

On January 1, 1986, the amount of lead additives allowed in gasoline in the U.S. was reduced to 0.1 gram per gallon, down from 1985's permissible level of 0.5 gram per gallon (and a reduction of more than 90 percent from the 1982 standard of 1.1 grams per gallon of gasoline). At year-end 1986, a total ban on lead additives by 1988 was under consideration by the Environmental Protection Agency.

Substitution by plastics has reduced the use of lead in building construction, electrical cable covering, and in cans and containers. Aluminum, tin, iron, and plastics compete with lead in packaging and protective coatings uses.

World Smelter (Primary & Secondary) Production of Lead   In Thousands of Metric Tons

Year	Aus-tralia[3]	Belgium[4]	Bul-garia	Canada[3]	China[2]	France	West Ger-many	Japan	Mexico[3]	Peru[3]	Spain	United States	United King-dom[3]	USSR	Yugo-slavia[3]	World Total
1978	356.0	76.5	120.0	245.9	160.0	151.4	305.0	293.9	215.4	74.3	122.2	1,337	253.4	620.0	140.4	5,133
1979	427.1	60.7	119.0	252.4	170.0	159.9	316.6	294.3	223.0	90.7	127.0	1,380	276.5	690.0	133.6	5,628
1980	393.9	83.9	119.0	234.6	175.0	162.5	301.4	315.6	189.0	84.9	120.7	1,224	241.4	700.0	124.7	5,397
1981	401.8	88.2	119.0	238.2	175.0	163.9	362.3	332.3	194.7	84.2	117.1	1,139	224.5	715.0	120.5	5,384
1982	428.7	80.9	118.0	238.9	175.0	145.1	350.4	311.9	179.4	82.0	131.6	1,088	209.3	730.0	109.0	5,296
1983	405.9	84.4	116.0	242.0	195.0	152.3	352.5	317.2	195.8	72.7	143.8	1,018	226.0	745.0	127.1	5,282
1984[1]	399.8	101.5	116.0	252.0	195.0	142.8	357.2	337.1	199.8	75.3	160.0	1,029	227.4	755.0	130.0	5,452
1985[2]	395.4	87.6	116.0	239.5	195.0	168.7	356.5	351.6	200.0	86.9	155.0	1,082	194.9	760.0	150.0	5,527

[1] Preliminary.   [2] Estimated.   [3] Refined & bullion.   [4] Includes scrap.   *Source: Bureau of Mines*   T.355

Consumption of Lead in the United States by Products   In Thousands of Metric Tons

Year	Ammu-nition	Bear-ing Metals	Pipes, Traps & Bends[2]	Cable Cover-ing	Calking Lead	Casting Metals	Glass & Ceramic Pdt's.	Paints	Sheet Lead	Solder	Storage Battery Grids, Post, etc.	Oxides	Gaso-line Ad-ditives	Type-Metal	Brass and Bronze	Total Consump-tion
1978	55.8	9.5	10.5	13.9	9.9	3.6	— 91.6 —		12.6	68.4	412.6	466.7	178.3	10.8	16.5	1,432.7
1979	53.2	9.6	7.2	16.4	8.0	22.7	48.8	26.7	20.4	54.3	375.6	438.8	186.9	10.0	18.7	1,358.3
1980	48.7	7.8	8.6	13.4	5.7	19.0	45.4	20.7	19.8	41.4	302.2	343.1	127.9	9.0	14.0	1,070.3
1981	49.5	6.9	8.8	12.1	5.5	18.6	44.3	16.3	19.4	29.7	342.2	428.0	111.4	7.8	13.3	1,167.1
1982	44.2	6.1	8.6	15.2	4.1	25.1	34.5	13.4	15.2	28.5	312.6	391.7	119.2	2.8	11.4	1,075.4
1983	43.7	5.8	13.1	10.5	3.6	16.2	39.7	15.4	14.2	28.5	382.3	424.6	89.1	2.5	11.0	1,148.5
1984	47.8	4.7	13.7	12.3	4.0	15.8	46.1	17.4	14.7	24.4	426.3	439.2	78.9	2.2	7.0	1,207.0
1985[1]	50.2	5.4	11.9	15.5	2.3	19.4	44.1	14.1	14.8	21.4	468.7	372.2	45.7	1.6	7.8	1,148.3
1986[3]	45.0	3.0	12.0	16.0	.5	10.0			10.0	12.0	— 600.0 —				6.0	1,000.0

[1] Preliminary.   [2] Building.   [3] Estimate.   *Source: Bureau of Mines*   T.358

Salient Statistics of Lead in the United States   In Thousands of Metric Tons

Year	Net Import Reliance as a % of Apparent Consumption	Production of Refined Lead From					Total Value of Refined Mil. $	Secondary Lead Recovered				Total Value of Secondary Mil. $	Dec. 31 Stocks		Avg. Price (¢ per Lb.)	
		Domestic Ores[2]	Foreign Ores[2]	Total Primary	Secondary Sources	Total		As Refined Metal	In Antimonial Lead	In Other Alloys	Total		Producers' Stocks[3]	Consumers' Stocks	New York	London
1976	15	515.8	76.5	592.3	—	592.3	301.6	282.1	310.2	66.8	659.1	335.7	110.4	117.6	23.10	20.46
1977	13	486.7	62.0	548.7	.1	548.8	371.4	303.1	383.4	71.1	757.6	512.8	91.1	121.4	30.70	28.00
1978	12	501.6	63.5	565.2	1.2	566.4	419.3	282.6	409.9	76.5	769.2	570.7	98.7	125.2	33.65	29.86
1979	5	530.0	45.6	575.6	2.9	578.5	668.0	352.2	378.8	70.3	801.4	930.0	89.3	153.2	52.64	54.52
1980	5[5]	508.2	39.4	547.6	2.1	549.7	512.6	315.2	306.7	53.7	675.6	632.4	126.0	126.2	42.46	41.21
1981	1	440.2	55.1	495.3	1.7	497.1	398.9	282.2	304.4	54.6	641.1	516.3	140.2	123.2	36.53	33.30
1982	3	459.9	52.3	512.2	.7	512.8	288.4	240.5	284.4	46.4	571.3	321.7	125.5	97.2	25.54	24.66
1983	14	459.3	55.2	514.6	.6	515.2	245.9	189.6	271.6	42.3	503.5	240.7	106.7	100.8	21.68	19.27
1984	16	330.2	65.4	395.6	1.0	396.6	222.8	263.4	327.8	42.1	633.4	266.3	135.1	97.1	25.55	20.12
1985[1]	0	416.1	71.4	487.5		488.0	204.9	263.3	288.0	43.0	594.2	249.8	128.0	93.1	19.07	17.84
1986[4]				400.0		400.0						590.0		60.0	21.00	

[1] Preliminary.   [2] And base bullion.   [3] At primary smelters & refineries.   [4] Estimates.   [5] Net exporter.   *Source: Bureau of Mines*   T.357

U.S. Mine Production of Recoverable Lead   In Thousands of Metric Tons

Year	Arizona	California	Colorado	Idaho	Illinois	New York	Missouri	Montana	Nevada	New Mexico	Oklahoma	Utah	Virginia	Washington	Wisconsin	Total U.S.[2]
1976	.3	.1	24.3	48.7	N.A.	2.9	454.5	.1	.5	N.A.	N.A.	14.8	1.8	N.A.	N.A.	553.0
1977	.3	—	20.9	42.9	N.A.	2.5	453.8	.1	.7	N.A.	N.A.	9.7	2.0	1.1	N.A.	537.5
1978	.4	N.A.	15.2	44.8	N.A.	1.0	461.8	.1	.7	N.A.	—	2.5	1.8	N.A.	N.A.	529.7
1979	.4	N.A.	7.6	42.6	N.A.	.5	472.1	.3	—	N.A.	—	N.A.	1.6	—	N.A.	525.6
1980	.2	N.A.	10.3	38.6	N.A.	.9	497.2	.3	—	—	—	—	1.6	N.A.	—	550.4
1981	1.0	N.A.	11.4	38.4	N.A.	1.0	389.7	.2	N.A.	N.A.	—	1.7	1.6	—	—	445.5
1982	.4	N.A.	N.A.	N.A.	N.A.	1.1	474.5	.7	N.A.	N.A.	—	N.A.	—	N.A.	—	512.5
1983	.2	N.A.	N.A.	25.9	N.A.	1.3	409.3	1.2	—	.3	—	—	—	—	—	449.3
1984	N.A.	N.A.	N.A.	N.A.	N.A.	N.A.	278.3	N.A.	—	N.A.	—	N.A.	—	—	—	322.7
1985[1]	.6	—	N.A.	33.7	N.A.	N.A.	371.0	.8	—	N.A.	—	—	—	—	—	414.0
1986[3]							320.0									360.0

[1] Preliminary.   [2] Includes Alaska.   [3] Estimate.   *Source: Bureau of Mines*   T.356

U.S. Foreign Trade of Lead   In Thousands of Metric Tons

Year	Exports					Imports for Consumption					General Imports From:						
	Ore & Concentrate	Unwrought Lead[3]	Wrought Lead[4]	Scrap	Total	Ores, Flue Dust or Fume & Mattes	Base Bullion	Pigs & Bars	Reclaimed Scrap, Etc.	Value Million $	Ore, Flue Dust & Matte			Pigs & Bars			
											Australia	Peru	Canada	Australia	Mexico	Peru	Canada
1977		4.3	4.7	77.5	86.5	88.8	7.3	230.1	3.5	196.9	16.6	6.6	16.0	19.9	71.8	30.4	75.4
1978		3.2	5.1	98.6	106.9	61.9	4.3	225.4	3.3	203.0	6.5	6.3	19.6	16.3	80.2	25.7	70.4
1979		7.4	3.3	119.7	130.4	44.4	1.7	182.6	4.0	248.3	1.9	12.4	12.8	17.3	73.6	17.9	
1980	27.6	156.5	8.0	119.7	284.2	29.6	.3	81.3	2.9	116.5	3.0	18.0	8.5	11.3	28.6	3.3	34.9
1981	33.0	16.8	6.5	59.4	82.7	27.2	.4	100.1	2.7	110.5	2.2	14.1	23.5	10.9	33.7	2.9	50.8
1982	29.1	51.0	4.6	51.8	136.5	18.9	—	94.9	4.8	69.9	7.7	14.5	4.8	7.3	23.5	8.3	49.8
1983	20.1	17.7	2.8	50.9	95.4	19.8	.1	134.4	4.2	89.9	10.0	22.7	6.1	10.9	34.9	10.1	72.7
1984	11.9	5.0	2.5	45.1	73.5	29.9	—	161.5	5.0	104.2	17.0	22.7	14.1	10.9	39.5	9.2	94.9
1985[1]	10.0	25.4	2.0	59.9	107.3	2.6	.8	131.4	3.2	59.0	12.3	15.2	5.2	3.6	33.8	5.2	90.1
1986[2]	6.0			65.0		1.0		120.0	2.5		6.0	8.0	40.0		25.0	2.0	85.0

[1] Preliminary.   [2] Estimates.   [3] And lead alloys.   [4] Blocks, Pigs, etc.   *Source: Bureau of Mines*   T.359

LEAD

Average Price of Pig Lead, U.S. Primary Producers (Common Corroding)[1]   In Cents Per Pound

Year	Jan.	Feb.	Mar.	Apr.	May	June	July	Aug.	Sept.	Oct.	Nov.	Dec.	Average
1980	51.06	50.00	49.52	45.34	36.00	34.19	35.95	40.95	42.43	45.00	44.06	40.43	42.91
1981	34.13	30.63	35.32	37.68	37.10	38.23	41.25	44.64	42.52	37.59	34.34	31.75	37.10
1982	29.90	28.89	27.98	26.57	26.50	25.89	27.88	27.45	26.64	23.12	21.48	20.12	26.03
1983	21.60	20.87	20.43	21.00	20.10	19.34	19.30	19.38	22.24	25.62	26.00	25.69	21.80
1984	26.38	26.00	26.45	27.00	26.55	29.00	32.14	30.13	25.68	24.04	26.42	23.11	26.91
1985	20.45	19.76	19.24	20.48	20.50	20.00	19.88	19.32	19.44	18.97	19.06	19.05	19.68
1986	18.70	18.41		18.93	19.58	22.41	22.63		23.43	25.53	27.93	28.37	22.25

[1] N.Y. Delivery.   *Source: American Metal Market*

T.360

Refiners Production[1] of Lead in the United States   In Thousands of Short Tons

Year	Jan.	Feb.	Mar.	Apr.	May	June	July	Aug.	Sept.	Oct.	Nov.	Dec.	Total
1980	56.9	49.3	54.1	47.5	47.0	47.1	52.0	48.2	50.2	52.2	48.4	53.5	606.4
1981	58.0	53.6	58.2	52.7	35.0	24.4	33.0	45.1	43.7	46.1	39.4	44.0	533.2
1982	50.3	45.2	44.0	36.1	54.3	53.0	44.2	46.4	49.2	50.6	50.8	48.6	572.6
1983	57.0	50.9	52.8	48.9	47.2	42.0	39.5	45.3	41.2	50.0	50.9	46.4	572.3
1984	51.5	51.4	43.0	40.0	39.2	26.2	28.4	29.1	25.3	40.8	28.0	26.5	429.2
1985	43.1	50.3	56.3	52.7	53.4	50.9	32.5	46.6	44.9	39.3	30.1	44.5	544.5
1986	47.4	41.6	49.4	40.2	40.2	26.5	16.9	31.3	27.5	28.6	28.5	30.1	408.2

[1] Represents refined lead produced from domestic ores by primary smelters plus small amount of secondary material passing through these smelters. Includes GSA metal purchased for remelt.   *Source: American Bureau of Metal Statistics, Inc.*

T.362

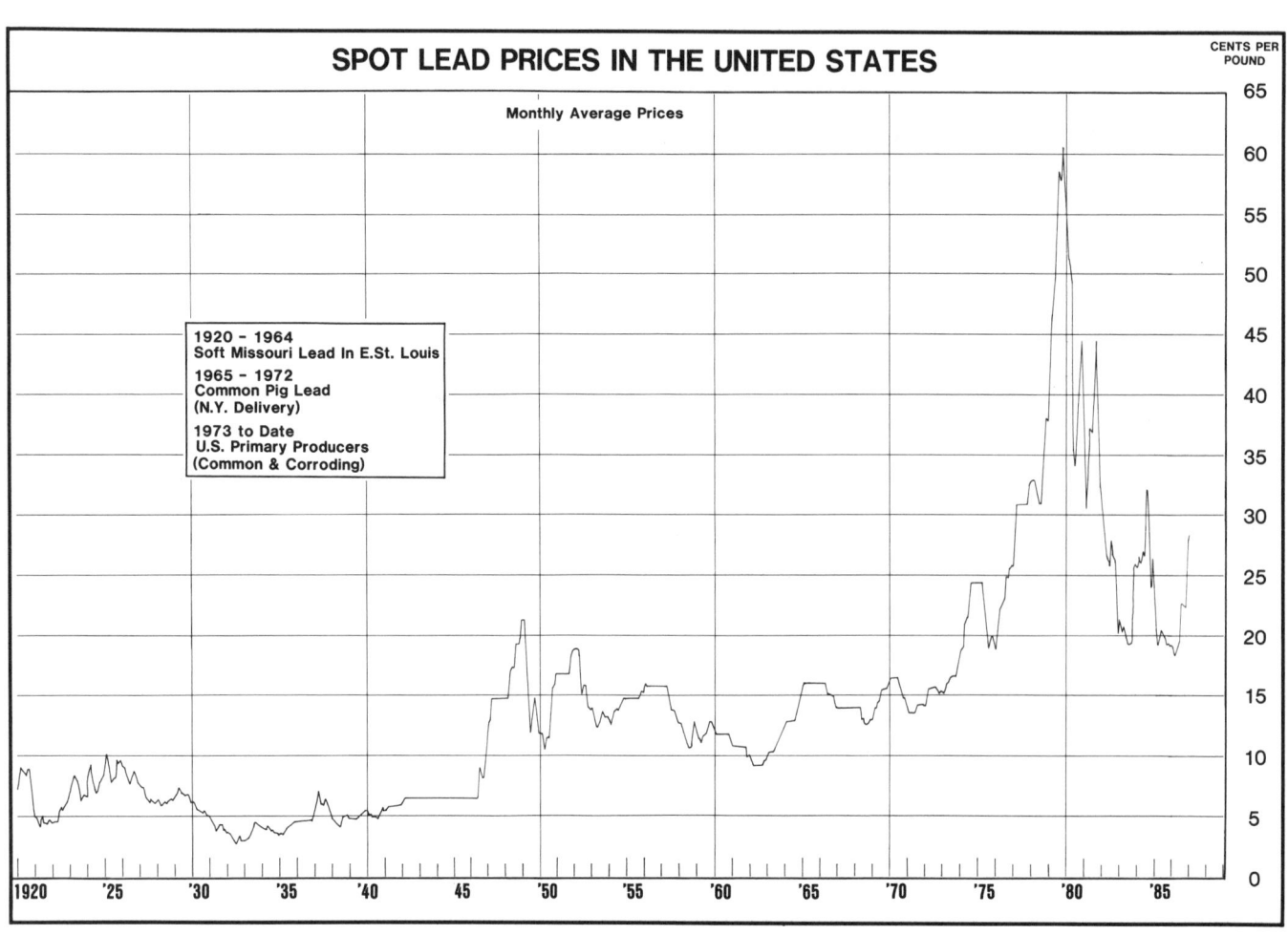

SPOT LEAD PRICES IN THE UNITED STATES

CENTS PER POUND

Monthly Average Prices

1920 - 1964
Soft Missouri Lead In E.St. Louis

1965 - 1972
Common Pig Lead
(N.Y. Delivery)

1973 to Date
U.S. Primary Producers
(Common & Corroding)

U.S. Mine Production of Recoverable Lead   In Thousands of Metric Tons[2]

Year	Jan.	Feb.	Mar.	Apr.	May	June	July	Aug.	Sept.	Oct.	Nov.	Dec.	Total
1978	49.8	45.0	57.1	49.4	54.3	40.1	35.5	47.6	49.5	55.5	50.0	49.1	528.8
1979	48.4	44.7	43.1	37.3	42.0	42.6	41.5	49.5	35.2	50.5	46.8	44.1	525.6
1980	51.4	50.3	49.8	48.9	49.9	46.1	43.4	41.5	39.4	48.6	39.7	41.3	550.4
1981[2]	42.6	40.9	43.4	26.7	27.8	17.4	31.8	38.2	48.0	47.5	39.8	41.3	445.5
1982	40.3	43.2	48.4	44.1	41.8	42.4	36.8	42.7	41.4	44.7	41.8	45.1	512.5
1983	44.9	39.6	37.3	36.7	35.9	28.4	35.3	43.2	37.4	37.1	38.3	34.9	449.2
1984[1]	41.8	42.6	46.2	20.9	24.0	12.2	24.8	23.4	18.6	22.4	19.5	25.4	321.9
1985[1]	31.4	32.9	37.2	38.8	36.7	32.1	34.1	34.4	30.4	36.5	32.1	32.6	409.4
1986[1]	40.2	36.1	38.0	33.8	24.9								

[1] Preliminary.   [2] Data prior to 1981 are in thousands of short tons.   *Source: Bureau of Mines*   T.359A

Total Stocks of Lead[1] in the United States at Refiners, at End of Month   In Thousands of Short Tons

Year	Jan.	Feb.	Mar.	Apr.	May	June	July	Aug.	Sept.	Oct.	Nov.	Dec.
1980	67.8	75.0	71.6	83.8	90.8	82.7	66.3	53.8	35.2	29.2	46.5	60.9
1981	86.6	92.3	88.9	87.8	71.2	61.6	59.9	52.6	38.5	49.1	57.5	62.8
1982	65.4	67.2	65.9	60.1	65.1	73.2	70.8	64.9	71.4	72.9	78.0	79.0
1983	83.3	91.2	84.9	89.0	100.6	98.6	95.3	82.1	61.3	56.6	51.6	58.9
1984	63.3	70.3	76.1	81.5	84.2	83.5	84.9	78.4	64.8	66.2	53.0	49.7
1985	48.2	59.6	79.3	90.4	107.2	128.9	125.0	118.2	114.1	102.4	90.6	93.1
1986	96.1	104.1	116.4	115.8	116.7	105.9	89.1	81.0	57.8	41.9	30.0	22.5

[1] Stocks at own plant & elsewhere.   *Source: American Bureau of Metal Statistics, Inc.*   T.364

Total[1] Lead Consumption in the United States   In Thousands of Metric Tons

Year	Jan.	Feb.	Mar.	Apr.	May	June	July	Aug.	Sept.	Oct.	Nov.	Dec.	Total
1982	98.7	87.9	97.2	94.5	84.7	88.4	72.4	96.7	88.3	98.3	81.5	86.8	1,075
1983	91.5	74.0	83.1	85.9	83.8	96.3	79.3	102.6	115.7	112.3	102.7	121.4	1,149
1984	112.7	94.1	96.8	89.5	87.3	96.4	82.7	97.3	96.7	103.2	96.9	95.1	1,207
1985	87.3	101.5	100.7	90.1	86.0	77.0	67.8	101.8	100.4	106.3	90.7	82.4	1,130
1986	96.7	85.4	79.6	90.8	86.0	84.1							

[1] Represents total consumption of primary & secondary lead as metal, in chemicals, or in alloys.   *Source: Bureau of Mines*   T.365

U.S. Lead Recovered from Scrap (Lead Content)   In Thousands of Metric Tons

Year	Jan.	Feb.	Mar.	Apr.	May	June	July	Aug.	Sept.	Oct.	Nov.	Dec.	Total
1979	54.6	60.5	65.1	64.1	62.0	65.2	51.3	58.1	58.2	65.0	60.7	54.3	801.4
1980	59.2	55.4	59.6	59.1	51.2	57.1	45.9	52.2	56.0	50.2	58.1	54.9	675.6
1981	46.5	43.9	43.8	42.5	44.1	46.7	46.4	49.1	52.5	50.9	52.2	48.7	641.1
1982	45.5	48.2	48.0	47.6	46.1	44.8	34.4	44.2	41.9	44.6	41.9	41.5	571.3
1983	41.3	37.4	41.0	41.3	42.5	37.3	37.2	39.6	43.4	48.9	48.4	45.7	503.5
1984[1]	44.4	48.6	47.6	48.5	46.6	46.7	44.5	50.0	49.0	51.7	48.1	41.3	582.8
1985[1]	44.6	31.4	46.4	43.9	44.7	34.9	41.1	45.5	50.8	53.9	54.2	43.4	531.8
1986[1]	49.8	52.9	53.2	50.2	59.1	46.0							

[1] Preliminary.   *Source: Bureau of Mines*   T.366

Domestic Shipments[1] of Lead in the United States by Refiners   In Thousands of Short Tons

Year	Jan.	Feb.	Mar.	Apr.	May	June	July	Aug.	Sept.	Oct.	Nov.	Dec.	Total
1980	40.5	37.6	38.9	28.8	30.1	35.3	36.6	48.0	60.1	55.6	31.0	38.6	481.0
1981	31.9	42.5	51.7	48.8	41.9	33.4	34.2	51.7	55.1	35.5	28.2	24.2	479.0
1982	39.3	35.8	37.0	30.7	40.9	39.3	41.8	57.8	62.0	54.5	55.6	39.0	544.1
1983	43.5	33.8	44.3	34.6	36.4	26.7	26.9	35.5	38.5	39.1	40.8	29.6	435.2
1984	46.6	43.8	36.6	34.6	36.7	29.1	36.4	53.4	48.9	51.2	41.9	41.9	501.2
1985	44.8	38.9	36.6	41.5	36.7	29.1	36.4	53.4	48.9	51.2	41.9	41.9	501.2
1986	44.5	33.5	37.1	40.9	39.3	37.3	33.7	39.3	50.7	44.6	40.4	37.6	478.8

[1] Includes GSA metal.   *Source: American Bureau of Metal Statistics, Inc.*   T.363

Lumber & Plywood

Total output of lumber in the U.S. during 1986 was an estimated 35.2 billion board feet, down more than five percent from 1985. Softwoods accounted for about five-sixths of total production, as in previous years. Gross stocks, roughly 6.6 billion board feet at the close of 1985, were little changed from that figure in late 1986. Just under three-fourths (73 percent) of stocks were softwoods.

Imports constitute a major element of domestic supply of lumber, running at about 38 percent of American production. The projected volume of imports of all types of lumber during 1986 was approximately 14 billion board feet, almost exactly the same as in 1985. About 75 percent of all imports of wood products originated in Canada, but the U.S. also buys a substantial amount of hardwood plywood from Indonesia and Taiwan, and it maintains a lively, if smaller, trade with Brazil and Mexico.

Statistics for the first half of 1986 indicated that U.S. exports of wood products were up nearly eight percent from the same period a year before. In dollar terms, the major export (accounting for nearly 38 percent of total value) was softwood logs, predominantly of Southern pine; upward of 60 percent of all such sales went to Japan. Softwood lumber exports constituted 21 percent of the total, with Japan taking nearly 39 percent of all such shipments. The other major American export was hardwood lumber, which generated 11 percent of the total export value.

Japan remained the most important market for U.S. exports and forest products. Shipments originating from the U.S. were valued at about $1.1 billion in 1986. The value of U.S. forest-product exports to Japan increased slightly in 1985 and was expected to remain relatively flat or to increase modestly in 1986. There were a number of favorable developments in the outlook for U.S. forest-product exports to Japan, despite stagnation of overall demand for wood in the Japanese market. Most important was the substantial strengthening of the yen versus the U.S. dollar.

In addition, U.S./Japan talks resulted in a commitment by the Japanese government to reduce import duties on forest products in 1987 and brought about progress on several standards and certification issues. On the other hand, competition from some third-country suppliers, especially Indonesia for plywood and the USSR for wood chips, intensified.

China is another large importer of U.S. wood products. For the first half of 1986, shipments originating from the U.S. were estimated at $123.3 million, off 28 percent from the year-ago period. Increased domestic supplies, a high 1985 import level, and reduced foreign exchange availability were cited as reasons for the drop. Total Chinese lumber imports for 1986 were expected to be off 10 percent. USDA projected that China will be unable to attain self-sufficiency in lumber for the next 15 years, and that the log import market is bright, especially for traditional suppliers like the U.S.

Domestic demand for lumber and plywood began 1986 on a strong note and should continue to be strong through most of the year, excepting the fall. Increased demand was spurred by high volume of residential construction, stimulated in some part by falling short- and long-term interest rates. The number of new housing starts in 1986 increased almost four percent from last year to total 1.87 units.

The producers' price index number (1967=100) for dressed Douglas fir fell from 336.6 in 1985 to 330.0 in November, 1986, a slide of two percent. Dressed Southern pine stood at 300.6 in 1985, but had dipped to 289.0 in November, 1986. However, by year-end, the demand for lumber increased and 1986 ended with prices slightly higher than year-ago. The index number for other softwoods, notably Western pine, rose from 378.7 in 1985 to 407.0 in late 1986, a jump of more than seven percent.

The main events affecting the U.S. lumber industry during 1986 had to do with trading relations between this country and Canada. In May, the Reagan Administration imposed a 35-percent tariff on red cedar shakes and shingles imported from Canada. Its justification was that imports were seriously injuring U.S. manufacturers of the same products, and that domestic producers needed time to become competitive with their Canadian counterparts. The tariff itself was designed to fall in stages over a period of five years, at the end of which it would be zero. Although the Canadian government promptly retaliated, imposing tariffs upon a variety of U.S. products imported into Canada, the U.S. International Trade Commission in late June ruled unanimously that this country's softwood lumber industry "is being materially injured, or threatened with material injury, by reason of softwood lumber imports from Canada."

During December, 1986, there were concerns that the U.S. might impose a 15-percent duty on imports of Canadian softwood lumber, the source of about one-third of the U.S. requirement. Canada imposed a 15-percent tax on its lumber exports, starting in January, 1987, to forestall the U.S. duty. The duty was urged by U.S. lumber producers, who alleged that Canadian provinces subsidize their lumber industry through low prices for timber cut on provincially-owned land.

Futures Market

Lumber futures are traded on the Chicago Mercantile Exchange (CME).

Salient Statistics of Lumber in the United States

Year	Lumber	Pulp Products	Plywood & Veneer	Other Pdts.[2]	Total[2]	Imports	Exports	Consumption	Fuelwood Consumption	Consumption Consum. All Pdt's.	All Eastern Hardwoods	Douglas Fir	Southern Pine	Western Hemlock	Ponderosa Pine	Maple
					In Million Cubic Feet								$ Per 1,000 Board Ft.			
1976	5,585	3,805	1,355	375	11,925	2,840	1,870	12,895	600	13,495	34.90	176.20	87.00	79.70	101.80	36.60
1977	5,950	3,645	1,425	385	11,960	3,310	1,795	13,700	1,030	14,730	37.90	225.90	100.30	89.30	131.40	41.20
1978	6,155	3,745	1,460	400	12,240	3,755	1,845	14,485	1,570	16,055	41.10	250.30	134.50	113.60	164.70	57.40
1979	6,115	4,110	1,370	410	12,510	3,655	2,135	14,470	2,270	16,740	46.80	394.40	155.20	200.80	239.00	33.90
1980	5,300	4,390	1,175	390	11,645	3,250	2,350	12,995	3,115	16,110	52.40	432.20	155.40	212.70	206.10	37.40
1981	4,610	4,125	1,180	350	10,710	3,165	2,090	11,985	3,650	15,635	50.90	350.20	172.00	163.40	195.20	41.50
1982	4,635	3,980	1,135	345	10,825	3,015	1,995	11,840	3,685	15,525	56.40	118.20	127.20	44.50	66.90	34.30
1983	5,730	4,180	1,365	400	12,395	3,705	2,105	13,995	4,120	18,115	60.10	161.60	140.60	62.20	104.00	25.00
1984[1]											90.10	132.90	139.40	61.80	122.70	48.60

[1] Preliminary. [2] Excludes fuelwood. Includes cooperage logs, poles & piling, fence posts, etc. *Sources: National Lumber Manufacturers Ass'n.: U.S. Dept. of Commerce; Forest Service*

T.367

United States Lumber Shipments   In Millions of Board Feet

Year	Jan.	Feb.	Mar.	Apr.	May	June	July	Aug.	Sept.	Oct.	Nov.	Dec.	Total
1977	2,683	2,873	3,362	3,364	3,314	3,387	3,077	3,358	3,296	3,269	2,859	2,983	37,899
1978	2,699	2,741	3,158	3,133	3,355	3,548	3,087	3,357	3,250	3,262	3,116	2,907	37,948
1979	2,813	2,756	3,279	3,107	3,329	3,087	3,128	3,408	3,106	3,224	2,777	2,589	36,909
1980	2,707	2,791	2,538	2,343	2,512	2,530	2,454	2,716	2,708	2,851	2,494	2,350	31,371
1981	2,424	2,379	2,752	2,755	2,633	2,765	2,395	2,431	2,260	2,382	2,045	1,989	29,132
1982	1,637	1,837	2,148	2,336	2,308	2,513	2,363	2,450	2,260	2,506	2,353	2,162	25,960
1983	2,435	2,290	2,632	2,683	2,775	2,764	2,537	2,669	2,737	2,795	2,404	2,445	31,358
1984	2,589	2,603	3,022	2,875	2,852	2,993	2,756	2,950	2,688	3,154	2,922	2,397	37,180
1985[1]	2,666	2,602	3,013	3,496	3,349	3,031	2,944	3,294	3,162	3,221	2,828	2,809	36,887
1986[1]	2,955	2,899	3,478	3,321	3,538	3,498	2,979						

[1] Preliminary. *Source: National Lumber Manufacturers' Association*

T.368

Stocks (Gross) of Lumber in the United States, Beginning of Month   In Millions of Board Feet

Year	Jan.	Feb.	Mar.	Apr.	May	June	July	Aug.	Sept.	Oct.	Nov.	Dec.
1977	5,086	5,171	5,228	5,325	5,197	5,133	4,964	4,854	4,787	4,859	4,876	4,855
1978	4,850	4,963	5,128	5,201	5,190	5,038	4,877	4,705	4,632	4,669	4,740	4,731
1979	4,795	4,811	4,932	4,964	4,975	4,868	5,003	4,893	4,843	4,875	5,063	5,207
1980	5,342	5,301	5,374	5,721	5,769	5,568	5,534	5,570	5,659	5,776	5,832	5,826
1981	5,805	5,883	6,065	6,098	6,123	6,213	6,015	6,103	6,232	6,284	6,285	6,075
1982	5,910	6,016	6,068	6,042	5,983	5,915	5,853	5,867	5,977	6,163	5,986	5,881
1983	5,724	5,770	5,950	5,997	5,924	5,824	5,772	5,817	5,858	5,870	5,862	5,964
1984	5,866	6,021	6,097	6,178	6,287	6,283	6,257	6,186	6,176	6,265	6,239	6,327
1985[1]	6,150	6,299	6,415	6,488	6,282	6,198	6,445	6,535	6,555	6,603	6,770	6,792
1986[1]	6,632	6,769	6,916	6,784	6,826	6,697	6,361	6,393				

[1] Preliminary. *Source: National Lumber Manufacturers' Association*

T.369

Lumber Production[1] in the United States   In Millions of Board Feet

Year	Jan.	Feb.	Mar.	Apr.	May	June	July	Aug.	Sept.	Oct.	Nov.	Dec.	Total
1977	2,822	2,930	3,388	3,260	3,253	3,160	2,975	3,290	3,368	3,268	2,839	2,944	37,667
1978	2,843	2,904	3,222	3,127	3,203	3,333	2,988	3,263	3,285	3,333	3,102	2,931	37,896
1979	2,877	2,877	3,306	3,119	3,219	3,143	3,018	3,355	3,131	3,412	2,914	2,631	37,445
1980	2,798	2,855	2,879	2,257	2,307	2,486	2,479	2,783	2,818	2,903	2,480	2,329	31,858
1981	2,523	2,542	2,818	2,780	2,651	2,588	2,483	2,554	2,307	2,379	1,831	1,765	29,216
1982	1,810	1,891	2,148	2,281	2,251	2,338	2,376	2,560	2,445	2,333	2,247	2,004	25,795
1983	2,484	2,481	2,682	2,623	2,645	2,718	2,585	2,714	2,748	2,787	2,504	2,345	31,479
1984	2,740	2,678	3,104	2,983	2,828	2,968	2,685	2,933	2,776	3,154	2,814	2,295	37,390
1985[2]	2,727	2,718	3,085	3,296	3,256	3,101	3,034	3,299	3,196	3,387	2,851	2,649	37,164
1986[2]	3,092	3,046	3,347	3,362	3,405	3,355	2,961						

[1] Adjusted with Census reports on lumber production. [2] Preliminary. *Source: National Lumber Manufacturers' Association*

T.374

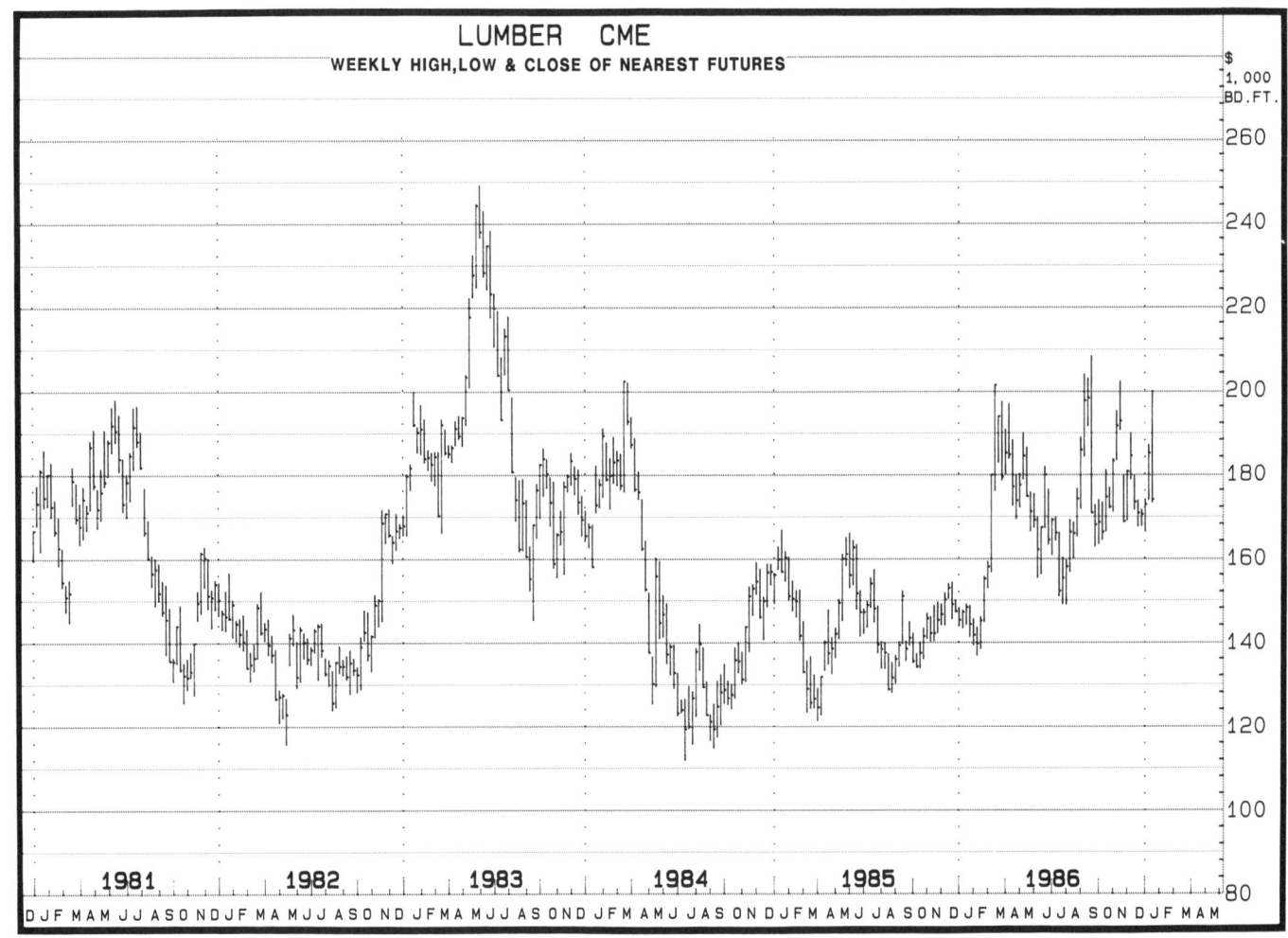

LUMBER CME
WEEKLY HIGH, LOW & CLOSE OF NEAREST FUTURES

Month–End Open Interest of Lumber Futures at Chicago   In Contracts

Year	Jan.	Feb.	Mar.	Apr.	May	June	July	Aug.	Sept.	Oct.	Nov.	Dec.
1979	8,420	9,059	7,851	7,127	8,055	7,380	8,901	11,039	10,426	10,664	10,125	10,260
1980	10,839	10,587	9,948	10,130	11,452	11,736	12,461	11,644	13,734	14,251	12,829	9,338
1981	8,882	9,053	8,029	8,102	7,639	8,161	8,554	7,586	7,690	8,809	8,808	9,067
1982	9,328	8,982	6,990	7,460	6,578	5,648	4,629	5,789	6,088	8,282	10,490	9,915
1983	10,492	10,610	10,793	11,425	9,070	8,187	7,963	8,552	8,324	6,771	6,595	7,512
1984	8,673	8,614	8,973	8,810	7,487	7,631	7,519	8,157	7,757	8,955	9,374	9,949
1985	9,702	8,984	8,447	9,045	9,764	9,224	8,708	8,346	7,397	6,965	6,687	6,383
1986	5,783	6,936	9,571	9,471	6,342	5,519	5,039	6,356	4,784	5,673	5,646	5,844

Source: Chicago Mercantile Exchange   T.370

Volume of Trading of Lumber Futures at Chicago   In Contracts

Year	Jan.	Feb.	Mar.	Apr.	May	June	July	Aug.	Sept.	Oct.	Nov.	Dec.	Total
1979	60,964	57,594	52,316	43,097	46,530	50,265	56,421	62,923	56,421	71,581	63,777	39,980	649,478
1980	59,063	61,288	73,412	86,057	81,960	68,528	76,296	65,740	73,660	76,984	59,076	58,376	838,676
1981	57,173	45,937	54,295	60,517	51,007	58,879	49,427	49,428	45,592	57,021	55,044	51,614	635,934
1982	51,268	45,193	44,717	44,116	40,828	47,512	34,624	35,432	29,835	47,761	51,046	44,387	516,619
1983	54,976	56,706	51,520	48,327	77,107	73,554	62,053	76,322	68,019	68,228	44,266	49,925	731,003
1984	51,170	70,031	57,075	68,314	88,009	59,592	60,156	65,739	60,035	61,012	52,496	59,939	753,568
1985	71,719	55,737	56,718	65,762	62,766	57,422	43,525	39,151	36,517	34,703	29,556	27,972	581,548
1986	29,570	34,647	61,718	64,176	44,778	49,929	35,203	42,212	44,961	35,847	28,912	30,577	502,530

Source: Chicago Mercantile Exchange   T.371

High, Low & Closing Prices of May Lumber Futures at Chicago   In Dollars per 1,000 Board Feet

Year of Delivery		Year Prior to Delivery										Delivery Year					Life of Delivery Range
		Mar.	Apr.	May	June	July	Aug.	Sept.	Oct.	Nov.	Dec.	Jan.	Feb.	Mar.	Apr.	May	
1980	High	—	—	—	215.0	217.0	227.0	239.5	241.0	227.5	230.2	244.4	242.2	219.3	183.0	160.0	244.4
	Low	—	—	—	208.5	211.0	214.0	222.0	197.7	201.2	216.5	215.3	215.0	181.5	153.1	146.5	146.5
	Close	—	—	—	212.7	214.6	222.7	233.5	206.3	222.8	218.4	234.1	216.3	185.5	161.5	152.2	—
1981	High	221.0	210.2	222.0	225.5	233.5	222.0	215.5	214.0	220.0	210.7	205.2	198.3	181.4	190.4	181.0	233.5
	Low	176.0	164.0	202.0	210.6	218.0	191.9	195.3	194.2	205.7	175.5	185.3	169.5	164.3	163.2	167.1	163.2
	Close	178.1	204.5	220.8	218.5	219.1	196.9	198.5	207.4	208.5	194.5	195.8	169.8	169.6	178.4	175.5	—
1982	High	—	—	—	220.3	214.3	201.5	186.0	183.0	182.8	180.0	166.5	153.1	151.9	145.2	127.5	220.3
	Low	—	—	—	204.6	199.0	183.3	160.0	157.1	162.4	163.4	147.6	142.7	137.5	120.6	115.5	115.5
	Close	—	—	—	211.0	199.3	184.0	163.2	164.8	179.2	169.1	154.0	142.9	142.4	126.8	122.6	—
1983	High	192.7	186.5	178.4	171.0	168.5	170.9	169.3	179.6	191.7	195.3	209.5	206.6	194.6	193.6	221.7	209.5
	Low	180.0	172.0	170.0	151.5	154.8	155.2	157.6	157.9	178.6	181.1	189.8	190.7	183.8	182.7	191.5	151.5
	Close	185.0	174.0	175.5	157.5	158.6	166.0	159.7	178.7	185.9	191.0	204.9	190.7	184.6	193.2	217.2	—
1984	High	237.1	240.1	245.5	234.5	231.0	221.5	213.7	217.6	209.4	205.0	194.3	199.7	201.9	188.2	150.4	245.5
	Low	228.8	228.6	222.9	221.0	214.0	200.4	195.3	198.5	196.8	189.5	184.0	182.0	186.0	148.2	125.1	125.1
	Close	231.8	239.5	230.6	228.5	214.8	207.4	213.0	199.3	202.8	194.2	185.7	197.0	186.7	148.6	130.8	—
1985	High	219.0	215.5	187.0	178.7	167.5	176.2	165.0	171.3	174.1	174.0	176.7	163.0	148.3	147.4	149.9	225.0
	Low	214.0	185.6	167.0	160.5	147.4	153.5	151.0	154.0	165.9	158.5	163.0	146.6	121.1	122.5	136.1	121.1
	Close	215.5	185.6	175.5	166.0	154.2	155.5	157.5	169.5	170.8	173.3	164.0	147.0	124.2	137.4	148.7	—
1986	High	164.5	173.0	176.4	176.0	170.5	158.7	154.9	158.2	160.5	161.9	156.6	161.9	197.0	196.5	189.5	197.0
	Low	153.0	154.0	162.0	165.5	154.5	145.2	145.6	147.7	153.0	155.0	143.3	140.0	159.1	169.0	175.1	140.0
	Close	155.0	163.0	171.1	168.1	156.9	150.3	152.7	157.4	157.9	158.1	144.3	159.9	183.9	177.4	180.6	—
1987	High	173.0	172.5	172.0	174.5	169.4	177.1	179.0	176.0	172.1	173.5						
	Low	160.0	161.1	163.2	162.3	155.5	159.0	162.0	162.0	163.0	159.5						
	Close	167.0	166.0	166.3	163.5	159.9	172.0	166.6	170.5	165.6	160.0						

Source: Chicago Mercantile Exchange   T.377

Residential Construction Contracts Awarded (All Types) in U.S.   In Millions of Dollars

Year	Jan.	Feb.	Mar.	Apr.	May	June	July	Aug.	Sept.	Oct.	Nov.	Dec.	Total
1976	2,168	2,557	3,636	4,017	3,932	4,175	4,190	4,201	3,824	4,119	3,761	3,264	44,169
1977	2,967	3,519	5,328	5,503	5,803	6,043	5,703	6,198	5,641	5,534	5,359	4,340	62,017
1978	3,925	3,863	6,333	6,850	7,801	7,917	6,823	7,120	6,496	7,080	5,973	4,715	74,949
1979	4,530	4,588	6,984	7,185	8,084	7,309	6,882	7,075	6,184	6,808	4,704	4,173	74,557
1980	4,055	4,365	4,435	4,318	4,410	5,067	6,139	6,092	6,255	6,804	5,847	5,540	63,668
1981	4,227	4,167	5,957	6,617	5,855	5,805	5,810	4,726	4,704	4,718	3,648	3,677	60,164
1982	2,991	3,045	4,542	4,645	5,060	5,674	5,188	5,354	5,560	5,548	5,784	5,401	59,210
1983	5,080	4,942	7,945	7,859	8,594	10,223	8,532	9,113	8,698	8,223	7,604	6,596	93,567
1984	6,809	6,989	9,085	9,518	10,831	9,879	9,093	9,365	8,090	8,340	7,614	5,774	101,389
1985[1]	6,354	5,881	9,374	9,443	10,331	8,819	10,608	9,971	9,465	9,598	8,015	6,976	106,771
1986[1]	6,623	6,602	9,069	11,791	11,252	10,977	10,840	10,145	9,950				

[1] Preliminary.   *Source: F. W. Dodge Co.*   T.372

United States Imports of Sawmill Products   In Millions of Board Feet

Year	Jan.	Feb.	Mar.	Apr.	May	June	July	Aug.	Sept.	Oct.	Nov.	Dec.	Total
1976	477	527	627	701	669	573	890	680	781	715	759	779	8,178
1977	691	721	906	890	996	999	934	920	938	858	956	911	10,698
1978	865	840	939	915	1,173	1,117	1,194	1,119	1,014	1,091	979	954	12,199
1979	925	761	998	925	1,237	1,011	1,010	1,043	999	924	909	771	11,513
1980	727	923	896	655	730	830	876	804	863	867	892	799	9,859
1981	756	848	966	980	992	934	842	465	660	755	728	591	9,518
1982	530	585	601	792	848	888	874	888	962	758	916	781	9,421
1983	879	933	1,055	885	1,153	1,099	1,048	1,090	1,057	1,118	1,092	885	12,293
1984	941	1,135	1,108	1,098	1,073	1,172	1,202	1,191	1,298	1,185	1,104	1,108	13,614
1985	967	1,203	1,212	420	1,431	1,445	1,318	1,308	1,307	1,395	1,146	1,039	14,191
1986	1,113	1,159	1,325	1,380	1,438	1,411	1,594	1,272					

Source: Department of Commerce   T.373

LUMBER & PLYWOOD

Average Index Price of Softwood Plywood—Western $ per Thousand Board Feet 1967 = 100

Year	Jan.	Feb.	Mar.	Apr.	May	June	July	Aug.	Sept.	Oct.	Nov.	Dec.	Average
1979	354.3	351.7	351.5	345.6	329.8	304.1	319.1	324.3	327.6	327.4	309.4	300.4	328.8
1980	293.8	308.0	302.3	256.9	275.4	301.7	324.5	346.2	324.0	324.2	330.3	343.3	310.9
1981	326.4	330.0	323.3	332.2	319.7	329.4	322.1	311.0	301.9	283.7	286.7	296.7	313.6
1982	291.3	288.4	288.7	283.5	279.2	287.6	282.3	278.8	274.9	272.5	276.5	284.6	282.4
1983	292.0	299.9	302.3	302.3	304.4	327.5	325.4	314.4	302.3	307.1	303.4	308.7	307.5
1984	312.4	320.1	318.0	308.7	289.7	288.8	290.3	308.6	305.2	307.2	302.4	302.4	304.5
1985	301.2	291.1	287.0	285.5	303.9	319.7	324.5	320.1	304.6	308.0	301.6	300.5	304.0
1986	300.0	298.2	312.2	329.5	321.1	311.0	311.5	307.9	310.9	310.1			

Source: Bureau of Labor Statistics (0831–01)   T.379

Average Index Price of Softwood Yellow Southern Pine (Dressed) Flooring[1] (C & Better)   1967 = 100

Year	Jan.	Feb.	Mar.	Apr.	May	June	July	Aug.	Sept.	Oct.	Nov.	Dec.	Average
1979	307.0	306.4	315.7	319.0	315.8	315.2	320.7	333.7	343.6	344.4	341.1	328.2	324.2
1980	322.0	322.2	317.2	281.2	280.1	287.3	296.4	304.1	295.1	282.3	286.9	293.7	297.4
1981	291.9	292.2	294.7	308.4	313.9	309.5	297.0	291.6	279.4	273.6	267.0	279.7	291.6
1982	278.0	273.4	273.4	285.3	283.1	298.4	305.1	288.6	287.5	279.3	284.9	293.4	285.9
1983	303.0	314.8	319.3	321.3	325.5	334.9	330.0	323.4	308.3	313.5	316.2	328.2	319.9
1984	334.0	337.8	336.1	334.5	320.4	317.1	318.8	318.4	308.5	305.4	302.4	304.8	319.9
1985	303.4	294.2	295.8	292.4	326.4	347.0	321.1	297.1	288.0	283.4	279.6	279.5	300.7
1986	288.8	288.8	304.1	324.5	317.0	306.1	302.8	302.7	291.0	287.9			

[1] Flooring. C and better, F. G., 1″ × 4″ × S/L.   *Source: Bureau of Labor Statistics* (0811–02)   T.381

Average Index Price of Ponderosa Pine[1] Softwood Lumber—No. 2   Dec. 1980 = 100[2]

Year	Jan.	Feb.	Mar.	Apr.	May	June	July	Aug.	Sept.	Oct.	Nov.	Dec.	Average
1976	154.01	177.50	198.52	209.92	189.73	165.91	161.57	168.63	182.50	198.68	198.57	206.15	184.31
1977	227.16	232.18	245.58	251.21	239.98	216.44	219.96	232.57	236.48	235.28	215.40	226.17	231.53
1978	247.58	263.85	264.90	267.57	240.07	251.25	232.33	236.92	254.23	267.17	N.A.	317.01	237.07
1979	304.49	332.11	366.87	371.17	342.59	338.16	306.16	301.95	309.48	316.41	277.35	240.42	317.26
1980	252.62	291.36	314.97	242.34	215.48	252.06	310.05	327.35	304.06	293.25	306.22	340.83	287.55
1981[2]	102.9	102.3	103.7	107.8	111.2	110.4	106.9	103.6	100.0	93.0	90.6	93.4	102.2
1982	N.A.	95.0	97.6	99.0	97.7	97.3	98.3	95.6	91.7	87.9	86.1	90.8	94.5
1983	N.A.	N.A.	N.A.	N.A.	N.A.	N.A.	N.A.	103.8	88.3	90.1	N.A.	91.3	93.4
1984	93.6	101.3	102.5	97.0	87.7	89.5	87.6	89.6	89.5	89.4	91.6	93.9	92.8
1985	95.6	97.5	98.4	94.9	92.2	103.3	98.7	94.9	89.7	93.6	95.3	97.5	96.0
1986	98.9	98.3	96.5	101.8	99.5	94.4	90.4	88.8	94.1	94.2			

[1] No. 3 1″ × 12″, B.L. (6′ and over).   [2] Prices prior to 1981 are for Ponderosa Pine in $ per Ths. Board Feet.   *Source: Bureau of Labor Statistics* (0811–0312.99)   T.380

Average Index Price of Douglas Fir Softwood Lumber—Dimension, Construction, Dried, 2″ × 4″, R.L.[1]   1967 = 100[2]

Year	Jan.	Feb.	Mar.	Apr.	May	June	July	Aug.	Sept.	Oct.	Nov.	Dec.	Average
1976	175.43	178.29	184.90	180.05	176.06	171.45	187.49	195.59	215.08	207.79	204.02	218.77	191.24
1977	228.38	225.50	232.09	226.05	225.42	213.79	230.93	242.51	256.92	237.27	218.03	227.70	230.38
1978	238.08	241.81	246.28	238.48	238.48	245.28	245.00	272.06	274.74	266.66	271.51	262.40	253.39
1979[2]	357.2	360.1	371.0	381.1	381.8	378.3	387.4	408.4	424.0	410.4	378.7	368.8	383.9
1980	363.3	367.1	358.8	327.1	329.6	353.2	358.7	360.0	357.1	354.5	352.9	353.4	353.0
1981	347.2	330.4	321.8	332.7	328.5	333.1	320.1	318.3	296.8	277.6	268.0	267.0	311.8
1982	266.4	259.4	258.5	265.6	262.1	271.8	277.8	268.9	269.6	261.8	259.9	272.5	266.2
1983	312.1	370.3	376.2	375.5	390.2	404.7	407.0	381.4	345.3	332.0	318.7	324.7	361.5
1984	322.8	351.7	369.7	364.3	335.8	322.8	307.8	309.2	312.5	301.6	312.8	325.8	328.1
1985	332.9	341.5	353.1	345.0	358.9	386.6	379.4	343.3	313.7	299.2	283.8	301.9	336.6
1986	314.2	303.6	316.1	348.0	358.2	331.1	341.8	339.3	345.4	332.4			

[1] Dried, S4S, mixed carlots, f.o.b. mill, rail shipment.   [2] Prices prior to 1979 are in $ per Ths. Board Feet.   *Source: Bureau of Labor Statistics* (0811–01)   T.382

Magnesium

1986 domestic production of magnesium is estimated to be unchanged from 1985's 150,000 short tons. During the year, three companies were engaged in the production of magnesium metal, one of the lightest of metals with good strength properties.

Magnesium metal is produced in the U.S. either by electrolytic or silico-thermal methods. There are two plants that use salt-diffusion techniques in an electrolytic recovery process and one company that mines dolomite ores for magnesium metal ore to be separated by silico-thermal recovery methods.

The U.S. is essentially self-sufficient in magnesium metal production; imports are an insignificant part of the consumption picture. The world's largest producer of magnesium metal, the U.S. is also a net exporter of about one-third of its annual production. The USSR is the second-largest producer with approximately 95,000 tons of annual production. Total world production is estimated at 350,000 tons.

Because of its strong structural characteristics, magnesium is being used more extensively in the automotive industry. Recent advances in improving the corrosion-resistant properties of magnesium has doubled its use in autos in each of the last two years.

More than half (54 percent) of magnesium consumption is in the manufacture of aluminum-base alloys; castings and wrought products account for 16 percent and a variety of other uses accounts for less than ten percent each.

Domestic consumption in 1986 was estimated unchanged from 1985's apparent consumption of 140,000 tons. (Apparent consumption is defined as primary metal production plus recovery from old scrap and net import reliance.)

Resources from which magnesium metal may be recovered are almost unlimited and are globally widespread. Resources of dolomite and magnesium-bearing evaporite minerals are enormous. Magnesium-bearing brines are estimated to be in the billions of tons; magnesium can be recovered from sea water at places along world coastlines where the degree of salinity is highest.

World Production of Magnesium (Primary and Secondary)   In Short Tons

	Primary										Secondary Production		
Year	Canada	China	France	Italy	Japan	Norway	USSR	United States	Yugoslavia	World Total[1]	Japan	United Kingdom	United States	USSR
1975	4,217	1,100	8,303	6,993	9,412	42,259	66,000	N.A.		138,284				
1976	6,715	5,500	8,857	9,740	12,335	42,778	69,000	119,957	—	274,882	8,379	3,000	30,553	N.A.
1977	8,414	5,500	9,570	9,663	10,379	42,070	72,000	125,958	—	283,554	8,360	3,000	32,684	N.A.
1978	9,159	6,600	9,370	10,668	12,304	43,166	77,000	149,463	0	317,755	12,057	3,000	36,228	N.A.
1979	9,937	6,600	9,968	9,653	12,531	48,697	79,000	162,464	0	338,850	18,058	3,000	37,222	8,000
1980	10,199	7,700	10,282	8,693	10,199	48,890	83,000	169,477	0	348,440	26,314	3,000	40,461	8,000
1981	9,370	7,700	8,006	11,900	6,247	52,472	86,000	153,782	4,254	339,731	31,345	2,100	46,256	9,000
1982	8,700	7,700	10,593	10,960	6,123	39,598	89,000	102,197	4,697	279,568	23,887	1,940	43,232	9,000
1983	6,600	7,700	12,208	8,473	6,643	32,897	91,000	115,431	5,252	286,204	14,343	1,900	46,329	9,000
1984[2]	8,800	7,700	14,299	8,257	7,830	54,343	94,000	159,207	4,700	360,236	17,258	N.A.	48,357	9,000
1985[1]	7,700	7,700	14,300	8,667	9,323	60,000	96,000	149,614	5,000	360,504	23,000	N.A.	45,523	9,000

[1] Estimate.   [2] Preliminary.   *Source: Bureau of Mines*   T.383

Salient Statistics of Magnesium in the United States   In Short Tons

Year	Primary (Ingot)	Production Secondary New Scrap	Production Secondary Old Scrap	Production Total	Exports[2]	Imports for Consumption	Consumer Stocks Dec. 31[3]	$ Price per Pound[4]	Castings Structural Products	Wrought Structural Products	Total	Alumin. Alloys	Other Uses[5]	Total
1975	120,203	18,090	9,783	27,873	32,591	7,903	19,664	.82	9,488	9,666	19,154	46,670	28,343	94,167
1976	119,957	19,024	11,529	30,553	13,444	14,907	17,295	.87–.92	7,051	10,241	17,292	54,320	32,841	104,453
1977	125,958	20,170	12,524	32,694	28,061	5,964	11,838	.96–.99	7,201	12,632	19,833	56,086	27,657	103,576
1978	149,463	22,135	14,093	36,228	41,807	6,668	12,583	.99–1.01	7,651	11,075	18,726	58,798	31,434	108,958
1979	162,464	23,340	13,882	37,222	54,280	4,754	13,901	1.01–1.09	7,460	11,562	19,022	60,549	29,273	108,844
1980	169,477	22,907	17,554	40,461	56,761	3,757	14,393	1.07–1.25	5,847	11,620	17,467	54,490	23,831	95,788
1981	153,782	22,073	24,183	46,256	34,855	6,897	11,367	1.25–1.34	4,951	10,376	15,327	50,518	25,616	91,461
1982	102,197	19,801	23,431	43,232	39,613	4,784	10,268	1.34	3,600	10,128	13,728	39,878	20,993	74,599
1983	115,431	21,591	24,738	46,329	46,690	6,350	11,329	1.38	3,341	11,435	14,776	46,026	21,174	81,976
1984[6]	159,207	21,594	26,763	48,357	48,337	9,381	6,920	1.43–1.48	4,193	10,246	14,439	48,673	26,775	89,887
1985[1]	149,614	19,579	25,944	45,523	40,322	9,271	6,168	1.48–1.53	5,000	11,949	16,949	40,850	25,703	83,502
1986[1]	125,000				44,000	9,400		1.29–1.53						

[1] Estimate.   [2] Metal & alloys in crude form, & scrap.   [3] Primary magnesium. Gov't. agencies continue to hold quantities of primary magnesium.   [4] Magnesium ingots (99.8%) f.o.b. Valasco, Texas.   [5] Distributive or sacrificial purposes.   [6] Preliminary.   *Source: Bureau of Mines* T.384

Manganese

Manganese, a hard metallic element, provides an oxide used as an alloying agent in steel. The USSR and South Africa account for more than 80 percent of the world's identified resources of manganese; the USSR contributes about 43 percent of the total. World production in 1986 was estimated at 27 million tons (gross weight), up five percent from 1985. Production in the USSR was estimated unchanged at 11 million tons; South African output was expected to increase eight percent to 4.1 million tons.

There was no U.S. production of ore of 35 percent or more manganese during 1986; the country relied on imports and stock drawdowns. U.S. imports for 1986 were projected to be about 193,000 tons, almost two percent more than last year. Gabon supplied 50 percent of U.S. imports, Brazil 18 percent, and Australia 14 percent. As of October, 1986, silicomanganese imports surpassed those for all of 1985. The U.S. is also a large importer of ferromanganese.

U.S. exports of manganese ore totaled 40,499 tons by October, 1986, one percent higher than in all of 1985. Mexico was the largest importer of manganese from the U.S. and constituted 72 percent of the U.S. export market, followed by Canada with 15 percent. Ferromanganese exports for this same period were estimated at 3,900 tons, compared with 8,000 tons in 1985; 53 percent of U.S. exports went to Canada, 32 percent to West Germany.

Average consumption rates for managanese ferroalloys increased modestly, along with a small advance in the raw steel production rate, according to the Bureau of Mines. Year-to-date U.S. consumption of manganese was 340,000 tons by October, 1986. Average daily consumption rate of ferromanganese was 785 tons; the rates for silicomanganese and manganese metal were 255 tons and 50 tons per day, respectively. Most manganese ore was consumed by 20 firms with plants located principally in the eastern and midwestern U.S. Most of the ore was upgraded to ferroalloys and metal for steel production; the remainder was used in pig iron, dry cell batteries and various chemicals. Industry stocks of manganese ore at the end of October, 1986, were 367,000 tons.

U.S. end uses of manganese ore in 1985 were broken down as follows: construction, 27 percent; transportation, 22 percent; machinery, 16 percent; and others, 35 percent. The Bureau of Mines predicts negligible annual growth in U.S. demand for manganese through 1990. Demand for the metal is closely linked with trends in U.S. raw steel production. There is no satisfactory substitute for manganese in its major applications.

Manganese is included in the government stockpile. As of October, 1986, no sales of manganese from the stockpile in 1986 were reported by the General Service Administration.

World Production of Manganese Ore   (Gross Weight) In Thousands of Short Tons

Year	Aus-tralia[3] 37–53[5]	Brazil 38–50	Bulgaria 29	China 30	Gabon 50–53	Ghana 30–50	Hungary[4] 30–33	India 10–54	Japan 24–27	Mexico 27–50	Morocco 50–53	South Africa 30–48+	USSR 30–31	Yugo-slavia 25–45	World Total
1980	2,204	2,515	54	1,760	2,366	275	91.0	1,865	87.7	492.9	144.8	6,278	10,750	33	29,086
1981	1,555	2,251	50	1,760	1,640	246	78.0	1,682	96	637	121	5,555	10,090	34	25,967
1982	1,238	2,580	50	1,760	1,667	176	91	1,642	86	561	106	5,750	10,830	30	26,701
1983	1,510	2,306	50	1,760	2,047	191	65	1,455	83	386	81	3,181	10,890	35	24,190
1984[1]	2,016	2,969	50	1,760	2,336	296	74	1,192	68	525	63	3,361	11,100	30	26,027
1985[2]	2,192	2,976	50	1,760	2,592	338	72	1,257	23	511	48	3,969	10,900	28	26,922

[1] Preliminary.   [2] Estimated.   [3] Metallurgical Ore.   [4] Concentrate.   [5] Ranges of percentage of manganese.
Source: Bureau of Mines   T.385

Salient Statistics of Manganese in the United States   In Thousands of Short Tons (Gross Weight)

Year	Net Import Reliance as a % of Apparent Consump-tion	Manganese Ore (35% or More Mn) Consumption by Use — Alloys and Metal	Pig Iron Steel	Dry Cells, Misc.	Imports For Con-sumption	Con-sump-tion	Stocks, Dec. 31[2]	Ferromanganese Domestic Produc-tion	Imports for Consump-tion	Ex-ports	Con-sump-tion	Manganiferous Ore[3] Ship-ments	Value Mil. $[4]	Silico-manganese Prod-uction	Ship-ments
1980	98	727.5	131.5	211.7	698	1,071	1,030	189.5	605.7	11.7	789.1	173.9	2.4	188	162
1981	98	744.8	147.8	184.0	639	1,077	1,036	192.7	671.2	14.9	820.9	174.8	2.9	173	173
1982	99	412.3	83.9	112.6	238	609	751	119.0	492.7	10.3	439.2	31.5	.3	69	83
1983	99	274.3	105.5	150.9	368	531	617	86	341.6	8.4	446.3	33.5	.2	N.A.	63
1984	98	N.A.	117.0	N.A.	338	615	582	N.A.	409.3	6.8	492.2	88.4	9	N.A.	N.A.
1985[1]	100	N.A.	90.0	N.A.	387	545	589	N.A.	366.9	6.9	466.0	20.0		N.A.	N.A.
1986[5]					410				135.0						

[1] Preliminary.   [2] Including bonded warehouses; excludes Gov't stocks; also excludes small tonnages of dealers' stocks.   [3] 5 to 35% Manganese.   [4] Combined value for total Manganese ore & Manganiferous ores.   [5] Estimate.   *Source: Bureau of Mines*   T.386

Manganese Ore (35% or More Mn) Imported[2] into the U.S.   In Thousands of Short Tons (Mn Content)

Year	Angola	Zaire	Brazil	Congo (Brazz.)	Canada	Ghana	India	Mexico	Morocco	Gabon	Australia	Turkey	South Africa	Total	Value Mill. $
1977	—	14.7	111.6	—	—	—	—	34.9	17.1	245.2	13.8	—	16.9	454	56.4
1978	—	13.2	52.1	9.5	—	—	—	18.4	14.5	127.0	32.6	—	11.0	278.2	33.6
1979	—	—	51.7	22.5	—	—	—	2.1	10.7	49.2	55.3	—	52.1	243.6	27.5
1980	—	—	33.6	—	—	—	—	18.6	5.3	79.9	106.0	—	86.4	329.8	46.4
1981	—	—	38.9	—	—	—	—	25.8	13.6	90.6	34.3	—	97.5	300.7	42.6
1982	—	—	3.0	—	1.7	—	—	1.5	5.0	23.2	18.8	—	57.9	111.1	16.2
1983	—	—	39.1	—	—	—	—	25.6	—	85.5	15.1	—	12.7	178.1	19.9
1984	—	—	44.3	—	—	—	—	16.3	—	66.1	21.0	—	17.3	165.0	16.0
1985[1]	—	—	59.8	—	—	—	—	21.8	.1	64.1	43.1	—	—	188.8	22.6
1986[3]	—	—	40.0					15.0	.2	100.0	30.0		17.0	200.0	

[1] Preliminary.   [2] Imported for consumption.   [3] Estimate.   *Source: Dept of Commerce*   T.387

United States General Imports[1] of Manganese Ore   In Thousands of Long Tons—Manganese Content

Year	Jan.	Feb.	Mar.	Apr.	May	June	July	Aug.	Sept.	Oct.	Nov.	Dec.	Total
1977	71	53	29	48	121	119	62	87	110	49	21	64	884
1978	94	50	113	50	71	55	82	42	97	62	64	63	842
1979	62	50	60	57	85	122	61	34	85	53	105	76	850
1980	109	56	54	66	97	68	54	67	60	38	57	69	795
1981	22	76	55	70	111	78	68	55	14	25	32	15	477
1982	65	49	65	55	22	58	35	33	14	25	32	15	483
1983	61	29	37	20	38	45	50	28	46	56	39	35	483
1984	39	63	33	64	33	68	46	52	31	37	33	35	535
1985	43	66	81	130	35	63	80	53	41	61	97	50	828
1986	66	104	53	98	51	47	75	79	93	58			

[1] General imports of ore, concentrates manganiferous ore, manganese alloys & metals.   *Source: Department of Commerce*   T.388

Production of Ferromanganese in U.S., & Materials Used in Its Manufacture

Year	Ferromanganese Produced Manganese Contained			Silico-Manganese Production (Gr. Wt.) Sh. Tns.	Materials Consumed (Short tons) Manganese Ore		Manganese Ore Used Per Ton of Ferromanganese & Silico-manganese	Ferromanganese shipments (Sh. Tons)
	Short Tons	Per Cent	Short Tons		Foreign	Domestic		
1977	334,134	78.8	263,136	120,000	889,296	35,769	1.9	
1978	272,530	80.6	219,707	142,000	740,906	90,660	1.9	
1979	317,102	80.2	254,389	165,000	785,664	125,130	1.8	
1980	189,472	79.7	150,982	188,000	691,250	34,877	1.9	194
1981	192,690	80.0	154,156	173,000	684,857	57,722	2.0	188
1982	119,000	82.0	97,500	69,000	—412,000—		2.2	98
1983	86,000	81.0	109,000	N.A.	—283,000—		N.A.	109
1984	N.A.	82.0	N.A.	N.A.	—N.A.—		N.A.	N.A.
1985[1]	N.A.	81.0	N.A.	N.A.	—N.A.—		N.A.	N.A.

[1] Preliminary.   *Source: Bureau of Mines*   T.390

Average Price of Ferromanganese[1] (78% Mn-F.O.B. Plant)   In Dollars Per Gross Ton—Carloads

Year	Jan.	Feb.	Mar.	Apr.	May	June	July	Aug.	Sept.	Oct.	Nov.	Dec.	Average
1976	432½	432½	432½	432½	432½	432½	432½	432½	432½	432½	425	417½	430.63
1977	417½	417½	417½	399½	399½	399½	399½	399½	399½	399½	399½	399½	404.00
1978	399½	399½	399½	399½	422.17	425	425	425	425	425	425	425	416.26
1979	440	440	440	465	490	490	490	490	490	493	510	510	479.04
1980	510	510	510	510	510	510	510	510	510	510	510	510	510.00
1981	510	510	510	510	510	510	510	510	510	510	510	510	510.00
1982	510	510	510	510	510	510	510	510	510	510	510	510	510.00
1983	510	510	510	510	510	510	510	510	510	510	510	510	510.00
1984	510	510	510	510	510	510	510	510	510	—No Quotes—			510.00

[1] Domestic standard.   *Source: American Metal Market.*   T.389

Meats

On a retail-weight basis, total U.S. red meat and poultry consumption in 1986 was estimated at 214 pounds per person, just under the record 215 pounds of 1985. Per-person purchases of 79 pounds of beef and 58 pounds of pork, combined with stable lamb, mutton and veal consumption, brought total red meat consumption to 141 pounds, two percent below 1985. Chicken consumption per person was forecast at 63 pounds, up from 58 pounds in 1985, and turkey consumption rose almost 12 percent to 13.5 pounds. Total poultry consumption was estimated at 73.4 pounds per person, a five-percent increase from last year.

Poultry consumption is likely to continue to expand through 1987, even though USDA expects per capita meat consumption to fall about one percent from 1986 levels. Beef consumption is expected to decline almost seven percent as supplies decrease from a year ago; pork consumption may drop about three percent. 1987 poultry consumption is projected to increase seven percent, chicken about five percent and turkey 17 percent.

Higher meat prices in 1986 and a sluggish economy hindered continued growth in consumption; the BLS Retail Price Index advanced almost seven percent from September, 1985, to September, 1986. Retail beef prices increased three percent, pork prices 15 percent and poultry prices 16 percent in the same period. The rise in beef and pork prices was attributed to a sharp drop in pork production, low pork stocks, and a slight increase in beef supplies. Poultry prices benefited from increased fast-food demand.

Total meat production for 1986 was estimated at 56.6 billion pounds, up one percent from last year. The largest gains were seen in turkeys (13 percent) and broilers (four percent). Poultry production was up six percent at an estimated 17.8 billion pounds. Red meat output, on the other hand, was down one percent to 38.7 billion pounds. Although beef production was up two percent from a year ago, both pork and lamb brought the complex lower, off five and seven percent, respectively. USDA is projecting total meat output in 1987 to be down one percent from 1986. The largest increase is expected in turkey production (15 percent), while the largest decline is expected in veal (eight percent).

Consumers purchased an annual average of 204 pounds of meat and poultry per person starting in 1982. Although this year's decline will probably be followed by another decrease in 1987, the USDA has noted that the consumption mix is likely to change sharply with continue rise in the amount of poultry consumed and a decrease in the consumption of pork and beef.

World Total Meat[1] Production   In Millions of Metric Tons

Year	Argentina	Australia	Bel. & Lux.	Canada	Czechoslovakia	Denmark	France	West Germany	Japan	Italy	New Zealand	Poland	Brazil	South Africa	United Kingdom	United States	U.S.S.R.
1972	2.6	2.4	.8	1.5	.7	.9	3.0	3.6	1.1	1.8	1.0	1.6	2.8	.8	2.1	16.8	10.0
1973	2.6	2.3	.9	1.5	.8	1.0	3.0	3.4	1.1	1.9	1.0	1.8	3.3	.7	2.1	15.8	9.9
1974	2.6	1.9		1.6			3.4	3.8	1.2	2.0		2.0	2.9		2.3	17.1	10.5
1975	2.8	2.4	.9	1.6	.8	1.0	3.4	3.8	1.3	1.7	1.0	2.1	3.0	.8	2.3	16.7	11.0
1976	3.2	2.7	.9	1.7	.8	1.0	3.5	3.9	1.4	1.9	1.2	2.4	3.1	.8	2.1	18.1	10.0
1977	3.3	2.0	.7	1.7	.9	1.0	3.4	3.9	1.5	2.0	1.1	2.3	3.4	.8	2.2	18.0	12.7
1978	3.5	2.8	.9	1.7	1.3	1.1	3.5	4.1	1.7	2.0	1.1	2.7	3.1	.8	2.2	17.5	13.3
1979	3.5	2.5	1.0	1.7	1.3	1.2	3.7	4.2	1.8	2.1	1.1	2.7	3.0	.9	2.2	17.1	13.2
1980	3.3	2.3	1.0	1.9	1.3	1.2	3.7	4.3	1.9	2.2	1.1	2.6	3.2	.9	2.3	17.7	12.6
1981	3.4	2.2	1.0	1.9	1.3	1.2	3.7	4.3	1.9	2.2	1.2	2.0	3.2	.8	2.3	17.7	12.7
1982	2.7	2.5	1.0	1.9	1.2	1.2	3.5	4.2	1.9	2.2	1.1	2.3	3.4	.9	2.2	17.0	12.7
1983[2]	2.5	2.1	1.0	1.9	1.3	1.3	3.5	4.2	1.9	2.3	1.2	2.2	3.4	.8	2.4	17.8	13.6
1984[2]	2.7	1.9	1.1	1.9	1.4	1.3	3.8	4.4	2.0	2.3	1.1	2.1	3.1	.8	2.4	17.8	13.8

[1] Production of beef & veal, mutton & lamb, goat meat, & pork. Horsemeat included from 1976.   [2] Preliminary.
Source: Foreign Agricultural Service, U.S.D.A.

T.395

World Per Capita Consumption of Meat[1] (Total Red Meat)   In Kilograms

Year	Argentina	Australia	Austria	Canada	Denmark	France	West Germany	Ireland	New Zealand	Poland	Switzerland	United Kingdom	United States	Uruguay	U.S.S.R.
1972	74	101	63	73	58	64	67	63	102	47	65	64	88	88	41
1973	79	91	63	71	53	63	65	60	104	49	66	59	81	85	40
1974	87	100	65	73	51	65	67	64	98	74	64	58	87	100	44
1975	99	109	68	73	54	66	67	67	103	73	64	58	83	100	45
1976	101.3	110.2	69.9	79.3	59.8	68.4	69.2	63.6	100.0	66.6	66.2	55.4	88.6	88.8	47.1
1977	101.2	110.1	71.1	76.8	58.7	69.4	69.6	62.4	107.2	65.5	69.5	58.1	87.2	96.8	51.0
1978	105.6	103.4	72.2	73.8	67.2	72.2	72.9	63.0	104.5	58.9	70.0	58.2	84.8	102.9	51.3
1979	103.0	88.3	73.4	71.1	66.9	74.2	74.3	64.9	100.2	57.8	70.2	59.9	81.7	81.5	51.7
1980[2]	103.3	83.8	74.3	73.6	71.0	75.1	75.7	65.9	98.1	56.6	76.8	58.2	83.9	94.0	49.8
1981[3]	103.2	77.7	74.9	72.4	72.1	74.5	75.7	65.9	97.9	48.2	77.9	56.1	80.0	95.1	47.9

[1] Summation of previous individual meat tables plus horse meat.   [2] Preliminary.   [3] Forecast.   *Source: Foreign Agricultural Service, U.S.D.A.*

T.396

Total Red Meat Imports (Carcass Weight Equivalent[2]) of Importing Countries   In Thous. of Metric Tons

Year	Belgium & Lux.	Canada	Czecho-slovakia	France	South Korea	W. Ger-many	Greece	Italy	Japan	Nether-lands	Spain	Switz-erland	Un. King-dom	United States	USSR
1977	121.2	194.3	21.4	556.2		627.0	110.9	612.9	649.0	175.3	59.2	26.0	1,280	1,100	496.2
1978	143.9	172.9	21.0	630.4		633.0	142.0	632.1	665.4	187.5	112.3	33.8	1,276	1,296	132.0
1979	99	140	21	541	108	648	140	684	610	149	124	25	1,245	1,348	469
1980	91	111	21	590	15	700	134	722	486	168	27	23	1,122	1,210	706
1981	88	110	21	579	45	687	80	690	612	146	16	31	1,072	1,058	786
1982	79	112	29	618	82	692	157	824	546	119	28	25	1,137	1,175	679
1983[1]	107	121	25	676	78	728	216	832	599	108	26	27	1,072	1,212	779
1984[3]	107	132	15	682	37	751	219	725	645	101	44	22	1,015	1,280	615

[1] Preliminary.   [2] Excludes fat, offals & live animals.   [3] Forecast.   Source: Foreign Agricultural Service, U.S.D.A.   T.397

Total Red Meat Exports (Carcass Weight Equivalent[2]) of Principal Countries   In Thousands of Metric Tons

Year	Argen-tina	Aus-tralia	Brazil	Canada	Den-mark	France	Ire-land	Mex-ico	Nether-lands	N. Zea-land	Poland	United States	USSR	Uru-guay	Yugo-slavia
1977	669.6	1,335	240.0	112.1	695.6	312.2	363.8	34.1	697.2	790.9	131.8	236.0	49.2	134.6	88.0
1978	823.7	1,377	178.1	117.1	753.4	267.2	359.3	46.6	751.6	724.7	141.0	256.6	38.0	118.8	113.4
1979	728	1,306	111	133	832	306	342	7	785	783	155	211	33	84	82
1980	487	1,087	170	182	857	362	453	1	843	796	141	195	35	128	98
1981	508	966	281	207	905	415	324	1	932	817	60	240	53	185	72
1982	546	1,184	361	247	909	401	311	13	879	846	52	213	32	182	107
1983[1]	438	947	404	242	945	387	341	14	957	938	93	225	25	236	83
1984[3]	264	667	510	268	967	472	335	4	1,054	786	85	227	25	145	90

[1] Preliminary.   [2] Excludes fat, offals & live animals.   [3] Forecast.   Source: Foreign Agricultural Service, U.S.D.A.   T.398

United States Meat Exports by Type of Product   In Metric Tons

Year	Beef and Veal Fresh or frozen	Canned	Pick-led or cured	Goat, lamb and mut-ton, fresh or frozen	Pork Fresh or frozen	Hams and shoul-ders, cured or cooked	Bacon	Other pork, pick-led, salted or other-wise cured	Other pork, canned	Sau-sage, bolo-gna, and frank-furters	Varie-ty meats fresh or fro-zen[1]	Other meats[2]	Total
1977	40,982		517	1,755	116,282	2,941	1,216	2,919	1,810	3,426	173,060	8,198	353,106
1978	51,710	2,296	1,263	1,375	84,120	3,934	1,655	7,524	2,932	3,653	185,831	6,801	353,095
1979	53,823	1,625	1,955	562	83,058	3,380	912	8,912	1,123	3,003	163,930	4,664	331,946
1980	55,003	1,995	2,505	595	69,966	3,327	820	8,438	1,667	3,296	200,417	7,427	355,454
1981	68,608	2,826	3,235	972	86,652	2,363	1,079	9,130	1,662	3,819	209,981	7,949	397,870
1982	78,781	3,028	3,858	676	58,541	1,358	774	7,514	1,289	3,404	230,344	5,291	394,857
1983	86,962	1,584	4,500	632	62,141	1,794	601	5,581	695	3,139	218,311	3,795	389,735
1984[3]	105,995	1,936	3,598	878	46,098	1,474	621	3,837	513	2,603	217,019	3,605	388,177

[1] Edible animal organs.   [2] Includes sausage ingredients, cured (excluding canned); meat and meat products canned (n.e.s.); and baby food, canned.   [3] Preliminary.   Source: Foreign Agricultural Service. Compiled from reports of the U.S. Department of Commerce   T.399

Production and Consumption of Red Meats in the United States (Carcass Weight)

Year	Beef Comm. Produc-tion Mil. Lbs.	Consumption Total	Per Capita Lb.	Veal Comm. Produc-tion Mil. Lbs.	Consumption Total	Per Capita Lb.	Lamb & Mutton Comm. Produc-tion Mil. Lbs.	Consumption Total	Per Capita Lb.	Pork (Excluding Lard) Comm. Produc-tion Mil. Lbs.	Consumption Total	Per Capita Lb.	All Meats Produc-tion Mil. Lbs.	Consumption Total	Per Capita Lb.
1978	24,242	25,998	117.9	599	645	2.9	301	343	1.6	13,393	13,293	60.3	38,119	40,279	182.7
1979	21,262	23,522	105.5	411	450	2.0	282	332	1.5	15,270	15,353	68.8	37,225	39,657	177.8
1980	21,469	23,320	103.4	379	410	1.8	310	345	1.5	16,431	16,574	73.5	38,590	40,648	180.2
1981	22,214	23,756	104.3	415	438	1.9	327	360	1.6	15,719	15,927	69.9	38,675	40,481	177.8
1982	22,366	23,998	104.3	423	457	1.99	356	381	1.65	14,121	14,425	62.6	37,266	39,261	170.5
1983	23,060	24,710	106.2	428	457	1.97	367	388	1.67	15,117	15,369	66.1	38,972	40,924	175.9
1984	23,418	24,900	106.1	479	503	2.14	371	398	1.70	14,720	15,396	65.6	38,988	41,197	175.5
1985[1]	23,557	25,342	106.9	499	527	2.22	352	386	1.63	14,728	15,648	66.0	39,136	41,903	176.8
1986[2]	23,900	25,500	106.8	503	532	2.20	329	371	1.60	13,968	14,847	62.0	38,741	41,302	171.6

[1] Preliminary.   [2] Estimate.   Source: Economic Research Service, U.S.D.A.   T.400

MEATS

U.S. Imports of Meats and Meat Preparations   In Millions of Pounds

Year	Jan.	Feb.	Mar.	Apr.	May	June	July	Aug.	Sept.	Oct.	Nov.	Dec.	Total
1978	138	155	183	202	181	167	161	137	182	184	201	181	2,072
1979	201	184	214	201	190	214	168	141	142	143	188	193	2,178
1980	196	152	166	134	173	154	208	170	133	207	167	191	2,052
1981	171	167	131	155	140	153	162	168	180	167	120	118	1,832
1982	127	106	160	169	167	215	158	234	246	194	124	114	2,015
1983	208	177	170	178	187	176	189	181	171	169	123	104	2,030
1984	180	167	171	198	161	128	209	198	189	226	175	159	2,160
1985[1]	193	179	207	213	214	221	230	232	226	198	196	201	2,511
1986[1]	225	196	197	179	180	213	260	232					

[1] Preliminary.   *Source: Dept. of Commerce*   T.401

United States Meat Imports by Type of Product   In Metric Tons

Year	Beef and Veal — Fresh or frozen[1]	Beef and Veal — Canned, including sausage	Beef and Veal — Other prepared or preserved[2]	Lamb, mutton, and goat, except canned	Pork — Fresh and frozen	Pork — Canned[3]	Pork — Other prepared or preserved[2]	Sausage, all types[4]	Mixed sausage	Other meats n.s.p.f.[5]	Variety meats, fresh or frozen	Total
1977	564,894	43,124	25,618	9,885	12,215	120,388	534	2,209	1,387	3,725	2,591	786,570
1978	675,415	46,779	28,689	17,447	27,891	126,045	1,285	2,082	1,743	4,350	2,454	934,180
1979	713,354	45,890	28,721	19,714	46,268	113,518	1,575	2,434	1,849	5,619	4,695	983,637
1980	642,268	42,729	17,799	15,482	93,143	98,529	1,990	2,929	2,230	5,957	4,562	927,618
1981	544,610	34,932	23,303	14,384	98,226	94,102	1,496	1,935	2,103	7,896	3,560	826,547
1982	607,184	37,747	17,402	8,649	125,282	96,831	1,547	2,372	2,242	7,373	2,823	909,452
1983	565,997	59,073	16,766	8,752	121,707	125,593	2,300	2,176	1,911	8,396	3,935	916,604
1984[6]	516,960	57,863	19,864	8,693	207,703	142,423	3,372	2,243	2,121	7,129	5,707	974,078

[1] Includes prepared items.   [2] Includes pickled and cured.   [3] Includes canned hams, shoulders, and bacon.   [4] Includes fresh and cured sausages.   [5] Mostly mixed luncheon meats.   [6] Preliminary.   *Source: Foreign Agricultural Service. Compiled from reports of the U.S. Department of Commerce.*   T.402

U.S. Exports of Meat and Meat Preparations   In Millions of Pounds

Year	Jan.	Feb.	Mar.	Apr.	May	June	July	Aug.	Sept.	Oct.	Nov.	Dec.	Total
1977	100	100	103	113	110	103	112	110	125	106	109	124	1,315
1978	109	101	115	108	108	99	93	119	131	124	119	111	1,338
1979	102	95	117	99	100	124	103	109	119	135	119	155	1,378
1980	101	108	144	132	139	164	145	129	136	165	144	154	1,663
1981	143	141	169	148	189	180	128	144	123	174	154	153	1,847
1982	129	147	124	131	167	147	111	108	112	133	143	115	1,566
1983	114	104	136	133	115	118	121	99	130	127	134	119	1,449
1984	112	104	134	106	114	103	128	119	123	139	121	119	1,422
1985[1]	119	110	118	112	116	116	130	139	118	139	122	123	1,461
1986[1]	124	123	123	132	139	121	125	147					

[1] Preliminary.   *Source: Dept. of Commerce*   T.403

Average Wholesale Prices of Meats   In Cents Per Pound

Year	Composite Retail Price — of Beef (Choice)	Composite Retail Price — of Pork[4]	Composite Retail Price — of Veal	Composite Retail Price — of Lamb (Choice)	Steer Beef Carcass, Choice, Centr. U.S.	Fresh Beef, Steer Carcasses Choice, E. Coast	Lamb Carcasses Choice & Prime (55-65 Lb.) East Coast	Pork, Fresh Loins, (8-14 lbs.) N.Y.	Hams[2] N.Y. Fancy Skinned, Smoked 14-17 Lb.	Cured Pork Cuts, Picnics, (Smoked) 4-8 Lb.[1]	Live Broilers Georgia
1977	148.4	125.4	175.3	186.8	62.69	66.2	108.73	95.25	86.5	57.03	23.7
1978	181.9	143.6	209.5	219.6	80.43	83.9	120.68	109.15	99.63	70.08	26.0
1979	226.3	144.1	282.3	245.7	101.62	101.1	127.74	107.65	99.38	69.91	26.0
1980	237.6	139.4	309.5	252.7	104.44	104.4	134.98	101.14	88.99	67.01	27.0
1981	238.7	152.4	314.5	252.4	99.84	99.8	127.67	113.70	95.55	68.38	26.5
1982	242.5	175.4	N.A.	N.A.	101.31	101.3	122.15	127.66	111.98	78.19	25.0
1983[3]	238.1	169.8			97.83	97.8	125.86	115.90	75.60	N.A.	27.0
1984[3]	239.6	162.0			100.11	100.1	131.89	115.73	78.22		32.0
1985[3]	232.6	162.0			90.76	91.3	145.93	113.60	67.65		28.2

[1] At NY.   [2] Prior to 1978 prices are composite averages.   [3] Preliminary.   [4] Sold as retail cuts (ham, bacon, loin, etc.).
Sources: Bureau of Labor Statistics; Department of Agriculture   T.404

Average Wholesale Price of Steer Beef Carcass, Choice[1], at Midwest Markets   In Cents per Pound

Year	Jan.	Feb.	Mar.	Apr.	May	June	July	Aug.	Sept.	Oct.	Nov.	Dec.	Average
1976	66.68	62.22	56.97	65.85	63.56	62.45	58.20	57.05	57.24	58.36	60.85	62.52	61.00
1977	60.04	58.92	57.12	60.54	64.44	62.62	63.65	62.49	63.04	65.87	65.47	68.10	62.69
1978	68.74	71.08	74.88	81.43	88.48	85.95	84.81	79.94	81.96	82.14	80.98	84.75	80.43
1979	93.57	97.47	104.59	108.61	108.64	103.56	99.85	94.13	101.91	98.32	103.22	105.53	101.62
1980	102.26	103.70	103.15	99.41	102.00	105.18	110.11	111.96	107.97	105.49	101.44	100.57	104.40
1981	99.80	96.10	94.32	99.68	103.32	106.52	107.20	103.90	102.96	96.02	94.56	93.70	99.80
1982	97.40	101.20	103.80	109.50	115.10	111.20	102.60	100.80	95.50	93.00	92.90	92.62	101.30
1983	93.90	96.55	100.62	107.76	105.00	102.47	97.72	95.01	92.10	91.24	91.57	99.82	97.83
1984	105.74	102.86	105.14	103.50	99.62	98.54	101.26	97.61	94.37	92.38	99.08	101.22	100.11
1985	99.50	97.42	92.00	89.20	89.52	88.48	82.22	80.02	81.14	91.11	99.68	98.84	90.76
1986	92.26	86.82	85.04	83.34	86.42	83.58	89.25	90.98	90.50	91.80	95.70		

[1] 500–600 pounds.   *Source: Economic Research Service, U.S.D.A.*   T.405

Production[2] (Commercial Slaughter) of All Meats[1] in the U.S.   In Millions of Pounds—Carcass Weight

Year	Jan.	Feb.	Mar.	Apr.	May	June	July	Aug.	Sept.	Oct.	Nov.	Dec.	Total
1976	3,267	2,907	3,515	3,109	2,928	3,150	3,048	3,350	3,467	3,497	3,453	3,367	39,060
1977	3,237	3,084	3,551	3,195	3,122	3,298	2,925	3,404	3,354	3,345	3,416	3,241	39,172
1978	3,215	3,045	3,342	3,079	3,269	3,081	2,883	3,274	3,139	3,355	3,345	3,094	38,119
1979	3,280	2,756	3,090	2,879	3,130	2,990	2,958	3,329	2,876	3,556	3,306	3,074	37,225
1980	3,398	3,050	3,099	3,315	3,311	3,089	3,070	3,016	3,221	3,577	3,097	3,349	38,590
1981	3,417	3,014	3,389	3,299	3,071	3,118	3,041	3,044	3,247	3,433	3,185	3,417	38,675
1982	3,152	2,894	3,296		——9,097——			——9,165——			——9,659——		37,266
1983	3,151	2,787	3,269	3,051	3,163	3,299	3,002	3,440	3,435	3,523	3,472	3,383	38,974
1984	3,219	3,092	3,349	3,079	3,411	3,205	3,045	3,362	3,111	3,672	3,324	3,119	38,987
1985[3]	3,420	2,938	3,161	3,294	3,486	3,085	3,277	3,402	3,252	3,544	3,123	3,145	39,131
1986[3]	3,482	2,937	3,133	3,478	3,387	3,157	3,282	3,181	3,259				

[1] Except for pork production & lard.   [2] Represents the total dressed carcass weight of livestock slaughtered under Federal inspection, exclusive of meats from condemned animals.   [3] Preliminary.   *Source: Agricultural Marketing Service, U.S.D.A.*   T.406

Cold Storage Holdings of All[1] Meats in the United States, at End of Month   In Millions of Pounds

Year	Jan.	Feb.	Mar.	Apr.	May	June	July	Aug.	Sept.	Oct.	Nov.	Dec.
1976	643.4	652.8	703.1	724.3	740.9	698.1	645.4	597.6	637.7	687.8	725.9	733.3
1977	745.4	759.6	776.4	823.0	802.4	723.4	629.4	568.6	579.0	532.1	565.2	566.6
1978	559.1	571.6	658.4	753.0	759.8	720.6	644.9	581.0	598.1	639.0	715.4	723.6
1979	728.4	710.9	762.5	783.4	797.0	755.0	685.6	580.7	549.1	604.5	656.9	706.2
1980	735.3	712.6	695.4	715.5	706.5	641.9	578.5	514.3	510.0	584.2	678.6	749.6
1981	790.3	782.9	775.9	817.2	795.2	716.6	628.6	538.9	508.6	546.8	552.2	578.2
1982	553.4	524.2	536.0	—	—	503.9	—	—	473.9	—	—	553.8
1983	573.4	571.0	576.3	607.6	619.2	595.5	569.8	543.3	535.3	576.7	667.6	679.3
1984	692.9	707.7	738.1	777.5	818.9	776.3	713.8	627.6	646.2	674.9	681.4	696.0
1985[2]	735.0	702.9	721.2	772.7	784.9	758.6	738.2	677.1	654.2	645.2	633.0	607.4
1986[2]	616.8	615.3	622.5	663.0	673.9	640.8	620.3	573.0	543.1	574.4	569.3	

[1] Includes beef and veal, mutton and lamb, pork and products, rendered pork fat, and miscellaneous meats. Excludes lard.   [2] Preliminary.   *Source: Crop Reporting Board, U.S.D.A.*   T.407

Cold Storage Holdings of Frozen Beef[1] in the United States   In Millions of Pounds

Year	Jan. 1	Feb. 1	Mar. 1	Apr. 1	May 1	June 1	July 1	Aug. 1	Sept. 1	Oct. 1	Nov. 1	Dec. 1
1976	349.8	342.8	355.7	390.6	390.8	399.7	395.3	382.6	362.8	382.4	405.0	429.6
1977	453.5	474.6	475.4	472.9	472.0	447.4	412.6	374.0	350.1	345.8	301.1	291.5
1978	315.6	313.1	318.4	357.2	376.0	388.2	372.3	336.5	315.7	332.2	348.4	388.2
1979	405.4	423.7	405.0	427.4	410.1	411.9	395.7	369.6	324.2	296.7	308.2	321.9
1980	350.3	367.3	357.6	335.1	296.6	277.9	256.5	242.5	228.6	219.7	243.8	279.0
1981	328.2	361.3	347.8	341.5	339.4	328.6	297.5	272.6	245.2	234.9	244.6	232.2
1982	256.7	249.1	223.3	211.9	—	—	189.7	—	—	247.7	—	—
1983	294.4	303.1	307.0	299.1	277.3	265.2	254.0	252.3	267.4	268.2	278.0	316.0
1984	325.0	338.0	332.5	325.7	324.6	312.8	303.2	301.7	290.0	319.6	326.0	340.1
1985[2]	357.7	375.1	347.0	334.0	328.0	300.9	292.5	319.7	310.6	308.4	294.9	302.3
1986[2]	317.4	318.4	302.3	297.1	301.2	318.5	321.6	337.0	318.4	291.6	292.3	299.0

[1] Includes frozen beef, cured beef, and beef in process of cure.   [2] Preliminary.   *Source: Crop Reporting Board, U.S.D.A.*   T.408

Mercury

Two countries account for about half the world's mercury production—the USSR and Spain. The U.S., often the third-largest producer, accounted for 10–15 percent of world production. In recent years, China's output may have exceeded that of the U.S. The world's largest mine is in Spain; it provides virtually all of that nation's production, estimated at 45,000 flasks in 1985. Last year, the mine was temporarily shut down, apparently owing to weak prices; production was estimated at 60 percent below the previous year.

The U.S. typically consumes more than a quarter of world output and is dependent upon imports to meet a sizable portion of domestic needs. During the past decade, net imports have varied from about 27–62 percent of apparent consumption. Mercury can be recovered from secondary sources; the higher the price, the greater the willingness is to bear recovery costs.

Mercury has important industrial applications. Demand, however, appears to have been adversely affected by publicity over mercury pollution. Demand also reflects economic conditions; sluggish economies in industrialized nations last year likely had an unfavorable impact. Batteries account for about half mercury's consumption, while manufacture of chlorine and caustic soda accounts for another 10–15 percent. Mercury's use in paints has been declining and now apparently accounts for less than half the 8,600 flasks used in the U.S. in 1980. Use in electrical applications appears to be holding, especially in mercury vapor lights which have greater life expectancy than ordinary lights. Preliminary consumption statistics for January–September, 1986, totaled 38,655 flasks, compared with 53,483 for all 1985. This suggests total use last year of 50,000 flasks, the lowest since 1983. The largest decline was apparently in battery use, which totaled 18,436 flasks through September, versus 29,782 for all of 1985.

The U.S. government maintains a mercury stockpile. At mid-year 1986, 169,226 flasks were in the National Defense Stockpile. Department of Energy's stockpile then totaled 32,144 flasks; that agency sold 15 flasks of secondary mercury during the second quarter. Private consumers and dealers were estimated to have 7,788 flasks on hand at mid-1986, versus 8,587 at year-end, 1985. Mine producers were estimated to have 20,000 flasks on hand during early 1986.

Mercury prices, basis New York, have been declining since 1981, when the $450/flask area was neared. Ten years ago, prices hovered around $125. Mercury prices declined during most of 1986. The average New York dealer's prices fell steadily in mid-year, from a June average of $262.33/flask to $173.10 in September. For the first three quarters of 1986, the average price was $240.19, versus $307.44 during the same 1985 period. No formal pact attempts to stabilize prices; the roller-coaster price pattern reflects demand for and supply of mercury at any given time. During the past year, total available supplies have exceeded demand.

World Mine Production of Mercury   In Flasks of 34.5 Kilograms (76 Pounds)

Year	Algeria	China[1]	Czecho-slovakia	Dom. Rep.	Fin-land	Italy	Mexico	Spain	Turkey	United States	USSR[1]	W. Ger-many	Yugo-slavia	World Total
1980	24,403	20,000	4,612	159	2,170	96	4,206	43,038	4,461	30,657	62,000	1,624	—	197,426
1981	25,000	20,000	4,438	77	1,949	7,427	6,962	46,008	5,915	27,904	63,000	2,205	—	210,885
1982	11,000	20,000	4,380	49	2,068	4,612	8,558	48,808	7,129	25,760	64,000	1,537	—	197,901
1983	10,000	20,000	4,177	40	1,857	—	6,411	41,075	4,665	25,070	64,000	2,005	1,500	180,800
1984[1]	23,000	20,000	4,409	30	2,292	—	11,140	44,093	5,274	19,048	64,000	2,000	2,000	195,286
1985[2]	25,000	20,000	4,400	20	2,300	—	10,000	45,000	6,000	16,530	65,000	—	2,000	196,250

[1] Estimate.   [2] Preliminary.   *Source: Bureau of Mines*   T.409

Salient Statistics of Mercury in the United States   In Flasks (76 Pounds Each)

Year	Net Import Reliance as a % of Apparent Consumption	Ore Treated (1,000 Short Tons)	Mercury Produced[2] Flasks	Pounds per Ton of Ore	Production Mine	Second-ary	Stocks, Dec. 31 Pro-ducers	Consum-ers & Dealers	Total	Ex-ports	U.S. Imports (For Consumption) From: Total	Alg-eria	Canada	Italy	Mex-ico	Spain	Japan
1980	27	356.0	30,623	6.5	30,657	16,806	11,095	21,974	33,069	N.A.	9,416	—	843	—	989	3,352	3,813
1981	44	262.4	27,888	8.1	27,904	11,244	11,783	15,556	27,339	—	12,408	—	112	—	104	4,989	2,372
1982	32	301.0	25,704	6.5	25,760	4,473	13,598	15,229	28,827	—	8,916	—	5	—	182	1,404	4,345
1983	30	335.4	25,033	5.7	25,070	13,751	18,323	12,695	31,018	—	12,786	1,795	4	500	1,590	3,408	511
1984	58	216.2	19,014	6.7	19,048	5,673	19,964	7,291	27,255	—	25,327	8,201	14	800	21	11,749	500
1985[1]	57	182.4	16,337	6.8	16,530	5,943	19,398	8,587	27,985	—	18,890	1,938	5	—	214	7,955	2,502
1986[3]					9,500		7,000				20,000						

[1] Preliminary.   [2] Excludes mercury produced from placer operation & from clean-up activity at furnaces & other plants.   [3] Estimate.
Source: Bureau of Mines   T.412

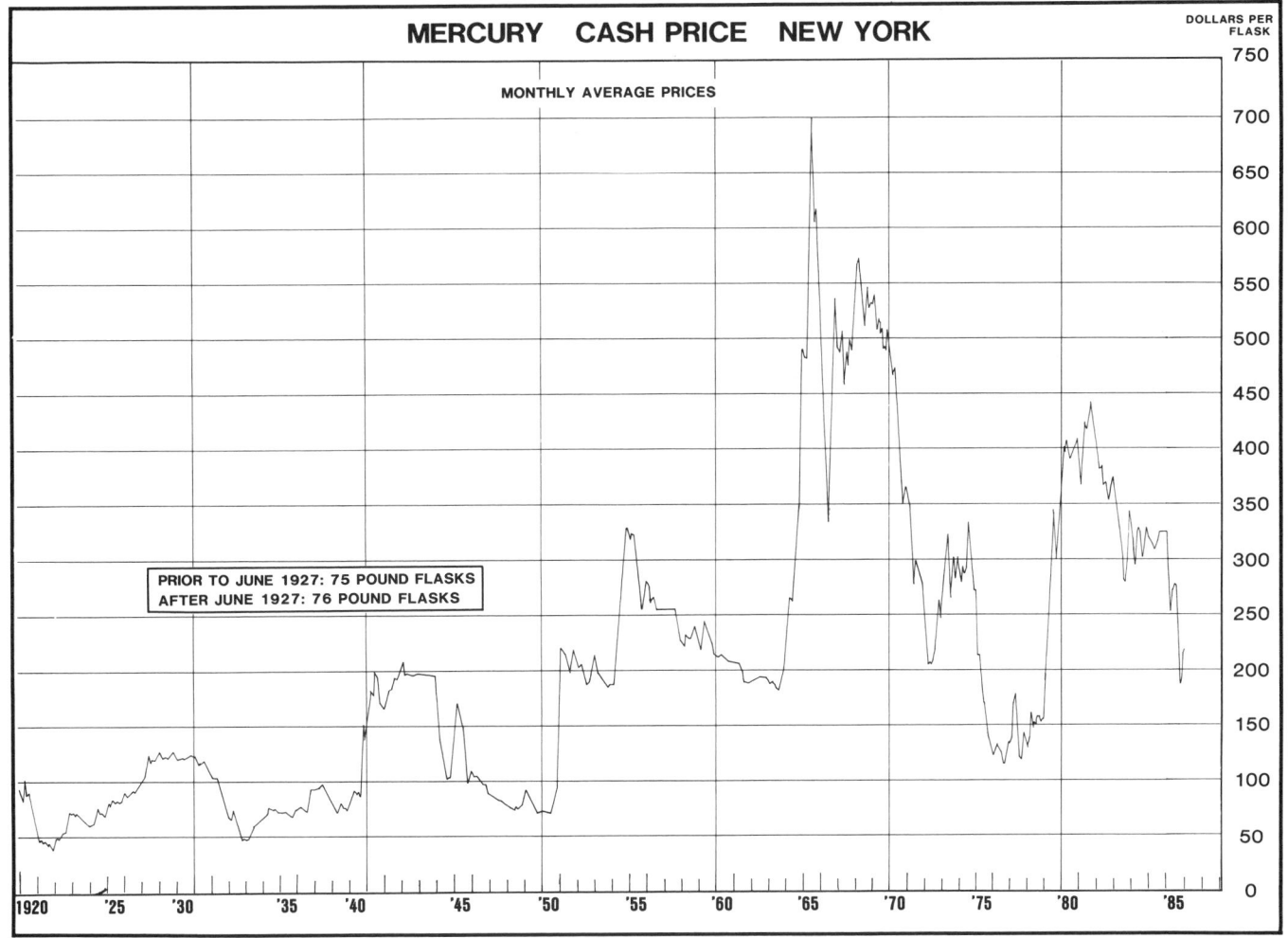

MERCURY CASH PRICE NEW YORK

Average Price of Mercury in New York   In Dollars Per Flask of 76 Pounds

Year	Jan.	Feb.	Mar.	Apr.	May	June	July	Aug.	Sept.	Oct.	Nov.	Dec.	Average
1980	383.75	399.90	420.00	406.81	398.33	389.57	397.11	397.26	402.62	407.83	404.56	376.19	396.72
1981	366.00	386.79	411.18	423.41	418.50	423.07	433.75	441.14	436.55	425.91	421.84	413.07	416.77
1982	405.00	380.92	390.76	384.32	365.88	367.50	364.29	343.30	352.55	373.21	373.75	374.29	372.98
1983	366.67	346.18	338.91	327.62	316.31	300.23	282.25	279.02	299.05	339.29	344.50	331.69	322.64
1984	318.67	295.68	300.45	324.26	328.27	325.48	314.64	302.09	317.18	329.07	327.13	320.08	316.92
1985	317.30	315.00	314.38	309.34	297.27	309.45	316.74	324.61	325.00	325.00	325.00	325.00	316.98
1986	285.68	261.97		272.50	277.50	276.07	260.00		181.91	193.80	215.19	219.43	242.85

Source: American Metal Market

T.410

Mercury Consumed in the United States   In Flasks

Year	Bat-teries	Chlo-rine & Caustic Soda	Cata-lysts	Dental Equip.	Elec-trical Light-ing	Gen-eral Lab. Use	Meas-uring Control Instrum.	Other Instru-ments + Relat.	Paints	Wiring Devices & Switches	Other	Grand Total
1980	27,829	9,470	765	1,779	1,036	363	3,049	190	8,621	3,062	790	58,983
1981	29,441	7,323	815	1,613	1,043	328	5,671	253	7,049	2,641	242	59,244
1982	24,880	6,243	499	1,019	826	281	3,064	194	6,794	2,004	984	48,943
1983	23,350	8,054	484	1,597	1,273	280	2,465	N.A.	6,047	2,316	1,356	49,138
1984	29,700	7,347	359	1,432	1,487	269	2,856	N.A.	4,651	2,730	1,404	54,669
1985[1]	29,782	6,700	497	1,960	1,726	446	2,654	N.A.	4,892	2,843	267	53,483
1986[2]	24,000	7,000		1,500	1,200	450	2,000		5,000	3,000	310	52,000

[1] Preliminary.   [2] Estimate.   *Source: Bureau of Mines*

T.413

Milk

According to preliminary USDA data, worldwide milk production for the 38 major producing countries was expected to expand less than one percent in 1986, to 420.3 million tonnes. This compares with 417.4 million tonnes in 1985. With milk production nearly unchanged in the U.S. and the European Community (EC), the rise in output is due mainly to continued expansion in the USSR; milk production there was projected to increase almost two percent in 1986, as greater productivity offset a decline in cow numbers. Other production gains were seen in India, Mexico, China and New Zealand. The EC accounted for 26 percent of estimated world milk production in 1986, the USSR 24 percent, the U.S. 16 percent, and Oceania three percent.

The major event of 1986 was the institution of the Dairy Termination Program (DTP) authorized as part of the 1985 Farm Bill. Commonly referred to as the buy-out program, the DTP offered cash payments to dairy farmers who contracted to give up dairying for a period of at least five years. Farmers were paid to sell all their dairy cattle for slaughter or export, to have no ownership interest in milk production or dairy cattle for five years, and to ensure that their production facilities would not be used for dairying purposes during those years.

Some 14,000 contracts were accepted under the buy-out program by the time it began in early 1986. The producers concerned had marketed more than 12 billion pounds of milk during 1985, just under nine percent of the domestic total. After mid-year 1986, milk production declined about 2–4 percent from year-earlier rates, as the population of cows fell on the order of three percent—a result of the DTP and a decline in the number of heifers per 100 cows (from more than 45 during 1984–85 to 43.3 in

1986). For 1986 as a whole, though, output of milk was estimated at 146 billion pounds, or approximately one percent greater than in 1985.

On the demand side, there was no major change in the forces that are combining to alter long-standing patterns of fluid-milk consumption. Spurred by advice from medical professionals to reduce intake of animal fats, consumers further lowered their usage of whole milk, in favor of low-fat milk. Production of non-fat dry milk rose more than eight percent during January–July 1986, compared with the same period a year before; canned whole-milk output fell more than 10 percent. Total demand for milk was little affected, however, by the shifts in consumption patterns. USDA reported that, for the first seven months of 1986, commercial usage of milk rose four percent above the level of the year before. The Department credited the gain to lower real (inflation-adjusted) retail prices, continued economic growth, and expanded promotion of the product.

The combination of a curtailed rate of output growth and rising demand produced increased prices at both the wholesale and retail levels. Prices at 1986's ending were expected to be 2–4 percent higher than 12 months earlier. USDA's preliminary forecast was that 1987 output will decline by 1–3 percent from the rate in 1986, while commercial usage of milk will rise by about the same amount. The Department also projects that retail dairy prices will decline through the first half of 1987, as wholesale prices drop toward support prices lowered by federal law, including the Gramm-Rudman-Hollings budget reduction act. But, USDA also expects rising retail prices during 1987's second half, and on balance, retail prices in 1987 are expected to be an average 1–3 percent higher than in 1986.

World Fluid Milk Production (Cow's Milk)   In Millions of Metric Tons

Year	Australia	Brazil	Canada	Czecho-slovakia	Den-mark	Fin-land	West Germany	USSR	India	Nether-lands	New Zealand	France	Poland	Switzerland	United Kingdom	United States
1980	5.6	10.3	7.9	5.9	5.1	3.3	24.8	90.6	15.5	12.0	6.8	26.9	16.7	3.7	16.0	58.3
1981	5.3	10.5	8.0	5.9	5.0	3.2	24.9	88.9	14.0	12.1	6.7	26.8	15.3	3.7	15.9	60.3
1982	5.4	10.1	8.3	5.9	5.2	3.2	25.5	91.0	14.9	12.7	6.8	27.4	15.3	3.7	16.7	61.5
1983	5.7	10.7	8.0	6.5	5.4	3.2	26.9	96.5	16.0	13.2	6.9	27.9	16.1	3.7	17.3	63.4
1984	6.1	10.8	8.2	6.8	5.2	3.2	26.2	97.9	17.1	12.8	7.6	27.6	16.8	3.9	16.6	61.4
1985[1]	6.2	10.4	8.2	6.9	5.1	3.1	25.7	98.2	18.5	12.6	7.9	27.0	16.5	3.8	16.6	65.2
1986[2]	6.2	9.8	8.1	6.9	5.1	3.0	26.0	100.0	20.0	12.3	8.2	27.2	15.4	3.7	16.6	65.3

[1] Preliminary.   [2] Estimate.   *Source: Foreign Agricultural Service, U.S.D.A.*   T.414

U.S. Milk-Feed Price Ratio[1]   In Pounds

Year	Jan.	Feb.	Mar.	Apr.	May	June	July	Aug.	Sept.	Oct.	Nov.	Dec.	Average
1980	1.54	1.57	1.55	1.55	1.53	1.50	1.47	1.42	1.40	1.43	1.40	1.39	1.48
1981	1.39	1.39	1.41	1.39	1.35	1.36	1.40	1.43	1.48	1.53	1.56	1.54	1.44
1982	1.55	1.53	1.53	1.51	1.46	1.47	1.47	1.50	1.57	1.61	1.62	1.60	1.53
1983	1.59	1.56	1.55	1.49	1.45	1.43	1.45	1.41	1.36	1.39	1.36	1.34	1.45
1984	1.33	1.33	1.34	1.32	1.32	1.32	1.35	1.40	1.48	1.56	1.62	1.59	1.42
1985[2]	1.57	1.57	1.55	1.51	1.47	1.45	1.44	1.47	1.51	1.56	1.55	1.53	1.51
1986[2]	1.52	1.50	1.48	1.46	N.A.	N.A.	1.51	N.A.	N.A.	1.72			

[1] Pounds of 16% protein ration equal in value to one pound of milk.   [2] Preliminary.   *Source: Economics & Statistics Service, U.S.D.A.*   T.420

Milk Cows & Cattle and Milk Production in the U.S.

Year	Number of Milk Cows on Farms[2] (Thousands)	Production Per Milk Cow[3] Milk (Pounds)	Milk Fat (Pounds)	Total Milk Production[3] Quantity Billion Pounds	% of Fat in All Milk Produced	MilkFat Mil. Lbs.	Milk Sold to Plants & Dealers Quantity Billion Pounds	$ Per 100 Lbs.	Milk Sold Directly to Consumers Quantity Million Quarts	¢ Per Quart	Milk Utilized Bill. Lbs.	Farm Value of All Milk Mill. $	Per Capita Consumption in pounds Milk-Fat Basis	Fluid Milk [4]
1979	10,734	11,492	420	123.4	3.66	4,512	119.4	12.02	692.7	42.3	120.9	14,942	548	232
1980	10,799	11,891	435	128.4	3.65	4,692	124.6	13.05	683.5	45.3	126.1	16,876	544	227
1981	10,898	12,183	444	132.8	3.64	4,836	129.0	13.77	684.7	48.3	130.5	18,415	542	222
1982	11,011	12,306	450	135.5	3.65	4,950	131.9	13.61	597.8	48.1	133.1	18,559	560	216
1983	11,098	12,585	460	139.7	3.66	5,105	136.1	13.58	563.4	48.4	137.3	19,081	577	215
1984[1]	10,833	12,506	458	135.5	3.66	4,964	131.2	13.46	539.7	49.2	132.4	18,343	582	217
1985[1]	11,025	13,031		143.7										
1986[5]	10,860	13,330		144.8										

[1] Preliminary. [2] Average number on farms during year excluding heifers not yet fresh. [3] Excludes milk sucked by calves & milk produced by cows not on farms. [4] And cream (milk fat basis). [5] Estimate. *Source: Crop Reporting Board, U.S.D.A.* T.415

Utilization of Milk in the United States   In Millions of Pounds (Milk Equivalent)

Year	Butter from Whey Cream	Creamery Butter[1]	Cheese[6]	Cottage Cheese (Creamed)	Condensed Whole Milk	Evaporated Milk[5]	Dry Whole Milk Products	Frozen Dairy Products[2]	Fluid Consumption Nonfarm	Farm[5]	Fed to Calves	Other Mfg. Products[4]
1980	2,998	22,826	33,925	1,016	524	1,594	607	11,926	50,855	943	1,395	909
1981	3,192	24,614	36,546	977	639	1,669	686	11,964	50,215	886	1,418	821
1982	3,365	24,987	38,903	950	704	1,490	758	12,135	49,346	839	1,521	656
1983[3]	3,554	25,788	41,006	941	648	1,525	823	12,598	49,705	842	1,527	663
1984[7]	3,406	21,471	38,718	932	724	1,419	880	12,660	50,624	824	2,250	488

[1] Excludes whey butter. [2] From milk and cream only. [3] Preliminary. [4] Includes dry cream, malted milk, dry part skim milk, dry ice cream mix. [5] Data include evaporated & sweetened condensed milk. [6] American & other. [7] Estimate. *Source: Crop Reporting Board, U.S.D.A.* T.416

Milk Production on Farms in the United States   In Millions of Pounds

Year	Jan.	Feb.	Mar.	Apr.	May	June	July	Aug.	Sept.	Oct.	Nov.	Dec.	Total
1980	10,320	9,972	10,945	11,024	11,697	11,335	11,075	10,792	10,353	10,461	10,055	10,494	128,525
1981	10,803	10,149	11,519	11,531	12,078	11,552	11,361	11,106	10,625	10,763	10,393	10,890	132,770
1982	11,106	10,361	11,700	11,607	12,191	11,781	11,618	11,370	10,939	11,053	10,644	11,135	135,505
1983	11,443	10,707	12,029	11,956	12,616	12,261	12,046	11,672	11,218	11,400	10,979	11,345	139,672
1984	11,373	10,856	11,713	11,660	12,219	11,710	11,487	11,205	10,784	10,913	10,524	11,006	135,450
1985	11,291	10,525	11,929	12,082	12,885	12,532	12,588	12,388	11,857	12,058	11,564	11,968	143,667
1986[1]	12,192	11,314	12,726	12,656	13,186	12,675	12,409	12,028	11,481	11,546	11,110		

[1] Preliminary. *Source: Crop Reporting Board, U.S.D.A.* T.417

Average Price Received by U.S. Farmers for All Milk[2] (Sold to Plants)   In Dollars Per Cwt.

Year	Jan.	Feb.	Mar.	Apr.	May	June	July	Aug.	Sept.	Oct.	Nov.	Dec.	Average[1]
1980	12.80	12.80	12.80	12.70	12.60	12.50	12.60	12.80	13.20	13.70	14.00	14.10	13.00
1981	14.10	14.00	13.80	13.70	13.50	13.40	13.40	13.50	13.70	14.00	14.00	14.00	13.80
1982	14.00	13.80	13.70	13.50	13.20	13.20	13.20	13.30	13.60	13.80	13.90	13.90	13.59
1983	13.90	13.80	13.60	13.60	13.30	13.20	13.20	13.30	13.50	13.80	13.90	13.70	13.58
1984	13.60	13.40	13.30	13.10	13.00	12.90	13.00	13.20	13.60	14.00	14.30	14.00	13.46
1985	13.90	13.70	13.30	12.90	12.50	12.20	12.10	12.10	12.30	12.60	12.60	12.60	12.75
1986[3]	12.50	12.40	12.20	12.00	12.00	11.90	12.00	12.20	12.70	13.10	13.40	13.40	12.48

[1] Weighted average. [2] Adjusted for seasonal variation. [3] Preliminary. *Source: Crop Reporting Board, U.S.D.A.* T.418

Farm Price of Milk[1] Eligible for Fluid Market   In Dollars Per Hundred Pounds

Year	Jan.	Feb.	Mar.	Apr.	May	June	July	Aug.	Sept.	Oct.	Nov.	Dec.	Average
1980	13.00	13.00	12.90	12.80	12.70	12.70	12.70	13.00	13.40	13.90	14.10	14.30	13.23
1981	14.20	14.20	14.00	13.80	13.70	13.60	13.60	13.70	13.90	14.20	14.20	14.20	13.95
1982	14.10	14.00	13.80	13.60	13.40	13.30	13.40	13.40	13.70	13.90	14.10	14.10	13.80
1983	14.00	14.00	13.80	13.70	13.50	13.30	13.30	13.50	13.70	13.90	14.10	13.90	13.75
1984	13.80	13.50	13.40	13.20	13.10	13.00	13.10	13.30	13.80	14.10	14.40	14.20	13.61
1985	14.20	13.90	13.50	13.00	12.60	12.30	12.20	12.30	12.30	12.70	12.70	12.70	12.90
1986	12.70	12.50	12.30	12.10	12.00	11.90	12.00	12.20	12.80	13.30	13.50	13.60	12.60

[1] MILK, Standard Grade, 3.5% milkfat. Weighted average price per 100 pounds (f.o.b. city). *Source: Crop Reporting Board, U.S.D.A.* T.419

Molasses

World industrial molasses production in 1986/87 was expected to expand three percent from the previous season's 33.6 million tonnes. Brazil is the world's largest producer of molasses. Production there remained at 4.8 million tonnes in 1985/86, unchanged from 1984/85, and was projected to stay at this level in 1986/87.

Output in the USSR, the second-largest producer, was down in 1985/86, but was forecast to recover substantially in 1986/87. The USSR is self-sufficient in molasses production; all output is for domestic consumption. USDA estimates almost half of production is utilized for spirits, 30 percent for livestock feed, 15 percent for baking yeast, and the remainder for food acids, solvents, and other uses.

1986/87 output in India was projected to be 15 percent higher than the 2.6 million tonnes produced in 1985/86. Exports were expected to be about 100,000 tonnes, a 200-percent increase over last year, due to increased supplies. About 60 percent of India's output is for table use and the remainder for industrial use. Production levels for 1986/87 were expected to be consistent with those of 1985/86 in Cuba, the European Community (EC), and Poland, while a slight increase was expected in Mexico.

In the U.S., molasses imports dropped in 1985/86 to levels not seen since 1982/83. Major sources of imports included Brazil, South Africa and Australia. For January–September, 1986, the average price of blackstrap molasses (cane) at New Orleans was $72.32 per ton. This figure was 51 percent higher than the year-ago average for the same period.

Domestic output in 1986/87 was projected to remain the same as the previous year's two million tonnes. The overall outlook for 1986/87 is for further gains in global supply.

World Production of Molasses (Industrial)   In Thousands of Metric Tons

Crop Year	Argentina	Brazil	Cuba[2]	France	W. Germany	India	Italy	Mexico	Philippines	Poland	Australia	Thailand	China	United States	USSR	World Total
1978–9	818	5,000	1,296	952	685	2,564	365	1,410	818	657	577			2,148	3,306	32,688
1979–0	789	4,800	1,185	958	653	1,582	390	1,260	818	653	598			2,054	3,062	30,052
1980–1	654	5,400	1,111	1,013	657	2,129	410	1,145	860	430	713			2,012	2,669	30,941
1981–2	565	4,520	1,200	1,404	836	3,400	500	1,373	941	665	719	1,736		2,051	2,385	34,384
1982–3	541	5,110	1,050	1,364	807	3,700	370	1,270	957	758	726	1,316		1,900	2,530	35,139
1983–4	560	5,130	1,150	1,072	605	2,500	380	1,390	928	816	718	1,230	1,275	2,015	2,723	32,981
1984–5	702	4,800	1,150	1,165	640	2,500	380	1,400	744	708	736	1,356	1,130	2,012	3,200	33,755
1985–6[1]	854	4,800	1,150	1,110	650	2,600	330	1,440	590	699	658	1,275	1,540	2,014	2,900	33,594
1986–7[3]	1,000	4,800	1,150	970	650	3,000	440	1,460	600	700	693	1,300	1,710	2,015	3,100	34,749

[1] Preliminary.   [2] Includes hi-test molasses.   [3] Estimate.   *Source: Foreign Agricultural Service, U.S.D.A.*   T.421

U.S. Annual Average Prices of Molasses, by Types (F.O.B. Tank Car or Truck)   In Dollars Per Ton[1]

Year	Blackstrap New Orleans	South Florida	Baltimore	Minneapolis	Omaha	Calif. Ports	Colorado	Beet Molasses Wyo. & Montana	Ore., Utah & Idaho	Citrus Molasses Florida
1977	40.55	42.45	47.00	54.35	58.75	42.90	41.45	45.20	55.10	50.65
1978	51.50	52.40	59.25	67.30	72.55	54.00	60.40	58.35	60.95	61.05
1979	82.95	85.50	91.20	107.90	107.75	84.05	85.30	82.65	N.A.	79.40
1980	96.50	96.80	106.75	124.45	128.85	101.70	95.60	96.55	N.A.	103.65
1981	84.90	90.00	99.30	111.20	119.40	89.20	85.30	95.20	N.A.	103.10
1982	48.00	56.55	64.15	70.85	81.90	60.50	69.40	63.70	44.50	86.90
1983	55.85	63.10	73.05	77.00	91.90	70.40	79.45	67.25	60.55	89.20
1984[2]	60.65	71.00	77.65	81.00	91.90	71.95	82.50	78.75	70.65	97.50
1985[2]	50.30	59.80	64.65	72.85	N.A.	61.90	N.A.	N.A.	N.A.	N.A.
1986										

[1] Per ton prices are based on 171 gallons for blackstrap, beet and corn molasses and on 175 gallons for citrus molasses. Prices represent sales F.O.B. terminal to the general feed trade and do not include sales made under various pricing arrangements above or below prices generally available to the ultimate user. Ton—2,000 lbs. Gallon—U.S. gallon. Prices are now rounded off to the nearest 5 cents.   [2] Preliminary.   *Source: Molasses Market News, Annual Summary, AMS, U.S.D.A. Denver Colorado, and Molasses Market News, Weekly, various issues*   T.423

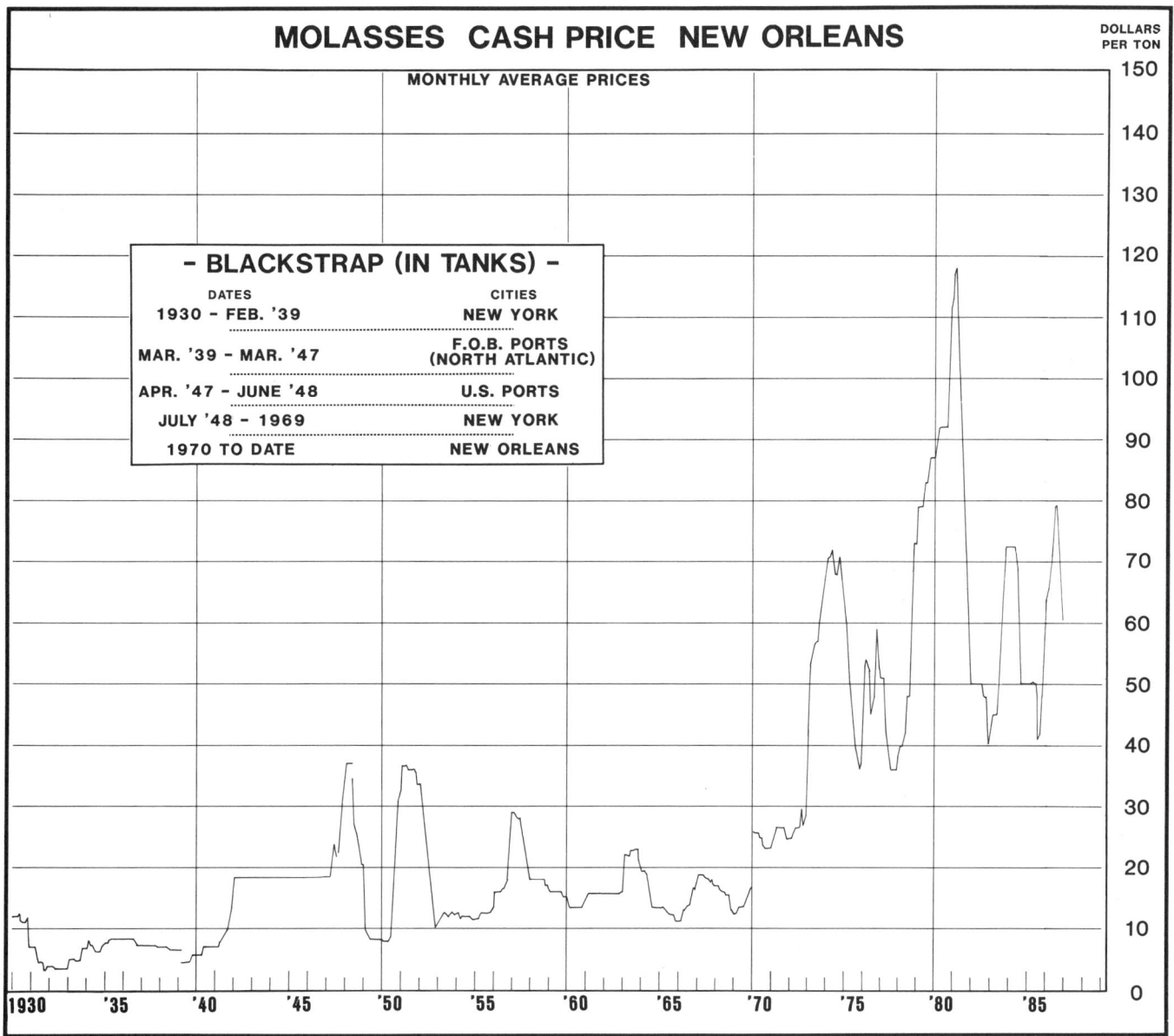

MOLASSES CASH PRICE NEW ORLEANS

DOLLARS PER TON

MONTHLY AVERAGE PRICES

- BLACKSTRAP (IN TANKS) -

DATES	CITIES
1930 - FEB. '39	NEW YORK
MAR. '39 - MAR. '47	F.O.B. PORTS (NORTH ATLANTIC)
APR. '47 - JUNE '48	U.S. PORTS
JULY '48 - 1969	NEW YORK
1970 TO DATE	NEW ORLEANS

Wholesale Price of Blackstrap Molasses (Cane) at New Orleans   In Dollars Per Ton

Year	Jan.	Feb.	Mar.	Apr.	May	June	July	Aug.	Sept.	Oct.	Nov.	Dec.	Average
1982	50.00	50.00	50.00	50.00	50.00	50.00	50.00	48.00	48.00	44.00	40.00	41.00	47.60
1983	44.00	45.00	45.00	45.00	47.50	49.40	53.75	61.50	68.75	72.50	72.50	72.50	56.45
1984	72.50	72.50	72.50	72.50	70.70	68.75	59.00	50.00	50.00	50.00	50.00	50.10	61.55
1985	50.00	50.00	50.00	50.00	50.00	47.75	41.00	41.90	48.00	53.75	57.50	63.50	50.28
1986	65.00	65.60	68.50	71.00	73.75	79.00	79.13	76.60	72.30	68.10	60.25		

Source: Economics Service, U.S.D.A.

T.424

Molybdenum

Molybdenum continued in oversupply in 1986 and, as a result, domestic production fell behind 1985's full-year pace. For the nine months ended September, 1986, production was 70.7 million pounds, compared with full-year 1985 output of 108.4 million pounds. Estimated production for 1986 is 100.0 million pounds.

There is little substitutability for molybdenum in its major applications as an alloying element in steels, cast iron, and nonferrous metals. Demand for molybdenum is expected to show annual increases of less than one percent a year; 1986's estimated 30 million pounds of consumption would equal 1985's offtake. Industry is also exploring new materials that would benefit from molybdenum's alloying properties.

Identified world resources of molybdenum amount to about 19 billion pounds in the U.S. and about 46 billion pounds worldwide. Molybdenum occurs both as the metal sulfate in its own right and as a metal sulfide in low-grade copper deposits. While data on world production are not currently available for 1986, it was estimated at 209.5 million pounds in 1985.

The U.S. is a major exporter of the metal. In 1985, it exported 78.0 million pounds, and 1986's total should be close to that amount. However, due to soft world demand, mining companies have been cutting production. In 1986, Cyprus Minerals Company, a major domestic producer, cut back output at its Thompson Creek Mine in Colorado to about 45 percent of capacity and reduced its workforce by 35 percent. Because of some drawdown in stocks, U.S. prices rebounded from their depressed 1985 levels. At the end of 1985, molybdenum oxide prices were between $2.80 and $2.90 a pound, but by the end of 1986, they had risen to about $3.45 a pound.

Three firms operating in California, Colorado, Idaho and New Mexico mine molybdenum in the U.S.; the U.S. company AMAX is the world's largest molybdenum miner. There are also eight secondary producers in the U.S. which recover molybdenum as a coproduct of ores of copper, tungsten, and uranium. After the U.S., Chile is the world's second-largest producer of molybdenum, followed by Canada, Peru, and Mexico. Centrally planned economies also produce commercially important amounts.

In the U.S., some molybdenum is retrieved from recycling. Some secondary molybdenum in the form of metal or super-alloy is recovered; an indeterminate quantity of molybdenum is reclaimed from spent catalysts as well.

World Mine Production of Molybdenum   In 1,000 Pounds (Contained Molybdenum)

Year	Bulgaria	Canada[3]	Chile	China	Japan	Mexico	Mongolia	Niger	Peru	Philippines	South Korea	United States	USSR	World Total
1977	330	36,526	24,112	3,300	401	2			1,005	—	223	122,408	21,400	209,707
1978	330	30,739	29,092	4,440	163	24			1,607	121	485	131,843	21,800	220,604
1979	330	24,634	29,895	4,400	154	105			2,637	311	417	143,967	22,500	229,350
1980	330	26,892	30,133	4,400	123	163	1,070	269	5,926	201	661	150,686	22,900	243,754
1981	330	28,329	33,863	4,400	163	994	1,460	249	5,485	207	1,023	139,900	23,600	240,003
1982	375	30,779	44,198	4,400	214	11,442	1,830	93	6,378	150	796	84,381	24,300	209,336
1983	420	22,474	33,651	4,400	214	12,932	2,120	88	5,794	86	313	33,593	24,500	140,585
1984[1]	420	25,479	37,172	4,400	324	8,938	2,200	73	6,788	—	348	103,664	24,700	214,506
1985[2]	420	16,730	40,543	4,400	215	8,150	2,200	73	8,439	—	660	108,409	24,900	215,139

[1] Preliminary.   [2] Estimate.   [3] Shipments.   *Source: Bureau of Mines*   T.425

U.S. Salient Statistics of Molybdenum   In 1,000 Pounds (Contained Molybdenum)

| | | Concentrate | | | | | | Primary Products[3] | | | | | | | |
| | | Shipments | | | | | | Net Production | | | Shipments | | | | |
Year	Production	Total (Includes Exports)	Value Mill. $	For Exports	Consumption	Imports for Consumption	Stocks Dec. 31[2]	Grand Total	Molybdic Oxide[4]	Molybdenum Metal Powder	Sodium Molybdate	To Domestic Destinations	For Exports	Consumption	Producers' Stocks Dec. 31
1977	122,408	124,974	450.4	29,666	91,041	1,976	9,161	90,520	68,671	4,142	1,275	100,626	33,332	54,557	10,141
1978	131,843	130,694	608.0	31,183	96,375	2,705	8,980	96,052	83,220	4,194	1,489	105,921	35,353	61,091	7,996
1979	143,967	143,504	871.1	36,405	103,152	2,329	9,520	101,752	79,035	4,946	1,541	109,419	35,773	60,388	8,502
1980	150,686	149,311	1,344	35,026	108,206	1,825	18,101	106,284	84,554	4,904	1,142	95,391	35,557	53,265	27,007
1981	139,900	118,916	945.5	32,735	80,725	1,988	35,043	105,824	59,645	3,513	96	64,368	20,004	50,189	44,961
1982	84,381	76,135	504.1	21,870	49,444	3,115	38,510	65,381	35,354	3,304	121	47,884	23,375	27,665	49,402
1983	33,593	48,805	166.6	18,979	27,014	1,673	11,637	37,533	11,148	3,667	191	50,562	19,877	27,225	28,352
1984	103,664	102,405	326.8	41,687	54,843	28	12,450	79,689	40,186	4,302	N.A.	65,527	24,553	34,792	22,155
1985[1]	108,409	111,936	347.8	38,646	N.A.	112	9,322	87,436	48,750	3,734	N.A.	73,861	36,268	33,451	21,014

[1] Preliminary.   [2] At mines & at plants making molybdenum products.   [3] Comprises ferromolybdenum, molybdic oxide, & molybdenum salts & metal.   [4] Includes molybdic oxide briquets, molybdic acid, & molybdenum trioxide.   *Source: Bureau of Mines*   T.426

Nickel

The last operating U.S. nickel mine and smelter closed for an indefinite period in August, 1986. The company said the operation was unprofitable, even after it had installed new technology to handle the ore. Total U.S. production in 1985 was estimated at 6,900 short tons; 1986 may have surpassed that, but no figures are currently available.

Domestic nickel consumption in the first ten months of 1986 was 158.9 million pounds, about 15 percent lower than 186 million pounds in the same 1985 period.

Plastics and other lighter-weight metals have cost nickel its market share. The auto industry once used as much as five pounds of nickel plating and nickel metal per car; current use in autos is negligible. Coinage use has dropped as well, with only four nations currently using nickel coin. The largest use of nickel stainless steel is in kitchen sinks, a quickly eroding market. Approximately 42 percent of the primary nickel consumed in 1986 went into stainless steel and alloy steel production; 36 percent went into nonferrous alloys, and 18 percent into electroplating.

In the first ten months of 1986, imports of nickel were 220.3 million pounds, compared with 1985's same-period total of 267.7 million pounds. The largest supplier was Canada with just over 50 percent (113.7 million pounds), followed by Norway and Australia.

In 1985, world production of nickel was estimated at 857,000 short tons and, using current production data, 1986's total should be close to that figure. The continuing over-abundance of world nickel production capacity has kept prices considerably below those required to operate many mines on a profitable basis. In late 1986, nickel cathode prices were $1.44 to $1.78 a pound, down from 1985's $2.28 a pound.

Identified world resources, in deposits averaging one percent nickel or more, contain 143 million tons of nickel. World resources of lower-grade nickel are large. Besides land recovery, there are extensive deposits of nickel on the Pacific Ocean floor, where it occurs in nodules along with manganese.

In 1986, depressed oil prices spurred the USSR to expand nickel sales to free-market economies. In late 1986, the U.S.-USSR Commercial Commission agreed in principle on a resolution of the issue of the U.S. embargo on imports of Soviet nickel. Analysts felt this represented a potential opening up of the U.S. market to the USSR. It is estimated that Soviet sales of nickel to free-market economies in 1986 totaled 55,000 short tons and are trending upwards. Some analysts warn that such shipments by the Soviets could undermine other producers' efforts to curtail output and could result in continued low world nickel prices.

World Mine Production of Nickel   In Thousands of Short Tons of Contained Nickel

Year	Australia[3]	Bots-wana	Brazil	Canada	Cuba	Domin. Repub.	Finland[3]	Greece	Indo-nesia	New Caledonia	Philip-pines	South Africa	United States	USSR	Zim-babwe	World Trade
1978	90.8	17.7	4.0	141.4	36.7	15.8	7.9	20.4	34.6	71.8	32.5	31.6	13.5	164.0	17.3	725.4
1979	76.8	17.8	3.3	139.4	34.3	27.7	6.4	22.2	41.1	88.2	36.7	33.3	15.1	166.0	16.1	756.5
1980	81.9	17.0	2.5	203.7	40.3	18.0	7.2	16.8	58.7	95.5	51.9	28.3	14.7	170.0	16.6	858.9
1981	82.0	18.2	7.2	176.6	42.5	20.6	7.6	17.2	53.8	86.1	32.2	29.1	12.1	174.0	14.4	800.0
1982	96.5	19.6	15.9	97.6	39.8	5.9	7.0	5.5	50.6	66.3	21.6	24.3	3.2	182.0	14.7	681.7
1983	84.5	20.1	17.2	141.2	41.5	21.6	5.9	18.5	54.4	50.9	15.3	22.6	—	187.0	11.2	735.4
1984[1]	83.7	19.3	23.9	192.0	35.1	26.4	7.6	18.4	52.5	63.0	15.0	27.6	14.5	192.0	11.3	832.6
1985[2]	93.7	20.0	26.0	167.0	35.7	29.0	7.2	19.0	54.0	80.4	30.3	27.6	6.1	198.0	11.0	856.7

[1] Preliminary.   [2] Estimate.   [3] Content of nickel sulfate and concentrates.   *Source: Bureau of Mines*   T.427

Salient Statistics of Nickel in the United States   In Short Tons

Year	Net Import Reliance as a % of Apparent Consumption	Production Plant[4]	Secondary[3]	Alloy Steels	Cast Irons	Copper Base Alloys	Electroplating Anodes	Nickel Alloys	Stainless & Heat Resisting Steels	Super Alloys	Chemicals	Total	Stocks, Dec. 31 At Consumers' Plants	At Producer Plants	Imports Nickel & Pdt's (Gross Weight)	Exports	Avg. N.Y. Price Free Mkt. $ Lb.
1978	80	36,298	44,182	17.2	4.3	7.0	27.3	39.6	60.5	15.7	1.9	180,723	20,443		234,352	36,293	
1979	75	44,181	57,404	20.2	4.7	8.5	28.5	41.1	69.6	17.6	1.2	196,293	19,518	28,500	177,205	50,810	
1980	76	44,225	49,291	16.9	4.0	8.8	18.8	27.4	54.7	19.2	1.5	156,299	15,231	60,000	189,188	56,675	2.85
1981	75	48,805	52,076	16.5	3.7	10.6	22.3	10.6	50.6	13.5	2.0	144,851	22,508	100,000	209,008	46,836	2.65
1982	76	44,956	42,968	10.0	1.9	4.3	20.9	17.9	32.2	11.0	2.0	103,981	18,853	62,000	129,787	57,029	2.24
1983	75	33,400	49,852	9.8	1.1	6.3	22.6	24.9	47.0	11.5	2.0	127,845	20,448	38,500	152,333	43,913	2.20
1984	68	44,933	55,167	11.9	1.5	6.7	24.8	29.4	45.8	12.9	2.2	136,861	20,934	37,300	176,715	58,525	2.22
1985[2]	68	36,382	57,183	9.6	3.1	14.9	24.9	25.3	68.0	13.6	2.1	119,907	19,106	13,300	157,690	51,429	2.26

[1] Exclusive of scrap.   [2] Preliminary.   [3] From purchased scrap (ferrous & nonferrous).   [4] Smelter & refinery.   *Source: Bureau of Mines* T.428

Oats

U.S. oats production in 1986/87 is estimated by USDA at 384 million bushels, the smallest crop in decades. This year's crop is 26 percent below a year ago. Oats production has been in a declining trend for many years, due in part to a falling horse population. As farms have adopted more mechanization, the need to feed farm animals has declined. Additionally, new crops such as sunflowers have proven to be more profitable than oats.

Planted acreage this season was 14.8 million acres, 11 percent above 1985/86. Despite the increase in plantings, harvested acreage amounted to only 7.5 million acres. Much of the acreage planted to oats was used as a cover crop on diverted acreage and not harvested. Additionally, wet weather resulted in a sharp decline in yields. The national average yield was 54.9 bushels per acre, down 14 percent from a year ago. In Minnesota, yields fell 23 bushels per acre from the year-ago level. Because of poor harvest weather, high-quality oats are likely to remain in short supply.

Season's beginning stocks of oats in 1986/87 were 183 million bushels, about the same as a year earlier. Imports were projected by USDA at 30 million bushels, making the total supply 596 million bushels, 18 percent less than a year ago. This is the smallest supply of oats on record.

Usage is projected by USDA to decline by 11 percent to 487 million bushels. Feeding usage is the largest source of disappearance and should account for 400 million bushels in 1986/87. This is 13 percent less than a year ago and is due to relatively high oat prices versus corn, as well as to dairy herd liquidation. Use of oats for food is expected to remain steady at 85 million bushels. Ending stocks of oats are projected at 109 million bushels, reflecting a decline of 40 percent from a year ago. The ratio of ending stocks to total use will be at a record low level.

U.S. Government Price Support

The national average loan rate for oats in 1987 is 94 cents per bushel, while the target price is $1.60 per bushel. The loan rate is down from 99 cents per bushel in 1986, though the target price remains the same. To participate in the 1987 program, oat producers must reduce base acreage by 20 percent. They will have the option of paid diversion on an additional 15 percent of acreage.

Futures Markets

Oats futures are traded on the Chicago Board of Trade (CBOT) and the Winnipeg Commodity Exchange (WCE).

World Production of Oats In Thousands of Metric Tons

Crop Year	Argentina	Aus-tralia	Canada	China	Den-mark	France	Nether-lands	Poland	Spain	Swe-den	Tur-key	United States	USSR	Un. King.	West Germany	World Total
1975–6	433	1,141	4,466		367	1,948	158	2,920	609	1,345	390	9,551	12,495	795	3,445	47,044
1976–7	530	1,073	4,831		256	1,402	103	2,695	505	1,251	400	7,930	18,113	764	2,497	48,744
1977–8	570	991	4,303	1,515	288	1,928	94	2,561	421	1,416	370	10,901	18,407	790	2,714	51,508
1978–9	676	1,763	3,621	1,500	206	2,203	140	2,492	553	1,550	370	8,730	18,507	706	4,049	51,753
1979–0	522	1,411	2,978	1,600	163	1,845	109	2,186	456	1,524	370	7,643	15,200	542	3,697	45,165
1980–1	433	1,128	3,028	1,800	160	1,927	94	2,245	680	1,567	355	6,652	15,544	601	3,249	44,543
1981–2	339	1,617	3,188	1,700	176	1,774	115	2,731	445	1,816	325	7,391	15,000	620	3,200	45,343
1982–3	637	848	3,637	1,660	178	1,802	136	2,608	443	1,663	330	8,602	15,500	575	3,777	47,866
1983–4	593	2,296	2,773	1,650	86	1,395	61	2,377	464	1,268	320	6,923	17,000	466	2,489	45,141
1984–5[1]	610	1,469	2,669	1,680	150	1,876	58	2,600	790	1,924	315	6,875	16,300	550	2,973	46,447
1985–6[2]												7,559				

[1] Preliminary. [2] Estimated. *Source: Foreign Agricultural Service, U.S.D.A*   T.434

United States Official Oat Crop Production Reports In Thousands of Bushels

Year	July 1	Aug. 1	Sept. 1	Dec.	Final	Year	July 1	Aug. 1	Sept. 1	Dec.	Final
1979	509,761	530,967	531,232	534,386	526,551	1983	519,002	504,201	472,541	477,303	476,961
1980	449,504	440,655	450,660	457,593	458,263	1984	454,747	455,190	472,460	471,921	473,661
1981	528,118	522,408	509,457	508,083	509,167	1985	498,953	519,028	537,443	518,626	520,800
1982	580,288	591,478	599,008	616,981	620,509	1986		443,183	413,025	383,553	

Source: Crop Reporting Board, U.S.D.A.   T.431

Production of Oats in the United States, by States   In Millions of Bushels

Year	Illi-nois	Indi-ana	Iowa	Michi-gan	Minne-sota	Mis-souri	Ne-braska	New York	No. Da-kota	Ohio	Ore-gon	Penn-sylvania	So. Da-kota	Texas	Wis-consin	Cali-fornia
1979	15.6	6.4	63.0	18.9	84.9	2.0	21.2	18.0	37.0	20.3	4.0	18.4	94.4	16.8	55.9	4.1
1980	14.0	5.9	62.0	20.1	82.7	2.0	15.6	17.9	13.5	19.4	4.1	19.0	66.0	12.6	58.7	4.3
1981	13.5	5.5	59.5	21.1	90.1	4.6	15.8	17.9	44.2	17.0	4.6	20.0	70.5	18.9	52.6	3.6
1982	11.8	6.7	54.2	28.4	97.9	3.3	26.7	18.2	55.7	23.5	6.4	19.8	123.5	10.7	49.3	3.4
1983	12.6	4.6	38.3	15.6	77.0	2.5	13.6	11.4	63.6	15.4	6.0	16.2	79.2	24.0	45.1	2.9
1984	11.4	5.0	47.4	21.7	78.0	1.6	15.7	10.6	50.0	13.9	6.6	16.0	86.8	8.8	53.3	3.5
1985	12.5	7.6	57.8	26.1	77.0	5.8	25.6	17.7	44.5	26.4	9.2	21.0	79.5	15.0	51.5	3.0
1986[1]	13.8	6.4	37.8	17.0	40.0	5.0	21.2	13.7	42.4	12.2	8.6	16.7	42.0	8.4	52.7	3.2

[1] Preliminary.   *Source: Crop Reporting Board, U.S.D.A.*   T.437

Oats Supply and Utilization in the United States

Year June–May	Acreage		Yield	Production	Imports	Total supply	Feed & resid-ual	Food & indus-trial	Seed	Ex-ports	Total use	Ending stocks	Farm price	Nat. avg. supp. rate
	Planted	Harvested												
	—Mil. acres—		Bu/acre					—Mil. bu—					—$/bu.—	
1980/81	13.4	8.7	53.0	459	1.3	697	432	41.0	33.0	13.3	520	177	1.79	1.16
1981/82	13.6	9.4	54.2	510	1.6	688	453	41.2	35.4	6.6	536	152	1.89	1.24
1982/83	14.0	10.3	57.8	593	3.9	748	441	41.7	43.3	3.0	529	220	1.49	1.31
1983/84	20.3	9.1	52.6	477	30.1	727	466	40.9	36.6	2.1	546	181	1.67	1.36
1984/85	12.4	8.2	58.0	474	34.0	689	433	41.0	33.2	1.3	509	180	1.69	1.31
1985/86	13.3	8.2	63.7	521	27.5	728	460	44.0	39.0	2.2	545	183	1.25	1.31
1986/87[2]	14.7	7.0	54.9	384	30.0	597	400	—85.4—		2.0	488	109	1.10	.99

[1] Preliminary.   [2] Estimate.   *Source: Economic Research Service, U.S.D.A.*   T.430

Quarterly Supply and Distribution of Oats in the United States   In Millions of Bushels

Year & Periods Begin. June 1	Supply				Disappearance								Stocks		
	Begin-ning Stocks	Produc-tion	Im-ports	Total Supply	Domestic Use					Ex-ports	Total Disap.	Gov't. Owned[2]	Pri-vately Owned[3]	Total Stocks
					Food	Alc. Bever.	Seed	Feed	Total					
1983–4	219.8	477.0	30.1	726.9	40.9	—	36.6	466.2	543.7	2.1	545.8	1.5	179.6	181.1
June–Sept.	219.8	477.0	11.7	708.5	15.8	—	1.9	184.8	202.5	.8	203.3	1.1	504.1	505.2
Oct.–Dec.	505.2	—	4.9	510.1	9.9	—	1.9	118.8	130.6	.7	131.3	1.4	377.4	378.8
Jan.–Mar.	378.8	—	10.6	389.4	10.5	—	7.4	101.2	119.1	.3	119.4	1.5	268.5	270.0
Apr.–May	270.0	—	2.9	272.9	4.7	—	25.4	61.4	91.5	.3	91.8	1.5	179.6	181.1
1984–5[1]	181.1	473.7	34.0	688.8	41.0	—	33.2	433.4	507.6	1.3	508.9	1.6	178.3	179.9
June–Sept.	181.1	473.7	5.8	660.6	15.7	—	1.9	167.3	184.9	.6	185.5	1.5	473.6	475.1
Oct.–Dec.	475.1	—	9.1	484.2	10.0	—	5.3	110.5	125.8	.3	126.1	1.6	356.5	358.1
Jan.–Mar.	358.1	—	12.1	370.2	10.4	—	5.6	97.6	113.6	.2	113.8	1.5	254.9	256.4
Apr.–May	256.4	—	7.0	263.4	4.9	—	20.4	58.0	83.3	.2	83.5	1.6	178.3	179.9
1985–6[4]	179.9	518.6	25.0	723.5	—	80.0	—	475.0	550.0	1.6	556.6			166.9
June–Sept.	179.9	518.6	5.8	704.3	15.7	—	2.0	175.2	192.9	.4	193.3	1.8	509.2	511.0
Oct.–Dec.	511.0	—	6.2	517.2	10.0	—	5.0	123.1	138.1	.5	138.6			378.6
Jan.–Mar.														

[1] Preliminary.   [2] Uncommitted inventory.   [3] Includes quantity under loan & farmer-owned reserve.   [4] Estimate.   T.436
Source: Economic Research Service, U.S.D.A.

Volume of Trading in Oats Futures at Chicago Board of Trade   In Millions of Bushels

Year	July	Aug.	Sept.	Oct.	Nov.	Dec.	Jan.	Feb.	Mar.	Apr.	May	June	Total
1978–9	103.8	121.3	120.0	149.0	141.0	67.7	59.3	93.9	51.6	95.4	87.1	135.7	1,225.3
1979–0	127.8	111.6	76.1	98.6	96.0	47.1	56.9	85.3	53.8	81.1	131.5	144.8	1,110.6
1980–1	200.4	183.9	199.6	197.1	167.9	151.0	124.8	170.2	129.2	136.4	120.5	162.2	1,943.2
1981–2	125.3	134.6	117.0	144.5	264.9	221.0	166.7	184.7	204.3	223.6	196.5	247.9	2,231.0
1982–3	221.0	218.9	151.2	113.2	127.6	82.5	121.1	154.0	141.3	213.6	159.1	159.7	1,863.2
1983–4	160.1	254.5	180.4	95.1	102.4	57.9	58.9	91.9	77.1	89.8	59.8	76.6	535.0
1984–5	64.7	88.7	38.5	41.0	48.8	39.5	46.1	38.1	33.7	33.7	30.9	31.2	534.9
1985–6	42.6	55.6	37.2	57.0	53.9	35.2	54.7	41.7	41.9	62.0	59.2	62.3	603.3
1986–7	42.0	45.6	47.0	47.2	93.6	107.6							

Source: Chicago Board of Trade   T.440

OATS

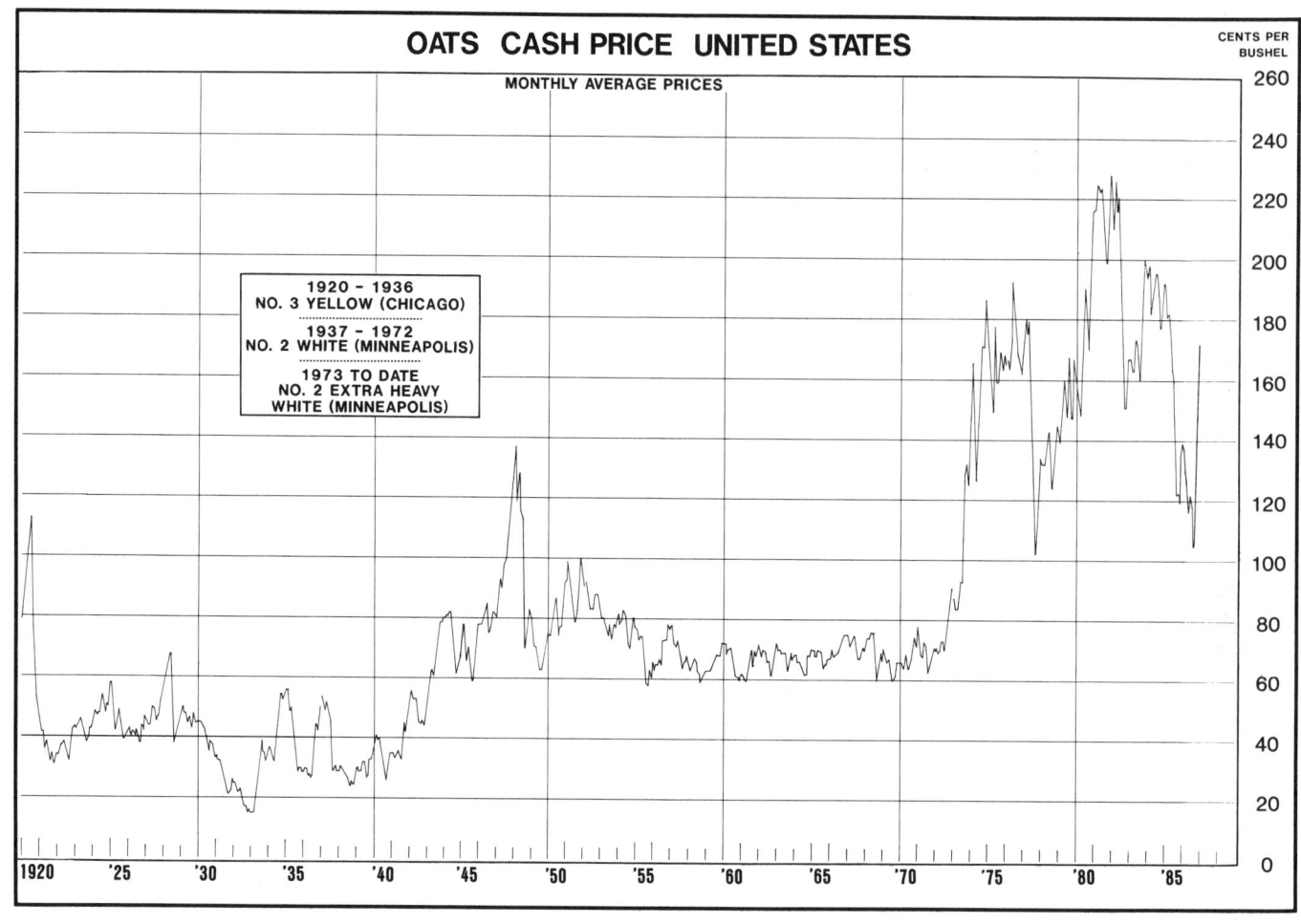

OATS CASH PRICE UNITED STATES

CENTS PER BUSHEL

MONTHLY AVERAGE PRICES

1920 – 1936
NO. 3 YELLOW (CHICAGO)

1937 – 1972
NO. 2 WHITE (MINNEAPOLIS)

1973 TO DATE
NO. 2 EXTRA HEAVY
WHITE (MINNEAPOLIS)

Average Cash Price[1] of No. 2 Heavy White Oats at Minneapolis   In Cents Per Bushel

Year	July	Aug.	Sept.	Oct.	Nov.	Dec.	Jan.	Feb.	Mar.	Apr.	May	June	Average[1]	No. 2 Heavy White, Portland	Tole-do
1977–8	115	102	111	117	134	132	132	132	133	140	143	136	127	144	136
1978–9	124	128	136	139	147	140	147	154	160	148	155	168	143	179	137
1979–0	160	147	155	165	167	159	152	150	148	152	162	188	157	187	160
1980–1	180	170	186	196	215	216	220	225	223	221	223	218	204	242	217
1981–2	202	199	202	209	228	210	223	226	216	221	216	212	214	236	223
1982–3	187	153	151	151	167	167	167	163	163	173	171	167	169	218	155
1983–4	160	179	194	200	197	194	198	182	188	189	196	192	187	195	201
1984–5	184	177	179	184	192	187	181	182	179	173	165	159	181	212	192
1985–6	144	123	124	119	132	139	137	130	127	116	122	118	131	163	108
1986–7[2]	105	112	129	139	172									126	82

[1] Weighted average of reported daily cash sales.   [2] Preliminary.   *Source: Economic Research Service, U.S.D.A.*   T.435

Month-End Open Interest of Oats at the Chicago Board of Trade & Winnipeg Commodity Exchange

Year	Jan.	Feb.	Mar.	Apr.	May	June	July	Aug.	Sept.	Oct.	Nov.	Dec.	Mar.	June	Sept.	Dec.
					Chicago (In Millions of Bushels)								Winnipeg (In Contracts)			
1979	31.1	32.8	24.4	29.8	25.4	28.8	27.0	32.2	29.2	28.6	26.2	25.8	2,515	2,778	3,085	2,635
1980	23.8	23.2	17.5	23.2	21.2	25.8	35.3	41.3	41.6	39.5	37.6	27.6	2,827	2,315	3,178	3,598
1981	36.2	36.7	27.0	25.2	27.8	29.7	25.3	23.9	29.0	45.6	42.4	34.6	3,295	2,625	2,203	1,863
1982	36.5	39.6	40.5	40.5	43.4	45.8	43.4	32.6	30.5	31.4	23.7	21.5	1,298	1,185	1,155	1,225
1983	30.8	35.8	43.3	45.1	48.8	42.5	49.8	48.2	41.8	36.7	26.0	22.1	1,202	1,313	3,170	1,978
1984	21.8	24.3	23.7	21.5	21.0	21.5	24.2	23.1	23.3	22.4	20.8	18.7	1,529	3,127	3,551	1,073
1985	19.4	19.0	16.5	16.2	14.5	14.9	16.7	16.6	15.8	21.3	19.3	19.3	1,028	1,248	1,581	1,028
1986	18.5	18.7	20.8	19.3	16.5	14.9	15.3	16.8	13.7	18.9	25.2	30.3	421	513	607	1,700

Source: Chicago Board of Trade & Winnipeg Commodity Exchange

T.438

OATS

High, Low & Closing Prices of May Oats Futures at the Chicago Board of Trade In Cents per Bushel

Year of Delivery		Year Prior to Delivery								Delivery Year					Life of Delivery Range
		May	June	July	Aug.	Sept.	Oct.	Nov.	Dec.	Jan.	Feb.	Mar.	Apr.	May	
1981	High	189	191	219½	217½	227	228	244½	244	232½	237	225¾	229½	232¼	244¼
	Low	181	179½	189	197½	207½	210	216½	210½	210½	212	206½	206	201	179½
	Close	183	189	212½	217	218	221	243½	226¾	216¼	224¼	223	213	224½	—
1982	High	231½	230	222½	217	194½	207	222½	212	209½	213¼	206	221¾	215	231½
	Low	226¼	212½	210	193	180½	185¼	197¾	177½	193¾	191½	186	202¾	200¼	177½
	Close	229¼	215	216	194½	185¾	205¾	206	200¼	207¾	199	203¼	208	207	—
1983	High	196	185	182½	177½	175	172¼	184½	179¾	181¼	175½	169	172½	163½	196
	Low	188½	173½	164	158½	163½	161	165½	172	172¼	149	151	151¾	154	149
	Close	189	176½	167¾	171	170¼	164	177½	174½	174½	149¼	160¼	155¾	157¼	—
1984	High	185	183½	200	226	220	206	199½	192¼	188	181½	185½	189¼	193	226
	Low	179½	177	181	189½	199¼	193	184½	180½	178	163	169	169¾	171½	163
	Close	179½	181½	197½	200	206	193	184½	188¾	180	168¾	185½	171	193	—
1985	High	—	191	185¾	181½	175	179¾	180¾	179¾	177½	174½	173¼	170	164	191
	Low	—	181	175	171	171	173	176	172½	169¼	167½	167¼	160¼	156¾	156¾
	Close	—	190	178½	172¼	173½	179	179	176¾	172¼	170¼	167¾	160½	160½	—
1986	High	163	161	150½	135	135¾	138¾	141¾	143½	142	129	122½	109	119	163
	Low	160	149¾	133½	127½	128	130½	134¾	133½	121½	118	106¾	94¼	101½	94¼
	Close	161	150¾	133¾	130	135	138½	135¼	142¼	124¼	120	108¼	109	108½	—
1987	High	116½	119	117½	123	128¾	135¼	150¾	155¾						
	Low	116¼	112½	110	115	120½	126	134¼	136						
	Close	116¼	115½	113¼	122¾	128	133¾	146	155¾						

Source: Chicago Board of Trade T.439

Average Price Received by U.S. Farmers for Oats In Cents Per Bushel

Year	July	Aug.	Sept.	Oct.	Nov.	Dec.	Jan.	Feb.	Mar.	Apr.	May	June	Average[1]
1979–0	133	124	129	131	141	131	139	137	134	138	143	148	136
1980–1	150	153	163	165	184	192	198	201	208	205	205	199	179
1981–2	184	172	174	178	188	194	197	199	202	199	199	188	189
1982–3	157	139	135	132	140	144	146	148	149	154	154	151	149
1983–4	146	145	155	162	167	173	181	188	181	182	184	180	167
1984–5	168	162	160	169	164	172	174	169	168	168	160	159	169
1985–6	131	116	110	108	114	120	118	116	114	114	121	110	125
1986–7	90	86	99	111	122								

[1] Weighted average by sales. *Source: Crop Reporting Board, U.S.D.A.* T.433

Oats Under Price Support Through the End of the Month
(Cumulative Total from Current Season's Crop) In Millions of Bushels

Year	July	Aug.	Sept.	Oct.	Nov.	Dec.	Jan.	Feb.	Mar.	Apr.	May	June	Total
1977–8	7.8	30.0	48.5	54.9	59.5	62.3	65.3	67.1	73.2	76.1	77.9	78.9	78.9
1978–9	.5	8.2	14.9	18.5	21.2	22.4	23.9	24.2	24.5	24.7	24.8	24.8	24.8
1979–0	—	2.2	5.0	7.1	8.7	9.5	10.5	11.0	11.6	12.1	12.2	12.2	12.2
1980–1	—	1.8	3.4	4.4	4.9	5.7	6.0	6.1	6.2	6.3	6.3	6.3	6.3
1981–2	.6	3.4	6.1	7.4	8.0	8.7	9.3	9.5	9.6	9.6	9.6	9.6	9.6
1982–3	.1	1.2	4.0	5.8	6.9	7.7	8.3	8.5	8.8	9.0	9.1	9.1	9.1
1983–4	.1	1.0	1.4	2.8	3.1	3.2	3.4	3.5	3.5	3.6	3.6	3.6	3.6
1984–5	—	.9	2.1	2.6	2.8	3.0	3.1	3.1	3.1	3.1	3.1	3.1	3.1
1985–6	.1	1.0	2.3	3.6	4.0	4.3	4.6	4.8	4.9	5.2	5.3	5.3	5.3
1986–7	.2	1.8	4.1	5.9	6.7								

Source: U.S. Department of Agriculture T.432

Olive Oil

World production of olive oil in 1986/87 is projected by USDA to decline 9 percent, to 1.51 million tonnes. Italy and Spain alternate as the world's largest producer, with output showing high variability. For instance, between the 1983 and 1984 seasons, Spain's production rose 151 percent, while Italy's fell 53 percent. Greece, Tunisia, and Turkey are also important olive oil producers. Most crops appear to have recovered from a severe freeze in 1984/85 which sharply cut Italy's crop. The olive oil harvest begins in mid-November in the northern area of the Mediterranean and somewhat later in the southern regions. By March, most of the harvest is complete. This season, increased production is expected in Spain and Turkey, while Italy will be down somewhat.

World trade in olive oil in 1986/87 is expected to increase only slightly to 410,000 tonnes, a rise of 10,000 tonnes from a year ago. It appears that the large output of last year has reduced demand somewhat. Spain, the world's largest exporter, saw its exports fall sharply in the past year due to improved crops in other countries. Greece is also an important exporter. Italy is a net importer of olive oil, but is also the largest exporter of oil to the U.S.

Consumption of olive oil in 1986/87 is projected by USDA at 1.64 million tonnes, 5 percent less than a year ago. Italy is the largest consumer of olive oil, supplementing domestic production with imports from Turkey and Tunisia. On average, Italy uses about one third of the world's supply. The peak in world consumption came in 1983/84 when 1.8 million tonnes were used.

With the decline in production, ending stocks are expected to fall to 680,000 tonnes, a decrease of 7 percent from 1985/86. Spain holds most of the available stocks. On joining the European Community in January 1986, Spain was given five years to phase out its olive oil policies which favor its use over soyoil.

World Production of Olive Oil (Pressed Oil)[2]   In Thousands of Metric Tons

Crop Year[2]	Al-geria	Greece	Italy	Jordan	Leba-non	Argen-tina	Moroc-co	Portu-gal	Spain	Syria	Tunisia	Turkey	Libya	Israel	World Total
1972–3	15	249	340	6	7	28	21	48	440	33	70	154		2	1,422
1973–4	16	192	543	—	8	22	30	42	447	14	130	53		—	1,520
1974–5	8	237	433	7	14	19	26	48	333	44	117	110		—	1,414
1975–6	18	257	633	1	5	17	38	36	455	33	180	96		5	1,788
1976–7	15	224	301	5	12	12	30	36	390	56	85	150		—	1,334
1977–8	5	234	688	2	6	14	15	30	361	38	130	60		4	1,594
1978–9	14	240	419	7	6	15	20	40	500	66	83	160	5	0	1,590
1979–0	10	203	626	1	15	22	39	66	433	42	85	52	4	5	1,599
1980–1	18	321	606	10	2	11	23	32	479	83	145	170	8	2	1,921
1981–2	15	229	515	5	12	14	34	23	300	44	70	60	8	4	1,350
1982–3[1]	13	324	430	8	5	9	30	79	666	97	58	170	10	4	1,911
1983–4[3]	10	230	824	10	4	10	22	9	266	31	155	40	10	3	1,650
1984–5[3]	15	185	390	8	6	9	28		667	72	110	80	8	4	1,630
1985–6[3]		220	400					35	325	62	110	60			1,240

[1] Preliminary.   [2] Total pressed oil in marketing year ending Oct. 31; excludes sulfur oil extracted from residues.   [3] Forecast.
Source: Foreign Agricultural Service, U.S.D.A.; Oil World.   T.441

Average Unit Value of U.S. Olive Oil Imports   In Thousand Dollars Per Metric Ton

Year	Jan.	Feb.	Mar.	Apr.	May	June	July	Aug.	Sept.	Oct.	Nov.	Dec.	Average
1984	1,336	1,313	1,301	1,307	1,424	1,357	1,379	1,342	1,438	1,361	1,397	1,284	1,353
1985	1,256	1,169	1,215	1,235	1,256	1,249	1,251	1,257	1,308	1,333	1,292	1,338	1,263
1986	1,402												

Source: U.S. Bureau of the Census

World Olive Oil Supply and Distribution   In Thousands of Metric Tons

Crop Year	Production	Exports	Imports	Consumption	Ending Stocks
1980–1	1,921	267	260	1,663	864
1981–2	1,337	204	296	1,593	700
1982–3	1,911	356	401	1,649	1,007
1983–4	1,656	302	340	1,857	844
1984–5[1]	1,637	436	433	1,812	666
1985–6[2]	1,306	356	372	1,634	354

[1] Preliminary.   [2] Forecast.   *Source: Foreign Agricultural Service, U.S.D.A.*

Onions

Salient Statistics of Onions in the United States

Crop Year	Stocks—Jan. 1 (1,000 Cwt.) Common Storage	Cold Storage	Total Stocks	Acres Harvested Acres	Yield Per Acre Cwt.	Production 1,000 Cwt.	Price Per Cwt. Dollars	Farm Value $1,000	Domestic Exports	Imports	Per Capita[2] — Utilization — (Lbs.)	Frozen
									Mil. Pounds			
1979	6,556	66	6,622	123,910	312	38,602	6.98	237,432	156.7	157.4	17.23	.74
1980	7,752	99	7,851	113,160	296	33,526	11.40	347,054	256.6	132.8	14.29	.68
1981	6,235	78	6,313	112,030	314	35,155	14.70	475,470	420.1	135.5	14.07	.7
1982	5,560	35	5,595	125,920	332	41,861	8.24	307,501	140.7	165.9	18.19	.8
1983		29		123,040	315	38,762	12.40	431,906	183.2	204.9	16.71	.6
1984		23		129,350	338	43,657	10.60	422,538	273.9	247.9	18.42	.7
1985[1]		27		122,760	367	45,059	9.08	347,247	121.6	263.7	19.42	
1986[1]				115,140	373	42,935	9.75	371,411				

[1] Preliminary. [2] Onions & shallots. Includes 0.1 lbs. of shallots in each year. [3] Year beginning July. *Source: Economic Research Service, U.S.D.A.*
T.443

Production of Onions in the United States   In Thousands of Hundredweight (Cwt.)

Year	Spring Texas	California	Arizona	Total (All)	Summer New Mexico	Texas	California	Colorado	Idaho	Michigan	Minnesota	New York	Oregon	Total (All)	Grand Total
1980	3,569	1,683	623	5,875	1,131	1,764	6,000	2,460	2,453	1,800	201	4,433	4,538	27,601	33,476
1981	2,700	2,160	512	5,372	1,242	1,488	7,025	2,925	2,625	2,446	199	3,933	4,460	29,649	35,021
1982	3,492	2,805	876	7,173	1,643	1,544	10,395	3,255	2,475	2,336	168	4,550	4,821	34,464	41,637
1983	3,800	2,166	656	6,622	1,248	1,643	9,179	3,432	2,475	2,573	158	2,793	5,292	32,140	38,762
1984	3,348	2,734	805	6,887	1,365	1,560	9,819	4,636	2,323	2,933	156	3,384	6,785	36,770	43,657
1985	3,230	3,510	564	7,304	1,463	943	9,250	5,355	3,740	2,535	194	3,960	6,785	37,755	45,059
1986[1]	3,600	2,886	660	7,146	1,733	1,537	9,684	4,590	3,710	1,653	208	3,456	5,913	35,789	42,935

[1] Preliminary.   *Source: Crop Reporting Board, U.S.D.A.*
T.444

Cold Storage Stocks of Fresh Onions in the United States   In Thousands of Pounds

Year	Jan. 1	Feb. 1	Mar. 1	Apr. 1	May 1	June 1	July 1	Aug. 1	Sept. 1	Oct. 1	Nov. 1	Dec. 1
1980	9,913	8,446	6,430	4,070	1,124	442	1,967	954	1,298	2,089	2,265	4,901
1981	7,777	6,972	4,422	3,730	1,247	591	1,828	649	143	719	665	3,219
1982	3,474	3,963	3,319	1,813	—	—	275	—	—	952	—	—
1983	4,183	4,407	4,116	2,988	1,042	235	325	724	385	785	1,348	8,826
1984	8,648	7,006	2,527	343	1,230	556	527	1,212	5,270	5,618	5,354	6,949
1985	7,465	5,518	4,454	2,248	810	4,806	2,804	1,280	6,205	6,526	5,890	6,128
1986[1]	5,171	5,325	2,572	1,573	545	1,769	1,627	1,001	346	2,116	4,693	7,787

[1] Preliminary.   *Source: Crop Reporting Board, U.S.D.A.*
T.445

Average Price Received by Farmers for Onions in the U.S.   In Dollars Per Hundred Pounds (Cwt.)

Year	Jan.	Feb.	Mar.	Apr.	May	June	July	Aug.	Sept.	Oct.	Nov.	Dec.	Average[2]
1980	4.73	4.34	5.32	6.94	10.00	10.70	9.19	10.30	10.30	10.90	11.50	14.20	12.40
1981	15.40	17.20	23.60	26.10	22.40	18.10	17.70	15.40	11.50	12.80	14.80	14.60	16.40
1982	17.60	17.40	13.20	12.70	12.60	9.43	11.90	12.60	7.83	7.12	6.90	6.35	8.89
1983	5.13	6.35	7.59	10.70	10.60	9.62	10.70	10.90	10.80	11.00	12.90	18.30	13.90
1984	17.30	19.40	25.20	25.30	13.90	11.00	14.00	13.60	11.00	9.52	10.30	11.90	11.70
1985	10.20	8.91	7.95	9.12	13.00	9.90	19.60	11.20	7.61	6.40	6.97	8.19	9.75
1986[1]	6.21	6.31	6.83	9.11	9.53	10.90	11.10	9.70	9.25	10.40	12.70	11.10	9.43

[1] Preliminary.   [2] Seasonal Average.   *Source: Crop Reporting Board, U.S.D.A.*
T.448

Orange Juice

Due to favorable weather, U.S. orange production in 1985/86 was up 11 percent (to 176.2 million boxes) after last year's freeze-damaged crop. In Florida, orange output was 119.2 million boxes, 15 percent above the 1984/85 season; citrus growers there are still recovering from freezes that have occurred in four of the last five winters. Even though supplies are bigger than last year, they are still some 23 percent below the 1975–80 average. This past season's large crop weakened prices for fresh oranges. The frozen concentrated orange juice (FCOJ) yield remained unchanged from last year at 1.38 gallons per box. But, the larger Florida orange crop has resulted in a pack of 132 million gallons of FCOJ, up 12 percent from last season. Lower FCOJ prices in 1986 increased demand. Florida FCOJ movement in 1986 was 8 percent higher than the previous year.

Imports into the U.S. (mostly from Brazil) were down 15 percent last year, a direct result of larger U.S. supplies. While Brazil had a record 1985/86 orange crop of 230 million boxes, its exports of FCOJ were down 16 percent from last year. During the season, Brazil significantly lowered its FCOJ prices in order to expand export sales, from $1800/tonne (f.o.b. Santos) to $800–$900/tonne. Nonetheless, Brazilian shipments fell and the country's citrus industry suffered losses in 1985/86, following several years of good exports. In October, 1986, the Department of Commerce preliminarily ruled that Brazilian FCOJ exports to the U.S. had violated anti-dumping laws, saying the country's exports had come into the U.S. at less than fair value. A final agency decision is scheduled for March, 1987. If a tariff is instituted, it may limit Florida's 1986/87 FCOJ imports from Brazil and would be supportive for futures.

Futures Market

FCOJ futures are traded on the Citrus Associates of the New York Cotton Exchange (NYCE).

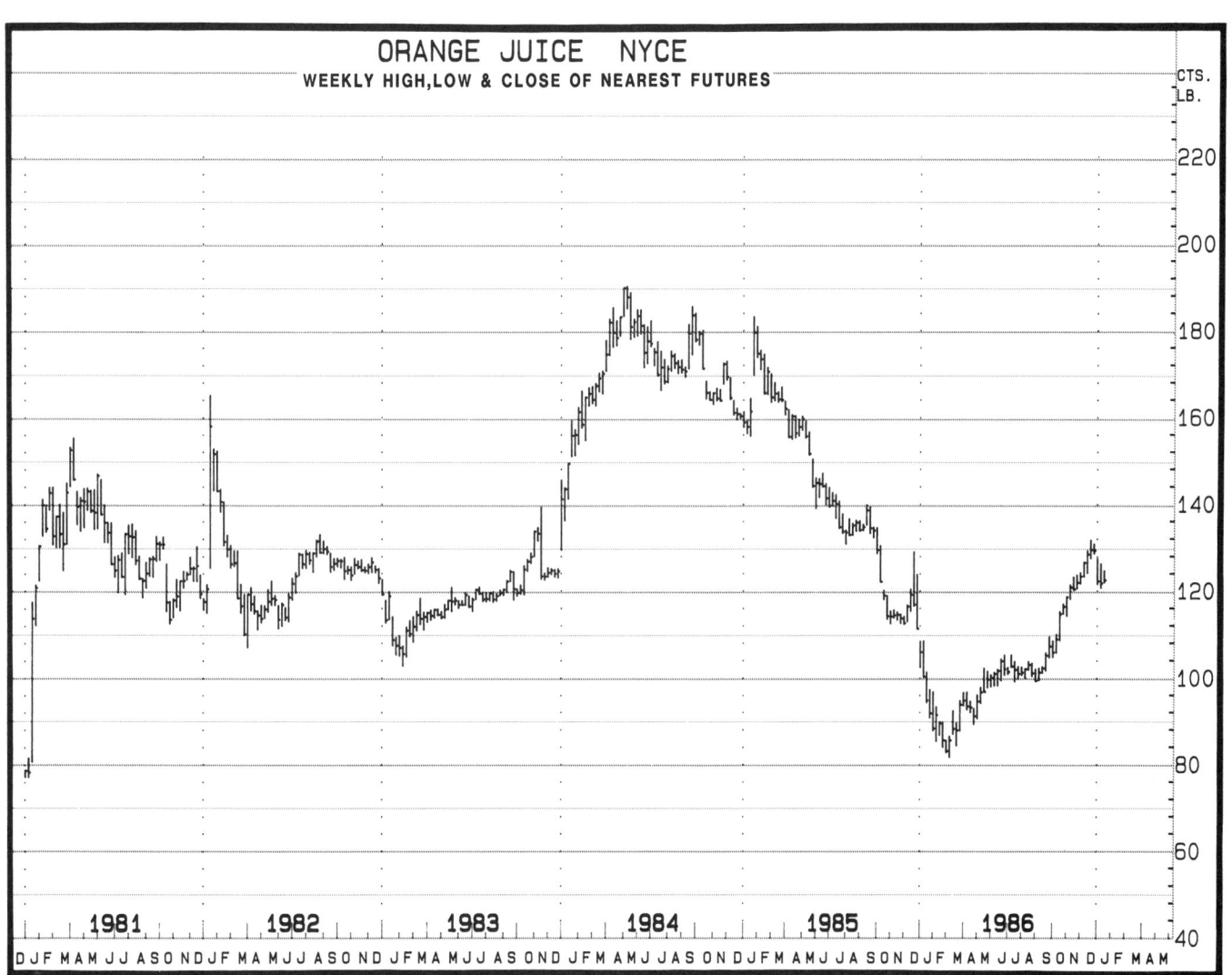

ORANGE JUICE NYCE
WEEKLY HIGH, LOW & CLOSE OF NEAREST FUTURES

ORANGES AND ORANGE JUICE

World Production of Oranges[3]   In Thousands of Metric Tons

Season	Egypt	Argentina	Brazil	Australia	Greece	Israel	Italy	Japan	Mexico	Morocco	Spain	Turkey	South Africa	United States	World Total[3]
1978–9		925	6,471	451	506	992	1,959	3,637	1,398	827	2,526	806	600	8,310	24,050
1979–0		921	9,282	448	360	943	2,104	3,945	1,810	1,024	2,597	835	565	10,734	38,502
1980–1		905	9,872	381	561	812	2,057	3,229	1,720	965	2,605	862	569	9,514	36,725
1981–2[3]	895	606	9,942	421	704	1,105	1,752	37	1,650	695	1,629	675	546	7,025	28,666
1982–3	1,201	639	9,210	392	665	889	1,498	52	1,380	670	1,652	656	510	8,827	29,294
1983–4[1]	1,243	500	9,588	459	691	950	2,299	60	1,220	731	2,077	600	491	6,573	28,687
1984–5[2]	1,255	600	10,812	436	787	884	1,850	59	865	735	1,235	540	491	6,095	27,915
1985–6[2]														6,815	

[1] Preliminary.   [2] Estimate.   [3] Data prior to 1981–82 include tangarines.   *Source: Foreign Agricultural Service, U.S.D.A.*   T.449

U.S. Salient Statistics of Oranges & Orange Juice

Season	Arizona	California	Florida	Texas	Total	Farm Price $ Per Box	Farm Value Million $	Carry-in	Pack	Total Supply	Total Season Movem.	Frozen Concentrates	Juice	Sections & Salads	Other Processed	Total Processed	Yield Per Box (Gall.)
	Million Boxes							in Million Gallons				Million Boxes					
1976–7	4.0	45.3	186.8	6.9	243.0	3.34	811.2	29.7	178.7	196.2	180.9	148.7	27.3	.4	8.8	185.2	1.07
1977–8	2.6	42.6	167.8	6.1	220.1	5.45	1,198.7	29.1	185.0	200.8	185.1	132.2	25.3	.4	8.1	166.0	1.23
1978–9	2.9	37.3	164.0	6.4	210.6	6.15	1,296.0	33.5	206.2	221.9	206.1	130.2	22.8	.3	6.5	159.8	1.34
1979–0	3.5	59.4	206.7	4.0	273.6	4.76	1,304.2	37.4	256.4	293.8	239.0	174.9	24.4	.3	7.0	206.6	1.34
1980–1	2.6	65.3	172.4	4.3	244.6	4.85	1,327.7	57.3	249.6	306.9	240.6	145.3	19.6	.2	6.4	171.5	1.21
1981–2	3.1	41.9	125.8	5.9	176.7	5.30	1,295.3	69.0	214.9	283.9	230.5	105.2	16.3	.2	4.5	126.1	1.28
1982–3	3.8	76.1	139.6	5.7	225.2	6.61	1,167.8	53.4	228.4	281.8	239.0	114.6	18.1	.2	2.7	135.5	1.48
1983–4	1.8	48.5	116.7	2.5	169.5	5.85	1,317.1	42.8	239.9	282.7	228.3	94.5	17.0	—	2.9	114.4	1.29
1984–5	2.5	52.4	103.9	0	158.8	7.69	1,304.3	54.4	209.6	264.0	215.7	86.1	14.9	—	1.9	102.9	1.38
1985–6[1]	2.3	54.8	119.0	.3	176.4	9.78	1,459.3	48.2				96.1				114.6	1.38
1986–7[3]	2.3	67.0	129.0	.9	199.2		1,074.1										1.44

[1] Preliminary.   [2] Fruit ripened on trees, but destroyed prior to picking is not included.   [3] Estimate.
Source: Economic Research Service, U.S.D.A. Florida Citrus Processors Assoc.   T.450

U.S. Cold Storage Stocks of Orange Juice Concentrate[2]   In Millions of Pounds (Gallon Equivalent)

Year	Jan. 1	Feb. 1	Mar. 1	Apr. 1	May 1	June 1	July 1	Aug. 1	Sept. 1	Oct. 1	Nov. 1	Dec. 1
1978	392.8	511.5	617.1	617.3	744.4	854.7	883.1	811.6	720.2	549.6	485.4	359.8
1979	506.5	762.3	996.6	995.0	1,044.4	1,186.5	1,228.4	1,116.4	926.2	704.6	560.1	466.6
1980	559.0	827.2	1,062.5	1,124.8	1,221.4	1,429.7	1,500.3	1,369.3	1,182.4	963.7	842.7	679.5
1981	722.4	907.1	1,053.2	1,180.1	1,264.4	1,502.2	1,491.3	1,307.8	1,178.8	1,022.2	892.2	759.1
1982	753.1	957.0	1,172.3	1,300.7	—	—	1,406.2	—	—	846.5	—	—
1983	835.9	1,028.1	1,016.2	963.3	1,187.0	1,408.0	1,318.6	1,192.4	960.8	810.7	684.8	595.0
1984	631.1	785.7	956.3	976.3	920.1	998.2	903.2	780.4	707.0	595.8	557.3	564.8
1985	651.6	883.4	1,050.6	1,102.7	1,188.6	1,229.5	1,063.7	1,036.1	912.4	882.2	778.8	656.0
1986[1]	679.2	888.4	966.8	911.5	1,031.6	1,047.5	1,056.9	920.3	855.3	715.4	577.8	536.3

[1] Preliminary.   [2] Adjusted to 42° BRIX basis (9.896 lbs./gal.) beg. 1/1/81; prev. 43.4°.   *Source: Crop Reporting Board, U.S.D.A.*   T.451

Month–End Open Interest of Frozen Concentrated Orange Juice Futures   In Thousands of Contracts

Year	Jan.	Feb.	Mar.	Apr.	May	June	July	Aug.	Sept.	Oct.	Nov.	Dec.
1978	8,973	10,002	10,611	11,980	12,381	12,878	11,964	13,950	12,781	12,878	9,212	9,073
1979	7,916	8,503	6,734	7,887	7,223	8,261	8,058	8,116	6,510	7,101	8,423	10,428
1980	7,612	6,501	6,126	6,390	6,210	5,923	6,186	6,920	8,046	9,063	9,239	9,582
1981	7,980	10,787	12,018	11,354	11,667	11,925	10,675	9,751	9,454	7,991	7,654	8,037
1982	9,519	8,634	6,580	6,238	6,227	5,808	6,007	6,395	5,666	5,775	7,106	9,359
1983	9,720	7,136	6,229	6,267	6,225	6,264	5,969	6,413	6,487	6,155	5,732	7,186
1984	8,873	10,650	11,676	11,733	11,295	12,965	11,646	10,350	10,039	9,356	9,339	8,542
1985	7,854	6,680	6,452	6,373	5,885	5,504	4,895	4,300	4,756	5,701	7,156	12,951
1986	8,763	7,782	7,827	6,469	7,013	7,295	6,908	6,682	7,470	8,774	9,460	11,290

Source: Citrus Assoc. of the N.Y. Cotton Exchange   T.456

High, Low & Closing Prices of May Orange Juice[1] Futures at New York   In Cents per Pound

Year of Delivery		Mar.	Apr.	May	June	July	Aug.	Sept.	Oct.	Nov.	Dec.	Jan.	Feb.	Mar.	Apr.	May	Life of Delivery Range
					Year Prior to Delivery								Delivery Year				
1982	High	149.50	151.50	150.95	149.40	144.75	145.90	140.00	139.50	129.30	133.50	156.90	146.40	133.00	120.50	120.00	156.90
	Low	136.00	140.25	144.80	138.75	134.00	134.00	134.25	126.00	122.30	119.00	119.50	129.00	106.75	110.90	113.50	94.00
	Close	146.45	148.45	150.70	138.75	142.90	137.25	136.95	126.10	127.70	122.55	146.20	130.30	115.10	113.30	117.70	—
1983	High	142.85	130.20	132.00	130.00	130.20	133.50	133.25	130.30	128.60	129.05	122.00	112.80	114.75	115.50	120.50	163.75
	Low	122.00	121.95	126.05	123.80	126.50	127.60	129.00	125.55	126.00	121.25	105.70	103.10	107.30	113.10	113.60	103.10
	Close	127.50	126.50	127.75	130.00	128.25	133.50	129.50	126.90	127.00	121.85	107.70	110.35	114.70	113.70	119.70	—
1984	High	106.90	104.95	104.30	108.50	110.00	111.30	114.25	121.00	122.50	149.00	159.50	167.20	177.40	186.40	190.00	190.00
	Low	104.00	100.50	101.40	103.30	106.90	109.20	110.85	109.00	119.70	121.10	141.00	155.00	160.00	174.10	177.75	100.50
	Close	104.80	102.05	103.70	106.60	108.80	110.95	112.45	120.50	121.75	146.00	156.75	163.00	174.20	186.15	177.75	—
1985	High	170.00	176.00	181.50	179.50	168.50	172.00	185.00	181.75	172.90	170.00	183.50	178.00	170.35	161.40	159.90	185.00
	Low	155.00	166.50	174.50	167.00	164.90	167.00	167.50	166.50	166.80	162.40	159.20	166.60	160.30	154.70	151.00	114.90
	Close	165.60	176.00	178.65	168.00	166.90	169.70	181.20	166.90	169.90	163.90	178.60	168.10	161.60	158.20	151.20	—
1986	High	166.25	160.50	152.45	140.90	133.45	127.00	128.90	128.10	116.60	131.50	113.25	92.95	95.70	96.40	101.00	178.40
	Low	160.35	152.50	136.70	133.10	124.00	122.95	122.65	111.95	113.00	107.25	88.30	83.50	82.60	89.00	93.10	82.60
	Close	161.30	152.50	140.00	133.15	124.65	122.95	128.50	114.45	114.55	108.15	89.00	84.30	95.60	92.75	96.55	—
1987	High	91.40	94.75	101.85	109.95	110.00	108.70	109.50	120.20	123.70	134.80						
	Low	84.50	90.50	92.95	100.40	101.10	105.80	106.80	108.00	119.50	123.95						
	Close	91.40	92.75	100.80	108.25	107.70	106.20	108.25	119.70	123.65	125.10						

[1] Frozen concentrated orange juice.   *Source: Citrus Associates of the N.Y. Cotton Exchange, Inc.*   T.455

Volume of Trading of Frozen Concentrated Orange Juice Futures   In Contracts

Year	Jan.	Feb.	Mar.	Apr.	May	June	July	Aug.	Sept.	Oct.	Nov.	Dec.	Total
1979	25,080	17,387	15,162	11,378	11,661	15,526	14,326	16,014	15,010	15,141	12,889	15,239	184,813
1980	21,982	13,010	22,555	9,337	6,742	7,914	8,308	9,715	11,800	16,276	13,042	22,183	162,864
1981	35,041	32,755	49,107	39,785	32,611	35,459	32,944	29,979	22,927	25,435	19,747	31,392	387,182
1982	28,968	25,524	27,139	17,038	12,206	21,501	14,577	14,242	8,424	9,606	8,647	19,188	207,070
1983	28,122	20,345	11,754	6,704	7,614	7,823	4,881	4,531	5,621	9,690	6,409	10,773	124,267
1984	33,189	36,206	34,643	32,774	26,882	30,273	23,803	15,246	36,508	23,693	11,737	12,410	317,364
1985	28,768	20,572	8,135	11,529	9,514	10,011	8,238	7,893	9,395	16,320	11,115	49,268	190,758
1986	39,756	24,971	21,413	13,209	13,909	14,979	10,469	9,887	10,940	17,513	9,551	24,946	211,543

Source: Citrus Assoc. of the N.Y. Cotton Exchange   T.452

Wholesale Index Price of Frozen Orange Concentrate[1]   1967 = 100

Year	Jan.	Feb.	Mar.	Apr.	May	June	July	Aug.	Sept.	Oct.	Nov.	Dec.	Average
1979	260.2	260.2	260.2	260.2	260.2	260.2	260.2	260.2	260.2	260.2	260.2	260.2	260.2
1980	260.2	260.2	260.2	254.3	254.3	249.2	249.2	249.2	249.2	249.2	236.5	236.5	250.7
1981	241.1	280.2	312.2	338.1	338.1	338.1	338.1	338.1	335.5	334.0	323.4	313.1	319.2
1982	312.9	337.7	334.5	326.5	315.4	308.4	308.7	307.1	307.8	307.7	307.5	303.2	315.5
1983	304.0	300.8	299.6	299.1	302.3	300.7	301.1	300.8	302.4	302.5	303.8	303.9	301.8
1984	316.4	361.6	373.3	380.3	385.2	395.0	387.6	392.4	403.7	410.2	408.3	407.8	385.2
1985	400.8	419.1	419.4	418.3	420.2	416.9	410.7	396.7	390.1	375.7	361.6	355.1	398.7
1986	328.5	324.6	307.2	297.0	296.3	296.7	300.5	296.5	295.4	304.1			

[1] Packer to wholesale distributor, or retail chain store, f.o.b. plant.   *Source: Bureau of Labor Statistics* (0242–0301.99)   T.454

Wholesale Price of Oranges (California) F.O.B. Packed Fresh   In Dollars Per Box

Year	Jan.	Feb.	Mar.	Apr.	May	June	July	Aug.	Sept.	Oct.	Nov.	Dec.	Average
1979	13.50	12.29	13.68	13.19	13.58	15.98	13.50	12.40	12.40	11.00	11.60	10.70	12.82
1980	9.72	9.72	10.60	9.54	9.21	9.39	9.52	9.52	9.50	9.54	13.40	11.60	10.11
1981	11.00	10.90	10.20	9.78	10.00	12.10	14.10	12.80	12.60	11.70	11.50	12.70	11.62
1982	13.50	13.80	13.50	14.20	17.20	17.50	18.70	20.30	28.30	28.40	16.50	12.80	17.89
1983	10.80	10.40	10.50	10.30	9.85	10.60	11.70	11.30	10.20	9.30	12.90	13.00	10.90
1984	13.10	12.00	11.60	12.60	19.20	22.40	22.50	23.30	24.40	24.40	19.30	18.50	18.61
1985	18.70	17.50	16.20	17.00	17.40	16.50	15.90	15.80	13.90	13.70	15.30	16.20	16.19
1986	15.10	13.70	13.80	12.90	13.10	12.10	12.40						

Source: Economic Research Service, U.S.D.A.   T.453

Palm Oil

Palm oil is the second-largest vegetable oil by volume produced in the world. USDA projects 1986/87 world palm oil production at 8.34 million tonnes, nearly three percent more than a year ago. World production has increased rapidly during the last 15 years; the annual rate of growth averages nearly nine percent. Malaysia is the largest producer; this season's crop of 4.8 million tonnes will account for 58 percent of total production. Indonesia, the second-largest producer, has been expanding production rapidly. Others are also expanding, but not at the rate of Malaysia.

World consumption of palm oil is expected to reach 8.29 million tonnes in 1986/87, an increase of over three percent from a year ago. The continuing increase in palm oil use accounts for a significant part of the increase in world oil use; this season, palm oil will make up nearly 17 percent of global vegetable oil consumption. In recent years, palm oil has traded at a discount to other oils, which has greatly improved its competitive position. U.S. imports of palm oil have expanded sharply, due mostly to low prices.

World exports of palm oil are projected by USDA to reach 5.61 million tonnes, a five-percent increase from a year ago. In line with production, exports have expanded rapidly. Malaysia is the major exporter; 1986/87 exports are estimated at 4.3 million tonnes. This would comprise 77 percent of world trade. Much of the world's consumption of edible oils occurs in Asian countries like India, Pakistan, and Bangladesh. Malaysia's and Indonesia's geographic proximity to these markets provide an important advantage in world trade. Palm oil is the world's most heavily traded oil, with exports this season exceeding soyoil exports by almost 77 percent. Palm-oil producing countries export virtually all of their crop.

Ending stocks of palm oil in 1986/87 are projected at 1.2 million tonnes, slightly higher than a year ago.

World Palm Oil Statistics   In Thousand Metric Tons

Crop Year	Malaysia	Colombia	China	Indonesia	Ivory Coast	Papua N. Guin.	Zaire	Nigeria	World Total	Malaysia	Indonesia	Ivory Coast	E.C.-10	Singapore	Zaire	Papua N. Guin.	World Total
				Production									Exports				
1980	2,693	75	100	702	182	39	171	520	4,828	2,434	503	80	121	679	10	36	3,721
1981	3,351	80	106	752	147	45	175	520	5,950	2,654	196	63	111	423	5	44	3,860
1982	3,179	87	112	884	160	80	175	525	5,910	2,869	260	68	94	502	5	77	3,680
1983	3,322	104	115	983	162	85	159	530	6,290	2,821	346	58	139	420		80	3,540
1984[1]	3,817	118	110	1,055	167	110	157	540	6,950	3,256	128	56	132	763		105	4,420
1985[1]	4,774	120	110	1,148	165	120	160	550	8,120	4,240	120	53	138	400		115	5,460
1986[2]	5,000	131	110						8,530	4,400							5,690

[1] Preliminary.   [2] Projected.   *Source: Economic Research Service, U.S.D.A.*   T.457

Palm Oil—U.S. Supply & Distribution   In Millions of Pounds

Year Begin. Oct.	Imports	Supply Stocks Oct. 1	Total Supply	Shortening	Margarine	Salad or Cooking Oil	Other	Total	Non-Food Uses	Total Disappearance	Exports (& Shipments)	Palm Kernel Oil ¢ Per Pound	U.S. Ports C.I.F. ¢ Lb.	Malaysia[2] U.S. $ Metric Ton
					Food Uses	Utilization							Prices	
1980-1	324	42	242	188						299	9	42.8	28.1	
1981-2	218	58	276	192						218	10	42.8	27.1	
1982-3	282	47	329	206						286	4		20.8	406
1983-4[1]	413	69	482	270						402	29		24.6	767
1984-5[1]	373	51	424	226						370	0		34.1	569
1985-6[1]	611	53	664	271						590	0		27.2	274
1986-7[3]	770	73	843							780	0			271

[1] Preliminary.   [2] Malaysia FOB; RBD.   [3] Estimate.   *Source: Economic Research Service, U.S.D.A.*   T.458

Average Wholesale Palm Oil Prices, CIF, Bulk, U.S. Ports   In Cents Per Pound

Year	Jan.	Feb.	Mar.	Apr.	May	June	July	Aug.	Sept.	Oct.	Nov.	Dec.	Average
1980	32.0	32.4	31.8	29.6	27.8	28.1	27.6	26.5	25.5	22.3	27.1	26.9	28.1
1981	27.5	28.3	25.5	27.5	27.6	N.A.	N.A.	25.0	24.7	N.A.	N.A.	N.A.	27.1
1982	N.A.	N.A.	24.0	23.7	24.4	22.3	18.9	18.6	19.3	18.0	19.0	20.0	20.8
1983	19.5	19.0	18.8	19.8	20.7	19.5	20.6	26.2	30.6	31.1	32.0	37.5	24.6
1984	40.5	38.2	36.6	37.0	43.0	36.3	28.2	28.4	30.3	28.3	32.4	29.8	34.1
1985	28.3	29.0	29.5	34.3	34.6	31.6	28.7	25.1	23.5	21.7	19.9	19.7	27.2
1986	18.4	15.6	13.3	14.3	14.1	14.1	13.2	12.1	11.7				

Source: Economic Research Service, U.S.D.A.   T.459

Paper

The U.S. paper industry began to recover in 1986 after a disappointing showing in 1985. The industry's turnaround was fairly broad-based and exceeded many analysts' expectations. Market pulp mills operated at full capacity through part of the year; pulp prices jumped by 20 percent. The strong recovery was also apparent in record shipments of corrugated boxes. Similarly, primary paper board production set new records as board mills increased output to meet strong demand. The weaker dollar had a positive impact on trade in the industry throughout 1986. Estimated total imports held steady at $7.7 billion, while exports rose 13 percent to an estimated $4.4 billion. This resulted in a negative trade balance, 13 percent smaller than in 1985.

The Department of Commerce forecast U.S. paper and paper board production at about 70 million tons, up four percent from 1985. Improved capacity utilization rate (93 percent) and recovery in prices were cited as reasons. Paper imports, which disrupted the price structure of domestic writing and printing paper in 1985, slackened in 1986. With the exception of newsprint, imports of all printing and writing paper in 1986 declined 10 percent from last year. Imports were a major source of supply in some paper grades, accounting for over 60 percent of newsprint, seven percent of total coated paper, and five percent of uncoated and writing papers. The decline in the value of the dollar prompted exports to increase to approximately 4.7 million tons, up an estimated 15 percent over last year.

Barring the return of a stronger dollar, the basic supply/demand elements should remain the same as in 1986. The Department of Commerce projects shipments by paper industries will rise three percent in 1987 and that industry growth will stem from improved economic conditions and a broadening of the export gains of 1986.

Shipments of (Paper Products) Shipping Containers[1]   In Millions of Square Feet Surface Area

Year	Jan.	Feb.	Mar.	Apr.	May	June	July	Aug.	Sept.	Oct.	Nov.	Dec.	Total
1982	18,896	18,706	21,147	19,957	18,777	20,084	18,677	20,462	20,650	21,025	19,179	17,646	235,185
1983	19,987	18,628	21,828	20,491	20,719	22,044	19,588	22,692	22,335	23,557	21,032	19,873	252,539
1984	21,889	21,903	23,777	22,111	23,082	22,489	21,257	23,759	21,605	24,852	21,103	19,496	267,547
1985[2]	23,127	20,337	21,708	20,491	22,582	22,345	21,545	23,441	22,037	25,515	20,726	19,594	264,128
1986[2]	24,075	21,306	22,567	25,174	23,365	23,449	23,976	23,726					

[1] Corrugated & solid fiber.   [2] Preliminary.   *Source: National Paperboard Association*   T.463

Index Price of Coated Printing Paper, No. 3   (Dec. 1973 = 100)

Year	Jan.	Feb.	Mar.	Apr.	May	June	July	Aug.	Sept.	Oct.	Nov.	Dec.	Average
1982	203.8	204.9	203.8	202.7	202.7	202.7	201.4	200.0	203.3	203.0	203.5	203.5	203.0
1983	203.5	203.6	203.5	204.2	204.2	204.3	204.3	203.7	210.8	210.9	211.7	211.8	206.4
1984	213.3	220.3	220.9	223.2	223.2	224.2	224.8	224.8	224.8	224.8	233.6	233.6	224.3
1985	234.2	234.6	234.6	234.6	234.6	234.6	234.6	234.6	234.6	234.6	234.6	234.2	234.5
1986[1]	234.2	233.8	233.8	233.8	233.8	233.2	233.2	233.2	233.2	233.8			

[1] Preliminary.   *Source: Bureau of Labor Statistics* (0913–0113.99)   T.470

Salient Statistics of Newsprint in the United States and Canada   In Thousands of Metric[3] Tons

Year	Pro-duction	Ex-ports	Imports[3] By Countries of Origin — Canada	Finland	Italy	Nor-way	Swe-den	U.K.	Others	Total	Con-sumption	Stocks, Dec. 31 At Mills	At Pub-lishers[2]	Canada Pro-duction	Ex-ports	Stocks At Mills
1982	4,574	275	6,485	11	0	19	0	0	16	6,531	10,107	86	854	8,109	7,120	256
1983	4,688	265	6,845	17		33	21			6,919	10,587	99	790	8,486	7,470	303
1984	5,025	258	7,688	31		63	86			7,899	11,431	60	874	9,013	8,133	298
1985[1]	4,924	279	8,129	47		78	131	18		8,472	11,580	57	910	8,988	8,275	290

[1] Preliminary.   [2] Reporting only to A.N.P.A.; group represents about 75%.   [3] Data for imports are in thousands of short tons.
Source: Newsprint Service Bureau, A.P.I.   T.464

Average Price of Newsprint Rolls   (Index: 1967 = 100)

Year	Jan.	Feb.	Mar.	Apr.	May	June	July	Aug.	Sept.	Oct.	Nov.	Dec.	Average
1982	316.8	318.1	318.1	321.1	322.4	319.4	318.4	318.4	318.4	318.4	299.8	299.8	315.8
1983	299.1	299.1	299.1	299.1	299.1	299.1	295.0	305.8	310.4	310.4	309.6	309.6	303.0
1984	309.6	309.6	316.0	314.8	314.8	314.8	334.5	331.2	331.2	332.5	334.9	333.2	323.1
1985	334.3	332.4	332.4	332.6	332.9	333.7	333.0	334.9	333.9	329.3	329.8	330.2	332.5
1986[1]	324.1	324.5	324.3	324.1	324.1	323.1	323.6	322.2	322.3	333.6			

[1] Preliminary.   *Source: Bureau of Labor Statistics* (0913–0291.99)   T.468

PAPER

U.S. Production & Consumption & Foreign Trade of Woodpulp — In Thous. of Short Tons[6]

Year	Dissolving Pulp	Sulfite Bleached	Sulfite Unbleached	Sulfate Bleached	Sulfate Paper Grades[2]	Sulfate Unbleached	Soda	Groundwood	Semi-Chemical	Defibrated[3]	Screenings, Damaged, etc.	Total Wood Pulp	Wood Pulp[4]	Waste Paper[5]	Pulpwood[6]	Exports	Imports
1980	1,508	—1,911—		17,561	40,430	19,735	N.A.	4,579	4,043	N.A.		50,560	N.A.	14,520	79,703	3,805	4,051
1981	1,365	—1,797—			—41,376—			5,320	3,924			51,982		15,409	79,747	3,678	4,086
1982	1,093	—1,434—			—39,478—			5,063	3,700			49,333		13,565	79,039	3,395	3,894
1983	1,261				—42,358—			5,067	3,851			52,537		14,696	85,442	3,674	4,093
1984	1,206				—44,690—			5,506	4,069			55,470		15,926	87,646	3,694	4,490
1985[1]	1,174				—43,696—			5,251	4,050			54,170		15,290	85,744	3,794	4,466

[1] Preliminary. [2] Chemical pulp. [3] Or exploded. [4] Does not include wood pulp consumption by plants classified outside paper & board industries. [5] Waste paper; straw; rags; cotton fibre; manila stock; etc. [6] Data for pulpwood expressed in thousands of cords of 128 cu. ft.—roughwood basis. Pulpwood includes slabs, chips, & millwaste. *Sources: Bureau of the Census; American Paper Institute.* T.465

Paper and Board Production in the United States — In Thousands of Short Tons

Year	Newsprint[5]	Coated (Shipments)	Tissue Paper	Uncoated Free Sheet (Shipments)	Coarse[2]	Sanitary[2]	All Paper Total	Other Bleached Paperboard	Corrugating Material	Unbleac. Kraft	All Paperboard Total	Wet Machine Board	Construction[3] Construction (Paper)	All Construction Total	Total All Types
1980	4,239	4,673	4,375	8,326	5,327	4,298	30,195	1,794	5,864	14,249	30,952	138	1,369	4,390	65,834
1981	4,752	4,940	4,518	8,234	5,700	4,600	31,030	1,900	6,000	14,800	31,232	160	1,200	3,847	66,440
1982	4,574	4,974	4,438	8,184			30,422				29,065				
1983	4,688	5,716	4,789	9,060			32,823				32,177				
1984	5,025	6,281	4,921	9,474	6,249	4,921	34,411				34,039				
1985[1]	4,924	5,642	4,941	9,991	5,875	4,941	34,021				33,034				

[1] Preliminary. [2] Shipments. [3] Paper & board. *Source: Bureau of the Census* T.467

Index Price of Wood Pulp, Bleached Sulphate Softwood — 1967 = 100

Year	Jan.	Feb.	Mar.	Apr.	May	June	July	Aug.	Sept.	Oct.	Nov.	Dec.	Average
1982	408.1	406.9	406.9	392.4	386.6	383.8	362.0	357.9	354.4	347.9	347.2	346.9	375.0
1983	333.7	330.7	322.3	319.2	321.4	323.2	328.5	331.4	333.3	342.4	353.3	351.2	332.5
1984	354.8	385.0	387.8	417.8	439.2	440.2	439.1	437.3	434.3	431.1	423.4	404.5	416.2
1985	385.4	366.0	352.1	337.6	331.8	330.7	332.2	328.9	323.3	320.7	317.2	316.3	336.8
1986	313.3	321.1	318.8	345.0	354.6	363.1	385.4	385.1	399.3	396.5			

Source: Bureau of Labor Statistics (0911–0211.09) T.469

Index Price of Shipping Sack Paper[1] — Dec. 1973 = 100

Year	Jan.	Feb.	Mar.	Apr.	May	June	July	Aug.	Sept.	Oct.	Nov.	Dec.	Average
1979	168.2	168.2	171.0	178.6	178.6	178.6	178.6	178.6	178.6	185.7	187.3	187.3	178.3
1980	176.5	183.7	188.3	195.5	195.5	195.5	192.2	194.2	194.2	194.2	N.A.	194.2	191.3
1981	203.2	213.0	217.4	221.2	224.5	224.5	224.5	224.5	224.5	224.5	223.4	219.5	220.4
1982	219.5	222.2	220.7	220.7	216.3	207.2	207.2	207.2	207.2	213.9	213.9	213.9	214.2
1983	220.7	222.9	222.9	N.A.	222.9	226.7	226.7	226.7	230.7	230.7	231.8	231.8	226.8
1984	231.8	238.8	247.2	247.2	247.8	247.8	241.1	241.1	241.1	241.1	241.1	233.0	240.3
1985	233.0	233.0	225.7	223.9	227.5	222.7	211.0	211.0	211.0	211.0	211.0	211.0	219.3
1986[2]	211.0	211.0	211.0	218.0	218.0	218.0	218.0	218.0	218.0	226.8			

[1] Unbleached kraft. [2] Preliminary. *Source: Bureau of Labor Statistics (0913–0304.99)* T.471

Index Price of Paperboard — 1967 = 100

Year	Jan.	Feb.	Mar.	Apr.	May	June	July	Aug.	Sept.	Oct.	Nov.	Dec.	Average
1985	287.2	285.9	285.7	284.2	280.4	273.7	267.8	265.8	266.0	265.8	266.4	266.7	274.6
1986	264.6	265.7	267.0	267.6	269.0	268.5	270.5	274.1	276.8	280.9			

Source: Bureau of Labor Statistics (0914)

Peanuts and Peanut Oil

World peanut production in 1986/87 was estimated at 20.30 million tonnes, marginally below the previous season. Declines in Chinese and U.S. output more than offset production gains in India, the Sudan, and Brazil. The crop in China was expected to decline 11 percent from 1985/86 to 5.9 million tonnes. One major growing area in the country had very dry weather; another received excessive rains. India's output was pegged at 5.90 million tonnes, up six percent from the season before with increased acreage. U.S. production was expected to decline 16 percent because of drought. In Senegal, output was forecast to fall by 15 percent, to 500,000 tonnes, due to insufficient rains; Sudan's crop was expected to be 14 percent higher at 250,000 tonnes.

The 1986/87 world crush was projected at 10.88 million tonnes, down three percent from the year before. USDA forecast global peanut oil production at 3.10 million tonnes, off three percent; world meal output was expected to decline four percent to 4.40 million tonnes.

World peanut exports in 1986/87 were forecast to rise marginally to 35.56 million tonnes. Shipments by the U.S., the leading exporter, were anticipated to decline as other suppliers' shipments rose. Projected global ending stocks of 29.55 million tonnes in 1986/87 were virtually unchanged from the year-before level.

In the U.S., the 1986/87 crop, placed at 3.45 million pounds, was severely affected by the drought in the Southeast. As a result, production fell to the lowest level in three years.

The domestic crush in 1986/87 was placed at only 379 million pounds, down more than 50 percent from the previous season. The large 1985/86 crush resulted in abundant U.S. peanut oil stocks.

U.S. peanut exports were forecast to fall in 1986/87 for the first time in many years, because of increased trade competition from China, India, Brazil, and South Africa. Exports were pegged at 900 million pounds, down 14 percent from 1985/86 shipments. In 1985/86, the U.S. accounted for 41 percent of the world peanut trade. Leading U.S. peanut customers include the European Community (EC), Canada, and Japan. In September, 1986, USDA announced a $4.5 million program to expand peanut exports to EC countries. U.S. peanut oil exports in 1986/87 were expected to decline from the previous year's level.

U.S. food use of peanuts has been gradually rising in recent years. Of total domestic use of shelled, edible peanuts in 1985/86, peanut butter accounted for 49 percent, salted peanuts for 25 percent, and candy for 22 percent.

Peanut stocks in the U.S. have declined from the peak of 1.42 billion pounds at 1984/85's end. Stocks at the beginning of 1986/87 were 845 million pounds.

World peanut prices trended higher during 1986, as reflected in the climb in Rotterdam prices. In December, 1986, the average monthly price of peanuts CIF Rotterdam was $975/tonne, compared with $691/tonne in December, 1985. During 1986, Rotterdam prices reached a peak in October of $1,585/tonne.

U.S. Government Support Program

The national quota for peanuts in 1986 was established at 1.356 million short tons. The national average quota support level for 1986 crop peanuts was $607.47, up from $559.00 in 1985. Additional 1986-crop peanuts were supported at $149.75 a short ton. Results of a January, 1986 vote by peanut growers on poundage quotas and price supports indicated that over 97 percent were in favor of this type of program.

World Production of Peanuts (in the Shell)   In Thousands of Metric Tons

Crop Year	Argentina	Brazil	Burma	China (mainland)	India	Indo-nesia	Mali	Nigeria	South Africa	Senegal	Sudan	Taiwan	Thai-land	United States	Zaire (Congo)	World Total
1978–9	672	465	384	2,377	6,208	708	107	341	179	1,053	815	92	102	1,793	295	17,832
1979–0	337	545	337	2,822	5,768	783	57	377	348	673	852	86	122	1,800	295	17,339
1980–1	243	310	431	3,600	5,005	791	92	560	309	521	707	82	130	1,045	320	16,200
1981–2	270	305	564	3,826	7,223	728	80	610	116	878	840	83	146	1,806	310	19,900
1982–3	250	250	541	3,916	5,282	795	80	580	89	1,109	497	63	145	1,560	310	17,620
1983–4	329	220	523	3,951	7,284	747	90	400	72	568	460	98	135	1,495	310	18,610
1984–5[1]	260	340	656	4,810	6,740	755	90	570	200	560	390	90	130	1,998	310	20,050
1985–6[1]	300	220	660	6,660	5,200	762			130	590	340			1,870		20,420
1986–7[2]	310	270		6,100	5,900				220	500	400			1,564		20,670

[1] Preliminary.   [2] Estimated.   *Source: Foreign Agricultural Service, U.S.D.A.*   T.474

177

PEANUTS AND PEANUT OIL

Salient Statistics of Peanuts in the United States

Crop Year	Acreage Planted (1,000 Acres)	Acreage Harvested For Nuts (1,000 Acres)	Average Yield Per Acre In Lbs.	Production Picked and Threshed 1,000 Lbs.	Season Farm Price ¢ Lb.	Farm Value Million Dollars	Thousand Pounds (Yr. Beg. Aug.) Exports Unshelled	Exports Shelled	Imports Unshelled	Imports Shelled
1974–5	1,520	1,472	2,491	3,667,604	17.9	657,987	17,703	548,083	127	466
1975–6	1,532	1,500	2,564	3,846,722	19.6	754,491	22,708	318,229	207	290
1976–7	1,549	1,518	2,464	3,739,190	20.0	746,675	24,765	580,496	432	66
1977–8	1,545	1,512	2,456	3,715,055	21.0	780,869	64,284	705,032	413	148
1978–9	1,541	1,509	2,619	3,952,384	21.1	833,885	94,612	713,701	413	139
1979–0	1,546	1,520	2,611	3,968,485	20.6	819,276	64,810	762,304	424	140
1980–1	1,521	1,400	1,645	2,302,762	25.1	578,635	33,071	353,677	3,597	3,710
1981–2	1,514	1,489	2,675	3,981,850	26.9	1,069,526	77,803	375,029	6	4,632
1982–3	1,311	1,277	2,693	3,440,255	25.1	862,686	51,321	473,406	846	1,323
1983–4	1,411	1,374	2,399	3,295,530	24.7	814,579	39,509	529,942	298	1,715
1984–5	1,563	1,531	2,878	4,405,745	27.9	1,229,190				
1985–6[1]	1,490	1,467	2,810	4,122,787	23.0	948,221				
1986–7[2]	1,505	1,520	2,216	3,368,950	28.0	943,292				

[1] Preliminary. [2] Estimate. *Source: Economic Research Service, U.S.D.A.*

T.475

Peanuts Supply & Disposition (Farmers' Stock Basis) & Support Program in the United States

Crop Year Begin. Aug. 1	Supply Production[3]	Supply Imports	Supply Stocks Aug. 1	Total	Disposition Exports & Shipments (Million Pounds)	Crushed for Oil	Seed, Loss & Residual	Domestic Food Use Military	Domestic Food Use Civilian	Civilian per Capita Lbs.	Support Price ¢ per lb.	Additional	Government Support Program Amount Put under Support Quantity Mil. Lbs.	% of Prod.	Owned by CCC July 31 Mi. Lbs.
1975–6	3,847	1	1,146	4,993	434	1,447	313	—	1,740	8.7	19.70		1,136	29.5	958
1976–7	3,739	1	1,060	4,800	783	1,108	666	—	1,635	8.4	20.70		854	22.8	0
1977–8	3,715	1	608	4,324	1,025	487	556	—	1,675	8.5	21.50		535	14.4	2
1978–9	3,952	1	581	4,534	1,141	527	521	—	1,759	9.2	21.00	12.5	515	12.9	—
1979–0	3,968	1	586	4,555	1,057	571	522	—	1,777	9.3	21.00	15.0	709	17.9	—
1980–1	2,303	401	628	3,332	503	446	505	—	1,465	9.0	22.75	12.5	337	14.6	—
1981–2	3,982	2	413	4,397	576	573	795	—	1,696		22.75	12.5	835	20.9	2
1982–3	3,440	2	757	4,199	681	342	463	—	1,849		27.50	10.0	539	15.7	—
1983–4	3,296	2	864	4,162	744	387	579	—	1,841		27.50	9.3	367	11.1	—
1984–5	4,406	2	611	5,019	860	625	218	—	1,892		27.50	9.3	1,370	30.9	—
1985–6[1]	4,123	2	1,424	5,549	1,043	812	876	—	1,973		27.95	7.4			
1986–7[2]	3,369	2	845	4,295	900	379	546	—	1,990		30.37	7.5			

[1] Preliminary. [2] Estimate. [3] Production is on a net weight basis. *Source: Economic Research Service, U.S.D.A.*

T.476

U.S. Production of Peanuts (Harvested for Nuts) by States   In Millions of Pounds

Crop Year	Alabama	Arkansas	Florida	Georgia	Louisiana	Mississippi	New Mexico	No. Car.	Oklahoma	So. Car.	Tennessee	Texas	Virginia	U.S. Total
1974	474.4	—	170.5	1,661.5	—	6.0	13.0	384.3	217.7	31.0	—	413.3	295.9	3,668
1975	535.6	—	177.7	1,726.6	—	13.5	20.2	373.7	232.3	29.5	—	463.6	284.6	3,847
1976	513.6	—	165.0	1,554.3	—	12.3	21.7	440.7	246.0	24.6	—	463.6	309.0	3,739
1977	589.1	—	170.5	1,499.1	—	11.6	25.4	444.1	267.6	31.2	—	394.5	293.0	3,715
1978	551.8	—	182.1	1,725.3	—	13.1	24.1	465.4	207.0	35.7	—	436.5	311.6	3,952
1979	584.9	—	179.9	1,704.8	—	12.4	25.3	378.5	264.0	32.3	—	533.0	253.5	3,968
1980	265.0	—	143.0	994.6	—	7.5	22.4	291.3	140.2	14.3	—	293.3	129.8	2,303
1981	602.7	—	178.0	1,655.5	—	12.7	24.9	555.6	189.3	39.0	—	393.3	330.8	3,982
1982	522.2	—	153.0	1,517.5	—	—	25.2	417.2	174.6	30.0	—	325.1	275.5	3,440
1983	454.5	—	166.8	1,568.0	—	—	25.6	318.3	176.5	25.0	—	362.3	198.6	3,296
1984	648.6	—	246.4	2,160.0	—	—	32.2	449.5	189.0	39.2	—	371.3	269.7	4,406
1985	590.0	—	216.0	1,921.3	—	—	32.0	452.0	171.0	34.2	—	422.6	283.7	4,123
1986[1]	436.0	—	224.1	1,397.5	—	—	30.0	414.7	190.0	24.0	—	396.0	256.7	3,369

[1] Preliminary. *Source: Crop Reporting Board, U.S.D.A.*

T.477

Disappearance and Reported Uses of Peanuts and Products in the U.S.   In Millions of Pounds

Year Begin. Aug. 1	Apparent Disappear.[2] Shelled Peanuts — Edible Grades	Oil Stock[3]	Total All Grades	(Milled Peanut Prod.) Cleaned (In Shell)	Crude Peanut Oil[4]	Cake & Meal[4]	Reported Used (Shelled Peanuts—Raw Basis) Edible Grades Used in — Peanut — Candy	Salted	Sandwich Spread	Butter[5]	Other Products	Roasting Stocks	Total	Oil Stock Crushed For Oil, Cake & Meal	Total All Grades
1976–7	1,700	783.2	2,483	163.2	342.9	460.7	235.0	253.8	24.2	617.9	17.8		1,149	833.2	1,982
1977–8	1,895	461.2	2,356	190.6	179.1	208.9	235.2	274.2	28.2	623.8	18.7		1,180	366.2	1,546
1978–9	1,955	426.9	2,382	210.9	161.6	227.9	268.4	291.6	28.1	664.9	19.1		1,272	396.0	1,668
1979–0	1,979	503.9	2,483	201.4	175.3	228.4	258.4	284.9	30.3	700.0	19.3		1,293	429.1	1,722
1980–1	1,097	306.0	1,403	120.3	143.5	189.6	237.9	205.5	24.1	588.6	19.7		1,076	335.5	1,411
1981–2	1,096	377.6	2,283	200.7	155.7	233.7	255.9	278.0	22.7	653.7	15.3		1,226	431.5	1,657
1982–3				206.4		145.5	284.2	308.1	21.9	677.6	17.0	155	1,464	256.4	
1983–4[1]				173.0		149.9	298.1	302.0	24.3	671.4	15.5	130	1,441	291.1	
1984–5[1]							291.0	309.0	26.0	697.0	19.0	159	1,501		
1985–6[1]							314.0	359.0	25.0	701.0	23.0				

[1] Preliminary.   [2] Includes in transit, exports and domestic use, except for oil stock for which disappearance is assumed to equal crushings.   [3] Graded & ungraded oil stock only.   [4] Relates to peanut oil mills only.   [5] Peanuts used in peanut butter by mfrs. for own use in candy is included under peanut candy.   *Source: Statistical Reporting Service, U.S.D.A.*   T.481

World Imports of Peanut Oil (Crude & Refined) into Specified Countries   In Thousands of Metric Tons

Crop Year	Algeria	Australia	Austria	Belgium-Lux.	Venezuela	Canada	Dominican Rep.	France	West Germany	Hong Kong	Italy	Singapore	Netherlands	Switzerland	Portugal	United Kingdom	Total
1977	5	4	2	29	64	7	15	217	37	23	31	2	8	—	—	16	
1978–9	—	1	2	35	66	6	2	221	40	25	46	2	21	20	—	15	454
1979–0	—	2	2	42	1	5	—	247	39	29	42	2	34	20	—	17	490
1980–1	—	—	3	33	—	5	—	161	26	28	20	3	23	10	—	12	327
1981–2		1		44		4		194	28	26	34		21	15		15	389
1982–3		2		57		4		223	25	28	37		24	12		17	447
1983–4		0		42		4		154	22	25	27		20	10		10	336
1984–5		3		42		3		124	21	32	37		12	10		10	303
1985–6[1]				37				135	20	30	50		20	10		12	324
1986–7[2]				32				135	20	30	40		15	10		10	300

[1] Preliminary.   [2] Estimate.   *Source: Foreign Agricultural Service, U.S.D.A.*   T.482

Production, Consumption, Stocks and Foreign Trade of Peanut Oil in the U.S.   In Millions of Pounds

Year	Production Crude	Refined	Consumption In Refining	In End pdt's.	Stocks—Dec. 31 Crude	Refined	Imports for Consumption	Exports Crude	Refined
1977	252.0	249.7	257.2	243.9	91.5	7.6	—	71.8	9.7
1978	145.2	171.9	178.0	169.0	7.3	4.7	—	32.9	7.6
1979	183.0	130.1	134.3	120.4	22.6	7.3		14.4	1.2
1980	182.4	170.6	166.7	165.3	7.5	4.3		46.0	1.6
1981	141.6	122.8	133.5	115.3	12.9	5.2		38.1	2.7
1982[1]	N.A.	148.0	162.1	150.2	N.A.	4.5		45.5	.6
1983[1]	N.A.	165.0	178.5	169.4	N.A.	2.9		67.4	.4
1984[1]	108.2	136.4	144.6	131.9	11.1	3.3			
1985[1]	146.7	119.3	125.2	N.A.	17.1	3.5			

[1] Preliminary.   *Source: Bureau of Census*   T.483

PEANUTS AND PEANUT OIL

Utilization of Peanut Oil in the United States   In Thousands of Pounds

Year Begin. Aug.	Shortening	Margarine	Cooking and Salad Oils	Other Edible	Total Food Uses	Non-Food Uses	Factory Consumption	Foots & Loss	Domestic Disappearance
1975–6	27,000	28,000	150,000	59,000	264,000	12,000	232,000	9,000	276,000
1976–7	29,000	27,000	143,000	26,000	225,000	8,000	218,000	6,000	232,000
1977–8	20,000	—	211,000	−47,000	183,000	11,000		8,000	194,000
1978–9	16,000		96,000						120,000
1979–0[1]			148,000						193,000
1980–1[2]			100,000						150,000
1981–2[2]			136,000		139,000				
1982–3[2]			157,000		174,000				
1983–4[2]			119,000		131,000				
1984–5[2]					118,405				
1985–6[2]					125,782				

[1] Preliminary.   [2] Estimate.   *Source: Bureau of the Census*   T.484

Average Price Received by Producers in U.S. for Peanuts in the Shell   In Cents Per Pound

Year	Sept.	Oct.	Nov.	Dec.	Jan.	Feb.	Mar.	Apr.	May	June	July	Aug.	Average[1]
1975–6	19.7	19.8	19.6	18.7	—	—	—	—	—	—	—	19.1	19.6
1976–7	19.8	19.9	20.0	20.0	20.2	—	—	—	—	—	—	21.3	20.0
1977–8	20.9	20.9	20.4	20.4	21.0	—	—	—	—	—	—	21.2	21.0
1978–9	20.8	21.4	21.0	20.8	21.2	—	—	—	—	—	—	21.2	21.1
1979–0	21.4	20.3	20.4	20.4	20.4	—	—	—	—	—	—	—	20.6
1980–1	22.5	23.2	27.9	37.3	47.7	—	—	—	—	—	—	—	25.1
1981–2	28.9	26.7	25.1	25.8	24.9	—	—	—	—	—	—	25.7	26.9
1982–3	25.1	24.9	25.3	26.1	22.9	—	—	—	—	—	—	27.1	25.1
1983–4	25.2	24.3	24.5	25.4	27.1	—	—	—	—	—	—	27.3	24.1
1984–5	27.6	25.6	25.4	24.4	24.1	—	—	—	—	—	—	22.1	24.8
1985–6[2]	22.5	23.3	24.0	23.1	22.4	19.8	—	—	—	—	—	29.6	23.5
1986–7[2]	26.1	27.7	30.6	30.9									

[1] Weighted average by sales.   [2] Preliminary.   *Source: Crop Reporting Board, U.S.D.A.*   T.479

Crude Peanut Oil Produced[2] in the United States   In Millions of Pounds

Year	Jan.	Feb.	Mar.	Apr.	May	June	July	Aug.	Sept.	Oct.	Nov.	Dec.	Total
1976	26.6	32.6	44.3	51.1	56.9	66.5	47.6	41.5	39.0	31.5	24.6	24.5	486.6
1977	20.7	24.7	35.5	33.0	32.8	30.1	24.7	22.4	6.9	6.1	10.5	4.4	252.0
1978	9.7	9.2	11.1	18.0	18.1	18.1	10.4	16.6	7.7	10.3	6.3	9.5	145.2
1979	11.7	14.2	22.5	18.6	23.0	15.5	8.2	10.8	4.5	4.5	6.1	7.7	183.0
1980	6.2	15.1	16.7	25.9	30.7	22.9	23.5	21.2	5.9	2.1	6.3	5.9	182.4
1981	6.1	6.0	10.5	17.3	19.1	19.5	13.6	9.8	5.3	9.7	12.0	12.7	141.6
1982	11.3	11.1	19.4	26.3	22.3	19.0	15.0	11.8	N.A.	N.A.	N.A.	N.A.	N.A.
1983	N.A.	N.A.	N.A.	N.A.	N.A.	N.A.	N.A.	N.A.	N.A.	N.A.	N.A.	N.A.	N.A.
1984	12.1	13.3	10.8	12.5	10.1	8.9	5.1	5.3	4.3	9.9	8.6	7.3	108.2
1985	9.8	13.9	15.8	15.5	14.5	12.4	10.4	10.0	10.1	9.2	10.2	14.9	146.7
1986[1]	19.2	21.1	19.9	20.8	24.0	26.4	14.2	9.6	N.A.	4.1	9.1		

[1] Preliminary.   [2] Not seasonally adjusted.   *Source: Statistical Reporting Service, U.S.D.A.*   T.473

Average Price of Domestic Crude Peanut Oil (in Tanks) F.O.B. Southeast Mills   In Cents Per Pound

Year	Oct.	Nov.	Dec.	Jan.	Feb.	Mar.	Apr.	May	June	July	Aug.	Sept.	Average
1978–9	45.1	49.7	46.0	51.4	47.4	37.9	40.9	41.2	36.5	39.0	37.0	35.5	42.3
1979–0	34.4	31.1	29.5	25.9	25.8	22.9	20.5	22.4	23.1	26.9	33.2	36.0	27.6
1980–1	35.8	48.7	49.1	47.7	39.3	34.1	34.0	37.1	38.0	38.1	43.2	40.3	40.5
1981–2	34.5	34.5	30.9	27.3	31.4	23.3	29.1	29.9	26.2	24.7	22.7	22.5	28.1
1982–3	22.9	25.2	26.1	25.6	25.7	24.1	25.1	26.4	26.4	26.7	30.7	50.5	28.0
1983–4	50.7	48.8	48.1	47.3	46.5	48.4	52.6	58.2	59.1	57.7	54.8	39.2	47.3
1984–5	36.7	41.2	41.4	39.2	38.8	40.3	49.6	46.2	40.7	39.7	37.6	33.9	40.4
1985–6	38.3	42.2	36.1	29.5	22.6	21.5	24.4	27.6	28.0	27.5	30.5	28.3	29.7

Source: Agricultural Marketing Service, U.S.D.A.   T.485

Pepper

Global consumption of pepper, the world's most important spice, has been running ahead of output for several years, requiring a drawdown of inventories to cover the shortfall. The latter was aggravated in 1985, when unfavorable growing conditions in Indonesia reduced production; India's 1985 crop was also smaller than in prior years. In Brazil and Malaysia, the other two major producers of pepper, output also declined in 1985 and 1986. Brazilian growers, hampered by a credit shortage and high costs of production, failed to make new plantings and thus cut back their cultivation. Farmers in Malaysia responded to higher prices for other crops, such as cocoa, by shifting production.

Although reliable data are lacking, it is believed that global stocks of pepper are at an extremely low level, relative to demand. Exports from all sources, for instance, declined 14 percent in 1984 from their level the year before, and further declines are probably recorded in 1985 and 1986. Because of the tight supply situation, the U.S. in 1986 stepped up its imports from India. Ordinarily, India's exports flow predominantly into Eastern Europe under trade agreements, but during 1986's crop season, the U.S. contracted to buy more than 12,000 tons of pepper from India, a three-fold increase over the amount imported during each of the preceding two years.

New York spot prices in early 1986 were being quoted at around $2.42 per pound for Lampong and Malabar black pepper, compared with $1.30 the year before. Prices were not expected to decline in the near term; it takes three to four years for new plants to produce. Also exacerbating the tight supply situation, the U.S. Food and Drug Administration in early 1986 "blocklisted" (detained for inspection at U.S. ports) all pepper shipped from both India and Brazil. In India's case, the action was taken after a pesticide was discovered during random inspection of incoming products. The blocklisting of Brazilian pepper was triggered by discovery of salmonella contamination in some shipments.

Because a bumper crop was harvested in India in 1986 and production in Indonesia partially rebounded from the weather-caused decline during 1984/85's crop season, world supplies were expected to be somewhat larger in 1987.

World Exports of Pepper (Black & White) and Prices

| | Exports (metric tons) | | | | | | | New York Spot Prices (¢ per pound) | | | | | |
| | | | | | | | | — Indonesian — | | — Brazilian — | | Indian | |
Year	Brazil	India	Indonesia	Singapore[2]	Madagascar	Sarawak	Sri Lanka	Lampong Black	Muntok White	Black	White	Malabar Black	Telli-cherry[3]
1974	15,491	28,569	15,188		2,241	28,933	337						
1975	17,944	24,399	14,525		3,461	29,815	96						
1976	19,986	17,813	29,481		2,958	34,850	10						
1977	17,099	25,892	30,856		3,748	26,795	635						
1978	29,505	19,370	37,090	40,904	1,566	30,780	1,205	93.7	132.6	91.9	129.7	93.9	112.2
1979	25,186	20,545	24,986	38,395	1,894	36,118	876	87.6	120.9	83.3	116.3	87.6	102.5
1980	31,964	26,795	29,345	33,233	1,674	30,709	945	68.8	101.5	62.3	100.0	80.4	103.8
1981	46,895	18,636	33,996	30,098	1,440	28,696	2,042	66.3	84.8	62.1	84.7	69.2	83.7
1982	44,539	20,454	36,327	26,459	1,796	25,010	1,238	72.1	96.7	65.5	96.2	76.0	86.5
1983	30,363	27,982	45,061	N.A.	2,801	23,481	1,120	72.1	96.7	65.5	96.2	76.0	86.5
1984[1]	36,499	21,000	33,817		2,804	16,502	2,202	98.6	153.9	96.5	152.8	98.9	115.2
1985[1]								169.6	190.6	167.4	190.4	169.6	185.3

[1] Preliminary. [2] Reexports. *Source: Foreign Agricultural Service, U.S.D.A.*

T.486

United States Imports of Pepper from Specified Countries   In Metric Tons

| | Black Pepper | | | | | | | | | | White Pepper | | | | | | |
Year	Brazil	Mexico	Sri Lanka (Ceylon)	Spain	India	Indonesia	Malaysia	Singapore	China	Total	Brazil	China	W. Germany	Indonesia	Malaysia	Singapore	Total
1975	6,436		41		6,708	4,613	4,487	773	10	23,156	170	—		1,514	63	59	1,813
1976	6,609		—		359	11,774	4,037	1,321	3	24,128	53	—		2,118	56	128	2,362
1977	5,282		157		4,890	9,466	3,140	478	—	23,540	40			2,765	42	63	2,920
1978	10,472		186		1,880	10,595	2,293	604	6	26,142	285	—		1,994	64	28	2,382
1979	9,704		281	—	627	10,898	2,644	156	61	24,482	414	10	—	2,159	51	94	2,756
1980	10,075	131	3,194														
1981	14,716	75	2,503														
1982	14,887	10	172	—	848	11,620	172	63	3	27,811	423	1	5	2,194	—	95	2,721
1983	13,047	—	256	—	2,498	12,327	25	120	3	28,346	571	17	6	2,460	—	65	3,130
1984	10,369	3	158	34	4,024	9,814	131	322	378	27,421	246	260	10	3,805	100	100	4,762
1985[1]	12,227	3	158	34	4,024	9,814	131	322	378	27,421	246	260	10	3,805	100	100	4,762
1986																	

[1] Preliminary. *Source: Foreign Agricultural Service, U.S.D.A.*

T.487

PEPPER

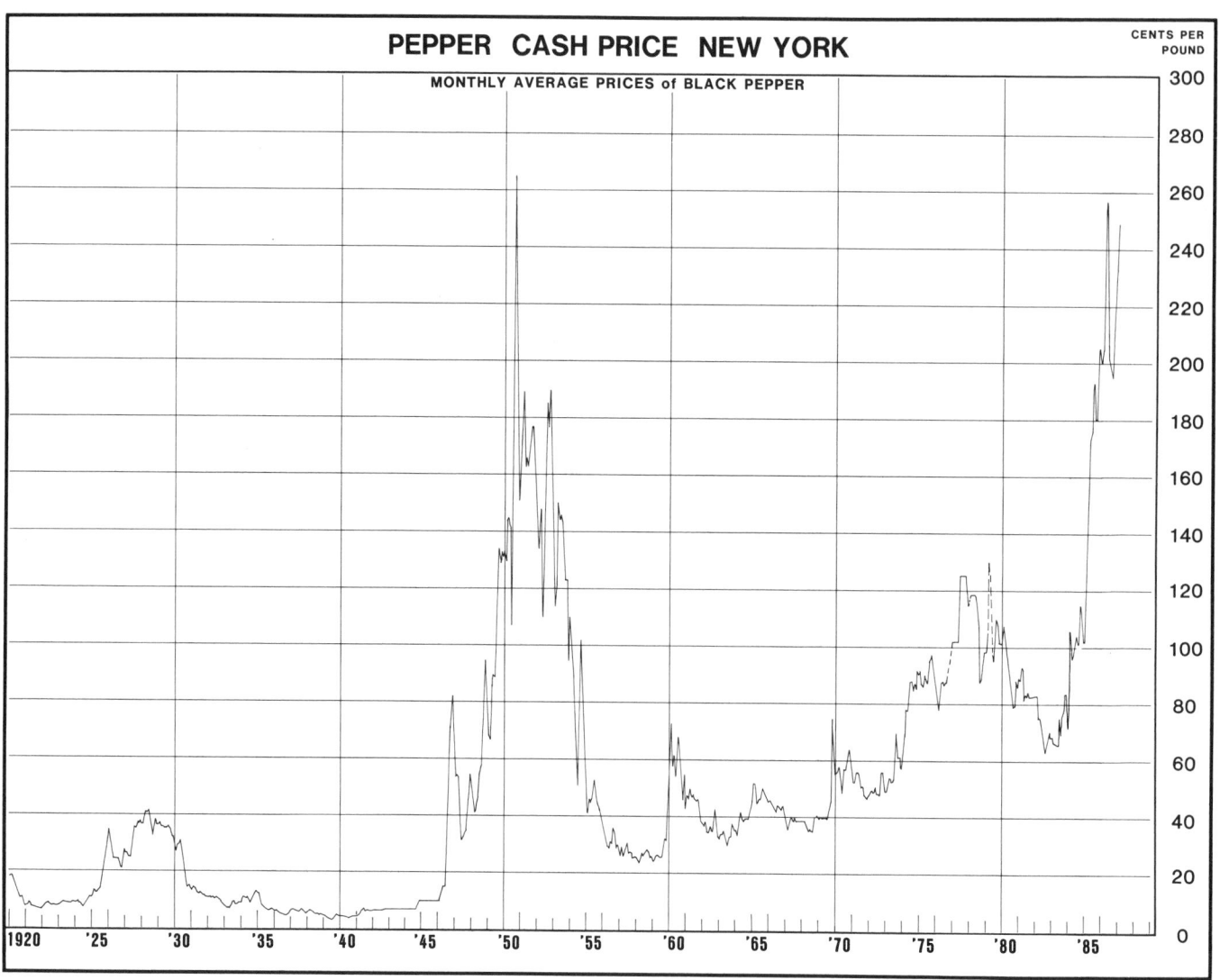

PEPPER CASH PRICE NEW YORK
MONTHLY AVERAGE PRICES of BLACK PEPPER

CENTS PER POUND

Average Black Pepper Prices in New York   In Cents Per Pound

Year	Jan.	Feb.	Mar.	Apr.	May	June	July	Aug.	Sept.	Oct.	Nov.	Dec.	Average
1973	49.3	52.0	54.0	53.0	52.5	53.0	65.0	70.0	61.0	61.0	57.5	61.0	57.4
1974	64.0	70.0	78.0	78.0	85.0	88.0	88.0	85.0	87.5	85.5	92.0	91.0	82.7
1975	91.5	87.0	86.0	90.0	89.0	87.5	88.5	95.0	97.0	94.0	87.5	85.0	89.8
1976	81.0	79.0	77.5	88.0	88.0	87.0	87.5	87.5	N.A.	N.A.	N.A.	102.0	86.4
1977	102.0	102.0	102.0	102.0	125.0	125.0	125.0	125.0	125.0	125.0	114.5	N.A.	115.7
1978	118.5	118.5	118.5	118.5	117.5	109.0	107.5	88.0	88.5	95.5	98.5	98.5	106.4
1979	105.0	N.A.	130.0	N.A.	N.A.	95.0	97.0	110.0	108.0	108.0	102.0	101.3	106.3
1980	108.0	101.0	96.3	93.0	87.0	84.3	82.8	79.0	79.0	88.0	86.5	89.3	89.5
1981	88.5	93.3	92.0	81.0	83.0	82.3	84.0	82.5	82.3	82.3	82.5	82.5	84.7
1982	82.5	82.5	75.0	75.0	70.0	69.0	67.0	63.0	69.0	70.5	68.5	68.3	71.7
1983	68.3	66.5	66.3	65.5	65.5	65.5	75.0	69.3	76.3	77.3	83.5	83.5	71.9
1984	105.7	102.0	95.7	97.0	100.7	102.0	103.7	101.3	109.0	115.3	107.3	102.3	103.5
1985	114.0	124.3	145.0	173.3	175.7	190.7	192.7	180.0	180.0	193.0	205.0	200.0	172.8
1986	208.0	217.0	257.0	226.0	201.0	199.0	197.0	195.0	210.0	231.0	233.0	249.0	218.6

Source: Bureau of Labor Statistics (0289–0131);   *N.Y. Wall St. Journal*

T.488

Petroleum

Total domestic field production of crude oil in 1986 averaged around 8.8 million barrels per day, according to incomplete data for the year. Imports of crude oil during the year averaged 4 million barrels per day, up sharply (about 25 percent) from 1985. Imports of other petroleum products increased from an average of 1.87 million barrels per day in 1985 to 1.9 million barrels in 1986, reflecting a rise of roughly three percent. U.S. exports of crude oil and petroleum products fell by about 13 percent from the prior year. Therefore, net imports rose, particularly during the later months of 1986, by about 50 percent.

A significant development in 1986 was that, for the first time since 1977, the percentage of petroleum products supplied to the U.S. from abroad increased. In peak year 1977, imports constituted 46.5 percent of domestic supply; they receded year by year through 1985, when they accounted for 27.3 percent. But, by mid-1986, the figure had risen to 33.5 percent. What is more, the fraction of domestic supply originating in OPEC countries reversed its downward trend: after dropping from an average of 33.5 percent in 1977 to 11.6 percent in 1985, it rose to more than 17 percent in the summer of 1986. The share originating in Arabian OPEC countries was only 3.0 percent in 1985, but rocketed to 7.2 percent by July, 1986.

The main reason for 1986's striking changes in imports and exports was the steep slide in prices of crude oil and its by-products that began in November, 1985. That slide was set in motion by Saudi Arabia's decision to supply substantially greater amounts of crude to international markets and, through that effort, to "punish" some of its rival sellers who had been undercutting OPEC's agreed-upon pricing structure. Whereas the refiners' average acquisition cost of imported crude oil averaged $37.05 per barrel in 1981, the figure fell to $26.60 in December, 1985, and to only $11.87 in August, 1986. The price to refiners of domestic crude nose-dived; it averaged $34.33 per barrel in 1981, $26.91 in December, 1985, and $11.95 in August, 1986.

The precipitous decline in prices failed to bring about a rise in domestic consumption, since demand for petroleum products is price-inelastic in the short run. Usage of petroleum in the residential and commercial sector in 1986 remained at its 1985 level, about 2.5 quadrillion (10 to the 15th power) Btu. In the industrial sector, usage fell from 7.7 quadrillion Btu in 1985 to an estimated 6.7 quadrillion in 1986. And, in the transportation sector, 1986 usage was estimated at 17.8 quadrillion Btu, as against 19.5 quadrillion the year before.

In the outlook for 1987, the price of crude is expected to be somewhat higher and the rate of output somewhat lower than in 1986. The members of OPEC reached an accord in late 1986 to reduce production and to support the price of crude at $18.00 per barrel. Moreover, with prices down substantially from their level of a few years ago, consumers have the incentive and the time to substitute petroleum for competing sources of energy. On the other hand, agreements by cartels such as OPEC are unstable and tend to break down when demand for their product is stagnant or falling—and there are abundant signs of slowing growth in the major oil-consuming economies.

Futures Market

Futures contracts in crude oil, heating oil, and unleaded gasoline are traded on the New York Mercantile Exchange (NYMEX).

World Production of Crude Petroleum, by Specified Countries   In Thousand Barrels Per Day

Year	Algeria	Canada	China	Libya	Iran	Iraq	Kuwait	Nigeria	Mexico	Indonesia	United Kingdom	USSR	Saudi Arabia	United States	Venezuela	World Total
1978	1,161	1,313	2,082	1,983	5,242	2,563	2,131	1,897	1,209	1,635	1,082	10,950	8,301	8,707	2,166	59,868
1979	1,154	1,496	2,122	2,092	3,168	3,477	2,500	2,302	1,461	1,591	1,568	11,187	9,532	8,552	2,356	62,353
1980	1,012	1,435	2,114	1,787	1,662	2,514	1,656	2,055	1,936	1,577	1,622	11,460	9,900	8,597	2,168	59,225
1981	805	1,285	2,012	1,140	1,380	1,000	1,125	1,433	2,313	1,605	1,811	11,552	9,815	8,572	2,102	55,546
1982	710	1,271	2,045	1,150	2,214	1,012	823	1,295	2,748	1,339	2,065	11,615	6,483	8,649	1,895	52,900
1983	660	1,356	2,120	1,105	2,440	1,005	1,064	1,241	2,689	1,343	2,291	11,684	5,086	8,688	1,801	52,654
1984	638	1,438	2,296	1,087	2,174	1,209	1,157	1,388	2,780	1,412	2,480	11,576	4,663	8,879	1,798	53,834
1985[2]	643	1,465	2,480	1,059	2,201	1,433	1,016	1,471	2,735	1,258	2,530	11,250	3,388	8,971	1,674	52,954
1986[1]	600	1,470	2,600	1,000	1,900	1,650	1,300	1,500	2,400	1,300	2,550	11,300	4,800	8,800	1,650	55,000

[1] Estimate.   [2] Preliminary.   *Source: Energy Information Administration*

T.489

PETROLEUM

United States Crude Oil[1] Supply & Disposition

Yearly Average	Field Production Total Domestic	Alaskan	Total	Imports SPR[4]	Other	Stock Withdrawal[3] SPR[4]	Other	Unaccounted for Crude Oil	Disposition Refinery Inputs	Exports	Ending Stocks[2] Total	SPR[5]	Other Primary
				Thousands barrels per day							Million barrels		
1981	8,572	1,609	4,396	256	4,141	−336	46	83	12,470	228	594	230	363
1982	8,649	1,696	3,488	165	3,323	−174	38	71	11,774	236	644	294	350
1983	8,688	1,714	3,329	234	3,096	−234	20	114	11,685	164	723	379	344
1984	8,879	1,722	3,426	197	3,229	−195	− 4	185	12,044	181	796	451	345
1985	8,971	1,825	3,201	118	3,083	−117	67	145	12,002	204	814	493	321
1986[6]	8,800	1,850	4,100	50	4,050	− 50	− 60	300	12,700	150	850	510	340
Aug.	8,708	1,871	4,826	51	4,775	− 51	293	−222	13,274	233	838	505	333
Sept.	8,671	1,870	4,984	47	4,937	− 47	−169	−134	13,098	160	844	506	338
Oct.	8,773	1,877	4,317	37	4,281	− 36	−166	− 59	12,636	151	850	508	343

[1] Includes lease condensate. [2] Stocks are totals as of end of period. [3] A negative number indicates an increase in stocks and a positive number indicates a decrease. [4] Strategic Petroleum Reserve. [5] Stocks of Alaskan crude oil in transit were included beginning in January 1981. Stock withdrawals are calculated using new basis levels. [6] Preliminary. *Source: Energy Information Administration* T.489a

Production[1] of Crude Petroleum in the United States In Millions of Barrels of 42 Gallons

Year	Jan.	Feb.	Mar.	Apr.	May	June	July	Aug.	Sept.	Oct.	Nov.	Dec.	Total
1981	264.7	240.9	267.0	256.7	263.5	258.9	263.5	266.1	258.1	265.4	257.6	266.1	3,129
1982	263.8	243.7	268.7	257.7	269.2	259.4	268.4	267.6	261.0	269.7	260.9	266.5	3,157
1983	269.6	245.2	269.7	263.3	267.6	260.0	267.7	269.1	263.5	271.9	263.1	260.3	3,171
1984	274.9	257.4	268.8	265.9	277.6	265.6	275.4	273.1	269.8	276.1	269.4	275.8	3,250
1985[2]	276.8	250.0	276.7	265.3	278.0	270.7	277.4	272.9	268.6	278.1	267.1	279.9	3,275
1986[2]	277.2	250.3	277.1	264.4	273.0	263.7	270.8						

[1] Represents oil transported from producing properties, plus that remaining on properties & consumed on leases. [2] Preliminary.
Source: Bureau of Mines T.500

United States Production of Gasoline[1] In Millions of Barrels

Year	Jan.	Feb.	Mar.	Apr.	May	June	July	Aug.	Sept.	Oct.	Nov.	Dec.	Total
1981	209.1	177.3	193.3	184.2	191.0	187.7	199.8	206.2	198.0	200.2	197.7	205.0	2,349
1982	191.8	165.7	186.5	183.4	196.7	203.5	210.7	200.1	196.5	194.9	188.9	203.2	2,322
1983	188.7	164.3	183.7	186.7	199.0	200.6	208.8	203.7	199.3	192.7	199.7	196.1	2,323
1984	187.7	184.1	197.6	196.4	207.0	199.6	200.9	199.5	196.2	198.7	202.1	201.4	2,371
1985[2]	183.0	165.7	187.9	190.4	203.2	204.2	211.5	212.3	189.8	197.8	195.2	206.7	2,352
1986[2]	202.8	177.2	188.6	195.8	220.7	214.1	217.4						

[1] Gasoline and naphtha from crude petroleum and natural gasoline used at refineries. [2] Preliminary. *Source: Bureau of Mines* T.502

United States Domestic Consumption of Gasoline In Millions of Barrels

Year	Jan.	Feb.	Mar.	Apr.	May	June	July	Aug.	Sept.	Oct.	Nov.	Dec.	Total
1981	200.1	177.1	196.4	199.1	205.9	212.0	212.7	206.9	200.6	204.9	191.9	207.9	2,416
1982	185.5	174.0	201.2	207.7	207.1	206.1	211.4	206.1	196.9	198.8	197.6	203.6	2,396
1983	187.8	168.9	212.5	194.4	205.8	210.8	210.7	216.0	202.8	205.2	198.8	212.9	2,427
1984	194.6	181.4	202.8	201.1	214.7	214.1	212.5	220.9	198.3	209.2	204.7	203.7	2,458
1985[1]	197.0	183.1	206.2	208.8	218.9	210.8	218.3	225.6	199.8	214.6	203.7	211.4	2,503
1986[1]	201.7	180.8	216.9	213.5	217.9	217.0	234.2						

[1] Preliminary. *Source: Bureau of Mines* T.503

Stocks of Finished Gasoline on Hand in the United States, at End of Month In Millions of Barrels

Year	Jan.	Feb.	Mar.	Apr.	May	June	July	Aug.	Sept.	Oct.	Nov.	Dec.
1981	229.1	232.4	234.5	225.2	214.8	196.1	187.9	190.9	193.4	193.1	203.3	206.2
1982	215.9	211.2	200.7	181.0	175.6	179.5	185.0	187.6	193.3	194.6	191.9	196.8
1983	210.0	209.2	185.4	185.4	188.0	185.4	192.3	187.4	191.8	189.5	198.4	187.8
1984	188.0	199.3	204.8	209.7	212.7	206.5	202.2	188.3	196.5	195.5	201.2	207.9
1985[1]	200.4	192.6	188.9	184.4	183.6	188.5	194.4	190.4	189.7	182.3	185.6	192.4
1986[1]	203.5	209.0	187.2	176.7	191.5	199.7	192.7					

[1] Preliminary. *Source: Bureau of Mines* T.504

Crude Petroleum Refinery Operations Ratio[1]   In Percent of Capacity

Year	Jan.	Feb.	Mar.	Apr.	May	June	July	Aug.	Sept.	Oct.	Nov.	Dec.	Average
1980	82	80	77	76	75	77	74	73	74	71	73	76	76
1981	72	71	68	66	67	68	67	71	68	67	68	69	69
1982	67	65	66	66	69	75	75	71	74	71	71	70	70
1983	68	65	66	70	72	75	75	74	78	73	75	70	72
1984	73	76	75	75	77	77	76	78	78	76	77	76	76
1985[2]	75	74	74	76	78	79	81	78	77	79	80	81	78
1986[2]	80	78	76	81	86	86	84						

[1] Based on the ratio of the daily avg. crude runs to stills to the rated capacity of refineries per day.   [2] Preliminary.   *Source: Bureau of Mines*
T.496

Production of Major Refined Petroleum Products in Continental U.S.   In Millions of Barrels

Year	As-phalt[2]	Avia-tion Gasol.	Fuel Oil Dis-tillate	Fuel Oil Resid-ual	Gaso-line[4]	Petro-Chemical Feedstocks	Special Naph-thas	Miscel. pdt's.	Jet Fuel	Kero-sene	Liquified Gases[7] (For Fuel)	Lubri-cants	Liquefied Gases[3] Total	Liquefied Gases[3] at L.P.G.[5]	Liquefied Gases[3] at L.R.G.[6]
1979	168.8	13.7	1,151	615.6	2,515	252.1	36.6	42.7	369.2	66.8	84.7	71.0	568.0	443.9	124.1
1980	141.2	12.8	974.1	578.4	2,394	254.6	36.5	38.5	365.6	50.1	87.0	65.1	561.8	440.9	120.8
1981	123.5	11.5	953.8	482.1	2,349				353.2	43.6		60.6	573.4	458.6	114.8
1982	119.4	8.9	951.3	390.4	2,322				357.0	42.0		51.6	557.5	459.0	98.5
1983	135.7	9.2	896.5	310.9	2,323				373.2	40.0		53.8	599.2	479.6	119.6
1984	141.3	9.1	981.2	326.2	2,371				414.3	41.8		58.3	620.9	488.2	132.7
1985[1]	146.3	9.3	980.9	322.0	2,352				433.9	34.5		53.1	622.0	479.3	142.6

[1] Estimated.   [2] 5.5 barrels = 1 short ton.   [3] Includes ethane & ethylene.   [4] Finished.   [5] Gas processing plants.   [6] Refineries.   [7] Liquified refinery gases.   *Source: Bureau of Mines*
T.490

Stocks of Petroleum & Products in the United States on January 1   In Millions of Barrels

Year	Crude Petro-leum	Strate-gic Reserve	Total	As-phalt[2]	Avia-tion Gasol.	Fuel Oil Distil-late	Fuel Oil Resid-ual	Finished Gasoline	Refined Products Petro-Chemical Feedstocks	Jet Fuel	Kero-sene	Liquefied Gases[3]	Lubri-cants	Road Oil	Wax[4]	Unfinished Oils (Net)[5]
1980	430.3	91.2	778.6	18.9	2.7	228.7	95.6	239.9	4.0	38.5	15.8	110.7	12.5	.3	.7	117.7
1981	482.9	107.8	745.3	18.8	2.3	205.4	91.5	213.5	5.9	42.4	11.4	128.0	13.6	.3	.5	
1982	593.8	230.3	712.5	19.6	2.7	191.5	78.0	206.2		41.1	11.0	134.7	14.3			176.8
1983	643.6	293.8	628.3	15.9	2.3	178.6	66.2	196.8		36.8	10.4	94.0	12.5			158.1
1984	722.9	379.1	569.2	18.8	2.3	140.3	48.5	187.8		38.6	7.9	100.6	12.1			161.5
1985	795.9	450.5	620.6	17.2	2.7	161.1	53.0	207.9		42.0	11.9	100.8	12.7			139.8
1986[1]	814.2	493.3	556.6	21.2	2.1	143.7	50.4	192.4		40.5	7.5	73.5	11.8			148.0

[1] Preliminary.   [2] 5.5 bbls. = 1 s. ton.   [3] Includes ethane & ethylene at plants & refineries.   [4] 1 bbl. = 280 lbs.   [5] And misc. products.
Source: Bureau of Mines
T.493

Stocks of Crude Petroleum[1] in the United States at Beginning of Month   In Millions of Barrels

Year	Jan.	Feb.	Mar.	Apr.	May	June	July	Aug.	Sept.	Oct.	Nov.	Dec.
1980	430.3	448.7	457.2	458.6	471.0	474.6	472.7	469.9	478.4	469.2	475.1	475.4
1981	482.9	486.4	494.2	513.8	531.7	543.8	547.8	559.0	546.7	555.2	578.0	588.5
1982	593.8	606.2	613.0	609.2	610.4	609.5	608.3	612.8	626.5	618.6	635.6	647.5
1983	643.6	660.4	669.4	666.8	678.9	679.4	683.0	675.8	700.5	707.7	716.2	712.7
1984	722.9	733.1	727.4	728.2	742.5	763.6	766.6	771.8	764.1	756.3	779.8	786.9
1985[2]	795.9	793.5	785.6	790.7	806.7	828.3	820.6	810.5	805.6	806.6	803.6	812.4
1986[2]	814.2	826.3	827.3	837.8	836.9	828.7	827.2	845.2				

[1] Total gasoline-bearing in the U.S.   [2] Preliminary.   *Source: Bureau of Mines*
T.501

U.S. Production of Residual Fuel Oil and Distillate Fuel Oils   In Millions of Barrels

Year	Jan.	Feb.	Mar.	Apr.	May	June	July	Aug.	Sept.	Oct.	Nov.	Dec.	Total
1981	142.6	122.4	121.1	112.1	114.0	112.0	110.6	120.5	117.1	115.4	118.3	129.8	1,436
1982	118.6	101.1	105.7	105.7	116.2	114.1	116.7	107.6	110.0	117.6	115.5	112.9	1,342
1983	102.1	83.8	87.7	93.3	104.8	101.2	104.5	103.1	107.0	108.1	105.8	106.0	1,207
1984	110.1	112.2	104.4	95.7	107.4	111.9	108.2	107.3	106.7	111.5	112.9	119.3	1,307
1985[1]	111.6	98.7	99.2	100.8	107.0	100.4	104.7	103.4	102.0	118.3	121.1	131.1	1,303
1986[1]	118.8	95.8	107.1	111.5	116.9	106.5	110.4						

[1] Preliminary.   *Source: Bureau of Mines*
T.505

PETROLEUM

Exports[2] of Petroleum and Products from the United States In Thousands of Barrels[1]

| | | | | Kerosene (Incl. Range Oil) | Refined Products | | | | | | | | | |
| | | | | | Fuel Oil | | Lubricants | | | | | | | |
Year	Crude	Total Refined	Finished Gasoline		Distillate	Residual	Grease	Oil	Wax	Coke	Asphalt	Liquified Gases	Misc. Oils
1978	57,728	74,329	470	40	1,202	4,634	288	9,399	543	40,438	138	7,238	171
1979	85,707	86,149	155	25	1,079	3,266	279	8,275	836	53,270	181	5,414	163
1980	104,908	94,289	494	32	1,238	12,232	246	8,322	736	49,872	247	7,826	210
1981	83,200	133,900	700		1,900	43,200	7,000						
1982	86,300	211,200											
1983	59,900	209,900											
1984	66,200	196,900											
1985[3]	74,500	209,900											
1986[4]	53,000	217,000											

[1] 42 gallons per barrel. [2] Includes shipments from Noncontiguous Territories. [3] Preliminary. [4] Estimate. *Source: Bureau of Mines* T.494

Imports[2] of Petroleum & Products into the United States In Thousands of Barrels (42 Gallons Per Barrel)

| | | | | Refined Products | | | | | | | | | | |
| | | | | Fuel Oil | | Finished Gasoline | | | Liquified Pet. Gases | Lubri-cants | Petro-chemical Feed-stocks | Special Naph-thas | Un-finished Oils | Wax |
Year	Crude	Total Refined	As-phalt	Dis-tillate	Re-sidual		Jet Fuel	Kero-sene						
1978	2,329,700	722,900	907	63,288	494,640	69,518	31,346	4,031	40,889	2,978	2,994	1,750	9,913	—
1979	2,400,900	685,600	1,448	70,489	420,144	66,006	28,566	3,298	62,576	3,441	3,934	3,480	21,372	0
1980	1,946,200	582,500	1,414	51,900	343,600	51,071	29,521	3,690	56,711	2,667	10,245	3,354	19,659	0
1981	1,654,200	534,200		63,100	292,100									
1982	1,352,400	514,000		34,000	283,100									
1983	1,317,800	525,900		63,500	255,200									
1984	1,368,800	620,200		99,400	249,200									
1985[1]	1,308,600	540,300		73,100	186,300									
1986[3]	1,500,000	575,000		75,000	220,000									

[1] Preliminary. [2] Includes shipments to Noncontiguous Territories. [3] Estimate. *Source: Bureau of Mines* T.495

Average Price of Crude Petroleum at Wells[1] Index (1967 = 100)

Year	Jan.	Feb.	Mar.	Apr.	May	June	July	Aug.	Sept.	Oct.	Nov.	Dec.	Average
1977	262.9	274.2	270.0	271.0	271.0	271.8	270.8	273.3	276.1	278.6	282.9	288.1	274.2
1978	288.8	289.7	293.4	294.3	295.5	298.9	301.9	302.7	305.7	307.5	310.5	312.4	300.1
1979	316.4	322.3	324.2	326.2	335.7	356.4	370.6	385.7	422.1	436.7	450.4	470.8	376.5
1980	513.6	515.1	522.8	533.9	540.1	549.0	551.4	566.8	571.3	579.6	600.6	632.8	556.4
1981	704.4	842.7	842.8	842.5	839.9	815.9	798.9	796.8	796.8	788.2	785.9	787.2	803.5
1982	787.2	770.3	744.8	717.9	717.8	718.2	718.4	718.4	718.3	735.3	733.6	720.0	733.4
1983	719.7	692.9	678.0	678.0	678.0	677.9	675.7	675.1	675.7	675.7	675.6	674.4	681.4
1984	675.6	675.6	675.6	673.9	673.9	673.3	672.6	671.1	670.6	669.8	655.8	649.4	669.8
1985	631.2	615.1	615.5	617.6	620.9	620.1	618.9	614.1	615.5	618.5	621.4	624.3	619.4
1986[2]	618.1	489.0	353.1	300.7	293.0	300.8	272.6	261.9	310.7	308.3	307.3		

[1] Buyers posted prices. [2] Preliminary. *Source: Bureau of Labor Statistics* (0561) T.497

Average Wholesale Prices of Gasoline[1] (Regular Grade—Leaded) Index (Feb. 1973 = 100)

Year	Jan.	Feb.	Mar.	Apr.	May	June	July	Aug.	Sept.	Oct.	Nov.	Dec.	Average
1977	239.9	240.4	245.6	249.5	254.5	258.9	261.2	260.5	259.6	257.5	256.3	255.8	253.6
1978	255.1	252.8	252.0	253.0	255.5	260.5	266.4	271.3	275.1	278.1	277.5	282.7	265.0
1979	287.0	292.3	299.9	313.0	331.6	349.3	371.0	397.7	422.1	439.2	488.3	459.6	367.6
1980	481.1	517.5	560.4	585.4	595.5	598.6	601.1	602.9	599.6	591.5	590.8	596.1	576.7
1981	607.5	632.9	683.2	694.7	690.4	685.6	677.4	668.4	666.4	666.1	661.7	657.7	666.0
1982	651.7	642.3	621.1	578.6	555.7	582.7	628.8	636.3	628.4	617.2	608.7	598.5	612.5
1983	576.7	551.4	533.5	515.3	537.2	559.5	566.6	571.2	566.3	559.2	548.2	535.8	551.7
1984	518.3	512.4	517.9	520.5	532.6	531.0	520.9	504.6	500.3	509.8	511.3	502.0	515.1
1985	480.5	458.4	467.2	493.9	522.5	535.7	539.3	526.7	513.6	506.1	520.1	523.0	507.3
1986[2]	486.5	427.7	327.8	310.4	348.4	361.4	286.6	282.5	311.9	284.5	283.9		

[1] Excludes aviation. [2] Preliminary. *Source: Bureau of Labor Statistics* (0571–02) T.498

High, Low & Closing Prices of December Crude Oil Futures in New York   In Dollars Per Barrel

Year of Delivery		Year Prior to Delivery			Delivery Year											Life of Delivery Range
		Oct.	Nov.	Dec.	Jan.	Feb.	Mar.	Apr.	May	June	July	Aug.	Sept.	Oct.	Nov.	
1984	High	—	29.75	29.55	29.60	30.50	30.56	30.42	31.60	30.89	30.34	30.29	30.02	29.92	28.87	31.60
	Low	—	28.60	27.50	28.20	28.85	30.05	30.15	30.10	29.62	28.01	28.31	29.23	26.93	28.30	26.93
	Close	—	29.00	28.20	29.15	30.03	30.35	30.15	30.85	30.25	28.19	29.72	29.89	28.46	28.44	—
1985	High	29.50	27.93	27.20	25.95	26.50	27.60	28.60	26.65	26.25	26.49	27.68	28.65	30.40	31.82	31.82
	Low	26.99	26.56	25.91	23.90	25.00	25.90	26.55	26.10	24.58	24.93	25.60	26.12	27.84	29.93	23.90
	Close	27.66	26.72	25.91	25.35	25.45	27.42	26.77	26.50	25.50	25.66	27.40	28.63	30.38	31.72	—
1986	High	25.60	26.45	25.66	22.05	19.23	15.85	14.85	15.30	13.80	12.70	15.92	16.52	15.85	15.83	26.45
	Low	23.80	24.74	22.18	19.15	15.05	11.69	11.20	13.00	12.70	10.40	11.28	13.90	13.52	14.68	10.40
	Close	25.33	24.74	22.21	19.19	15.44	11.69	12.82	13.56	12.82	11.28	15.85	14.93	15.27	15.08	—

Source: N.Y. Mercantile Exchange   T.502a

Month–End Open Interest of Crude Oil Futures in New York   In Contracts

Year	Jan.	Feb.	Mar.	Apr.	May	June	July	Aug.	Sept.	Oct.	Nov.	Dec.
1984	23,168	27,650	28,142	26,647	23,970	28,635	37,349	32,245	32,236	37,613	39,896	49,201
1985	63,458	57,479	44,532	45,875	50,450	57,820	52,134	53,743	64,731	64,981	58,099	61,161
1986	66,522	64,007	72,083	92,863	98,292	102,404	131,234	97,455	100,805	114,505	100,041	121,248

Source: N.Y. Mercantile Exchange   T.502b

Volume of Trading of Crude Oil Futures in New York   In Thousands of Contracts

Year	Jan.	Feb.	Mar.	Apr.	May	June	July	Aug.	Sept.	Oct.	Nov.	Dec.	Total
1984	108.7	130.7	121.5	106.2	136.4	134.5	154.9	200.4	111.2	243.3	174.7	217.7	1,840.3
1985	385.3	263.3	298.5	272.6	290.1	342.2	329.8	269.7	339.8	365.9	337.9	386.8	3,980.9
1986	520.1	490.9	560.0	691.4	677.0	612.7	858.4	701.6	666.7	986.4	604.4	941.8	8,313.5

Source: N.Y. Mercantile Exchange   T.502c

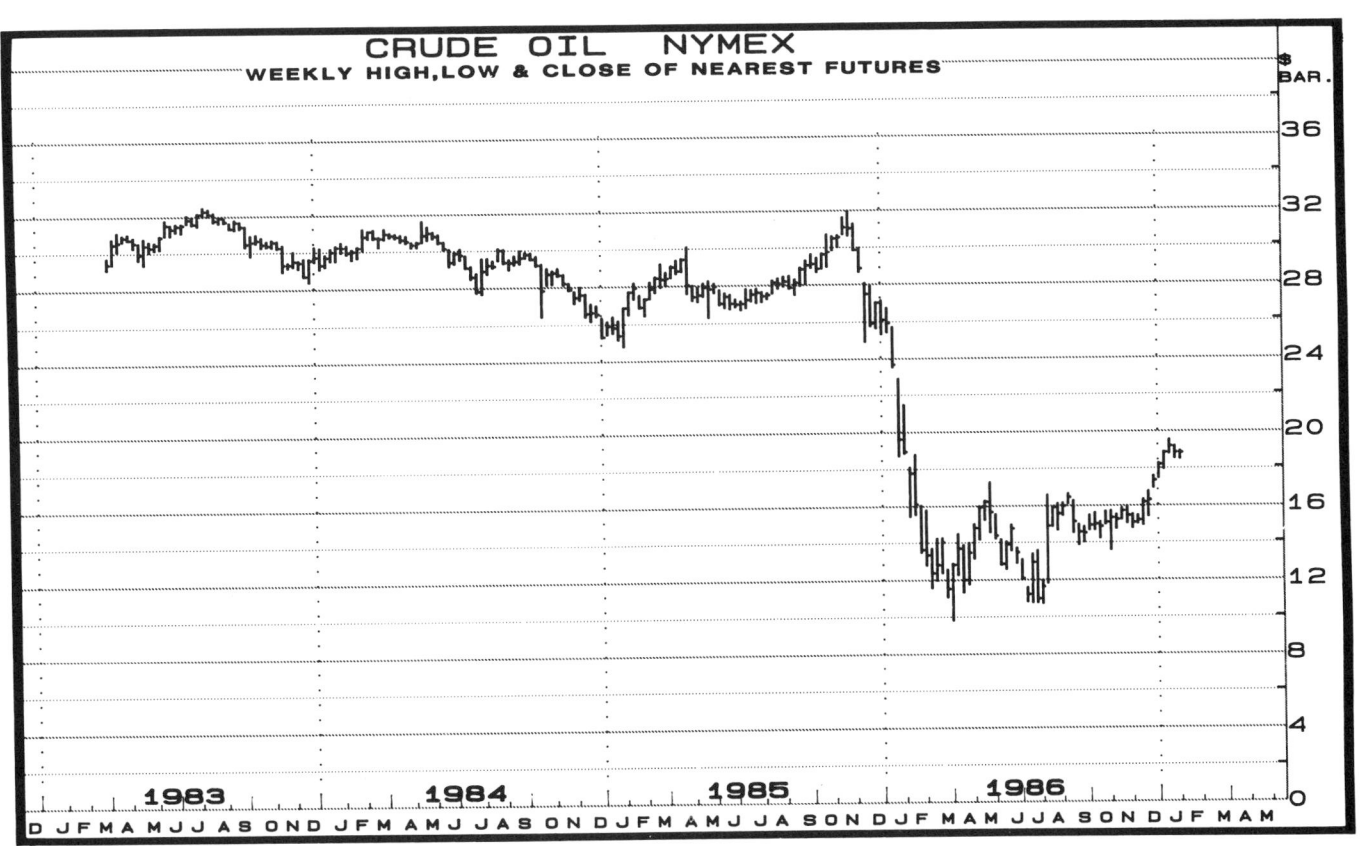

187

Plastics

The basic raw materials of the plastics-synthetic resins industries are petroleum and natural gas. Naptha, derived from crude oil, is converted into such resins as nylon, polycarbonates, silicones, polyesters, polystyrene, and phenolics. Natural gas is an important feedstock source of ethylene and propylene, which are essential in the production of low- and high-density polyethylene, polyvinyl chloride, and polypropylene. These large-volume plastics account for more than 70 percent of total production.

Incomplete statistics on U.S. demand for and supply of plastics materials and resins during 1986 indicate that domestic output and imports continued their long-term upward trend. The value of domestic shipments, expressed in 1982 dollars, was forecast at just under $21 billion for 1986, up nearly five percent from 1985 and up almost one-third from 1981. No figure for the value of imports in 1986 had been projected by the U.S. Department of Commerce (DOC) at this writing, but they were expected to rise substantially in 1986, as they had in the four preceding years: +15 percent in 1983, +42 percent in 1984, and +16 percent in 1985. The principal reason for this surge was a decline in prices of foreign-produced plastics. The primary foreign suppliers to the U.S. are Japan, Canada, and West Germany. The value of U.S. exports dropped in 1985, after rising for three successive years, and was expected to fall again in 1986. Factors contributing to this development included a sharp increase in U.S. prices of exported plastics, entrance of Saudi Arabia into the world market, and slowing growth in many industrialized economies.

The DOC reports that many growth opportunities remain for plastics, among them displacement of rival materials in other domestic markets.

Prospects are bright, notes the Department, for specialty applications, such as oil cans, grocery sacks, fuel tanks, barrier packaging, half-gallon dairy bottles, and aseptic packaging. However, some reductions in domestic demand could occur in the electronics and automotive markets, as a result of shrinking demand for electronics products and continued growth in automobile imports.

The prospects for U.S. exports of plastics are less optimistic. Producers in the Middle East, Canada, Mexico, and other oil-producing countries have a favorable cost position with respect to feedstocks. These foreign producers are aggressively entering the "commodity" plastics field and building up their capacity to produce high-volume plastics materials. They could soon become major competitors to U.S. producers trying to generate sales abroad.

World Production of Plastics and Resins[3] (Condensation, Polymerization, Etc.)   In Thous. of Metric Tons

Year	Australia	Austria	Czecho-slovakia	France	Germany East	Germany West	Italy	Japan	Netherlands	Poland	Belgium	Hungary	USSR	United Kingdom	United States
1976	407	404	580	1,769	679	7,088	2,266	4,952	1,723	559	824	186	3,216	2,556	13,261
1977	480	430	738	1,834	734	6,270	2,538	4,978	1,783	583	1,471	144	3,300	2,710	11,232
1978	522	434	810	1,885	762	6,703	2,466	5,882	1,962	596	1,682	209	3,516	2,621	12,380
1979	618	437	853	2,220	779	7,255	2,562	6,964	2,012	571	1,969	289	3,504	2,647	13,866
1980	709	487	894	2,052	859	6,710	2,464	6,422	1,975	667	1,835	324	3,636	2,260	12,418
1981	700	504	913	2,480	998	6,600	2,154	5,936	2,393	588	1,940	307	3,696	2,051	13,664
1982	715	454	961		989	6,275	2,142	5,986	2,502	600	2,023	322	4,057	1,966	13,009
1983		550	1,004		1,045	7,031	2,436	6,504	2,777	526	2,246	337	4,392	1,800	14,790
1984[1]		613	1,034	2,694	1,057	7,408	2,731	7,424	2,641	600	2,374	377	4,500	1,900	15,505
1985[2]		625	1,075	2,900	1,050	7,700	2,700	7,400	2,500	590	2,500	390	4,700	1,800	

[1] Preliminary.   [2] Estimate.   [3] Refers to production of thermoplastic & thermosetting resins & plastic materials obtained by chemical transformation of natural organic substances or by chemical synthesis.   *Source: United Nations*   T.506

Production of Important Synthetic Plastics & Resin Materials in the U.S.   In Millions of Pounds

Year	Phenolic Resins	Polyethlene & Copolymers	Poly-propylene	Polystyrene & Copolymers	Polyvinyl Chloride & Copolymers	Year	Phenolic Resins	Polyethlene & Copolymers	Poly-propylene	Polystyrene & Copolymers	Polyvinyl Chloride & Copolymers
1978	1,926	11,259	3,055	5,989	5,878	1983	1,460	14,053	4,457	6,254	6,256
1979	1,779	12,408	3,824	6,327	6,211	1984	1,656	14,621	5,216	6,857	6,828
1980	1,745	11,720	3,699	5,540	5,485	1985	1,423	15,386	5,180	5,652	6,894
1981	1,688	12,604	4,008	5,915	5,618	1986[1]	1,430	15,900	5,700	5,700	7,300
1982	1,398	12,548	3,515	5,609	5,397	1987					

Note: Data included in the table does not cover all Plastics production. Various types of Plastics production of lesser importance are not included because statistics are not available on a consistent basis. Also, many individual firms do not make their production figures known.   [1] Estimate.
Sources: U.S. Tariff Commission, Bureau of Census   T.507

Average Wholesale Price Index of Plastic Materials in the United States (1967 = 100)

Year	Jan.	Feb.	Mar.	Apr.	May	June	July	Aug.	Sept.	Oct.	Nov.	Dec.	Average
Plastic Resins and Materials (066)													
1980	270.4	272.1	274.5	287.6	288.4	287.6	285.7	281.5	276.5	276.1	276.2	274.1	279.2
1981	274.7	276.1	279.4	285.1	287.9	290.0	295.9	297.5	296.8	299.5	293.2	294.2	289.2
1982	286.1	297.3	285.5	286.0	283.2	282.1	280.9	282.2	281.6	281.6	281.4	281.4	284.1
1983	283.8	283.1	282.1	285.4	288.0	289.1	291.3	293.7	302.6	299.1	297.9	301.5	291.5
1984	305.2	305.0	306.2	307.8	310.6	311.1	310.6	310.3	311.8	309.4	309.0	306.2	308.6
1985	305.2	306.9	306.3	306.1	305.4	307.1	307.5	306.4	305.1	300.7	300.3	299.3	304.7
1986[1]	297.1	302.4	301.8	296.6	295.6	295.2	296.7	294.6	291.8	292.7	295.5		
PE Resin, Low, Pkg. Firm (0662-0301.99)													
1980	257.2	260.9	N.A.	275.1	270.8	264.0	259.4	254.4	249.4	249.3	251.8	250.9	258.5
1981	251.5	251.2	252.5	263.0	263.0	263.7	280.7	N.A.	279.8	279.9	N.A.	247.3	263.3
1982	207.5	208.1	209.7	224.5	202.1	197.2	184.3	185.3	184.2	183.9	184.7	184.7	196.4
1983	204.9	205.2	193.9	215.4	215.4	N.A.	236.2	236.2	237.8	251.6	250.9	250.9	227.1
1984	272.1	272.6	272.1	272.1	272.1	272.1	272.1	272.1	272.1	272.1	272.1	272.1	272.1
1985	272.1	272.1	272.1	272.1	272.1	272.1	272.1	272.1	272.1	206.8	206.8	206.8	255.8
1986[1]	224.7	224.7	224.7	224.7	224.7	224.7	224.7	N.A.	N.A.	224.0	224.5		
Thermoplastic Resins (0662) — Dec. 1980 = 100													
1981	100.2	101.0	102.6	104.6	105.8	106.6	109.3	110.1	109.7	110.5	107.2	107.6	106.3
1982	103.5	104.2	103.2	103.5	102.1	101.5	100.9	101.5	101.3	101.3	101.3	101.1	102.1
1983	102.4	102.1	101.5	103.4	104.7	105.2	106.3	107.3	111.6	109.6	108.8	110.6	106.1
1984	112.3	112.0	112.5	112.8	113.4	114.0	113.8	113.6	114.4	113.2	113.0	111.7	113.1
1985	111.1	112.0	111.7	111.5	111.3	111.9	111.9	111.4	110.6	108.3	108.1	107.8	110.6
1986[1]	106.6	109.4	109.0	106.9	106.3	105.9	106.7	105.6	104.3	104.9	106.3		
Polystyrene Resin, Rubber Modified (0662-0602.99)													
1980	283.5	N.A.	278.8	291.4	291.9	293.2	288.0	287.6	282.1	286.0	287.3	289.4	287.2
1981	290.2	294.2	291.7	299.2	299.2	305.2	303.1	N.A.	N.A.	292.6	298.9	299.7	297.4
1982	297.8	297.8	297.8	N.A.	294.2	293.9	291.2	291.2	291.2	N.A.	291.0	290.9	293.7
1983	299.6	287.8	287.8	287.8	N.A.	N.A.	N.A.	N.A.	N.A.	N.A.	N.A.	N.A.	290.8
1984	N.A.	N.A.	N.A.	N.A.	N.A.	N.A.	302.5	301.6	300.8	300.2	298.9	298.2	300.7
1985	296.9	295.6	295.0	295.7	296.9	297.6	297.6	297.6	296.2	296.2	296.2	295.6	296.4
1986[1]	307.3	307.3	304.2	N.A.	275.7	275.7	291.7	N.A.	N.A.	N.A.	N.A.		
Thermosetting Resins (0663)—Dec. 1980 = 100													
1981	101.4	101.1	101.4	104.0	104.5	105.4	106.6	106.5	106.6	107.7	107.6	108.2	105.1
1982	108.0	107.9	108.1	108.1	108.0	108.6	108.7	108.8	108.9	108.8	108.9	109.2	108.4
1983	109.0	108.8	108.9	108.5	108.4	108.6	108.7	109.4	110.1	110.8	111.5	111.5	109.5
1984	112.2	112.7	113.1	113.3	116.1	114.6	114.4	114.6	114.5	114.4	114.2	114.2	114.0
1985	114.1	114.1	114.2	114.1	114.0	114.6	114.9	115.0	115.3	115.7	115.7	115.1	114.7
1986[1]	115.3	115.0	115.1	113.7	113.5	114.0	114.0	114.0	113.8	113.2	113.3		
Phenolic Molding Compound (0663-0201.99)													
1980	239.7	239.7	244.3	249.9	251.3	251.3	250.4	240.2	240.2	240.2	240.2	240.2	244.0
1981	N.A.	N.A.	N.A.	N.A.	N.A.	N.A.	254.2	254.2	254.2	254.2	254.2	254.2	254.2
1982	254.2	254.2	254.2	254.2	254.6	254.6	254.6	254.5	254.5	254.5	254.5	254.5	254.4
1983	249.6	245.7	245.7	245.7	245.7	245.7	245.7	245.9	246.0	246.0	245.6	245.7	246.1
1984	245.6	245.8	246.3	252.1	259.5	260.2	259.4	259.4	259.7	259.6	259.2	259.2	255.5
1985	259.2	259.2	259.2	259.2	259.2	259.2	259.2	268.1	268.1	268.1	268.1	268.1	262.9
1986[1]	268.1	267.3	267.3	259.2	252.4	252.4	252.4	252.4	252.4	252.4	252.4		

[1]Preliminary.   *Source: Bureau of Labor Statistics*

T.508

Platinum-Group Metals

The platinum group (PGM) consists of six related metals: platinum, palladium, iridium, osium, rhodium and ruthenium. Platinum and palladium represent 95 percent of supply. All six metals share the same properties of high melting point and resistance to acid, but subtle differences lend each to special applications. Platinum is favored for jewelry fabrication and investor hoarding, as well as in industry.

Platinum prices made a stellar performance in 1986. Spot prices rose from $341 per ounce, at the beginning of the year, to a high of $675 in September. Fueling the rise was an expected shortfall in supplies if South Africa, the world's leading producer, were to curtail shipments to the West. As it happened, the shortfall was overestimated. While demand for platinum rose moderately, supplies and inventories proved to be adequate. Turmoil in South Africa waxed and waned, but serious disruption never materialized. However, a phenomenal take-off in investor demand occurred in 1986. Increased participation by speculators brought breadth and depth to the platinum market.

Three major South African companies—Rustenburg, Impala and Western—produce about 80 percent of Western world supplies. In January, 1986, a miner's strike at Impala gave the market impetus for an upsurge in prices. Even after the strike ended, platinum prices continued a sustained upward drive. Higher platinum prices encouraged Rustenburg and Impala to utilize existing capacity to the fullest extent. As a result, total shipments from South Africa in 1986 may show a net gain over 1985.

After three consecutive years of decline, 1986 platinum shipments by the USSR, the second-largest producer in the world, were expected to show an increase from the 230,000-ounce level of 1985. There was speculation that the USSR would increase sales of platinum to make up for revenue lost from plunging oil prices. However, there was no indication that the Soviets had, in fact, stepped up exports in the first half of 1986.

A steady stream of platinum supplies was always available to fabricators in 1986, especially when South African materials tightened. Given the level of demand in 1986, Johnson Matthey Limited estimated that centrally planned economies supplied about 20 percent of new platinum to the Western world, or about 240,000–300,000 ounces.

Production of PGM occurs in the U.S. on a very small scale. The Bureau of Mines estimated that domestic mine production in 1986 totaled 10,000 ounces, while apparent consumption totaled 3.3 million ounces. The bulk of domestic supply—92 percent—comes from imports. About 45 percent of U.S. imports were from South Africa, 16 percent from England, and 13 percent from the USSR. U.S. exports of PGM during the first three quarters of 1986 were 580,000 ounces, an 18-percent decline from the same year-ago period. Stocks of PGM held by refiners, importers and dealers, as of September 30, 1986, were 1.2 million ounces, compared with 1.1 million the year before. The principal end-usages of PGM in the U.S. during 1986 were: automotive (chiefly in catalytic converters), 50 percent; electronic, 17 percent; and dental and medical, 16 percent. The Stillwater Complex in southern Montana holds palladium-rich deposits. A project to develop Stillwater is expected to yield 75,000 ounces of palladium and 25,000 ounces of platinum annually; the start-up date is planned for mid-1987.

In 1986, platinum supplies in Western countries are estimated to reach 2.8 million ounces. This outstrips demand—including sales to Comecon (Soviet bloc) countries and China—by 60,000 ounces. Since a good portion of the 400,000 ounces of platinum demanded by investors in 1986 represents a transfer of inventories, the industrial world is apparently not running short of needed supplies. As a maturing investment vehicle, platinum tends to respond to currency and financial market conditions. At year-end 1986, inflation in the U.S., Western Europe and Japan was still under control; competitive real returns on interest-bearing investments were difficult to beat. Given these conditions and considerations, platinum prices may well trend lower in 1987.

Futures Market

Platinum and palladium futures are traded on the New York Mercantile Exchange (NYMEX).

World Mine Production of Platinum-Group Metals   In Troy Ounces

Year	Australia	Zimbabwe	Finland	Canada	Colombia[3]	Ethiopia	Japan	South Africa	USSR	United States	Yugo-slavia	World Total[1]
1979	9,645	—	1,643	197,943	12,933	108	34,637	3,017,000	3,200,000	7,300	5,916	6,487,125
1980	12,603	9,774	900	410,757	14,345	113	41,334	3,100,000	3,250,000	3,348	4,919	6,848,093
1981	14,989	7,500	3,601	382,658	14,804	125	36,269	3,110,000	3,350,000	7,318	3,601	6,930,865
1982	15,767	4,469	8,809	228,425	11,886	125	43,273	2,600,000	3,500,000	8,033	3,480	6,424,098
1983	13,900	4,090	4,469	223,925	10,303	125	58,582	2,600,000	3,600,000	6,257	3,311	6,524,770
1984	13,900	1,994	2,154	348,216	10,106	125	53,325	3,500,000	3,700,000	14,635	3,119	7,647,755
1985[2]	16,000	2,100	2,200	350,000	11,400	125	65,919	3,700,000	3,800,000	N.A.	3,550	7,951,294

[1] Estimate.   [2] Preliminary.   [3] Placer platinum.   *Source: Bureau of Mines*   T.509

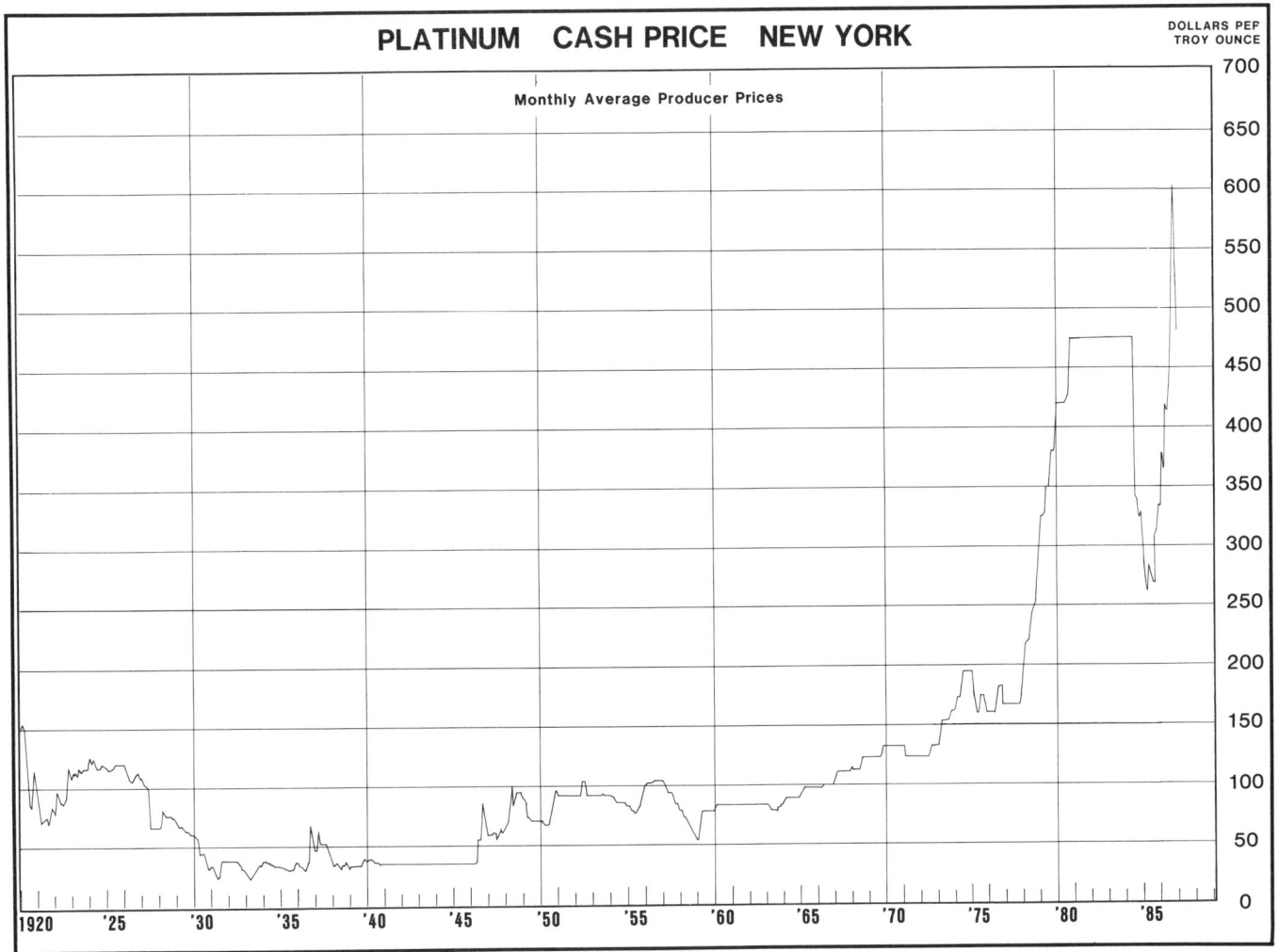

PLATINUM CASH PRICE NEW YORK

DOLLARS PEP TROY OUNCE

Monthly Average Producer Prices

Platinum-Group Metals Sold to Consuming Industries in the United States   In Thousands of Troy Ounces

Year	Automotive Plati-num	Automotive Others[2]	Chemical Plati-num	Chemical Others[2]	Electrical Plati-num	Electrical Others[2]	Dental & Medical Plati-num	Dental & Medical Others[2]	Jewelry & Decorative Plati-num	Jewelry & Decorative Others[2]	Petroleum Plati-num	Petroleum Others[2]	All Platinum-Group Metals Plati-num	All Platinum-Group Metals Palla-dium	All Platinum-Group Metals Other[2] Metals	Total
1973			239.0	334.1	117.4	551.1	27.9	136.3	22.4	38.9	123.6	20.3	658.5	1,012.5	160.9	1,833.9
1974	350.0	15.0	350.0	150.0	98.6	452.6	25.5	125.7	23.0	35.3	139.5	26.7	943.7	886.1	151.2	1,981.0
1975	273.0	97.0	148.8	166.9	73.6	153.1	17.1	115.9	22.9	29.5	108.0	5.4	698.6	541.5	68.6	1,308.7
1976	481.0	194.9	83.6	154.7	89.3	197.5	26.9	140.4	23.4	14.8	59.1	7.7	851.1	657.1	94.9	1,603.1
1977	354.3	125.9	84.4	196.6	90.2	254.5	27.1	113.9	34.7	22.1	74.8	13.6	789.8	700.5	102.0	1,592.3
1978	597.5	201.8	149.7	186.5	106.4	346.5	44.1	208.0	25.8	25.1	108.4	19.2	1,196.3	917.9	145.4	2,259.6
1979	803.2	248.3	98.6	264.9	115.8	457.4	27.1	244.9	27.7	21.6	170.0	27.9	1,408.9	1,132.6	214.5	2,756.0
1980	517.1	214.2	119.0	165.6	150.1	376.1	25.8	245.4	51.0	22.6	144.0	26.7	1,118.2	912.0	175.7	2,205.9
1981	446.7	160.6	78.1	152.4	111.7	388.3	18.7	255.8	27.6	19.6	88.3	22.9	872.6	889.2	158.8	1,920.7
1982	477.8	144.8	63.6	200.6	90.0	348.4	22.8	312.1	16.0	12.7	21.6	21.7	780.1	926.3	166.8	1,873.3
1983	508.5	191.8	65.4	99.8	74.7	404.8	16.7	261.7	10.3	10.6	38.0	51.1	796.7	921.8	195.4	1,914.0
1984	722.0	350.3	73.5	108.7	99.2	452.8	18.6	349.0	9.5	11.0	28.0	92.7	1,029.2	1,257.5	184.1	2,470.8
1985[1]	811.0	370.3	85.2	87.4	115.8	359.1	24.6	352.6	16.0	11.9	28.8	81.0	1,217.8	1,186.0	191.4	2,595.2
1986[3]	—1,100.0—		—180.0—		—460.0—		—330.0—		—20.0—		—100.0—		1,200.0	1,100.0	200.0	2,500.0

[1] Preliminary.   [2] Palladium, iridium, osmium, rhodium, & ruthenium.   [3] Estimate.   *Source: Bureau of Mines*   T.512

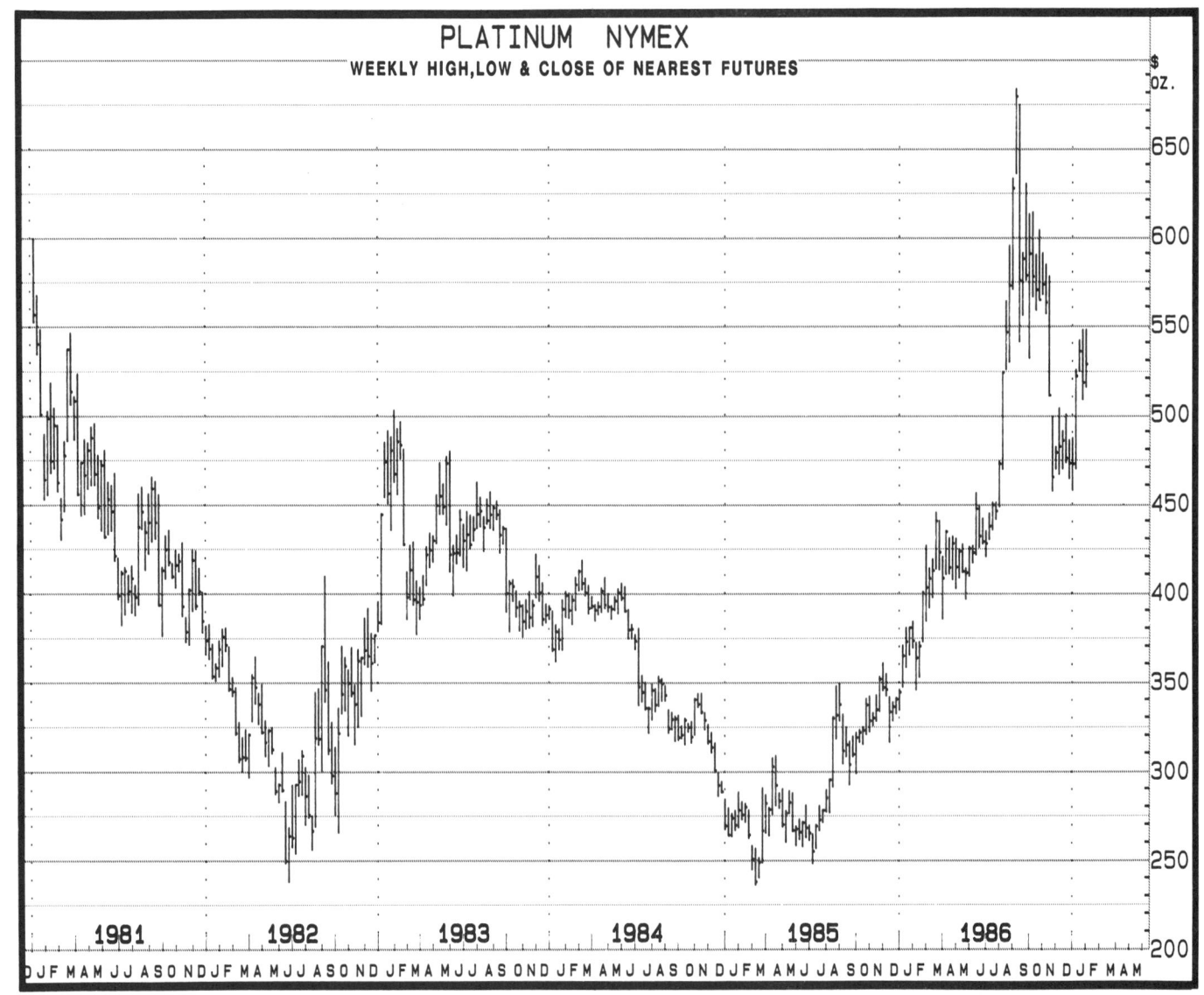

PLATINUM NYMEX
WEEKLY HIGH,LOW & CLOSE OF NEAREST FUTURES

Average Merchant's Prices of Platinum in New York In Dollars Per Troy Ounce

Year	Jan.	Feb.	Mar.	Apr.	May	June	July	Aug.	Sept.	Oct.	Nov.	Dec.	Average
1973	132.50	141.97	152.50	152.50	152.50	152.50	152.50	152.50	155.24	160.50	160.50	160.50	152.18
1974	162.68	172.50	172.50	172.50	174.55	195.00	195.00	195.00	195.00	195.00	195.00	195.00	184.98
1975	195.00	180.53	175.00	163.06	160.00	160.00	162.73	175.00	175.00	172.17	160.00	160.00	169.87
1976	160.00	160.00	160.00	160.00	160.00	163.54	175.60	182.50	182.50	182.50	167.00	167.00	168.39
1977	167.00	167.00	167.00	167.00	167.00	167.00	167.00	167.00	167.00	167.00	167.65	174.81	167.71
1978	186.55	206.58	217.07	220.00	220.00	227.73	237.89	241.74	250.23	253.18	284.00	300.00	237.08
1979	303.41	325.00	325.00	327.38	350.00	350.00	350.00	357.83	380.00	380.00	380.00	393.33	351.83
1980	420.00	420.00	420.00	420.00	420.00	420.00	420.00	425.24	475.00	475.00	475.00	475.00	436.77
1981	475.00	475.00	475.00	475.00	475.00	475.00	475.00	475.00	475.00	475.00	475.00	475.00	475.00
1982[1]	369.26	361.95	322.46	338.95	314.43	278.26	286.90	290.41	334.98	324.58	346.65	370.95	328.32
1983	441.07	468.34	400.17	410.38	446.69	420.23	431.63	438.30	431.93	399.87	389.33	399.70	423.14
1984	375.11	391.38	398.47	395.17	388.95	386.31	345.55	336.03	327.36	324.65	328.45	309.11	383.88
1985	275.76	274.37	255.36	287.23	273.24	267.94	269.52	303.91	304.59	321.73	334.53	327.75	291.33
1986[2]	377.74	365.14	413.35	418.97	413.82	432.76	439.46		602.30	580.37	519.99	481.02	465.31

[1] Prior to 1982 prices are for *producer* prices.   [2] Preliminary.   *Source: American Metal Market*   T.511

Salient Statistics of Platinum and Allied Metals in the U.S.   In Troy Ounces

Year	Net Import Reliance as a % of Apparent Consump.	Production Crude[5]	Refinery New Metal	Refinery Secondary Metal	Stocks as of Dec. 31[1] Platinum	Stocks as of Dec. 31[1] Palladium	Stocks as of Dec. 31[1] Other	Total	Imports for Consumption	Value of Imports Mil. $	Exports Platinum	Exports Other Groups[3]	Exports Other[6]
1979	89	7,300	8,392	309,022	305,605	323,865	131,812	761,282	3,479,128	840.5	207,832	522,195	189,218
1980	87	3,348	2,300	330,923	502,185	353,002	118,074	973,261	3,501,782	1,177	289,454	302,457	173,053
1981	83	7,318	5,607	391,637	401,389	398,933	117,856	918,178	2,849,617	800.3	391,194	258,745	213,426
1982	81	8,033	7,078	344,160	604,632	384,184	117,812	1,106,628	2,493,706	553.9	175,805	262,764	423,576
1983	89	6,257	5,884	303,165	433,457	412,178	97,513	943,148	3,218,022	752.8	184,599	261,188	782,967
1984	89	15,000	14,433	339,526	648,130	524,924	145,593	1,318,647	4,474,106	1,118.1	220,885	375,802	565,543
1985[2]	92	N.A.	3,987	258,650	564,363	478,348	148,603	1,191,314	3,989,594	1,025.7	187,013	339,254	362,384
1986[4]					650,000	450,000	100,000	1,200,000					

[1] In hands of refiners, importers, & dealers.   [2] Preliminary.   [3] Palladium, rhodium, iridium, osmium, ruthenium & osmium metals & alloys.   [4] Estimate.   [5] From crude platinum placers & byproduct platinum-group metals.   [6] Ore & concentrates, waste, scrap & sweepings.
Source: Bureau of Mines   T.513

High, Low & Closing Prices of April Platinum Futures in New York   In Dollars per Ounce

Year of Delivery		Feb.	Mar.	Apr.	May	June	July	Aug.	Sept.	Oct.	Nov.	Dec.	Jan.	Feb.	Mar.	Apr.	Life of Delivery Range
1983	High	429.6	390.0	400.0	356.0	329.5	333.0	358.1	415.0	392.0	385.0	405.0	499.3	502.0	428.0	433.0	502.0
	Low	388.0	342.6	352.0	318.0	263.0	280.5	271.5	291.0	285.2	320.0	352.0	393.0	396.3	376.5	393.0	263.0
	Close	395.0	357.2	352.0	315.2	306.4	303.3	333.1	294.4	355.1	384.3	392.6	498.7	396.3	392.6	424.0	—
1984	High	526.0	461.0	459.5	495.0	465.0	474.0	470.0	464.5	421.0	426.0	422.0	398.5	410.0	417.5	407.2	528.0
	Low	423.3	410.0	433.5	458.0	422.0	439.0	439.5	404.0	382.0	380.0	389.5	369.0	382.0	388.0	384.0	364.3
	Close	423.3	425.6	453.4	468.5	441.5	457.7	453.6	415.8	383.0	417.2	399.5	391.3	403.8	392.2	397.0	—
1985	High	438.5	447.5	440.0	427.5	433.5	402.0	370.5	352.2	345.0	350.0	328.0	289.5	282.0	290.0	308.0	447.5
	Low	415.0	422.0	414.0	411.5	401.0	343.0	350.5	335.0	327.8	322.0	291.0	265.5	244.5	236.0	263.5	236.0
	Close	433.5	426.0	417.4	426.2	402.9	349.7	361.3	336.1	331.7	323.0	293.0	280.5	249.3	281.4	281.5	—
1986	High	—	308.5	329.8	303.9	293.9	298.5	357.0	333.0	345.0	362.5	356.0	385.0	425.8	444.5	434.0	444.0
	Low	—	279.5	290.5	273.0	275.5	261.2	287.0	297.5	311.0	326.5	321.0	340.0	345.2	391.2	385.0	261.2
	Close	—	307.3	290.5	281.5	278.6	297.7	338.9	309.5	327.9	349.0	346.2	372.7	402.3	399.1	426.9	—
1987	High	430.0	448.5	446.0	434.5	463.3	475.0	620.1	689.5	622.0	586.0	506.7					
	Low	361.0	400.0	398.0	404.0	425.5	432.0	471.0	546.4	564.5	459.5	462.0					
	Close	409.4	412.9	430.3	433.1	441.9	473.6	620.1	558.6	576.2	481.7	476.2					

Source: N.Y. Mercantile Exchange   T.514

Month–End Open Interest of Platinum Futures in New York   In Contracts

Year	Jan.	Feb.	Mar.	Apr.	May	June	July	Aug.	Sept.	Oct.	Nov.	Dec.
1980	8,200	8,409	6,209	5,434	6,369	7,943	7,797	8,286	14,239	12,140	12,026	11,911
1981	9,410	8,946	9,441	7,709	8,130	7,891	5,520	6,446	8,421	7,055	8,601	7,839
1982	6,278	7,524	8,686	8,302	10,326	9,337	11,137	12,853	14,141	13,002	15,547	15,620
1983	19,927	23,506	15,197	15,878	18,375	15,918	16,934	15,671	15,413	12,450	13,227	13,384
1984	12,692	13,912	13,805	15,244	15,852	17,254	15,775	15,766	17,288	14,826	14,753	15,525
1985	15,210	14,131	13,256	12,096	11,668	11,371	11,677	16,492	13,149	13,068	17,969	14,853
1986	18,163	20,490	19,938	15,768	16,582	18,748	18,749	25,939	23,364	19,152	18,204	17,707

Source: N.Y. Mercantile Exchange   T.515

Volume of Trading of Platinum Futures in New York   In Thousands of Contracts

Year	Jan.	Feb.	Mar.	Apr.	May	June	July	Aug.	Sept.	Oct.	Nov.	Dec.	Total
1980	35.2	28.5	41.7	21.4	26.6	37.6	40.8	26.7	59.7	41.0	34.8	35.9	429.7
1981	36.5	29.7	56.1	36.7	30.8	44.7	37.9	39.1	63.9	35.4	33.2	46.6	490.5
1982	32.5	29.5	48.4	42.4	33.1	46.6	55.8	76.9	84.8	70.8	70.0	78.1	669.0
1983	126.0	117.0	107.9	71.9	106.2	115.4	75.9	77.0	79.2	61.5	57.2	57.9	1,035.4
1984	44.7	43.7	68.9	54.5	44.9	53.8	55.2	38.4	52.2	35.9	38.3	40.7	571.1
1985	41.0	26.2	53.5	48.8	43.1	42.2	40.3	98.1	82.7	68.6	64.8	84.0	693.3
1986	101.3	114.7	139.8	100.3	77.0	122.2	75.4	189.8	289.4	164.8	136.6	113.3	1,624.6

Source: N.Y. Mercantile Exchange   T.516

PALLADIUM NYMEX
WEEKLY HIGH,LOW & CLOSE OF NEAREST FUTURES

Average Dealer[1] Price of Palladium in the United States   In Dollars Per Troy Ounce

Year	Jan.	Feb.	Mar.	Apr.	May	June	July	Aug.	Sept.	Oct.	Nov.	Dec.	Average
1975	124.32	105.00	93.92	90.50	73.27	57.71	55.86	58.30	50.52	47.60	44.00	44.00	70.42
1976	42.00	39.62	37.56	38.50	41.58	48.50	55.75	50.28	53.25	52.99	59.20	52.38	47.63
1977	54.06	58.10	57.82	55.20	52.97	45.18	44.90	42.36	42.20	43.07	48.83	51.97	49.72
1978	55.10	64.86	64.18	59.33	60.82	60.42	59.53	61.86	60.09	71.58	70.74	73.25	63.48
1979	76.14	103.35	95.56	93.97	105.53	124.33	121.40	117.45	136.94	143.63	141.95	163.42	118.62
1980	220.00	262.80	259.83	194.79	169.74	169.56	199.55	203.88	212.74	204.72	185.85	155.69	203.10
1981	134.38	112.18	117.82	110.42	102.90	94.76	83.61	85.86	85.50	79.08	72.13	69.51	95.68
1982	67.70	67.53	66.99	69.43	68.51	59.27	57.35	57.76	64.50	59.99	74.03	86.14	66.60
1983	116.05	124.33	99.55	114.67	130.60	128.66	143.83	147.65	152.21	145.35	147.71	160.69	134.28
1984	157.30	161.10	159.26	161.03	156.25	154.07	140.98	135.83	136.94	140.07	146.47	136.72	148.84
1985	120.87	127.88	114.45	114.77	108.67	99.15	94.79	102.49	97.25	101.55	101.32	94.50	106.48
1986[2]	103.02	102.17	110.00	108.28	109.13	110.35	111.96		141.99	136.11	123.30	117.80	116.99

[1] Based on wholesale quantities, prompt delivery.   [2] Estimate.   *Source: American Metal Market*

T.510

Pork Bellies

Pork bellies, the layer of meat and fat from the underside of the hog, are cured and smoked to produce bacon. An average hog, marketed at around 225 pounds, will yield two bellies, each weighing eight to 18 pounds, depending upon the animal's slaughter weight. Bellies generally account for about 12 percent of a hog's live weight and a somewhat larger percentage of the total cut-out value. Profit margins for hog processors reflect the value of all pork products, including ham and loins as well as bacon. Even when overall cut-out value is profitable, the price of any one product may be independently weak because of seasonally-reduced demand or other reasons. Typically, consumer bacon demand is strongest during the summer months.

Futures prices for pork bellies trended higher during 1986, in reaction to smaller-than-expected hog supplies. Belly prices tend to follow the hog market. A surprisingly bullish quarterly hog report in mid-1986 indicated fewer hogs on hand than expected; evidence of the curtailed supply triggered a 20-cent /lb. advance in belly prices from late June to late July. Much of the gain was then lost during the August–October period. The hog report abetted a mid-year tendency for belly prices to move higher and followed early 1986 forecasts suggesting that bellies might have a contra-seasonal slide in mid-year. Thus, belly prices were under some pressure during the spring and the positive reaction to the June pig crop report was strong. Initial forecasts for 1987 were somewhat similar to a year earlier, including expectations of larger hog supplies and increased belly production and the possibility of a contra-seasonal decline in mid-1987.

Pork belly prices in January, 1986, averaged 61.27 cents/lb. (12–14 lb. weight) and drifted to a low of 49.45 cents by April. Prices averaged 90.08 cents in July. Retail bacon prices during January averaged $1.94/lb. and eased to $1.87 in April. The dip in retail prices was filtered into the retail level.

Generally, belly prices during the course of a full year are sensitive to the inventory of bellies in cold storage and to net movement in or out (which tends to reflect demand, although a better measure is the quantity of bellies being sliced into bacon). The USDA's monthly cold-storage report showed a sharp drawdown during the second half of 1986, from 61.5 million pounds on hand July 1, 1986, to 13 million on October 1, the lowest for that date since 1982.

Futures Markets

Pork belly futures and options are traded on the Chicago Mercantile Exchange (CME). The size of the futures and options contracts is now 40,000 pounds, revised last year from 38,000 pounds.

United States Quarterly Sliced Bacon Production[1]   In Millions of Pounds

Year	Retail	Commercial	Total	Year	Retail	Commercial	Total
1982	1,000.7	500.8	1,501.5	1984[2]	1,038.0	693.6	1,731.6
I	246.3	120.9	367.2	I	253.6	176.4	430.0
II	247.2	128.0	375.3	II	246.8	162.2	409.0
III	273.5	129.2	402.6	III	268.8	166.4	435.2
IV	233.7	122.7	356.4	IV	268.8	188.6	457.4
1983	1,113.6	562.8	1,676.4				
I	248.6	127.7	376.2				
II	250.8	140.8	391.6				
III	260.6	152.1	412.8				
IV	353.6	142.2	495.7				

[1] Smoked, dried or cooked. Under Federal Inspection.   [2] Preliminary.   *Source: Agricultural Marketing Service, USDA*   T.517a

U.S. Frozen Pork Belly Storage Stocks   (In Thousand Pounds, as of First of the Month)

Year	Jan.	Feb.	Mar.	Apr.	May	June	July	Aug.	Sept.	Oct.	Nov.	Dec.
1976	44,722	37,386	38,526	51,176	60,144	63,799	49,258	25,773	8,689	5,858	9,708	24,946
1977	42,906	38,338	36,364	52,806	69,539	80,658	62,695	29,901	9,640	5,241	4,230	20,642
1978	23,747	19,013	15,738	39,631	70,976	82,343	75,027	44,787	21,015	7,482	20,013	40,964
1979	54,367	39,432	37,172	57,744	69,689	86,065	78,935	53,373	21,800	11,077	17,739	42,156
1980	70,201	69,635	67,800	85,444	98,163	106,869	96,967	68,616	34,410	21,867	42,186	72,127
1981	97,365	90,181	94,661	104,357	125,469	132,568	117,795	72,998	36,094	16,228	18,060	35,058
1982	54,639	46,167	41,855	66,061	—	—	72,593	—	—	7,558	—	—
1983	31,292	33,592	33,400	44,304	54,510	64,671	63,468	48,409	26,642	15,672	20,047	52,924
1984	78,648	71,568	78,169	95,009	112,205	127,527	115,034	85,630	43,626	22,321	24,048	38,333
1985	57,361	53,623	51,633	68,315	83,836	96,040	88,367	61,397	35,764	20,158	29,787	47,427
1986[1]	51,314	47,633	51,218	62,508	68,325	65,895	61,547	40,333	20,797	12,941	17,022	24,530

[1] Preliminary.   *Source: Crop Reporting Board, U.S.D.A.*   T.517

PORK BELLIES

Wkly Fed. Inspected Hog Slaughter

1985[2] Week Ending	(In Thousand Head)			
	1985	1984	1983	1982
Jan. 1	1,238	1,350	1,204	1,428
7	1,295	1,418	1,457	1,881
14	1,679	1,708	1,564	1,656
21	1,615	1,625	1,561	1,643
28	1,528	1,577	1,519	1,623
Feb. 5	1,565	1,543	1,350	1,552
12	1,582	1,571	1,467	1,650
19	1,508	1,578	1,491	1,484
26	1,539	1,579	1,544	1,652
Mar. 5	1,608	1,656	1,646	1,698
12	1,635	1,791	1,584	1,676
19	1,638	1,691	1,546	1,663
26	1,647	1,681	1,558	1,705
Apr. 2	1,642	1,695	1,607	1,609
9	1,569	1,695	1,738	1,606
16	1,623	1,728	1,704	1,608
23	1,676	1,642	2,694	1,656
30	1,662	1,588	1,659	1,640
May 7	1,702	1,635	1,642	1,596
14	1,699	1,664	1,607	1,610
21	1,705	1,579	1,558	1,553
28	1,580	1,578	1,390	1,532
June 4	1,361	1,367	1,617	1,279
11	1,592	1,591	1,528	1,561
18	1,561	1,541	1,510	1,467
25	1,535	1,431	1,557	1,416
July 2	1,476	1,438	1,348	1,394
9	1,171	1,105	1,538	1,162
16	1,523	1,445	1,493	1,434
23	1,427	1,378	1,535	1,352
30	1,400	1,305	1,476	1,357
Aug. 6	1,474	1,382	1,540	1,398
13	1,556	1,406	1,535	1,391
20	1,524	1,409	1,473	1,424
27	1,531	1,479	1,613	1,400
Sept. 3	1,601	1,502	1,435	1,411
10	1,429	1,396	1,772	1,286
17	1,690	1,657	1,716	1,527
24	1,667	1,679	1,732	1,418
Oct. 1	1,681	1,679	1,841	1,501
8	1,644	1,699	1,844	1,482
15	1,686	1,701	1,895	1,536
22	1,620	1,754	1,844	1,599
29	1,654	1,736	1,927	1,614
Nov. 5	1,668	1,754	1,955	1,620
12	1,654	1,742	1,981	1,677
19	1,654	1,681	1,593	1,650
26	1,697	1,446	1,944	1,310
30	1,328	1,812	1,941	1,676
Dec. 3	1,656	1,792	1,804	1,523
10	1,566	1,692	1,465	1,588
17	1,655	1,687	1,350	1,278
24	1,153	1,238		
1986[2]				
Jan. 1	1,153	1,295		
8	1,250	1,679		
15	1,635	1,615		
22	1,654	1,528		
29	1,563	1,565		

Weekly Pork Belly Storage Movement

1985[2] Week Ending	Stocks[1] in Thousands of Pounds			Net Move-ment
	In	Out	On Hand	
Jan. 5	2,407	1,008	50,546	+1,399
12	2,398	1,885	51,059	+513
19	1,561	2,242	50,378	−681
26	1,074	2,164	49,288	−1,090
Feb. 2	706	2,499	47,495	−1,793
9	377	2,302	45,570	−1,925
16	956	655	45,871	+301
23	423	772	45,521	−349
Mar. 2	644	491	45,674	+153
9	2,027	200	47,501	+1,827
16	2,971	67	50,405	+2,904
23	3,722	201	53,926	+3,521
30	6,281	107	60,100	+6,174
Apr. 6	4,504	24	64,580	+4,480
13	3,128	149	67,559	+2,979
20	3,498	386	70,671	+3,112
27	2,497	156	73,012	+2,341
May 4	3,131	101	76,042	+3,030
11	2,620	70	78,592	+2,550
18	2,847	45	81,394	+2,802
25	2,804	154	84,044	+2,650
June				
July				
Aug.				
Sept.				
Oct.				
Nov.				
Dec.				
1986[2]				
Jan.				
Feb.				

[1] Total approved Chi. Merc. Exch. warehouses.   [2] Preliminary.   *Sources: U.S. Department of Agriculture; Chicago Mercantile Exchange*   T.518

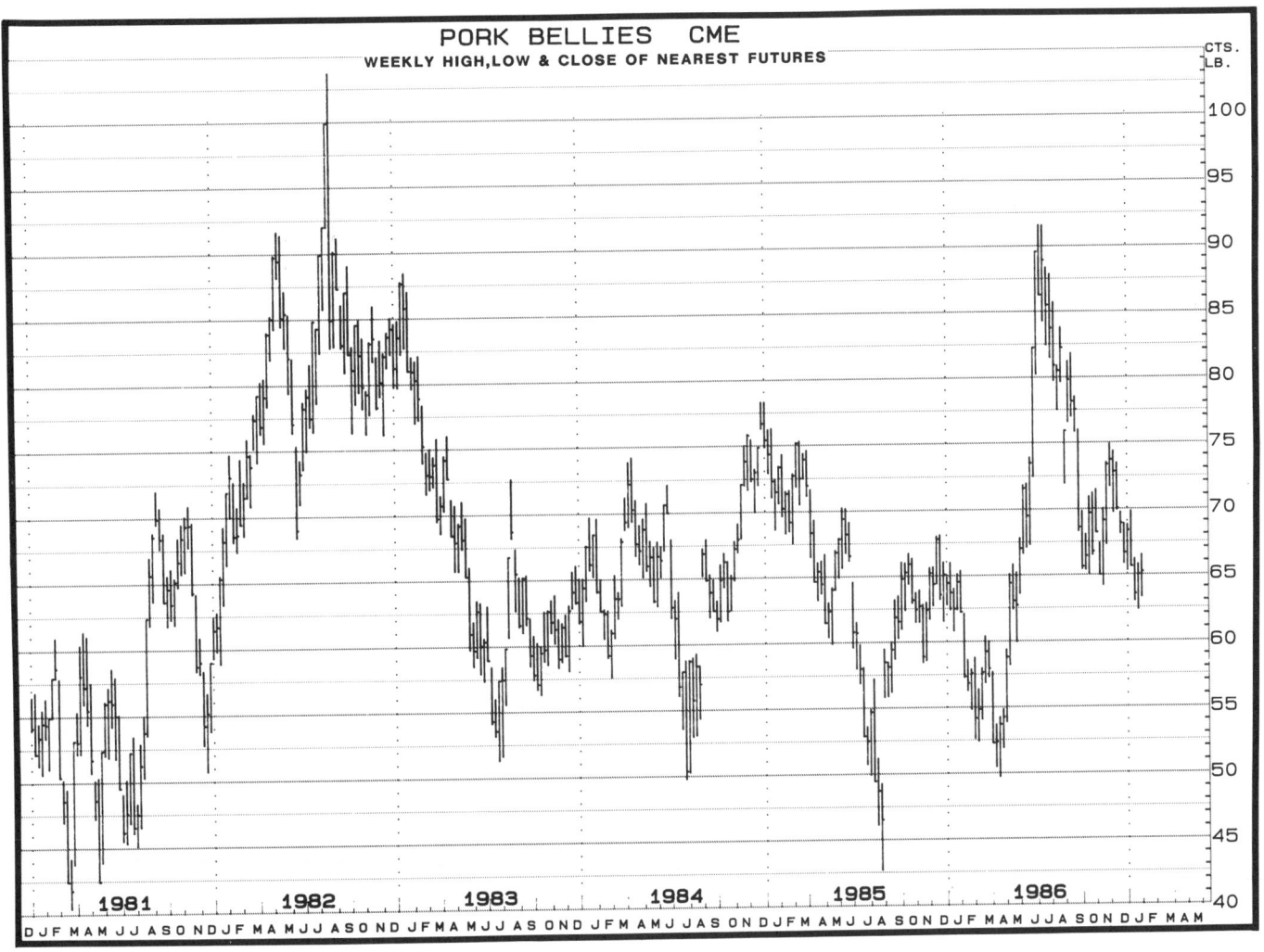

PORK BELLIES CME
WEEKLY HIGH, LOW & CLOSE OF NEAREST FUTURES

Month-End Open Interest of Pork Bellies Futures at Chicago   In Contracts

Year	Jan.	Feb.	Mar.	Apr.	May	June	July	Aug.	Sept.	Oct.	Nov.	Dec.
1980	29,631	28,195	18,212	22,939	28,404	26,944	20,025	14,983	18,242	23,098	26,231	22,480
1981	15,687	12,471	12,821	16,714	15,825	18,911	11,550	10,058	10,424	14,088	16,425	13,643
1982	21,542	21,666	21,048	28,063	25,765	17,940	14,203	14,799	16,090	19,063	18,596	18,521
1983	19,654	16,510	17,563	16,850	16,870	17,242	12,162	12,268	16,042	16,976	20,242	20,247
1984	18,836	17,434	19,114	18,332	17,379	17,250	9,453	7,387	8,925	9,763	13,265	13,507
1985	14,452	14,784	12,561	12,580	11,355	10,731	8,452	6,590	6,914	7,904	9,134	8,103
1986	7,821	7,826	7,145	8,987	10,530	10,838	8,567	7,698	7,915	9,432	11,453	11,057

Source: Chicago Mercantile Exchange   T.520

Volume of Trading of Pork Bellies Futures at Chicago   In Contracts

Year	Jan.	Feb.	Mar.	Apr.	May	June	July	Aug.	Sept.	Oct.	Nov.	Dec.	Total
1980	191,920	206,539	189,881	183,876	165,844	206,669	198,256	169,404	167,355	220,435	178,821	176,622	2,250,945
1981	176,243	154,438	135,527	179,503	157,342	199,013	187,785	131,619	139,272	171,480	194,561	170,944	1,997,697
1982	196,040	216,333	263,431	265,863	301,763	248,825	217,434	229,207	188,129	224,449	227,482	232,688	2,811,674
1983	276,556	229,198	207,543	225,034	226,617	227,522	218,813	169,113	132,894	154,642	159,982	175,363	2,403,277
1984	221,795	182,080	186,817	159,774	207,820	173,066	187,619	119,469	77,028	121,926	148,940	121,711	1,908,045
1985	173,488	137,334	133,509	148,489	149,809	135,319	136,026	89,784	77,326	99,291	85,377	91,634	1,457,386
1986	92,033	81,768	75,830	96,642	106,958	100,331	109,981	78,967	91,470	87,712	91,779	86,868	1,100,339

Source: Chicago Mercantile Exchange   T.521

PORK BELLIES CASH PRICE CHICAGO

MONTHLY HIGH & LOW PRICES FOR FRESH OR F.F.A.. 12 - 14 POUNDS

High, Low & Closing Prices of May Pork Bellies Futures at Chicago In Cents per Pound

Year of Delivery		Mar.	Apr.	May	June	July	Aug.	Sept.	Oct.	Nov.	Dec.	Jan.	Feb.	Mar.	Apr.	May	Life of Delivery Range
					Year Prior to Delivery									Delivery Year			
1981	High	58.50	52.60	49.75	54.50	61.60	66.25	73.30	75.15	75.15	77.05	59.60	63.00	55.30	61.35	52.65	77.05
	Low	49.75	46.15	43.35	41.32	53.50	57.40	59.25	63.47	67.70	58.05	53.65	52.55	41.90	52.15	42.45	41.32
	Close	51.10	48.40	43.45	53.90	59.30	59.50	68.47	71.20	75.15	58.05	57.70	52.55	55.05	52.15	48.77	—
1982	High	69.15	75.50	72.70	75.90	69.40	72.10	72.50	70.22	71.40	63.75	73.55	75.80	77.85	85.10	91.50	91.50
	Low	54.50	70.15	63.00	64.10	61.75	64.12	62.70	62.95	59.25	51.90	61.12	67.55	69.00	74.75	84.15	51.90
	Close	69.15	70.15	72.70	64.10	65.15	64.95	65.15	68.85	61.05	62.70	73.55	70.37	75.15	84.92	84.95	—
1983	High	73.85	77.95	79.20	77.00	75.00	82.90	85.45	82.05	83.10	83.30	86.30	81.55	76.40	75.90	70.90	86.30
	Low	70.20	71.65	74.00	65.25	67.25	69.02	75.37	75.80	74.25	74.35	78.15	74.25	68.50	65.60	64.45	64.45
	Close	72.60	77.55	79.00	72.72	74.35	82.10	82.40	77.80	80.75	79.70	79.70	74.25	70.60	67.80	65.05	—
1984	High	65.40	65.95	65.90	61.90	64.75	71.55	66.80	64.40	65.60	67.40	71.30	68.10	71.07	74.10	70.65	74.10
	Low	61.25	62.80	60.00	56.00	54.70	61.50	59.50	58.35	60.32	60.40	62.12	59.25	60.55	65.50	64.35	54.70
	Close	64.90	64.72	61.00	57.15	61.90	65.37	59.37	64.22	62.30	63.62	67.27	60.70	69.22	65.82	65.42	—
1985	High	79.95	80.50	79.00	82.47	77.70	69.50	67.70	68.52	76.50	79.00	79.15	74.90	75.40	71.52	66.30	82.47
	Low	67.00	74.95	73.80	75.40	63.70	63.15	61.05	62.50	67.90	70.75	70.75	67.47	70.20	63.10	59.80	59.80
	Close	78.50	75.30	74.65	77.75	64.75	66.80	62.62	68.15	76.40	78.52	72.75	70.72	71.82	65.65	65.65	—
1986	High	75.60	75.25	74.57	75.27	70.00	64.35	64.85	67.52	66.65	67.80	66.90	63.45	61.67	58.55	65.75	75.60
	Low	69.00	70.55	69.80	69.70	59.50	57.05	57.25	62.35	60.00	63.00	62.35	54.40	54.37	49.65	57.65	49.65
	Close	75.35	73.70	74.12	70.30	62.95	59.65	64.85	63.65	66.45	64.90	63.50	55.85	55.87	58.55	59.85	—
1987	High	63.15	63.20	62.50	70.80	78.20	76.40	79.87	69.70	72.95	72.20						
	Low	61.50	58.40	59.20	58.20	64.92	69.85	66.37	63.90	63.00	65.20						
	Close	62.77	62.20	61.10	66.92	75.40	73.85	66.45	66.25	71.62	65.77						

Source: Chicago Mercantile Exchange

T.519

Potatoes

USDA estimated plantings of the 1986 U.S. fall potato crop at 1.06 million acres, 11 percent less than 1985. Harvested acreage was down 10 percent and yield per acre was off two percent. Fall crop production was estimated at 311 million cwt. (hundredweight) in 1986, off 12 percent from last year's record high, and one percent short of 1985 output.

Large supplies from the 1985 fall potato crop, coupled with forecast low fresh-market potato prices and a slowdown in processor demand, signaled continued market weakness and placed pressure on growers to reduce fall acreage. Poor weather also contributed to the decline.

Storage of fall potatoes in the 15 major producing states totaled 204 million cwt. on December 1, 1986, down 13 percent from 1985, but one percent above 1984. Stocks in the three Eastern states fell 32 percent from 1985 to 22 million cwt. As of December

1, 1986, the Central states stored 44.9 million cwt. of potatoes, 18 percent less than 1985. Storage in the Western states fell by seven percent.

Disappearance in the 15 states from harvest to December 1, 1986, dropped 11 percent to 96.8 million cwt. Shrinkage and loss were 15.2 million cwt., versus 20.4 million in 1985.

One developing trend has been change in the allocation of acreage among seasons. Acreage share devoted to fall production has grown from 77 percent in 1970 to 85 percent in 1986; the other three seasons' shares have declined.

Futures Market

Round white potato futures are traded on the New York Mercantile Exchange. This contract will cease trading in May, 1987.

Salient Statistics of Potatoes in the United States

	Acreage		Yield Per Harv. Acre Cwt.	Total Prod- uction Mil. Cwt.	Farm Disposition — Used Where Grown			Farm Price $ Cwt.	Value of		Stocks on Jan. 1[4] 1,000 Cwt.	Foreign Trade		Consumption[2]	
					Seed & Feed	Shrinkage & Loss	Sold[3]		Prod.[5]	Sales		Dom. Exports	Im- ports	Per Capita —In Lbs.—	
Year	Planted	Har- vested			Million Cwt.				Million $			Ths. Cwt.		Fresh	Pro- cessed
	— 1,000 Acres —														
1980	1,182	1,148	265	303.9	6.4	23.4	273.1	6.55	1,979	1,788	176,020	1,996	1,407	44.2	61.5
1981	1,263	1,232	276	340.6	6.0	26.1	306.5	5.41	1,819	1,660	147,010	2,807	2,470	43.6	65.3
1982	1,303	1,267	280	355.1	7.3	31.0	316.8	4.45	1,563	1,411	164,380	2,256	3,484	48.5	65.3
1983	1,272	1,243	269	333.9	6.0	24.7	303.3	5.82	1,936	1,765	178,980	1,957	2,702	45.9	67.1
1984	1,337	1,301	279	362.6	5.7	30.1	326.7	5.69	2,046	1,858	165,330	1,484	2,536	44.7	68.1
1985[1]	1,409	1,361	299	407.1	8.1	52.8	346.2	3.92	1,571	1,357	173,380	1,023	2,991	49.9	
1986[1]	1,247	1,216	290	352.3							202,800				

Note: 60 pounds equals one bushel. [1] Preliminary. [2] Fresh & processed. [3] For all purposes, including food, seed processing livestock feed. [4] Merchantable stocks held by growers & local dealers. [5] Farm weight basis. Excludes canned & frozen potatoes.
Source: National Agricultural Statistics Service, U.S.D.A.   T.522

Utilization of Potatoes in the United States   In Millions of Cwt.

Crop Year	Table Stock		Sales									Used on Farms Where Grown	Total
			For Processing						Other Sales				
		Chips, Shoestrings	For dehy- dration	Frozen French Fries	Other Frozen Pdt's	Canned Potatoes	Other Canned Pdt's[2]	Starch & Flour	Live- stock Feed	Seed	Total Sales		
1980	96.8	37.9	28.2	67.2	13.7	2.1	2.0	2.2	3.9	19.2	273.1	29.8	302.9
1981	112.0	39.3	29.9	79.8	16.8	2.5	1.7	2.3	3.6	20.4	308.3	32.3	340.6
1982-3	120.3	40.7	27.7	76.0	17.3	2.7	1.8	4.6	6.2	19.5	316.8	38.3	355.2
1983-4	107.3	43.3	26.8	74.4	19.7	2.1	2.0	3.0	3.8	20.9	303.3	30.6	333.9
1984-5	113.8	42.3	27.8	87.4	20.3	2.6	1.8	3.4	4.7	22.6	326.7	35.9	362.6
1985-6[1]	126.2	42.3	30.0	94.7	17.9	2.2	1.6	3.5	8.1	19.8	346.2	60.9	407.1

[1] Preliminary.   [2] Hash, stews, soups.   [3] Includes 12.0 sold for livestock feed & starch under the U.S.D.A. diversion program.
Source: Crop Reporting Board, U.S.D.A.   T.531

POTATOES

Potato Crop Production Estimates, Stocks & Disappearance in the U.S.   In Millions of Cwt.

Year	Crop Production Estimates Total Crop Oct. 1	Nov. 1	Dec.	Fall Crop Oct. 1	Nov. 1	Dec. 1	Total Storage Stocks[2] Dec. 1	Following Year Jan. 1	Feb. 1	Mar. 1	Apr. 1	May 1	Disappearance of Previous Fall Crop Until Dec. 1	Following Year Jan. 1	Feb. 1	Mar. 1	Apr. 1
1980	296.9	296.9	301.0	260.7	260.7	264.6	172.0	147.0	122.1	97.7	72.7	44.5	84.1	110.0	135.0	160.0	186.0
1981	329.9	329.9	333.7	287.1	287.1	290.7	193.6	164.4	137.8	111.8	82.3	50.8	93.6	121.0	149.0	175.0	204.0
1982	350.0	350.0	349.3	306.9	308.9	305.0	206.5	179.0	150.2	122.5	90.1	57.3	92.3	121.0	149.0	178.0	209.0
1983	329.8	329.8	325.7	292.7	292.7	325.7	192.5	165.3	138.9	112.7	81.7	50.4	90.7	117.0	143.0	169.0	200.1
1984	358.8	358.8	361.6	310.0	310.0	312.2	201.4	173.4	144.8	118.4	86.4	52.5	130.0	159.0	187.0	217.0	251.0
1985[1]	—	400.4	404.1	—	346.1	340.8	235.5	202.8	171.5	138.7	104.5	65.4	139.0	171.0	203.0	238.0	277.0
1986[1]	—	352.3	352.3	—	307.5	301.0	204.2										

[1] Preliminary.   [2] Held by growers & local dealers in the fall producing areas.   *Source: Crop Reporting Board, U.S.D.A.*   T.525

United States Potato Production by Seasonal Groups   In Millions of 96.8 Cwt.

Year	Winter	Spring Florida	Calif.	Total Spring	Summer Va.	Total	Fall Maine	Wisc.	Minn.	Colo.	No. Dak.	Wash.	Idaho	Oregon	Total Fall
1980	2.4	3.6	8.8	17.1	1.5	17.0	25.0	16.0	9.9	11.0	15.7	43.9	79.8	19.7	266.4
1981	2.2	5.3	10.3	20.8	2.3	20.0	26.5	18.2	13.3	11.6	20.1	52.9	84.5	21.7	295.6
1982	2.3	5.7	9.6	21.0	2.5	22.8	27.0	22.6	11.5	12.8	17.3	52.8	91.8	21.1	309.1
1983	2.2	5.1	8.3	18.3	1.0	18.7	22.6	18.9	10.3	14.0	20.5	54.1	86.0	20.7	294.7
1984	2.6	6.7	11.1	23.8	1.5	23.1	21.4	21.4	13.8	17.2	20.6	56.9	86.6	23.5	313.1
1985	2.7	6.6	10.6	23.0	3.3	27.8	28.2	24.1	14.1	17.9	23.6	63.6	102.5	26.9	353.6
1986[1]	3.0	6.8	7.4	19.8	1.1	22.0	21.0	20.1	13.7	18.2	21.6	60.2	87.3	23.2	310.8

[1] Preliminary, December estimate.   *Source: Crop Reporting Board, U.S.D.A*   T.524

United States Potatoes Processed[1], Eight States   In Thousands of Cwt.

States	Storage Season	to Dec. 1	to Jan. 1	to Feb. 1	to Mar. 1	to Apr. 1	to May 1	Entire Season
Idaho and	1983–4	15,755	20,445	24,785	29,540	35,155	40,640	53,810
Malheur Co.,	1984–5	19,000	24,310	29,200	34,010	39,510	44,650	57,410
Oreg.	1985–6	17,830	22,980	26,660	32,170	37,910	43,240	55,220
	1986–7	13,210						
Maine[2]	1983–4	1,160	1,745	2,260	2,780	3,370	3,970	5,125
	1984–5	1,820	2,410	3,015	3,520	4,330	5,185	6,830
	1985–6	2,215	2,935	3,845	4,630	5,540	6,280	8,660
	1986–7	2,120						
Wash. and other	1983–4	16,245	19,920	23,690	28,250	33,280	37,455	45,800
areas, Oreg.	1984–5	20,745	24,690	29,345	33,560	38,815	43,380	51,670
	1985–6	21,725	25,665	29,450	34,450	39,990	45,110	57,430
	1986–7	21,530						
Other States[3]	1983–4	4,305	6,005	7,755	9,600	11,615	13,400	16,320
	1984–5	5,695	7,510	9,210	10,930	12,745	14,715	21,005
	1985–6	6,470	7,990	9,900	12,020	13,860	16,095	22,245
	1986–7	6,240						
Total	1983–4	37,465	48,115	58,490	70,170	83,420	95,465	121,055
	1984–5	47,260	58,920	70,770	82,020	95,400	107,930	136,915
	1985–6	48,240	59,570	69,855	83,270	97,300	110,725	143,555
	1986–7	43,100						

[1] Total quantity received and used for processing regardless of the state in which the potatoes were produced. Does not include quantities used for potato chips in Maine, Mich., Minn., N. Dak. or Wis.   [2] Includes Maine grown potatoes only.   [3] Mich., Minn., N. Dak. and Wis.
Source: Crop Reporting Board, U.S.D.A.   T.524a

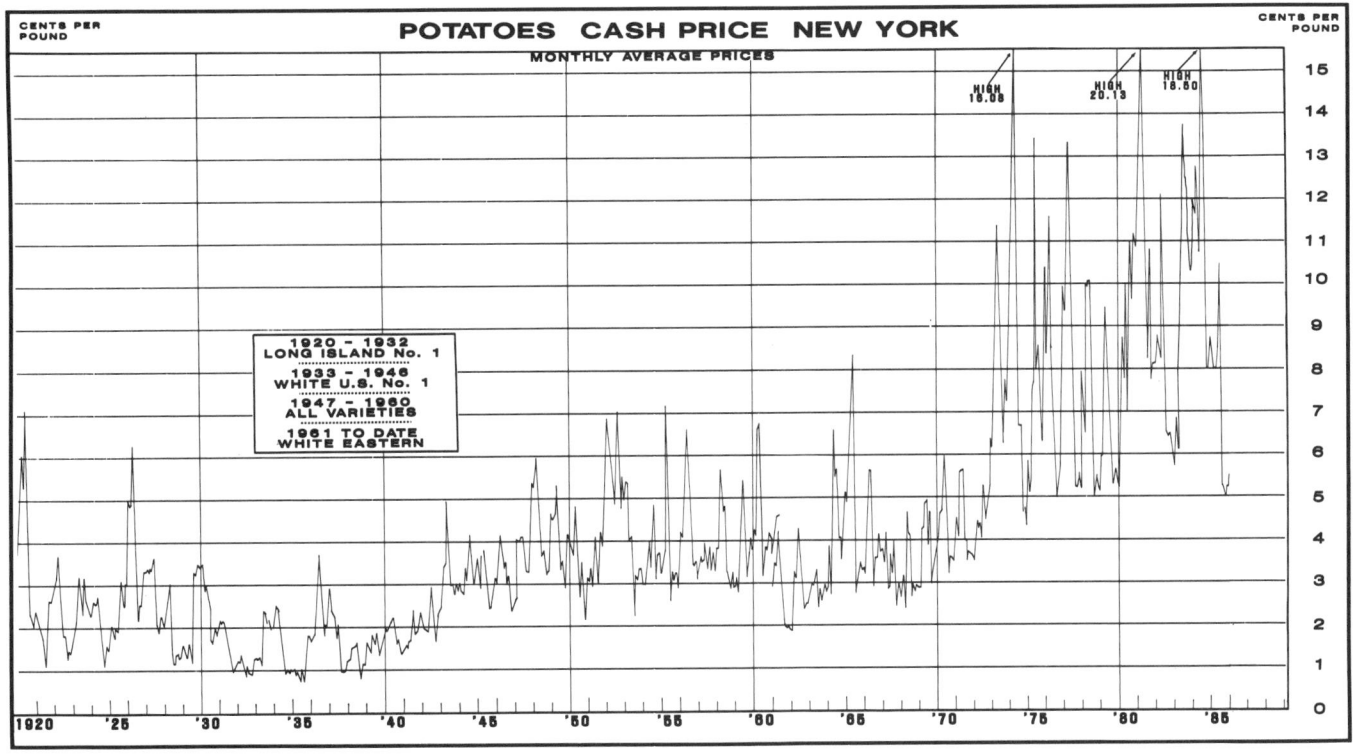

POTATOES CASH PRICE NEW YORK

MONTHLY AVERAGE PRICES

1920 – 1932
LONG ISLAND No. 1
1933 – 1946
WHITE U.S. No. 1
1947 – 1960
ALL VARIETIES
1961 TO DATE
WHITE EASTERN

U.S. Cold Storage Stocks of All Frozen Potatoes (First of Month)   In Millions of Pounds

Year	Jan.	Feb.	Mar.	Apr.	May	June	July	Aug.	Sept.	Oct.	Nov.	Dec.
1984	773.0	754.8	783.9	827.6	808.2	843.3	840.4	626.8	516.5	635.3	821.3	884.2
1985[1]	892.3	900.0	943.4	1,003.3	1,023.6	1,081.6	1,058.4	828.2	735.4	861.4	1,014.2	1,020.2
1986[1]	1,012.3	907.0	950.4	1,017.3	1,025.7	1,126.5	1,096.9	958.1	733.4	771.2	904.1	941.7

[1] Preliminary.   *Source: Crop Reporting Board, U.S.D.A.*   T.529

Month–End Open Interest of Potato Futures at New York   In Contracts

Year	Jan.	Feb.	Mar.	Apr.	May	June	July	Aug.	Sept.	Oct.	Nov.	Dec.
1984	1,449	1,498	1,191	665	947	1,459	1,745	2,098	2,213	2,092	1,863	1,870
1985	2,010	2,280	1,684	907	407	635	1,164	1,566	1,611	1,678	1,585	1,720
1986	1,994	2,080	2,290	2,704	1,903	997	1,133	1,160	1,422	1,808	1,339	1,451

Source: N.Y. Mercantile Exchange   T.532

Volume of Trading in Maine Potato Futures, on N.Y. Mercantile Exchange   In Contracts

Year	Jan.	Feb.	Mar.	Apr.	May	June	July	Aug.	Sept.	Oct.	Nov.	Dec.	Total
1984	1,930	1,894	3,161	2,893	1,297	2,372	2,578	1,819	1,665	3,865	1,795	1,326	26,595
1985	1,311	1,777	2,505	2,155	1,550	743	1,464	1,215	1,143	1,639	848	553	16,903
1986	672	1,044	786	1,358	2,525	1,101	1,373	807	1,312	2,435	1,510	1,675	16,558

Source: New York Mercantile Exchange.   T.526

U.S. Average Price Received by Farmers for Potatoes   In Dollars Per Cwt.

Year	Jan.	Feb.	Mar.	Apr.	May	June	July	Aug.	Sept.	Oct.	Nov.	Dec.	Avg.[1]
1984	6.43	6.29	6.55	6.69	7.04	7.52	9.72	8.75	4.87	4.26	4.60	4.90	5.69
1985	5.22	5.31	5.40	5.80	6.44	6.67	5.78	3.97	3.65	3.51	3.46	3.26	3.91
1986[2]	3.11	3.30	3.50	4.24	4.09	4.89	7.21	6.25	4.50	4.27	4.64	4.65	4.55

[1] Annual weighted average by sales.   [2] Preliminary.   *Source: Statistical Reporting Service, U.S.D.A.*   T.530

POTATOES

High, Low & Closing Prices of May[1] Potato Futures at New York   In Cents per Pound

Year of Delivery		Feb.	Mar.	Apr.	May	June	July	Aug.	Sept.	Oct.	Nov.	Dec.	Jan.	Feb.	Mar.	Apr.	Life of Delivery Range
							Year Prior to Delivery							Delivery Year			
1982	High	—	11.87	11.49	10.25	10.22	10.86	10.99	10.80	10.50	8.77	8.77	8.99	9.39	8.25	—	11.87
	Low	—	11.05	9.70	9.40	8.85	8.93	10.02	9.96	8.14	8.17	7.72	7.75	8.22	7.40	—	7.40
	Close	—	11.14	9.85	10.21	9.04	10.50	10.20	10.11	8.37	8.48	7.85	8.64	8.27	7.80	—	—
1983	High	—	—	10.74	10.65	10.20	9.75	9.13	8.72	8.49	6.90	6.83	7.41	6.69	6.23	—	10.74
	Low	—	—	9.71	9.85	8.52	8.44	8.49	8.20	6.20	6.10	6.28	6.37	5.82	5.46	—	5.46
	Close	—	—	10.50	10.01	8.74	8.73	8.70	8.25	6.25	6.56	6.57	6.50	5.82	5.87	—	—
1984	High	—	—	—	—	5.00	5.39	6.10	6.25	5.25	5.85	6.48	6.28	5.75	5.97	5.12	6.48
	Low	—	—	—	—	4.17	4.40	5.20	5.67	4.55	5.30	5.71	5.68	5.38	5.24	4.53	4.17
	Close	—	—	—	—	4.40	5.30	5.74	6.00	4.75	5.85	6.38	5.62	5.75	5.29	4.53	—
1985	High	—	—	—	4.18	4.75	4.50	4.18	4.15	3.90	3.57	3.60	3.54	3.83	3.67	3.20	4.75
	Low	—	—	—	3.82	3.90	4.00	3.97	3.84	3.21	3.39	3.26	3.31	3.40	3.19	3.05	3.05
	Close	—	—	—	3.96	4.35	4.13	3.98	3.84	3.52	3.55	3.37	3.47	3.63	3.20	3.16	—
1986	High	—	—	—	—	—	2.85	2.82	2.47	2.36	2.25	2.22	2.25	2.03	1.99	1.81	2.85
	Low	—	—	—	—	—	2.70	2.40	2.33	2.11	2.12	2.15	2.03	1.82	1.77	1.75	1.75
	Close	—	—	—	—	—	2.70	2.40	2.33	2.22	2.20	2.16	2.03	1.95	1.77	1.75	—
1987[1]	High	4.08	4.25	4.25	4.28	4.20	4.98	5.20	5.81	6.10	5.80	5.32					
	Low	4.00	4.08	4.13	3.75	3.87	3.84	4.57	5.10	5.30	4.91	4.81					
	Close	4.08	4.20	4.25	3.88	3.97	4.60	5.05	5.77	5.52	5.07	5.25					

[1] Prior to 1986 prices are for the April contract.   *Source: N.Y. Mercantile Exchange*

T.528

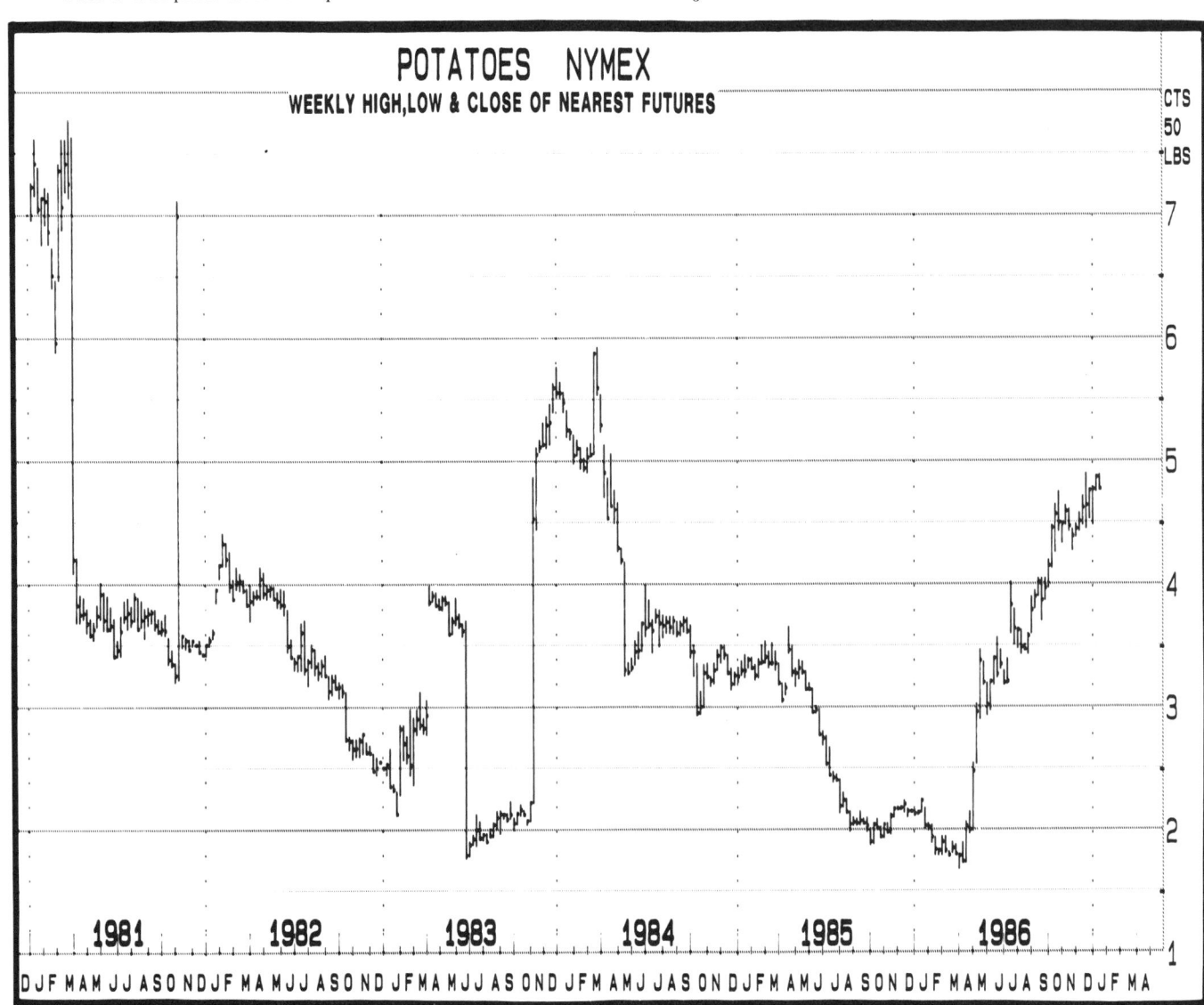

POTATOES NYMEX

WEEKLY HIGH, LOW & CLOSE OF NEAREST FUTURES

CTS 50 LBS

1981   1982   1983   1984   1985   1986

DJFMAMJJASONDJFMAMJJASONDJFMAMJJASONDJFMAMJJASONDJFMAMJJASONDJFMA

Rapeseed

World rapeseed production in 1986/87 is projected by USDA to reach a record 20.08 million tonnes, up six percent from last year's record harvest. Major increases in China, Canada, India and Poland, four of the larger producers, account for the season's gains. The European Community (EC) was the only region to experience production declines, as a result of poor sowing conditions in France last fall and a cold, damp spring in much of the EC. China, the largest producer, saw production increase five percent to 5.9 million tonnes; while Canada, second-largest, recorded an 11-percent increase. Rapeseed now comprises over 10 percent of world oilseed output.

Despite the record supply, world trade is expected to decline slightly. USDA projects 1986/87 exports of 3.46 million tonnes, down about two percent from a year ago, due to China and India, where increased production will be used in the domestic market. Reduced rapeseed availability in the EC, however, could result in increased exports by Canada and Poland. Poland traditionally supplies rapeseed to England and West Germany in times of shortage.

With the increase in world production, ending stocks are expected to increase substantially. By the end of the 1986/87 marketing year, rapeseed stocks should reach a record 2.13 million tonnes, 57 percent more than in 1985/86, according to USDA.

The world rapeseed crush is expected to increase to 17.76 million tonnes, up four percent from 1985/86. (The oil content in rapeseed is twice as high as in soybeans.) With the increased crush, world rapeseed oil production is expected to grow by nearly four percent, to 6.45 million tonnes. Rapeseed accounts for about 13 percent of total world oil production. While China and India are the world's largest producers, neither is an exporter and India is the world's largest importer. The major exporters are West Germany, France and Canada.

World exports of rapeseed oil are projected by the USDA to increase only modestly, to 1.34 million tonnes, compared to 1.3 million tonnes a year ago. In recent years, producers have been growing low erucic acid varieties, which makes the oil fit for human consumption. (A notable result of this is the increase in use in the U.S. One major vegetable oil processor recently announced it would market a brand of cooking oil containing only rapeseed oil.) In Europe, production of this type of rapeseed is slowly expanding due to the use of subsidies.

World rapeseed meal production is projected by USDA to total 10.81 million tonnes, up four percent from a year ago. Worldwide consumption is expected to come to 10.73 million tonnes, up almost three percent from a year ago. Over the last few years, consumption of rapeseed meal has been growing fairly rapidly, but is expected to slow. Nonetheless, South Korea and Japan should expand imports in 1986/87. In South Korea, where soybean meal imports are limited to 100,000 tons for 1986, feed millers are importing rapeseed meal. China is the world's largest producer and user of rapeseed meal, consuming 26 percent of the world supply. Rapeseed meal is also widely used in India, the EC and Eastern Europe; it has limited feeding use for poultry and pigs, but can be used extensively in cattle rations.

Global trade in rapeseed meal is projected to expand to 1.66 million tonnes, eight percent more than a year ago. The major exporters are West Germany, France and Canada. Ending stocks of rapeseed meal are projected by USDA to reach 250,000 tonnes, slightly less than a year ago.

Futures Market

Rapeseed futures are traded on the Winnipeg Commodity Exchange (WCE).

World Production of Rapeseed (In Thousands of Metric Tons)

Year[2]	Canada	China	Czecho-slovakia	Denmark	France	East Germany	West Germany	India	United Kingdom	Bangla-desh	Pakistan	Poland	Sweden	Yugo-slavia	World Total
1972	2,155	1,000	107	51	722	234	249	1,433		106	301	430	327		6,624
1973	1,300	1,050	117	92	661	246	242	1,808		98	287	512	339		7,001
1974	1,207	1,075	85	112	690	200	301	1,692		107	293	523	351		7,022
1975	1,163	1,090	115	115	532	250	194	2,300		110	305	726	327		7,989
1976	1,749			90	561							980	279		
1977	1,973	1,180	162	77	388	308	282	1,650	142	134	236	708	236	40	7,890
1978	3,497	1,868	166	91	568	318	331	1,860	155	137	248	691	289	73	10,721
1979	3,411	2,402	80	150	510	201	321	1,428	198	118	247	233	264	93	10,080
1980	2,484	2,384	214	225	1,103	277	377	2,002	300	122	252	572	285	68	11,104
1981	1,849	4,065	200	290	990	284	363	2,382	325	123	238	496	282	65	12,345
1982	2,225	5,656	178	335	1,147	307	535	2,207	580	120	246	433	320	79	14,804
1983	2,609	4,287	314	309	906	259	599	2,608	565	131	217	555	318	103	14,259
1984[1]	3,428	4,205	300	474	1,305	303	662	3,030	925	140	234	911	327	124	16,906
1985[2]	3,508	5,610	285	575	1,385	380	803	3,000	895	145	242	1,081	320	120	18,950
1986[3]	3,900	5,900	275	600	972	393	868	3,300	835	150	250	1,260	328	110	20,050

[1] Preliminary. [2] Harvest generally occurs in the first half of the calendar year given in all major producing countries except Canada.
[3] Estimate. *Source: Foreign Agricultural Service, U.S.D.A.*

T.533

RAPESEED

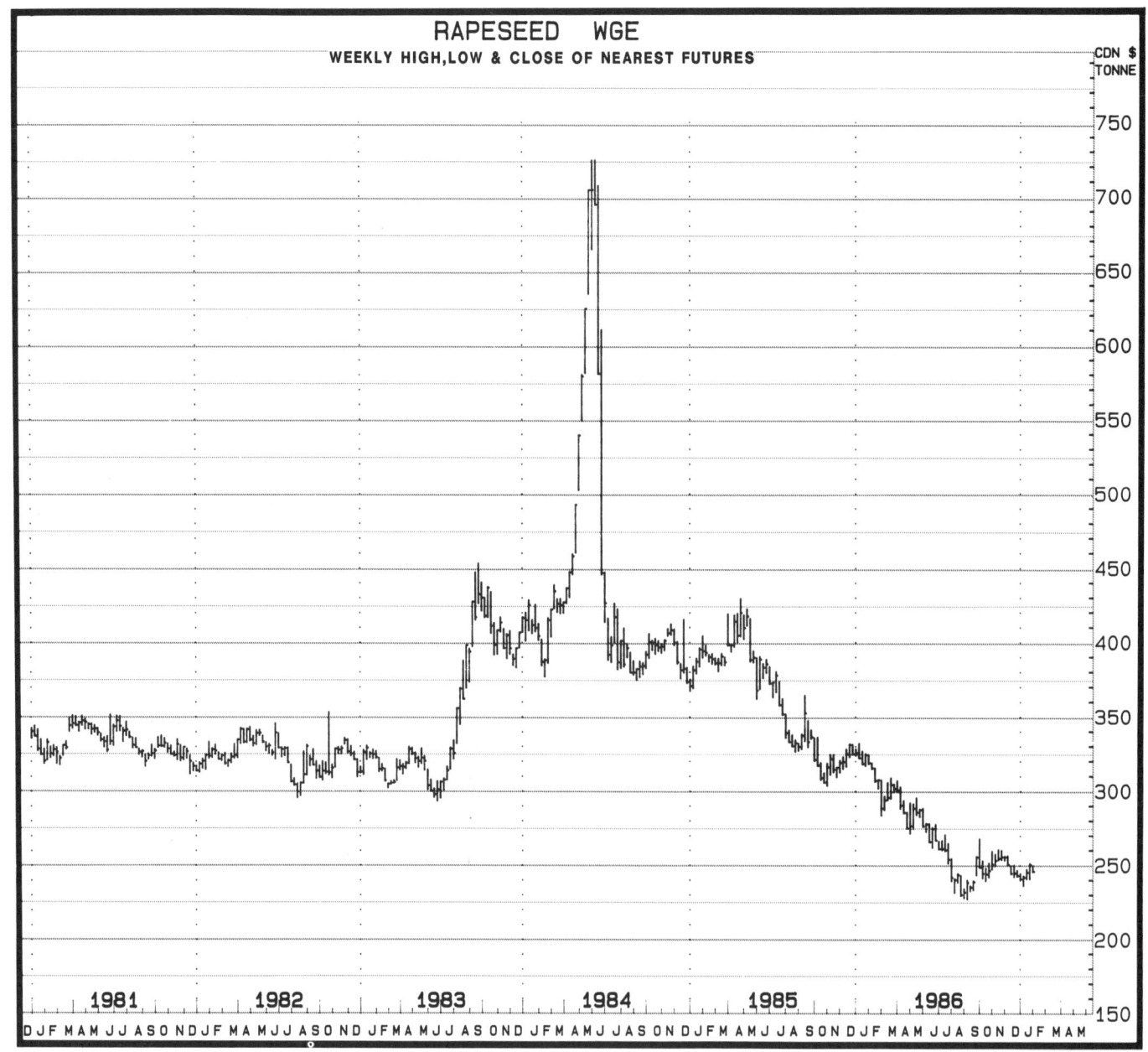

RAPESEED WGE
WEEKLY HIGH, LOW & CLOSE OF NEAREST FUTURES

CDN $ / TONNE

1981 1982 1983 1984 1985 1986

World Supply & Distribution of Rapeseed & Products   In Thousands of Metric Tons

Crop Year	Rapeseed					Rapeseed Meal					Rapeseed Oil				
	Pro-duction	Exports	Imports	Crush	Ending Stocks	Pro-duction	Exports	Imports	Con-sumption	Ending Stocks	Pro-duction	Exports	Imports	Con-sumption	Ending Stocks
1979–80	10,081	2,102	2,403	8,714	1,708	5,206	520	640	5,316	149	3,365	643	571	3,295	159
1980–81	11,104	2,305	2,366	10,477	1,489	6,297	808	636	6,075	199	3,933	814	756	3,914	210
1981–82	12,345	2,142	2,216	11,959	911	7,331	845	683	7,182	186	4,383	824	775	4,404	140
1982–83	14,804	2,469	2,540	13,826	740	8,449	768	871	8,500	238	4,991	841	790	4,925	155
1983–84	14,259	2,524	2,697	13,313	647	8,132	1,192	1,316	8,204	290	4,860	972	964	4,808	199
1984–85	16,906	3,123	3,289	15,325	1,080	9,387	1,461	1,443	9,422	237	5,590	1,277	1,213	5,524	201
1985–86[1]	18,995	3,540	3,540	17,100	1,360	10,410	1,530	1,610	10,440	280	6,230	1,300	1,340	6,210	270
1986–87[1]	20,008	3,460	3,390	17,760	2,130	10,810	1,660	1,580	10,760	250	6,450	1,340	1,280	6,370	290

[1] Preliminary.   *Source: Foreign Agricultural Service, U.S.D.A.*

T.534a

High, Low & Closing Prices of June Rapeseed Futures in Winnipeg   In Dollars per Tonne

Year of Delivery		Apr.	May	June	July	Aug.	Sept.	Oct.	Nov.	Dec.	Jan.	Feb.	Mar.	Apr.	May	June	Life of Delivery Range
					Year Prior to Delivery								Delivery Year				
1980	High	301.0	315.9	354.5	351.0	340.0	339.0	340.5	339.0	331.8	342.0	330.5	319.9	295.1	331.2	326.2	354.5
	Low	295.0	299.0	315.9	319.0	321.0	326.7	314.1	320.0	318.5	301.0	318.5	291.0	282.0	287.6	299.5	282.0
	Close	299.0	315.8	329.5	325.5	337.0	335.6	324.0	330.5	319.5	324.5	319.4	291.0	289.5	299.9	317.0	—
1981	High	—	—	—	370.0	383.5	389.0	382.5	375.5	387.5	375.9	351.8	350.6	350.5	348.3	338.3	389.0
	Low	—	—	—	367.5	360.0	365.0	359.1	391.0	325.5	334.0	337.9	334.5	340.0	337.4	326.0	325.5
	Close	—	—	—	367.5	372.5	368.5	376.0	387.0	368.0	337.0	345.8	350.0	347.5	339.1	327.2	—
1982	High	—	—	—	396.0	391.0	378.3	371.8	366.5	353.0	344.0	340.8	333.5	342.8	340.8	331.7	396.0
	Low	—	—	—	384.0	375.5	355.0	358.8	341.6	334.6	331.0	328.0	319.8	327.3	329.7	321.0	319.8
	Close	—	—	—	391.0	375.5	360.3	365.4	344.8	335.1	334.5	332.7	327.0	334.1	332.7	330.0	—
1983	High	—	—	—	—	361.0	366.3	345.5	349.1	340.0	335.9	329.0	321.0	329.3	328.1	308.5	366.3
	Low	—	—	—	—	346.0	332.0	332.6	339.6	322.3	323.1	311.5	311.8	311.0	309.5	292.8	292.8
	Close	—	—	—	—	354.2	337.0	342.5	340.3	325.6	329.1	311.7	316.0	324.7	309.9	297.2	—
1984	High	—	—	—	359.5	434.0	467.4	452.5	435.2	424.5	431.4	412.0	426.5	502.2	724.0	724.0	724.0
	Low	—	—	—	330.0	364.5	415.5	409.0	406.1	397.3	406.5	382.9	403.0	426.0	507.5	577.0	330.0
	Close	—	—	—	350.5	423.6	447.5	409.7	407.8	421.5	410.2	403.5	426.5	502.2	704.0	577.0	—
1985	High	—	—	—	443.9	434.5	417.5	424.1	427.9	417.5	408.8	404.5	402.5	429.2	422.0	389.7	443.9
	Low	—	—	—	409.5	413.5	406.5	414.9	415.3	389.8	388.0	395.5	391.4	393.2	361.5	379.0	361.5
	Close	—	—	—	413.0	413.7	416.5	417.7	416.8	390.5	397.4	397.4	397.5	408.6	367.0	381.9	—
1986	High	422.5	424.0	409.5	400.4	370.0	357.0	351.5	315.5	347.3	346.7	329.8	316.7	306.5	295.0	277.5	424.0
	Low	421.5	402.5	388.0	364.5	348.0	342.5	328.4	325.5	330.7	328.6	296.1	298.8	271.0	274.0	261.3	261.3
	Close	421.5	403.2	388.0	368.5	352.8	342.5	328.4	333.6	342.2	329.5	300.6	305.7	291.5	275.8	267.7	—
1987	High	—	—	—	290.7	270.0	284.0	277.0	278.0	269.4							
	Low	—	—	—	290.2	254.0	255.0	258.5	266.8	256.5							
	Close	—	—	—	270.2	258.6	279.8	270.8	268.6	258.1							

Source: Winnipeg Commodity Exchange   T.536

Wholesale Price of Rapeseed Oil, Refined (Denatured), in Tanks at N.Y.   In Cents Per Pound

Year	Jan.	Feb.	Mar.	Apr.	May	June	July	Aug.	Sept.	Oct.	Nov.	Dec.	Average
1974	17.5	18.4	21.0	21.0	30.6	45.0	45.0	45.0	46.2	47.5	45.8	59.0	36.8
1975	59.0	59.0	59.0	59.0	59.0	59.0	59.0	59.0	59.0	51.2	46.0	46.0	56.2
1976	46.0	46.0	46.0	46.0	46.0	46.0	46.0	44.2	39.0	39.0	39.0	39.0	43.5
1977	39.0	39.0	39.0	39.0	39.0	39.0	39.0	39.0	39.0	39.0	39.0	39.0	39.0
1978	39.0	39.0	39.0	39.0	39.0	39.0	39.0	39.0	39.0	39.0	39.0	39.0	39.0
1979	39.0	39.0	39.0	39.0	39.0	39.0	39.0	39.0	39.0	39.0	39.0	39.0	39.0
1980	47.0	47.0	47.0	47.0	47.0	47.0	47.0	46.0	46.0	46.0	46.0	46.0	46.6
1981	56.4	59.0	59.0	59.0	59.0	59.0	59.0	59.0	59.0	59.0	59.0	59.0	58.8
1982	57.0	55.0	56.8	57.5	56.0	56.0	56.0	56.0	55.7	55.3	55.3	55.3	50.0
1983	55.3	55.3	55.3	55.3	55.3	55.3	55.3	55.3	55.3	55.3	55.3	55.3	55.3
1984	55.3	55.3	55.3	55.3	55.5	55.5	55.2	55.2	55.2	55.2	55.2	55.2	55.3
1985	55.2	55.2	55.2	N.A.	N.A.	68.3	67.9	64.0	62.5	62.5	62.5	60.5	61.4
1986	60.0	60.0	60.0	60.0	60.0	60.0	60.0	60.0	60.0				

Source: Economic Research Service, U.S.D.A.   T.534

Month–End Open Interest of Rapeseed Futures in Winnipeg   In 20-Tonne Units

Year	Jan.	Feb.	Mar.	Apr.	May	June	July	Aug.	Sept.	Oct.	Nov.	Dec.
1978	9,288	11,435	11,869	11,908	14,442	14,300	17,778	20,456	17,960	18,672	16,707	15,299
1979	15,288	15,164	16,338	15,593	12,993	14,209	12,950	13,596	15,001	21,300	21,827	21,966
1980	15,718	17,516	13,392	14,285	17,722	17,254	17,126	17,108	18,827	22,036	21,911	20,504
1981	15,376	15,326	18,028	18,764	18,000	15,332	14,948	15,316	15,755	16,064	16,260	12,911
1982	13,532	14,970	9,952	12,230	15,997	11,554	12,623	16,948	13,904	15,503	17,992	20,555
1983	16,288	17,964	18,266	16,681	15,327	13,834	18,249	22,681	20,481	18,778	18,302	17,554
1984	14,170	16,807	13,980	13,743	15,220	14,025	14,348	15,822	17,967	15,893	18,046	19,361
1985	20,883	22,483	22,144	19,666	19,617	16,639	18,019	18,962	13,924	15,894	15,213	18,832
1986	15,083	21,017	19,412	21,161	23,154	17,457	17,478	24,836	22,087	32,220	28,293	27,989

Source: Winnipeg Commodity Exchange   T.535

Rayon and Other Synthetic Fibers

World Production of Rayon &/or Acetate Filament Yarn & Monofilaments In Thousands of Metric Tons

Year	United States	Bel./Neth-erlands	Brazil	Canada	France	W. Ger-many	E. Ger-many	Un. Kingdom	Italy	Japan	India	Poland	Spain	China	USSR	World Total
1977	160.0	36.2	28.8	11.0	20.8	63.7	36.0	62.6	44.4	107.4	58.9	28.6	15.0	61.0	295.0	1,172
1978	164.6	36.0	24.1	12.3	19.3	59.7	34.0	59.7	39.3	109.8	62.4	28.0	13.8	65.0	300.0	1,167
1979	169.4	36.1	24.4	14.1	18.5	58.1	35.0	59.2	38.4	114.3	60.5	27.2	12.6	68.0	298.0	1,176
1980	161.3	37.4	26.0	14.0	16.4	65.2	36.5	36.7	36.6	119.3	57.7	25.4	12.8	75.0	305.0	1,161
1981	138.6	38.3	21.0	13.5	11.0	65.0	37.0	27.0	35.1	118.7	55.9	19.5	12.6	80.0	300.0	1,104
1982	103.6	38.1	20.8	9.5	8.6	61.0	34.0	24.0	31.6	120.5	48.6	19.3	11.3	80.0	294.4	1,025
1983	119.7	41.1	18.4	10.0	8.4	59.0	35.0	25.0	29.3	116.8	46.2	18.2	10.5	85.0	300.0	1,043
1984[1]	108.4	41.1	17.7	10.0	7.5	66.0	35.2	21.0	30.6	110.8	44.2	19.5	7.2	87.0	307.0	1,038
1985[2]	92.8															

[1] Preliminary. [2] Estimate. *Source: Textile Organon*   T.537

World Production of Rayon &/or Acetate Staple & Tow In Thousands of Metric Tons

Year	United States	Austria	China	Czecho-slovakia	France	W. Ger-many	E. Ger-many	Un. King-dom	Italy	Japan	Po-land	Spain	Swe-den	India	USSR	World Total
1977	242.7	90.2	77.0	50.6	60.7	46.0	131.0	113.6	62.3	272.7	67.1	43.1	33.1	87.1	334.0	2,109
1978	245.7	96.0	80.0	49.5	55.2	49.0	129.2	124.4	46.9	279.4	65.4	46.6	36.9	92.0	335.0	2,148
1979	252.4	98.8	85.0	36.0	58.9	50.0	130.0	139.2	39.0	290.4	56.6	45.3	36.9	92.2	337.0	2,195
1980	204.3	100.6	95.0	34.9	49.6	46.0	132.0	109.3	27.5	278.0	61.0	40.1	34.9	74.7	345.0	2,081
1981	210.7	107.9	105.0	36.0	42.9	50.0	132.0	102.4	24.4	273.5	44.4	37.8	34.7	94.5	345.5	2,100
1982	161.5	100.8	105.0	35.5	36.9	50.0	127.8	89.2	14.2	258.8	45.1	31.8	38.0	52.8	340.5	1,917
1983	170.6	109.7	112.0	37.9	29.5	55.0	130.1	115.2	0	271.0	51.2	21.5	39.3	69.9	345.0	1,979
1984[1]	176.7	114.0	115.0	38.6	19.0	55.0	135.0	106.2	0	266.6	56.0	26.1	40.1	94.0	345.0	2,040
1985[2]	160.2															

[1] Preliminary. [2] Estimate. *Source: Textile Organon*   T.538

World[5] Production of Non-Cellulosic Man-Made Fibers (Except Olefin) In Thousands of Metric Tons

Year	Text. Glass Fiber[1]	United States Yarn[3]	United States Staple[4]	United States Total	Total[5]	Can-ada	China	France	W. Ger-many	Italy/Malta	Tai-wan	Japan	Korea	Bene-lux	USSR	United King-dom	World Total
1977	357	1,415	1,622	3,037	3,394	112.8		243.9	690.2	330.1	364.4	1,280	349.9	139.3	456.0	358.8	9,149
1978	419	1,467	1,751	3,218	3,637	123.1	136.6	246.4	729.4	354.4	464.2	1,376	432.5	142.7	475.0	406.4	10,034
1979	460	1,595	1,889	3,484	3,944	121.6	164.0	224.0	759.5	360.2	521.3	1,363	477.3	135.6	476.0	381.1	10,601
1980	393	1,412	1,831	3,243	3,635	122.0	248.0	192.0	720.1	354.8	557.8	1,357	536.4	104.3	550.0	287.6	10,476
1981	472	1,439	1,837	3,276	3,748	105.9	347.0	201.2	752.2	435.3	587.0	1,329	610.4	105.7	572.8	249.3	10,827
1982	408	1,121	1,482	2,603	3,011	97.0	369.0	190.1	701.9	428.7	630.9	1,304	612.4	89.8	593.8	204.3	10,140
1983	530	1,294	1,715	3,009	3,539	112.3	400.0	198.3	757.6	455.1	737.4	1,318	663.9	83.2	622.0	227.7	11,074
1984[6]	632	1,260	1,677	2,937	3,569	121.3	701.0	193.8	771.0	518.9	865.9	1,369	746.2	85.5	644.0	235.5	11,893
1985[7]		1,400	1,600	3,000													

[1] Textile glass fiber of all types, including some staple. [2] Acrylic fiber, nylon, polyester, saran, etc. [3] Includes monofilaments as well as some saran staple. [4] Includes tow, but does not include some saran staple. [5] The textile glass fiber data are included in the U.S. total & excluded from the rest of the world data. [6] Preliminary. [7] Estimate. *Source: Textile Organon*   T.539

Man-Made Fiber Production in the United States In Millions of Pounds

Year	Rayon Yarn Indust.	Rayon Yarn Textile	Acet. Yarn	Total Yarn	Staple & Tow Rayon	Staple & Tow Ace-tate	Staple & Tow Total	Total	Non-Cellulosic Fiber Yarn	Non-Cellulosic Fiber Staple	Non-Cellulosic Fiber Total	Total Ray. & Acet. & Non-Cel.	Textile Glass Fiber	Total Man-made Fiber	Producers' Waste — Shipments Rayon	Producers' Waste — Shipments Non-Cell.
1978	47.0	15.0	300.9	362.9	534.6	7.0	541.6	904.5	3,830.3	3,952.7	7,783.0	8,687.5	923.3	9,610.8	15.7	263.9
1979	41.7	15.1	316.6	373.4	549.4	7.0	556.4	929.8	4,154.3	4,282.3	8,436.6	9,336.4	1,014.4	10,380.8	17.2	238.6
1980	32.2	15.0	308.5	355.7	443.3	7.0	450.3	806.0	3,744.3	4,148.2	7,892.5	8,698.5	867.3	9,565.8	13.5	170.2
1981	33.4	15.1	257.0	305.5	460.6	4.0	464.6	770.1	3,814.8	4,191.1	8,005.9	8,776.0	1,041.1	9,817.1	15.3	174.2
1982	20.8	12.4	195.2	228.4	355.0	1.0	356.0	584.4	3,057.4	3,402.5	6,459.9	7,044.3	899.2	7,943.5	10.7	173.2
1983	25.0	11.2	227.6	263.8	374.8	1.4	376.2	640.0	3,567.8	3,970.6	7,538.4	8,178.4	1,167.2	9,335.9	9.4	214.1
1984	28.8	12.1	198.2	239.1	389.2	.4	389.6	628.7	3,524	3,947	7,472	8,100	1,394.0	9,494	11.4	216.9
1985[1]			204.6	352.7		.5	353.2	557.8	3,790	3,773	7,564	8,121	N.A.	N.A.	8.8	235.8

[1] Preliminary. *Source: Textile Organon*   T.543

U.S. Rayon and Acetate Distribution   In Millions of Pounds

	Yarn & Monofilaments								Staple & Tow & Fiber Fill						
	Producers' Shipments						Domestic		Producers' Shipments						Domestic
	To Domestic Consumers						Consump.		Domestic Consumers						Consump.
Year	Industrial	Textile	Acetate	Total	Export	Total	Import		Rayon	Acetate	Total	Export	Total	Import	
1979	—55.0—		288.4	343.4	31.8	375.2	13.3	356.7	442.4	7.0	449.4	100.1	549.5	16.5	465.9
1980	—47.5—		269.2	316.7	32.7	349.4	8.3	325.0	390.7	7.0	397.7	61.0	458.7	10.3	408.0
1981	—46.6—		226.3	272.9	34.8	307.7	10.7	283.6	396.9	4.0	400.9	59.8	460.7	16.8	417.7
1982	—30.1—		169.0	199.1	29.8	228.9	7.0	206.1	293.7	1.0	294.7	66.5	361.2	13.4	308.1
1983	—35.5—		197.6	233.1	28.2	261.3	8.7	241.8	333.5	1.4	334.9	43.9	378.8	13.6	348.5
1984	—38.2—		180.1	218.3	18.2	236.5	10.0	228.3	331.9	.4	332.3	52.1	384.4	17.0	349.3
1985[1]			187.1		23.0	210.1	13.9	201.0	323.7	.5	324.2	35.0	359.2	12.3	336.5

[1] Preliminary.   *Source: Textile Organon*   T.540

U.S. Domestic Shipments of Synthetic Fibers   In Millions of Pounds

	Yarn & Monofilaments							Staple & Tow						
	Cellulosic			Non-Cellulosic				Rayon	Nylon	Non-Cellulosic				Textile
						Polyester &				Acrylic & Mod-	Olefin &			Glass
Year	Rayon	Acetate	Total	Nylon	Olefin[2]	Other	Total[3]	Rayon	Nylon	Acrylic	Vinyon	Polyester	Total	Fiber
1979	55.0	288.4	343.4	1,631	624.2	1,525	3,798	442.4	913.2	546.6	119.3	2,134	3,714	922.6
1980	47.5	269.2	316.7	1,539	611.7	1,363	3,532	390.7	711.2	585.3	115.0	2,071	3,483	874.4
1981	46.6	226.3	272.9	1,404	628.3	1,430	3,483	396.9	696.4	494.1	132.0	2,005	3,328	982.0
1982	30.1	169.0	199.1	1,166	577.0	1,135	2,894	293.7	673.3	457.9	138.9	1,768	3,038	875.6
1983	35.5	197.6	233.1	1,392	698.6	1,294	3,385	333.5	897.1	492.2	183.4	2,099	3,672	1,166.1
1984	38.2	180.1	218.3	1,438	725.6	1,145	3,309	331.9	814.4	446.7	240.9	1,992	3,494	1,273.8
1985[1]			187.1	1,417	937.6	1,204	3,559	323.7	830.3	458.7	279.7	1,873	3,441	N.A.

[1] Preliminary.   [2] Includes film fiber.   [3] Includes Saran & Spandex.   *Source: Textile Organon*   T.541

U.S. Mill Consumption of Fiber & Products & Per Capita Consumption

| | Mill Consumption (Million Pounds) | | | | | | | | | | | Per Capita[4] Consumption (Pounds) | | | | |
Year	Yarn & Monofila-ments	Staple & Tow	Total R. & A.[2]	Noncel-lulosic Fiber	Textile Glass Fiber	Waste	Total Man-made[3]	Cotton	Wool	Silk	Grand Total	Non-cell. Man-made Fibers	Rayon & Ac-etate	Cotton	Wool	Total All Fibers
1979	356.7	465.9	822.6	7,692	922.6	130.4	8,697	3,066	134.4	1.5	11,899	34.9	3.7	14.9	1.0	52.9
1980	325.0	408.0	733.0	7,145	874.4	83.0	8,064	3,064	137.8	1.5	11,266	32.2	3.3	14.6	.9	49.3
1981	283.6	417.7	701.3	7,007	982.0	129.8	7,862	2,731	152.7	2.0	10,748	31.1	3.1	14.4	1.0	46.7
1982	206.1	308.1	514.2	6,131	875.6	132.8	6,775	2,479	129.5	2.0	9,386	26.9	2.2	13.5	.9	40.5
1983	241.8	348.5	590.3	7,396	1,166.1	197.2	8,164	2,796	162.5	2.0	11,124	32.4	2.5	16.8	1.2	47.5
1984	228.3	349.3	577.6	7,202	1,273.8	188.0	7,946	2,668	163.2	3.0	10,781	31.2	2.4	16.8	1.4	45.7
1985[1]	201.0	336.5	537.5	7,466	N.A.	209.0	8,011	2,793	134.7	3.0	10,942	31.9	2.3	17.7	1.4	46.5

[1] Preliminary.   [2] Rayon and acetate.   [3] Man-made fiber data include only glass fiber for textile end uses.   [4] Mill consumption adjusted for raw fiber equivalent of net U.S. trade in textile mfg.   *Source: Textile Economics Bureau; Economic Research Service, U.S.D.A.*   T.542

United States Imports of Manmade Fiber Manufactures   In Millions of Pounds

Year	Jan.	Feb.	Mar.	Apr.	May	June	July	Aug.	Sept.	Oct.	Nov.	Dec.	Total
1981	46.72	38.55	43.81	45.53	57.83	58.01	66.66	69.32	56.77	67.24	49.12	39.51	639.08
1982	53.18	48.07	47.74	40.14	67.85	91.93	77.34	100.05	82.75	70.14	68.76	59.16	807.10
1983	79.98	71.92	76.53	73.20	86.99	105.55	98.14	108.25	98.34	106.84	85.83	77.93	1,069.5
1984	100.34	118.86	110.21	110.50	114.35	122.45	169.47	127.72	114.80	98.79	80.51	74.56	1,342.6
1985	96.34	116.29	116.16	90.56	122.22	123.98	136.98	118.98	139.60	132.32	122.32	114.33	1,491.0
1986	142.31	130.04	132.47	125.18	147.02	159.71	179.65						

Source: Department of Commerce   T.544

Producer Price Index of Gray Synthetic Broadwovens   (Dec. 1975 = 100)

Year	Jan.	Feb.	Mar.	Apr.	May	June	July	Aug.	Sept.	Oct.	Nov.	Dec.	Average
1981	139.5	138.8	139.7	141.7	142.0	144.2	144.2	145.6	145.7	145.0	144.3	144.4	142.9
1982	146.2	145.2	144.6	144.2	143.8	143.9	143.3	143.0	142.3	142.7	142.3	142.5	143.7
1983	144.9	144.3	144.7	145.5	146.1	146.3	146.5	147.4	147.7	149.3	151.7	151.0	147.0
1984	148.8	151.2	152.3	152.4	153.5	153.3	153.3	153.6	151.9	152.5	151.0	150.1	152.1
1985	149.4	148.1	147.3	147.0	148.0	147.2	146.4	146.1	146.2	146.6	147.0	147.1	147.2
1986[1]	147.7	147.3	147.2	147.9	147.2	147.4	147.5	148.0	145.4	144.4	144.2		

[1] Preliminary.   *Source: Bureau of Labor Statistics.* (0337-03)   T.545

207

Rice

World rough rice production in 1986/87 was estimated at 466.7 million tonnes, down one percent from the previous season. In the last 15 years, world output has risen almost 50 percent, with large yield increases and slightly higher planted acreage. China, still the largest producer, was expected to provide 37 percent of 1986/87 output; the crop was forecast at 172 million tonnes, up two percent from 1985/86, but below the excellent harvest of 1984/85.

In India, the second major producer, the 1986/87 crop was estimated at 90 million tonnes, off seven percent from the year before. Indonesia's output was forecast at 38.2 million tonnes, down two percent. Other major producers were Bangladesh, Vietnam, and Japan. Brazil and the U.S. were the largest non-Asian producers. Brazilian output was estimated unchanged at 10 million tonnes. The U.S. crop was expected to fall four percent, to 5.95 million tonnes, as farmers participating in the rice program allowed more of their acreage to remain idle.

According to USDA, world milled rice utilization in calendar 1986 was 317.7 million tonnes, one percent lighter than in 1985. Use in China, the world's largest consumer, declined five percent to 117.2 million tonnes, partly due to substitution of wheat. Indian consumption expanded 10 percent to 62.4 million tonnes; use in Indonesia rose about four percent to 26.2 million tonnes.

1986 world exports grew 10 percent from 1985 to 12.6 million tonnes. Thailand, the leading exporter, shipped 4.3 million tonnes, compared with 4 million in 1985. Pakistani exports increased 10 percent to 1.1 million tonnes. U.S. shipments were 21 percent higher at 2.3 million tonnes. Major U.S. rice customers were Brazil and Iraq.

The leading importer in 1986 remained the European Community (1.4 million tonnes, up eight percent from 1985). Iran's imports rose by 17 percent, to 700,000 tonnes, after having retreated the year before. Imports by Iraq and Saudi Arabia held steady at 500,000 tonnes each. Brazil reportedly stepped up its imports.

At year-end 1986, global stocks (milled basis) were 24.3 million tonnes, up 10 percent from 1985. India held 37 percent of world stocks, Indonesia 12 percent, and the U.S. 10 percent.

U.S. prices dropped by over 50 percent after a marketing loan, established under the 1985 Farm Bill, went into effect on April 15, 1986. 1986/87 U.S. market prices were expected to vary with world prices and to range from $3.20–$4.00/cwt., versus an average $6.72/cwt. in 1985/86.

The 1986/87 U.S. support program held the target price at $11.90/cwt. The loan rate was lowered nine percent to $7.20 and a loan repayment rate was set at $3.60. Acreage reduction was raised to 35 percent from 20 percent the previous season.

Futures Market

Rice futures are traded on the Chicago Rice and Cotton Exchange.

World Rice[3] Supply & Distribution In Millions of Metric Tons

Year	Production U.S.	Non-U.S.	Total	Exports U.S.	Non-U.S.	Total	Imports U.S.	Non-U.S.	Total	Utilization U.S.	Non-U.S.	Total	Stocks (End) U.S.	Non-U.S.	Total
1983	7.0	412.5	419.5	2.3	9.6	11.9	—	11.9	11.9	2.0	287.6	289.6	2.3	15.0	17.3
1984	4.5	448.2	452.7	2.1	10.4	12.6	—	12.6	12.6	1.8	306.3	308.1	1.5	15.8	17.2
1985	6.3	462.7	469.0	1.9	9.6	11.5	—	11.5	11.5	1.9	312.5	314.5	2.0	20.0	22.1
1986[1]	6.2	459.3	465.5	2.3	10.3	12.6	—	12.6	12.6	2.1	313.6	315.7	2.5	20.6	23.1
1987[2]	6.0	461.5	467.5	2.6	9.3	11.9	—	11.9	11.9	2.2	318.0	320.2	2.0	19.1	21.1

[1] Preliminary. [2] Forecast. [3] Production is on rough basis; the rest are on milled basis. *Source: Foreign Agricultural Service, U.S.D.A.* T.547a

World Production of Rough Rice In Millions of Metric Tons

Crop Year	Brazil	Burma	China	Vietnam	India	Japan	Indo-nesia	Rep. of Korea	Bang-ladesh	Philip-pines	Pakistan	Taiwan	Thai-land	United States	World Total
1982–3	7.8	14.4	161.2	13.8	70.7	12.8	33.6	7.3	21.3	7.7	5.2	3.3	16.9	7.0	419.5
1983–4	9.0	14.4	168.9	14.7	90.2	13.0	35.3	7.6	21.8	7.8	5.0	3.3	19.5	4.5	452.7
1984–5	9.0	14.8	178.3	15.4	88.0	14.8	38.1	8.0	21.9	8.2	5.0	2.9	19.9	6.3	469.0
1985–6[1]	10.0	14.9	168.5	15.0	91.5	14.6	39.0	7.9	22.8	8.7	4.4	2.9	19.7	6.2	465.5
1986–7[2]	10.0	15.0	172.0		90.0	14.1	39.0	7.7	23.2		4.8		19.2	6.0	467.5

[1] Preliminary. [2] Estimate. *Source: Foreign Agricultural Service, U.S.D.A.* T.547

World Exports of Rice (Milled Basis), by Country of Origin In Thousands of Metric Tons

Year	Aus-tralia	Argentina	Guy-ana	Burma	P.R. China	Egypt (U.A.R.)	Uru-guay	Pakistan	EC-12	Japan	India	Taiwan	Thailand	United States	World Total
1982	530	92	35	701	470	22	227	794	887	318	633	307	3,620	2,487	11,823
1983	281	68	45	750	580	21	189	1,299	847	321	200	533	3,700	2,331	11,925
1984	370	115	47	727	1,168	50	155	1,050	772	102	200	210	4,528	2,129	12,567
1985[1]	450	165	35	450	1,010	16	231	962	908	0	200	40	3,993	1,906	11,508
1986[2]	400	145	35	600	900	50	220	1,100	1,045	0	200	275	4,400	2,300	12,605

[1] Preliminary. [2] Estimate. *Source: Foreign Agricultural Service, U.S.D.A.* T.552

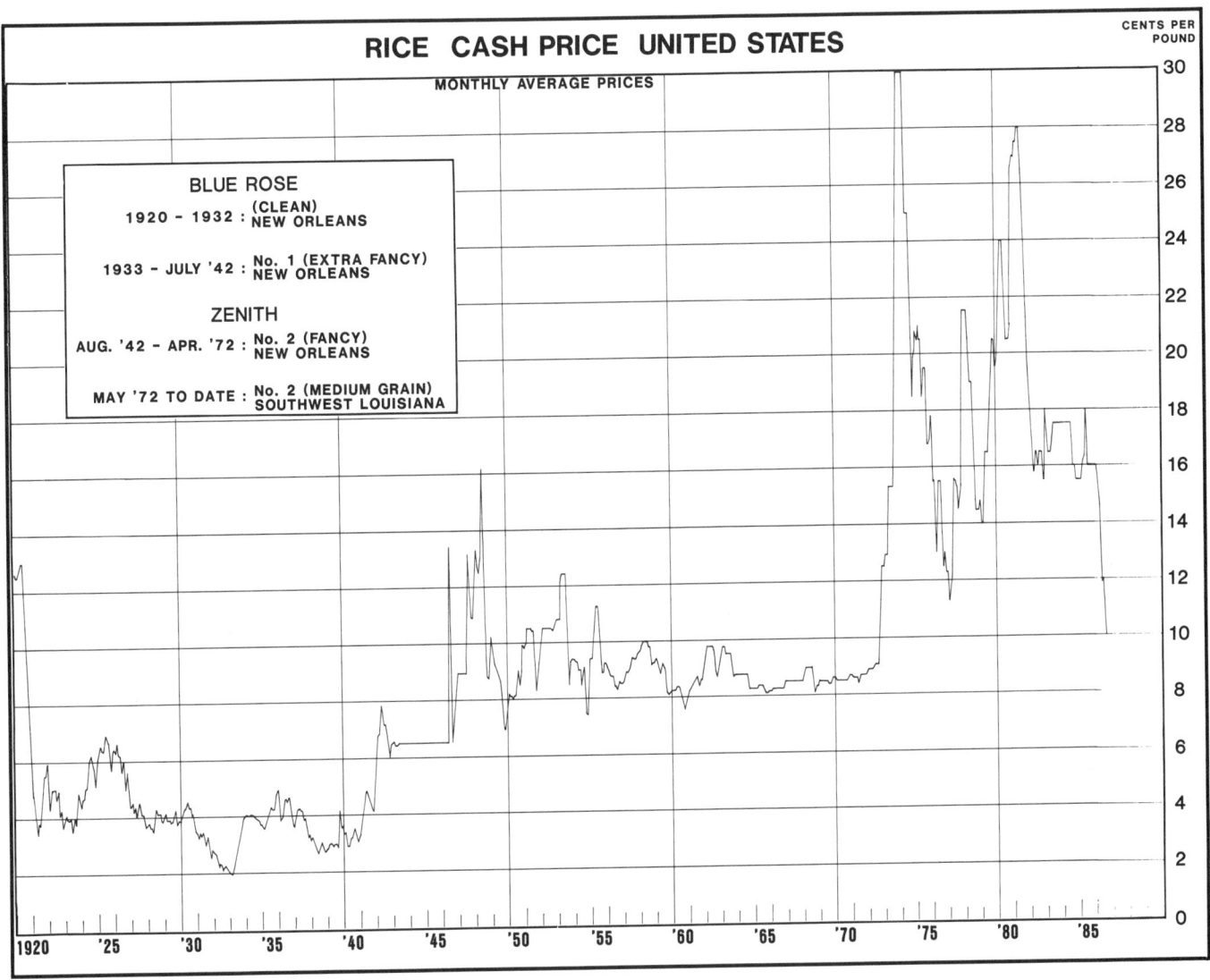

RICE CASH PRICE UNITED STATES

MONTHLY AVERAGE PRICES

CENTS PER POUND

BLUE ROSE
1920 - 1932 : (CLEAN) NEW ORLEANS

1933 - JULY '42 : No. 1 (EXTRA FANCY) NEW ORLEANS

ZENITH
AUG. '42 - APR. '72 : No. 2 (FANCY) NEW ORLEANS

MAY '72 TO DATE : No. 2 (MEDIUM GRAIN) SOUTHWEST LOUISIANA

Average Wholesale Price of Rice No. 2 (Medium Grain)[1] Southwest Louisiana   Dollars per cwt. bagged

Year	Aug.	Sept.	Oct.	Nov.	Dec.	Jan.	Feb.	Mar.	Apr.	May	June	July	Average
1978–9	17.5	14.5	14.5	14.5	14.8	14.0	14.0	14.0	16.5	16.5	16.5	16.5	15.3
1979–0	19.0	20.0	20.5	20.5	19.5	20.0	22.0	23.5	24.0	24.0	22.0	21.0	21.3
1980–1	20.5	20.8	21.6	24.4	26.4	27.0	27.1	27.5	27.6	28.0	28.0	27.8	25.6
1981–2	26.4	24.2	22.9	21.2	20.0	18.8	17.8	16.1	16.0	16.4	16.2	16.0	19.3
1982–3	16.5	16.5	16.5	16.7	17.8	17.3	16.5	16.5	16.5	17.1	17.5	17.5	16.9
1983–4	17.5	17.5	17.5	17.5	17.5	17.5	17.5	17.5	17.5	17.5	17.5	17.5	17.5
1984–5	16.0	16.0	15.5	15.5	15.5	15.5	15.5	16.0	16.2	16.3	18.0	16.2	16.0
1985–6[2]	16.0	16.0	16.0	16.0	16.0	16.0	15.7	15.5	14.6	11.9	12.0	11.3	14.8
1986–7[2]	10.0												

[1] U.S. No. 2—Broken not to exceed 4%.   [2] Preliminary.   *Source: Bureau of Labor Statistics* (0213–0101)   T.549

U.S. Rice (Rough) Production by Type and Variety   In Thousands of Cwt.

Year	Long Grain	Medium Grain	Short Grain	Total	Year	Long Grain	Medium Grain	Short Grain	Total
1979	80,692	40,421	10,834	131,947	1983	64,318	27,388	8,014	99,720
1980	86,851	51,407	7,892	146,150	1984	96,029	35,304	7,477	138,810
1981	110,426	61,497	10,819	182,742	1985	100,938	28,680	6,424	136,042
1982	93,424	51,342	8,871	153,637	1986[1]	96,353	30,460	4,453	131,266

[1] Preliminary.   *Source: Crop Reporting Board, U.S.D.A.*   T.548

RICE

Salient Statistics of Rice, Rough & Milled (Rough Equivalent) in the United States   In Thousands of Cwt.

Year Beginning August	Supply: Stocks Aug. 1	Supply: Pro-duction	Supply: Im-ports[2]	Supply: Total Supply	Distribution Domestic: Food[3]	Distribution Domestic: Indus-try[4]	Distribution Domestic: Seed	Distribution: Total	Distribution: Exports	Owned By CCC Aug. 1	Total Under Price Support	Gov't Support: Loan Rate Rough: Long	Gov't Support: Loan Rate Rough: Med & Short	Gov't Support: Loan Rate: Milled Long	Gov't Support: Loan Rate: All Classes
1981–2	16,493	182,742	—	199,500	42,500	12,700	4,400	68,600	82,000	—	42,848				8.01
1982–3	48,987	153,637	—	203,100	37,300	13,500	3,200	62,900	68,900	17,500	65,375	8.86	7.74	14.75	8.14
1983–4	71,440	99,720	—	171,900	33,200	12,800	3,300	54,900	70,300	22,320	40,950	9.12	7.58	14.96	8.14
1984–5[1]	46,909	138,810	—	187,300	35,800	13,900	2,800	60,500	62,100	25,000	55,200	9.12	6.80	14.96	8.00
1985–6[5]	64,700	136,042	—	200,742	37,400	14,000	2,600	66,900	58,700			8.86	6.60	14.53	8.00
1986–7[5]	77,300	131,266	—	208,566				67,000	80,000			7.57	6.45	12.44	7.20

[1] Preliminary. [2] Consists mostly of broken rice. [3] Includes shipments to territories and military food use. [4] Primarily for beer-production. [5] Projected. *Source: Agricultural Marketing Service, U.S.D.A.*   T.551

Acreage, Yield, Production, and Prices of Rice in the United States

Crop Year	Acreage Harvested (1,000 Acres): Southern States	Acreage Harvested: California	Acreage Harvested: United States	Yield Per Harvested Acre (In Lbs.): California	Yield Per Harvested Acre: United States	Production 1,000 Cwt.: Southern States	Production: California	Production: United States	Farm Value of Pro-duction $1,000	Farm Price of Rough Rice $ Per Cwt.	Wholesale Prices ($ Per Cwt.): Arkansas[2]	Wholesale Prices: Houston[3]
1980–1	2,747	565	3,312	6,440	4,413	109,764	36,386	146,150	1,873,007	12.80	25.30	25.55
1981–2	3,199	593	3,792	6,900	4,819	141,818	40,924	182,742	1,654,413	9.05	19.40	21.15
1982–3	2,727	535	3,262	6,700	4,710	117,740	35,848	153,637	1,246,608	8.11	16.80	18.70
1983–4	1,841	328	2,169	7,040	4,598	76,631	23,089	99,720	874,004	8.76	17.35	19.88
1984–5	2,352	450	2,802	7,120	4,954	106,750	32,060	138,810	1,118,809	8.06	16.23	18.69
1985–6[1]	2,102	400	2,502	7,400	5,437	106,448	29,594	136,042	914,202	6.72	15.22	16.84
1986–7[1]	2,193	340	2,533	7,700	5,626	105,086	26,180	131,266	472,558	3.60		

[1] Preliminary. [2] F.O.B. mills, Arkansas, medium. [3] Houston, Texas (long grain). *Source: Economic Research Service, U.S.D.A.*   T.550

U.S. Exports of Milled Rice[1] by Country of Destination   In Thousands of Metric Tons

Crop Year	Belg.-Lux.	South Africa	Cana-da	Un. Kingd.	South Korea	Niger-ia	Indo-nesia	Italy	Bangla-desh	Liberia	Saudi Arabia	Switzer-land	Iraq	Iran	Total Exports
1979–0	85.0	105.5	77.6	30.1	574.7	137.9	225.1	42.5	—	61.9	169.5	63.3	309.6	31.1	2,706
1980–1	101.6	112.4	93.3	19.3	1,048.8	283.2	138.8	11.5	—	85.1	257.0	69.5	71.4	—	3,028
1981–2	118.4	114.1	101.0	30.5	281.6	412.8	15.8	201.4	22.6	88.4	277.7	91.1	221.1	147.2	2,682
1982–3	114.9	109.3	100.6	26.2	187.8	168.7	63.4	11.6	67.3	91.3	279.1	57.2	279.2	—	2,219
1983–4[2]	135.3	154.5	94.1	4.2	98.9	—	81.6	51.0	55.7	83.5	285.7	65.1	274.8	0	2,358
1985–6[2]															1,943

[1] No adjustment of brown & parboiled rice has been made; treated as milled rice. [2] Preliminary. *Source: Bureau of the Census, Dept. of Commerce*   T.553

Exports of Rice from the United States   In Millions of Pounds[1] (Clean Basis)

Year	Aug.	Sept.	Oct.	Nov.	Dec.	Jan.	Feb.	Mar.	Apr.	May	June	July	Total
1980–1	419	577	409	474	730	533	613	809	688	794	497	371	6,914
1981–2	453	470	532	583	458	479	515	399	487	661	538	370	5,945
1982–3	809	320	431	199	307	241	316	490	446	438	550	360	4,907
1983–4	488	624	460	378	359	299	220	462	432	420	431	314	4,587
1984–5	384	567	331	343	307	236	292	411	315	355	296	336	4,173
1985–6	380	489	417	290	283	277	163	249	208	212	450	603	4,021
1986–7	778												

[1] 162 pounds rough—100 pounds clean. *Source: Department of Commerce*   T.554

Average Price Received by Farmers for Rice (Rough) in the U.S.   In Dollars Per 100 Pounds (Cwt.)

Year	Aug.	Sept.	Oct.	Nov.	Dec.	Jan.	Feb.	Mar.	Apr.	May	June	July	Average[1]
1980–1	10.60	10.20	10.90	11.60	13.10	13.20	13.00	13.40	13.80	13.30	11.90	12.80	12.80
1981–2	11.80	10.70	10.20	9.86	9.34	9.34	9.46	9.46	8.54	8.55	8.54	8.25	9.05
1982–3	7.31	7.75	7.73	7.78	8.06	8.05	8.26	7.99	8.23	8.23	7.88	7.95	8.11
1983–4	8.41	8.48	8.80	8.80	8.66	8.57	8.85	8.63	8.49	8.24	8.20	8.18	8.76
1984–5	8.22	8.17	8.08	8.13	8.08	8.09	7.72	8.17	8.20	7.91	7.83	7.54	8.06
1985–6[2]	7.86	7.55	7.73	7.84	7.71	7.90	7.86	7.60	5.80	5.01	4.83	4.47	6.72
1986–7[2]	3.82	3.82	3.90	3.93	3.91								

[1] Weighted average by sales. [2] Preliminary. *Source: Crop Reporting Board, U.S.D.A.*   T.555

Rubber

World natural rubber production for the first seven months of 1986 was forecast at 2.6 million tonnes, almost unchanged from the same period in 1985. Global production of synthetic rubber for the first seven months was projected at 5.3 million tonnes, almost three percent higher than in the same 1985 period. World stocks of natural rubber in producing countries as of January, 1986, were estimated at 495,000 tonnes, about 10 percent below the 545,000 tonnes on hand a year earlier. World stocks of natural rubber in consuming countries at 1986's beginning were 805,000 tonnes, off 11 percent from the year before. Data on world consumption of natural rubber in 1986 were not available at this writing; usage amounted to 4.3 million tonnes in 1985.

The world's largest producer and exporter of natural rubber is Malaysia, accounting for 35 percent of global output. 1985 production was estimated at 1.5 million tonnes, down two percent from 1984. Exports were pegged at 1.50 million tonnes, compared with nearly 1.59 million in 1984.

Indonesia is the second-largest producer and exporter of natural rubber contributing 25 percent to global output. For 1986, production there was forecast at 1.22 million tonnes, compared to 1.05 million in 1985. However, low prices and competition from oil-based synthetics were expected to pare the 1986 outlook. The major importers of Indonesian natural rubber were the U.S., Singapore (for transhipment), the USSR, West Germany and Romania.

The U.S. produces no natural rubber, although it is the world's largest consumer, responsible for over 17 percent of world consumption. Imports of natural rubber through the first half of 1986 averaged about 65,000 tonnes a month. U.S. consumption of natural rubber was projected at 735,000 tonnes, compared with the 1985 estimate of 750,000 tonnes. Consumption of synthetic rubber was projected at 1.9 million tonnes, versus the previous year's 2.1 million. About 57 percent of total U.S. consumption of rubber was expected to be used for tires and tire products.

The U.S. was the second-largest producer of synthetic rubber in 1986, and the world's largest consumer. More than 10 percent of U.S. synthetic rubber is used for export. Production of synthetic rubber continued to be depressed in 1986 by reduced demand from the automotive industry, the largest market for tires and a major outlet for hose, belting and scores of component parts. The one major exception to falling production in recent years has been specialty elastomers, which rose 14 percent between 1979 and 1984, while total production of synthetic rubber fell 17 percent. Estimated growth rate for elastomer output is projected at 5–10 percent per annum.

The overall output of synthetic rubber has been adversely affected by longer-lasting radial tires, smaller tires and smaller rubber parts for cars, U.S. imports of automobiles containing tires and rubber components, imports of tires and rubber products, and substitution of newer materials for older rubbers. However, demand for several specialty rubbers has grown, notably in the automotive sector, and rubbers have been increasingly alloyed with plastics to form new materials.

Prospects for the synthetic and natural markets depend on the demand for rubber products in general and on the industry's ability to develop new rubber-based alloyed materials; growth areas include roofing and oil additives. Specialty rubbers and blends were expected to expand in international trade. On balance, slow growth is anticipated for the industry during the next five years, based on a number of sometimes conflicting forces. Tires will continue to be smaller and longer lasting, which tends to curtail demand. However, demand should be enhanced by gains in the driving-age population and in the amount of mileage driven. Exports may increase slightly and will continue to go primarily to Canada, with truck tires moving to some developing countries.

The fabricated products industry in the U.S. is composed of over 1,300 firms that make molded rubber mechanical goods, rubber compounds, medical sundries, etc. Fabricated products will continue to depend on automotive production and industrial activity. The industry's growth through the decade is estimated at 2.0–2.5 percent annually; alloying rubber and plastics to create products with improved properties will aid the industry's growth.

Prices generally trended lower during the first half of the 1980s. The spot price for crude rubber (smoked sheets) in New York reached a post–World War II high of 87 cents per pound in early 1980 and posted a low of 39 cents per pound in late 1985. The average spot price for 1986 was 43-cents per pound, slightly higher than the 42-cents figure of 1985.

Futures Markets

Rubber futures are listed for trading in Kuala Lumpur and Tokyo.

RUBBER

World Rubber Production[1]   In Thousands of Metric Tons

Year	Sri Lanka	India	Indo-nesia	Malaysia	Natural Philip-pines	Thai-land	Liberia	Brazil	China	World Total	Canada	West Germany	Japan	Synthetic United States	United Kingdom	USSR	World Total
1978	155.7	133.0	902.5	1,582	56.6	467.0	72.5	23.7	101.6	3,770	248.3	407.0	1,029	2,662	293.7	1,950	8,955
1979	152.7	147.2	905.0	1,570	63.3	531.2	75.0	25.0	108.3	3,870	282.5	418.5	1,107	2,720	277.7	2,025	9,370
1980	133.2	155.4	1,020	1,530	69.9	501.1	77.5	27.8	113.0	3,850	252.8	389.9	1,094	2,215	211.8	2,040	8,690
1981	123.9	150.7	867.5	1,510	75.3	504.0	77.5	30.3	127.7	3,705	263.3	396.8	1,010	2,225	226.2	2,000	8,525
1982	126.2	165.9	880.0	1,494	74.2	552.2	67.5	32.8	152.6	3,750	181.7	383.8	930.7	1,817	246.3	1,950	7,840
1983	140.0	168.0	997.2	1,564	75.0	587.2	65.0	35.2	172.4	4,025	182.0	418.0	1,003	1,987	262.3	1,970	8,300
1984[2]	141.9	183.9	1,115	1,529	84.0	628.6	76.0	36.0	190.0	4,260	217.8	437.6	1,161	2,219	288.8	2,125	9,100
1985[3]	145.0	186.0	1,050	1,500	85.0	640.0	78.0	38.0	195.0	4,280	215.0	435.0	1,165	2,100	275.0	2,300	9,070
1986																	

[1] Including rubber in the form of latex.   [2] Preliminary.   [3] Estimate.   *Source: Rubber Study Group*   T.556

World Consumption of Natural and Synthetic Rubber   In Thousands of Metric Tons

Year	Aus-tralia	Brazil	Canada	France	Natural West Germany	Japan	United Kingdom	United States	World Total	Canada	France	Synthetic West Germany	Japan	United Kingdom	United States	World Total
1978	41.1	72.5	89.1	163.2	184.9	355.0	139.2	770.8	3,750	203.9	296.2	429.5	741.0	313.4	2,519	8,860
1979	45.4	75.9	93.8	177.0	184.5	390.0	137.5	740.4	3,880	232.0	317.8	447.1	830.0	301.1	2,501	9,210
1980	42.2	81.1	80.0	187.7	179.7	427.0	130.8	585.0	3,760	200.0	341.9	421.3	885.0	248.2	1,980	8,780
1981	41.9	74.4	82.0	167.2	169.1	436.0	120.0	635.0	3,700	210.0	303.4	396.2	851.0	247.0	2,022	8,545
1982	36.4	67.8	76.0	156.8	171.2	439.0	118.0	585.0	3,680	182.0	265.2	386.9	797.0	238.0	1,765	8,000
1983	30.9	70.2	87.0	155.9	179.5	504.0	120.0	665.0	3,985	195.0	276.6	395.8	851.0	228.0	1,883	8,335
1984[1]	35.9	88.7	102.0	162.0	190.0	525.0	118.0	750.7	4,240	280.0	287.0	403.0	915.0	247.0	2,061	8,985
1985[2]	38.0	90.0	104.0	160.0	195.0	530.0	120.0	750.0	4,310	211.0	285.0	407.0	920.0	245.0	2,050	9,085
1986																

[1] Preliminary.   [2] Estimate.   *Source: Rubber Study Group*   T.557

World Stocks[1] of Natural Rubber, January 1   In Thousands of Metric Tons

Year	Brazil	Viet-nam	Sri Lanka	Indo-nesia	In Producing Countries Malaysia (Penin-sular)	Singa-pore	Thai-land	Total	Aus-tralia	Canada	China	France	In Consuming Countries (Commercial Stocks) West Germany	India	Japan	United Kingdom	United States	Total
1979	19.1	4.0	47.4	75.0	245.5	35.8	60.3	505.0	2.7	8.3	137.5	20.1	13.7	42.9	90.7	29.0	142.3	730
1980	20.8	4.0	61.3	75.0	240.1	51.1	44.7	515.0	3.8	7.3	135.0	20.3	13.5	54.6	76.5	27.6	144.6	735
1981	20.8	4.0	58.5	75.0	254.8	46.3	61.0	535.0	3.2	6.0	150.0	19.6	13.5	40.1	106.9	21.4	126.7	770
1982	19.6	4.0	33.7	75.0	286.3	43.8	60.0	535.0	2.7	9.9	140.0	16.8	14.5	45.9	116.9	20.0	131.9	830
1983	18.5	4.0	11.3	75.0	266.0	26.9	36.6	570.0	4.2	6.9	137.5	9.5	14.5	60.6	90.8	17.8	95.4	860
1984	15.3	5.0	9.6	75.0	254.9	32.2	39.6	545.0	1.8	7.4	187.5	9.0	14.5	47.4	81.0	16.8	80.8	880
1985[2]	11.2	6.0	10.2	95.0	228.8	36.8	41.3	545.0	2.8	8.5	192.5	4.0	15.0	58.0	70.7	15.8	96.4	900
1986[3]	11.0	6.0	13.4	90.0	173.0	28.5	35.0	495.0	3.0	10.0	158.0	4.0	12.0	45.0	72.0	10.0	81.0	805

[1] Exclusive of "Stock Afloat" and unreported gov't. stockpiles.   [2] Preliminary.   [3] Estimate.   *Source: Rubber Study Group* (London)   T.558

Net Exports of Natural Rubber from Producing Areas   In Thousands of Metric Tons

Year	Burma	Kampu-chea	Sri Lanka (Ceylon)	Indonesia	Malaysia (Penin-sular)	Sabah	Sarawak	Thailand	Viet-nam	Other Asia	Liberia	Nigeria	Other Africa	Papua New Guinea	World Total
1979		9.5	128.2	861.0	1,537	33.2	39.5	517.8	34.0	27.8	75.0	26.4	51.3	4.0	3,325
1980		—	120.9	976.1	1,416	30.9	35.2	456.8	33.3	33.3	76.5	14.6	59.2	4.0	3,270
1981		4.0	132.5	808.7	1,402	25.5	28.2	476.0	33.7	30.8	76.9	23.6	57.5	4.5	3,110
1982		7.5	131.3	801.4	1,317	21.7	15.9	546.7	32.3	24.2	67.5	26.8	57.8	2.3	3,065
1983		10.0	125.2	938.0	1,498	21.5	18.9	552.5	35.8	19.0	65.0	28.8	62.0	2.7	3,360
1984[1]		12.0	126.2	1,010	1,484	25.2	18.0	595.2	43.0	19.0	76.0	28.8	65.5	3.0	3,525
1985[2]		12.0	125.0	950.0	1,450	24.0	17.0	610.0	43.0	21.0	78.0	29.1	67.0	3.0	3,500

[1] Preliminary.   [2] Estimate.   *Source: Rubber Study Group* (London)   T.559

U.S. Imports of Natural Rubber (Includes Latex & Guayule)   In Thousands of Long Tons

Year	Jan.	Feb.	Mar.	Apr.	May	June	July	Aug.	Sept.	Oct.	Nov.	Dec.	Total[1]
1981	30.06	86.64	53.38	67.62	66.36	50.47	41.59	43.40	62.76	69.42	56.23	49.13	662.4
1982	50.99	59.33	45.71	53.86	56.19	63.39	38.67	54.35	40.60	54.36	51.37	49.45	618.3
1983	33.01	49.63	48.54	62.11	63.44	65.20	50.41	31.90	44.22	67.83	71.06	54.71	642.1
1984	87.84	57.82	75.45	69.18	70.25	41.45	73.81	56.23	67.46	61.95	62.36	62.21	786.0
1985[2]	71.64	71.68	88.04	63.98	84.66	48.09	59.97	45.30	40.73	69.44	71.81	64.49	779.8
1986[2]	63.64	70.32	76.62	83.12	47.64	54.01	68.96	44.47					

[1] Includes latex and guayule.   [2] Preliminary.   *Source: Department of Commerce*   T.560

Average Spot Crude Rubber Prices (Smoked Sheets[1]) in New York   In Cents Per Pound

Year	Jan.	Feb.	Mar.	Apr.	May	June	July	Aug.	Sept.	Oct.	Nov.	Dec.	Average
1981	71.3	69.0	65.0	59.0	58.0	57.0	56.0	54.0	50.4	—	45.6	48.3	57.6
1982	48.8	46.5	47.0	45.3	45.3	46.1	46.5	46.8	44.5	42.6	42.1	41.8	45.3
1983	44.0	48.5	57.8	57.8	56.8	54.5	58.3	59.3	60.5	60.5	58.3	—	56.0
1984	57.3	58.3	58.0	56.8	51.8	47.0	46.0	46.0	46.0	43.0	42.8	42.0	49.6
1985	42.3	42.3	41.8	42.3	40.8	42.0	40.3	41.8	41.8	43.8	42.5	39.8	41.8
1986	40.7	42.8	42.0	39.2	40.1	41.0	43.5	43.5	45.3	46.9	44.7	44.7	42.9

[1] No. 1, ribbed, plantation rubber.   *Source: Bureau of Labor Statistics* (07–11–02.01)   T.561

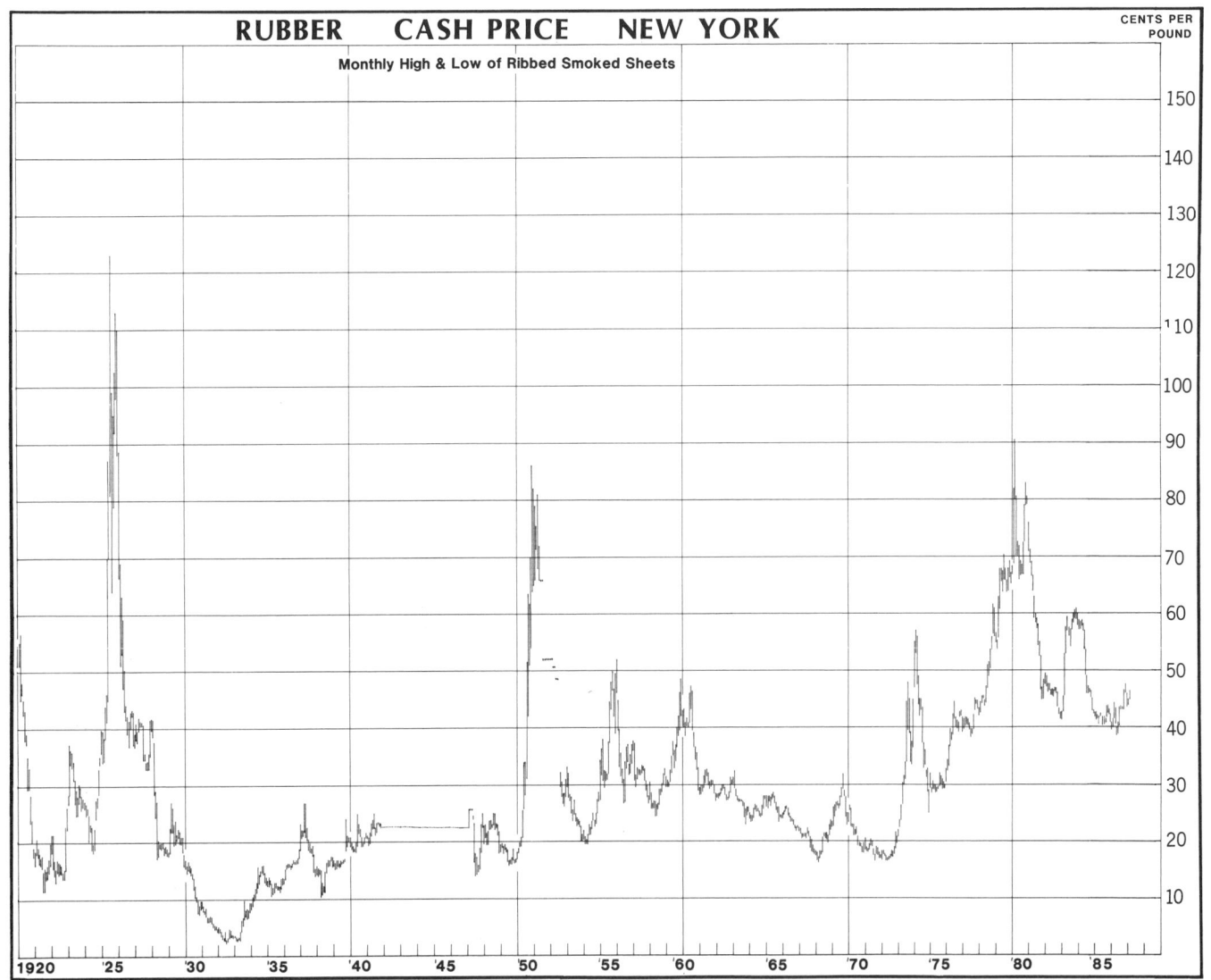

RUBBER   CASH PRICE   NEW YORK

Monthly High & Low of Ribbed Smoked Sheets

RUBBER

Consumption of Natural Rubber in the United States   In Thousands of Metric Tons

Year	Jan.	Feb.	Mar.	Apr.	May	June	July	Aug.	Sept.	Oct.	Nov.	Dec.	Total
1977	70.2	66.8	74.5	68.5	66.8	68.2	50.4	62.8	64.6	63.6	61.3	62.5	780.13
1978	59.2	61.1	63.8	61.2	68.0	61.9	51.7	69.1	65.6	69.5	70.9	62.8	764.65
1979	68.3	66.6	74.5	61.8	60.2	59.0	57.9	63.2	57.7	65.2	55.6	47.9	739.00
1980	63.0	57.3	55.7	46.9	42.3	41.3	38.8	43.2	49.4	49.5	50.3	48.7	586.15
1981	49.0	52.6	55.4	55.1	53.9	59.5	56.4	51.1	52.1	57.3	49.7	42.6	634.67
1982	55.3	59.9	50.2	57.8	63.3	68.9	32.7	65.6	48.8	53.3	48.9	56.0	660.61
1983	64.5	44.5	55.3	55.3	56.9	67.0	48.8	39.2	50.2	75.3	69.7	49.6	676.30
1984	73.8	56.8	83.1	68.2	65.1	42.4	73.9	56.1	63.7	58.3	55.4	54.1	750.70
1985[1]	71.8	65.7	91.5	51.7	89.0	45.2	55.4	47.3	68.1	47.2	65.7	52.4	774.70
1986[1]	59.4	71.8	71.3	81.9	45.5	54.6							

[1] Preliminary.   *Source: Rubber Manufacturers' Association*   T.562

Stocks of Natural Rubber in the United States, Beginning of Month   In Thousands of Metric Tons

Year	Jan.	Feb.	Mar.	Apr.	May	June	July	Aug.	Sept.	Oct.	Nov.	Dec.
1977	125.3	119.9	127.0	123.8	118.4	120.5	119.7	131.7	139.7	133.0	137.5	129.4
1978	127.6	123.3	116.4	117.1	115.6	122.8	123.4	125.4	126.1	127.7	133.5	124.0
1979	125.6	121.4	115.6	116.1	136.6	130.2	137.7	146.0	144.4	135.6	135.0	124.5
1980	132.1	131.4	135.3	141.4	152.4	145.7	147.4	149.9	138.5	132.9	129.5	123.1
1981	126.7	128.0	125.4	122.8	127.6	124.1	119.5	113.5	111.2	114.4	123.0	130.5
1982	142.4	127.1	126.5	121.3	116.6	110.8	105.4	110.2	97.7	89.0	90.2	95.4
1983	95.4	91.8	95.0	87.4	93.8	100.0	97.9	99.2	90.7	83.3	74.8	75.9
1984	80.8	95.2	95.7	87.7	87.8	91.4	88.5	87.0	84.8	86.2	87.3	91.3
1985[1]	96.4	94.3	97.3	91.4	101.9	95.9	95.6	97.9	93.9	84.9	81.1	85.1
1986[1]	95.2	97.0	96.9	100.4	98.6	98.6	96.7					

[1] Preliminary.   *Source: Rubber Manufacturers' Association*   T.563

Stocks of Synthetic Rubber in the United States, Beginning of Month   In Thousands of Metric Tons

Year	Jan.	Feb.	Mar.	Apr.	May	June	July	Aug.	Sept.	Oct.	Nov.	Dec.
1977	458.1	441.4	431.8	407.6	412.9	409.3	402.2	430.4	430.3	422.3	424.5	424.0
1978	426.8	441.0	427.9	434.5	446.9	441.4	433.1	456.5	445.1	435.8	425.3	419.9
1979	424.1	407.1	400.0	393.6	398.9	391.5	401.3	411.3	402.2	402.8	389.9	402.1
1980	402.9	439.9	436.2	427.6	452.2	445.1	429.2	391.2	372.3	339.7	325.4	328.9
1981	341.8	364.5	354.6	347.0	365.9	368.3	359.8	369.4	353.4	351.9	352.6	364.4
1982	349.0	333.3	336.8	349.2	358.3	364.4	352.9	342.8	326.6	304.3	318.8	294.6
1983	269.7	281.0	284.8	283.5	283.8	294.3	290.8	304.8	269.8	256.2	250.7	276.9
1984	277.9	284.1	277.2	277.0	294.6	305.0	302.3	309.3	300.6	312.0	301.4	285.9
1985[1]	272.6	281.2	271.8	288.6	294.0	292.5	286.4	295.8	413.5	397.3	374.9	367.0
1986[1]	349.0	352.8	353.0	397.7	403.0	238.6	247.5					

[1] Preliminary.   *Source: Department of Commerce*   T.564

Production of Synthetic Rubber in the United States   In Thousands of Metric Tons

Year	Jan.	Feb.	Mar.	Apr.	May	June	July	Aug.	Sept.	Oct.	Nov.	Dec.	Total
1977	204.0	193.0	213.1	204.8	211.5	201.8	191.3	198.8	201.7	205.6	195.4	196.6	2,418
1978	198.2	193.8	210.3	214.9	211.2	194.4	195.9	205.7	207.4	212.3	212.1	219.1	2,475
1979	207.9	200.8	232.1	216.7	223.3	210.7	202.9	202.8	210.0	213.8	206.0	207.6	2,535
1980	195.6	194.7	206.8	192.4	159.6	129.6	110.3	123.7	149.8	174.6	178.5	193.7	2,015
1981	193.5	169.7	200.4	180.9	175.9	158.2	161.5	159.7	168.4	170.0	157.7	125.5	2,021
1982	155.6	162.3	187.9	171.7	171.1	156.8	139.7	145.5	147.9	154.4	122.4	116.5	1,829
1983	155.2	153.9	170.1	160.5	171.1	164.6	154.4	146.7	159.6	174.5	189.4	160.2	1,936
1984	183.3	173.0	190.3	193.2	191.4	183.7	166.7	178.4	173.0	179.7	158.3	147.5	2,156
1985[1]	169.9	161.6	182.1	166.0	154.2	142.5	150.4	154.2	160.3	153.6	149.2	131.8	1,907
1986[1]	166.5	158.4	189.1	178.6	167.8	164.9							

[1] Preliminary.   *Source: Department of Commerce*   T.565

Consumption of Synthetic Rubber in the United States In Thousands of Metric Tons

Year	Jan.	Feb.	Mar.	Apr.	May	June	July	Aug.	Sept.	Oct.	Nov.	Dec.	Total
1977	217.6	203.6	232.6	203.1	218.8	208.6	161.1	209.8	209.0	205.7	190.9	203.4	2,464
1978	193.7	193.2	206.2	197.5	212.7	194.7	170.6	213.9	211.7	220.3	212.1	209.8	2,436
1979	226.0	201.4	224.4	201.5	212.0	179.6	176.5	202.3	187.9	202.8	174.5	163.3	2,341
1980	170.8	176.1	191.1	148.9	135.7	120.1	131.0	133.7	166.0	167.9	157.7	155.1	1,854
1981	153.0	166.7	194.0	144.9	167.1	154.1	144.7	165.0	163.5	163.8	141.1	131.9	1,890
1982	153.3	140.7	154.3	145.3	148.5	154.5	135.8	150.5	158.1	131.0	136.8	136.1	1,757
1983	131.7	140.2	158.2	146.3	146.2	156.7	135.6	170.3	170.5	180.4	158.2	147.2	1,828
1984	177.5	175.4	180.5	166.7	167.1	171.0	147.1	173.9	151.5	184.1	166.3	147.2	2,062
1985[1]	155.8	169.5	159.6	154.8	152.7	143.6	139.8	150.6	171.6	174.3	154.0	140.3	1,875
1986[1]	160.7	146.9	175.7	157.6	163.9	148.0							

[1] Preliminary.   *Source: Department of Commerce*   T.566

Exports of Synthetic Rubber from the United States In Thousands of Long Tons

Year	Jan.	Feb.	Mar.	Apr.	May	June	July	Aug.	Sept.	Oct.	Nov.	Dec.	Total
1977	19.11	20.97	24.34	21.48	22.06	20.78	24.72	14.86	26.15	14.59	13.80	17.13	239.98
1978	16.94	18.86	22.55	19.48	24.90	22.28	19.35	20.04	20.77	22.22	23.81	23.77	254.96
1979	23.62	22.29	27.74	29.43	28.74	34.61	34.51	39.37	34.90	38.61	36.53	34.76	385.11
1980	31.46	34.48	41.98	41.68	46.88	37.33	36.54	30.46	25.51	33.45	30.72	32.31	422.78
1981	31.21	31.65	38.73	31.77	32.00	28.55	26.27	21.97	24.40	23.94	22.49	21.65	334.63
1982	27.76	23.46	31.18	26.53	24.73	25.23	20.40	22.04	22.83	21.13	20.47	18.86	284.62
1983	20.24	18.61	24.44	24.91	31.66	24.37	20.15	21.08	22.01	20.14	23.75	23.67	275.01
1984	24.12	22.22	28.09	29.13	29.42	28.02	29.58	30.24	29.95	25.54	25.92	25.68	327.91
1985	23.86	22.68	28.94	26.23	30.38	27.25	22.21	24.95	27.60	25.33	22.13	25.44	306.93
1986	23.49	27.66	24.00	35.39	25.71	25.04	26.34	31.77					

Source: Department of Commerce   T.567

Production of Auto. Pneumatic Casings[2] & Truck & Bus Retail Sales[1] in the U.S. In Ths. of Casings

| Year | Total Production of Tires | | | | | | | | | | | | | Sales[1] |
	Jan.	Feb.	Mar.	Apr.	May	June	July	Aug.	Sept.	Oct.	Nov.	Dec.	Total	
1977	20,638	20,094	22,640	20,087	19,512	20,734	15,050	19,495	19,321	18,926	17,716	17,425	231,638	3,675
1978	18,290	18,319	18,987	18,828	19,148	18,946	15,108	19,245	19,155	20,497	18,299	18,869	223,406	4,110
1979	20,352	19,592	21,807	18,609	18,544	15,603	14,904	16,911	15,985	17,775	14,480	12,340	206,687	3,480
1980	15,188	15,059	15,082	13,678	11,370	10,716	10,206	12,057	13,911	15,790	12,861	13,346	159,263	2,487
1981	15,434	15,614	16,805	15,438	15,157	15,447	14,321	15,443	15,894	16,604	13,750	11,855	181,762	2,260
1982	14,866	15,387	17,051	15,077	14,856	15,669	12,293	14,835	15,528	15,381	13,585	13,972	178,500	2,559
1983	15,497	14,992	15,370	16,325	15,653	15,473	12,570	16,440	16,360	16,734	15,136	15,483	186,923	3,129
1984	16,749	17,498	19,122	16,988	18,043	18,557	15,546	18,078	17,333	19,136	16,645	15,682	209,375	3,485
1985[3]	18,381	17,375	18,704	17,388	16,781	15,216	12,989	16,635	16,844	17,626	15,198	13,786	195,972	3,913
1986[3]	16,306	15,966	16,968	16,037	15,003	14,647	14,203	16,112						

[1] Domestic & imports, in thousands.   [2] Passenger cars, buses, trucks & motorcycle tires.   [3] Preliminary.
Sources: Rubber Manufacturers' Association; Motor Vehicle Manufacturing Association   T.568

Stocks of Auto. Pneumatic Casings & Passenger[1] Car Retail Sales in the U.S. In Ths. of Casings

| Year | Total Stocks of Tires | | | | | | | | | | | | Sales[1] |
	Jan. 1	Feb. 1	Mar. 1	Apr. 1	May 1	June 1	July 1	Aug. 1	Sept. 1	Oct. 1	Nov. 1	Dec. 1	
1977	34,768	39,010	43,212	45,616	45,832	46,231	44,887	43,460	45,229	44,542	43,841	45,176	11,185
1978	47,181	51,523	54,621	51,986	50,006	49,277	46,293	44,280	44,057	41,796	40,135	40,394	11,312
1979	43,472	47,212	51,284	52,223	53,540	53,033	46,362	49,397	48,422	46,002	44,357	44,546	10,671
1980	44,873	46,760	49,993	50,471	49,220	46,972	42,817	40,079	37,057	33,730	32,112	32,363	8,979
1981	33,298	41,226	44,402	45,217	44,713	43,480	41,445	39,998	39,601	38,986	39,487	41,112	8,536
1982	40,863	42,904	46,254	47,817	46,583	45,337	43,475	40,763	40,192	38,685	38,116	38,436	7,980
1983	39,955	43,839	45,483	50,287	51,921	42,395	39,622	36,989	35,541	32,854	31,530	31,676	9,182
1984	33,340	35,450	37,615	38,529	38,026	37,693	37,678	36,365	37,199	37,685	37,277	37,995	10,394
1985[2]	39,623	41,948	45,905	48,875	49,168	49,063	46,909	44,349	43,553	41,514	40,425	40,023	11,039
1986[2]	39,823	40,717	43,499	45,359	44,519	44,741	40,009	38,036	36,836				

[1] Domestic & imports, in thousands.   [2] Preliminary.   *Sources: Rubber Manufacturers' Association; Motor Vehicle Mfg. Association*   T.569

Rye

Rye is a cereal grass, providing grain used for livestock feed and for making flour and whiskey. U.S. production in 1986/87 is estimated at 20 million bushels, down two percent from the previous season. U.S. domestic output peaked at 33 million bushels in 1984/85, but has since declined as planted area and yields have fallen. Major producing states include South and North Dakota, Minnesota, and Georgia.

Domestic use of rye in 1986/87 is forecast to retreat slightly to 22.3 million bushels, from 23.5 million last season. More than half of this season's utilization is for animal feed.

U.S. imports are forecast at 1 million bushels, down from 1.7 million in 1985/86. The U.S also exports some rye and is expected to ship about 200,000 bushels in 1986/87.

Domestic stocks reached a record during 1984/85, with a carryout of 19.9 million bushels. Since then, there has been a slight stock drawdown. The 1986/87 carry-in was about 18.6 million bushels, while the season's carryout is forecast at 17.4 million bushels.

World output in 1985 was 29.6 million tonnes; no global production data for 1986 were available at this writing. The leading producer, accounting for over one-third of world output, is the USSR. Poland, East and West Germany, Czechoslovakia, and Canada also grow large quantities. World exports in 1985 amounted to 868,000 tonnes, most of which was supplied by Poland, Canada, and Denmark. The world's largest importer is Japan, which purchased 263,100 tonnes in 1985. East and West Germany, Finland, and the Netherlands are also noteworthy importers.

U.S. Government Price Support

The U.S. price-support loan rate for rye was $1.63 per bushel in 1986, down from $2.17 the year before. There is no target price for rye.

Futures Market

Rye futures are traded on the Winnipeg Commodity Exchange (WCE).

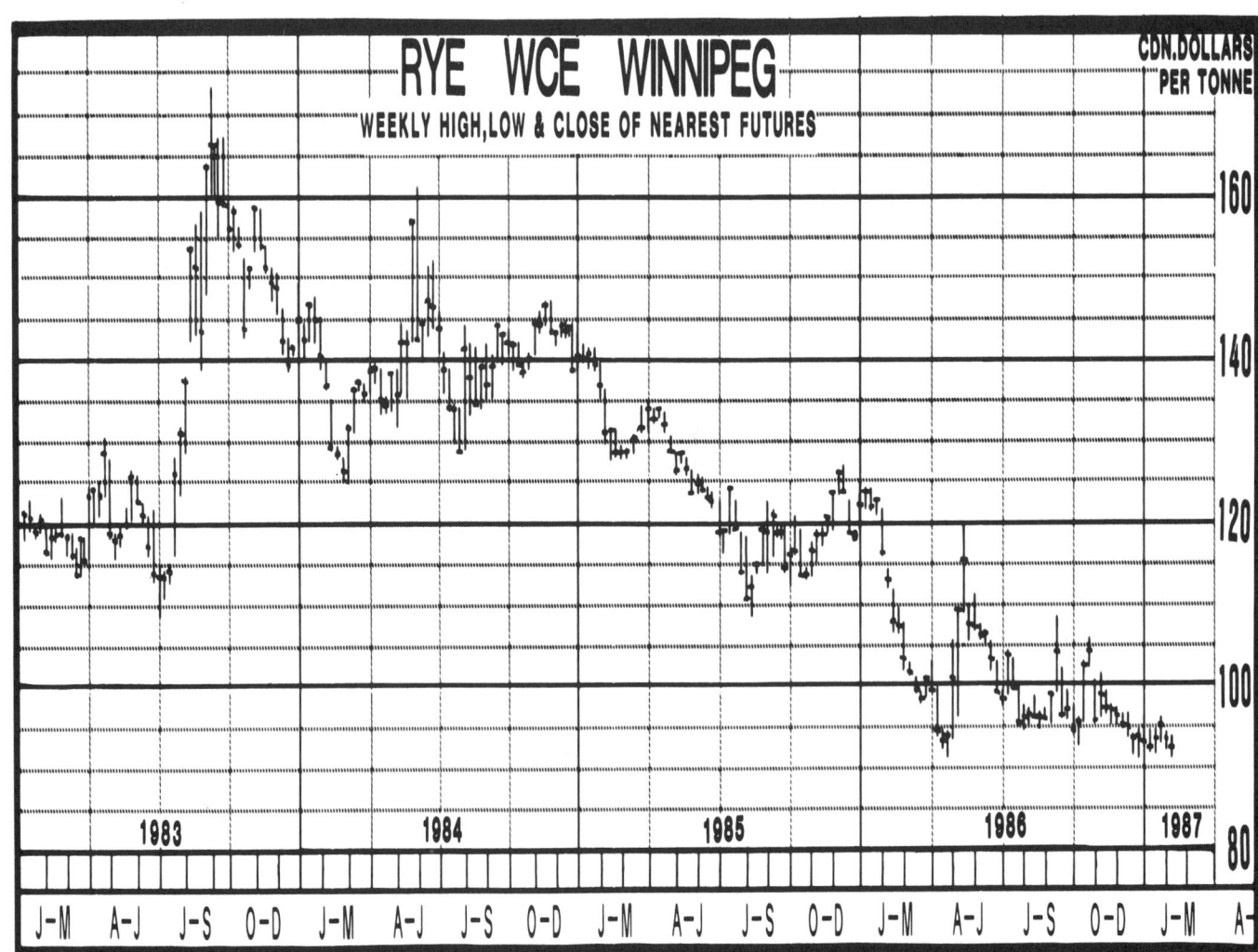

RYE WCE WINNIPEG
WEEKLY HIGH, LOW & CLOSE OF NEAREST FUTURES
CDN. DOLLARS PER TONNE

World Production of Rye   In Thousands of Metric Tons

Crop Year	Argentina	Austria	Canada	Czecho-slovakia	Denmark	France	Germany West	East	Hungary	Netherlands	Poland	Spain	Turkey	USSR	United States	World Total
1980–1	155	383	448	575	199	405	2,184	1,917	139	39	6,566	284	525	10,205	419	25,268
1981–2	149	320	927	544	208	342	1,793	1,797	116	29	6,731	212	520	9,500	478	24,373
1982–3	148	348	933	583	235	327	1,703	2,119	120	26	7,792	169	430	14,000	496	30,108
1983–4	130	348	828	751	315	293	1,646	2,092	136	26	8,781	253	380	14,600	689	31,421
1984–5[1]	140	381	663	710	608	359	1,983	2,502	170	25	9,500	325	360	13,400	825	32,747
1985–6[2]															524	
1986–7[2]															454	

[1] Preliminary.   [2] Estimate.   *Source: Foreign Agricultural Service, U.S.D.A.*   T.570

Salient Statistics of Rye in the United States

Year Begin. June 1	Supply						Disappearance							Total Disappearance	Acreage		Yield Per Harvested Acre Bushels
	Stocks, June 1						Domestic Use										
	Privately Owned[2]	Gov't.[3]	Total Stocks	Production	Imports	Total Supply	Food	Industry	Seed	Feed[5]	Total	Exports			Planted	Harvested for Grain	
						Thousands of Bushels									Mil. Acres		
1980–1	12,000	192	11,970	15,958	10	27,900	3,515	2,050	4,150	6,600	16,400	7,494	23,900	2,488	650	24.6
1981–2	4,000	145	4,030	18,187	432	22,600	3,458	2,242	4,160	8,200	18,100	1,529	19,600	2,566	685	26.6
1982–3			3,012	19,533	3,043	25,600	3,315	2,256	4,400	9,600	19,600	194	19,800	2,533	677	28.9
1983–4			5,822	27,116	1,600	34,500	3,500	2,100	4,800	11,800	22,200	1,000	23,200	2,707	896	30.3
1984–5			11,300	32,463	600	44,400	3,500	2,000	4,500	14,100	24,100	400	24,500	2,971	981	33.1
1985–6[1]			19,900	20,637	1,700	42,200	3,500	2,100	4,600	13,300	23,500	100	23,600	2,563	717	28.8
1986–7[4]			18,600	17,892	1,000	39,900	3,500	2,000	4,500	12,300	22,300	200	22,500	2,364	660	27.1

[1] Preliminary.   [2] Includes total loans.   [3] Uncommitted, gov't only.   [4] Forecast.   [5] Residual; approximates total feed use.
Source: Economics Research Service, U.S.D.A.   T.571

Production of Rye in the United States   In Thousands of Bushels

Year	Illinois	Indiana	Kansas	Michigan	Minnesota	Georgia	Nebraska	No. Dakota	Ohio	Oklahoma	Oregon	So. Dakota	Virginia	Texas	Wisconsin	So. Carolina
1979	391	208	504	625	2,275	2,310	770	4,200	155	910	144	5,700	384	513	368	609
1980	368	182	210	504	1,900	1,995	666	1,470	231	816	150	4,030	325	494	368	616
1981	336	234	252	532	2,883	2,730	924	2,560	150	680	150	3,220	364	475	408	726
1982	299	260	240	522	3,300	1,470	1,269	2,400	155	736	116	4,680	364	504	300	621
1983	336	270	220	600	4,960	1,470	1,265	4,320	210	780	100	8,740	312	450	300	320
1984	308	336	312	588	6,650	1,760	1,392	5,400	175	704	140	10,800	378	240	216	546
1985	256	308	300	651	3,300	2,070	1,242	2,640	172	828	111	4,440	312	400	234	532
1986[1]	210	280	210	713	1,050	1,785	1,035	3,680	175	840	111	4,140	364	190	168	391

[1] Preliminary.   *Source: Crop Reporting Board, U.S.D.A.*   T.572

Month-End Open Interest of Rye Futures in Winnipeg   In 20 Tonne Units

Year	Jan.	Feb.	Mar.	Apr.	May	June	July	Aug.	Sept.	Oct.	Nov.	Dec.
1980	4,648	5,028	5,379	6,172	3,313	5,229	5,348	4,839	5,814	6,106	4,250	3,428
1981	3,876	4,811	3,704	3,640	2,948	3,368	5,028	6,440	5,251	2,516	4,404	3,828
1982	3,739	3,622	3,219	3,583	4,426	3,008	2,268	4,286	5,250	4,052	3,773	3,244
1983	3,227	3,628	3,097	4,625	4,834	4,935	7,883	7,915	3,665	4,494	3,110	3,054
1984	2,224	4,566	3,980	3,883	3,731	3,023	2,888	5,430	7,098	6,320	5,894	4,158
1985	4,267	4,826	4,175	4,227	3,893	3,919	4,031	5,022	4,872	5,478	4,289	3,786
1986	4,287	4,335	3,302	4,211	3,039	2,553	2,900	3,447	3,377	2,862	2,437	2,032

Source: Winnipeg Commodity Exchange   T.577

RYE

U.S. Rye Crop Production Reports and CCC Operations   In Thousands of Bushels

Year Begin. June 1	Official Crop Reports				National Average —Support Rate—		Placed Under Loan	Direct Pur- chases	Total	Acqu- ired by CCC	Ending Carry- over[1]	Total Stocks Ending May 31		
	July 1	Aug. 1	Dec. 1	Final	$ Per Bushel	% of Parity						CCC Uncom- mitted	Privately Owned[3] Under Loan[4]	Other
1977–8	17,787	18,242	16,998	16,543	1.70	61	—	—	900	—	4,418	—	—	—
1978–9	28,518	28,567	26,160	24,065	1.70	56	—	—	3,000	—	4,137	—	—	—
1979–0	23,638	23,736	24,549	21,887	1.79	49			2,000	—	8,973		—	
1980–1	15,784	16,189	16,265	15,958	1.91	51			450	—	11,970		—	
1981–2	16,743	17,083	18,621	18,187	2.04	48			500	—	4,030			
1982–3	20,119	19,924	20,817	19,533	2.17	48			1,700	1,400	3,012			
1983–4	26,058	25,698	28,152	27,116	2.25	47			5,300	4,600	5,822			
1984–5[2]	29,903	30,184	32,392	32,463	2.17	45			10,000	8,900	11,300			
1985–6[2]	19,255	19,298	20,637	20,637	2.17	47					19,900			
1986–7[2]	—	17,892			2.17						18,600			

[1] Old-crop rye under loan at end of crop year.   [2] Preliminary.   [3] Derived by subtracting CCC stocks & loans outstanding from ending carryover.   [4] Includes previous crops under reseal.   *Source: Economic Research Service, U.S.D.A.*   T.573

RYE   CASH   PRICE   MINNEAPOLIS

CENTS PER BUSHEL

Monthly Average Prices No. 2 RYE

Average Price of Cash Rye No. 2 at Minneapolis   In Cents per Bushel

Year	July	Aug.	Sept.	Oct.	Nov.	Dec.	Jan.	Feb.	Mar.	Apr.	May	June	Average
1979–0	279	247	235	257	249	235	245	235	235	218	244	266	247
1980–1	297	287	292	307	344	340	352	363	389	387	396	394	346
1981–2	352	330	356	371	374	334	394	414	375	426	410	397	378
1982–3	342	276	286	260	261	256	251	246	231	250	244	232	261
1983–4	227	256	265	256	254	252	251	245	250	260	258	244	252
1984–5	227	209	207	206	221	227	231	230	235	236	235	248	226
1985–6	210	215	223	233	248	259	246	228	226	226	219	178	226
1986–7	156	151	160	168	173								

Source: Economic Research Service, U.S.D.A.   T.575

High, Low & Closing Prices of May Rye Futures in Winnipeg   In Canadian Dollars per Tonne

Year of Delivery		Year Prior to Delivery							Delivery Year					Life of Delivery Range
		June	July	Aug.	Sept.	Oct.	Nov.	Dec.	Jan.	Feb.	Mar.	Apr.	May	
1980	High	154.00	188.00	167.50	189.40	191.00	181.00	175.00	192.50	195.00	205.50	196.50	195.50	205.50
	Low	117.50	148.50	139.50	159.40	171.50	170.50	160.80	163.50	182.00	176.00	173.80	168.50	117.50
	Close	143.50	158.00	159.40	184.00	181.50	172.10	169.40	183.00	186.00	187.60	178.50	195.50	—
1981	High	193.50	205.90	194.50	205.70	231.00	250.50	244.00	242.00	244.50	242.50	232.50	199.50	250.50
	Low	170.50	189.00	182.10	192.00	201.80	228.00	216.50	223.00	225.50	223.40	176.00	186.70	170.50
	Close	192.90	194.00	194.20	203.00	230.00	242.80	237.00	225.50	244.50	230.20	189.50	194.00	—
1982	High	167.00	181.50	215.90	233.50	218.00	195.60	187.00	185.20	187.30	171.00	178.00	180.90	233.50
	Low	151.20	154.90	183.50	211.20	193.00	181.50	169.80	168.70	169.50	158.50	160.00	163.40	151.20
	Close	151.20	181.50	215.90	217.70	194.20	183.40	171.00	182.00	169.50	160.30	170.00	165.50	—
1983	High	162.00	162.00	152.50	150.50	139.50	140.20	133.00	126.30	123.20	123.00	130.00	126.00	162.00
	Low	162.00	152.00	138.00	133.80	128.00	129.00	121.00	119.80	116.40	115.30	118.10	116.50	115.30
	Close	162.00	152.50	145.00	133.80	128.20	130.20	121.00	123.10	120.50	122.70	118.70	122.50	—
1984	High	—	—	174.00	176.00	173.30	165.80	158.30	150.00	141.00	140.00	139.30	157.00	176.00
	Low	—	—	154.40	169.50	154.40	156.60	146.00	140.70	125.10	129.20	134.00	131.50	125.10
	Close	—	—	170.10	170.50	162.50	157.70	148.90	141.00	129.30	138.20	135.50	151.50	—
1985	High	—	—	156.00	158.70	156.90	157.20	154.80	145.40	142.30	134.60	133.80	128.80	158.70
	Low	—	—	152.20	152.90	152.20	153.00	145.20	143.00	132.00	132.30	128.30	122.80	122.80
	Close	—	—	153.00	157.70	152.70	154.10	145.20	143.00	132.60	133.70	128.30	122.80	—
1986	High	—	—	131.70	130.80	128.00	132.50	134.00	126.90	118.40	107.00	102.20	116.00	131.70
	Low	—	—	121.50	124.50	121.40	125.00	126.30	119.50	106.60	100.70	91.70	96.30	91.70
	Close	—	—	128.30	124.50	125.00	132.10	126.30	119.70	107.50	102.50	100.50	107.20	—
1987	High	—	—	101.00	102.50	105.00	104.50	103.00						
	Low	—	—	100.50	97.40	99.50	100.80	96.00						
	Close	—	—	101.00	100.40	101.00	103.10	98.20						

Source: Winnipeg Commodity Exchange   T.576

Rye Under Price Support Through the End of the Month
(Cumulative Total from Current Season's Crop)   In Thousands of Bushels

Year	July	Aug.	Sept.	Oct.	Nov.	Dec.	Jan.	Feb.	Mar.	Apr.	May	June	Total
1979–0	5	338	765	1,106	1,313	1,397	1,592	1,653	1,790	1,882	1,900	1,905	1,905
1980–1	—	97	240	297	348	384	396	399	402	406	406	406	
1981–2	36	264	359	398	424	439	448	456	456	456	456	456	
1982–3	7	344	771	1,008	1,096	1,193	1,324	1,369	1,588	1,709	1,711	1,712	
1983–4	83	1,819	2,228	3,533	3,885	4,199	4,577	4,862	5,141	5,228	5,254	5,256	
1984–5	68	3,581	6,661	8,224	8,653	8,911	9,655	9,830	9,996	10,078	10,066	10,070	
1985–6	567	1,769	2,836	3,516	3,728	3,816	3,955	3,996	4,012				
1986–7	147	1,337	2,249	4,627	5,022								

Source: U.S. Department of Agriculture   T.578

Salt

World salt production was estimated at 188,000 short tons in 1986, an increase of 0.5 percent over 1985. The U.S. continued as the largest producing country, accounting for about 40,000 short tons, or 21 percent of global output. The USSR and China each accounted for about 10 percent of production. West Germany contributed nearly seven percent and Canada six percent.

Partial data for 1986 suggest U.S. consumption was 46,000 short tons, 15 percent above output. The difference was made up by imports, estimated at 6,-000 tons; 40 percent originated in Canada, 25 percent in Mexico, and 15 percent in the Bahamas. Salt from brine and in bulk are subjected to an American tariff. For most-favored nations, salt from brine pays a rate of 3.7 percent *ad valorem* and in bulk, 0.4 percent *ad valorem*. For all other nations, rate from brine is 20 percent *ad valorem* and in bulk, 26 percent. Salt in other forms enters the U.S. from most-favored nations duty-free; that from other nations is assessed at 11 cents per hundredweight.

The average value per ton, f.o.b. mine, for vacuum and open pan salt climbed from about $80 in 1981 to $92.62 in 1984, then receded to $90 in 1985; prices in 1986 were not expected to change much. Solar salt's average value per ton ranged from $18.37 to $21.47 during 1981–85, settling at $20 in 1985. The average value per ton of salt from brine, in contract, peaked at $6.21 in 1982 and then slid steadily to $4.50 in 1985; a further decline seemed likely during 1986.

World Production of All Salt In Thousands of Short Tons

Year	Brazil	Canada	China	France	West Germany	India	Italy	Japan	Mexico	Nether- lands	Poland	Spain	United Kingdom	United States	USSR	World Total
1978	3,637	7,112	21,528	6,926	13,953	7,385	5,436	1,183	6,212	3,240	4,843	3,714	8,058	42,896	15,983	185,462
1979	3,918	7,585	16,281	8,882	16,634	7,756	6,249	1,189	6,800	4,355	4,882	3,801	8,620	45,820	15,763	191,107
1980	4,231	7,748	19,048	7,831	12,562	8,828	5,806	1,226	7,248	3,818	4,997	3,868	7,887	40,351	16,094	186,156
1981	3,974	7,981	20,194	7,315	13,824	9,845	5,039	1,105	8,767	3,944	4,708	4,072	7,408	38,907	16,755	189,198
1982	4,105	8,752	18,060	7,389	12,102	7,763	5,074	1,065	6,130	3,517	4,251	3,626	8,418	37,894	17,416	179,923
1983[1]	4,615	9,482	17,780	7,662	11,466	7,730	5,007	1,323	6,287	3,444	3,997	3,481	6,957	34,573	17,857	175,563
1984[2]	4,690	11,347	17,600	7,860	12,300	8,306	4,688	1,300	6,600	4,000	4,000	3,400	7,160	39,225	18,200	185,132
1985[2]		11,500	18,000	7,800	12,300	8,300	4,600		6,500		4,000		7,100	39,700	18,500	186,900

[1] Preliminary. [2] Estimate. *Source: Bureau of Mines*   T.581

Salient Statistics of the Salt Industry in the United States In Thousands of Short Tons

Year	Net Import Reliance as a % of Apparent Consumption	Avg. Value F.O.B. Mine Vacuum & Open Pan $ Ton	Evaporated (Mfg.) Bulk Open & Vacu- um Pans	Solar	Pressed Blocks	Total Evapor- ated	Rock Salt Bulk	Pressed Block	Total Salt Rock	Salt in Brine	Total Salt	Value[3] Mil- lion $	Im- ports for Con- sump- tion	Exports Total	Exports To Canada	Ap- parent Con- sump- tion
1978	10	58.86	3,463	2,001	381	5,845	14,630	58	14,688	22,336	42,869	499.3	5,380	776	750	47,473
1979	10	61.64	3,726	2,104	391	6,221	14,827	64	14,891	24,681	45,793	538.4	5,275	697	681	50,371
1980	7	76.44	3,587	2,334	393	6,314	11,742	65	11,806	22,231	40,352	656.2	5,263	831	800	44,784
1981	8	79.68	3,500	2,298	404	6,201	11,809	62	11,871	20,835	38,907	637.6	4,319	1,046	1,011	42,180
1982	11	86.72	3,379	2,478	447	6,305	13,431	72	13,503	18,086	37,894	671.4	5,451	1,001	957	42,344
1983	18	87.39	3,309	1,962	408	5,680	9,867	73	9,941	18,952	34,573	597.1	5,997	517	475	40,053
1984[1]	15	92.62	3,322	2,345	542	6,209	13,276	71	13,348	19,669	39,225	675.1	7,545	820	792	45,950
1985[2]	12	90.00									39,700		6,600	1,200		45,100

[1] Preliminary. [2] Estimate. [3] Values are f.o.b. mine or refinery & do not include cost of cooperage or containers. [4] Or Grainers. *Source: Bureau of Mines*
T.582

Salt Sold or Used by Producers in the U.S. by Classes & Consumers or Uses In Thousands of Short Tons

Year	Chlorine, Caustic Soda Ash	Flour Proces- sors	Tex- tile & Dyeing	Meat Packers, Tanners, Etc.[2]	Can- ning	Bak- ing	U.S. Govt.	Feed Dealers	Feed Mixers	Rubber	Oil	Paper & Pulp	Metals	Water Soften- er Mfg.[3]	Grocery Stores	Flour Proc.	High- way Use
1978	23,735	91	182	540	254	111	86	1,197	654	96	451	221	346	764	1,057	91	8,487
1979	26,200	95	188	546	280	119	78	1,194	723	99	550	194	356	810	1,140	95	8,742
1980	23,941	92	177	546	287	113	121	1,172	662	95	709	230	272	686	995	92	6,389
1981	22,241	82	180	491	230	109	126	1,147	646	113	820	246	299	700	1,021	82	6,725
1982	18,861	83	165	550	204	109	152	967	699	51	1,035	209	294	718	1,053	83	9,053
1983	19,950	86	171	531	211	114	563	977	628	45	918	274	242	707	987	86	5,041
1984[1]	19,701	79	135	537	242	124	1,131	923	590	41	860	307	309	892	859	79	7,610

[1] Preliminary. [2] Also casing mfg. [3] Also service companies. *Source: Bureau of Mines*
T.583

Sheep & Lambs

Beginning sheep inventories in the 29 major sheep-raising countries in 1986 were projected at 690 million head, only marginally higher than in 1985. Australia accounted for 22 percent of the total, the Soviet Union claimed 20 percent, and New Zealand 10 percent. In all three countries, the year-over-year change in beginning inventories was negligible.

World production of sheepmeat was forecast to decline in 1986, after increasing over the last three years. World trade was also expected to fall. Australian exports were projected to expand by 10 percent; New Zealand was projected to show exports down three percent in 1986. The two again supplied over 70 percent of the world's exports. World consumption was forecast to decline slightly in 1986.

Production of sheepmeat in New Zealand was ex-pected to decrease by roughly eight percent in 1986. New Zealand has been having difficulty exporting sheepmeat to its major markets in Europe because of an increase in production throughout the European Community. To expand exports, New Zealand has started promoting further-processed lamb products in several Pacific Rim nations and exports of live sheep to Iran and Mexico. New Zealand produces sheep primarily for meat consumption; Australia produces them for wool. Australian sheep inventories expanded in 1986 as farmers continued restocking for wool production. As a result, sheepmeat production also increased.

U.S. lamb prices reached record highs again in 1986, and were quite volatile. 1986 prices averaged $68–$69 per cwt., about the same as last year.

World Sheep Numbers in Specified Countries   In Millions of Head

Year	India	Argentina	Aus-tralia	Brazil	Peru	France	New Zealand	Spain[2]	Turkey	United Kingdom	United States	South Africa	Uru-guay	USSR	China[4]	World
1980	40.5	32.0	136.0	18.0	13.5		63.5	16.1	46.0	21.7	12.7	34.9	23.3	143.6		653
1981	40.7	30.0	134.4	18.0	13.5		68.8	16.5	48.6	21.6	12.9	33.8	24.1	141.6	187.0	657
1982	48.0	29.0	138.0	18.0	13.0	13.1	69.9	17.1	49.6	22.2	13.0	33.6	23.2	142.4		671
1983	49.5	33.5	133.2			12.1	70.3	17.5	50.0	22.9	12.1	32.0	23.3	142.2		672
1984	51.1	33.8	139.2			11.9	70.3	17.6	49.0	23.3	11.5	31.3	23.3	145.3		685
1985	52.8	29.3	149.7			11.6	69.7	17.5	48.5	23.9	10.4	30.3	22.8	142.9		689
1986[1]	54.5	28.9	156.3			11.2	67.8	17.3	48.0	24.5	9.9	29.5	24.8	140.5		692
1987[3]	55.5	28.5	160.0			10.6	73.2	17.4	47.5	25.2	10.0	29.6	26.7	140.0		704

[1] Preliminary.   [2] One year old & older.   [3] Estimate.   [4] Mainland.   *Source: Foreign Agricultural Service, U.S.D.A.*   T.584

Salient Statistics of Sheep & Lambs in the United States

Year	On Hand Jan. 1 — Mil. Head —	Lambs Saved — Mil. Head —	In Shipments	Market-ings[2] Ths. Head	Slaughter Farm	Slaughter Total[4]	Production Mil. Lbs.	Market-ings[2] Mil. Lbs.	Value of Production	Cash Receipts[3]	Value of Home Consumption Millions of Dollars	Gross Income	Farm Value (1/1) All	$ per Head
1979	12.4	8.0	2,143	7,683	172	5,189	704.6	812	406.8	470.4	11.8	482.2	891.0	72.10
1980	12.7	8.3	2,216	8,138	166	5,742	746.3	852	402.7	470.8	11.6	482.4	992.1	78.20
1981	12.9	8.8	1,885	8,613	189	6,197	772.4	884	359.1	416.1	12.3	428.4	903.3	69.80
1982	13.0	8.6	2,115	9,482	195	6,643	785.4	1,033	355.7	445.1	13.0	458.1	739.6	57.00
1983	12.1	8.2	1,838	8,924	171	6,792	767.6		356.7	426.4	10.6	437.0	628.6	51.80
1984	11.5	7.8	1,848	8,799	141	6,900	692.2		375.6	465.5	11.1	476.6	598.9	58.10
1985[1]	10.4	7.4				6,300							637.9	61.10
1986[1]	9.9												669.9	67.40

[1] Preliminary.   [2] Excludes interfarm sales.   [3] Includes receipts from marketings & from sales of farm slaughter meats.   [4] Includes all commercial & farm.   *Source: Crop Reporting Board, U.S.D.A.*   T.585

Sheep and Lambs on Farms in the United States, January 1   Thousands of Head

Year	Minnesota	Cali-fornia	Colorado	Idaho	Missouri	Montana	New Mexico	Ohio	South Dakota	Texas	Utah	Wyoming	Iowa	Total[2]	Total[1] Stock
1979	255	1,150	795	466	126	475	604	350	740	2,415	486	1,080	380	12,365	10,786
1980	264	1,175	870	468	123	574	660	320	783	2,400	625	1,050	408	12,687	11,065
1981	295	1,205	810	512	138	595	650	310	780	2,360	650	1,110	437	12,936	11,287
1982	335	1,210	710	498	133	616	615	313	750	2,400	636	1,130	485	12,966	11,402
1983	300	1,115	750	429	126	560	610	295	680	2,225	590	1,060	457	12,140	10,385
1984	255	1,115	690	383	128	564	589	265	740	1,970	568	1,090	425	11,487	9,769
1985[3]	255	1,065	675	313	123	515	538	265	639	1,810	515	860	360	10,443	8,847
1986[3]	213	1,065	600	320	101	423	525	275	540	1,810	484	819	350	9,932	8,440

[1] Stock sheep & lambs; does not include sheep & lambs on feed for market.   [2] Includes sheep & lambs on feed for market and stock sheep & lambs.   [3] Preliminary.   *Source: Crop Reporting Board, U.S.D.A.*   T.586

SHEEP AND LAMBS

Average Wholesale Price of Lambs at Omaha   In Dollars Per 100 Pounds

Year	Jan.	Feb.	Mar.	Apr.	May	June	July	Aug.	Sept.	Oct.	Nov.	Dec.	Average
1979	73.75	71.25	61.25	70.50	70.75	65.00	61.52	60.62	67.00	64.50	65.00	67.75	66.58
1980	64.60	62.71	64.64	56.12	67.62	65.78	66.99	66.98	64.88	61.77	55.67	53.13	59.81
1981	50.00	53.50	55.25	59.25	65.00	66.42	57.33	54.10	48.53	49.86	45.27	45.10	52.23
1982	48.92	51.58	58.52	58.67	62.56	60.28	56.16	50.71	48.93	46.92	45.46	47.62	53.03
1983	53.50	58.50	59.75	58.75	59.00	53.00	51.12	49.25	48.50	51.75	56.00	57.75	54.74
1984	60.50	58.75	58.75	60.50	62.25	61.75	61.50	62.76	63.58	63.35	62.98	60.08	61.39
1985[1]		66.92	67.75	69.50	74.25	72.56	71.98	71.42	68.94	63.32	62.50	60.62	68.41
1986[1]	61.75	68.50	67.00	68.00	80.75	74.71	70.50	66.16	62.45	57.23	65.17		

[1] Preliminary.   *Source: Economic Research Service, U.S.D.A.*   T.587

Federally Inspected Slaughter of Sheep & Lambs in the United States   In Thousands of Head

Year	Jan.	Feb.	Mar.	Apr.	May	June	July	Aug.	Sept.	Oct.	Nov.	Dec.	Total
1979	391	354	431	425	421	371	384	415	410	455	386	389	4,833
1980	448	419	470	466	454	400	420	427	466	510	415	468	5,363
1981	488	426	488	512	426	440	439	467	546	558	476	522	5,789
1982	510	490	570	———	1,493	———	———	1,577	———	———	1,634	———	6,273
1983	509	457	616	509	508	508	497	585	595	580	510	536	6,412
1984	540	548	586	592	558	500	511	561	528	588	524	514	6,549
1985[1]	544	473	564	512	494	423	485	496	480	554	460	490	5,976
1986[1]	507	441	524	477	417	406	432	426	495	495	401		

[1] Preliminary.   *Source: Economic Research Service, U.S.D.A.*   T.588

Cold Storage Holdings of Lamb and Mutton, on 1st of Month   In Thousands of Pounds

Year	Jan.	Feb.	Mar.	Apr.	May	June	July	Aug.	Sept.	Oct.	Nov.	Dec.
1979	11,716	10,965	10,827	12,022	12,072	12,897	11,483	11,943	11,763	10,951	11,697	11,071
1980	10,751	10,302	9,464	7,945	8,475	8,995	10,229	10,263	8,880	8,336	8,165	9,779
1981	9,142	8,997	7,843	7,823	10,196	10,403	12,297	12,564	13,694	13,311	12,676	11,362
1982	10,540	9,569	8,449	8,783	—	—	8,266	—	—	8,571	—	—
1983	8,653	7,682	7,673	8,218	8,331	8,839	8,691	7,717	8,815	8,622	9,092	10,270
1984	10,701	8,312	7,542	8,057	9,123	8,839	8,678	8,404	8,026	8,889	8,403	7,890
1985	7,066	7,339	6,840	6,547	7,644	8,068	8,931	9,193	9,541	9,237	10,033	12,525
1986[1]	12,766	11,615	13,813	11,811	12,754	12,742	14,068	14,318	15,459	14,450	14,641	13,803

[1] Preliminary.   *Source: Crop Reporting Board, U.S.D.A.*   T.589

Average Price Received by Farmers for Sheep in the U.S.   In Dollars per 100 Pounds

Year	Jan.	Feb.	Mar.	Apr.	May	June	July	Aug.	Sept.	Oct.	Nov.	Dec.	Average[1]
1979	26.20	26.30	28.10	31.00	27.90	24.00	25.10	24.30	26.50	27.20	26.30	25.00	26.30
1980	27.40	30.50	26.90	21.90	21.70	20.30	17.80	19.40	21.40	18.90	19.90	20.80	21.30
1981	27.40	29.00	26.10	23.40	19.50	20.30	23.00	20.40	20.30	19.70	19.10	19.20	21.20
1982	25.10	21.30	27.20	22.20	21.00	22.00	21.00	18.60	16.50	15.20	15.30	16.80	19.50
1983	21.30	21.90	20.80	17.40	15.20	14.50	16.20	15.50	12.80	13.80	15.10	17.00	15.70
1984	18.20	19.80	18.70	16.30	13.00	13.80	16.80	17.30	15.90	15.20	18.10	24.30	16.40
1985[2]	26.50	24.10	26.20	24.70	22.90	22.00	27.20	26.10	25.30	21.50	23.60	26.60	23.90
1986[2]	29.90	26.10	23.00	24.90	24.10	25.90	26.70	26.40	27.30	25.50	26.20	27.00	26.10

[1] Weighted average by quantities sold.   [2] Preliminary.   *Source: Crop Reporting Board, U.S.D.A.*   T.590

Average Price Received by Farmers for Lambs in the U.S.   In Dollars per 100 Pounds

Year	Jan.	Feb.	Mar.	Apr.	May	June	July	Aug.	Sept.	Oct.	Nov.	Dec.	Average[1]
1979	74.10	69.90	64.90	70.40	69.70	66.40	64.00	61.40	66.70	65.70	64.90	66.90	66.70
1980	66.40	64.40	67.10	59.20	60.30	64.60	65.30	65.80	66.70	64.30	59.90	58.40	63.60
1981	54.10	55.40	56.50	58.80	63.10	65.00	59.50	56.20	50.40	50.60	47.40	47.50	54.90
1982	50.40	53.30	60.30	61.50	63.50	57.80	56.30	52.90	50.90	49.10	47.70	50.90	53.10
1983	55.50	60.50	63.20	61.50	59.60	54.20	49.80	48.30	47.50	50.90	55.80	58.90	53.90
1984	60.00	59.20	58.20	60.60	59.50	57.50	58.60	61.00	61.80	62.40	63.30	61.90	60.10
1985[2]	63.40	64.70	68.00	68.40	72.40	69.70	70.80	70.80	70.20	67.80	66.00	62.70	67.70
1986[2]	63.90	67.00	64.90	69.10	76.30	74.00	71.90	69.50	67.60	62.50	69.30	73.00	69.10

[1] Weighted average by quantities sold.   [2] Preliminary.   *Source: Crop Reporting Board, U.S.D.A.*   T.591

Silk

World production of raw silk and waste was 65,000 tonnes in 1985; there were no estimates of 1986 output at this writing. Output in China, the leading producer, was estimated at 40,000 tonnes in 1985. Chinese production has been on an uptrend in recent years; export opportunities have improved with rising world demand. Japanese output in 1985 was about 10,000 tonnes. Silk, once the second major crop in Japan after rice, has declined in importance in the last two decades with falling output. The USSR and North Korea each produced about 4,000 tonnes of silk in 1985; India was also a major supplier.

Global trade in raw silk amounts to about 30,000 tonnes annually. Shipments by China, the major exporter, have expanded in recent years and currently amount to over 17,000 tonnes annually. World prices are strongly influenced by Chinese prices. Other major exporters are India, North Korea, and Hong Kong. The largest importers are Japan, Hong Kong, and Italy, all of which are prominent silk textile producers. The U.S. imports over 700 tonnes of raw silk each year.

Salient Statistics of Silk in the United States

Year	World Produc- tion (Raw) Million Lbs.	U.S. Unmanufactured[1] Imports[2] (By Country of Origin)										U.S. Silk Imports[2] Raw Waste —Mil. Lbs.—		Mill Consumption	
		Total Imports	Brazil	United Kingdom	Hong Kong	India	Italy	Japan	Switzer- land	China	Korea			Total Mil. Pounds	Per Capita Pounds
					Thousands of Pounds										
1971	90	1,702	38	—	—	—	345	1,154	—	—	74	.3	1.4	1.7	.10
1972	93	2,139	76	—	—	—	227	1,339	—	—	106	.6	1.6	2.1	—
1973	95	3,342	79	13	—	—	472	2,197	—	—	15	.6	2.8	3.3	—
1974	99	2,593	145	0	—	—	397	1,476	—	—	107	.4	2.2	2.6	—
1975	104	968	176	1	—	—	0	386	—	353	0	.6	.4	1.0	—
1976	106	2,653	247	1	—	—	98	1,727	—	457	—	.7	1.9	2.8	—
1977	108	1,621	106	0	—	—	0	1,230	—	268	0	.4	1.2	1.6	—
1978	112	1,989	182	0	—	107	1	918	—	607	119	.7	1.3	2.0	—
1979	121	1,565	193	—	—	—	—	602	—	747	—	.8	.8	1.5	—
1980	123	1,053	139	—	5	—	—	108	—	713	71	.5	.6	1.5	—
1981	126	1,983	176	—	29	—	223	175	—	1,280	0	.8	1.2	2.0	—
1982[3]	121	4,219	224	—	94	—	223	256	—	3,311	0	1.4	2.8	2.0	—
1983[4]	121													2.0	—
1984[4]	121													3.0	
1985[4]														3.0	

[1] In skeins, wild or tussah, cocoons, and waste.   [2] Imports for consumption.   [3] Preliminary.   [4] Estimate.
Sources: Department of Commerce; Textile Organon

T.592

Raw Silk Deliveries in the U.S.   In Bales (132 Lbs.—60 Kilos)

Year	Jan.	Feb.	Mar.	Apr.	May	June	July	Aug.	Sept.	Oct.	Nov.	Dec.	Total
1971	247	205	187	277	228	129	192	241	247	355	165	253	2,726
1972	233	184	308	198	141	195	182	445	529	209	229	313	3,166
1973[1]	556	355	450	499	393	119	577	214	71	93	105	246	3,678
1974	124	305	233	277	175	288	269	139	97	302	151	96	2,456
1975	190	188	410	393	394	219	380	219	505	585	225	641	4,349
1976	925	469	689	362	251	579	337	358	422	268	222	159	5,041
1977	352	239	242	212	254	259	322	311	370	424	322	433	3,740
1978	321	394	424	382	397	299	316	341	401	280	468	214	4,237
1979	501	302	687	353	471	418	407	756	492	490	368	518	5,763
1980	312	644	422	507	366	285	257	332	342	365	265	323	4,420
1981	471	380	471	446	322	529	300	259	348	414	487	611	5,038
1982	450	489	662	398	234	369	495	403	364	226	514	317	4,921
1983	280	506	390	462	717	377	377	264	474	534	529	587	324	5,444
1984	715	537	455	315	636	655	229	672	532	562	391	538	6,237
1985	462	689	344	480	415	N.A.	N.A.	N.A.	N.A.	N.A.	N.A.	N.A.	—

[1] Includes re-exports from 1973.   *Source: International Silk Association*

T.593

Silver

World silver production during 1986, according to a preliminary estimate by the Bureau of Mines, was 406 million troy ounces, up five percent from 1985. The largest-producing country was Mexico, accounting for one-sixth of total world output. Peru provided one-seventh, followed by the USSR with 12 percent, the U.S. with 11 percent, and Canada with just under 10 percent. At the start of 1986, the world's reserve base was estimated at 11 billion troy ounces. About 17 percent of that amount is in the U.S., 1.5 percent in the USSR, and 13 percent each in Mexico and Canada. Because two-thirds of global silver resources are interred in common with copper, lead, and zinc, substantial increases in the size of the reserve base are expected in the immediate future, as new sources of those base materials are discovered.

Extrapolation of actual output in the U.S. between January and July, 1986, yielded a figure of about 28 million troy ounces for the year. If that amount was realized, total extraction during 1986 was well below the figure for 1985, when approximately 39.4 million troy ounces were brought to the surface. Much of the decline was attributed to the closing of U.S. silver mines. In late April, 1986, two of the larger U.S. mines, the Sunshine Mine and Lucky Friday (which together produced some 9–10 million troy ounces of silver in 1985) were closed because of low prices and labor disputes. Depressed prices continued throughout 1986 and the mines remained closed. U.S. output was accounted for by 17 states, including New York, South Carolina, Michigan and Tennessee, none of which enjoys a reputation for silver mining. The largest single contributor to annual production was Idaho, providing some 39 percent of output; Nevada contributed another 15 percent, Montana 13 percent, and Arizona nearly 11 percent.

Imports into the U.S. were arriving, by the end of August, 1986, at the annual rate of 126.3 million troy ounces. More than 87 percent of imported silver was refined bullion; ore and precipitates accounted for nine percent of the remainder. Exports from the U.S. were running at the annual rate of 24.3 million troy ounces, about equal to the amount shipped the year before. Approximately 50 percent of exports were in the form of waste and scrap; another 41 percent were refined bullion. The principal sources for imports were Mexico (42 percent) and Canada (36 percent), followed by Peru (11 percent) and Belgium-Luxembourg (9 percent).

1986 U.S. apparent consumption was projected at 170 million ounces. Consumption by end use was: photography, 48 percent; electrical and electronic products, 25 percent; sterlingware, electroplates ware, and jewelry, 12 percent. The photographic industry was mainly in New York; other end-use manufacturers were in Connecticut, Rhode Island and New Jersey. From a 1983 base, U.S. Bureau of Mines estimated demand will increase at an average annual rate of 0.8 percent through 1990.

Silver prices eased during the first seven months of 1986, but later rebounded. Data from Handy & Harman show that in New York the average spot price per troy ounce was $6.05 in January, 1986, but had fallen to $5.00 by July; prices advanced to $6.00 in August and ended the year at around $5.40. Activity was in line with spot price movements. Speculator and investment activity, as distinguished from industrial demand, continued to be the primary factors in price movement in 1986. Fluctuations in the value of the U.S. dollar, weak oil prices, banking industry problems and sales of silver by private investors were among the factors which influenced prices during the year.

Futures Markets

Silver futures are traded on New York's Commodity Exchange (COMEX), Chicago Board of Trade (CBOT) and Chicago's MidAmerica Exchange (MidAm). They are also traded on the London Metal Exchange (LME) and the Winnipeg Commodity Exchange (WCE).

World Mine Production of Silver, by Selected Countries — In Millions of Fine Ounces (Troy Ounces)

Year	Argentina	Australia	Bolivia[1]	Canada	West Germany	Honduras	Japan	Mexico	Morocco	Peru	Poland	United States	USSR[2]	Yugoslavia	Zaire (Congo)	World Total[2]
1976	2.25	25.03	5.34	41.20	1.03	3.18	9.30	42.64	2.05	35.58	17.8	34.33	44.0	4.63	2.47	316.4
1977	2.45	27.53	5.81	42.24	1.06	2.82	9.60	47.03	2.82	39.73	20.7	38.17	45.0	4.68	2.73	331.3
1978	2.16	26.12	6.29	40.73	.80	2.79	9.66	50.78	3.13	37.02	21.9	39.39	46.0	5.13	4.39	345.0
1979	2.21	26.76	5.74	36.87	1.04	2.43	8.68	52.17	3.28	39.25	22.6	37.90	46.0	5.21	3.89	348.1
1980	2.36	24.65	6.10	33.34	1.06	1.77	8.60	50.05	3.15	44.42	24.63	32.33	46.0	4.79	2.73	342.8
1981	2.52	23.91	6.39	36.30	1.13	1.82	9.01	52.92	2.12	46.94	20.58	40.68	46.5	4.44	2.58	361.6
1982	2.68	29.16	5.47	42.25	1.28	2.10	9.84	59.18	2.64	53.48	21.12	40.25	46.9	3.34	1.75	383.0
1983	2.50	33.21	6.03	35.56	1.17	2.59	9.88	63.61	2.85	55.88	21.80	43.43	47.2	3.99	1.29	392.1
1984[3]	1.66	31.18	4.56	42.66	1.23	2.65	10.40	75.34	2.41	56.52	23.92	44.59	47.4	4.05	1.23	415.2
1985[2]	1.60	35.00	4.00	38.89	1.23	2.68	10.90	69.00	2.73	60.40	24.00	39.36	47.9	5.02	1.20	412.3
1986[2]												32.70				

[1] Exports.   [2] Estimate.   [3] Preliminary.   *Source: Bureau of Mines*

T.594

SILVER   CASH PRICE   NEW YORK

HANDY & HARMAN MONTHLY AVERAGE PRICES

HIGH JAN. 38.27   FEB. 35.09

Average Price of Silver in New York (Handy & Harman)   In Cents per Troy Ounce (.999 Fine)

Year	Jan.	Feb.	Mar.	Apr.	May	June	July	Aug.	Sept.	Oct.	Nov.	Dec.	Average
1972	147.3	150.4	153.6	157.2	158.3	156.9	173.6	184.6	177.7	181.1	183.3	197.6	168.5
1973	201.7	223.6	230.9	220.7	240.1	262.1	270.6	263.7	267.5	288.6	286.0	313.7	256.0
1974	363.7	535.9	532.6	503.6	543.2	489.6	441.6	443.1	404.9	483.0	469.4	439.1	470.8
1975	419.3	437.0	434.5	420.9	453.8	448.9	470.5	492.5	451.6	432.9	433.2	408.5	442.0
1976	406.3	408.6	418.9	435.1	448.9	481.2	478.0	423.7	429.5	422.5	437.3	434.7	435.4
1977	440.9	452.7	484.2	477.7	469.2	444.3	449.8	444.4	453.9	476.3	482.8	470.6	462.3
1978	493.4	493.6	526.8	511.6	512.0	531.6	533.1	549.5	557.5	591.8	586.5	593.0	540.0
1979	625.5	741.7	745.4	749.3	836.6	853.8	913.5	933.4	1,395.9	1,678.1	1,655.3	2,179.3	1,109.0
1980	3,827.2	3,508.5	2,413.3	1,384.1	1,253.3	1,574.8	1,606.0	1,589.7	2,014.4	2,018.1	1,864.8	1,639.3	2,063.3
1981	1,475.2	1,306.5	1,236.9	1,091.7	1,084.8	1,000.1	863.1	892.3	1,003.6	925.1	854.7	843.2	1,048.1
1982	803.1	826.8	721.3	731.1	667.4	557.8	649.7	713.6	872.5	948.8	991.8	1,058.6	795.0
1983	1,239.6	1,396.4	1,061.9	1,169.4	1,295.3	1,174.9	1,208.8	1,209.6	1,191.5	984.1	883.7	912.1	1,143.9
1984	818.2	912.7	965.1	922.1	897.2	874.4	741.6	761.3	726.3	731.7	748.9	669.4	814.1
1985	609.8	607.0	601.4	645.8	628.0	617.0	610.4	624.7	605.4	619.0	613.3	588.8	619.2
1986	605.3	587.4											

Source: Handy & Harman

T.595

225

SILVER

World[2] Silver Consumption — In Millions of Troy Ounces

Year	Canada	France	W. Germany	India	Italy	Japan	Un. Kingdom	United States	World Total	Canada	France	W. Germany	Austria	Mexico	United States	World Total	World Total
			Industrial Uses									**Coinage**					
1973	8.6	14.3	64.7	13.0	41.5	69.0	31.0	195.9	477.8	1.4	.1	9.5	6.6		.9	29.2	507.0
1974	9.6	15.5	59.9	15.0	38.6	46.5	25.0	177.0	409.4	8.9	.1	8.8	5.6		1.0	27.9	436.9
1975	10.6	21.2	38.9	13.0	28.9	46.4	28.0	157.7	376.8	10.4	5.2	4.3	13.4	—	2.7	38.8	415.6
1976	9.5	19.0	50.8	18.0	32.1	60.7	28.0	170.5	437.5	8.4	6.7	2.9	6.9	—	1.3	29.7	467.2
1977	8.8	20.6	59.5	17.6	33.8	63.2	32.2	153.6	433.6	.3	6.9	2.6	3.0	4.2	.4	23.4	457.0
1978	9.0	22.2	47.2	20.0	41.8	64.8	29.0	160.2	442.6	.3	11.1	3.6	4.5	6.3	.1	36.3	478.9
1979	8.1	21.5	46.1	19.0	31.1	66.4	26.5	157.2	434.2	.3	7.7	3.7	5.0	5.0	.1	27.8	462.0
1980	8.7	20.2	29.1	19.0	21.8	61.7	20.5	124.7	354.5	.2	—	—	4.3	6.1	.1	13.7	368.2
1981	9.4	20.6	33.8	19.0	12.9	59.8	18.5	116.6	344.0	.2	—	—	3.0	—	—	9.0	353.0
1982	9.0	18.6	35.9	22.5	9.6	63.2	20.0	118.8	351.8	.3	—	—	4.0	—	2.5	12.8	364.6
1983	8.9	18.6	30.3	21.8	9.0	71.5	18.0	116.3	349.6	.4	—	—	2.0	—	19.2	19.6	369.2
1984	9.0	17.0	30.1	25.7	11.6	78.7	19.0	114.8	362.9	.3	—	—	—	2.0	3.4	8.7	371.6
1985[1]	9.1	18.0	31.7	25.7	14.5	77.2	19.0	118.6	373.9	.3			—	3.0	.4	8.7	382.6

[1] Preliminary.   [2] Non-communist areas only.   *Source: Handy & Harman*

T.597

SILVER COMEX
WEEKLY HIGH, LOW & CLOSE OF NEAREST FUTURES

U.S. Mine Production of Recoverable Silver   In Thousands of Troy Ounces

Year	Ari-zona	Cali-fornia	Colo-rado	Idaho	Ore-gon	Mis-souri	Mon-tana	Nevada	New Mexico	New York	Ten-nessee	So. Dakota	Utah	Alaska	Total
1978	6,638	58	4,217	18,379		2,056	2,918	804	895	21	N.A.	N.A.	2,885		39,385
1979	7,479	64	2,809	17,144	2	2,201	3,302	560	N.A.	11	N.A.	58	2,454	N.A.	37,896
1980	6,268	49	2,987	13,695	1	2,357	2,024	940	21	N.A.	51	2,203	8	32,329
1981	8,055	53	3,009	16,546	7	1,837	2,989	3,039	1,632	29	N.A.	56	2,883	2	40,683
1982	6,309	34	1,934	14,830	—	2,241	6,169	3,142	805	27	N.A.	26	4,343	2	40,248
1983	4,492	27	2,146	17,684	1	2,021	5,708	5,179	N.A.	33	N.A.	62	4,567	4	43,431
1984	4,247	N.A.	2,200	18,869	N.A.	1,401	5,653	6,477	N.A.	N.A.	N.A.	50	N.A.	N.A.	44,592
1985[1]	4,885	115	549	18,828	—	1,635	4,010	4,947	N.A.	N.A.	N.A.	63	N.A.	N.A.	39,357
1986[2]	4,375	104	400	13,000	—	1,370	4,400	4,850				70			32,700

[1] Preliminary.   [2] Forecast.   *Source: Bureau of Mines*   T.599

U.S. Consumption of Silver, by End Use   In Thousands of Troy Ounces

Year	Bear-ings	Brazing Alloys & Solders	Cata-lysts	Dental & Medical	Electro-plated Ware	Electrical & Electronic Products Batteries	Contacts & Con-ductors	Jewelry	Mirrors	Photo-graphic Ma-terials	Ster-ling Ware	Coins, Medal-lions[2]	Total Net Industrial Consump-tion	Coinage	Total Consump-tion
1978	373	10,987	8,197	2,033	7,274	6,029	30,756	6,766	1,862	64,299	17,908	2,727	160,165	45	160,210
1979	332	10,912	5,637	2,295	8,065	4,583	33,506	5,358	1,850	65,978	13,088	4,676	157,258	168	157,426
1980	649	8,508	3,035	2,212	4,350	5,976	27,796	5,893	672	49,825	9,082	4,693	124,694	72	124,766
1981	297	7,718	3,830	1,709	3,904	3,803	26,411	5,368	581	51,025	4,407	2,622	116,670	179	116,849
1982	228	7,384	2,418	1,688	3,254	4,167	27,730	6,260	970	51,769	6,579	1,832	118,840	1,846	120,686
1983	170	5,837	2,424	1,532	3,154	2,800	26,298	6,885	970	51,827	7,022	2,979	116,464	2,128	118,592
1984	260	5,889	2,448	1,569	3,542	2,671	25,633	5,773	970	55,322	3,638	2,564	114,841	2,665	117,506
1985[1]	183	5,590	2,409	1,485	3,660	2,470	27,517	5,779	970	57,895	3,527	2,514	118,559	355	118,914
1986[3]	260	6,350	2,300	1,650	3,000	3,700	30,400	7,700	970	57,100	4,050	3,500	126,000	500	126,500

[1] Preliminary.   [2] Includes commemorative objects.   [3] Estimate.   *Source: Bureau of Mines*   T.598

Commodity Exchange, Inc. (COMEX) Warehouse Stocks of Silver   In Millions of Ounces

Year	Jan. 1	Feb. 1	Mar. 1	Apr. 1	May 1	June 1	July 1	Aug. 1	Sept. 1	Oct. 1	Nov. 1	Dec. 1
1978	68.7	70.0	72.3	74.2	73.4	70.8	72.8	73.6	72.4	66.7	64.3	63.0
1979	58.2	52.0	51.8	49.2	50.3	55.5	54.1	48.9	47.3	51.8	60.3	70.2
1980	74.8	76.0	77.8	83.1	84.2	82.3	82.0	81.7	82.6	82.2	87.1	86.1
1981	86.9	86.8	85.4	84.6	85.7	85.1	86.6	85.4	78.8	78.1	76.0	77.3
1982	77.6	76.3	78.5	77.1	79.9	78.0	72.4	66.2	60.0	60.7	59.2	80.6
1983	91.2	90.9	106.4	96.8	91.3	69.8	91.1	93.7	113.6	129.3	129.4	129.6
1984	127.4	123.7	116.8	117.2	115.3	114.3	121.8	120.3	116.2	115.0	113.4	115.4
1985	118.9	121.5	122.3	106.6	106.0	104.2	133.7	140.8	141.0	143.6	149.2	153.7
1986	155.2	142.3	145.9	151.3	154.9	144.6	151.9	150.7	158.6	156.8	138.1	145.1
1987	144.9											

Source: Commodity Exchange of New York (COMEX)   T.600

United States Production[1] of Refined Silver from All Sources   In Thousands of Troy Ounces

Year	Jan.	Feb.	Mar.	Apr.	May	June	July	Aug.	Sept.	Oct.	Nov.	Dec.	Total
1977	13,196	10,114	13,173	13,335	13,260	14,100	5,781	7,840	10,412	13,643	13,002	14,966	143,125
1978	10,694	12,699	12,503	10,871	12,196	12,000	10,186	12,214	10,727	12,666	11,526	12,721	141,003
1979	10,592	10,888	13,070	11,451	11,938	11,600	12,433	9,837	9,118	12,476	12,221	17,008	155,723
1980	18,088	17,548	17,673	16,941	10,400	14,800	6,676	11,583	10,785	10,603	10,578	14,553	166,326
1981	12,889	12,000	11,352	11,889	10,402	11,500	10,433	10,114	10,533	9,954	8,105	11,589	130,783
1982	9,043	8,407	10,300	8,856	9,095	8,840	7,781	8,518	7,872	8,307	9,607	11,655	108,252
1983	9,121	8,533	9,063	9,653	7,663	10,210	8,579	8,342	7,886	8,738	9,880	12,058	112,200
1984	7,094	8,414	8,446	9,827	10,423	8,921	8,879	11,226	8,971	8,386	10,200	13,920	116,400
1985	8,414	7,930	8,645	9,238	9,344	9,850	8,578	9,885	8,191	8,429	8,987	11,467	109,000
1986	7,897	7,835	7,340	8,727	7,547	7,129	3,988	6,404	6,932	7,869			

[1] Output of commercial bars .999 fine, including U.S. Mint purchases of crude. Production is from both foreign and domestic silver.
Sources: American Bureau of Metal Statistics; The Silver Institute, Inc.   T.603

SILVER

Highest and Lowest Prices of December Silver Futures at New York (Comex)   In Dollars per Ounce

Year of Delivery		Yr. Prior to Delivery Nov.	Dec.	Jan.	Feb.	Mar.	Apr.	May	June	July	Aug.	Sept.	Oct.	Nov.	Dec.	Life of Delivery Range
1979	High	6.558	6.538	7.160	8.405	8.230	8.363	9.360	9.235	9.975	10.935	16.900	18.130	19.400	25.750	25.750
	Low	6.205	6.260	6.360	6.990	7.453	7.625	8.310	8.640	8.842	8.985	11.150	15.910	15.850	18.650	5.585
	Close	6.465	6.514	7.089	8.140	7.839	8.363	9.091	8.960	9.293	10.860	16.800	16.790	18.820	25.500	—
1980	High	20.528	30.910	44.370	42.150	39.780	20.270	14.750	20.200	20.090	17.140	24.180	22.280	20.320	19.020	44.370
	Low	17.540	20.705	31.910	35.200	21.270	13.860	11.450	16.975	17.570	15.900	16.670	18.540	17.580	13.370	7.564
	Close	20.528	30.910	37.645	38.640	21.270	13.860	14.530	19.240	17.840	16.840	21.250	19.100	18.590	16.610	—
1981	High	23.525	22.615	18.800	15.900	14.670	13.580	12.700	11.840	9.780	10.260	11.800	10.050	9.410	9.050	43.750
	Low	20.875	17.190	14.600	13.750	12.800	11.900	11.210	9.080	8.770	8.730	8.490	9.000	7.870	7.980	7.970
	Close	22.015	18.190	15.165	13.720	13.135	12.205	11.685	9.180	9.032	9.720	9.380	9.250	8.205	7.985	—
1982	High	10.700	10.150	9.490	9.860	8.820	8.390	7.540	6.680	7.720	8.660	9.975	10.070	11.010	11.180	17.975
	Low	9.110	9.040	8.730	8.650	7.600	7.350	6.670	5.110	5.800	6.320	7.700	8.020	8.950	10.020	5.110
	Close	9.280	9.185	9.182	8.622	7.870	7.470	6.675	6.406	6.965	8.040	8.240	10.090	10.090	11.140	—
1983	High	11.900	12.350	15.238	16.070	12.180	13.380	14.420	13.320	13.110	13.250	12.740	10.780	9.860	10.040	16.070
	Low	9.900	11.070	11.840	12.666	10.710	11.440	12.680	11.513	11.720	11.750	11.010	8.630	8.320	8.440	6.146
	Close	11.090	11.910	15.238	12.666	11.382	12.715	13.640	12.055	12.225	12.410	11.070	8.630	9.620	8.810	—
1984	High	10.860	11.100	9.780	10.730	10.970	10.490	9.970	10.130	8.739	8.390	7.900	7.865	7.900	17.165	17.550
	Low	9.220	9.400	8.470	9.290	9.930	9.465	9.110	8.700	7.060	7.200	7.120	7.120	6.950	6.245	6.245
	Close	10.649	9.867	9.329	10.420	10.541	9.555	9.835	8.817	7.274	7.660	7.620	7.280	7.019	6.573	—
1985	High	8.745	7.850	6.930	6.850	7.250	7.200	7.015	6.740	6.615	6.630	6.320	6.530	6.318	6.120	12.300
	Low	7.700	6.800	6.300	5.930	5.900	6.440	6.180	6.200	5.990	6.230	5.960	6.075	6.040	5.700	5.700
	Close	7.736	6.860	6.832	6.059	7.106	6.480	6.392	6.309	6.460	6.370	6.095	6.125	6.077	5.865	—
1986	High	6.840	6.650	6.830	6.450	6.140	5.795	5.495	5.660	5.295	5.780	6.020	5.835	5.820	5.515	7.990
	Low	6.540	6.130	6.070	5.930	5.370	5.170	5.030	5.100	5.060	5.150	5.155	5.520	5.210	5.270	5.030
	Close	6.609	6.263	6.443	5.968	5.395	5.342	5.434	5.256	5.214	5.230	5.569	5.654	5.389	5.290	—
1987	High	6.210	5.850													
	Low	5.520	5.580													
	Close	5.717	5.714													

Source: Commodity Exchange of N.Y. (COMEX)   T.596

Month–End Total Open Interest of Silver Futures at New York (COMEX) & Chicago   In Thous. of Contracts

Year	At New York (COMEX) Jan. 1	Feb. 1	Mar. 1	Apr. 1	May 1	June 1	July 1	Aug. 1	Sept. 1	Oct. 1	Nov. 1	Dec. 1	At Chicago (1,000 oz.[1]) Jan. 1	Apr. 1	July 1	Oct. 1
1978	287.8	245.4	242.4	226.0	217.8	208.6	196.2	212.6	214.4	239.1	277.5	304.8	275.9	240.2	230.0	235.4
1979	299.5	242.9	218.7	203.5	185.7	170.0	153.3	154.5	156.2	167.3	144.3	133.4	252.8	180.5	166.6	156.7
1980	123.6	77.7	63.4	48.5	27.1	23.8	22.9	25.1	24.5	29.8	35.0	36.0	88.9	23.6	22.9	24.0
1981	32.0	27.6	24.3	25.7	26.1	28.8	29.4	31.0	31.0	29.9	32.3	27.5	28.0	21.2	29.8	16.3
1982	27.6	27.5	25.0	29.3	28.3	27.0	'27.3	29.0	27.2	24.6	30.0	31.0	7.1	8.6	7.0	12.5
1983	33.9	44.6	54.3	45.9	50.1	57.1	42.8	42.7	48.1	53.0	51.7	55.4	19.4	32.6	35.8	35.1
1984	59.9	62.0	64.3	71.6	64.5	66.5	58.2	64.8	61.3	64.1	73.2	76.2	32.0	37.8	42.7	35.0
1985	81.5	84.3	76.1	74.3	70.1	77.3	73.5	72.5	70.1	76.1	86.6	85.3	27.1	23.2	25.1	21.4
1986	86.7	82.2	79.5	78.9	73.0	75.6	66.6	72.3	69.4	69.8	92.0	90.5	18.5	16.6	12.9	12.9
1987	89.4												12.4			

[1] 1,000 oz. contract from 1/82. Prior data are for 5,000 oz. contract.   *Source: Commodity Exchange of N.Y. (COMEX); Chicago Board of Trade*
T.601

Volume of Trading in Silver Futures at New York (COMEX)   In Thousands of Contracts

Year	Jan.	Feb.	Mar.	Apr.	May	June	July	Aug.	Sept.	Oct.	Nov.	Dec.	Total
1978	330.0	270.7	391.0	287.5	244.9	247.2	254.1	316.2	192.0	469.0	438.0	381.4	3,822
1979	460.0	388.3	304.6	367.3	545.3	480.5	383.9	404.1	283.1	191.7	178.6	111.1	4,081
1980	167.7	76.2	143.5	94.0	46.6	63.3	45.6	41.8	100.9	92.9	97.1	90.6	1,059
1981	70.7	71.0	74.9	72.6	58.0	97.4	77.4	116.0	171.9	121.4	136.6	172.8	1,241
1982	112.8	193.9	211.5	192.9	99.7	217.4	263.1	317.2	258.0	288.9	350.6	372.8	2,869
1983	502.7	601.4	446.6	452.9	516.1	623.7	454.3	656.5	492.0	569.0	596.9	512.7	6,433
1984	570.8	698.8	695.7	629.9	626.7	587.4	554.7	601.5	431.3	449.2	534.2	362.3	6,698
1985	531.8	488.0	518.4	449.8	424.8	377.9	377.7	388.5	267.7	314.0	332.8	349.9	4,821
1986	394.0	368.9	277.6	438.8	280.1	336.1	187.9	317.8	454.6	286.7	338.9	168.2	3,850

Source: Commodity Exchange of N.Y. (COMEX)   T.602

Soybean Meal

Soybean meal remains the most important protein meal produced in the world. For the 1986/87 season, the USDA projects world soybean meal production at 62.03 million tonnes, an increase of nearly three percent over 1985/86. With world production of all protein meals expected to reach 105.51 million tonnes in 1986/87, soybean meal will comprise about 59 percent of the total. While the share of meal production held by soybean meal remains about steady, other protein meals such as rapeseed and sunflowerseed have increased their share.

World protein meal use in 1986/87 is projected by USDA to outstrip production again, as has been the case in the previous three years. Consumption of soybean meal is estimated at 62.65 million tonnes, an increase of almost two percent from a year ago. Use of rapeseed meal will also rise; cottonseed meal and sunflowerseed meal use will decline. Much of the increase in world use of soybean meal will originate in the U.S., where poultry production is rising sharply.

Global exports of all protein meals are projected by USDA to reach 33.51 million tonnes in 1986/87, the third year of increases in world trade. Soybean meal exports are estimated at 22.69 million tonnes, less than a one-percent rise from a year ago. Brazil is the world's largest exporter and is currently projected to ship 7.5 million tonnes. Argentina will also increase exports to 3.3 million tonnes. The major importers of soybean meal are France, West Germany and the Eastern European countries.

U.S. production of soybean meal in 1986/87 is estimated by USDA to total 25.49 million tons, a two-percent increase from last season. The total supply is projected at 25.70 million tons, a one-percent rise from a year ago, and the largest supply since 1982/83. Domestic use of soybean meal is projected at 19.50 million tons, a two-percent increase from last season. High protein animal units are only slightly higher than a year ago, with declining hog numbers offset by gains in poultry production. Less availability of competing meals such as cottonseed will also improve soybean meal use; working against increased use is a huge supply of corn and a generally mild winter in the Corn Belt.

U.S. exports of soybean meal in 1986/87 are currently projected by the USDA to total 5.98 million tons, two percent less than a year ago. The major markets for U.S. meal are the Netherlands, Italy and West Germany. Venezuela and Canada are also important markets. Early in the season, soybean meal exports were large, helped by reduced South American availabilities, a favorable meal/feed wheat price ratio in the European Community, and a sharp decline in the value of the dollar. With large soybean crops expected in Brazil and Argentina, meal exports from those sources will increase during the spring and early summer. This, in turn, is expected to pressure U.S. exports.

While total use of soybean meal is projected to increase slightly to 25.4 million tonnes, increased supplies will more than offset this. Ending stocks on September 30, 1987, are projected at 300,000 tons, compared to 212,000 tons at the end of last season.

Futures Market

Soybean meal futures are traded on the Chicago Board of Trade (CBOT).

World Soybean Meal Supply & Distribution   In Thousands of Metric Tons

Season Year	Production Brazil	China	EC-12	United States	Total	Exports Brazil	United States	Total	Imports France	Total	Consumption EC-12	United States	Total	Stocks Brazil	United States	Total
1981-2	9,940	1,520	N.A.	22,348	57,250	8,347	6,266	20,780	3,503	20,970	N.A.	16,071	57,920	610	159	1,940
1982-3	10,607	1,370	11,780	24,230	60,520	8,239	6,449	23,290	3,330	23,180	18,100	17,510	59,810	680	430	2,530
1983-4	9,702	1,430	10,330	20,646	55,510	7,706	4,860	21,400	3,399	22,590	17,680	15,980	56,100	984	231	3,130
1984-5	10,170	1,350	9,820	22,250	58,160	8,440	4,460	22,290	3,290	23,030	18,060	17,670	59,280	720	350	2,750
1985-6[1]	9,660	1,510	10,230	22,630	60,300	7,380	5,450	22,550	3,450	23,410	18,150	17,340	61,430	600	190	2,490
1986-7[2]	9,970	1,590	10,410	23,120	62,030	7,500	5,350	22,690	3,440	23,240	18,070	17,690	62,650	470	270	2,420

[1] Preliminary. [2] Forecast. *Source: Foreign Agricultural Service, U.S.D.A.*   607a

Supply and Distribution of Soybean Meal in the United States   In Thousands of Short Tons

Year Begin. Oct.	Supply — Production For Stocks Oct. 1	Total	For Animal Feed	For Edible Protein Pdt's.	Total Supply	Distribution Domestic Feed[2]	Exports	Total	$ Ton Decatur 44% Solvent	$ Tonne Decatur 44% Solvent	$ Tonne Brazil FOB 45-46% Protein
1981-2	163	24,634	23,500	308	24,797	17,714	6,908	24,622	182.52	201	212
1982-3	175	26,714			26,889	19,306	7,109	26,415	187.19	206	213
1983-4	474	22,756			23,230	17,615	5,360	22,975	188.20	207	203
1984-5	255	24,529			24,784	19,480	4,917	24,397	125.40	138	141
1985-6[1]	387	24,957			25,344	19,125	6,007	25,132	155.00	171	175
1986-7[3]	212	25,488			25,700	19,500	5,900	25,400	140-160	169	180

[1] Preliminary. [2] Includes small quantities used for industrial purposes, estimated at 30,000 tons annually. [3] Estimate.
Source: Economic Research Service, U.S.D.A.   T.606

SOYBEAN MEAL CBOT
WEEKLY HIGH, LOW & CLOSE OF NEAREST FUTURES

Stocks (at Oil Mills) of Soybean Cake & Meal in the United States   In Thousands of Short Tons

Year	Oct. 1	Nov. 1	Dec. 1	Jan. 1	Feb. 1	Mar. 1	April 1	May 1	June 1	July 1	Aug. 1	Sept. 1
1975–6	358.3	396.1	441.4	371.4	378.1	419.5	358.3	358.8	462.8	369.8	406.9	350.5
1976–7	354.9	423.5	427.7	353.9	384.7	429.9	412.6	449.0	408.3	390.7	399.0	270.4
1977–8	228.3	270.0	239.8	245.1	251.7	239.7	227.3	308.2	263.3	191.1	262.6	234.1
1978–9	242.9	210.4	178.2	260.5	215.1	198.4	210.4	231.6	207.4	205.3	232.2	140.3
1979–0	224.3	204.1	164.2	207.7	158.7	160.6	219.1	193.9	265.0	262.0	232.4	225.1
1980–1	189.7	211.1	350.0	221.8	209.7	214.4	232.2	184.4	254.0	209.7	156.1	199.7
1981–2	233.8	309.2	314.8	279.4	315.7	324.9	190.3	172.1	309.3	224.9	209.1	189.7
1982–3	175.2	342.8	349.6	332.3	400.2	422.8	341.0	356.1	341.5	272.3	365.2	378.5
1983–4	474.1	419.3	466.8	391.1	475.8	446.7	460.7	418.6	427.2	391.2	355.5	242.7
1984–5	255.4	236.1	285.7	336.8	319.6	334.1	444.6	429.8	495.8	569.6	562.5	458.0
1985–6[1]	386.9	318.4	369.2	358.4	372.4	281.3	386.6	300.8	282.4	278.7	250.6	298.3

[1] Preliminary.   *Sources: Economic Research Service, U.S.D.A.; Bureau of the Census*

T.613

U.S. Exports of Soybean Cake & Meal by Country of Destination   In Thousands of Metric Tons

Yr. Beg. Oct. 1	Egypt	Ven-ezuela	Canada	Den-mark	France	West Germany	Spain	Ireland	Italy	Nether-lands	Philip-pines	Poland	United Kingdom	Yugo-slavia	Total
1978–9			416.0	65.6	355.1	717.6	253.5	117.9	691.1	748.1	—	243.0	66.8	57.9	5,998
1979–0			355.9	48.5	270.2	1,013	58.0	74.1	855.7	1,490	41.1	400.0	69.0	152.9	7,196
1980–1			331.2	.1	8.0	710.3	21.6	.5	684.3	1,502	0	312.3	56.9	191.4	6,154
1981–2	10.4	518.0	339.6	0	62.6	630.9	82.3	15.8	947.3	2,201	69.7	0	106.9	84.7	6,266
1982–3	22.5	464.0	401.4	3.5	3.7	1,073	28.6	21.2	953.5	2,066	82.5	57.1	72.7	80.1	6,449
1983–4	14.3	527.2	427.6	0	0	1,154	63.0	4.6	493.0	693.1	293.8	278.5	2.5	8.1	4,862
1984–5	87.0	686.5	489.9	0	0	195.9	73.5	16.2	499.0	905.0	195.6	117.2	56.2	51.3	4,457
1985–6[1]	200.0	542.5	607.3	9.9	15.0	576.0	74.5	4.7	658.2	1,221	164.0	0	59.7	128.8	5,450

[1] Preliminary.   *Source: Bureau of the Census, U.S. Dept. of Commerce*   T.607

Average Price of Soybean Meal[1] (44% Solvent) at Decatur   In Dollars per Short Ton (Bulk)

Year	Jan.	Feb.	Mar.	Apr.	May	June	July	Aug.	Sept.	Oct.	Nov.	Dec.	Average
1981	223.50	212.50	210.40	222.00	221.00	200.90	204.10	202.25	190.00	180.75	178.40	187.50	202.78
1982	191.00	191.00	183.60	190.25	192.40	183.60	181.90	169.00	160.80	157.00	173.40	178.50	179.37
1983	179.75	177.10	177.30	186.75	185.75	175.50	189.30	232.80	233.60	228.60	224.70	216.60	200.64
1984	201.90	184.40	196.40	190.00	187.40	174.40	157.60	151.60	144.90	141.60	135.20	136.75	166.84
1985	135.25	125.20	125.90	117.90	111.50	110.25	144.00	121.40	130.60	138.30	142.50	145.00	126.43
1986	153.25	152.25	163.70	157.00	157.90	158.90	161.00	163.50	165.20	151.90	154.00		

Source: Consumer Marketing Service, U.S.D.A.   T.608

Production of Soybean Cake & Meal in the U.S.   In Thousands of Short Tons

Crop Year	Oct.	Nov.	Dec.	Jan.	Feb.	Mar.	Production April	May	June	July	Aug.	Sept.	Total	Meal in Form of Soybeans[2]
1979–0	2,214	2,359	2,431	2,477	2,319	2,379	2,129	2,167	1,922	1,990	1,945	1,896	26,227	21,118
1980–1	2,253	2,291	2,179	2,133	1,838	2,074	1,976	1,896	1,709	1,681	1,726	1,763	23,518	
1981–2	2,502	2,326	2,451	2,266	2,077	2,050	1,931	2,066	1,844	1,684	1,620	1,819	24,634	
1982–3	2,386	2,581	2,679	2,628	2,221	2,259	1,950	1,993	1,956	1,934	2,053	2,075	26,714	
1983–4	2,288	2,049	2,123	2,220	1,872	2,029	1,760	1,872	1,665	1,629	1,690	1,559	22,756	
1984–5	2,108	2,326	2,381	2,226	1,887	2,024	1,958	2,101	1,953	1,934	1,832	1,802	24,530	
1985–6[1]	2,218	2,288	2,380	2,344	1,925	2,160	2,008	2,037	1,879	1,980	1,863	1,879	24,958	

[1] Preliminary.   [2] Calculated at 47.5 lbs of meal per bushel.   *Sources: Economic Research Service, U.S.D.A.; Bureau of Census.*   T.609

Month–End Open Interest of Soybean Meal Futures at the Chicago Board of Trade   In Contracts

Year	Jan.	Feb.	Mar.	Apr.	May	June	July	Aug.	Sept.	Oct.	Nov.	Dec.
1979	48,076	54,316	54,873	48,923	49,678	56,627	47,847	47,804	49,348	56,178	52,426	50,072
1980	49,490	53,379	51,143	47,016	46,603	47,769	50,797	61,261	66,805	82,421	84,051	64,965
1981	53,077	50,584	47,002	51,831	45,160	50,909	45,901	48,379	48,152	47,619	48,140	38,804
1982	41,034	39,700	43,830	45,035	45,481	45,877	47,094	50,823	46,833	44,740	47,300	46,016
1983	50,744	44,808	52,979	46,653	42,893	40,900	50,340	66,826	64,266	64,124	63,461	60,248
1984	55,566	54,875	64,511	58,259	74,576	61,051	48,893	48,410	43,264	47,877	46,919	37,167
1985	39,110	43,110	45,164	48,579	54,103	53,405	41,451	44,260	40,703	46,091	42,925	46,875
1986	43,681	48,404	49,219	49,060	46,708	53,813	50,539	51,857	50,791	56,566	57,794	56,475

Source: Chicago Board of Trade   T.610

Volume of Trading of Soybean Meal Futures at the Chicago Board of Trade   In Thousands of Contracts

Year	Jan.	Feb.	Mar.	Apr.	May	June	July	Aug.	Sept.	Oct.	Nov.	Dec.	Total
1980	172.6	159.2	152.1	183.0	159.1	183.9	370.8	281.5	371.9	413.6	369.3	401.7	3,219
1981	261.9	203.1	220.9	254.3	218.4	294.8	301.8	241.3	276.3	219.0	242.8	304.4	3,040
1982	219.6	238.1	258.6	279.7	197.3	244.0	229.9	225.1	198.8	241.0	233.4	218.9	2,784
1983	269.2	248.0	252.7	272.9	238.6	259.5	320.5	528.2	447.6	349.4	413.1	271.8	3,872
1984	298.8	283.3	299.6	355.5	449.0	424.0	382.2	307.5	271.2	246.3	266.7	237.3	3,822
1985	252.1	232.6	244.5	283.9	285.0	277.3	420.9	250.7	268.5	287.5	292.3	243.9	3,339
1986	260.2	252.9	218.2	289.3	260.6	242.1	292.5	274.1	222.7	292.3	209.3	234.8	3,049

Source: Chicago Board of Trade   T.611

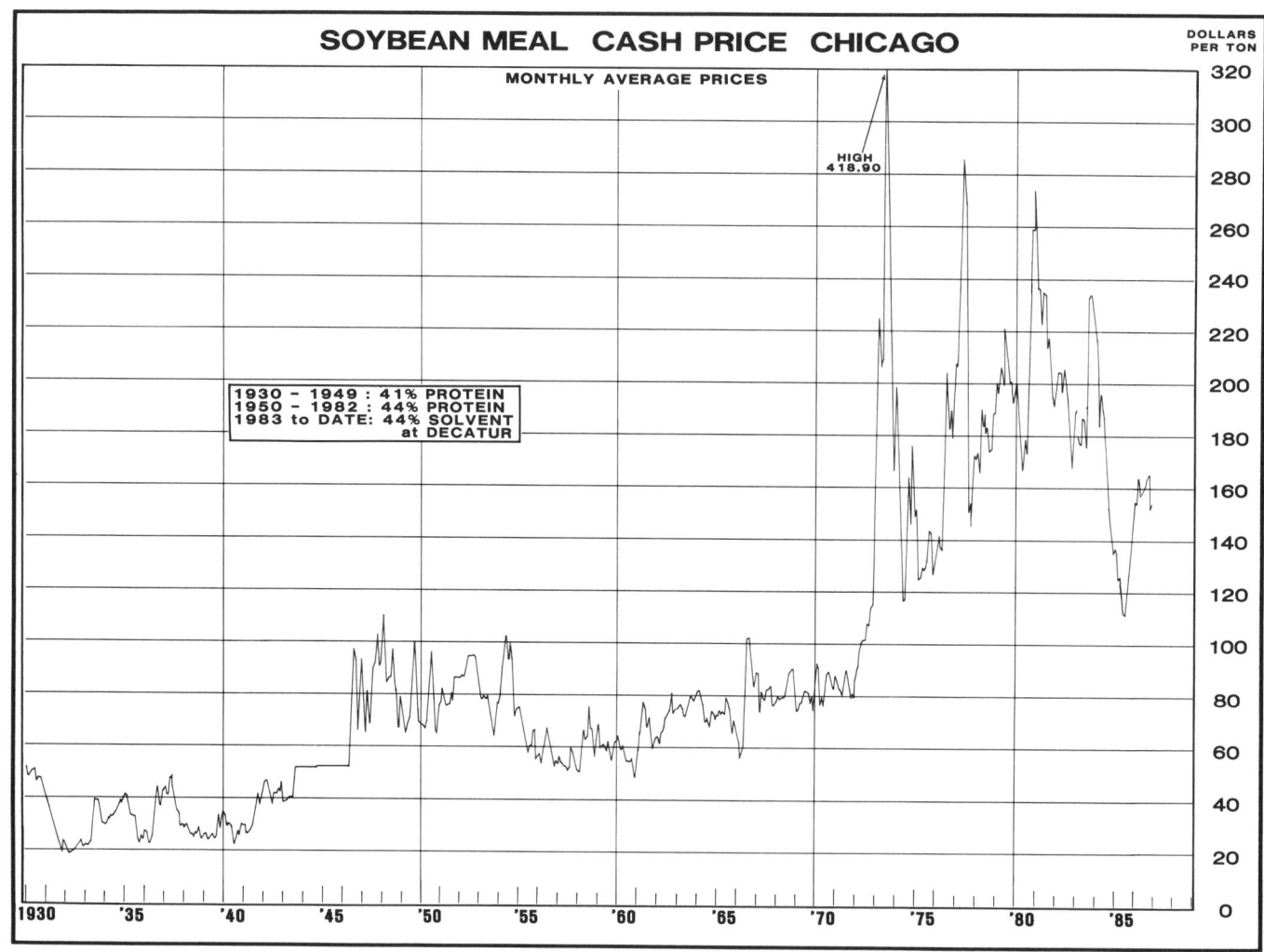

SOYBEAN MEAL CASH PRICE CHICAGO

MONTHLY AVERAGE PRICES

DOLLARS PER TON

1930 – 1949 : 41% PROTEIN
1950 – 1982 : 44% PROTEIN
1983 to DATE: 44% SOLVENT
at DECATUR

HIGH 418.90

High, Low & Closing Prices of May Soybean Meal Futures on the Chicago Board of Trade $ per Ton

Year of Delivery		Mar.	Apr.	May	June	July	Aug.	Sept.	Oct.	Nov.	Dec.	Jan.	Feb.	Mar.	Apr.	May	Life of Delivery Range
						Year Prior to Delivery							**Delivery Year**				
1981	High	206.5	200.5	201.0	205.0	238.0	242.5	265.0	299.0	300.5	294.8	259.5	232.5	224.0	231.7	230.2	300.5
	Low	193.0	191.0	191.5	190.3	205.0	217.0	241.0	244.3	275.0	220.7	213.7	214.5	205.2	216.9	214.0	190.3
	Close	195.2	195.5	192.0	205.0	229.6	242.5	251.7	290.2	292.7	249.0	220.7	215.2	220.8	226.9	214.0	—
1982	High	—	261.5	252.0	242.0	241.0	230.0	218.0	210.5	206.5	203.5	197.0	197.7	188.5	196.0	196.5	261.5
	Low	—	248.5	234.5	221.0	223.0	207.0	203.5	201.8	194.1	181.5	187.8	182.7	178.4	186.2	188.0	181.5
	Close	—	249.5	239.0	225.0	231.5	209.0	206.5	203.5	197.3	188.3	195.9	186.1	187.7	190.9	189.0	—
1983	High	—	215.0	210.0	205.5	199.0	195.5	176.0	169.0	180.5	178.5	186.0	186.1	192.8	193.3	190.3	215.0
	Low	—	203.0	201.5	197.0	189.5	171.0	165.3	160.3	166.5	171.3	174.1	170.6	172.5	183.3	176.1	160.3
	Close	—	209.5	201.5	197.7	192.0	174.0	166.5	166.0	178.0	175.2	185.6	171.4	189.7	189.4	181.3	—
1984	High	219.5	217.5	213.0	198.0	229.0	267.5	261.0	246.0	249.6	229.5	221.5	201.5	210.0	205.4	199.0	267.5
	Low	213.5	207.5	194.2	185.0	194.0	218.8	229.0	229.5	220.0	212.2	193.2	188.9	200.5	182.5	183.0	182.5
	Close	215.2	211.5	194.2	195.0	216.2	244.0	240.0	232.0	226.7	225.0	197.4	200.7	202.9	183.8	198.4	—
1985	High	—	204.5	195.7	201.0	197.0	180.0	172.0	175.0	173.3	165.5	154.0	147.0	141.5	137.0	124.9	204.5
	Low	—	196.0	190.5	188.2	169.5	167.5	160.0	160.5	163.0	150.1	145.6	129.5	130.1	120.1	118.5	118.5
	Close	—	196.0	198.0	200.5	171.3	171.0	162.0	169.7	164.8	151.1	147.6	130.3	138.1	120.5	118.6	—
1986	High	—	162.5	154.3	151.5	158.0	139.5	145.2	151.9	152.5	157.0	160.5	161.5	163.9	159.5	156.5	163.9
	Low	—	152.8	145.0	143.0	135.5	132.5	134.0	139.0	136.0	141.5	150.0	150.3	153.5	150.5	144.3	132.5
	Close	—	152.8	146.2	143.7	137.0	135.5	141.0	151.0	145.0	153.4	154.0	161.2	153.7	157.2	149.6	—
1987	High	—	165.5	169.7	154.0	158.5	155.4	157.1	155.5	151.8	149.0						
	Low	—	149.7	152.0	146.5	143.0	148.0	152.1	148.7	148.6	141.5						
	Close	—	165.2	153.2	146.5	154.7	155.3	155.0	151.8	149.0	145.5						

Source: Chicago Board of Trade

T.612

Soybean Oil

1986/87 world soybean oil production is estimated by USDA to reach 14.08 million tonnes, an increase of almost three percent from 1985/86. Soybean oil should have a 28-percent share of world vegetable and marine oil production, up slightly from a year ago. World soybean oil production has been rising since 1983/84. The U.S. share of world output is expected to be 38 percent this year. Other major producers are Brazil and the European Community.

World soybean oil consumption has been rising since 1983/84 and is projected to reach 14.03 million tonnes this season. While soybean oil use has been increasing, consumption of other oils has been rising at a much faster rate. Palm oil use this season is projected to be 43 percent higher than in 1983/84, while rapeseed oil consumption should be 33 percent higher than three years ago.

Soybean oil exports are projected by USDA to reach 3.17 million tonnes or 19 percent of world vegetable oil trade. Following palm oil, soybean oil is the second most widely traded oil.

World stocks of vegetable and marine oils at the end of 1986/87 are projected by USDA to total 5 million tonnes, five percent less than last season. World ending stocks of soybean oil are expected to total 1.52 million tonnes.

U.S. soybean oil production in 1986/87 is estimated by USDA at 11.88 billion pounds, up over two percent from last season. With carry-in stocks of 947 million pounds, the total supply of soybean oil will be 12.82 billion pounds, five percent more than a year ago and the highest level since 1982/83. Ample stocks and low prices should expand use.

Changes in domestic consumption are directly related to income and population growth. Some of the largest yearly increases in use came during strong growth in gross national product. Domestic demand for soyoil indicates that lower prices alone will not prompt much additional use. Another important factor is competition from other oils. The availability of domestically produced cottonseed, peanut and sunflowerseed oil is projected to fall 25 percent from a year ago. With smaller livestock herds, supplies of animal fats will also be lower. Offsetting this are increased imports of foreign oils like palm and coconut. Overall, domestic use is projected by USDA at 10.40 billion pounds, three percent more than a year ago.

U.S. soyoil exports are projected by USDA at 1.20 billion pounds, a decline of about five percent from last season and the lowest export total since 1975/76. U.S. exports have trended lower since the 1979/80 season, with increasing competition from foreign oils. The sharpest competitor is palm oil produced in Malaysia. Due to Malaysia's proximity to large markets like India, Pakistan and Bangladesh, it has a competitive advantage in exports. India, the second-largest market for U.S. soybean oil in 1983/84, no longer buys any U.S. oil. Since most U.S. exports are made on credit terms to developing countries, a weaker dollar has little effect on exports.

Ending stocks of soybean oil in 1986/87 are estimated by USDA to climb to 1.225 billion pounds, 29 percent above a year ago.

Futures Market

Soybean oil futures are traded on the Chicago Board of Trade (CBOT).

World Supply & Demand of Soybean Oil   In Thousands of Metric Tons

Season Crop Year	Production Brazil	Production EC-12	Production United States	Production Total	Exports Brazil	Exports United States	Exports Total	Imports India	Imports Total	Consumption Brazil	Consumption EC-12	Consumption India	Consumption United States	Consumption Total	Stocks[3] United States	Stocks[3] Total
1981-2	2,406		4,980	12,730	852	942	3,510	460	3,440	1,542		550	4,320	12,950	500	1,370
1982-3	2,564	2,580	5,462	13,570	1,020	918	3,810	537	3,650	1,612	1,550	540	4,472	13,230	572	1,540
1983-4	2,352	2,320	4,932	12,820	987	830	3,970	810	3,900	1,510	1,410	760	4,354	13,020	327	1,280
1984-5	2,460	2,220	5,202	13,310	980	750	3,660	400	3,490	1,550	1,420	570	4,500	13,060	290	1,360
1985-6[1]	2,350	2,280	5,270	13,710	450	570	3,160	220	3,120	1,990	1,410	490	4,560	13,510	430	1,520
1986-7[2]	2,440	2,320	5,390	14,090	450	540	3,170	300	3,110	2,100	1,450	500	4,720	14,030	560	1,520

[1] Preliminary.   [2] Forecast.   [3] End of season.   *Source: Foreign Agricultural Service, U.S.D.A.*   T168b

Production, Consumption, Stocks and Foreign Trade of Soybean Oil in the U.S.   In Millions of Pounds

Year	Production Crude	Production Refined	Consumption In Refining	Consumption In End Pdt's.	Stocks December 31 Crude	Stocks December 31 Refined	Imports for Consumption	Exports Crude	Exports Refined
1977	8,836	7,790	8,092	7,451	524.0	340.0	.2	1,427.3	81.3
1978	10,625	8,618	8,955	8,175	623.1	347.5	—	1,560.8	77.8
1979	11,504	9,110	9,456	8,656	656.6	373.5	—	———2,489———	
1980	12,097	8,982	9,300	8,585	1,369.6	368.2	—	———2,417———	
1981	11,301	9,461	9,817	9,024	1,680.2	343.6	—	———1,805———	
1982	11,183	9,671	10,042	9,307	1,241.1	345.6	—	———2,057———	
1983[1]	11,653	9,590	9,939	9,418	1,559.3	360.0	—	———1,732———	
1984[1]	11,004	9,716	9,986	9,932	500.2	276.9	—		
1985[1]	11,496	9,863	10,200	10,499	969.4	1,132	—		

[1] Preliminary.   *Source: Bureau of Census*   T.614

SOYBEAN OIL

U.S. Exports of Soybean Oil,[1] by Country of Destination In Thousands of Metric Tons

Yr. Beg. Oct. 1	Aus-tralia	Colom-bia	Cana-da	Venez-uela	Ecua-dor	Ethi-opia	Haiti	Peru	India	Israel	Mex-ico	Moroc-co	Paki-stan	Pana-ma	Egypt	Grand Total
1976–7	20.1	27.3	26.0		16.2		17.2	57.3	252.2	3.1	15.4	3.0	119.2	12.5	1.4	702
1977–8	21.0	44.1	27.7		26.0		13.8	68.6	247.7	6.3	29.6	5.6	95.8	8.3	6.1	933
1978–9	16.2	84.1	20.9		22.4		17.2	29.4	181.1	9.8	5.1	6.0	163.3	19.0	13.9	1,059
1979–0	16.4	82.6	14.8		35.3		22.8	36.2	427.7	9.6	31.4	2.3	147.4	19.0	6.0	1,220
1980–1	16.5	60.3	7.8		38.6		22.4	41.2	61.8	5.2	21.6	5.0	125.7	14.7	3.4	740
1981–2	22.6	77.4	5.4	42.7	36.2		8.8	46.8	68.4	.3	91.1	9.7	259.9	21.7	6.9	942
1982–3	5.0	69.5	7.5	55.9	50.4		20.4	70.2	54.9	.4	16.3	9.0	236.7	16.4	3.5	918
1983–4	.3	24.8	9.8	50.5	41.1		12.5	24.9	169.4	.5	68.1	2.5	216.1	15.7	3.6	827
1984–5	.2	22.2	12.9	51.9	44.7	24.0	16.1	11.4	62.8	.9	45.4	3.8	168.4	8.0	3.9	753
1985–6[2]	.2	8.9	6.1	17.1	16.7	17.3	9.5	1.6	37.6		49.1	3.2	274.9	2.8	4.9	570

[1] Crude & refined oil combined as such. [2] Preliminary. *Source: The Bureau of the Census, U.S. Dept. of Commerce.* T.615

Supply & Distribution of Soybean Oil in the U.S. In Millions of Pounds

Year Begin. Oct.	Produc-tion	Stocks Oct. 1	Exports & Ship-ments	Total Domestic	Short-ening	Mar-garine	Cooking & Salad Oils	Other Edible	Total Food	Paint & Varnish	Resins & Plastics	Fatty Acids	Other Inedi-ble	Total Non-Food	Total Disap-pearance
1976–7	8,578	1,251	1,607	7,454	2,189	1,568	3,165	25	6,947	85	83	26	36	507	9,058
1977–8	10,288	771	2,137	8,273	2,279	1,585	3,325	29	7,621	87	79	42	33	549	10,330
1978–9	11,323	729	2,411	8,942	2,480	1,593	3,825								11,276
1979–0	12,105	776	2,690	8,981	2,680	1,643	4,060								11,671
1980–1	11,270	1,210	1,631	8,610	2,675	1,666	4,226	43	8,610						10,744
1981–2	10,979	1,736	2,077	9,536	2,991	1,723	4,368	51	9,133						11,612
1982–3	12,040	1,103	2,025	9,857	2,944	1,615	4,668	58	9,284						11,882
1983–4	10,872	1,261	1,824	9,588	3,207	1,494	4,442	101	9,245						11,412
1984–5	11,468	721	1,660	9,917	3,655	1,589	4,800	129	10,172						11,577
1985–6[1]	11,628	632	1,257	10,063	3,155	1,591	4,259	129	9,139						11,320
1986–7[2]	11,880	940	1,200	10,300											11,500

[1] Preliminary. [2] Forecast. *Source: Economic Research Service, U.S.D.A.* T.623

U.S. Production of Crude Soybean Oil In Millions of Pounds

Year	Oct.	Nov.	Dec.	Jan.	Feb.	Mar.	Apr.	May	June	July	Aug.	Sept.	Total
1976–7	807.4	804.0	805.7	786.7	791.2	823.7	747.3	682.4	631.1	566.6	553.6	578.2	8,578
1977–8	821.9	922.3	931.5	911.9	809.5	943.3	866.9	908.2	795.1	777.9	815.8	783.3	10,287
1978–9	984.3	974.8	1,050	989.1	902.3	982.2	939.6	964.7	930.5	899.9	856.7	849.9	11,324
1979–0	1,020	1,068	1,102	1,115	1,065	1,098	993.7	1,010	901.6	927.8	913.8	890.1	12,105
1980–1	1,080	1,078	1,024	1,011	887.8	991.3	954.2	914.9	830.7	815.8	827.2	855.6	11,271
1981–2	1,125	1,018	1,070	995.6	917.7	912.1	866.8	930.2	828.4	765.6	732.0	818.3	10,979
1982–3	1,079	1,145	1,191	1,167	997.0	1,015	881.3	908.9	891.3	888.0	930.2	945.3	12,040
1983–4	1,081	957.7	990.9	1,053	896.9	972.7	846.7	906.3	803.5	788.8	819.4	755.9	10,872
1984–5	995.5	1,072	1,096	1,027	879.0	946.0	917.6	983.3	918.9	912.6	868.8	853.4	11,470
1985–6[1]	1,040	1,053	1,096	1,086	894.8	1,005	935.4	953.3	881.9	909.5	875.3	886.7	11,618
1986–7[1]	1,163	1,172											

[1] Preliminary. *Source: Bureau of the Census* T.618

U.S. Production of Refined Soybean Oil In Millions of Pounds

Year	Oct.	Nov.	Dec.	Jan.	Feb.	Mar.	Apr.	May	June	July	Aug.	Sept.	Total
1977–8	700.1	764.2	745.0	705.6	653.2	801.4	738.0	732.1	649.9	636.8	725.3	679.9	8,532
1978–9	782.8	747.7	765.7	753.3	681.7	768.9	760.1	835.4	742.8	748.3	762.8	693.0	9,043
1979–0	805.9	797.6	760.3	801.9	760.5	767.7	687.1	712.8	669.0	720.3	760.7	764.5	9,038
1980–1	784.1	760.5	763.1	741.6	706.3	833.9	741.2	754.9	812.9	765.4	813.3	812.1	9,289
1981–2	833.6	840.9	805.2	768.7	767.6	866.4	754.5	817.3	866.3	775.4	811.7	794.0	9,702
1982–3	824.6	827.8	795.1	784.1	727.1	841.8	800.9	843.1	824.0	778.7	837.7	828.8	9,714
1983–4	839.2	747.2	737.1	797.9	813.2	841.8	763.8	859.5	794.6	767.9	752.2	760.9	9,475
1984–5	907.6	835.5	821.2	838.7	796.1	835.5	865.0	899.5	773.1	763.9	806.2	794.4	9,937
1985–6[1]	865.7	834.8	790.0	804.2	751.1	819.5	794.6	808.5	816.8	780.2	830.1	834.8	9,730
1986–7[1]	900.4												

[1] Preliminary. *Source: Bureau of the Census* T.617

Soybean Oil Consumption in End Products in the U.S.   In Millions of Pounds

Year	Jan.	Feb.	Mar.	Apr.	May	June	July	Aug.	Sept.	Oct.	Nov.	Dec.	Total
1976	658.0	617.6	687.3	623.4	625.9	634.6	626.8	635.1	623.7	621.3	609.1	613.8	7,577
1977	571.5	591.2	694.5	597.1	611.0	553.8	517.9	629.8	621.5	658.6	682.3	721.9	7,451
1978	664.1	648.8	771.7	686.5	662.4	640.5	596.2	699.8	672.5	715.9	709.3	707.5	8,175
1979	695.1	636.2	755.3	682.4	775.0	701.6	711.4	744.8	700.9	781.4	742.2	730.1	8,656
1980	750.7	719.4	762.9	671.6	693.6	683.7	671.2	754.5	737.1	719.1	682.6	738.7	8,585
1981	698.7	680.7	775.1	722.3	728.7	774.0	741.1	755.1	796.4	796.8	783.6	749.3	9,002
1982	740.0	737.7	809.6	715.2	761.0	834.6	775.2	811.9	820.5	799.9	763.1	733.2	9,302
1983	761.6	702.2	827.3	765.9	814.9	830.3	745.1	847.0	894.3	812.7	711.4	705.2	9,418
1984	827.6	821.7	837.8	781.1	857.4	824.4	744.7	772.2	780.6	932.0	883.4	856.1	9,919
1985	989.0	804.0	867.1	885.9	940.8	810.5	825.9	856.1	863.7	922.4	864.2	869.3	10,508
1986[1]	836.7	794.0	889.7	884.4	850.3	856.8	835.1	843.1	890.3	930.3			

[1] Preliminary.   *Source: Bureau of the Census*   T.624

U.S. Exports of Soybean Oil (Crude & Refined)   In Millions of Pounds

Year	Jan.	Feb.	Mar.	Apr.	May	June	July	Aug.	Sept.	Oct.	Nov.	Dec.	Total
1976	32.6	120.2	89.6	55.5	160.9	74.4	77.6	41.8	151.5	100.8	107.7	75.8	1,088
1977	103.7	92.3	236.4	103.3	209.4	159.9	154.2	72.0	66.0	108.8	185.5	175.3	1,667
1978	113.1	141.8	252.6	218.9	176.4	147.2	165.5	108.8	193.4	96.8	154.8	175.4	1,945
1979	219.1	249.8	199.0	185.6	107.3	299.0	166.2	187.4	159.1	127.8	208.5	261.9	2,371
1980	173.4	250.0	325.4	269.6	327.3	194.6	109.7	175.7	171.2	112.5	84.7	120.5	2,315
1981	116.0	113.8	202.8	76.1	109.6	108.8	93.1	291.7	97.9	187.2	146.6	184.3	1,698
1982	43.9	176.7	126.5	148.5	103.3	208.0	270.2	237.4	244.1	181.1	174.9	142.0	2,057
1983	124.0	225.9	90.4	305.7	127.5	94.1	208.9	125.1	225.1	55.1	54.7	95.5	1,732
1984	161.3	289.9	258.9	163.3	208.3	157.3	140.0	73.0	156.3	200.3	214.6	189.6	2,068
1985	66.7	198.3	184.9	66.9	52.4	138.8	174.4	70.1	102.8	125.4	38.1	74.3	923.3
1986[1]	80.6	100.7	92.8	124.0	50.7	115.1	44.6	187.7	223.4				

[1] Preliminary.   *Source: Dept. of Commerce*   T.619

U.S. Stocks of Soybean Oil (Crude & Refined) at Factory & Warehouses   In Millions of Pounds

Year	Oct. 1	Nov. 1	Dec. 1	Jan. 1	Feb. 1	Mar. 1	April 1	May 1	June 1	July 1	Aug. 1	Sept. 1
1976–7	1,251	1,351	1,432	1,488	1,606	1,616	1,493	1,485	1,361	1,174	1,037	942.5
1977–8	771.1	756.4	771.1	864.0	913.8	856.5	803.8	822.2	828.7	834.4	820.8	777.5
1978–9	728.6	813.4	837.1	970.6	932.2	942.8	1,004	987.3	1,043	922.9	915.4	815.1
1979–0	775.8	819.8	867.3	1,030	1,155	1,205	1,176	1,184	1,145	1,226	1,305	1,263
1980–1	1,210	1,428	1,677	1,738	1,900	1,976	2,017	2,119	2,166	2,139	2,024	1,783
1981–2	1,736	1,790	1,884	2,024	2,160	2,141	2,141	2,112	2,018	1,889	1,647	1,398
1982–3	1,103	1,208	1,305	1,587	1,713	1,700	1,842	1,600	1,552	1,546	1,411	1,408
1983–4	1,261	1,453	1,661	1,919	1,907	1,583	1,520	1,380	1,203	1,012	989.6	871.0
1984–5	720.5	597.2	580.1	777.1	883.6	723.9	715.6	666.0	706.7	731.9	724.2	715.7
1985–6[1]	640.1	636.1	810.4	969.4	1,167	1,181	1,247	1,219	1,360	1,225	1,321	1,152
1986–7[1]	946.6	967.5										

[1] Preliminary.   *Source: Bureau of the Census*   T.616

Average Prices of Crude Domestic Soybean Oil (in Tank Cars) F.O.B. Decatur   In Cents per Pound

Year	Oct.	Nov.	Dec.	Jan.	Feb.	Mar.	Apr.	May	June	July	Aug.	Sept.	Average
1975–6	21.4	18.9	16.8	16.2	16.3	16.6	16.3	15.8	17.6	20.9	20.4	22.5	18.3
1976–7	20.7	21.8	21.0	20.9	22.4	26.5	29.6	31.3	28.3	23.8	21.1	19.2	23.9
1977–8	18.8	21.0	22.6	20.9	21.6	26.6	26.8	28.8	26.9	25.9	26.3	27.8	24.5
1978–9	26.7	23.7	25.8	25.8	27.3	26.9	26.7	27.8	27.4	29.1	29.2	30.0	27.2
1979–0	27.9	27.8	26.2	23.6	23.4	22.1	20.3	20.8	21.6	26.2	25.9	26.1	24.3
1980–1	25.1	26.7	23.7	23.0	22.0	23.1	23.4	21.6	21.3	22.8	20.8	19.4	22.7
1981–2	19.7	19.9	18.9	18.4	18.2	18.5	19.7	20.6	19.4	19.0	17.9	17.4	19.0
1982–3	17.4	17.6	16.6	16.4	17.3	17.7	19.3	19.8	19.4	21.6	30.2	34.3	20.6
1983–4	30.7	28.1	27.3	28.3	27.2	30.1	32.1	39.0	36.0	31.0	29.0	28.0	30.6
1984–5	30.6	31.9	28.4	28.0	29.6	31.4	33.6	32.5	32.5	29.1	24.1	22.5	29.5
1985–6	20.7	20.6	21.4	20.6	18.6	17.6	17.7	17.8	16.8	16.2	14.3	13.9	18.0
1986–7	14.6	14.7											

Source: Bureau of Labor Statistics   T.620

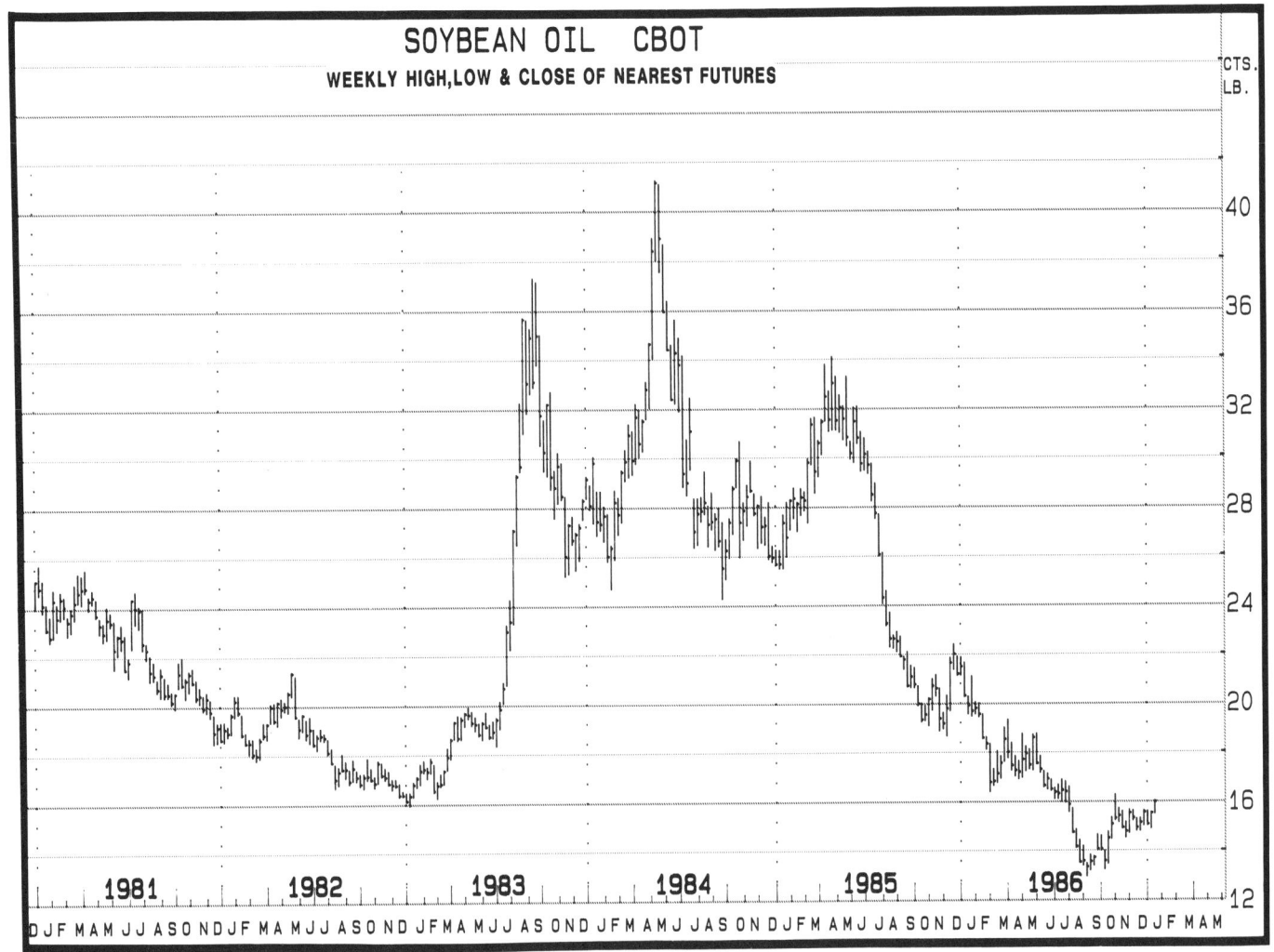

SOYBEAN OIL CBOT
WEEKLY HIGH, LOW & CLOSE OF NEAREST FUTURES

High, Low & Closing Prices of May Soybean Oil Futures on the Chicago Board of Trade ¢ per lb.

Year of Delivery		Mar.	Apr.	May	June	July	Aug.	Sept.	Oct.	Nov.	Dec.	Jan.	Feb.	Mar.	Apr.	May	Life of Delivery Range
						Year Prior to Delivery								Delivery Year			
1982	High	28.60	29.02	28.10	26.50	27.90	25.90	24.50	24.25	23.25	21.85	21.01	21.08	19.45	20.25	20.90	29.02
	Low	27.13	27.75	26.30	24.70	24.85	23.50	22.52	22.45	21.20	19.65	19.70	18.72	18.26	18.88	19.70	18.26
	Close	28.60	27.75	26.35	25.02	25.90	23.60	22.87	23.00	21.21	19.76	20.88	19.13	18.88	19.83	20.72	—
1983	High	—	—	22.90	21.65	20.42	19.90	19.35	18.60	18.40	17.75	17.96	18.30	18.59	19.64	19.85	22.90
	Low	—	—	21.66	20.30	19.73	18.15	18.00	17.50	17.25	16.91	16.61	16.65	16.80	18.54	18.92	16.61
	Close	—	—	21.66	20.32	19.73	18.85	18.00	17.60	17.48	16.91	17.91	16.74	18.56	19.61	19.29	—
1984	High	—	21.60	21.60	20.75	25.25	34.00	35.85	22.60	30.70	30.10	30.60	28.82	31.55	33.70	41.15	41.15
	Low	—	20.75	19.27	19.75	20.50	25.05	29.90	28.35	26.20	26.50	27.00	25.05	27.72	29.70	31.97	19.27
	Close	—	21.53	20.20	20.75	24.30	32.75	31.00	28.88	27.74	30.08	27.68	28.25	29.82	32.47	39.87	—
1985	High	—	—	29.95	30.10	27.15	27.45	26.50	25.75	26.10	25.60	27.20	27.70	30.60	34.00	33.27	34.00
	Low	—	—	28.10	26.92	23.15	24.35	22.80	23.85	23.78	23.95	24.40	26.30	26.15	30.05	30.65	22.80
	Close	—	—	28.88	27.92	24.35	26.70	23.80	25.07	24.55	24.61	26.67	27.26	30.52	32.53	32.93	—
1986	High	24.40	27.85	27.45	25.80	25.40	24.20	22.65	22.15	21.60	23.04	22.50	20.30	19.27	19.25	18.50	27.85
	Low	24.40	24.40	24.40	24.20	23.90	22.30	21.45	20.02	19.25	19.30	19.91	16.76	16.96	16.90	17.22	16.76
	Close	24.40	27.20	24.53	24.86	24.25	22.60	22.20	20.92	19.60	22.01	20.14	17.06	19.24	18.65	17.50	—
1987	High	20.60	20.90	19.75	18.71	18.40	17.35	15.80	16.75	16.35	16.40						
	Low	18.38	18.48	18.50	17.65	17.20	14.75	14.40	14.60	15.27	15.70						
	Close	20.60	19.95	18.68	17.65	17.20	14.90	15.43	15.95	16.19	15.77						

Source: Chicago Board of Trade

T.622

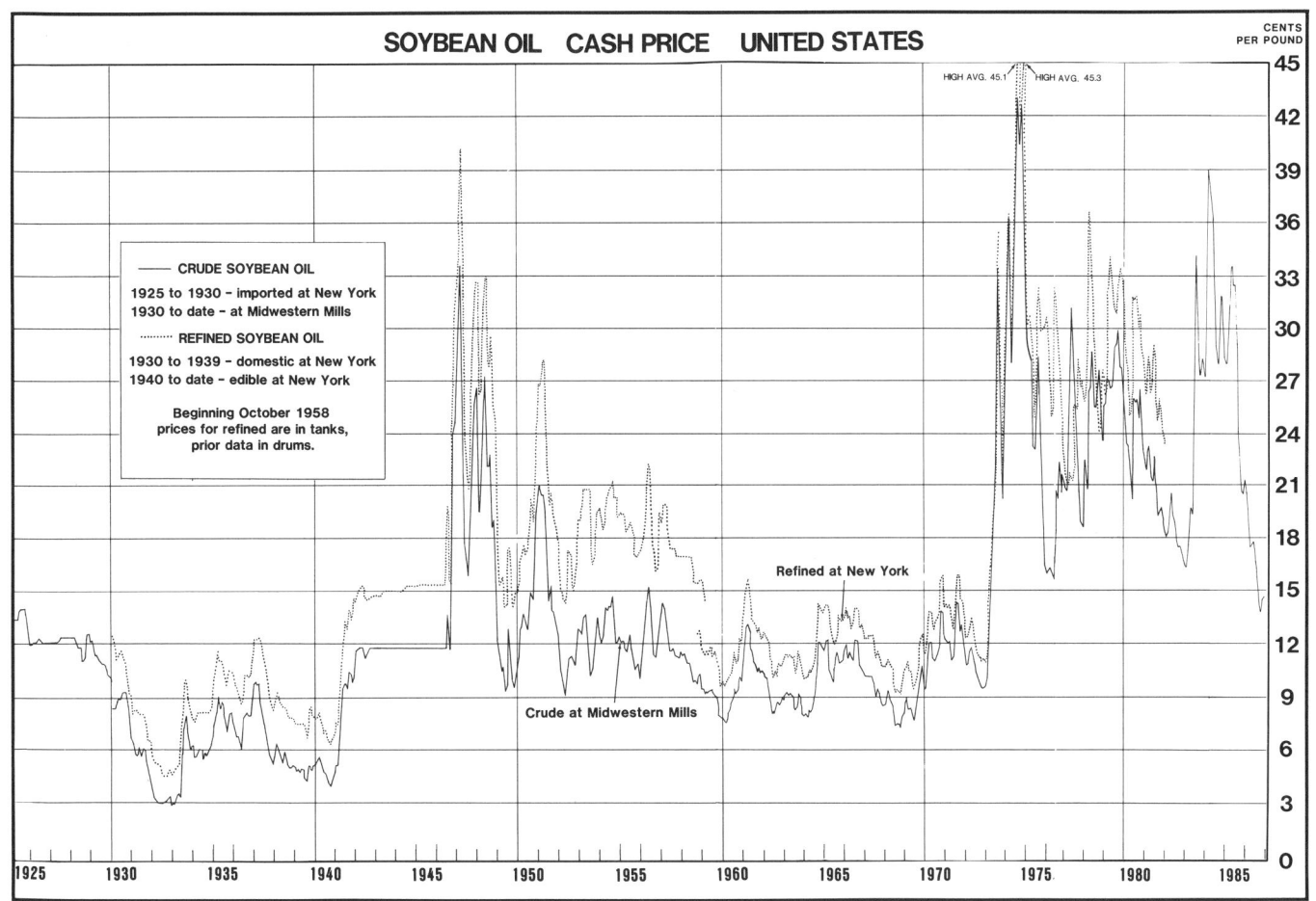

SOYBEAN OIL   CASH PRICE   UNITED STATES

CENTS PER POUND

CRUDE SOYBEAN OIL
1925 to 1930 – imported at New York
1930 to date – at Midwestern Mills
REFINED SOYBEAN OIL
1930 to 1939 – domestic at New York
1940 to date – edible at New York

Beginning October 1958
prices for refined are in tanks,
prior data in drums.

HIGH AVG. 45.1   HIGH AVG. 45.3

Refined at New York

Crude at Midwestern Mills

Month–End Open Interest of Soybean Oil Futures of the Chicago Board of Trade   In Contracts

Year	Jan.	Feb.	Mar.	Apr.	May	June	July	Aug.	Sept.	Oct.	Nov.	Dec.
1978	40,175	44,145	49,994	49,592	55,292	52,682	52,230	49,553	50,322	60,842	57,363	54,133
1979	50,713	57,729	57,893	55,657	57,820	64,671	58,852	58,258	60,854	67,778	65,893	64,374
1980	62,515	63,472	59,707	52,805	61,089	65,949	64,710	63,908	66,723	75,815	91,407	71,527
1981	58,671	65,580	57,956	67,241	56,968	63,400	54,007	56,847	49,411	50,786	54,232	48,295
1982	53,029	53,375	49,824	53,395	57,366	58,151	56,863	50,574	44,091	41,930	45,976	50,290
1983	49,329	49,360	57,446	59,894	58,635	55,678	53,842	71,341	73,946	79,303	74,817	67,695
1984	58,227	54,536	53,081	60,190	65,570	58,857	49,323	46,848	41,617	40,386	43,856	40,264
1985	38,534	44,803	48,093	60,717	58,629	59,856	41,451	56,313	48,963	45,951	44,186	48,361
1986	50,584	55,010	57,640	57,825	54,035	61,808	62,011	59,429	53,720	66,372	72,037	63,797

Source: Chicago Board of Trade   T.625

Volume of Trading of Soybean Oil Futures at the Chicago Board of Trade   In Thousands of Contracts

Year	Jan.	Feb.	Mar.	Apr.	May	June	July	Aug.	Sept.	Oct.	Nov.	Dec.	Total
1978	209.5	183.4	312.7	266.8	258.1	278.6	215.2	236.3	204.3	285.4	257.3	201.7	2,909
1979	215.0	291.5	233.8	254.4	212.3	321.7	313.0	252.5	262.0	311.6	222.3	191.6	3,082
1980	200.7	210.3	177.1	185.0	198.2	216.9	361.8	284.8	329.9	332.6	327.0	343.7	3,168
1981	243.8	231.1	237.9	254.0	221.7	274.8	355.1	233.7	240.2	235.0	228.1	292.1	3,047
1982	219.1	245.6	239.8	272.2	277.7	270.7	264.5	294.9	260.5	195.4	307.4	221.6	3,049
1983	273.6	244.1	264.4	273.2	233.1	288.9	332.6	452.3	445.4	378.7	355.5	316.7	3,859
1984	358.3	346.5	337.7	360.0	513.7	436.7	353.6	280.8	244.2	269.5	288.0	220.5	4,010
1985	264.2	256.0	311.6	405.0	416.4	308.7	341.1	281.5	233.0	270.0	281.5	278.4	3,647
1986	263.1	235.9	254.0	311.7	273.8	262.0	296.0	237.9	202.7	324.8	261.4	259.6	3,183

Source: Chicago Board of Trade   T.626

Soybeans

Soybeans, the most important oilseed produced globally, should comprise over 50 percent of 1986/87 world oilseed production. Projected world oilseed output is 196.5 million tonnes; soybeans should account for 98.8 million tonnes. According to USDA, world production of soybeans should increase by about three percent. Cottonseed, the next major oilseed, should show production down 10 percent to 27.4 million tonnes. A significant development this year is a record world rapeseed crop. Since 1982/83, world soybean production has risen six percent; rapeseed production has increased over 35 percent.

The U.S. is the world's largest producer of soybeans, although its share has declined recently as production in Brazil, Argentina, and Paraguay has risen. USDA projects these countries will account for 25 percent of 1986/87 world production. Brazil's severe drought last year reduced the crop to 13.4 million tonnes. USDA also expects large crops in Argentina and Paraguay. The Argentine crop of 7.7 million tonnes should be five percent above 1985/86; Paraguay's crop should total 900,000 tonnes.

World soybean trade should be more active than a year ago. 1986/87 global exports are projected at 27.3 million tonnes, up over five percent from 1985/86. The U.S. is the leading exporter, with a market share this season projected at almost 76 percent. South American producers tend to crush their crops and export soybean oil and meal to increase export earnings. The leading importers of soybeans are West Germany, the Netherlands, Spain, Japan and the Soviet Union.

The 1986/87 world crush is projected by USDA to be 78.88 million tonnes, up over three percent from last season. Major processors are the U.S., Brazil, the European Community (EC) and Argentina. World ending soybean stocks are estimated at 25.2 million tonnes, an increase of over 12 percent from a year ago; since 1983/84, world stocks have risen by 88 percent. Over the same period, the U.S. share has grown significantly. This season, USDA projects the U.S. will hold 66 percent of world stocks.

The USDA estimates 1986/87 U.S. production at 2.01 billion bushels, down four percent from a year ago. Acreage harvested fell three percent to 59.9 million, the smallest since 1977. In recent years, there has been a significant shift of acreage out of the Southeastern states; poor weather and pests have sharply cut the profitability of growing soybeans.

1985/86 national average yield was 33.8 bushels per acre, slightly below last season's record yield, but still above the recent average. Average yield in the Southeastern states was 19.3 bushels per acre.

U.S. carry-in stocks were a record 536 million bushels. Total domestic supply of soybeans was estimated at a record 2.545 billion bushels, over five percent above 1985/86.

Despite low prices, disappearance is projected to increase only marginally. The soybean crush is estimated at 1.08 billion bushels, up three percent from a year ago. USDA notes that, on a historical basis, current projected crush as a percentage of total supplies is below average. Early in the season, the crush was supported by heavy demand for soybean meal. As larger South American crops approach maturity, demand for meal should slow and the crushing rate should ease.

Soybean exports are projected at 760 million bushels, almost three percent above 1985/86. Primary export markets for U.S. soybeans are Japan, the EC and Taiwan. Over the first half of the season, exports have benefited from reduced South American availabilities and a much weaker dollar. With South American crops expected to return to normal or above-normal size, U.S. exports in spring and summer should slow significantly. Exports to the EC have benefited from the dollar's decline against Continental currencies, but larger world supplies of vegetable oils may discourage European crushers from importing more soybeans.

USDA projects carryout of soybeans on August 31, 1987, at a record 615 million bushels. Record supplies and low prices indicate producers will actively use the price-support loan program. Additionally, the Commodity Credit Corporation (CCC) inventory is expected to increase. Current policy allows the CCC to resell inventory at prices above the loan rate.

U.S. Government Support Program

The price-support loan rate for 1986 crop soybeans is $4.77 per bushel. There is no target price or farmer-owned reserve for soybeans.

Futures Markets

Soybean futures and options are traded on the Chicago Board of Trade (CBOT).

World Production of Soybeans   In Thousands of Metric Tons

Year of Harvest[3]	Argentina	Brazil	Canada	China	Colombia	India	Indonesia	Japan	South Korea	Mexico	Romania	Paraguay	Thailand	United States	USSR	World Total
1978	3,700	10,240	516	7,565	137		680	190	293	330	230	549	100	50,898	634	77,266
1979	3,600	15,156	671	7,460	154	350	653	192	257	680	383	575	102	61,722	467	93,705
1980	3,500	15,200	690	7,940	89	442	704	174	216	280	448	600	105	48,772	525	80,910
1981	4,150	12,835	607	9,325	99	467	514	212	257	680	268	600	131	54,435	450	86,020
1982	4,200	14,750	848	9,030	127	491	580	226	233	550	301	520	113	59,610	500	93,570
1983	7,000	15,400	722	9,765	85	583	625	217	226	600	259	550	172	44,518	560	83,150
1984[1]	6,750	18,280	936	9,690		750	660	238	254	550	410	950	240	50,644	425	93,010
1985[3]	7,300	13,400		10,500								600		57,113		96,290
1986[3]	7,700	16,200		11,000								900		54,207		98,780

[1] Preliminary.   [2] Projected.   [3] Split year includes Northern Hemisphere crops harvested in the late months of the first year shown combined with Southern Hemisphere crops harvested in the early months of the following year.   *Source: Foreign Agricultural Service, U.S.D.A.*   T.627

U.S. Soybean Price Support Program & Official Crop Production Reports   In Millions of Bushels

| Year | Quantity Put Under Support | Deliveries to C.C.C. | Sept. 1 Stocks | | National Avg. Support | | (In Thousands of Bushels) Crop Production Reports | | | | | |
			Total	Gov't. Owned	% of Parity	$ Per Bu.	August 1	September 1	October 1	November 1	December 1	Final
1974	34.6	—	170.8	—	37	2.25	1,314,232	1,315,792	1,262,352	1,243,912	1,233,425	1,216,287
1975	—	—	188.2	—	—None—		1,457,672	1,442,422	1,473,782	1,519,882	1,521,370	1,548,344
1976	22.5	—	244.9	—	34	2.50	1,344,343	1,274,263	1,249,713	1,252,148	1,287,560	1,288,608
1977	97.5	—	102.9	—	46	3.50	1,602,065	1,644,220	1,647,315	1,682,705	1,761,755	1,767,267
1978	64.2	—	161.0	—	51	4.50	1,765,024	1,772,364	1,792,064	1,810,389	1,870,181	1,868,754
1979	122.1	—	174.1	—	45	4.50	2,129,254	2,174,179	2,213,289	2,235,869	2,267,647	2,260,655
1980	133.2	—	358.5	.1	43	5.02	1,880,342	1,831,172	1,757,272	1,774,742	1,817,097	1,797,543
1981	221.5	—	313.0	.5	40	5.02	2,017,468	2,089,418	2,106,568	2,076,998	2,030,452	1,989,110
1982	396.6	—	254.5	20.9	39	5.02	2,293,420	2,313,880	2,300,345	2,299,520	2,276,976	2,190,297
1983	100.2	—	344.6	5.8	39	5.02	1,843,459	1,534,969	1,517,019	1,536,519	1,595,437	1,635,772
1984	280.0	—	175.7	—	39	5.02	2,035,370	2,027,565	1,971,700	1,901,565	1,860,783	1,860,863
1985[1]			316.1			5.02	1,959,439	2,062,889	2,108,379	2,129,034	2,098,531	
1986[1]			536.3			5.02	1,979,773	1,979,773	1,991,763	2,009,333		
1987[1]						4.77						

[1] Preliminary.   *Source: Crop Reporting Board, U.S.D.A.*   T.628

Soybean Stocks in the United States   In Thousands of Bushels

| Year | On Farms | | | | Off Farms | | | | Total Stocks | | | |
	Jan. 1	April 1	June 1[2]	Sept. 1	Jan. 1	April 1	June 1[2]	Sept. 1	Jan. 1	April 1	June 1[2]	Sept. 1
1973	429,071	145,333	33,855	9,415	437,924	358,372	145,352	50,222	866,995	503,705	179,207	59,637
1974	608,160	331,885	151,104	64,545	552,756	405,943	190,865	106,337	1,160,916	737,828	341,969	170,882
1975	483,869	331,241	165,324	75,114	505,392	323,317	191,704	109,922	989,261	654,558	357,028	185,036
1976	590,466	411,366	253,963	86,150	665,689	456,283	300,938	158,781	1,256,155	867,649	554,901	244,931
1977	473,120	227,723	92,374	32,748	559,045	390,214	243,335	70,168	1,032,165	617,937	335,709	102,916
1978	672,861	393,684	207,102	59,000	652,400	455,448	298,815	102,044	1,325,261	849,132	505,917	161,044
1979	699,556	412,570	241,255	61,509	692,534	467,646	284,850	112,579	1,392,090	880,216	526,105	174,088
1980	890,091	600,648	396,040	128,596	877,896	580,322	378,144	229,880	1,767,987	1,180,970	774,184	358,476
1981	732,384	527,222	363,317	153,571	792,792	493,892	317,603	159,436	1,525,176	1,021,114	680,920	313,007
1982	882,826	565,792	354,097	117,749	727,478	460,128	292,268	136,732	1,610,304	1,025,920	646,365	254,481
1983	1,008,139	643,134	424,658	118,574	754,560	504,529	365,966	226,060	1,762,699	1,147,663	790,624	344,634
1984	620,171	374,237	179,601	67,912	670,384	415,765	292,085	107,784	1,290,555	790,002	471,686	175,696
1985	766,335	487,369	326,596	143,221	655,724	408,632	281,821	172,836	1,422,059	896,001	608,417	316,057
1986[1]	927,395	599,246	411,740	167,090	837,884	576,738	437,186	369,175	1,765,279	1,175,984	848,926	536,265

[1] Preliminary.   [2] Data prior to 1976 are as of July 1.   *Source: Crop Reporting Board, U.S.D.A.*   T.629

U.S. Commercial Stocks of Soybeans on the First of the Month   In Millions of Bushels

Year	Jan.	Feb.	Mar.	Apr.	May	June	July	Aug.	Sept.	Oct.	Nov.	Dec.
1973	39.1	32.0	56.8	59.7	48.9	31.8	22.8	16.6	12.1	10.5	30.4	35.6
1974	33.6	32.0	35.3	36.2	27.3	21.2	21.2	20.3	18.0	14.3	51.6	55.4
1975	48.1	43.3	40.5	31.1	18.0	12.8	16.6	13.0	12.6	14.2	60.2	62.5
1976	52.0	55.7	57.1	51.7	42.5	37.0	32.5	30.4	21.3	27.9	54.4	52.2
1977	46.8	49.5	51.1	52.3	55.4	50.0	38.7	19.6	8.5	10.9	43.6	50.9
1978	46.2	44.3	41.8	49.1	47.9	42.7	30.6	23.0	10.7	13.0	58.3	63.2
1979	60.9	57.6	62.0	60.8	52.5	40.7	37.6	31.2	19.3	11.5	77.6	84.9
1980	76.5	71.5	73.2	72.3	56.5	52.6	53.2	51.8	44.8	51.5	80.6	79.5
1981	73.1	71.1	69.0	53.1	45.3	35.7	24.7	19.0	11.2	12.6	40.7	51.7
1982	50.6	50.4	41.1	39.9	34.7	67.4	21.5	18.4	11.5	12.8	43.9	53.5
1983	53.6	58.2	57.5	55.7	55.9	44.7	34.9	35.8	42.5	47.0	78.8	83.0
1984	77.2	74.4	65.2	58.6	49.2	41.1	35.4	20.8	7.9	6.7	23.3	41.7
1985	41.1	44.0	38.2	33.3	22.8	14.7	12.7	11.3	6.9	9.6	47.6	60.9
1986	61.7	63.9	57.3	53.6	40.2	30.5	24.9	24.5	24.8	30.1		

Source: Foreign Agricultural Service, U.S.D.A.   T.630

SOYBEANS

Salient Statistics of Soybeans in the United States

Crop Year	Planted Alone — 1,000 Acres	Acreage Harvested — 1,000 Acres	Yield Per Acre (Bus.)	Farm Price ($ Bu.)	Farm Value (Million Dollars)	Pounds Per Bushel Crushed — Yield of Oil	Pounds Per Bushel Crushed — Yield of Meal	U.S. Exports — Grand Total	Bel.-Luxem.	Spain	Canada	W. Germany	Japan	Nether-lands	Tai-wan	U.S.S.R.
1974–5	53,507	51,341	23.7	6.64	8,079	10.51	47.48	420.7	5.6		26.9	51.0	96.9	77.7	24.4	0
1975–6	54,550	53,617	28.9	4.92	7,622	10.94	47.27	555.1	17.7		28.0	45.6	118.1	130.5	32.8	11.4
1976–7	50,226	49,401	26.1	6.81	8,776	11.09	47.81	15,351	411	1,030	462	1,520	3,219	3,007	697	825
1977–8	58,760	57,830	30.6	5.88	10,383	10.39	47.34	19,061	475	1,532	264	1,521	3,636	4,086	854	744
1978–9	64,708	63,663	29.4	6.66	12,450	11.07	47.63	20,117	420	1,475	352	1,486	3,865	4,012	1,271	1,178
1979–0	71,632	70,343	32.1	6.28	14,204	10.74	48.01	23,818	584	2,203	392	1,318	3,868	6,035	780	813
1980–1	70,037	67,813	26.5	7.57	13,601	11.09	47.93	19,712	670	1,383	345	1,791	3,816	3,839	1,063	
1981–2	67,810	66,163	30.1	6.04	12,005	10.72	47.86	25,285	1,404	3,855	310	2,135	4,196	5,349	1,059	683
1982–3	70,884	69,442	31.5	5.69	12,463	10.76	47.88	24,634	1,259	2,313	324	1,813	4,580	4,648	1,300	199
1983–4	63,779	62,525	26.2	7.81	12,775	11.26	47.36	20,215	882	1,800	248	967	4,394	2,988	1,382	408
1984–5	67,755	66,113	28.1	5.78	10,757	11.05	47.15	16,279	658	1,084	140	718	3,828	2,857	1,389	
1985–6[1]	63,130	61,584	34.1	5.10	10,705	11.34	47.87	20,142	784	1,519	130	934	4,293	3,056	1,506	1,519
1986–7[3]	61,835	59,513	33.8	4.70	9,442			20,680								

[1] Preliminary. [2] Data prior to 1976–7 are in millions of bushels. [3] Forecast. *Source: Crop Reporting Board, U.S.D.A.* T.631

Supply and Distribution of Soybeans in the United States   In Millions of Bushels

Crop Year Begin. Sept. 1	Supply — Stocks, Sept. 1 — Farms	Mills, Elevators[2]	Total	Production	Total Supply	Crushings	Exports	Seed	Feed	Residual	Total Distribution
1973–4	9.4	50.2	59.6	1,547.5	1,607.1	821.3	539.1	56.1	1.2	18.7	1,436.4
1974–5	64.5	106.3	170.9	1,216.3	1,387.2	701.3	420.7	57.2	1.0	21.7	1,198.9
1975–6	75.1	109.9	188.2	1,548.3	1,736.5	865.1	555.1	53.5	1.2	15.7	1,490.6
1976–7	86.2	158.8	244.9	1,288.6	1,533.5	790.2	564.1	61.0	1.0	13.3	1,429.6
1977–8	32.7	70.2	102.9	1,767.3	1,870.2	926.7	700.5	68.0	1.0	13.0	1,703.6
1978–9	59.0	102.0	161.0	1,868.8	2,029.8	1,018	739.0	75.0	1.0	23.0	1,856.0
1979–0	61.5	112.6	174.1	2,260.7	2,437	1,123	875.0	———81———			2,079
1980–1	128.6	229.9	358.5	1,797.5	2,156	1,020	724.0	———99———			1,843
1981–2	153.6	159.4	313.0	1,989.1	2,302	1,030	929.0	———89———			2,048
1982–3	117.7	136.7	254.5	2,190.3	2,444	1,108	905	———86———			2,099
1983–4	118.6	226.1	344.6	1,635.8	1,981	983	743	———79———			1,805
1984–5	67.9	107.8	175.7	1,860.9	2,037	1,030	598	———93———			1,721
1985–6[1]	143.2	172.8	316.1	2,098.5	2,415	1,053	740	———86———			1,879
1986–7[3]	167.1	369.2	536.3	2,009.3	2,545	1,080	760	———90———			1,930

[1] Preliminary. [2] Also warehouses. [3] Estimates. *Source: Economic Research Service, U.S.D.A.* T.632

Production of Soybeans for Beans in the U.S., by Selected States   In Millions of Bushels

Year	Ark.	So. Car.	Ill.	Ind.	Iowa	La.	Mich.	Minn.	Miss.	Mo.	N. Car.	Ohio	Tenn.	Nebr.	Ky.
1973	116.3	23.0	281.3	135.1	263.5	34.8	16.6	127.3	60.5	126.9	34.8	89.8	36.9	36.3	26.0
1974	81.7	24.0	202.6	97.3	199.1	44.0	13.2	84.0	46.3	93.5	30.5	79.8	31.9	28.2	25.0
1975	117.5	30.4	299.5	121.6	237.0	48.0	15.9	98.6	70.2	113.6	33.4	102.3	46.3	32.4	29.7
1976	82.1	21.4	249.5	111.5	200.0	63.0	11.6	66.4	71.5	84.0	24.6	95.0	40.5	19.6	28.9
1977	105.8	26.7	336.3	144.3	251.3	63.0	21.6	133.8	78.5	148.8	29.0	120.0	52.2	40.7	40.9
1978	115.2	32.3	309.5	144.2	283.1	76.0	21.6	146.2	81.7	155.0	40.3	127.7	56.9	42.5	40.8
1979	144.2	39.8	379.1	159.1	306.4	93.8	30.3	162.6	118.9	183.6	45.8	144.8	70.7	54.7	54.0
1980	65.3	20.8	309.9	157.7	318.4	67.0	30.4	149.9	61.6	135.5	34.7	135.4	45.9	53.1	36.0
1981	99.0	31.0	351.5	151.8	326.0	64.2	29.1	139.2	75.6	155.6	46.3	99.8	61.1	78.7	47.9
1982	105.6	39.6	354.2	173.3	306.6	75.4	35.3	169.1	92.3	171.0	52.5	133.2	61.0	78.8	51.3
1983	70.3	23.6	267.0	122.5	278.6	68.1	33.8	151.8	58.9	103.0	33.0	105.0	31.5	59.0	24.5
1984	101.4	29.8	284.1	150.1	264.6	66.8	32.1	172.9	76.8	108.7	46.5	137.6	48.1	66.3	42.3
1985	98.1	24.6	382.5	185.1	309.7	44.1	34.6	160.0	70.7	180.4	39.1	160.6	45.3	85.0	41.8
1986[1]	68.0	14.4	375.9	161.5	361.2	39.9	28.5	174.6	45.0	183.6	36.8	153.3	37.5	95.6	32.1

[1] Preliminary. *Source: Crop Reporting Board, U.S.D.A.* T.633

High, Low & Closing Prices of May Soybean Futures at the Chicago Board of Trade   In Cents per Bushel

Year of Delivery		Year Prior to Delivery											Delivery Year					Life of Delivery Range
		Mar.	Apr.	May	June	July	Aug.	Sept.	Oct.	Nov.	Dec.	Jan.	Feb.	Mar.	Apr.	May	
1980	High	744½	747	760	859	823	773	790	788	739½	726½	704	710½	669½	611	624	859
	Low	735	719½	734	749	730½	720	729½	695	702	686½	653	656½	582½	569½	589½	569½
	Close	737½	739¾	756	764	738¾	757¾	762½	709¾	723¼	687¼	695½	657½	583	594½	612	—
1981	High	741½	713½	710	750	859	855½	933	997½	1,006	1,001	882	798½	788½	812½	785	1,006
	Low	696½	681	684	680	744	783	842	847½	937	765½	735	754½	719½	757½	733	680
	Close	699	692	695¾	750	822	854½	873¼	966½	997½	843½	751½	761	783½	778½	741	—
1982	High	894	922	883	832½	853½	807	751	739	721	696¼	677	683	642	670¾	669½	922½
	Low	859	872	820	772	787	722	703½	705	670	619	637	617½	605½	639½	647	605
	Close	888½	873	829	788½	812½	730	715¼	714¼	678¼	641¼	674½	632¾	640	651¾	666	—
1983	High	713	729½	723½	704½	678½	664½	611½	588	607¾	595½	620	622	643¾	655½	643	746
	Low	667½	698	687½	670	651	593½	572½	558½	570½	576¼	577	572½	577½	620¼	610¼	558½
	Close	696	716½	687½	671	654¾	601	574¼	568¼	594	581¾	618½	575½	637	640¼	621½	—
1984	High	718	732	720	678	794	984	996	927	903½	853	825	768	815	813	894	996
	Low	645	695½	659	630	657½	760	859½	831	791	775½	738	706	762	765	768½	630
	Close	714	719	659½	660	761	930	890	851	822	843½	747½	765	789	771	888	—
1985	High	773	777	784	797	764	700	675	678	676½	640½	624	619½	614	609¾	590¾	797
	Low	753	737	744½	736	940	643½	601	623	623	597¼	581¾	572	570¾	585	568	568
	Close	768½	737	777	761	646½	675	627	659¾	634¼	599	613¼	573	605½	588	568	—
1986	High	645	650	637	616	618	560½	560½	551½	557	567	566½	537	523¼	527¼	519½	527	650
	Low	608½	631	583½	577	547	531¼	532	534¼	549	504		542½	529¼	527¼	519½	527	504
	Close	643½	636½	590½	583	555¼	541	547½	548¾	513	554		523¾	541½	544	534½	—
1987	High	554	574	574	536	541½	529½	513¾	514	512	511¼					
	Low	535½	522	529½	509½	504½	492	491¾	493¼	501	489					
	Close	544¾	564½	529½	510	525	502	508½	509	510½	498¼					

Source: Chicago Board of Trade

T.634

Soybean Stocks at U.S. Mills on First of Month   In Millions of Bushels

Crop Year	Sept.	Oct.	Nov.	Dec.	Jan.	Feb.	Mar.	Apr.	May	June	July	Aug.
1975–6	27.4	26.8	116.6	137.2	131.5	121.1	109.8	101.3	92.8	79.4	80.5	66.3
1976–7	48.7	63.0	127.5	159.8	154.2	147.5	146.5	140.3	126.8	108.6	83.4	50.9
1977–8	23.4	20.3	101.5	123.9	113.0	94.4	87.3	102.8	90.2	76.3	54.5	44.6
1978–9	37.9	31.9	138.4	149.4	127.3	112.4	124.0	120.9	96.7	71.1	73.0	55.6
1979–0	37.5	39.2	166.5	184.5	163.3	145.4	130.7	118.6	95.8	79.7	75.7	73.9
1980–1	56.9	80.4	166.0	172.0	138.7	125.9	105.4	97.2	84.4	67.8	49.2	43.9
1981–2	33.4	31.5	105.8	135.2	114.5	99.8	84.6	79.2	72.2	60.8	51.2	43.6
1982–3	30.0	29.0	114.2	145.5	125.1	116.2	98.5	96.2	84.6	69.8	62.0	55.4
1983–4	58.6	63.9	124.5	142.3	124.0	125.3	114.8	105.3	94.2	101.7	83.4	57.7
1984–5	35.3	19.7	53.9	116.4	98.4	85.9	65.8	69.7	65.2	53.4	47.6	36.0
1985–6	26.7	25.7	92.8	113.4	119.9	124.6	97.5	84.9	67.6	53.2	40.7	39.8
1986–7	28.5	38.4										

Sources: Economic Research Service, U.S.D.A.

T.635

Soybean Exports from the United States   In Millions of Bushels

Year	Sept.	Oct.	Nov.	Dec.	Jan.	Feb.	Mar.	Apr.	May	June	July	Aug.	Total
1975–6	24.3	62.7	61.5	49.6	51.8	52.2	52.3	50.5	49.5	47.2	29.2	24.3	555.1
1976–7	22.2	60.1	67.4	56.7	50.9	59.9	58.4	57.0	55.1	31.0	27.2	18.1	564.1
1977–8	15.0	77.6	87.7	57.0	52.6	54.4	66.6	72.7	79.3	63.4	34.7	39.3	700.5
1978–9	38.0	87.6	101.7	70.6	77.0	53.2	83.5	67.7	46.8	40.9	32.7	39.7	739.2
1979–0	40.9	88.9	118.1	78.3	85.8	73.0	69.4	81.3	74.2	58.7	49.1	57.7	875.2
1980–1	41.4	60.3	75.0	74.5	73.6	55.5	103.2	60.0	69.6	41.8	29.6	41.8	724.3
1981–2	50.9	100.8	103.7	73.6	84.3	89.4	79.0	85.7	90.6	59.8	53.8	57.5	929.1
1982–3	58.0	94.4	93.6	90.1	86.3	87.2	84.4	73.3	58.5	67.7	51.6	60.2	905.2
1983–4	53.9	67.6	69.2	74.5	80.4	79.7	78.8	68.5	56.8	41.1	39.2	30.7	686.6
1984–5	19.0	40.9	93.5	84.8	70.3	72.6	59.8	60.4	33.1	18.2	19.2	26.3	598.2
1985–6[1]	31.5	55.3	79.6	94.1	84.7	92.1	88.7	80.4	57.2	28.7	26.6	21.0	740.1
1986–7[1]	30.2												

[1] Preliminary.   *Source: Bureau of the Census*

T.636

SOYBEANS CBOT
WEEKLY HIGH, LOW & CLOSE OF NEAREST FUTURES

Month–End Open Interest of Soybean Futures at Chicago Board of Trade In Millions of Bushels

Year	Jan.	Feb.	Mar.	Apr.	May	June	July	Aug.	Sept.	Oct.	Nov.	Dec.
1978	470.3	438.0	499.4	483.9	553.5	491.8	452.8	485.8	562.2	726.6	720.1	775.1
1979	613.9	719.0	642.0	576.1	562.2	584.4	514.4	477.1	534.9	564.7	630.4	704.3
1980	533.2	540.0	502.2	449.6	513.5	615.0	703.5	784.4	880.4	1,069.6	1,102.7	1,056.4
1981	645.7	586.9	565.0	551.4	523.3	513.6	470.3	455.7	449.1	523.2	491.4	426.6
1982	400.8	391.6	435.2	422.1	399.1	377.0	400.2	353.7	357.7	422.9	433.3	424.7
1983	465.3	413.9	485.7	507.5	428.5	401.2	547.5	714.3	745.7	684.1	648.2	603.2
1984	548.3	548.9	556.2	494.5	577.1	428.7	316.2	275.1	287.0	339.4	351.2	343.2
1985	359.5	359.2	327.9	311.9	320.2	321.5	329.9	331.6	307.9	390.1	370.5	386.4
1986	373.3	376.5	385.4	371.7	328.7	323.2	287.7	296.3	309.7	426.5	408.7	392.2

Source: Chicago Board of Trade

T.642

Volume of Trading in Soybean Futures at the Chicago Board of Trade   In Millions of Bushels

Year	Jan.	Feb.	Mar.	Apr.	May	June	July	Aug.	Sept.	Oct.	Nov.	Dec.	Total
1978	2,978	2,224	5,057	4,121	3,820	3,742	2,662	2,965	2,561	4,754	3,992	3,511	42,386
1979	3,701	5,038	4,123	3,856	3,686	5,485	4,184	2,843	2,920	3,946	3,115	2,674	45,572
1980	3,222	2,916	2,808	3,035	2,911	3,602	6,803	5,226	6,562	7,706	7,025	7,024	58,841
1981	5,808	4,074	4,796	4,585	3,917	4,737	4,821	3,897	3,626	4,087	3,765	4,337	52,450
1982	3,120	3,497	4,478	4,484	3,517	4,245	4,017	3,822	3,197	4,014	4,282	3,198	45,828
1983	3,942	3,820	4,247	4,375	4,259	4,409	6,224	8,799	7,852	8,071	6,793	5,609	68,402
1984	5,550	5,247	6,008	4,945	7,300	6,323	5,314	4,045	2,505	3,687	3,427	2,463	56,813
1985	3,315	2,749	2,657	2,821	2,766	3,309	3,779	2,581	2,525	3,364	3,881	3,213	36,961
1986	3,692	2,484	2,435	2,976	2,546	2,199	2,925	2,049	1,812	3,266	2,473	1,811	30,668

Source: Commodity Futures Trading Commission   T.638

Soybeans Under Price Support Through the End of the Month
(Cumulative Total from Current Season's Crop)   In Thousands of Bushels

Year	Sept.	Oct.	Nov.	Dec.	Jan.	Feb.	Mar.	Apr.	May	June	July	Aug.
1977-8	360	13,135	47,879	68,269	89,128	93,293	96,234	96,808	97,048	97,146	—	—
1978-9	0	6,403	31,008	43,015	58,278	61,489	62,365	63,146	63,508	65,087	—	—
1979-0	11	9,507	39,559	67,372	101,052	106,135	113,638	119,860	121,684	122,013	—	—
1980-1	22	11,705	28,541	67,744	100,809	116,167	125,480	130,236	132,346	133,160	—	—
1981-2	1,044	26,019	81,377	138,202	191,386	208,285	216,412	219,743	144,165	221,303		
1982-3	861	50,145	203,031	311,105	363,696	382,536	391,432	393,567	394,727	395,893		
1983-4	0	9,098	32,869	62,736	84,526	92,974	98,945	100,030	100,656	100,817		
1984-5	0	46,349	99,437	174,002	242,526	258,174	268,812	271,353	274,051	275,687		
1985-6	1,056	86,633	265,929	408,793	482,658	499,223	506,818	511,462	513,089	513,954		
1986-7	313	34,971	154,207									

Source: U.S. Department of Agriculture   T.639

Soybeans Crushed (Factory Consumption) in the U.S.   In Millions of Bushels—One Bushel = 60 Pounds

Year	Sept.	Oct.	Nov.	Dec.	Jan.	Feb.	Mar.	Apr.	May	June	July	Aug.	Total
1976-7	68.8	72.9	73.4	72.7	72.2	71.6	74.4	67.1	61.2	56.2	50.6	49.1	790.2
1977-8	51.9	75.8	85.3	86.6	85.3	75.4	86.5	80.1	82.7	72.4	70.8	73.9	926.7
1978-9	71.4	89.3	89.6	96.4	90.6	81.5	89.0	83.3	86.9	82.8	80.6	76.4	1,018
1979-0	75.9	95.8	101.4	104.4	106.6	100.0	102.2	92.0	93.8	82.7	84.9	83.7	1,123
1980-1	81.0	97.8	98.5	94.1	92.2	79.6	88.7	85.4	82.3	73.4	72.3	74.6	1,020
1981-2	75.4	104.5	97.6	102.5	94.9	86.7	85.1	81.0	86.6	77.1	70.6	67.8	1,030
1982-3	76.0	100.2	108.1	111.9	110.0	93.0	94,6	81.8	83.7	81.5	81.6	85.7	1,108
1983-4	86.6	96.4	86.6	89.4	93.8	79.2	86.0	74.6	79.4	70.6	69.0	71.1	982.7
1984-5	65.5	89.2	98.9	101.1	94.5	80.8	85.6	83.2	89.3	82.7	82.0	77.5	1,030
1985-6[1]	76.5	94.3	96.7	100.8	99.6	81.4	91.6	84.4	86.3	79.6	83.1	78.4	1,053
1986-7[1]	79.5												

[1] Preliminary.   *Source: Bureau of the Census*   T.641

Average Price Received by Farmers for Soybeans in the U.S.   In Cents Per Bushel

Year	Sept.	Oct.	Nov.	Dec.	Jan.	Feb.	Mar.	Apr.	May	June	July	Aug.	Average
1976-77	665	590	611	656	681	706	783	905	924	813	652	548	681
1977-78	517	528	561	568	575	553	620	649	477	669	640	621	588
1978-79	620	626	641	649	658	699	716	706	706	736	736	707	666
1979-80	681	635	630	627	639	620	594	563	576	591	675	718	628
1980-81	759	768	818	780	780	750	759	760	740	705	713	671	757
1981-82	621	606	603	600	613	604	604	617	627	612	599	559	604
1982-83	522	506	534	546	556	566	582	609	606	590	627	757	565
1983-84	828	796	780	774	785	728	768	783	812	799	695	650	781
1984-5	609	608	602	582	591	577	588	588	570	562	542	510	585
1985-6	499	485	492	500	516	518	523	522	525	519	511	498	
1986-7	486	455	477										

Source: Crop Reporting Board   T.637

243

SOYBEANS

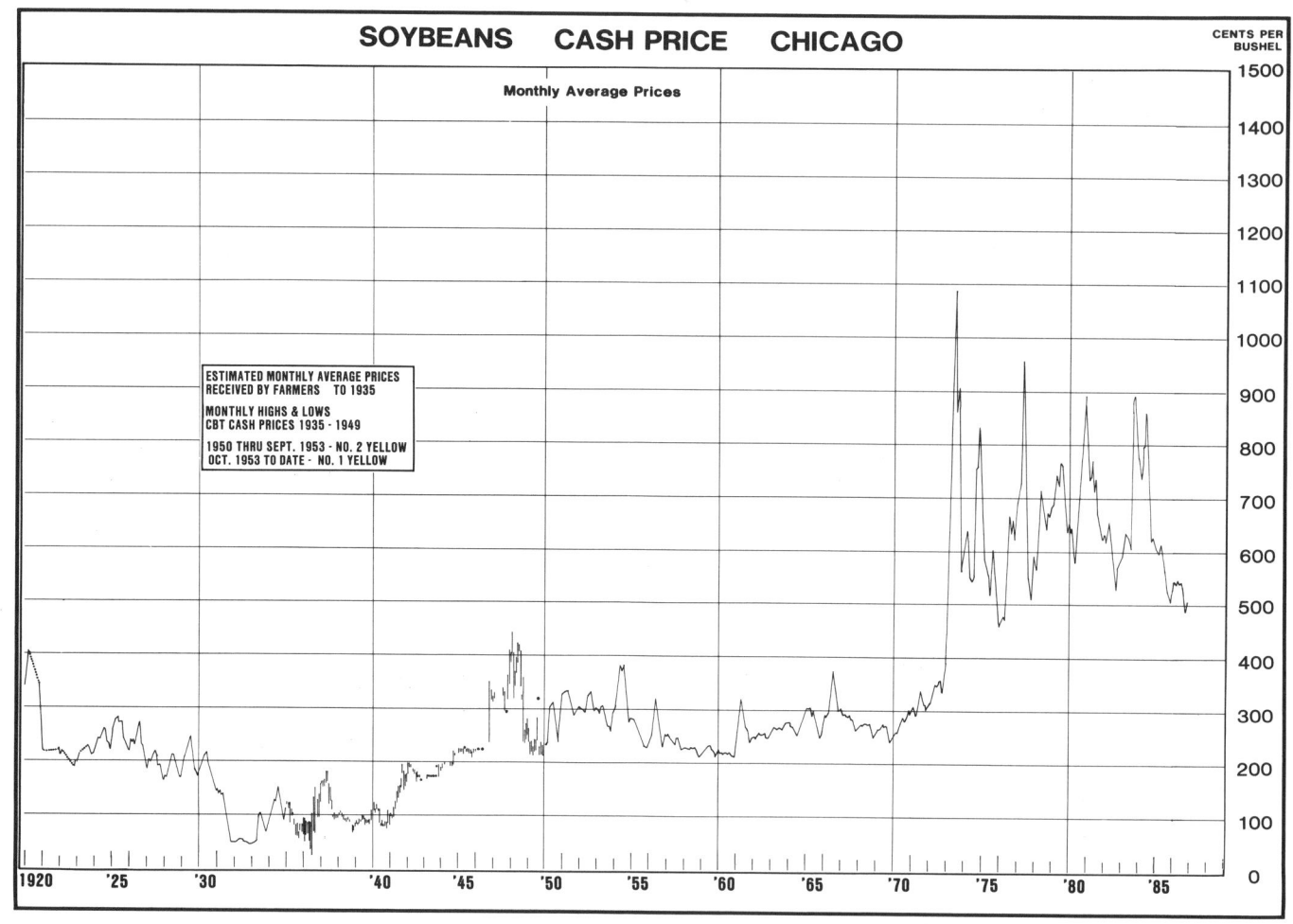

SOYBEANS   CASH PRICE   CHICAGO

Monthly Average Prices

CENTS PER BUSHEL

ESTIMATED MONTHLY AVERAGE PRICES
RECEIVED BY FARMERS   TO 1935

MONTHLY HIGHS & LOWS
CBT CASH PRICES 1935 - 1949

1950 THRU SEPT. 1953 - NO. 2 YELLOW
OCT. 1953 TO DATE - NO. 1 YELLOW

Average Cash Price of No. 1 Yellow Soybeans at Illinois Processor   In Cents per Bushel

Year	Oct.	Nov.	Dec.	Jan.	Feb.	Mar.	Apr.	May	June	July	Aug.	Sept.	Average
1976–7	622	655	686	706	726	825	960	942	825	640	549	516	721
1977–8	507	584	594	573	565	658	681	701	676	662	647	642	624
1978–9	672	668	681	689	728	745	727	721	768	764	728	704	716
1979–0	656	652	653	636	642	607	580	604	610	722	745	813	660
1980–1	827	891	773	757	734	737	772	758	713	736	694	644	753
1981–2	630	628	623	630	624	616	642	656	631	620	573	540	618
1982–3	526	570	573	581	586	598	635	627	606	659	846	893	640
1983–4	846	820	777	767	737	797	798	861	791	685	663	621	764
1984–5	627	625	607	604	597	608	613	595	588	565	528	519	598
1985–6	505	519	532	545	538	547	540	544	543	533	500	496	529
1986–7	489	508											

Source: Agricultural Marketing Service, U.S.D.A.

T.643

Stock Index Futures

The bull market for securities which began in August, 1982, continued during 1986, despite several alarums and excursions. The New York Stock Exchange's (NYSE) composite index began the year at about 120, raced upward during the first quarter to a peak at 138 at the end of March, then fought its way in brief upward thrusts, interrupted by equally brief downturns, to the year's high of approximately 146 in late August. Two weeks later, the Index plunged a total of 10 points on two successive days, provoking fears that the bull market's charmed life was over. But, the Index quickly resumed its rise, returning—despite another brief slide in late November—to 146 in late December. These movements were accompanied by a high volume of trading, one that averaged in the vicinity of 125 million shares per day for the year as a whole and that on five separate occasions exceeded 200 million shares per day.

The most popular futures contract was, as has been since 1982, the S&P 500 Index traded at the Chicago Mercantile Exchange. In a distant second place, in terms of volume, was the NYSE Composite Index contract traded at the New York Futures Exchange. At the end of January, 1986, open interest in the S&P 500 stood at roughly 64,000 contracts; by the end of November, following nearly unbroken increase in each month's ending figure, open interest stood at more than 144,000. Similarly, open interest in NYSE Composite futures rose from just over 10,000 at January, 1986's close to almost 21,000 by the end of November.

A major factor affecting stock indices was a continuation of the downtrend, started in 1985, of the entire interest rate structure. Falling rates on fixed-income obligations of varying maturities helped to make equities a more attractive investment than they had been a year or so earlier, when debt instruments had effective yields in double digits. Investment in equities, and in stock-index futures contracts, was also stimulated by the widespread expectation that the general inflation rate would remain low by recent standards, improving prospects for rising corporate earnings. A factor leading to increased volume of trading of both securities and stock index futures was continued growth in program trading. The reference here is to computer-assisted transactions for hedging institutional investment portfolios or for arbitraging between the stock markets and the stock-index futures markets. It was widely believed that program trading in 1986 was a major cause for the much-increased volatility in the stock indices and in the price of different stock-index futures contracts.

Futures Markets

The S&P 500 Index futures contract is traded on the Chicago Mercantile Exchange (CME). The New York Stock Exchange Composite Index is traded on the New York Futures Exchange (NYFE). The CME is home for the Maxi Major Market Index (MMI) contract and the Value Line Index contract is traded on the Kansas City Board of Trade (KCBOT). The Financial Times Index is traded on the London International Financial Futures Exchange (LIFFE), the Nikkei Stock Average on the Singapore Monetary Exchange (SIMEX), and the Toronto Stock Exchnge 300 Composite Index contract on the Toronto Futures Exchange (TFE).

Month–End Open Interest of NYSE Composite Stock Index Futures at New York in Contracts

Year	Jan.	Feb.	Mar.	Apr.	May	June	July	Aug.	Sept.	Oct.	Nov.	Dec.
1982	—	—	—	—	4,024	4,384	4,646	4,690	5,722	5,459	7,753	5,273
1983	6,841	10,781	6,583	9,120	10,426	9,397	11,354	10,032	8,066	10,303	9,461	8,539
1984	9,348	9,874	8,571	8,454	9,376	7,957	7,918	10,968	9,710	9,181	7,745	7,149
1985	11,062	10,884	9,804	9,438	13,672	9,677	12,102	10,388	7,218	7,011	8,131	9,381
1986	10,164	13,992	15,320	13,809	15,902	10,503	11,662	11,883	21,880	18,816	20,740	9,306

Source: New York Futures Exchange
T.643E

Month–End Open Interest of KC Value Line Stock Index Futures at Kansas City in Contracts

Year	Jan.	Feb.	Mar.	Apr.	May	June	July	Aug.	Sept.	Oct.	Nov.	Dec.
1982	—	1,402	3,679	3,176	3,803	4,250	5,065	5,858	3,456	3,235	3,094	2,777
1983	3,292	3,942	2,879	2,948	4,482	4,487	4,408	3,654	3,381	3,476	3,924	4,498
1984	4,019	5,032	3,241	3,235	3,669	3,041	3,811	5,305	3,000	4,195	5,244	3,888
1985	7,563	7,332	5,741	6,197	8,634	6,556	11,707	10,695	7,576	7,765	11,926	16,844
1986	16,536	19,310	15,129	15,568	14,607	8,603	7,941	7,442	6,478	6,625	6,543	8,735

Source: Kansas City Board of Trade
T.643F

Month–End Open Interest of Maxi[1] Major Market Stock Index Futures at Chicago (CBT) in Contracts

Year	Jan.	Feb.	Mar.	Apr.	May	June	July	Aug.	Sept.	Oct.	Nov.	Dec.
1984	Futures trading began July 23, 1984						5,423	5,846	7,610	11,594	14,211	13,515
1985	17,427	12,779	14,688	14,577	9,328	5,660	9,247	3,884	5,000	3,923	7,169[1]	3,453
1986	4,350	5,973	7,760	5,028	7,290	8,765	8,407	7,524	8,351	7,558	7,268	4,713

[1] Data prior to Nov. 1985 are for the major market index. (Not the maxi.)   *Source: Chicago Board of Trade*   T.643H

STOCK INDEX FUTURES

High, Low & Closing Prices of the December S&P 500 Stock Index Futures at Chicago IMM

Year of Delivery		Yr. Prior to Del. Dec.	Jan.	Feb.	Mar.	Apr.	May	June	July	Aug.	Sept.	Oct.	Nov.	Dec.	Life of Delivery Range
1983	High	147.20	152.60	156.50	158.00	166.70	170.70	175.05	173.70	167.50	172.60	174.25	169.70	167.55	175.05
	Low	138.00	140.60	144.75	151.10	151.90	162.50	161.90	168.85	160.65	165.50	164.15	164.20	161.75	138.0
	Close	143.00	149.20	152.40	154.05	166.40	164.30	171.35	165.00	165.95	168.25	165.45	166.50	161.75	—
1984	High	175.00	177.30	171.50	166.75	166.20	167.70	160.55	158.90	173.95	174.60	174.40	172.90	169.50	179.20
	Low	169.95	170.65	158.60	154.60	159.70	153.90	153.95	150.70	155.40	166.30	162.75	163.90	161.55	150.70
	Close	173.85	171.00	162.50	165.35	166.00	155.60	157.35	154.90	170.20	170.10	168.60	164.55	165.51	—
1985	High	181.05	191.25	194.90	196.50	191.90	198.00	199.10	200.85	195.75	191.40	190.45	204.50	213.85	213.85
	Low	178.40	175.40	188.75	187.00	186.20	185.35	191.55	192.20	188.75	180.65	182.10	189.10	200.40	175.40
	Close	178.40	189.75	193.55	190.20	187.20	186.40	196.65	193.85	189.90	182.80	189.25	202.40	210.90	—
1986	High	220.90	223.30	237.20	249.50	252.10	254.80	255.30	257.25	256.85	256.40	244.80	249.95	256.05	257.25
	Low	215.70	209.50	218.00	230.20	232.40	235.60	241.20	234.40	232.95	226.10	229.80	235.20	244.75	209.50
	Close	219.30	220.50	234.90	247.30	239.55	252.20	254.25	237.55	254.35	230.60	244.70	248.65	249.60	—
1987	High	251.75													
	Low	243.20													
	Close	244.55													

Source: Chicago Mercantile Exchange, International Monetary Market.

High, Low & Closing Prices of the December NYSE Composite Stock Index Futures at New York

Year of Delivery		Yr. Prior to Delivery Nov.	Dec.	Jan.	Feb.	Mar.	Apr.	May	June	July	Aug.	Sept.	Oct.	Nov.	Dec.	Life of Delivery Range
1983	High	85.70	85.35	88.20	90.25	91.00	95.90	98.25	101.45	100.75	96.80	99.85	100.50	97.75	96.90	101.45
	Low	78.80	80.20	81.50	83.80	87.00	87.65	93.65	94.30	95.00	92.70	95.50	94.65	94.10	93.80	60.25
	Close	84.00	83.30	86.70	88.05	88.65	95.75	95.65	99.35	95.55	95.80	97.30	95.45	96.30	94.95	—
1984	High	102.25	101.15	102.65	99.30	95.90	95.45	96.20	92.55	91.50	100.40	100.85	100.90	9.85	97.90	103.55
	Low	98.25	98.50	98.70	91.00	91.90	91.80	88.55	88.80	86.70	89.35	95.85	93.80	94.45	93.20	86.70
	Close	100.95	99.85	99.00	93.90	95.15	95.35	89.55	90.70	89.00	98.30	98.05	97.40	94.90	95.56	—
1985	High	—	104.15	110.90	112.95	113.75	111.55	115.15	115.50	117.20	115.45	111.05	110.05	117.95	123.25	123.25
	Low	—	103.20	101.20	109.60	108.55	108.05	107.60	111.80	111.55	109.60	104.45	105.15	109.20	115.65	101.20
	Close	—	103.55	110.25	112.25	110.85	108.70	114.30	114.40	112.55	110.20	105.70	109.35	116.75	121.30	—
1986	High	—	127.05	129.10	136.30	144.20	145.35	146.55	146.70	148.00	147.65	146.65	141.05	143.30	146.50	148.00
	Low	—	124.85	121.00	126.90	133.55	134.60	135.60	139.00	133.90	133.90	128.00	131.80	135.15	139.90	121.00
	Close	—	126.45	127.15	134.90	142.60	138.15	144.70	145.95	136.55	145.95	132.60	140.95	142.35	142.65	—
1987	High	—	144.50													
	Low	—	140.30													
	Close	—	139.70													

Source: New York Futures Exchange.

High, Low & Closing Prices of the December Value Line Stock Index Futures at K.C. Board of Trade

Year of Delivery		Yr. Prior to Delivery Nov.	Dec.	Jan.	Feb.	Mar.	Apr.	May	June	July	Aug.	Sept.	Oct.	Nov.	Dec.	Life of Delivery Range
1983	High	165.65	168.50	175.50	181.00	184.25	192.80	204.80	213.35	211.70	200.90	206.45	205.60	201.30	199.05	213.35
	Low	150.30	155.55	160.80	168.10	177.20	178.20	189.65	199.50	199.75	192.25	196.70	189.25	189.30	192.45	111.40
	Close	161.55	163.20	172.65	177.20	180.60	192.60	200.60	209.95	201.15	197.80	200.25	190.75	197.85	194.05	—
1984	High	—	—	210.80	200.60	191.95	188.20	189.00	180.35	177.70	191.50	193.40	191.70	188.15	180.95	210.80
	Low	—	—	201.00	184.00	185.60	181.35	173.00	174.60	164.45	170.00	183.50	179.05	175.60	172.65	164.45
	Close	—	—	201.00	187.60	188.85	186.25	175.15	177.30	169.40	188.75	187.60	183.75	175.90	177.98	—
1985	High	—	—	—	211.55	215.45	209.15	213.00	210.50	217.05	209.80	202.60	196.00	209.70	216.65	216.65
	Low	—	—	—	209.50	204.70	201.80	200.30	202.00	205.20	200.80	188.80	188.60	194.60	205.30	188.60
	Close	—	—	—	211.40	207.30	201.80	209.10	207.70	206.95	202.20	190.20	194.85	207.55	213.70	—
1986	High	—	226.25	228.35	235.30	250.00	251.90	251.60	247.65	250.10	237.60	240.00	231.00	233.60	235.60	251.90
	Low	—	219.00	217.50	224.20	235.20	236.00	237.00	240.70	221.30	218.70	210.80	215.50	220.90	226.50	210.80
	Close	—	222.00	223.65	235.30	246.90	240.30	248.00	245.80	222.45	235.15	218.80	230.65	230.00	231.00	—

Source: Kansas City Board of Trade.

High, Low & Closing Prices of the September Major Market Maxi[1] Stock Index Futures at Chicago BOT

Year of Delivery		Jan.	Feb.	Mar.	Apr.	Delivery Year May	June	July	Aug.	Sept.	Life of Delivery Range
1984	High			Futures Trading				222⅛	247	245⅞	247
	Low			Began July 23, 1984				215	222¼	234⅞	215
	Close							221⅞	241⅜	235½	—
1985	High	—	—	264⅞	264	265	266⅝	267½	265½	259	267½
	Low	—	—	259	255¼	251⅝	257¾	261¼	255½	248⅞	248⅞
	Close	—	—	262¼	256¼	264¼	263¼	264¼	256¾	250½	—
1986[1]	High	287.00	299.00	272.60	353.50	362.10	365.70	366.90	368.80	368.00	368.80
	Low	272.60	272.60	272.60	272.60	333.90	348.60	336.00	336.00	335.00	272.60
	Close	272.60	272.60	272.60	340.70	357.40	363.65	342.75	364.20	336.65	—

[1]Prices prior to Jan. 1986 are for the major market stock index. *Source: Chicago Board of Trade* T.643G

Month-End Open Interest of S&P 500 Stock Index Futures at Chicago IMM in Contracts

Year	Jan.	Feb.	Mar.	Apr.	May	June	July	Aug.	Sept.	Oct.	Nov.	Dec.
1982	—	—	—	1,613	6,780	9,603	15,482	13,840	12,901	12,625	16,601	11,681
1983	15,748	22,841	17,766	25,556	30,796	25,013	28,616	29,747	24,129	29,329	27,967	25,349
1984	34,012	38,441	27,931	33,389	34,200	28,395	33,971	31,973	31,610	46,104	53,530	42,191
1985	58,332	62,142	57,664	58,131	72,642	58,890	60,612	60,718	53,629	65,568	74,909	62,879
1986	63,660	86,224	78,431	73,268	99,371	83,100	112,015	107,016	125,304	138,262	144,347	95,433

Source: International Monetary Market (Chicago) T.643D

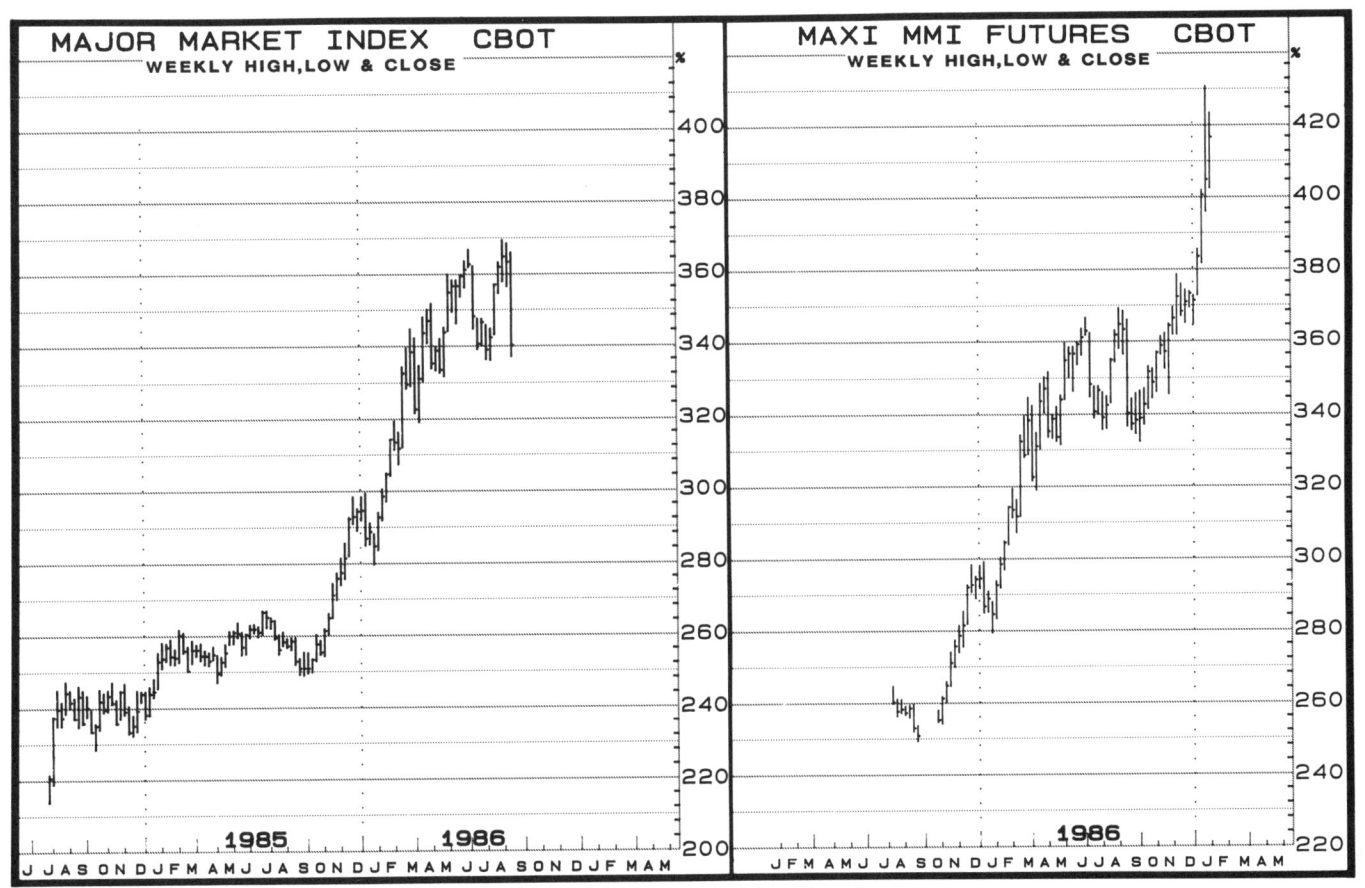

STOCK INDEX FUTURES

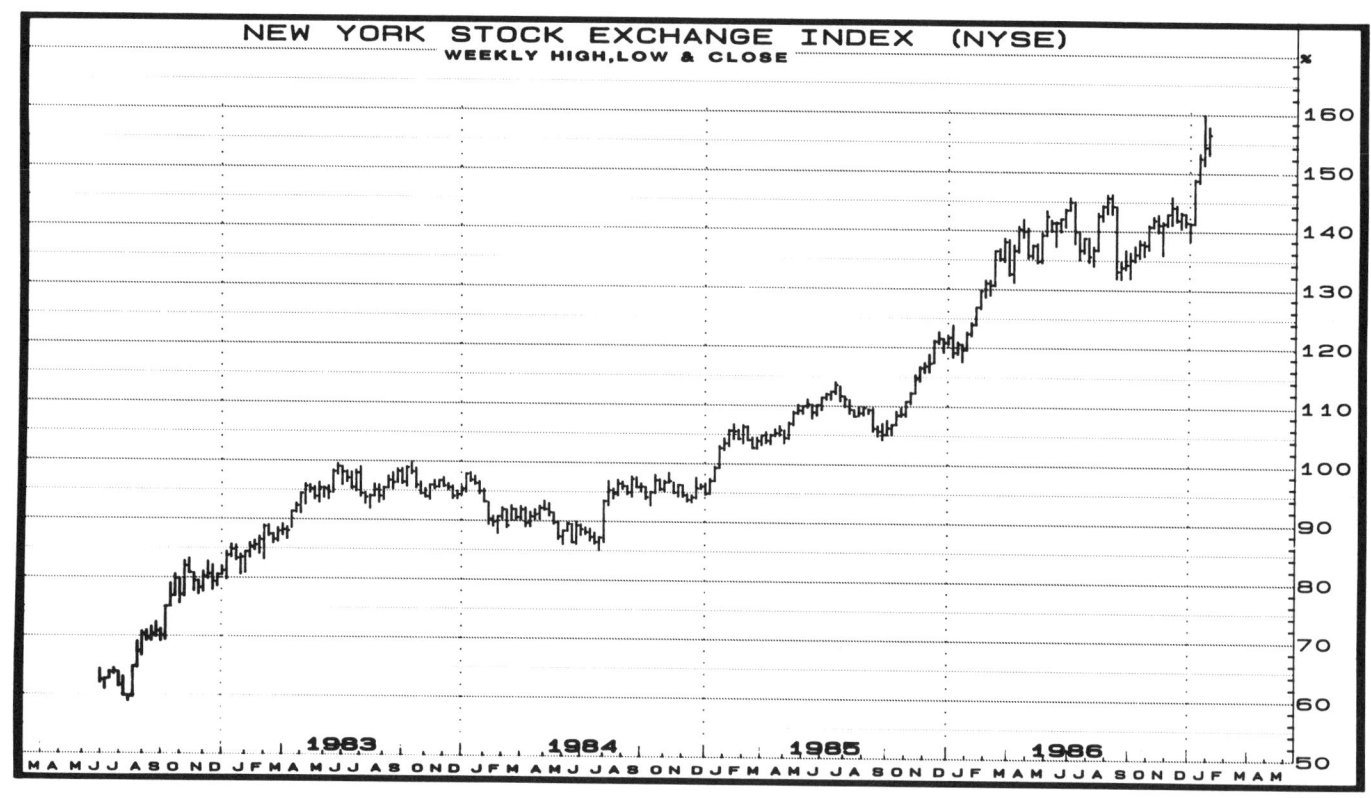

NEW YORK STOCK EXCHANGE INDEX (NYSE)
WEEKLY HIGH, LOW & CLOSE

1983   1984   1985   1986

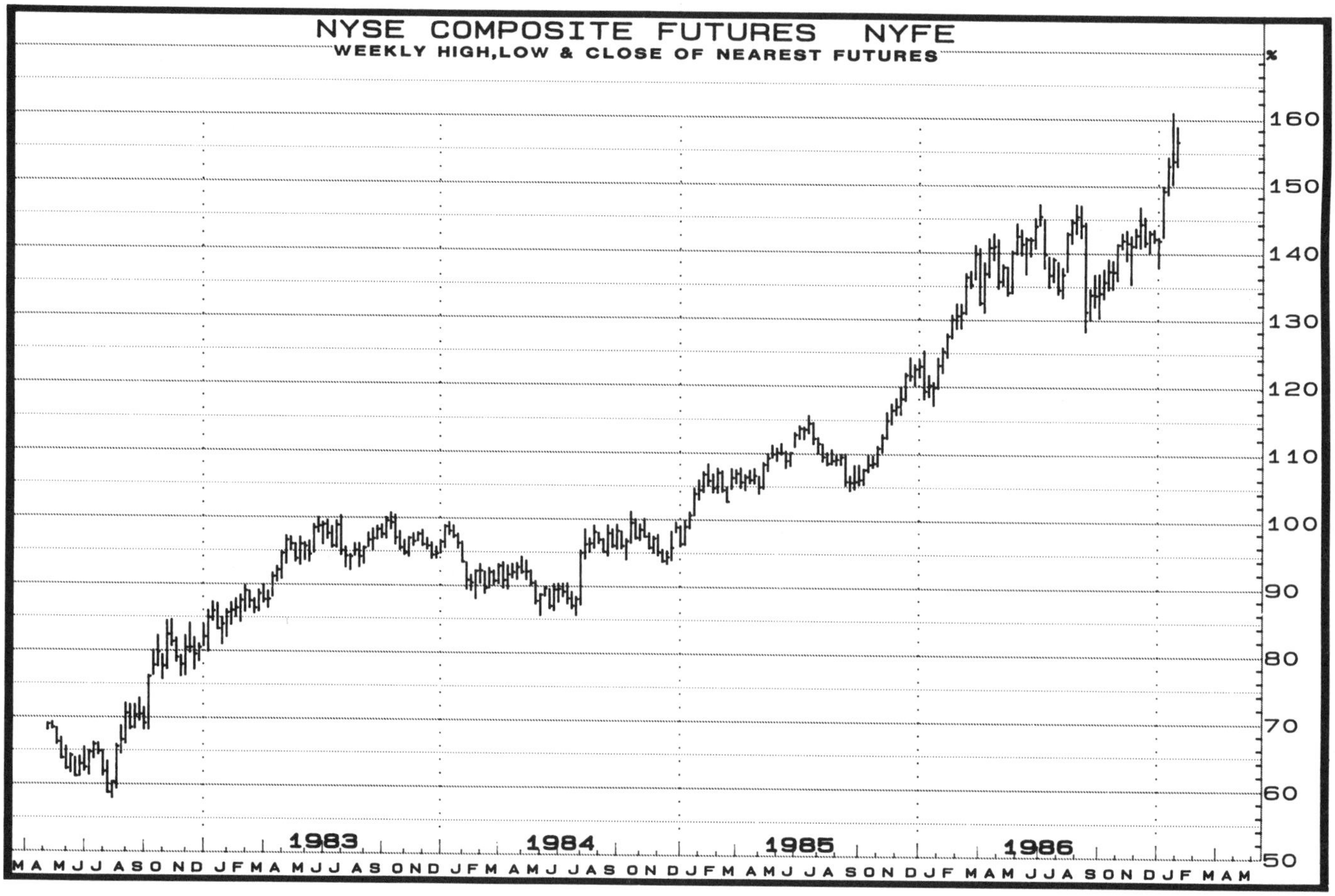

NYSE COMPOSITE FUTURES   NYFE
WEEKLY HIGH, LOW & CLOSE OF NEAREST FUTURES

1983   1984   1985   1986

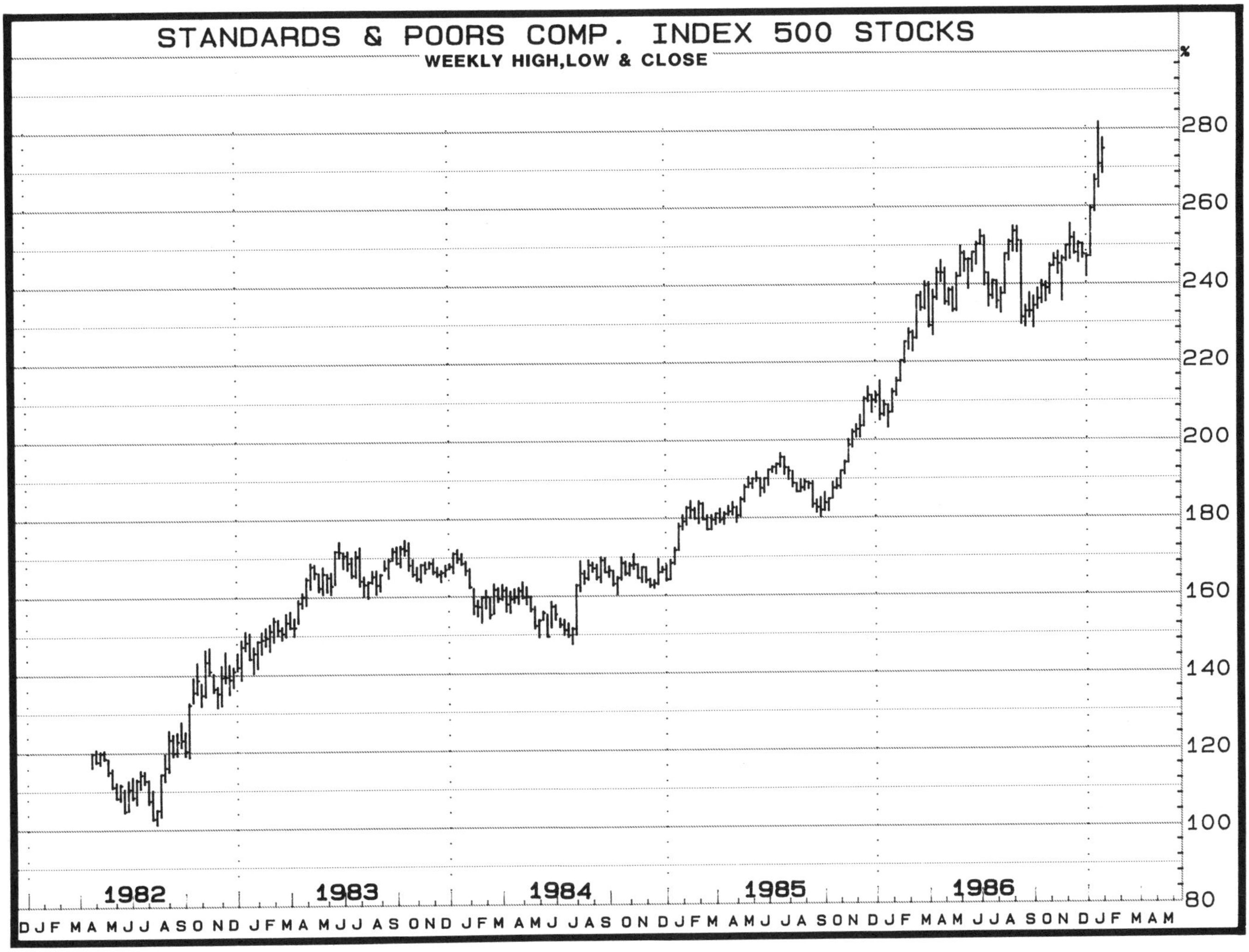

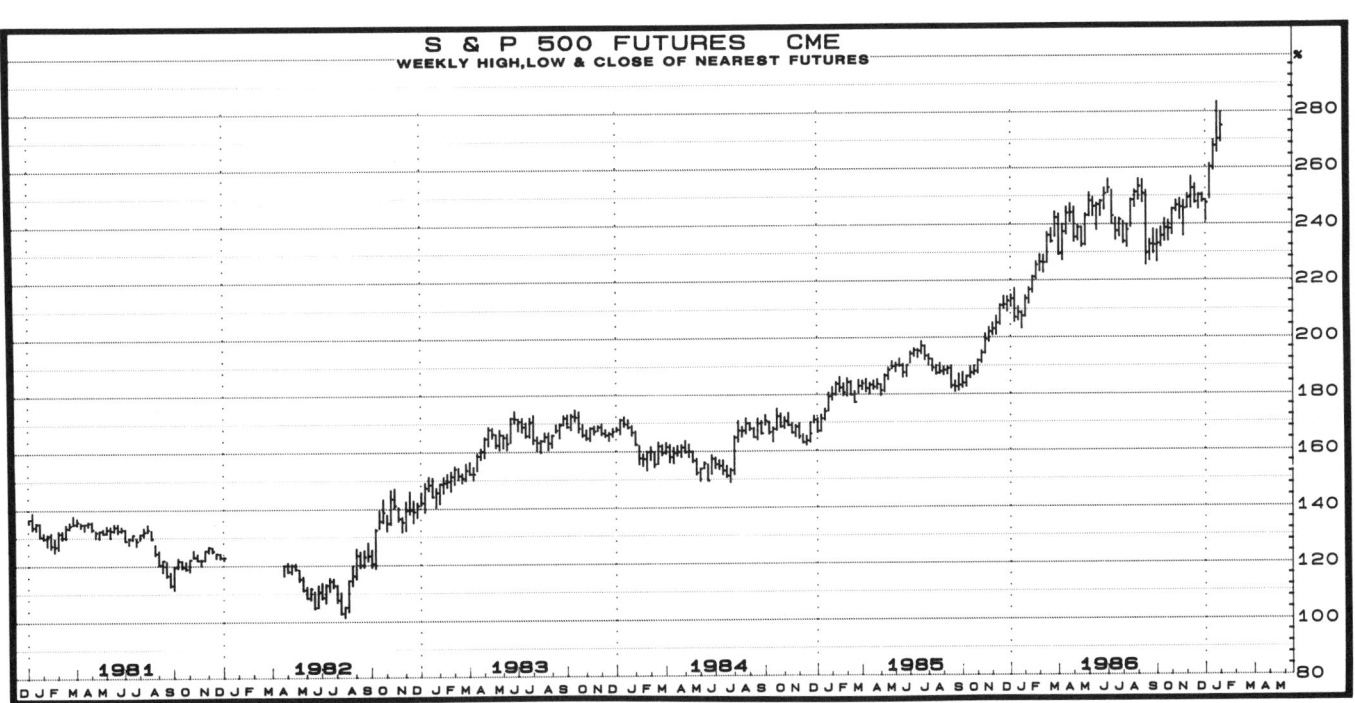

STANDARDS & POORS COMP. INDEX 500 STOCKS
WEEKLY HIGH, LOW & CLOSE

S & P 500 FUTURES   CME
WEEKLY HIGH, LOW & CLOSE OF NEAREST FUTURES

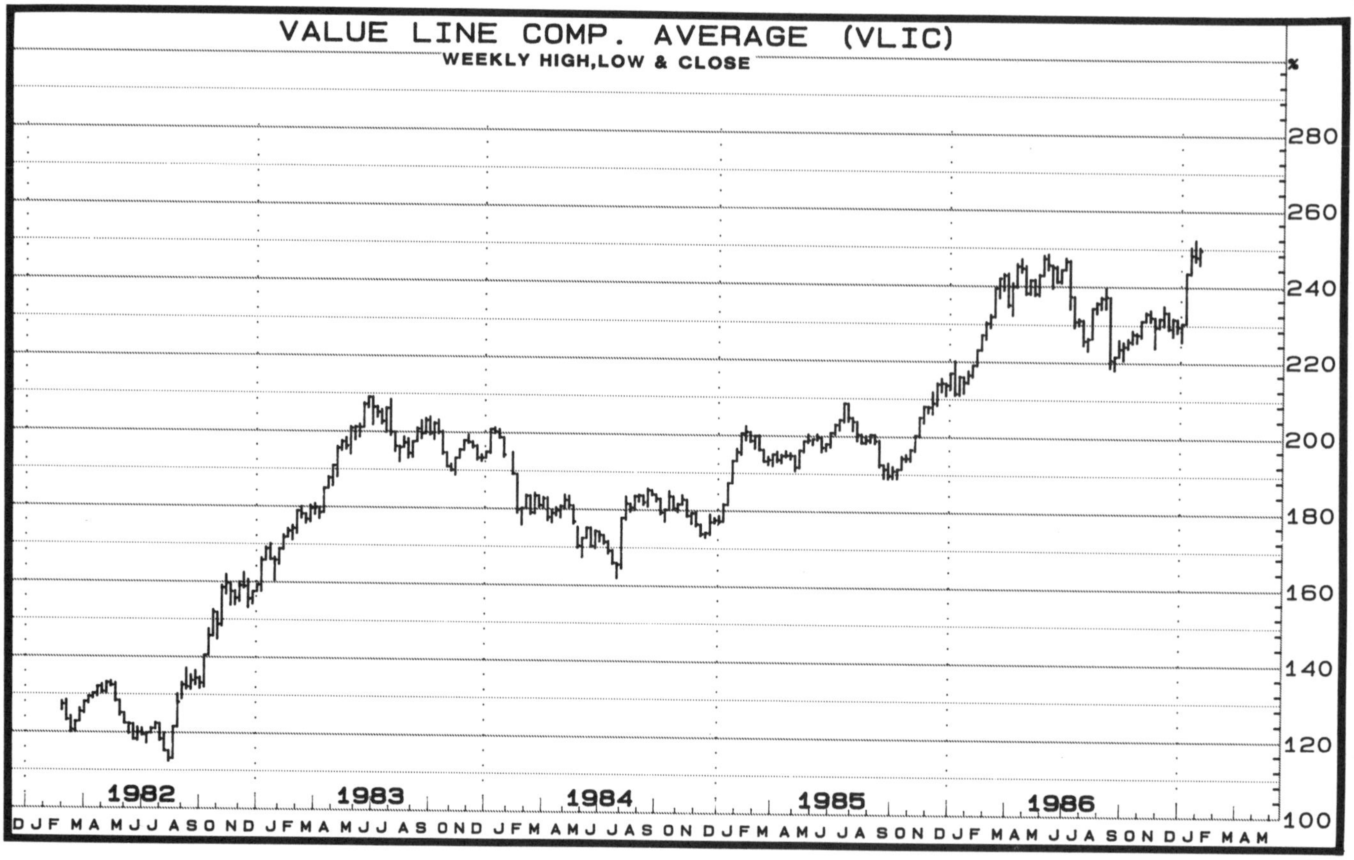
VALUE LINE COMP. AVERAGE (VLIC)
WEEKLY HIGH,LOW & CLOSE
%
280
260
240
220
200
180
160
140
120
100
1982
1983
1984
1985
1986
D J F M A M J J A S O N D J F M A M J J A S O N D J F M A M J J A S O N D J F M A M J J A S O N D J F M A M J J A S O N D J F M A M

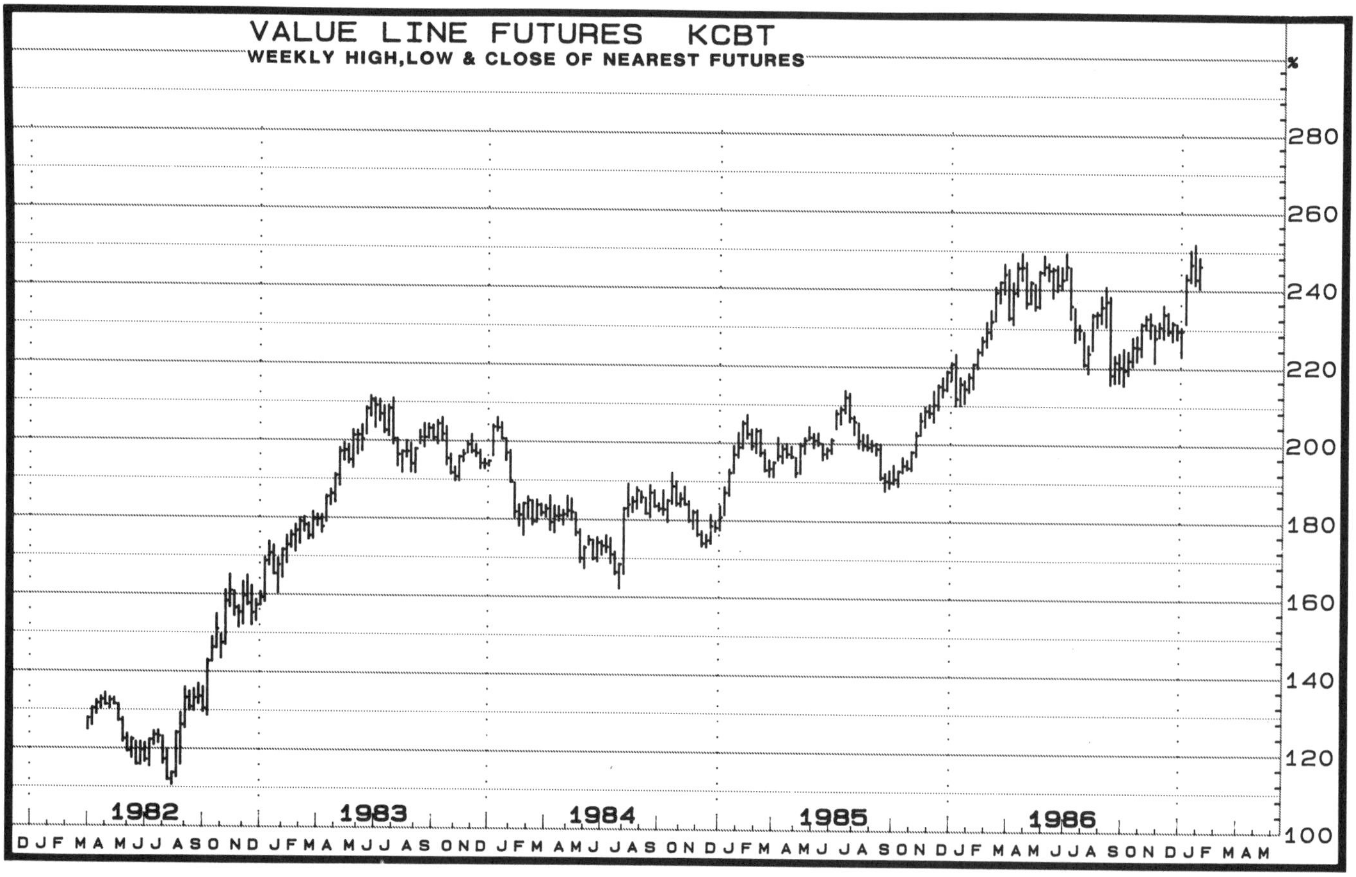
VALUE LINE FUTURES KCBT
WEEKLY HIGH,LOW & CLOSE OF NEAREST FUTURES
%
280
260
240
220
200
180
160
140
120
100
1982
1983
1984
1985
1986
D J F M A M J J A S O N D J F M A M J J A S O N D J F M A M J J A S O N D J F M A M J J A S O N D J F M A M J J A S O N D J F M A M

Sugar

World centrifugal sugar production in 1986/87 was estimated by USDA at 100.1 million tonnes (raw basis). Initial forecasts, somewhat higher, were trimmed due to reduced output in the USSR. Global production in 1985/86 totaled 98.1 million tonnes. Generally, cane accounts for more than 60 percent of world output. For the current crop year, cane was estimated at 64.4 million tonnes, four percent more than the previous season. Beet was estimated at 35.7 million tonnes, down two percent from 1985/86. Chemically, there is no major difference between cane and beet sugar, but the latter is grown in cooler climates and the refining process requires some additional steps.

Brazil is the world's largest producer; 1986/87 cane production was estimated at 9.1 million tonnes, up 11 percent from 1985/86. Cuba's production was expected to total 7.6 million tonnes, up .5 million from a year earlier. Beet production in the USSR was estimated at 7.7 million tonnes, down seven percent from 1985/86. Dry growing conditions adversely affected yields, but improved processing was expected to curtail the loss seen between the fields and refining factories. U.S. production was forecast at 5.8 million tonnes, up six percent from 1985/86. Beet and cane production were placed at 2.9 million tonnes, the former up eight percent and the latter up four percent from 1985/86. The area allocated to beets totaled about 1.2 million acres; cane acreage was placed at .8 million. India is the largest Asian producer. China's output has been increasing; the crop was estimated at 5.5 million tonnes this year, compared with 8.7 million tonnes in India. In Western Europe, France and Germany's beet production generally accounts for about half the area's total production. In Eastern Europe (excluding the USSR), Poland is consistently the largest producer.

World consumption in 1986/87 was estimated at 99.7 million tonnes, up 2 million from 1985/86, and was expected to allow a small increase in world stocks (as of August 31, 1987) of about 400,000 tonnes. Consumption was expected to remain stable or to decline slightly in North America, the Caribbean and Western Europe, owing to substitution of sugar with alternative sweeteners; increases were expected in the USSR, Eastern Europe, and Asia.

Brazil's use of sugar for conversion into gasohol was expected to help maintain consumption there at about 6.3 million tonnes. This season's world increase in offtake is attributed to population growth, a number of improved economies and low prices.

World ending stocks are now calculated using 1980/81 as a base year to reflect the difference between production and consumption and do not take into account import and export estimates. Thus, the apparent 1985/86 ending stock figure of 46.4 million tonnes, reflecting a 46-million carryover from 1984/85, represents a stocks-to-use ratio of 47.5 percent, which was expected to increase this season.

Monthly world prices declined during much of 1986, averaging 7.46 cents/pound in May and sliding to 4.67 cents in September. Weakened import demand during the third quarter, higher-than-expected world output, and uncertainty over U.S. sugar policy reinforced the lower price trend. Prices rebounded in October to 5.42 cents. The recovery was not expected to be sustained or to bring any significant price strength during 1986/87, because of continued high world stocks and a stock-to-use ratio of nearly 50 percent, the highest in several years.

Nearby futures prices of domestic raw sugar (contract No. 14, c.i.f./duty paid, New York) held fairly constant during much of 1986 within a range of 20.87–21.02 cents/pound. These prices compared with the 1985/86 market stabilization price (MSP) of 21.50 cents. For 1986/87, the MSP was set at 21.78 cents, and consists of a loan rate of 18 cents, adjusted average transportation costs of 2.93 cents, interest of 0.65 cents and an incentive factor of 0.20 cents. The New York Coffee, Sugar, and Cocoa Exchange discontinued trading in the No. 12 domestic sugar futures market during 1986 and inaugurated a No. 14 contract. The difference is largely one of quality; the No. 14 is more stringent.

Futures/Options Markets

World and domestic raw sugar contracts are traded on the New York Coffee, Sugar, and Cocoa Exchange. World raw sugar futures are also traded on the London United Terminal Sugar Market. In addition, white sugar futures are traded on the Paris International Sugar Market and in London. The New York Futures Exchange has submitted to the Commodity Futures Trading Commission a white sugar futures contract for approval for trading during 1987. The contract would be the No. 15 and would trade with the world contract (No. 11) and the domestic raw sugar contract (No. 14). The rationale for the contract is that an increasing portion of world trade is now being conducted in white sugar and a broader means for hedging is necessary. Options against the No. 11 world contract are also traded on the New York Coffee, Sugar and Cocoa Exchange.

World Production of Sugar (Centrifugal Sugar–Raw Value)   In Thousands of Metric Tons

Crop Year	Australia Cane	Brazil Cane	China	Cuba Cane	South Africa Cane	India Cane	Indo- nesia Cane	Philip- pines Cane	Poland Beet	West Germany	United States[3] Beet	United States[3] Cane	USSR Beet	Mexico	France	World All
1982–3	3,535	9,300	4,132	7,200	2,256	9,508	1,731	2,521	2,009	3,591	2,483	1,712	7,392	3,078	4,833	101,342
1983–4	3,414	9,400	3,825	8,330	1,462	7,042	1,762	2,381	2,141	2,726	2,575	2,700	8,700	3,242	4,153	96,542
1984–5	3,548	9,300	4,627	8,100	2,514	7,071	1,767	1,878	3,146		2,644	2,645	8,587	3,436	4,301	100,183
1985–6[2]	3,552	8,200	5,535	7,100	2,247	7,983	1,725	1,400	1,809	3,432	2,719	2,756	8,250	3,630	4,323	98,079
1986–7[1]	3,300	9,100	5,480	7,600	2,268	8,730	1,800	1,500	1,700	3,450	2,945	2,855	7,700	3,670	3,575	100,129

[1] Estimated.   [2] Preliminary.   [3] From 1983, data include continental beet & cane and Hawaiian cane.
Source: Foreign Agricultural Service, U.S.D.A.

T.644

SUGAR

United States Sugar (Cane & Beet) Supply and Utilization   In Thousands of Short Tons (Raw Value)

Year	Production Cane	Production Beet	Production Total	Offshore Receipts For-eign	Offshore Receipts Terri-tories	Offshore Receipts Total	Begin-ning Stocks	Total Supply	Total Use	Ex-ports	Net Changes in Invisible Stocks	Refin. Loss Adjust.[3]	Imp. Blends & Mix-tures	Domestic Disappearance Military & Civilian Total	Domestic Disappearance Military & Civilian Per Capita
1977	2,666	3,423	6,089	6,138	102	6,240	3,498	15,827	11,336	22	201	14	—	11,099	94.2
1978	2,535	3,067	5,602	4,683	52	4,735	4,491	14,828	11,074	48	29	108	—	10,889	91.4
1979	2,727	3,066	5,793	5,027	47	5,074	3,754	14,621	10,921	73	-12	103	—	10,756	89.3
1980	2,684	3,052	5,736	4,495	178	4,673	3,701	14,110	11,028	689	72	78	—	10,189	83.6
1981	3,043	3,182	6,225	5,025	48	5,073	3,082	14,380	10,919	1,191	-94	53	—	9,769	79.4
1982	2,776	3,160	5,936	2,964	80	3,044	3,461	12,441	9,373	137	30	53	—	9,153	73.6
1983	3,094	2,588	5,682	3,186	67	3,253	3,068	12,003	9,433	300	249	72	—	8,812	70.2
1984	2,831	3,059	5,890	3,559	24	3,583	2,570	12,043	9,038	429	89	58	8	8,454	66.7
1985[1]	3,100	2,869	5,969	2,872	74	2,946	3,005	11,920	8,794	464	-31	122	15	8,035	62.8
1986[2]	3,150	3,150	6,300	2,089	60	2,149	3,126	11,575	8,417	365	—	50	25	7,800	60.4
1987[2]							3,158								

[1] Preliminary.   [2] Estimate.   [3] Residual.   *Source: Agricultural Marketing Service, U.S.D.A.*   T.645

Sugar Cane for Sugar & Seed and Production of Cane Sugar and Molasses in the United States

Year	Acreage Har-vested 1,000 Acres	Yield of Cane per Acre Tons	Production for Sugar 1,000 Tons	Production for Seed 1,000 Tons	Production Total 1,000 Tons	Farm Price $ per Ton	Farm Value of Cane used for Sugar 1,000 Dollars	Farm Value of Cane used for Sugar & Seed 1,000 Dollars	Sugar Production Raw Value Total 1,000 Tons	Sugar Production Raw Value Per Ton of Cane Lbs.	Refined Basis 1,000 Tons	Molasses Made Black-strap (80° Brix) 1,000 Gallons	Molasses Made Edible 1,000 Gallons	Molasses Made Total 1,000 Gallons
1976	747	37.6	26,919	1,201	28,120	13.70	408,403	425,342	2,724	202	2,545	179,180	2,574	180,730
1977	759	35.3	25,730	1,100	26,830	18.50	454,217	474,257	2,684	209	2,508	N.A.	2,538	164,894
1978	744	35.0	24,821	1,176	25,997	19.40	483,905	507,069	2,612	210	2,441		2,750	161,810
1979	733	36.2	25,410	1,122	26,532	26.00	661,212	690,544	2,700	213	2,524		2,900	164,581
1980	733	36.8	25,582	1,381	26,963	38.50	984,559	1,035,990	2,728	213	2,550		1,900	163,341
1981	755	36.3	26,165	1,243	27,408	24.90	650,721	681,983	2,833	217	2,647		2,100	182,656
1982	742	40.1	28,450	1,321	29,770	26.50	755,038	789,896	3,063	215	2,863		1,550	177,041
1983	768	36.7	27,201	960	28,161	27.80	755,574	781,393	2,930	215	2,739		1,850	177,725
1984[1]	741	36.6	26,008	1,332	27,340	N.A.	N.A.	N.A.	3,007	231	2,811		1,800	175,573
1985[1]	770	36.6	26,877	1,336	28,213				3,033	226	2,816			176,322
1986[1]	801	37.8			30,255				3,150					

[1] Preliminary.   *Source: Statistical Reporting Service, U.S.D.A.*   T.646

U.S. Sugar Beets, Beet Sugar, Pulp, & Molasses Produced from Sugar Beets & Raw Sugar Spot Prices

Year of Harvest	Sugar Beets Acreage Planted 1,000 Acres	Sugar Beets Acreage Harv. 1,000 Acres	Sugar Beets Yield Per Har. Acre Tons	Sugar Beets Production 1,000 Tons	Sugar Beets Price[1] Dollars	Sugar Beets Farm Value $1,000	Sugar Production Refined Basis 1,000 Sh. Tons	Sugar Production Equivalent "Raw Value"[2] 1,000 Sh. Tons	Raw Sugar Prices World[4] Intern. Agreem. Cents Per Lb.	Raw Sugar Prices Cof., Sugar Exch. World Cents Per Lb.	Raw Sugar Prices N.Y. Duty Paid Cents Per Lb.	Whole-sale List Price HFCS (42%) No. East
1977	1,273	1,216	20.6	25,007	24.20	604,399	2,905	3,108	8.10	8.11	11.00	13.05
1978	1,305	1,269	20.3	25,788	25.20	649,846	3,074	3,289	7.81	7.82	13.93	12.32
1979	1,161	1,120	19.6	21,996	33.90	745,273	2,691	2,879	9.65	9.66	15.56	13.54
1980	1,231	1,190	19.8	23,502	47.20	1,108,974	2,943	3,149	28.66	29.02	30.11	24.27
1981	1,252	1,228	22.4	27,538	29.20	803,569	3,166	3,388	16.89	16.93	19.73	21.94
1982	1,054	1,027	20.3	20,894	35.40	740,342	2,558	2,737	8.40	8.42	19.92	16.82
1983	1,081	1,056	19.9	20,992	37.00	777,718	2,522	2,699	8.46	8.49	22.04	18.46
1984	1,124	1,096	20.2	22,134	33.90	750,162	2,715	2,905	5.21	5.18	21.74	20.41
1985[3]	1,125	1,103	20.5	22,636			2,759	2,997	4.06	4.04	20.34	19.38
1986[3]	1,238	1,188	20.8	24,768				3,250	6.02			

[1] Includes support payments, but excludes Sugar beet payments.   [2] Refined sugar multiplied by factor of 1.07.   [3] Preliminary.   [4] International Sugar Agreement, World Price.   *Source: Statistical Reporting Service, U.S.D.A.*   T.647

Raw Sugar N.Y. Spot Price (C.I.F., Duty/Fee Paid, Contract #12 & #14)   In Cents per Pound

Year	Jan.	Feb.	Mar.	Apr.	May	June	July	Aug.	Sept.	Oct.	Nov.	Dec.	Average
1980	19.66	24.69	21.18	22.67	31.89	32.10	28.75	33.14	36.03	41.70	39.28	30.29	30.11
1981	29.57	26.07	23.81	19.91	17.43	18.95	19.10	17.42	15.49	15.66	16.28	17.07	19.73
1982	18.16	17.77	17.13	17.89	19.57	21.03	22.15	22.45	20.88	20.44	20.79	20.83	19.92
1983	21.23	21.76	21.86	22.43	22.60	22.54	22.09	22.55	22.20	21.94	21.83	21.47	22.04
1984	21.51	21.90	22.00	22.03	22.01	22.06	21.89	21.72	21.70	21.56	21.40	21.10	21.74
1985	20.72	20.38	20.91	20.97	21.09	21.27	21.23	20.59	19.51	18.68	18.89	19.89	20.34
1986	20.67	21.01	20.95	20.85	20.88	20.99	20.97	20.87					

Sources: Economic Research Service, U.S.D.A.; N.Y. Coffee & Sugar Exchange

T.648

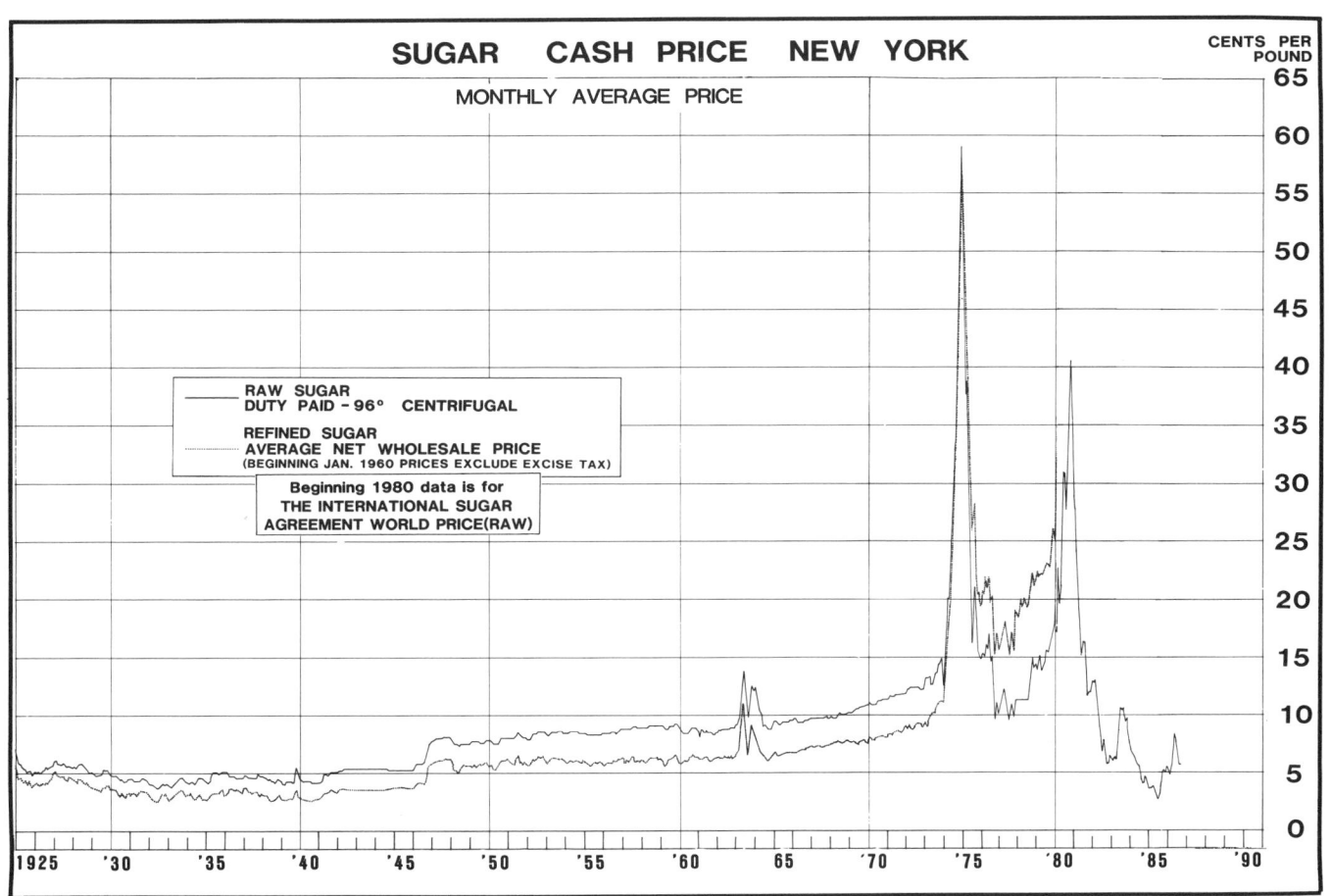

SUGAR

United States Production & Imports of Edible Syrups   In Thousands of Gallons

Year	Production[2] Sirups Corn	Maple	Refiners'	Edible Molasses	Honey	Total	Imports Maple Sirup	Edib. Molas. & Cane Sirup	Honey	Total
1978	751,809	1,154	2,571	2,750	19,466	777,750	811	2,077	4,727	7,615
1979	845,741	1,219	2,524	2,900	20,160	872,544	857	2,944	4,948	8,749
1980	941,056	973	1,983	1,900	16,871	962,783	855	3,422	4,143	8,420
1981	1,073,933	1,410	1,446	2,100	15,703	1,094,592	1,046	2,040	6,530	9,616
1982	1,212,759	1,292	1,003	1,550	18,666	1,235,270	1,154	2,566	7,767	11,487
1983	1,334,557	1,150	1,000	1,850	17,314	1,355,871	1,287	2,336	9,277	12,900
1984[1]	1,501,377	1,366	1,000	1,800	13,936	1,519,479	1,248	3,495	10,869	15,612
1985[1]								4,164		

[1] Preliminary.   [2] Production of cane syrup, sorghum syrup, & edible molasses is of the fall of the preceding year.
Source: Agricultural Marketing Service, U.S.D.A.   T.652

U.S. Exports & Domestic Consumption of Edible Syrups, Corn Sugar & Sugar   In Thousands of Gallons

Year	Exports Corn Sirup	Honey	Total	Indicated Domestic Consumption Sirups Corn	Maple	Cane & Refin. & Edib. Mol.	Honey	Total	Per Capita Consumption in Pounds Corn Sweet-ners[2]	Cal-oric Sweet-eners	Aspar-tame	Sacc-harin	Sugar U.S. Grown	Cane	Total	Total All Sweet-eners
1979	1,207	747	1,954	844,534	2,076	8,368	24,361	879,339	36.8	127.1	0	7.0	47.6	62.8	89.3	
1980	3,498	722	4,220	937,558	1,828	7,620	20,292	967,298	40.2	125.0	0	7.7	51.2	56.8	83.6	132.8
1981	2,916	777	3,693	1,071,017	2,456	5,586	21,456	1,100,515	44.5	125.1	.2	8.0	47.1	53.8	79.4	133.3
1982	791	721	1,512	1,211,968	2,446	5,119	25,712	1,245,245	48.2	123.2	1.0	8.4	49.8	48.4	73.7	132.6
1983	1,223	630	1,853	1,333,334	2,437	5,186	25,961	1,366,918	52.2	124.6	3.5	9.5	47.1	47.9	71.1	137.6
1984	656	627	1,283	1,500,721	2,614	6,295	24,178	1,533,808	57.9	126.9	5.8	10.0			67.6	142.7
1985[1]									65.0	129.7	11.0	6.0			63.3	146.7
1986[1]									66.2	128.5					60.9	

[1] Preliminary.   [2] Corn syrup & dextrose.   *Source: Agricultural Marketing Service, U.S.D.A.*   T.653

Sugar Deliveries and Stocks in the United States   In Thousands of Short Tons, Raw Value

Year	Deliveries by Primary Distributors Cane[1] Sugar Re-fineries	Beet Sugar Fac-tories	Importers of Direct Consump-tion Sugar	Cane Sugar Mills[1]	Total	Sales of Refined Sugar For Export	Total Domestic Consump-tion[2]	Stocks (January 1) Cane Sugar Re-fineries	Beet Sugar Fac-tories	Comm. Credit Corp.	Re-finers Raws	Main-land Cane Mills	Total
1979	7,565	3,191	84	18	10,069	73	10,756	257	1,560		510	641	2,968
1980	7,024	3,165	7	45	9,933	689	10,189	315	1,205	432	691	1,068	3,279
1981	6,618	3,151	17	24	10,207	1,191	9,769	272	1,286	20	832	658	3,048
1982	6,127	3,026	46	24		137	9,153	272	1,296	20	844	931	3,344
1983	5,910	2,902				300	8,812	262	1,417	—	510	701	2,897
1984	5,722	2,732				429	8,454	225	1,103	—	528	592	2,448
1985[3]	4,937	3,062				464	8,035	214	1,430	—	473	762	2,879
1986[3]	4,586	2,906				365	7,800	199	1,189	220	523	834	2,964

[1] Sugar for direct consumption only.   [2] Includes deliveries for U.S. military forces at home and abroad.   [3] Preliminary estimate.
Source: Department of Agriculture   T.654

Sugar, Refined—Deliveries by Type of Product of Buyer in the U.S.   In Thousands of Short Tons

Year	Bakery & Cereal Pdts.	Bever-ages	Confec-tionery[3]	Insti-tutions	Dairy Products	Proc-essed Foods	Other Food Uses	Retail Gro-cers[4]	Whole-sale Grocers[5]	Other Uses[6]	Total De-liveries	In Con-sumer Size Pckgs.	To Indus-trial Users
1978	1,308	2,608	912	230	531	689	412	1,180	1,996	161	10,027	2,267	909
1979	1,289	2,441	911	276	480	681	483	1,239	2,038	126	9,934	2,410	867
1980	1,337	2,161	932	303	450	535	589	1,169	1,881	120	9,477	2,347	703
1981	1,306	1,852	983	259	459	484	581	1,161	2,001	126	9,212	2,425	737
1982	1,296	1,583	940	177	404	450	526	1,086	1,951	106	8,519	2,310	727
1983	1,387	1,248	1,087	195	385	454	431	1,168	1,713	131	8,199	2,314	567
1984	1,404	908	1,115	209	408	433	416	1,100	1,744	127	7,863	2,274	570
1985[1]	1,494	340	1,059	204	456	428	441	1,045	1,874	131	7,472	2,185	734
1986[6]	1,422	280	1,030	150	440	380	456	986	1,692	130	6,966	2,150	528

[1] Preliminary.   [2] Used largely for pharmaceuticals & some tobacco.   [3] And related products.   [4] Chain stores, supermarkets.   [5] Jobbers, sugar dealers.   [6] Forecast.   *Source: Stat. Rep. Serv., U.S.D.A.*   T.649

World Stocks of Centrifugal Sugar as of Sept. 1   In Thousands Metric Tons (Raw Value)

Sugar-Making Season	Australia	Brazil	France	West Germany	India	Italy	Japan	Mexico	Netherlands	Philippines	Sweden	Iran	United Kingdom	United States & Ins. Areas	Total
1976-7	328	1,746	174	165	737	337	98	642	139	744	138	207	139	2,399	10,574
1977-8	534	1,286	706	202	732	562	104	198	199	1,607	127	304	253	2,718	12,820
1978-9	383	1,516	947	305	1,448	859	350	134	207	1,290	140	364	234	3,375	15,843
1979-0	687	3,008	962	537	1,934	758	421	138	222	1,214	108	354	455	3,549	19,122
1980-1	555	1,959	899	535	386	833	497	192	196	727	93	325	625	2,904	14,353
1981-2	499	2,234	415	300	706	663	212	167	181	158	75	275	706	2,508	12,322
1982-3	364	918	1,212	416	3,354	570	377	587	128	269	317	151	503	1,399	14,253
1983-4	433	1,056	1,565	550	4,999	479	340	1,112	178	220	350	201	204	1,252	17,937
1984-5[1]	613	1,056	725	385	3,029	385	350	981	117	209	281	251	209	802	13,546

[1] Preliminary.   Source: Foreign Agricultural Service, U.S.D.A.   T.650

Month-End Open Interest of World Sugar (#11) Futures at New York   In Contracts

Year	Jan.	Feb.	Mar.	Apr.	May	June	July	Aug.	Sept.	Oct.	Nov.	Dec.
1978	41,918	32,736	30,260	31,558	34,902	34,186	35,419	34,381	30,702	31,290	30,439	31,498
1979	35,004	34,529	36,200	31,824	36,521	39,646	44,938	58,184	61,442	73,701	87,182	92,007
1980	103,041	87,843	68,667	61,126	69,666	68,554	68,996	70,993	71,316	79,313	76,754	64,740
1981	61,522	57,087	59,025	54,898	62,330	61,022	66,730	64,604	52,740	60,761	66,399	72,326
1982	76,623	60,990	65,457	57,719	61,332	51,267	54,706	51,737	42,363	50,682	61,916	64,406
1983	78,889	76,429	83,851	88,011	99,100	94,091	94,216	94,245	80,360	81,261	83,302	84,059
1984	81,806	73,634	92,503	84,925	92,769	89,393	90,897	98,425	76,056	85,413	86,508	80,550
1985	91,973	81,892	84,390	78,336	94,570	81,969	91,489	92,291	85,946	84,583	97,145	93,355
1986	96,382	85,112	118,580	111,625	95,088	86,064	85,427	91,764	82,851	84,290	84,340	92,574

Source: Coffee, Sugar & Cocoa Exch., Inc., N.Y.   T.660

Volume of Trading of World Sugar (#11) Futures at New York   In Contracts

Year	Jan.	Feb.	Mar.	Apr.	May	June	July	Aug.	Sept.	Oct.	Nov.	Dec.	Total
1978	61,854	70,103	86,634	79,359	65,623	98,323	75,940	116,271	115,808	99,632	75,243	71,983	1,016,773
1979	72,961	107,951	76,267	82,804	64,224	132,200	121,474	142,006	192,200	255,858	278,458	256,919	1,783,342
1980	381,805	354,441	338,118	245,233	309,417	277,846	271,884	279,149	317,170	295,673	250,627	255,379	3,576,702
1981	233,217	237,286	212,519	240,420	212,708	241,736	192,142	203,404	247,160	138,529	137,768	183,438	2,470,327
1982	166,913	209,386	199,263	217,689	138,377	177,657	176,641	144,980	151,639	140,262	160,656	154,657	2,037,020
1983	207,678	249,392	198,034	261,939	396,435	396,267	272,150	329,129	283,827	214,897	231,757	160,436	3,201,941
1984	192,451	205,499	252,489	227,150	175,268	213,491	163,955	228,279	263,419	234,008	154,735	124,579	2,449,549
1985	273,316	265,967	215,540	210,046	193,527	237,904	263,842	338,816	323,387	224,856	216,340	249,398	3,012,929
1986	308,004	268,053	382,053	519,027	343,746	289,900	281,124	235,535	328,830	258,744	173,612	195,126	3,583,814

Source: Coffee, Sugar & Cocoa Exch., Inc., N.Y.   T.661

United States Deliveries[1] of All Sugar by Primary Distributors   In Thousands of Short Tons, Raw Value

Year	Jan.	Feb.	Mar.	Apr.	May	June	July	Aug.	Sept.	Oct.	Nov.	Dec.	Total
1979	838	774	964	811	893	947	923	1,103	860	924	879	840	10,756
1980	794	848	866	772	943	882	910	904	909	825	717	818	10,189
1981	——2,208——			——2,532——			——2,400——			——2,305——			9,770
1982	——2,083——			——2,418——			——2,349——			——2,252——			9,153
1983	——2,078——			——2,195——			——2,349——			——2,190——			8,812
1984	——2,029——			——2,121——			——2,238——			——2,066——			8,454
1985[2]	——1,909——			——1,972——			——2,150——			——2,004——			8,035
1986[2]	——1,834——			——1,913——									

[1] Includes for domestic consumption and for export.   [2] Preliminary.   Source: Department of Agriculture   T.659

SUGAR

Centrifugal Sugar (Raw Value) Imported into Selected Countries   In Thousands of Metric Tons

Crop Year	Algeria	Canada	Chile	France	West Germany	Israel	Japan	Malay-sia	Mor-occo	Nigeria	Iran	United Kingdom	China	United States	USSR	World Total[2]
1976	354	895	98	136	169	131	2,439	336	263		626	2,101	638	4,136	3,760	22,593
1977	431	1,064	342	110	108	153	2,708	336	389	329	277	1,870	1,676	5,290	4,776	25,949
1978	437	1,030	317	117	152	195	2,284	398	294	595	875	1,689	1,438	3,616	3,993	23,843
1979	513	1,010	294	103	146	256	2,605	418	279	530	746	1,424	985	4,437	4,080	24,827
1980	569	859	433	69	150	119	2,265	510	332	709	785	1,404	946	3,802	4,981	26,480
1981–2	535	929	194	376	186	180	2,209	432	350	600	755	1,307	1,060	3,196	6,883	28,935
1982–3	600	993	249	357	183	207	1,770	500	307	570	650	1,050	2,480	2,865	5,926	28,452
1983–4[1]	565	843	200	363	180	190	1,870	511	360	650	650	1,500	1,362	3,442	5,600	27,839
1984–5[3]	565	930	81	360	175	190	1,870	500	360	650	650	1,300	1,000	3,187	5,250	26,260

[1] Preliminary.   [2] Excludes U.S. trade with Territories.   [3] Forecast.   *Source: Foreign Agricultural Service, U.S.D.A.*   T.655

Centrifugal Sugar (Raw Value) Exported from Selected Countries   In Thousands of Metric Tons

Crop Year	Australia	Brazil	Czecho-slovakia	Cuba	Dom. Re-public	France	Thai-land	Mau-ritius	Peru	Philip-pines	South Africa	Taiwan	Un. King-dom	USSR	World Total[2]
1976	2,016	1,252	71	5,764	977	1,422	1,124	584	284	1,467	860	519	285	79	22,818
1977	2,558	2,518	171	6,238	1,101	1,816	1,657	637	434	2,443	1,384	599	178	87	28,271
1978	2,482	2,005	306	7,231	901	2,357	1,040	579	275	1,142	719	365	93	174	26,088
1979	2,002	1,860	242	7,269	986	2,347	1,190	641	181	1,150	884	387	76	244	26,373
1980	2,410	2,615	186	6,191	794	2,750	479	655	53	1,745	785	403	100	164	27,290
1981–2	2,620	2,984	160	7,734	816	3,226	2,419	560	63	1,314	851	380	122	268	33,044
1982–3	2,687	2,984	250	6,792	816	3,066	1,560	628	92	1,407	1,027	181	390	165	31,701
1983–4[1]	2,600	3,100	175	7,100	864	3,300	1,366	624	120	965	424	150	240	250	30,670
1984–5[3]	2,860	2,800	200	7,000	900	3,000	2,100	575	130	950	990	10	175	300	30,220

[1] Preliminary.   [2] Excludes U.S. trade with Territories.   [3] Forecast.   *Source: Agricultural Marketing Service, U.S.D.A.*   T.656

Spot Raw Sugar International Sugar Agreement World Price   In Cents per Pound

Year	Jan.	Feb.	Mar.	Apr.	May	June	July	Aug.	Sept.	Oct.	Nov.	Dec.	Average
1979	7.57	8.23	8.46	7.82	7.85	8.14	8.52	8.85	9.90	11.94	13.68	14.93	9.65
1980	17.16	22.69	19.64	21.24	30.94	30.80	27.70	31.77	34.89	40.53	37.81	28.79	28.66
1981	27.78	24.09	21.81	17.83	15.06	16.38	16.34	14.76	11.65	12.04	11.97	12.98	16.89
1982	12.90	13.07	11.26	9.58	8.11	6.84	7.80	6.77	5.76	5.93	6.52	6.31	8.40
1983	6.03	6.43	6.20	6.71	9.24	10.74	10.53	10.56	9.43	9.69	8.33	7.67	8.46
1984	6.97	6.64	6.42	5.99	5.61	5.53	4.54	4.05	4.16	4.65	4.38	3.55	5.21
1985	3.62	3.70	3.83	3.42	2.82	2.78	3.18	4.39	5.14	5.01	5.48	5.34	4.06
1986[1]	4.86	5.57	6.95	8.33	7.63	6.33	5.55	5.57	4.68	5.39	5.93	5.66	6.02

[1] Preliminary.   *Source: Sugar Division, Commodity Stabilization Service*   T.657

Average Refined Cane Sugar[1] (Wholesale)—Chicago-West   In Cents per Pound

Year	Jan.	Feb.	Mar.	Apr.	May	June	July	Aug.	Sept.	Oct.	Nov.	Dec.	Average
1979		19.15			19.15			19.15			21.27		19.68
1980		28.71			36.30			41.17			47.00		38.30
1981		35.50			27.47			25.43			24.63		28.95
1982		27.50			26.77			28.20			28.00		27.62
1983		24.53			26.53			26.96			26.56		26.09
1984		26.62			26.42			25.35			24.24		25.66
1985		23.31			23.26			23.40			22.75		23.18
1986		23.34			23.27								

[1] These are f.o.b. basis prices in 100-lb. paper bags, not delivered prices. To obtain delivered prices, add freight "prepays" & deduct discounts & allowances.   *Source: Economics & Statistics Service, U.S.D.A.*   T.658

High, Low & Closing Prices of March World Sugar (#11) At New York   In Cents per Pound

Year of Delivery		Dec.	Jan.	Feb.	Mar.	Apr.	May	June	July	Aug.	Sept.	Oct.	Nov.	Dec.	Delivery Year		Life of Delivery Range
															Jan.	Feb.	
1983	High	15.15	15.25	15.05	13.68	12.51	10.50	9.35	10.74	8.97	8.22	7.85	8.33	8.28	6.84	7.34	15.25
	Low	13.98	14.03	13.49	12.18	10.28	9.24	8.28	8.37	7.83	7.05	6.60	7.27	6.80	6.05	6.08	6.05
	Close	14.71	14.90	13.65	12.49	10.52	9.25	9.33	8.78	7.96	7.11	7.84	8.32	6.85	6.20	6.28	—
1984	High	9.95	8.92	9.45	9.00	9.77	14.48	13.50	13.16	13.44	11.96	11.94	10.10	9.62	8.29	7.66	14.48
	Low	8.75	8.48	8.11	8.08	8.72	9.60	11.33	10.84	11.60	10.98	9.33	8.82	7.99	7.26	5.65	5.65
	Close	8.98	8.62	8.17	9.00	9.64	14.48	12.52	12.79	11.63	10.94	9.36	9.57	8.18	7.50	5.73	—
1985	High	11.50	10.25	9.60	9.44	9.12	8.39	7.70	6.74	6.08	6.17	6.27	6.05	5.35	4.84	4.45	13.60
	Low	10.06	9.38	8.63	8.74	8.28	7.19	6.61	5.62	4.94	5.05	5.33	5.08	4.02	4.01	3.74	3.74
	Close	10.16	9.56	8.75	9.04	8.40	7.45	6.73	5.72	5.80	5.44	5.83	5.28	4.16	4.32	4.10	—
1986	High	7.40	7.12	6.43	6.05	5.21	4.69	4.33	5.45	5.59	6.20	6.15	6.39	6.56	6.13	6.52	8.27
	Low	6.02	6.13	5.70	5.05	4.58	3.98	3.34	3.59	4.41	5.17	5.25	5.73	5.38	4.97	5.60	3.34
	Close	6.22	6.31	5.83	5.06	4.17	4.28	3.63	5.22	5.13	5.65	6.14	6.13	5.62	5.92	6.28	—
1987	High	7.68	7.60	7.50	9.48	9.67	9.50	8.30	7.54	7.62	6.53	7.10	7.30	7.07			
	Low	6.70	6.45	6.95	7.33	8.31	7.65	6.70	6.17	6.15	5.83	5.75	6.45	5.99			
	Close	6.96	7.36	7.37	9.43	9.43	8.00	7.51	7.20	6.16	6.28	6.90	6.60	6.16			
1988	High	8.01															
	Low	7.17															
	Close	7.30															

Source: Coffee, Sugar & Cocoa Exchange, Inc., N.Y.   T.662

SUGAR "11" NYCSC
WEEKLY HIGH, LOW & CLOSE OF NEAREST FUTURES

Sulfur

Data for the first 10 months of 1986 indicate that total supply of Frasch and recovered sulfur was smaller for the year as a whole than in 1985. Production was roughly 9.8 million metric tons, as against 10.3 million tons in 1985. Frasch output was especially reduced, at about 3.4 million tons for the first 10 months of 1986, compared with 4.2 million tons during the same period the year earlier. Sulfur recovered by petroleum refineries was up more than 25 percent year-over-year. Imports were 36 percent lower in 1986 than in 1985; the annual rate of elemental sulfur shipments averaged 9.7 million tons in 1986, down marginally from 9.9 million tons in 1985.

Based on preliminary data, domestic consumption of Frasch and recovered sulfur was about 9.3 million tons, 13 percent below the 1985 level. By the same token, consumption of elemental sulfur in late 1986 was running at an annual rate that was 14 percent less than in the previous year. Exports provided a partial offset to the slump in domestic usage: through the end of 1986's third quarter they were running at an annual rate of nearly 1.8 million tons, 32 percent greater than in 1985.

With supply greater than consumption, one would expect prices of Frasch and recovered sulfur to be under downward pressure. The average export price per metric ton for American sulfur in late 1986 was $133, compared with $139 in 1985. However, the average value of an imported metric ton was some $11 higher in 1986 than the year before.

World Production of Sulfur [All Forms]   In Thousands of Metric Tons

Year	Canada	Chile	China	France	West Germany	Isreal	Italy	Japan	Mexico	Poland	Spain	Turkey	USSR	United States	Yugoslavia	World Total
1979	7,027	104	2,000	2,288	1,649	10	571	2,891	2,125	5,195	1,224	107	9,240	12,101	395	53,227
1980	7,260	115	2,200	2,216	1,799	10	604	2,784	2,217	5,535	1,236	126	9,590	11,866	457	54,983
1981	6,799	143	2,300	2,042	1,732	10	544	2,609	2,178	5,003	1,268	131	9,900	12,145	490	53,550
1982	6,280	137	2,300	2,035	1,821	10	489	2,595	1,916	5,130	1,167	109	9,750	9,787	557	50,870
1983	6,577	131	2,850	1,910	1,322	10	490	2,613	1,702	5,180	1,204	112	9,650	9,290	481	50,530
1984[1]	6,606	86	2,650	1,862	1,530	10	400	2,592	1,985	5,210	1,231	119	9,700	10,652	464	52,607
1985[2]	6,748	109	2,900	1,694	1,605	10	481	2,510	2,190	5,096	1,259	125	9,725	11,609	496	54,856

[1] Preliminary.   [2] Estimate.   [3] Content of ore.   *Source: Bureau of Mines*

T.663

Salient Statistics of Sulfur in the United States   In Thousands of Metric Tons of Sulfur Content

Year	Frasch-Process Total	Native Sulfur[2] Mines Louisiana	Texas	Recovered Elemental Brimstone	Pyrites (Includ. Coal Brasses)	By-product Sulfuric Acid[3]	Other Sulf. Acid Compounds	Production (All Forms)	Imports Pyrites & Sulfur	Producers' Stocks Dec. 31[4]	Exports (Elemental)	Apparent Consumption (All Forms)	FAASCH	Recovered	Average
1979	6,357	2,460	3,897	4,070	400	1,167	107	12,101	2,494	4,239	1,963	13,739	59.87	48.23	55.75
1980	6,390	2,309	4,081	4,073	322	1,003	78	11,866	2,523	3,094	1,673	13,659	97.36	74.13	89.06
1981	6,348	2,440	3,908	4,259	307	1,159	72	12,145	2,522	3,546	1,392	12,785	121.11	97.97	111.48
1982	4,210	1,312	2,898	4,404	265	828	80	9,787	1,905	4,218	961	10,059	120.79	97.89	108.27
1983	3,202	1,286	1,915	4,955	N.A.	831	302	9,290	1,695	3,223	992	10,988	100.76	76.22	87.24
1984	4,193	1,937	2,257	5,214	N.A.	962	283	10,652	2,557	2,419	1,334	12,679	109.20	80.02	94.31
1985[1]	5,011	2,071	2,940	5,313	N.A.	957	328	11,609	2,104	2,799	1,365	11,968	122.62	92.11	106.46
1986[5]	4,500			6,000				12,000	1,400	2,850	2,000	12,000			

[1] Preliminary.   [2] Or sulfur ore.   [3] Basis 100%, produced at Cu, Zn, & Pb plants.   [4] Frasch & recovered.   [5] Estimates.   *Source: Bureau of Mines*

T.664

Sulfur Consumption & Foreign Trade of the United States   In Thousands of Metric Tons

Year	Net Import Reliance as a % of Apparent Consumption	Native Sulfur (Frasch)	Recovered Sulfur Shipm.	Total Pyrites Shipments	Smelter Acid Prod. Shipm.	Other Prod.[2] Shipm.	Total	Imports of Recovered Sulfur	Sales to Consumers of Frasch Sulfur	Imports of Frasch Sulfur	Exports Quantity	Exports Value Ths. $	Imports Quantity	Imports Value Ths. $
1979	11	6,773	4,108	400	1,167	107	13,739	1,265	7,507	1,229	1,963	142,966	2,494	94,147
1980	14	6,717	4,115	322	1,003	78	13,659	1,533	7,400	990	1,673	185,866	2,523	138,852
1981	5	5,550	4,207	307	1,159	72	12,785	1,666	5,910	856	1,392	187,407	2,522	209,766
1982	4	3,557	4,344	265	828	80	10,059	1,215	3,598	690	961	122,143	1,905	164,885
1983	15	4,114	5,041	N.A.	831	302	10,988	1,091	4,111	604	992	109,298	1,695	129,110
1984	16	4,812	5,210	N.A.	962	283	12,679	1,835	5,001	722	1,334	156,067	2,557	200,189
1985[1]	5	4,416	5,266	N.A.	957	328	11,968	1,380	4,678	724	1,365	189,248	2,104	199,240

[1] Preliminary.   [2] Includes hydrogen sulfide, liquid sulfur dioxide.   [3] Crude sulfur equivalent.   *Source: Bureau of Mines*

T.665

Sunflowerseed and Oil

World sunflowerseed production is projected by USDA at 18.91 million tonnes in 1986/87—a two-percent decline from 1985/86. Sunflower production makes up almost 10 percent of world oilseed output. Among major producers, the USSR will have a crop of 4.6 million tonnes, 12 percent less than a year ago; Argentina's crop is estimated at 3.5 million tonnes, 15 percent less than a year ago. Only Eastern Europe and the European Community (EC) are projected to have larger crops. The EC has been rapidly expanding production through price supports. U.S. production, on a steady decline, is estimated to be 1.09 million tonnes, down 24 percent from 1985/86; harvested acreage fell 35 percent.

World exports are expected to increase about four percent to 1.87 million tonnes. The U.S. had been the major exporter; France has now taken the lead. In 1980, U.S. share of world trade was 77 percent; by 1985, it had fallen to 28 percent. Much of the decline can be traced to increased competition from the EC. Major importers are Mexico, West Germany and the Netherlands. Ending 1986/87 stocks are projected at 70,000 tonnes, up 19 percent from a year ago.

World crush in 1986/87 is forecast at 16.49 million tonnes, virtually unchanged from a year ago. Major processors are the USSR, Argentina, and China. Projected world production of meal is 7.59 million tonnes, down one percent from 1985/86. Argentina dominates export trade, expected to reach 1.8 million tonnes. Differential export taxes offer Argentine crushers strong incentive to export meal; recently, Argentina has had about 75 percent of the market. Major importers are West Germany, Denmark and Great Britain.

World meal consumption in 1986/87 is estimated at 7.46 million tonnes, down slightly from a year ago. The USSR is the largest consumer, followed by China. Ending stocks are projected at 180,000 tonnes, a slight increase from a year ago.

Global production of sunflowerseed oil in 1986/87 is estimated by USDA at 6.52 million tonnes, less than one percent higher than a year ago. Major producers are the USSR and Argentina. World exports are projected at 1.99 million tonnes, down five percent from 1985/86. Argentina is the largest exporter, with about 45 percent of the world market; internal tax policies promote export of oil. Other important exporters include Hungary, the Netherlands and the U.S., where exports have been on a steady decline in recent years. Importers are Egypt, the USSR, and Cuba. World consumption is projected at 6.49 million tonnes, up less than one percent from a year ago. The USSR is the largest consumer of oil, followed by Spain and Turkey. Ending stocks are expected to be 310,000 tonnes, down 16 percent from 1985/86.

World Production of Sunflowerseed   In Thousands of Metric Tons

Crop Year	Argentina	Australia	Bulgaria	Burma	China	France	Hungary	India	Romania	South Africa	Spain	Turkey	United States	USSR	Yugoslavia	World Total
1982-3	2,400	104	511	70	1,286	650	582	230	847	202	750	600	2,419	5,341	202	16,682
1983-4	2,200	170	454	112	1,340	828	592	300	700	180	750	685	1,451	5,063	139	15,494
1984-5	3,400	293	453	139	1,704	957	600	365	851	238	1,100	710	1,698	4,527	154	17,878
1985-6[1]	4,100	210	354	145	1,900	1,389	669	300	710	263	915	700	1,430	5,234	234	19,360
1986-7[2]	3,500	194	475	145	1,750	1,682	780	400	850	325	770	1,030	1,086	4,600	448	18,910

[1] Preliminary.   [2] Estimate.   *Source: Foreign Agricultural Service, U.S.D.A.*   T.668

Sunflowerseed Statistics in the United States

Crop Year Begin Sept.	Acres Harvested In Ths.	Yield per Harv. Acre Pounds	Farm Price $ Metric Ton	Value of Production Mil. $	Supply Production	Supply Imports	Supply Stocks Sept. 1	Supply Total	Crushings	Exports	Disappearance Non-Oil Usage	Seed	Residual	Total
								In Thousands of Metric Tons						
1982-3	4,724	1,129	196	474.1	2,419	40	143	2,602	766	1,348	——191——			2,305
1983-4	3,063	1,044	289	419.3	1,451	31	297	1,779	590	1,047	——104——			1,741
1984-5	3,692	1,014	245	416.0	1,698	26	38	1,762	567	997	——108——			1,672
1985-6[1]	2,844	1,109	172	246.0	1,430	26	90	1,546	674	365	——305——			1,344
1986-7[1]	1,844	1,298	146	158.6	1,086	27	202	1,315	510	375	——140——			1,025

[1] Preliminary.   *Source, Economic Research Service, U.S.D.A.*   T.666

Sunflowerseed Statistics in the United States   In Metric Tons

Crop Year Begin. Oct.	Sunflowerseed Oil — Supply Stocks Oct. 1	Supply Production	Supply Total	Disappearance Exports	Disappearance Domestic	Disappearance Total	Price $ per Metric Ton (Crude Mpls.)	Sunflowerseed Meal — Supply Stocks Oct. 1	Supply Production	Supply Total	Disappearance Exports	Disappearance Domestic	Disappearance Total	Price $ per Metric Ton 28% Protein
1982-3	12	303	315	229	43	272	495	4	434	438	—	433	433	112
1983-4	43	204	247	188	53	241	741	5	265	270	25	240	265	123
1984-5	6	219	225	130	65	195	661	5	321	326	14	307	321	58
1985-6[1]	30	270	300	205	66	271	421	5	370	375	44	326	370	76
1986-7[1]	29	201	230	125	70	195	360	5	280	285	30	250	280	72

[1] Preliminary.   [2] Estimate.   *Source: Economic Research Service, U.S.D.A.*   T.667

Tall Oil

Tall Oil—Supply & Distribution in the U.S. In Millions of Pounds

Year Beginning Oct. 1	Supply (Crude) Pro-duction	Stocks Oct. 1	Total Supply	Ex-ports	To U.S. Territ.	Soap	Paint & Varnish	Lino-leum & Oil-cloth	Resins & Plastics	Other Drying Oils	Lubri-cants & Similar Oils	Fatty Acids	Other	Total Nonfood Products
1976-7	1,181	148	1,329	176		7								1,015
1977-8	350	169	519	168		3								230
1978-9	1,267	150	1,417	107		3	8		5			1,141	96	1,254
1979-0[1]	1,353	150	1,503			3	11		10		6	1,208	74	1,312
1980-1[1]	1,336	155	1,491			4	11		15		5	1,206	94	1,334
1981-2[2]	1,190	137	1,327			3	16		17		4	1,096	48	1,185
1982-3[2]	1,557	151	1,708				33		25			1,096	64	1,228
1983-4[2]	1,293	217	1,510											
1984-5[2]	1,321	113	1,434											
1985-6[2]	1,354	126	1,480											

[1] Preliminary.   [2] Estimated.   *Source: Agricultural Marketing Service, U.S.D.A.*   T.669

U.S. Tall Oil Consumption in Inedible Products   In Millions of Pounds

Year	Jan.	Feb.	Mar.	Apr.	May	June	July	Aug.	Sept.	Oct.	Nov.	Dec.	Total
1977	81	88	103	97	99	95	87	97	85	110	100	91	1,134
1978	85	103	105	108	117	112	95	107	100	100	100	94	1,226
1979	97	102	111	119	125	123	90	85	107	117	105	103	1,284
1980	97	114	113	125	111	118	95	104	111	116	113	104	1,321
1981	110	110	107	110	128	124	97	112	104	104	108	83	1,203
1982	95.4	107.4	121.8	105.2	96.8	95.6	84.7	95.8	88.3	94.4	84.3	66.9	1,136
1983	100.0	96.3	106.9	92.8	98.7	109.1	98.1	114.0	93.7	94.1	95.0	82.6	1,181
1984	100.8	100.7	105.6	97.8	104.2	113.6	117.2	105.2	111.2	100.6	95.7	85.2	1,238
1985[1]	84.1	87.4	94.3	90.4	84.6	85.8	91.7	95.3	91.7	97.6	88.2	85.1	1,076
1986[1]	86.3	93.1	106.0	106.1	95.3	99.5	93.7	101.4	91.1	103.8			

[1] Preliminary.   *Source: Statistical Reporting Service, U.S.D.A.*   T.670

Tall Oil Production in the United States   In Millions of Pounds

Crop Year		Oct.	Nov.	Dec.	Jan.	Feb.	Mar.	Apr.	May	June	July	Aug.	Sept.	Total
1983-4	Crude	107.9	105.4	93.4	99.5	116.3	125.6	111.7	117.8	109.0	105.1	106.1	95.4	1,293.2
	Refined	12.1	14.8	9.9	13.0	11.6	13.4	12.0	13.4	10.7	13.0	12.9	12.6	149.4
1984-5	Crude	112.8	110.7	109.2	95.2	104.0	121.4	116.4	108.4	112.1	117.1	107.8	105.8	1,320.9
	Refined	12.9	11.7	10.9	10.2	9.9	11.8	9.9	10.3	9.7	7.3	10.0	10.5	125.1
1985-6[1]	Crude	115.5	103.5	102.9	120.2	113.8	126.6	124.0	111.7	108.4	107.7	107.9	111.8	1,354.0
	Refined	9.8	9.2	8.7	8.4	8.0	7.9	8.1	8.7	8.2	8.2	9.4	9.7	104.3
1986-7[1]	Crude	114.3												
	Refined	9.3												

[1] Preliminary.   *Source: Bureau of the Census*   T.0578

Tall Oil Stocks in the United States   In Millions of Pounds

Crop Year		Oct. 1	Nov. 1	Dec. 1	Jan. 1	Feb. 1	Mar. 1	Apr. 1	May 1	June 1	July 1	Aug. 1	Sept. 1
1983-4	Crude	217.2	205.4	185.7	186.2	164.6	160.1	168.9	179.7	190.2	163.3	149.0	123.6
	Refined	19.9	18.8	18.1	17.4	16.3	15.9	15.5	12.9	11.7	9.2	11.1	11.1
1984-5	Crude	112.8	101.9	103.0	109.5	108.7	117.0	117.3	126.4	113.8	121.1	141.8	131.4
	Refined	9.9	10.9	12.6	13.0	13.6	17.7	18.3	21.9	22.9	23.8	25.9	29.4
1985-6[1]	Crude	125.9	125.1	158.7	167.6	154.1	160.7	182.7	173.4	181.1	175.5	184.1	169.7
	Refined	19.7	19.7	19.9	21.2	18.5	19.3	25.3	27.9	27.6	26.5	25.3	30.1
1986-7[1]	Crude	177.8	168.3										
	Refined	29.1	27.9										

[1] Preliminary.   *Source: Bureau of the Census*   T.0578A

Tallow and Greases

USDA projected 1986 world tallow and grease production at 6.4 million tonnes, off three percent from the record level of 1985. The decline reflected reduced cattle and hog slaughter, notably in the U.S. Tallow and grease consumption was also projected to decline, though negligibly. This was primarily due to the increased use of cheaper palm oil as a tallow substitute. The U.S. was the largest consumer of tallow, responsible for 31 percent of world consumption. Other major consumers were the Soviet Union, the European Community (EC), Egypt and Japan.

Edible tallow is primarily a byproduct of the commercial beef industry and, in the U.S., must be federally inspected to be termed edible. It is used in some processed foods and is a substitute good for soybean oil, other vegetable oils and lard, competing on a price basis. Inedible tallow and grease is a major raw material for fatty acids and is used extensively in animal feeds. It is also used in some lubricants.

The U.S. is the world's largest producer of edible and inedible tallow and greases, accounting for 50 percent of total world production. USDA estimated 1986 tallow production at 3.5 million tonnes, off four percent from a year ago. Inedible tallow constituted about 78 percent of production, and edible tallow the remaining 22 percent. Domestic disappearance of tallow was down 5.5 percent, while exports increased by 1.5 percent.

The largest importers of U.S. tallow were Egypt, Mexico, Spain and Pakistan, constituting 36 percent of the U.S. export market. In Egypt, tallow imports fell in 1985 and continued lower in 1986, due to a shortage of foreign exchange and competition from palm and coconut oils. Egyptian imports are expected to increase in 1987, however, with rising demand in the soap manufacturing industry. The U.S. supplies all of Mexico's tallow imports, 90 percent of which is inedible; those imports jumped from 54,000 tonnes in 1983 to 115,000 tonnes in 1986. 1987 imports are expected to decline due to an increase in domestic production and a decline in consumption.

The EC maintained its quota on tallow imports from the U.S. in 1986; the group had imposed a quota of 107,000 tonnes per year as retaliation for the U.S. decision to implement unilateral restrictions on semi-finished steel products originating in the EC.

In 1987, U.S. production of tallow is projected to decrease six percent to 3.2 million tonnes. U.S. exports are expected to remain unchanged; domestic consumption should decline about six percent.

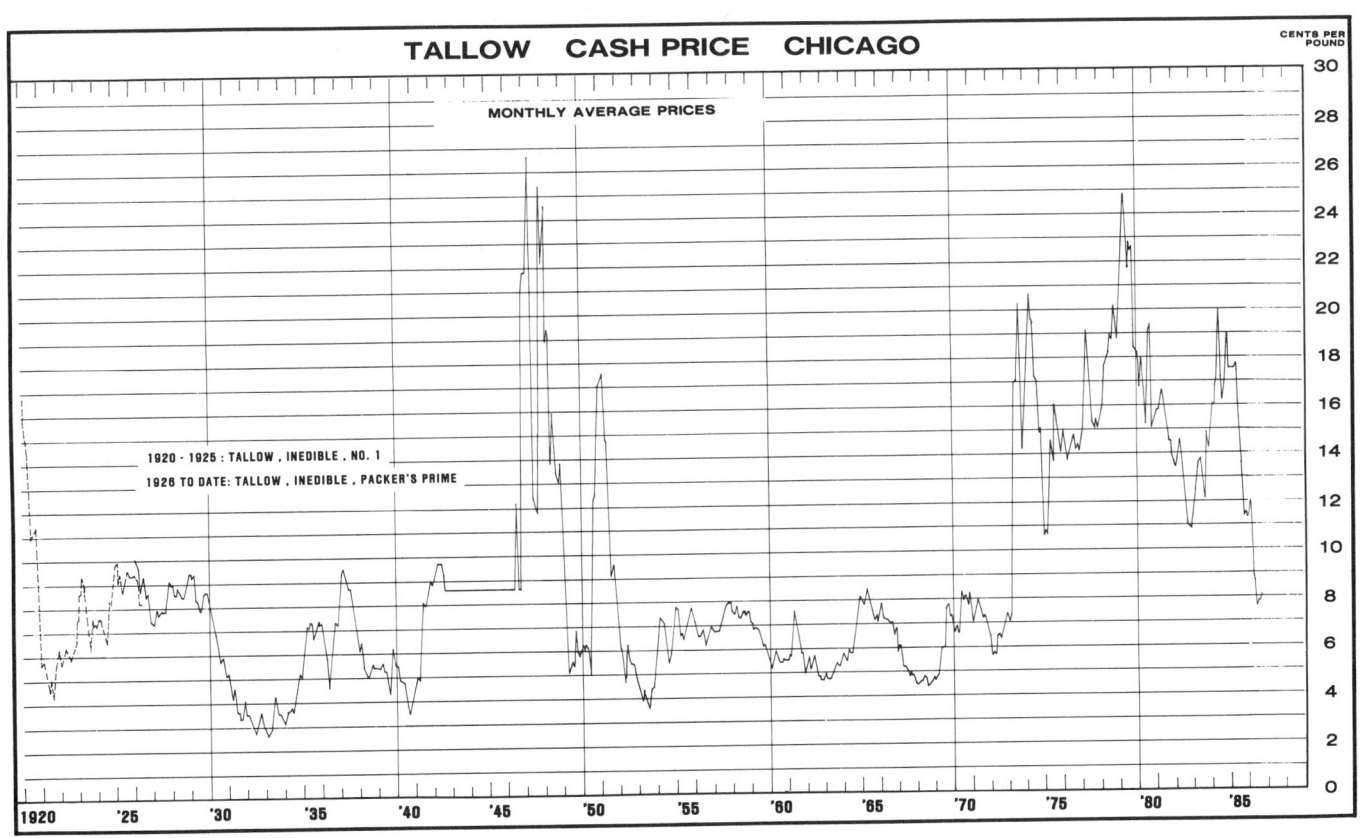

TALLOW CASH PRICE CHICAGO

CENTS PER POUND

MONTHLY AVERAGE PRICES

1920 - 1925 : TALLOW , INEDIBLE , NO. 1
1926 TO DATE: TALLOW , INEDIBLE , PACKER'S PRIME

TALLOW AND GREASES

World Production of Tallow and Greases (Edible and Inedible)   In Thousands of Metric Tons

Year	Argen-tina	Aus-tralia	Brazil	Canada	Colom-bia	USSR	France	W. Ger-many	Italy	Jap-an	Mexico	Nether-lands	New Zealand	United Kingdom	United States	Eastern Europe	World Total
1977	312	400	233	217	22	333	230	186	100		31	83	120	152	2,770	131	5,675
1978	342	397	214	270	23	343	232	205	95		33	88	98	153	2,638	135	5,644
1979	331	334	200	203	26	345	243	221	100		32	90	112	188	3,058	137	6,171
1980	308	309	200	204	29	340	220	235	105		33	94	118	235	3,157	132	6,273
1981	313	309	210	213	33	355	205	235	106	193	52	96	125	218	3,290	140	6,357
1982	276	316	220	220	32	350	188	232	96	196	47	91	125	218	3,228	138	6,241
1983	255	319	230	215	28	355	192	235	94	197	64	89	138	222	3,351	132	6,350
1984	274	300	200	214	30	360	190	250	110	198	69	98	131	238	3,275	136	6,412
1985[1]	293	305	220	212	30	370	180	250	115	212	69	103	156	230	3,373	142	6,509
1986[2]	289	325	200	205	30	375	176	256	117	208	63	106	133	213	3,320	134	6,403

[1] Preliminary.   [2] Estimate.   *Source: Foreign Agricultural Service, U.S.D.A.*   T.672

Salient Statistics of Tallow and Greases (Inedible) in the United States   In Millions of Pounds

Year	Pro-duction	Im-ports	Stocks Jan. 1	Total	Exports & Ship-ments	Soap	Feed	Fatty Acids	Lubri-cants & Oils	Other	Total[2]	Edible, (Loose) Chi-cago	Inedible Chicago No. 1	Bleach-able Fancy
1977	6,106	4	355	6,465	2,885	737	1,330	764	128	158	3,180	21.2	13.6	17.1
1978	5,815	3	344	6,162	2,698	695	1,390	——1,099——			3,220	22.8	16.0	19.8
1979	5,836	3	347	6,183	2,795	663	1,239	——1,215——			3,117	26.2	18.8	
1980	5,916	—	390	6,306	3,254	666	1,246	813	69	177	2,979	21.6	14.3	
1981	6,124	0	413	6,537	3,134	520	1,323				2,985	30.3	15.3	
1982	6,026	0	451	6,477	3,035	545	1,418				2,898	N.A.	12.8	
1983[1]	6,129	0	368	6,497	2,931	574	1,397				2,813	N.A.	13.5	
1984[4]	5,881	0	322	6,203	2,325	623	1,346				2,941	N.A.	17.5	
1985[4]	5,827	0	368	6,195		535	1,361				2,781	20.1		
1986[4]			362											

[1] Preliminary.   [2] Includes small amounts used in drying-oil products in some years.   [3] Estimate.   *Sources: Economic Research Service, U.S.D.A.; Bureau of Labor Statistics*   T.673

Edible Tallow: Supply, Disappearance, and Price, U.S.   In Million Pounds, Rendered Basis

Calendar year	Stocks Jan. 1	Production	Total	Domestic	Exports	Total	Direct use	Baking or Fry-ing Fats	Per capita Lb.	Price[1] ¢ Lb.
1978	42	835	877	802	20	822		808		22.8
1979	55	905	960	853	50	903	87	713	.4	26.2
1980	57	1,043	1,101	957	88	1,047	242	648	1.1	21.6
1981	56	1,130	1,188	992	142	1,134	225	724	1.0	30.3
1982	54	1,110	1,163	1,030	75	1,106	303	679	1.3	N.A.
1983	59	1,260	1,319	1,166	107	1,273	480	632	2.0	N.A.
1984	46	1,340	1,386	1,295	54	1,349	395	821	1.7	N.A
1985[2]	36	1,599	1,635	1,515	80	1,595	458	1,004	1.9	20.1

[1] Loose, average wholesale, Chicago.   [2] Preliminary.   *Source: Economic Research Service, U.S.D.A.*   T.673A

Average Wholesale Price of Tallow, Inedible, No. 1 Packers (Prime), C.A.F. Chicago   In Cents per Pound

Year	Jan.	Feb.	Mar.	Apr.	May	June	July	Aug.	Sept.	Oct.	Nov.	Dec.	Average
1977	14.7	14.9	15.9	17.6	19.2	17.6	16.9	15.3	15.0	15.5	15.3	15.0	16.1
1978	15.4	16.0	17.3	17.8	17.9	18.2	18.9	18.7	19.5	19.8	20.1	18.8	18.4
1979	19.8	20.8	22.9	24.8	24.1	21.7	22.8	22.4	22.6	20.9	18.4	18.2	21.6
1980	18.1	16.7	17.5	18.0	16.8	15.2	16.8	19.0	19.4	17.5	20.4	19.0	17.9
1981	15.8	15.8	16.0	16.5	15.6	16.0	15.2	15.0	14.5	14.5	13.9	13.6	13.6
1982	13.4	13.4	14.1	14.4	14.5	14.3	13.6	12.0	11.4	11.0	11.0	10.8	12.8
1983	11.4	12.0	12.5	13.6	13.8	13.2	12.1	13.7	14.9	14.2	14.8	15.1	13.4
1984	16.0	16.0	16.8	17.0	19.1	20.0	17.1	16.2	16.9	17.9	19.0	17.5	17.5
1985	17.5	17.5	17.5	17.7	16.1	14.3	13.6	12.1	11.4	11.5	11.3	11.5	14.3
1986	12.0	11.8	9.4	8.9	8.7	7.6	7.8	7.8	8.1				

Source: Economic Research Service, U.S.D.A.   T.674

Tea

World tea production for 1985 was estimated at 2.26 million tonnes, four percent higher than the 1984 harvest; estimates for 1986 were not available at this writing. India is the world's largest producer, accounting for 30 percent of global output. Production in that country was estimated at 675,000 tonnes in 1985, up five percent from the year before and an all-time record. The rise in output reflected favorable growing conditions in northern India, where nearly 75 percent of the country's tea is grown, as well as increased usage of fertilizers and pesticides and improved managerial practices.

China is the world's second-largest tea producer. Output there was estimated at 390,000 tonnes in 1985, down six percent from the record 413,000 in 1984. The decline was attributed to poor weather during early 1985. Sri Lankan production was up three percent in 1985 to an estimated 215,000 tonnes. Favorable weather and increased fertilizer application were cited as reasons for the rise. Warm and wet weather during Kenya's growing season lifted output there to a record 150,000 tonnes, 29 percent above the drought-reduced harvest of 1984.

For the first eight months of 1986, U.S. imports of tea were projected at 136 million pounds, up 15 percent from the 118 million pounds imported during the year-ago period. U.S. imports of tea from some traditional suppliers, such as Sri Lanka and Kenya, have declined significantly over a period of several years. Argentina has become the largest supplier to the U.S. market in response to increased demand for lesser-quality, lower-priced teas.

About 80 percent of U.S. tea consumption is in iced teas, which face strong competition from beverages such as soft drinks and beer. Herbal teas have also provided increased competition. Just over 61 percent of all tea sold in the U.S. is in the form of tea bags; 18 percent is in instant tea and another 17 percent in the form of instant mixes. World tea prices in 1985 declined from the record-high levels of 1984, as supplies moved into closer balance with demand, following several years of stock drawdowns.

World Tea Production, in Major Producing Countries In Thousands of Metric Tons

Year	Argentina	China	Sri Lanka (Ceylon)	India	Indonesia	Iran	Japan	Kenya	Malawi	Mozambique	Bangladesh	Taiwan	Turkey	Tanzania	USSR	World Total
1972	24.0	N.A.	213.5	456.0	49.8	22.0	94.8	53.3	20.7	18.7	23.8	26.2	46.5		71.3	1,197
1973	23.1	N.A.	211.3	472.0	54.5	23.0	101.0	56.6	23.6	18.8	27.6	28.6	43.2		74.8	1,236
1974	26.0	N.A.	204.0	492.1	51.7	25.0	95.2	53.4	23.3	17.6	32.2	24.2	42.8		80.8	1,245
1975	29.0	N.A.	213.7	487.1	56.8	23.0	105.4	56.7	26.2	13.1	29.0	26.1	55.6		86.3	1,284
1976	33.0	N.A.	196.6	511.8	61.1	22.0	100.1	62.0	28.3	13.8	33.3	24.8	59.5		92.0	1,316
1977	21.6	252.0	208.6	556.3	64.3	24.0	102.3	86.3	31.7	17.0	38.0	26.3	84.1		106.4	1,709
1978	26.3	268.0	199.0	563.8	73.2	23.0	104.7	93.4	31.7	18.1	38.0	25.9	86.5		111.2	1,755
1979	32.1	277.1	206.4	551.9	73.3	21.0	98.0	93.3	32.6	19.7	35.9	27.1	102.0		117.6	1,782
1980	40.0	304.0	191.4	569.6	98.7	20.0	102.3	89.9	29.9	22.3	40.0	24.5	95.9	17.1	129.8	1,857
1981	33.0	343.0	210.1	560.0	110.2	20.0	102.3	90.9	32.0	23.3	41.3	25.2	42.6	15.9	136.5	1,870
1982	40.0	397.0	187.8	560.7	91.7	25.0	98.5	96.0	38.5	25.8	40.9	24.1	68.0	16.2	139.8	1,939
1983	45.0	401.0	179.3	589.0	115.0	25.0	102.7	119.7	32.0	12.0	43.7	24.3	101.0	15.6	145.6	2,044
1984[1]	46.0	414.0	208.1	645.1	126.4	25.0	92.5	116.2	37.5	14.1	38.2	24.4	113.7	16.5	148.0	2,171
1985[2]	46.0	440.0	214.1	657.3	130.0	25.0	100.0	147.2	40.0	15.0	43.4	24.5	110.0	16.5	150.0	2,266

[1] Preliminary. [2] Estimate. *Source: Foreign Agricultural Service, U.S.D.A.* T.677

World Tea Exports from Producing Countries In Thousands of Metric Tons

Year	Sri Lanka (Ceylon)	China	India	Indonesia	Japan	Malaysia	Bangladesh	Taiwan	Total Asia	Kenya	Mozambique	Malawi	Total Africa	Argentina	Grand Total
1972	190.1	42.0	209.8	38.5	1.9	.8	13.2	21.3	535.8	47.4	18.4	19.9	129.3	18.9	688.7
1973	205.5	50.2	188.2	35.6	2.2	.6	20.3	21.1	547.0	51.5	17.9	22.1	137.4	18.0	709.0
1974	185.1	63.6	205.9	50.2	1.8	.6	21.2	17.2	563.6	49.6	17.2	23.8	134.3	24.1	728.3
1975	212.4	61.3	219.4	46.0	2.2	.5	24.1	20.1	592.3	52.6	12.2	24.2	132.6	17.4	747.5
1976	199.7	61.2	237.3	47.5	3.2	.5	30.7	21.1	608.7	59.3	12.9	29.6	142.2	25.1	782.7
1977	185.5	81.8	229.6	51.3	3.5	.5	26.0	20.8	611.1	70.2	12.9	29.9	158.6	26.9	803.1
1978	192.6	86.9	176.1	56.2	3.4	.6	30.9	20.4	576.7	85.0	16.7	30.6	178.1	31.0	795.1
1979	187.5	106.8	199.6	53.6	3.1	.6	31.9	19.3	616.0	94.0	18.2	31.0	180.5	29.6	834.9
1980	184.5	108.0	224.0	74.2	2.7	.6	31.0	18.2	657.1	74.8	18.0	31.3	156.4	33.5	856.1
1981	182.8	92.0	241.2	71.3	2.7	.2	29.2	15.9	648.5	75.6	18.0	31.5	159.6	25.8	842.8
1982	181.1	115.8	189.9	63.7	2.5	.3	34.4	10.1	605.6	80.4	18.0	37.1	172.2	33.1	820.6
1983	157.9	136.9	208.5	68.6	2.1	.3	30.0	11.6	625.3	100.6	13.3	36.1	191.5	44.7	870.1
1984[1]	204.2	151.3	217.0	85.7	2.8	.3	23.1	11.9	705.9	91.3	7.7	37.1	179.6	43.2	938.6

[1] Preliminary. *Source: Foreign Agricultural Service, U.S.D.A.* T.678

TEA

Salient Statistics of Tea in the United States In Thousands of Metric Tons

Year	Brazil	Argentina	Sri Lanka (Ceylon)	China	India	Indonesia	Japan	Kenya[2]	Mozambique	Netherlands	Malawi	Taiwan	Total	Sales by U.S. Retail Stores — Tea Bags	Loose Tea	Instant Tea	Instant Mixes	Total Quantity
1973		1.1	19.7	.6	8.2	13.3	2.1	8.4	3.1	5.1	2.7	3.2	78.9	30.8	5.1	19.4	8.2	63.5
1974		1.8	19.6	1.2	7.5	13.3	1.9	7.9	3.1	6.4	3.2	3.3	80.9	31.5	4.6	18.7	8.7	63.5
1975		1.8	18.3	2.0	6.8	12.9	1.7	8.4	2.7	2.4	2.2	4.0	72.3	31.6	4.1	19.8	8.0	63.5
1976		2.1	21.1	3.0	8.0	11.6	3.2	10.7	2.0	1.3	4.1	4.8	82.2	33.8	4.2	19.6	8.5	66.2
1977		4.9	16.6	4.2	12.3	14.7	3.4	9.5	2.3	3.0	5.6	5.7	92.1	36.2	5.2	20.0	10.7	72.1
1978	2.0	6.7	14.0	2.9	1.7	10.7	3.2	8.2	1.4	4.1	4.2	3.0	68.8	35.5	4.4	18.7	11.7	70.3
1979	3.5	7.0	14.7	6.5	5.9	11.2	2.9	9.4	2.4	4.7	2.5	2.3	79.2	36.1	4.1	18.0	11.7	69.9
1980	2.8	10.3	12.2	8.0	4.2	13.9	2.5	6.8	5.0	5.9	2.1	3.1	83.8	37.9	3.7	17.1	12.1	70.8
1981	3.5	10.0	13.0	7.1	4.7	14.7	2.5	5.5	4.2	7.7	2.4	4.2	86.3	39.7	3.3	15.9	12.0	70.8
1982	3.5	12.2	12.4	6.9	2.9	14.0	2.4	6.9	4.0	6.1	1.4	3.8	82.8	40.6	3.0	14.9	11.7	70.3
1983	3.9	15.1	8.1	6.4	2.9	14.4	1.8	4.5	3.5	4.7	1.3	3.5	77.3	41.9	2.7	14.9	13.1	72.6
1984	3.6	18.1	9.4	9.6	3.8	15.5	2.1	3.9	2.2	4.8	.9	6.3	88.3	40.7	2.3	13.3	12.2	64.5
1985[1]	4.3	15.2	9.8	10.9	2.9	12.8	2.1	4.2	.7	4.2	.9	2.2	79.2	41.0	2.1	12.6	11.4	67.1

[1] Preliminary. *Sources: Statistical Reporting Service, U.S.D.A.; Bureau of Census*   T.675

United States Imports of Tea In Thousands of Pounds

Year	Jan.	Feb.	Mar.	Apr.	May	June	July	Aug.	Sept.	Oct.	Nov.	Dec.	Total
1971	13,226	12,360	15,073	18,078	15,128	16,529	20,150	25,141	19,427	4,631	3,828	11,862	175,432
1972	12,914	16,907	10,276	10,165	12,885	16,563	10,835	11,581	12,830	14,348	11,460	10,731	151,495
1973	15,481	14,295	15,399	14,107	17,423	12,425	13,660	12,614	12,527	16,878	16,506	11,997	173,314
1974	11,675	14,974	16,583	17,177	18,122	17,489	21,788	16,432	13,954	10,460	7,735	11,844	178,326
1975	14,297	12,200	15,486	13,648	14,694	12,170	9,915	11,276	12,404	17,594	13,940	11,843	159,287
1976	11,842	12,309	15,779	15,805	13,053	13,893	14,259	15,051	19,224	15,683	16,133	18,273	181,304
1977	16,059	15,064	22,389	23,302	27,345	22,335	22,252	15,932	9,994	9,702	7,213	10,924	203,012
1978	9,023	12,791	18,648	15,450	17,523	8,286	13,141	13,788	9,390	12,502	8,877	12,332	151,751
1979	14,797	10,568	15,584	13,822	13,556	14,352	13,361	14,809	15,841	16,992	15,432	15,578	174,690
1980	18,749	17,562	17,456	18,501	15,871	16,460	14,099	11,883	11,870	14,271	12,126	15,936	184,786
1981	12,891	18,354	14,696	19,220	18,990	17,736	14,586	19,128	13,205	15,855	13,473	12,121	190,254
1982	15,055	15,464	13,787	13,176	16,518	14,309	14,286	15,598	17,425	16,207	18,222	12,567	182,613
1983	13,748	15,092	14,170	15,799	16,018	10,931	12,159	11,747	15,025	16,531	13,600	15,631	170,451
1984	15,599	15,956	20,235	18,031	17,546	12,803	22,287	12,023	14,169	20,946	12,386	12,585	194,565
1985	16,238	13,856	15,491	13,342	15,337	15,054	15,586	12,745	14,942	14,878	13,656	13,493	174,617
1986	16,923	13,219	21,719	19,002	15,747	14,970	19,732	14,626					

Source: Department of Commerce   T.679

London Auction Tea Prices In U.S. Cents per Pound

Year	Jan.	Feb.	Mar.	Apr.	May	June	July	Aug.	Sept.	Oct.	Nov.	Dec.	Average
1980	102.4	105.7	102.4	100.4	104.2	106.8	100.9	102.5	95.1	92.4	101.3	98.1	101.0
1981	98.6	101.2	100.5	97.9	94.7	90.4	84.6	80.0	81.7	87.4	91.3	91.6	91.7
1982	92.0	94.2	88.5	84.7	84.8	83.3	79.9	80.8	86.7	91.4	89.8	96.1	87.7
1983	98.5	93.1	89.8	92.1	91.0	85.2	86.6	90.6	99.0	117.4	158.8	163.8	105.5
1984	194.2	169.0	166.7	160.4	161.3	144.8	130.3	133.2	154.1	164.2	155.2	147.9	156.8
1985	143.1	127.3	110.4	98.6	75.2	74.6	71.5	72.2	73.3	78.7	80.2	75.3	90.0
1986	82.1	85.7	91.5	91.3									

Source: International Tea Committee   T.679a

Tin

Tin prices continued their precipitous fall, begun when the International Tin Council (ITC) declared its inability to continue its buffer stockpile tin purchasing program. On October 24, 1985, tin was quoted at $6.06 a pound, the result of ITC buffer stocks being withheld from the market. By October, 1986, the price was about $3.53 a pound.

The ITC is an unchartered agency organized to support the price of tin. It was strongly influenced by the government of Malaysia, the world's largest producer, which viewed tin as a semi-precious metal. Over a period of years, Malaysia engineered a number of squeezes in the London Metals Exchange (LME) tin market; prices were kept firm, thereby underpinning a high international support price of 29.15 Malaysian dollars per kilogram.

By the fall of 1985, the ITC had acquired a stockpile of about 85,000 tonnes, but could not pay for additional tin it had contracted on the LME. This caused the LME to halt tin trading. On March 12, 1986, the exchange settled all outstanding tin contracts and effectively closed the LME tin contract. Suits were instituted by a number of large brokerage firms which dealt in the physical metal and suffered large losses against the LME and the ITC. As of early 1987, there had been no settlement.

The ITC announced an end to all export and production quotas for its 22 members. This gave official sanction to practices that had been honored more in the breach than in reality, since above-quota sales were one reason for the large stockpile purchases which eventually broke the ITC.

This action cleared the way for producers to dispose of more than 40,000 tonnes of tin in concentrates held at minehead. Although the international tin agreement is not to expire until June, 1987, it is now, in effect, defunct.

The release of concentrates into the market and the sale of tin held as collateral by banks kept prices on the defensive in 1986; the outlook is poor.

Estimated 1986 U.S. apparent consumption of tin was 52,000 tonnes, slightly above 1985's 50,200 tonnes. More than 67 percent of domestic consumption is supplied by imports of metal and ore. Primary consumption in January–September, 1986, was 28,400 tonnes, compared with 1985's final primary consumption of 37,128 tonnes. Secondary consumption for the same three quarters of 1986 was 9,500 tonnes; final 1985 secondary consumption was 12,590 tonnes. Imports for consumption for the first nine months of 1986 were 26,937 tonnes of metal and 2,696 tonnes of concentrates, compared with full-year 1985 imports of 33,830 tonnes and 1,636 tonnes, respectively.

Brazil continued to be the major tin metal supplier in the U.S. Malaysia was the second leading supplier; in 1985, it did not rank among the top five. U.S. tin ore imports through the first nine months of 1986 were running at a rate twice that of 1985. In the same period, Brazil had exported 7,803 tonnes of tin metal to the U.S., compared with full-year 1985 exports of 11,021 tonnes. Malaysia had exported 5,148 tonnes, compared with 379 tonnes in all of 1985. Bolivia also showed rapid export growth, moving to 4,073 tonnes and third place from 1985's total exports of 1,815 tonnes.

During 1986, the Bolivian government attempted to reorganize its COMIBOL mining organization into five separate companies and to lay off 25 percent of COMIBOL's 21,000 workers. The government was forced to declare a state of emergency, eventually lifted. But, because of the labor unrest in Bolivia, industry analysts expect tin mine output there, which has declined steadily in recent years, to show a steeper drop in 1986.

U.S. tin resources, located primarily in Alaska, are insignificant when compared with those of the rest of the world. World resources are located principally in southeastern Asia, Australia, Bolivia, Brazil, China, and the USSR. Sufficient resources are available to sustain present production rates well into the next century.

World Mine Production of Tin (Content of Ore)   In Thousands of Metric Tons

Year	Australia	Bolivia[1]	Brazil	Burma	China[3]	Indonesia	Japan	Malaysia	Nigeria	Rwanda	South Africa	Thailand	United Kingdom	USSR	Zaire (Congo)	World Total
1981	12.3	29.8	8.3	1.4	15.0	35.4	.6	59.9	3.2	1.8	2.8	31.5	3.9	21.0	2.5	238.0
1982	12.1	26.8	8.2	1.7	15.0	33.8	.5	52.3	2.4	1.7	3.0	26.1	4.2	21.0	2.3	219.9
1983	9.3	25.3	13.3	1.6	15.0	26.6	.6	41.4	1.6	1.5	2.7	19.9	4.0	22.0	2.2	196.9
1984[2]	7.7	19.9	20.0	2.0	15.0	23.2	.5	41.3	1.7	1.6	2.3	21.9	5.2	23.0	2.7	198.4
1985[3]	7.0	18.0	22.0	1.8	15.0	22.1	.5	36.9	1.7	1.2	2.2	20.0	5.3	23.0	2.9	191.1

[1] Exports.   [2] Preliminary.   [3] Estimate.   *Source: Bureau of Mines*   T.682

World Smelter Production of Tin   In Thousands of Metric Tons

Year	Australia	Thailand	Bolivia	Brazil	China	Zaire (Congo)	West Germany	Indonesia	Japan	Malaysia	Nigeria	Portugal	South Africa	United Kingdom	United States	USSR	Total
1981	4.3	32.6	20.0	7.8	15.0	.5	1.8	32.5	1.3	70.3	2.5	.9	2.6	6.9	2.0	23.0	235.9
1982	3.1	25.5	19.0	9.3	15.0	.4	.6	29.8	1.3	62.8	2.8	.4	2.9	8.2	3.5	24.0	221.0
1983	2.9	18.5	14.2	13.0	15.0	.2	.4	28.4	1.3	53.3	1.2	.2	2.7	6.5	2.5	24.0	199.8
1984[2]	2.9	20.0	15.8	18.9	15.0	.2	.4	22.5	1.4	46.9	1.3	.2	1.6	6.8	4.0	25.0	199.7
1985[3]	2.7	19.0	12.0	21.0	15.0	.2	.4	21.2	1.4	47.0	1.4	.2	1.4	7.2	3.0	25.0	193.7

[1] Imports into the U.S. of tin concentrates (tin content).   [2] Preliminary.   [3] Estimate.   *Source: Bureau of Mines*   T.683

TIN

Tin Foreign Trade of the United States   In Metric[5] Tons

Year	Exports (Metal[2])	Concentrates[3] (Ore) Total All Ore	Bolivia	Peru	Imports (For Consumption) Total All Metal	Australia	Belgium	Bars, Blocks, Pigs, etc.[4] (Metal) Bolivia	Brazil	China	Indonesia	Malaysia	Nigeria	Singapore	Thailand	United Kingdom
1976	2,338	5,733	5,733	—	45,055	—	—	1,978	—	—	4,972	26,981	—	15	6,885	284
1977	5,480	6,724	6,667	—	47,774	—	—	3,358	2,380	381	5,294	27,084	2	207	7,780	513
1978	4,692	3,873	3,541	—	46,776	—	155	5,768	1,810	1,571	5,664	23,448	—	230	6,865	468
1979	569	4,529	3,745	—	48,355	—	100	5,387	933	185	5,429	23,448	—	1,070	10,440	550
1980	595	840	528	—	45,982	145	190	5,597	2,031	858	6,477	15,548	770	864	12,414	416
1981	2,361	232	—	232	45,874	552	—	8,277	1,129	2,032	7,096	13,163	520	656	11,967	46
1982	5,769	1,961	192	1,416	27,939	334	10	4,340	2,409	2,632	5,744	2,364	124	600	9,116	55
1983	1,340	969	257	341	34,048	390	45	5,739	5,604	1,938	6,004	4,704	265	1,029	7,436	18
1984	1,429	3,272	271	2,502	41,224	288	137	5,438	10,220	1,640	4,985	6,622	60	781	9,531	583
1985[1]	1,478	1,636	22	1,506	33,830	266	—	1,815	11,021	4,513	4,587	379	—	1,886	6,373	48

[1] Preliminary.   [2] Ingots, Pigs & Bars. Excludes re-exports from 1979.   [3] Tin content.   [4] Also grain, or granulated.
Source: Department of Commerce

T.684

United States Tin (Pig) Consumption (Total)   In Metric Tons

Year	Jan.	Feb.	Mar.	Apr.	May	June	July	Aug.	Sept.	Oct.	Nov.	Dec.	Total
1976	5,170	4,930	5,825	5,415	5,490	5,965	5,240	5,380	5,680	6,395	5,950	5,700	62,928
1977	5,600	5,500	6,800	5,800	5,800	6,000	5,200	5,800	5,900	5,400	5,000	5,100	60,732
1978	5,400	5,000	5,500	5,200	5,700	5,400	4,600	5,200	5,200	5,300	5,400	4,900	61,531
1979	5,400	5,500	6,400	5,400	5,400	5,300	4,900	4,900	5,000	5,500	5,000	4,600	62,465
1980	5,500	5,300	5,750	5,300	4,600	4,100	3,700	3,900	4,150	4,300	4,050	3,750	56,362
1981	4,300	4,400	4,100	4,600	4,400	4,350	3,900	4,200	3,950	3,900	3,400	2,950	54,373
1982	3,400	3,300	3,750	5,100	5,000	5,100	4,900	4,700	4,700	4,600	4,500	4,400	53,450
1983	4,400	4,700	4,900	4,700	4,700	4,800	4,300	4,600	4,700	4,800	4,400	4,800	55,800
1984[1]	4,600	4,300	5,300	3,900	4,500	4,400	4,100	4,400	4,100	4,000	3,300	3,500	50,400
1985[1]	4,000	3,900	4,600	4,500	4,600	4,400	4,200	4,400	4,300	4,500	4,200	4,000	51,600
1986[1]	4,300	4,000	4,200	4,500	4,400	4,400	4,100						

[1] Preliminary.   *Source: Bureau of Mines.*

T.681

United States Tin Stocks (Pig—Industrial)   In Metric Tons

Year	Jan. 1	Feb. 1	Mar. 1	Apr. 1	May 1	June 1	July 1	Aug. 1	Sept. 1	Oct. 1	Nov. 1	Dec. 1
1976	9,642	9,395	8,624	9,189	7,855	6,963	8,375	9,623	8,749	7,871	7,929	7,213
1977	7,282	8,032	7,883	5,874	6,157	5,644	4,720	6,305	5,557	5,378	9,124	7,272
1978	8,441	7,626	6,628	6,291	7,785	8,139	7,846	7,817	7,260	5,774	4,975	5,666
1979	5,040	4,594	4,254	5,891	6,097	5,938	6,317	6,270	6,096	5,058	4,901	4,244
1980	4,238	7,720	6,882	7,527	5,443	7,263	6,592	6,544	6,051	5,180	5,208	5,086
1981	5,504	5,968	5,745	5,229	5,725	5,978	6,227	6,465	5,663	5,710	5,325	5,563
1982	5,988	3,872	3,490	3,829	5,222	4,953	4,653	3,888	2,910	2,940	2,970	3,437
1983	3,152	4,609	3,513	3,815	4,026	3,527	3,634	3,931	4,091	3,604	3,074	3,180
1984[1]	3,020	2,968	2,268	2,840	2,646	3,119	2,795	2,688	2,837	2,495	2,512	2,326
1985[1]	2,592	2,766	2,283	2,407	2,228	2,853	3,042	2,762	2,663	2,985	4,121	4,913
1986[1]	5,665	5,310	4,692	3,097	4,127	3,987	4,032	4,166				

[1] Preliminary.   *Source: Bureau of Mines*

T.680

TIN CASH PRICE NEW YORK

Monthly Average Prices
STRAITS TIN

CENTS PER POUND

NOT AVAILABLE SINCE 9/85

NO QUOTES

EX-DOCK TIN AT N.Y. FROM 1/84

Average Price of Ex–Dock Tin in New York[1]   In Cents per Pound

Year	Jan.	Feb.	Mar.	Apr.	May	June	July	Aug.	Sept.	Oct.	Nov.	Dec.	Average
1976	312.39	326.00	349.07	358.80	377.00	390.30	424.27	411.27	405.40	406.77	414.84	423.25	383.34
1977	470.54	514.16	522.97	485.28	491.93	482.15	518.71	559.51	558.47	619.25	626.16	613.36	538.76
1978	591.19	595.93	557.48	537.85	570.58	600.95	606.21	641.80	679.66	739.69	758.84	695.86	631.34
1979	684.56	724.57	746.14	740.06	745.18	760.14	712.31	739.93	762.03	785.54	801.23	830.88	756.87
1980	836.46	866.39	900.23	872.21	861.84	845.19	836.95	834.61	861.92	832.92	788.67	751.36	840.73
1981	739.94	705.76	691.70	677.38	652.07	652.77	680.22	746.06	777.36	798.70	813.00	801.59	728.05
1982	787.41	749.93	669.51	649.58	662.35	643.00	638.00	636.33	644.33	627.94	627.93	630.18	663.88
1983	648.90	653.89	669.18	692.29	683.36	670.54	663.13	653.10	649.31	650.65	653.02	636.71	660.34
1984[1]	590.60	592.10	603.40	605.10	601.70	602.20	593.50	594.70	590.20	578.60	574.40	566.10	591.10
1985	542.10	532.00	533.80	559.10	557.70	576.30	594.90	593.80	578.60	580.50	N.Q.	N.Q.	564.90
1986	N.Q.	N.Q.	N.Q.	275.00	265.00	260.30	260.50	—	260.70	267.50	292.80	308.30	280.20

[1] Data prior to 1984 are for Straits (Alloyer Price).   *Source: American Metal Market*

T.685

Secondary Tin Recovered in the United States   In Metric Tons

Year	Tin-plate Scrap Treated (Ths. Tons)	Tin Recovered at Detinning Plants — As Metal	In Com-pounds[2]	Total	Weight of Tin Com-pounds Produced	Avg. Quantity of Tin Recov. Per Ton of Tin-Scrap (Kilog.)	Avg. Delivered cost of Tinplate Scrap. $ per Metric Ton	Tin Recovered by Form of Recovery — Tin Metal	Bronze & Brass	Solder	Type Metal	Babbitt	Anti-Monial Lead	Chemi-cal Com-pounds	Misc.[3]	Grand Total
1976	685.5	1,195	424	1,619	1,348	2.36		1,467	8,319	4,513	668	495	548	424	12	16,446
1977	667.4	1,376	365	1,741	1,516	2.61		1,668	10,397	4,094	708	694	565	365	12	18,503
1978	714.9	1,324	463	1,787	1,803	2.50	60.04	1,565	12,419	4,363	1,038	521	712	463	19	21,100
1979	841.4	1,536	433	1,969	1,256	2.34	90.73	1,767	12,090	5,282	584	441	867	433	29	21,493
1980	766.9	1,457	321	1,778	1,533	2.32	89.38	1,703	10,402	4,423	525	378	856	321	30	18,638
1981	668.0	1,328	265	1,593	1,220	2.38	102.42	1,587	8,894	3,035	576	261	791	265	29	15,438
1982	464.6	810	447	1,257	1,754	2.37	56.16	1,067	6,971	2,723	222	237	1,015	447	101	12,783
1983	486.5	928	182	1,110	1,284	1.98	60.60	1,180	8,517	3,072	172	185	803	182	94	14,205
1984	492.8	824	301	1,125	1,498	2.24	68.01	1,107	9,146	3,653	142	123	894	301	51	15,417
1985[1]	460.1	931	186	1,117	338	2.38	53.69	1,302	8,847	3,565	122	88	791	186	10	14,911

[1] Preliminary.   [2] Tin content.   [3] Includes foil, cable lead & terne metal.   *Source: Bureau of Mines*   T.687

U.S. Consumption of Primary and Secondary Tin   In Metric Tons

Year	Net Import Reliance as a % of Apparent Consumption	Industry Stocks Jan. 1[2]	Net Receipts — Primary	Secondary	Scrap	Total	Available Supply	Stocks Dec. 31 (Total Available Less Total Processed)	Total Processed	Consumed in Mfg. Pdt's.
1976	85	19,510	49,995	2,019	10,189	62,203	81,713		64,819	62,928
1977	82	16,894	48,215	4,025	10,604	62,844	79,738		62,880	60,732
1978	79	16,858	46,821	2,541	10,499	59,861	76,719		63,135	61,531
1979	80	13,584	50,126	2,636	10,659	63,421	77,005		64,067	62,465
1980	79	7,075	43,545	2,461	7,709	53,715	60,790	3,593	57,197	56,362
1981	77	8,835	41,162	5,692	8,050	54,904	63,739	8,640	55,099	54,373
1982	68	8,717	35,843	6,507	7,830	50,180	58,897	12,328	46,569	46,295
1983	73	7,549	36,494	5,412	7,435	49,341	56,890	11,098	45,792	45,547
1984	74	7,740	39,388	6,096	7,323	52,807	60,547	10,788	49,759	49,441
1985[1]	72	8,478	38,936	8,904	7,917	55,757	64,235	14,295	49,940	49,726

[1] Preliminary.   [2] Includes tin in transit in the U.S.   *Source: Bureau of Mines*   T.686

Consumption of Tin in the United States by Finished Products   In Metric Tons of Contained Tin

Year	Alloys	Tin-plate[2]	Solder	Babbitt	Bronze & Brass	Collap. Tubes & Foil	Tinning	Chemi-cals[3]	Tin Powder	Type Metal	Bar Tin & Anodes	White Metal	Other	Total Primary	Secondary
1976		20,766	17,728	2,423	7,656	694	2,308	5,621	1,208	216	758	2,347		51,767	11,161
1977		18,539	17,315	2,093	8,606	787	2,323	5,727	1,287	202	578	1,655		47,596	13,136
1978		17,280	17,770	2,346	9,048	673	2,431	4,557	1,360	171	424	1,484		48,403	13,128
1979	2,428	17,929	18,022	2,243	8,690	686	2,584	4,797	1,435	140	567	1,258	1,686	49,496	12,969
1980	134	16,346	15,618	2,380	7,478	526	2,577	N.A.	1,109	N.A.	486	914	8,794	44,342	12,020
1981	2,435	13,306	15,799	3,844	7,041	561	2,491	4,417	983	52	455	1,201	1,788	40,229	14,144
1982	N.A.	11,134	13,142	1,915	4,400	N.A.	1,887	N.A.	906	N.A.	509	1,177	11,225	33,019	13,276
1983	N.A.	9,462	14,120	2,881	4,583	N.A.	1,759	N.A.	793	N.A.	654	937	10,358	34,301	11,246
1984	N.A.	8,825	17,249	2,684	4,998	N.A.	1,748	N.A.	1,057	N.A.	526	958	11,396	37,819	11,622
1985[1]	N.A.	9,322	18,616	1,488	4,329	N.A.	1,511	N.A.	977	7	466	937	12,073	37,136	12,590
1986[4]														38,000	12,600

[1] Preliminary. [2] Includes small quantity of secondary pig tin & tin acquired in chemicals. [3] Including tin oxide. [4] Estimated.
Source: Bureau of Mines   T.688

Titanium

Titanium has been referred to as a space-age metal; its uses have been heavily centered in aerospace applications. Approximately 65 percent of titanium metal consumed in the U.S. is used in jet engines, airframes, and space and missile applications. About 20 percent is used in the chemical processing industry, power generation, and in marine and military equipment applications. Another 17 percent is used in steel and other alloys.

For the nine months ended September, 1986, production of titanium sponge totaled 12,921 short tons, compared with the full-year 1985 total of 23,257 short tons. Ingot production in the same 1986 nine-month period totaled 26,750 short tons, compared with full-year 1985 production of 35,902 short tons.

For the three quarters ended September, 1986, domestic titanium sponge consumption was 14,875 short tons; full-year 1985 consumption was 21,606 short tons.

Total imports of titanium metal of all descriptions were 4,053 short tons for the first nine months of 1986, compared with 5,478 short tons for all of 1985. Imports accounted for about six percent of total nine-month consumption of all descriptions—almost 70,000 short tons. This compared with full-year 1985 consumption of 97,164 tons.

Titanium dioxide pigment was produced by five companies in the U.S.; the largest use was in paints, varnishes and lacquers. The pigment was also used in the paper and plastics industries. Domestic titanium dioxide pigment production on a gross-weight basis was 684,864 short tons in the first nine months of 1986; full-year 1985 production totalled 848,627 short tons.

1986 world production figures for titanium sponge metal were not available at this writing, but 1985 production is estimated at 99,000 tons. The USSR is the world's largest titanium producer, with about 50 percent of the total. The U.S. and Japan each account for about 25 percent of total output.

The titanium source for domestic sponge production is rutile. Pigment production sources are ilmenite, slag and rutile. For aircraft and space use, there is no substitute for titanium, which is as strong as steel but lighter in weight; neither is there a cost-effective substitute for titanium dioxide pigment.

Average Titanium Prices in the United States

Year	Ilmenite—54% T_iO_2 F.O.B. Atlantic Seaboard— $ per Long Ton	Slag, 85% T_iO_2 F.O.B. Richards Bay, South Africa $ Lg. Ton	Ilmenite Domestic F.O.B. Titen, Fla. — $ per Long Ton —	Rutile F.O.B. Eastern Ports, Last Quarter (Spot) $ per Short Ton	Synthetic F.O.B. Mobile, Ala. — $ per Short Ton —	Titanium Metal Sponge	Titanium Dioxide Pigments Anatase	Titanium Dioxide Rutile
						Dec. 31 in $ per pound		
1976	55			510		2.70	0.410	0.465
1977	55			360		2.98	0.435	0.485
1978	50			340		3.28	0.460	0.510
1979	50		—	390		3.98	0.530	0.590
1980	55		—	440	310	7.02	0.570	0.630
1981	70–75		39	450–475	340	7.65	0.690	0.750
1982	70–75	170–180	44–45	450–475	350	5.55	0.690	0.750
1983	70–75	187–198	44–45	400–430	350	5.55	0.690	0.750
1984	70–75	200	44–45	460–490	350	5.55	0.690	0.750
1985	N.A.	212	50–56	N.A.	350	5.55–5.85	.72–.73	0.780
1986[1]		225–230	50–56	350–360	350	3.75–4.30	.72–.73	0.780

[1] Preliminary.   *Source: U.S. Bureau of Mines*   T.690

TITANIUM

World Production of Titanium Ilmenite Concentrates[2]   In Thousands of Short Tons

Year	Australia	Brazil	Canada[2]	China	Finland	India	Japan[3]	Malaysia (Exports)	Norway	South Africa[3]	Sri Lanka (Ceylon)	United States[4]	USSR	World Total[2]
1977	1,139	14.6	763.2	—	137.5	151.4	1.4	169.4	913.3	—	37.6	638.5	440.0	4,418
1978	1,383	22.1	937.0	N.A.	145.4	178.1	.2	205.9	845.5	100.0	36.4	589.8	450.0	4,912
1979	1,327	14.5	525.8	N.A.	131.9	161.9	.2	220.3	903.7	316.0	61.0	639.3	450.0	4,752
1980	1,553	18.6	934.4	N.A.	175.3	185.1	N.A.	208.3	912.5	379.0	37.4	556.6	460.0	5,420
1981	1,478	17.5	836.9	150.0	178.0	179.1	N.A.	190.4	727.1	408.0	88.2	542.4	470.0	5,266
1982	1,289	12.5	737.4	150.0	185.0	168.6	N.A.	111.6	608.2	420.0	75.3	263.4	475.0	4,496
1983	998.2	33.6	700.0	154.0	180.7	148.2	N.A.	245.5	612.8	460.0	90.1	N.A.	480.0	4,108
1984[1]	1,231	45.1	800.0	154.0	184.0	154.3		259.0	729.0	460.0	112.5	N.A.	485.0	4,662
1985[6]	1,340	50.0	930.0	154.0	150.0	187.0		303.0	810.5	480.0	110.0	N.A.	490.0	5,064

[1] Preliminary.   [2] Includes Ti slag containing approx. 70% TiO_2.   [3] Represents titanium slag.   [4] Includes a mixed product containing ilmenite, leucoxene, & rutile.   [5] Includes slag & concentrate.   [6] Estimate.   *Source: Bureau of Mines*   T.692

World Production of Titanium Rutile Concentrates   In Short Tons

Year	South Africa	Australia	USSR	Brazil	Sierra Leone	India	Sri Lanka (Ceylon)	United States	World Total
1977	5,000	358,561	10,000	141	—	6,053	1,078	N.A.	380,833
1978	20,000	283,376	10,000	402	—	6,239	12,673	N.A.	332,690
1979	46,000	302,620	11,000	484	8,267	5,445	16,176	N.A.	389,992
1980	53,000	343,639	11,000	472	52,356	5,908	14,097	N.A.	480,472
1981	55,000	254,432	11,000	190	55,992	7,397	14,662	N.A.	398,673
1982	52,000	243,277	11,000	258	52,590	6,374	7,950	N.A.	373,449
1983	62,000	174,404	11,000	510	79,146	6,100	9,821	N.A.	342,081
1984[1]	62,000	200,048	11,000	454	100,641	6,600	7,129	N.A.	387,872
1985[2]	61,000	225,000	11,000	500	89,000	7,700	7,700	N.A.	401,900

[1] Preliminary.   [2] Estimate.   *Source: Bureau of Mines*   T.691

World Production of Titanium Sponge Metal & U.S. Consumption of Titanium Concentrates

Year	Production of Titanium (in short tons) Sponge Metal[1]						U.S. Consumption of Titanium Concentrates, by Products (in short tons) Ilmenite (TiO_2 Content)			Rutile (TiO_2 Content)			
	China	USSR	United Kingdom	Japan	United States	Total	Pigments	Misc.	Total	Welding Rod Coatings	Pigments	Misc.	Total
1978		39,000	2,400	10,115	N.A.	—	467,410	8,038	475,448	8,427	195,431	41,326	245,184
1979		43,000	2,600	14,000	N.A.	—	475,342	11,886	478,228	9,947	230,776	52,189	292,912
1980		45,000	2,600	21,257	N.A.	—	502,108	11,207	513,315	6,876	211,599	59,407	277,882
1981	2,000	42,000	2,600	27,500	26,419	100,519	501,301	9,721	511,022	6,944	192,779	66,873	266,596
1982	1,500	44,000	2,600	18,600	15,600	82,300	345,618	6,775	352,393	5,275	184,403	35,435	225,113
1983	2,000	45,000	2,000	11,600	13,966	74,000	468,279	6,006	474,285	3,649	210,949	35,820	250,418
1984[3]	2,000	46,000	2,500	16,938	24,326	92,000	492,658	6,319	498,977	3,911	231,808	62,920	298,639
1985[2]	2,000	47,000	2,000	23,000	23,257	99,000	474,561	6,450	481,011	4,881	239,893	41,714	286,488
1986[2]					18,000								

[1] Unconsolidated metal in various forms.   [2] Estimated.   [3] Preliminary.   *Source: Bureau of Mines*   T.689

Salient Statistics of Titanium[4] in the United States   In Short Tons

Year	Ilmenite Production (Gross Wt.)	Ilmenite Shipments (TiO_2)	Imports[3]	Stocks Dec. 31 (TiO_2)	Titanium Slag Consumption (TiO_2)	Imports[3]	Stocks (TiO_2)	Rutile Imports[3,4]	Stocks Dec. 31 (TiO_2)	Exports of Titanium Products Ores & Concentrates	Scrap	Dioxide & Pigments	Ingots, Billets, Etc.
1977	638,503	331,139	334,990	494,658	106,201	150,564	44,464	123,800	136,935	22,679	3,394	16,336	1,050
1978	589,751	352,842	308,671	510,430	91,490	149,172	75,097	289,617	172,685	N.A.	5,453	39,341	1,340
1979	639,292	389,535	184,478	462,415	106,346	111,210	56,917	283,479	119,947	9,903	4,967	51,456	1,984
1980	556,646	358,181	357,488	584,280	133,933	194,994	127,981	281,605	147,670	17,830	3,300	45,795	3,278
1981	542,357	310,854	236,217	543,114	186,020	268,825	150,706	202,373	153,770	7,297	3,280	62,432	4,203
1982	263,391	145,725	348,366	470,776	168,433	247,845	103,667	163,325	165,762	21,682	4,287	72,823	2,196
1983	N.A.	N.A.	259,328	254,237	127,267	138,708	61,026	111,578	122,189	4,391	5,379	91,702	1,371
1984	N.A.	N.A.	409,605	128,507	152,534	209,839	52,397	180,508	96,186	8,651	4,109	106,124	2,071
1985[1]	N.A.	N.A.	506,804	147,357	199,610	291,828	83,711	179,663	109,319	27,759	6,760	101,954	2,248
1986[2]			500,000			310,000		180,000		5,000	13,500	105,000	2,300

[1] Preliminary.   [2] Estimate.   [3] For consumption.   [4] Natural & synthetic.   *Source: Bureau of Mines*   T.693

Tobacco

Total 1986 U.S. tobacco production was forecast at 1.19 billion pounds, 21 percent below 1985 and the lowest since 1936. Effective marketing quotas for flue-cured tobacco were reduced seven percent; those for burley were cut 10 percent. Acreage under cultivation fell 12 percent, to a low point untouched since 1974. Because of the smaller crop, domestic supplies were down eight percent from a year earlier; both carry-in stocks and production were down. The largest producing states were North Carolina (39 percent of total production), Kentucky (31 percent) and Tennessee (10 percent), accounting for 80 percent of U.S. tobacco output.

U.S. tobacco use during 1986/87 was expected to exceed production with domestic consumption increasing and exports on the decline. January–October U.S. exports of unmanufactured tobacco were off 19 percent from the same period last year. Export prospects for 1987 were a little brighter (assuming a good-quality crop) due to lower U.S. prices and the weakening dollar. In the first 10 months of 1986, U.S. imports of tobacco for consumption increased 11 percent from a year earlier. Imported tobacco constituted 33 percent of that used in cigarettes and 43 percent of that used in other products. Imports in 1987 were expected to decline slightly.

Flue-cured tobacco is the most common type grown in the U.S., accounting for nearly 52 percent of U.S. output. The quality of the flue-cured tobacco crop in 1986 was not as good as last year because of poor growing conditions. Harvested acreage was down 12 percent and yields were off eight percent. Reduced carry-in stocks and a smaller crop lowered the flue-cured supply to 2.62 billion pounds, nine percent below last year. Flue-cured exports declined from last year's 435 million pounds. Reasons for the decline were stagnant or declining cigarette consumption, reduced leaf use per cigarette, quotas and tariffs that discriminated against U.S. tobacco, and ample world supplies. Domestic use, on the other hand, was projected to have increased, possibly offsetting reduced exports and raising total disappearance from last year's level. The Flue-Cured Stabiliza-

tion Cooperative sold 272 million pounds during January–November, 1986, while loan receipts reached 55 million. By January 1, 1987, unsold loan stocks had fallen sharply from the 745 million pounds held a year earlier.

Burley is the second major type of tobacco grown in the U.S., accounting for 39 percent of production. The quality of the burley crop was lower than last year, with less good tobacco and more fair- and low-quality. Growers reduced acreage 13 percent; yields were also down 13 percent. The 1986 crop, estimated at 435 million pounds as of December 1, was the lowest since 1943 and 20 percent below last year. The 1986/87 burley supply is about 3.3 times probable disappearance. In addition, manufacturers and dealers held 250 million pounds of foreign-grown burley on October 1, about the same as a year earlier. During the year ended September 30, 1986, burley disappearance totaled 476 million pounds, 3.5 percent above the previous period. Domestic use rose 5.5 percent and exports fell by two percent. Although lower U.S. prices and a weaker dollar supported burley exports, stagnant cigarette consumption in major importing countries combined with other factors to hold shipments below the previous year. West Germany and Japan were the major importers of U.S. burley.

Fire-cured tobacco, the third major type grown in the U.S., accounts for three percent of production. The 1986 fire-cured crop was estimated at about 37 million pounds, off 27 percent from last year. Despite this drop in output, the large carry-in kept supplies only 5.5 million pounds below 1985. Disappearance in 1985/86 was estimated at 42.5 million pounds, 8 million above the previous season. Use of fire-cured tobacco had been boosted for several years by rising snuff consumption. However, due to the imposition of a Federal excise tax on smokeless tobacco products in mid-1986, the banning of radio and television advertising and the requirement for health warning labels, snuff and chewing consumption has begun to decline. As a result, domestic use of dark fire-cured is likely to decline over the next few years.

World Production of Leaf Tobacco   In Thousands of Metric Tons (Farm Sales–Weight[3])

Year	United States	Brazil	Canada	China	USSR	France	Greece	India	Indonesia	Italy	Japan	Pakistan	Philippines	Turkey	World Total[1]
1976	971.0	276.1	81.5	1,370	318.0	61.4	140.0	349.8	88.4	108.6	176.2	60.7	89.0	324.0	6,038
1977	870.0	310.0	104.3	1,389	307.0	43.6	118.9	418.8	83.7	109.7	173.2	72.6	84.3	248.0	5,892
1978	919.8	330.0	115.6	1,452	282.0	50.5	130.3	493.6	82.5	109.7	172.0	76.3	79.2	292.6	6,097
1979	693.3	401.0	78.9	941	301.0	50.6	127.2	453.8	141.2	136.6	153.3	69.9	85.3	214.3	5,701
1980	810.9	364.0	107.9	845	289.0	46.5	116.8	438.5	185.5	125.5	141.4	71.0	78.2	228.3	5,199
1981	936.3	325.0	112.4	1,497	273.0	42.8	127.4	440.8	109.7	131.0	137.7	67.6	80.9	168.0	5,939
1982	904.7	378.0	70.2	2,179	307.0	44.5	131.4	520.1	111.4	145.0	139.4	68.3	90.4	207.7	6,878
1983	648.2	378.0	111.7	1,400	382.7	44.5	112.6	594.2	130.1	156.0	136.7	65.5	91.7	228.3	6,065
1984[2]	783.8	373.0	90.2	1,500	345.5	35.9	140.2	450.0	118.0	147.0	137.0	78.5	105.2	210.0	6,125
1985[1]	685.5														
1986[1]	540.0														

[1] Estimated.   [2] Preliminary.   [3] Farm Sales–weight is about 10% above dry weight which is normally reported in trade statistics.
Source: Foreign Agricultural Service, U.S.D.A.

T.694

TOBACCO

Production and Consumption of Tobacco Products in the United States

Year	Plug	Twist	Loose-leaf	Total	Cigarettes (Billion)	Cigars[2]	Smoking Tobacco (Million Lbs.)	Snuff	Cigars[2] (Number)	Cigarettes (Number)	Cigars[2] (Pounds)	Cigarettes (Pounds)	Smoking Tobacco (Pounds)	Chewing Tobacco	Total Pdt.'s
	Chewing Tobacco — Million Pounds								Consumption[3] Per Capita[4]						
1978	15.9	2.1	64.6	94.6	695.9	3.80	36.4	25.1	63.4	3,967	1.05	6.89	.60		8.10
1979	15.3	2.0	71.7	102.3	704.4	3.60	32.8	23.7	56.0	3,861	.92	7.00	.50		8.12
1980	17.3	1.9	72.1	106.0	714.1	3.45	32.2	24.3	51.1	3,849	.84	6.78	.48		7.98
1981	17.9	1.8	70.3	90.0[5]	736.5	3.43	30.3	42.5[5]	48.9	3,836	.81	6.52	.46	1.13	7.59[5]
1982	15.7	1.7	73.0	90.4	694.2	3.20	28.3	43.8	45.2	3,739	.74	6.45	.42	1.09	7.46
1983	14.1	1.7	71.0	86.8	667.0	3.56	28.0	46.7	43.8	3,488	.72	6.19	.40	1.05	7.19
1984	12.7	1.7	74.4	88.8	668.8	3.50	24.5	49.4	41.9	3,446	.69	5.89	.35	1.05	6.85
1985[1]	11.4	1.5	74.0	86.9	665.3	3.13	22.1	48.8	38.2	3,370	.63	5.91	.32	1.01	6.83
1986[6]	9.2	1.4	72.4	83.0	658.5	2.95	18.5	48.5	36.3	3,275	.60	5.73	.29	.97	6.61

[1] Preliminary. [2] Large cigars & cigarillos. [3] Consumption of tax-paid tobacco products; Represents unstemmed equivalent of tobacco used in the manufacture of these products. [4] 18 years old & over. [5] New classifications. [6] Estimate.
Sources: Bureau of the Census; Internal Revenue Service

T.695

Production of Tobacco in the United States   In Millions of Pounds

Year	Conn.	Florida	Georgia	Indiana	Kentucky	Maryland	Massachusetts	North Car.	Ohio	Pa.	South Car.	Tenn.	Virginia	Wisconsin	W. Virg.
1978	5.0	22.1	125.7	15.5	469.7	30.6	1.5	849.7	22.5	25.2	150.5	142.1	135.2	20.3	2.7
1979	4.9	23.2	101.0	11.9	343.1	22.0	1.5	621.4	14.1	17.7	117.7	104.8	109.6	25.1	1.7
1980	5.3	20.4	110.6	16.8	420.7	25.3	1.9	762.4	20.0	24.7	125.5	111.9	106.9	26.0	1.8
1981	5.6	22.8	121.0	18.8	509.6	33.0	2.0	795.9	22.9	27.3	149.6	161.5	157.8	26.4	2.4
1982	4.2	21.0	105.6	20.2	589.4	37.5	.9	700.7	31.9	25.9	124.2	178.2	125.4	20.1	3.6
1983	3.4	17.6	96.4	13.0	324.6	29.7	.8	546.9	17.7	22.0	112.9	118.2	99.1	16.7	3.8
1984	2.8	17.9	85.5	18.8	530.1	30.4	.8	590.0	26.5	22.4	105.5	154.6	115.9	16.4	4.5
1985	3.3	16.3	82.1	14.6	428.4	26.6	.8	556.5	16.9	21.9	98.9	127.4	91.1	17.6	3.4
1986[1]	3.1	13.4	68.3	12.8	322.2	22.5	.7	444.7	14.2	20.4	77.9	74.9	74.9	14.7	3.3

[1] Preliminary, December estimate. *Source: Crop Reporting Board, U.S.D.A.*

T.696

Salient Statistics of Tobacco in the United States

Year	Acres Harvested 1,000 Acres	Yield Per Acre Lbs.	Production Million Lbs.	Farm Price ¢ Lb.	Farm Value Mil. $	Exports[2]	Imports[3]	Cigarettes	Cigars & Cheroots	Chewing Tobacco & Snuff	Smoking Tobacco[5]	Jan. 1	April 1	July 1	Oct. 1
						Tobacco (July–June) Mil. Lbs.		Millions		Metric Tons		Stocks of Leaf Tobacco[4] All Types Billion Pounds			
1978	963.7	2,101	2,025	132.4	2,679	671.9	359.7	74,359	166	47	12,639	5,008	4,781	4,451	4,728
1979	827.7	1,844	1,527	141.1	2,154	617.4	398.1	79,717	177	43	8,289	5,071	4,914	4,518	4,740
1980	920.5	1,939	1,786	152.3	2,720	553.4	439.8	81,998	354	124	6,103	4,974	4,608	4,284	4,548
1981	976.0	2,113	2,064	170.6	3,520	584.9	384.9	82,582	181	191	9,105	4,850	4,617	4,285	4,699
1982	912.7	2,185	1,994	176.4	3,517	553.4	434.0	73,585	181	887	10,345	5,080	4,909	4,675	5,034
1983	789.2	1,811	1,429	174.7	2,495	526.5	515.9	60,698	130	1,073	15,036	5,367	5,288	4,900	5,209
1984	791.7	2,183	1,728	180.7	3,120	519.8	425.1	56,517	104	1,162		5,357	5,247	4,987	5,186
1985[1]	688.0	2,196	1,511	165.0	2,518	541.6	449.1	58,900	101			5,444	5,186		
1986[1]	602.3	1,977	1,190			533.6		67,500	70						

[1] Preliminary. [2] Domestic. [3] For consumption. [4] Owned by dealer & mfgrs., converted to a farm-sales weight equivalent. [5] In packages & in bulk & other. *Source: Agricultural Marketing Service, U.S.D.A.*

T.700

Tobacco Production in the U.S., by Types   In Million Pounds (Farm–Sales Weight)

Types	11–14	31	32	21	22–23	35–36	37	41	42–44	72	51–52	54–55	61
1978	1,232	626	30.6	6.8	51.4	22.2	.9	25.2	3.0	.1	2.6	20.3	3.8
1979	946	446	22.0	5.4	39.6	16.1	.6	17.7	2.0	.1	2.4	25.1	4.0
1980	1,086	561	26.2	3.6	32.7	16.2	.4	24.7	2.4	.1	2.6	26.0	4.5
1981	1,170	730	46.4	5.2	32.4	15.7	.7	27.3	2.4	.1	3.5	26.4	4.1
1982	1,006	822	42.0	5.5	47.7	19.9	.7	21.4	3.5		3.5	20.1	1.6
1983	821.3	481.4	37.4	4.6	32.5	14.3	.4	14.2	1.9		2.5	16.7	1.7
1984	864.6	712.2	38.1	6.1	50.5	19.0	.6	14.6	2.2		1.9	16.4	1.7
1985	800.3	573.3	32.9	4.5	45.9	15.2	.2	15.6	1.7		2.1	17.6	2.0
1986[1]	663.5	424.9	26.9	3.0	32.4	10.5	.2	14.7	1.0		2.0	14.2	1.9

[1] Preliminary. *Source: Crop Reporting Board, U.S.D.A.*

T.701

U.S. Exports of Unmanufactured Tobacco   In Millions of Pounds (Declared Weight)

Year	Aus-tralia	Belg.-Luxem.	Den-mark	Egypt	France	W. Ger-many	Thailand	Ireland	Japan	Nether-lands	Norway	Italy	Sweden	Switzer-land	United Kingdom	Total U.S. Exports
1978	12.4	16.9	27.1	24.5	9.8	53.2	18.2	5.3	102.3	34.2	4.2	41.0	17.5	26.2	148.8	700.0
1979	12.4	5.4	16.4	3.8	11.5	67.7	18.8	6.9	95.9	29.3	5.7	34.8	13.7	19.3	68.2	567.4
1980	13.4	7.9	17.5	17.4	4.5	100.7	22.6	3.6	82.1	44.9	6.8	30.7	15.4	20.1	32.5	598.7
1981	12.6	9.5	11.1	16.1	6.1	83.2	18.4	3.9	117.0	28.6	4.2	26.5	9.9	22.2	39.4	584.5
1982	10.1	15.2	16.8	22.0	5.3	68.2	27.7	4.7	110.3	25.1	3.6	28.1	8.7	26.7	30.7	572.0
1983	9.7	9.6	20.2	21.6	7.3	58.0	9.1	3.2	114.1	28.4	5.7	32.2	12.4	16.8	27.8	524.4
1984	8.2	9.4	19.8	37.4	5.1	66.0	14.6	8.0	92.1	22.3	4.7	31.3	11.5	25.3	31.8	542.7
1985[1]	7.3	11.5	16.2	41.2	9.9	76.7	17.8	7.3	102.0	20.9	3.3	28.7	15.8	23.9	18.4	548.9
1986[2]	9.0	10.5	15.0	5.0	10.0	85.0	15.0	6.0	110.0	40.0	4.0	27.0	10.0	20.0	18.0	450.0

[1] Preliminary.   [2] Estimate.   *Source: Bureau of the Census*   T.702

U.S. Salient Statistics for Flue-Cured Tobacco (Types 11–14)

Crop Year	Acres Har-vested 1,000	Yield Acre 100 Lbs.	Market-ings	Stocks, July 1	Total Supply	Exports	Dom. Disap-pearance	Total Disap-pearance	Farm Price ¢ Lb.	Crop Value Mil. $	Parity Price[2] ¢ Lb.	Price Support Level ¢ Lb.	Placed Under Gov't. Loan Mil. Lb.	Under Loan July 1 Mil. Lb.
1977	589.3	19.2	1,124	2,075	3,199	539	608	1,147	117.6	1,329	162.0	113.8	195.6	556.9
1978	602.1	20.5	1,206	2,052	3,258	599	584	1,183	135.0	1,663	176.0	121.0	64.1	534.0
1979	502.8	18.8	946	2,075	3,021	520	563	1,083	140.0	1,324	203.0	129.3	72.0	564.0
1980	555.1	19.6	1,086	1,965	3,052	509	530	1,039	144.5	1,569	222.0	141.5	137.2	554.4
1981	540.6	21.6	1,144	2,013	3,157	523	489	1,012	166.4	1,947		158.7	105.9	595.8
1982	472.3	21.3	994	2,145	3,139	456	479	935	178.5	1,774		169.9	259.9	518.7
1983–4	409.8	20.0	855	2,205	3,060	453	442	894	177.9	1,521		169.9	194.8	688.4
1984–5	392.0	22.1	850	2,165	3,015	481	454	935	181.1	1,539		169.9	159.2	797.5
1985–6[1]	357.1	22.4	789	2,080	2,870	435	477	912	171.9	1,361		169.9	132.2	833.1
1986–7[3]	326.8	20.3	675	1,958	2,633							143.8		790.4

[1] Preliminary.   [2] As of applicable date when support level was computed.   [3] Estimate.   *Source: Agricultural Marketing Service, U.S.D.A.*   T.697

U.S. Salient Statistics for Burley Tobacco (Type 31)

Crop Year	Acres Har-vested 1,000	Yield Per Acre 100 Lbs.	Market-ings	Stocks, Oct. 1	Total Supply	Exports	Dom. Disap-pearance	Total Disap-pearance	Farm Price ¢ Lb.	Crop Value Mil. $	Parity Price[2] ¢ Lb.	Support Level ¢ Lb.	Placed Under Gov't. Loan Mil. Lb.	Under Loan on Oct. 1 Mil. Lb.
1977	268.6	23.0	613	1,217	1,830	117	495	611	120.0	741	166.0	117.3	57.0	54.9
1978	261.4	24.0	618	1,218	1,836	121	503	624	131.2	822	184.0	124.7	67.7	113.5
1979	238.1	18.7	446	1,212	1,658	133	499	632	145.2	700	210.0	133.3	7.3	155.4
1980	276.6	20.3	558	1,026	1,583	106	478	583	165.9	930	236.0	145.9	.0	66.3
1981	331.2	22.0	726	1,000	1,726	141	464	605	180.7	1,318		163.6	.8	0
1982	346.2	23.7	777	1,121	1,898	135	444	579	181.0	1,406		175.1	269.2	.7
1983–4	292.6	16.5	527	1,319	1,845	112	389	501	177.3	934		175.1	255.6	226.1
1984–5	315.7	22.6	674	1,344	2,018	154	403	556	187.6	1,264		175.1	200.3	377.2
1985–6[1]	255.1	22.5	542	1,462	2,004	160	395	555	159.4	877		148.8	82.7	548.9
1986–7[3]	221.4	19.2	465	1,449	1,914							148.8		580.0

[1] Preliminary.   [2] As of applicable date when support level was computed.   [3] Estimate.   *Source: Agricultural Marketing Service, U.S.D.A.*   T.698

Exports[1] of Tobacco from the United States   In Millions of Pounds

Year	Jan.	Feb.	Mar.	Apr.	May	June	July	Aug.	Sept.	Oct.	Nov.	Dec.	Total
1977	76.8	53.0	54.7	31.3	38.0	41.5	49.7	47.5	66.3	17.9	49.5	102.4	628.6
1978	52.5	55.6	73.2	40.9	32.3	29.2	42.7	52.3	41.3	85.8	95.8	86.3	687.8
1979	35.6	50.1	57.1	51.8	42.2	25.3	38.0	29.5	30.1	41.6	78.9	81.5	561.8
1980	28.0	52.5	80.1	54.6	53.2	43.0	40.9	28.3	32.3	47.6	64.4	66.6	591.5
1981	44.8	32.8	53.7	49.4	44.6	40.1	31.3	27.4	45.5	63.2	86.8	55.6	575.3
1982	31.7	39.4	62.1	41.8	54.0	37.2	23.9	30.2	24.8	74.5	92.2	50.5	562.3
1983	24.2	38.3	46.0	44.0	33.6	32.7	28.6	36.0	26.4	51.7	87.9	60.3	509.8
1984	42.0	40.2	43.3	32.4	26.5	28.9	14.8	18.4	39.1	68.0	97.9	77.1	528.5
1985[2]	34.6	48.5	48.1	54.1	15.8	14.2	20.4	39.2	41.1	48.1	85.4	89.3	538.6
1986[2]	21.6	31.9	48.8	45.9	28.4	22.4	16.4	23.7					

[1] Represents unmanufactured tobacco, including stems, trimmings and scrap.   [2] Preliminary.   *Source: Department of Commerce*   T.699

Tung Oil

Tung oil is derived from tung nuts, a tree crop, and is used as an industrial lubricant and a drying oil. Total world output each year ranges between 95,000 and 105,000 tonnes, of which three-fourths originates in China. Other significant producers and exporters of tung oil are Argentina and Paraguay.

All U.S. requirements for tung oil are obtained from imports, which in recent years have been 12.4–14.0 million pounds. Stocks on hand at factories and warehouses averaged around 2.8 million pounds during 1986, 38 percent higher than during 1985. Domestic supply is consumed mainly in industrial applications. In 1984, the latest year for which relevant data were available, total factory consumption amounted to 12.4 million pounds, of which 41 percent went into paint and varnish, and 36 percent was used in resins and plastics.

The average monthly price of tung oil (imported drums, f.o.b. New York) fell throughout the first nine months of 1986, starting the year at 52.0 cents per pound and skidding to only 33.0 cents in September. Prices were well below the average of 66.1 cents per pound during 1985, when the average monthly price ranged from the high of 81 cents per pound during January through April to the low of 52.5 cents in December.

Supply and Distribution of Tung Oil in the United States   In Thousands of Pounds

Year	Stocks Jan. 1	Production	Imports	Exports[2]	Total Supply	Apparent Disappearance	Factory Consumption (Crop Yr. Beg. Oct.) — Total	Paint & Varnish	Resins & Plastics	Other Inedible Prods	Oil Acquired By CCC
1977	2,300	—	18,821	1,200	19,900	16,900	20,100				
1978	3,000		17,912				13,500	7,200	3,700	2,600	
1979	1,200		20,038				15,700	10,400	3,000	2,300	
1980	3,500		16,239				16,600	8,300	3,700	4,600	
1981	2,800		15,033				14,600	5,800	3,200	5,600	
1982[1]	2,200		14,398				12,700	5,300	2,800	4,000	
1983[1]	2,217		13,635				19,700	5,600	3,400	10,800	
1984[3]	3,137		13,929				12,400	5,100	4,500	2,900	
1985[3]	2,546										
1986[3]	3,514										

[1] Preliminary.   [2] Also including re-exports.   [3] Estimate.   *Source: Economic Research Service, U.S.D.A.*   T.703

U.S. Consumption of Tung Oil in Inedible Products   In Thousands of Pounds

Year	Jan.	Feb.	Mar.	Apr.	May	June	July	Aug.	Sept.	Oct.	Nov.	Dec.	Total
1985	1,110	1,079	887	1,039	818	1,197	1,303	1,096	1,105	1,068	911	891	12,504
1986	884	964	959	989	923	1,093	976	895	949	1,081			

Source: Bureau of the Census

U.S. Stocks of Tung Oil at Factories & Warehouses   In Thousands of Pounds

Year	Jan. 1	Feb. 1	Mar. 1	Apr. 1	May 1	June 1	July 1	Aug. 1	Sept. 1	Oct. 1	Nov. 1	Dec. 1
1983	2,217	3,124	1,612	1,697	1,768	2,706	2,901	2,742	2,406	1,103	1,948	1,845
1984	3,137	2,867	3,042	2,634	2,609	2,102	1,815	1,802	1,476	1,192	2,113	2,029
1985[1]	2,546	2,589	2,353	1,642	1,707	1,599	1,564	2,163	2,272	1,526	1,798	2,617
1986[1]	3,514	3,347	2,651	3,036	2,847	2,255	2,691	2,742	2,151	2,212	3,286	

[1] Preliminary.   *Source: Bureau of the Census*   T.703A

Average Price of Tung Oil[1] (Imported-Drums) F.O.B. New York   In Cents per Pound

Year	Jan.	Feb.	Mar.	Apr.	May	June	July	Aug.	Sept.	Oct.	Nov.	Dec.	Average
1977	65.5	72.7	97.0	142.4	147.0	147.0	128.2	100.0	100.0	100.0	100.0	100.0	108.3
1978	100.0	100.0	100.0	100.0	100.0	100.0	100.0	87.5	87.5	87.5	68.5	66.4	91.4
1979	68.9	68.9	67.9	69.0	69.0	69.0	69.0	69.0	62.5	55.0	51.0	51.0	64.2
1980	51.0	55.1	55.8	53.0	51.1	48.3	45.2	43.7	46.6	56.5	65.5	67.2	53.3
1981	69.6	68.0	64.0	60.3	62.9	64.5	64.0	64.0	62.1	60.3	58.5	58.5	63.1
1982	61.4	69.5	68.2	66.5	68.3	69.4	66.9	63.5	60.6	60.5	60.5	60.5	64.6
1983	60.5	57.0	57.0	61.9	86.4	102.5	102.5	107.3	133.4	136.0	138.0	138.0	98.4
1984	138.0	138.0	138.0	138.0	138.0	134.0	134.0	117.0	106.9	89.0	81.0	81.0	119.2
1985	81.0	81.0	81.0	81.0	81.0	N.A.	52.0	53.0	55.0	55.0	55.0	52.5	66.1
1986	52.0	46.5	46.1	44.5	43.5	40.1	36.5	34.8	33.0				

[1] Carlots, imported, f.o.b. New York.   *Source: Economic Research Service, U.S.D.A.*   T.704

Tungsten

Preliminary data report consumption of tungsten concentrate at 4,870 tonnes in 1986, as against 6,840 tonnes in 1985. Net production of intermediate products (metal powder, carbide powder, and chemicals) was an estimated 6,600 tonnes in 1986 versus 8,200 in 1985. Production of ammonium paratungstate was estimated down 19 percent from 1985.

1986 U.S. imports of tungsten concentrate and intermediate products originated from China, Bolivia, and Germany. About half were in the form of concentrate; 26 percent were ammonium tungstates; and nine percent tungsten carbide. U.S. exports went mainly to the Netherlands, Israel, and Germany: metal powder constituted about 54 percent; 25 percent were tungsten carbide; 14 percent were compound, wire, unwrought tungsten and alloy in crude form.

1986 tungsten and products prices were depressed. In 1981, the average value f.o.b. U.S. mine of a short ton of tungsten trioxide was $130.25, in 1985, $68, and in November, 1986, only $44.34.

In October, 1986, the U.S. General Services Administration received no bid on its offer to sell tungsten concentrate from the national-defense stockpile.

World Concentrate Production of Tungsten   In Metric Tons of Contained Tungsten[3]

Year	Japan	Argen-tina	Australia	Bolivia	Brazil	Burma	China	Rep. of Korea	Canada	Portugal	Spain	Thailand	USSR	United States	World Total
1981	631	11	3,517	2,779	1,576	825	13,500	2,739	1,993	1,395	437	1,209	8,850	3,605	50,269
1982	604	17	2,618	2,534	1,524	844	12,500	2,420	2,842	1,358	545	855	9,000	1,521	46,921
1983	475	41	2,015	2,449	1,026	930	12,500	2,480	328	1,183	517	562	9,100	980	40,821
1984[1]	477	37	1,772	1,893	1,037	1,096	13,500	2,702	3,715	1,493	565	741	9,100	1,203	46,478
1985[2]	526	36	1,912	1,551	1,175	945	15,000	2,572	3,100	1,751	530	586	9,200	996	46,989

[1] Preliminary.   [2] Estimate.   [3] Conversion Factors: WO_3 to W, multiply by 0.7931; 60% WO_3 to W, multiply by 0.4758.
Source: Bureau of Mines

T.706

Salient Statistics of Tungsten in the U.S.   In Metric Tons of Contained Tungsten

Year	Net Import Reliance as a % of Apparent Consumption	Produc-tion[1]	Ship-ments from Mines[1]	Total Con-sump-tion	Steel Tool	Steel Stainless & Heat Assisting	Alloy Steel[3]	Super-alloys	Cutting & Wear Resistant Materials	Pdt's. Made from Metal Powder	Miscel-laneous	Chemicals & Ceramic	Exports	Consumers & Dealers	Pro-ducers[1]
1981	50	3,605	3,545	9,839									79	671	108
1982	42	1,521	1,575	4,506									305	1,765	54
1983	52	980	1,016	5,181	196	46	12	215	4,097	1,553	220	71	1	1,085	47
1984	70	1,203	1,173	8,577	516	81	38	5	6,386	2,036	983	139	129	959	46
1985[2]	68	996	983	6,838	326	76	19	13	5,033	1,858	674	85	124	1,077	60
1986[4]				4,600	200				1,500	1,000	1,200		125	800	

Consumption of Tungsten Products by End Uses — columns: Tool, Stainless & Heat Assisting, Alloy Steel[3], Super-alloys, Cutting & Wear Resistant Materials, Pdt's. Made from Metal Powder, Miscellaneous, Chemicals & Ceramic. Stocks at End of Year (Concentrate): Consumers & Dealers, Producers[1].

[1] Primary concentrates.   [2] Preliminary.   [3] Other than tool.   [4] Estimate.   *Source: Bureau of Mines*

T.707

U.S. Imports[1] of Tungsten Ores & Concentrates and Ferrotungsten   In Metric Tons[4] (Tungsten Content)

Year	Australia	Bolivia	Brazil	Canada	South Korea	Mexico	Portugal	Spain	Thailand	Peru	Total 1,000 Pounds	Value Mil. $	Austria	Port-ugal	West Germany	Total 1,000 Lbs.
1982	16	643	247	1,259	9	246	239	—	134	114	3,528	46.7	11	43	3	69
1983	28	662	78	649	117	215	339	—	142	199	2,861	25.7	25	19	—	48
1984	133	1,302	149	1,464	16	196	606	22	774	605	5,807	51.7	93	65	38	285
1985[2]	414	627	69	1,371	4	183	555	11	472	282	4,746	36.7	27	41	1	93
1986[3]	200	500	30	400		220	300		250	250	2,100					

Tungsten Ores and Concentrates Imported (For Consumption). Ferrotungsten Imported.

[1] Imports for consumption.   [2] Preliminary.   [3] Estimate.   *Source: Bureau of Mines*

T.708

Tungsten Prices   In U.S. Dollars

Year	U.S.[1] Markets	European Markets	Total (Mil. $)	Avg. per Unit of WO_3	Avg. per Kilogram of Tungsten	Year	U.S.[1] Markets	European[1] Markets	Total (Mil. $)	Avg. per Unit of WO_3	Avg. per Kilogram of Tungsten
1980	131.07	129.87	50.6	146.49	18.47	1983	85.00	81.00	10.5	82.17	10.36
1981	130.25	129.16	62.2	139.21	17.55	1984	85.00	87.00	13.4	90.63	11.43
1982	106.00	107.00	22.1	111.06	14.00	1985[3]	68.00	71.00	9.1	73.77	9.30

Reported Value, F.O.B. U.S. Mine[2].

[1] Conc., Stu WO_3, Average (a short ton unit [stu] of tungsten trioxide [WO_3] contains 15,862 pounds of tungsten).   [2] Values apply to finished concentrate & are in some instances f.o.b. custom mill.   [3] Preliminary.   *Source: Bureau of Mines*

T.709

Turkeys

For the first three quarters of 1986, federally inspected turkey slaughter increased 13 percent over the year-ago period; turkey meat production was up nine percent. The 1986 turkey crop was estimated at 203 million head, up 10 percent from 1985. North Carolina continued to hold its position as top producer, with 39.1 million head, followed by Minnesota (34.2 million), California (21.9 million), Arkansas (16.5 million) and Virginia (14.3 million). These states accounted for over 60 percent of the turkeys produced in the U.S. during 1986. Low feed prices, relatively strong demand, and favorable returns to producers encouraged increased production.

January–September, 1986 U.S. exports of whole turkey and turkey parts totaled 17 million pounds, six percent below last year. Exports of turkey parts were down nine percent; whole turkey exports increased five percent. Egypt was the largest importer, followed by West Germany. West Germany has been sharply expanding domestic turkey production, but the weaker U.S. dollar has encouraged continued imports of U.S. turkeys.

The weighted average wholesale price of turkeys was 80 cents per pound during the third quarter of 1986, up slightly from 78 cents last year. The higher prices were the result of retailers contracting for their needs early this year.

Cold storage stocks of frozen turkey on October 1, 1986, were 511 million pounds, up 15 percent from the year-ago period. Stocks were large relative to the past few years; there were only two years since 1960 when larger amounts of turkey were in storage. Whole turkey stocks were up 16 percent and stocks of

other turkey up 11 percent. With higher stocks and higher production, the supply of turkey for consumption was substantially above last year.

Per capita consumption of turkey in 1986 is expected to average 13.5 pounds, up 12 percent from 1985. The fourth quarter is usually the largest consumption period, with 40 percent of turkey disappearance occuring at this time. Projected per capita disappearance for October–December, 1986 is 5.5 pounds, or 41 percent of the annual total.

With abundant grain supplies in 1987, feed prices will likely be below 1986 and will help to reduce production costs, providing incentive to expand output in 1987. The number of poults placed in September, 1986, which will be ready for slaughter in early 1987, was 28 percent above last year. This increase will give a big boost to slaughter early in 1987. Producers will likely continue the expansion through 1987, although USDA estimates that the rate of increase will be below that indicated by the September placements. 1987 output of turkey meat is expected to be 15–17 percent above the year-earlier level.

Wholesale prices for 8–16 pound young hen turkeys in 1987 are expected to average slightly below 1986, as production increases. Further processed turkey products are expected to enjoy good demand, with a smaller red-meat supply and higher meat prices; this should help to support turkey prices. Turkey should also continue to substitute for red meat as a filler in frankfurters and bologna. With pork supplies lower in most of 1987, and smaller supplies of cows and nonfed cattle, processing meat will likely be priced higher.

Salient Statistics of Turkeys in the U.S.

Year	Breeder Hens on Farms—Dec. 1 Number	$ Value Per Head In Millions	Raised	(Liveweight) Produced Million —Lbs.—	Farm Price ¢ Lb.	Gross Income Million $	Production	Commercial Storage Jan. 1	Exports & Shipments	Military	Consumption — Civilian — Total	Per Capita Lb.	Production Costs Live-Weight— Feed	Total	Wholesale Ready-to-Cook Total Costs	3-City Composite Price
1977	3.0	11.39	136.4	2,563	35.5	910	2,023	203	56	11	1,992	9.3	22.6	31.6	51.4	56.2
1978	3.4	12.53	138.9	2,655	43.6	1,157	2,098	168	57	15	2,019	9.2	22.1	31.7	51.7	68.8
1979	3.7	13.57	156.5	2,958	41.1	1,214	2,343	175	57	19	2,204	9.9	25.3	35.8	58.2	67.0
1980	3.7	14.11	164.9	3,077	41.3	1,272	2,425	240	81	16	2,370	10.5	26.1	37.1	61.0	66.0
1981	3.5	15.35	159.9	3,264	38.2	1,248	2,574	198	68	15	2,450	10.7	30.2	41.2	66.1	64.0
1982	3.4	14.60	164.5	3,175	39.5	1,255	2,522	238	56	12	2,489	10.8	24.5	36.3	60.1	63.6
1983	3.2	17.59	170.7	3,336	38.0	1,269	2,635	204	54	13	2,609	11.2	26.6	39.8	65.4	63.5
1984[1]	3.2	16.54	171.2	3,386	48.9	1,655	2,685	162	33	13	2,676	11.4	29.0	42.0	69.0	72.0
1985[2]			185.3	3,702	47.2	1,747	2,942	125	27	13	2,870	12.1	21.4	35.1	60.1	77.3
1986[2]			203.2				3,305	150	25	14	3,241	13.5				

[1] Preliminary. [2] Estimate. *Source: Economic Research Service, U.S.D.A.* T.710

Turkey Per Capita Consumption in the U.S. by Quarters In Pounds

Year	First	Second	Third	Fourth	Total	Year	First	Second	Third	Fourth	Total
1979	1.5	1.9	2.3	4.2	9.9	1983	2.1	2.2	2.5	4.4	11.2
1980	1.8	2.0	2.7	4.0	10.5	1984	2.0	2.2	2.7	4.5	11.4
1981	1.6	1.9	2.5	4.6	10.7	1985[1]	2.1	2.3	2.9	4.9	12.1
1982	1.8	2.1	2.6	4.3	10.7	1986[1]	2.4	2.5			

[1] Preliminary. *Source: Economic Research Service, U.S.D.A.* T.711

Wholesale Price of Turkeys[3] (Hens, 8–16 lbs.) N.Y.   In Cents per Pound

Year	Jan.	Feb.	Mar.	Apr.	May	June	July	Aug.	Sept.	Oct.	Nov.	Dec.	Avg.	Yearly Average Price 4-Region Retail	Farm Price[2]
1973	45.1	48.6	56.0	57.7	60.6	67.8	69.4	81.1	86.0	84.2	80.2	71.2	67.3		34.8
1974	60.7	54.2	51.9	45.3	48.4	52.5	52.6	55.8	55.7	54.4	56.3	58.8	53.9		28.8
1975	59.0	56.7	55.9	52.0	52.6	56.5	59.5	61.8	64.3	66.8	69.9	70.0	60.3		34.8
1976	69.0	69.0	69.9	70.0	70.6	71.0	71.0	71.0	71.0	71.0	72.8	73.0	70.8		31.7
1977	72.5	70.2	68.8	68.8	69.0	70.1	72.1	73.2	73.6	74.6	75.5	78.2	72.2		35.5
1978	78.5	78.5	78.9	79.0	82.2	86.1	86.8	87.0	87.0	89.1	91.6	90.7	84.6		43.6
1979	91.0	90.8	90.0	89.5	90.9	91.0	91.0	91.5	91.4	93.1	94.5	92.9	91.5		41.9
1980[1]	62.3	57.8	56.8	54.1	53.3	55.5	63.3	67.2	74.5	77.0	75.0	67.0	63.6		40.0
1981	59.4	60.7	63.8	61.2	63.5	66.2	66.8	61.8	59.5	56.4	57.3	51.7	60.7	97.7	38.4
1982	53.6	55.8	56.0	55.8	58.8	61.8	64.1	64.1	68.0	69.6	67.2	54.2	60.8	92.6	39.5
1983	53.6	54.9	56.0	54.4	56.6	60.9	58.5	57.6	65.0	65.1	67.0	76.1	60.5	91.7	46.6
1984	72.2	64.7	66.1	67.0	66.8	67.0	68.6	72.4	76.2	82.6	91.5	97.3	74.4	98.7	48.0
1985	74.0	65.6	67.0	64.6	62.6	68.1	72.8	78.4	82.4	90.2	93.1	86.9	75.5	105.2	47.2
1986	60.2	61.7	63.9	64.6	67.1	73.8	77.8	80.5	88.7						

[1] Prior to 1980 prices are for frozen eviscerated tom turkeys (N.Y.C.); heaviest weights.   [2] Live weight.   [3] Ready-to-cook.   T.713
Source: Economic Research Service, U.S.D.A.

Certified Federally Inspected Turkey Slaughter in the U.S.   In Millions of Lbs.

Year	Jan.	Feb.	Mar.	Apr.	May	June	July	Aug.	Sept.	Oct.	Nov.	Dec.	Total
1974	97.3	59.8	58.9	80.1	113.2	159.7	213.1	237.2	220.2	261.1	215.2	119.9	1,836
1975	64.9	47.1	54.4	68.7	81.9	138.4	193.2	203.3	229.0	257.5	220.2	157.5	1,716
1976	76.3	61.7	68.6	79.9	106.5	182.2	213.9	243.8	252.8	256.6	261.5	146.4	1,950
1977	70.5	58.7	80.3	78.9	110.0	176.5	189.6	244.4	238.2	250.3	246.8	148.2	1,892
1978	81.8	59.7	86.3	80.8	129.3	189.5	199.9	248.8	230.9	271.2	248.9	156.3	1,983
1979	99.3	77.2	95.0	112.3	157.3	195.9	219.2	267.7	233.0	297.5	261.9	165.5	2,182
1980	—378.6—			—528.3—			—711.6—			—713.9—			2,232
1981	—398.1—			—553.2—			—785.2—			—772.6—			2,509
1982	—410.4—			—527.9—			—761.5—			—759.1—			2,459
1983	—462.2—			—581.5—			—760.3—			—759.0—			2,563
1984	—432.3—			—589.3—			—777.2—			—775.3—			2,574
1985	—482.1—			—628.3—			—854.6—			—834.8—			2,800
1986[1]	—556.1—			—717.4—			—933.8—						

[1] Preliminary.   *Source: Economic Research Service, U.S.D.A.*   T.714

Storage Stocks of Turkeys (Frozen) in the United States   In Millions of Pounds

Year	Jan. 1	Feb. 1	Mar. 1	Apr. 1	May 1	June 1	July 1	Aug. 1	Sept. 1	Oct. 1	Nov. 1	Dec. 1
1973	208.1	188.4	152.6	115.4	91.3	88.1	137.1	199.4	261.2	350.7	450.5	321.1
1974	281.0	274.0	250.5	235.9	225.0	227.4	265.8	335.8	431.8	528.7	554.6	372.0
1975	275.0	267.1	239.9	207.3	180.2	162.7	193.2	248.6	328.6	409.8	472.4	286.2
1976	195.2	186.8	160.7	140.7	114.5	120.8	177.3	261.8	370.3	459.7	512.3	298.8
1977	203.4	190.3	167.8	142.3	130.3	138.2	201.4	253.6	329.9	409.3	444.5	269.4
1978	167.9	168.2	136.6	113.0	101.1	103.9	152.8	213.6	301.2	373.3	425.4	236.2
1979	175.1	170.7	154.7	135.7	128.0	153.1	200.9	272.5	382.5	432.3	445.5	281.2
1980	240.0	246.8	225.0	208.9	206.6	233.8	286.6	325.8	384.0	398.8	528.1	257.6
1981	198.0	208.3	207.9	220.7	228.7	256.2	327.3	400.8	466.0	532.1	528.1	305.1
1982	238.4	236.9	236.4	232.8	—	—	281.7	—	—	435.8	—	—
1983	203.9	193.8	187.7	185.3	192.3	210.5	255.7	323.5	384.3	432.2	460.1	251.6
1984	161.8	161.5	145.8	144.4	142.2	180.9	226.3	278.2	331.3	390.6	415.4	195.7
1985	125.3	124.1	129.5	131.1	157.0	183.7	243.3	304.7	387.8	444.5	484.1	208.2
1986[1]	150.2	156.8	161.3	150.0	186.3	226.8	294.0	388.1	449.3	511.6	543.5	255.4

[1] Preliminary.   *Source: Crop Reporting Board, U.S.D.A.*   T.712

Uranium

In 1985, after five years of image and price problems, the domestic uranium mining industry was declared nonviable by the U.S. Department of Energy. Some U.S. producers attempted to maintain operations; most domestic mines closed properties by phasing out or abandonment. The industry demise negatively affected the economies of Wyoming and New Mexico.

The 1979 accident at Three Mile Island was a major blow to the nuclear power complex in the U.S. Since then, there have been no domestic orders for nuclear power plants and more than 100 orders have been canceled. The 1986 reactor meltdown in Chernobyl in the Soviet Ukraine also is likely to keep demand for nuclear power subdued in the foreseeable future.

In 1979, the U.S. had more than 220,000 workers in the uranium industry, but in 1986, there were fewer than 3,500. With 1985 production estimated at around 5,500 short tons, output is down dramatically from the 1979/80 peaks of 20,000 tons. Prices, too, have fallen sharply, tumbling from 1979's $43.70 a pound to 1985's $14.45. By June of 1986, prices had recovered somewhat, possibly due to a drawdown in spot supplies, to about $17.20 a pound.

The domestic mining industry's troubles are also related to dumping of cheap yellowcake by other producing nations acting in concert. In the middle 1970s, U.S. producers had a virtual monopoly on the sale of uranium to non-communist nations. Currently, two European consortia supply two-thirds of the market with low-cost production from Canada, South Africa, Niger and Australia.

Canada accounts for 35 percent of world production; South Africa supplies about 13 percent and Central Africa about 11 percent. Even with reduced production, the U.S. provides about 12 percent of total world output of 45,000 tons.

Prospects continue to look negative for the domestic uranium industry. Oil prices have fallen from their early-decade highs and the major rationale for nuclear power stations, cheap power, is no longer considered valid. Also, large cost overruns in building projects, as well as continued public skepticism about nuclear safety, will keep the industry under pressure.

There have been periodic attempts to encourage Congress to do something to help the uranium industry. While some hope has come from that quarter, there has been nothing concrete. In 1984, the Atomic Energy Commission removed all restrictions against foreign uranium being used in U.S. reactors. No further changes are contemplated.

Free-World Production of Uranium Oxide (U$_3$O$_8$) Concentrate   In Thousands of Short Tons

Year	Argentina	Australia	Canada	Spain	Namibia	Gabon	France	Portugal	Niger	Brazil	Sweden	South Africa	United States	World Total
1979	.2	.9	8.9		5.0		3.1		4.7	0		6.2	18.7	49.6
1980	.2	2.0	9.3		5.3		3.4		5.3	0		8.0	21.8	57.2
1981	.2	3.7	10.0		5.2		3.3		5.7	.1		8.0	19.2	57.1
1982	.2	5.7	10.5		4.9		3.7		5.5	.4		7.6	13.4	53.7
1983[2]	.3	4.8	9.8		4.8		4.2		5.2	.4		7.5	10.6	49.3
1984[2]		5.2	14.6		4.3		4.1					7.5	7.8	49.5
1985[2]		4.3	14.3		4.3		4.0					6.1	5.6	44.9

[1] Less than 50 tons.   [2] Preliminary.   *Source: Bureau of Mines, Dept. of Energy; NUEXCO.*   T.720

Month–End Uranium (U$_3$O$_8$) Transaction Values[1]

	Jan.	Feb.	Mar.	Apr.	May	June	July	Aug.	Sept.	Oct.	Nov.	Dec.
1976	—	—	—	—	39.60	39.70	39.70	40.40	40.30	40.60	40.70	40.70
1977	41.30	41.30	41.40	41.50	42.80	42.90	43.00	42.60	42.50	42.80	42.90	42.90
1978	43.10	43.30	43.70	43.60	43.60	43.20	43.30	43.40	43.40	43.60	43.40	43.70
1979	43.60	43.80	43.70	43.40	43.60	43.70	43.70	43.60	43.60	43.60	43.50	42.30
1980	42.00	39.30	38.60	38.40	37.90	37.60	37.30	31.60	30.60	29.00	28.70	27.70
1981	27.20	27.20	27.00	25.70	25.70	24.50	24.40	24.30	23.90	24.10	24.10	24.00
1982	24.00	23.70	23.40	22.60	22.70	21.50	20.30	19.10	17.30	17.00	17.55	18.80
1983	19.35	20.00	21.35	21.40	22.35	22.45	23.50	23.60	23.65	23.65	23.85	23.85
1984	23.05	22.50	19.25	17.90	17.00	16.50	16.60	16.40	16.55	16.05	15.90	15.90
1985	16.20	15.70	15.05	14.90	14.45	14.60	14.75	15.10	15.10	15.75	15.80	16.55

[1] Transaction value is a weighted average price of recent natural uranium sales transactions, based on prices paid in transactions closed within the previous three-month period for which delivery is scheduled within one year of the transaction date; at least 10 transactions; and transactions involving a sum total of at least 2 million pounds of U$_3$O$_8$ equivalent.   *Source: NUEXCO.*

Vanadium

U.S. vanadium production data for 1986 and 1985 are withheld by the Bureau of Mines to avoid disclosing proprietary data belonging to the five active domestic vanadium extractors. Production of vanadium in 1984 is estimated to have been 1,617 tons.

In late 1986, the Bureau of Mines announced that an experimental leaching technique, which involves the use of sulfuric acid as a solvent for the extraction of vanadium and uranium from Idaho phosphorite ores, was commercially successful. The new technology represents a substantial boost to the recovery capabilities of the U.S. mining industry; estimated vanadium recovery with leaching, following roasting of the ore, produces extraction rates of 98–99 percent. U.S. vanadium reserves recoverable from this process were estimated at 125,000 tons with a total reserve base of 500,000 tons.

1985 world production of vanadium is estimated at 35,500 tons. 1986 should show little change. South Africa produces about 40 percent of the total; the Soviet Union provides 30 percent of annual world output, and China 16 percent.

World resources of vanadium exceed 140 billion pounds, but because the metal is generally recovered as a byproduct or coproduct, demonstrated resources of the element are not fully indicative of available supplies. While resources are adequate to supply current domestic needs, a substantial part of U.S. demand is met by foreign material which is cheaper than domestic vanadium.

Reported U.S. vanadium consumption in 1985 was 4,450 tons, with apparent consumption, including processing losses from low-grade imports, estimated to be 5,300 tons. Complete data on U.S. consumption by end use were not available from the Bureau of Mines, but it was estimated that 1986 consumption would be about 4,500 tons.

Despite a bleak near-term outlook, consumption of vanadium is expected to show long-term growth, as demand for high-strength, low-alloy steels and other high-performance materials accelerates. From a 1981 base, U.S. demand for vanadium is expected to increase at an average annual rate of two percent through 1990.

World Production of Vanadium from Ores and Concentrates   In Short Tons (of Contained Vanadium)

Year	USSR	Chile	China	Finland	Australia	Norway	South West Africa[1]	South Africa	United States[1]	Other[4]	World Total
1978	10,000	760	2,200	3,092	—	510	485	12,400	4,272	1,697	35,416
1979	10,000	510	4,000	3,051	—	630	—	13,600	5,520	2,337	39,648
1980	10,500	300	5,000	3,135	—	540	—	16,428	4,806	2,230	42,939
1981	10,500	140	5,000	3,431	77	380	—	13,908	5,126	2,587	41,149
1982	10,500	—	5,000	3,470	25	120	—	12,911	4,098	2,267	38,391
1983	10,500	—	5,000	3,516	—	—	—	9,737	2,171	1,671	32,595
1984[2]	10,500	—	5,000	3,376	—	—	—	13,798	1,617	2,471	36,762
1985[3]	10,500	—	5,000	2,716	—	—	—	15,449	N.A.	3,535	37,200

[1] Recoverable vanadium.   [2] Preliminary.   [3] Estimate.   [4] Production from petroleum residues, ashes, & spent catalysts. Mainly in Japan & the United States.   *Source: Bureau of Mines*

T.722

Salient Statistics of Vanadium in the United States   In Short Tons of Contained Vanadium

Year	Vanadium in Ores & Concentrates — Mine Production	Recoverable Vanadium	Prod. of Vanad. Pentoxide (V_2O_5)	Consumer Stocks Dec. 31	Tool Steel	Cast Irons	High Strength Low Alloy	Non-ferrous Alloys	Chemicals	Carbon	Full Alloy	Total	$ Per Lb. Van. Pentoxide[3]	General Imports[5]	Ore & Concentrates[4]	Ferro-Vanadium (Gross Weight)
1978	4,446	1,309														
1979	5,841	880														
1980	5,832	4,806	9,829	879	653	54	1,986	728	59	1,114	1,420	6,139	3.54	1,786	960	803
1981	5,852	5,126	11,367	683	584	42	2,123	852	56	1,278	1,832	6,863	3.52	2,435	463	435
1982	4,093	4,098	8,689	326	273	20	1,148	461	29	698	811	3,496	3.50	1,112	2,000	326
1983	N.A.	2,171	4,344	374	426	10	966	505	19	577	716	3,277	3.50	58	2,802	775
1984	N.A.	1,617	4,678	449	610	18	1,636	905	22	683	816	4,761	3.50	633	4,029	469
1985[1]	N.A.	N.A.	N.A.	360	522	22	1,383	788	14	1,135	944	4,883	3.50	303	1,852	454

Vanadium Consumed by Uses[2]

[1] Preliminary.   [2] Represent about 90% of the total consumption.   [3] Dealer export.   [4] Also includes fused vanadium oxide.   [5] Ores, slags, residues.   [6] Estimate.   *Source: Bureau of Mines*

T.723

279

Wheat

World wheat production in 1986/87 is projected by USDA to increase over four percent, to 521.7 million tonnes. U.S. production fell significantly; larger crops were grown in other major producing countries. In Canada, a record crop of 31.9 million tonnes was harvested, over 31 percent higher than a year ago. China, the world's largest wheat producer, grew a crop of 89 million tonnes, four percent more than a year earlier. The Soviet Union's crop was 11 percent larger (87 million tonnes). India, traditionally an importer, produced 47 million tonnes, seven percent more than last season.

Global use is expected to total 505 million tonnes, three percent more than a year ago. The trend has been higher for many years. China and the Soviet Union are the largest users; both countries will increase consumption this year. World exports are projected by USDA to total 84.7 million tonnes, off less than one percent from a year ago. The U.S. is the major exporter of wheat, but its share of world trade—this season expected to be 31 percent—has been declining. Canada, the second-largest exporter, will have a market share of seven percent. Australia is expected to ship 14 million tonnes, a 13-percent decline from a year ago; Argentina's exports of 4.5 million tonnes would represent a yearly decline of 26 percent.

The Soviet Union, the largest importer of wheat, this season is expected to take only 12 million tonnes, 24 percent less than a year ago, 38 percent under the five-year average, and the smallest total since 1978/79. China is the second-largest importer with projected imports of 6.5 million tonnes, a two percent decline from last year. China's wheat imports have been trending lower since domestic production has expanded.

World ending stocks of wheat are projected by USDA to reach 154.4 million tonnes, over 12 percent above a year ago. This is a record stock level and extends the trend which began in 1980/81.

U.S. production of wheat in 1986/87 is estimated by USDA at 2.08 billion bushels, 14 percent less than last season and the smallest crop since 1978/79. Harvested acreage was 60.48 million acres, 6 percent less than a year ago. National average yield was 43.3 bushels per acre. In hard red winter wheat, grown in the Great Plains states, production was 1.02 billion bushels, 17 percent less than a year ago. The soft red winter wheat crop, grown in the Corn Belt and the Southeast, totaled only 288 million bushels, a 22-percent decline from a year ago. The hard red spring wheat crop, produced in the Dakotas and Minnesota, totaled 440 million bushels, four percent below 1985/86. White wheat and durum crops were also smaller than a season ago.

Record carrying stocks of 1.9 billion bushels mean that supply will increase to 3.99 billion bushels, three percent over a year ago. With larger supplies and lower prices, domestic use is expected to expand eight percent to 1.13 billion bushels. Food use will rise to 690 million bushels, as the trend toward increased consumption of bread products continues. In late 1986, U.S. flour mills ground record amounts of wheat. Feed use of wheat is projected by USDA at 350 million bushels, a 28-percent increase from last season. Part of the increase is due to expanding poultry production.

Wheat exports represent the largest source of usage. The trend since 1981/82 has been lower; this season is expected to show a break in that trend. USDA currently projects 1986/87 wheat exports of 975 million bushels, an increase of over six percent from a year ago. Primary markets for U.S. wheat are Japan, South Korea, Egypt, Algeria and Morocco. The Soviet Union, the largest market during 1984/85, reduced imports of U.S. wheat significantly during 1985/86. In part, this was due to a larger domestic crop and ample availabilities from other suppliers. China, the largest market for U.S. wheat in 1982/83, has also reduced imports substantially due, primarily, to record levels of domestic production.

Ending stocks in 1986/87 are projected by USDA to reach 1.89 billion bushels, down one percent from a year ago, but still 32 percent above the level of 1984/85. With active use of the price support loan program and a growing CCC inventory, free stocks of wheat will comprise less than half of total stocks. Stocks of soft red winter wheat will be tightest due to smaller supplies.

Government Loan Program

For 1987 crop wheat, the price support loan rate has been reduced to $2.28 per bushel, the lowest rate allowed under the Farm Bill. In 1986, the loan rate was $2.40. The target price remains unchanged at $4.38. Qualified producers will be eligible to receive a maximum deficiency payment of $2.10 per bushel, if prices average less than $2.28 over the first five months of the marketing year. To qualify for program benefits, producers must reduce planted acreage by 27.5 percent, the largest cutback allowed under the Farm Bill.

Futures Markets

Wheat futures and options on futures are traded at Chicago Board of Trade (CBOT), Kansas City Board of Trade (KCBOT), and Minneapolis Grain Exchange (MGE).

World Production of Wheat   In Thousands of Metric Tons

Crop Year	Argentina	Australia	Canada	China	France	West Germany	India	Italy	Pakistan	Spain	Turkey	United Kingdom	USSR	United States	World Total[1]
1982-3	15,000	8,900	26,700	68,400	25,368	8,632	37,500	8,903	11,300	4,410	13,800	10,315	84,300	75,300	477,500
1983-4	12,800	22,000	26,500	81,400	24,828	8,998	42,800	8,514	12,400	4,330	13,300	10,880	77,500	65,900	489,500
1984-5	13,200	18,700	21,200	87,800	33,125	10,223	45,500	9,478	10,900	6,044	13,300	14,900	68,600	70,600	511,300
1985-6[2]	8,500	16,100	24,300	85,800			44,200						78,100	66,000	499,100
1986-7[1]	9,600	16,000	31,300	89,000			47,000						81,000	56,518	513,600

[1] Estimated.   [2] Preliminary.   *Source: Foreign Agricultural Service, U.S.D.A.*

T.724

World Wheat Supply & Demand   In Millions of Metric Tons/Hectares

	Area Harvested	Yield	Production	World Trade	Utilization Total	Ending Stocks	Stocks as % of Util
1981/82	238.7	1.88	449.5	101.3	443.6	87.0	19.6
1982/83	237.7	2.01	477.5	98.7	462.2	102.3	22.1
1983/84	229.1	2.14	489.5	102.0	482.3	109.5	22.7
1984/85	231.3	2.21	511.3	106.9	495.1	125.7	25.4
1985/86[1]	229.2	2.18	499.1	85.0	488.0	136.8	28.0
1986/87[2]	228.5	2.25	513.6	86.6	507.3	143.1	28.2

[1] Preliminary. [2] Estimate. *Source: Foreign Agricultural Service, U.S.D.A.*

T.724a

Salient Statistics of Wheat in the United States

Crop Year	Planting Intentions —1,000 Acres—	Acreage Harvested Winter	Spring 1,000 Acres	All	Avg.—All Yield Per Acre In Bushels	Used for Seed	Fed to Livestock (Million Bushels)	Sold	Value of Production Ths. $	Domestic Exports[2] Million Bushels	Imports[3]	Flour In Pounds	Cereal
1981-2	88,251	58,476	22,166	80,642	34.5		Not Available		10,172,242	1,771	2.8	116	3.1
1982-3	86,232	57,633	20,304	77,937	35.5				9,813,015	1,509	7.6	119	3.1
1983-4	76,419	47,584	13,806	61,390	39.4				8,532,790	1,429	4.0	116	3.1
1984-5	79,213	51,513	15,415	66,928	38.8				8,755,000	1,424	9.0	118	3.1
1985-6[4]	75,575	47,953	16,781	64,734	37.5				7,652,000	915	15.0	123	
1986-7[4]	71,834	43,115	17,368	60,483	34.3					1,150	5.0		

[1] Civilian only. [2] Includes flour milled from imported wheat. [3] Total wheat, flour & other products. [4] Preliminary. [5] Year beginning June. *Source: Economic Research Service, U.S.D.A.*

T.728

Supply and Distribution of Wheat in the United States   In Millions of Bushels

Crop Yr. Beginning June	Supply On Farms	Stocks, June 1 Mills, Ele- vators[3]	Total Stocks	Produc- tion	Im- ports[4]	Total Supply	Domestic Disappearance Food	Seed	Indus- try	Resid- ual[5]	Feed (On Farms Where Grown)	Total Dom- estic Disap.	Exports[4]	Total Disap- pear- ance
1982-3	576.2	583.2	1,159.4	2,765.0	7.6	3,932	616.4	97.0	—		194.9	908.3	1,508.6	2,417
1983-4	668.9	846.1	1,515.1	2,419.8	4.0	3,939	642.6	100.0	—		369.1	1,111.7	1,428.6	2,540
1984-5	591.7	806.7	1,398.6	2,595.5	9.4	4,004	650.9	93.0	—		409.5	1,153.4	1,424.2	2,578
1985-6[1]	582.1	843.2	1,425.2	2,424.1	14.7	3,865	678.1	88.0	—		283.2	1,049.3	915.3	1,965
1986-7[2]	681.1	1,223.9	1,905.0	2,076.7	5.2	4,070	690.0	85.0	—		300.0	1,075.0	1,150.0	2,225

[1] Preliminary. [2] Estimated. [3] Also warehouses and all off-farm storage not otherwise designated, including flour mills. [4] Imports & exports are for wheat, including flour & other products in terms of wheat. [5] Approximate feed use. *Source: Economic Research Service, U.S.D.A.* T.737

Stocks, Production, and Exports of Wheat, by Classes   In Millions of Bushels

Year Beginning June	Hard Spring June 1 Stocks	Produc- tion	Ex- ports[2]	Durum[3] June 1 Stocks	Produc- tion	Ex- ports[2]	Hard Winter June 1 Stocks	Produc- tion	Ex- ports[2]	Soft Red Winter June 1 Stocks	Produc- tion	Ex- ports[2]	White June 1 Stocks	Produc- tion	Ex- ports[2]
1982-3	346	492	239	106	146	59	538	1,243	679	60	590	325	109	294	207
1983-4	408	323	221	136	73	62	754	1,198	704	74	504	222	143	322	220
1984-5	314	409	183	99	103	61	745	1,251	717	74	531	253	167	301	210
1985-6[1]	371	460	166	100	113	53	717	1,230	395	64	368	149	173	254	152
1986-7[4]	496	503	170	123	102	60	1,004	1,029	630	79	289	130	198	242	160

[1] Preliminary. [2] Includes flour made from U.S. wheat & shipments to territories. [3] Includes "Red Durum." [4] Estimate.
Source: Economic Research Service, U.S.D.A.

T.727

Seeded Acreage, Yield and Production of All Wheat in the United States

Year	Seeded Acreage—1,000,000 Acres — Winter	Not Durum	Durum	All	Yield Per Harvested Acre—In Bushels— Winter	Not Durum	Durum	All	Production—1,000,000 Bushels — Winter	Not Durum	Durum	All
1982	65.5	16.4	4.3	86.2	36.0	33.8	34.9	35.5	2,073.6	545.5	145.9	2,765.0
1983	62.1	11.7	2.6	76.4	41.8	31.7	29.3	39.4	1,988.3	358.5	73.0	2,419.8
1984	63.4	12.5	3.3	79.2	40.0	35.3	32.1	38.8	2,060.3	431.1	103.4	2,594.8
1985[2]	57.8	14.6	3.2	75.6	38.1	35.4	36.4	37.5	1,827.6	485.0	112.5	2,425.1
1986[1]	53.9	15.0	2.9	71.8	35.2	32.0	33.1	34.3	1,517.7	466.0	93.0	2,076.7

[1] Preliminary. [2] Estimate. *Source: Crop Reporting Board, U.S.D.A.*

T.726

WHEAT

Production of Winter Wheat in the United States   In Millions of Bushels

Year	Colo-rado	Idaho	Illinois	Indiana	Kansas	Michi-gan	Missouri	Mon-tana	Nebraska	Ohio	Okla-homa	Ore-gon	Pa.	Texas	Wash.	So. Dakota
1978	57.3	41.8	33.4	28.9	300.0	16.4	28.6	83.7	81.6	42.1	145.8	47.3	7.1	54.0	117.0	18.2
1979	67.6	35.7	53.8	44.4	410.4	31.6	70.4	57.4	86.7	63.4	216.6	48.0	7.3	138.0	94.6	10.5
1980	107.2	51.9	75.4	53.9	420.0	35.2	89.0	54.8	108.3	67.1	195.0	72.0	9.3	130.0	143.0	20.9
1981	83.9	55.7	92.5	62.1	305.0	41.5	115.5	89.3	104.4	72.6	172.8	73.2	9.7	183.4	161.3	30.4
1982	81.5	53.0	67.5	43.3	458.5	23.0	74.8	80.6	101.5	51.6	227.7	59.4	8.2	144.0	125.4	36.3
1983	117.0	55.6	64.4	49.5	448.2	35.8	70.3	79.1	98.9	58.8	150.5	62.0	7.6	161.0	162.5	51.3
1984	110.4	56.7	70.4	48.3	431.2	45.6	84.1	67.0	81.0	48.4	190.8	66.2	8.4	150.0	148.8	61.2
1985	134.6	46.1	36.8	37.1	433.2	45.0	49.9	22.4	89.7	58.9	165.0	51.8	10.1	187.2	115.2	44.1
1986[1]	92.8	52.7	36.1	30.1	336.6	30.6	18.8	66.0	76.0	48.3	150.8	51.3	9.7	120.0	102.9	57.0

[1] Preliminary, December estimate.   *Source: Crop Reporting Board, U.S.D.A.*

T.734

United States Official Winter Wheat Crop Production Reports   In Thousands of Bushels

Crop Year	Previous December	May 1	June 1	July 1	August 1	Sept. 1	Current December	Final
1977–8	1,438,015	1,477,455	1,526,000	1,539,029	1,526,029	1,528,844	1,526,713	1,540,419
1978–9	1,321,068	1,284,375	1,308,000	1,801,705	1,248,405	1,243,685	1,248,272	1,222,446
1979–0	1,441,306	1,390,848	1,427,000	1,560,768	1,602,901	1,595,591	1,608,897	1,601,234
1980–1	1,567,817	1,711,010	1,757,170	1,848,000	1,870,000	1,878,000	1,891,251	1,895,383
1981–2	1,977,079	2,078,137	2,013,607	2,092,692	2,064,845	2,059,205	2,098,719	2,103,538
1982–3	2,128,133	2,063,336	2,131,214	2,124,854	2,095,554	2,106,149	2,108,246	2,073,560
1983–4	Discontinued	1,893,241	1,882,916	1,937,388	1,963,243	1,976,843	1,993,888	1,988,304
1984–5		1,979,366	1,972,776	2,021,918	2,045,088	2,036,028	2,060,646	2,060,266
1985–6		1,974,228	1,892,438	1,854,254	1,842,884	1,839,284	1,827,195	
1986–7		1,603,127	1,578,277	1,553,026	1,532,526	1,532,526		

Source: Crop Reporting Board, U.S.D.A.

T.736

Production of All Spring Wheat in the United States   In Millions of Bushels

| Year | Durum Wheat | | | | | | | Other Spring Wheat | | | | | | | | | Total |
	Ari-zona	Cali-fornia	Minne-sota	Mon-tana	North Dakota	South Dakota	Total Durum	Colo-rado	Idaho	Minne-sota	Mon-tana	North Dakota	Ore-gon	South Dakota	Utah	Wash-ington	
1978	6.4		3.8	8.7	102.1	3.8	133.3	2.0	33.6	87.8	53.7	180.1	4.6	44.0	1.4	11.2	419.8
1979	5.3		2.8	6.8	84.5	3.6	106.7	2.6	38.4	85.8	52.3	165.1	9.3	46.0	1.6	23.4	426.2
1980	12.4	7.8	3.4	7.6	73.2	4.1	108.4	3.1	44.2	96.9	57.4	105.5	5.4	37.4	1.4	17.2	370.5
1981	18.3	14.7	5.4	11.0	130.8	5.8	185.9	4.0	34.1	134.0	72.5	197.4	4.2	52.8	1.4	7.0	509.3
1982	7.0	11.6	3.0	9.9	110.8	3.5	145.9	3.5	41.8	120.8	89.9	209.3	4.1	58.8	1.6	13.4	545.5
1983	5.0	6.3	1.2	4.1	54.3	2.1	73.0	5.1	36.1	75.1	53.7	135.0	3.6	36.4	1.4	10.1	358.5
1984	7.2	9.4	1.6	3.6	78.6	3.1	103.4	4.6	24.7	103.7	34.1	183.6	2.8	61.7	1.6	11.6	431.1
1985	3.9	7.4	1.7	1.4	95.5	2.6	112.5	4.8	25.9	130.4	26.4	212.0	4.2	64.5	1.6	13.1	485.0
1986[1]	4.2	6.5	1.3	3.4	76.0	1.7	93.0	3.6	26.2	102.7	67.5	192.2	5.1	51.3	1.5	13.3	466.0

[1] Preliminary.   *Source: Crop Reporting Board, U.S.D.A.*

T.735

Wheat Under Price Support Through the End of the Month
(Cumulative Total from Current Season's Crop)   In Millions of Bushels

Year	July	Aug.	Sept.	Oct.	Nov.	Dec.	Jan.	Feb.	Mar.	Apr.	May	June	Total
1978–9	53.0	105.7	154.6	183.1	202.5	213.4	237.5	242.8	251.0	254.0	254.3	255.0	255.0
1979–0	6.5	30.1	55.6	82.8	103.3	115.5	138.2	145.4	161.0	176.4	179.4	180.5	180.5
1980–1	35.7	56.6	99.2	126.5	142.2	183.3	228.6	261.0	297.4	328.0	328.0	329.4	329.4
1981–2	84.6	164.4	254.8	296.1	314.1	344.7	392.3	411.7	427.4	443.3	444.5	445.8	
1982–3	106.7	206.5	335.2	414.0	467.2	501.1	579.1	606.1	629.4	638.6	640.9	643.4	
1983–4	196.3	335.2	357.5	462.8	494.7	520.4	571.5	595.4	619.2	627.5	629.1	630.3	
1984–5	48.8	104.9	195.5	213.4	225.6	237.7	263.5	270.2	275.7	279.7	280.1	280.8	
1985–6	269.5	414.2	567.7	679.0	714.3	740.7	787.0	803.8	813.5	825.0	827.3	828.1	
1986–7	81.7	155.7	274.6	400.5	441.6								

Source: Economic Research Service, U.S.D.A.

T.729

United States Grindings of Wheat by Mills   In Millions of Bushels (of 60 Pounds Each)

Year	July	Aug.	Sept.	Oct.	Nov.	Dec.	Jan.	Feb.	Mar.	Apr.	May	June	Total
1979-0	52.1	59.0	52.4	58.9	55.7	50.6	55.0	50.4	49.1	47.2	49.8	47.8	628.0
1980-1	51.8	53.0	54.8	58.4	54.6	56.9	53.9	51.1	55.3	53.4	52.2	52.6	648.0
1981-2	51.2	53.3	54.6	55.6	51.0	50.2	54.8	53.9	57.8	51.4	50.0	51.2	635.0
1982-3	53.4	57.0	55.4	57.5	54.9	55.9	55.7	53.6	60.1	54.8	59.1	57.7	675.1
1983-4	56.2	66.1	62.9	59.4	57.2	56.0	55.7	57.5	58.4	54.0	60.1	54.6	698.1
1984-5[1]	51.8	59.2	55.2	58.7	56.3	53.1	56.9	57.3	58.9	55.0	58.1	53.6	673.8
1985-6[1]	54.6	60.9	59.5	65.1	63.7	56.0	61.1	60.1	55.4	57.7	58.9	58.4	711.4
1986-7[1]	60.7	66.1											

[1] Preliminary. *Source: Bureau of the Census*   T.744

U.S. Wheat Foreign Trade and Domestic Disappearance   In Millions of Bushels

Year Begin. June	Imports (Grain Only)					Exports (Grain Only)					Domestic Disappearance				
	June-Aug.	Oct.-Dec.	Jan.-Mar.	Apr.-May	Total	June-Aug.	Oct.-Dec.	Jan.-Mar.	Apr.-May	Total	June-Aug.	Oct.-Dec.	Jan.-Mar.	Apr.-May	Total
1978-9	.6	.5	.5	.3	1.9	493	309	225	168	1,194	327	195	177	138	837
1979-0	.7	.5	.5	.4	2.1	511	388	283	194	1,375	277	167	209	130	783
1980-1	.8	.6	.6	.5	2.5	375	379	399	360	1,514	194	243	171	174	783
1981-2	.7	.8	.7	.6	2.8	424	486	415	446	1,771	295	233	147	173	847
1982-3	1.2	3.0	2.6	.8	7.6	411	337	394	367	1,509	285	252	180	191	908
1983-4	1.1	.9	1.0	1.0	4.0	347	360	369	353	1,429	356	339	216	201	1,112
1984-5[1]	4.6	1.8	1.2	1.8	9.4	399	486	335	204	1,424	439	337	204	174	1,154
1985-6[1]	3.5	5.1	2.7	3.5	14.8	249	253	224	189	915	401	312	166	170	1,049

[1] Preliminary. *Source: Crop Reporting Board, U.S.D.A.*   T.730

Wheat Government Loan Program Data in the United States   Loan Rates (Cents Per Bushel)

Crop Year Beginning June	Total Support Rate	National Avg.[1]	Target Rate	Corn Belt (Soft Red Winter)	Central & So. Plains (Hard Winter)	No. Plains (Spr. & Dur.)	Pacific North-West (White)	Placed Under Loan	Put in Reserve (June 1)	Repaid Loans (June 1)	Delivered to CCC	Ending Carry-over	CCC Uncommitted	CCC Loans	Farmer-Owned Reserve	Privately Owned
1978-9	340	235	340	234	228	236	241	255.1	23.9	231.2	—	924.1	—		14.6	873.0
1979-0	340	250	340	248	243	251	257	180.5	39.7	140.8	—	902.0	99.3	259.9	714.2
1980-1	363	300	363	300	294	302	308	329.4	205.1	123.2	—	989.1	54.6	359.6	789.4
1981-2	381	320	381	320	313	321	329	452.2	239.8	180.7	61.1	1,159	112.0	560.4	696.1
1982-3	405	355	405	356	347	357	365	646.0	573.1	9.9	9.3	1,515	65.2	1,060.6	1,323.1
1983-4	430	365	430	366	356	368	375	635.0			192.0	1,399	379.1	611.2	1,210.5
1984-5[2]	438	330	438	332	323	334	343	300.0				1,425	175.0	654.1	1,047.6
1985-6[3]	438	330	438	332	323	334	343					1,900	677.7	433.3	1,298.3
1986-7[3]	438	240	438									1,845			

Total Stocks Ending May 31 — Outstanding — Millions of Bushels

[1] The national average loan rate at the farm as a percentage of the parity-priced wheat at the beginning of the marketing year. [2] Preliminary. [3] Estimate. *Source: Agricultural Marketing Service, U.S.D.A.*   T.741

Exports of Wheat (Only) from the United States   In Millions of Bushels

Year	July	Aug.	Sept.	Oct.	Nov.	Dec.	Jan.	Feb.	Mar.	Apr.	May	June	Total
1978-9	106.1	131.9	118.3	113.0	92.3	90.0	70.4	67.1	75.5	77.0	76.8	102.2	1,120.6
1979-0	133.3	117.8	129.6	149.0	108.9	114.9	82.7	89.5	94.7	98.3	88.6	96.2	1,305.5
1980-1	123.6	139.6	136.0	116.2	112.2	131.9	129.9	124.4	128.8	127.7	76.0	124.5	1,470.8
1981-2	138.1	145.4	194.1	156.9	127.5	137.4	124.2	138.7	159.1	147.4	114.8	155.7	1,739.3
1982-3	117.9	124.0	130.8	98.5	94.1	88.5	143.1	146.3	131.1	111.8	95.3	112.0	1,393.0
1983-4	115.8	87.5	119.2	114.8	102.3	128.4	118.3	111.0	118.7	94.3	111.7	104.8	1,326.8
1984-5[1]	133.3	146.0	242.4	136.9	96.1	131.4	105.3	81.8	57.4	65.0	55.8	79.1	1,330.5
1985-6[1]	63.6	85.6	72.0	85.6	81.3	60.5	68.6	67.7	60.1	54.0	46.3	79.5	824.8
1986-7[1]	104.0	113.4											

[1] Preliminary. *Source: Department of Commerce*   T.738

WHEAT

United States Wheat and Wheat Flour Imports and Exports   In Thousands of Bushels

Year Beginning June	Imports — Wheat Suitable for Milling	Imports — Wheat Unfit for Human Consumption	Flour	Other Pdt's.[2] (Wheat Equivalent)	Total	Sales for Foreign Currency[3]	Long-Term $ & Conver. for Cur. Credit Sales	Gov't. to Gov't. Donations[4]	Donations Thru Voluntary Relief Agencies	Barter for Strategic Materials	Mutual Security (A.I.D.)[5]	Total Specified Gov't. Programs
1979–80	155	50	62	1,869	2,136	—	107,288	8,724	7,064	—	2,147	125,218
1980–81	128	58	200	2,148	2,534	—	101,052	9,659	7,158	—	153	118,022
1981–82	59	14	357	2,423	2,853	—	110,046	14,312	8,614	—	—	132,972
1982–83	3,901	35	624	3,036	7,596	—	113,322	22,081	8,724	—	6,805	150,932
1983–84[1]	67	11	336	3,426	3,840	—	119,838	6,000	4,915	—	—	130,753

[1] Preliminary.   [2] Includes macaroni, semolina & similar pdt's.   [3] Authorized by title, I, P.L. 480.   [4] Author, by title II, P.L. 480.   [5] Foreign Assist. Act of 1961.   *Source: Economic Research Service, U.S.D.A.*
T.732

Wheat Stocks in the United States   In Millions of Bushels

Year	On Farms Jan. 1	On Farms Apr. 1	On Farms June 1	On Farms Sept. 1[2]	Off Farms Jan. 1	Off Farms Apr. 1	Off Farms June 1	Off Farms Sept. 1[2]	Total Stocks Jan. 1	Total Stocks Apr. 1	Total Stocks June 1	Total Stocks Sept. 1[2]
1981	754.0	539.1	414.4	1,197.7	1,150.3	790.1	574.7	1,529.8	1,904.2	1,329.1	989.1	2,727.5
1982	948.7	742.6	576.2	1,402.3	1,223.4	809.0	583.2	1,567.2	2,172.1	1,551.6	1,159.4	2,969.5
1983	1,150.5	870.8	668.9	1,235.9	1,355.6	991.2	846.1	1,719.3	2,506.2	1,862.0	1,515.1	2,955.2
1984	1,015.4	771.2	591.7	1,217.3	1,311.0	986.9	807.0	1,522.7	2,326.4	1,758.1	1,398.6	2,740.0
1985[1]	930.3	713.4	582.1	1,248.4	1,210.8	953.7	843.2	1,722.7	2,141.0	1,667.1	1,425.2	2,971.1
1986[1]	1,011.2	799.4	681.1	1,291.0	1,515.0	1,330.6	1,223.9	1,824.1	2,526.1	2,130.0	1,905.0	3,115.1

[1] Preliminary.   [2] Data prior to Sept. 1986 are as of Oct 1.   *Source: Crop Reporting Board, U.S.D.A.*
T.731

Commercial Stocks of Domestic Wheat[1] in the United States, at First of Month   In Millions of Bushels

Year	July	Aug.	Sept.	Oct.	Nov.	Dec.	Jan.	Feb.	Mar.	Apr.	May	June
1981–2	312.2	427.0	472.0	487.4	476.9	425.8	395.6	352.4	285.1	254.3	218.2	204.9
1982–3	256.8	401.4	471.5	500.7	493.9	454.2	442.5	404.9	360.4	333.8	300.9	267.5
1983–4	285.0	403.1	462.1	477.0	442.0	385.4	334.9	294.9	273.0	255.1	236.6	212.4
1984–5	265.2	423.0	413.7	409.4	387.8	352.8	309.9	268.0	248.5	239.8	215.1	221.4
1985–6	312.5	434.8	474.8	510.9	504.2	473.9	446.3	435.7	413.0	400.3	399.0	407.2
1986–7	437.5	483.7	494.7	475.9								

[1] Domestic wheat in store in public and private elevators in 39 markets and wheat afloat in vessels or barges at lake and seaboard ports, the first Saturday of the month.   *Source: Department of Agriculture*
T.746

Comparative Average Cash Wheat Prices   In Dollars per Bushel

Crop Year— June to May	Received by U.S. Farmers	No. 2 Soft Red Winter Chicago	No. 1 Hd. Red Ordin. Prot. Kansas City	No. 2 Soft Red Winter St. Louis	Minneapolis No. 1 Dark Northern Spring	Minneapolis No. 1 Hard Amber Durum	No. 1 Soft Portland Oregon	No. 2 Western White Pacific N.W.	No. 2 White Soft Toledo	Export Prices Australia Std. White	Export Prices Canada Vanc. No. 1 CWRS	Export Prices Argentina	Export Prices U.S. Gulf No. 2 H.W.	Export Prices Rotterdam[3] C.I.F. U.S. No. 2 Hd. Winter
1981–2	3.65	3.74	4.27	3.66	4.29	4.61	4.20	3.82	3.70	175	212	169	177	194
1982–3	3.55	3.32	3.94	3.32	4.09	4.25	4.39	3.93	3.33	160	187	166	162	178
1983–4	3.53	3.56	3.84	3.62	4.30	4.83	3.95	3.58	3.48	161	185	138	158	186
1984–5[1]	3.38	3.51	3.74	3.57	4.06	4.44	3.82	3.44	3.42	153	186	135	153	176
1986–7[1]	3.16	3.22	3.28	3.26	3.94	4.07	3.72	3.34		141	178	106	138	167

[1] Preliminary.   [2] Estimate.   *Source: Economic Research Service, U.S.D.A.*
T.733

Open Interest of All Wheat Futures Contracts at Chicago,[1] K.C. & Mpls.   In Millions of Bushels

Year	Jan.	Feb.	Mar.	April	May	June	July	Aug.	Sept.	Oct.	Nov.	Dec.	Kansas City[3] Jan. 1	Kansas City[3] July 1	Minn.[2] Jan. 1
1981	291.1	236.5	211.7	209.8	243.0	283.1	324.4	329.5	337.3	384.7	368.7	312.9	142.6	80.7	28.7
1982	335.9	274.7	244.5	234.9	253.2	235.5	277.6	254.8	238.9	218.7	186.8	182.3	137.0	97.7	28.7
1983	193.9	155.5	194.9	172.2	191.7	223.0	294.0	348.1	329.7	300.3	282.3	304.3	118.5	106.0	21.3
1984	291.5	281.3	288.9	248.4	256.7	215.3	246.6	233.0	217.9	222.5	209.9	213.3	89.0	92.8	23.7
1985	197.9	191.7	176.2	189.6	201.6	191.4	189.2	186.3	163.4	152.3	144.2	158.9	95.4	130.9	21.6
1986	167.4	162.8	164.1	183.5	167.0	190.9	178.0	165.7	191.6	165.4	143.5	115.8	63.0	101.0	23.4
1987													59.1		19.7

[1] Chicago Board of Trade.   [2] Minneapolis Grain Exchange.   [3] Kansas City Board of Trade.   *Source: Commodity Futures Trading Commission*
T.748

United States Wheat Quarterly Supply and Disappearance   In Millions of Bushels

Year & Begin. June 1	Supply Begin-ning Stocks	Pro-duction	Im-ports[2]	Total Supply	Disappearance — Domestic Use Food	Alc. Bever-ages	Seed	Feed[3]	Total	Ex-ports[2]	Total Disap-pear-ance	Ending Stocks Gov't. Owned[4]	Pri-vately Owned[5]	Total Stocks
1979-0	924.1	2,134	2.1	3,060	596.1	—	101.0	86.0	783.1	1,375	2,158	141.7	760.3	902.0
June–Sept.	824.1	2,134	.7	3,059	198.5	6	33.0	45.6	277.1	511.0	788.1	49.9	2,221	2,271
Oct.–Dec.	2,271	—	.5	2,271	157.9	6	37.0	-27.7	167.2	387.9	555.1	49.6	1,667	1,716
Jan.–Mar.	1,716	—	.5	1,717	145.1	6	1.0	62.8	208.9	282.7	491.6	63.3	1,162	1,225
Apr.–May	1,225		.4	1,226	94.6	.1	30.0	5.3	129.9	193.6	323.5	141.7	760.3	902.0
1980-1	902.0	2,381	2.5	3,285	610.5	—	113.0	59.0	782.5	1,514	2,296	199.7	789.4	989.1
June–Sept.	902.0	2,381	.8	3,284	197.2	6	38.0	56.6	291.8	518.4	810.2	201.1	2,272	2,474
Oct.–Dec.	2,474	—	.6	2,474	167.1	6	43.0	-11.6	198.5	371.4	569.9	203.1	1,701	1,904
Jan.–Mar.	1,904	—	.7	1,905	150.1	6	1.0	24.3	175.4	400.4	575.8	202.6	1,127	1,329
Apr.–May	1,329	—	.4	1,330	96.1	6	31.0	-10.3	116.8	223.6	340.4	199.7	789.4	989.1
1981-2	989.1	2,785	2.8	3,777	602.4	6	110.0	134.8	847.2	1,771	2,618	190.3	969.1	1,159
June–Sept.	989.1	2,785	.7	3,775	202.5	6	37.0	186.4	425.9	621.8	1,048	191.6	2,536	2,728
Oct.–Dec.	2,728	—	.8	2,728	159.0	6	45.0	-75.2	128.8	427.4	556.2	190.6	1,982	2,172
Jan.–Mar.	2,172	—	.8	2,173	151.7	6	1.0	27.6	180.3	441.0	621.3	189.1	1,362	1,551
Apr.–May	1,552	—	.5	1,552	89.2	6	27.0	-4.0	112.2	280.5	392.7	190.3	969.1	1,159
1982-3	1,159	2,765	7.6	3,932	616.4	6	97.0	194.9	908.3	1,509	2,417	192.0	1,323	1,515
June–Sept.	1,159	2,765	1.2	3,926	206.4	6	37.0	167.1	410.5	545.6	956.1	190.6	2,779	2,970
Oct.–Dec.	2,970	—	3.0	2,973	161.8	6	40.0	-28.1	173.7	292.6	466.3	185.4	2,321	2,506
Jan.–Mar.	2,506	—	2.7	2,509	151.4	—	1.0	52.4	204.8	442.1	646.9	185.2	1,677	1,862
Apr.–May	1,862	—	.7	1,863	96.8	—	19.0	3.5	119.3	228.3	347.6	192.0	1,323	1,515
1983-4	1,515	2,420	4.0	3,939	642.6		100.0	369.1	1,112	1,429	2,540	188.1	1,211	1,399
June–Sept.	1,515	2,420	1.2	3,936	214.2	—	37.0	254.4	505.6	475.3	980.9	157.5	2,798	2,955
Oct.–Dec.	2,955	—	.9	2,956	163.7	—	41.0	62.4	267.1	362.6	629.7	165.6	2,161	2,326
Jan.–Mar.	2,326	—	1.1	2,328	163.0	—	1.0	41.0	205.0	364.4	569.4	167.1	1,591	1,758
Apr.–May	1,758	—	.8	1,759	101.7	—	21.0	11.3	134.0	226.3	360.3	188.1	1,211	1,399
1984-5	1,399	2,595	9.4	4,003	651.0	—	93.0	409.5	1,154	1,424	2,578	377.6	1,048	1,425
June–Aug.	1,399	2,595	4.6	3,998	157.8	—	1.0	279.9	438.7	399.2	837.9	278.1	2,882	3,160
Sep.–Nov.	3,160	—	1.8	3,162	168.5	—	65.0	103.9	337.4	486.0	823.4	359.4	1,979	2,339
Dec.–Feb.	2,339	—	1.2	2,340	164.2	—	4.0	35.5	203.7	335.2	538.9	375.7	1,415	1,801
Mar.–May	1,801	—	1.8	1,803	160.5	—	23.0	- 9.8	173.7	203.7	377.4	377.6	1,048	1,425
1985-6[1]	1,425	2,425	14.8	3,865	678.1	—	88.0	283.2	1,049	915.4	1,965	601.7	1,298	1,900
June–Aug.	1,425	2,425	3.5	3,854	165.8	—	1.0	234.1	400.9	249.1	650.0	406.7	2,797	3,204
Sep.–Nov.	3,204	—	5.1	3,209	185.6	—	63.0	63.7	312.3	252.9	565.2	517.1	2,126	2,643
Dec.–Feb.	2,650	—	2.7	2,646	164.2	—	3.0	-1.3	165.9	224.4	390.3	526.3	1,730	2,256
Mar.–May	2,256	—	3.5	2,259	162.5	—	21.0	-13.3	170.2	189.0	359.2	601.7	1,298	1,900
1986-7[7]	1,900	2,077	5.0	4,070	690.0	—	85.0	300.0	1,075	1,150	2,225			1,845
June–Aug.	1,900	2,077												

[1] Preliminary.   [2] Imports & exports include flour and other products expressed in wheat equivalent.   [3] Residual.   [4] Uncommitted, Gov't. only.   [5] Includes total loans.   [6] Less than 50,000 bushels.   [7] Projected.   *Source: Economics Research Service, U.S.D.A.*   T.740

Wheat Supply and Distribution in Canada, Australia and Argentina   In Millions of Metric Tons

Crop Year	Canada (Yr. Beg. Aug. 1) Supply Stocks Aug. 1	New Crop	Total Supply	Disappearance Domes-tic	Ex-ports[1]	Australia (Yr. Beg. Dec. 1) Supply Stocks Dec. 1	New Crop	Total Supply	Disappearance Domes-tic	Ex-ports[1]	Argentina (Yr. Beg. Dec. 1) Supply Stocks Dec. 1	New Crop	Total Supply	Disappearance Domes-tic	Ex-ports[1]
1976-7	8.2	23.6	31.8	5.0	13.4	2.7	11.7	14.4	2.8	9.5	.7	11.0	11.7	4.2	5.9
1977-8	13.3	19.9	33.2	5.1	16.0	2.1	9.4	11.5	2.6	8.1	1.6	5.7	7.3	4.3	1.8
1978-9	12.1	21.1	33.2	5.3	13.1	.8	18.1	18.9	2.5	11.7	1.2	8.1	9.3	4.1	4.1
1979-0	14.9	17.2	32.1	5.5	15.9	4.6	16.2	20.8	3.4	13.2	1.1	8.1	9.2	4.0	4.8
1980-1	10.7	19.3	30.0	5.2	16.3	4.3	10.9	15.2	3.5	9.6	.4	7.8	8.2	4.0	3.8
1981-2	8.6	24.8	33.4	5.2	18.4	2.0	16.4	18.4	2.6	11.0	.4	8.3	8.7	4.3	3.6
1982-3	9.8	26.7	36.5	5.1	21.4	4.8	8.9	13.7	4.1	7.3	.8	15.0	15.8	4.8	9.9
1983-4	10.0	26.5	36.5	5.6	21.8	2.3	22.0	24.3	3.4	13.3	1.1	12.8	13.9	4.7	7.8
1984-5	9.2	21.2	30.2	5.2	17.6	7.5	18.7	26.2	3.0	14.7	1.3	13.2	14.5	4.6	9.4
1985-6[2]	7.6	24.3	31.9	5.7	17.7	8.5	16.1	24.6	3.0	16.0	.5	8.5	9.0	4.4	4.3
1986-7[3]	8.5	31.3	39.8	5.6	18.0	5.6	16.0	21.6	3.0	14.5	.3	9.6	9.9	4.5	5.1
1987-8[3]	16.2					4.1					.3				

[1] Including flour.   [2] Preliminary.   [3] Forecast.   *Source: Foreign Agricultural Service, U.S.D.A.*   T.725

285

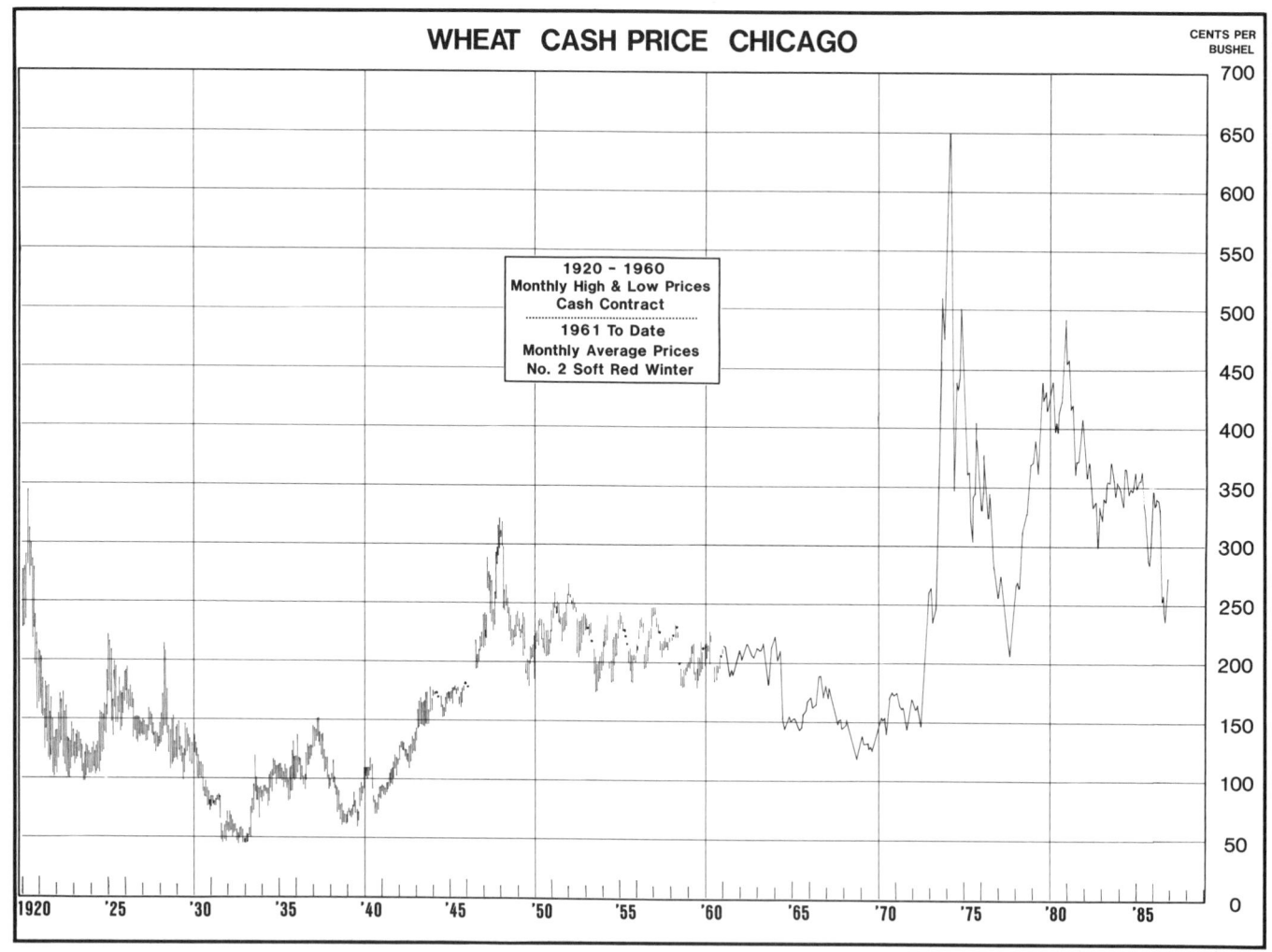

WHEAT CASH PRICE CHICAGO

CENTS PER BUSHEL

1920 – 1960
Monthly High & Low Prices
Cash Contract

1961 To Date
Monthly Average Prices
No. 2 Soft Red Winter

Average Price of No. 2 Soft Red Winter (30 Days) Wheat at Chicago In Dollars per Bushel

Year	June	July	Aug.	Sept.	Oct.	Nov.	Dec.	Jan.	Feb.	Mar.	Apr.	May	Average
1977–8	2.29	2.20	2.08	2.20	2.27	2.59	2.65	2.69	2.64	2.82	3.11	3.14	2.56
1978–9	3.18	3.22	3.32	3.42	3.51	3.68	3.68	3.73	3.88	3.79	3.60	3.86	3.57
1979–0	4.36	4.39	4.23	4.28	4.30	4.13	4.26	4.36	4.39	4.18	3.96	4.04	4.24
1980–1	3.96	4.17	4.21	4.38	4.70	4.92	4.54	4.57	4.34	4.15	4.18	3.80	4.33
1981–2	3.60	3.70	3.70	3.87	3.97	4.08	3.86	3.77	3.57	3.59	3.70	3.43	3.74
1982–3	3.31	3.36	3.35	3.18	2.98	3.33	3.23	3.32	3.40	3.36	3.51	3.55	3.32
1983–4	3.53	3.59	3.71	3.62	3.56	3.42	3.55	3.47	3.34	3.57	3.65	3.65	3.56
1984–5	3.51	3.44	3.49	3.47	3.51	3.62	3.49	3.51	3.55	3.55	3.63	3.34	3.51
1985–6	3.27	3.09	2.87	2.83	3.04	3.33	3.46	3.34	3.37	3.40	3.39	3.25	3.22
1986–7	2.52	2.58	2.44	2.36	2.57	2.73							

Source: Agricultural Marketing Service, Grain Division, U.S.D.A.

T.745

Stocks of Wheat Flour Held by Mills in the United States In Thousands of Sacks (100 Pounds)

Year	Jan. 1	April 1	July 1	Oct. 1	Year	Jan. 1	April 1	July 1	Oct. 1
1977	1,334	4,248	4,167	3,537	1982	3,460	3,384	3,744	3,563
1978	4,160	4,096	3,459	3,342	1983	4,276	3,760	3,490	3,599
1979	3,214	3,477	3,895	3,813	1984	3,805	3,780	3,763	3,833
1980	3,975	3,323	4,268	3,716	1985[1]	4,230	4,303	5,040	5,052
1981	3,842	3,897	3,895	4,222	1986[1]	4,847	4,466	4,786	

[1] *Preliminary. Source: Department of Commerce*

T.755

High, Low & Closing Prices of May Wheat Futures on the Chicago Board of Trade In Cents per Bushel

Year of Delivery		Year Prior to Delivery Apr.	May	June	July	Aug.	Sept.	Oct.	Nov.	Dec.	Delivery Year Jan.	Feb.	Mar.	April	May	Life of Delivery Range
1982	High	526	510	489	491	484½	465	476½	478½	453½	412	400½	375½	382½	360	526
	Low	500	479	447	455	446½	447	455	444½	384	382	360½	345	357	342	342
	Close	506	487	454	476	449½	458	474¼	447¾	400¾	391¾	366¾	370¼	357	354	—
1983	High	444¼	434½	411	403½	399	390½	354¼	368¼	355	356¾	363½	370½	366¼	360½	444¼
	Low	423	406¼	388½	381	374	343¼	327¼	338½	333¼	330½	318½	322¼	338¼	341¾	318½
	Close	431	406¼	395	392	383¼	349½	337¾	353¾	338½	351½	321½	360¼	351¼	346¾	—
1984	High	415	403	388	401¼	441	432	392½	376	365½	359	333¾	375	380	397	441
	Low	396	380¼	375¾	372½	397	386	364¾	347½	347	329¾	324½	330	349½	348½	324½
	Close	399	380¼	379½	398	431¼	390½	369½	355	360½	334	331¼	374	350¾	396½	—
1985	High	383½	405	392½	387	388	363	363½	362½	349¼	347¾	350	361¼	371½	349½	405
	Low	372	367¼	373½	369	355¼	350	351¼	347¼	334½	332½	333¾	335½	345	319¾	319¾
	Close	372	390½	385½	381½	357	353¾	361	349	341	343½	336¼	356½	349	320¾	—
1986	High	350	338¼	328¾	316	305	303	315	319½	326½	320½	294	312	328	360	360
	Low	335	316	314	286½	284	286½	294½	305¼	308½	281	274	285¼	275½	300	274
	Close	338¼	316	314	291¾	291½	300	311½	311¼	321	288¼	286¼	304¼	328	358	—
1987	High	283	300	255¼	250	253	250½	261½	267	269½						
	Low	244	248	239	233¼	241½	237	244	252½	258						
	Close	283	249	239	245¼	246½	244¼	255½	267	260¾						

Source: Chicago Board of Trade T.750

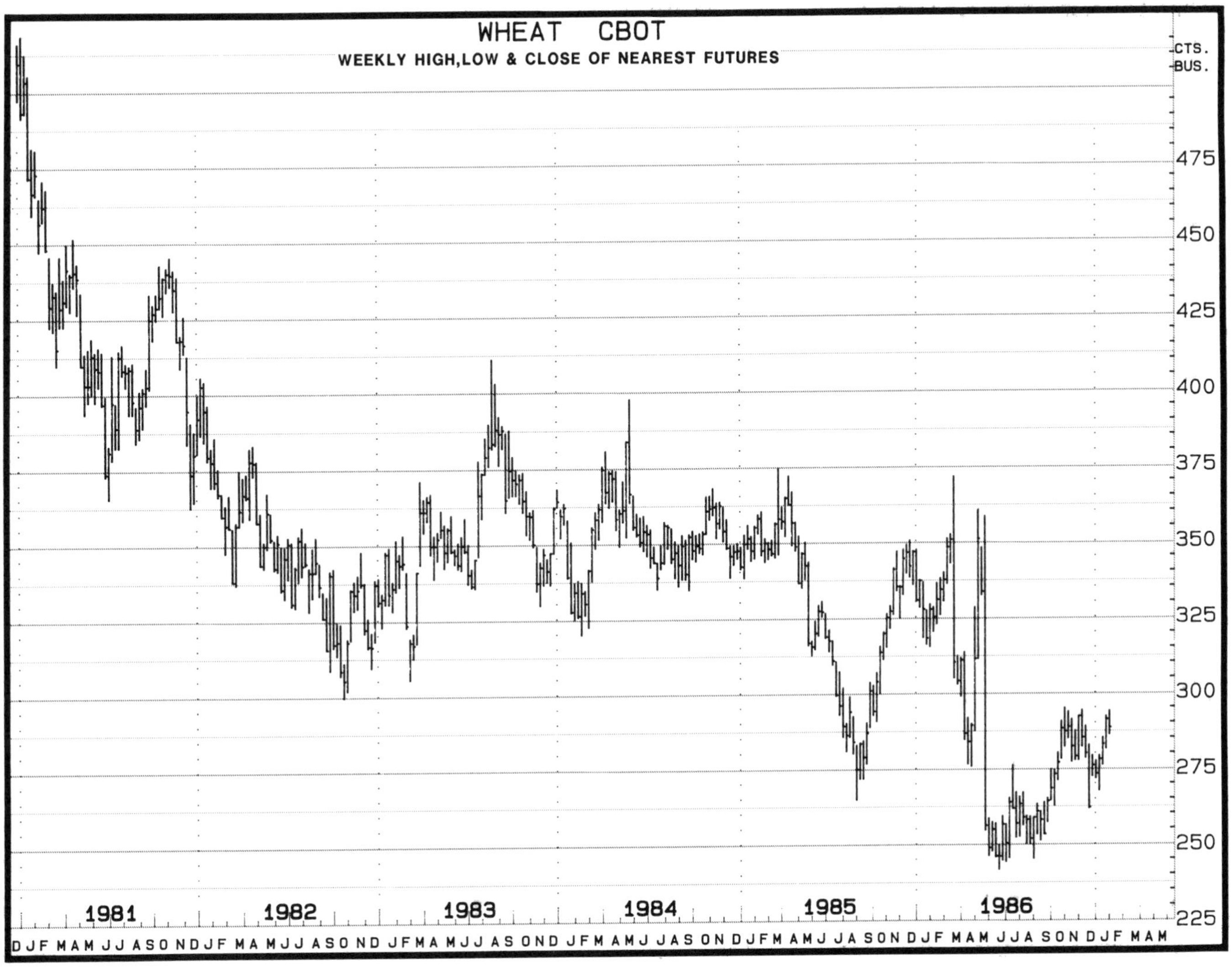
WHEAT CBOT
WEEKLY HIGH,LOW & CLOSE OF NEAREST FUTURES
CTS. BUS.
475
450
425
400
375
350
325
300
275
250
225
1981
1982
1983
1984
1985
1986
D J F M A M J J A S O N D J F M A M J J A S O N D J F M A M J J A S O N D J F M A M J J A S O N D J F M A M J J A S O N D J F M A M J J A S O N D J F M A M

WHEAT

Average Price of No. 1 Hard Winter (Ordinary Protein) Wheat, at Kansas City   In Cents per Bushel

Year	July	Aug.	Sept.	Oct.	Nov.	Dec.	Jan.	Feb.	Mar.	Apr.	May	June	Average
1978–9	314	314	324	342	348	339	342	350	352	353	364	417	338
1979–0	434	412	426	439	453	451	433	432	407	390	410	407	425
1980–1	421	431	445	470	489	454	460	447	435	448	436	424	445
1981–2	425	414	419	431	446	435	433	426	425	428	422	406	427
1982–3	374	370	375	361	386	398	400	408	418	421	405	392	392
1983–4	371	388	390	384	382	385	381	371	385	393	372	380	383
1984–5	367	380	389	386	385	376	376	374	367	362	342	338	374
1985–6	317	303	307	315	335	342	332	330	336	345	340	280	328
1986–7	250	248	253	260	268								

Source: Agricultural Marketing Service, U.S.D.A.   T.739

Average Price of No. 1 Dark Northern Spring Wheat at Minneapolis (14% Protein)   In Cents per Bushel

Year	July	Aug.	Sept.	Oct.	Nov.	Dec.	Jan.	Feb.	Mar.	Apr.	May	June	Average
1978–9	311	313	326	341	347	332	330	336	342	345	373	432	335
1979–0	442	419	429	445	429	417	407	408	402	396	431	433	421
1980–1	469	455	456	482	495	477	481	478	467	480	477	456	471
1981–2	450	425	423	429	438	422	428	421	416	425	420	413	429
1982–3	416	396	402	400	408	396	393	392	408	440	440	439	409
1983–4	438	434	433	433	425	421	417	408	424	437	445	445	430
1984–5	434	407	397	403	402	392	390	392	394	409	402	399	406
1985–6	377	356	376	391	409	416	397	390	400	417	403	317	394
1986–7	300	286	285	298	309								

Source: Agricultural Marketing Service, U.S.D.A.   T.742

Average Price[1] Received by Farmers for Wheat in the U.S.   In Cents per Bushel

Year	July	Aug.	Sept.	Oct.	Nov.	Dec.	Jan.	Feb.	Mar.	Apr.	May	June	Average[2]
1979–0	389	374	387	398	394	381	374	378	364	358	369	369	382
1980–1	381	394	399	419	432	422	421	417	409	407	395	370	391
1981–2	362	362	365	377	385	380	378	370	367	368	364	339	365
1982–3	326	334	338	343	348	351	357	357	366	375	373	350	355
1983–4	334	361	365	361	354	348	350	340	349	363	366	346	353
1984–5	328	343	343	343	345	338	338	338	338	334	329	309	338
1985–6	293	289	300	309	323	325	319	315	328	336	302	247	316
1986–7	225	226	228	230	237								

[1] Weighted average by sales.   [2] Includes an allowance for unredeemed loans at average loan values.
Source: Statistical Reporting Service, U.S.D.A.   T.743

Average Wholesale Price Index of Wheat Flour (Spring[1])   June 1983 = 100

Year	July	Aug.	Sept.	Oct.	Nov.	Dec.	Jan.	Feb.	Mar.	Apr.	May	June	Average
1983–4	99.9	99.6	100.0	98.4	96.6	96.1	96.4	95.8	97.0	99.3	98.8	100.6	98.2
1984–5	99.5	96.9	96.9	97.3	97.7	96.8	98.2	98.7	98.3	100.3	97.0	96.3	97.8
1985–6	95.2	93.1	93.7	94.9	96.6	96.7	96.2	96.4	96.4	94.8	99.7	92.8	95.5
1986–7	87.5	87.0	85.5	86.7									

[1] Standard patent.   *Source: Bureau of Labor Statistics (0212–0301.99)*   T.758

World Wheat Flour Production   In Thousands of Metric Tons

Year	Argentina	Australia[2]	Canada	France	India[3]	Mexico	Israel	Japan	W. Germany	Egypt	Poland	South Africa	Un. Kingdom	United States	Yugoslavia
1978	2,524	1,062	1,951	3,385	2,660	1,814	490	4,013	2,447	3,480	2,324	940	3,848	12,606	2,388
1979	2,482	1,039	1,978	3,467	1,636	1,951	476	4,150	2,528	3,492	2,533	901	3,785	12,884	2,400
1980	2,438	1,044	1,930	3,488	2,410	2,147	455	4,184	2,713	3,188	2,642	890	3,702	12,822	2,404
1981	2,456	1,069	1,900	3,481	2,327	2,422	464	4,184	2,601	3,512	2,815	718	3,596	12,884	2,330
1982	2,550	1,086	1,750	3,454	2,404	2,484	498	4,367	2,480	3,550	2,827	726	3,504	13,049	2,442
1983	2,678	1,055	1,702	4,386	3,092	2,435	506	4,356	2,280	3,686	2,539	694	3,420	13,883	2,414
1984[1]	2,851	1,138		4,632	3,328	2,446	516	4,439	3,500	3,707		727	3,604	13,584	2,350
1985[4]		1,100		4,600	3,200	2,400	530	4,350	3,700	3,600		690	3,800	13,700	2,250

[1] Preliminary.   [2] Twelve months ending June 30 of the year stated.   [3] Represents 60 percent of the total production.   [4] Estimate.
Source: United Nations   T.752

Wheat and Flour—Price Relationships at Milling Centers (In Dollars)

Crop Year (June-May)	At Kansas City					At Minneapolis				
	Cost of Wheat to Produce 100 lb. Flour[1]	Bakery Flour Per 100 lb.[2]	Wholesale Price of By-Products Obtained 100 lb. Flour[3]	Total Products Actual	Over Cost of Wheat	Cost of Wheat to Produce 100 lb. Flour[1]	Bakery Flour Per 100 lb.[2]	Wholesale Price of By-Products Obtained 100 lb. Flour[3]	Total Products Actual	Over Cost of Wheat
1978–9	7.85	7.89	1.47	9.36	1.51	7.76	8.22	1.34	9.56	1.80
1979–0	9.85	10.02	1.70	11.72	1.87	9.73	10.26	1.51	11.77	2.04
1980–1	10.30	10.38	1.99	12.37	2.07	10.95	11.00	1.78	12.78	1.83
1981–2	9.81	10.37	1.57	11.94	2.13	9.80	10.67	1.41	12.08	2.28
1982–3	9.46	10.22	1.52	11.74	2.28	9.45	10.54	1.26	11.80	2.35
1983–4	9.45	9.99	1.83	11.69	2.37	9.84	10.75	1.59	12.33	2.49
1984–5	8.91	9.78	1.32	11.10	2.18	9.31	10.84	1.01	11.85	2.54
1985–6[4]	8.28	9.25	1.20	10.45	2.17	9.07	11.32	.91	12.23	3.16
Jun.–Sep.	8.01	8.89	1.10	9.99	1.98	8.68	10.96	.78	11.74	3.06
Oct.–Dec.	8.37	9.10	1.39	10.48	2.11	9.24	11.61	1.06	12.67	3.43
Jan.–Mar.	8.37	9.33	1.10	10.43	2.06	9.05	11.69	.83	12.53	3.48
Apr.–May	8.38	9.70	1.21	10.91	2.53	9.30	11.04	.95	11.99	2.69

[1] Cost of 2.28 bushels. [2] Quoted as 95% patent at K.C. & standard patent at Minn., bulk basis. [3] Assumes 50–50 millfeed distribution between bran & shorts or middlings, bulk basis. [4] Preliminary. *Source: Economic Research Service, U.S.D.A.* T.751

United States Wheat Flour Production   In Millions of Sacks (100 Pounds Each)

Year	July	Aug.	Sept.	Oct.	Nov.	Dec.	Jan.	Feb.	Mar.	Apr.	May	June	Total
1979–0	23.5	26.3	23.3	26.1	24.8	22.7	24.6	22.6	22.2	21.2	22.8	21.4	281.5
1980–1	23.1	24.0	24.8	26.3	24.4	25.2	24.2	22.8	25.0	24.0	23.4	23.5	290.7
1981–2	23.3	23.7	24.2	24.7	22.8	22.3	24.5	24.0	25.8	22.9	22.3	22.9	283.4
1982–3	23.6	25.2	24.7	25.5	24.4	25.0	24.9	23.8	27.3	24.6	26.2	25.5	300.7
1983–4	25.1	29.4	27.9	26.6	25.4	24.9	24.8	25.5	25.9	24.1	26.6	24.3	310.5
1984–5[1]	22.8	26.0	24.4	26.3	25.1	23.7	25.5	25.6	26.3	24.7	26.1	24.1	300.6
1985–6[1]	24.3	27.3	26.8	29.1	28.4	25.2	27.4	27.1	25.2	25.9	26.4	26.2	319.3
1986–7[1]	27.0	29.5											

[1] Preliminary. *Source: Bureau of the Census* T.754

United States Wheat Flour Exports   In Thousands of 100 Pound Sacks

Year	July	Aug.	Sept.	Oct.	Nov.	Dec.	Jan.	Feb.	Mar.	Apr.	May	June	Total
1979–0	1,669	2,489	2,218	1,223	842	1,971	1,018	1,300	2,713	867	918	1,606	18,833
1980–1	894	2,137	1,396	1,034	522	609	980	1,896	2,241	2,932	1,724	2,350	18,715
1981–2	987	1,420	724	284	117	184	605	2,165	2,336	2,858	1,760	944	14,384
1982–3	352	1,196	698	593	824	185	1,587	3,734	2,692	4,256	3,193	4,172	23,482
1983–4	3,293	3,095	3,621	3,469	1,122	395	830	883	2,842	2,802	3,213	2,457	28,022
1984–5[1]	1,716	285	433	1,122	121	222	138	2,384	1,857	2,663	1,548	693	13,182
1985–6[1]	850	381	132	131	1,079	2,569	1,374	2,312	2,171	2,526	888	2,089	16,502
1986–7[1]	2,044	2,791											

[1] Preliminary. *Source: Department of Commerce* T.756

Supply and Distribution of Wheat Flour in the United States   In Thousands of Cwt.

Year	Wheat Ground 1,000 Bu.	Milfeed Production 1,000 Tons	Flour Production[1]	Flour & Product Imports[2]	Total Supply	Exports Flour	Exports Products[2]	Domestic Disappearance	Total Population July 1 Millions	Per Capita Disappearance Pounds
			1,000 Cwt.							
1978	621,321	4,860	277,950	773	278,723	22,170	43	256,510	222.6	115
1979	636,375	4,945	284,051	823	284,874	20,927	86	263,861	225.1	117
1980	628,599	4,866	282,655	904	283,559	17,378	54	266,127	227.7	117
1981	634,381	5,045	283,966	1,166	285,132	18,655	84	266,393	229.8	116
1982	667,841	5,573	297,288	1,496	298,784	20,926	154	277,704	232.1	119
1983	686,983	5,563	306,066	1,109	307,175	34,969	150	272,056	234.3	116
1984	674,665	5,420	299,476	1,179	300,655	21,752	160	278,743	236.7	118
1985[3]	698,355	5,502	313,001	1,144	314,145	20,766	140	293,239	237.8	123

[1] Commercial production of wheat flour, whole wheat, industrial and durum flour and farina reported by Bureau of Census. [2] Imports and exports of macaroni products (flour equivalent). [3] Preliminary. *Source: Economics & Statistics Service, U.S.D.A.* T.753

Wool

1986/87 world wool production was estimated at 3.7 billion pounds, unchanged from the previous season, according to USDA in November, 1986. Production in Australia was expected to rise by 2.5 percent to 1.17 billion pounds, greasy, due to an increase in the country's sheep herd. In New Zealand, herd size has been reduced, and wool output was expected to decline by about one percent in 1986/87 to 780 million pounds, greasy. Nonetheless, wool production continues to be a lucrative activity there, more so than sheep-meat production. Wool output in both the Soviet Union and China, two major producing countries, has apparently declined in recent years.

World wool carry-in stocks in 1986/87 were 423 million pounds, up 12 percent from the year before. Much of the carry-in was held by the Australian Wool Corporation. While wool demand has been sluggish in a number of industrialized countries, it has expanded in China and the USSR. Consequently, world consumption has been rising in recent years. 1986/87 world raw exports are expected to be about 3 billion pounds, slightly above the year-before level.

U.S. wool production, declining in recent years with a smaller herd, was estimated at 42 million pounds in 1986, compared with 47 million in 1985. Reduced U.S. consumption of lamb and mutton has resulted in lower sheep numbers, causing less wool output. Other reasons for declining U.S. wool output are rising labor costs and competition from man-made fibers.

U.S. imports of raw wool during 1986 were expected to expand to 100 million pounds from 80 million in 1985, boosted by increasing demand for fine-quality wool. Australia and New Zealand continued to be the principal U.S. suppliers. Mill use of wool in the U.S. was forecast to rebound to 140 million pounds, after having dipped to 117 million in 1985. The decline in 1985 was attributed largely to competition from imported sweaters of both wool and man-made fibers. U.S. usage of wool rated as 60 and finer expanded in 1986, with part of the increase due to large orders for fine quality grades of women's coating fabrics. U.S. exports were pegged at 1 million pounds, down from 1.4 million the previous season. During the year, stocks were expected to rise marginally to 52 million pounds at year-end, versus 51 million in 1985.

The 1985 Farm Bill extended price supports for wool through 1990. Shorn wool is supported at 77.5 percent of an amount arrived at by formula, as set forth in the Wool Act of 1954. In 1986, the shorn wool support price was $1.78 per pound. In recent years, wool support payments have accounted for about 20 percent of sheep producers' incomes.

Futures Market

Greasy merino wool futures are traded on the Sydney Futures Exchange, and New Zealand crossbred futures are traded in London.

World Production of Wool[3]   In Thousands of Metric Tons (Greasy Basis)

Year	Brazil	Argen-tina	Aus-tralia	China	France	Morocco	India	New Zealand	Spain	Turkey	South Africa	United Kingdom	United States	Uru-guay	USSR	World[1] Total
1973	36.5	179.2	700.9		21.4	23.0	30.1	284.8	31.8	47.3	113.3	49.4	72.0	53.0	433.0	2,355
1974	34.4	183.4	793.5		21.7	19.0	30.5	294.1	34.0	52.4	114.6	49.9	64.7	55.0	461.0	2,495
1975	31.3	190.2	757.4		21.9	20.0	31.0	311.8	29.0	53.0	114.3	50.3	58.6	60.0	463.0	2,481
1976	30.3	176.3	702.7	61.0	22.0	21.0	32.0	302.5	28.6	53.9	110.5	49.9	53.8	60.4	432.0	2,457
1977	26.9	172.0	677.4	61.0	22.4	20.0	33.1	310.8	28.0	54.1	113.4	48.0	49.9	62.2	455.0	2,465
1978	28.0	170.8	709.2	61.0	22.6	12.0	34.2	310.8	29.0	56.7	113.4	49.2	46.2	65.8	460.0	2,433
1979	31	166	709	153	26	21	35	357	29	59	110	48	48	72	412	2,553
1980[2]	35	163	700	176	27	22	35	381	28	61	112	50	49	79	464	2,641
1981[2]	33	163	716	180	27	22	35	363	21	62	112	42	50	79	482	2,653
1982[1]			701					370							471	
1983[1]			672					370							474	

[1] Estimated.   [2] Preliminary.   [3] Includes shorn, pulled, & wool exported on skins.   *Source: Foreign Agricultural Service, U.S.D.A.*   T.760

Wool Goods[1] Production in the United States   In Millions of Square Yards

Year	First Quarter	Second Quarter	Third Quarter	Fourth Quarter	Total Year	Year	First Quarter	Second Quarter	Third Quarter	Fourth Quarter	Total Year
1980	45.2	46.8	31.9	34.4	158.3	1984[2]	48.6	44.3	29.7	36.7	159.4
1981	50.6	52.9	39.0	35.5	178.1	1985[2]	43.2	39.5	24.3	34.0	138.3
1982	41.0	36.3	20.2	23.6	121.1	1986[2]	37.7	38.8			
1983	36.0	41.8	28.8	37.0	143.5	1987					

[1] Woolen and worsted woven goods, except woven felts.   [2] Preliminary.   *Source: Bureau of Census*   T.763

Salient Statistics of Wool in the United States

Year	Sheep & Lambs Shorn[2] Ths.	Weight per Fleece Lbs.	Shorn Wool Production Ths. Lbs.	Price per Lb.	Value of Production Mil. $	Pulled Wool Production — Avg. Weight per Skin Lbs.	Pulled Wool Production — Total	Total Wool Production[4]	Apparel Wool (Clean Content) — Domestic Prod.	Apparel Wool (Clean Content) — Exports Domestic Wool	Apparel Wool (Clean Content) — Imports for Consumption[4]	Total New Supply[3]	Carpet Wool Imports for Cons.	Mill Consumption — Apparel	Mill Consumption — Carpet
											— Thousand Pounds —				
1979	13,069	8.02	104,867	86.3	90.5	3.20	900	105,767	56,022	313	20,283	75,992	22,047	106,533	10,513
1980	13,263	7.95	105,419	88.1	92.8	3.10	1,050	106,469	56,426	304	30,491	86,613	25,992	113,423	10,020
1981	13,493	8.14	109,787	94.4	103.7	3.05	1,150	110,937	58,806	307	48,106	106,605	26,145	127,752	10,896
1982	13,199	8.04	106,129	68.6	72.8	N.A.	N.A.	106,129	56,800	1,351	39,988	94,673	21,433	105,857	9,825
1983	12,865	8.00	102,886	61.3	63.0			103,886	55,100	1,014	49,371	102,681	28,688	126,729	13,851
1984[1]	12,300	7.80	95,900	79.5	73.9			96,900	51,100	488	63,271	110,857	30,906	128,982	13,088
1985[1]	11,200	7.83	88,000	63.3	55.7			89,000	47,200	1,400	50,164	95,964	29,308	106,051	10,562
1986[1]														129,000	11,000

[1] Preliminary. [2] Includes sheep shorn at commercial feeding yards. [3] Production minus exports plus imports; stocks not taken into consideration. [4] Apparel wool includes all dutiable wool; carpet wool includes all duty-free wool. *Sources: Economics Service, U.S.D.A.; Dept. of Commerce*

T.766

Consumption of Apparel Wool in the United States   In Millions of Pounds (Clean Basis)

Year	Jan.	Feb.	Mar.	Apr.	May	June	July	Aug.	Sept.	Oct.	Nov.	Dec.	Total
1980	11.3	10.2	9.8	11.4	9.2	8.3	7.5	8.4	7.7	10.8	8.8	10.0	113.4
1981	10.2	11.0	12.9	10.8	10.2	12.8	8.4	10.1	11.4	9.4	9.4	11.2	127.8
1982	9.4	9.6	12.9	9.2	8.3	9.4	5.9	8.0	8.4	7.2	7.8	9.6	105.9
1983	8.5	9.3	12.4	10.2	9.4	13.0	8.5	10.0	12.3	10.7	10.7	11.8	126.7
1984	10.6	12.0	14.1	11.3	11.9	13.0	8.2	9.9	11.2	8.5	8.9	9.4	129.0
1985[1]	9.3	8.3	9.8	8.8	9.3	10.5	6.5	8.1	10.4	8.6	8.8	8.9	106.1
1986[1]	12.6	11.1	11.6	13.5	10.8	11.4							

[1] Preliminary.   *Source: Bureau of the Census*

T.767

Average Wool Prices[1]—Australian—64's, Type 62, Duty Paid—U.S. Mills   In Cents per Pound

Year	Jan.	Feb.	Mar.	Apr.	May	June	July	Aug.	Sept.	Oct.	Nov.	Dec.	Average
1980	292	310	306	299	310	321	311	306	311	306	320	321	309
1981	319	312	307	314	316	319	323	320	316	316	317	312	316
1982	301	303	313	323	336	321	304	294	287	276	269	267	299
1983	273	271	266	266	262	262	260	262	263	271	270	266	266
1984	268	276	279	276	271	269	255	259	247	249	255	251	263
1985	246	233	236	227	234	229	230	226	224	224	217	222	219
1986	231	229	231	238	252	242	—	229	224				

[1] Raw, clean basis.   *Source: U.S. Dept. of Agriculture*

T.768

Average Wool Prices—Domestic[1]—Graded Territory, 64's, Staple 2¾'' & Up—U.S. Mills   ¢/Lb.

Year	Jan.	Feb.	Mar.	Apr.	May	June	July	Aug.	Sept.	Oct.	Nov.	Dec.	Average
1973	188.0	232.5	302.5	233.8	233.5	257.5	260.0	275.0	275.0	263.0	241.9	237.5	250.0
1974	236.0	222.5	197.5	185.0	174.0	178.8	166.5	161.2	162.5	156.5	141.2	130.8	176.0
1975	116.2	112.5	113.8	134.0	150.6	155.6	153.8	171.2	172.5	172.5	172.5	177.5	150.2
1976	177.5	177.5	173.5	176.2	177.5	177.5	182.5	182.5	187.5	192.5	192.5	187.5	182.1
1977	187.5	187.5	182.5	182.5	182.5	182.5	182.5	182.5	182.5	182.5	182.5	182.0	183.3
1978	182	178	178	181	184	192	192	192	195	197	202	202	190
1979	202	202	206	220	220	218	218	218	220	230	233	233	218
1980	238	253	256	231	225	233	245	251	253	253	253	253	245
1981	253	268	274	278	278	283	283	283	283	283	283	283	278
1982	275	263	244	240	240	240	240	240	240	—	—	—	247
1983	—	—	193	193	193	198	219	223	225	225	225	228	212
1984	230	230	230	245	234	230	230	230	230	221	218	214	228
1985	205	195	185	182	191	193	193	193	193	193	193	193	192
1986	193	189	180	188	198	198	193	190	190				

[1] Raw, shorn, clean basis.   *Source: U.S. Dept. of Agriculture*

T.769

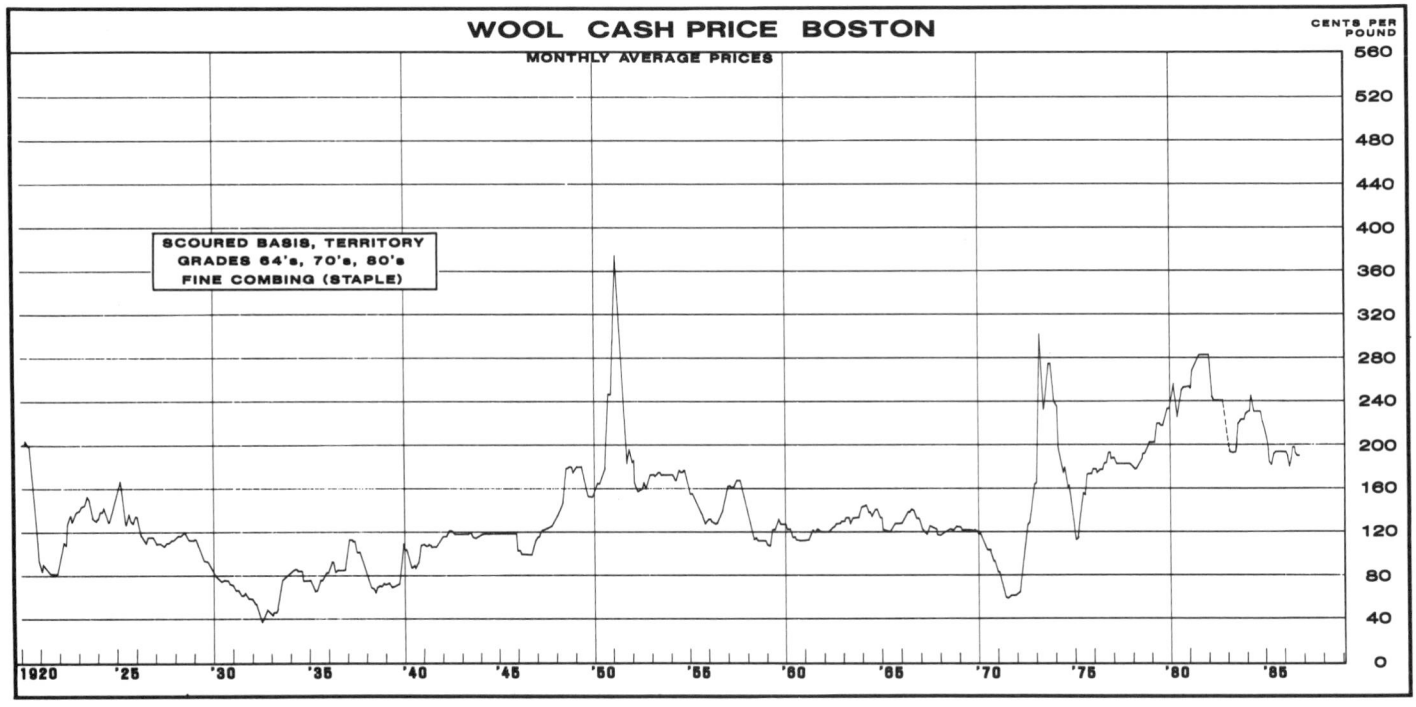

WOOL CASH PRICE BOSTON

MONTHLY AVERAGE PRICES

SCOURED BASIS, TERRITORY
GRADES 64's, 70's, 80's
FINE COMBING (STAPLE)

Wool: Mill Consumption, by Grades in the U.S., Scoured Basis   In Millions of Pounds

Year	Woolen System 60's & Finer	Woolen System 50's Up to 60's	Woolen System Total	Apparel Wool[1] Worsted System 60's & Finer	Worsted System Coarser Than 60's	Worsted System Total	All Total	Carpet Wool[2]
1981	35.2	29.3	64.5	41.2	22.0	63.3	127.8	10.9
1982	23.8	24.6	48.4	36.2	21.3	57.5	105.9	9.8
1983	30.5	30.2	60.7	42.4	23.6	66.0	126.7	13.9
1984	32.9	32.2	65.2	39.7	24.1	63.8	129.0	13.1
1985[3]	28.0	27.7	55.7	33.6	16.7	50.3	106.1	10.6
1986[4]							129.0	11.0

[1] Domestic & duty-paid foreign.   [2] Duty-free foreign.   [3] Preliminary.   [4] Estimate.   *Source: Economic Research Service, U.S.D.A.*   T.762

United States Imports[1] of Unmanufactured Wool (Clean Yield)   In Millions of Pounds

Year	Jan.	Feb.	Mar.	Apr.	May	June	July	Aug.	Sept.	Oct.	Nov.	Dec.	Total
1982	8.0	6.3	6.6	4.9	6.0	6.6	4.0	4.2	4.7	2.9	3.6	3.7	61.4
1983	6.0	6.2	5.0	6.7	4.9	7.5	6.5	5.8	5.1	8.5	8.0	8.9	78.1
1984	11.2	9.0	7.8	7.8	10.4	6.7	9.6	6.4	6.0	6.9	5.6	6.8	94.2
1985	10.7	5.8	6.0	5.7	7.1	4.9	7.3	4.5	6.9	7.1	5.5	8.0	79.5
1986	10.2	8.8	7.6	7.5	8.0	8.6	7.8	6.3					

[1] Data are imports for consumption.   *Source: Department of Commerce*   T.764

Price Received by Farmers for Shorn[2] Wool in the U.S.   In Cents per Pound

Year	Jan.	Feb.	Mar.	Apr.	May	June	July	Aug.	Sept.	Oct.	Nov.	Dec.	Average[1]
1982	73.1	72.9	63.6	83.6	76.5	68.0	77.0	64.2	56.5	70.7	54.7	55.5	68.4
1983	50.0	57.1	56.0	65.7	65.0	63.5	62.7	59.6	57.2	66.4	70.1	64.1	61.3
1984	58.4	67.1	79.3	87.9	86.5	86.6	82.3	78.5	74.3	80.2	67.5	69.4	79.5
1985	59.2	58.7	61.0	67.9	68.5	69.8	64.0	60.2	59.5	66.6	58.5	56.8	63.3
1986[3]	54.3	55.8	61.7	67.8	75.2	73.5	70.7	68.8	72.1	68.2	62.3	62.0	66.0

[1] Weighted average.   [2] Grease basis.   [3] Preliminary.   *Source: Crop Reporting Board, U.S.D.A.*   T.765

Zinc

Through October, 1986, domestic zinc mine production was eight percent below that for the same period of 1985. Despite increased monthly output late in the year, domestic mine production in 1986 is likely to be the lowest since 1906.

U.S. smelter production of slab zinc fell in November, 1986, and for those 11 months of the year was down about 11 percent from the same 1985 period, according to the American Bureau of Metal Statistics. Based on smelter production through November, 1986, domestic slab zinc production will likely be the lowest since the early 1930s.

In May, 1986, seven of the nation's 15 largest domestic zinc producing mines did not operate. And in mid-May, a Buick, Missouri lead-zinc mine, the second-largest U.S. zinc mine in 1985, was closed down for economic evaluation. This came on top of several temporary mine closures in April, 1986.

U.S. recoverable mined zinc totaled 168,160 tonnes for January–October, 1986, compared with total 1985 mined zinc of 226,545 tonnes. For the first 10 months of 1986, Tennessee was the leading domestic producer of mined zinc with 83,929 tonnes; Missouri was next with 33,808, and six other states produced some 50,425 tonnes for the period.

Reported slab zinc consumption for the same 1986 period totaled 568,829 tonnes, compared with full-year 1985's total of 764,752 tonnes. Apparent total 10-month consumption in 1986 is estimated at 825,900 tonnes, compared to full-year 1985 consumption of 940,600 tonnes.

For the first 10 months of 1986, imports of zinc ore and concentrates for consumption totaled 71,347 tonnes, compared with full-year 1985 imports of 90,186 tonnes. Slab zinc imports for the period were 553,737 tonnes, versus full-year 1985 imports of 610,000.

Canada continues to be the major supplier of imported zinc ore and concentrates with a 10-month 1986 total of 25,445 tonnes; full-year 1985 total was 47,200 tonnes. From January to October, 1986, Peru picked up its export pace considerably with 24,848 tonnes, compared with all of 1985's 13,402 tonnes. Honduras and Mexico were other important U.S. suppliers.

Canada was also the main source for imports of blocks, pigs or slab zinc to the U.S., sending 302,969 tonnes across the border; its full-year 1985 exports were 383,618 tonnes. The ten-month U.S. imports total was 553,737 tonnes, compared with 610,762 tonnes imported in all of 1985.

Identified zinc resources of the world are estimated at about 1.8 billion tons. Available data on sphalerite-bearing coals in mid-continent U.S. indicate a resource potential of many millions of tons of zinc that could be recovered as a byproduct of coal mining, with limited modification of existing technology. Preliminary evaluations suggest that some coals on other continents may have similar zinc resources.

Aluminum, plastics, and magnesium are the major substitutes for die-casting uses. Aluminum and plastic sheet and molded plastics substitute for formed products and galvanized sheet. Aluminum, magnesium, titanium and zirconium are significant competitors of zinc in chemicals and pigments.

Environmental concerns in zinc industry are associated more with coproducts which have toxic implications for the environment. These coproducts are lead, cadmium, and sulphur. Waste rock, effluents, gases and fume are well controlled by modern technology. In some mines, the tailings and waste rock are sold as crushed rock and agricultural limestone.

Futures Market

In 1986, two zinc futures contracts traded on the London Metal Exchange (LME).

Salient Statistics of Zinc in the United States — In Thousands of Metric Tons

Year	Net Import Reliance as a % of Apparent Consumption	Production of Slab Zinc Primary Domestic	Primary Foreign	Total	Value Mil. $[6]	Redistilled Secondary	Total Production	Dec. 31 Stocks at Producer Plants	Consumer Plants	Gov't. Stockpile	Total All Stocks	Zinc Slab	Consumption Base Scrap[2] Ores[2]	Zinc[3]	Copper	Aluminum[4]	Total
1976	59	346.4	106.1	452.6	359	62.2	514.7	88.0	109.9	349.4		1,028.9	91.8	138.4	139.2	.5	1,394
1977	57	322.2	86.2	408.4	309	45.9	454.3	83.8	86.5	347.8		999.5	86.5	139.6	139.6	.6	1,368
1978	66	267.4	139.3	406.7	207	34.8	441.5	37.9	99.3	345.9		1,050.6	90.0	73.2	141.5	.5	1,442
1979	63	255.3	217.1	472.5	220	53.2	525.7	59.1	92.6	345.7		1,000.6	79.7	146.7	166.4	.9	1,394
1980	60	231.9	108.6	340.5	262	29.4	369.9	22.6	69.6	342.4	125.8	811.1	59.0	133.0	138.2	1.1	1,142
1981	65	259.8	86.7	346.5	307	50.2	396.8	44.7	81.9	340.6	195.4	840.9	60.6	149.3	138.7	.7	1,189
1982	58	193.3	34.9	228.2	257	74.3	302.5	34.2	77.6	340.6	159.2	709.5	35.5	93.1	114.3	.7	953.1
1983	65	210.3	25.4	235.7	251	69.4	305.1	23.9	89.0	340.6	148.1	805.9	38.3	131.7	144.0	.7	1,121
1984	68	197.9	55.2	253.1	271	78.1	331.2	46.3	72.5	340.6	137.6	848.9	47.6	157.9	159.5	.7	1,215
1985[1]	69	172.8	63.2	236.0	202	75.6	311.6	32.4	58.9	340.6	118.5	764.8	42.3	140.6	147.2	.6	1,095
1986[5]							225.0	10.0	45.0		100.0	620.0					800.0

[1] Preliminary. [2] Recoverable zinc content. [3] Excludes redistilled slab & zinc produced by remelting. [4] Aluminum & magnesium-base scrap. [5] Estimate. [6] Domestic ores (recoverable content). *Source: Bureau of Mines*

T.770

293

ZINC

World Smelter Production of Zinc   In Thousands of Metric Tons

Year	Aus-tralia	Bel-gium	Canada	France	W. Ger-many	Italy	Japan	Mexico	Nor-way	Peru	Po-land	Spain	USSR	United Kingdom[3]	United States	World Total
1977	256.4	258.2	494.9	238.3	354.8	169.4	805.0	174.4	69.8	66.9	228.0	156.6	815.0	81.5	454.3	5,812
1978	294.8	241.5	495.4	231.2	306.8	177.6	792.7	173.1	71.6	62.9	222.0	177.0	850.0	73.6	441.5	5,882
1979	310.4	252.6	580.4	248.6	355.5	202.3	789.4	161.7	77.8	68.2	209.0	182.7	880.0	76.7	525.7	6,260
1980	306.0	247.6	591.6	252.8	370.6	206.4	735.2	143.9	79.4	63.8	217.0	151.7	895.0	86.7	369.9	6,049
1981	300.4	234.7	618.6	257.1	366.6	180.9	670.2	126.5	80.3	126.2	167.1	179.5	905.0	81.6	396.8	6,081
1982	295.9	228.3	511.9	243.8	335.0	158.6	662.4	127.0	79.0	160.7	165.4	181.8	920.0	79.3	302.5	5,866
1983	303.0	262.6	617.0	249.5	356.5	155.9	701.3	175.7	90.7	154.0	170.3	189.9	930.0	87.7	305.1	6,201
1984[1]	306.4	270.7	683.2	258.8	356.4	169.7	754.5	167.0	94.2	149.0	176.0	207.4	945.0	85.6	331.2	6,463
1985[2]	292.9	277.0	692.4	247.0	367.8	215.6	740.0	170.0	92.7	162.8	180.0	205.3	950.0	74.3	311.6	6,567

[1] Preliminary.   [2] Estimated.   [3] Some secondary metal included.   *Source: Bureau of Mines*   T.771

U.S. Mine Production of Recoverable Zinc   In Thousands of Metric Tons

Year	Arizona	Colorado	Idaho	Illinois	Mis-souri	Montana	Pennsyl-vania	New Mexico	New York	New Jersey	Ten-nessee	Utah	Virginia	Wash-ington	Wis-consin	Total U.S.
1977	4.0	36.5	28.1	N.A.	74.1	.1	20.7	N.A.	64.3	30.4	82.0	16.1	12.0	5.1	N.A.	407.9
1978	N.A.	22.2	32.4	N.A.	59.0	.1	19.1	N.A.	26.5	28.9	87.9	3.5	11.0	N.A.	N.A.	302.7
1979	N.A.	9.9	29.7	N.A.	61.7	.1	21.4	N.A.	12.1	31.1	85.1	N.A.	11.4	—	N.A.	267.3
1980	N.A.	13.8	27.7	N.A.	62.9	.1	22.6	N.A.	33.6	28.9	111.8	N.A.	12.0	—	N.A.	317.1
1981	.1	N.A.	N.A.	N.A.	52.9	—	24.7	N.A.	36.9	16.2	117.7	1.6	9.7	—	—	312.4
1982	—	N.A.	N.A.	N.A.	63.7	N.A.	24.8	—	52.3	16.8	121.3	—	—	—	—	303.2
1983	—	N.A.	N.A.	N.A.	57.0	—	16.8	—	56.7	16.5	110.0	—	—	—	—	275.3
1984	—	N.A.	N.A.	N.A.	45.5	—	—	—	N.A.	N.A.	116.5	N.A.	—	—	—	252.8
1985[1]	—	N.A.	N.A.	N.A.	49.3	—	—	—	N.A.	N.A.	104.5	—	—	—	—	226.5
1986[2]					37.0						95.0					200.0

[1] Preliminary.   [2] Estimated.   *Source: Bureau of Mines*   T.772

Consumption of Slab Zinc in the United States, by Industries and Grades   In Thousands of Metric Tons

Year	Total	By Industries							By Grades					
		Gal-vanizers	Brass Products	Zinc-Base Alloy[2]	Rolled Zinc	Zinc Oxide	Light-Metal Alloys	Other	Special High Grade	High Grade	Contin.[5] Galvan. Grade	Contrd.[4] Lead Grade	Prime Western	Remelt
1976	1,028.9	392.9	150.8	387.4	27.1	35.4	5.2	30.1	500.1	101.1	21.0	94.8	310.7	1.2
1977	999.5	396.4	128.3	367.1	27.4	38.5	5.6	36.1	492.6	91.0	19.7	101.2	293.7	1.2
1978	1,050.6	454.0	141.5	354.1	24.9	37.2	11.0	27.8	491.3	109.7	21.8	98.4	327.7	1.7
1979	1,000.6	452.8	141.4	314.1	22.0	35.5	12.9	21.9	443.1	108.6	22.5	86.8	336.8	2.8
1980	811.1	379.2	98.8	254.2	21.1	27.0	11.1	19.6	354.3	76.2	18.5	70.3	290.3	1.6
1981	840.9	411.0	113.0	243.4	23.2	25.7	8.2	16.5	361.5	97.6	18.2	80.3	275.3	1.2
1982	709.5	342.0	81.1	197.8	37.2	32.4	8.3	10.7	324.8	84.6	24.5	68.7	204.9	2.0
1983	805.9	373.2	107.9	212.9	56.3	36.2	12.5	6.9	406.7	91.0	62.6	60.8	179.1	5.6
1984	848.9	375.6	125.6	232.6	56.9	37.0	14.9	6.2	449.1	100.3	53.9	55.4	184.5	5.6
1985[3]	764.8	361.4	77.9	218.3	48.0	39.7	15.2	4.3	420.6	87.4	37.1	39.3	174.8	5.5
1986[1]	700.0	320.0	70.0	170.0	30.0	18.0	—10.0—		420.6					

[1] Estimated.   [2] Die casters.   [3] Preliminary.   [4] Controlled.   [5] Continuous.   *Source: Bureau of Mines*   T.773

Zinc Foreign Trade of the United States   In Metric Tons

Year	Imported for Consumption							Zinc Ore & Manufactures Exported						
								Blocks, Pigs, Anodes, etc.		Wrought & Alloys				
	Ores[1]	Blocks, Pigs, Slabs	Zinc Fume	Waste & Scrap	Dross, & Skim-mings	Dust, Powder & Flakes	Total Value Thous. $	Un-wrought	Un-wrought Alloys	Sheets, Plates & Strips	Angles Bars, Rods, etc.	Waste & Scrap	Dust (Blue Powder)	Zinc Ore & Con-cen-trates
1978	106,315	622,470	60	3,310	7,436	8,978	434,376	723	554	2,262	860	14,986	1,803	10,973
1979	87,499	524,130	28	3,259	4,454	3,586	434,677	279	366	1,824	1,451	28,149	966	20,095
1980	182,370	410,163	25	3,470	4,062	3,928	401,134	302	485	2,103	804	29,542	4,512	54,457
1981	245,710	612,007	184	5,782	7,629	7,993	676,299	323	378	1,500	1,160	30,046	5,003	54,232
1982	66,809	456,233	11	2,653	7,104	5,864	409,896	341	863	995	1,028	29,424	2,066	77,289
1983	63,156	617,679	631	3,900	6,508	6,533	533,398	427	662	957	1,046	28,255	1,914	60,168
1984	86,172	639,228	314	6,259	5,027	7,572	683,211	760	588	975	840	39,146	2,933	30,579
1985[2]	90,186	610,900	—	3,247	4,942	8,681	559,434	1,011	1,240	776	1,434	43,947	2,037	23,264
1986[3]	70,000	640,000						1,300				70,000		5,000

[1] Zinc content.   [2] Preliminary.   [3] Estimate.   *Source: Bureau of Mines*   T.774

U.S. Mine Production of Recoverable Zinc In Thousands of Metric Tons

Year	Jan.	Feb.	Mar.	Apr.	May	June	July	Aug.	Sept.	Oct.	Nov.	Dec.	Total
1979	23.3	21.7	23.8	21.1	23.0	21.9	20.9	25.4	18.7	23.8	22.2	21.7	267.3
1980	28.7	26.8	28.6	27.2	25.9	27.4	24.9	25.5	24.4	28.6	24.3	24.8	317.1
1981	25.5	25.7	28.5	26.3	25.6	23.9	24.2	25.2	28.9	28.7	26.0	23.9	312.4
1982	24.3	24.7	26.3	23.4	25.6	27.0	21.3	27.4	26.1	27.8	25.9	23.3	303.2
1983	25.2	23.0	25.6	23.1	22.5	21.1	20.2	24.0	23.1	23.9	21.9	21.7	275.3
1984[1]	23.2	25.0	26.9	21.8	22.7	19.9	19.2	16.2	15.1	21.5	21.2	19.0	252.8
1985[1]	19.7	21.8	23.6	17.8	18.9	18.8	13.9	14.2	14.8	19.1	16.3	18.8	217.5
1986[1]	20.4	18.4	19.6	15.3	12.2	14.2							

[1] Preliminary.   *Source: Bureau of Mines*   T.774A

U.S. Consumption of Slab Zinc by Fabricators   In Thousands of Metric Tons

Year	Jan.	Feb.	Mar.	Apr.	May	June	July	Aug.	Sept.	Oct.	Nov.	Dec.	Total
1979	88.4	89.3	96.9	88.4	94.1	90.3	73.6	84.5	72.4	82.4	76.4	71.4	1,000.6
1980	80.4	80.3	82.8	74.1	61.0	55.5	46.8	58.2	66.7	74.6	72.3	70.5	811.1
1981	74.5	73.6	77.3	74.3	73.6	77.2	64.4	72.4	70.2	66.2	59.8	52.0	840.9
1982	55.1	55.3	60.0	57.8	58.8	65.8	56.3	60.7	61.4	60.8	53.7	50.8	709.5
1983	61.8	59.9	68.8	66.7	64.1	65.7	55.8	64.5	67.2	65.5	70.1	63.7	805.9
1984[1]	69.4	70.2	76.8	72.1	73.1	71.1	62.8	67.6	65.1	69.2	64.9	62.4	848.9
1985[1]	65.3	64.4	62.8	61.0	66.0	59.0	52.6	55.9	56.8	58.9	55.8	52.1	711.8
1986[1]	55.4	56.3	59.9	56.2	57.8	59.1							

[1] Preliminary.   *Source: Bureau of Mines*   T.774B

Stocks of Slab Zinc[1] (at Smelter) in the United States, at Beginning of Month   In Thousands of Short Tons

Year	Jan.	Feb.	Mar.	Apr.	May	June	July	Aug.	Sept.	Oct.	Nov.	Dec.
1980	47.5	34.0	31.9	31.4	36.9	42.8	42.1	35.4	30.1	23.4	20.6	20.6
1981	18.4	18.8	20.9	17.6	17.2	17.9	20.9	22.9	21.5	27.0	34.9	38.1
1982	40.4	45.4	46.1	44.0	39.0	30.8	22.6	16.5	17.6	22.0	23.7	27.1
1983	24.2	24.4	21.4	19.8	21.2	22.4	22.2	15.0	10.6	16.0	17.8	18.4
1984	18.4	15.9	17.4	16.5	22.0	27.9	37.4	43.4	44.4	49.0	40.5	36.1
1985	48.2	48.1	46.0	37.8	35.6	35.3	35.3	35.6	37.8	39.9	35.8	37.3
1986	39.2	33.6	28.8	28.0	21.6	17.0	12.5	10.0	10.3	8.2	9.6	11.8
1987	17.1											

[1] Figures include zinc produced from foreign ores as well as domestic ores.   *Source: American Bureau of Metal Statistics, Inc.*   T.777

Smelter Production of Slab Zinc[1] in the United States (Includes GSA Metal)   In Thousands of Short Tons

Year	Jan.	Feb.	Mar.	Apr.	May	June	July	Aug.	Sept.	Oct.	Nov.	Dec.	Total
1979	45.7	46.1	52.9	51.1	49.9	43.0	44.0	42.0	39.8	46.0	43.4	33.5	537.4
1980	30.5	30.6	34.8	32.1	31.9	28.5	20.8	26.7	28.6	31.0	29.9	33.2	358.6
1981	33.4	31.5	34.5	34.1	32.2	30.8	33.0	33.5	29.4	29.8	29.3	25.3	376.8
1982	26.7	23.8	23.6	21.3	23.7	23.7	20.6	22.4	26.5	27.3	20.6	19.9	280.3
1983	20.0	22.8	25.0	24.7	25.9	24.0	17.6	25.6	25.1	26.5	27.3	24.1	288.5
1984	25.5	24.3	23.9	28.4	27.3	30.1	27.0	26.0	25.4	25.4	25.2	31.2	319.7
1985	30.9	28.5	33.2	28.2	26.9	21.3	23.6	26.9	27.4	30.7	27.2	27.1	331.8
1986	28.2	21.3	21.3	23.2	26.5	25.0	25.7	24.4	25.0	26.6	24.1	26.2	297.5

[1] Smelter & refinery production from domestic & foreign ores.   *Source: American Bureau of Metal Statistics, Inc.*   T.775

Domestic Shipments of Slab Zinc[1] in the United States   In Thousands of Short Tons

Year	Jan.	Feb.	Mar.	Apr.	May	June	July	Aug.	Sept.	Oct.	Nov.	Dec.	Total
1979	44.2	47.9	53.5	44.1	47.7	44.5	37.4	35.7	40.3	47.3	33.7	37.9	514.3
1980	44.5	44.2	36.8	32.7	26.4	22.6	21.5	33.4	34.0	37.6	32.7	33.3	399.6
1981	35.6	31.1	32.3	37.4	32.6	30.2	30.0	31.5	30.8	24.3	21.4	22.0	359.2
1982	24.4	18.8	22.9	23.4	28.7	31.9	28.7	28.6	25.4	23.0	18.9	16.5	291.3
1983	22.9	22.6	28.0	26.3	24.4	22.8	17.9	32.8	29.5	21.2	25.5	23.5	297.3
1984	28.0	22.8	24.8	22.9	21.4	20.5	20.9	25.1	20.8	33.8	29.7	19.1	289.9
1985	30.9	30.6	41.4	30.5	27.1	21.3	23.4	24.7	25.3	34.8	25.6	25.2	340.7
1986	33.9	26.2	22.1	29.6	31.1	29.5	28.2	24.1	27.1	25.1	21.9	20.9	319.7

[1] Does not include export shipments & gov't. account shipments.   *Source: American Bureau of Metal Statistics, Inc.*   T.776

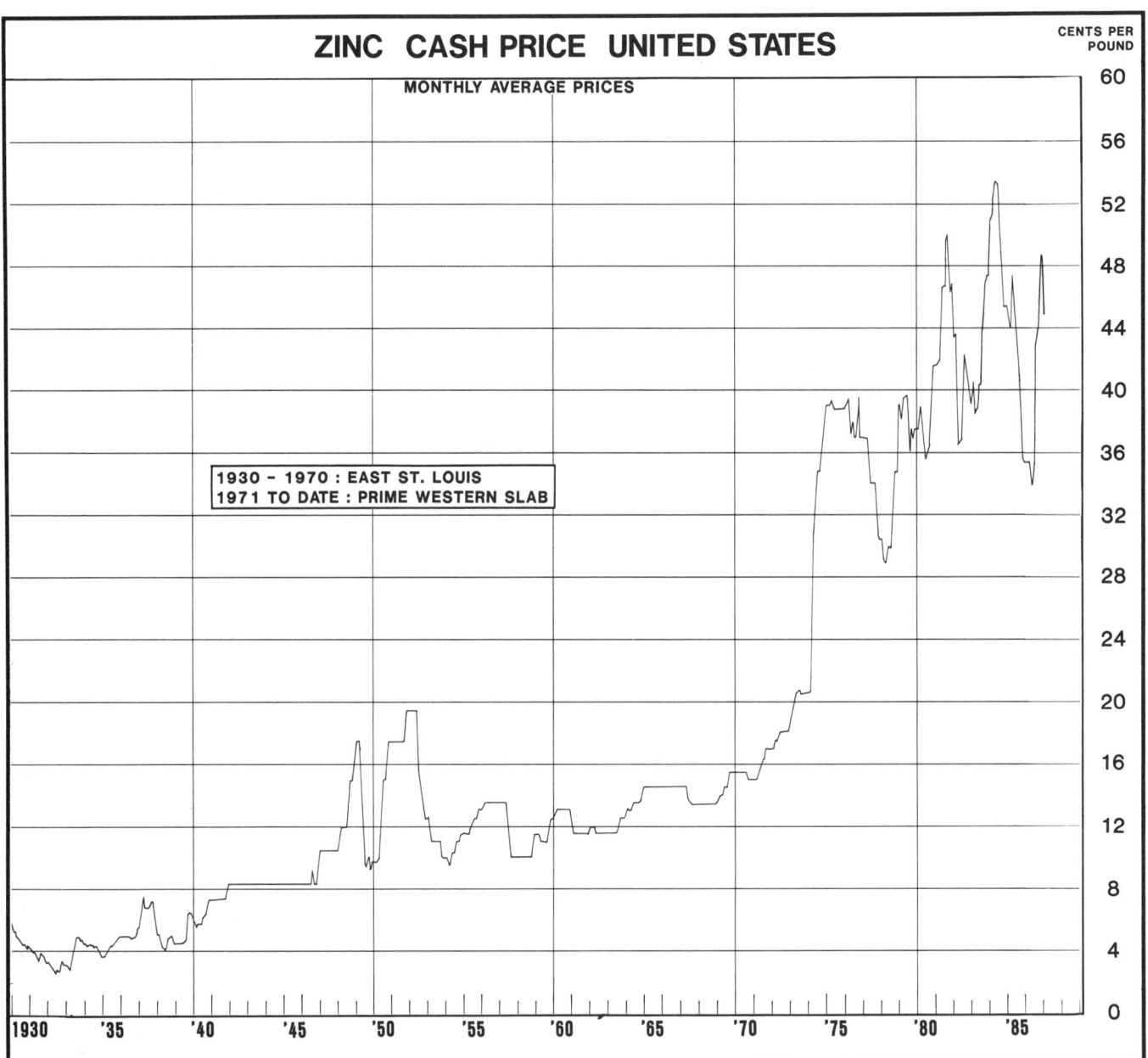

ZINC CASH PRICE UNITED STATES

CENTS PER POUND

MONTHLY AVERAGE PRICES

1930 – 1970 : EAST ST. LOUIS
1971 TO DATE : PRIME WESTERN SLAB

Average Price of Zinc, Prime Western Slab (Delivered U.S. Basis)   In Cents per Pound

Year	Jan.	Feb.	Mar.	Apr.	May	June	July	Aug.	Sept.	Oct.	Nov.	Dec.	Average
1975	39.25	39.07	38.75	38.75	38.75	38.75	38.75	38.75	38.75	39.66	38.75	38.75	38.89
1976	37.26	37.00	37.00	37.00	37.00	37.00	37.00	38.75	39.50	37.00	37.00	37.00	37.38
1977	37.00	37.00	37.00	37.00	35.64	34.00	34.00	34.00	34.00	31.74	30.66	30.50	35.21
1978	30.50	30.26	29.00	29.00	29.00	29.95	30.00	31.92	32.75	33.66	34.75	34.75	31.30
1979	35.00	36.90	38.09	39.50	39.50	39.55	39.63	36.82	36.03	37.50	36.88	37.50	37.74
1980	37.50	38.70	38.92	38.50	37.50	36.55	35.50	35.98	37.46	38.48	39.69	41.63	38.03
1981	41.63	41.63	42.13	43.73	46.55	46.63	46.67	49.74	49.88	46.41	46.75	43.65	45.45
1982	43.31	43.56	43.56	36.39	36.64	36.69	38.86	40.00	42.21	42.50	40.80	38.99	39.95
1983	40.20	40.35	38.38	38.73	40.38	40.38	41.51	44.03	46.38	47.09	49.38	49.38	43.02
1984	51.10	51.38	52.84	53.38	53.26	52.61	50.13	48.97	47.16	45.38	45.38	45.38	49.75
1985	44.65	44.01	46.05	47.38	47.38	46.44	42.67	41.38	40.63	38.38	35.56	35.38	42.49
1986	35.38	35.38		33.86	35.38	39.85	43.02		45.53	48.09	48.72	44.92	40.74

Source: American Metal Market   T.778